Dictionary of Literary Biography

1 *The American Renaissance in New England*, edited by Joel Myerson (1978)

2 *American Novelists Since World War II*, edited by Jeffrey Helterman and Richard Layman (1978)

3 *Antebellum Writers in New York and the South*, edited by Joel Myerson (1979)

4 *American Writers in Paris, 1920-1939*, edited by Karen Lane Rood (1980)

5 *American Poets Since World War II*, 2 parts, edited by Donald J. Greiner (1980)

6 *American Novelists Since World War II, Second Series*, edited by James E. Kibler Jr. (1980)

7 *Twentieth-Century American Dramatists*, 2 parts, edited by John MacNicholas (1981)

8 *Twentieth-Century American Science-Fiction Writers*, 2 parts, edited by David Cowart and Thomas L. Wymer (1981)

9 *American Novelists, 1910-1945*, 3 parts, edited by James J. Martine (1981)

10 *Modern British Dramatists, 1900-1945*, 2 parts, edited by Stanley Weintraub (1982)

11 *American Humorists, 1800-1950*, 2 parts, edited by Stanley Trachtenberg (1982)

12 *American Realists and Naturalists*, edited by Donald Pizer and Earl N. Harbert (1982)

13 *British Dramatists Since World War II*, 2 parts, edited by Stanley Weintraub (1982)

14 *British Novelists Since 1960*, 2 parts, edited by Jay L. Halio (1983)

15 *British Novelists, 1930-1959*, 2 parts, edited by Bernard Oldsey (1983)

16 *The Beats: Literary Bohemians in Postwar America*, 2 parts, edited by Ann Charters (1983)

17 *Twentieth-Century American Historians*, edited by Clyde N. Wilson (1983)

18 *Victorian Novelists After 1885*, edited by Ira B. Nadel and William E. Fredeman (1983)

19 *British Poets, 1880-1914*, edited by Donald E. Stanford (1983)

20 *British Poets, 1914-1945*, edited by Donald E. Stanford (1983)

21 *Victorian Novelists Before 1885*, edited by Ira B. Nadel and William E. Fredeman (1983)

22 *American Writers for Children, 1900-1960*, edited by John Cech (1983)

23 *American Newspaper Journalists, 1873-1900*, edited by Perry J. Ashley (1983)

24 *American Colonial Writers, 1606-1734*, edited by Emory Elliott (1984)

25 *American Newspaper Journalists, 1901-1925*, edited by Perry J. Ashley (1984)

26 *American Screenwriters*, edited by Robert E. Morsberger, Stephen O. Lesser, and Randall Clark (1984)

27 *Poets of Great Britain and Ireland, 1945-1960*, edited by Vincent B. Sherry Jr. (1984)

28 *Twentieth-Century American-Jewish Fiction Writers*, edited by Daniel Walden (1984)

29 *American Newspaper Journalists, 1926-1950*, edited by Perry J. Ashley (1984)

30 *American Historians, 1607-1865*, edited by Clyde N. Wilson (1984)

31 *American Colonial Writers, 1735-1781*, edited by Emory Elliott (1984)

32 *Victorian Poets Before 1850*, edited by William E. Fredeman and Ira B. Nadel (1984)

33 *Afro-American Fiction Writers After 1955*, edited by Thadious M. Davis and Trudier Harris (1984)

34 *British Novelists, 1890-1929: Traditionalists*, edited by Thomas F. Staley (1985)

35 *Victorian Poets After 1850*, edited by William E. Fredeman and Ira B. Nadel (1985)

36 *British Novelists, 1890-1929: Modernists*, edited by Thomas F. Staley (1985)

37 *American Writers of the Early Republic*, edited by Emory Elliott (1985)

38 *Afro-American Writers After 1955: Dramatists and Prose Writers*, edited by Thadious M. Davis and Trudier Harris (1985)

39 *British Novelists, 1660-1800*, 2 parts, edited by Martin C. Battestin (1985)

40 *Poets of Great Britain and Ireland Since 1960*, 2 parts, edited by Vincent B. Sherry Jr. (1985)

41 *Afro-American Poets Since 1955*, edited by Trudier Harris and Thadious M. Davis (1985)

42 *American Writers for Children Before 1900*, edited by Glenn E. Estes (1985)

43 *American Newspaper Journalists, 1690-1872*, edited by Perry J. Ashley (1986)

44 *American Screenwriters, Second Series*, edited by Randall Clark, Robert E. Morsberger, and Stephen O. Lesser (1986)

45 *American Poets, 1880-1945, First Series*, edited by Peter Quartermain (1986)

46 *American Literary Publishing Houses, 1900-1980: Trade and Paperback*, edited by Peter Dzwonkoski (1986)

47 *American Historians, 1866-1912*, edited by Clyde N. Wilson (1986)

48 *American Poets, 1880-1945, Second Series*, edited by Peter Quartermain (1986)

49 *American Literary Publishing Houses, 1638-1899*, 2 parts, edited by Peter Dzwonkoski (1986)

50 *Afro-American Writers Before the Harlem Renaissance*, edited by Trudier Harris (1986)

51 *Afro-American Writers from the Harlem Renaissance to 1940*, edited by Trudier Harris (1987)

52 *American Writers for Children Since 1960: Fiction*, edited by Glenn E. Estes (1986)

53 *Canadian Writers Since 1960, First Series*, edited by W. H. New (1986)

54 *American Poets, 1880-1945, Third Series*, 2 parts, edited by Peter Quartermain (1987)

55 *Victorian Prose Writers Before 1867*, edited by William B. Thesing (1987)

56 *German Fiction Writers, 1914-1945*, edited by James Hardin (1987)

57 *Victorian Prose Writers After 1867*, edited by William B. Thesing (1987)

58 *Jacobean and Caroline Dramatists*, edited by Fredson Bowers (1987)

59 *American Literary Critics and Scholars, 1800-1850*, edited by John W. Rathbun and Monica M. Grecu (1987)

60 *Canadian Writers Since 1960, Second Series*, edited by W. H. New (1987)

61 *American Writers for Children Since 1960: Poets, Illustrators, and Nonfiction Authors*, edited by Glenn E. Estes (1987)

62 *Elizabethan Dramatists*, edited by Fredson Bowers (1987)

63 *Modern American Critics, 1920-1955*, edited by Gregory S. Jay (1988)

64 *American Literary Critics and Scholars, 1850-1880*, edited by John W. Rathbun and Monica M. Grecu (1988)

65 *French Novelists, 1900-1930*, edited by Catharine Savage Brosman (1988)

66 *German Fiction Writers, 1885-1913*, 2 parts, edited by James Hardin (1988)

67 *Modern American Critics Since 1955*, edited by Gregory S. Jay (1988)

68 *Canadian Writers, 1920-1959, First Series*, edited by W. H. New (1988)

69 *Contemporary German Fiction Writers, First Series*, edited by Wolfgang D. Elfe and James Hardin (1988)

70 *British Mystery Writers, 1860-1919*, edited by Bernard Benstock and Thomas F. Staley (1988)

71 *American Literary Critics and Scholars, 1880–1900,* edited by John W. Rathbun and Monica M. Grecu (1988)

72 *French Novelists, 1930–1960,* edited by Catharine Savage Brosman (1988)

73 *American Magazine Journalists, 1741–1850,* edited by Sam G. Riley (1988)

74 *American Short-Story Writers Before 1880,* edited by Bobby Ellen Kimbel, with the assistance of William E. Grant (1988)

75 *Contemporary German Fiction Writers, Second Series,* edited by Wolfgang D. Elfe and James Hardin (1988)

76 *Afro-American Writers, 1940–1955,* edited by Trudier Harris (1988)

77 *British Mystery Writers, 1920–1939,* edited by Bernard Benstock and Thomas F. Staley (1988)

78 *American Short-Story Writers, 1880–1910,* edited by Bobby Ellen Kimbel, with the assistance of William E. Grant (1988)

79 *American Magazine Journalists, 1850–1900,* edited by Sam G. Riley (1988)

80 *Restoration and Eighteenth-Century Dramatists, First Series,* edited by Paula R. Backscheider (1989)

81 *Austrian Fiction Writers, 1875–1913,* edited by James Hardin and Donald G. Daviau (1989)

82 *Chicano Writers, First Series,* edited by Francisco A. Lomelí and Carl R. Shirley (1989)

83 *French Novelists Since 1960,* edited by Catharine Savage Brosman (1989)

84 *Restoration and Eighteenth-Century Dramatists, Second Series,* edited by Paula R. Backscheider (1989)

85 *Austrian Fiction Writers After 1914,* edited by James Hardin and Donald G. Daviau (1989)

86 *American Short-Story Writers, 1910–1945, First Series,* edited by Bobby Ellen Kimbel (1989)

87 *British Mystery and Thriller Writers Since 1940, First Series,* edited by Bernard Benstock and Thomas F. Staley (1989)

88 *Canadian Writers, 1920–1959, Second Series,* edited by W. H. New (1989)

89 *Restoration and Eighteenth-Century Dramatists, Third Series,* edited by Paula R. Backscheider (1989)

90 *German Writers in the Age of Goethe, 1789–1832,* edited by James Hardin and Christoph E. Schweitzer (1989)

91 *American Magazine Journalists, 1900–1960, First Series,* edited by Sam G. Riley (1990)

92 *Canadian Writers, 1890–1920,* edited by W. H. New (1990)

93 *British Romantic Poets, 1789–1832, First Series,* edited by John R. Greenfield (1990)

94 *German Writers in the Age of Goethe: Sturm und Drang to Classicism,* edited by James Hardin and Christoph E. Schweitzer (1990)

95 *Eighteenth-Century British Poets, First Series,* edited by John Sitter (1990)

96 *British Romantic Poets, 1789–1832, Second Series,* edited by John R. Greenfield (1990)

97 *German Writers from the Enlightenment to Sturm und Drang, 1720–1764,* edited by James Hardin and Christoph E. Schweitzer (1990)

98 *Modern British Essayists, First Series,* edited by Robert Beum (1990)

99 *Canadian Writers Before 1890,* edited by W. H. New (1990)

100 *Modern British Essayists, Second Series,* edited by Robert Beum (1990)

101 *British Prose Writers, 1660–1800, First Series,* edited by Donald T. Siebert (1991)

102 *American Short-Story Writers, 1910–1945, Second Series,* edited by Bobby Ellen Kimbel (1991)

103 *American Literary Biographers, First Series,* edited by Steven Serafin (1991)

104 *British Prose Writers, 1660–1800, Second Series,* edited by Donald T. Siebert (1991)

105 *American Poets Since World War II, Second Series,* edited by R. S. Gwynn (1991)

106 *British Literary Publishing Houses, 1820–1880,* edited by Patricia J. Anderson and Jonathan Rose (1991)

107 *British Romantic Prose Writers, 1789–1832, First Series,* edited by John R. Greenfield (1991)

108 *Twentieth-Century Spanish Poets, First Series,* edited by Michael L. Perna (1991)

109 *Eighteenth-Century British Poets, Second Series,* edited by John Sitter (1991)

110 *British Romantic Prose Writers, 1789–1832, Second Series,* edited by John R. Greenfield (1991)

111 *American Literary Biographers, Second Series,* edited by Steven Serafin (1991)

112 *British Literary Publishing Houses, 1881–1965,* edited by Jonathan Rose and Patricia J. Anderson (1991)

113 *Modern Latin-American Fiction Writers, First Series,* edited by William Luis (1992)

114 *Twentieth-Century Italian Poets, First Series,* edited by Giovanna Wedel De Stasio, Glauco Cambon, and Antonio Illiano (1992)

115 *Medieval Philosophers,* edited by Jeremiah Hackett (1992)

116 *British Romantic Novelists, 1789–1832,* edited by Bradford K. Mudge (1992)

117 *Twentieth-Century Caribbean and Black African Writers, First Series,* edited by Bernth Lindfors and Reinhard Sander (1992)

118 *Twentieth-Century German Dramatists, 1889–1918,* edited by Wolfgang D. Elfe and James Hardin (1992)

119 *Nineteenth-Century French Fiction Writers: Romanticism and Realism, 1800–1860,* edited by Catharine Savage Brosman (1992)

120 *American Poets Since World War II, Third Series,* edited by R. S. Gwynn (1992)

121 *Seventeenth-Century British Nondramatic Poets, First Series,* edited by M. Thomas Hester (1992)

122 *Chicano Writers, Second Series,* edited by Francisco A. Lomelí and Carl R. Shirley (1992)

123 *Nineteenth-Century French Fiction Writers: Naturalism and Beyond, 1860–1900,* edited by Catharine Savage Brosman (1992)

124 *Twentieth-Century German Dramatists, 1919–1992,* edited by Wolfgang D. Elfe and James Hardin (1992)

125 *Twentieth-Century Caribbean and Black African Writers, Second Series,* edited by Bernth Lindfors and Reinhard Sander (1993)

126 *Seventeenth-Century British Nondramatic Poets, Second Series,* edited by M. Thomas Hester (1993)

127 *American Newspaper Publishers, 1950–1990,* edited by Perry J. Ashley (1993)

128 *Twentieth-Century Italian Poets, Second Series,* edited by Giovanna Wedel De Stasio, Glauco Cambon, and Antonio Illiano (1993)

129 *Nineteenth-Century German Writers, 1841–1900,* edited by James Hardin and Siegfried Mews (1993)

130 *American Short-Story Writers Since World War II,* edited by Patrick Meanor (1993)

131 *Seventeenth-Century British Nondramatic Poets, Third Series,* edited by M. Thomas Hester (1993)

132 *Sixteenth-Century British Nondramatic Writers, First Series,* edited by David A. Richardson (1993)

133 *Nineteenth-Century German Writers to 1840,* edited by James Hardin and Siegfried Mews (1993)

134 *Twentieth-Century Spanish Poets, Second Series,* edited by Jerry Phillips Winfield (1994)

135 *British Short-Fiction Writers, 1880–1914: The Realist Tradition,* edited by William B. Thesing (1994)

136 *Sixteenth-Century British Nondramatic Writers, Second Series,* edited by David A. Richardson (1994)

137 *American Magazine Journalists, 1900–1960, Second Series,* edited by Sam G. Riley (1994)

138 *German Writers and Works of the High Middle Ages: 1170–1280,* edited by James Hardin and Will Hasty (1994)

139 *British Short-Fiction Writers, 1945–1980,* edited by Dean Baldwin (1994)

140 *American Book-Collectors and Bibliographers, First Series,* edited by Joseph Rosenblum (1994)

141 *British Children's Writers, 1880–1914,* edited by Laura M. Zaidman (1994)

142 *Eighteenth-Century British Literary Biographers,* edited by Steven Serafin (1994)

143 *American Novelists Since World War II, Third Series,* edited by James R. Giles and Wanda H. Giles (1994)

144 *Nineteenth-Century British Literary Biographers,* edited by Steven Serafin (1994)

145 *Modern Latin-American Fiction Writers, Second Series,* edited by William Luis and Ann González (1994)

146 *Old and Middle English Literature,* edited by Jeffrey Helterman and Jerome Mitchell (1994)

147 *South Slavic Writers Before World War II,* edited by Vasa D. Mihailovich (1994)

148 *German Writers and Works of the Early Middle Ages: 800–1170,* edited by Will Hasty and James Hardin (1994)

149 *Late Nineteenth- and Early Twentieth-Century British Literary Biographers,* edited by Steven Serafin (1995)

150 *Early Modern Russian Writers, Late Seventeenth and Eighteenth Centuries,* edited by Marcus C. Levitt (1995)

151 *British Prose Writers of the Early Seventeenth Century,* edited by Clayton D. Lein (1995)

152 *American Novelists Since World War II, Fourth Series,* edited by James R. Giles and Wanda H. Giles (1995)

153 *Late-Victorian and Edwardian British Novelists, First Series,* edited by George M. Johnson (1995)

154 *The British Literary Book Trade, 1700–1820,* edited by James K. Bracken and Joel Silver (1995)

155 *Twentieth-Century British Literary Biographers,* edited by Steven Serafin (1995)

156 *British Short-Fiction Writers, 1880–1914: The Romantic Tradition,* edited by William F. Naufftus (1995)

157 *Twentieth-Century Caribbean and Black African Writers, Third Series,* edited by Bernth Lindfors and Reinhard Sander (1995)

158 *British Reform Writers, 1789–1832,* edited by Gary Kelly and Edd Applegate (1995)

159 *British Short-Fiction Writers, 1800–1880,* edited by John R. Greenfield (1996)

160 *British Children's Writers, 1914–1960,* edited by Donald R. Hettinga and Gary D. Schmidt (1996)

161 *British Children's Writers Since 1960, First Series,* edited by Caroline Hunt (1996)

162 *British Short-Fiction Writers, 1915–1945,* edited by John H. Rogers (1996)

163 *British Children's Writers, 1800–1880,* edited by Meena Khorana (1996)

164 *German Baroque Writers, 1580–1660,* edited by James Hardin (1996)

165 *American Poets Since World War II, Fourth Series,* edited by Joseph Conte (1996)

166 *British Travel Writers, 1837–1875,* edited by Barbara Brothers and Julia Gergits (1996)

167 *Sixteenth-Century British Nondramatic Writers, Third Series,* edited by David A. Richardson (1996)

168 *German Baroque Writers, 1661–1730,* edited by James Hardin (1996)

169 *American Poets Since World War II, Fifth Series,* edited by Joseph Conte (1996)

170 *The British Literary Book Trade, 1475–1700,* edited by James K. Bracken and Joel Silver (1996)

171 *Twentieth-Century American Sportswriters,* edited by Richard Orodenker (1996)

172 *Sixteenth-Century British Nondramatic Writers, Fourth Series,* edited by David A. Richardson (1996)

173 *American Novelists Since World War II, Fifth Series,* edited by James R. Giles and Wanda H. Giles (1996)

174 *British Travel Writers, 1876–1909,* edited by Barbara Brothers and Julia Gergits (1997)

175 *Native American Writers of the United States,* edited by Kenneth M. Roemer (1997)

176 *Ancient Greek Authors,* edited by Ward W. Briggs (1997)

177 *Italian Novelists Since World War II, 1945–1965,* edited by Augustus Pallotta (1997)

178 *British Fantasy and Science-Fiction Writers Before World War I,* edited by Darren Harris-Fain (1997)

179 *German Writers of the Renaissance and Reformation, 1280–1580,* edited by James Hardin and Max Reinhart (1997)

180 *Japanese Fiction Writers, 1868–1945,* edited by Van C. Gessel (1997)

181 *South Slavic Writers Since World War II,* edited by Vasa D. Mihailovich (1997)

182 *Japanese Fiction Writers Since World War II,* edited by Van C. Gessel (1997)

183 *American Travel Writers, 1776–1864,* edited by James J. Schramer and Donald Ross (1997)

184 *Nineteenth-Century British Book-Collectors and Bibliographers,* edited by William Baker and Kenneth Womack (1997)

185 *American Literary Journalists, 1945–1995, First Series,* edited by Arthur J. Kaul (1998)

186 *Nineteenth-Century American Western Writers,* edited by Robert L. Gale (1998)

187 *American Book Collectors and Bibliographers, Second Series,* edited by Joseph Rosenblum (1998)

188 *American Book and Magazine Illustrators to 1920,* edited by Steven E. Smith, Catherine A. Hastedt, and Donald H. Dyal (1998)

189 *American Travel Writers, 1850–1915,* edited by Donald Ross and James J. Schramer (1998)

190 *British Reform Writers, 1832–1914,* edited by Gary Kelly and Edd Applegate (1998)

191 *British Novelists Between the Wars,* edited by George M. Johnson (1998)

192 *French Dramatists, 1789–1914,* edited by Barbara T. Cooper (1998)

193 *American Poets Since World War II, Sixth Series,* edited by Joseph Conte (1998)

194 *British Novelists Since 1960, Second Series,* edited by Merritt Moseley (1998)

195 *British Travel Writers, 1910–1939,* edited by Barbara Brothers and Julia Gergits (1998)

196 *Italian Novelists Since World War II, 1965–1995,* edited by Augustus Pallotta (1999)

197 *Late-Victorian and Edwardian British Novelists, Second Series,* edited by George M. Johnson (1999)

198 *Russian Literature in the Age of Pushkin and Gogol: Prose,* edited by Christine A. Rydel (1999)

199 *Victorian Women Poets,* edited by William B. Thesing (1999)

200 *American Women Prose Writers to 1820,* edited by Carla J. Mulford, with Angela Vietto and Amy E. Winans (1999)

201 *Twentieth-Century British Book Collectors and Bibliographers,* edited by William Baker and Kenneth Womack (1999)

202 *Nineteenth-Century American Fiction Writers,* edited by Kent P. Ljungquist (1999)

203 *Medieval Japanese Writers,* edited by Steven D. Carter (1999)

204 *British Travel Writers, 1940–1997,* edited by Barbara Brothers and Julia M. Gergits (1999)

205 *Russian Literature in the Age of Pushkin and Gogol: Poetry and Drama,* edited by Christine A. Rydel (1999)

206 *Twentieth-Century American Western Writers, First Series,* edited by Richard H. Cracroft (1999)

207 *British Novelists Since 1960, Third Series,* edited by Merritt Moseley (1999)

208 *Literature of the French and Occitan Middle Ages: Eleventh to Fifteenth Centuries,* edited by Deborah Sinnreich-Levi and Ian S. Laurie (1999)

209 *Chicano Writers, Third Series,* edited by Francisco A. Lomelí and Carl R. Shirley (1999)

210 *Ernest Hemingway: A Documentary Volume,* edited by Robert W. Trogdon (1999)

211 *Ancient Roman Writers,* edited by Ward W. Briggs (1999)

212 *Twentieth-Century American Western Writers, Second Series*, edited by Richard H. Cracroft (1999)

213 *Pre-Nineteenth-Century British Book Collectors and Bibliographers*, edited by William Baker and Kenneth Womack (1999)

214 *Twentieth-Century Danish Writers*, edited by Marianne Stecher-Hansen (1999)

215 *Twentieth-Century Eastern European Writers, First Series*, edited by Steven Serafin (1999)

216 *British Poets of the Great War: Brooke, Rosenberg, Thomas. A Documentary Volume*, edited by Patrick Quinn (2000)

217 *Nineteenth-Century French Poets*, edited by Robert Beum (2000)

218 *American Short-Story Writers Since World War II, Second Series*, edited by Patrick Meanor and Gwen Crane (2000)

219 *F. Scott Fitzgerald's* The Great Gatsby: *A Documentary Volume*, edited by Matthew J. Bruccoli (2000)

220 *Twentieth-Century Eastern European Writers, Second Series*, edited by Steven Serafin (2000)

221 *American Women Prose Writers, 1870–1920*, edited by Sharon M. Harris, with the assistance of Heidi L. M. Jacobs and Jennifer Putzi (2000)

222 *H. L. Mencken: A Documentary Volume*, edited by Richard J. Schrader (2000)

223 *The American Renaissance in New England, Second Series*, edited by Wesley T. Mott (2000)

224 *Walt Whitman: A Documentary Volume*, edited by Joel Myerson (2000)

225 *South African Writers*, edited by Paul A. Scanlon (2000)

226 *American Hard-Boiled Crime Writers*, edited by George Parker Anderson and Julie B. Anderson (2000)

227 *American Novelists Since World War II, Sixth Series*, edited by James R. Giles and Wanda H. Giles (2000)

228 *Twentieth-Century American Dramatists, Second Series*, edited by Christopher J. Wheatley (2000)

229 *Thomas Wolfe: A Documentary Volume*, edited by Ted Mitchell (2001)

230 *Australian Literature, 1788–1914*, edited by Selina Samuels (2001)

231 *British Novelists Since 1960, Fourth Series*, edited by Merritt Moseley (2001)

232 *Twentieth-Century Eastern European Writers, Third Series*, edited by Steven Serafin (2001)

233 *British and Irish Dramatists Since World War II, Second Series*, edited by John Bull (2001)

234 *American Short-Story Writers Since World War II, Third Series*, edited by Patrick Meanor and Richard E. Lee (2001)

235 *The American Renaissance in New England, Third Series*, edited by Wesley T. Mott (2001)

236 *British Rhetoricians and Logicians, 1500–1660*, edited by Edward A. Malone (2001)

237 *The Beats: A Documentary Volume*, edited by Matt Theado (2001)

238 *Russian Novelists in the Age of Tolstoy and Dostoevsky*, edited by J. Alexander Ogden and Judith E. Kalb (2001)

239 *American Women Prose Writers: 1820–1870*, edited by Amy E. Hudock and Katharine Rodier (2001)

240 *Late Nineteenth- and Early Twentieth-Century British Women Poets*, edited by William B. Thesing (2001)

241 *American Sportswriters and Writers on Sport*, edited by Richard Orodenker (2001)

242 *Twentieth-Century European Cultural Theorists, First Series*, edited by Paul Hansom (2001)

243 *The American Renaissance in New England, Fourth Series*, edited by Wesley T. Mott (2001)

244 *American Short-Story Writers Since World War II, Fourth Series*, edited by Patrick Meanor and Joseph McNicholas (2001)

245 *British and Irish Dramatists Since World War II, Third Series*, edited by John Bull (2001)

246 *Twentieth-Century American Cultural Theorists*, edited by Paul Hansom (2001)

247 *James Joyce: A Documentary Volume*, edited by A. Nicholas Fargnoli (2001)

248 *Antebellum Writers in the South, Second Series*, edited by Kent Ljungquist (2001)

249 *Twentieth-Century American Dramatists, Third Series*, edited by Christopher Wheatley (2002)

250 *Antebellum Writers in New York, Second Series*, edited by Kent Ljungquist (2002)

251 *Canadian Fantasy and Science-Fiction Writers*, edited by Douglas Ivison (2002)

252 *British Philosophers, 1500–1799*, edited by Philip B. Dematteis and Peter S. Fosl (2002)

253 *Raymond Chandler: A Documentary Volume*, edited by Robert Moss (2002)

254 *The House of Putnam, 1837–1872: A Documentary Volume*, edited by Ezra Greenspan (2002)

255 *British Fantasy and Science-Fiction Writers, 1918–1960*, edited by Darren Harris-Fain (2002)

256 *Twentieth-Century American Western Writers, Third Series*, edited by Richard H. Cracroft (2002)

257 *Twentieth-Century Swedish Writers After World War II*, edited by Ann-Charlotte Gavel Adams (2002)

258 *Modern French Poets*, edited by Jean-François Leroux (2002)

259 *Twentieth-Century Swedish Writers Before World War II*, edited by Ann-Charlotte Gavel Adams (2002)

260 *Australian Writers, 1915–1950*, edited by Selina Samuels (2002)

261 *British Fantasy and Science-Fiction Writers Since 1960*, edited by Darren Harris-Fain (2002)

262 *British Philosophers, 1800–2000*, edited by Peter S. Fosl and Leemon B. McHenry (2002)

263 *William Shakespeare: A Documentary Volume*, edited by Catherine Loomis (2002)

264 *Italian Prose Writers, 1900–1945*, edited by Luca Somigli and Rocco Capozzi (2002)

265 *American Song Lyricists, 1920–1960*, edited by Philip Furia (2002)

266 *Twentieth-Century American Dramatists, Fourth Series*, edited by Christopher J. Wheatley (2002)

267 *Twenty-First-Century British and Irish Novelists*, edited by Michael R. Molino (2002)

268 *Seventeenth-Century French Writers*, edited by Françoise Jaouën (2002)

269 *Nathaniel Hawthorne: A Documentary Volume*, edited by Benjamin Franklin V (2002)

270 *American Philosophers Before 1950*, edited by Philip B. Dematteis and Leemon B. McHenry (2002)

271 *British and Irish Novelists Since 1960*, edited by Merritt Moseley (2002)

272 *Russian Prose Writers Between the World Wars*, edited by Christine Rydel (2003)

273 *F. Scott Fitzgerald's* Tender Is the Night: *A Documentary Volume*, edited by Matthew J. Bruccoli and George Parker Anderson (2003)

274 *John Dos Passos's* U.S.A.: *A Documentary Volume*, edited by Donald Pizer (2003)

275 *Twentieth-Century American Nature Writers: Prose*, edited by Roger Thompson and J. Scott Bryson (2003)

276 *British Mystery and Thriller Writers Since 1960*, edited by Gina Macdonald (2003)

277 *Russian Literature in the Age of Realism*, edited by Alyssa Dinega Gillespie (2003)

278 *American Novelists Since World War II, Seventh Series*, edited by James R. Giles and Wanda H. Giles (2003)

279 *American Philosophers, 1950–2000*, edited by Philip B. Dematteis and Leemon B. McHenry (2003)

280 *Dashiell Hammett's* The Maltese Falcon: *A Documentary Volume*, edited by Richard Layman (2003)

281 *British Rhetoricians and Logicians, 1500–1660, Second Series*, edited by Edward A. Malone (2003)

282 *New Formalist Poets*, edited by Jonathan N. Barron and Bruce Meyer (2003)

283 *Modern Spanish American Poets, First Series*, edited by María A. Salgado (2003)

284 *The House of Holt, 1866–1946: A Documentary Volume*, edited by Ellen D. Gilbert (2003)

285 *Russian Writers Since 1980,* edited by Marina Balina and Mark Lipovetsky (2004)

286 *Castilian Writers, 1400–1500,* edited by Frank A. Domínguez and George D. Greenia (2004)

287 *Portuguese Writers,* edited by Monica Rector and Fred M. Clark (2004)

288 *The House of Boni & Liveright, 1917–1933: A Documentary Volume,* edited by Charles Egleston (2004)

289 *Australian Writers, 1950–1975,* edited by Selina Samuels (2004)

290 *Modern Spanish American Poets, Second Series,* edited by María A. Salgado (2004)

291 *The Hoosier House: Bobbs-Merrill and Its Predecessors, 1850–1985: A Documentary Volume,* edited by Richard J. Schrader (2004)

292 *Twenty-First-Century American Novelists,* edited by Lisa Abney and Suzanne Disheroon-Green (2004)

293 *Icelandic Writers,* edited by Patrick J. Stevens (2004)

294 *James Gould Cozzens: A Documentary Volume,* edited by Matthew J. Bruccoli (2004)

295 *Russian Writers of the Silver Age, 1890–1925,* edited by Judith E. Kalb and J. Alexander Ogden with the collaboration of I. G. Vishnevetsky (2004)

296 *Twentieth-Century European Cultural Theorists, Second Series,* edited by Paul Hansom (2004)

297 *Twentieth-Century Norwegian Writers,* edited by Tanya Thresher (2004)

298 *Henry David Thoreau: A Documentary Volume,* edited by Richard J. Schneider (2004)

299 *Holocaust Novelists,* edited by Efraim Sicher (2004)

300 *Danish Writers from the Reformation to Decadence, 1550–1900,* edited by Marianne Stecher-Hansen (2004)

301 *Gustave Flaubert: A Documentary Volume,* edited by Éric Le Calvez (2004)

302 *Russian Prose Writers After World War II,* edited by Christine Rydel (2004)

303 *American Radical and Reform Writers, First Series,* edited by Steven Rosendale (2005)

304 *Bram Stoker's* Dracula: *A Documentary Volume,* edited by Elizabeth Miller (2005)

305 *Latin American Dramatists, First Series,* edited by Adam Versényi (2005)

306 *American Mystery and Detective Writers,* edited by George Parker Anderson (2005)

307 *Brazilian Writers,* edited by Monica Rector and Fred M. Clark (2005)

308 *Ernest Hemingway's* A Farewell to Arms: *A Documentary Volume,* edited by Charles Oliver (2005)

309 *John Steinbeck: A Documentary Volume,* edited by Luchen Li (2005)

310 *British and Irish Dramatists Since World War II, Fourth Series,* edited by John Bull (2005)

311 *Arabic Literary Culture, 500–925,* edited by Michael Cooperson and Shawkat M. Toorawa (2005)

312 *Asian American Writers,* edited by Deborah L. Madsen (2005)

313 *Writers of the French Enlightenment, I,* edited by Samia I. Spencer (2005)

314 *Writers of the French Enlightenment, II,* edited by Samia I. Spencer (2005)

315 *Langston Hughes: A Documentary Volume,* edited by Christopher C. De Santis (2005)

316 *American Prose Writers of World War I: A Documentary Volume,* edited by Steven Trout (2005)

317 *Twentieth-Century Russian Émigré Writers,* edited by Maria Rubins (2005)

318 *Sixteenth-Century Spanish Writers,* edited by Gregory B. Kaplan (2006)

319 *British and Irish Short-Fiction Writers 1945–2000,* edited by Cheryl Alexander Malcolm and David Malcolm (2006)

320 *Robert Penn Warren: A Documentary Volume,* edited by James A. Grimshaw Jr. (2006)

321 *Twentieth-Century French Dramatists,* edited by Mary Anne O'Neil (2006)

322 *Twentieth-Century Spanish Fiction Writers,* edited by Marta E. Altisent and Cristina Martínez-Carazo (2006)

323 *South Asian Writers in English,* edited by Fakrul Alam (2006)

324 *John O'Hara: A Documentary Volume,* edited by Matthew J. Bruccoli (2006)

325 *Australian Writers, 1975–2000,* edited by Selina Samuels (2006)

326 *Booker Prize Novels, 1969–2005,* edited by Merritt Moseley (2006)

327 *Sixteenth-Century French Writers,* edited by Megan Conway (2006)

328 *Chinese Fiction Writers, 1900–1949,* edited by Thomas Moran (2007)

329 *Nobel Prize Laureates in Literature, Part 1: Agnon–Eucken* (2007)

Dictionary of Literary Biography Documentary Series

1 *Sherwood Anderson, Willa Cather, John Dos Passos, Theodore Dreiser, F. Scott Fitzgerald, Ernest Hemingway, Sinclair Lewis,* edited by Margaret A. Van Antwerp (1982)

2 *James Gould Cozzens, James T. Farrell, William Faulkner, John O'Hara, John Steinbeck, Thomas Wolfe, Richard Wright,* edited by Margaret A. Van Antwerp (1982)

3 *Saul Bellow, Jack Kerouac, Norman Mailer, Vladimir Nabokov, John Updike, Kurt Vonnegut,* edited by Mary Bruccoli (1983)

4 *Tennessee Williams,* edited by Margaret A. Van Antwerp and Sally Johns (1984)

5 *American Transcendentalists,* edited by Joel Myerson (1988)

6 *Hardboiled Mystery Writers: Raymond Chandler, Dashiell Hammett, Ross Macdonald,* edited by Matthew J. Bruccoli and Richard Layman (1989)

7 *Modern American Poets: James Dickey, Robert Frost, Marianne Moore,* edited by Karen L. Rood (1989)

8 *The Black Aesthetic Movement,* edited by Jeffrey Louis Decker (1991)

9 *American Writers of the Vietnam War: W. D. Ehrhart, Larry Heinemann, Tim O'Brien, Walter McDonald, John M. Del Vecchio,* edited by Ronald Baughman (1991)

10 *The Bloomsbury Group,* edited by Edward L. Bishop (1992)

11 *American Proletarian Culture: The Twenties and The Thirties,* edited by Jon Christian Suggs (1993)

12 *Southern Women Writers: Flannery O'Connor, Katherine Anne Porter, Eudora Welty,* edited by Mary Ann Wimsatt and Karen L. Rood (1994)

13 *The House of Scribner, 1846–1904,* edited by John Delaney (1996)

14 *Four Women Writers for Children, 1868–1918,* edited by Caroline C. Hunt (1996)

15 *American Expatriate Writers: Paris in the Twenties,* edited by Matthew J. Bruccoli and Robert W. Trogdon (1997)

16 *The House of Scribner, 1905–1930,* edited by John Delaney (1997)

17 *The House of Scribner, 1931–1984,* edited by John Delaney (1998)

18 *British Poets of The Great War: Sassoon, Graves, Owen,* edited by Patrick Quinn (1999)

19 *James Dickey,* edited by Judith S. Baughman (1999)

See also DLB 210, 216, 219, 222, 224, 229, 237, 247, 253, 254, 263, 269, 273, 274, 280, 284, 288, 291, 294, 298, 301, 304, 308, 309, 315, 316, 320, 324

Dictionary of Literary Biography Yearbooks

1980 edited by Karen L. Rood, Jean W. Ross, and Richard Ziegfeld (1981)

1981 edited by Karen L. Rood, Jean W. Ross, and Richard Ziegfeld (1982)

1982 edited by Richard Ziegfeld; associate editors: Jean W. Ross and Lynne C. Zeigler (1983)

1983 edited by Mary Bruccoli and Jean W. Ross; associate editor Richard Ziegfeld (1984)

1984 edited by Jean W. Ross (1985)

1985 edited by Jean W. Ross (1986)

1986 edited by J. M. Brook (1987)

1987 edited by J. M. Brook (1988)

1988 edited by J. M. Brook (1989)

1989 edited by J. M. Brook (1990)

1990 edited by James W. Hipp (1991)

1991 edited by James W. Hipp (1992)

1992 edited by James W. Hipp (1993)

1993 edited by James W. Hipp, contributing editor George Garrett (1994)

1994 edited by James W. Hipp, contributing editor George Garrett (1995)

1995 edited by James W. Hipp, contributing editor George Garrett (1996)

1996 edited by Samuel W. Bruce and L. Kay Webster, contributing editor George Garrett (1997)

1997 edited by Matthew J. Bruccoli and George Garrett, with the assistance of L. Kay Webster (1998)

1998 edited by Matthew J. Bruccoli, contributing editor George Garrett, with the assistance of D. W. Thomas (1999)

1999 edited by Matthew J. Bruccoli, contributing editor George Garrett, with the assistance of D. W. Thomas (2000)

2000 edited by Matthew J. Bruccoli, contributing editor George Garrett, with the assistance of George Parker Anderson (2001)

2001 edited by Matthew J. Bruccoli, contributing editor George Garrett, with the assistance of George Parker Anderson (2002)

2002 edited by Matthew J. Bruccoli and George Garrett; George Parker Anderson, Assistant Editor (2003)

Concise Series

Concise Dictionary of American Literary Biography, 7 volumes (1988–1999): *The New Consciousness, 1941–1968; Colonization to the American Renaissance, 1640–1865; Realism, Naturalism, and Local Color, 1865–1917; The Twenties, 1917–1929; The Age of Maturity, 1929–1941; Broadening Views, 1968–1988; Supplement: Modern Writers, 1900–1998.*

Concise Dictionary of British Literary Biography, 8 volumes (1991–1992): *Writers of the Middle Ages and Renaissance Before 1660; Writers of the Restoration and Eighteenth Century, 1660–1789; Writers of the Romantic Period, 1789–1832; Victorian Writers, 1832–1890; Late-Victorian and Edwardian Writers, 1890–1914; Modern Writers, 1914–1945; Writers After World War II, 1945–1960; Contemporary Writers, 1960 to Present.*

Concise Dictionary of World Literary Biography, 4 volumes (1999–2000): *Ancient Greek and Roman Writers; German Writers; African, Caribbean, and Latin American Writers; South Slavic and Eastern European Writers.*

Dictionary of Literary Biography® • Volume Three Hundred Twenty-Nine

Nobel Prize Laureates in Literature, Part 1: Agnon–Eucken

Samuel Beckett's Nobel Prize diploma (art by Gunnar Brusewitz, calligraphy by Kerstin Anckers; © The Nobel Foundation, 1969)

Dictionary of Literary Biography® • Volume Three Hundred Twenty-Nine

Nobel Prize Laureates in Literature, Part 1: Agnon–Eucken

A Bruccoli Clark Layman Book

Detroit • New York • San Francisco • New Haven, Conn. • Waterville, Maine • London • Munich

Dictionary of Literary Biography
Volume 329: Nobel Prize Laureates in Literature,
Part 1: Agnon–Eucken

Advisory Board
John Baker
William Cagle
Patrick O'Connor
George Garrett
Trudier Harris
Alvin Kernan

Editorial Directors
Matthew J. Bruccoli and Richard Layman

© 2007 Thomson Gale, a part of The Thomson Corporation.

Thomson and Star Logo are trademarks and Gale is a registered trademark used herein under license.

For more information, contact
Thomson Gale
27500 Drake Rd.
Farmington Hills, MI 48331-3535
Or you can visit our Internet site at
http://www.gale.com

ALL RIGHTS RESERVED
No part of this work covered by the copyright hereon may be reproduced or used in any form or by any means—graphic, electronic, or mechanical, including photocopying, recording, taping, Web distribution, or information storage retrieval systems—without the written permission of the publisher.

For permission to use material from this product, submit your request via Web at http://www.gale-edit.com/permissions, or you may download our Permissions Request form and submit your request by fax or mail to:

Permissions Department
Thomson Gale
27500 Drake Rd.
Farmington Hills, MI 48331-3535
Permissions Hotline:
248-699-8006 or 800-877-4253, ext. 8006
Fax: 248-699-8074 or 800-762-4058

While every effort has been made to ensure the reliability of the information presented in this publication, Thomson Gale does not guarantee the accuracy of the data contained herein. Thomson Gale accepts no payment for listing; and inclusion in the publication of any organization, agency, institution, publication, service, or individual does not imply endorsement of the editors or publisher. Errors brought to the attention of the publisher and verified to the satisfaction of the publisher will be corrected in future editions.

LIBRARY OF CONGRESS CATALOGING-IN-PUBLICATION DATA

Nobel prize laureates in literature.
    v. cm. — (Dictionary of literary biography ; v. 329-)
"A Bruccoli Clark Layman book."
Includes bibliographical references and index.
ISBN-13: 978-0-7876-8147-0
ISBN-10: 0-7876-8147-4 (hardcover : alk. paper)
1. Literature, Modern—20th century—Bio-bibliography—Dictionaries.
2. Literature, Modern—21st century—Bio-bibliography—Dictionaries.
3. Nobel Prizes. 1. Thomson Gale (Firm)
PN171.P75N58 2006
809'.04—dc22
    [B]
            2006018605

Printed in the United States of America
10 9 8 7 6 5 4 3 2 1

Contents

Plan of the Series xv

Introduction xvii
Park Bucker

Shmuel Yosef Agnon (1887–1970) 3
Dvir Abramovich

    1966 Nobel Prize in Literature Presentation Speech 15
        by Anders Österling, Member of the Swedish Academy

    Agnon: Banquet Speech 16

Vicente Aleixandre (1898–1984) 19
Santiago Daydí-Tolson

    1977 Nobel Prize in Literature Presentation Speech 29
        by Dr. Karl Ragnar Gierow, of the Swedish Academy (Translation from the Swedish)

    Aleixandre: Banquet Speech 30

    Press Release: The Nobel Prize in Literature 1977 31

Aleixandre: Nobel Lecture, 12 December 1977 33

Ivo Andrić (1892–1975) 36
Vasa D. Mihailovich

    1961 Nobel Prize in Literature Presentation Speech 45
        by Anders Österling, Permanent Secretary of the Swedish Academy

    Andrić: Banquet Speech 47

Miguel Ángel Asturias (1899–1974) 49
Oralia Preble-Niemi

    1967 Nobel Prize in Literature Presentation Speech 61
        by Anders Österling, Permanent Secretary of the Swedish Academy

    Asturias: Banquet Speech 62

Asturias: Nobel Lecture, 12 December 1967 64

Samuel Beckett (1906–1989) 69
Julian A. Garforth

    1969 Nobel Prize in Literature Presentation Speech 87
        by Dr. Karl Ragnar Gierow, of the Swedish Academy (Translation from the Swedish)

Contents

Saul Bellow (1915–2005) 89
Keith M. Opdahl

   1976 Nobel Prize in Literature Presentation Speech 103
      by Dr. Karl Ragnar Gierow, of the Swedish Academy (Translation from the Swedish)

   Bellow: Banquet Speech 105

Bellow: Nobel Lecture, 12 December 1976 106

Jacinto Benavente (1866–1954) 111
Montserrat Alás-Brun

   1922 Nobel Prize in Literature Presentation Speech 124
      by Per Hallström, Chairman of the Nobel Committee of the Swedish Academy

   Benavente: Banquet Speech 126

Henri Bergson (1859–1941) 127
Philip B. Dematteis

   1927 Nobel Prize in Literature Presentation Speech 141
      by Per Hallström, President of the Nobel Committee of the Swedish Academy

   Bergson: Banquet Speech 143

Bjørnstjerne Bjørnson (1832–1910) 144
Hans H. Skei

   1903 Nobel Prize in Literature Presentation Speech 153
      by C. D. af Wirsén, Permanent Secretary of the Swedish Academy

   Bjørnson: Banquet Speech 154

Heinrich Böll (1917–1985) 156
Reinhard K. Zachau

   Böll: Autobiographical Statement 173

   1972 Nobel Prize in Literature Presentation Speech 173
      by Dr. Karl Ragnar Gierow, Permanent Secretary of the Swedish Academy (Translation from the Swedish)

   Böll: Banquet Speech 174

Böll: Nobel Lecture, 2 May 1973 177

Joseph Brodsky (Iosif Aleksandrovich Brodsky) (1940–1996) 184
Alyssa Dinega Gillespie

   1987 Nobel Prize in Literature Presentation Speech 202
      by Professor Sture Allén, of the Swedish Academy (Translation from the Swedish)

   Brodsky: Banquet Speech 203

   Press Release: The Nobel Prize in Literature 1987 204

Brodsky: Nobel Lecture, 8 December 1987 205

Pearl S. Buck (1892–1973) 210
Tracy Simmons Bitonti

   1938 Nobel Prize in Literature Presentation Speech 221
      by Per Hallström, Permanent Secretary of the Swedish Academy

   Buck: Banquet Speech 224

Buck: Nobel Lecture, 12 December 1938 226

Ivan Bunin (1870–1953) 235
Julian W. Connolly

    Bunin: Autobiographical Statement 246

    1933 Nobel Prize in Literature Presentation Speech 246
        by Per Hallström, Permanent Secretary of the Swedish Academy

    Bunin: Banquet Speech 249

Albert Camus (1913–1960) 250
Catharine Savage Brosman

    1957 Nobel Prize in Literature Presentation Speech 267
        by Anders Österling, Permanent Secretary of the Swedish Academy

    Camus: Banquet Speech 268

Elias Canetti (1905–1994) 271
Thomas H. Falk and Dagmar C. G. Lorenz

    1981 Nobel Prize in Literature Presentation Speech 283
        by Dr. Johannes Edfelt, of the Swedish Academy (Translation from the Swedish)

    Canetti: Banquet Speech 284

Giosuè Carducci (1835–1907) 286
Thomas E. Peterson

    1906 Nobel Prize in Literature Presentation Speech 299
        by C. D. af Wirsén, Permanent Secretary of the Swedish Academy

Camilo José Cela (1916–2002) 303
Lucile C. Charlebois

    1989 Nobel Prize in Literature Presentation Speech 318
        by Professor Knut Ahnlund, of the Swedish Academy (Translation from the Swedish)

    Cela: Banquet Speech 319

    Press Release: The Nobel Prize in Literature 1989 319

Cela: Nobel Lecture, 8 December 1989 321

Sir Winston Churchill (1874–1965) 327
Laurence Kitzan

    1953 Nobel Prize in Literature Presentation Speech 342
        by Sigfrid Siwertz, Member of the Swedish Academy

    Churchill: Banquet Speech 344

J. M. Coetzee (1940–) 346
Michael Marais and Merritt Moseley

    2003 Nobel Prize in Literature Presentation Speech 363
        by Per Wästberg of the Swedish Academy (Translation from the Swedish)

    Coetzee: Banquet Speech 364

    Press Release: The Nobel Prize in Literature 2003 365

Coetzee: Nobel Lecture, 7 December 2003 366

Contents

Grazia Deledda (1871–1936) 370
    Stefania Lucamante and E. Ann Matter

    Deledda: Autobiographical Statement 381

    1926 Nobel Prize in Literature Presentation Speech 382
        by Henrik Schück, President of the Nobel Foundation

José Echegaray (1832–1916) 385
    Judy B. McInnis

    1904 Nobel Prize in Literature Presentation Speech 397
        by C. D. af Wirsén, Permanent Secretary of the Swedish Academy

T. S. Eliot (1888–1965) 402
    Jewel Spears Brooker

    1948 Nobel Prize in Literature Presentation Speech 418
        by Anders Österling, Permanent Secretary of the Swedish Academy

    Eliot: Banquet Speech 420

Odysseus Elytis (1911–1996) 422
    Marinos Pourgouris

    1979 Nobel Prize in Literature Presentation Speech 430
        by Dr. Karl Ragnar Gierow, of the Swedish Academy (Translation from the Swedish)

    Elytis: Banquet Speech 432

    Press Release: The Nobel Prize in Literature 1979 433

Elytis: Nobel Lecture, 8 December 1979 435

Rudolf Eucken (1846–1926) 439
    Uwe Dathe

    1908 Nobel Prize in Literature Presentation Speech 449
        by Harald Hjärne, Director of the Swedish Academy

Eucken: Nobel Lecture, 27 March 1909 453

Nobel Laureates in Literature, 1901–2005 461

Contributors 463

Index 467

Plan of the Series

... Almost the most prodigious asset of a country, and perhaps its most precious possession, is its native literary product—when that product is fine and noble and enduring.

Mark Twain*

The advisory board, the editors, and the publisher of the *Dictionary of Literary Biography* are joined in endorsing Mark Twain's declaration. The literature of a nation provides an inexhaustible resource of permanent worth. Our purpose is to make literature and its creators better understood and more accessible to students and the reading public, while satisfying the needs of teachers and researchers.

To meet these requirements, *literary biography* has been construed in terms of the author's achievement. The most important thing about a writer is his writing. Accordingly, the entries in *DLB* are career biographies, tracing the development of the author's canon and the evolution of his reputation.

The purpose of *DLB* is not only to provide reliable information in a usable format but also to place the figures in the larger perspective of literary history and to offer appraisals of their accomplishments by qualified scholars.

The publication plan for *DLB* resulted from two years of preparation. The project was proposed to Bruccoli Clark by Frederick G. Ruffner, president of the Gale Research Company, in November 1975. After specimen entries were prepared and typeset, an advisory board was formed to refine the entry format and develop the series rationale. In meetings held during 1976, the publisher, series editors, and advisory board approved the scheme for a comprehensive biographical dictionary of persons who contributed to literature. Editorial work on the first volume began in January 1977, and it was published in 1978. In order to make *DLB* more than a dictionary and to compile volumes that individually have claim to status as literary history, it was decided to organize volumes by topic, period, or genre. Each of these freestanding volumes provides a biographical-bibliographical guide and overview for a particular area of literature. We are convinced that this organization—as opposed to a single alphabet method—constitutes a valuable innovation in the presentation of reference material. The volume plan necessarily requires many decisions for the placement and treatment of authors. Certain figures will be included in separate volumes, but with different entries emphasizing the aspect of his career appropriate to each volume. Ernest Hemingway, for example, is represented in *American Writers in Paris, 1920–1939* by an entry focusing on his expatriate apprenticeship; he is also in *American Novelists, 1910–1945* with an entry surveying his entire career, as well as in *American Short-Story Writers, 1910–1945, Second Series* with an entry concentrating on his short fiction. Each volume includes a cumulative index of the subject authors and articles.

Between 1981 and 2002 the series was augmented and updated by the *DLB Yearbooks*. There have also been nineteen *DLB Documentary Series* volumes, which provide illustrations, facsimiles, and biographical and critical source materials for figures, works, or groups judged to have particular interest for students. In 1999 the *Documentary Series* was incorporated into the *DLB* volume numbering system beginning with *DLB 210: Ernest Hemingway*.

We define literature as the *intellectual commerce of a nation:* not merely as belles lettres but as that ample and complex process by which ideas are generated, shaped, and transmitted. *DLB* entries are not limited to "creative writers" but extend to other figures who in their time and in their way influenced the mind of a people. Thus the series encompasses historians, journalists, publishers, book collectors, and screenwriters. By this means readers of *DLB* may be aided to perceive literature not as cult scripture in the keeping of intellectual high priests but firmly positioned at the center of a nation's life.

DLB includes the major writers appropriate to each volume and those standing in the ranks behind them. Scholarly and critical counsel has been sought in deciding which minor figures to include and how full their entries should be. Wherever possible, useful refer-

---

*From an unpublished section of Mark Twain's autobiography, copyright by the Mark Twain Company ences are made to figures who do not warrant separate entries.

Each *DLB* volume has an expert volume editor responsible for planning the volume, selecting the figures for inclusion, and assigning the entries. Volume editors are also responsible for preparing, where appropriate, appendices surveying the major periodicals and literary and intellectual movements for their volumes, as well as lists of further readings. Work on the series as a whole is coordinated at the Bruccoli Clark Layman editorial center in Columbia, South Carolina, where the editorial staff is responsible for accuracy and utility of the published volumes.

One feature that distinguishes *DLB* is the illustration policy—its concern with the iconography of literature. Just as an author is influenced by his surroundings, so is the reader's understanding of the author enhanced by a knowledge of his environment. Therefore *DLB* volumes include not only drawings, paintings, and photographs of authors, often depicting them at various stages in their careers, but also illustrations of their families and places where they lived. Title pages are regularly reproduced in facsimile along with dust jackets for modern authors. The dust jackets are a special feature of *DLB* because they often document better than anything else the way in which an author's work was perceived in its own time. Specimens of the writers' manuscripts and letters are included when feasible.

Samuel Johnson rightly decreed that "The chief glory of every people arises from its authors." The purpose of the *Dictionary of Literary Biography* is to compile literary history in the surest way available to us—by accurate and comprehensive treatment of the lives and work of those who contributed to it.

The *DLB* Advisory Board

Introduction

Park Bucker
University of South Carolina, Sumter

On 10 December 1896, Alfred Nobel–inventor, manufacturer, and amateur author–died in Paris following a massive cerebral hemorrhage. He left behind neither widow nor children, few family heirs, and even fewer close friends. He had spent his adult life as an expatriate, seldom returning to his native Sweden. Through the manufacture and marketing of his own inventions (particularly the mixing of nitroglycerin with silica to form a malleable paste called dynamite) Nobel had amassed a fortune of 33 million Swedish krona (SEK), which translates to $9 million in 1900, and $200 million in 2005.

Unlike many other self-made millionaires of the nineteenth century, Nobel had not attempted to offset class resentment against his fortune, or to alter his image of "death merchant," with acts of ostentatious philanthropy. He avoided publicity. The eccentric millionaire rarely allowed himself to be photographed, citing his "hog-bristled beard" and "unredeemed ugliness." Nobel intended his charitable endowment to be formed from the bulk of his estate and established posthumously. Written without legal advice, Nobel's will created what became the world's most celebrated–and remunerative–annual awards for individual achievement in the fields of science, literature, and world peace.

Aside from granting several small legacies, the will stipulates:

> With the residue of my convertible estate I hereby direct my executors to proceed as follows: They shall convert my said residue of property into money, which they shall then invest in safe securities; the capital thus secured shall constitute a fund, the interest accruing from which shall be annually awarded in prizes to those persons who shall have contributed most materially to benefit mankind during the year immediately preceding. The said interest shall be divided into five equal amounts, to be apportioned as follows: one share to the person who shall have made the most important discovery or invention in the domain of physics; one share to the person who shall have made the most important chemical discovery or improvement; one share to the person who shall have made the most important discovery in the domain of physiology or medicine; one share to the person who shall have produced in the field of literature the most distinguished work of an idealistic tendency; and, finally, one share to the person who shall have most or best promoted the fraternity of nations and the abolition or diminution of standing armies and the formation or increase of peace congresses. The prizes for physics and chemistry shall be awarded by the Swedish Academy of Science in Stockholm, the one for physiology or medicine by the Caroline Medical Institute in Stockholm; the prize for literature by the Swedish Academy in Stockholm, and that for peace by a committee of five persons to be elected by the Norwegian Storthing. I declare it to be my express desire that, in awarding these prizes, no consideration whatever be paid to the nationality of the candidates, that is to say, the most deserving be awarded the prize, whether of Scandinavian origin or not.

The will generated great controversy among potential heirs and governments: France claimed Nobel as a citizen and therefore wanted to tax the estate. In order for the award to be established, the respective organizations listed in the will had to agree to accept Nobel's gift and the responsibility of administering it. The Swedish and soon-to-be-independent Norwegian governments formed the Nobel Foundation to administer the estate and make the required investments. The separate societies were left to interpret Nobel's ambiguous directives according to their own preconceptions and ideologies.

In a previous will Nobel had left part of his estate to establish prizes for scientific advancement and peace, but not literature. Embittered by business reverses and lawsuits in the latter part of his life, Nobel wrote poetry and a philosophical prose tragedy, *Nemesis*. Composed shortly before his death and heavily influenced by Percy Bysshe Shelley's *The Cenci* (1819), the play was printed while the author suffered from his final illness. After Nobel's death, his family attempted to destroy the entire printed edition, because they feared the amateur play would harm his reputation as a prize-giver; but three copies survived. The heroine of *Nemesis*, Beatrice Cenci, advances one of Nobel's themes: "The lyrics of our wonderful poets became for me entrancing and consoling echoes of the spiritual world of feeling and thought." This late interest in literary composition and its role in society may have prompted Nobel to revise his will.

Unlike the objective fields of physics, chemistry, or medicine—in which reasonable observers can generally agree on the scientific breakthroughs or discoveries that merit recognition—literature is an art form dependent on a common language and culture, and it defies qualitative distinctions. In naming the Swedish Academy (unschooled in international literary trends) as the arbiter of the literary prize, Nobel inadvertently insured a bureaucratic and ill-informed selection process in which idealistic meritocratic principles fell prey to compromise and pettiness and too often resulted in mediocre choices. A few times the Swedish Academy has successfully fulfilled Nobel's wishes in honoring the distinguished creators of recent masterpieces: William Butler Yeats (1923), George Bernard Shaw (1925), and Eugene O'Neill (1936). Ernest Hemingway, who should have been recognized following the publication of *A Farewell to Arms* (1929) or *For Whom the Bell Tolls* (1940), did not receive this award until 1954, after the publication of the minor novella *The Old Man and the Sea* (1952). Similarly, T. S. Eliot did not receive his award until 1948, twenty-six years after publication of *The Waste Land* (1922). The reasons for an author's selection often have stemmed not from "distinguished work" beneficial to mankind, but rather from internal prejudices, and from external geopolitical and cultural concerns.

Why the Nobel Prize Remains Important

If the prize for literature routinely rewards controversial or nondeserving authors, why does it continue to hold the world's attention? The nonwinners who enjoyed strong international reputations during their lifetimes (including Leo Tolstoy, Mark Twain, Henrik Ibsen, James Joyce, Theodore Dreiser, Graham Greene, Robert Frost, and Vladimir Nabokov) are often more impressive than the actual laureates. Aside from the fact that the world's media feeds on controversy, three reasons may explain the continued relevance of the award.

Money. The Nobel Prize cash award—called "dynamite money" by American novelists (and nonwinners) John O'Hara and Kurt Vonnegut—often relieves the winner of economic pressures, especially when combined with the subsequent worldwide boost in book sales. As outlined by Nobel's will, the winner or winners in each category share equally each year in the interest accrued by the Foundation's investments. The first winners in 1901 received 150,782 SEK or $40,000, roughly equivalent to $800,000 in twenty-first-century dollars. The cash amounts decreased for the first twenty years of the prize. In 1923 the Academy awarded the lowest amount in its history: 114,935 SEK, or $30,000. The Nobel Foundation received tax-exempt status in 1946 from Sweden and in 1953 from the United States, which allowed the endowment income to increase greatly. By the early 1970s each award brought more than $100,000; through years of profitable investments by the Nobel Foundation, the award reached almost a million dollars by 1990. The 2004 winner, Austrian author Elfriede Jelinek, received ten million SEK or $1.28 million. See Table A.

YEAR	WINNER	SEK	$
1907	Rudyard Kipling	138,796	40,000
1923	William Butler Yeats	114,935	30,000
1930	Sinclair Lewis	172,947	46,000
1948	T. S. Eliot	159,773	32,000
1954	Ernest Hemingway	190,214	35,000
1964	Jean-Paul Sartre (refused)	273,000	53,000
1970	Aleksandr Solzhenitsyn	400,000	77,000
1976	Saul Bellow	681,000	180,000
1992	Derek Walcott	6,500,000	1,200,000
1993	Toni Morrison	6,700,000	880,000
1999	Günter Grass	7,900,000	960,000
2005	Harold Pinter	10,000,000	1,276,000

Table A: Sample amounts illustrate the increased income of Nobel's estate

Since its inception and throughout its history, the Nobel Prize has offered the largest cash award of any literary prize. The established American literary prizes offer a small fraction of the Nobel payout: the PEN/Faulkner Award ($15,000), the National Book Award ($10,000), and the Pulitzer Prize ($10,000). In the British Isles, prize-winning authors do significantly better: the British Man Booker Prize pays £50,000 ($86,000), and the IMPAC Dublin Literary Award, a relative newcomer to the field, pays €100,000 ($118,500).

In addition to a check, the laureate receives a certificate and a gold medal bearing the portrait of Alfred Nobel. Since 1961 every winner has also been commemorated on a series of Swedish postage stamps. The Academy usually requires that the recipient attend the ceremony in Stockholm to receive the money prize (it will mail the gold medal and certificate) but has made allowances for illness. Although Shaw did not accept his prize in person, the Academy did agree to the playwright's request that the money be used to establish the Anglo-Swedish Literary Foundation to finance the publication of English translations of classic Swedish literature, particularly the works of Shaw's favorite Swedish author—and non–Nobel Prize winner—August Strindberg. A highly successful author at age sixty-nine, Shaw explained to the Nobel judges that "The money is a lifebelt thrown to a swimmer who has already reached the shore in safety!"

Global Scope. Most literary prizes are restricted to specific nationalities or languages. But Nobel's will directed that "no consideration whatever be paid to the nationality of the candidates." With its first selection, the Academy deliberately chose an author from a non-Scandinavian country (French poet Sully Prudhomme), so that the prize would not be perceived as a Scandinavian award. In 1913, Indian poet Rabindranath Tagore became the first non-European to win the prize (the first American did not win until seventeen years later, when Sinclair Lewis received the award). Although winners include authors from every continent other than Antarctica, 75 percent of laureates have been from Europe (13 percent from France). The United States has the second highest percentage of winners at 10 percent. Even when the Academy selects a non-European, the recipient often writes in a European language (Tagore translated his poems from his native Bengali into English). Four Africans have received the prize: Wole Soyinka (Nigeria, 1986), Naguib Mahfouz (Egypt, 1988), Nadine Gordimer (South Africa, 1991), and J. M. Coetzee (South Africa, 2003). But only one, Mahfouz, wrote in a language native to Africa—the other three composed in English. In recent decades the Academy has tried to broaden its scope to include non-European-language authors, such as Chinese novelist and playwright Gao Xingjian, who was selected in 2000.

Prestige by Association. In a commercial culture, some of the prestige of the prize obviously emanates from the amount of the monetary award, but the Nobel Prize in Literature achieves a great deal of cachet by its association with the other Nobel awards. Each December, the winner in Literature receives the award on the same stage as that year's winners in Medicine, Physics, Chemistry, Economics (added in 1969), and World Peace. Nobel's will characterizes these winners as having contributed "most materially to benefit mankind." Linking literature to the sciences and peace argues that the written word fulfills an ennobling good for humanity analogous to finding the cure for a disease or ending a war. It also argues for literature as civilization's most "beneficial" art form. The prize places a poet, playwright, or novelist on the same level as Albert Einstein and Martin Luther King Jr. The winner also shares in the glory of past recipients in Literature as the new member of an exclusive club of geniuses.

A Nobel Prize can do more than provide another award to an already recognized genius: its prestige and global notoriety can also revive the career of a neglected or forgotten author. For the rest of the recipient's life, the mention of his or her name is usually preceded by the phrase "Nobel Prize–winning author." The 1949 award to William Faulkner simultaneously resurrected and cemented the novelist's literary reputation. Although his work was popular in Europe—especially France—Faulkner's American reputation had waned, and many of his books had gone out of print. After his Nobel Prize, other awards followed. In 1951 he received the National Book Award (for *Collected Stories of William Faulkner,* 1950) and the French Legion of Honor. In 1955 he received the Pulitzer Prize (his first) and another National Book Award for his 1954 novel, *A Fable.*

How the Prize Is Administered

Nobel specifically charged the Swedish Academy in Stockholm to select the prize for literature. The Swedish Academy was founded on the model of the French Academy to work for the "purity, vigor, and majesty" of the Swedish language; their main purpose now is overseeing the Nobel process. It is made up of eighteen Swedish citizens who serve lifetime appointments and select their own successors, subject to approval by the king of Sweden. Members in 1900 were primarily minor academics and government officials. The current makeup includes more than eight authors as well as linguists, literary scholars, and historians. Once elected, a member may not resign, but may refuse to attend meetings or vote. One Academy member publicly "resigned" in protest over the 1983 award to British novelist William Golding. In 1989 two other members similarly withdrew in protest against the Academy's refusal to denounce Iran's call for the execution of British novelist Salman Rushdie.

The Swedish statutes that created the Nobel Foundation in 1900 instituted procedural guidelines for awarding the prizes. As per Nobel's will, the Swedish Academy awards the prize for literature defined as "not only belle-lettres, but also other writings which, by virtue of their form and style, possess literary value."

The public perceives the Nobel Prize in Literature as a lifetime achievement award for the author's career, but Nobel's will specifies that the recipient be the author of a "distinguished work" produced "during the year immediately preceding." The statute modifies Nobel's stipulation to include "older works only if their significance has not become apparent until recently." The Swedish Academy has largely ignored Nobel's directive to honor a single work produced in the preceding year throughout the history of the award. The Academy regularly singles out a specific book or work in its selection rationale even though the winning author may have written the "masterwork" many years previously. The Academy drew particular attention, for example, to Lewis's *Babbitt* (1922), to 1962 winner Steinbeck's *The Grapes of Wrath* (1939), to 1969 winner Samuel Beckett's *En attendant Godot* (1952; translated by Beckett as *Waiting for Godot*, 1954), and to 1999 winner Grass's *The Tin Drum* (1959) as the primary justification for their authors' recognition. In the presentation speech for 2005 winner Harold Pinter, the Academy mentioned only four plays: *The Dumb Waiter* (1957), *The Birthday Party* (1957), *The Hothouse* (1958), and *Mountain Language* (1988).

The Academy can suspend awarding the prize if no nominated author matches its criteria, but must name a winner at least every five years. (The Nobel Foundation suspended granting awards during parts of World Wars I and II). Each prize-giving academy must select a three- to five-member nominating committee of its own members, charged with making a final recommendation to its respective academy. The statutes leave up to each academy the criteria by which nominations are made. The committee's deliberations and reports are held confidential.

According to Swedish law, the right to nominate shall be enjoyed by:

1. Members of the Swedish Academy and of other academies, institutions and societies which are similar to it in construction and purpose;

2. Professors of literature and of linguistics at universities and university colleges;

3. Previous Nobel Prize Laureates in Literature;

4. Presidents of those societies of authors that are representative of the literary production in their respective countries.

Posthumous nominations are not allowed. The Academy receives an average of two hundred literary-prize nominations each year by the 1 February deadline. The Academy's Nobel committee makes a recommendation to the full Academy membership for an October vote. For most of the history of the prize, the committee made a single recommendation. Since the 1970s, every committee member prepares a report and advances a few candidates, allowing the Academy members a slightly larger choice than a single recommendation by the committee. By the end of May, the Academy has whittled down the committee's suggestions to five finalists, allowing the summer for members to review the candidates' work. To win, a nominee must receive more than half of the votes cast. Since the nominating committee filters proposals and makes recommendations to the Academy for approval, this small group has historically held considerable—some critics have charged disproportionate—power and influence.

A first-time nominee can no longer win the award, but rather must be the veteran of earlier nomination processes. The Academy instituted this convention after the controversial choice of American novelist Pearl S. Buck in 1938. She had been nominated in September of that year by senior Academy member Dr. Sven Hedin, who was the Academy's sole Asian authority (and whose American publisher was Buck's husband). Some critics believed that the full Academy did not take time to give her due consideration but selected her in deference to Hedin.

How the Prize Fails to Accomplish Its Purpose

The weakness of the selection process for the Nobel Prize in Literature lies in its reliance on the secretive committee structure of an eighteen-member national academy. Committees may be an effective method to select winners in the sciences, but the assessment of an aesthetic activity is inherently subjective. The Academy's insularity also limits the selection process. The philosophies and personal prejudices of the members unavoidably affect their decision. The two greatest Scandinavian writers of the late nineteenth century—Ibsen and Strindberg—were both denied membership and Nobel Prizes by the Academy. (Although Norwegian, Ibsen was eligible for membership in the

Swedish Academy until 1905, when Norway became independent from Sweden.)

A committee also breeds compromise. After European critics expressed outrage over the first two less-than-stellar laureates (Sully Prudhomme and German historian Theodor Mommsen), the Academy felt external pressure to honor Ibsen. But C. D. af Wirsén, the permanent secretary of the Academy and chairman of the nominating committee, forcefully opposed Ibsen's nomination as contrary to Nobel's intention to honor work of an "idealistic tendency." The culturally conservative Wirsén distrusted Ibsen's social criticism in such works as *Ghosts* (1881) and *An Enemy of the People* (1882). Despite the secretary's opposition, many members still wished to recognize the newly independent Norway and hoped to diffuse Wirsén's objections by pairing Ibsen with another Norwegian playwright, Bjørnstjerne Bjørnson. Wirsén dismissed the proposal as political grandstanding. Bjørnson received the award in 1903; Ibsen died in 1906.

Committees also like balance, or at the least, the appearance of fairness. Although the practice is never publicly admitted, most observers agree that the Academy makes a habit of granting awards in reference to who has won and not won previously. Individuals from the same country or who write in the same language rarely win in succession. The Academy will put off an author for later consideration "to spread the award around." Deserving authors often die before their turn comes. After Steinbeck won in 1962, O'Hara recognized he would never win the award because the Academy would not honor another American fiction writer within his lifetime. O'Hara died in 1970. The next American winner was Saul Bellow in 1976.

In direct conflict with Nobel's will, the Academy often honors an author's national heritage rather than the quality of his or her art. The list of prizewinners suggests an equitable veneer to selections in that every nationality or race will eventually get recognition, as if to answer the questions "When will it be Country X's turn?" or "When will we have a winner from Minority Y?" The Academy fulfills these socially conscious requirements with authors it regards as representative of their entire national or ethnic literature. In honoring Icelandic novelist Halldór Laxness–the first and only Icelander to receive the prize–the 1955 certificate praised him for renewing "the great narrative art of Iceland." Critics labeled the dual award to German poet Nelly Sachs and Israeli novelist Shmuel Yosef Agnon in 1966 as the "Jewish Award" (Polish-born Jewish American author Isaac Bashevis Singer won in 1978.) The Academy celebrated Agnon for taking his "motifs from the life of the Jewish people" and praised Sachs for interpreting "Israel's destiny with touching strength." In 1988 the Academy attempted cultural balance in selecting the Egyptian Mahfouz and lauding him for forming "an Arabian narrative art that applies to all mankind." He remains the only winner from the Arab world.

One aspect in which the Academy obviously has not exhibited balance is the genre in which an author writes. Almost two-thirds of the laureates have been primarily writers of narrative fiction, eclipsing poets and playwrights. Historians and philosophers rarely won in the first half-century of the prize; the last philosopher to win was Bertrand Russell (1950), and the last historian Sir Winston Churchill (1953). The reason for this dominance by fiction writers may be the result of the language barrier. The Academy considers the works of almost all of the nominees in translation. Although many members of the Academy surely read other languages, the availability of good Swedish translations is known to strengthen a nominee's chances. A novel is more easily appreciated in translation than the condensed imagery of poetry, and a high degree of theatrical sophistication is required to evaluate a play script properly. But even novelists can run into difficulty: one of the reasons given by Nobel historian Burton Feldman for the failure of American novelist Henry James to win in 1911 over Belgian playwright Maurice Maeterlinck is that his dense prose style did not translate well into Swedish.

The language barrier is also given as a reason for the dominance of European-language laureates over Asian and African authors. In defense of the apparent Eurocentrism in the history of the prize, Academy member Artur Lundkvist wrote an article titled "Nobelpris åt vem?" for *Svenska Dagbladet* (12 October 1977) in which he defined the award as a "Western institution" that "cannot reasonably be distributed on a basis other than Western evaluations." He derided the literary output of non-European nations and cultures:

> The academy is often reproached for thus neglecting the literatures of Asia and Africa and other "remote" parts. But I doubt if there is so far very much to find there. It is a question of literatures that (with certain exceptions, particularly in the case of Japan) as far as can be judged have not achieved that level of development (artistic, psychological, linguistic) that can make them truly significant outside their given context.

Lundkvist's controversial comments expose one of the major weaknesses of the prize: the Academy's small, homogenous membership makes its selections especially vulnerable to the personal prejudices of its members. Lundkvist (elected in 1968) boasted that Greene–a finalist in 1967–would never win the Nobel Prize while Lundkvist was an Academy member. (Despite Lundkvist's boast, an Academy member cannot veto a selection.) Lundkvist maintained that Greene was too well known and respected to need the award, as its purpose was to draw "attention to achievements that have not been sufficiently regarded and to a high degree deserve recognition." Greene never won the prize. Both Lundkvist and Greene died in 1991. A review of other winners during Lundkvist's tenure reveals his preference for Spanish-language authors. Lundkvist championed Chilean poet Pablo Neruda, who became the first South American winner in 1971; Lundkvist was his Swedish translator. Other Spanish-language laureates advocated by Lundkvist include Spanish poet Vicente Aleixandre (1977), Colombian novelist Gabriel García Márquez (1982), Spanish novelist Camilo José Cela (1989), and Mexican poet and critic Octavio Paz (1990).

Ten women have won the Nobel Prize in Literature. Only the Peace Prize has more female winners with eleven. Seven women have won for Physiology or Medicine, three for Chemistry, and two for Physics (the first woman to win a Nobel Prize in any field was Marie Curie for Physics in 1903). In 1909 Swedish novelist Selma Lagerlöf won the Nobel Prize in Literature, and her major distinction today is in being the first female winner in that category. In selecting female authors the Swedish Academy followed the same pattern it had with male writers: it first awarded the prize to a Scandinavian, then other Europeans before choosing an American. After Italian novelist Grazia Deledda won in 1926 and Norse novelist Sigrid Undset in 1928, Buck became the first American woman to win the literary prize in 1938. Her award generated much controversy, as many critics considered her novels and memoirs set in China as not worthy of worldwide recognition. Most Nobel observers expected Willa Cather to be the first female American winner. In 1945 Chilean poet Gabriela Mistral became the first Latin American author to receive the prize. The first South African author to be honored was novelist Gordimer in 1991. Between 1945 and 1991, the only other female winner was Sachs, who shared the 1966 prize with Agnon. In 1993, novelist Toni Morrison became the first and only African American Nobel laureate for literature. Two Eastern European women were honored in recent years: Polish poet Wisława Szymborska in 1996 and Austrian author Jelinek in 2004.

After the Peace Prize, the Nobel Prize in Literature is the award most tightly entangled with international controversy and geopolitical intrigue. As with any subjective award, the winners reflect the attitudes and anxieties of their age: Irish poet Yeats won in 1923, one year after his country became an independent nation, for his poetry that "gives expression to the spirit of a whole nation"; Finnish novelist Frans Eemil Sillanpää won in 1939 as his country resisted the encroachment of the Soviet Union; American Bellow won the same year as the United States celebrated its bicentennial; and Polish expatriate poet Czesław Miłosz won in 1980 as Polish workers struck against their Communist government.

When Steinbeck won in 1962, several observers—including Steinbeck—expressed dismay that he had won out over such eligible American authors as John Dos Passos, Frost, and Tennessee Williams. One Swedish source later reported that the Nobel judges regarded an award for the author of *The Grapes of Wrath* "at least in part, as a social gesture in support of the tormented South." The Swedish Academy had apparently conflated the Depression-era hardship of white migrant workers with the civil rights movement of the 1950s.

Award Trends

After the formation of the Nobel Foundation and the scheduling of awards, most European literary critics agreed that the first prize for literature should go to Russian novelist Tolstoy. His works were regarded as the greatest literary product of nineteenth-century Europe and as exhibiting the "idealistic tendency" that Nobel prescribed for his awards. Tolstoy's masterpieces *War and Peace* (1865–1869) and *Anna Karenina* (1875–1877) had appeared more than a quarter century earlier; in 1900 he was living as a rural religious extremist, publicly denouncing all government and church institutions as ungodly. Secretary Wirsén interpreted Nobel's injunction of "idealism" rigidly as a conformity to traditional forms of government, worship, and societal norms. He could not countenance the award going to someone he considered an anarchist. Academy apologists use the excuse that the Russian author was not properly nominated in the first year of balloting—a situation that was remedied by many non-Academy nominators the next year. But Tolstoy himself relieved the pressure on Wirsén by stating in a letter to supporters that he was glad not to receive the prize and thus could avoid the temptation of a cash award that could "bring nothing but evil."

No such international outcry erupted for the Academy's failure to recognize Twain. American literature was not yet considered—either by the Academy or other European nominating academies—within the scope of "distinguished work."

Wirsén's tenure (1901–1912) as the award's first custodian is noteworthy not so much for its winners as for its also-rans (Tolstoy, Ibsen, Strindberg, James). The one winner from this period who continues to enjoy popular acclaim is British author Kipling, the first English-language writer to receive the award. He represented the Victorian values Wirsén hoped to preserve. In his presentation address Wirsén praised Kipling as the heir to Alfred Tennyson and described the award as a national tribute to all English authors: "homage to the literature of England, so rich in manifold glories."

The Academy did not want to appear to be taking sides among the combatants of World War I by honoring authors with high political or nationalistic profiles. This "neutrality" accounts for the Scandinavian awards during this period: Sweden, 1916; Denmark, 1917; Sweden, 1920.

The first indication that the Academy was addressing the relevant modern literature of its day is the 1923 award to Yeats. Yet, the Academy's tribute does not celebrate Yeats as a modernist but rather for his "fairy poetry" of twenty years previous. A future Nobel laureate, the then-unknown Hemingway, used the occasion of Yeats's award to criticize the Academy for its omissions. In an article written from Paris for the *Toronto Star Weekly* Hemingway praises Yeats as the greatest living English-language poet with the possible exception of Ezra Pound. Hemingway does not advance any other American as a contender, announcing that Sherwood Anderson "was headed in that direction, but he has swerved a long way off now." He champions English novelist Thomas Hardy (who was a finalist against Yeats) as the "ghost that must haunt the Nobel Prize-givers' consciences." He also advocates Polish-born English novelist Joseph Conrad as a much more fitting recipient of the prize than the 1905 winner Henryk Sienkiewicz, the Polish author of *Quo Vadis* (1895).

Unlike Yeats, who won his award for his early writings, Shaw (a nominee for several years) finally secured his prize with a recent work. His pre–World War I plays are filled with cynical observations about human nature, ideas that the conservative Academy usually did not celebrate. In *Major Barbara* (1905) Shaw depicts an Alfred Nobel–like munitions millionaire who expresses a revolutionary Machiavellian-Socialist philosophy. But the Academy rested its rationale for Shaw's award on his play *Saint Joan* (1923) as excusing the author's suspect and nonidealistic politics. In his presentation speech, secretary Per Hallström explained: "If from this point we look back on Shaw's best works, we find it easier in many places, beneath all his sportiveness and defiance, to discern something of the same idealism that has found expression in the heroic figure of Saint Joan."

Many observers speculated about who would be the first American author to win the prize. By 1930 several critics believed the United States's "turn" had come. Dreiser campaigned for the award as early as 1911 and lobbied for the support of critic H. L. Mencken. In 1926, a year after he published his naturalistic masterwork *An American Tragedy,* Dreiser toured Sweden to discuss translations of his works with publishers, believing they had influence on Academy members. Dreiser's main rival was Lewis, who won primarily because his novels—eleven were in Swedish translation in 1930—were best-sellers in Scandinavia, whereas Dreiser's were not. Neither author was considered by the Academy for his celebration of native values or the national character (unlike Kipling or Yeats) but rather for his harsh criticism of American life. As with other "first" winners, the Academy praised Lewis as a representative of his country:

> Yes, Sinclair Lewis is an American. He writes the new language—American—as one of the representatives of 120,000,000 souls. He asks us to consider that this nation is not yet finished or melted down; that it is still in the turbulent years of adolescence. The new great American literature has started with national self-criticism. It is a sign of health.

In his acceptance speech, Lewis offered the Swedish audience a primer on contemporary American literature, championing such authors as Anderson, Cather, O'Neill, Thornton Wilder, Hemingway, Dos Passos, Thomas Wolfe, and Faulkner. Three of the authors on his list eventually won the Nobel Prize. Although Lewis admitted that Dreiser was not a popular author because of his despairing characters and "cumbersome" style, he praised his rival as his greatest literary mentor: "Now to me, as to many other American writers, Dreiser more than any other man, marching alone, usually unappreciated, often hated, has cleared the trail from Victorian and Howellsian timidity and gentility in American fiction to honesty and boldness and passion of life."

In the post–World War II period of the Nobel Prize, the Academy tried to make up for past omissions. It recognized three masters of modernism well past the peak of their careers: American/British poet Eliot (1948) and American novelists Faulkner (1949) and Hemingway (1954). The major modernist author that the Academy deliberately chose not to honor belatedly was American poet—and fascist—Pound.

During the 1950s the Academy engaged in its own version of the Cold War politics, alternating awards between left- and right-wing authors. Many observers criticized the selection of Churchill in 1953 as a blatantly political award, a concession for not having awarded him the Nobel Peace Prize earlier. In a 12 May 1955 letter to critic and fellow Academy member Sten Selander, Swedish diplomat Dag Hammarskjöld questioned whether such an award made the Swedish Academy "a literature committee in the Foreign Office?"

While the judges did sometimes select a politically conservative author such as Churchill, they apparently could not abide any candidate with a connection to prewar fascism. When Pound was considered for an award in the 1950s, he would have been an extremely controversial choice. The poet was then committed to an insane asylum instead of prison for his treasonable acts as a supporter of Benito Mussolini in World War II. Hammarskjöld worked for Pound's release but did not advocate awarding him the Nobel Prize. In a 24 July 1959 letter to fellow Academy member Pär Lagerkvist, Hammarskjöld argued that an award to Pound should be denied because the author's anti-Semitism "ought to exclude the possibility of a prize that is after all intended to lay weight on the 'idealistic tendency' of the recipient's efforts. I do not know exactly what the words 'idealistic tendency' mean, but at least I do know what is diametrically opposed to what they can reasonably be assumed to signify."

The Academy also denied Argentine author Jorge Luis Borges the prize, allegedly for being photographed shaking the hand of Chilean dictator General Augusto Pinochet. Lundkvist blocked Borges's nomination because, he argued in an interview with Karl Vennberg in *Svenska Dagbladet* (20 December 1979), "When it comes to his political blunders, this time in a fascist direction, these make him in my opinion unsuitable on ethical and human grounds for a Nobel Prize."

But the Academy held no such qualms in recognizing former Communist or pro-Stalinist authors. The Soviet Union created the Stalin Peace Prize (renamed the Lenin Peace Prize in 1956) in 1949 as a counterpart to the Nobel Prize. It was awarded by a government-appointed committee to individuals who had "strengthened peace among peoples." The first recipient was Laxness, six years before he won the Nobel Prize. Neruda received this prize in 1953, effusively praising Joseph Stalin the following year as "the high noon, the fulfillment of men and peoples." Academy member Gunnar Ekelöf suspected Neruda, a former Chilean diplomat assigned to Mexico, of complicity in the 1940 assassination of Russian exile Leon Trotsky. Ekelöf successfully blocked Neruda's candidacy for a Nobel Prize until Ekelöf's death in 1968. His membership passed to Lundkvist, and Neruda won three years later. In his 1963 *Memoirs* Neruda renounced his Stalinism, but he wrote the poems praised by the Nobel committee during his period of Stalinist devotion.

The most public Cold War skirmish associated with the Nobel Prize in Literature occurred in 1964, when the Academy selected French author and celebrated leftist Jean-Paul Sartre, who refused the award—and the money—claiming that the prize was anti-Soviet and "an honor restricted to Western writers and Eastern rebels." The "Eastern rebel" to which Sartre referred may have been 1958 laureate Boris Pasternak, author of *Doctor Zhivago* (1957), an historical novel of the Russian Revolution. His selection angered Soviet authorities, who refused to allow the author to travel to Stockholm for his award. In 1965, the year after the Academy members chose Sartre—and perhaps in answer to his charge—they selected Russian novelist and suspected plagiarist Mikhail Sholokhov, who was openly supportive of the Soviet regime. The Kremlin allowed Sholokhov to accept his prize. Guatemalan novelist Miguel Ángel Asturias received the Lenin Peace Prize in 1965, the year before he received his Nobel award.

Once the Cold War culture wars subsided, the Academy began to make less overtly political choices. Exasperated by the celebrity selections of Hemingway and Churchill, Hammarskjöld wrote to Selander in the mid 1950s, "Oh—if only we could show a touch of daring." The 1969 selection of Beckett, best known for the absurdist play *Waiting for Godot,* quashed the assumption that laureates must express an idealistic outlook for the human race. Since then the Academy has cast its favor far afield from its Eurocentric background, particularly toward Latin American authors, though they usually compose in a European language. Perhaps the most unconventional choice came in 1997 with the selection of Italian postmodern comedian Dario Fo. His acceptance lecture—"Against Jesters Who Defame and Insult"—was a free-form improvisation combining text, illustrations, and theatrical performance. Charlie Chaplin had been nominated several years previous, but his candidacy was dismissed by the committee because his movie scripts were not published texts.

The Also-Rans

Why Russian American novelist Nabokov never won remains a mystery. Fellow Russian émigré and Nobel laureate Aleksandr Solzhenitsyn was known to have nominated him. Perhaps, like the Polish-born English-language author Conrad, he defied easy categorization; Nabokov wrote in three languages. But most critics agree that the most glaring omission from the list of laureates is Joyce. The reasons for his failure to win the award are not clear.

YEAR	WINNER	ALSO NOMINATED
1902	Theodor Mommsen	Leo Tolstoy
1903	Bjørnstjerne Bjørnson	Henrik Ibsen
1906	Giosuè Carducci	Mark Twain, Rainer Maria Rilke
1908	Rudolf Eucken	Algernon Swinburne
1911	Maurice Maeterlinck	Henry James
1923	William Butler Yeats	Thomas Hardy
1930	Sinclair Lewis	Theodore Dreiser
1936	Eugene O'Neill	Sigmund Freud
1938	Pearl S. Buck	Margaret Mitchell
1944	Johannes V. Jensen	Willa Cather, W. Somerset Maugham
1954	Ernest Hemingway	Robert Frost
1955	Halldór Laxness	Tennessee Williams
1967	Miguel Ángel Asturias	Graham Greene
1968	Yasunari Kawabata	Yukio Mishima, Mao Tse Tung
1969	Samuel Beckett	Eugene Ionesco
1973	Patrick White	Vladimir Nabokov

Table B: Noteworthy nominees who were passed over for the Nobel Prize in Literature

The Academy's claim that he was never nominated is not credible. Joyce achieved a high international reputation during his lifetime—*Ulysses* was published in 1922. Since Joyce died in 1941, he did not survive to the Academy's postwar period of reprieve for previously unrecognized modernist writers. Before 1940 the only modernists the judges embraced were dramatists (the Italian Luigi Pirandello in 1934 and the American O'Neill in 1936). Desmond Fitzgerald, a minister of the newly independent Ireland, wrote to Joyce in 1923 proposing to nominate him for a Nobel Prize. Joyce replied that not only would he not win, but such a public nomination would probably result in Fitzgerald's being removed from office. In 1946, Academy member—and Buck proponent—Hedin was asked if Joyce had ever been considered for the prize. He responded "Joyce? Who is he?"

The difficulty encountered with Williams's nomination in 1955 is instructive both for its revelation of the role that marketing and self-promotion play in the selection process, and as a cautionary tale for future nominees. Only one American dramatist had won the prize previously, and the atmosphere seemed promising for Williams. His dramas of poetic realism had received international productions and were acclaimed in Sweden. O'Neill's tragedies (heavily influenced by Strindberg) had achieved similar Scandinavian success. Williams's chances appeared strong until a public-relations fiasco played out on the Academy's doorstep. Lilla van Saher—an ambitious Hungarian émigré labeled a dominatrix by Williams—had persuaded the playwright to come to the Swedish capital and court the local press. In a 1981 interview in *Paris Review*, Williams described the disastrous press conference:

> Well, she had all the press there. She was like a field marshal! "You over that way! You over there! You do not approach Mr. Williams until I give you the signal!" Barking out orders. Oh, it was just terrifying. The next morning the newspapers all came out saying Mr. Williams arrived in Stockholm preceded by a very powerful press agent! And my agent . . . said, "You know, you've been nominated for the Nobel Prize but now it's finished."

For a list of other nominees who did not win, see Table B.

Prospects

A cynic might look for the next winner to come from a previously unrecognized country or ethnicity. Guessing who the Academy will select becomes an annual October literary parlor game. The Academy still may not have recovered from the public-relations disaster of 1974 to select another Swedish author. In that year novelist Eyvind Johnson and poet/novelist Harry

Martinson—both members of the Swedish Academy—shared the prize, winning over finalists Greene and Nabokov.

But who deserves to win? If the Academy does indeed believe in the geographic "sharing" of the prize, then American dramatists deserve their "turn." A North American playwright has not won in almost seventy years. Americans August Wilson (who died in October 2005 on the eve of the prize announcement) and Edward Albee have both generated groundbreaking and influential work for decades. If the Academy believes in a genre balance, then dramatists merit even greater recognition; among the 101 Nobel laureates in Literature to 2004, only 10 have been playwrights. In 2005 the Academy increased that number to 11 when it chose British playwright Pinter. His selection, like Hemingway's and Eliot's, honors the author's past achievements and innovations rather than recent creations. In the 1960s and 1970s Pinter was a major force in world drama, but he has not enjoyed a large success in more than two decades. His political activism since the 1990s against American foreign policy may also have increased his chances among politically liberal Academy members.

A committee, particularly a small one, always dislikes the obvious selection because it diminishes its power. The Swedish Academy will probably continue to make surprising, unexpected (even unwarranted) choices.

Sources

Arthur, Anthony. *Literary Feuds: A Century of Celebrated Quarrels—From Mark Twain to Tom Wolfe*. New York: St. Martin's Press, 2002.

Devlin, Albert J., ed. *Conversations with Tennessee Williams*. Jackson & London: University Press of Mississippi, 1986, pp. 325–360.

Espmark, Kjell. *The Nobel Prize in Literature: A Study of the Criteria Behind the Choices*. Boston: G. K. Hall, 1986.

Feldman, Burton. *The Nobel Prize: A History of Genius, Controversy and Prestige*. New York: Arcade, 2000.

Hemingway, Ernest. "'Nobelman' Yeats," in his *Dateline: Toronto / The Complete* Toronto Star *Dispatches, 1920–1924*. Ed. William White. New York: Scribners, 1985, pp. 384–386.

The Nobel Foundation and Wilhelm Odelberg, eds. *Nobel: The Man and His Prizes*. Third edition. New York: American Elsevier, 1972.

Wallace, Irving. "The Nobel Prize Awards: Literature," in *The People's Almanac*. Garden City, N.Y.: Doubleday, 1975, pp. 1098–1105.

Acknowledgments

This book was produced by Bruccoli Clark Layman, Inc. Tracy Simmons Bitonti was the in-house editor.

Production manager is Philip B. Dematteis.

Administrative support was provided by Carol A. Cheschi.

Accountant is Ann-Marie Holland.

Copyediting supervisor is Sally R. Evans. The copyediting staff includes Phyllis A. Avant, Caryl Brown, Melissa D. Hinton, Philip I. Jones, Rebecca Mayo, and Nancy E. Smith.

Pipeline manager is James F. Tidd Jr.

Editorial associates are Elizabeth Leverton, Dickson Monk, and Timothy C. Simmons.

In-house vetter is Catherine M. Polit.

Permissions editor is Amber L. Coker. Permissions assistant is Crystal A. Gleim.

Layout and graphics staff includes Zoe R. Cook and Janet E. Hill.

Office manager is Kathy Lawler Merlette.

Photography editor is Mark J. McEwan.

Digital photographic copy work was performed by Joseph M. Bruccoli.

Systems manager is Donald Kevin Starling.

Typesetting supervisor is Kathleen M. Flanagan. The typesetting staff includes Patricia Marie Flanagan and Pamela D. Norton.

Library research was facilitated by the following librarians at the Thomas Cooper Library of the University of South Carolina: Elizabeth Suddeth and the rare-book department; Jo Cottingham, interlibrary loan department; circulation department head Tucker Taylor; reference department head Virginia W. Weathers; reference department staff Laurel Baker, Marilee Birchfield, Kate Boyd, Paul Cammarata, Joshua Garris, Gary Geer, Tom Marcil, Rose Marshall, and Sharon Verba; interlibrary loan department head Marna Hostetler; and interlibrary loan staff Bill Fetty and Nelson Rivera.

Dictionary of Literary Biography® • Volume Three Hundred Twenty-Nine

Nobel Prize Laureates in Literature, Part 1: Agnon–Eucken

Dictionary of Literary Biography

Shmuel Yosef Agnon
(8 August 1887 – 17 February 1970)

Dvir Abramovich
University of Melbourne

BOOKS: *Ve-Hayah he-'Akov le-Mishor* (Jerusalem: Y. H. Brener, 1912; Berlin: Jüdischer, 1919);

Giv 'at ha-Hol (Berlin: Jüdischer, 1919);

Be-Sod Yesharim (Berlin: Jüdischer, 1921);

Sipur Me-Hamat ha-Metsik (Berlin: Jüdischer, 1921);

'Al kapot ha-man'ul: Sipure ahavim (Berlin: Jüdischer, 1922);

Die Erzälung vom Toraschreiber (Berlin: Marx, 1923); original Hebrew version published as *Agadat ha-sofer* (Tel Aviv: Omanut, 1929);

Der Verstossene (Berlin: Jüdischer, 1923);

Polin (Tel Aviv: Hedim, 1924);

Ma'aseh ha-meshulah me-erets ha-Kedoshah (Tel Aviv: Kupat Ha-sefer, 1924);

Ma'aseh rabi Gadiel ha-Tinok (Berlin: Jüdischer, 1925);

Tsipori (Tel Aviv: Devir, 1926);

Sipur ha-Shanim ha-Tovot / Ma'aseh ha-Rav Veha-Orah (Tel Aviv, 1927);

Kol Sipurav shel Shmuel Yosef Agnon, volumes 1–6 (Berlin: Schocken, 1931–1935); volumes 7–11 (Jerusalem: Schocken, 1939–1952)—comprises volumes 1–2, *Hakhnasat Kalah* (1931), translated by Israel Meir Lask as *The Bridal Canopy* (Garden City, N.Y.: Doubleday, Doran, 1937); volume 3, *Me'az U-Me'atah* (1931); volume 4, *Sipure Ahavim* (1931); volume 5, *Sipur Pashut* (1935), translated by Hillel Halkin as *A Simple Story* (New York: Schocken, 1985); volume 6, *Be-shuvah va-nahat* (1935); volume 7, *Oreah natah la-lun* (1939), translated by Misha Louvish as *A Guest for the Night* (New York: Schocken, 1968; London: Gollancz, 1968); volume 8, *Elu Ve-Elu* (1941), selection translated by J. Weinberg and H. Russell as *A Dwelling Place of My People: Sixteen Stories of the Chassidim* (Edinburgh: Scottish Academic Press, 1983); volume 9, *Temol Shilshom* (1945), translated by Barbara Harshav as

Shmuel Yosef Agnon in London a few days after receiving the Nobel Prize in Literature, December 1966 (AP World Wide)

Only Yesterday (Princeton, N.J.: Princeton University Press, 2000); volume 10, *Samukh Ve-Nir'eh* (1950); and volume 11, *'Ad henah* (1952);

Bi-levav Yamim (Berlin: Schocken, 1935); translated by Lask as *In the Heart of the Seas: A Story of a Journey to the Land of Israel* (New York: Schocken, 1948);

Kovets Sipurim (Tel Aviv: Keren Yisra'el Mets, 1937);

Mi-dirah le-dirah (Jerusalem: Schocken, 1939);

Pi Shenaim o me-Husar Yom (Tel Aviv, 1939);

Sefer Ha-Ma'asim (Jerusalem: Schocken, 1941);

Shevu'ath Emunim (Jerusalem: Schocken, 1943); translated by Walter Lever as "Betrothed," in *Betrothed, & Edo and Enam: Two Tales* (New York: Schocken, 1966; London: Gollancz, 1966);

'Al Berl Katsenelson (Tel Aviv: Schocken, 1944);

Sipurim ve-agadot (Tel Aviv: Schocken, 1944);

Kelev Hutsot (Merhavyah: Sifriyat Po'alim, 1950);

Kol Sipurav shel Shmuel Yosef Agnon, 8 volumes (Jerusalem: Schocken, 1953–1962)—comprises volume 1, *Hakhnasat Kalah* (1953); volume 2, *Elu Ve-Elu* (1953); volume 3, *'Al kapot ha-man'ul* (1953); volume 4, *Oreah natah la-lun* (1953); volume 5, *Temol Shilshom* (1953); volume 6, *Samukh Ve-Nir'eh* (1953); volume 7, *'Ad henah* (1953); and volume 8, *Ha-Esh ve-Ha'etsim* (1962);

'Ad olam (Jerusalem: Schocken, 1954); translated as *Forever More* (New York: Schocken, 1961);

Tehilla, and Other Israeli Tales, by Agnon and others, translated by Lask and others (London & New York: Abelard-Schuman, 1956);

Pen-ishom ha-mavet (Tel Aviv, 1960);

Shene Talmide hakhamim she-hayu be'irenu. Agadat ha-sofer, edited by Naftali Ginaton (Jerusalem: Schocken, 1967);

Sipure Yom ha-Kipurim, edited by Ginaton (Jerusalem: Schocken, 1967);

Sipurim: Yalkut le-vet ha-sefer ha-yesodi, edited by Ginaton (Jerusalem: Schocken, 1967);

Selected Stories of S. Y. Agnon [text in Hebrew, commentary in English], edited by Samuel Leiter (New York: Tarbuth Foundation, 1970);

Shirah, edited by Emunah Yaron (Jerusalem: Schocken, 1971; expanded edition, 1974; expanded edition, 1978); translated by Zeva Shapiro as *Shira* (New York: Schocken, 1989);

Ir u-Melo'ah (Jerusalem: Schocken, 1973);

Be-Hanuto shel Mar Lublin (Jerusalem: Schocken, 1974);

Lifnim Min Ha-Homah (Jerusalem: Schocken, 1975);

Me-'atsmi el 'atsmi (Jerusalem: Schocken, 1976);

Yidishe verk, edited by Dov Sadan (Jerusalem: The Yiddish Department, Hebrew University/The Council for Jewish Culture in Israel, 1977);

Pithe devarim (Jerusalem: Schocken, 1977);

Mivhar Sipurim, edited by Ginaton and Zvi Massad (Jerusalem: Schocken, 1978);

Korot Batenu (Jerusalem: Schocken, 1979);

Sefer Ha-Otiyot (Jerusalem: Schocken, 1983); bilingual edition translated by Robert Friend as *Agnon's Alef bet: Poems* (Philadelphia: Jewish Publication Society, 1998);

Takhrikh shel Sipurim, compiled by Yaron (Jerusalem: Schocken, 1984);

Bi-demi Yameha: Ve-'od Sipurim (Jerusalem: Schocken, 1991);

Kol Sipurav shel Sh. Y. Agnon, 9 volumes (Jerusalem: Schocken, 1998–).

Editions in English: *Twenty-One Stories*, edited by Nahum Norbert Glatzer (New York: Schocken, 1970; London: Gollancz, 1970);

A Book That Was Lost and Other Stories, edited by Alan L. Mintz and Anne Golomb Hoffman (New York: Schocken, 1995);

Yafo Yefat Yamim: Leket mi-tokh Sipurav shel Sh. Y. Agnon / Jaffa, Belle of the Seas: Selections from the Works of S. Y. Agnon [bilingual edition], selected by David Sharir, translated by Barbara Harshav (Jerusalem: Schocken, 1998).

OTHER: *Das Buch von den polnischen Juden*, edited by Agnon and Ahron Eliasberg (Berlin: Jüdischer, 1916);

Moaus Zur: Ein Chanukkahbuch, edited by Agnon (Berlin: Jüdischer, 1918);

Sefer, sofer, ve-sipur: Sipurim 'al sofrim ve-'al sefarim, edited by Agnon (Jerusalem, 1938; expanded, Jerusalem: Schocken, 1978); selections published as *Sifrehem shel Tsadikim* (Jerusalem: Schocken, 1961);

Yamim Nora'im, edited by Agnon (Jerusalem: Schocken, 1938);

Atem re'item, edited by Agnon (Jerusalem: Schocken, 1959); translated by Michael Swirsky as *Present at Sinai: The Giving of the Law* (Philadelphia: Jewish Publication Society, 1994).

Shmuel Yosef Agnon is one of the greatest modern Hebrew writers and an important prose writer of the twentieth century. Critics have described his achievements as singular and his art as universal. Dedicating himself to his craft, the self-effacing writer raised Hebrew literature to a global plane, blending authentic Jewish heritage with European sources to present instructive tales that posit a moral and legal conundrum reflective of the modern condition. He was a 1966 recipient (sharing the honor with Nelly Sachs) of the Nobel Prize in Literature, the first granted to a Hebrew writer. His contribution to the Jewish state is manifested elsewhere than just in the literary realm. Annually, on Yom Kippur, the holiest day in Judaism, hundreds of thousands of synagogue congregants cite the Prayer for the Welfare of the State of Israel, written in 1948 by Agnon together with Chief Rabbis Yitzhak Herzog and Ben Zion Uziel.

Agnon has been feted as one whose standing is akin to that of William Shakespeare in England; he has been memorialized on the fifty-shekel note as well as on the first commemorative banknote to celebrate Israel's fiftieth anniversary of independence. A Tel Aviv street bears his name, and on the occasion of the hundredth anniversary of his birth, the Israeli Parliament convened a special session to honor the wordsmith. In 2002, when the National Yiddish Book Centre listed their one hundred greatest works of modern Jewish literature, Agnon's three novels occupied the fourth, fifth, and sixth places. In addition, his novels and stories appear frequently as compulsory reading in Israeli schools.

Yet, outside Israel, Agnon is virtually unknown. This obscurity is principally because of the formidable difficulties involved with translating his idiosyncratic and allusive Hebrew, which is bristling with wordplays and acrostics and interlarded with quotations, echoes, and references from a vast array of biblical sources. One of his translators, Hillel Halkin, remarked in a 1989 article by Matt Nesvisky that Agnon "was in a class by himself . . . there's so much going on in his language. To impersonate Agnon in English, a translator has to exercise his ingenuity to the utmost." The difficulty of getting across in English the full flavor and profundity of the Agnon prose may be one reason why the broad, lasting international appreciation accorded to other modernist giants has not been forthcoming, despite the Nobel Prize. Sharon Green notes also that Agnon's virtuosity lay in his ability to "hold in creative tension the Jewish religious tradition and the secular modern world, both of which he shows to be needed for Jews to thrive," and that "The dialectical tension in his work is probably the reason why many readers find his works enigmatic." Moreover, his highly allusive style, subtle turns of thought, and purposeful ambiguity pose an intimidating challenge to the reader.

More than anyone else, Agnon advanced the idea of creating not only a new literature in Hebrew, but a new culture composed of a synthesis of Eastern European traditions and modern Israeli norms. Agnon was an interpreter of Jewish life, serving as a cultural conduit between the subjective experiences of Eastern European Jewry and its historical national memory. He chronicled both the disappearing world of European orthodox Jewry and the emerging milieu of the Zionist pioneers, the majority of whom were revolting against the long-established tenets of that orthodoxy. Green maintains that the "uniqueness of Agnon is that he was able to capture the richness of traditional life, while at the same time he was absolutely clear sighted about the dangers such a life holds for Jewish survival in modern times."

Sources usually give Agnon's birth date as 17 July or 26 July 1888, but biographer Dan Laor puts the date at 8 August 1887. Agnon was born Shmuel Yosef Halevi Czaczkes in the Jewish town of Buczacz in eastern Galicia, then part of Austria-Hungary (now Buchach, Ukraine), although in his Nobel acceptance speech he noted that he regarded himself as "one who was born in Jerusalem." He was born to a middle-class family of rabbis and scholars; his father, Shalom Mordechai Halevi, a qualified rabbi, worked as a fur merchant and was a fervent and educated disciple of the Hasidic rebbe of Chortov. His presence was deeply influential on the boy: "All I know," Agnon maintained (according to biographer Laor), "I learned from my father." In his address at the state banquet delivered in honor of the Nobel laureates, Agnon revealed that he composed his first poem at age five out of longing for his father, who was often away. His father, together with a local rabbi, taught the boy Talmud as well as the teachings of the Jewish philosopher Maimonides. From his mother, Esther Farb, whose family belonged to the stream of Mitnagdim (a Jewish movement whose strict rationalism stood in sharp contrast to the emotive mysticism of the Hasidim), he acquired a knowledge of German literature. Agnon's drama is a blend of these divergent views.

While the shtetl was the universe of his childhood, where he was immersed in religious education, his work was shaped by the clashing forces of a transitional world. The period of Agnon's youth was a time of turmoil, when the pogroms in Russia following the assassination of Czar Alexander II in 1881 wreaked havoc on the Jews. Consequently, a considerable flow of Jews poured out westward to Europe, with a smaller stream choosing Palestine as their destination.

He decided to become a writer when he was eight and published his first poem in Yiddish when he was fifteen. Over the next three years (1903–1906) he produced about seventy literary works in Hebrew and Yiddish that were published in Galicia in journals such as *Hamitzpeh* and *Hayarden* (in 1977, the Hebrew University published the collection of stories and poems he composed in Yiddish during those years). In 1907, at age nineteen, he left the shtetl and came to Palestine as part of the great wave of emigration (known as the second Aliyah) and settled in Jaffa and Jerusalem. There, the budding writer served as the first secretary of the Jewish Court in Jaffa and was confronted with the contradictory confluence of Judaic tradition, the cosmopolitan Western culture of the twentieth century, and modern Hebrew literature. Temporarily jettisoning his religious habits during his first stay in Palestine, he published his first story, "Agunot" (Forsaken Wives), in 1908 in the journal *Ha-Omer*. Concerning star-crossed couples in Jerusalem, the tale displays the style of writing seen in the author's later work. The story not only enhanced his nascent reputation but also gave him his pseudonym, which he adopted as his official family name in 1924: Agnon is taken from *agunot,* a term applied to women who have been abandoned by their husbands and are left in a state of limbo since they cannot remarry.

Critics have suggested that the name "Agnon" is aimed at braiding the author's destiny to that of the Jewish people. Agnon perceived himself as trapped in a similar situation as the abandoned women—caught between different universes but belonging to neither, a fractured position dramatized in his writing. Baruch Hochman says that it is no accident that Agnon appropriated that name:

> The very word is redolent of loss, but also of the infinite yearning and ineffable tenderness elicited by loss. All of Agnon's work was to pivot on such feeling. First there was the sort of loss rendered in this tale: of loved ones torn away in the midst of life, by chance, by fate, by death or desire. Then there was historical loss: the submergence of the world of origins to which one's feelings are bound, in the abyss of history. Finally, there was metaphysical loss: of transcendental objects of desire in the bewilderment of modernity.

Ruth Wisse proffers another reading: "The adoption of the Hebrew name suggests that the writer will always remain within the bounds of tradition but without full security, like that afforded a wedded spouse."

Agnon repeatedly tied parts of his autobiography to the annals of Jewish history. For example, he liked to claim (inaccurately) that he was born on the Ninth of Av, the momentous date that marks the destruction of the two Jewish temples, as well as the supposed time when the future messiah will be born. Additionally, he connected the two occasions his house was wrecked (in 1924 by fire, and in 1929 by rioters) to the obliteration of the two temples. Similarly, in his fiction, one can discern semi-autobiographical aspects. Buczacz, his childhood town, serves as the backdrop in several stories, appearing under the fictional name of Szybuzs, which translates as "error" in Hebrew. Szybuzs functions as the all-purpose metaphor for the fading mythical space the shtetl once occupied in the diaspora.

In 1912 Agnon published his first novella, *Ve-Hayah he-'Akov le-Mishor* (And the Crooked Shall Be Made Straight), with the support of his friend, the writer Yosef Haim Brenner. The work was noticed by several literary specialists, and the aspiring writer was urged by Arthur Rupin, a major figure in the Zionist movement, to broaden his horizons in Berlin. In 1913 Agnon traveled to Germany, where for the next eleven years he gained a reputation as a litterateur, mainly because of his mastery of the German language and the impressive fiction he began publishing in Berlin. During his sojourn in Berlin, he served as a research assistant to academics, gave Hebrew lessons, and worked for a publisher of Jewish-themed books, all the while attending lectures on philosophy and the social sciences.

During these restless years, living also in Munich, Leipzig, and Wiesbaden, he helped found the journal *Der Jude* (The Jew) and edited the *Juedischer Verlag* (Jewish Publisher). Embraced by the Jewish intelligentsia, in 1913, while in Berlin, Agnon met Shlomo Zalman Schocken, a self-made businessman and philanthropist who became an admirer of the young man and consequently financed the publication of his books. Schocken's extraordinary support (in the form of a writing stipend) permitted Agnon to live free from financial worries and to concentrate comfortably on writing. Schocken Publishing, which still publishes Agnon's work, relocated to Tel Aviv in the 1930s after the Nazis closed it down, and later the firm opened an office in New York. Schocken, together with Gershom Gustav Schocken, the editor of the Israeli daily *Ha'aretz* (owned by the Schocken family), organized the lobby that eventually led to the awarding of the Nobel.

When in the summer of 1916 Agnon was summoned for a medical checkup in anticipation of conscription into the Austrian army, he was horrified by the possibility of military service. He ingested a large number of pills and chain-smoked in an effort to make himself sick enough to avoid the draft. Dismissed by the medical board, he nevertheless was required to stay in the hospital for several months afterward.

In 1920 Agnon met and married Esther Marx, the feisty daughter of a well-to-do orthodox family that initially opposed the union, believing she was marrying a man below her status. The couple, who were married for fifty years (until Agnon's death), had a son and a daughter, both born in Germany. In 1983 Agnon's daughter, Emunah Yaron, gathered and edited letters that Agnon and his wife exchanged. The book, *Esterlain Yekirati* (Darling Esther), is a cornucopia of intimate details, shining a new light on the political situation in Jerusalem as well as Agnon's longing for his wife and affection for his two children. The letters are written in the same lyrical prose one finds in Agnon's stories.

Although he had begun writing in Yiddish as a child, Agnon chose to write his major works in Hebrew, the ancient holy tongue that had been moribund for hundreds of years until revived and turned into a reemerging language by Eliezer Ben Yehuda at the end of the nineteenth century and the beginning of the twentieth century. In a 1995 *Buffalo News* article, Mark Shechner observes that to write in Hebrew in 1908 was "to draw one's language and frame of reference from traditional liturgy and to envision a future based on sacred time and space in which Judaism would not be simply preserved but renewed and transformed." Unlike other pioneers of secular fiction, such as I. L. Peretz, Isaac Bashevis Singer, Sholem Aleichem, and Isaac Babel, who turned to Yiddish, Russian, and German, Agnon elected for Hebrew because he wanted to write for a future nation that would be located in Eretz Israel (The Land of Israel) rather than in Europe or the United States. Agnon had been an ardent Zionist since he was seventeen, and championing Hebrew as the modern language of his writing corresponded to the philosophical tenets of Zionism and enlightenment, two movements that promoted Hebrew as the language of emancipation and argued for Western modernization as the road to rebuilding the Jewish nation.

Submerged in biblical and talmudic teachings, Agnon filled his works with pious folktales, Hasidic-like parables, Gothic romances, and stream-of-consciousness plots—reminiscent of European literature in the manner of Jorge Luis Borges and Bruno Schulz—that underscore the sufferings and history of the Jewish people. As a host of theorists have observed, Agnon's whole output is crossed with references to Scandinavian, Russian, and French literature, pointing to the fact that he read widely and was conversant with European novelists such as Gustave Flaubert (whose virtues he exalted in correspondence), Miguel de Cervantes, Schulz, and Stefan Zweig. Yet, Agnon insisted in his Nobel acceptance speech that he was influenced primarily by "the Bible, Mishna, Talmud, Midrash and Rashi's commentary on the Bible," the next influences being "the medieval halachic commentators, Hebrew poets and philosophers led by Maimonides." Certainly, Agnon drew much inspiration from Rabbi Nachman of Bratslav, a master storyteller who paved the way for Agnon to write rabbinically themed tales in a secular world where every action carries symbolic overtones. He edited several wide-ranging anthologies of rabbinical texts, such as *Yamim Nora'im* (1938, Days of Awe), a cluster of folktales inspired by the Jewish festivals; *Atem re'item* (1959, Ye Have Seen), which brings together material extending from the Bible to the Hasidic scribes of the nineteenth century; and *Sifrehem shel Tsadikim* (1961, Book of the Righteous), selections from *Sefer, sofer, ve-sipur* (1938, Book, Writer, Story), a volume of Hasidic lore.

Straddling the worlds of the sacred and the modern as an orthodox Jew, Agnon often depicted religion as the only bulwark against the moral disorder of contemporary society. Gershon Shaked, who labels Agnon a revolutionary traditionalist, maintains that the revolutionary aspect can be attributed to the tendency in Agnon to show that the new social order sweeping through Europe was in truth a type of anarchy that disoriented the Jews. In a headnote for *Tehilla, and Other Israeli Tales* (1956), Israel Meir Lask explained:

Agnon's stories of life a hundred years ago and more ago are shrouded in a mellow nostalgia, a family chronicle warmness similar to that of a grandmother telling the tales of her clan. The closer he comes to the contemporary scene, however, the less pleased with his subject matter he appears to be. His tales of life fifty years ago are marked by an almost photographic realism while when he comes to the present day a certain undercurrent of asperity can be detected in the apparent serenity that characterizes all he writes.

Agnon also did not refrain from criticizing an unchecked single-mindedness to one's faith. One such example is *Agadat ha-sofer* (1923, The Tale of the Scribe). It concerns a pious Jewish scribe who devotes all of his energy to his craft and thus neglects his suffering wife, who remains childless. The story ends with the righteous man's death, following that of his wife, though he manages to complete a Torah scroll in her memory. Alongside Agnon's total identification with the yeshiva world, one can also detect a certain ambivalence that doggedly avoids superfluous sentimentality. One invariable element that informs the Agnon imagination is that an over-reliance on modern attitudes on the one hand, and an exclusive belief in the moral certainty brought forth by tradition on the other, can imprison as much as it can liberate.

Aloof and reserved, Agnon rarely sought the limelight and refrained from articulating his social and political views. He was intensely serious about his religion and vigorously defended the orthodox world against what he viewed as unfair attacks. Shortly before traveling to Stockholm to receive the Nobel Prize, he consulted rabbis as to whether or not it was appropriate for him to leave the Holy Land for the occasion. Concurrently, he retained close ties to the less religiously observant literary and scholarly communities. Yet, he did not shy away from disapproving of the religious community, especially when religious parties entered the political fray. He was disappointed that the Jewish experience was diluted and condensed to a simple political credo. Thus, his nationalist belief in the Greater Land of Israel according to the Bible stemmed from his religious philosophy and thinking rather than any political outlook. In fact, Agnon belonged to the Land of Israel movement, founded in 1967, which believed that the whole of the land of Israel included Western Palestine.

A coterie of Agnon experts believe that his strength lies chiefly in short fiction, a form that encases the midrashic sketch and the Hasidic yarns. Agnon's lengthier opuses resemble his short fiction: the novels are structured as vignettes braided together thematically. *Sefer Ha-Ma'asim* (1941, The Book of Deeds) is a multistranded collection of twenty-one stories characterized by expressionism, Surrealism, and stream of consciousness that tell of the anguished suffering of the Jews in Europe. The intensity of the plots led the critic Nahum Norbert Glatzer to observe (in his afterword to *Twenty-One Stories*, 1970) that Agnon "must have felt compelled to abandon the form of the well-composed tale for the experience of chaos." Agnon's stories chronicle and reflect an inward and reclusive mood, at times melancholic, embodied by a cast of forlorn intellectuals, neurotic husbands, and remorseful scholars and philosophers. These characters are rendered powerless by personal angst and sexual immobility. The affinity with Franz Kafka is unmistakable. Although Agnon denied any suggestion that he was influenced by contemporary writers (insisting he had never read Kafka, even though the latter's collected writings sat on a bookshelf in Agnon's study), Kafka's signature elements of irony, dream-like sequences, and skepticism are much to the fore in Agnon's writings, fused with his religious doubt. A portion of the author's Nobel acceptance speech conveys the image of a solitary artist aloof and ignorant of present-day modes: "Some see in my books the influences of authors whose names, in my ignorance, I have not even heard, while others see the influences of poets whose names I have heard but whose writings I have not read."

Also evident in the Agnon universe is Jerusalem; a systematic check of his works reveals that the name Jerusalem is mentioned 2,600 times. In many ways, Jerusalem serves as the central axis of Agnon's life and canvas. When he arrived in Jerusalem in 1924, after spending twelve years in Europe, he rented a room and immediately headed for the Western Wall. Arriving at dusk, he covered his face and wept. David Patterson believes that amid Agnon's anguished sense of exile and rupture from tradition, Jerusalem personified the one stable positive element, stating that in Agnon's tales the city is "endowed with a personality of her own, and becomes a symbol for all that is meaningful and permanent and harmonious in life. It is as though the holy city alone contains the seeds which might restore that wholeness of spirit and oneness that are slipping through the nerveless fingers of our unhappy generations." Seminal critics such as Baruch Kurzweil and Dov Sadan, who did much to enhance Agnon's reputation, determined early on that Jerusalem was the soul and purpose in the Agnon canon, that it epitomized an absolute value within his world.

Agnon repeatedly declaimed his abiding love for Jerusalem, as in *Oreah natah la-lun* (1939; translated as *A Guest for the Night*, 1968): "My life and soul I shall give for you the holy city / Asleep and awake, you shall have my entire happiness." Many of his tales and novels are set in the old city and depict Jerusalem in a loving, reverential fashion. In *Tehilla* (originally published in Hebrew in 1950 and translated in *Tehilla, and Other Israeli Tales*, 1956), for instance, Agnon draws a direct parallel between the 104-year-old eponymous heroine, whose name radiates admiration (since it has biblical origins and means "praise"), and the city. Like Jerusalem, Tehilla is blessed with long life and embodies the supreme ideals of piety, holiness, and pride, usually associated with Israel's eternal capital. The opening paragraph, although referring to Tehilla, can just as well be a paean to Jerusalem:

> Now there used to be in Jerusalem a certain old woman, as comely an old woman as you have seen in your eyes. Righteous she was, and wise she was, and gracious and humble; for kindness and pity were the light of her eyes, and every wrinkle in her face told of blessing and peace. I know that women should not be likened to angels: yet her I would liken to an angel of God. She had in her, besides, the vigor of youth; so that she wore old age like a mantle, while in herself there was seen no trace of her years.

Agnon lived in the southern neighborhood of Talpiot for forty years, working from a small library-turned-office that is now a museum visited by tourists and the site of monthly lectures on his work. He followed a strict and spartan routine, rising early to say his morning prayers and then ascending the stairs to the private, tiny area where he toiled until noon. He would sometimes work all day and into the night. Near a stove, he stood at a polished wood podium writing by hand. Biographer Laor reports that Agnon stood to write, in order, as Agnon put it, "to grab the exact word I want from all those flying around the room." Only after he was diagnosed with a heart condition in 1951 did he sit to work. For the serious and seasoned artist, writing was a craft of precision. Aharon Megged, a renowned Israeli writer, says that Agnon would get angry when someone criticized him. Seldom satisfied with his handiwork, he labored for months, even years, amending and substituting words and phrases in many versions, delivering the full flavor of his linguistic richness and own inimitable archaic Hebrew (sometimes tagged as "Agnonit" for its distinctiveness). Accordingly, there are in existence many manuscripts and widely disparate versions of his collected works, including one in eleven volumes (1931–1952) and another in eight volumes (1959–1962).

When Agnon worked, no one was allowed into the study, and his wife, Esther, had to ensure that there was absolute quiet. Laor records that the street on which Agnon lived was blocked off to traffic by the city council, while a sign hanging at the head of the street proclaimed to all passersby: "No cars are to enter. Agnon is Writing."

A true lover of old books, he routinely patronized secondhand bookshops, purchasing rare editions (sometimes dating back to the seventeenth century) with money he steadily set aside. During his spell in Germany, he acquired old Jewish books for the private library of his patron, Schocken. Books and their traumatic loss figure prominently in the writer's life. In the summer of 1924, while he was still living in Bad Homburg, Germany, a fire consumed his large private library, including valuable manuscripts and "Bitzror ha-hayim" (In the Bond of Life), a nearly completed autobiographical novel whose publication was imminent. Also destroyed was a compilation of Hasidic legends that Agnon had assembled with his friend Martin Buber. The causes for the mysterious fire have never been explained (the fifty-shekel note that bears his portrait includes on the other side a précis of that event). Agnon, who was in the hospital for a hernia operation at the time, lost 4,000 Hebrew books. This disaster had a lasting impact on Agnon, who saw the fire as an omen. In the wake of this misfortune, he became convinced that his stopover in exile was too long, and in 1924 he returned to Palestine, where, as he revealed in his Nobel Prize address, he wrote "all that God has put into my heart and into my pen."

During the bloody Arab riots of 1929, his rented home in Jerusalem was invaded and looted. Although he had managed to save most of his cherished books and writings, once again thousands of volumes were ruined and damaged. Agnon wrote about this calamity in the 1941 tale "Me'oyev Le'ohev" (From Foe to Friend), a multifaceted, allegorical narrative about a mighty battle waged by a persistent wind (an all-purpose metaphor for the Arabs) and a determined settler who wishes to live in the suburb of Talpiot. Shattered, Agnon asked his friend, architect Fritz Kornberg, to design a new dwelling in Talpiot for him and his family, which was completed in 1931 and is now a museum. On the wall of Agnon's house remains an inscription that encapsulates his intense feelings about his home: "I have built myself a house and planted myself a garden." The feeling of homelessness, of losing one's dwelling, or simply not having a house where one can lodge, is a strong current in Agnon's work, serving as a metaphor for the precarious situation of the Jew.

The wandering, homeless Jew and his relationship with the world is at the heart of Agnon's first novel, *Hakhnasat Kalah* (1931; translated as *The Bridal Canopy*, 1937), a folk epic first published as a story in 1920, rich in scale and ambitious in its thematic perspective. Formally, *Hakhnasat Kalah* resembles a patchwork of stories within stories, separate pieces stitched together around the main narrative and bound by such themes as marriage, charity, generosity, the role of providence, and rootlessness. Often compared to Cervantes's *Don Quixote de La Mancha* (1605), Agnon's novel is concerned with the travels of the Hasidic Reb Yudel and his companion Notte through the towns and villages of nineteenth-century Galicia as he attempts to find a dowry for his daughters. Welding fantasy and realism, the adventures of the two peripatetic principals and the characters they encounter, each with a vivid story to tell, allow Agnon to paint a mosaic of Jewish and Gentile life, replete with folk-like vignettes, tragic tales, and homiletical wisdom. Looming large throughout is the emphasis placed on unwavering faith in the creator, as shown by Yudel's piety and love for his fellow man. In a wider context, the novel is a meditation on the decline of religious life in Poland, utilizing a religious protagonist whose worldview is obtrusively at odds with his secular surroundings but who maintains throughout his simple faith in God. Yudel's fidelity is rewarded when upon his return, he finds a buried treasure, giving him the wealth to provide for his daughters.

In Hochman's words, a key element in the novel is "the search for a past, a probing into a once-upon-a-time way of life. In *Hakhnasat Kalah* Agnon is the literary archivist of Galician Jewry, the comprehensive preserver of a now destroyed civilization." Critics, dazed by the mighty stream of digressions and Jewish lore that clog the main plot, have now realized that Agnon, who included *Hakhnasat Kalah* in his collected works (the 1931–1952 *Kol Sipurav shel Shmuel Yosef Agnon*), intended this project to serve as a thematic and aesthetic index for his later creations. Scholars have argued that in this novel Agnon sought to show (early in his career) that his future landmark projects would be fundamentally different from what his literary forebears had done, in both Hebrew and European letters.

Sipur Pashut (translated as *A Simple Story,* 1985), Agnon's 1935 novel, is anything but simple; it is a social treatise that dramatizes the conflict of Jewish middle-class mores with European modernist ideas of religious and sexual freedom, as well as rebellion against indurate boundaries of behavior. At the same time, it is a perceptive social allegory melded with a character study of the dilemmas entailed in human existence and the sacrifices man must make to fit into a rigidly defined world. David Ghitelman writes that "*A Simple Story* is, in the order of Thomas Mann's *Death in Venice* or Andre Gide's *The Immoralist,* a complex and resonant meditation on the comforts of civilization versus its inevitable discontents."

Set in the first decade of the twentieth century in an East European backwater (the town of Szybuzs), *Sipur Pashut* follows the life of Hirshl Horowitz, the only son of wealthy shopkeepers. He falls in love with Blume Nacht, his poor second cousin, who is sent to live with Hirshl's parents and work as a housekeeper following the death of her mother. Hirshl, a classic schlemiel who relishes the warmth of his middle-class family, is forced by his dominant and overbearing mother, Tzirel, to repress his yearnings for Blume and marry the pre-matched, shallow Mina Ziemlich (daughter of a wealthy landowner). Hirshl's blistering affection for the woman who captured his heart, however, is not quelled but rather increases, resulting in restlessness, insomnia (he undertakes nocturnal walks hoping to catch a glimpse of Blume, only to see her vision at a lighted window), and eventually mental disintegration. The breakdown scenes are revelatory of an inner journey into the netherland of the psyche, coupled with chilling historical flashbacks to Jewish milestones of exile and destruction. Woven into the architecturally precise tale is a multihued portrait of the Jewish community in the Austro-Hungarian Empire at the dawn of the twentieth century, depicting the respite and success the Jews of Galicia benefited from under the tough czarist rule.

Aware of their son's pining, Hirshl's manipulative parents send him to a sanitarium at a distant city, relieved to learn that the townsfolk believe this move is a clever scam to help Hirshl avoid the draft. There, the frustrated young man is treated by Dr. Langsham, whose unconventional methods involve Freudian regressive therapy that takes the patient back to his childhood. Singing his patient nostalgic lullabies he remembers from the small Jewish village he grew up in and abandoned, the eccentric psychiatrist shows Hirshl that the only cure for the soul is a return to one's simple roots of Jewish spiritualism and living. As the novel draws to a close, Hirshl reconciles with his wife, rejoicing in parenthood and finding emotional and sexual contentment, seemingly embodying Agnon's affirmation of marriage as the bedrock of society.

What is the unsuspecting reader to make of Hirshl's final acceptance of the conformity to bourgeois existence? Is Agnon mocking a weak-willed character who, after being tempted by the chaos of thwarted, forbidden love, does not think for himself? Halkin, who first translated the book into English, views *Sipur Pashut* as an antimodernist tract, arguing that the conclusion of the novel ventures beyond the typical modernist aversion to bourgeois mores by suggesting that sexual desire is a destructive force and that middle-class values are what provide vitally needed constancy. By contrast, Robert Alter in *The New York Times Book Review* (22 December 1985) contended that there is "more irresolution in the novel" and that "to the end Agnon makes us painfully aware of the terrible price Hirshl pays for his final normality."

Agnon's talent was at its peak in *Oreah natah la-lun*, an unsettling, nightmarish account of the spiritual and material decline of European Jewry after World War I, as related by an unnamed narrator returning to his native town. The apocalyptic novel, first serialized in the newspaper *Ha'aretz*, from 18 October 1938 to 7 April 1939, was inspired by Agnon's visit to Buczacz in 1930, after a sixteen-year absence, which provoked a Marcel Proust–like flood of childhood memories that constitutes one of the pillars of the work and explains the concatenation of the past and the present.

Upon his arrival at his hometown of Szybuzs, the hero discovers a community in decline, devoid of faith and ravaged by the war—the antithesis to the congregation of yore. As a teenager, Agnon had occasionally called his hometown "a city of the dead," and in *Oreah natah la-lun* this sentiment overhangs every scene and action. Agnon tips his metaphorical hat when his protagonist on arrival meets crippled watchmen and later a Jew-hating beggar, signifying the degradation of the place. Acute religious emptiness permeates diaspora life: the synagogues are almost barren, and those attending services do so out of routine, even presenting the guest with the key for the Bet Midrash (Jewish house of study), for which they have no further use. Starkly painful in tone and atmosphere, the tale records the despair Agnon felt and portends the desolation of Jewish life that followed. Nonetheless, the conclusion of the book is laced with optimism: prior to leaving, the narrator presents a newborn baby at a circumcision ceremony with a substitute key for the Bet Midrash. This hopeful message for the future is given added resonance in an essential scene in which the hero, now back in Palestine, finds the original key he thought he lost. Asserting that *Oreah natah la-lun* is Agnon's most important opus, Judith Romney Wegner writes that the novel constitutes an historical document of protest: "It is the author's testament to the inability of European Jewry to find an adequate replacement for the traditional culture that for centuries had sustained Jewish self identification and raison d'etre in an alien world. Agnon bears witness to the disappointment of the *maskilim* (enlightened ones) who had hoped to forge a modern Jewish identity compatible with the Age of Reason, as well as to his own profound disillusionment with the failure of the *Haskalah* (enlightenment)."

Arguably Agnon's capstone, *Temol Shilshom* (1945, The Day Before Yesterday; translated as *Only Yesterday*, 2000) was the first of his novels to be located in Palestine, and although set during the second Aliyah, it was in fact written in the shadow of the Holocaust—evidenced in the interconnected motifs of death and rebirth it tackles. Alter explained in his 1985 review that Agnon dealt with the grim reality of the Shoah indirectly because of his fabulist proclivities: "he preferred to approach the menace of recent history obliquely, often displacing the raw terror of contemporary experience into various kinds of symbolic images and parabolic intimations that could be held at an intellectual distance." Alter adds that "the utter bleakness . . . of this novel's vision of man and God may be, after all, a direct response to the nightmare of Hitler years."

Temol Shilshom begins with a wish-fulfillment journey, proceeds with a series of picaresque adventures, dwells on love and loss, and finally ends on a tragic note. The buried themes of the book are about how often people fail to actualize their dreams and how bewildered they feel when they stumble against tragedy. Like many of Agnon's stories, *Temol Shilshom* deals with the twisted threads of life that expose fairy tales as mere fictions and show existence to be a whirlpool of dark, unfulfilled desires. Finally, it is about how the romantic images of places and ideologies rarely resemble their true state.

A reconstruction of early pioneer society, the novel is an insightful and sour critique of the Zionist endeavor that also examines the elegiac and dark undertow of human existence following the national and personal exile of the Jewish nation. Cosmic imagery, prophetic images, and apocalyptic messages abound as the novel seeks to reference and encompass the universal destiny and suffering of all people. The novel was recognized as such a gigantic achievement in world literature that in 1956 the critic Edmund Wilson, who compared Agnon to Kafka and Marc Chagall, publicly called for the author to be given the Nobel Prize, noting that "Agnon is a classic . . . one is ready to accept him as a true representative of that great line of Jewish writers that begins with the authors of Genesis." The metaphysically loaded novel is a companion piece to Agnon's earlier tour de force, *Oreah natah la-lun*.

Temol Shilshom is the story of Yitzhak Kumer, a naive pioneer who travels from Galicia to Turkish-controlled Palestine, along with the massive wave of immigrants leaving the moribund world of the shtetl between the first decade of the twentieth century and the outbreak of World War II, intending to rebuild the Holy Land through backbreaking work. These pioneers were mainly secular idealists, intent on upholding the values of Jewish labor and resurrecting the Hebrew language. The dreamy-eyed Kumer, who left his Hasidic family in Szybuzs for Zion, is impelled by the pioneer rhetoric and craves to plough its soil, make the desert bloom, and be revived by the place. An iconic emblem of the Zionist pioneers who strained to become the new Jews and build a new national Jewish home, he is also the quintessential schlemiel, denuded of self-reflection or will, hopelessly romantic and devoted to the doctrine that all of his fellow immigrants are brothers linked by a shared cause. Before long, the brutal economics of the times are exposed when Kumer, like his brethren, discovers that the Jewish farmers of the colonies prefer the docile Arab laborers, as they are cheaper and already familiar with working the land. It soon becomes apparent that the reality is far removed from the Zionist ideal as settlers struggle to adapt to the cultural and social conditions of the harsh environment.

In response, Kumer settles in the bustling, secular Jaffa, where he becomes a peripatetic sign painter (painting is a metaphor in the book for the covering up of reality), while at the same time casting off the shackles of his religious upbringing. Despite eventually becoming a capable housepainter, Kumer lives with a recurring sense of failure for not working the land. In Jaffa, Kumer is agonized by the titanic choice between the secular and traditional worlds. With remarkable care for detail, and drawing on his memories of his own time there, Agnon paints Jaffa as a sensual, lively center, abrim with young lovers, would-be revolutionaries, writers, crooked politicians, and charlatans.

Over the course of his sojourn in Jaffa, the virginal Kumer meets and falls in love with Sonya Zweering, the seductive, dangerously sexual female figure who appears frequently in Agnon's corpus. For her part, Sonya treats the affair as a casual fling, whereas Yitzhak is so infatuated with the alluring female that he flagellates himself for not having done the honorable thing and married her. Crushed after Sonya capriciously ends their short-lived romance, Kumer moves to Jerusalem and into the arms of the virtuous Shifra, the only daughter of Reb Faish, an extreme fanatic of Me'ah She'arim who specializes in excommunications.

Jerusalem is the converse of Jaffa. It is a bastion of religious Jews and manipulative rabbis who are mostly anti-Zionists, enmeshed in shtetl-like surroundings. Amos Oz, in his 2000 collection of essays on Agnon, observes that Jerusalem is shown to be fossilized and empty, a portrayal filled with scathing barbs and irony. Still, Kumer is inveigled by Jaffa's charm, to which he comes back once more, but ultimately chooses Jerusalem. The return to Jerusalem also signals a resumption of his religious observance and an abandonment of his Zionist ideals. And although he marries Shifra, Kumer struggles to reconcile the spiritual vacuity of the present with the nostalgic image of the past.

Much of the drama of the novel comes from a subplot involving Balak, a dog on whose back Kumer, in an act of childish playfulness, paints the words "Mad Dog." The stray animal, up until then a staid fixture on the streets of Me'ah She'arim, begins to suffer persecution by the inhabitants of the community, who heed the warning daubed on his fur. Pelted with stones, Balak is forced to flee his beloved neighborhood, where he scoured for kosher meat left by the butchers, and instead must eat disgraceful scraps from the Gentiles. The author imagines the dog's thoughts, as Balak comments on the people he encounters and the enigma of mankind, in a prose made up of different Hebrew architectonics. Whenever the narrative focus switches to Balak, the plot assumes a

Kafkaesque turn intermingled with magic realism. Balak, who wanders through the maze of Christian and Muslim quarters in the city, needs to call on all of his wiliness to survive the panic-seized residents. Soon, he emerges as a celebrated point of discussion in the diaspora, a cause for newspaper articles and debates and an object for various theories about his real import.

After a while, the exiled animal sets out to avenge his fate on the man who marked him and who is responsible for all his anguish. In the end, the two heroes meet for the second and last time. The mongrel bites Kumer, who dies a grotesque death from rabies (even though the dog did not have rabies when Kumer labeled him). Agnon underlines the biblical leitmotiv of the binding of Isaac near the coda of the book, when the hero, like the biblical Isaac, bound with ropes, squirms in pain like a dog from the torturous agony of his disease. Kumer's catastrophic and disproportionate punishment, coupled with God's silence in the face of such violence, served as Agnon's literary reaction to the German atrocities taking place. Nonetheless, the resolution of the book offers optimism—in a crucial scene, set a day after Kumer's funeral, a life-giving rain comes down to end the excruciating drought that has eroded the sun-baked land.

There have been many interpretations as to what Balak stands for. On one level, he may be said to be Kumer's bestial alter ego, embodying the primal and repressed desires the hero does not dare articulate. On another level, he can be read as a modern-day Job, suffering from inexplicable cosmic injustice and determined to decipher the mysteries of his bitter woes (at one point, he mutters "where is heaven?"). And on still another, he may, as Oz suggests, represent the motifs of desertion and displacement as well as the eternal search for love and home.

While the narrative obviously leads in many different directions, one operating tenet is the parallel drawn between Balak and Kumer. Both pine for the past—Kumer for the home that he was raised in, bursting with the sweetness of tradition and daily observance, Balak for the kosher food of Me'ah She'arim. Both feel despairingly lonely. Both search for meaning in their particular universe. And both have been deceived by the trickeries of life. After all, rather than building the land and being rebuilt by it, Kumer is destroyed in the end.

Agnon received many prestigious literary awards. He won the Usshiskin Prize for *Temol Shilshom* in 1950 and the prestigious Israel Prize for his collected stories in 1954 and 1958, as well as the Bialik Prize for Literature bestowed by the city of Tel Aviv, in 1935 and again in 1951. In 1962 the city of Jerusalem made him an honorary citizen. Then, in 1966, came the Nobel Prize.

Agnon's supporters, including Shlomo Schocken and professor Hugo Berman, had campaigned for a Nobel nomination for him in 1947, following the success of *Temol Shilshom*. Although this attempt and others failed, the publication in English of *Betrothed, & Edo and Enam: Two Tales* in the summer of 1966 coincided with a wave of international critical acclaim for his earlier work that contributed to his winning the prize.

In his Nobel presentation speech, Swedish Academy member Anders Österling lauded Agnon's reputation as the foremost writer in modern Hebrew literature, noting that Agnon is "endowed with remarkable gifts of humor and wisdom, and with a perspicacious play of thought combined with naive perception—in all, a consummate expression of the Jewish character." At the banquet held after the official Nobel ceremony, Ingvar Andersson of the Swedish Academy commented to Agnon: "We honour in you a combination of tradition and prophecy, of saga and wisdom."

At the end of his life Agnon was completely debilitated by strokes and died of a final stroke in the town of Rehovot on 17 February 1970. He was buried on The Mount of Olives in Jerusalem. Since the 1970s, his daughter has been collecting and publishing his voluminous writings, something her prolific father was reluctant to do while alive. As a result, there are now more works in print than there were in the author's lifetime.

Shirah (1971; translated as *Shira*, 1989), Agnon's swan song, was unfinished at the time of his death and was edited by his daughter according to her father's instructions. Agnon had worked on *Shirah* for twenty-five years and left a tangle of related materials. With no ending vouchsafed in the original, two chapters were subsequently added in 1974 and 1978 editions as the designated conclusion. This intricately plotted, penetrating novel works on many levels in probing the most grand of themes: the nature of art; love and obsession; evil; death; and beauty. Beverly Fields adds that Agnon undertakes some of the most perennial European motifs: "among them Thomas Mann's concept of life as a disease of matter, with art as the ultimate disease, and the legends of Faust, Prometheus and the Wandering Jew." Fields also points out that the main character's name—Manfred Herbst—calls to mind George Gordon, Lord Byron's 1817 verse drama *Manfred*, conjuring up resonances of those legends.

Shirah tells the story of Herbst, a German-born history professor immersed in German culture, who teaches at the Hebrew University of the 1930s. While in the hospital where his wife, Henrietta, is giving birth to their third child, he meets Shirah, a sickly, mannish, and enigmatic nurse (whose name means "poetry") with whom he begins a brief affair that later develops into a tormenting, erotic infatuation when she disappears.

The novel astonished many for its overt pattern of secularism and candid descriptions of sexual obsession and existential angst. There was wide-ranging amazement at the lack of admiration for the sacred world, and surprise at a central character's scorn for tradition. Agnon populates his pages with secular German immigrants whose cultural affiliations are to the German republic they escaped from, rather than to the devout and pious Jews of Jerusalem, where they have made their home. There is a wealth of social detail conveyed through Agnon's collage of eccentric characters, including madmen, prophets, and poets who roam the streets of the Rehavia and Talpiot neighborhoods. In the background is a skein of historical references (the independence underground movements, Arab terrorism) that imbues the personal patchwork with a political strand. Palestine is under the rule of the British mandate, and the tumultuous conflict between Arab nationalism and Zionist nationalism is a prominent theme, particularly when Herbst is shot and his daughter Tamara joins one of the Jewish resistance movements.

Herbst's inability to finish a book is fused with his search for Shirah, whom he finally finds as a patient in a leper hospital in the 1974 edition. The disquieting relationship offers Herbst no contentment. His morbid fantasies about Shirah lead to a creative and emotional block and prevent him from completing his book. (In a case of art imitating life, Herbst's passion for collecting and organizing books parallels Agnon's own fixation.) The 1974 ending is laden with parable: after being afflicted with leprosy himself, Herbst decides to remain and care for Shirah. In the 1978 version, he deduces Shirah's fate and confesses his infidelity to his wife. Alan L. Mintz argues that the primary reason why the novel was not concluded is that the dialectic between Shirah as an unattainable object of desire and an allegorical container for "art, eros, purity, spirituality can simply not be accommodated by the worldly resources of the novel as a genre."

The macabre elements of the narrative are symbolic. For instance, Herbst's main area of study is Byzantine burial customs, while Shirah is enfolded by images of disease and death. Alter has opined that the answer to Shirah's identity lies in her name, averring that Herbst's fixation is with a pagan spirit of poetry. A repeated symbolic and visual trope in *Shirah* is the hero's death wish and self-destructive sexual desire, fully articulated through an undercurrent of dreams that afflict the respected academician. Herbst leads a double existence, born out of a lust for the inexplicably fascinating nurse who shatters the married man's sterile routine and domestic boredom. Driven to escape his austere life with the dull but devoted Henrietta, the hero is dominated by a libido that erotically enslaves him to the bold Shirah. Above all, *Shirah* is at once an exploration of modern man's fascination with death and the crumbling moral structure of society. Both themes are ones Agnon investigates with compassion and restraint, marshaling his customary novelistic devices of dreams and allusions while tempering his irony.

Hand in hand with his major novels, Agnon published about six new short stories every year, which were featured in the Hebrew daily *Ha'aretz*. In 1995 Agnon's short fiction was showcased in a new translation of twenty-five of his stories into English, titled *A Book That Was Lost and Other Stories*. The representative sampling of moral fables, autobiographical sketches, and psychologically perspicuous delineations spotlights Agnon's scope, ambition, and his keen ear and eye, thus illustrating the reasons he is appreciated and remembered for his shorter writings. The deceptively uncomplicated tales are cleverly subversive and derisive of the writer's own cultural domain. Profound loss and the disruptive collapse of relationships touch many of the eclectic story lines. In "The Doctor's Divorce," a young physician is wracked with regret and suffering for the absurd jealousy that drove his wife away; in "The Kerchief," a narrator reminisces about the demise of his childhood naiveté, exploring memory through his mother's Sabbath kerchief; and in "Two Pairs," a precious *tefillin* (set of phylacteries) is destroyed in a fire. The volume also displays the same strain that was so significant in Agnon's novels: an enchantment with the village of his birth, which was annihilated by the Nazis. On a broad scale, the single, unified community of Buczacz was for Agnon an example of how all people could peacefully live together.

Another central aspect in *A Book That Was Lost and Other Stories* is that the act of writing and reflection emerges as a recuperative, symbolic way to deal with the loss experienced by the characters. One striking occurrence of this theme is in the title story, in which the narrator stumbles upon an unpublished rabbinic commentary and attempts to send the manuscript from Buczacz to the national library in Jerusalem. The Yeshiva student saves enough pennies to post the book but later discovers that the manuscript, a touchstone for the intellectual traditions of the old world, never made it to the Holy Land. Yet, writing the story counteracts and compensates for the commentary that seems to be in continuous transit.

Preeminent author Oz, who holds the Agnon Chair at Ben Gurion University in southern Israel, believes that every Israeli author is connected to Agnon, who set the bar so high that most aspire to only once reach his marvelous heights. Oz acknowledges Agnon as one of his literary mentors, as do A. B. Yehoshua, Aharon Appelfeld, and the late Yehuda Amichai. This admiration is further proof that Agnon is still a father figure and mentor to scores of Israeli authors, exerting an irresistible influence on his successors.

Haim Be'er, author of a 1992 study of Agnon's relationships with two other Hebrew authors (Hayyim Nahman Bialik and Brenner), notes: "Agnon is the centre of our cultural discourse. His work is the most frequent subject of Hebrew literary research. He stands at the juncture of trends and conflicts which make up our life today–Jewish and Hebrew culture, tradition, faith and Jerusalem. Through Agnon, you can relate to a variety of themes." Arnold Band, one of the first critics to examine Agnon's fiction, contends that Agnon resists easy pigeonholing, that for some readers he was "the epitome of traditional Jewish-folk literature; for others, he is the most daring of modernists. For the older reader, Agnon conjures up memories of Jewish life in Eastern Europe; for the younger reader, he wrestles with the central universal problems of our agonized century." Anne Golomb Hoffman, in commentary for *A Book That Was Lost and Other Stories*, concurs: "Agnon's is a restless writing. . . . He has been read by some as a pious storyteller, by others as a modern ironist. He is both and more."

Letters:

Esterlain Yekirati: Mikhtavim 684–691 (1924–1931), edited by Emunah Yaron (Jerusalem: Schocken, 1983);

Sh. Y. Agnon – Sh. Z. Shoken: Hilufe Igrot (676–719) (Jerusalem: Schocken, 1991);

Mi-sod Hakhamim: Mikhtavim 1909–1970: Agnon, Brener, Bi'alik, Lahover, Katsnelson, Sadan (Jerusalem: Schocken, 2002).

Biography:

Dan Laor, *Hayey Agnon: Biographia* (Jerusalem: Schocken, 1998).

References:

David Aberbach, *At the Handles of the Lock: Themes in the Fiction of S. Y. Agnon* (Oxford: Oxford University Press, 1984);

Robert Alter, *After the Tradition: Essays on Modern Jewish Writing* (New York: Dutton, 1969);

Alter, *Hebrew and Modernity* (Bloomington: Indiana University Press, 1994);

Arnold J. Band, *Nostalgia and Nightmare: A Study in the Fiction of S. Y. Agnon* (Berkeley: University of California Press, 1968);

Hillel Barzel, *Sipure ahavah shel Shmuel Yosef 'Agnon: 'iyune mehkar* (Ramat Gan: University of Bar Ilan, 1975);

Haim Be'er, *Gam ahavatam gam sinatam: Bialik, Brenner, Agnon-maarachot yahasim* (Tel Aviv: Am Oved, 1992);

Nitza Ben-Dov, *Agnon's Art of Indirection: Uncovering Latent Content in the Fiction of S. Y. Agnon* (Leiden & New York: Brill, 1993);

Ben-Dov, *Ahavot lo meusharot: tiskul eroti, Omanut vemavet beyetzirat Agnon* (Tel Aviv: Am Oved, 1997);

Beverly Fields, "The Poetry of Truth in S. Y. Agnon's Final Novel, Tragedy Must Be Acted Out," *Chicago Tribune*, 31 December 1989, p. 4;

Harold Fisch, *S. Y. Agnon* (New York: Ungar, 1975);

David George, "A New Social Order," *Jerusalem Post*, 4 January 1991, p. 26;

David Ghitelman, "A Schlemiel Falls in Love," *Newsday*, 2 February 1986, p. 17;

Sharon Green, *Not a Simple Story: Love and Politics in a Modern Hebrew Novel* (Lanham, Md.: Lexington Books, 2002);

Daniel Grossberg, "An Introduction to Modern Israeli Literature," *Midstream*, 49 (May–June 2003): 28–31;

Baruch Hochman, *The Fiction of S. Y. Agnon* (Ithaca, N.Y.: Cornell University Press, 1970);

Stephen Katz, *The Centrifugal Novel: S. Y. Agnon's Poetics of Composition* (Madison, N.J. & London: Fairleigh Dickinson University Press, 1999);

Shalom Kremer, *Realism ve-shvirato* (Tel Aviv: Agudat Hasofrim/Masada,1968);

Baruch Kurzweil, *Masot as sipurei Agnon* (Jerusalem: Schocken, 1963);

Curt Leviant, "Mirror of the Jewish Past," *Congress Bi-Weekly*, 25 September 1967, pp. 20–21;

Yair Mazor, *The Dynamics of Motifs in S. Y. Agnon's Works* (Tel Aviv: Dekel Academic Press, 1979);

Aharon Megged, "Bepardeso Shel Agnon," in his *Shulhan na-ketivah* (Tel Aviv: Am Oved, 1989);

Alan L. Mintz, *Translating Israel: Contemporary Hebrew Literature and Its Reception in America* (Syracuse, N.Y.: Syracuse University Press, 2001);

Matt Nesvisky, "'Hillel Halkin' Master of the Translator's Trade," *Jerusalem Post*, 26 May 1989, p. 5;

Amos Oz, *The Silence of Heaven: Agnon's Fear of God* (Princeton, N.J.: Princeton University Press, 2000);

Menachem Ribalow, *The Flowering of Modern Hebrew Literature: A Volume of Literary Evaluation* (London: Vision Press, 1959);

Dov Sadan, *Al Shay Agnon* (Tel Aviv: Hakibutz Hameuchad, 1959);

Gershon Shaked, *Omanut ha Sippur shel S. Y. Agnon* (Tel Aviv: Sifriat Poalim, 1973); translated by Jeffrey M. Green as *Shmuel Yosef Agnon: A Revolutionary Traditionalist* (New York & London: New York University Press, 1989);

Mark Shechner, "A Storyteller For the Whole World: Collection Shines New Light on Israeli Writer S. Y. Agnon," *Buffalo News*, 6 August 1995, p. 8G;

Judith Romney Wegner, "*A Guest for the Night:* Epitaph on the Perished Hopes of the *Haskalah*," in *Studies in the Fiction of S. J. Agnon,* edited by David Patterson and Glenda Abramson (Boulder, Colo.: Westview Press, 1994), pp. 107–127;

Samuel Werses, *Relations Between Jews and Poles in S. Y. Agnon's Work* (Jerusalem: Magnes Press/Hebrew University of Jerusalem, 1994);

Edmund Wilson, *Red, Black, Blond and Olive: Studies in Four Civilizations: Zuni, Haiti, Soviet Russia, Israel* (London: W. H. Allen, 1956);

Ruth Wisse, *The Modern Jewish Canon: A Journey Through Language and Culture* (New York: Free Press, 2000);

Leon I. Yudkin, ed., *Agnon: Text and Contexts in English Translation* (New York: M. Wiener, 1988).

Papers:

The major collection of Shmuel Yosef Agnon's papers is the Agnon Archive at the National Library in Jerusalem.

1966 Nobel Prize in Literature Presentation Speech

by Anders Österling, Member of the Swedish Academy

This year's Nobel Prize in Literature has been awarded to two outstanding Jewish authors—Shmuel Yosef Agnon and Nelly Sachs—each of whom represents Israel's message to our time. Agnon's home is in Jerusalem, and Miss Sachs has been an immigrant in Sweden since 1940, and is now a Swedish subject. The purpose of combining these two prizewinners is to do justice to the individual achievements of each, and the sharing of the prize has its special justification: to honour two writers who, although they write in different languages, are united in a spiritual kinship and complement each other in a superb effort to present the cultural heritage of the Jewish people through the written word. Their common source of inspiration has been, for both of them, a vital power.

Shmuel Agnon's reputation as the foremost writer in modern Hebrew literature has gradually penetrated linguistic barriers which, in this case, are particularly obstructive. His most important works are now available in Swedish under the title *I havets mitt* (In the Heart of the Seas). Agnon, now seventy-eight years old, began writing in Yiddish but soon changed to Hebrew, which, according to experts, he handles with absolute mastery, in a taut and sonorous prose style of extraordinary expressiveness. He was only twenty when he left his native town in East Galicia, where, as the scion of an old and respected family, he had been brought up in a scholarly tradition. He felt drawn to Palestine, where now, as an aged classical author, he can look back on the long struggle for national reestablishment, and where the so-called cultural Zionism possesses in him one of its finest creative champions.

Agnon's unique quality as a writer is apparent chiefly in the great cycle of novels set in his native town of Buczacz, once a flourishing centre of Jewish piety and rabbinical learning, now in ruins. Reality and legend stand side by side in his narrative art. *Hakhnasat Kalah,* 1922 (The Bridal Canopy), is one of his most characteristic stories, in its ingenious and earthy humour, a Jewish counterpart to *Don Quixote* and *Till Eulenspiegel.* But, perhaps, his greatest achievement is his novel *Oreah natah la-lun,* 1939 (A Guest for the Night), which tells of a visit to Buczacz, the war-ruined city of his childhood, and of the narrator's vain attempts to assemble the congregation for a service in the synagogue. Within the framework of a local chronicle we see a wonderful portrayal of destinies and figures, of experience and meditation. The lost key to the prayer house, which the traveller finds in his knapsack only after his return to Jerusalem, is, for Agnon, a symbolic hint that the old order can never be rebuilt in the Diaspora, but only under the protection of Zionism. Agnon is a realist, but there is always a mystical admixture which lends to even the greyest and most ordinary scenes a golden atmosphere of strange fairy-tale poetry, often reminiscent of Chagall's motifs from the world of the Old Testament. He stands out as a highly original writer, endowed with remarkable gifts of humour and wisdom, and with a perspicacious play of thought combined with naive perception—in all, a consummate expression of the Jewish character.

Nelly Sachs, like so many other German-Jewish writers, suffered the fate of exile. Through Swedish intervention she was saved from persecution and the threat of deportation and was brought to this country. She has since then worked in peace as a refugee on Swedish soil, attaining the maturity and authority that are now confirmed by the Nobel Prize. In recent years she has been acclaimed in the German world as a writer of convincing worth and irresistible sincerity. With moving intensity of feeling she has given voice to the worldwide tragedy of the Jewish people, which she has expressed in lyrical laments of painful beauty and in dramatic legends. Her symbolic language boldly combines an inspired modern idiom with echoes of ancient biblical poetry. Identifying herself totally with the faith and ritual mysticism of her people, Miss Sachs has created a world of imagery which does not shun the terrible truth of the extermination camps and the corpse factories, but which, at the same time, rises above all hatred of the persecutors, merely revealing a genuine sorrow at man's debasement. Her purely lyrical production is now collected under the title *Fahrtins Staublose*, 1961 (Journey to the Beyond), which comprises six interconnected works written during a twenty-year creative period of increasing concentration. There is also a series of dramatic poems, equally remarkable in their way, under the joint title *Zeichen im Sand*, 1961 (Signs in the Sand), the themes of which might have been taken from the dark treasure house of Hassidic mysticism, but which, here, have taken on new vigour and vital meaning. Let it suffice here to mention the mystery play *Eli* (1950) about an eight-year-old boy who is beaten to death by a German soldier in Poland when he blows on his shepherd's pipe to call on heaven's help when his parents are taken away. The visionary cobbler Michael manages to trace the culprit to the next village. The soldier has been seized by remorse and, at the encounter in the forest, he collapses without Michael's having to raise his hand against him. This ending denotes a divine justice which has nothing to do with earthly retribution.

Nelly Sachs's writing is today the most intense artistic expression of the reaction of the Jewish spirit to suffering, and thus it can indeed be said to fulfill the humane purpose underlying Alfred Nobel's will.

Doctor Agnon—according to the wording of the diploma, this year's Nobel Prize in Literature has been awarded to you for your "profoundly distinctive narrative art with motifs from the life of the Jewish people." We should be happy if you would consider this international distinction as a sign that your writing need not be isolated within the boundary of its language, and that it has proved to have the power to reach out beyond all confining walls, and to arouse mankind's sympathy, understanding, and respect. Through me, the Swedish Academy conveys its sincere congratulations, and I now ask you to receive the Prize from the hands of His Majesty, the King.

Miss Nelly Sachs—you have lived a long time in our country, first as an obscure stranger and then as an honoured guest. Today the Swedish Academy honours your "outstanding lyrical and dramatic writings, which interpret Israel's destiny with touching strength." On an occasion like this it is natural also to recall the invaluable interest you have shown in Swedish literature, a token of friendship which, in turn, has found a response in the desire of our Swedish writers to translate your work. Offering you the congratulations of the Swedish Academy, I ask you now to receive this year's Nobel Prize in Literature from the hands of His Majesty, the King.

[©The Nobel Foundation, 1966).]

Agnon: Banquet Speech

Introductory remarks by Ingvar Andersson of the Swedish Academy at the Nobel Banquet at the City Hall in Stockholm, 10 December 1966:

Shmuel Yosef Agnon, Nelly Sachs—This year's literary Prize goes to you both with equal honour for a literary production which records Israel's vicissitudes in our time and passes on its message to the peoples of the world.

Mr. Agnon—In your writing we meet once again the ancient unity between literature and science, as antiquity knew it. In one of your stories you say that some will no doubt read it as they read fairy tales, others will read it for edification. Your great chronicle of the Jewish people's spirit and life has therefore a manifold message. For the historian it is a precious source, for the philosopher an inspiration, for those who cannot live without literature it is a mine of never-failing riches. We honour in you a combination of tradition and prophecy, of saga and wisdom.

Miss Sachs—About twenty years ago, through the Swedish poet Hjalmar Gullberg, I first learned of your fate and your work. Since then you have lived with us in Sweden and I could talk to you in our own language. But it is through your mother tongue that your work reflects a historical drama in which you have participated. Your lyrical and dramatic writing now belongs to the great laments of literature, but the feeling of mourning which inspired you is free from hate and lends sublimity to the suffering of man. We honour you today as the bearer of a message of solace to all those who despair of the fate of man.

We honour you both this evening as the laurel-crowned heroes of intellectual creation and express our conviction that, in the words of Alfred Nobel, you have conferred the greatest benefit on mankind, and that you have given it clearsightedness, wisdom, uplift, and beauty. A famous speech at a Nobel banquet—that of William Faulkner, held in this same hall sixteen years ago—contained an idea which he developed with great intensity. It is suitable as a concluding quotation which points to the future: "I do not believe in the end of man."

Agnon's speech (Translation)

Our sages of blessed memory have said that we must not enjoy any pleasure in this world without reciting a blessing. If we eat any food, or drink any beverage, we must recite a blessing over them before and after. If we breathe the scent of goodly grass, the fragrance of spices, the aroma of good fruits, we pronounce a blessing over the pleasure. The same applies to the pleasures of sight: when we see the sun in the Great Cycle of the Zodiac in the month of Nissan, or the trees first bursting into blossom in the spring, or any fine, sturdy, and beautiful trees, we pronounce a blessing. And the same applies to the pleasures of the ear. Through you, dear sirs, one of the blessings concerned with hearing has come my way.

It happened when the Swedish Chargé d'Affaires came and brought me the news that the Swedish Academy had bestowed the Nobel Prize upon me. Then I recited in full the blessing that is enjoined upon one that hears good tidings for himself or others: "Blessed be He, that is good and doeth good." "Good," in that the good God put it into the hearts of the sages of the illustrious Academy to bestow that great and esteemed Prize upon an author who writes in the sacred tongue; "that doeth good," in that He favoured me by causing them to choose me. And now that I have come so far, I will recite one blessing more, as enjoined upon him who beholds a monarch: "Blessed art Thou, O Lord, our God, King of the Universe, Who hast given of Thy glory to a king of flesh and blood." Over you, too, distinguished sages of the Academy, I say the prescribed blessing: "Blessed be He, that has given of His wisdom to flesh and blood."

It is said in the Talmud (Tractate Sanhedrin 23a): "In Jerusalem, the men of discrimination did not sit down to dine in company until they knew who their companions were to be"; so I will now tell you who am I, whom you have agreed to have at your table.

As a result of the historic catastrophe in which Titus of Rome destroyed Jerusalem and Israel was exiled from its land, I was born in one of the cities of the Exile. But always I regarded myself as one who was born in Jerusalem. In a dream, in a vision of the night, I saw myself standing with my brother-Levites in the Holy Temple, singing with them the songs of David, King of Israel, melodies such as no ear has heard since the day our city was destroyed and its people went into exile. I suspect that the angels in charge of the Shrine of Music, fearful lest I sing in wakefulness what I had sung in dream, made me forget by day what I had sung at night; for if my brethren, the sons of my people, were to hear, they would be unable to bear their grief over the happiness they have lost. To console me for having prevented me from singing with my mouth, they enable me to compose songs in writing.

(Out of respect for the time, the rest of my words will be read in translation only.)

I belong to the Tribe of Levi; my forebears and I are of the minstrels that were in the Temple, and there is a tradition in my father's family that we are of the lineage of the Prophet Samuel, whose name I bear.

I was five years old when I wrote my first song. It was out of longing for my father that I wrote it. It happened that my father, of blessed memory, went away on business. I was overcome with longing for him and I made a song. After that I made many songs, but nothing has remained of them all. My father's house, where I left a roomful of writings, was burned down in the First World War and all I had left there was burned with it. The young artisans, tailors, and shoemakers, who used to sing my songs at their work, were killed in the First World War and of those who were not killed in the war, some were buried alive with their sisters in the pits they dug for themselves by order of the enemy, and most were burned in the crematories of Auschwitz with their sisters, who had adorned our town with their beauty and sung my songs with their sweet voices.

The fate of the singers who, like my songs, went up in flame was also the fate of the books which I later wrote. All of them went up in flame to Heaven in a fire which broke out one night at my home in Bad Homburg as I lay ill in a hospital. Among the books that were burned was a large novel of some seven hundred pages, the first part of which the publisher had announced he was about to bring out. Together with this novel, called *Eternal Life,* was burned everything I had written since the day I had gone into exile from the Land of Israel, including a book I had written with Martin Buber as well as four thousand Hebrew books, most of which had come down to me from my forebears and some of which I had bought with money set aside for my daily bread.

I said, "since the day I had gone from the Land of Israel," but I have not yet related that I had dwelt in the Land of Israel. Of this I will now speak.

At the age of nineteen and a half, I went to the Land of Israel to till its soil and live by the labour of my hands. As I did not find work, I sought my livelihood elsewhere. I was appointed Secretary of the Hovevei Zion (Lovers of Zion) Society and Secretary of the Palestine Council—which was a kind of parliament-in-the-making and I was also the first Secretary of the voluntary Jewish Magistrate's Court. Through these offices it was my privilege to get to know almost every Jewish person, and those whom I did not come to know through these offices I came to know through love and a desire to know my brethren, the members of my people. It is almost certain that in those years there was not a man, woman, or infant in the Land of Israel whom I did not know.

After all my possessions had been burned, God gave me the wisdom to return to Jerusalem. I returned to Jerusalem, and it is by virtue of Jerusalem that I have written all that God has put into my heart and into my pen. I have also written a book about the Giving of the Torah, and a book on the Days of Awe, and a book on the books of Israel that have been written since the day the Torah was given to Israel.

Since my return to the Land of Israel, I have left it twice: once in connection with the printing of my books by the late Zalman Schocken, and once I travelled to Sweden and Norway. Their great poets had implanted love and admiration for their countries in my heart, and I decided to go and see them. Now I have come a third time, to receive your blessing, sages of the Academy.

During the time I have dwelt in Jerusalem, I have written long stories and short ones. Some have been printed; most I still have in manuscript.

I have already told how my first songs came out of longing for my father. The beginnings of my studies also came to me from my father, as well as from the Rabbinical Judge of our town. But they were preceded by three tutors under whom I studied, one after the other, from the time I was three and a half till I turned eight and a half.

Who were my mentors in poetry and literature? That is a matter of opinion. Some see in my books the influences of authors whose names, in my ignorance, I have not even heard, while others see the influences of poets whose names I have heard but whose writings I have not read. And what is my opinion? From whom did I receive nurture? Not every man remembers the name of the cow which supplied him with each drop of milk he has drunk. But in order not to leave you totally in the dark, I will try to clarify from whom I received whatever I have received.

First and foremost, there are the Sacred Scriptures, from which I learned how to combine letters. Then there are the Mishna and the Talmud and the Midrashim and Rashi's commentary on the Torah. After these come the *Poskim*—the later explicators of Talmudic Law—and our sacred poets and the medieval sages, led by our Master Rabbi Moses, son of Maimon, known as Maimonides, of blessed memory.

When I first began to combine letters other than Hebrew, I read every book in German that came my way, and from these I certainly received according to the nature of my soul. As time is short, I shall not compile a bibliography or mention any names. Why, then, did I list the Jewish books? Because it is they that gave me my foundations. And my heart tells me that they are responsible for my being honoured with the Nobel Prize.

There is another kind of influence, which I have received from every man, every woman, every child I have encountered along my way, both Jews and non-Jews. People's talk and the stories they tell have been engraved on my heart, and some of them have flown into my pen. It has been the same way with the spectacles of nature. The Dead Sea, which I used to see every morning at sunrise from the roof of my house, the Arnon Brook in which I used to bathe, the nights I used to spend with devout and pious men beside the Wailing Wall—nights which gave me eyes to see the land of the Holy One, Blessed be He—the Wall which He gave us, and the city in which He established His name.

Lest I slight any creature, I must also mention the domestic animals, the beasts and birds from whom I have learned. Job said long ago (35:11): "Who teacheth us more than the beasts of the earth, And maketh us wiser than the fowls of heaven?" Some of what I have learned from them I have written in my books, but I fear that I have not learned as much as I should have, for when I hear a dog bark, or a bird twitter, or a cock crow, I do not know whether they are thanking me for all I have told of them, or calling me to account.

Before I conclude my remarks, I will say one more thing. If I have praised myself too much, it is for your sake that I have done so, in order to reassure you for having cast your eyes on me. For myself, I am very small indeed in my own eyes. Never in all my life have I forgotten the Psalm (131:1) in which David said: "Lord, my heart is not haughty, nor mine eyes lofty; neither do I exercise myself in great matters, or in things too high for me." If I am proud of anything, it is that I have been granted the privilege of living in the land which God promised our forefathers to give us, as it is written (Ezekiel 37:25): "And they shall dwell in the land that I have given unto Jacob my servant, wherein your fathers have dwelt; and they shall dwell therein, even they, and their children, and their children's children forever."

Before concluding, I would say a brief prayer: He who giveth wisdom unto the wise and salvation unto kings, may He increase your wisdom beyond measure and exalt your sovereign. In his days and in ours may Judah be redeemed and Israel dwell in safety. May a redeemer come to Zion, may the earth be filled with knowledge and eternal joy for all who dwell therein, and may they enjoy much peace. May all this be God's will. Amen.

[©The Nobel Foundation, 1966. Shmuel Yosef Agnon is the sole author of his speech.]

Vicente Aleixandre
(26 April 1898 – 14 December 1984)

Santiago Daydí-Tolson
University of Texas at San Antonio

This entry was expanded by Daydí-Tolson from his Aleixandre entry in *DLB 108: Twentieth-Century Spanish Poets, First Series*.

BOOKS: *Ambito* (Málaga: Litoral, 1928);
Espadas como labios (Madrid: Espasa-Calpe, 1932);
Pasión de la tierra (Mexico City: Fábula, 1935);
La destrucción o el amor (Madrid: Signo, 1935; revised, 1944); selections translated by Stephen Kessler as *Destruction or Love* (Santa Cruz, Cal.: Green Horse Three, 1976);
Sombra del paraíso (Madrid: Adán, 1944); translated by Hugh A. Harter as *Shadow of Paradise* (Berkeley: University of California Press, 1987);
Vida del poeta: El amor y la poesía (Madrid: Real Academia Española, 1950);
Mundo a solas (Madrid: Clan, 1950); translated by Lewis Hyde and David Unger as *World Alone* (Great Barrington, Mass.: Penmaen Press, 1982);
Nacimiento último (Madrid: Ínsula, 1953);
Historia del corazón (Madrid: Espasa-Calpe, 1954);
Algunos caracteres de la nueva poesía española (Madrid: Instituto de España/Góngora, 1955);
Mis poemas mejores (Madrid: Gredos, 1956; augmented, 1968);
Los encuentros (Madrid: Guadarrama, 1958);
Poesías completas (Madrid: Aguilar, 1960);
Poemas amorosos (Buenos Aires: Losada, 1960; enlarged, 1970);
Picasso (Málaga: Guadalhorce, 1961);
En un vasto dominio (Madrid: Revista de Occidente, 1962);
Presencias (Barcelona: Seix Barral, 1965);
Retratos con nombre (Barcelona: Bardo, 1965);
Dos vidas (Málaga: Guadalhorce, 1967);
Poemas de la consumación (Barcelona: Plaza & Janés, 1968);
Obras completas (Madrid: Aguilar, 1968; revised and enlarged, 2 volumes, 1978);
Antología del mar y la noche, edited by Javier Lostalé (Madrid: Al-Borak, 1971);
Poesía superrealista: Antología (Barcelona: Barral, 1971);

Vicente Aleixandre (from Obras completas, *volume 1 [1977]; Thomas Cooper Library, University of South Carolina)*

Sonido de la guerra (Valencia: Fomento de Cultura, 1972);
Diálogos del conocimiento (Barcelona: Plaza & Janés, 1974);
Antología total, edited by Pere Gimferrer (Barcelona: Seix Barral, 1975);

Antología poética, edited by Leopoldo de Luis (Madrid: Alianza, 1977);

Poemas paradisiacos, edited by José Luis Cano (Madrid: Cátedra, 1977);

Poesía (1924–1967) (Madrid: Aguilar, 1977);

Antología: Verso y prosa (Barcelona: Planeta, 1979);

Antología esencial, edited by Alejandro Duque Amusco (Barcelona: Orbis, 1983);

Nuevos poemas varios, edited by Irma Emiliozzi and Amusco (Barcelona: Plaza & Janés, 1987);

Prosas recobradas, edited by Amusco (Barcelona: Plaza & Janés, 1987);

En gran noche: Ultimos poemas, edited by Carlos Bousoño and Amusco (Barcelona: Seix Barral, 1991);

Miré los muros: Textos inéditos y olvidados, edited by Mario Hernández and Driss El-Fakhour (Madrid: Ediciones de la Universidad Autónoma de Madrid, 1991);

Poesías completas, edited by Amusco (Málaga: Visor Libros, 2001);

Prosas completas, edited by Amusco (Málaga: Visor Libros, 2002).

Editions in English: *Twenty Poems,* translated by Lewis Hyde and Robert Bly (Madison, Minn.: Seventies Press, 1977);

A Longing for the Light: Selected Poems of Vicente Aleixandre, translated by Hyde (New York: Harper & Row, 1979);

The Crackling Sun, translated by Louis Bourne (Madrid: Sociedad General Española de Librería, 1981);

A Bird of Paper, translated by Willis Barnstone and David Garrison (Athens: Ohio University Press, 1982);

Destruction or Love, translated by Robert G. Mowry (Selinsgrove, Pa.: Susquehanna University Press, 2000).

OTHER: Gerardo Diego, ed., *Poesía española,* introduction by Aleixandre (Madrid: Signos, 1932; revised, 1934).

The 1977 Nobel Prize in Literature was awarded to Vicente Aleixandre for "a creative poetic writing which illuminates man's condition in the cosmos and in present-day society, at the same time representing the great renewal of the traditions of Spanish poetry between the wars," as the citation read. These words continue to be a valid representation of what is essential in Aleixandre's contribution to literature as a twentieth-century Spanish author. At the time of the awarding of the Nobel Prize, Aleixandre's name was little known outside Hispanic literary circles; his poetic work was seen as stylistically and conceptually too complex, and consequently too difficult to understand, by the general reading public. This perceived difficulty constitutes a characterizing factor in the current appreciation of the poet as a figure of exceptional poetic quality. An undisputed master of the previous century, Aleixandre is well recognized by critics and by the newer generation of Spanish poets as an influential voice. For most people, though, the Spanish "Generation of 1927," of which Aleixandre is a representative member, is most often associated with the much more popular figure of Federico García Lorca, whose surrealistic book *Poeta en Nueva York* (1940; translated in *The Poet in New York and Other Poems of Federico García Lorca,* 1940) has much in common with Aleixandre's poetic views, objectives, and techniques.

Since the 1920s, when he began to frequent the literary *tertulias* (conversational gatherings) in Madrid, Aleixandre was always an important part of Spain's literary scene, although not a poet for the general public. Because his health was poor, he had to maintain permanent residence in Madrid, with only a few short trips, mostly within Spain; his home in the neighborhood of the Ciudad Universitaria (University Campus) became the meeting place for Spanish and Spanish American writers for several years before the Spanish Civil War (1936–1939). García Lorca and Pablo Neruda were regular visitors and close friends of the poet. As one of the members of the prestigious Generation of 1927, Aleixandre was involved in the innovative changes that characterized the best poetry in Spain during the conflict-filled last years of the monarchy and the short period of the Republic. He survived the civil war, and, unlike other surviving poets of the generation, he did not leave Spain for a life of exile in a foreign country. He lived, during Francisco Franco's regime, the interior exile of an intellectual who was opposed to the political dictatorship.

After the civil war, Aleixandre became again a central figure in Spanish literary circles: poets and critics began to visit the ailing master, whose house resumed its function as a meeting place for writers and intellectuals. The younger generation saw in Aleixandre a connecting link with the older, pre-civil-war poets who had died or were living in exile. He was seen as a model by those who began to write during the first years of dictatorship: he represented the continuity of literary excellence in postwar Spain. Because he always considered himself part of a larger scheme, the Nobel Prize awarded to him may be seen to represent international recognition not only of his personal work but also of the best literature written in Spain since the great period before the war.

In his Nobel Prize acceptance speech, a text that summarizes aptly Aleixandre's main ideas about his art, he states that poetry is, above all, tradition: the poet is a link between past and future—a truism made evident in his own case. His life covers a period of Spanish literary history that extends from the masterful Generation of 1898 to the developments of the 1980s, including a period of poetry akin to the politicized social poetry preferred in Spain in the 1950s and 1960s. As a young man he was involved in a group of poets including, besides García Lorca and Neruda, Luis Cernuda, Pedro Salinas, Rafael Alberti, and Miguel Hernández. As a mature writer Aleixandre was given the opportunity and the responsibility of helping the younger generations searching for a poetic inheritance half lost after the civil war. In his old age he acquired the inspiring presence of a master, the consecrated poet in whom tradition finds its continuity.

Aleixandre's works are the poetic reflection of the circumstances in which he lived. From his first published poems, written during a period of highly technical and aesthetically demanding literature, to his last collection of dramatic monologues, *Diálogos del conocimiento* (1974, Dialogues of Knowledge), his poetry evolved in harmonious correspondence with the main transformations in Spanish lyric poetry. He had a clear understanding of the historical character of all artistic creation, and his own writing reflects his recognition of what was essential in the main currents of Spanish poetic art at different historical moments. This ability to transform his poetic diction in accordance with the times was not the result of an inordinate interest in aesthetic fashion, but it was the natural consequence of his conception of poetry and the poet.

From a theoretical position well within a tradition of contemporary poetry, Aleixandre defined the poet as a prophet or a seer. Reminiscent of the Platonic idea of poetic inspiration, this conception and the practice it condones have their most immediate antecedent in Surrealism, although they can be traced back to early Romanticism. This visionary interpretation of the poet as a means for other voices to express themselves, as a spiritually superior being who can be in touch with the cosmos and with humankind's essence, is directly related to the total immersion of the individual writer in a tradition. Thus, in theoretical terms, Aleixandre saw himself as *the poet,* the nameless speaker through whom all humanity talks; in his writings he even refers directly to himself as "the poet," instead of using the first-person pronoun. Many of his works convey a degree of anonymity, a feeling that the lyrical voice in his poems does not belong to any definite persona, much less to the author. This absence of an identifiable speaker is a central characteristic of his poetic discourse and defines much of its originality within the development of contemporary Spanish poetry.

Born in Seville on 26 April 1898, Vicente Aleixandre Merlo grew up in a period of extremely active political and intellectual life in his country. He spent his boyhood in Málaga, a fact that explains his later images of the sea and the paradisiacal world of infancy in an old provincial town on the Mediterranean. In 1909, when he was eleven years old, his parents, Cirilo and Elvira Merlo Aleixandre, moved the family (including Vicente's sister) to Madrid, where Vicente completed his high-school and university studies.

Although during his school years he was an avid reader, he avoided reading poetry; he was then under the impression that such a form of literature neither provided much enjoyment nor had much intellectual value. But by the age of eighteen he had become a fervent enthusiast of poetry. His acquaintance with another young poet, Dámaso Alonso, whom he met the summer of 1917 while vacationing in Ávila, had changed his attitude. Alonso, who would not accept his friend's refusal to read poetry, introduced him to the work of Rubén Darío, the Latin American master of modernism. Many years later, in a prologue to the second edition of *La destrucción o el amor* (1935, selections translated as *Destruction or Love,* 1976), Aleixandre recalled that the reading of Darío's poems produced a revolution in his spirit. He had discovered true poetry and felt infused with his great passion, one that never abandoned him throughout the remainder of his life. During that same summer vacation he began to write, but his first publications did not appear until ten years later. While studying for his professional degrees in business and law at the University of Madrid, he cultivated in silence his personal vocation, probably unaware of his talents. In 1919, after graduating from the university, he began to teach at the school of business there. For a while he devoted himself to his profession and wrote on economic subjects. A trip in 1923 to Paris and London was of little consequence to his literary career. He never married or had children.

When he began to write his first book in the 1920s, the masters of the Generation of 1898 were at the peak of their careers, and among the younger writers one could already find salient names, such as Jorge Guillén, Alberti, and Cernuda. His own generation, which would be known as the Generation of 1927, was bewildered by the new aesthetic, philosophical, and scientific ideas of post–World War I Europe. The climate in the literary circles frequented by Aleixandre in those days was one of curiosity, renovation, and activity. In Madrid the literary cafés, theaters, art galleries, the Ateneo, and the important Residencia de Estudiantes were the meeting places for writers, artists, and philosophers from Spain and abroad. In the friendly atmosphere of common intellectual and aesthetic interest, Aleixandre found his first admiring readers and the motivation to become a writer.

It is particularly revealing that Aleixandre was awakened to his own poetic gifts after reading Darío's poems, because a spiritual correspondence existed between the two writers. For the young poet-to-be, Darío's works represented not only the manifold possibilities of language but most of all the poetic view that defines man as a passionate creature consumed by love. In Darío's writings poetic language reaches a level of communicativeness directly related to the poet's ability to create a purely fictional reality representing, in metaphorical terms, an otherwise inexpressible understanding of man and existence. No less important for such poetic effectiveness of language in Darío's works is the general tone of passionate materialism, an essential sensuality not at all alien to an unquenchable desire for spiritual transcendence. These aspects of Darío's literary accomplishments inspired Aleixandre.

But the influence of the Latin American modernist is not seen in Aleixandre's first published poems. These works were the result of a more immediate influence: Aleixandre wrote them when he had an intense literary relationship with other young poets who declared their interest in Juan Ramón Jiménez and the theories of "pure" poetry. Aleixandre's participation in the group's literary experimentation and theoretical discussions explains the influence of their taste on *Ambito* (Ambit), his first collection of poems, published in 1928. Aleixandre's career as a poet began in 1926 when a few of his friends sent to *Revista de Occidente* (Western Review), the new periodical founded by José Ortega y Gasset, the poems Aleixandre himself did not care to publish. They appeared that same year; the book, consisting of a tightly knit collection of interrelated poems, soon followed.

Ambito constitutes a basis for later developments in his art. A careful critical reading demonstrates that, although *Ambito* has many debts to other poets respected highly at the time, this first collection displays some of the peculiar characteristics of Aleixandre's work. In comparison with his later books, *Ambito* seems at first particularly different—its external characteristics are a good imitation of Jiménez's techniques. Like many other young poets of his generation, Aleixandre wrote under the dictates of a rigorous concept of style and composition. Most of the thirty-five poems in *Ambito* are written in traditional verse; but the combination of different meters in some poems is the first indication of the poet's inclination toward free verse, a form that came to characterize his personal style.

The other important aspect of the book is its irrational imagery, suggestive of Surrealism and directly communicative of a cosmic vision of man and nature as identical in essence. Love in its widest sense is central to these compositions; it constitutes, in the poet's view, the only possible way for man to achieve the desired fusion with all matter. *Ambito* represents Aleixandre's first attempt to conform to the requisites of being a poet of his time; it is the product of several years of apprenticeship in the active workshop of his generation—the cultural life of Madrid. But it is also the result of the poet's seclusion and dedication to poetry after contracting tubercular nephritis, a chronic illness that curtailed his activities starting in 1925.

Pasión de la tierra (1935, Earth Passion), the first good example of Aleixandre's characteristic poetic language, is even more the result of the serious illness. It represents a new awareness of the mysterious character of human nature, gained through personal experience and study. By 1928 Aleixandre was reading the works of Sigmund Freud and James Joyce, two authors influential in his own decision to look for a new form of literary experimentation. Although *Pasión de la tierra* was finished in 1929, it remained practically unknown until 1946, by which time Aleixandre was established as the most representative member of his generation still living in Spain. Only a few copies of the 1935 Mexican first edition reached Spain before the civil war, and consequently, in spite of its revolutionary nature, the book did not have any noticeable influence on the literary developments of the period it represents so well. Had it been published immediately after Aleixandre finished writing it, *Pasión de la tierra* would likely have become one of the major Surrealist books in Spanish literature.

In *Ambito*, Aleixandre was able to resolve every stylistic problem by using the well-known and already established solutions—he was working within the predetermined patterns of a tradition. In *Pasión de la tierra* the fixed channels of poetic expression were totally disrupted: language itself lacks the normal semantic values that render it meaningful. These seemingly incoherent prose poems express within the limitations imposed by language the new reality revealed by psychoanalysis and by writers such as Jean-Nicolas-Arthur Rimbaud and Joyce. *Ambito* and *Pasión de la tierra* appear to be the works of two completely different poets, one a "purist" poet of aesthetic restraint and technical control, the other a vanguardist writer who follows the Surrealist practice of automatic writing. The decision to adopt a Surrealistic form of expression came as a result of Aleixandre's well-informed confidence in the value of psychoanalytical theories and in the effectiveness of automatic writing. By accepting the theoretical principles behind the Surrealistic method, he was stating his revolt against established poetic objectives and methods. His interest in aesthetic experimentation common to the period was in response to the need for new techniques to express his new awareness of himself.

Between the carefully measured and well-combined verses of *Ambito* and the entirely loose prose poetry of *Pasión de la tierra,* there is a difference not only in external form and poetic techniques but more significantly in the perspective of the speaker, his attitude, and tone of voice. Once traditional diction is attacked, the attitude of the speaker changes from dutiful acceptance of the norm to rebellious freedom. In *Pasión de la tierra* this freeing force appears in the external form of prose, releasing the new verbal flux. The model for this form had already been set forth convincingly by Joyce; Aleixandre adapted it to a still deeper search into the human psyche and its world of fascinating dreams, fears, and desires. The reasons for writing poetry in such a manner are to be found in his emotional experiences at the time. His life was centered around his innermost experiences, as illness had made him more aware of mortality. Compelled by this realization, he began a desperate and obsessive search within himself for life and its meaning.

Surrealism offered a theoretical basis and more effective ways to express his new awareness. The idealized experience of cosmic union presented in *Ambito* lacks the powerful conviction found in *Pasión de la tierra*. In the first book the perspective and the attitude of the poet are constrained by traditional principles, whereas they are free from any limitations in the latter.

Prose is the form that best reproduces the free flow of speech, the uncontrolled stream of oneiric visions created by a web of apparently unrelated images. A return to versification in Aleixandre's next book, *Espadas como labios* (1932, Swords like Lips), is a significant change. The transcription of the Surrealistic, associative images into verse suggests that he was still hesitant about which form best suited his expressive needs. He never again used prose for poetic purposes, but the experiment with it in *Pasión de la tierra* left him with a keener sense of prosody. The shorter compositions in *Espadas como labios* are in traditional metrics. The main rhythmic patterns and the general tone are not new; they lack the strangeness and novelty of *Pasión de la tierra*. These poems are the products of controlled writing and reproduce a measured attitude even when the images allude to strong emotions; from this duality emerges a feeling of tension. The longer poems instead use a freer form of versification in accordance with a freer attitude of the speaker, who allows his emotional state to appear in the poem. This second type of composition, akin to both verse and prose, was improved in Aleixandre's next book, *La destrucción o el amor,* and became characteristic of most of Aleixandre's subsequent works.

Aleixandre's free verse, or versicle, is constituted by several types of repetitions, with the exception of regular rhyme and isosyllabism. Repetition is found in the phonic, the syntactical, and the semantic levels of the poems, and observable correspondences with the traditionally established meters are only circumstantial. Essential to Aleixandre's verse are several stylistic devices, which, by stressing repetition, underline the value of resonance and rhythm. *Espadas como labios* includes some of them, and in *La destrucción o el amor* they become defining characteristics. These reiterative techniques include anaphora, alliteration, and assonance; another technique used for the same effect is apposition. These richly rhythmic, dualistic patterns convey the indecisiveness of the speaker in naming things. In some cases the poet seems to stutter in confusion, or tries unsuccessfully to put his vision into words in different ways. Behind this attitude of bewilderment there is a clear sense of the mysterious interrelation of all aspects of reality. Thus, the most characteristically Aleixandrian of all these devices is the use of the conjunction *or,* not as a disjunctive but as a means of connecting two terms. The constant use of this conjunction—present even in the title of the book—provides many pairings. Duality becomes identity, and variety is a sign of unity.

Only a detailed analysis of the poems would give an adequate idea of all the possibilities of free verse in expressing the various attitudes and emotional states of the speaker. This type of versification has its first antecedent in the combination of traditional verses used in *Ambito;* the experience with prose in *Pasión de la tierra* taught the poet how to extend the common Spanish metric patterns into a much more flexible rhythmic use of the language. Free verse became for Aleixandre the best medium to communicate his particular conception of humankind and destiny. In *La destrucción o el amor* one finds the application of Aleixandre's ideas about poetry as he stated them in his commentary for the 1934 edition of Gerardo Diego's *Poesía española*. In the first edition, published in 1932, Aleixandre had expressed his doubts about the function and value of poetry in modern society; two years later he had a more positive outlook. Without intending an explanation of poetry, Aleixandre offers a few principles of a coherent poetic theory closely related to a general cosmic vision of humankind and nature. For him all elements of creation are only different manifestations of the one and only universal entity. In *La destrucción o el amor* he underlines this meaning through chaotic enumerations including terms referring to human aspects as well as to animate and inanimate nature: "Flor, risco o duda, o sed o sol o látigo: / el mundo todo es uno, la ribera y el párpado" (Flower, rock or doubt, or thirst or whip: / all in the world is one, the riverbank and the eyelid). Aleixandre's conception of the unity of all existing matter and of the power of love to effect this unification finds its contemporary equivalents in philosophy, theology, psychology, and natural sciences.

As in *Pasión de la tierra*, Aleixandre is driven in *La destrucción o el amor* by the desire for authenticity; he looks for poetic revelation in the subconscious, where words change their everyday meaning. It is the poet's duty to listen to the messages of the cosmos and to make of them a sensible and communicating expression.

In *La destrucción o el amor*, Aleixandre is still using a form of automatic writing, except that in this case he no longer writes the utterances of an unconscious self but rather has become the mouthpiece for all life and matter communicating itself through the deep consciousness of a man who acts under inspiration as a sibyl, a bridge between human understanding and the cosmos. In *La destrucción o el amor*, Aleixandre's poetry reaches a vaguely ancient tone of pagan pantheism with mythical overtones. The poet's journey toward the attainment of the ideal takes him to the depths of existence as lived and experienced by the inner man. At this point the emotionally cautious and aesthetically restrained songs of *Ambito* have changed drastically to primal screams.

The poet's conception of reality is clearly stated in *La destrucción o el amor*. The personal view of Aleixandre in this epoch of his life is the poetically coherent exposition of his Surrealistic approach to knowledge. In this book Aleixandre has conceived a metaphorical world, a purely literary construction, through which his own interpretative view becomes evident. This world of primitive nature and oneiric images is reminiscent of *Pasión de la tierra,* but *La destrucción o el amor* has a more logical structure and a clearer language. By this time Aleixandre was moving toward a more easily understandable lyric language: this new diction reflects not only the deeper levels of subconscious knowledge but also the conscious need for order and intelligible communication.

By 1936, at the beginning of the Spanish Civil War, Aleixandre was thirty-eight years old and had survived a dangerous illness. For ten years he had suffered physical shortcomings; life and death, pleasure and pain, and desire and fear had been for him omnipresent opposites that had to affect his outlook. As a chronically ill man he was more aware than others of biological determinants; he could see in his own body the slow and unremitting process of decay and dissolution. He contemplated the different available explanations for human life and death. Aleixandre's first books, the ones written before the war, are imbued with an anguished search for a meaningful explanation for existence. Irrationalism in this case is more a method than an objective in itself. Confusion and chaos are the conditions of a mind in a state of total uncertainty, but in the mass of images that fill these Surrealistic books it is possible to discern the elements that in further works develop into a more logical understanding. With a more mature sense of his accomplishments, and aware of the circumstances surrounding him, Aleixandre had begun, in 1934, a new book, *Mundo a solas* (published in 1950; translated as *World Alone,* 1982). It is a sad and pessimistic book in which he depicts humankind's loss of the primeval elemental state.

During the three years of the civil war, Aleixandre wrote sparingly, although he contributed war poems to Republican publications. It was a time of sorrow and devastation; his own house was half destroyed in the fighting in Madrid. At the end of the conflict, peace brought life back to the shattered garden and rooms of the house, but many of those who frequented it in the prewar years were gone: García Lorca was dead; Cernuda, Guillén, Neruda, and many others had left Spain; and Hernández was in prison, where he died a few years later. Still faithful to his old friends and ideals, Aleixandre wrote a poem to Hernández's memory, a tacit criticism of the new political regime. But while the memories of those who had gone lingered in the renovated house where Aleixandre continued living his reclusive life, a new group of writers started to replace them and came to visit the poet. They did not form a generational group, nor a school following the dictates of a leader; these new visitors were the first among many postwar Spanish poets who saw in Aleixandre the inspiration of the master. The author of revolutionary Surrealist books had reached maturity. Coincidentally, in 1944, an important year for the history of postwar Spanish poetry because of the publication of *Hijos de la ira* (Children of Wrath) by Alonso, Aleixandre published his first book in almost ten years, *Sombra del paraíso* (translated as *Shadow of Paradise,* 1987).

Sonnets and other neoclassical pastiches, inspired by the stale desire to believe in the reborn greatness of the empire, were the main expressions of poetry in the early days of the Franco regime. The long free verses, the sensuous images, and the musically ample rhythms of Aleixandre's new book were a much-needed exception. His worldview was made concrete in the imagery of the poems. With *Mundo a solas,* which only appeared in 1950 as a document of past experiences, Aleixandre wanted to express his sad realization that humans lived in a fallen state; this same idea, reminiscent of religious explanations for human inadequacy in nature, is fully developed in *Sombra del paraíso,* but with important differences. The first volume conveys in violent overtones a negative view; the dominant chord in *Sombra del paraíso* is a more complex and richly evocative feeling of human totality. This difference between the two books, one written immediately before the war, the other during the first years of peace, is indicative of two stages in Aleixandre's understanding of reality. The first stage includes the five books written in the prewar years; they are the work of youth and convey an impression of disorder and confusion. The second stage, which begins with *Sombra del paraíso,* introduces a more harmonious, if nostalgic, view of the universe and corresponds to the mature years of the poet.

This change in Aleixandre's outlook did not happen suddenly because of the war, nor did it come as a total surprise—it is a sign of the writer's maturity reached after years of poetic meditation on life and death. Essential to this new understanding of the relationship between humankind and the universe are Aleixandre's conceptions of poetry and the poet. Although in essence they are the same ones he professed in 1934, the intensity of the conviction and its purposefulness make them appear new. What years before had been a supposition and a wish was now an accepted fact, a definite ordering of the multiple components. The poet, for Aleixandre, continues to be a seer, a person who can reveal to others that ultimate knowledge of the otherwise inexpressible truth. Aleixandre represents the poet as a gigantic being whose feet are deep inside the earth and whose head is up above, touching the sky.

Sombra del paraíso can be compared with Romantic works. Everything in it is designed to underline the emotion of remembrance and the hope of recovering a lost paradisiacal state. From the conception of poetry and the poet to the images and versification, *Sombra del paraíso* stands out in contemporary Spanish letters as a document of people's eager acceptance of a degraded existence that is only a pale shadow of the original one. The speaker addresses nature, the cosmos, and other men as if he were indeed the gigantic poet of magnificent voice depicted in his own Surrealistic image.

At this point in Aleixandre's literary career his work had reached its originality by a constant effort to relate poetry and the personal search for meaning. He had applied with conviction the theory of poetic knowledge as learned from Surrealism and its predecessors. *La destrucción o el amor* and *Sombra del paraíso* are two examples of poetry understood as a spiritual vocation, as a method to reach a higher form of consciousness. Partly because of his delicate health and his inability to lead a normal, active life, Aleixandre had not had other interests or devotions outside poetry; everything in his reclusive life depended on it and found meaning in it. As in the case of a religious believer, Aleixandre's particular belief provided an order and interpretation to all creation. This virtually religious conviction does not correspond in Aleixandre's case to an already provided answer that the individual readily accepts and embraces. He went step-by-step in a personal search for an explanation of existence; this spiritual journey he described metaphorically in his commentary for *Mis poemas mejores* (1956, My Best Poems) as an aspiration toward light.

Up to the publication of *Sombra del paraíso* the image of light pervades all Aleixandre's work and carries with it a meaning of knowledge representative of the writer's own definition of his poetic aim. This predominance of light finds its correspondence in his prose texts about poetry in which the poet is described as "illuminator, provider of light." Aleixandre's books are closely related to each other; together they form an extended structure in which there is a continuity of purpose, a slow development in his view of reality and its poetic manifestation, both represented by a growing luminosity. This light is particularly bright in *Sombra del paraíso,* the collection standing at the center of Aleixandre's whole production: it is the culmination of a process but also provides the basis for the developments that follow in the subsequent collections.

The novelty of the next book Aleixandre wrote, *Historia del corazón* (1954, The Heart's History), which took almost ten years to finish, lies in its central subject—concrete, everyday reality. His ideas about the cosmic indistinctness of all things and of the equalizing powers of love are applied in this book in a much more restricted way—they refer only to people in society. Aleixandre explains this transformation by saying that *Historia del corazón* presupposes a new view and a new conception. But, more than a new conception, the book illustrates the last stage in the developmental process that Aleixandre's poetry had been following from the first compositions he wrote under the influence of Jiménez to the poems of *Sombra del paraíso.* That process was one of clarification, the journey to light that takes the poet from the universality of a cosmic view to the realization of the most immediate destiny of humankind.

In the 1950s Aleixandre achieved harmony with his world and with himself. Love, on the other hand, the all-encompassing force of identification, took on the form of social love. And his voice became the voice of collective humankind, as is clearly stated in the title of his poem "El poeta canta por todos" (The Poet Sings for Everyone). An obvious consequence of this attitude is the need to stress the importance of communication, a conviction sustained also by the social poets of the same period.

With the abandonment of the visionary images found in his prewar books, the vague feeling of awe before the mystery of life and the almost-sacred tone of the oracle also vanished. His interest in humankind, common people, brought other aspects of everyday reality into Aleixandre's perspective and affected greatly his inspiration and discourse. The imagined reader or listener, the poetic personae, and the settings of the poems all point to a different attitude. They also bring to the forefront a factor Aleixandre started to consider only in relation to human life—the day-to-day passage of time. The attention focused on purely realistic aspects had to be complemented by an interest in realistic language—a language much nearer to everyday discourse while still maintaining a poetic force. Visionary imagery comes to be replaced in *Historia del corazón* by common images imbued with a profoundly emotional understanding, acceptance, and exaltation of human life in a communal world:

> Aquí también entré, es esta casa.
> Aquí vi a la madre cómo cosía.
> Una niña, casi una mujer (alguien diría: qué alta, qué guapa se está poniendo),
> alzó sus grandes ojos oscuros, que no me miraban.
> Otro chiquillo, una menuda sombra, apenas un grito, un ruidillo por el suelo,
> tocó mis piernas suavemente, sin verme.
> Fuera, a la entrada, un hombre golpeaba, confiado, en un hierro.
>
> (Here I also went into this house.
> Here I saw how the mother was sewing.
> A girl, almost a woman [someone would say: how tall she is, how beautiful she is becoming]
> raised her large dark eyes that did not look at me.
> Another child, a little shadow, only a cry, a subtle noise around the floor,
> touched my legs, softly, not seeing me.
> Outside, at the entrance, a man was beating, confidently, a piece of metal.)

The basic principles of free verse again constitute the stylistic basis for these new compositions. Every form of repetition is tried in order to create the appropriate tone of chants, hymns, elegies, and songs. The poems cover the complete range of subjects listed by Aleixandre in the prologue to the 1944 edition of *La destrucción o el amor* as those that every poet writing for the majority of people should embrace as central: the essentially unifying aspects of love, sadness, hate, and death. He did not include in his list, as he certainly does in his poetry, the joy of living and the sensuous awareness of the real.

At the time of writing *Historia del corazón*, Aleixandre had reached his full emotional and intellectual maturity. Public recognition, underlined by his election to the Spanish Royal Academy in 1950, is also an indication of his complete adjustment to circumstances and of his involvement in literary activities. He had become more of a public man as he was invited to give lectures and read his poems. He published some of his nearly forgotten works, prepared anthologies and new editions of his works, contributed to poetical publications, and was extensively interviewed and honored. Some of Aleixandre's most important theoretical texts are from this period and include *Algunos caracteres de la nueva poesía española* (1955, Some Characteristics of the New Spanish Poetry) and the notes to the anthology *Mis poemas mejores*.

His point of view on poetics became a guiding principle among Spanish poets. Aleixandre knew how to interpret the times, and his principles appeared as appropriate to the circumstances and the needs of that particular historical time. In his prologue to *Mis poemas mejores,* Aleixandre explains that, starting with *Historia del corazón,* he believed the poet was the expression of difficult human life and that the poet's voice either comes from his extended communitarian heart, comforted by love, or is gathered from the mass of the people. Aleixandre had followed a similar path—only at a slower pace—to the one taken by other writers of his generation who, having practiced Surrealism in the years before World War II, had later written a poetry committed to their immediate social situation. Another Nobel Prize winner comes to mind in this regard—the Chilean Neruda, who was one of Aleixandre's close friends while living in Madrid as a diplomat. For him the evolution from visionary to realistic poetry was sudden and ideologically inspired. A comparison of these poets shows many differences, but they have in common their awareness of nature and cosmos, people and society, love and death, and the never-forgotten visionary origin of their understanding of reality. Only poets such as they, modern-day seers and inheritors of a lyric tradition, could have written fully poetic realist works. In post-civil-war Spain, Aleixandre's *Historia del corazón, En un vasto dominio* (1962, In a Vast Domain), and *Retratos con nombre* (1965, Portraits with Names) are good examples of this new social sensibility caused by political circumstances.

En un vasto dominio has an introductory poem that, mirroring a growing concern among the poets of the day, offers another declaration of poetic principles. The attraction poets have toward *ars poetica* seems unusually conspicuous in post-civil-war Spanish poetry, particularly during the period when the social realist style was predominant. Aleixandre himself paid less attention to the subject in his books prior to *Sombra del paraíso*. The preoccupation with poetics can be accounted for, at least in this brief period, by the

Manuscript of one of Aleixandre's last poems (from Ínsula *[January–February 1985], Thomas Cooper Library, University of South Carolina; by permission of the Estate of Vicente Aleixandre)*

nature of literary creativity under a dictatorship. Realistic poets, whose manifest social awareness was limited at the most to a personal testimony of their attitude toward the troubled world, felt the psychological need to explain their social value as poets to themselves and to others. Aleixandre was sensitive to the fact that there are unavoidable limitations in communication with all people through poetry, but he did not seem to see these facts changing the essentially communal character of the authentic poet, who continues to be the same as the one he had described years before. His keeping intact the previous conception of the poet as a bard of cosmic dimensions had an influence on his understanding of realism and its social function. Unlike the poets who confused the levels of poetic understanding with the most obvious everyday social and individual experiences, he saw reality in a wider perspective.

"Para quien escribo" (To Whom I Write), the introductory poem in *En un vasto dominio*, uses simple, direct language, as befits the style of realistic writing; most of the emotional impact comes from the rhythmic organization of the plain discourse. The long lines are separated from one another in stanza-like units characterized by enumeration and repetitions: "Escribo para el enamorado para el que pasó con su angustia en los ojos; para el que le oyó para el que al pasar no miró para el que finalmente cayó cuando preguntó y no le oyeron" (I write for the one in love for the one who walked by with anguish in his eyes; for the one who heard him; for the one who passed by and did not look; for the one who fell at last when he asked and no one listened). The similarities of the compositions in the book to some of Walt Whitman's can be attributed not solely to the metrical form but also the inspired conception of poetry and worldview that in both writers leads to a comparable expression. By listing the different types of people to whom he writes or does not intend to write, Aleixandre conveys in his first poem his basic tenets. Two of those for whom he does not write are "the gentleman with the stiff jacket" who has "furious moustaches" and raises his disapproving finger "among the sad waves of music," and the lady hidden inside a car, her lorgnettes shining "like cold lightning." These are unequivocal references to a false world of social disguise and cruel lack of sensibility, a constant motif in Aleixandre's view of creation: some forms of life are false, and, therefore, to him nonexistent. On the other hand, he writes for people who perhaps will never have the opportunity, nor the interest, to read his work: "Para todos escribo. Para los que no me leen sobre / Todo escribo" (I write for everybody. I write particularly for those who do not read my poetry). This comment coincides with a common concern among social poets who knew that they were writing for those who by education and social standing would never read their poetry. This awareness is not the full idea behind Aleixandre's verse; he was stating once more his long-sustained belief in the universal character of the poet who is fused into the totality of humankind. Thus, to tie this interpretation in with the cosmic vision of his earlier books, natural elements are also included in the list of those for whom he writes.

Toward the end of the 1960s Aleixandre abandoned most of the elements that characterize his realistic work. Social and political circumstances had changed in Spain, making it unnecessary to sing any longer the hymns of human solidarity. Furthermore, old age had finally come to him, and with it came also more of the luminosity so cherished from the beginning. A more meditative attitude set the tone of his poems. They are grouped in two major books: *Poemas de la consumación* (1968, Poems of Consumption) and *Diálogos del conocimiento*. These collections constitute a final development in the long process of the poet's growing understanding of the world. They are at the same time undeniably his and so novel that they fall well within the parameters of the new Spanish poetry. In his old age the master was able to renew himself because his experience had taught him the need to be open to inspiration. This inspiration came in different forms as he was able to grasp new meanings and interpret anew the presence of the world.

Poemas de la consumación and *Diálogos del conocimiento* reintroduce as a poetic method the almost hermetic image of his Surrealist period that had been abandoned by the mature poet in order to attain the much-desired ideal of communication. Aleixandre brought together in his last books all his capacities as a writer. He found himself in possession of revealed truth and could not pass the opportunity to try for the last time to put his inner visions into words. From the time of his initial experiments in *Ambito*, he had been dealing with poetry as a form of knowledge, as a method of apprehending the essences lost to science. He tried from the beginning to construct a worldview, a system of poetic ideas to account for reality. Consequently most of the critical approaches to his work had tried to explain, discuss, compare, or interpret its philosophical aspects. *Poemas de la consumación* and *Diálogos del conocimiento* add a new, still more complex chapter to the already comprehensive system.

Poemas de la consumación includes several brief poems in short, almost traditional hendecasyllabic meter. This style of concision reproduces the succinct discourse of a wise man who does not need many words to state his ideas. Light and darkness—day and night—are once more central to Aleixandre's conception and find their correlatives in the polarities of youth and old age, the point of realization from which the book develops as a meditation on man's temporal condition. The poems are for the most part a series of short, aphoristic sentences as expressed by a detached speaker. The poet, who to a certain extent is an objective voice, transmits the emotional feeling of ultimate, wistful wisdom.

This objective voice of knowledge changes to specific voices in *Diálogos del conocimiento,* as the poems are made up of the contrasting speeches of different characters. The structural polarity seen in *Poemas de la consumación* assumes in this volume the form of long compositions that reproduce the words of two, in some cases three, speakers who sustain opposing views but do not seem to pay attention to each other's monologues. As if they were entranced by their own intellectual and emotive convictions, they talk in the same epigrammatic manner that the unspecified speaker uses in *Poemas de la consumación*. In both cases the attitudes of the speakers and their tones of voice give the impression of ancient oracles. Several other factors help to produce in *Diálogos del conocimiento* the effect of entrancement. First in importance is the philosophical character of the book, which explains the abundance of apothegmatic statements. Images are also used in a similar axiomatic way. Many statements are contradictory or hermetic, and images are irrational, adding still more to the mysterious and gnomic tone. Reiterations give density and rhythm to the book; of particular interest are the several references to earlier texts by Aleixandre, whose work acquires in such a way the fullness of a complete and self-contained system.

After a flurry of journalistic interest caused by his 1977 Nobel Prize, Aleixandre returned to a less visible position, although he maintained his profile as one of the masters of Spanish lyrical poetry. By the time he received the Nobel Prize, Aleixandre was old (ill health prevented him from attending the ceremony), and the award had little effect on his life. The initial media exposure did not lead to increased critical attention, particularly outside Spain, and he did not write much more. He died on 14 December 1984.

The analysis and evaluation of Vicente Aleixandre's contribution to Spanish and universal letters is an ongoing process; as critical readings enhance with time the quality of his art, Aleixandre's poetry becomes an essential component of Spanish culture. Critics have most often admired in him his ability to put into highly emotional poetic language a few basically profound ideas about being. A poet with an almost religious penchant for meditation and hymn singing, Aleixandre has been praised for his understanding of the mysterious, for the poetic knowledge underlining his poetry, and for his capacity to communicate his luminous visions through verbal images.

Letters:

Epistolario, edited by José Luis Cano (Madrid: Alianza, 1986);

Correspondencia a la generación del 27 (1928–1984), edited by Irma Emiliozzi (Madrid: Castalia, 2001);

Cartas de Vicente Aleixandre a José Antonio Muñoz Rojas (1937–1984), edited by Emiliozzi, transcribed by María del Carmen Martínez Pereira (Valencia: Pre-Textos, 2005).

Biographies:

Antonio Colinas, *Conocer: Vicente Aleixandre y su obra* (Barcelona: Dopesa, 1977);

Leopoldo de Luis, *Vida y obra de Vicente Aleixandre* (Madrid: Espasa-Calpe, 1978);

José Luis Cano, *Los cuadernos de Velintonia: Conversaciones con Vicente Aleixandre* (Barcelona: Seix Barral, 1986).

References:

Carlos Bousoño, *La poesía de Vicente Aleixandre,* third edition, revised (Madrid: Gredos, 1977);

Vicente Cabrera and Harriet Boyer, eds., *Critical Views on Vicente Aleixandre's Poetry* (Lincoln, Nebr.: Society of Spanish and Spanish-American Studies, 1979);

José Luis Cano, ed., *Vicente Aleixandre* (Madrid: Taurus, 1977);

Santiago Daydí-Tolson, ed., *Vicente Aleixandre: A Critical Appraisal* (Ypsilanti, Mich.: Bilingual Press/Editorial Bilingüe, 1981);

Giancarlo Depretis, *Lo zoo di spechi (Il perceptive ambivalente nella poesia di V. Aleixandre)* (Turin: Facoltà di Magisterio, 1976);

Francisco Javier Díez de Revenga, *La poesía de Vicente Aleixandre: Testimonio y conciencia* (Málaga: Centro Cultural Generación del 27, 1999);

Hernán Galilea, *La poesía superrealista de Vicente Aleixandre* (Santiago, Chile: Editorial Universitaria, 1971);

Vicente Granados, *La poesía de Vicente Aleixandre (Formación y evolución)* (Madrid: Cupsa, 1977);

Robert Havart, ed., *A Companion to Spanish Surrealism* (London: Tamesis, 2004);

José Olivio Jiménez, *Vicente Aleixandre: Una aventura hacia el conocimiento* (Madrid: Júcar, 1982);

Gabrielli Morelli, *Linguaggio poetico del primo Aleixandre* (Milan: Gilardino-Giolardica, 1972);

Daniel Murphy, *Vicente Aleixandre's Stream of Consciousness* (Lewisburg, Pa.: Bucknell University Press, 2001);

Darío Puccini, *La palabra poética de Vicente Aleixandre* (Barcelona: Ariel, 1979);

Kessel Schwartz, *Vicente Aleixandre* (New York: Twayne, 1970).

1977 Nobel Prize in Literature Presentation Speech

by Dr. Karl Ragnar Gierow, of the Swedish Academy (Translation from the Swedish)

Your Majesties, Your Royal Highnesses, Ladies and Gentlemen,

This year's Nobel Prize winner in Literature, Vicente Aleixandre, is hard to understand and in one way controversial. The latter may be due to the former. For even his devoted admirers offer varying interpretations of his poetry. It is doubtful if anyone has yet been able to sum it up properly, one reason being that fifty years after Aleixandre's debut his writing still seems to be forging ahead. His two most remarkable collections of poems, the twin crowns of his career to date, appeared in 1968 (*Poemas de la consumación*) and 1974 (*Diálogos del conocimiento*).

On one point, however, all are agreed: Aleixandre's place and importance in the spiritual life of Spain. In the history of literature he is part of the current that broke into Spanish poetry in the 1920s with unequalled breadth and force. One of the names of the vigorous avant garde was the Pleiades. It is all the more suitable as no one with the naked eye can make out the correct number in the group of stars that we colloquially call The Seven Sisters. There are many more of them, and in the firmament of Spanish poetry these Pleiades are usually numbered at around twenty-five—a brilliant cluster of lyric talent. Among those who came to shine the brightest and the longest is Vicente Aleixandre.

The affinity of the new style with French surrealism is striking. There are those in Spain who prefer to call it apparent. They are sometimes reluctant to stress the points in common, asserting their unconformity all the more strongly. The Spanish declaration of independence is not without ground. The Second Golden Age, which is another name for the breakthrough and epoch of the Pleiades, referred directly and expressly to the first, Spain's century-long age of greatness, the baroque. When the young guard banded together to strike their big blow they chose as a standard to celebrate the 300th anniversary of Luis de Góngora, the creator of the hair-splitting "estilo culto" who originated and gave his name to the ingeniously and extravagantly ornamented gongorism. Virtuoso pastiches on Spanish baroque poetry in frills, and beside them folk-song variations of rustic themes, were characteristic elements in the renewal during the 1920s south of the Pyrenees, and they distinguish it undeniably from the manifestos up by the Seine.

When this vital generation of poets, with Lorca at the head, stormed the Spanish Parnassus, Aleixandre too was busy with his pen. He was then writing about the need of rationalization and pension and insurance problems on the Spanish railways, where he was employed. But in 1925 something happened which was to determine the whole of his existence and still does today. He was taken seriously ill with renal tuberculosis. It changed his life in two ways. He had to leave his employment and he could take another position with communications of a different kind: those of poetry. When the Góngora anniversary was celebrated he had not yet published his first volume of verse, but he had printed poems in the Pleiades' magazines and was already a member of the group. He was perhaps the one least concerned about the connexion with "the golden century" and to that extent also the one who came closest to the new doctrines from Paris. This may be the background to a somewhat defiant declaration by one of his poet friends that Spanish surrealism had given French surrealism what it had always lacked–a great poet: Vicente Aleixandre. But he has never been a mediator in this literary frontier dispute. Against the basic article of faith "l'ecriture automatique" he has reiterated his belief in "la conciencia creadora," creative consciousness. He went his own way.

In extremely simplified terms it is the way from a cosmic vision to a realistic close-up. One of Aleixandre's conclusive collections of poems is called *La destrucción o el amor* (Destruction or Love). The title is thematically pregnant with meaning and certain Aleixandre connoisseurs have taken it to mean an Either-Or, to quote Kierkegaard: without love all that is left to us is destruction. But the word "or" can mean not only two alternative contrasts but also an explanatory addition, and what the title then says is: Destruction, in other words love. It would agree better with the perspective of creation in its entirety that these poems, and those that followed, aim at depicting and that Aleixandre has been striving for ever since his debut with *Ambito*. "Man is an element in the cosmos and in his being does not differ from it," as he himself says. Love is destruction, but destruction is a result of or an act of love, of self-effacement, of man's innate yearning to be received back into the world order from which, as a living being, he has been separated and cast out–"segregado–degradado." His decease therefore has nothing of despair at a meaningful life meeting with a meaningless death. Only with death does life acquire its meaning and is complete; it is the last birth, *Nacimiento último,* as one of the later collections of poems is called. Aleixandre does not hesitate to carry his vision to the paradoxical extreme: "Man does not exist." In other words: so long as he is alive, he is actually unborn.

But out of the conviction that man is an element in a cosmic whole grows of necessity the awareness that our short life on earth is also a part of the same course of events. It is that knowledge which has brought Aleixandre back to "the tellurian world," as he calls it, given his continued writings a proximity to life, an openness and directness which formerly he was not capable of or did not strive for, and has made his last two books, mentioned in the introduction to this presentation, the peak of his work hitherto. On his way there, but conscious of where he was heading, he wrote in *Historia del corazón* a poem called "Entre dos oscuridades un relámpago," A Lightning Between Two Darknesses. In it is the earth, in it is man, and life must be affirmed so long as we have it. Intentionally or not one of the gifted dreamers of our time here quotes the words of another visionary when the meaning of the play is to be explained:

> "We are such stuff as dreams are made on, and our little life is rounded with a sleep."

Outwardly too Aleixandre went his own way. When the civil war came he was bedridden and listened to the bombs exploding. Lorca was murdered, other poet friends died in prison, and when the remainder went into exile at the end of the war, a constellation scattered to the four winds, they had to leave the invalid behind. But mentally as well Aleixandre survived the regime. He never submitted to it and went on with his writing, frail but unbroken, thereby becoming the rallying-point and source of power in Spain's spiritual life that we today have the pleasure of honouring.

The Swedish Academy deeply regrets that owing to his state of health Mr. Aleixandre can't be here today. But as his representative we greet his friend and younger colleague, Mr. Justo Jorge Padrón, and I ask you, Mr. Padrón, to convey to Mr. Aleixandre our warmest congratulations and to receive the Nobel Prize for Literature, awarded to him, from the hands of His Majesty the King.

[© The Nobel Foundation, 1977.]

Aleixandre: Banquet Speech

As Aleixandre was unable to be present at the Nobel Banquet, 10 December 1977, the speech of thanks was read by Mr. Jorge Padrón (in Spanish):

Majestades, Altezas Reales, Señoras y Señores,

En esta reunión tan grata para todos, unos, la mayoría, están aquí son su presencia física; alguna como yo con su asistencia espiritual. La voz me la presta dignamente Justo Jorge Padrón, a quien doy las gracias muy sinceras. En una reunión como ésta en que nos congregamos, de un modo u otro hombres de procedencias diversas, todos en la convocatoria del Nobel y su llamamiento radicalmente humanista, yo sienta más que nunca lo que en otra parte he expresado: que dicha alta distincion es antes que nada un simbolo de la solidaridad humana. El quiere colaborar en el progreso humano subrayando los pasos que los hombres dan en las más diferentes actividades, todas conducentes al adelantamiento de la comunicación y de la solidaridad en un destino común.

En este alto propósito de Nobel, bajo techo compartido que aquí nos reúne, yo alzo espiritualmente mi copa por el pueblo que lo ha hecho posible por todos los que lo componen. Sea pues mi brindis por este faro de Europa, ejemplo en el esfuerzo por la libertad, justicia y progreso. Levanto pues mi vaso, en la compania de ustedes, por el pueblo sueco y, con él, por quien altamente lo representa en este instante: la Academia Sueca.

[© The Nobel Foundation, 1977. Vicente Aleixandre is the sole author of his speech.]

Translation by Carla Breidenbach:

Your Majesties, Your Royal Highnesses, Ladies and Gentlemen,

At such an event so pleasant for all, some, the majority are physically present; others, like me, are with you in spirit. The honorable Jorge Padrón delivers this speech in my absence, and for this I send him my most sincere thanks. In a gathering such as this at which we all congregate in one way or another, men from diverse backgrounds, all at the summons of the Nobel and its radically humanistic calling, I feel more than ever that which I have expressed elsewhere: that this great distinction is more than anything a symbol of human solidarity. The desire to collaborate in human progress underlines the steps that man takes in his different endeavors, all conducive to the advancement of communication and solidarity toward a common goal.

In this great purpose of the Nobel, under the roof that unites us here today, I, in spirit, raise my glass to all the people who have made this possible. Let my toast be for the beacon that is Europe, example in the quest for liberty, justice, and progress. I lift my glass, in your company, for the Swedish nation and, with it, for those who represent it so highly at this moment: the Swedish Academy.

Press Release: The Nobel Prize in Literature 1977

from the Office of the Permanent Secretary of the Swedish Academy

When Vicente Aleixandre published his first volume of verse in 1928, *Ambito,* he was already closely associated personally with the greatly gifted Spanish poets who have given this epoch in Spanish literature the name, "The Second Golden Age." In its conception of poetry's essence and mode of expression, the vigorous group had something in common with the surrealism that had appeared in France and spread its manifestations from there. Iberian literary circles, however, preferred to assert their independence and drew a literary borderline along the Pyrenees. They were kindred but not allied, and south of the border, the differences were stressed by giving other names to the corresponding impulses in style—ultraism, creationism. It has also happened that the similarities have been recognized and the Gallic term accepted, but the admission has been worded in a challenging way: Spanish surrealism has given the French surrealism what it has lacked—a poet. The poet referred to was Vicente Aleixandre.

There was in fact good reason for the literary frontier dispute. It could be claimed that the Spanish current had not only taken a divergent course but also had another origin. When this unusually promising generation of Spanish writers banded together to strike their big blow, it was no coincidence that they did so at a spectacular ceremony they themselves had staged on the three hundredth anniversary of Góngora's death. They share the extravagantly ornamented imagery and the abrupt allusion technique with the French surrealists, but to an equal degree, with the baroque style, especially in its Spanish variant. Furthermore, the penchant for hairsplitting and clear-cut antitheses on the one hand, and for motifs from everyday life on the other, which characterizes much in Spanish modernism and builds on its tradition from the first golden age, is actually incompatible with "l'écriture automatique," the basic article of faith in the new doctrine from the Seine. And some of the Spaniards did voice their mistrust in this form of inspiration and communication; one of them was, and is, Aleixandre.

His first collection of poems appeared the year after the Góngora anniversary. This means that he was not one of the standard-bearers for the re-orientation of Spanish poetry; that march was well on the move. But he was already one of the company. He had contributed to their magazines and he was their contemporary. Precocity is hardly Aleixandre's literary characteristic, whereas constant renewal is. He won his place in the group immediately, and it was his own. It was confirmed as time went on, and his position became more and more prominent, founded on a prolific production with masterpieces such as *La destrucción o el amor,* 1935 (Destruction or Love), *Sombra del paraiso,* 1944 (The Shadow of Paradise), *Nacimiento último,* 1953 (The Last Birth), and *En un vasto dominio,* 1962 (In a Vast Dominion), as perhaps the most important.

There is no formula that sums up this continuously developing poetry, extensive both in time and choice of subject. But if we seek a recurrent impression, a theme which manifests itself in Aleixandre's work at different stages and in various ways, we can call it: the strength to survive. It is true also of his physical life, his personal existence. In 1925, three years before his début, he fell ill with severe and never-cured renal tuberculosis; since then he has, in brief, been bedridden or a captive at his desk. The civil war came, and from his bed he listened to the bombs exploding. When it was over and his friends and fellow-writers went into exile, they had to leave the invalid behind. But mentally, too, he survived the Franco regime, never submitting, and thus becoming a rallying-point and key figure in what remained of Spain's spiritual life.

Exemplary, revered, and a guide, frail but unbroken, Aleixandre showed even in his writings the same strength to survive and, what is more, always to renew himself, to explore other means and motifs. His inspiration has neither weakened nor dried up—on the contrary, he has attained a simplicity of expression and a warm openness both to existence and to the reader, which formerly he was not capable of or did not strive for. In this way, strangely enough, his two most recent collections of poems—*Poemas de la consumación* (Poems about Perfection) from 1968, and perhaps, above all, *Diálogos del conocimiento* (Dialogues of Insight), published as recently as three years ago—form the peak hitherto of Vicente Aleixandre's half century-long writing career.

[© The Nobel Foundation, 1977.]

Aleixandre: Nobel Lecture, 12 December 1977

(Translation)

At a moment like this, so important in the life of a man of letters, I should like to express in the most eloquent words at my command the emotion that a human being feels and the gratitude he experiences in the face of an event such as that which is taking place today. I was born in a middle-class family, but I had the benefit of its eminently open and liberal outlook. My restless spirit led me to practise contradictory professions. I was a teacher of mercantile law, an employee in a railway company, a financial journalist. From early youth this restlessness of which I have spoken lifted me to one particular delight: reading and, in time, writing. At the age of 18 the apprentice poet began to write his first verses, sketched out in secret amid the turmoil of a life which, because it had not yet found its true axis, I might call adventurous. The destiny of my life, its direction, was determined by a bodily weakness. I became seriously ill of a chronic complaint. I had to abandon all my other concerns, those which I might call corporal, and to retreat to the countryside far from my former activities. The vacuum thus created was soon invaded by another activity which did not call for physical exertion and could easily be combined with the rest that the doctors had ordered me to take. This unforgettable, all-conquering invasion was the practice of letters; poetry occupied to the full the gap in activity. I began to write with complete dedication and it was then, only then, that I became possessed by the passion which was never to leave me.

Hours of solitude, hours of creation, hours of meditation. Solitude and meditation gave me an awareness, a perspective which I have never lost: that of solidarity with the rest of mankind. Since that time I have always proclaimed that poetry is communication, in the exact sense of that word.

Poetry is a succession of questions which the poet constantly poses. Each poem, each book is a demand, a solicitation, an interrogation, and the answer is tacit, implicit, but also continuous, and the reader gives it to himself through his reading. It is an exquisite dialogue in which the poet questions and the reader silently gives his full answer.

I wish I could find fitting words to describe what a Nobel Prize means to the poet. It cannot be done; I can only assure you that I am with you body and soul, and that the Nobel Prize is as it were the response, not gradual, not tacit, but collected and simultaneous, sudden, of a general voice which generously and miraculously becomes one and itself answers the unceasing question which it has come to address to mankind. Hence my gratitude for this symbol of the collected and simultaneous voice to which the Swedish Academy has enabled me to listen with the senses of the soul for which I here publicly render my devoted thanks.

On the other hand, I consider that a prize such as I have received today is, in all circumstances, and I believe without exception, a prize directed to the literary tradition in which the author concerned—in this case myself—has been formed. For there can be no doubt that poetry, art, are always and above all tradition, and in that tradition each individual author represents at most a modest link in the chain leading to a new kind of aesthetic expression; his fundamental mission is, to use a different metaphor, to pass on a living torch to the younger generation which has to continue the arduous struggle. We can conceive of a poet who has been born with the highest talents to accomplish a destiny. He will be able to do little or nothing unless he has the good fortune to find himself placed in an artistic current of sufficient strength and validity. Conversely, I think that a less gifted poet may perhaps play a more successful role if he is lucky enough to be able to develop himself within a literary movement which is truly creative and alive. In this respect I was born under the protection of benign stars inasmuch as, during a sufficiently long period before my birth, Spanish culture had undergone an extremely important process of swift renewal, a development which I think is no secret to anyone. Novelists such as Galdós; poets like Machado, Unamuno, Juan Ramón Jiménez and, earlier, Becquer; philosophers like Ortega y Gasset; prose writers such as Azorín and Baroja; dramatists such as Valle-Inclán; painters like Picasso and Miró; composers such as de Falla: such figures do not just conjure themselves up, nor are they the products of chance. My generation saw itself aided and enriched by this warm environment, by this source, by this enormously fertile cultural soil, without which perhaps none of us would have become anything.

From the tribune in which I now address you I should like therefore to associate my words with this generous nursery ground of my compatriots who from another era and in the most diverse ways formed us and enabled us, myself and my friends of the same generation, to reach a place from which we could speak with a voice which perhaps was genuine or was peculiar to ourselves.

And I do not refer only to these figures which constitute the immediate tradition, which is always the one most visible and determinative. I allude also to the other tradition, the one of the day before yesterday, which though more distant in time was yet capable of establishing close ties with ourselves; the tradition formed by our classics from the Golden Age, Garcilaso, Fray Luis de León, San Juan de la Cruz, Gongora, Quevedo, Lope de Vega, to which we have also felt linked and from which we have received no little stimulation. Spain was able to revive and renew herself thanks to the fact that, through the generation of Galdós, and later through the generation of 1898, she as it were opened herself, made herself available, and as a result of this the whole of the nourishing sap from the distant past came flowing towards us in overwhelming abundance. The generation of 1927 did not wish to spurn anything of the great deal that remained alive in this splendid world of the past which suddenly lay revealed to our eyes in a lightning flash of uninterrupted beauty. We rejected nothing, except what was mediocre; our generation tended towards affirmation and enthusiasm, not to scepticism or taciturn restraint.

Everything that was of value was of interest to us, no matter whence it came. And if we were revolutionaries, if we were able to be that, it was because we had once loved and absorbed even those values against which we now reacted. We supported ourselves firmly on them in order to brace ourselves for the perilous leap forward to meet our destiny. Thus it should not surprise you that a poet who began as a surrealist today presents a defence of tradition. Tradition and revolution—here are two words which are identical.

And then there was the tradition, not vertical but horizontal, which came to help us in the form of a stimulating and fraternal competition from our flanks, from the side of the road we were pursuing. I refer to that other group of young people (when I too was young) who ran with us in the same race. How fortunate I was to be able to live and perform, to mould myself in the company of poets so admirable as those I came to know and devote myself to with the right of a contemporary! I loved them dearly, every one. I loved them precisely because I was seeking something different, something which it was only possible to find through differences and contrast in relation to these poets, my comrades. Our nature achieves its true individuality only in community with others, face to face with our neighbours. The higher the quality of the human environment in which our personality is formed, the better it is for us. I can say that here, too, I have had the good fortune to be able to realize my destiny through communion with one of the best companies of men of which it is possible to conceive. The time has come to name this company in all its multiplicity: Federico García Lorca, Rafael Alberti, Jorge Guillén, Pedro Salinas, Manuel Altolaguirre, Emilio Prados, Dámaso Alonso, Gerardo Diego, Luis Cernuda.

I speak then of solidarity, of communion, as well as of contrast. If I do so, it is because such has been the feeling that has been most deeply implanted on my soul, and it is its heartbeat that, in one way or another, can be heard most clearly behind the greater part of my verse. It is therefore natural that the very way in which I look upon humanity and poetry has much to do with this feeling. The poet, the truly determinative poet, is always a revealer; he is, essentially, a seer, a prophet. But his "prophecy" is of course not a prophecy about the future; for it may have to do with the past: it is a prophecy without time. Illuminator, aimer of light, chastiser of mankind, the poet is the possessor of a Sesame which in a mysterious way is, so to speak, the word of his destiny.

To sum up, then, the poet is a man who was able to be more than a man: for he is in addition a poet. The poet is full of "wisdom"; but this he cannot pride himself on, for perhaps it is not his own. A power which cannot be explained, a spirit, speaks through his mouth: the spirit of his race, of his peculiar tradition. He stands with his feet firmly planted on the ground, but beneath the soles of his feet a mighty current gathers and is intensified, flowing through his body and finding its way out through his tongue. Then it is the earth itself, the deep earth, that flames from his glowing body. But at other times the poet has grown, and now towards the heights, and with his brow reaching into the heavens, he speaks with a starry voice, with cosmic resonance, while he feels the very wind from the stars fanning his breast. All is then brotherhood and communion. The tiny ant, the soft blade of grass against which his cheek sometimes rests, these are not distinct from himself. And he can understand them and spy out their secret sound, whose delicate note can be heard amidst the rolling of the thunder.

I do not think that the poet is primarily determined by his goldsmith's work. Perfection in his work is something which he hopes gradually to achieve, and his message will be worth nothing if he offers mankind a coarse and inadequate surface. But emptiness cannot be covered up by the efforts of a polisher, however untiring he may be.

Some poets—this is another problem and one which does not concern expression but the point of departure—are poets of "minorities." They are artists (how great they are does not matter) who owe their individuality to devoting themselves to exquisite and limited subjects, to refined details (how delicate and profound were the poems that Mallarmé devoted to fans!), to the minutely savoured essences in individuals expressive of our detail-burdened civilization.

Other poets (here, too, their stature is of no importance) turn to what is enduring in man. Not to that which subtly distinguishes but to that which essentially unites. And even though they see man in the midst of the civilization of his own times, they sense all his pure nakedness radiating immutably from beneath his tired vestments. Love, sorrow, hate or death are unchanging. These poets are radical poets and they speak to the primary, the elemental in man. They cannot feel themselves to be the poets of "minorities." Among them I count myself.

And therefore a poet of my kind has what I would call a communicative vocation. He wants to make himself heard from within each human breast, since his voice is in a way the voice of the collective, the collective to which the poet for a moment lends his passionate voice. Hence the necessity of being understood in languages other than his own. Poetry can only in part be translated. But from this zone of authentic interpretation the poet has the truly extraordinary experience of speaking in another way to other people and being understood by them. And then something unexpected occurs: the reader is installed, as through a miracle, in a culture which in large measure is not his own but in which he can nevertheless feel without difficulty the beating of his own heart, which in this way communicates and lives in two dimensions of reality: its own and that conferred on it by the new home in which it has been received. What has been said remains equally true if we turn it round and apply it not to the reader but to the poet who has been translated into another language. The poet, too, feels himself to be like one of those figures encountered in dreams, which exhibit, perfectly identified, two distinct personalities. Thus it is with the translated author, who feels within himself two personae: the one conferred on him by the new verbal attire which now covers him and his own genuine personae which, beneath the other, still exists and asserts itself.

Thus I conclude by claiming for the poet a role of symbolic representation, enshrining as he does in his own person that longing for solidarity with humankind for which precisely the Nobel Prize was founded.

[©The Nobel Foundation, 1977. Vicente Aleixandre is the sole author of the text.]

Ivo Andrić
(9 October 1892 - 13 March 1975)

Vasa D. Mihailovich
University of North Carolina

See also the Andrić entry in *DLB 147: South Slavic Writers Before World War II*

BOOKS: *Ex Ponto* (Zagreb: Književni jug, 1918);
Nemiri (Zagreb: Sv. Kugli, 1920);
Put Alije Djerzeleza (Belgrade: S. B. Cvijanović, 1920);
Pripovetke I (Belgrade: Srpska književna zadruga, 1924);
Pripovetke (Belgrade: Srpska književna zadruga, 1931);
Pripovetke II (Belgrade: Srpska književna zadruga, 1936);
Izabrane pripovetke (Sarajevo: Svjetlost, 1945);
Na Drini ćuprija (Belgrade: Prosveta, 1945); translated by Lovett F. Edwards as *The Bridge on the Drina* (New York: Macmillan, 1959; London: Allen & Unwin, 1959);
Travnička hronika (Belgrade: Državni izdavački zavod Jugoslavije, 1945); translated by Kenneth Johnstone as *Bosnian Story* (London: Lincolns-Prager / New York London House & Maxwell, 1959);
Gospodjica (Sarajevo: Svjetlost, 1945); translated by Joseph Hitrec as *The Woman from Sarajevo* (New York: Knopf, 1965; London: Calder & Boyars, 1966);
Most na Žepi: Pripovetke (Belgrade: Prosveta, 1947);
Pripovijetke (Zagreb: Matica Hrvatska, 1947);
Nove pripovetke (Belgrade: Kultura, 1948);
Priča o vezirovom slonu (Zagreb: Nakladni zavod Hrvatske, 1948); expanded as *Priča o vezirovom slonu, i druge pripovetke* (Belgrade: Rad, 1960);
Priča o kmetu Simanu (Zagreb: Novo pokoljenje, 1949; expanded edition, Sarajevo: Svjetlost, 1960);
Pod gradićem: Pripovetke o zivotu bosanskog sela (Sarajevo: Seljačka knjiga, 1952);
Prokleta avlija (Novi Sad: Matica srpska, 1954); translated by Johnstone as *Devil's Yard* (New York: Grove, 1962; London: Calder, 1964);
Panorama (Belgrade: Prosveta, 1958);
Sabrana djela Ive Andrića, 16 volumes, edited by Vera Stojić, Petar Džadžić, Muharem Pervić, and Radovan Vučković (Belgrade: Prosveta / Zagreb:

Ivo Andrić (right) receiving the 1961 Nobel Prize in Literature from King Gustav VI Adolf of Sweden (AP World Wide)

Mladost / Sarajevo: Svjetlost, 1963–1976)—comprises volume 1, *Na Drini ćuprija*; volume 2, *Travnička hronika*; volume 3, *Gospodjica*; volume 4, *Prokleta avlija*; volume 5, *Nemirna godina*; volume 6, *Žeđ*; volume 7, *Jelena, žena koje nema*; volume 8, *Znakovi*; volume 9, *Deca*; volume 10, *Staze, lica, predeli*; volume 11, *Ex Ponto, Nemiri, Lirika*; volume 12, *Istorija i legenda: Eseji, ogledi i članci*; volume 13, *Umetnik i njegovo delo*; volume 14, *Znakovi pored puta*; volume 15, *Kuća na osami i druge pripovetke*; and volume 16, *Omer paša Latas*;

Ljubav u kasabi: Pripovetke (Belgrade: Nolit, 1966);

Aska i vuk: Pripovetke (Belgrade: Prosveta, 1968);

Eseji i kritike, edited by Ljubo Jandrić (Sarajevo: Svjetlost, 1976);

Sveske, volume 17 of *Sabrana djela Ive Andrića* (Sarajevo: Svjetlost, 1982).

Editions in English: "The Žepa Bridge," translated by L. Vidaković, *Slavonic Review,* 14 (1926): 398–405;

"Gjerzelez at the Inn," translated by N. B. Jopson, *Slavonic and East European Review,* 14 (July 1935): 13–19;

"Gerzelez at the Gypsy Fair," translated by Jopson, *Slavonic and East European Review,* 14 (April 1936): 556–563;

The Vizier's Elephant: Three Novellas, translated by Drenka Willen (New York: Harcourt, Brace & World, 1962);

Bosnian Chronicle, translated by Joseph Hitrec (New York: Knopf, 1963);

"The Story of a Bridge," "Miracle at Olovo," and "Neighbors," translated by Michael Scammel in *Death of a Simple Giant and Other Modern Yugoslav Stories,* edited by Branko Alan Lenski (New York: Vanguard, 1965), pp. 19–53;

"The Climbers" and "The Bridge on the Žepa," in *Yugoslav Short Stories,* translated by Svetozar Koljević (London & New York: Oxford University Press, 1966), pp. 185–236;

The Pasha's Concubine and Other Tales, translated by Hitrec (New York: Knopf, 1968);

"Death in Sinan's Monastery," translated by James Barham, *Southern Humanities Review,* 21, no. 4 (1987): 329–339;

The Development of Spiritual Life in Bosnia under the Influence of Turkish Rule, translated by Želimir B. Juričić and John F. Loud (Durham, N.C.: Duke University Press, 1990);

Conversation with Goya; Bridges; Signs, translated by Celia Hawkesworth and Andrew Harvey (London: Menard Press with the School of Slavonic and East European Studies, University of London, 1992);

The Damned Yard and Other Stories, translated by Hawkesworth and others (London & Boston: Forest Books, 1992)—includes "A Letter from the Year 1920," translated by Lenore Grenoble;

The Days of the Consuls, translated by Hawkesworth and Bogdan Rakić (London & Boston: Forest Books, 1992).

Ivo Andrić is one of the best-known writers in the South Slav literatures. In short stories and several novels he presents the people of Bosnia, a small area in the heart of Europe, with several nationalities and four religions. He documents its long, mostly turbulent history with a plethora of remarkable characters. By immortalizing them, he has thrown light on this region that has so often erupted in violence and internecine struggle. Andrić was able to couch these events and characters in highly artistic forms that have fascinated readers all over the world and earned him a Nobel Prize in Literature, which he received in 1961.

He was born Ivan Andrić on 9 October 1892 in Dolac, a small town near Travnik in central Bosnia. Both his parents were Catholics. His father, Ivan Antun Andrić, a coppersmith, moved his family to Sarajevo soon after Andrić's birth. When his father died of tuberculosis in 1894, his impoverished mother, Katarina Andrić (née Pejić), moved with her only child to Višegrad, a town on the Drina River. Andrić completed elementary school in Višegrad and high school in Sarajevo. He attended universities in Zagreb, Vienna, and Kraków, sponsored by Hrvatsko Kulturno Društvo "Naprednok" in Sarajevo. Because of his radical nationalistic activities, he was arrested by the Austrians as a member of the revolutionary group Young Bosnia and spent three years in prison. He was released in 1917 because of poor health and a lack of evidence against him. In prison he wrote his first work, a book of prose poems, *Ex Ponto* (1918), followed two years later by a similar volume, *Nemiri* (Unrest).

After World War I, Andrić entered the diplomatic service of the new Kingdom of Yugoslavia and served for two decades in various capitals. In 1923 he was a vice consul in Graz but was in danger of losing his position because he had not completed his university studies. He enrolled that fall at the University of Graz, and in 1924 he received his doctorate after defending his dissertation, written in German: "Die Entwicklung des geistigen Lebens in Bosnien unter der Einwirkung der türkischen Herrschaft" (translated as *The Development of Spiritual Life in Bosnia under the Influence of Turkish Rule,* 1990). He returned to diplomatic service, throughout which he continued to write.

In the first twenty years of his literary career, he wrote almost exclusively short fiction, settling early upon the short story as the genre most appropriate to him. The main features of his narrative style are already discernible in his first stories, and there is relatively little change in his basic worldview or in his literary craftsmanship during the five decades of his development.

The setting of Andrić's work is most frequently Bosnia, with its plethora of races, nationalities, religions, and creeds. The narrow region of Bosnia, however, widens by implication into the whole country, indeed the entire world. Although Andrić frequently concentrates on the Turkish or Islamic element, he encompasses all nationalities and faiths. He often portrays Catholic characters also, whereas the third large group, the Orthodox Jews, remains somewhat in the background.

Andrić prefers to dwell on the distant past. For that reason many of his stories, as well as his novels, are called chronicles. In his treatment of minute detail he is scrupulously faithful to the historical sources, but he gives them artistic form. In stories dealing with the present, Andrić loses some of his ability to create lasting characters or convincing narratives. He is trying to solve the riddles of human existence by reference to the legends of the past. His constant journeys into the past do not signify an escape from the present reality but rather a keen understanding of the unity of time and space in the history of the Bosnian people.

Andrić's characters display an acute sense of loneliness and are imbued with a pervasive silence about themselves. They seem to have difficulty in coming to an understanding with their fellowman. A typical Andrić character spends his life in the search for lost identity and in trying to find his rightful place. As a symbol of the utter loneliness of his characters, Andrić uses the *kasaba* (a small, forsaken Bosnian town off the main roads). Life in a *kasaba* is torpid, desolate, and bleak. Strong individuals are condemned to futility and withering away. When their pent-up passion or frustration erupts, these individuals come to a tragic end, pulling others into the abyss as well.

Basically, life in Andrić's world is a reflection of the tragic element in human existence. His characters show an immense capacity for suffering. Sporadic happiness is but an illusion. Weak men vegetate under the spell of the strong, and strong men (in whom Andrić is most interested) are in constant rebellion against their lot. The disparity between their powers and the limited opportunities provided by their surroundings drives them mad. In his first story, *Put Alije Djerzeleza* (1920; translated as "The Journey of Ali Djerzelez," 1968), Andrić immediately raises the question of the meaning of human existence amid evil and suffering, a theme on which he will expound in many of his works. A legendary Bosnian figure (a hero of popular Muslim ballads), Alija vacillates between reality and dream, action and futility. This ambivalence results from Alija's desire to elevate himself from the torpor of confinement into a world of feeling and beauty to which he thinks he belongs. But the pragmatic life takes its revenge: Alija becomes "ridiculous and glorious" at the same time. The fact that he subjugates everything to his insatiable sexual drive underscores the frustration of his strong personality. In the merciless ridicule that vengeful weaklings heap upon Alija, and in the rejection of his passion by the women of his choice, Andrić sees the tragic aspect of human destiny.

In another early story, "Ćorkan i Švabica" (1921, Ćorkan and a German Girl), Andrić again stresses a divergence of the two worlds in an individual. In most people's eyes Ćorkan, a grave- and ditchdigger, is a hapless fool, a target of practical jokes in the *kasaba;* in his own eyes, however, he is a thwarted poet of lofty sentiments, an incorrigible dreamer, and an admirer of feminine charms and beauty. Thus, stark, drab reality clashes once more with the delicate, peculiarly refined world of a Bosnian Don Quixote who, almost invariably, ends up misunderstood and miserable.

The efforts of people like Alija and Ćorkan to extricate themselves from their confinement are almost never successful. One by one they succumb to their fate, although not without a fierce struggle. Being pitted against an unknown adversary produces in Andrić's characters a twofold reaction: in many of them it has called forth a deep-seated fear of life and people; in others it has engendered a venomous hatred against life and one's fellowman. The fear is found even among the children, whom Andrić often depicts, as if to show the primordial origin of this crippling sentiment. As Andrić mentions in "Mila i Prelac" (1936, Mila and Prelac), "Man has only to be born into this world and to open his eyes, and there is no end to what could happen to him." And in "Ćilim" (1948, The Rug) he writes, "Fear triumphs, bending man like grass whenever possible."

This fear is often coupled with a vague feeling of guilt for having been born and for being what one is. Andrić's stories often feature people who are mentally or physically handicapped or are otherwise suffering, who all carry deep in themselves a heavy burden of guilt, as if imposed upon them by fate. The guilt complex assumes many forms. It may be guilt because the character possesses an irresistible power of seduction, as in the case of the village beauty Anika in "Anikina vremena" (1931; translated as "Anika's Times," 1962), a power that ultimately leads to collective destruction. Or the guilt may arise from one's inability to suppress effectively the call of the flesh, as in "Smrt u Sinanovoj tekiji" (1936; translated as "Death in Sinan's Monastery," 1987). The source of guilt may go back for generations and transcend logical boundaries, as in the story "Ekskurzija" (1955, Excursion). It is often an underlying feeling of inextricable debt to some unknown power for bestowing joy and sorrow, love and hatred—a feeling that only adds to the helplessness of Andrić's characters.

This fear of life and feeling of guilt often result from the unjust persecution and needless suffering of Andrić's characters. Entirely blameless people are punished, sometimes even only for thinking about an evil deed or for trying to avoid it. For example, a boy whose revenge-seeking friends damage his house is punished by his father without investigation in "Prozor" (1953, The Window).

Hatred in the people of Bosnia sometimes reaches pathological proportions. In "Mustafa Madžar" (1923; translated as "Mustapha Magyar," 1968), one of Andrić's most striking characters repeats vitriolically that "the world is full of rot." A fearless warrior, he hates everyone and is, in turn, hated and feared by everybody. He ultimately dies a senseless death at the hands of a decrepit gypsy. The hatred is not always so spontaneous and irrational. Sometimes it is deliberately fostered by the conflicting variety of nationalities, races, and religions, which, under specific historical circumstances, pits one segment of the population against another or against all the rest. In Andrić's words, Bosnia is a land of hatred. It appears, as he writes in "Pismo iz godine 1920" (1946; translated as "A Letter from 1920," 1992), "as a self-sustained force that has an end in itself. . . . It is simply an agent of self-destruction."

Andrić's basic philosophy seems extremely skeptical and pessimistic; yet, Andrić does not negate life, despite its shortcomings. He firmly believes that there exists an unknown formula that governs the relationship between joys and sorrows. He conceives of life as a constant struggle between the opposites in nature, especially in the human soul. He said in one of his prose poems from *Ex Ponto,* "I am constantly watching the flower and the bloom and yet cannot help thinking about man." Ubiquitous enmities and contradictions may, and often do, lead to individual tragedies but not to an unequivocal denial of life. If a clarification of the apparent senselessness of human existence cannot be obtained, there is still hope in a struggle against evil, no matter how futile such efforts may seem.

Andrić attempts to solve the problem of the meaning of life ontologically. His favorite metaphor in this respect is a bridge that connects opposites: myth and reality, the unlimited and limited, East and West. A manifest proof of human vitality and indestructibility amid apparent contradiction and decay in nature, a bridge is also a lasting monument of the human quest for art and beauty. It is not by reason and force that man conquers fate but by synthesis, silence, and beauty. The white, slender silhouette of a bridge represents for Andrić "an unusual thought gone astray and arrested in this strange wilderness," which thus becomes at the same time a conqueror of evil and chaos, as he writes in "Most na Žepi" (1925; translated as "The Žepa Bridge," 1926).

Another illustration of Andrić's attempt to solve the basic problem of the meaning of man's existence is found in an unusual allegorical story, "Aska i vuk" (1953, Aska and the Wolf). Aska, a young lamb, has lost its way in the woods and is confronted by a hungry wolf. The lamb begins to dance a highly artistic pantomime, which so intrigues the wolf that he not only forgets to eat the lamb but remains transfixed until he is ultimately slain. This dance from fear of death is transformed into a dance for life, thus symbolizing Andrić's belief that as long as man tries to live fully, his nothingness remains irrelevant. In his own words, "art and will to resist are victorious over all evil, and even death."

When World War II began, Andrić was an ambassador in Berlin. Because he disagreed with the Yugoslav government's joining Adolf Hitler's tripartite pact, he resigned in March 1941, thus ending his diplomatic career. Hitler captured Yugoslavia in less than two weeks. Andrić spent the entire occupation in Belgrade, turning to writing novels in quiet and isolation. These four years, permeated by wholesale death and destruction, were the most productive in Andrić's literary career. He completed three novels and published them in 1945, the first postwar Yugoslav publications after the victory over the Germans.

Perhaps his most important work, the novel *Na Drini ćuprija* (1945; translated as *The Bridge on the Drina,* 1959), is an encompassing saga covering the history of Bosnia between 1566 and 1914. However, Andrić wrote the novel not as history but as a chronicle of life in Bosnia and of characters of several generations. The novel is replete with details about the life of the Bosnians under the Turkish occupation. The most important is the so-called blood tribute, a practice of the Turkish rulers during the several hundred years of their occupation of the Balkans. It meant taking boys away from their parents and raising them as the sultan's obedient servants, called janissaries. One such boy, taken from the Serbian village of Sokolovići in Bosnia in 1516 when he was only ten years old, later became Mehmed Pasha Sokolli and rose to the title of grand vizier—the highest position a non-Turk could attain in the Ottoman Empire. In memory of his childhood, he decided to build a bridge across the Drina River by the town of Višegrad, the last place where he had seen his mother when he was taken away.

The building of the bridge began in 1566, using slave labor conscripted in the Serbian villages nearby. The peasants not only resented having to work as slaves but also saw in the building of the bridge a sinister symbol of the Turkish might. For that reason they resisted its progress, often destroying at night what was built during the day. To frighten the distrusting and rebellious populace into submission and obedience, the builder Abidaga caught one of them, Radisav, and had him impaled at the site of the bridge. The excruciatingly painful process lasted several days.

The bridge was completed in 1571, a beautiful structure of eleven arches rising above the turbulent Drina, with a *kapia*—an elevated fixture in the middle of the bridge where people can sit and talk while drinking coffee—as a focal point. A caravansary was also built next to the bridge for tired travelers. Thus began the long influence of the bridge on every aspect of the lives of the people on the shores, who finally resigned themselves to it and learned even to like it because of its usefulness and its uncommon beauty. Mehmed Pasha was stabbed to death by a deranged dervish only a few years after the completion. Although he had accomplished many other things as a vizier, his name in Bosnia will forever be remembered by this bridge.

As the years and decades pass, life among the Muslims, Christians, and Jews keeps changing, but the bridge survives everything, shining "clean, young and unalterable, strong and lovely in its perfection, stronger than all that time might bring and men imagine to do." The novel chronicles events both on a larger scale—cholera and plague in the nineteenth century, the Austrian annexation of Bosnia in 1908, and the first bombs of World War I—and on an individual level, as when a beautiful girl, Fata, jumps from the *kapia* to her death during her wedding procession because her father is forcing her to marry a man she does not love. No matter how unquiet the waters that pass beneath the smooth and perfect arches of the bridge, nothing changes the bridge itself. It becomes a focal point of life in the town and surrounding villages.

The story is completely historical. The bridge was blown up during World War I, but it was rebuilt just as it was, and still stands. As a lifelong diplomat of the Kingdom of Yugoslavia, Andrić was also an astute student of history, and he often studied historical documents in preparation for writing his works. Even his doctoral thesis reveals his passion for history. *Na Drini ćuprija* encompasses the entire period of the Turkish rule of the Balkans, mirroring the birth and death of the Ottoman occupation of Bosnia. It is a broadly conceived panorama of cultural changes brought about by the Turkish reign and of the multicultural and multireligious state resulting from it. It also depicts inevitable and multifaceted conflicts in the area. The novel is, therefore, a good source of general information about Bosnia, although not a substitute for a scholarly history.

Andrić concludes half of the chapters with a short paragraph extolling the bridge as a symbol of the permanence of all life. Considering the constant changes taking place around the bridge, its permanence serves as a comforting and life-affirming value. Andrić imparts another symbolic meaning to the bridge by calling it a thing of beauty, a reflection of man's age-old desire to create beauty and enrich life. The inborn need of man to express himself in arts found its fulfillment in the creation of this beautiful edifice that defies transience. The final symbolic interpretation of the bridge lies in its spanning the two shores, as if connecting two worlds, the East and the West, and different nationalities, religions, and cultures of Bosnia. As a diplomat who saw the main key to success in the art of compromise, Andrić used the metaphor of the bridge to underline the need for minimizing the differences for the sake of living in harmony. The strife in Bosnia in the 1990s clearly shows what happens when the plea that Andrić built into his novel is unheeded.

Travnička hronika (1945, The Travnik Chronicle); translated as *Bosnian Story,* 1959; as *Bosnian Chronicle,* 1963; and as *The Days of the Consuls,* 1992) is a chronicle of life in Travnik, a provincial Turkish capital in Bosnia, in the first two decades of the nineteenth century. Travnik was an administrative seat at the westernmost border of the Ottoman Empire and the residence of a vizier. The facts that the French had occupied nearby Dalmatia and that the Turks had been forced to retreat from Hungary made Travnik important beyond its true political and strategic value. The French sent in 1806 a consul, Jean Baptiste-Etienne Daville, to keep an eye on the Turks. This act, in turn, prompted the Austrians to send their own consul, Josef von Mitterer. Both find themselves under the constant vigil of the distrustful Turks. Non-Turkish inhabitants welcome them in their own ways: Catholic Croats are friendly toward their neighbor, von Mitterer, while shunning Daville; the Jews, of whom there is a small number, like Daville; while the Orthodox Serbs distrust both, pinning their hopes on Russia, which is expected to send their consul also. Yet, they are all powerless under the Turkish domination. Daville, a middle-aged diplomat who writes classical poetry and tries to keep the semblance of civilization in a backwater town where the lifestyle resembles that of the Middle Ages, finds it difficult to function, yet he endures for the sake of his idol Napoleon Bonaparte and for the glory of France. Von Mitterer has it somewhat easier since Bosnia is closer to Austria, and the non-Turkish population is more sympathetic. Both of them, however, have to deal primarily with Turkish viziers, who wield all power and can thwart all their efforts by various means. The work of the two Western consuls is further complicated by the necessity of playing against each other. The entire novel chronicles the lives and endeavors of these participants in world politics in a most unlikely place.

Even though the two consuls and their families eventually adjust to the unusual life in Travnik, both have difficulties leading a normal life, especially Daville's gentle wife, who during their stay loses a child and gives birth to two others. Yet, being more practical and more religious than her husband, she is better equipped to cope with life in a foreign land. When, finally, Napoleon's fortunes turn sour and Daville's mission is terminated, both he and his wife are glad to leave, as are von Mitterer and his family. The chronicle of the attempts of the Western powers to intrude in the life of this strange but fascinating country comes to an end, and Travnik again recedes into the darkness of a life outside of history, leaving its people to remember for a long time "the days of the consuls."

The main theme of the novel is the contrast between the West and the East. The comparatively enlightened world of the West, represented by the consuls, is countered by the backward, mysterious, dark world of the East as it existed in the Turkish empire. Even though the opposing sides are not in an open conflict, the behavior of the players involved points to a tacit rivalry that is just as intense. The distrust with which the Westerners are met, not only by the Turkish officials but also by the people on the street, can only be explained by a deep-seated enmity. The antagonism goes beyond the political and national differences; it goes to the core of the way of life and thinking of the two worlds. Philosophical fatalism, resignation, deep mistrust of everything foreign, and a basic disregard for the rights of individuals—considered normal among the people of the East and the Turkish Empire—are pitted against the more open, compassionate, rational, and law-oriented ways of the West.

Andrić presents this drama not so much by musings and discussions about history but through the interplay of the characters, who are forced into situations beyond anything they have experienced before. This focus, in turn, adds a special dimension to the novel. That this novel is not simply an historical chronicle but primarily a story of the people caught in the maelstrom of history is further demonstrated by the psychological studies Andrić provides for most of his characters. In all of his works he is at his best when he illuminates the deepest recesses of the minds and hearts of his protagonists, no matter to what race, nationality, class, or creed they belong. This approach makes the novel more interesting than if it were strictly an historical chronicle. Thus, Travnik, its historical significance at the time notwithstanding, becomes a backdrop for several human dramas that make up the core of the novel. Even though almost all events and personalities can be traced back to historical sources, which Andrić had researched diligently, the historical events—the Napoleonic Wars, the reforms of Selim the Third, and the first Serbian uprising—are never in the forefront. In the last analysis, however, the actions of the characters are futile, because everything is decided for them elsewhere; the actors are like puppets directed by remote control, so to speak, achieving little by themselves as far as history is concerned.

Another important theme is the role of women in the novel. Unlike in many of his other works, Andrić sharply differentiates between oriental women, who are little more than objects of men's pleasure, and the emancipated Western women, who are equal partners, with their own rights. Furthermore, the universal meaning of the novel can be seen as the need for perseverance in a hopeless, dead-end situation. This theme is symbolized by Daville's hope at the end of the novel, before leaving Travnik, that "the right road" will eventually be found, his contrary Bosnian experience notwithstanding.

Like many other works, this novel serves Andrić in part as a vehicle for his own thoughts and ideas about life and history. Furthermore, just as the bridge on the Drina is the symbol of bridging the differences between worlds, Travnik is a symbol of the *kasaba* in the backwaters of an empire, where little is happening, yet people continue to strive against all odds. Thus, even though the picture Andrić presents is often bleak and melancholy, life pulses beneath the surface with full vigor. His mastery of a penetrating psychological study of his characters against the backdrop of events over which they have little control, yet somehow survive and move forward, has reached in *Travnička hronika* its highest peak.

His next novel, *Gospodjica* (1945, Miss; translated as *The Woman from Sarajevo,* 1965), has several fascinating aspects: Andrić's concentration on one character and the resulting depth of portraiture; the brilliant penetration into the psyche of a woman unusual in many ways; the author's strange attachment to this character, an attitude Andrić has shown in few other works; and the setting in a more modern time rather than the distant past. For these reasons, *Gospodjica,* though less acclaimed critically than most of Andrić's other works, has a significance of its own.

At the beginning of the novel, Rajka Radaković, a middle-aged spinster, lives in Belgrade, where she has moved after World War I from her native Sarajevo. She has lived alone with her mother since she was fifteen, when her beloved father, a well-known businessman from Sarajevo, died bankrupt and in disgrace. The story of her happy childhood and unhappy youth is told in flashbacks. An only child, withdrawn and overly serious for her age, she felt secure while her father was alive. Just before he died prematurely, he warned her to "save, save always, everywhere and in everything" and not to trust people because "all our feelings and concerns for others show our weaknesses only." This admonition marks the beginning of an aberration in the character of little Rajka that eventually grows to monstrous proportions. She takes her father's advice literally and from an early age begins a life of excessive thrift and self-denial bordering on obsession.

As soon as she becomes of age, Rajka takes over her father's business and with a remarkable dexterity rebuilds the family fortune, mainly through lending money at exorbitant rates. She denies her mother and herself all normal pleasures save for the most basic needs. She isolates herself and, little by little, turns away all family friends and most of the relatives. Her life centers exclusively on money matters, out of a pathological fear that she will suffer the same financial ruin as her father. That insecurity, coupled with some peculiar strains in her character—excessive egotism, selfishness, miserliness, insensitivity to the needs of others, and a lack of normal human drives—follows her throughout her life until she ruins everyone she associates with and, ultimately, herself.

There is only one occasion when she lets her guard down and allows herself to be sidetracked from her single-minded direction. An attractive and pleasant young man, a war hero, needs money to obtain an automobile dealership and asks Rajka for it. Because he resembles her younger uncle, whom she loved and who had died young and penniless mainly because of his irresponsibility, Rajka lends him a sizable amount of money against her better judgment. When, after patiently waiting for him to return the money, she discovers that he has been squandering it on women and the easy life, she is almost crushed, but she recovers. She is also reaffirmed in her belief that no one is to be trusted and that one must think of oneself exclusively. The most disturbing aspect of this affair is her realization that she let her emotions guide her even after so many years of conditioning herself to the opposite. This experience makes Rajka even more suspicious of everything, so much so that she develops a persecution mania. She is ultimately frightened to death when she imagines an intruder has come to rob her, and she dies of a heart attack, all alone. Her body is discovered two days later by a mailman.

The greatest merit of the novel lies in the focused portrait of the protagonist. Rajka is an archetype, the quintessential miser, in a long line of similar characters in world literature, such as Plautus's *Aulularia,* Moliere's *L'Avare* (1668, The Miser), and Jovan Sterija Popović's *Kir Janja* (1837), with some inevitable differences. Her pathological miserliness derives from a sense of insecurity, which came about primarily from her father's failure in business. Rajka apparently has no redeeming qualities; Andrić seems to want to soften such a harsh conclusion, however, by offering an explanation for her affliction. She desires to avenge and redeem her father, who was ruined financially and eventually died from grief because his business morality was based on trust in others and on a desire to help rather than to amass wealth. Rajka's justification for her behavior, stemming from the experience of her father as she understood it, is rather simple: the world is basically evil, selfish, insensitive, even cruel; it kills soft and honest people like her father but is subservient before hard and unscrupulous people like herself. Therefore, she has become avaricious, insensitive, and even cruel only to protect herself from an evil world. And if she avenges her father's untimely death in the process, it would give her an added satisfaction.

These two traits—her desire for revenge and her insecurity complex—have combined to create a monster of a human being. Still, Andrić ultimately does not leave her without some positive qualities. The need to avenge her father is an understandable human quality after all, and her insecurity is also all too human. Moreover, when the young man needs help, she for once shows understanding and compassion; yet, she is bitterly deceived, thus confirming her distrust and forcing her to shun people for the rest of her life.

Andrić approaches the theme of avarice from a purely psychological angle, as a character trait of one person only and not of a social class, race, or nationality. Rajka's trait is not an easily recognizable stereotype, as with William Shakespeare's Shylock in *The Merchant of Venice* (1600), for example. Hers is an individual aberration, and as such, is all the more convincing. It is also interesting that she is the only woman among the prototypes of a miser and the only heroine of a novel, while all the others are dramatis personae. Finally, Rajka has a few more sympathetic qualities than other archetypal misers, thus she is developed more fully as an individual.

The change of political system in Yugoslavia in 1945 presented Andrić with a problem. Even though he was always interested in politics, he was by nature reclusive and cautious, and as a diplomatic servant he was reluctant to make public his opinions and preferences. Yet, the new regime insisted that everyone who was not anticommunist should render his or her services in the rebuilding of the country after enormous destruction, so Andrić agreed. Honored and feted, he served in many public posts, even though it was against his nature. To be sure, Andrić was careful not to step over the boundaries of decency. At the same time, the regime was careful not to press him more than necessary. The relationship of mutual understanding lasted for the rest of his life.

Manuscript page from Andrić's 1945 historical novel Travnicka hronika *(translated as* Bosnian Story, *1959), which depicts the lives of two foreign consuls in the nineteenth-century provincial Turkish capital of Travnik, in Bosnia (Ivo Andrić Foundation, Belgrade; from Radovan Popovic,* Ivo Andrić–A Writer's Life, *1989; Davis Library, University of North Carolina–Chapel Hill)*

Andrić's short novel (treated by some critics as a novella) *Prokleta avlija* (1954; translated as *Devil's Yard*, 1962; as *Damned Yard*, 1992) is one of the best of his post–World War II works. The yard, actually the Turkish prison near Istanbul, is envisioned as a microcosm. Its inhabitants, both the rulers and the ruled, represent the full scale of man's diversity and of his problems. Amid the cruel world of the warden, Karadjoz, and his perverse notion that it is easier to release an innocent man from the prison than to hunt him, if necessary, in the dark corners of Istanbul, there lives as a prisoner a young scholar and a dreamer, Ćamil, whose only crime is his "subversive" interest in an authoritarian historical figure. In the clash between the ruthless wielder of naked force and the gentle champion of pure spirit, the warden claims the head of the imprisoned scholar, but the latter emerges as moral victor. The tempting allusions to present-day politics notwithstanding, Andrić's philosophy here tends to transcend the real and the obvious and to elevate the question of the meaning of human existence to a universal level. Fear, guilt, hatred, loneliness, indeed all evil, are conquered within the walls of human imprisonment. Though life may be accursed and walled in, its creative forces emerge as much stronger than the adversities or the adversaries.

Among Andrić's late short stories, "Priča o vezirovom slonu" (1947; translated as "The Vizier's Elephant," 1962) stands out. The sultan's vizier is never seen in public; instead, his elephant, an animal unheard of in Bosnia save in a circus, parades every day through the town, displaying a blatant proof of the vizier's terrifying presence. The animal is not really responsible for its various pranks among the townspeople, nor is the vizier in the town of his own will. The chain of responsibility is extended into infinity, revealing the absurdity of the entire situation. This vivid metaphor of ruthless authoritarianism also lends itself possibly to the allegory pertaining to the present.

In 1958 Andrić married Milica Babić, a widowed costume designer for the National Theatre in Belgrade with whom he had been in love for many years. The marriage lasted until her death ten years later.

Winning the Nobel Prize in Literature in 1961 had an enormous effect upon Andrić the man and the artist. As he was the only South Slav writer to receive this prestigious award, it was highly gratifying for him. The outpouring of congratulations and respect attested that he now truly belonged to world literature. He was already famous, but after the Nobel Prize he became even more useful to the regime, which enhanced its reputation by taking credit for any citizen's success. However, as modest and withdrawn as he was for his entire life and career, he took the prize in stride. He continued to write as before, at a somewhat lesser pace, but the publication and republication of his works skyrocketed not only in his home country but also around the world. Andrić's Nobel Prize also spurred a larger interest in all Serbian literature, and translations into other languages increased significantly. Andrić donated his prize money to several local libraries.

Andrić spent the last years of his life struggling with poor health but continuing to write. He succumbed to illness on 13 March 1975. Of all of his late works, one stands out: the novel *Omer paša Latas* (Omer-pasa Latas), published posthumously in 1976. It was envisioned as a concluding part of the "Bosnian trilogy," together with *Na Drini ćuprija* and *Travnička hronika*. It was supposed to be the story of a famous Turkish military leader of Serbian descent, who was uncommonly brave and who crushed many rebellions in the Ottoman Empire. Andrić never completed it, however, and since it was left unfinished, it is difficult to pass any definitive judgment about it. Since Andrić used his favorite method of going meticulously through historic documents to lend his work the utmost authenticity, one can only guess what *Omer paša Latas* would have added to the trilogy: confirmation of earlier standpoints or their revision. Knowing his attachment to his beloved Bosnia, it is possible that this novel would have been a finishing touch on a grand literary edifice.

Two other unfinished works published posthumously, *Znakovi pored puta* (1976, Signs by the Roadside) and *Kuća na osami* (1976, The House by Itself), are collections of short stories and meditative pieces. Although interesting in themselves, they represent only glimpses of what they could have been had they been completed.

When Andrić received the Nobel Prize, the citation praised "the epic force with which he has traced themes and depicted human destinies from his country's history." In his banquet speech he commented that "the storyteller and his work serve no purpose unless they serve, in one way or another, man and humanity." These words sum up Andrić's philosophy concerning his literary output. It can be safely said that he has fulfilled his mission of a witness to the existence and history of his country, small by space and numbers, but important to Andrić within his artistic vision.

Letters:

Letters, translated and edited by Želimir B. Juričić (Toronto: Serbian Heritage Academy, 1984);

Pisma (1912-1973): Privatna pošta, edited by Miroslav Karaulac (Novi Sad: Matica srpska, 2000).

Bibliographies:

Gordana Popović, *Ivo Andrić: Bibliografija dela, prevoda i literature* (Belgrade: Srpska akademija nauka i umetnosti, 1974);

Vasa D. Mihailovich and Mateja Matejic, *A Comprehensive Bibliography of Yugoslav Literature in English 1593-1980* (Columbus, Ohio: Slavica, 1984), pp. 38-41; supplements, (1988), p. 26; (1992), pp. 26-27; (1999), pp. 16-17.

Biographies:

Petar Džadžić, *Ivo Andrić* (Belgrade: Nolit, 1957); translated into English by Marija Stansfild-Popović (Belgrade: Committee for Foreign Relations of the FPR Yugoslavia, 1960);

Miroslav Karaulac, *Rani Andrić* (Belgrade: Prosveta / Sarajevo: Svjetlost, 1980);

Radovan Popović, *Ivo Andrić: Život* (Belgrade: Jugoslovenska Revija, 1989); translated by Karin Radovanović as *Ivo Andrić–A Writer's Life* (Belgrade: Jugoslovenska Revija, 1989);

Vanita Singh Mukerji, *Ivo Andrić: A Critical Biography* (Jefferson, N.C. & London: McFarland, 1990).

References:

Miloš I. Bandić, *Ivo Andrić: Zagonetka vedrine* (Novi Sad: Matica srpska, 1963);

Gun Bergman, *Turkisms in Ivo Andrić's 'Na Drini Ćuprija' Examined from the Points of View of Literary Style* (Uppsala: Almquist & Wiksells, 1969);

Thomas Butler, "Reflections of Ottoman Rule in the Works of Petar Kočić, Ivo Andrić and Meša Selimović," *Serbian Studies,* 11 (1997): 66-75;

Mary P. Coote, "Narrative and Narrative Structure in Ivo Andrić's *Devil's Yard*," *Slavic and East European Journal,* 21 (Spring 1977): 56-63;

Jovan Deretić, "Tematska središta u strukturi Andrićeve pripovetke," *Književna istorija,* 5 (1972): 208–233;

Vojislav Djurić, ed., *Ivo Andrić* (Belgrade: Institut za teoriju književnosti i umetnosti, 1962);

Thomas Eekman, "The Later Stories of Ivo Andrić," *Slavonic and East European Review,* 48 (July 1970): 341–356;

Alan Ferguson, "Public and Private Worlds in *Travnik Chronicle*," *Modern Language Review,* 70 (October 1975): 830–838;

E. D. Goy, "The Work of Ivo Andrić," *Slavonic and East European Review,* 41 (June 1963): 301–326;

Celia Hawkesworth, *Ivo Andrić: Bridge between East and West* (London: Athlone Press, 1984);

Hawkesworth, "Ivo Andrić's Unobtrusive Narrative Technique with Special Reference to *Kuća na osami*," *Annali dell' Istituto Orientale di Napoli,* 20, no. 1 (1979): 131–153;

Želimir B. Juričić, *The Man and the Artist: Essays on Ivo Andrić* (Lanham, Md.: University Press of America, 1986);

Ante Kadić, "The French in *The Chronicle of Travnik*," *California Slavic Studies,* 1 (1960): 134–169;

J. Kragalott, "Turkish Loanwords as an Element of Ivo Andrić's Literary Style in *Na Drini ćuprija*," *Balkanistica,* 2 (1975): 65–82;

Albert Lord, "Ivo Andrić in English Translation," *American Slavic and East European Review,* 23 (September 1964): 563–573;

John Loud, "Between Two Worlds: Andrić the Storyteller," *Review of National Literatures,* 5, no. 1 (1974): 112–126;

Loud, "*Zanos* in the Early Stories of Ivo Andrić," dissertation, Harvard University, 1971;

Claudio Marabini, "La Narrativa di Ivo Andrić," *Nuova antologia di lettere, arti e scienze,* 499 (1967): 474–490;

Vasa D. Mihailovich, "The Basic World View in the Short Stories of Ivo Andrić," *Slavic and East European Journal,* 10 (Summer 1966): 173–177;

Mihailovich, "The Reception of the Works of Ivo Andrić in the English-Speaking World," *Southeastern Europe,* 9 (1982): 41–52;

Regina Minde, *Ivo Andrić. Studien ueber seine Erzaehlkunst* (Munich: Otto Sagner, 1962);

Dragan Nedeljković, ed., *Delo Ive Andrića u kontekstu evropske književnosti i kulture* (Belgrade: Zadužbina I've Andrića, 1981);

Predrag Palavestra, *Knjiga o Andriću* (Belgrade: BIGZ & SKZ, 1992);

Lorna Mintz Peterson, "The Development of Narrative Technique in Ivo Andrić," dissertation, Yale University, 1973;

Njegoš M. Petrović, *Ivo Andrić, L'homme et l'oeuvre* (Ottawa: Les Editions Lemeac, 1969);

Branko Popović, "Istorija i poezija u Andrićevom delu," *Književna istorija,* 5 (1972): 193–207;

Felicity Rosslyn, "The Short Stories of Ivo Andrić: Autobiography and the Chain of Proof," *Slavonic and East European Review,* 67 (January 1989): 29–41;

Isidora Sekulić, "Istok u pripovetkama Iva Andrića," *Srpski književni glasnik,* 10 (1923): 502–511;

Dragoljub Stojadinović, *Romani Iva Andrića* (Priština: Jedinstvo, 1970);

Vida Taranovski-Johnson, "Bosnia Demythologized: Character and Motivation in Ivo Andrić's Stories 'Mara Milosnica' and 'O starim i mladim Pamukovićima,'" *Die Welt der Slaven,* 25 (1981): 98–108;

Taranovski-Johnson, "Ivo Andrić's *Kuća na osami*: Memories and Ghosts of the Writer's Past," in *Fiction and Drama in Eastern and Southeastern Europe,* edited by Henrik Birnbaum and Eekman (Columbus, Ohio: Slavica, 1980), pp. 239–250;

Wayne S. Vucinich, ed., *Ivo Andrić Revisited: The Bridge Still Stands* (Berkeley, Cal.: International and Area Studies Publications, 1995);

Radovan Vučković, *Velika sinteza* (Sarajevo: Svjetlost, 1974);

Jan Wierzbicki, *Ivo Andrić* (Warsaw: Wiedza Powszechna, 1965).

Papers:

Ivo Andrić's manuscripts and correspondence are housed at the Serbian Academy of Science and Art and at the Documentation Center of the Ivo Andrić Foundation in Belgrade, Serbia. His apartment in Belgrade is now a memorial museum.

1961 Nobel Prize in Literature Presentation Speech

by Anders Österling, Permanent Secretary of the Swedish Academy

The Nobel Prize in Literature has been awarded this year to the Yugoslav writer, Ivo Andrić, who has been acknowledged in his own country as a novelist of unusual stature, and who in recent years has found an increasingly wide audience as more and more of his works have come to be translated. He was born in 1892 to a family of artisans that had settled in Bosnia, a province still under Austrian rule when he was a child.

As a young Serbian student, he joined the national revolutionary movement, suffered persecution, and was imprisoned in 1914 when the war broke out. Nevertheless, he studied at several universities, finally obtaining his degree from Graz. For several years he served his country in the diplomatic service; at the outbreak of the Second World War he was the Yugoslav ambassador in Berlin. Only a few hours after his return to Belgrade, the city was bombed by German planes. Forced to retreat during the German occupation, Andrić nevertheless managed to survive and to write three remarkable novels. These are generally called the Bosnian trilogy, although they have nothing in common but their historical setting, which is symbolized by the crescent and the cross. The creation of this work, in the deafening roar of guns and in the shadow of a national catastrophe whose scope then seemed beyond calculation, is a singularly striking literary achievement. The publication of the trilogy did not take place until 1945.

The epic maturity of these chronicles in novel form, especially of his masterpiece *Na Drini ćuprija* (The Bridge on the Drina), 1945, was preceded by a phase during which Andrić, speaking in the first person of the lyric poet, sought to express the harsh pessimism of his young heart. It is significant that in the isolation of his years in prison he had found the greatest consolation in Kierkegaard. Later, in the asceticism of strict self-discipline, he discovered the way that could lead him back to what he called "the eternal unconscious and blessed patrimony," a discovery that also signified the introduction into his work of the objective epic form which he henceforth cultivated, making himself the interpreter of those ancestral experiences that make a people conscious of what it is.

Na Drini ćuprija is the heroic story of the famous bridge which the vizier Mehmed Pasha had built during the middle of the sixteenth century near the Bosnian city of Višegrad. Firmly placed on its eleven arches of light-coloured stone, richly ornamented, and raised in the middle by a superstructure, it proudly perpetuated the memory of an era throughout the following eventful centuries until it was blown up in the First World War. The vizier had wanted it to be a passage that would unite East and West in the centre of the Ottoman Empire. Armies and caravans would cross the Drina on this bridge, which for many generations symbolized permanence and continuity underneath the contingencies of history. This bridge became the scene for every important event in this strange corner of the world. Andrić's local chronicle is amplified by the powerful voice of the river, and it is, finally, a heroic and bloody act in world history that is played here.

In the following work, *Travnička hronika* (Bosnian Story), 1945, the action takes place at the time of the Napoleonic Wars. Here we witness the rivalry between the Austrian and French consuls in a desolated, old-fashioned city where a Turkish vizier has established his residence. We find ourselves in the midst of events which bring together tragic destinies. The discontent which stirs among the bazaars in the alleys of Travnik; the revolts of the Serbo-Croatian peasants; the religious wars between Mohammedans, Christians, and Jews—all of this contributes to create the atmosphere that, after a century of tension, was going to be rent by the lightning at Sarajevo. Again, Andrić's power is revealed in the breadth of his vision and the masterly control of his complex subject matter.

The third volume, *Gospodjica* (The Woman from Sarajevo), 1945, is different; it is a purely psychological study of avarice in its pathological and demoniac aspect. It tells the story of a merchant's daughter who lives alone in Sarajevo. Her bankrupt father had told her on his death-bed to defend her interests ruthlessly, since wealth is the only means of escape from the cruelties of existence. Although the portrait is strikingly successful, Andrić here confines himself to a subject that does not permit him a full display of his great narrative gifts. They are revealed fully, however, in a minor work that should receive at least a brief mention: *Prokleta avlija* (Devil's Yard), 1954. A story set in an Istanbul prison, it is as colourful in its pattern as an Oriental tale and yet realistic and convincing.

Generally speaking, Andrić combines modern psychological insight with the fatalism of the *Arabian Nights*. He feels a great tenderness for mankind, but he does not shrink from horror and violence, the most visible proof to him of the real presence of evil in the world. As a writer he possesses a whole network of original themes that belong only to him; he opens the chronicle of the world, so to speak, at an unknown page, and from the depth of the suffering souls of the Balkan slaves he appeals to our sensibility.

In one of his novellas, a young doctor recounting his experiences in the Bosnia of the 1920s says, "If you lie awake one whole night in Sarajevo, you learn to distinguish the voices of the Sarajevian night. With its rich and firm strokes the clock of the Catholic cathedral marks the hour of two. A long minute elapses; then you hear, a little more feeble, but shrill, the voice of the Orthodox Church, which also sounds its two strokes. Then, a little more harsh and far away, there is the voice of the Beg Mosque clock; it sounds eleven strokes, eleven ghostly Turkish hours, counted after the strange division of time in those far-off regions. The Jews have no bell to toll their hours, and God alone knows what time it is for them, God alone knows the number indicated on the calendar of the Sephardims and the Ashkenazims. Thus, even in the deep of the night, when everybody sleeps, the world is divided; it is divided over the counting of the lost hours of a night that is coming to an end."

Perhaps this suggestive nocturnal atmosphere also gives a key to the chief problems that have dominated Andrić's work. The study of history and philosophy has inevitably led him to ask what forces, in the blows and bitterness of antagonisms and conflicts, act to fashion a people and a nation. His own spiritual attitude is crucial in that respect. Considering these antagonisms with a deliberate and acquired serenity, he endeavours to see them all in the light of reason and with a profoundly human spirit. Herein lies, in the last analysis, the major theme of all his work; from the Balkans it brings to the entire world a stoic message, as our generation has experienced it.

Dear Sir—It is written on your diploma that the Nobel Prize has been bestowed upon you "for the epic force with which you have traced themes and depicted human destinies from your country's history." It is with great satisfaction that the Swedish Academy honours in you a worthy representative of a linguistic area which, up to now, has not appeared on the list of laureates. Extending to you our most sincere congratulations, I ask you to receive from the hands of His Majesty, the King, the Prize awarded to you.

[© The Nobel Foundation, 1961.]

Andrić: Banquet Speech

Introductory remarks by G. Liljestrand, Member of the Royal Academy of Sciences, at the Nobel Banquet at the City Hall in Stockholm, 10 December 1961:

Dr. Andrić, as a chronicler and a novelist, you have told us about your countrymen, their life and toil, their misfortunes and endurance, in peace as well as in war. You have yourself fought for their freedom and right to live their own life. Just as the bridge on the Drina brought East and West together, so your work has acted as a link, combining the culture of your country with that of other parts of our planet, a task, well worthy of a diplomat, who is also a great author.

Andrić's speech (Translation)

In carrying out the high duties entrusted to it, the Nobel Committee of the Swedish Academy has this year awarded the Nobel Prize in Literature, a signal mark of honour on the international scene, to a writer from a small country, as it is commonly called. In receiving this honour, I should like to make a few remarks about this country and to add a few considerations of a more general character about the storyteller's work to which you have graciously awarded your Prize.

My country is indeed a "small country between the worlds," as it has aptly been characterized by one of our writers, a country which, at break-neck speed and at the cost of great sacrifices and prodigious efforts, is trying in all fields, including the field of culture, to make up for those things of which it has been deprived by a singularly turbulent and hostile past. In choosing the recipient of this award you have cast a shining light upon the literary activity of that country, at the very moment when, thanks to a number of new names and original works, that country's literature is beginning to gain recognition through an honest endeavour to make its contribution to world literature. There is no doubt that your distinction of a writer of this country is an encouragement which calls for our gratitude; I am happy to have the opportunity to express this gratitude to you in this place and at this time, simply but sincerely.

It is a more difficult and more delicate task to tell you about the storyteller's work which you have honoured with your Prize. In fact, when it comes down to a writer and his work, can we expect him to be able to speak of that work, when in reality his creation is but a part of himself? Some among us would rather consider the authors of works of art either as mute and absent contemporaries or as famous writers of the past, and think that the work of art speaks with a clearer and purer voice if the living voice of the author does not interfere. This attitude is neither uncommon nor particularly new. Even in his day Montesquieu contended that authors are not good judges of their own works. I remember reading with understanding admiration Goethe's rule: "The artist's task is to create, not to talk"; and many years later I was moved to find the same thought brilliantly expressed by the greatly mourned Albert Camus.

Let me then, as seems fitting to me, concentrate in this brief statement on the story and the storyteller in general. In thousands of languages, in the most diverse climes, from century to century, beginning with the very old stories told around the hearth in the huts of our remote ancestors down to the works of modern storytellers which are appearing at this moment in the publishing houses of the great cities of the world, it is the story of the human condition that is being spun and that men never weary of telling to one another. The manner of telling and the form of the story vary according to periods and circumstances, but the taste for telling and retelling a story remains the same: the narrative flows endlessly and never runs dry. Thus, at times, one might almost believe that from the first dawn of consciousness throughout the ages, mankind has constantly been telling itself the same story, though with infinite variations, to the rhythm of its breath and pulse. And one might say that after the fashion of the legendary and eloquent Scheherazade, this story attempts to stave off the executioner, to suspend the ineluctable decree of the fate that threatens us, and to prolong the illusion of life and of time. Or should the storyteller by his work help man to know and to recognize himself? Perhaps it is his calling to speak in the name of all those who did not have the ability or who, crushed by life, did not have the power to express themselves. Or could it be that the storyteller tells his own story to himself, like the child who sings in the dark in order to assuage his own fear? Or finally, could the aim of these stories be to throw some light on the dark paths into which life hurls us at times and to tell us about this life, which we live blindly and unconsciously, something more than we can apprehend and comprehend in our weakness? And thus the words of a good storyteller often shed light on our acts and on our omissions, on what we should do and on what we should not have done. Hence one might wonder whether the true history of mankind is not to be found in these stories, oral or written, and whether we might not at least dimly catch the meaning of that history. And it matters little whether the story is set in the present or in the past.

Nevertheless, some will maintain that a story dealing with the past neglects, and to a certain degree turns its back on, the present. A writer of historical stories and novels could not in my opinion accept such a gratuitous judgment. He would rather be inclined to confess that he does not himself know very well when or how he moves from what is called the present into what we call the past, and that he crosses easily—as in a dream—the threshold of centuries. But in the end, do not past and present confront us with similar phenomena and with the same problems: to be a man, to have been born without knowing it or wanting it, to be thrown into the ocean of existence, to be obliged to swim, to exist; to have an identity; to resist the pressure and shocks from the outside and the unforeseen and unforeseeable acts—one's own and those of others—which so often exceed one's capacities? And what is more, to endure one's own thoughts about all this: in a word, to be human.

So it happens that beyond the imaginary demarcation line between past and present the writer still finds himself eye to eye with the human condition, which he is bound to observe and understand as best he can, with which he must identify, giving it the strength of his breath and the warmth of his blood, which he must attempt to turn into the living texture of the story that he intends to translate for his readers, in such a way that the result be as beautiful, as simple, and as persuasive as possible.

How can a writer arrive at this aim, by what ways, by what means? For some it is by giving free rein to their imagination, for others it is by studying with long and painstaking care the instructions that history and social evolution afford. Some will endeavour to assimilate the substance and meaning of past epochs, others will proceed with the capricious and playful nonchalance of the prolific French novelist who once said, "What is history but a peg to hang my novels on?" In a word, there are a thousand ways and means for the novelist to arrive at his work, but what alone matters and alone is decisive is the work itself.

The author of historical novels could put as an epigraph to his works, in order to explain everything to everyone, once and for all, the old saying: "Cogitavi dies antiquos et annos aeternos in mente habui" (I have pondered the days of yore and I have kept in mind the years of eternity). But with or without epigraph, his work, by its very existence, suggests the same idea.

Still, these are ultimately nothing but questions of technique, tastes, and methods, a fascinating intellectual pastime concerning a work or having vaguely to do with it. In the end it matters little whether the writer evokes the past, describes the present, or even plunges boldly into the future. The main thing is the spirit which informs his story, the message that his work conveys to mankind; and it is obvious that rules and regulations do not avail here. Each builds his story according to his own inward needs, according to the measure of his inclinations, innate or acquired, according to his conceptions and to the power of his means of expression. Each assumes the moral responsibility for his own story and each must be allowed to tell it freely. But, in conclusion, it is to be hoped that the story told by today's author to his contemporaries, irrespective of its form and content, should be neither tarnished by hate nor obscured by the noise of homicidal machines, but that it should be born out of love and inspired by the breadth of ideas of a free and serene human mind. For the storyteller and his work serve no purpose unless they serve, in one way or another, man and humanity. That is the essential point. And that is what I have attempted to bring out in these brief reflections inspired by the occasion and which, with your permission, I shall conclude as I began them, with the repeated expression of a profound and sincere gratitude.

[© The Nobel Foundation, 1961. Ivo Andrić is the sole author of his speech.]

Miguel Ángel Asturias
(19 October 1899 – 9 June 1974)

Oralia Preble-Niemi
University of Tennessee at Chattanooga

This entry was expanded by Preble-Niemi from her Asturias entry in *DLB 290: Modern Spanish American Poets, Second Series*. See also the Asturias entry in *DLB 113: Modern Latin-American Fiction Writers, First Series*.

BOOKS: *Sociología guatemalteca: El problema social del indio* (Guatemala City: Sánchez y de Guise, 1923); translated by Maureen Ahern as *Guatemalan Sociology: The Social Problem of the Indian* (Tempe: Arizona State University Center for Latin American Studies, 1977);

Rayito de estrella (Paris: Imprimerie Française de l'Edition, 1925);

La arquitectura de la vida nueva (Guatemala City: Goubaud, 1928);

La barba provisoria (Havana, 1929);

Leyendas de Guatemala (Madrid: Oriente, 1930);

Émulo Lipolidón, fantomima (Guatemala City: Américana, 1935);

Sonetos (Guatemala City: Américana, 1936);

Alclasán, fantomima (Guatemala City: Américana, 1940);

Con el rehén en los dientes: Canto a Francia (Guatemala City: Zadik, 1942);

Anoche, 10 de marzo de 1543 (Guatemala City: Ediciones del Aire, 1943);

El Señor Presidente (Mexico City: Costa-Amic, 1946; Buenos Aires: Losada, 1948); translated by Frances Partridge as *The President* (London: Gollancz, 1963); translation republished as *El Señor Presidente* (New York: Atheneum, 1963);

Poesía: Sien de alondra (Buenos Aires: Argos, 1949);

Hombres de maíz (Buenos Aires: Losada, 1949); translated by Gerald Martin as *Men of Maize* (New York: Delacorte/Seymour Lawrence, 1975);

Viento fuerte (Buenos Aires: Ministerio de Educación Pública, 1950); translated by Darwin Flakoll and Claribel Alegría as *Cyclone* (London: Owen, 1967); translated by Gregory Rabassa as *Strong Wind* (New York: Delacorte, 1968);

Ejercicios poéticos en forma de soneto sobre temas de Horacio (Buenos Aires: Botella al Mar, 1951);

Miguel Ángel Asturias (right) receiving the 1967 Nobel Prize in Literature from King Gustav VI Adolf of Sweden (photograph © Bettmann/CORBIS)

Alto es el Sur: Canto a la Argentina (La Plata, Argentina: Talleres gráficos Moreno, 1952);

Carta aérea a mis amigos de América (Buenos Aires, 1952);

El papa verde (Buenos Aires: Losada, 1954); translated by Rabassa as *The Green Pope* (New York: Delacorte, 1971);

Bolívar: Canto al Libertador (San Salvador: Ministerio de Cultura, 1955);

Soluna: Comedia prodigiosa en dos jornadas y un final (Buenos Aires: Losange, 1955);

Week-end en Guatemala (Buenos Aires: Losada, 1956);

La audiencia de los confines (Buenos Aires: Ariadna, 1957);

Messages Indiens (Paris: Seghers, 1958);

Los ojos de los enterrados (Buenos Aires: Losada, 1960); translated by Rabassa as *The Eyes of the Interred* (New York: Delacorte, 1973; London: Cape, 1974);

Las estrellas, las rosas, y la lámpara, prosas escritas entre 1927 y 1930: Unas palabras de Miguel Ángel Asturias, edited by Enrique Muñoz Meany (Guatemala City: Ediciones Revista de Guatemala, 1960);

El alhajadito (Buenos Aires: Goyanarte, 1961); translated by Martin Shuttleworth as *The Bejeweled Boy* (Garden City, N.Y.: Doubleday, 1971);

Mulata de tal (Buenos Aires: Losada, 1963); translated by Rabassa as *The Mulatta and Mr. Fly* (London: Owen, 1963); translation republished as *Mulata* (New York: Delacorte, 1967);

Rumania, su nueva imagen (Xalapa, Mexico: Universidad Veracruzana, 1964);

Teatro: Chantaje, Dique seco, Soluna, La audiencia de los confines (Buenos Aires: Losada, 1964);

Sonetos de Italia (Milan: Instituto Editoriale Cisalpino, 1965);

Clarivigilia primaveral (Buenos Aires: Losada, 1965);

El espejo de Lida Sal (Mexico City: Siglo Veintiuno, 1967); translated by Gilbert Alter-Gilbert as *The Mirror of Lida Sal: Tales Based on Mayan Myths and Guatemalan Legends* (Pittsburgh: Latin American Literary Review, 1997);

Torotumbo; La audiencia de los confines; Mensajes indios (Barcelona: Plaza y Janés, 1967);

Latinoamérica y otros ensayos (Madrid: Guadiana, 1968);

Obras completas, 3 volumes (Madrid: Aguilar, 1968);

Comiendo en Hungría, by Asturias and Pablo Neruda (Barcelona: Lumen, 1969); translated by Barna Balogh as *Sentimental Journey around the Hungarian Cuisine* (Budapest: Corvina, 1969);

Maladrón (Buenos Aires: Losada, 1969);

Trois des quatre soleils, translated by Claude Couffon (Geneva: Skira, 1971); original Spanish version published as *Tres de cuatro soles (edición crítica),* edited by Dorita Nouhaud (Paris: Klincksieck / Madrid: Fondo de Cultura Económica, 1977);

The Talking Machine, translated by Beverly Koch (Garden City, N.Y.: Doubleday, 1971);

El problema social del indio y otros textos, edited by Couffon (Paris: Centre de Recherches de l'Institut d'Etudes Hispaniques, 1971);

Novelas y cuentos de juventud, edited by Couffon (Paris: Centre de Recherches de l'Institut d'Etudes Hispaniques, 1971);

América, fábula de fábulas y otros ensayos, edited by Richard J. Callan (Caracas: Monte Ávila, 1972);

Viernes de dolores (Buenos Aires: Losada, 1972);

Juárez (Mexico City: Comisión Nacional para la Conmemoratión del Centenario del Fallecimiento de don Benito Juárez, 1972);

Sinceridades, edited by Epaminondas Quintana (Guatemala City: Académica Centroamericana, 1980);

El hombre que lo tenía todo, todo, todo; La leyenda del Sombrerón; La leyenda del tesoro del Lugar Florido (Barcelona: Bruguera, 1981);

El árbol de la cruz, edited by Aline Jacquart and Amos Segala (Nanterre: ALLCA XX/Université Paris X, Centre de Recherches Latino-Américaines, 1993);

Miguel Ángel Asturias, raíz y destino: Poesía inédita (1917–1924), edited by Marco Vinicio Mejía (Guatemala City: Artemis Edinter, 1999).

Editions and Collections: *Obras escogidas,* 3 volumes (Madrid: Aguilar, 1955–1966);

Mi mejor obra: Autoantología (Mexico City: Organización Editorial Novaro, 1973);

El Señor Presidente: Edición crítica, edited by Ricardo Navas Ruiz and Jean-Marie Saint-Lu (Paris: Klincksieck, 1978);

Viernes de dolores: Edición crítica, edited by Iber H. Verdugo (Paris: Klincksieck / Madrid: Fondo de Cultura Económica, 1978);

Hombres de maíz: Edición crítica, edited by Gerald Martin (Paris: Klincksieck / Madrid: Fondo de Cultura Económica, 1981);

Viajes, ensayos y fantasías, edited by Richard J. Callan (Buenos Aires: Losada, 1981);

París 1924–1933: Periodismo y creación literaria, edited by Amos Segala (Nanterre: ALLCA XX/Université Paris X, Centre de Recherches Latino-Américaines, 1988);

Con la magia de los tiempos (Guatemala City: Ministerio de Cultura y Deportes/Herederos de Miguel Ángel Asturias, 1999);

El hombre que lo tenía todo, todo, todo (Guatemala City: Editorial Piedra Santa Arandi, 2000);

Cuentos y leyendas, edited by Mario Roberto Morales (Madrid: ALLCA XX, 2000).

OTHER: "Maximón, divinidad de agua dulce," in *Terres Latines, Année 2* (N.p., 1946), pp. 25–36;

Poesía precolombina, edited by Asturias (Buenos Aires: Compañía General Fabril, 1960);

"La novela latinoamericana es testimonio de nuestro tiempo," in *Inostrannaia literatura,* 9 (Moscow, 1966), pp. 25–36.

TRANSLATIONS: *Los dioses, los héroes y los hombres de Guatemala Antigua; o El libro del Consejo, Popol Vuh de los indios quichés,* translated by Asturias and J. M. González de Mendoza from the French translation by Georges Raynaud (Paris: París-Americana, 1927); republished as *El libro del consejo* (Mexico City: Universidad Nacional Autónoma, 1939);

Anales de los Xahil de los indios cakchiqueles, translated by Asturias and González de Mendoza from the French translation by Raynaud (Paris, 1928; revised edition, Guatemala City: Tipografía Nacional, 1937).

Guatemalan author Miguel Ángel Asturias was recognized with the Nobel Prize in Literature in 1967 for his prolific and innovative literary production in multiple genres. His worldwide fame came primarily because of his narratives in both the novel and short-story genres. In the preface to his 1970 study of Asturias, Richard J. Callan identifies Asturias's considerable contributions to the world of letters: "there are some who see in his works on political and social dictatorship the finest novels of protest we have. For others, his fanciful tales of Indian and Spanish folklore, told in the rich and ambiguous language of dreamwork, have the inexhaustible value of poetry." In subsequent decades many critical essays and books have been written about Asturias's narrative, focusing on some aspect of that nutshell statement. In fact, few of his works are exempt from the qualities to which Callan refers. Even his narratives of harshest reality include passages of lyric language and move in a magical atmosphere.

The reason for Asturias's inclusion of these qualities in so much of his writing may be found in his essay "Heine o la poesía comprometida" (Heine or Committed Poetry, included in *América, fábula de fábulas y otros ensayos* [America, Fable of Fables and Other Essays], 1972) about the works of fellow poet Heinrich Heine. In it he posits that protest literature "usa de sus espejos mágicos para limpiar el mundo, para dar otra extensión a la existencia del hombre" (uses its magic mirrors to clean the world, to give another dimension to man's existence).

Almost all critics of his literature note Asturias's masterful use of language. Interviewers Luis Harss and Barbara Dohmann state that for Asturias, "language lives a borrowed life. Words are echoes or shadows of living beings. The faith in the power of words . . . is reminiscent of an ancient belief that words are doubles of objects in the external world and are therefore an animated part of it. The rhythms of speech are instinctual and subliminal. And the subliminal is close to the mythical." They further assert that in his texts "metaphor is magic, it conjures up the unconscious." Asturias's novels are narrated in a language that many believe to be the result of the influence of Surrealism, to which he was exposed during his early years in Europe. Asturias, however, denied this connection and asserted that his style was influenced instead by the indigenous Latin American way of thinking; as he told scholar Marta Pilón de Pacheco, "el surrealismo de mis libros corresponde un poco a la mentalidad indígena, mágica y primitiva, a la mentalidad de esta gente que está siempre entre lo real y lo soñado, entre lo real y lo imaginado, entre lo real y lo que se inventa. Y creo que es esto lo que forma el eje principal de mi pretendido surrealismo" (the surrealism of my books corresponds somewhat to a magical and primitive indigenous mentality, to the mentality of these people who are always between the real and the dreamed, between the real and the imagined, between the real and the invented. And I believe that it is this that forms the main axis of my so-called surrealism). He elaborated further about the link critics like to forge between that "indigenous mentality" and magical realism in an interview with Gunther W. Lorenz: "Las alucinaciones, las impresiones que el hombre obtiene de su medio tienden a transformarse en realidades. . . . No se trata de una realidad palpable, pero sí de una realidad que surge de una determinada imaginación mágica" (The hallucinations, the impressions that man gets from his environment tend to transform themselves into realities. . . . It is not a question of a palpable reality, but it is one of a reality that emerges from a specific magical imagination).

Asturias was born on 19 October 1899 in the Parroquia Vieja (Old Parish) neighborhood of Guatemala City. His father was Ernesto Asturias, a lawyer; his mother was María Rosales de Asturias, a teacher. His younger brother, Marco Antonio, was born in 1901. Because of problems with the despotic president Manuel Estrada Cabrera, in 1904 his father moved the family to Salamá, a commercial center in the province of Baja Verapaz near the farm of his maternal grandparents, where they visited frequently. Asturias began school there in 1906 and completed the first three grades before the family returned in 1908 to Guatemala City, where he finished his elementary schooling at Father Pedro Jacinto Palacios's school and the Domingo Savio school. He began his secondary education in 1912 at the Central National Institute for Boys and finished with a secondary-school diploma in 1916. At the Institute he met the great Nicaraguan poet Rubén Darío, who was just nine months from his death. Prior to this encounter, Asturias's hobby had been painting; but subsequently he turned to literature.

Poetry is the genre in which Asturias first began writing. His earliest poems date from 1917, but they remained unpublished until 1999, when Marco Vinicio Mejía published them in *Miguel Ángel Asturias, raíz y destino: Poesía inédita (1917–1924)* (Miguel Ángel Asturias, Reason and Destiny: Unpublished Poems [1917–1924]). In many of these poems the quality of modernist musicality is unquestionable. Asturias himself collected the poetry he wrote between 1918 and 1948 and published it under the title of *Poesía: Sien de alondra* (1949, Poetry: The Lark's Temple). The poems of the earlier years are intimate in content, expressing the poet's deepest feelings about his family, and have traditional Hispanic meter and rhyme forms. To a limited degree the astonishing imagery associated with Surrealism is already present in the earlier poems, as is evident in "Ronda de andares" (Round of Wanderings, published in the 1918–1928 section of *Poesía: Sien de alondra*): "Haré la cabecita de mi hijo / con un nido de pájaros" (I will make my son's little head / with a birds' nest). Some of the later poetry gathered in *Poesía: Sien de alondra* is avant-garde, with imagery, rhythms, and parallel constructions that betray the influence of ancient indigenous writings. Asturias admitted this influence in "The Latin American Novel: Testimony of an Epoch," his Nobel lecture: "the parallelism in the indigenous texts allows an exercise of nuances that we find hard to appreciate but which undoubtedly permitted a poetic gradation destined to induce certain states of consciousness which were taken to be magic." An evolution from traditional forms to avant-garde, Surrealist forms can be traced through the dated parts of *Poesía: Sien de alondra*.

Asturias's poetry reflects the cultural duality that surrounded him in his formative years. There are poems, such as his sonnets, that only someone who was immersed in European culture could have written. There are also poems—such as "Tecún Umán," "Señor del agua" (Man of Water), "Marimba tocada por indios" (Marimba Played by Indians), "Habla el gran lengua" (The Great Interpreter Speaks), and "Cerbatanero" (Blowgunner), from *Poesía: Sien de alondra*, and the book-length poem *Clarivigilia Primaveral* (1965; Springtime Clear Vigil; *clarivigilia* is a neologism, made up of *claro*, clear or bright, and *vigilia*, vigil)—that only someone acquainted with Mayan culture could write. Asturias gained a firsthand acquaintance with that culture in early childhood as he listened to Lola Reyes, a Mayan servant in his home, tell traditional indigenous and mestizo tales; later, he read the ancient Maya-Quiché texts in the French translations made of them by Professor Georges Raynaud. Giuseppe Bellini identifies in Asturias's poetic works "los módulos y los ritmos propios de la antigua poesía maya, especialmente en la reiteración, la metáfora, la imagen simbólica, el paralelismo, creando una atmósfera de sugestiva eficacia, evocadora de mundos remotos, proyectados en el tiempo presente" (the modules and the rhythms peculiar to ancient Mayan poetry, especially in the reiteration, metaphor, symbolic image, and parallelism that create an atmosphere of suggestive efficacy, evocative of remote worlds projected onto present time).

In Asturias's plays the influence of the literary movements of the times is especially discernible. Asturias's earliest play, written when he was seventeen, is still in typescript form, annotated in the margins in his own hand. According to María del Carmen Meléndez de Alonzo, this play, "El loco de la aurora" (The Madman of the Dawn), betrays the influence of the *Modernista* movement. Elements of the Surrealist movement as well as *Modernismo* can also be found in *Rayito de estrella* (1925, Little Star Ray), his first "fantomima" (a neologism composed of *fantasía*, fantasy, and *mima*, mime). The term Asturias used to name this "new genre" is an early example of his penchant for wordplay and the creation of neologisms to achieve new meanings. Surrealism and the use of neologisms are also integral parts of his other "fantomimas," *Émulo Lipolidón* (1935), *Alclasán* (1940), and *Soluna: Comedia prodigiosa en dos jornadas y un final* (1955, Soluna: Prodigious Play in Two Days and an Ending; *soluna* is a neologism made up of *sol*, sun, and *luna*, moon). In all of them there is a Surrealistic, dream-like quality that prevents reality from completely descending on the action. Although the "fantomimas" are dialogue-based works, at times it is difficult in some of them to determine who is speaking. The experimentation he had started with *Rayito de estrella* evolved significantly; it became apparent that his "fantomimas" were "laboratory pieces," works in which Asturias tried out the avant-garde linguistic strategies that eventually enriched his more extensive works.

Asturias graduated from the Central National Institute for Boys in 1917 and entered the School of Medicine of the University of San Carlos in Guatemala City, but in 1918 he transferred to the School of Juridical and Social Sciences there. In 1920 José Candida Piñol y Batres, the bishop of Granada, Nicaragua, delivered a series of lectures denouncing dictatorship, basing himself on Christian doctrine. Piñol y Batres's words resonated with many citizens of Guatemala, which had been ruled by the dictator Estrada Cabrera since 1898, and the lectures led to the formation of the Unionist Party. A general attitude of belligerence ensued; antigovernment manifestos were issued, and on 11 March 1920 there was a massive demonstration against Estrada Cabrera, in which the Association of Unionist Students, a group originally formed by Asturias, David Vela, and other classmates as the Asociación de Estudiantes Universitarios (Association of University students) participated. This outpouring was bloodily repressed. The ensuing armed struggle between supporters and opponents of the dictator came to be known as the "Semana Trágica" (Tragic Week), and the fighting came to an end with the overthrow of Estrada Cabrera on 14 April 1920. During the ensuing short-lived rule of Carlos Herrera y Luna, Asturias was active in civic and political matters.

Asturias's first paying job consisted of writing for several magazines, including *Studium,* which he founded with Vela and which continued in publication until it was suspended when the university was closed by the government of General José María Orellana in April 1924. He also wrote for *El Estudiante* (The Student) and *La Cultura* (Culture). As a fourth-year law student Asturias represented the Asociación de Estudiantes Universitarios at the commemoration of Mexican independence. In Mexico he met the Spanish man of letters Ramón del Valle Inclán, who exerted great influence on him. He also was exposed to the populist ideas of José Vasconcelos, at that time Mexico's minister of education.

When the Colombian poet Porfirio Barba Jacob, who lived in Guatemala and Mexico for many years, proposed the creation of the Popular University, Vasconcelo's populist ideas resonated in the proposal and attracted Asturias's attention. In 1922 Asturias was among the founders of the Popular University of Guatemala; in addition to teaching workers to read, he taught grammar and gave weekly lectures there. This university expanded and eventually had branches in several provinces; it operated until the dictator Jorge Ubico closed it in 1932. In 1922 Asturias and some of his university friends wrote the lyrics of "La chalana" (The Shrewd Woman), a battle song that became popular among Guatemalan university students.

According to most of his biographers, Asturias received his law degree at the University of San Carlos in 1923. However, in his notes for *Miguel Ángel Asturias, raíz y destino,* Mejía asserts that Asturias in fact attended the Estrada Cabrera National University, since the University of San Carlos "practicamente no existió con ese nombre en los períodos comprendidos de 1831 a 1855 y de 1875 a 1945" (in practical terms, did not exist under that name during the periods included from 1831 to 1855 and from 1875 to 1945). Asturias's first work in the essay genre is the thesis he presented for graduation, *Sociología guatemalteca: El problema social del indio* (1923; translated as *Guatemalan Sociology: The Social Problem of the Indian,* 1977). It was awarded the Premio Gálvez (Gálvez Prize) given by the university for the best thesis of the year and was immediately published. Its sociological focus on the disadvantaged indigenous people of his country is repeated in many of his later essays. The work is flawed, however, by the essentially racist attitude toward the Indians that his *Ladino* (term used in Guatemala to designate those who do not consider themselves Mayas) upbringing ingrained in his consciousness.

Asturias briefly wrote for the newspaper *Tiempos Nuevos* (New Times) before being imprisoned for a few days by the dictator Orellana because of the subversive tone of many of his columns. On his release in 1924 he left Guatemala for his political safety. In September he traveled to London, accompanied by a family friend, former Peruvian senator José Antonio Encina, and financed by his father, whose intention was that Asturias would study economics there. Instead, Asturias soon left for Paris, where in 1925 he began studying Mayan religions at the Sorbonne with Raynaud, the director of studies on religions of Pre-Columbian America at the School of Higher Learning. In Paris he became a correspondent for *El Imparcial* (The Impartial) in Guatemala and for several newspapers in Mexico; during the ten years he spent in Paris, he sent more than four hundred articles to *El Imparcial.* A collection of these essays, *Paris 1924–1933: Periodismo y creación literaria* (Paris 1924–1933: Journalism and Literary Creation), was published in 1988. These works manifest the evolution of Asturias's thought and the ideological and cultural components evident in his later narrative texts.

In addition to journalistic articles and essays, he also contributed interviews with some of Spain's greatest contemporary authors. In 1925 he traveled to Italy to represent Prensa Latina (Latin Press) at a conference there. Asturias established friendships with some of the most influential writers of the time, including Miguel de Unamuno, Vicente Blasco Ibáñez, James Joyce, André Breton, and Tristan Tzara. In 1927 Asturias and J. M. González de Mendoza published their Spanish translation of Raynaud's French version of the *Popol Vuh,* the sacred book of the Quiché Indians, under the title *Los dioses, los héroes y los hombres de Guatemala Antigua; o El libro del Consejo, Popol Vuh de los indios quichés* (Gods, Heroes, and Men of Ancient Guatemala; or, The Book of the Council, Popol Vuh of the Quiché Indians).

He returned to Guatemala for a visit in 1928, stopping in Cuba on the way to attend a conference for journalists. During that visit he published *La arquitectura de la vida nueva* (1928, Architecture of the New Life), a book based on four lectures he had delivered at the Popular University, the National School for Boys, the Society of Mutual Human Assistance, and the Union of Commercial Employees. When he returned to Paris, he and González de Mendoza translated and published Raynaud's French version of *Anales de los Xahil de los indios cakchiqueles* (1928, The Annals of the Xahils of the Cakchiquel Indians).

In 1929 Asturias ended his studies in Paris, and in his position as a correspondent to several Latin American newspapers he traveled all over Western Europe as well as to the Middle East, spending significant periods of time in both Italy and Greece. In Spain he made the acquaintance of the poets of the avant-garde "Generation of 1927," which included Rafael Alberti, Vicente Aleixandre, Dámaso Alonso, Luis Cernuda, Rosa Chacel, Gerardo Diego, Federico García Lorca, Jorge Guillén, Pedro Salinas, and María Zambrano.

Callan's claim about Asturias's "rich and ambiguous language of dreamwork" is substantiated by some of the tales in *Leyendas de Guatemala* (Legends of Guatemala), a 1930 collection of short stories based on Guatemalan folklore. This book establishes the hybridization of Guatemala's folk culture (both Indian and Spanish) and the transculturation of the belief systems of the indigenous population and the Spaniards who conquered them. A 1932 French version by Francis de Miomandre (pseudonym of François Durand), with a letter by the French poet Paul Valéry as preface, was awarded the Sylla Monsegur Prize for the best translation from Spanish to French for that year.

In 1932 Asturias traveled to Egypt and Palestine. During these travels he wrote poetry and worked on a short story with the title "Los mendigos políticos" (The Political Beggars), which eventually became the novel *El Señor Presidente* (1946; translated as *The President*, 1963, and as *El Señor Presidente*, 1963). Although his family's economic situation gave him the means to live in France without deprivation until 1933, the worldwide economic crisis of those years prevented his father's continued financial support of him in Paris, and Asturias returned to Guatemala. At that time the dictator Ubico headed the government, and aware of the potential implications of the content of *El Señor Presidente*, Asturias opted not to take the manuscript with him when he returned to Guatemala. This decision delayed publication of the novel for thirteen years.

On his return to Guatemala in 1933 he became a professor of literature in the School of Juridical Sciences of Guatemala at the University of San Carlos. On 1 May 1934 he founded the newspaper *Éxito* (Success), which was published for only one year. When *Éxito* ceased publication he began working for the government newspaper *El Liberal Progresista* (The Progressive Liberal). When he published his second "fantomima," *Émulo Lipolidón*, he dedicated it to some of the friends he had left in Europe–Alberti, Miomandre, Alfonso Reyes, Mariano Brull, Eugène Jolas, Georges Pillement, Luis Cardoza y Aragón, Alejo Carpentier, and Arturo Uslar Pietri. In this Surrealist play Asturias continued to play with language, using neologisms, sound repetitions, and onomatopoeia. In 1936 the Spanish Civil War began, and Asturias declared his support for the Republican cause. He also published poems that he had written in the preceding years as *Sonetos* (1936, Sonnets).

Asturias was fired from *El Liberal Progresista* in 1937, again for the subversive tone of his writings, but in June 1938 he and his friend Francisco Soler y Pérez founded a radio news program, "Diario del Aire" (Newspaper of the Air). In 1939 he married Clemencia Amado; his father died; and his first child, Rodrigo, was born. Asturias's second son, Miguel Ángel, was born in 1941, and the following year Asturias was elected to the Guatemalan legislature. That same year he published *Con el rehén en los dientes: Canto a Francia* (1942, With the Hostage in His Teeth: Song to France), a book-length poem about the German occupation of France. Also in 1942 he took part in the Congreso Mariano Nacional (National Marian Conference) with the poem "Con el rehén en los dientes," which received an award offered by the conference. His lifelong friendship with Chilean poet Pablo Neruda began that year when Neruda spent a few days in Asturias's home. In 1943 Asturias published *Anoche, 10 de marzo de 1543* (Last Night, 10 March 1543), a poem commemorating the fourth centenary of the founding of Guatemala.

Ubico resigned in 1944, and Asturias found himself isolated and ostracized by those who considered him a collaborator with the deposed regime because he had been appointed by Ubico and had served as a deputy in the National Assembly. He ceased broadcasting the "Diario del Aire." In 1945 a democratic government was established in Guatemala under the presidency of Juan José Arévalo. Asturias returned home from Mexico (where he had resided since Ubico's resignation) for a few months, and while he was there Arévalo named him cultural attaché to the Guatemalan Embassy in Mexico. After moving to that country, Asturias continued working on *El Señor Presidente*, the novel begun in 1922. With the increased freedom in Guatemala, Asturias felt secure enough in 1946 to publish privately, with the financial assistance of his mother and a cousin, the novel held so long in abeyance; it was eventually published commercially by Losada in 1948.

El Señor Presidente protests against dictatorship. Its setting is not specific but could reflect many Latin American countries of the middle of the twentieth century. This novel portrays a prototypical military dictator and the repression, humiliation, unjust imprisonment, degradation, and even the murders of his opponents or of those who momentarily displease him. A nightmarish horror permeates this novel both in the scenes it depicts and in the actions it relates. Although many critics regard this novel as a representation of a generic Latin American dictatorship, it is also widely accepted that it is based on the dictatorship of Estrada Cabrera, who controlled Guatemala for twenty years. Its theme of tyrannical dictatorship has engrossed the reading public in Guatemala and abroad, precisely because it is a theme that has resonated in the reality of Guatemala and other Latin American countries for many decades. *El Señor Presidente* may be responsible for Asturias's great fame throughout the Americas and eventually the world, because it is much more than just a novel of political criticism. There are passages of poetic language, and in *América, fábula de fábulas y otros ensayos* Asturias acknowledged his use of legends from Mayan culture to create myth in the novel. In fact, Callan finds in it a series of archetypes deeply rooted in universal mythologies.

In 1947, Asturias returned from Mexico for a few months in Guatemala, and Arévalo named him cultural attaché to the Guatemalan Embassy in Argentina. Two years later he became minister adviser, a post he held until 1952. Prior to taking up his new position in Argentina, Asturias divorced his wife; he retained custody of his sons. Asturias's mother died in 1948, moving him to write the poem "Madre, tú me inventaste" (Mother, You Invented Me): "antes tú y yo / y después, tú y yo solos . . . / Hizo frío. / La sombra de tu pelo le quedó a la noche" (before you and I / and afterward, you and I alone . . . / It was cold. / The shadow of your hair suited the night). The poem was included in *Poesía: Sien de alondra,* which he published with a prologue by the Mexican poet and scholar Alfonso Reyes after visiting Neruda in Chile. He regretted the exclusion of some of his poems in the selection made by his friends Alberti and Antonio Salazar, saying, "los quiero como se quiere a los malos hijos" (I love them as one loves one's bad children).

In November 1949 Asturias published the novel *Hombres de maíz* (1949; translated as *Men of Maize,* 1975), which according to Jorge Campos was the author's own favorite. In *Hombres de maíz,* Asturias protests the unscrupulous despoiling of Guatemala by those who exploit it for mercenary reasons. The novel delves into the religious respect of the indigenous people for the land and the elements of their rituals still surviving in contemporary Guatemalan society, illustrating the conflict between the unchanged ritual observances of these people and the materialism of the modern world. Some critics perceive a lack of unity among the six parts of the novel, but René Prieto argues that the "unifying principle is thematic and not dependent on character or chronological development but, rather, on three pivotal elements—fire, water, and corn—which harness the six tales together." The general consensus is that *Hombres de maíz* is a novel of remythification in which the "men of maize" return to their mythic origin in order to be worthy of returning to the land.

Asturias next spent four months in Guatemala doing research for the novels of his "banana trilogy": *Viento fuerte* (1950; translated as *Cyclone,* 1967, and as *Strong Wind,* 1968), *El papa verde* (1954; translated as *The Green Pope,* 1971), and *Los ojos de los enterrados* (1960; translated as *The Eyes of the Interred,* 1973). Asturias in fact planned a tetralogy; the fourth novel, tentatively titled "Bastardo" (Bastard) and later "Dos veces bastardo" (Two Times a Bastard), was never finished, although his son Miguel Ángel declared after Asturias's death that in his last days, his father had been working on it. As a unit, these novels constitute a sharp criticism of the agricultural exploitation of Guatemala—and, by extension, of all of Central and South America's resources—by the United States and other foreign powers. The trilogy presents the problems inherent in the exploitation of Guatemala's banana industry, represented in the novels by the Tropical Banana Company and by wealthy American plantation owners, wealthier absent stockholders, or even a president who colludes with the exploiters to Guatemala's detriment. Asturias was alluding to the United Fruit Company, which exploited that country's rich agricultural resources from 1906 until 1954, when the Guatemalan government expropriated the plantations.

In these novels he offers various solutions to the problems posed. On the one hand, he proposes reality-based solutions, such as establishing a banana-producing cooperative in which the locals unite under the guidance of altruistic American plantation owners, organizing worker unions that retaliate for the atrocities of the plantation owners by going on strike, or killing locals who betray their cause. On the other hand, he offers solutions more in keeping with the magical realism that is so often attributed to his narrative, such as the destruction of the banana plantations by a hurricane conjured by a shaman who invokes the powers of Huracán and Cabracán—respectively, the Giant of the Winds and the Giant of the Earth in Quiché mythology. In the final analysis, Asturias believed that solutions to his country's problems could not be formulated by outsiders but would have to be undertaken by Guatemalans themselves.

When he finished the research for the "banana trilogy," he returned to Buenos Aires, and in 1950 he traveled to Montevideo, Uruguay, to marry Blanca Mora y Araujo, an Argentine whom he had met in Buenos Aires when she was writing a thesis on his literary works. *Viento Fuerte,* the first novel of the trilogy, was published that same year.

In 1951 Asturias published a collection of seventeen rather traditional sonnets, *Ejercicios poéticos en forma de sonetos sobre temas de Horacio* (Poetic Exercises in the Form of Sonnets on Themes by Horace), dedicating it to his wife. The following year he traveled to Bolivia at the invitation of its president, Paz Estenssoro, who had just led a victorious revolution there. Also in 1952 the

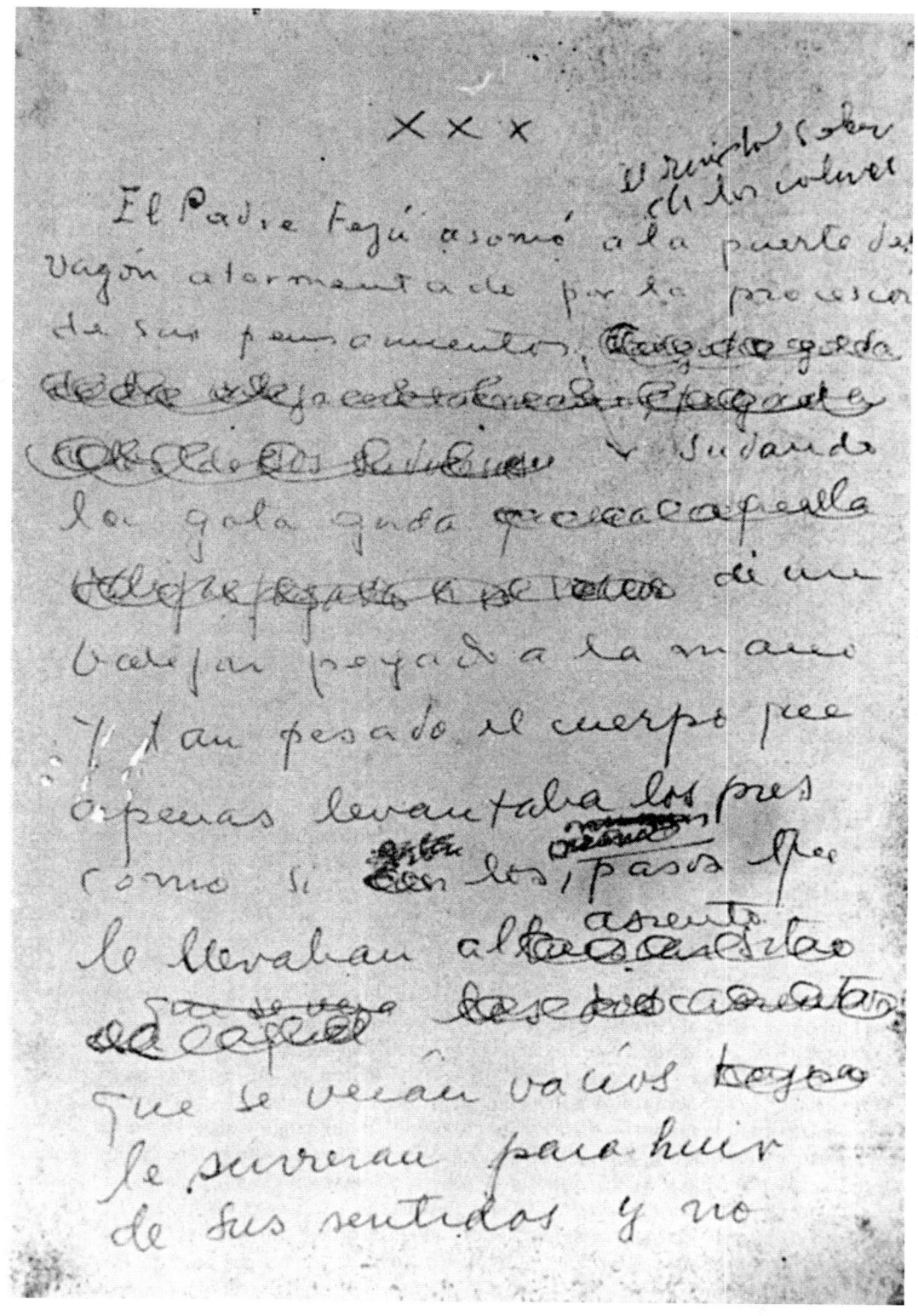

Page from the manuscript for Asturias's 1960 novel, Los ojos de los enterrados (translated as The Eyes of the Interred, 1973), the third book in a trilogy about foreign exploitation of the banana industry in Guatemala (from Jimena Saenz, Genio y figura de Miguel Ángel Asturias, 1974; University of Kentucky Library)

new president of Guatemala, Jacobo Arbenz Guzmán, named Asturias minister adviser in Paris. The French translation of *El Señor Presidente* was published there and received the International Prize of the French Book Club. In 1953 Arbenz recalled Asturias to Guatemala and named him ambassador to El Salvador. Early in 1954 Asturias traveled to Caracas as a delegate to the tenth Conferencia Interamericana (Inter-American Conference). He was visiting in Guatemala in June of that year when Colonel Carlos Castillo Armas led a revolution against the Arbenz government, which was accused by American fruit interests of communist influences; Castillo Armas became the country's next president. Asturias returned to San Salvador and renounced his diplomatic position, as is customary in diplomatic circles, whereupon Castillo Armas stripped him of his citizenship. Asturias traveled to Panama, visited Neruda in Chile, and settled in Buenos Aires, where he remained in exile until 1962. Also in 1954 he published the second novel of the "banana trilogy," *El papa verde*, in Buenos Aires. In 1955 he published *Soluna*, a Surrealist play with its stylistic roots in the "fantomima," and the poem *Bolívar: Canto al Libertador* (Bolivar: Song to the Liberator). He also did occasional translations for the Losada publishing company during this year. In 1956 he began publishing a regular column, "Buenos Aires de día y de noche" (Buenos Aires by Day and by Night), in the Caracas newspaper *El Nacional*.

Callan's claim about the political and social content of Asturias's novels is equally valid with respect to Asturias's short fiction. This claim is especially true of the short stories in *Week-end en Guatemala* (1956, Weekend in Guatemala), a collection that is an indictment of the political and economic machinations of the United States that led to Castillo Armas's overthrow of Arbenz. Asturias dedicated this volume to his wife.

In 1957 he published the play *La audiencia de los confines* (1957, The Royal Tribunal of the Borderlands), which is characterized by realism and a tone of protest. It presents the sixteenth-century priest Bartolomé de las Casas, who advocated better treatment of the Indians in the Spanish colonies. The play highlights the duality of cultures and sets forth the struggle between them that is the heritage of Guatemala and all of Latin America. The stage directions indicate Asturias's desire to emphasize this duality and to indicate which side he favored; the directions call for a stage set divided into two areas, one a dark room in a Spanish-built castle in the New World, the other an Indian temple in the middle of a bright, sunny jungle.

This text is the only one of his works that Asturias ever reworked after it had been published. According to Meléndez de Alonso, in 1971, after *La audiencia de los confines* had been not only published but also staged, Asturias modified it significantly. She contends that in effect Asturias prepared the manuscript of a new play titled "Las Casas: El Obispo de Dios" (Las Casas: God's Bishop), based on the prototext of *La audiencia de los confines*. The changes he made are significant and include increasing the number of battles, explaining the origin and function of the maiden's stone (used to summon sacrificial virgins to the altar), describing the function of Musén-Ca (guardian of the virgins selected to be sacrificed to the God of Corn), blaming the Spaniards as instigators and manipulators of the Indians' uprising, emphasizing the Spaniards' lust for riches, inserting several poetic passages, abbreviating the stage directions, inserting a scene with characters not listed in the dramatis personae, and replacing a female character with a male one. The latter change was most probably prompted by Asturias's desire to avoid the cultural anachronism she represented in the social circumstances depicted in the play. The new play remains in manuscript form.

Also in 1957 Asturias took a long trip to India, where he attended a writers conference. He then visited China and Russia, where he took part in a comparative literature seminar in Moscow. Toward the end of the year he traveled through France, Spain, and finally to Brazil. In 1959 President Miguel Ydígoras Fuentes restored Asturias's Guatemalan citizenship and passport. He then traveled to Buenos Aires, where he met Fidel Castro, and in September he traveled to Cuba at Castro's invitation to attend festivities commemorating the first anniversary of the Cuban Revolution. He then continued to Guatemala to celebrate his sixtieth birthday in the city of his birth. While there he lectured on the Latin American novel.

Returning to Buenos Aires, in 1960 Asturias published *Los ojos de los enterrados*, the final novel in the "banana trilogy." The title of this book refers to an indigenous belief that the dead keep their eyes open in their graves until justice is done on Earth; in the novel, justice will be done when the fruit company is destroyed and the dictator finally falls. Also in 1960 Asturias compiled and published the anthology *Poesía precolombina* (Pre-Columbian Poetry). The following year he published the novel *El alhajadito* (1961; translated as *The Bejeweled Boy*, 1971), based on a legend from the colonial period. In 1962 the Argentine president Arturo Frondizi was overthrown, and Asturias was briefly detained in error by Frondizi's successor, José María Guido. On his release Asturias left Argentina for Europe. He traveled in France and Italy and received medical treatment in Romania for poor health that had been aggravated by his imprisonment in Argentina. In 1962 the English translation of *El Señor Presidente* received the William Faulkner Foundation Prize for the best Latin American novel.

Asturias returned to Buenos Aires in 1963 and published *Mulata de tal* (1963; translated as *The Mulatta and Mr. Fly,* 1963, and as *Mulata,* 1967), an important novel that is not a work of protest but that conforms with the "ambiguous language of dreamwork" proposed by Callan. It is a novel of communitarian values, unorthodox eroticism, and mythic resonance. In it priests fight against devils, and Catholic rituals confront the rituals of Mayan mythology. The reality of the novelistic world is in constant flux as nature changes in the convulsions of an earthquake and the characters undergo impossible physical changes or incarnate serially as different characters.

In 1964 he published *Rumania, su nueva imagen* (Romania, Its New Image) about his travels in that country, and *Teatro* (Theater), a collection of four plays, two of which had been published previously. He also lectured in several Italian cities and traveled in Scandinavia, where he lectured at several universities. He then attended an international writers' colloquium in Berlin.

In 1965 he published *Clarivigilia primaveral,* his book-length poem dealing with Mayan myths of origin and the traditional Indian artisans and their art forms. The inspiration for this work may be found in Asturias's essay "De sueño y barro: Arte de los mayas de Guatemala" (Of Dream and Clay: The Art of the Maya of Guatemala), included in *América, fábula de fábulas y otros ensayos.* In it Asturias explains:

> En todas las mitologías, los dioses se preocupan por crear guerreros, sacerdotes, caudillos, hombres eminentes. No así en las creencias y mitos de aquellos que poblaron de obras de arte las ciudades de la América Media. Para éstos, artistas por los cuatro costados del ciclo, las divinidades del alba, las abuelas del día, se deleitan en la creación de pintores, poetas, escultores, músicos, danzarines, orfebres, acróbatas, plumistas, a quienes se llamaba magos o pequeños brujos, únicos que podían repetir el milagro de crear cosas de sueño.
>
> (In all mythologies, the gods took care to create warriors, priests, chiefs, eminent men. Not so in the beliefs and myths of those who populated the cities of Middle America with works of art. For them, artists on all four sides of the cycle, the divinities of dawn, the grandmothers of the day, are delighted in the creation of painters, poets, sculptors, musicians, dancers, goldsmiths, acrobats, feather smiths, who were called magi or little sorcerers, the only ones who could repeat the miracle of creating things from dream.)

The intertextuality of *Clarivigilia primaveral* goes beyond content and may be found in the form as well. Perhaps the earliest critic to point out this relationship was Bellini, who scarcely two years after its publication noted that Asturias's poem recalls the rhythms of ancient Mayan poetry, its reiterations, metaphors, symbolic images, and parallelism.

In 1965 Asturias traveled in Hungary with Neruda. He also traveled to Italy, where he directed the Columbianum, a conference on Christopher Columbus studies, in Genoa and organized another conference on Third World writers. That same year he represented the French PEN Club in Yugoslavia; he was a candidate for the presidency of that organization but lost. The second half of the decade of the 1960s was full of moments of recognition and honors bestowed on him by entities around the world. In 1966 he became president of the French PEN Club in Paris. He spent that summer in Romania, and in August he received the first of his world-level honors, the Lenin Peace Prize in Moscow. In April 1967 Asturias traveled to Guatemala to attend the second Congreso de la Comunidad de Escritores Latinoamericanos (Conference of the Community of Latin American Writers). During that visit the newly elected president Julio César Méndez Montenegro named him ambassador to France. That year he inaugurated an exhibit of Mayan art in several French cities. He also published a book that included two plays, *Torotumbo* and *La audiencia de los confines,* and the poems of *Mensajes indios* (Indian Messages).

On 19 October 1967 he was named winner of the Nobel Prize in Literature. His literary work attracted the attention of the critics at that time and probably prompted his nomination for the award, because of the way in which he combined in his novels and legends the Mayan heritage of his native Guatemala with the quality that has been called magical realism or Surrealism. At the same time, the courage implicit in his overt representation of the real-life horror of political life in the Guatemala of that time and his protest against external exploitation of that country's natural resources also drew the notice of readers. His innovative narrative techniques, which later were taken up by members of the Latin American Boom writers, also undoubtedly contributed to his recognition.

In speeches he delivered during various occasions linked to the Nobel Prize that year, Asturias acknowledged all of these qualities in his work, stating that, as did many Latin American writers of the time, he viewed his novels as instruments of political protest. The most noteworthy quality of his writing, as he suggested, is its capacity for revealing the true nature of the Guatemalan people, especially the indigenous folk. Speaking of his poetry, he acknowledged the deep influence of the lyric style of the ancient Mayan texts.

An unintended result of his recognition by the Nobel Prize has been, in the years since then, an overt effort to repeal the mythic status that Asturias achieved as a result of the intense focus on him and his work during the decade following the awarding of the prize. Later critics have taken issue with aspects of his life and works, ranging from the revelation that he had no Mayan blood, to claims that he had had little hand in the translation of the Popol-Vuh into Spanish. Some critics have disparaged the authenticity of his reformist attitude, while others reject the intensity of his love for everything indigenous in his later life and writings. Citing the racist aspects of Asturias's thesis, one particular Mayan poet from Guatemala refused to accept a national literary prize because the writer's name figured as part of the award title.

In November 1967 Asturias visited Italy and Germany to present the translations of his books. In December he departed for Sweden, where he received the Nobel Prize from King Gustaf Adolphus VI. That same year he published (first in France and then in Mexico) *El espejo de Lida Sal* (translated as *The Mirror of Lida Sal*, 1997), a collection of short stories that are realistic in setting and action and of legends written in the Surrealist or magical realist style.

In 1968 Asturias presided over the San Sebastián Film Festival in Spain. That same year, the Association of Guatemalan Journalists awarded him its Quetzal de Jade (Jade Quetzal), and the indigenous communities of Guatemala named him "only-begotten son of Tecún Umán" (referring to the Quiché prince who was killed in battle by Spanish conquistador Pedro de Alvarado in 1524) because of his recognition of the indigenous roots of that country's culture. He then traveled to Colombia, where he received the Gran Cruz de San Carlos (Great Cross of Saint Charles) and presided over the Festival of Latin American University Theater in Manizales. Invited by Senegal's president, Asturias visited that country in 1969, stopping in Madrid en route. He spent some time at the home of his doctor in Palma, Majorca, then underwent an undisclosed surgery in Paris. That same year he and Neruda published *Comiendo en Hungría* (1969; translated as *Sentimental Journey around the Hungarian Cuisine*, 1969), based on their travel in that country in 1965. Also in 1969 Asturias published the novel *Maladrón* (1969, Bad Thief), about a fictional religion whose followers worship Gestas, the unrepentant *mal ladrón* (bad thief) crucified with Christ. As a representative of the French PEN Club, he interviewed the astronauts of the Apollo 11 crew.

Several of Asturias's mature essays appear in *Latinoamérica y otros ensayos* (1968, Latin America and Other Essays) and *América, fábula de fábulas y otros ensayos*. The content of many of them is political; he speaks out about the repressive governments of Guatemala and about actions of the United States that he considered imperialistic. Other essays are philosophical, sociological, or anthropological in nature, while the bulk of them have a cultural focus. He favors literary topics, and his varied themes include the communications media, his theoretical musings about various literary genres, literary criticism of his own works and those of others, and religious beliefs, particularly that of the Quiché Indians.

When Méndez Montenegro died in office in 1970, Asturias renounced his position as ambassador to France, as is customary in the diplomatic establishment. Before leaving the country, he presided over the jury at the Cannes Film Festival; it was the first time that a Latin American author was named to this position. A few days later he served on the jury of the International Book Fair in Nice. Also in 1970 he attended the screening in Venice of a movie based on *El Señor Presidente*, directed by the Argentine screenwriter and director Marcos Madanes; Asturias was not satisfied with the movie, and it was never released commercially. Asturias then returned to Majorca, where he visited his good friend Camilo José Cela, who received the Nobel Prize in Literature in 1989. In Majorca he composed *Tres de cuatro soles* (1971, Three of Four Suns), a book about his system for literary creation that was published first in its French translation in Geneva (*Trois des quatre soleils*); the original Spanish version was published in 1977. In May 1972 he traveled to Israel, and in June of that year his semi-autobiographical novel *Viernes de dolores* (Holy Friday) was published in Argentina. The protest message in *Viernes de dolores* lies in its narration of the demonstrations and other antigovernment activities of a group of university students in Guatemala in the early 1920s. Asturias's alter ego in the novel is the student "Chirimoya" (Sweetsop), or "Moya" for short, nicknames by which Asturias's university friends addressed him.

Viernes de dolores was the last of his novels published during his life. In November of the same year he visited Mexico, where he was honored repeatedly. Thus ended the most prolific part of Asturias's career, and the period of his decline began.

Asturias met with the former Argentine president Juan Perón in Paris in 1973. His commitments related to being a Nobel laureate multiplied, and in April 1974 he traveled to Dakar for a conference; from there he went to Tenerife, then to Palma, Majorca, Seville, and finally Madrid. He prepared to travel to Argentina and to Chile, where Neruda had called him because he felt close to death; this trip never took place, however, because Asturias fell seriously ill. On 16 May 1974 he was admitted to the Clínica de la Concepción (Clinic of the Conception) in Madrid because of pulmonary insufficiency and intestinal blockage. When the government of Mexico learned of the critical state of Asturias's health, it sent a commission to Spain to invite him to travel to Mexico for his recovery; his condition was too critical for him to be moved, however. He attained some relief from the immediate symptoms, but on 9 June 1974 Asturias died from cancer, an adenocarcinoma of the intestine. His wife and son Miguel Ángel were at his bedside. In accordance with his will, the family had his remains taken for interment in the Père Lachaise Cemetery in Paris, where they were transported onboard Mexico's official airplane. He is still buried there, although many Guatemalans would like to repatriate the remains of the most illustrious of their compatriots.

The Asociación de Periodistas de Guatemala (Association of Guatemalan Journalists) was the first to react to the death of their longtime colleague and declared three days of mourning. The University of San Carlos also called for three days of mourning, as did *El Imparcial*, the newspaper in which Asturias had published his journalistic essays for fifty-three years. The newspaper also offered the means for the repatriation of Asturias's remains, a vain gesture, since Asturias had been an active opponent of General Carlos Arana Osorio, then the president. The Congress of Guatemala also decreed a three-day period of mourning for Guatemala's most acclaimed son. Groups and institutions with which Asturias had at some time in his life been linked gathered to render tribute to him; among them were the University of San Carlos de Guatemala, the municipal government of the City of Guatemala, the Academia Guatemalteca de la Lengua (Guatemalan Academy of the Language), the Asociación de Estudiantes Universitarios, and UNESCO. While his body lay in state, his coffin was draped with the white and azure Guatemalan flag; and, according to his expressed wishes, the staff that the indigenous communities of Guatemala had bestowed on him as "only-begotten son of Tecún Umán" accompanied him in his coffin.

Asturias left an almost finished novel that was published posthumously, *El árbol de la cruz* (1993, The Trunk of the Cross). According to Alain Sicard (in an essay included in a 1993 facsimile edition of the book), it is a novel about "un dictador, pero de un dictador cuya dictadura es menos política que metafísica, ya que su obsesión no es otra que la de abolir todo lo que, de cerca o de lejos, recuerda a Cristo: es decir, la Cruz, y en general y, según nuestra opinión, más significativa: la Muerte" (a dictator, but about a dictator whose dictatorship is less political than metaphysical, since his obsession is none other than that of abolishing everything that, from near or far, reminds one of Christ: that is to say, the Cross, and in general and, in our opinion, more significant: Death). Asturias's manuscript trails off in mid sentence and ends in a comma: "Se echó los almohadones encima," (He pulled the large pillows over himself,), thus ending on a note of poignancy the literary production of one of Latin America's most distinctive writers.

The deep admiration and respect that Guatemalans have for Asturias is best summed up in the title of the eulogy published by the writer Robert Paz y Paz in *La Nación* (10 June 1974): "No ha muerto, ha nacido a la inmortalidad" (He Has Not Died, He Has Been Born to Immortality). In his obituaries and other published eulogies, Asturias was repeatedly referred to as the "Gran Lengua" (Great Interpreter). Some critics take issue with the use of this term in connection with Asturias, arguing that he was ill-prepared to be such an interpreter, since he was not a Maya or even a mestizo, and minimizing his close relationships with the indigenous population of Guatemala. Asturias did use the term to refer to himself, however, knowing the significance it has within Mayan culture, as can be gleaned from his poem "Habla el gran lengua," in which the figure of the "Gran Lengua" resembles that of the *chilanes* in Mayan society, "prophets" who predicted the future and interpreted the will of the gods for the people. Other critics support the identification of Asturias as the "Gran Lengua." In the 1981 critical edition of *Hombres de maíz*, Gerald Martin describes Asturias as the "guardián de los misterios e intérprete del mundo de la magia y sus depósitos, las sagradas escrituras, los libros pintados y los bajorelieves simbólicos" (guardian of the mysteries and interpreter of the world of magic and its deposits, the sacred writings, the painted books and the symbolic bas-reliefs) of the Maya of Guatemala. Asturias's claim to the title of "Gran Lengua" lies not only in his sensitive presentation of a culture that was steeped in mystery for the rest of the world until he wrote about it, but also in his masterful and almost magical use of language. His awareness is clear in his answer to Pilón de Pacheco's question about whether he believed, as he often had his characters state, that words were foundational or magic: "Sí, y esto es absolutamente de carácter sagrado, indígena. La palabra para los indígenas fue y es lo más importante" (Yes, and that is absolutely of a sacred, Indian character. Words for the Indians were and are the most important thing).

Letters:

Cartas de amor entre M. Á. Asturias y Blanca Mora y Araujo (1948–1954), edited by Felipe Mellizo (Madrid: Ediciones de Cultura Hispánica, Instituto de Cooperación Iberoamericana, 1989).

Interviews:

Luis Harss and Barbara Dohmann, "Miguel Ángel Asturias, or the Land Where the Flowers Bloom," in their *Into the Mainstream: Conversations with*

Latin-American Writers (New York: Harper & Row, 1967), pp. 6–101;

Luis López Álvarez, *Conversaciones con Miguel Ángel Asturias* (Madrid: EMESA, 1974).

Bibliographies:

Pedro F. de Andrea, "Miguel Ángel Asturias: Anticipo bibliográfico," *Revista Iberoamericana*, 35, no. 67 (1969): 133–270;

Richard Moore, "Miguel Ángel Asturias: A Bio-Bibliography," *Bulletin of Bibliography*, 27, no. 4 (1970): 85–90, 107–111.

Biographies:

Atilio Jorge Castelpoggi, *Miguel Ángel Asturias* (Buenos Aires: La Mandrágora, 1961);

Claude Couffon, *Miguel Ángel Asturias* (Paris: Seghers, 1970);

Carlos Meneses, *Miguel Ángel Asturias* (Madrid: Júcar, 1975).

References:

Actas del Coloquio Internacional: Miguel Ángel Asturias, 104 años después, 2–4 de julio 2003, Universidad Rafael Landívar (Guatemala City: Abrapalabra, 2003);

Francisco Albizúrez Palma, *La novela de Asturias* (Guatemala City: Editorial Universitaria, 1975);

Ruth Alvarez de Scheel, *Análisis y estudio de algunos rasgos caracterizadores de "El Señor Presidente"* (Guatemala City: Ministerio de Cultura y Deportes, 1999);

Isabel Arredondo, *De brujos y naguales: La Guatemala imaginaria de Miguel Ángel Asturias* (Lewiston, N.Y.: Edwin Mellen Press, 1997);

Giuseppe Bellini, "La poesía de Miguel Ángel Asturias," *Revista Nacional de Cultura* (Caracas), 180 (April–June 1967): 125–127;

Richard J. Callan, *Miguel Ángel Asturias* (New York: Twayne, 1970);

Jorge Campos, "Miguel Ángel Asturias," *Ínsula*, 12, no. 133 (1957): 4;

Atilio Jorge Castelpoggi, *El poeta narrador: Miguel Ángel Asturias* (Buenos Aires: Prueba de Galera Ediciones, 1998);

Otto Raúl González, *Miguel Ángel Asturias, el gran lengua: La voz más clara de Guatemala* (Guatemala City: Editorial Cultura, 1999);

Stephen Henighan, *Assuming the Light: The Parisian Literary Apprenticeship of Miguel Ángel Asturias* (Oxford: Legenda, 1999);

Saúl Hurtado Heras, *Por las tierras de Ilóm: El realismo mágico en "Hombres de maíz"* (Mexico City: Universidad Autónoma del Estado de México, 1997);

Eladia León Hill, *Miguel Ángel Asturias: Lo ancestral en su obra literaria* (Eastchester, N.Y.: E. Torres, 1972);

Gunther W. Lorenz, *Diálogo con Latinoamérica: Panorama de una literatura del futuro*, translated by Dora Weidl Haas-De la Vega (Santiago de Chile: Pomaire, 1972);

María del Carmen Meléndez de Alonzo, "El reencuentro de Asturias con el padre Las Casas," *Letras de Guatemala: Revista Semestral* (Universidad de San Carlos de Guatemala), 20–21 (2000);

Marta Pilón de Pacheco, *Miguel Ángel Asturias: Semblanza para el estudio de su vida y obra, con una selección de poemas y prosas* (Guatemala City: Cultural Centroamericana, 1968);

Rafael Pineda Reyes, *Los misterios de Los hombres de maíz* (Guatemala City: Cultura, 1998);

René Prieto, *Miguel Ángel Asturias's Archaeology of Return* (Cambridge & New York: Cambridge University Press, 1993);

Teresita Rodríguez, *La problemática de la identidad en El Señor Presidente de Miguel Ángel Asturias* (Amsterdam & Atlanta: Rodopi, 1989);

Jimena Saenz, *Genio y figura de Miguel Ángel Asturias* (Buenos Aires: Editorial Universitaria de Buenos Aires, 1974).

Papers:

Miguel Ángel Asturias's personal papers and manuscripts are held in the Bibliothèque nationale de France (National Library of France). Collected newspaper articles published in *El Imparcial* (The Impartial) that were either written by Asturias or written about his literary works are held in the Archivo Histórico de Guatemala (Historical Archive of Guatemala) at the Centro de Investigaciones Regionales de Mesoamérica (Center for Regional Research of Mesoamerica).

1967 Nobel Prize in Literature Presentation Speech

by Anders Österling, Permanent Secretary of the Swedish Academy

This year the Nobel Prize in Literature has been awarded to the Guatemalan writer Miguel Ángel Asturias, a prominent representative of the modern literature of Latin America, in which such interesting developments are now taking place. Born in 1899 in the capital of Guatemala, Asturias became imbued, even as a child, with the characteristically Guatemalan love of nature and of the mythical world. He devoted to this native heritage, and to its libertarian spirit, a fervour which was to dominate his whole literary production. After studying law and folklore, he lived in France during the twenties, and, for a time, represented his country in the diplomatic service. He condemned himself to a long exile after the anti-democratic coup d'etat of 1954, but returned when the legitimate regime took office again. He is presently the Guatemalan Ambassador in Paris.

During the last few years, Asturias has gained international recognition, as his most important works came to be translated into various languages; today they can be read even in Swedish. His first work was a collection of Guatemalan legends, strange evocations of the Mayas' past, a treasure of images and symbols which has, ever since, been the inexhaustible source of his inspiration. But he did not get his real start as a writer until 1946, the year of the publication of the novel, *El Señor Presidente* (The President). This magnificent and tragic satire criticizes the prototype of the Latin American dictator who appeared in several places at the beginning of the century and has since reappeared, his existence being fostered by the mechanism of tyranny which, for the common man, makes every day a hell on earth. The passionate vigour with which Asturias evokes the terror and distrust which poisoned the social atmosphere of the time makes his work a challenge and an invaluable aesthetic gesture. The narrative, entitled, *Hombres de maíz* (Men of Maize) appeared three years later. It might be considered as a folktale whose chief inspiration is in the imagination but which, nevertheless, remains true to life. Its motifs are from the mythology of that tropical land where man must struggle simultaneously against a mysteriously beautiful but hostile nature and against unbearable social distortions, oppression, and tyranny. Such an accumulation of nightmares and totemic phantasms may overwhelm our sensibilities, but we cannot help being fascinated by a poetry so bizarre and terrifying.

With the trilogy of novels begun in 1950–*Viento Fuerte,* 1950 (Strong Wind), *El papa verde,* 1954 (The Green Pope), and *Los ojos de los enterrados,* 1960 (The Eyes of the Buried)–a new topical concern appears in Asturias's epic work: the theme of the struggle against the domination of American trusts, epitomized by the United Fruit Company, and its political and economic effects upon the contemporary history of the "Banana Republic." Here, again, we see the violent effervescence and the visionary vehemence which stem from the author's intense involvement in the situation of his country.

Asturias has completely freed himself from obsolete narrative techniques. Very early, he came under the influence of the new tendencies appearing in European literature; his explosive style bears a close kinship to French surrealism. It must be noted, however, that he always takes his inspiration from real life. In his impressive cycle of poems entitled *Clarivigilia primaveral,* 1965 (Bright and Awake in Spring), on which a Swedish critical study has just appeared, Asturias deals with the very genesis of the arts and of poetic creation, in a language which seems to have assumed the bright splendour of the magical quetzal's feathers and the glimmering of phosphorescent insects.

Latin America today can boast an active group of prominent writers, a multivoiced chorus in which individual contributions are not readily discernible. Asturias's work is nevertheless vast, bold, and outstanding enough to arouse interest outside of his own literary milieu, beyond a geographically limited area situated far away from us. One of the Indian legends Asturias alludes to evokes the belief that dead ancestors are forced to witness, with open eyes, the struggles and sufferings of their offspring. Only when justice is re-established, and the stolen soil restituted, will the dead finally be able to close their eyes and sleep peacefully in their tombs. It is a beautiful and poignant popular belief, and we can easily imagine that the militant poet has often felt upon him the gaze of his ancestors and has often heard the silent, symbolic appeal reaching to his heart.

Mr. Ambassador–you come from a distant country, but do not let this fact make you feel today that you are a stranger among us. Your work is known and appreciated in Sweden. We take pleasure in welcoming you as a messenger from Latin America, its people, its spirit, and its future. I congratulate you in the name of the Swedish Academy, which pays tribute to the "vividness of your literary work, rooted in national traits and Indian traditions." I now invite you to receive your Prize from His Majesty, the King.

[© The Nobel Foundation, 1967.]

Asturias: Banquet Speech

Introductory remarks by Hugo Theorell, professor at the Caroline Institute, at the Nobel Banquet at the City Hall in Stockholm, 10 December 1967:

One of our most competent literary critics has pointed out that this year's Nobel Prize winner in Literature, Miguel Ángel Asturias, in one of his most important books, *El Señor Presidente,* produces a strong effect by skilfully working with time and light–again our common "theme with variations." Asturias paints in dark colours–against this background the rare light makes a so much stronger impression with his passionate, but artistically well balanced, protest against tyranny, injustice, slavery, and arbitrariness. He transforms glowing indignation into great literary art. This is indeed admirable.

May times come when conditions like those condemned by Mr. Asturias belong to history; when human beings live peacefully and happily together. This was indeed what Alfred Nobel hoped to promote by his Prizes.

Mr. Asturias—We sincerely admire your literary craftsmanship, and we hope that your work will contribute to ending the shameful social conditions that you have described with such impressive intensity. We congratulate you on your Nobel Prize, which you so very much deserve.

Asturias's speech (Translation)

My voice on the threshold. My voice coming from afar. On the threshold of the Academy. It is difficult to become a member of a family. And it is easy. The stars know it. The families of luminous torches. To become a member of the Nobel family. To become an heir of Alfred Nobel. To blood ties, to civil relationship, a new consanguinity is added, a more subtle kinship, born of the spirit and the creative task. And this was perhaps the unspoken intention of the founder of this great family of Nobel Prize winners. To enlarge, through time, from generation to generation, the world of his own kin. As for me, I enter the Nobel family as the least worthy to be called among the many who could have been chosen.

I enter by the will of this Academy, whose doors open and close once a year in order to consecrate a writer, and also because of the use I made of the word in my poems and novels, the word which, more than beautiful, is responsible, a concern not foreign to that dreamer who with the passing of time would shock the world with his inventions—the discovery of the most destructive explosives then known—for helping man in his titanic chores of mining, digging tunnels, and constructing roads and canals.

I do not know if the comparison is too daring. But it is necessary. The use of destructive forces, the secret which Alfred Nobel extracted from nature, made possible in our America the most colossal enterprises. Among them, the Panama Canal. A magic of catastrophe which could be compared to the thrust of our novels, called upon to destroy unjust structures in order to make way for a new life. The secret mines of the people, buried under tons of misunderstanding, prejudices, and taboos, bring to light in our narrative—between fables and myths—with blows of protest, testimony, and denouncement, dikes of letters which, like sands, contain reality to let the dream flow free or, on the contrary, contain the dream to let reality escape.

Cataclysms which engendered a geography of madness, terrifying traumas, such as the Conquest: these cannot be the antecedents of a literature of cheap compromise; and, thus, our novels appear to Europeans as illogical or aberrant. They are not shocking for the sake of shock effects. It is just that what happened to us was shocking. Continents submerged in the sea, races castrated as they surged to independence, and the fragmentation of the New World. As the antecedents of a literature these are already tragic. And from there we have had to extract not the man of defeat, but the man of hope, that blind creature who wanders through our songs. We are peoples from worlds which have nothing like the orderly unfolding of European conflicts, always human in their dimensions. The dimensions of our conflicts in the past centuries have been catastrophic.

Scaffoldings. Ladders. New vocabularies. The primitive recitation of the texts. The rhapsodists. And later, once again, the broken trajectory. The new tongue. Long chains of words. Thought unchained. Until arriving, once again, after the bloodiest lexical battles, at one's own expressions. There are no rules. They are invented. And after much invention, the grammarians come with their language-trimming shears. American Spanish is fine with me, but without the roughness. Grammar becomes an obsession. The risk of anti-grammar. And that is where we are now. The search for dynamic words. Another magic. The poet and the writer of the active word. Life. Its variations. Nothing prefabricated. Everything in ebullition. Not to write literature. Not to substitute words for things. To look for word-things, word-beings. And the problems of man, in addition. Evasion is impossible. Man. His problems. A continent that speaks. And which was heard in this Academy. Do not ask us for genealogies, schools, treatises. We bring you the probabilities of a word. Verify them. They are singular. Singular is the movement, the dialogue, the novelistic intrigue. And most singular of all, throughout the ages there has been no interruption in the constant creation.

[© The Nobel Foundation, 1967. Miguel Ángel Asturias is the sole author of his speech.]

Asturias: Nobel Lecture, 12 December 1967

The Latin American Novel: Testimony of an Epoch
(Translation by The Swedish Trade Council Language Services)

I would have preferred this meeting to have been called a colloquium instead of lecture—a dialogue of doubts and assertions on the subject that concerns us. Let us start by analysing the antecedents of Latin American literature in general, focusing our attention on those aspects that have most connection with the novel. Let us follow the sources back to the millenarian origins of indigenous literature in its three great moments: Maya, Aztec and Inca.

The following question arises: Was there something resembling the novel among the indigenous peoples? I believe there was. The history of the original cultures of Latin America has more of what we in the western world call the novel than of history. It is necessary to bear in mind that the books of their history—their novels we would now say—were painted by the Aztecs and Mayas and preserved in a figurative form which we still do not understand by the Incas. This assumes the use of pictograms in which the voice of the reader—the indigenous do not distinguish between reading and reciting since for them it is the same thing—recited the text to the listeners in song form.

The reader, reciting stories or "great language," the only person who understood what the pictograms meant, carried out an interpretation, re-creating them for the enlightenment of those who listened. Later, these painted stories become fixed in the memory of the listeners and pass in oral form from generation to generation until the alphabet brought by the Spanish fixes them in their native tongues with Latin characters or directly in Spanish. In this way indigenous texts come to our knowledge with very little exposure to European corruption. The reading of these documents is what has allowed us to affirm that, among the native Americans, history has more of the characteristics of the novel than of history. They are accounts in which reality is dissolved in fable, legend, the trappings of beauty and in which the imagination, by dint of describing all the reality that it contains, ends up re-creating a reality that we might call surrealist.

This characteristic of the annulment of reality through imagination and the re-creation of a more transcendental reality is combined with a constant annulment of time and space as well as something more significant: the use and abuse of parallel expressions, i.e. the parallel use of different words to designate the same object, to convey the same idea and express the same feelings. I wish to draw attention to this point—the parallelism in the indigenous texts allows an exercise of nuances that we find hard to appreciate but which undoubtedly permitted a poetic gradation destined to induce certain states of consciousness which were taken to be magic.

If we return to the theme of the origin of a literary genre, similar to the novel, among the pre-Colombian peoples it is necessary to link the birth of this novel form with the epic. The heroic legend, exceeding the possibilities of historical fiction, was sung by the rhapsodists—the great voices of the tribes or "cuicanimes" who toured the cities reciting the texts in order that the beauty of their songs would be disseminated among the peoples like the golden blood of their gods.

These epic songs that are so abundant in pre-Columbian literature, and so little known, possess what we call "fictional plot" and what the Spanish friars and missionaries termed "tricks."

These fictional tales were originally the testimony of past epochs; the memory and fame of high deeds that others on hearing would desire to emulate, this literature of reality and fable is broken in the instant of servitude and remains as one of the many broken vessels of those great civilisations. Other narratives will follow—in this same documentary form—recounting not the evidence of greatness but of misery, not the testimony of liberty but of slavery, no longer the statements of the masters but those of the subjects and a new, emerging American literature attempting to fill the empty silences of an epoch.

However, the literary genres that flourished in the Iberian peninsulas—the realistic novel and the theatre—were not to put down roots here. On the contrary, it is the indigenous effervescence, the sap and the blood, river, sea and mirage that affects the first Spaniard to write the first great American "novel," for the "True

Story of the Events of the Conquest of New Spain" written by Bernal Diaz del Castillo deserves to be called no less. Is it not rather bold to describe as a "novel" what that soldier called not history but "true history"? But are not novels frequently the true history? I repeat the question: is it really boldness to describe as a novel the work of this illustrious chronicler?

To those who might call me daring in my description I would invite them to enter the cadenced and panting prose of this versatile foot soldier and they will notice how—on entering into it—they gradually forget that what happened was reality and it will seem to them increasingly a work of pure imagination. Indeed, even Bernal himself says no less, next to the very walls of Tenochtitlan: "this seemed to be the work of enchantment that is recounted in the book of Amadis!" But this is the work of a Spaniard—it will be said—although the only thing Spanish about it is its having been written by a "peninsular" resident in Santiago de los Caballeros de Guatemala—where that glorious manuscript is kept—and its having been composed in the old language of Castile although it partakes of that masquerade characteristic of indigenous literature. To Don Marcelino Menendez y Pelayo—this expert in classic Spanish literature—the taste of this prose is strange and the fact that it has been written by a soldier he finds surprising. It escapes this eminent writer that Bernal, at the age of eighty, had not only heard many texts of indigenous literature being recited, being influenced by it, but through osmosis had absorbed America and had already become American.

But there is another more impressive parenthesis. In their last sorrowful cantos the indigenous peoples—now subjugated—call for justice and Bernal Diaz Castillo expresses his deepest feelings in a chronicle which is a howl of protest at the oblivion into which they fell after being "fought and conquered."

As from this moment, all Latin American literature, in song and novel, not only becomes a testimony for each epoch but also, as stated by the Venezuelan writer Arturo Uslar Pietri, an "instrument of struggle." All the great literature is one of testimony and vindication, but far from being a cold dossier these are moving pages written by one conscious of his power to impress and convince.

Will the south give us a *mestizo*? The *mestizo* par excellence since—in order for nothing to be lacking—he was the first American exile: Inca Garcilaso. This Creole exile follows the indigenous voices already extinguished in his denunciation of the oppressors of Peru. The Inca offers us in his magnificent prose not only the native American—nor only the Spanish—but the mixture materialised in the fusion of the bloods, and in the same demand for life and justice.

To start with nobody discerns the "message" in the prose of Inca. This will be clarified during the struggle for independence. Inca will then appear with the dignity of the Indian that knew how to make fun of the empire of "the two knives"—that is to say civil and ecclesiastical censorship. The Spanish authorities, slow to fathom the message containing so much spirit, imagination and melancholy, wisely order the confiscation of the story of Inca Garcilaso where the Indians have "learned so many dangerous things."

Not only poetry and works of fiction bear witness. The least expected authors such as Francisco Javier Clavijero, Francisco Javier Alegre, Andres Calvo, Manuel Fabri, Andres de Guevara gave birth to a literature of exiles which is—and will continue to be—a testimony of its epoch.

Even the Guatemalan poet Rafael Landívar has his form of rebellion. His protest is silence—he calls the Spanish "Hispani" without qualifying the adjective. We refer to Landívar because, despite being the least known, he should be considered the standard bearer of American literature as the authentic expression of our lands, our people and landscapes. According to Pedro Henriquez-Urena, "among the poets of the Spanish colonies he is the first master of landscape, the first to break definitively with the conventions of the Renaissance and discover the characteristic features of nature in the New World—its flora and fauna, its countryside and mountains, its lakes and waterfalls. In his descriptions of customs, of the crafts and the games there is an amusing vivacity and—throughout the poem—a deep sympathy and understanding of the survival of the original cultures."

In 1781 in Modena, Italy, there appeared under the title of *Rusticatio Mexicana* a poetic work of 3,425 Latin hexameters, in 10 cantos, written by Rafael Landívar. One year later in Bologna the second edition appeared. The poet called by Menendez y Pelayo "the Virgil of the modern age" proclaimed to the Europeans the excellence of the land, the life and the peoples of America. He was concerned for the people of the Old World to know that El Jorullo, a Mexican volcano, could rival Vesuvius and Etna, that the waterfalls and caves of San Pedro Martir in Guatemala were the equals of the famous fountains of Castalia and Aretusa and referring to the cenzontle—the bird whose song has 400 tones—he elevated it above the realm of the nightingale.

He sings the praises of the countryside, of the gold and silver that was filling the world with valuable coins and the sugar loaves offered at royal tables.

His poem is not short of statistics concerning the riches of America. He cites the droves of cattle, the flocks of sheep, the herds of goats and pigs, the sources of medicinal waters, the popular games—some unknown in Europe—and he does not hide the glory of the cocoa and chocolate of Guatemala. But there is something that we should be aware of in the song of Landívar; namely his love of the indigenous. The Indian, for Landívar, is the race that succeeds in everything, he describes the marvels of the floating gardens created by the Indians, he holds them up as examples of charm and skill without forgetting their great sufferings. In this way he imparts poetic substance—in naturalistic poetry far from symbolism—to a fact that has always been denied: the superiority of the American Indian as farmer, as craftsman and worker.

To the image of the bad Indian, lazy and immoral that was so widely propagated in Europe and accepted in America by those who exploit it Landívar opposes the picture of the Indian on whose shoulders has weighed—and continues to weigh—the burden of labour in America. And he does not do it by simply stating it—in which case we would have the right or not of believing it. In his poem we see the Indian on board his charming canoe, transporting his goods or travelling and we admire him extracting the purple and scarlet, laying out the snowy worms that produce the silk, holding on stubbornly to the rocks in order to remove the beautiful shellfish, patiently and doggedly ploughing, cultivating the indigo plant, extracting the silver from his native mines, exhausting the golden veins. . . . The *Rusticatio* of Landívar confirms what we have said of the great American literature—it cannot accept a passive role while on our soil a famished people live in these abundant lands. In its content it is a form of novel in verse.

Fifty years later, Andres Bello was to renovate the American adventure in his famous "Silva," an immortal and perfect work in which the nature of the New World appears again with maize the leader—as haughty chief of the corn tribe—the cacao in "coral urns," the coffee plants, the banana, the tropics in all their vegetable and animal power, contrasting the impoverished inhabitant with this grandiose vision "of the rich soil."

Bello recalls Inca Garcilaso in his role as an exile, he is of the American lineage of Landívar, both represent the brilliant start of the great American odyssey in world literature. As from this moment the image of nature in the New World will awake in Europe an interest but it will never attain the incandescent fidelity that is achieved in the work of Landívar and Bello. A distorted vision of the marvels is offered us by Chateaubriand in "Atala" and "Les Natchez."

For the Europeans nature is a background without the gravitational force achieved by Creole romanticism. The romantics give nature a permanent presence in the creations of poets and novelists of the epoch. This is exemplified by José Maria de Heredia singing of the Niagara Falls and Estaban Echeverria describing the desert in "La Cautiva" to mention just two.

Latin American romanticism was not only a literary school but a patriotic flag. Poets, historians and novelists divide their days and nights between political activities and dreaming their creations. Never has it been more beautiful to be a poet in America! Amongst the poets influenced by the *Patria* converted in Muse are José Mármol, author of one of the most widely read novels in Latin America—*Amalia*. The pages of this book have been turned by our febrile and sweaty fingers when we suffered in our very bones the dictatorships that have plagued Central America. The critics, when referring to the novel of Mármol, point out inconsistencies and carelessness without realising that a work of this type is written with a madly beating heart—pulsations that leave in the sentence, in the paragraph, on the page that abnormal heartbeat reflecting the distortion of the life force that troubled the entire country. We are in the presence of one of the most passionate examples of the American novel. Despite the years *Amalia*—the imprecations of José Mármol—continue to move readers to such an extent as to represent an act of faith.

It is at this very moment that the voice of Sarmiento is heard posing his famous dilemma at the threshold of the century: "civilisation or barbarism." Indeed, Sarmiento himself will be startled when he becomes aware that "Facundo" turns his arms against him and against everyone, declaring himself to be the authentic representative of Creole America, of the America that refuses to die and attempts to break—with a breast already hardened—the antithetical scheme of civilisation and barbarism in order to find between these two extremes the point where the American peoples are able to find their authentic personality with their own essential values.

In the middle of the last century another romantic, no less passionate, appears in Guatemala: José Batres Montúfar. In the midst of tales of festive character the reader feels that he should forget the fiesta to listen to the poetry. The immortal José Batres Montúfar, with abundant charm tinged with bitterness, was able to get to the core of issues that already—in the middle of the past century—were highly charged.

Another voice was to ring out from north to south, that of José Martí. His presence was felt, whether as an exile or in his beloved Cuba, the fire of his speech as poet or journalist being combined with the example of his sacrifice.

The 20th century is full of poets, poets that have nothing more to say with very few exceptions. Among the latter stand out the immortal Rubén Darío and Juan Ramón Molina from Honduras. The poets flee from reality, maybe because this is one of the ways of being a poet. But there is nothing living in much of their work which instead tend towards garrulity.

They are ignorant of the clear lesson of the native rhapsodists, they are forgetful of the colonial craftsmen of our great literature, satisfied with the bloodless imitation of the poetry of other latitudes and ridicule those who sang the bold gestures of the liberation struggle, considering them dazzled by a local patriotism.

It is only when the First World War is passed that a handful of men—men and artists—embark on the reconquest of their own tradition. In their encounter with the indigenous peoples they drop anchor in their Spanish home port and return with the message that they have to deliver to the future.

Latin American literature will be reborn under other signs—no longer that of verse. Now the prose is tactile, plural and irreverent in its attitude to conventions—to serve the purpose of this new crusade whose first move was to plunge into reality not so as to objectify but rather to penetrate the facts in order to identify fully with the problems of humanity. Nothing human—nothing which is real—will be foreign to this literature inspired by contact with America. And this is the case of the Latin American novel. Nobody doubts that the Latin American novel is at the leading edge of its genre in the world. It is cultivated in all our countries, by writers of different tendencies, which means that in the novel everything is forged from American material—the human witness of our historic moment.

We, the Latin American novelists of today, working within the tradition of engagement with our peoples which has enabled our great literature to develop—our poetry of substance—also have to reclaim lands for our dispossessed, mines for our exploited workers, to raise demands in favour of the masses who perish in the plantations, who are scorched by the sun in the banana fields, who turn into human bagasse in the sugar refineries. It is for this reason that—for me—the authentic Latin American novel is the call for all these things, it is the cry that echoes down the centuries and is pronounced in thousands of pages. A novel that is genuinely ours; determined and loyal—in its pages—to the cause of the human spirit, to the fists of our workers, to the sweat of our rural peasants, to the pain for our undernourished children; calling for the blood and the sap of our vast lands to run once more towards the seas to enrich our burgeoning new cities.

This novel shares—consciously or unconsciously—the characteristics of the indigenous texts; their freshness and power, the numismatic anguish in the eyes of the Creoles who awaited the dawn in the colonial night, more luminous however than this night that threatens us now. Above all, it is the affirmation of the optimism of those writers that defied the Inquisition, opening a breach in the conscience of the people for the march of the Liberators.

The Latin American novel, our novel, cannot betray the great spirit that has shaped—and continues to shape—all our great literature. If you write novels merely to entertain—then burn them! This might be the message delivered with evangelical fervour since if you do not burn them they will anyway be erased from the memory of the people where a poet or novelist should aspire to remain. Just consider how many writers there have been who—down the ages—have written novels to entertain! And who remembers them now? On the other hand, how easy it is to repeat the names of those amongst us who have written to bear witness.

To bear witness. The novelist bears witness like the apostle. Like Paul trying to escape, the writer is confronted with the pathetic reality of the world that surrounds him—the stark reality of our countries that overwhelms and blinds us and, throwing us to our knees, forces us to shout out: WHY DO YOU PERSECUTE ME? Yes, we are persecuted by this reality that we cannot deny, which is lived in the flesh by the people of the Mexican revolution, embodied in persons such as Mariano Azuela, Agustin Yanez and Juan Rulfo whose convictions are as sharp as a knife; those who share with Jorge Icaza, Ciro Alegría, Jesús Lara the shout of protest against the exploitation and abandonment of the Indian; those who with Romulo Gallegos in "Done Bábara" create for us our Prometheus. Here is Horacio Quiroga who frees us from the nightmare of the tropics, a nightmare that is as peculiar to him as his style is American. "Los ros profundos" of José María Arguedas, the "Rio oscuro" of the Argentinian Alfredo Varela, "Hijo de hombre" of the Paraguayan Roa Bastos and "La ciudad y los perros" of the Peruvian Vargas Llosa make us see how the life-blood of the working people is drained in our lands.

Mancisidor takes us to the oil fields to which are drawn—leaving their homes—the inhabitants of "Cases muertas" of Miguel Otero Silva.... David Vinas confronts us with the tragic Patagonia, Enrique Wernicke sweeps us along with the waters that overwhelm whole communities while Verbitsky and María de Jesús lead us to the miserable shanty towns, the Dantesque and subhuman quarters of our great cities....

Teitelboim in "El hijo del salitre" tells us of the gruelling work in the saltpetre mines while Nicomedes Guzman makes us share in the lives of the children in the Chilean working class districts. We feel the countryside of El Salvador in "Jaragua" by Napoleón Rodríguez Ruiz and our small villages in "Cenizas del Izalco" by Flakol and Clarivel Alegria. We cannot think of the pampas without speaking of "Don Segundo Sombra" by Guiraldes nor speak of the jungle without "La voragine" of Eustasio Rivera, nor of the Negroes: without Jorge Amado, nor of the Brazilian plains without the "Gran Sertao" of Guimaraes Rosa, nor of the plains of Venezuela without Ramón Díaz Sánchez.

Our books do not search for a sensationalist or horrifying effect in order to secure a place for us in the republic of letters. We are human beings linked by blood, geography and life to those hundreds, thousands, millions of Latin Americans that suffer misery in our opulent and rich American continent. Our novels attempt to mobilise across the world the moral forces that have to help us defend those people. The *mestizo* process was already advanced in our literature and in rediscovering America it lent a human dimension to the grandiose nature of the continent. But this is a nature neither for the gods as in the texts of the Indians, nor a nature for heroes as in the writings of the romantics, but a nature for men and women in which the human problems will be addressed again with vigour and audacity.

As true Latin Americans the beauty of expression excites us and—for this reason—each one of our novels is a verbal feat. Alchemy is at work. We know it. It is no easy task to understand in the executed work all the effort and determination invested in the materials used—the words.

Yes, I say words—but by what laws and rules they have been transformed! They have been set as the pulse of worlds in formation. They ring like wood, like metals. This is onomatopoeia. In the adventure of our language the first aspect that demands attention is onomatopoeia. How many echoes—composed or disintegrated—of our landscape, our nature are to be found in our words, our sentences. The novelist embarks on a verbal adventure, an instinctive use of words. One is guided along by sounds. One listens, listens to the characters.

Our best novels do not seem to have been written but spoken. There is verbal dynamics in the poetry enclosed in the very word itself and that is revealed first as sound and afterwards as concept.

This is why the great Spanish American novels are vibrantly musical in the convulsion of the birth of all the things that are born with them.

The adventure continues in the confluence of the languages. Amongst the languages spoken by the people, in which the Indian languages are represented, there is an admixture of the European and Oriental languages brought by the immigrants to America.

Another language is going to rain its sparkle over sounds and words. The language of images. Our novels seem to be written not only with words but with images. Quite a few people when reading our novels see them cinematically. And this is not because they pursue a dramatic statement of independence but because our novelists are engaged in universalising the voice of their peoples with a language rich in sounds, rich in fable and rich in images.

This is not a language artificially created to provide scope for the play of the imagination or so-called poetic prose; it is a vivid language that preserves in its popular speech all the lyricism, the imagination, the grace, the high-spiritedness that characterise the language of the Latin American novel.

The poetic language which nourishes our novelistic literature is more or less its breath of life. Novels with lungs of poetry, lungs of foliage, lungs of rich vegetation. I believe that what most attracts non-American readers is what our novels have achieved by means of a colourful, brilliant language without falling into the merely picturesque, the spell of onomatopoeia cast by representing the music of the countryside and sometimes the sounds of the indigenous languages, the ancestral smack of those languages that flourish unconsciously in the prose that is used. There is also the importance of the word as absolute entity, as symbol. Our prose is distinguished from Castilian syntax because the word—in our novels—has a value of its own, just as it had in the indigenous languages. Word, concept, sound; a rich fascinating transposition. Nobody can understand our literature, our poetry if the power of enchantment is removed from the word.

Word and language enable the reader to participate in the life of our novelistic creations. Unsettling, disturbing, forcing the attention of the reader who—forgetting his daily life—will enter into the situations and personalities of a novel tradition that retains intact its humanistic values. Nothing is used to detract from mankind but rather to perfect it and this is perhaps what wins over and unsettles the reader, that which transforms our novel into a vehicle of ideas, an interpreter of peoples using as instrument a language with a literary dimension, with imponderable magical value and profound human projection.

[© The Nobel Foundation, 1967. Miguel Ángel Asturias is the sole author of the text.]

Samuel Beckett
(13 April 1906 – 22 December 1989)

Julian A. Garforth
Beckett International Foundation, University of Reading

See also the Beckett entries in *DLB 13: British Dramatists Since World War II; DLB 15: British Novelists, 1930–1959; DLB 233: British and Irish Dramatists Since World War II, Second Series; DLB 319: British and Irish Short-Fiction Writers, 1945–2000; DLB 321: Twentieth Century French Dramatists;* and *DLB Yearbook: 1990.*

BOOKS: *Whoroscope* (Paris: Hours Press, 1930);
Proust (London: Chatto & Windus, 1931; New York: Grove, 1957);
More Pricks than Kicks (London: Chatto & Windus, 1934; New York: Grove, 1970);
Echo's Bones and Other Precipitates (Paris: Europa Press, 1935);
Murphy (London: Routledge, 1938; New York: Grove, 1957); translated into French by Beckett (Paris: Bordas, 1947);
Molloy (Paris: Editions de Minuit, 1951); translated by Beckett and Patrick Bowles (Paris: Olympia Press, 1955; New York: Grove, 1955; London: Calder & Boyars, 1966);
Malone meurt (Paris: Editions de Minuit, 1951); translated by Beckett as *Malone Dies* (New York: Grove, 1956; London: Calder, 1958);
En attendant Godot (Paris: Editions de Minuit, 1952); translated by Beckett as *Waiting for Godot* (New York: Grove, 1954; London: Faber & Faber, 1956);
L'Innommable (Paris: Editions de Minuit, 1953); translated by Beckett as *The Unnamable* (New York: Grove, 1958; London: Calder, 1975);
Watt (Paris: Olympia Press, 1953; New York: Grove, 1959; London: Calder, 1963); translated into French by Beckett, Ludovic Janvier, and Agnès Janvier (Paris: Editions de Minuit, 1968);
Nouvelles et textes pour rien (Paris: Editions de Minuit, 1955); translated by Beckett as *Stories and Texts for Nothing* (New York: Grove, 1967);
All That Fall (New York: Grove, 1957; London: Faber & Faber, 1957); translated into French by Beckett

Samuel Beckett, 1987 (AP World Wide)

and Robert Pinget as *Tous ceux qui tombent* (Paris: Editions de Minuit, 1957);
Fin de partie, suivi de Acte sans paroles [I] (Paris: Editions de Minuit, 1957); translated by Beckett as *Endgame, Followed by Act Without Words* (New York: Grove, 1958; London: Faber & Faber, 1958);
From an Abandoned Work (London: Faber & Faber, 1958); translated into French by Beckett, Ludovic Janvier, and Agnès Janvier as *D'un ouvrage abandonné* (Paris: Editions de Minuit, 1967);

Molloy, Malone Dies, and The Unnamable: Three Novels (New York: Grove, 1958; London: Calder, 1959; Paris: Olympia Press, 1959);

Krapp's Last Tape and Embers (London: Faber & Faber, 1959); translated into French by Beckett and Pierre Leyris as *La Dernière bande, suivi de Cendres* (Paris: Editions de Minuit, 1960);

Krapp's Last Tape and Other Dramatic Pieces (New York: Grove, 1960)–comprises *Krapp's Last Tape, All That Fall, Embers, Act Without Words I,* and *Act Without Words II* (the last two translated from the French by Beckett);

Comment c'est (Paris: Editions de Minuit, 1961); translated by Beckett as *How It Is* (New York: Grove, 1964; London: Calder, 1964);

Happy Days (New York: Grove, 1961; London: Faber & Faber, 1962); translated into French by Beckett as *Oh les beaux jours* (Paris: Editions de Minuit, 1963);

Poems in English (London: Calder, 1961; New York: Grove, 1963);

Dramatische Dichtungen, 2 volumes, French and English texts by Beckett, German translations by Elmar Tophoven and Erika Tophoven (Frankfurt am Main: Suhrkamp, 1963, 1964)–includes in volume 1: *Acte sans paroles II [Act Without Words II],* original French version; *Cascando,* original French version, with English translation by Beckett; in volume 2: *Comédie [Play],* translated into French by Beckett;

Play and Two Short Pieces for Radio (London: Faber & Faber, 1964)–comprises *Play, Words and Music,* and *Cascando;*

Imagination morte imaginez (Paris: Editions de Minuit, 1965); translated by Beckett as *Imagination Dead Imagine* (London: Calder & Boyars, 1965);

Proust [by Beckett] *and Three Dialogues* [by Beckett and Georges Duthuit] (London: Calder, 1965);

Assez (Paris: Editions de Minuit, 1966); translated by Beckett as *Enough* in *No's Knife: Collected Shorter Prose, 1945–1966* (London: Calder & Boyars, 1967) and in *First Love and Other Shorts* (New York: Grove, 1974);

Bing (Paris: Editions de Minuit, 1966); translated by Beckett as *Ping* in *No's Knife: Collected Shorter Prose, 1945–1966* (London: Calder & Boyars, 1967) and in *First Love and Other Shorts* (New York: Grove, 1974);

Comédie et actes divers (Paris: Editions de Minuit, 1966)–comprises *Comédie, Va-et-vient, Cascando, Paroles et musique, Dis Joe,* and *Acte sans paroles II;* expanded edition (Paris: Editions de Minuit, 1972)–includes *Acte sans paroles I, Film,* and *Souffle;*

Eh Joe and Other Writings (London: Faber & Faber, 1967; New York: Grove, 1969)–comprises *Eh Joe, Act Without Words II,* and *Film;*

Come and Go (London: Calder & Boyars, 1967);

No's Knife: Collected Shorter Prose, 1945–1966 (London: Calder & Boyars, 1967)–comprises *The Expelled, The Calmative, The End, Texts for Nothing 1–13, From an Abandoned Work, Enough, Imagination Dead Imagine,* and *Ping;*

Têtes-mortes, translated by Beckett, Ludovic Janvier, and Agnes Janvier (Paris: Editions de Minuit, 1967)–comprises *D'un ouvrage abandonné, Assez, Imagination morte imaginez,* and *Bing;* expanded edition (Paris: Editions de Minuit, 1972)–includes *Sans;*

Cascando and Other Short Dramatic Pieces (New York: Grove, 1968)–comprises *Cascando, Words and Music, Eh Joe, Play, Come and Go,* and *Film;*

Film, Eh Joe in drei Sprachen (Frankfurt am Main: Suhrkamp, 1968)–includes *Film,* translated into French by Beckett;

Poèmes (Paris: Editions de Minuit, 1968);

Film (New York: Grove, 1969; London: Faber & Faber, 1972);

Sans (Paris: Editions de Minuit, 1969); translated by Beckett as *Lessness* (London: Calder & Boyars, 1970);

The Collected Works of Samuel Beckett, 16 volumes (New York: Grove, 1970);

Le Dépeupleur (Paris: Editions de Minuit, 1970); translated by Beckett as *The Lost Ones* (London: Calder & Boyars, 1972; New York: Grove, 1972);

Mercier et Camier (Paris: Editions de Minuit, 1970); translated by Beckett as *Mercier and Camier* (London: Calder & Boyars, 1974; New York: Grove, 1974);

Premier amour (Paris: Editions de Minuit, 1970); translated by Beckett as *First Love* (London: Calder & Boyars, 1973);

Breath and Other Shorts (London: Faber & Faber, 1971)–comprises *Breath, Come and Go, Act Without Words I, Act Without Words II,* and *From an Abandoned Work;*

Film, suivi de Souffle (Paris: Editions de Minuit, 1972)–includes *Souffle [Breath],* translated into French by Beckett;

Not I (London: Faber & Faber, 1973); translated into French by Beckett as *Pas moi* (Paris: Editions de Minuit, 1975);

Au loin un oiseau, text by Beckett, etchings by Avigdor Arikha (New York: Double Elephant Press, 1973); translated by Beckett as *Afar a Bird* in *For to End Yet Again and Other Fizzles* (London: Calder, 1976) and in *Fizzles* (New York: Grove, 1976);

First Love and Other Shorts (New York: Grove, 1974)–comprises *First Love, From an Abandoned Work,*

Enough, Imagination Dead Imagine, Ping, Not I, and *Breath;*

Still, text by Beckett, etchings by William Hayter (Milan: M'Arte Edizione, 1974);

Oh les beaux jours, suivi de Pas moi (Paris: Editions de Minuit, 1975);

I Can't Go On, I'll Go On: A Selection from Samuel Beckett's Work, edited by Richard W. Seaver (New York: Grove, 1976)–includes *That Time;*

Foirades = Fizzles, bilingual edition, text by Beckett, etchings by Jasper Johns (London: Petersburg Press, 1976);

Pour finir encore et autres foirades (Paris: Editions de Minuit, 1976); translated by Beckett as *For to End Yet Again and Other Fizzles* (London: Calder, 1976); translation published as *Fizzles* (New York: Grove, 1976);

All Strange Away (New York: Gotham Book Mart, 1976; London: Calder, 1979);

That Time (London: Faber & Faber, 1976); translated into French by Beckett as *Cette fois* (Paris: Editions de Minuit, 1978);

Footfalls (London: Faber & Faber, 1976); translated into French by Beckett as *Pas* (Paris: Editions de Minuit, 1977);

Ends and Odds: Eight New Dramatic Pieces (New York: Grove Press, 1976)–comprises *Not I, That Time, Footfalls, Ghost Trio, [Rough for] Theatre I, [Rough for] Theatre II, [Rough for] Radio I,* and *[Rough for] Radio II;* expanded as *Ends and Odds: Plays and Sketches* (London: Faber & Faber, 1977)–includes *. . . but the clouds . . . ;* expanded edition published as *Ends and Odds: Nine Dramatic Pieces* (New York: Grove Press, 1981);

. . . but the clouds . . . (London: Faber & Faber, 1977);

Collected Poems in English and French (London: Calder, 1977; New York: Grove, 1977); expanded as *Collected Poems 1930–1978* (London: Calder, 1984)–includes *Mirlitonnades;*

Pas suivi de quatre esquisses (Paris: Editions de Minuit, 1978)–comprises *Pas, Fragment de théâtre I, Fragment de théâtre II, Pochade radiophonique,* and *Esquisse radiophonique;*

Poèmes suivi de Mirlitonnades (Paris: Editions de Minuit, 1978);

Company (New York: Grove, 1980; London: Calder, 1980); translated into French by Beckett as *Compagnie* (Paris: Editions de Minuit, 1980);

Mal vu mal dit (Paris: Editions de Minuit, 1981); translated by Beckett as *Ill Seen, Ill Said* (New York: Grove, 1981; London: Calder, 1982);

Rockaby and Other Short Pieces (New York: Grove, 1981)–comprises *Rockaby, Ohio Impromptu, All Strange Away,* and *A Piece of Monologue;*

Berceuse; suivi de Impromptu d'Ohio (Paris: Editions de Minuit, 1982)–comprises *Berceuse [Rockaby]* and *Impromptu d'Ohio [Ohio Impromptu],* translated into French by Beckett;

Solo; suivi de Catastrophe (Paris: Editions de Minuit, 1982)–comprises *A Piece of Monologue,* translated by Beckett as *Solo,* and *Catastrophe;*

Catastrophe et autres dramaticules (Paris: Editions de Minuit, 1982)–comprises *Cette fois, Solo, Berceuse, Impromptu d'Ohio,* and *Catastrophe;* expanded edition (Paris: Editions de Minuit, 1986)–includes *Quoi où;*

Three Occasional Pieces (London: Faber & Faber, 1982)–comprises *A Piece of Monologue, Rockaby,* and *Ohio Impromptu;*

Quoi où (Paris: Editions de Minuit, 1983);

Worstward Ho (New York: Grove, 1983; London: Calder, 1983);

Disjecta: Miscellaneous Writings and a Dramatic Fragment, edited by Ruby Cohn (London: Calder, 1983; New York: Grove, 1984);

Collected Shorter Plays (London: Faber & Faber, 1984; New York: Grove, 1984)–includes *Quad, Nacht und Träume,* and Beckett's English translation of *Catastrophe;*

Collected Shorter Prose 1945–1980 (London: Calder, 1984);

Three Plays (New York: Grove, 1984)–comprises *Ohio Impromptu, Catastrophe,* and *What Where;*

The Complete Dramatic Works (London: Faber & Faber, 1986);

L'Image (Paris: Editions de Minuit, 1988);

Stirrings Still, text by Beckett, illustrations by Louis le Broquy (New York: Blue Moon, 1988; London: Calder, 1988);

Comment dire (Paris: Librairie Compagnie, 1989);

Nohow On: Company, Ill Seen Ill Said, Worstward Ho (London: Calder, 1989; New York: Grove, 1995);

As the Story Was Told: Uncollected and Late Prose (London: Calder, 1990; New York: Riverrun, 1990)–includes *The Capitol of the Ruins, The Image, All Strange Away, Heard in the Dark 1, Heard in the Dark 2, One Evening, As the Story Was Told, Neither, Stirrings Still,* and *What Is the Word;*

Dream of Fair to Middling Women, edited by Eoin O'Brien and Edith Fournier (Dublin: Black Cat, 1992; London: Calder, 1993; New York: Arcade, 1993);

Eleutheria (Paris: Editions de Minuit, 1995); translated from the French by Michael Brodsky as *Eleuthéria* (New York: Foxrock, 1995); translated by Barbara Wright (London: Faber & Faber, 1996).

Editions and Collections: *Proust,* translated into French by Edith Fournier (Paris: Editions de Minuit, 1990);

Quad, Ghost Trio, . . . but the clouds . . . , and *Nacht und Träume,* translated by Fournier as *Quad et Trio du fantôme, . . . que nuages . . . , Nacht und Träume; suivi de l'Epuise de Gilles Deleuze* (Paris: Editions de Minuit, 1992);

Endgame, edited by S. E. Gontarski, volume 2 of *The Theatrical Notebooks of Samuel Beckett* (London: Faber & Faber, 1992; New York: Grove, 1992)– includes a revised text;

Krapp's Last Tape, edited by James Knowlson, volume 3 of *The Theatrical Notebooks of Samuel Beckett* (London: Faber & Faber, 1992; New York: Grove, 1992)–includes a revised text;

Waiting for Godot, edited by Dougald McMillan and Knowlson, volume 1 of *The Theatrical Notebooks of Samuel Beckett* (London: Faber & Faber, 1993; New York: Grove, 1994)–includes a revised text;

More Pricks than Kicks, translated into French by Fournier as *Bande et sarabande* (Paris: Editions de Minuit, 1994);

The Complete Short Prose 1929-1989, edited by Gontarski (New York: Grove, 1995);

The Shorter Plays, edited by Gontarski, volume 4 of *The Theatrical Notebooks of Samuel Beckett* (London: Faber & Faber, 1999; New York: Grove, 1999)– includes revised texts of *Footfalls, Come and Go,* and *What Where;*

Shorts, 12 volumes (London: Calder, 1999);

Poems 1930-1989 (London: Calder, 2002).

PLAY PRODUCTIONS: *En attendant Godot,* Paris, Théâtre de Babylone, 5 January 1953; produced in English as *Waiting for Godot,* London, Arts Theatre Club, 3 August 1955; transferred to the Criterion Theatre, 12 September 1955; Miami, Coconut Grove Playhouse, 3 January 1956; New York, John Golden Theatre, 19 April 1956;

Fin de partie and *Acte sans paroles (I),* London, Royal Court Theatre, 3 April 1957; Paris, Studio des Champs-Elysées, 26 April 1957; translated into English by Beckett as *Endgame* and *Act Without Words I,* New York, Cherry Lane Theatre, 28 January 1958; London, Royal Court Theatre, 28 October 1958;

Krapp's Last Tape, London, Royal Court Theatre, 28 October 1958 [produced with *Endgame*]; New York, Provincetown Playhouse, 14 January 1960; translated into French by Beckett as *La Dernière bande,* Paris, Théâtre Récamier, 22 March 1960;

Act Without Words II, London, Institute of Contemporary Arts, 25 January 1960; Milwaukee, University of Wisconsin, 10 July 1962;

Happy Days, New York, Cherry Lane Theatre, 17 September 1961; London, Royal Court Theatre, 1 November 1962; translated into French by Beckett as *Oh les beaux jours,* Venice, Teatro del Ridotto, 28 September 1963; Paris, Odéon-Théâtre de France, 21 October 1963;

Play, translated into German by Elmar Tophoven and Erika Tophoven as *Spiel,* Ulm, Germany, Ulmer Theater, 14 June 1963; original English version produced as *Play,* New York, Cherry Lane Theatre, 4 January 1964; London, Old Vic Theatre, 7 April 1964; translated into French by Beckett as *Comédie,* Paris, Pavillon de Marsan, 11 June 1964;

Come and Go, translated into German by Elmar Tophoven and Erika Tophoven as *Kommen und Gehen,* Berlin, Schiller-Theater Werkstatt, 14 January 1966; translated into French by Beckett as *Va-et-vient,* Paris, Odéon-Théâtre de France, 28 February 1966; original English version produced as *Come and Go,* Dublin, Peacock Theatre, 28 February 1968; London, Royal Festival Hall, 9 December 1968; Milwaukee, University of Wisconsin, Performing Arts Center, 23 November 1970;

Breath, New York, Eden Theatre, 17 June 1969 [as part of *Oh! Calcutta!*]; Oxford, Oxford Playhouse, 8 March 1970;

Not I, New York, Lincoln Center, 22 November 1972; London, Royal Court Theatre, 16 January 1973; translated into French by Beckett as *Pas moi,* Paris, Théâtre d'Orsay, 3 April 1975;

That Time and *Footfalls,* London, Royal Court Theatre, 20 May 1976; Washington, D.C., Arena Stage, 3 December 1976; *Footfalls* translated into French by Beckett as *Pas,* Paris, Théâtre d'Orsay, 11 April 1978;

A Piece of Monologue, New York, La Mama Experimental Theatre Club, 14 December 1979;

Rockaby, Buffalo, State University of New York at Buffalo, 8 April 1981; London, Cottesloe Theatre (National Theatre), 9 December 1982; translated into French by Beckett as *Berceuse,* Paris, Centre Georges Pompidou, 14 October 1981;

Ohio Impromptu, Columbus, Ohio State University, 9 May 1981; Nottingham, University of Nottingham Dramatic Society, 22 June 1984; first professional production, Edinburgh, Edinburgh Festival, 13 August 1984; translated into French by Beckett as *Impromptu d'Ohio,* Paris, Théâtre du Rond-Point, 15 September 1983;

Catastrophe, Avignon, Avignon Festival, 21 July 1982; English version produced with *What Where,* New York, Harold Clurman Theatre, 15 June 1983; Edinburgh, Edinburgh Festival, 13 August 1984;

What Where, produced with *Catastrophe,* New York, Harold Clurman Theater, 15 June 1983; Edinburgh, Edinburgh Festival, 13 August 1984; original French version of *What Where* produced as *Quoi où,* Paris, Théâtre du Rond-Point, April 1986.

PRODUCED SCRIPTS: *All That Fall,* radio, BBC Third Programme, 13 January 1957;

Embers, radio, BBC Third Programme, 24 June 1959;

Words and Music, radio, BBC Third Programme, 13 November 1962;

Cascando, radio, RTF-France Culture, 13 October 1963; English version, BBC Third Programme, 6 October 1964;

Film, motion picture, Evergreen, 1965;

Eh Joe, television, Süddeutscher Rundfunk, 13 April 1966 [as *He, Joe*]; original English version, BBC 2, 4 July 1966; German version revised as *He, Joe,* Süddeutscher Rundfunk, 13 September 1979;

Rough for Radio II, radio, BBC Radio 3, 13 April 1976;

Shades, television, BBC 2, 17 April 1977—comprised *Ghost Trio, . . . but the clouds . . . ,* and *Not I;*

Quadrat 1 + 2, television, Süddeutscher Rundfunk, 8 October 1981; English version broadcast as *Quad,* BBC 2, 16 December 1982;

Nacht und Träume, television, Süddeutscher Rundfunk, 19 May 1983;

Was wo [What Where], television, Süddeutscher Rundfunk, 13 April 1986.

OTHER: "Dante, Bruno, Vico, Joyce," in *Our Exagmination Round His Factification for Incamination of Work in Progress,* by Beckett and others (Paris: Shakespeare and Company, 1929), pp. 3–22;

"From the Only Poet to a Shining Whore" in *Henry-Music,* by Henry Crowder and others (Paris: Hours Press, 1930), pp. 12–14;

"Hell Crane to Starling," "Casket of Pralinen for a Daughter of a Dissipated Mandarin," "Text," and "Yoke of Liberty," in *The European Caravan: An Anthology of the New Spirit in European Literature. Part 1, France, Spain, England and Ireland,* edited by Samuel Putnam, Maida Castelhun Darnton, George Reavey, and J. Bronowski (New York: Brewer, Warren & Putnam, 1931), pp. 475–480;

As the Story Was Told, in *Günter Eich zum Gedächtnis,* edited by Siegfried Unseld (Frankfurt am Main: Suhrkamp, 1973);

Ceiling, in Avigdor Arikha, *Arikha* (Paris: Hermann, 1985; London: Thames & Hudson, 1985), p. 12.

TRANSLATIONS: Selected translations, in *Negro: An Anthology,* edited by Nancy Cunard (London: Wishart, 1934);

Octavio Paz, comp., *Anthology of Mexican Poetry* (Bloomington: Indiana University Press, 1958);

Arthur Rimbaud, *Drunken Boat [Le bateau ivre]* (Reading: Whiteknights Press, 1976).

Samuel Beckett is the only Nobel laureate to appear in the cricketers' bible, *Wisden,* having represented a Dublin University side that toured England in 1925 and 1926. Beckett batted left-handed and bowled right-handed—an individual approach that was reflected in most aspects of his life, including his distinctive writing. The Nobel citation from the Swedish Academy states that his award was for "a body of work that, in new forms of fiction and the theatre, has transmuted the destitution of modern man into his exaltation." Beckett was, without doubt, one of the most significant writers of the twentieth century, and his influence and popularity live on into the twenty-first century.

Samuel Barclay Beckett was born at Cooldrinagh in Foxrock, County Dublin, on Good Friday, 13 April 1906. Friday the Thirteenth was a particularly appropriate date for this enigmatic figure, who had the reputation of being somber and secretive and who refused to give interviews about himself or his work, which appears to focus almost exclusively on the bleaker, darker side of existence. The popular myth of Beckett as a mysterious recluse was far from the truth, however, and hid a private but immensely gracious and caring person, whose generosity extended well beyond his immediate circle of friends to almost anyone he met.

Beckett was the second son of William Frank Beckett, a quantity surveyor, and his wife, Maria (née Roe), known as May, who was a nurse. The family was staunchly Protestant and middle-class, placing Beckett in the minority in the predominantly Catholic Dublin. Despite a turbulent relationship with his mother, who was strong-willed and protective, he had a relatively happy childhood in rural Foxrock, attending a kindergarten run by two elderly German sisters, Ida and Pauline Elsner, in the nearby village of Stillorgan. He was subsequently sent to Portora Royal School in Enniskillen, along with his elder brother, Frank. In addition to being gifted academically, Beckett had a lifelong love of sport, dating back to his school days, where he excelled at rugby, tennis, boxing, and cricket. When he entered Trinity College, Dublin, in 1923, Beckett's passion for sport was gradually superseded by his interests in art, music, and literature. Although he only drifted slowly toward the study of modern languages, having also studied English literature, he proved to be a talented linguist, graduating first in his year in

French and Italian. His French tutor, Thomas Brown Rudmose-Brown, introduced him to a wide range of classical and modern French literature, and his Italian studies provided his initial contact with Dante's *Divina commedia,* a source of interest throughout his life. His academic prowess was partnered with a passion for music-hall and vaudeville theater as well as the silent slapstick movies and early shorts of Charlie Chaplin, the Marx Brothers, and Buster Keaton. While at Trinity College, Beckett met his first love, fellow pupil Ethna MacCarthy, who inspired the poems "Alba" (first published in *Dublin Magazine* in 1931) and "Yoke of Liberty" (first published in *The European Caravan: An Anthology of the New Spirit in European Literature,* 1931). Although his feelings were not reciprocated, the two remained good friends until MacCarthy's death from cancer in 1959.

After he graduated, an academic career seemed the obvious option for the young, gifted linguist, and Beckett taught French for two terms at Campbell College, Belfast—an experience he hated. In November 1928 he assumed the position of *lecteur* at the Ecole Normale Supérieure in Paris, where he became friends with Thomas MacGreevy, his predecessor in the post, who introduced him to James Joyce and his circle. Beckett immersed himself completely in this artistic group, resulting in the inclusion of his essay "Dante, Bruno, Vico, Joyce" in *Our Exagmination Round His Factification for Incamination of Work in Progress* (1929), a volume celebrating the work that became Joyce's *Finnegans Wake* (1939). The essay, which also appeared in the literary journal *Transition* (Spring–Summer 1929), shows Beckett's clear admiration for Joyce's style but also allows him to exhibit his own ability to manipulate language. Beckett's first fictional work, "Assumption," appeared in the same issue of *Transition,* followed shortly afterward by his first independent publication: *Whoroscope* (1930), a poem based on the life of René Descartes, written as an entry for the Hours Press poetry competition organized by Nancy Cunard. The title shows Beckett's playfulness with language, being a pun on the word "whore" and the Greek "horo" (time/hour), as well as alluding to Descartes's famous refusal to reveal his exact date of birth, so that no astrologer could write an accurate horoscope predicting the date of his death.

In the autumn of 1930 Beckett returned to Dublin to take up a lectureship in modern languages at Trinity College, where he taught classes on the works of Jean Racine, Molière, Honoré de Balzac, Stendhal, Gustave Flaubert, and Marcel Proust. As his contribution to the Modern Languages Society's annual presentation at the Peacock Theatre, Beckett took his first steps toward becoming a playwright by collaborating with Georges Pelorson to create a one-act pastiche of Pierre Corneille's play *Le Cid* (1637), titled *Le Kid* (performed in 1931). Although Pelorson wrote most of the piece (and most Beckett scholars therefore no longer regard it as a work by Beckett), Beckett came up with the title, which was also a play on Chaplin's movie *The Kid* (1921). In complete contrast to this lighthearted parody, Beckett also published his highly regarded essay *Proust* (1931), a study of *A la recherche du temps perdu* (1913–1927, Remembrance of Things Past), showcasing Beckett's critical writing. In this book he analyzes the main Proustian concepts: time, "that double-headed monster of damnation and salvation"; involuntary memory, "an immediate, total and delicious deflagration"; and habit, "the ballast that chains the dog to his vomit."

As biographer James Knowlson records, Beckett did not take to the "grotesque comedy of lecturing," describing it as "teaching to others what he did not know himself." After suffering a virtual breakdown toward the end of 1931, Beckett realized that he was not cut out for the rigors of academic life but was more suited to the artistic lifestyle he had encountered in Paris in the company of Joyce. He subsequently resigned from his teaching post and decided to return to Paris in order to forge a career as a writer and translator.

During 1932 Beckett worked on a novel titled *Dream of Fair to Middling Women* (1992), which he had begun in Dublin. A complex mixture of critical theory and biographical detail, based loosely on Beckett's own turbulent lifestyle during his time at Trinity College, this novel presents the young writer with an opportunity to display his literary and linguistic knowledge. It follows the adventures of a young Irishman, Belacqua Shuah, whose name is lifted directly from Dante's *Purgatorio.* Full of foreign vocabulary and obscure literary allusions, it was perhaps too intellectual for its own good, and Beckett was unable to find a publisher for it. It was finally published after his death. In 1933, virtually broke and under pressure to leave Paris because of a clampdown on foreign residents, Beckett returned to Dublin. His father died on 26 June 1933, leaving Beckett feeling guilty and depressed at having failed him by resigning from the teaching post. His mental problems increased as the year progressed, and he moved to London, where he underwent psychotherapy for almost two years with Wilfred Bion at the Tavistock Clinic. During this period, Beckett read widely on psychology and psychoanalysis and visited Bethlem Royal Hospital, where a former school friend, Geoffrey Thompson, worked as a doctor. Beckett's own experience of psychotherapy and his interest in mental illness in general are reflected in much of his subsequent writing.

Beckett recycled some of the material from his unpublished novel in *More Pricks than Kicks* (1934), a collection of ten satirical short stories about the exploits of Belacqua Shuah. Written in a similarly highbrow literary style, the book was well received critically but sold poorly. Beckett also completed nineteen translations for Nancy Cunard's *Negro: An Anthology* (1934), realizing that translation might be one possible way to support himself. MacGreevy introduced Beckett to various figures in the publishing world in an attempt to aid his writing career. This assistance resulted in a series of reviews for literary journals, one of which, a review of *Mozart On the Way to Prague,* a 1934 translation of Eduard Mörike's *Mozart auf der Reise nach Prag* (1856), offers an early insight into Beckett's stance concerning language. In this review, included in *Disjecta: Miscellaneous Writings and a Dramatic Fragment* (1983), Beckett argues that Mörike's work is "at least short, which is nowadays so rare a quality in a literary work that one cannot refrain from commending this book for having contrived, in 20,000 words instead of in 200,000, to exhaust the inessential." This goal is precisely what many of Beckett's own subsequent protagonists are trying to achieve—"to exhaust the inessential." Beckett claims that "all writing, *qua* writing, is bound to fail," neatly summarizing his approach to his own creative process and his constant attempts to "Fail again. Fail better," as he wrote in *Worstward Ho* (1983). In addition to these literary reviews, he also published a collection of thirteen poems under the title *Echo's Bones and Other Precipitates* (1935).

In September 1934 Beckett moved to the World's End area of London, the setting for his next novel, *Murphy* (1938), which he completed in June 1936. Somewhat autobiographical in nature, the novel recounts the tale of the Irish "everyman" of the title: down on his luck, living in similar circumstances to Beckett, and torn between the spiritual and the physical. Probably Beckett's most accessible prose work, it is less overtly intellectual than his previous efforts, being what C. J. Ackerley and S. E. Gontarski in *The Grove Companion to Beckett* (2004) call "a gigantic joke made up of tiny ones." It has a wealth of entertaining characters and draws on Beckett's knowledge of Descartes and Flemish philosopher Arnold Geulincx as well as his own love of chess for its plot. Its most famous moment is Murphy's funeral wake, where, during a drunken argument, "the body, mind and soul of Murphy were freely distributed over the floor of the saloon." In a scene that mixes comedy and pathos, his ashes are swept away "with the sand, the beer, the butts, the glass, the matches, the spits, the vomit." Despite the potential appeal of the novel, Beckett remained unable to find a publisher for it for almost two years. After a promising start, his literary career now seemed to be struggling.

In September 1936, having recently become interested in art history, Beckett traveled to Germany with the intention of visiting various galleries. He was disappointed to find that the Nazis had removed all the modern paintings that they considered degenerate. This period in Germany was of great importance in Beckett's development as a writer, as he met a series of people who introduced him to the work of the most forward-thinking German artists and writers. Although the period was unproductive in terms of creative writing, Beckett kept a six-volume diary and a notebook during his travels. The notebook bears the inscription "Whoroscope," although its contents are unrelated to the poem of that title. It includes a wealth of information on Beckett's reading matter and thoughts during these six unhappy months, in particular outlining his attraction toward German philosophy and his growing interest in contemporary German literature. Around this time, Beckett also began working on a play about Samuel Johnson and his circle, which he titled "Human Wishes." Despite filling several notebooks with source material and drafts, he never published the play, and only a fragment appears in *Disjecta*.

On returning to Dublin, Beckett was called as a witness in a libel case involving his uncle, Harry Sinclair; Knowlson reports that during the trial, Beckett's artistic lifestyle was scrutinized and he was described as "that bawd and blasphemer from Paris." Having witnessed firsthand the intolerance of the Nazi regime toward writers and artists in Germany, Beckett made the decision to live in Paris for the rest of his life. His life as an exile did not begin well: on 5 January 1938 he was stabbed near the heart by a pimp and only narrowly escaped death. While recuperating in hospital, he was visited by Suzanne Deschevaux-Dumesnil, a French woman he had met ten years earlier. By 1939 they were living together, although they did not marry until 25 March 1961. Beckett spent the last years of the decade working on the French translation of *Murphy* with Alfred Péron. He also wrote several poems in French, which were published in *Les Temps Modernes* in 1946.

Beckett's decision that he preferred France at the outbreak of World War II to Ireland at peace was more than a mere gesture. As an Irishman living abroad, Beckett was, in theory, a neutral. But, having recently experienced the inhumanity of the Nazi regime in Germany, he felt unable to stand by and allow his French friends and colleagues to be persecuted. He was introduced to a Résistance cell by

Péron and was soon working as a translator and relaying messages. When the cell was infiltrated in August 1942, Beckett and Deschevaux-Dumesnil fled to Roussillon in the Vaucluse, where they spent the rest of the war in hiding. During their forced isolation, Beckett managed to complete a novel, *Watt* (1953), which he later described disparagingly (according to Lawrence Harvey) as "only a game . . . a means of staying sane and a way to keep [my] hand in." In contrast to *Murphy*, *Watt* is one of Beckett's least accessible works. It relates the story of the title character, first a servant in Mr. Knott's house and later resident of an institution, where he recounts his adventures to another inmate called Sam. The novel documents Watt's gradual mental deterioration and is full of complex lists, hypotheses, and calculations, based on probabilities and permutations, which can be perplexing for the reader. Completely different stylistically from his previous novels, *Watt* was Beckett's last work in English for several years. Beckett's experiences during the war altered his outlook on life dramatically, and his feelings of isolation, uncertainty, and danger are reflected in much of his postwar writing. Beckett was awarded the Croix de Guerre and the Médaille de la Reconnaissance Française for his Résistance work during the war. Yet, with his usual modesty, he dismissed his brave actions as merely "boy scout activities."

During a visit to Foxrock shortly after the war, Beckett experienced what he described as a "revelation," an episode he later drew on in *Krapp's Last Tape* (performed in 1958, published in 1959). At the root of this vision was the realization that he had to move away from Joyce's shadow and forge his own distinctive literary style. Knowlson notes that whereas Joyce regarded knowledge as a means to understand and control the world, Beckett's "own way was in impoverishment, in lack of knowledge and in taking away, in subtracting rather than adding." In an attempt to simplify his literary style, Beckett began writing in French in earnest. Forcing himself to write in a foreign language seemed the best way of avoiding what he viewed as the literary excesses of his earlier works. This dissatisfaction with his own language as an expressive medium has its roots in *Dream of Fair to Middling Women,* in which Beckett claims, "They have no style, they write without style, do they not. . . . Perhaps only the French can do it. Perhaps only the French language can give you the thing you want." He had clearly been harboring these feelings for some years. In a letter to a German friend, Axel Kaun, dated 9 July 1937 and included in *Disjecta,* Beckett writes: "It is indeed becoming more and more difficult, even senseless, for me to write an official English. And more and more my own language appears to me like a veil that must be torn apart in order to get at the things (or the Nothingness) behind it." In this letter he advocates the search for a new medium of expression: "Let us hope the time will come, thank God that in certain circles it has already come, when language is most efficiently used where it is being most efficiently misused."

These thoughts are the roots of his attempts to express the inexpressible—that which lies behind language. As he notes in *Watt,* "the only way one can speak of nothing is to speak of it as though it were something." Beckett wants to express his disgust with language through language itself, claiming he would like to commit "an assault against words in the name of beauty." Until he can achieve that goal, "I have the consolation, as now, of sinning involuntarily against a foreign language, as I should love to do with full knowledge and intent against my own." He is too proficient in his own language; grammar and syntax are no longer a challenge. Writing in a foreign language can offer him this challenge until he can find a way of "sinning" in his native tongue.

The first work Beckett completed in French, in 1946, was the novel *Mercier et Camier* (1970; translated by Beckett as *Mercier and Camier,* 1974), which follows the exploits of the two titular characters, who meet to undertake a journey that involves many distractions and deviations. Thematically and stylistically, it clearly prefigures *En attendant Godot* (1952; translated by Beckett as *Waiting for Godot,* 1954), with lines from the novel (such as "They didn't beat you?") resurfacing almost verbatim in the play. Beckett regarded the novel as a kind of apprentice work, in order to attune his ear to writing in French, and it remained unpublished until 1970. In early 1947 Beckett completed his first full-length play, the three-act *Eleutheria* (1995; translated as *Eleuthéria,* 1995), the title being the Greek term for freedom. It is an unwieldy satire, with many characters and a split set, making it difficult to stage. Perhaps aware of the structural failings of the play, Beckett remained adamant that it should not be published or performed throughout his life. It was eventually published six years after his death.

The only items Beckett did get published at this time were several poems and translations in *Transition,* the journal edited by Georges Duthuit. His most significant writings from this period are the *Three Dialogues,* which appeared in the December 1949 issue of *Transition* and were later published with *Proust* in 1965. Ostensibly a series of conversations between Beckett and Duthuit about three artists—Pierre Tal-Coat, André Masson, and Bram van Velde—the texts act as a kind of manifesto for Beckett to state his

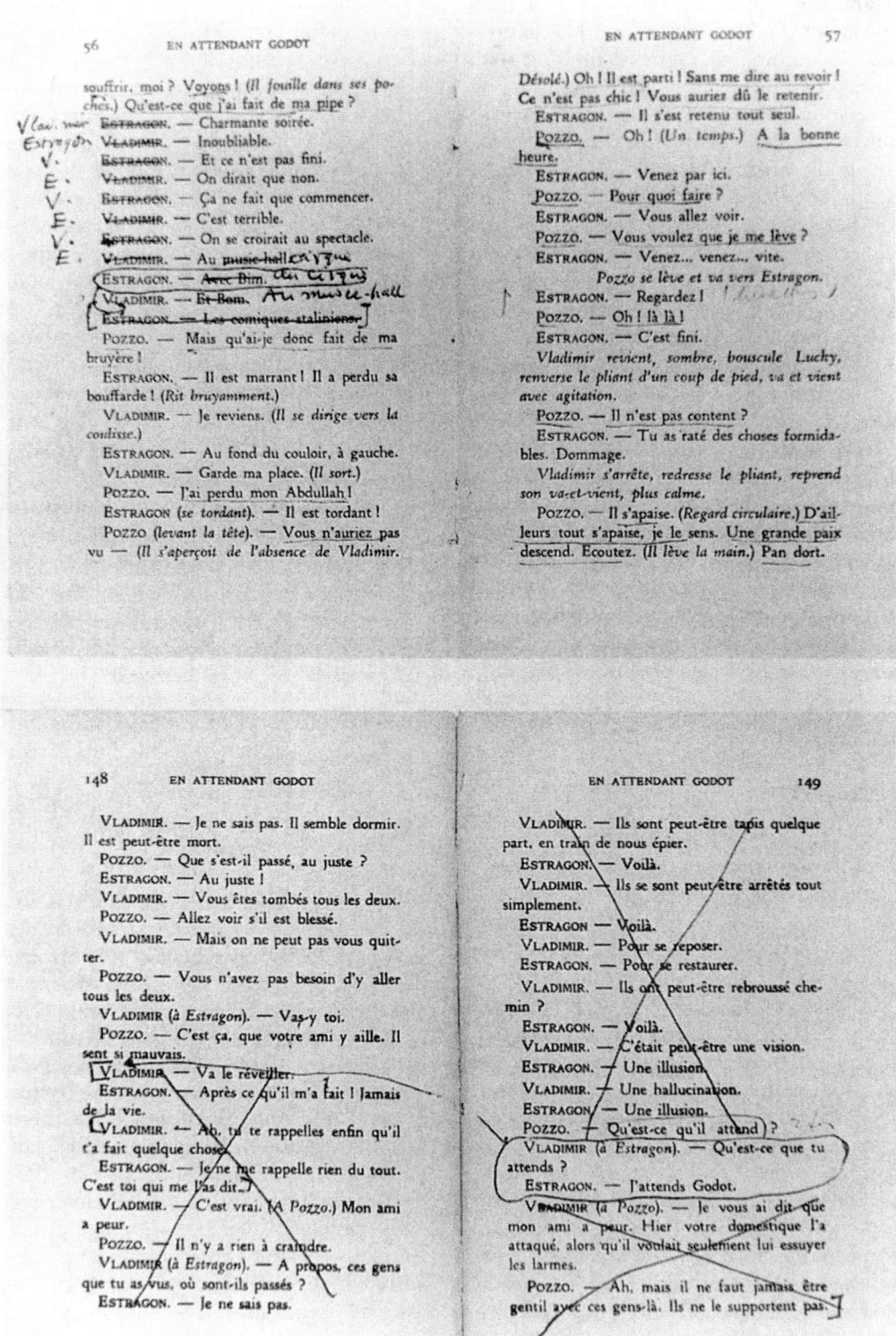

Pages from Beckett's working rehearsal copy for the first performance of En attendant Godot *(1952; translated by Beckett as* Waiting for Godot, *1954) in Paris, 1953. Many of Beckett's revisions were incorporated into the second published edition of the play (Sotheby's, 13 December 1990).*

views on art and the role of the artist. Beckett summarizes the problems facing a writer as "The expression that there is nothing to express, nothing with which to express, nothing from which to express, no power to express, no desire to express, together with the obligation to express." As far as Beckett is concerned, failure is the artist's lot; he claims he would be "the first to admit that to be an artist is to fail, as no other dare fail, that failure is his world and the shrink from it desertion."

The change to writing in French marked a burst of literary activity for Beckett–a period he referred to, according to biographer Deirdre Bair, as "the siege in the room"–and he began writing a dense prose trilogy comprising *Molloy* (1951; translated by Beckett and Patrick Bowles, 1955), *Malone meurt* (1951; translated by Beckett as *Malone Dies*, 1956) and *L'Innommable* (1953; translated by Beckett as *The Unnamable*, 1958). The composition of this trilogy also marked Beckett's move to the first-person monologue as the predominant style in his prose work. This shift allowed him to draw on his own mental and physical experiences to a much greater degree while still being able to retain a suitable distance from any biographical elements by writing in a foreign language. Beckett viewed the three novels as part of the same difficult yet rewarding compositional process.

Molloy was written relatively quickly in 1947 and concerns the eponymous hero's quest for his mother, a search that has Oedipal overtones: "I took her for my mother and she took me for my father." Like most literary quests, Molloy's journey eventually brings him back to himself. The novel is divided into two sections with a similar structure; in each the reader encounters a man in a room writing a report. In the first, Molloy recounts his story; in the second, Moran tells how he was sent to find Molloy. Despite the Freudian and Jungian overtones of the novel, a certain black humor is present throughout, with each narrator constantly questioning himself and undermining his previous utterances. Moran asks: "Does this mean I am freer now than I was? I do not know. I shall learn. Then I went back into the house and wrote, It is midnight. The rain is beating on the windows. It was not midnight. It was not raining." Beckett regarded *Molloy* as his first successful attempt at incorporating his personal experiences into his own fiction. In a 16 February 1961 article in *Nouvelles Littéraires,* Gabriel d'Aubarède claimed that Beckett summarized the change in his approach to writing thus: "*Molloy* and the others came to me the day I became aware of my own folly. Only then did I begin to write the things I feel."

Beckett began writing *Malone meurt* less than a month after completing *Molloy*. Planned as a companion piece, the novel was originally titled "L'Absent," giving an indication of the narrator's isolation from the world, a theme that is reinforced by the pun inherent in his name: Malone (M, alone). Like Molloy, Malone is a writer, alone in a room, aged, prostrate and immobile, who strives to recount four stories before death overcomes him: "one about a man, another about a woman, a third about a thing and finally one about an animal, a bird probably." The scene and tone of the novel are set in the opening line: "I shall soon be quite dead at last in spite of all." Malone feels a compulsion to write and to examine his past life and his current situation, in order to stave off the boredom of his daily existence and to understand himself more fully. For him, "Nothing is more real than nothing." The novel focuses on the act of writing, and Malone's storytelling acts as a metaphor for his life: as his pencil wears down, the sands of his own life trickle away. As long as he is able to write "a few lines to remind me that I too subsist," he can cling to the last vestiges of existence. As death approaches, Malone seems to find some kind of inner peace with the acceptance that the world is full of things he can never understand. Perhaps unwittingly, Beckett predicts the nature of his next novel and also much of his future writing, in which his characters become shadowy, nameless figures: "Then it will be all over with the Murphys, Merciers, Molloys, Morans and Malones, unless it goes on beyond the grave." The novel was turned down by several publishers, presumably because of its subject matter and style.

Unable to find a publisher for these two novels and finding himself in a creative dead end, Beckett turned to drama as a relaxation from this intense project and, between October 1948 and January 1949, he worked feverishly on a play he titled *En attendant Godot*–the work that brought him international fame and recognition as an author. Yet, as with his earlier works, Beckett struggled initially to find a publisher. This minimalist, ostensibly simple play–in which, famously, as Vivian Mercier observes, "nothing happens, *twice*"–marks a stark contrast from Beckett's recent prose work and represents the closest he had come to an embodiment of his search for a simpler, more precise linguistic style. The play is set in an unspecified location ("A country road. A tree. Evening.") and focuses on the dialogue between the two protagonists, Estragon and Vladimir, who are half-tramp, half-clown; the theme is perhaps best summarized by Estragon's opening line, "Nothing to be done." As they wait in vain for the mysterious

Godot to arrive, they fill what Beckett called "the terrible silence that is waiting to flood into this play like water into a sinking ship" with a succession of verbal and physical games, which range from slapstick routines to an earnest contemplation of suicide. A brief distraction occurs with the arrival of a second couple, Pozzo and Lucky, the former leading the latter by a rope round his neck, giving the impression of master and slave. After their departure a boy appears, informing them that Godot will not come today, but will definitely come tomorrow, renewing their fading hopes.

The shorter second act is a structural repetition of the first, with subtle but significant variations. Although the tree gains a few leaves in the interval, suggesting new life and hope, in contrast, when Pozzo and Lucky return, Pozzo is blind and Lucky is mute. The rope binding the two is much shorter, suggesting the power balance has been reversed, with Pozzo now reliant on Lucky as his guide. By not giving the play a specific setting, Beckett succeeds in making it completely universal. Existence is portrayed as a constant search for meaning and salvation, which are never found. Life equates with suffering and comprises a series of inane conversations designed to fill the time until death. Despite the ostensible bleakness of the situation, there is much humor in the play. Estragon and Vladimir do not lose their faith, and the bond between them remains as strong as ever at the close. Like an old married couple, they are unable to live together without bickering, yet are even less able to survive apart.

The play was published by Editions de Minuit in 1952 and received its premiere at the Théâtre de Babylone in Paris on 5 January 1953 to great critical success. Jean Anouilh described it in *Arts Spectacles* (27 February – 5 March 1953) as "Pascal's *Pensées* played by the Fratellini clowns." Beckett translated the play into English during 1953, and it premiered at the Arts Theatre Club in London in August 1955, directed by Peter Hall. Although it received mainly hostile reviews, the two leading theater critics of the era, Kenneth Tynan and Harold Hobson, championed it, helping to turn it into an intellectual success. In January 1956 the play had its American premiere in Miami, again to a hostile reception; but within a few months, it was playing on Broadway to large audiences, claiming its rightful position as one of the most significant plays of the twentieth century.

After this brief interlude that resulted in *En attendant Godot*, Beckett returned to writing the final part of his prose trilogy, *L'Innommable*. Originally titled "Mahood," after one of the names attributed to the narrator, this novel was begun in March 1949, with trepidation, after the mental and physical effort he had expended on the two previous novels—apparently in vain, since he still had not found a publisher for them. In a conversation with the artist Avigdor Arikha (quoted in Anne Atik, *How It Was: A Memoir of Samuel Beckett*, 2001), Beckett later described *The Unnamable* as an attempt "to try to tell one more time what it is to have been." The questioning tone of the novel is set by the opening line: "Where now? Who now? When now?" *The Unnamable* is a key work in Beckett's canon, as it prefigures much of his subsequent prose and drama in both style and content. It focuses on the desire to be silent, combined with the compulsion to speak: "Having nothing to say, no words but the words of others, I have to speak." This lack of "desire to express, together with the obligation to express," is something Beckett had already identified in the *Three Dialogues*. Prefiguring by more than twenty years the subject matter of his play *Not I* (performed in 1972, published in 1973), in which the character Mouth is forced to spout the words that are pent up within her, the narrator in *The Unnamable* is "compelled to speak" and has just as little control over language: "Where do these words come from that pour out of my mouth, and what do they mean?" Echoing the situation in *Waiting for Godot*, where Estragon and Vladimir find seemingly endless ways to continue their conversations, the narrator of *The Unnamable* argues that "the discourse must go on. So one invents obscurities. Rhetoric." As he explains, "the search for the means to put an end to things, an end to speech, is what enables the discourse to continue." In order to add to the narrator's confusion, Beckett uses several contradictory voices, with the result that language both comforts and terrorizes the narrator: "Ah if only this voice could stop, this meaningless voice which prevents you from being nothing, just barely prevents you from being nothing and nowhere." If the voices are silenced, then he will have peace; but the cessation of the voices also means the end of life, so it is a double-edged sword. The novel concludes with one of Beckett's most famous lines, which encapsulates the ethos of many of his characters who continue their struggle in the face of overwhelming odds: "where I am, I don't know, I'll never know, in the silence you don't know, you must go on, I can't go on, I'll go on."

In response to a request from his American publisher, Barney Rosset, Beckett reverted to English for his next composition, *From an Abandoned Work* (1958). It first appeared in *Trinity News* in June 1956, with many editorial modifications, and was the first example of Beckett's generosity toward his alma mater. As the title suggests, the text is resurrected from a longer, discarded piece. It is written in a conversational style, as the first-person narrator recounts three days chosen randomly from his life. The text seems to allude to Beckett's own experience of language learning: "I was very quick as a boy and picked up a lot of hard knowledge, Schimmel, nice word for an English speaker." Yet, the narrator is scathing about his proficiency in his mother tongue—"awful English this"—an unintentional, but apt, comment on the changes made by the *Trinity News* editors.

In the years following the success of *Waiting for Godot,* Beckett focused on dramatic writing, starting with *Fin de partie* (1957; translated by Beckett as *Endgame,* 1958), another play with a closed, nonspecific location, which has been interpreted as both a postapocalyptic bunker and the inside of the human brain. This nondescript, gray setting is populated by four characters, who appear to represent three generations of the same family. Bleaker and "more inhuman than *Godot*" (according to Beckett), with the action limited to this claustrophobic single room with two high windows that look out onto what remains of the deserted outside world, the play focuses on the love-hate relationship between Hamm and Clov, who are apparently father and son. Like Estragon and Vladimir, these two protagonists are an inseparable couple whose existence is a routine of verbal exchanges in order to pass the time. Beckett used the Latin phrase *nec tecum nec sine te* (neither with you nor without you) to describe their relationship. Clov's opening line, "Finished, it's finished, nearly finished, it must be nearly finished," is indicative of his desire to be free from Hamm. He yearns for "a world where all would be silent and still and each thing in its last place, under the last dust." Hamm, in contrast, merely regards Clov as an object of entertainment: "Since that's the way we're playing it . . . let's play it that way." The humor and the dialogue in this play are much darker than its predecessor, with physical and mental suffering more evident. The other two characters, Nagg and Nell, Hamm's parents, are reduced to living in dustbins. Yet, as Nell remarks, "Nothing is funnier than unhappiness." Like *Waiting for Godot, Endgame* has a loosely circular structure. Although there seems to be some kind of progression by the end of the play, with Clov apparently dressed to leave, it is merely an asymptotic approach toward an unattainable end. There is nothing to suggest that the action will not begin again the next day in exactly the same manner. The play premiered in French at the Royal Court Theatre in London on 3 April 1957, after censorship problems concerning several lines that the Lord Chamberlain regarded as blasphemous. By October of the following year, Beckett's English translation was playing in the same theater.

Around this time, Beckett was asked by the BBC to write a radio play, resulting in *All That Fall* (1957), which is set in Foxrock and features characters from the same background as himself; it was broadcast in January 1957. Radio also provided him with the inspiration for his next dramatic work. Having heard the Irish actor Patrick Magee reading extracts from *Molloy* and *From an Abandoned Work* as part of a BBC broadcast in December 1957, Beckett was inspired to write *Krapp's Last Tape,* the story of a lonely old man who spends his birthdays listening to recordings of his former self and making a new recording documenting the achievements of that year. By clever use of what was relatively new technology at the time, Beckett is able to present three incarnations of Krapp on the stage, as he listens to recordings from different eras of his life. Beckett utilizes Manichaean imagery to portray Krapp's constant struggle between good and bad, the spiritual and the physical, as he moves physically and metaphorically between light and dark, desperate to distance himself from his failed earlier self. At one point Krapp recounts a revelation he had—"that memorable night in March, at the end of the jetty, in the howling wind, never to be forgotten, when suddenly I saw the whole thing"—echoing Beckett's own revelation some years earlier. The play ends with a recording of the younger Krapp (at age thirty-nine) still playing: "Perhaps my best years are gone. When there was a chance of happiness. But I wouldn't want them back. Not with the fire in me now." His present condition is evidence that this fire burned out and came to nothing. The decade concluded with Beckett being awarded an honorary D.Litt. degree from Trinity College, Dublin in 1959. Around this time, he also began a relationship with Barbara Bray, a script editor at the BBC, which continued for many years.

Beckett's next play, *Happy Days* (1961), focuses on the ramblings of an elderly woman, Winnie, who is buried up to her waist in scorched grass in the first act and up to her neck in the second, as the earth literally engulfs her. Her only solace is "a capacious black bag, shopping variety," containing a range of implements—toothbrush, mirror, spectacles, and, rather ominously, a revolver, which she places on the mound in front of her as her final option. This visually striking image and the almost complete lack of physical action allows Beckett to focus attention on the words Winnie speaks. Despite the fact that everything is "running out," including her memory—"Words fail, there are times when even they fail"—Winnie struggles to remain optimistic, happy just to be acknowledged by her husband, Willie, who is hidden behind the mound and utters a mere handful of words throughout. Unable to remain silent, she needs an audience of some kind in order to be able to continue: "just to know that in theory you can hear me even though in fact you don't is all I need, just to feel you there within earshot." At the end of the play, Willie crawls to the front of the mound and reaches toward the gun. As the curtain falls on this tableau, it remains unclear whether he is simply reaching out to touch Winnie, or whether he intends to use the gun to kill her, or himself, and bring an end to their pitiful existence. A virtual monologue, lasting around an hour and a half, the play is the first of several to involve challenging female roles with which Beckett moves away from the physical and focuses on the verbal.

Beckett's next work for the stage, *Play* (performed and published in English, 1964), depicts the conventional love triangle of a man, his wife, and his mistress—perhaps reflecting his own situation with Deschevaux-Dumesnil and Bray—but in an unconventional manner. Written in English, but first performed and published in German (as *Spiel*), it premiered in Ulm in June 1963. The three characters, one male flanked by two females, are ensconced up to their necks in urns, as Beckett again forces the audience's attention to the verbal element by removing any physical attributes. Assuming the role of a fourth character, or inquisitor, a spotlight focuses on each head in turn, prompting it to speak at great speed and with little emotion—in stark contrast to the textual content. The entire play is repeated, stressing that there is no way out of the situation. The three characters are consigned to this living hell. One of the most significant lines is the male's question, "Am I as much as . . . being seen?"—indicating Beckett's interest in the concept of observation and perception, a theme initiated in *Happy Days*. He investigated this theme in greater depth in his next project, the screenplay *Film* (1965). Based on George Berkeley's maxim "esse est percipi" (to be is to be perceived), and silent throughout, with the exception of a "sssh!", the twenty-minute motion picture follows an old man (played by Buster Keaton) as he appears to be fleeing the attention of the camera, his face only becoming visible, briefly, at the conclusion. Beckett traveled to New York in the summer of 1964 to direct the piece, along with Alan Schneider. It premiered at the Venice Film Festival in September 1965 and also played at the New York Film Festival; it was Beckett's only venture into the medium of motion pictures.

After his success with *Film,* Beckett turned his attention to the small screen with his first television play, *Eh Joe* (broadcast in 1966; published in French as *Dis Joe* in 1966; published in English in 1967), written for the Irish actor Jack MacGowran. As part of the reductive process begun with *Play,* and with a similar thematic approach to *Film,* this work focuses, literally, on a solitary character sitting on a bed, as the camera moves ever closer. In contrast to the usual television convention, the voice heard by the audience is not that of MacGowran, but a female voice that echoes around his head, taunting him with memories of his past: "You know that penny farthing hell you call your mind. . . . That's where you think this is coming from, don't you?" This process of refinement and paring away continued with *Come and Go* (produced as *Kommen und Gehen,* 1966; published in French as *Va-et-vient,* 1966; published in English, 1967, performed in 1968), a brief, two-page text in which three shrouded women discuss what appear to be their grave illnesses or impending deaths. As each woman leaves the stage in turn, the remaining two discuss her apparent critical situation. By the end of this cycle, it becomes clear that each woman has a devastating secret to hide. This reductive process reached its logical conclusion in *Breath* (produced in 1969, published in 1971), a thirty-second piece comprising two cries, of birth and death, and a stage strewn with rubbish representing the detritus of life.

Despite his success as a dramatist, Beckett continued to write prose and poetry in both English and French, refining his prose style in the same way as his work for the theater and television. In 1961 he had published the groundbreaking novel *Comment c'est,* translated as *How It Is* (1964). Divided into three sections ("Before Pim," "With Pim," and "After Pim"), the novel appears to describe the emergence of an incipient form from formlessness. The French title of the novel reflects this theme, being a pun on the French verb *commencer* (to begin). Written as one long sentence with no punctuation, the text is divided into a succession of rhythmically organized segments that reflect the patterns of human speech. In a vein similar to Lucky's monologue in *Waiting for Godot,* the novel ends in a dramatic crescendo: "trouble the peace no more no answer the silence no answer die no answer DIE . . . screams I MAY DIE screams I SHALL DIE screams good."

As the 1960s progressed, Beckett's prose and drama decreased in length as he found increasingly successful ways to express the inexpressible. While his dramatic works tended to be written in English, he published several minimalist prose texts written in French, beginning with *Imagination morte imaginez* (1965; translated by Beckett as *Imagination Dead Imagine,* 1965). Taking its title from the first line of *All*

Strange Away (written the previous year but not published until 1976), this text opens with the ominous line, "No trace anywhere of life, you say." The narrator describes the construction of a white rotunda containing two motionless figures. Within "this little fabric" there are erratically fluctuating levels of light and heat, suggesting an unstable environment. Beckett's next prose work, *Assez* (1966; translated by Beckett as *Enough,* 1967), marks a return to a first-person narrator, who tells the reader, "All that goes before forget." Despite this command, he proceeds to recount what has not been forgotten. The title refers to the act of narration itself–the narrator has had enough of recounting. *Bing* (1966; translated by Beckett as *Ping,* 1967) reverts to the theme and style of *Imagination Dead Imagine,* as the narrator describes a single figure in a white box. Despite the narrator's claim at the start that "All [is] known," he spends the remainder of the text making minor modifications to repeated phrases, undermining this opening statement. The "bing"/"ping" of the title appears with increasing regularity as the text progresses, suggesting the emergence of a new life force. On the cover of the English translation of his next prose work, *Sans* (1969; translated by Beckett as *Lessness,* 1970) Beckett summarized its theme as "the collapse of some such refuge as that last attempted in *Ping* and with the ensuing situation of the refugee." Like his other recent novellas, *Lessness* is based on a structure of repetition and variation; but in place of the intense white heat and light, here everything is "ash grey" as in *Endgame.* The French texts of *Imagination Dead Imagine, Enough,* and *Ping,* along with Beckett's French translation of *From an Abandoned Work,* were gathered together as *Têtes-mortes* (1967), the title being a play on the French *tête-de-mort* (skull and crossbones). Their English counterparts appeared in *No's Knife: Collected Shorter Prose, 1945-1966* (1967).

The decade ended with Beckett being awarded the Nobel Prize in Literature in 1969, something he regarded not as an honor, but as a "catastrophe," as he was well aware of the impact the ensuing increase in celebrity and public recognition would have on his modest lifestyle. Beckett had been nominated for the award several times during the previous decade, but, as someone who valued his privacy highly, he was secretly relieved that these earlier nominations had been unsuccessful. He immediately went into hiding in Tunis, sending his French publisher, Jérôme Lindon, to Sweden to receive the prize. Beckett's main reason for accepting the award was to avoid appearing discourteous to the Swedish Academy. He also hoped that it would benefit financially the publishers who had supported him, particularly during his early years. He subsequently gave away the prize money (some $45,000) to artists and institutions, including the Library of Trinity College, Dublin. A 1971 volume of the *Collection des Prix Nobel de Littérature,* comprising *Malone meurt* and *Oh les beaux jours,* commemorated Beckett's success. It included illustrations by Avigdor Arikha and a cover designed by Pablo Picasso. Beckett regarded the pressures he associated with being awarded the Nobel Prize as contributing greatly to his lack of artistic creativity at the time; yet, friends and colleagues felt it did not alter his modest and generous nature.

Beckett began the 1970s with the publication of *Le Dépeupleur* (1970; translated by Beckett as *The Lost Ones,* 1972), the title of which is taken from Alphonse de Lamartine's poem "L'Isolement" (1820, Isolation). The piece depicts the existence of more than two hundred figures in a large cylinder. This environment, with its oscillating levels of light and heat, is an "abode where lost bodies roam each searching for its lost one." The figures climb ladders to alcoves in the upper section of the cylinder following a complex system of rules–but there is ultimately no escape from this closed system. As the text proceeds, the narrator becomes increasingly confused, admitting, "All has not been told and never shall be." Although portraying an ostensibly alien environment, the text is a clever parody of the human rat race.

Since the mid 1960s, Beckett had become increasingly involved with the direction of his stage and television drama. He had been particularly impressed by the patience and meticulousness of the German actors he had encountered when attending rehearsals for the world premiere of *Play* in Ulm in 1963 and while assisting with a German production of *Waiting for Godot* in Berlin in 1965. The following year he became involved with the production of his television play *Eh Joe* at the Süddeutscher Rundfunk (SDR) in Stuttgart, and in 1967 he was invited to direct a German-language production of *Endgame* in Berlin. Beckett had sufficient confidence in his command of the German language by this juncture to assume the role of director in this country. He felt that working with such enthusiastic and compliant actors might allow him to create a production that reflected his own precise plans for a particular play. Between 1967 and 1978, Beckett directed seven of his stage plays in German in Berlin to great acclaim– *Endgame* in 1967, *Krapp's Last Tape* in 1969, *Happy Days* in 1971, *Waiting for Godot* in 1975, *That Time* and *Footfalls* in 1976, and *Play* in 1978–exhibiting another side of his versatile, creative character. Although most of his directorial work took place at the Schiller-Theater Werkstatt in Berlin, he also directed stage productions in Paris and London as well as television productions at the BBC and the SDR in Stuttgart. As the years progressed, Beckett's ability as a director grew, as evidenced by his attention to detail in the directorial notebooks he compiled for the later productions. It is not surprising that Beckett chose to direct the majority of his drama in German—a precise, technical language that reflected his own fastidious approach to writing and directing. Although Beckett claimed his productions were not intended to be definitive interpretations, the versions he directed in Berlin represent an almost perfect embodiment of his wishes. As a result, they have become regarded as authoritative productions and have been re-created worldwide.

Although directing took up a great deal of his time, and despite increasing problems with his eyesight, Beckett continued to write, predominantly drama in English. His first play of the 1970s, *Not I* (1973), again focuses on the female voice. On this occasion, however, Beckett takes the premise of *Happy Days* a step further by removing all physical traits of the female form, leaving only a mouth visible in a spotlight, apparently floating high in the darkness, spouting a torrent of virtually unintelligible words. Inspired by Caravaggio's painting *The Beheading of St. John the Baptist* (1608) and also by a figure he had seen in Morocco clad in a djellaba, the piece lasts around fifteen minutes. The aim of Mouth's monologue is to avoid admitting that the tale she is relating is autobiographical: "what? . . . who? . . . no! . . . she!" A silent Auditor, dressed in a black djellaba, is present onstage to witness the stream of words. The physically and mentally demanding role of Mouth has become synonymous with Billie Whitelaw, who played the part under Beckett's direction in the British premiere at the Royal Court Theatre in 1973. She reprised the role for a BBC production of the play in 1976, in which the Auditor was removed, focusing the audience's attention exclusively on the raging mouth—a grotesque and unforgettable image.

Around the time of his seventieth birthday, in 1976, Beckett published two short plays, *That Time* and *Footfalls*. Combining elements of *Not I* and *Krapp's Last Tape*, *That Time* presents the face of a white-haired male character suspended high in the darkness. The man is apparently on his deathbed, listening to three voices, all his own, recounting different stories from three stages of his life: his youth by Voice B, his middle age by Voice A, and his old age by Voice C. At the close, a smile, "toothless for preference," appears on the Listener's face, suggesting perhaps relief that the voices have ceased their torment of him, perhaps acceptance of his impending death. In *Footfalls,* a female character, May, in a "worn grey wrap," paces back and forth across the stage in mental turmoil, "revolving it all in her poor mind." The disembodied voice of her mother speaks to her, possibly from beyond the grave, and May narrates a parallel story of a Mrs. Winter and her daughter, Amy (an anagram of May). As the play progresses, the lighting dims and the pacing slows, so that in the final scene, there is "no trace of May"—she all but disintegrates before the audience's eyes. The plays were premiered in a double bill, directed by Beckett and featuring Whitelaw, at the Royal Court Theatre on 20 May 1976. Beckett also directed the two plays in German at the Schiller-Theater Werkstatt in Berlin in October that year.

Beckett returned to the medium of television the following year, writing and helping to direct two plays at the BBC. The first, *Ghost Trio* (1977), is based on a section of Ludwig von Beethoven's *Piano Trio No. 5 in D Minor,* known as "The Ghost." The title of the second, *. . . but the clouds . . .* (1977), is taken from a line in William Butler Yeats's poem "The Tower" (1928). Both plays are structurally similar to *Eh Joe* in that they feature a lone male figure and a disembodied voice—female in the former, male in the latter. They were broadcast, along with the filmed version of *Not I* on BBC 2 on 17 April 1977, under the collective title *Shades*. German-language versions were recorded at the SDR and broadcast in Germany on 1 November 1977, along with the BBC version of *Not I*. In the last years of the decade, Beckett also wrote around three dozen short poems in French, which he gathered under the title *Mirlitonnades*—an invented, diminutive term, which is a play on *mirliton* (kazoo/toy flute) and *vers de mirliton* (doggerel), indicating their light, fragile nature. These brief verses were written on scraps of paper and transcribed into a tiny leather-bound notebook. Most are haiku-like in structure, being only a few lines in length. While their meanings can be translated literally, it is virtually impossible to convey the essence of the poems into English because of their succinct nature. They first appeared in *Poèmes suivi de Mirlitonnades* (1978) and subsequently in *Collected Poems 1930–1978* (1984), although only in French. As a group they remain among the few works that Beckett never attempted to render into English. By the end of the 1970s Beckett's profile was at a peak. The decade closed with *A Piece of Monologue* in 1979. This contemplation of death was written for the bilingual actor David Warrilow, who first performed it at the La Mama Experimental Theatre Club in December of that year. Originally titled "Gone," suggesting the passing of all but the lone figure reciting the monologue, it opens with the bleak phrase, "Birth was the death of him" and closes with the line, "Alone gone"—encapsulating a brief life cycle in just a handful of pages.

As Beckett approached his seventy-fifth birthday in 1981, he continued to divide his time between writing and directing. His first prose text of the decade was *Company* (1980), a loosely autobiographical novel that deals with the themes of solitude, the unreliability of memory, and the difference between the self and the other. Reminiscent of his recent stage and television plays, the novel describes a "man alone in the dark, listening to a voice he can't control and which he both dreads and longs to hear," as Katharine Worth describes it. The opening line sets the scene: "A voice comes to one in the dark. Imagine." The narrator's language has an archaic feel—"whence," "thither," "hitherto"—words from a bygone age. Beckett still clearly enjoys playing with language, as he introduces a character named "H. Aspirate. Haitch." His next work, *Mal vu mal dit* (1981; translated by Beckett as *Ill Seen, Ill Said*, 1981), is considered by Ruby Cohn as "The Beckett Masterwork" and features a white-haired woman clad in black, encircled by twelve mysterious figures and drawn toward a white tombstone. The novel explores the themes of existence, consciousness, and perception, as indicated by its title. The passage of time is again prominent, with one paragraph dedicated to a "close-up of a dial." Like much of Beckett's later prose, this piece has a structure of repetition and variation. Bleaker than its predecessor, it ends with the lines, "Not another crumb of carrion left. Lick chops and basta. No. One moment more. One last. Grace to breathe that void. Know happiness." *Worstward Ho* (1983) formed the final part of what has become regarded as Beckett's second prose trilogy, its title being a parody of Charles Kingsley's *Westward Ho!* (1855). Taking Edgar's speech in William Shakespeare's *King Lear* (circa 1606) that "The worst is not so long as one can say, This is the worst" as its starting point, it describes the (artist's) need to "Try again. Fail again. Fail better," echoing Beckett's comments in the *Three Dialogues* almost forty years earlier. It begins with the narrator urging himself, "On. Say on. Be said on. Somehow on" and ends with the ominous phrase, "Said nohow on." The three novels were published together under the title *Nohow On* in 1989.

Beckett continued to alternate between prose and drama and, in 1981, produced and published two short plays, *Rockaby* and *Ohio Impromptu*. The first features a woman being rocked gently in a rocking chair to the sound of her own recorded voice reciting a poem. Toward the end of the play, the rocking slows down to a halt and the woman apparently dies, as the words "time she stopped" are uttered. It was premiered at the State University of New York at Buffalo on 8 April 1981. *Ohio Impromptu* was written at the request of the Beckett scholar S. E. Gontarski for an international symposium on Beckett's work at Ohio State University, where it was premiered on 9 May 1981. Two almost identical white-haired figures, dressed in long gowns like figures from a Rembrandt painting, sit at a table as one reads from a book and the other listens. It ends with the poignant line, "Nothing is left to tell," suggesting that Beckett knew he was nearing the end of his creative life.

Beckett had continued to involve himself with television work, both at the BBC and the SDR in Stuttgart. In 1981 he wrote and directed *Quadrat 1 + 2* (the later English version is simply titled *Quad*). Described as "a piece for four players, light and percussion," the play has no dialogue but is merely a series of movements across and around the edges of a designated square. As they move diagonally across the square, the four players veer sharply as they approach the central point, suggesting it represents some kind of vortex or terrible danger. Beckett's most overtly political play, *Catastrophe* (1983), dedicated to the imprisoned Czech playwright Václav Havel, was premiered at the Avignon Festival on 21 July 1982. The play features a brutal theater director barking instructions at his assistant and an ostensibly meek actor, who appear to be trying to please their master. In the final scene, however, the actor raises his head and stares fixedly at the audience in a gesture of defiance that asserts his own individuality.

At the request of the SDR, Beckett wrote another television play, *Nacht und Träume,* based on Franz Schubert's 1825 *lied* of the same name, and returned to Stuttgart to direct a German-language version of the piece, which was broadcast on 19 May 1983. The medium of television seemed perfect for the stark, imposing images of his later, minimalist pieces. Later that year, his final play, *What Where,* premiered at the Harold Clurman Theatre in New York. Based on a series of interrogations to establish the "what" and the "where" of the title, the play ends with the prophetic lines: "Time passes. That is all. Make sense who may. I switch off." Beckett returned to the SDR one last time, in order to create a radical reworking of *What Where* for German television under the title *Was wo,* which was broadcast on his eightieth birthday, 13 April 1986. In this production, as in *Not I,* all physical attributes are removed except for the faces of the four characters, focusing the audience's attention on the stark, imposing image on the screen and the bleak words of the text.

Despite the apparent impasse suggested by the final lines of his recent prose and drama, Beckett produced two further works. *Stirrings Still* (1988), dedicated to Rosset, his American publisher, was published as a limited, illustrated edition of 226 copies, signed by Beckett and the illustrator Louis le Broquy, costing £1000. It also appeared in *The Guardian* on 3 March 1989, making it much more readily available to the public. Named after a line from *Company,* the text conveys a sense of farewell, of Beckett still stirring creatively but marking his intention to sign off. Beckett's last published work, the poem *Comment dire* (1989; translated by Beckett as *What Is the Word,* 1989), has also been included in collections of his prose, because of the nature of the text. Written in the Hôpital Pasteur after a fall and translated in the Tiers Temps nursing home, the piece echoes Beckett's own aphasia and is a meditation on the impossibility of language, reflecting his constant struggle throughout his literary career to find the appropriate words to "express the inexpressible." Beckett remained a bilingual author to the end, creating French and English versions of almost all his texts. Perhaps fittingly, the final line of his final published work reads, "what is the word."

By this juncture, Beckett was eighty-three and was suffering with severe respiratory problems that were diagnosed as emphysema. After moving into the Tiers Temps nursing home permanently, he fell ill on 6 December and died in the Hôpital St. Anne of respiratory failure on 22 December 1989, less than six months after his wife, who had been his partner and constant supporter since the late 1930s. (The couple had no children.) In keeping with his simple lifestyle, Beckett was laid to rest in a private ceremony shortly after Christmas in the Cimetière de Montparnasse in Paris.

Beckett is often described as being apolitical, as he never aligned himself or his work to any particular political movement or party. In reality, his political views were broadly left-wing. He championed the underdog and the victim, both in his work and also in real life. Although shy and self-absorbed as a young man, in later life he became noted for his caring and generous nature. Beckett was fiercely opposed to any form of censorship in his own work and that of others, offering practical and financial support to oppressed writers and directors in various countries. His refusal to be interviewed about himself or his work created an air of mystery and secrecy, which served to protect his privacy.

Although he is often depicted as a pessimist, Beckett's work has a thick vein of black humor running through it, as well as more obvious visual gags, particularly in his drama. Although apparently without hope or prospects, and often on the verge of death, his characters somehow find the strength to continue against all odds. Almost a century after Beckett's birth, the Nobel Academy's citation still holds true. His work is more popular than ever, and his influence on contemporary artists of all kinds is unquestionable.

Letters:

No Author Better Served: The Correspondence of Samuel Beckett and Alan Schneider, edited by Maurice Harmon (Cambridge, Mass.: Harvard University Press, 1998).

Bibliographies:

Raymond Federman and John Fletcher, *Samuel Beckett: His Works and His Critics: An Essay in Bibliography* (Berkeley & Los Angeles: University of California Press, 1970);

Robin J. Davis, Jackson R. Bryer, M. J. Friedman, and P. C. Hoy, eds., *Samuel Beckett: Calepins de bibliographie,* no. 2 (Paris: Lettres Modernes Minard, 1971);

Robin J. Davis, *Samuel Beckett: Checklist and Index of His Published Works, 1967-1976* (Stirling: University of Stirling, 1979);

Cathleen Culcotta Andonian, *Samuel Beckett: A Reference Guide* (Boston: G. K. Hall, 1989);

P. J. Murphy, Werner Huber, Rolf Breuer, and Konrad Schoell, eds., *Critique of Beckett Criticism: A Guide to Research in English, French and German* (Columbia, S.C.: Camden House, 1994);

Mary Bryden, Julian A. Garforth, and Peter Mills, *Beckett at Reading: Catalogue of the Beckett Manuscript Collection at the University of Reading* (Reading: Whiteknights Press/Beckett International Foundation, 1998).

Biographies:

Deirdre Bair, *Samuel Beckett: A Biography* (London: Cape, 1978);

Enoch Brater, *Why Beckett* (London: Thames & Hudson, 1989);

Anthony Cronin, *Samuel Beckett: The Last Modernist* (London: HarperCollins, 1996);

James Knowlson, *Damned to Fame* (London: Bloomsbury, 1996);

Gerry Dukes, *Samuel Beckett* (London: Penguin, 2001).

References:

C. J. Ackerley and S. E. Gontarski, *The Grove Companion to Samuel Beckett* (New York: Grove, 2004);

Richard L. Admussen, *The Samuel Beckett Manuscripts: A Study* (Boston: G. K. Hall, 1979);

Anne Atik, *How It Was: A Memoir of Samuel Beckett* (London: Faber & Faber, 2001);

David Bradby, *Beckett: Waiting for Godot* (Cambridge: Cambridge University Press, 2001);

Enoch Brater, *Beyond Minimalism: Beckett's Late Style in the Theater* (New York: Oxford University Press, 1987);

Mary Bryden, *Women in Samuel Beckett's Prose and Drama* (Basingstoke: Macmillan, 1993);

Richard Coe, *Samuel Beckett* (New York: Grove, 1967);

Ruby Cohn, *Back to Beckett* (Princeton, N.J.: Princeton University Press, 1973);

Cohn, *A Beckett Canon* (Ann Arbor: University of Michigan Press, 2001);

Cohn, *Just Play: Beckett's Theater* (Princeton, N.J.: Princeton University Press, 1980);

Steven Connor, *Samuel Beckett: Repetition, Theory and Text* (Oxford: Blackwell, 1988);

Raymond Federman, *Journey to Chaos: Samuel Beckett's Early Fiction* (Berkeley & Los Angeles: University of California Press, 1965);

John Fletcher, *The Novels of Samuel Beckett* (London: Chatto & Windus, 1964);

S. E. Gontarski, *The Intent of Undoing in Samuel Beckett's Dramatic Texts* (Bloomington: Indiana University Press, 1985);

Lawrence Graver and Raymond Federman, *Samuel Beckett: The Critical Heritage* (London: Routledge & Kegan Paul, 1979);

Lawrence Harvey, *Samuel Beckett: Poet and Critic* (Princeton, N.J.: Princeton University Press, 1970);

John Haynes and James Knowlson, *Images of Beckett* (Cambridge: Cambridge University Press, 2003);

Ludovic Janvier, *Pour Samuel Beckett* (Paris: Editions de Minuit, 1966);

Janvier, *Samuel Beckett par lui-même* (Paris: Editions du Seuil, 1969);

Journal of Beckett Studies (Univerity of Reading: Calder/Beckett Archive, 1975–1985; Tallahassee: Florida State University, 1989–);

Jonathan Kalb, *Beckett in Performance* (Cambridge: Cambridge University Press, 1989);

Hugh Kenner, *Samuel Beckett: A Critical Study* (New York: Grove, 1961);

James Knowlson and John Pilling, *Frescoes of the Skull: The Later Prose and Drama of Samuel Beckett* (London: Calder, 1979);

Knowlson, ed., *Happy Days: Samuel Beckett's Production Notebooks* (London: Faber & Faber, 1985);

Dougald McMillan and Martha Fehsenfeld, *Beckett in the Theatre* (London: Calder, 1988);

Anna McMullan, *Theatre on Trial: Samuel Beckett's Later Drama* (London: Routledge, 1993);

Vivian Mercier, *Beckett/Beckett* (New York: Oxford University Press, 1977);

John Minihan, *Samuel Beckett: Photographs* (London: Secker & Warburg, 1995);

Eoin O'Brien, *The Beckett Country: Samuel Beckett's Ireland* (London: Black Cat Press in association with Faber & Faber, 1986);

John Pilling, *Beckett Before Godot* (Cambridge: Cambridge University Press, 1997);

Pilling, *Samuel Beckett* (London: Routledge & Kegan Paul, 1976);

Rosemary Pountney, *Theatre of Shadows: Samuel Beckett's Drama, 1956–1976* (Gerrards Cross, U.K.: Colin Smythe, 1988);

Jean-Marie Rabaté, ed., *Beckett avant Beckett: Essais sur le jeune Beckett (1930–1945)* (Paris: Presses de l'Ecole Normale Supérieure, 1984);

Christopher Ricks, *Beckett's Dying Words: The Clarendon Lectures, 1990* (Oxford: Clarendon Press, 1993);

Samuel Beckett Today/Aujourd'hui (Amsterdam: Rodopi, 1992–);

Anthony Uhlmann, *Beckett and Poststructuralism* (Cambridge: Cambridge University Press, 1999);

Klaus Völker, *Beckett in Berlin* (Berlin: Frolich & Kaufmann, 1986);

Billie Whitelaw, *Billie Whitelaw . . . Who He?* (London: Hodder & Stoughton, 1995);

Katharine Worth, *Samuel Beckett's Theatre: Life Journeys* (Oxford: Clarendon Press, 1999);

Clas Zilliacus, *Beckett and Broadcasting: A Study of the Works of Samuel Beckett for and in Radio and Television* (Abo, Finland: Abo Akademi, 1976);

Nicholas Zurbrugg, *Beckett and Proust* (Gerrards Cross: Colin Smythe, 1988).

Papers:

The major collections of Samuel Beckett's papers are held at the Beckett International Foundation, University of Reading; Harry Ransom Humanities Research Center, University of Texas at Austin; and Trinity College, Dublin. Other collections are housed at John J. Burns Library, Boston College; Baker Library, Dartmouth College; The Lilly Library, Indiana University; Institut des Mémoires de l'Edition Contemporaine, Paris; Ohio State University Libraries, Columbus; Princeton University Library; Syracuse University, New York; University of Washington, St. Louis, Missouri; and The Beinecke Library, Yale University.

1969 Nobel Prize in Literature Presentation Speech

*by Dr. Karl Ragnar Gierow, of the Swedish Academy
(Translation from the Swedish)*

Your Majesty, Your Royal Highnesses, Ladies and Gentlemen,

Mix a powerful imagination with a logic in absurdum, and the result will be either a paradox or an Irishman. If it is an Irishman, you will get the paradox into the bargain. Even the Nobel Prize in Literature is sometimes divided. Paradoxically, this has happened in 1969, a single award being addressed to one man, two languages and a third nation, itself divided.

Samuel Beckett was born near Dublin in 1906. As a renowned author he entered the world almost half a century later in Paris when, in the space of three years, five works were published that immediately brought him into the centre of interest: the novel *Molloy* in 1951; its sequel, *Malone Meurt,* in the same year; the play *En attendant Godot* in 1952; and in the following year the two novels, *L'Innommable,* which concluded the cycle about *Molloy* and *Malone,* and *Watt.*

These dates simply record a sudden appearance. The five works were not new at the time of publication, nor were they written in the order in which they appeared. They had their background in the current situation as well as in Beckett's previous development. The true nature of *Murphy,* a novel from 1938, and the studies of Joyce (1929) and Proust (1931), which illuminate his own initial position, is perhaps most clearly seen in the light of Beckett's subsequent production. For while he has pioneered new modes of expression in fiction and on the stage, Beckett is also allied to tradition, being closely linked not only to Joyce and Proust but to Kafka as well, and the dramatic works from his debut have a heritage from French works of the 1890s and Alfred Jarry's *Ubu Roi.*

In several respects, the novel *Watt* marks a change of phase in this remarkable output. Written in 1942-44 in the South of France—whence Beckett fled from the Nazis, having lived for a long time in Paris—it was to be his last work in English for many years; he made his name in French and did not return to his native tongue for about fifteen years. The world around had also changed when Beckett came to write again after *Watt*. All the other works which made his name were written in the period 1945-49. The Second World War is their foundation; it was after this that his authorship achieved maturity and a message. But these works are not about the war itself, about life at the front, or in the French resistance movement (in which Beckett took an active part), but about what happened afterwards, when peace came and the curtain was rent from the unholiest of unholies to reveal the terrifying spectacle of the lengths to which man can go in inhuman degradation—whether ordered or driven by himself—and how much of such degradation man can survive. In this sense the degradation of humanity is a recurrent theme in Beckett's writing and to this extent, his philosophy, simply accentuated by elements of the grotesque and of tragic farce, can be described as a negativism that cannot desist from descending to the depths. To the depths it must go because it is only there that pessimistic thought and poetry can work their miracles. What does one get when a negative is printed? A positive, a clarification, with black proving to be the light of day, the parts in deepest shade those which reflect the light source. Its name is fellow-feeling, charity. There are precedents besides the accumulation of abominations in Greek tragedy which led Aristotle to the doctrine of catharsis, purification through horror. Mankind has drawn more strength from Schopenhauer's bitter well than from Schelling's beatific springs, has been more blessed by Pascal's agonized doubt than by Leibniz's blind rational trust in the best of all possible worlds has reaped—in the field of Irish literature, which has also fed Beckett's writing—a much leaner harvest from the whitewashed clerical pastoral of Oliver Goldsmith than from Dean Swift's vehement denigration of all humankind.

Part of the essence of Beckett's outlook is to be found here—in the difference between an easily-acquired pessimism that rests content with untroubled scepticism, and a pessimism that is dearly bought and which penetrates to mankind's utter destitution. The former commences and concludes with the concept that nothing is really of any value, the latter is based on exactly the opposite outlook. For what is worthless cannot be degraded. The perception of human degradation—which we have witnessed, perhaps, to a greater extent than any previous generation—is not possible if human values are denied. But the experience becomes all the more painful as the recognition of human dignity deepens. This is the source of inner cleansing, the life force nevertheless, in Beckett's pessimism. It houses a love of mankind that grows in understanding as it plumbs further into the depths of abhorrence, a despair that has to reach the utmost bounds of suffering to discover that compassion has no bounds. From that position, in the realms of annihilation, rises the writing of Samuel Beckett like a miserere from all mankind, its muffled minor key sounding liberation to the oppressed, and comfort to those in need.

This seems to be stated most clearly in the two masterpieces, *Waiting for Godot* and *Happy Days,* each of which, in a way, is a development of a biblical text. In the case of *Godot* we have, "Art thou he that should come, or do we look for another?" The two tramps are confronted with the meaninglessness of existence at its most brutal. It may be a human figure; no laws are as cruel as those of creation, and man's peculiar status in creation comes from being the only creature to apply these laws with deliberately evil intent. But if we conceive of a providence—a source even of the immeasurable suffering inflicted by, and on, mankind—what sort of almighty is it that we—like the tramps—are to meet somewhere, some day? Beckett's answer consists of the title of the play. By the end of the performance, as at the end of our own, we know nothing about this *Godot.* At the final curtain we have no intimation of the force whose progress we have witnessed. But we do know one thing, of which all the horror of this experience cannot deprive us: namely, our waiting. This is man's metaphysical predicament of perpetual, uncertain expectation, captured with true poetic simplicity: *En attendant Godot, Waiting for Godot.*

The text for *Happy Days*—"a voice crying in the wilderness"—is more concerned with the predicament of man on earth, of our relationships with one another. In his exposition Beckett has much to say about our capacity for entertaining untroubled illusions in a wilderness void of hope. But this is not the theme. The action simply concerns how isolation, how the sand rises higher and higher until the individual is completely buried in loneliness. Out of the suffocating silence, however, there still rises the head, the voice crying in the wilderness, man's indomitable need to seek out his fellow men right to the end, speak to his peers and find in companionship his solace.

L'Académie Suédoise regrette que Samuel Beckett ne soit pas parmi nous aujourd'hui. Cependant il a choisi pour le représenter l'homme qui le premier a découvert l'importance de l'oeuvre maintenant récompensée, son éditeur a Paris, M. Jérôme Lindon, et je vous prie, cher Monsieur, de vouloir bien recevoir de la main de Sa Majesté le Roi le Prix Nobel de littérature, décerné par l'Académie à Samuel Beckett.

(The Swedish Academy regrets that Samuel Beckett could not be with us today. However, he has chosen to represent him the man who was the first to discover the importance of the work now rewarded, his editor in Paris, Mr. Jérôme Lindon, and I ask you, dear Sir, to be willing to receive from the hand of His Majesty the King the Nobel Prize in Literature, awarded by the Academy to Samuel Beckett.)

[© The Nobel Foundation, 1969].

Saul Bellow

(10 June 1915 – 5 April 2005)

Keith M. Opdahl

This entry was expanded by Opdahl from his Bellow entry in *DLB 28: Twentieth-Century American-Jewish Fiction Writers*. See also the Bellow entries in *DLB 2: American Novelists Since World War II*; *DLB 299: Holocaust Novelists*; and *DLB Yearbook: 1982*.

BOOKS: *Dangling Man* (New York: Vanguard, 1944; London: Lehmann, 1946);

The Victim (New York: Vanguard, 1947; London: Lehmann, 1948);

The Adventures of Augie March (New York: Viking, 1953; London: Weidenfeld & Nicolson, 1954);

Seize the Day (New York: Viking, 1956; London: Weidenfeld & Nicolson, 1957);

Henderson the Rain King (New York: Viking, 1959; London: Weidenfeld & Nicolson, 1959);

Herzog (New York: Viking, 1964; London: Weidenfeld & Nicolson, 1965);

The Last Analysis: A Play (New York: Viking, 1965; London: Weidenfeld & Nicolson, 1966);

Mosby's Memoirs and Other Stories (New York: Viking, 1968; London: Weidenfeld & Nicolson, 1969);

Mr. Sammler's Planet (New York: Viking, 1970; London: Weidenfeld & Nicolson, 1970);

The Portable Saul Bellow, edited by Edith Tarcov (New York: Viking, 1974; Harmondsworth, U.K.: Penguin, 1977);

Humboldt's Gift (New York: Viking, 1975; London: Secker & Warburg, 1975);

To Jerusalem and Back: A Personal Account (New York: Viking, 1976; London: Secker & Warburg, 1976);

Nobel Lecture (Stockholm: United States Information Service, 1977; Greenwich Village, N.Y.: Targ Editions, 1979);

The Dean's December (New York: Harper & Row, 1982; London: Secker & Warburg, 1982);

Him with His Foot in His Mouth and Other Stories (New York: Harper & Row, 1984; London: Secker & Warburg, 1984);

More Die of Heartbreak (New York: Morrow, 1987; London: Alison, 1987);

Saul Bellow (center) receiving the 1976 Nobel Prize in Literature from King Carl XVI Gustaf of Sweden (AP Photo/Pool, Peter Knapp)

A Theft (New York: Penguin, 1989; London: Alison [Secker & Warburg], 1989);

The Bellarosa Connection (New York: Penguin, 1989; London: Penguin, 1989);

Something to Remember Me By: Three Tales (New York: Viking, 1991; London: Secker & Warburg, 1992);

It All Adds Up: From the Dim Past to the Uncertain Future (New York: Viking, 1994; London: Secker & Warburg, 1994);

The Actual (New York: Viking, 1997; London: Viking, 1997);

Ravelstein (New York: Viking, 2000; London: Viking, 2000);

Collected Stories (New York: Viking, 2001; London: Viking, 2001);

Bellow Novels 1944–1953 (New York: Library of America, 2003)—comprises *The Dangling Man, The Victim,* and *The Adventures of Augie March.*

PLAY PRODUCTIONS: *The Last Analysis,* New York, Belasco Theater, 1 October 1964;

Under the Weather, London, 7 June 1966; Spoleto, Italy, Festival of Two Worlds, 14 July 1966; New York, Cort Theatre, 27 October 1966–comprised *A Wen, Orange Soufflé,* and *Out from Under.*

OTHER: Isaac Bashevis Singer, "Gimpel the Fool," translated by Bellow, *Partisan Review,* 20 (May–June 1953): 300–313;

"Distractions of a Fiction Writer," in *The Living Novel,* edited by Granville Hicks (New York: Macmillan, 1957), pp. 1–20;

Noble Savage, edited by Bellow, Keith Botsford, and Aaron Asher, 5 volumes (New York: Meridian, 1960–1962);

Great Jewish Short Stories, edited by Bellow (New York: Dell, 1963);

"Literature," in *The Great Ideas Today,* edited by Mortimer Adler and Robert M. Hutchins (Chicago: Encyclopaedia Britannica, 1963), pp. 135–179;

"Zetland: By A Character Witness," in *Modern Occasions,* edited by Philip Rahv (Port Washington, N.Y.: Kennikat Press, 1974), pp. 9–30;

Allan Bloom, *The Closing of the American Mind,* foreword by Bellow (New York: Simon & Schuster, 1987).

SELECTED PERIODICAL PUBLICATIONS– UNCOLLECTED:

FICTION

"Two Morning Monologues," *Partisan Review,* 8 (May–June 1941): 230–236;

"A Sermon by Dr. Pep," *Partisan Review,* 16 (May–June 1949): 455–462;

"The Trip to Galena," *Partisan Review,* 17 (November–December 1950): 769–794;

"Address by Gooley MacDowell to the Hasbeens Club of Chicago," *Hudson Review,* 4 (Summer 1951): 222–227;

A Wen, Esquire, 63 (January 1965): 72–74ff.;

Orange Soufflé, Esquire, 64 (October 1965): 130–136.

NONFICTION

"The Jewish Writer and the English Literary Tradition," *Commentary,* 8 (October 1949): 366–367;

"Dreiser and the Triumph of Art," *Commentary,* 11 (May 1951): 502–503;

"Man Underground," *Commentary,* 13 (June 1952): 608–610;

"Laughter in the Ghetto," *Saturday Review of Literature,* 36 (30 May 1953): 15;

"Hemingway and the Image of Man" [review of Philip Young, *Ernest Hemingway*], *Partisan Review,* 20 (1953): 338–342;

"How I Wrote Augie March's Story," *New York Times Book Review,* 31 January 1954, pp. 3, 17;

"Deep Readers of the World, Beware!" *New York Times Book Review,* 15 February 1959, pp. 1, 34;

"Where Do We Go From Here: The Future of Fiction," *Michigan Quarterly Review,* 1 (Winter 1962): 27–33;

"Memoirs of a Bootlegger's Son," *Granta,* 41 (1992): 9–35;

"The Next Chapter," *National Review,* 52, no. 1 (24 January 2000): 34.

As an American winner of the Nobel Prize in Literature in 1976, Saul Bellow inherited the mantle of Ernest Hemingway and William Faulkner; but he never became a culture hero like those two nor a cult figure like Jorge Luis Borges or Gabriel García Márquez. When in 1979 *The New York Times Book Review* asked twenty leading intellectuals which books since 1945 would count among the hundred most important books in Western civilization, Bellow was not mentioned. However, when Philip Roth was asked who are "the great inventors of narrative detail and masters of narrative voice and perspective," he replied, "James, Conrad, Dostoevski and Bellow." In 1994 some of Britain's leading writers and critics told *The Sunday Times* that Bellow was "the greatest living novelist writing in English."

Bellow enjoyed the kind of reputation that is won by solid and accomplished work. He was a private person, and in his public appearances he was sometimes distant or moody. But as a writer he caught and articulated the sometimes hidden feelings of the modern era. Bellow showed what alienation actually is on a winter afternoon, or precisely how American culture crushes a mediocre man.

Bellow was born Solomon Bellow in Lachine, Quebec, on 10 June 1915, two years after his parents, Abraham and Liza Gordin Bellow, had emigrated from St. Petersburg, Russia (where their surname had been spelled "Belo," from *byelo,* Russian for *white*). His father was a daring and not always successful businessman who in Russia had imported Egyptian onions (Bellow describes him in an unpublished manuscript excerpted in "Memoirs of a Bootlegger's Son" [1992] as a "sharpie circa 1905") and in the New World attempted several often unconventional businesses. Solomon ("Solly") was their youngest child, with a sister and two brothers.

The Bellowses lived in a slum on St. Dominique Street "between a market and a hospital," Bellow has said; "I was generally preoccupied with what went on in it and watched from the stairs and windows." His father, who blamed himself for the family's poverty, worried that Solly would see too much; and the boy did witness violence and sexuality, saying later that the raw reality of St. Dominique Street made all else in his life seem strange and foreign. "Little since then has worked upon me with such force," Bellow wrote, and he returned to the scene in some of his novels. He lived amid the color and spirituality of an earlier era: Lachine was "a medieval ghetto . . . my childhood was in ancient times which was true of all orthodox Jews." By the age of four he knew the Book of Genesis in Hebrew.

Lachine was also a multilingual environment, and young Bellow learned Yiddish, French, and English, as well as Hebrew. Taken ill with peritonitis, he spent six months in the Royal Hospital (in the tuberculosis ward) with nothing to do but read. But by the time his family had moved to Humboldt Park in Chicago, when he was nine, he was healthy enough for sports as well as his many intellectual projects. Humboldt Park was a neighborhood of immigrants, filled with the cultural and intellectual activity of sidewalk orators, branch libraries, and mission houses. By the time he attended Tuley High School, Bellow had such friends as Isaac Rosenfeld, future newspaper columnist Sydney J. Harris, and David Peltz, who remembers that "Solly Bellows was the most precocious of the lot—a good runner on the track team, a fair swimmer, middling tennis player, but a remarkable writer even then."

Bellow's family continued to have financial problems. His mother died when he was fifteen, and when he was seventeen he and Harris ran away to New York for a few weeks to peddle their first novels, unsuccessfully. From 1933 to 1935 his father managed to find the money for Bellow to attend the University of Chicago, where he felt the dense cultural atmosphere to be suffocating. He left when a fatal accident involving his father's coal truck ruined what was left of the family finances. He was nevertheless able to transfer to Northwestern, where he founded a socialists' club and graduated in 1937 with honors in sociology and anthropology. He wished to study literature but was advised that anti-Semitism would thwart his career, and so he accepted a scholarship to study anthropology at the University of Wisconsin, where his professor told him he wrote anthropology like a good novelist. In Chicago on New Year's Eve 1937, Bellow married Anita Goshkin, a social worker, and abandoned his graduate work. "In my innocence," he said, "I had decided to become a writer."

It was a bold decision at that time, and such boldness has characterized Bellow's work ever since. His greatest strength as a novelist is his style, which is fluid and rich, picking up the rhythms and energy of Yiddish and the plain speech and sharply observed detail of the Midwest. His style is precise and implies an integrity that has at times gotten Bellow into trouble. In an era of experimentalism Bellow was a realist, claiming that "the development of realism in the nineteenth century is still the major event of modern literature." When alienation was popular, Bellow celebrated accommodation. He reacted to the popularity of the Jewish novel by turning to a WASP protagonist (in *Henderson the Rain King*, 1959), and he met America's new youth culture head-on with the creation of a seventy-year-old protagonist (in *Mr. Sammler's Planet*, 1970). Yet, in most of these ventures he was successful, largely because of his fertile imagination and clarity of mind.

Bellow's greatest difficulty as a writer lies in plot. He has confessed this difficulty, and many critics believe his novels to be formless. If Bellow's characters are colorful and his situations telling, he characteristically gives too much: too many ideas, too many characters, and too many memorable details for readers to discern a simple story or central focus. But Bellow is not as formless as he seems, since his point is often the subtle insight of the realist, so easily lost among his comic characters and rich descriptions, and he himself is a diligent craftsman, working through draft after draft. But the fact remains that his art is one of clearing and solidifying an abundance of materials, and when he has finished with the process, the reader is invited to do the same.

Indeed, this density of life is one of Bellow's central themes. So too is the malice or nastiness of his protagonist and those around him. Another theme is the experience of transcendence and the fact that the issues that confront people are ultimately metaphysical or religious, an element that provides one of the keys to Bellow's style: the sense of a special meaning or significance just out of reach adds another dimension to his precisely detailed physical world. A society that can invent the inner life but give it no nourishment, a universe that requires one to twist oneself to survive within its force, a protagonist seeking most of all to cure himself of some unknown malady—all of these are typical Bellow themes.

Bellow has insisted that he is not that exotic creature, the Jew who writes in English, but an American writer—a Western writer who happens to be Jewish. "I did not go to the public library to read the Talmud," Bellow says of his Chicago days, "but the novels and poems of Sherwood Anderson, Theodore Dreiser, Edgar Lee Masters, and Vachel Lindsay." Bellow nevertheless is singled out by Allen Guttmann in *The Jewish Writer in America* (1971) as portraying the full range of American Jewish experience. Bellow's comedy, intellectualism, moral preoccupation and alienation, his concern with the family and with rough Eastern European immigrants, his obsession with the past and with the dangers of an alien world, his emphasis on purity, his sense, as Alfred Kazin says, "of the unreality of this world as opposed to God's"—all of these elements bespeak his deep Jewish concern.

Certainly the fact that he was Jewish added a special tension to his decision to be a writer, for he entered a world dominated by WASPs from New England. He worked for the Work Projects Administration doing biographical sketches of Midwestern writers and then taught at Pestalozzi-Froebel Teacher's College in Chicago. He went to Mexico in 1940, writing the never-published novel "Acatla," and lived, he says, a bohemian life. But these years were not all gaiety: "I sat on a bridge table in a back bedroom of the apartment while all rational, serious, dutiful people were at their jobs or trying to find jobs, writing something." After lunch with his mother-in-law, in whose apartment he lived, he would walk the city streets. "If I had been a dog I would have howled," he has written. He managed in 1941 to place a short story in the *Partisan Review*, "Two Morning Monologues," about a young man waiting for the draft; the next year he placed another, "The Mexican General," about the assassination of Leon Trotsky, which happened on the day before Bellow was to meet with him. And in 1943 *Partisan Review* published part of his novel in progress.

Perhaps the most memorable quality of this first novel, published in 1944 as *Dangling Man*, is the tone of voice: modeled after that of Rainer Maria Rilke's *Die Aufzeichnungen des Malte Laurids Brigge* (1910; translated as *The Journal of My Other Self*, 1930), the voice is frank and honest, compensating for its self-pity by the depth and precision of its observation. Taking on Hemingway, the protagonist Joseph jibes at the hard-boiled: "If you have difficulties, grapple with them silently, goes one of their commandments. To hell with that! I intend to talk about mine, and if I had as many mouths as Siva has arms and kept them going all the time, I still could not do myself justice."

Like Bellow himself, Joseph has been kept dangling by his draft board, bound in the red tape surrounding his Canadian birth. His ostensibly formless journal is actually shaped by his increasing lack of self-control, as he records first the failure of his attempts to write or to prepare himself for the army, and then his disappointment with his friends, his wife, his in-laws, and his mistress. Wanting to forge a self that would be "a member of the Army, but not a *part* of it," he must watch himself become overwhelmed by a hundred trivial details, as his self-control leaves him and the nasty temper he has remarked in others comes to dominate. When he strikes his landlord and realizes that his sense of the strangeness and impermanence of the world has grown, he gives up, crying "Long live regimentation."

One anonymous critic for *Time* (8 May 1944) thought Joseph was a "stinker," but other reviewers gave the book a remarkably affirmative judgment. Edmund Wilson, Peter DeVries, Diana Trilling, and Delmore Schwartz all felt this first novel worthy of their attention. Wilson, in *The New Yorker* (1 April 1944), called it "one of the most honest pieces of testimony on the psychology of a whole generation," and George Mayberry proclaimed the creation of a complex character like Joseph "an event that is rare and wonderful in modern American writing." Subsequent critics have found the book narrow and Bellow's attitude toward Joseph uncertain. To some, Joseph at the end rejoins society; to others, he is totally defeated, surrendering his individuality. Bellow's novel is a lively and even memorable work, with many striking figures, even if the author himself has confessed that he cannot bear to reread it.

Bellow's own dangling was ended by the army for medical reasons, and in 1943 he began to work for Mortimer Adler's "Great Books" project for the *Encyclopaedia Britannica*, reading some 60 of the 443 works indexed. He joined the merchant marine, which stationed him in New York, and then worked for the Maritime Commission onshore. After the war Bellow decided to stay in New York, enjoying the intellectual life of Greenwich Village and the pleasures of fatherhood with the birth of his son Gregory. He reviewed books, edited, wrote reports for Penguin Books, and spent two days as movie reviewer for *Time*, until Whittaker Chambers reportedly picked a quarrel and fired him on the spot—an event he included in his next novel, *The Victim* (1947).

Joseph in *Dangling Man* had complained that upon awakening, when he read the newspaper and acknowledged the world, he went "in the body from nakedness to clothing and in the mind from relative purity to pollution." To Joseph the world is a war that can kill him. In *The Victim* this impurity pursues the protagonist Asa Leventhal as Kirby Allbee comes one hot summer night to accuse the solitary and anxious Leventhal of causing his ruin. Leventhal had quarreled with Allbee's boss, prompting Allbee's loss of his job, he claims, and thus his drinking and the loss of his wife. Bellow explores the intense and ambivalent relation between the two men, as Allbee presses deeper and deeper into Leventhal's life, taking money, a bed in his apartment, liberties with his mail, and finally a whore in Leventhal's own bed—an impurity that is still not the final one, since Allbee slips into the apartment late at night to attempt suicide in Leventhal's kitchen.

Was Leventhal responsible? A parallel plot suggests he was not, for he mistakenly assumes the blame for a death for which he had no responsibility. Both Leventhal and Allbee are victims of an oppressively dense world and of their inability to discern a clear order in it. Each argues for a version of reality that the other cannot accept. Allbee cannot bear the notion of an impersonal universe in which he might be harmed for no reason at all. He must find a scapegoat—a Jew. To Leventhal, on the other hand, such a "human" universe is ominous, frightening, a world in which he could be ruined overnight. Allbee appears inexplicably, emerging from a crowd in a park as an embodiment of the city streets, which Leventhal, like his immigrant forebears, considers full of impurity and danger: "He really did not know what went on about him," Leventhal thinks, "what strange things, savage things."

The Victim is a remarkable advance over *Dangling Man,* for though it is dense and claustrophic, it is also rich and full of honest life. It raised some eyebrows, coming as it did only two years after the Nazi death camps had been opened: was this the time to show that the psychology of Jew and bigot can be similar? To Theodore Ross in the *Chicago Jewish Forum,* Allbee and Leventhal are too much alike. Bellow had insisted on paying the Jew the same respect he would pay all human beings, neither more nor less, and in the Gentile Allbee he captured the unconscious subtleties of Jewish self-hatred, making him a messenger from not just a destructive world but Leventhal's own psyche. Leventhal's alienation is that of modern man, moreover; for by showing Jew and Gentile to be alike, Bellow shows that all people are Jews.

The Victim brought Bellow a Guggenheim Fellowship for 1948, freeing him from teaching at the University of Minnesota, where he had been in 1946 and 1947. In France on his fellowship he began "The Crab and the Butterfly," a third novel in the same serious vein as his first two, but found he needed some relief. He took to writing a "memoir" of Chicago—which in France had become exotic to him, he says—and by 1949 had turned to it almost exclusively. "Augie was my favorite fantasy," he has said of the Chicago book. "Every time I was depressed while writing the grim one I'd treat myself to a fantasy holiday." He wrote *The Adventures of Augie March* (1953) while on the move—in trains and cafés in Paris and Rome; in Minneapolis, where he returned to teach in 1949; in a cold-water flat in New York, where he lectured at New York University; at Princeton, where he was a Creative Writing Fellow; and even in the editorial offices at Viking Press. At some point he felt such revulsion with the "grim" work he had begun that he dumped some one hundred thousand words down an incinerator. (One chapter survived and was published as "Trip to Galena.")

Thus, *The Adventures of Augie March* begins as the opposite of Bellow's serious concerns, shifting to the first person from the third person of *The Victim* and from Leventhal's fears of the streets to Augie's celebration of them. Bellow had known someone like Augie: "He came of just such a family as I described. I hadn't seen him in 25 years, so the novel was a speculative biography." What was especially speculative was Bellow's definition of the young man as an enthusiast who is swept up by the people he loves, sometimes in a sexual swoon and at other times as an admiring disciple. Can a young man in a harsh world of force survive without weapons other than affection and tolerance and a lack of calculation? The answer lies in the adults who surround Augie and are as large and threatening as they would appear to a child. They exist with a Balzacian vigor and importance that testifies to human worth as they act upon their environment, but they also overwhelm the passive young Augie, who becomes another Bellow hero oppressed by the world.

Augie manages to survive at first. Augie's childhood is dominated by Grandma Lausch, whose world is every bit as dramatic and cynical as the czar's court, and whom Bellow describes as the equal of the great politicians of the world. The crippled Einhorn, for whom Augie works as a male nurse, is great too, even if his kingdom is a West Side neighborhood. Augie also serves the North Shore matron Mrs. Renling (until she wishes to adopt him) and acts as an aide-de-camp to his ambitious brother Simon, who marries into a wealthy family. In each case, Augie observes not only that "it wasn't so necessary to lie," as he says in the first chapter, rejecting Machiavellian cynicism, but also that these egotists finally do themselves in. Only Augie, larky, impetuous, sensual, accepting—the opposite of Bellow's usual protagonist and thus a true fantasy for Bellow—only Augie, it seems, is escaping a harsh and destructive world.

Yet, Augie does not escape, either, and readers can measure the progress of the novel by noting his responses. In the first chapter Augie is beaten up by neighborhood punks (including Augie's good friend) for being a Jew: "But I never had any special grief from it," Augie says, "or brooded, being by and large too larky and boisterous to take it to heart." By the middle of the novel, when Augie is beaten up in a labor strike, he flees, full of rage and terror. He goes to Mexico with his lover Thea, another Machiavellian who plans to hunt iguanas with a trained eagle, and suffers a concussion that makes him spend depressing weeks on the mend. When he cheats on Thea, she tells him he is not a man of love at all, but isolate or indifferent, a fact that Einhorn had earlier described as Augie's "opposition." The book ultimately becomes the memoir of a rather scarred and saddened middle-aged man who defines himself as one singing in the middle of a desolate and frozen farm field.

Reviewers in 1953 praised the novel for its energy and acceptance and stylistic fireworks. Even though *The Adventures of Augie March* won a National Book Award in 1954, Bellow himself had reservations, commenting that "I got stuck in a Sherwood Anderson ingenue vein: here are all these people and isn't life wonderful! By the last third of the book I wasn't feeling that way anymore." The novel is notable for the warm tone of its voice and the precision of its details. Bellow had grown up on the naturalistic work of Dreiser, John Dos Passos, and James T. Farrell, and he transforms it here into something less mechanical, less deterministic or external, focusing more on the perception and history and feeling of the inner protagonist—who finds a triumph, finally, in consciousness if not in love.

Bellow taught at Bard College in 1953 and 1954 and at the University of Minnesota the next year. He won a second Guggenheim Fellowship, which permitted him to spend 1955 in Nevada and California, and then, having terminated his troubled marriage, he was free to marry Sondra Tschacbasov and settle down—after almost two decades of moving about—in Dutchess County, New York, near Tivoli. During this period he also wrote the short works that make up his next book, *Seize the Day* (1956): "Looking for Mr. Green" (1951), "A Father to Be" (1955), "The Gonzaga Manuscripts" (1956), the title novella, and a one-act play, *The Wrecker* (1954). The novella *Seize the Day* reflects a pattern of variety in Bellow's work, as each novel seems to contrast in tone with its predecessor. While *The Adventures of Augie March* sprawls and attacks the world with energy, *Seize the Day* is tight and sets an elegiac tone.

The story recounts a day in the life of a failing middle-aged American, Tommy Wilhelm, who has made a series of poor decisions that land him jobless in his early forties at the once-grand, now-shabby Hotel Ansonia on the Upper West Side of New York, where his father lives in retirement. Tommy wants his father's help—and is denied. He wants his substitute father's help too, and this father, the sometime psychologist Tamkin, is the character Bellow finds most interesting in the tale, for "like most phony phonies, he is always somewhere near the truth. . . . But Tamkin's truths aren't really true." As he treats patients over the phone and spouts existential clichés, Tamkin promises to cure all of Tommy's troubles. He will make him strong, teaching him to "seize the day"—the very vagueness of which is Bellow's point—and he will make him financially comfortable, too, using Tommy's money to speculate on the grain market. Bellow begins the novella with Tommy emerging from his room, assuming a bold front. The first three sections cover Tommy's past and his breakfast with his father, and the second three his relations with Tamkin. In the last, climactic section, Tommy's disgusted father disowns him and Tamkin, having lost Tommy's savings, disappears.

Tommy's defeat makes many readers uncomfortable, and several reviewers termed *Seize the Day* an interim work, filling the time after *The Adventures of Augie March*. Since 1956 its reputation has grown steadily, however, until, as Kazin puts it, "none of his work is so widely and genuinely admired as this short novel." Herbert Gold called *Seize the Day* "one of the central stories of our day." Tommy is at once the ultimate antihero and a worthwhile man, and likable, with "a large, shaky, patient dignity." He is cheerful and without malice. He cares for his loved ones. More important, he is intelligently aware, undergoing his experience with depth and sensitivity.

The finest accomplishment of the story is the climactic scene. Tommy at one moment is on the New York streets, desperately looking for Tamkin and feeling the pressure of the crowd, "the inexhaustible current of millions of every race and kind pouring out, pressing round, of every age, of every genius, possessors of every secret," and at the next inside a funeral parlor, where it is suddenly "dark and cool" and where "men in formal clothes and black homburgs strode softly back and forth on the cork floor, up and down the center aisle." In a few moments he stands before the corpse of a man he has never known, and begins to cry. He sobs at first for the man, "another human creature," he thinks, but soon he cries for himself and for all his troubles. "Soon he was past words, past reason, coherence," Bellow writes; "The source of all tears had suddenly sprung open within him, black, deep." The other guests envy the dead man for having inspired such mourning, but Tommy does not stop. His grief becomes a strangely triumphant moment, as the flowers and lights and music fuse within him, pouring "into him where he had hidden himself in the center of a crowd by the great and happy oblivion of tears. He heard it and sank deeper than sorrow, through torn sobs and cries toward the consummation of his heart's ultimate need."

Critics disagree about Bellow's final meaning—puzzled, as Brendan Gill put it in *The New Yorker* (5 January 1957), by the sense that Tommy is "sobbing his heart out over his plight and yet feeling rather better than usual"—but almost all readers sense the authority of the scene. As Kazin says of the whole novella, "It has a quite remarkable intensity of effect without ever seeming to force one." The circumstance of Tommy finding his way to a stranger's funeral crystallizes Tommy's situation and needs. For he needs a father and has been denied, seeking help from people "dead" to him. He has sought all day to hide his failure, to put up a front, and here he is publicly reduced to truthfulness. Bellow himself has said that he wanted to dramatize the way New

Yorkers fulfill intimate emotional needs through strangers, and so Tommy turns from his psychologist (the professional stranger) to an unfamiliar corpse—and finally finds fulfillment. Since Tommy has had mystical promptings that his suffering somehow has a transcendent purpose, Bellow's point is also that Tommy sinks to a truer, more spiritual level of being accessible only when he is stripped of worldly pretensions.

Henderson the Rain King did not receive strong praise when it was published in 1959, but it did not diminish Bellow's reputation either. Bellow wrote it in Tivoli, New York, in 1957 (the year his second son, Adam, was born) and in 1958 at the University of Minnesota (an anchor for Bellow in these years and the place where he was friends with John Berryman), and then the next year in Europe on a two-year Ford Foundation grant. This book about a WASP millionaire's trip to a dream-like Africa illustrates the fertility and variety in Bellow's imagination and his desire, as he said later, to develop "a fiction that can accommodate the full tumult, the zaniness and crazed quality of modern experience."

Henderson is a gigantic man in body and emotion, six feet four inches tall, with "an enormous head, rugged, with hair like Persian lambs' fur. Suspicious eyes, usually narrowed. Blustering way. A great nose." He is heir to a fortune, a hard drinker, a bully, a fighter, and a man fleeing death. He is nasty to his wives and torments the neighbors. His rages finally scare the family cook to death, making him seek salvation in Africa, where, he says, "the world which I thought so mighty an oppressor has removed its wrath from me." Henderson (whose initials are the same as Hemingway's) is the militant, insecure American who attempts to prove his manhood by killing. He is also the intelligent and sensitive man who suffers from his knowledge of human limitation. Confessing that he is most like the character Henderson, "the absurd seeker of high qualities," Bellow comments that "what Henderson is really seeking is a remedy to the anxiety over death. What he can't endure is this continuing anxiety . . . which he is foolhardy enough to resist."

Although the novel has many realistic touches, it is essentially a fantasy, a trip deep within the Africa of Henderson's mind. He discovers first the Arnewi, a tribe that reacts to its environment with a soft, worshiping attitude, and then (after he has harmed the gentle Arnewi irremediably by blowing up their water supply) the Wariri, a fierce and manipulative tribe that beats its gods and threatens to kill its king. Part of Bellow's point is Henderson's desire to serve a community even though it involves often bizarre and dangerous conditions, as in the case of the marvelously relaxed Wariri king Dahfu, who has studied the works of Ralph Waldo Emerson, William James, and Wilhelm Reich and who will be unceremoniously strangled if he fails to satisfy any one of his forty wives. To make the anxious Henderson equally serene, Dahfu takes him into a lion's den, where he teaches him to emulate the lion. Dahfu's tribe believes that he is not completely king until he captures the soul of his dead father in a live lion. Although educated in the Western empirical tradition, which would scoff at such a view, Dahfu accepts these conditions and is killed by a lion as a result. When Henderson then feels himself cured or freed from the world's wrath, he stumbles in explaining the cause, for he claims it was not the lion's cruel indifference that freed him but the love of the Arnewi—a statement that grows more out of Bellow's desire than the events of the novel. Critics complained about the murky ending.

Bellow is bolder than he had been in his previous work (he dates his maturity as a writer from *Henderson the Rain King*), for he openly makes a connection between the force of the universe and a human or spiritual principle. But he once again sought variety, turning next to a realistic work. He spent much of 1959 in Europe and the next year at his country home in Dutchess County. With Keith Botsford and Aaron Asher he edited the periodical *Noble Savage*. He taught at the University of Puerto Rico and then, after his second divorce, settled down to his third marriage, with Susan Glassman, whom he wed in December 1961. With a new child on the way (Daniel, born in 1963) and a desire to return to his roots, Bellow left New York for Chicago, where he accepted a permanent position at the University of Chicago on the Committee on Social Thought.

In Chicago, Bellow sought greater freedom to work, a desire that bore fruit in 1964 with the publication of *Herzog* and the production of *The Last Analysis* (published in 1965). The play was a lighthearted episodic farce Bellow hoped would survive because of its entertaining qualities. The novel was more serious, embodying the theory he had announced in 1961 that a novelist must be permitted to deal with ideas. The play flopped, but the novel was a best-seller for six months. "I received two or three thousand letters from people pouring out their souls to me, saying 'This is my life, this is what it's been like for me,'" Bellow said after the publication of *Herzog*. "And then I understood that for some reason these themes were visited upon me, that I didn't always pick them, they picked me." Since the novel covered events similar to those of Bellow's life, portraying an intellectual professor devastated after being betrayed by his wife and friends, some of the interest in the novel was that of a roman à clef. But most of the people who bought it were not in on the gossip; the novel articulated their own anger, their own frustration—precisely that frame of mind that characterized the late 1960s as tempers flared over the issues of free speech, racial injustice, and war. As early as 1960, Bellow anticipated the mood of the coming decade.

The story consists of Moses Herzog's memories as he putters alone about his country home in western Massachusetts. Herzog remembers himself in New York, where he had stayed a few days after teaching a course, and then in Chicago, where he had lurked outside his estranged wife's apartment before suffering a minor auto accident and a brief incarceration, from which the police freed him to go home. If the geography is simple, however, the story is not. Since Herzog writes letters to many people and remembers all kinds of earlier events, the novel seems disorganized. Critics divide largely into those who forgive this disorganization (since it reflects Herzog's mind) and those who do not. And once again the protagonist feels somewhat better at the end of the novel, but the reader is not certain why. Yet, the truth is that the book, which Bellow rewrote at least thirteen times, is indeed well formed. Herzog decides early in the story to shift from an emotional "personal" life, such as the one in which his wife, Madeleine, abused him, to a more rational, civil, moderate one—he will shift, as he says in a letter to President Eisenhower, from Leo Tolstoy to Georg Wilhelm Friedrich Hegel. Much of the novel flows from this decision. He flies to Chicago contemplating the murder of his former wife and her lover in order to protect his daughter Junie, reportedly locked crying in a car outside Madeleine's apartment; but he decides once more (as the novel catches the realistic zigzags of a man trying on a new mode) that he is being extreme and indulging in personal "drama."

Each of the nine sections of the novel dramatizes Bellow's theme. After he is caught the next day with the gun in his pocket, Herzog finds himself standing before a police sergeant, next to Madeleine, who in pure hatred seeks to have him imprisoned: "Her voice went up sharply, and as she spoke, Herzog saw the sergeant take a new look at her, as if he were beginning to make out her haughty peculiarities at last." When the sergeant lets him go, Herzog receives a symbolic justice. The friends and relatives and even doctors who had witnessed his divorce had all failed him, but the civil authority had not. And having gotten justice, he feels better. One of the problems with the novel, however, is that he feels an ecstatic joy that goes far beyond fair treatment.

Herzog is notable for the controversy it caused. Bellow's second National Book Award winner, it was both praised and criticized. Kazin, who provided a dust-jacket blurb, called it Bellow's most brilliant novel; Gill in *The New Yorker* termed it "faultless." Other critics worried that Herzog pondered only himself, making the novel solipsistic. The key question is whether Herzog succeeds in making a character of himself as he looks back. Does Herzog get out of his own mind? His ability to see himself from the outside and with precise detail suggests that he does. Bellow's theme at any rate is something like solipsism, as Herzog is imprisoned in the "private" life.

However one evaluates the structure of the novel, *Herzog* is most notable for its style, which represents Bellow at his best. Since Herzog does a great deal of observing, the center of the novel is its descriptions. The prose is charged, full of the specifics and precisely defined impressions that create the feel of mid-1960s American life. Because Herzog is deflected from his course not by any insight or charged drama but by the sight of kindly Gersbach giving little Junie a bath, *Herzog* is a defense of the realistic mode, holding that the significant levels of life are often the common, whether in the home or outside in society—a view Herzog himself embraces (rejecting the fashionable existentialism) and then in his life dramatizes.

The Last Analysis, performed in fall 1964, was the culmination of Bellow's long interest in the theater. He had collaborated on a dramatization of *Seize the Day* (performed at the avant-garde workshop Theatre of Ideas, with Mike Nichols as Tommy) and had included a one-act play, *The Wrecker,* among the pieces in the collection *Seize the Day.* Bellow also seems to have been motivated financially, for his novels had not made him much money, and *Herzog* did not initially look like a best-seller. Zero Mostel was scheduled to play the lead in "Humanitis," as *The Last Analysis* was originally titled, and Bellow thought the play would be easy to write. He saw the theater as a form of freedom, since the stage required a more direct, less subtle approach.

By 1964, though, Bellow complained that he was writing himself into his grave. Mostel backed out, to be replaced by Sam Levene, and Bellow found playwriting more demanding than he had imagined. He persevered, however, presenting the story of a comedian who has slipped in his career because of his seriousness and who now, in his New York warehouse studio, seeks to combine laughter and home-style psychoanalysis. The protagonist, Bummidge, seeks a cure for "humanitis," and his technique, he says, is to act out "the main events of my life, dragging repressed material into the open by sheer force of drama." The Broadway version flopped after twenty-eight performances, receiving poor reviews.

Bellow's second effort in the theater did no better. For the production *Under the Weather* (1966), Bellow combined three one-act plays, two of which have been published: *A Wen,* a comedy about a scientist who has found the experience of winning the Nobel Prize less intense than the glimpse of a birthmark on a woman's thigh (a glimpse he seeks to duplicate, in middle age, with the same surprised lady); and *Orange Soufflé,* a somewhat darker comedy about a Polish whore who wants to move in with her elderly and wealthy WASP customer. *Under the Weather* was produced in London, Spoleto, and New York, but failed to catch on.

Bellow continued to teach in Chicago in the years following *Herzog,* although he took time out in 1967, the year in which he and Glassman divorced, to cover the Six-Day War for *Newsday* and in 1968 to receive the Croix de Chevalier des Arts et Lettres from France. He had begun the novel that became *Humboldt's Gift* (1975), but upon hearing an anecdote about an old man witnessing a pickpocket at work, shifted to the manuscript that became *Mr. Sammler's Planet.* He also found time to write two short stories, "The Old System" (1967) and "Mosby's Memoirs" (1968), to which he added "Leaving the Yellow House" (1957) and several previously published tales for *Mosby's Memoirs and Other Stories* (1968), a more or less "made" book designed to keep Bellow's name before the public and perhaps to capitalize on the success of *Herzog.*

The best story of the group is "The Old System," in which a well-known scientist, Samuel Braun (transparently Bellow himself), embodies a characteristic Bellow posture in the late 1960s and 1970s: the middle-aged man remembering his Jewish relatives, losing himself in a colorful and exotic past. The characters are mysterious to Braun, who loves them. He ponders their reality, their evolution, the strangeness of their being. They are in one sense crude and grasping immigrants from Eastern Europe who would embarrass a third-generation Jew. But they are also vital and proud. They seem to Braun to be more intensely alive, or at least more passionate, than his modern colleagues.

Mr. Sammler's Planet was well but somewhat absentmindedly received, as though the reviews praised Bellow by rote; a few years later the novel was attacked by radical young critics for political reasons, in part because Bellow had declared his independence from the liberal establishment in 1965 by attending the White House dinner that Robert Lowell, protesting the Vietnam War, had boycotted. In this novel, as in *Herzog,* Bellow seemed to test both his readers and his own powers, having chosen—in a decade obsessed with American youth—to write about an elderly man. Artur Sammler is an old Polish Jew who, having lived in London in the 1930s where he knew many of the Bloomsbury group, and having survived Nazi atrocities, has the civilized tastes of the intellectual English and the wisdom of the survivor. Around him he finds a host of modern young nieces, nephews, and acquaintances who reject all limits on their desire. They know no sexual bounds, no moral imperatives, no common civility. Sammler alone in New York quietly pursues something like duty. When his crazed daughter Shula steals a manuscript to help her father with his study of H. G. Wells, he doggedly seeks to return the manuscript. When his friend and benefactor Elya Gruner lies mortally ill in a hospital, Sammler alone pays homage.

The plot consists largely of the young interfering with these two tasks and is typified in the running story of Sammler's encounters with a black pickpocket, whose crimes he has witnessed on a bus and who follows Sammler to his apartment foyer to threaten the old man by exposing himself. Sammler mentions the incident to his opportunistic friend Feffer, and later (in too much of a coincidence) stumbles upon the pickpocket wrestling with Feffer, who has taken pictures of the crime. When Sammler asks his former son-in-law, Eisen, to intervene, Eisen hits to kill. In contrast to such madness, Sammler at the end praises his friend Gruner, who (although sometimes an abortionist for the mob) had known how to be kind and to do his duty. Gruner had met "the terms of his contract," Sammler concludes, "the terms of which, in his inmost heart, each man knows."

Mr. Sammler's Planet is full of the precise detail, honest feeling, and lively ideas that are Bellow's strengths. The character of Sammler, who has survived the Holocaust, having woken from a pile of corpses to kill fascists in his escape, is an excellent point of view from which to examine and judge American culture. Bellow captures better than anyone the feel of American society in the late 1960s, with its blend of social rebellion, sexuality, racial unrest, and personal aggrandizement. What mars the novel, finally, is Sammler's basic feeling of revulsion toward the world, both in its social form, which is cheap and distracting—Gruner's daughter worries about her sex life as her father dies—and in terms of all matter. Sammler has no use for the natural physical world, or what he calls "creatureliness. . . . Its low tricks, its doggish hind-sniffing charm." Sammler yearns to be "a soul released from Nature, from impressions, and from everyday life."

Mr. Sammler's Planet won a National Book Award in 1971. While continuing to teach at the University of Chicago (where he had become chairman of the Committee on Social Thought) and coping with the public and bitter dissolution of his third marriage, Bellow worked on two novels, segments of which were published in 1974. One of these was *Humboldt's Gift,* which became his seventh novel, won Bellow a Pulitzer Prize, and immediately preceded his 1976 Nobel Prize in Literature.

Many reviewers praised the book, and *Newsweek* did a cover story on "America's leading writer," but other critics were disappointed. "The book is not very real," Kazin confessed, in *The New York Review of Books* (3 December 1970), although large pieces of it were. Part of the trouble seemed to be the combination of the realistic and manic: Bellow attempted to work grotesque gangsters into a finely detailed world, and some critics felt it did not work.

The story is told from the point of view of Charles Citrine, a well-known dramatist who reminisces about his friendship with Humboldt, a poet who combines qualities of Berryman, with whom Bellow had been close friends at Minnesota, and Schwartz, whom Bellow had known in New York. Bellow began working on the novel in 1966, shortly after Schwartz died. Much of the story consists of Citrine's trying to hang onto his memories of Humboldt and do a little philosophical meditation while being harrassed by gangsters, lawyers, bimbos, and creeps—some funny and some not. All of them are typified by Cantabile, to whom Citrine owes money and who has Citrine's car smashed in by baseball bats and later forces the playwright to watch him defecate. A former wife is suing Citrine, and a mistress—the sensual Renata—is attempting to lead him to the altar. But during all these events, Citrine moves inward in memory and meditation.

What is interesting thematically in *Humboldt's Gift* is the equation within Citrine's inner life of his meditation of spirit and his memories of his friend. Both of these exist in saving opposition to the world, although Humboldt's actual gift combines the vulgar and the sublime, for it consists first of a movie scenario on which they had collaborated and which proceeds to earn Citrine a small fortune, and then of a scribbled sentence at the end of a farewell letter: "We are not natural beings but supernatural beings."

The chief critical issue with the novel, aside from Bellow's struggle to mesh his transcendental philosophy with commercial America, is its uneven quality: this novel includes writing as good as any that Bellow has done and also some of the worst that he has done. Bellow at his worst sounds like an amateur playwright providing background information as he moves his characters on and offstage. The later parts of the novel fall off, becoming talky and cranky, as though (as reportedly is the case) Bellow had taken to dictating his novel to a stenographer, or as though his troubled personal life had taken its toll. The best early parts of the book were written not too long after *Herzog*, while the later parts, developing some of the disenchantment with the real world Bellow expressed in *Mr. Sammler's Planet,* came after 1969.

Bellow's 1976 book, the journalistic *To Jerusalem and Back: A Personal Account,* was published after Bellow had accompanied his new wife, Alexandra Ionescu Tulcea, professor of mathematics at Northwestern University, to Israel. The author asked himself, what could a practitioner of the humanities add to the politics and propaganda and terror of the Israeli-Arab conflict? Could he penetrate the confusion and make some kind of contribution to solving Israel's troubles? The book describes Bellow's travels, his interviews with Israeli and American leaders, and his dinner conversations with the powerful and the humble, and then—and not least important—documents his reading and research into the problem.

Bellow's writing is lucid and detailed, and not without humor, as a Hasidim, for example, is offended by Bellow's eating habits and offers to send him money each month if he will return to orthodoxy. But the rational and well-meaning Bellow ultimately is forced to conclude that the situation is even more dangerous than he had supposed, for he finds that nations (and their leaders) do not act consistently with even their own self-interests. If only they recognized their goals and sought them ruthlessly, Bellow suggests, the struggle would have some order. But both Arab and Jew act irrationally, creating a volatile mix.

Shortly after returning to Chicago in the fall of 1976, Bellow learned that he had won the Nobel Prize in Literature. His acceptance speech, delivered in Sweden on 12 December 1976, provided valuable insight into his fiction. Successful art, Bellow told the king and queen of Sweden, offers "true impressions"—a phrase Bellow borrowed from Marcel Proust to describe intuitions of a spiritual reality. Such glimpses give humans their sense of meaning, of goodness, of value. They move people to believe that "the good we hang onto so tenaciously . . . is no illusion." They offer refuge from the distractions and impurity of the world—they are the stillness achieved by Tommy Wilhelm, the joy experienced by Eugene Henderson, the reason art is essential even in an age of science. The "true impression" is personal, buried within the individual and expressed only within the language of art. It is a hint, a glimpse, a feeling—Bellow is careful not to claim too much—discovered by the person within the work.

In these remarks Bellow reveals the true subject of his fiction, which is not society, much as those readers who value Bellow's social observation might have expected. His Nobel address did not stress his Jewish identity either, in spite of the many readers who view him as the quintessential Jewish American writer. In what must be the penultimate explanation of his work to the world, Bellow says his subject is the private experience of the individual. That experience takes place in America and belongs to a Jew, true enough. But it also involves sensations that lie deeper than social or ethnic identity. Before 1976 the Bellow protagonist experienced a level of physical sensation so intense that it itself became the story. The antagonist in the Bellow novel is the "world" with all its sensation and distraction. The world is impure, unclean, oppressive. Bellow embodies it in a person (Allbee of *The Victim*) or an animal (the lion in *Henderson the Rain King*). He gives the sensory world a geography (in the streets of New York) or a psychology (Herzog's masochism) or an image (Joseph's dream in *Dangling Man*). Whatever form the world might take, however, the intensity of sensation that makes it oppressive also hints at a spiritual level of reality.

But by the 1970s, Bellow's fiction had changed. Herzog's shift from the private to the public describes the evolution of Bellow's art, even though it took some time to become apparent. After *Humbolt's Gift*, the intensity of the oppressive world diminished as Bellow viewed it more and more in social or historic terms. Bellow moved from the meaning of matter to questions of social policy, from the hidden psychology of his protagonist to the dynamics of a dinner party. He shifted from an early lyricism to something more external and prosaic and in doing so became a different kind of writer.

After the Nobel ceremony, Bellow and his wife lived in an apartment overlooking the lake on the north side of Chicago, close to her job at Northwestern University. To meet his classes at the University of Chicago, Bellow drove down the Outer Drive. At this time he also wrote *The Dean's December* (1982), which is nothing less than an indictment of American society—on all levels. The blacks in American cities are in truth doomed, Bellow says; the whites show only a cruel indifference. Public officials are guilty of hypocrisy, and those unofficial public figures who have the opportunity to study the problem—journalists and experts and professors—are guilty of jargon and cant. "Many American writers cross the bar in their 60's and 70's," Bellow has said, "and become Grand Old Men, gurus or bones of the Robert Frost variety. This is how society eases us out." Bellow's concern for America is deep, but his tone is anything but grandfatherly.

The novelist delivers his views in a book that seems at first to be typical Bellow: an intelligent but fumbling protagonist has the leisure to reflect upon a shocking event in the past, providing not only the drama of a mind in action but also a fascinating exercise in perspective. Albert Corde, a dean of students at a Chicago college, has accompanied his sensible astronomer wife, Minna, to Bucharest, where her mother lies ill in a hospital. Petty Communist officials make it difficult for Minna to visit the dying woman, who is also a Communist official now fallen from grace, and finally permit Minna only one visit—she must choose the time. Corde's wife must suffer the thought of her mother dying alone.

As Minna hurries about the city seeking help, Corde passes the time in a chilly apartment remembering the problems he has left behind in Chicago. He had published a set of articles in *Harper's* on the black underclass of the city and had insisted upon the prosecution of two blacks for the murder of a white student. In both instances he has taken a controversial stand in a way administrators dare not do. He has alienated whites by reminding them of the millions of people they have abandoned. He has alienated the blacks by insisting that however victimized they may be, they must be responsible for their actions. The blacks are "startled souls," Bellow told an interviewer; "They cannot be reasoned with or talked to about anything."

To the liberal, Corde sounds suspiciously racist. To the conservative, he stirs up muddy waters. And to his provost, Corde has violated academic decorum: how dare he, as an officer of the university, wade into a messy social issue? To everyone else Corde is an aesthete, arguing that the problem is one of perception, since people have learned to evade the truth, shutting off experience. Like the nineteenth-century realistic novelists, to whom Bellow has confessed a debt, Corde believes that facing the truth can be a rare (and perhaps heroic) accomplishment. His articles (like the novel itself) are meant "to recover the world that is buried under the debris of false description or nonexperience."

Bellow provides several different sources of narrative interest. As readers await the outcome of Minna's struggle to visit her mother, they also await the outcome of the trial in Chicago (Had the white student sought kinky sex? Had he asked for trouble?) and the effect of Corde's articles on his career. His job hangs by a thread. The novel moves from Romania to Chicago, sometimes in Corde's memory and at other times in his articles or letters sent from America. In the two cities, the style of administrators, the ways of death, and the kinds of parties (a Romanian tea and a high-rise celebration of a dog's birthday), the novel sets contrasts that reveal and dramatize each society. The communist society is cold and harsh, as dreary administrators parcel out pain. The capitalistic society is hot and chaotic, as the slums grow out of control. In both countries good people struggle to be decent. Romanian women support one another, remembering the old European culture, while black heroes such as Rufus Ridpath, a prison warden, and Toby Winthrop, the founder of a drug rehabilitation center, struggle to stop the people from brutalizing themselves and one another. Corde's articles in *Harper's* (which Bellow excerpts in the novel) provide riveting accounts of the underclass and the officials who work with it.

Yet, much as one appreciates Bellow's style and ideas, the novel is a disappointment to read—or so many critics felt, as they wrote their mixed reviews. Those who called the book a success confessed that it was a near thing. Everything depends on the protagonist, said Robert Towers in *The New York Times Book Review,* concluding that Corde does work as a character: "Sentence by sentence, page by page, Saul Bellow is simply the best writer that we have." Other reviewers objected that Corde does not have the independent existence of Bellow's other protagonists—he is clearly a spokesman for Bellow. Many critics gave Bellow high marks for struggling with this difficult but crucial subject, while some readers, most notably David Evanier in the *National Review,* were put off by Bellow's subject, which they felt was stale. Others complained that the book is too grim (Christopher Lehmann-Haupt wrote in *The New York Times* that reaching the ending was "like not hitting one's head against the wall anymore") or too talky or too full of scolding. Those who praised it were exhilarated: "He gives Corde's thoughts such palpable immediacy, such convincing shifts in tone," wrote Dean Flower in the *Hudson Review,* "that sometimes one can only revel in Bellow's gifts."

Him with His Foot in His Mouth and Other Stories (1984) turns from the public realm to the private or personal one. It is essentially Bellow's third book of stories, following *Seize the Day* and *Mosby's Memoirs,* and, like those volumes, is a loose collection of short stories made significant by Bellow's style. Although he returns to many of his old themes (which now appear to be obsessive), he manages to make them fresh or immediate.

The title story is a letter of apology from Professor Shawmut to Miss Rose, a librarian Shawmut had insulted thirty-five years previously. Shawmut, now old and sick, has not done well, he confesses to his ancient victim. His impetuous tongue has insulted many people. But he too has been a victim, having innocently trusted a strong-willed, amoral character—his brother, who cheated him. Thus, Bellow once again portrays an innocent or gentle character in conflict with a robust Machiavellian. In "What Kind of Day Did You Have?," the weakest of the five stories, an attractive young matron is used by a famous and powerful art critic; in "Zetland: By a Character Witness" (originally published in 1974 as part of a novel in progress), the title character marries in defiance of his angry, brooding father. In the best story of the volume, "A Silver Dish," Woody Selbst remembers his father stealing from the Christian woman who had befriended Woody, a crime that costs Woody his place in the seminary and a career as a Christian minister—a fact his Jewish father foresaw. And in the last story, Ijah Metzger is surrounded by equally willful and amoral "Cousins," all of whom want something from him.

Although the collection was a best-seller and much praised by reviewers, it embodies Bellow's new characteristic weakness: the dialogue in "What Kind of Day Did You Have?" is wooden and the events somewhat contrived. But the volume features Bellow's strengths as well. One who wishes to know what it is like to ride a Chicago trolley need only read "A Silver Dish." As John Updike wrote in *The New Yorker* (22 February 1982) of *The Dean's December,* Bellow "is not just a very good writer, he is one of the rare writers who when we read them feel to be taking mimesis a layer or two deeper than it has gone before. His lavish, rippling notations of persons, furniture, habiliments, and vistas awaken us to what is truly there."

Bellow's interest in the transcendent may be found in these stories (one character believes that "The Divine Spirit . . . has withdrawn in our time from the outer, visible world"). But perhaps the most notable point about this volume is Bellow's concern with emotion. More than anything else, these stories are studies of human feeling, exploring the danger of emotion as well as its strength. Shawmut's love of his brother causes him to give the businessman all his money; Woody's love of his father makes him trusting; and Ijah's deep feeling for his cousins (or at least their parents) makes him a soft touch. Again and again Bellow portrays characters bound by their emotions and vulnerable before people who do not feel. "Pop never had these groveling emotions," Woody thinks; "There was his whole superiority. Pop had no such feelings."

Bellow believes that such emotion is also salvation, however. The emotional characters are sustained by their love, rising above petty concerns. They learn to control their feelings, when that is appropriate, and also to trust them. Ijah in "Cousins" reads the work of philosopher Martin Heidegger on emotion and perception. Even hate, Ijah notes, "increases lucidity, it opens a man up; it makes him reach out and concentrates his being so that he is able to grasp himself." To another character (in the title story), "redemption from *mere* nature is the work of feeling and of the awakened eye of the Spirit."

Bellow and Tulcea divorced in 1986, the year before Bellow published *More Die of Heartbreak,* his weakest novel. The story centers on the relationship between the narrator, Kenneth Trachtenberg, an assistant professor of Russian literature, and his uncle, the famous botanist Benn Crader, who combines high-minded thought with a comic failure with women. Crader has married Matilda Layamon, a beautiful woman twenty years his junior, who proves to be more interested in money than her husband. After a complicated and farcical plot involving a real-estate swindle, Crader escapes to the Antarctic.

To summarize the events of the story, however, is to give the wrong impression, since the book consists largely of rumination. Although most reviewers paid Bellow the respect he was due as a distinguished writer, it was clear they disliked the novel. "The characters are lost in a fog of discourse," as James Atlas put it in *Saul Bellow:*

A Biography (2000). They are also full of anger and misogyny.

In truth, Bellow by 1986 was confronted as a writer by a great many difficulties. He faced so many obstacles, in fact, that only his habit of writing every morning, no matter what else was going on in his life, enabled him to stay productive. Once Bellow had won the Nobel Prize, he became an even more public figure, asked to give speeches all over the country. He did so reluctantly, though many of the invitations involved honors that he could not easily turn down. Whether it was a conference on his novels in Haifa, Israel, or a literary prize (such as the National Medal of Arts in 1988), or a library named after him in his hometown of Lachine, Bellow found himself playing a highly public and distracting role.

His notoriety hurt in another way. When a judge sentenced him to ten days in jail in a 1977 legal dispute with his third wife (a sentence overturned by an Illinois appeals court), it made all the papers—and so did his increasingly conservative views. Bellow resented the loss of the economically just, culturally serious society envisioned by intellectuals in the early 1960s. He also rejected the relativism of French Deconstruction, championing a humanism that appeared old-fashioned. In contrast to the ethos of the time, Bellow believed in the universality of certain values and the greatness of certain masterpieces. He insisted on high culture as a value in itself, equal to any political cause; and he believed in the efficacy of language and the human mind. All of these views made him appear elitist, misogynistic, and—when he asked, "Who is the Tolstoi of the Zulus?"—racist. No one remembered his plea in *The Dean's December* for racial justice.

Bellow's advancing years also affected his work. He had always written out of his own experience, even when he used events that happened to others, but that experience now belonged to an aging male ruminating on his past. The rumination might be witty and full of observation; it might offer a rare seriousness and originality; but it still lacked the immediacy of a dramatized event. Instead of using dialogue and analysis to support his plot, Bellow now used his plots as an excuse for the protagonist's rumination. As the years passed, Bellow also lost the stamina to continue producing daring and different works, choosing to write novellas instead of novels, for example, and moving from a lyrical to a more rambling, discursive—and so less demanding—mode.

In 1989 Bellow married Janis Freedman, a graduate student in the Committee on Social Thought, achieving the marital happiness that had so far eluded him. He also wrote two novellas, *A Theft* and *The Bellarosa Connection*. When Viking Press felt they were too short to publish in hardcover (and when magazines claimed they were too long for a periodical), Bellow arranged to publish them as Penguin paperbacks. In *A Theft*, a female narrator, Clara Velde, dotes on an older male, the powerful Washington lawyer Ithiel Regler. Bellow had used a female point of view before, in some of his stories, but critics now complained that Clara sounded too much like the author himself. Nor did they much care for the plot, in which an emerald ring stolen by the boyfriend of an au pair is eventually returned. The story is not so much dramatized as explained.

In *The Bellarosa Connection,* published seven months later, Bellow used an unnamed, elderly Jewish American narrator to recount the experience of Harry Fonstein, who had been saved from the Holocaust by the generosity of Broadway producer Billy Rose. When after the war Harry sought to thank Rose personally, the celebrity refused to meet with him. Harry's wife, Sorella, contrives to blackmail Rose into accepting the thanks of her husband, but when she changes her mind, claiming that Rose is not worth the effort, the story collapses. Some years later the narrator attempts to contact the Fonsteins, only to discover that they are dead.

A third novella, *The Actual,* published in 1997, is considered better written that the earlier two. (Its opening sentence, for example—"It's easy enough to see what people *think* they're doing"—is much smoother and more engaging than that of *A Theft*: "Clara Velde, to begin with what was conspicuous about her, had short blond hair, fashionably cut, growing upon a head unusually big"). In *The Actual,* Bellow tells the story of the love of Harry Trellman for his schooltime crush, Amy Wustrin. The couple is brought together by the elderly Sigmund Adletsky, and Harry proposes to Amy while they arrange the reburial of Amy's first husband, Jay.

Bellow had turned to the novella because he found it comfortable, but critics complained that these fictions were relatively minor. The reviewers used phrases such as "interim report" and "a novelist's sketchbook," often worrying that the central action of the story—so clearly based on some anecdote—was thin.

In 1991 Bellow published another collection of short fiction (including "Zetland: By a Character Witness" and *The Bellarosa Connection*). In the title story, "Something to Remember Me By," the aging Louie tells his son about a shameful incident in his youth. While his mother was dying of cancer, Louie had taken up with a prostitute, who had stolen his money and clothes. Louie earned carfare by taking care of a drunken Gentile (when he could have been consoling his mother), and when he reached home, he was gratified to receive a beating from his father, since it meant his mother was still alive. This story won praise from reviewers.

Bellow and his wife moved from Chicago to Boston in 1993 and spent increasing amounts of time in Vermont, enjoying the house they had built there. Bellow also worked on the novel he had promised to write about his close friend Allan Bloom, conservative professor of philosophy at the University of Chicago, who died in 1992.

In 1999 Janis gave birth to Bellow's fourth child—a daughter, Naomi Rose—and in 2000 Bellow published *Ravelstein,* his homage to Bloom. This full-length novel recounts Bloom's success in the classroom and with his surprise best-seller, *The Closing of the American Mind* (1987), as well as the fact that he was homosexual and his death may have been AIDS-related, which had been a secret before the book appeared. When people objected to Bellow's revelation, he found himself once again embroiled in a public controversy.

Ravelstein is remarkable for its vivid writing. Although Bellow had aged and had almost died from toxic seafood (as he recounts in the novel), he had not lost his eye for detail. The novel is discursive, with little plot and lots of conversation, as the two aging men discuss subjects ranging from Judaism to the nature of love, and yet Bellow offers dramatic scenes more compelling than those found in the novellas. He depicts Ravelstein's bald head and dominant manner, his love of gossip and expensive trinkets, his table manners, and his theory of eros. Readers are shown his apartment, where most of the novel takes place, with its exquisite carpets and first-class CD player, and told the story of his best-selling polemic, which made him rich and famous. Ravelstein is one of Bellow's "reality instructors," tutoring his innocent friend Chick (Bellow's alter ego, himself a successful writer) in the ways of the world.

Though it is clear that Chick, the narrator, loves Ravelstein, the reader finds it hard to share that affection. Bellow gives him a vivid presence, but he does not make him likable or convince readers that he is brilliant. When Ravelstein ruins a $4,000 sport coat shortly after buying it, the reader cringes at such waste. When neighbors in Ravelstein's apartment complain about his loud music, he refuses to turn it down (though he later soundproofs his apartment). Ravelstein is careless with money, honest with friends, and generous with his time. But he is also snobbish, gossipy, egotistical, and selfish. Both he and Chick seem to be overly impressed with wealth and luxury. Bloom had asked for an accurate portrait, nothing held back, which is what Bellow provides.

Ravelstein was well received by reviewers and soon found its way onto *The New York Times* best-seller list. The fact that Bellow at eighty-five had published such an accomplished book pleased almost everyone, especially since Bellow's other publications during this period were collections of previously published work: *It All Adds Up: From the Dim Past to the Uncertain Future* (1994), a collection of Bellow's essays; *Collected Stories* (2001); and *Bellow Novels 1944–1953* (2003), the Library of America edition of Bellow's first three novels.

Saul Bellow died on 5 April 2005 at home in Brookline, Massachusetts, at the age of eighty-nine. In a tribute article for *Slate* magazine (8 April 2005), several novelists and critics offered their thoughts on Bellow's work and influence. Philip Gourevitch said that Bellow "was, consciously, and in every sense, an original." Norman Rush pointed out, "What Saul Bellow achieved in his art he achieved without tricks: no magic realism, typographical jiggering, no inanimate objects as narrators. His expansive, detailed, widely allusive, radically traditional mode of attack is pure." Clive James commented, "Bellow could do every tone of the American voice, and somewhere underneath his range of mimicry he had the basic tone, the deep rhythm of the American demotic that could bring even his most directly expository prose to poetic life." In another article for *Slate* (6 April 2005), Christopher Hitchens wrote: "despite the ethnic emphasis of much of his work, Bellow will always attract readers by the scope and universality and humor of his themes."

Interviews:

Gordon Lloyd Harper, "Saul Bellow: An Interview," in *Writers at Work: The "Paris Review" Interviews,* third series (New York: Viking, 1967), pp. 175–196;

Joseph Epstein, "A Talk with Saul Bellow," *New York Times Book Review,* 5 December 1976, pp. 3, 92–93;

Gloria Cronin and Ben Siegal, eds., *Conversations with Saul Bellow* (Jackson: University Press of Mississippi, 1994).

Bibliographies:

B. A. Sokoloff and Mark Posner, *Saul Bellow: A Comprehensive Bibliography* (Folcroft, Pa.: Folcroft Library Editions, 1972);

Marianne Nault, *Saul Bellow: His Works and His Critics* (New York: Garland, 1977);

Robert G. Noreen, *Saul Bellow: A Reference Guide* (Boston: G. K. Hall, 1978).

Biography:

James Atlas, *Saul Bellow: A Biography* (New York: Random House, 2000).

References:

Gerhard Bach, ed., *The Critical Response to Saul Bellow* (Westport, Conn.: Greenwood Press, 1995);

Malcolm Bradbury, *Saul Bellow* (New York: Methuen, 1982);

Jean Braham, *A Sort of Columbus: The American Voyages of Saul Bellow's Fiction* (Athens: University of Georgia Press, 1984);

John J. Clayton, *Saul Bellow: In Defense of Man* (Bloomington: Indiana University Press, 1968);

Sarah Blacher Cohen, *Saul Bellow's Enigmatic Laughter* (Urbana: University of Illinois Press, 1974);

Robert Detweiler, *Saul Bellow: A Critical Essay* (Grand Rapids, Mich.: Eerdmans, 1967);

Robert R. Dutton, *Saul Bellow* (New York: Twayne, 1982);

Daniel Fuchs, *Saul Bellow: Vision and Revision* (Durham, N.C.: Duke University Press, 1984);

David D. Galloway, *The Absurd Hero in American Fiction: Updike, Styron, Bellow, Salinger* (Austin: University of Texas Press, 1966; revised, 1970);

Michael K. Glenday, *Saul Bellow and the Decline of Humanism* (New York: St. Martin's Press, 1990);

Lelia Goldman, *Saul Bellow's Moral Vision: A Critical Study of Jewish Experience* (New York: Irvington, 1983);

Eugene Hollahan, ed., *Saul Bellow and the Struggle at the Center,* Georgia State Library Studies, 12 (New York: AMS, 1996);

Peter Hyland, *Saul Bellow* (New York: St. Martin's Press, 1992);

Alfred Kazin, "My Friend Saul Bellow," *Atlantic Monthly* (January 1965);

Robert Kiernan, *Saul Bellow* (New York: Continuum, 1990);

Claude Levy, *Les Romans de Saul Bellow: Tactiques Narrative et Strategies Oedipiennes,* Etudes Anglo-Americaines, 5 (Paris: Klincksieck, 1983);

Irving Malin, *Saul Bellow's Fiction* (Carbondale: Southern Illinois University Press, 1969);

Malin, ed., *Saul Bellow and the Critics* (New York: New York University Press, 1967);

D. T. Max, "With Friends Like Saul Bellow," *New York Times Magazine* (16 April 2000) <http://partners.nytimes.com/library/magazine/home/20000416mag-ravelstein.html>;

Judie Newman, *Saul Bellow and History* (New York: St. Martin's Press, 1984);

Keith M. Opdahl, *The Novels of Saul Bellow: An Introduction* (University Park: Pennsylvania State University Press, 1967);

Ellen Pifer, *Saul Bellow Against the Grain* (Philadelphia: University of Pennsylvania, 1990);

M. Gilber Porter, *Whence the Power? The Artistry and Humanity of Saul Bellow* (Columbia: University of Missouri Press, 1974);

Eusebio Rodriques, *Quest for the Human: An Exploration of Saul Bellow's Fiction* (Lewisburg, Pa.: Bucknell University Press, 1981);

Earl Rovit, *Saul Bellow* (Minneapolis: University of Minnesota Press, 1967);

Rovit, ed., *Saul Bellow: A Collection of Critical Essays* (Englewood Cliffs, N.J.: Prentice-Hall, 1975);

Saul Bellow Journal (1981–);

Brigitte Scheer-Schaetzler, *Saul Bellow* (New York: Ungar, 1972);

Edmond Schraepen, *Saul Bellow and His Work* (Brussels: Vrije Universitet Brussel, 1978);

Tony Tanner, *Saul Bellow* (Edinburgh & London: Oliver & Boyd, 1965; New York: Barnes & Noble, 1965);

Stanley Trachtenberg, ed., *Critical Essays on Saul Bellow* (Boston: G. K. Hall, 1979);

Harriet Wasserman, *Handsome Is: Adventures with Saul Bellow* (New York: Fromm, 1997);

Jonathan Wilson, *Herzog: The Limit of Ideas,* Twayne's Masterworks Series, 46 (Boston: Twayne, 1990);

Wilson, *On Bellow's Planet: Readings From the Dark Side* (Rutherford, N.J.: Fairleigh Dickinson University Press, 1985).

Papers:

Except for that for *Mr. Sammler's Planet,* which is at the New York Public Library, Saul Bellow's manuscripts are at Regenstein Library of the University of Chicago. This extensive collection includes manuscripts from most of the novels, many different working drafts, letters, and memorabilia. Several manuscripts of *Seize the Day* are at the Harry Ransom Humanities Research Center, University of Texas at Austin.

1976 Nobel Prize in Literature Presentation Speech

by Dr. Karl Ragnar Gierow, of the Swedish Academy
(Translation from the Swedish)

Your Majesties, Your Royal Highnesses, Ladies and Gentlemen,

When Saul Bellow published his first book, the time had come for a change of climate and generation in American narrative art. The so-called hard-boiled style, with its virile air and choppy prose, had now slackened into an everyday routine, which was pounded out automatically; its rigid paucity of words left not only much unsaid but also most of it unfelt, unexperienced. Bellow's first work, *Dangling Man* (1944), was one of the signs portending that something else was at hand.

In Bellow's case emancipation from the previous ideal style took place in two stages. In the first he reached back to the kind of perception that had found its already classic guides in Maupassant, Henry James and Flaubert perhaps most of all. The masters he followed expressed themselves as restrainedly as those he turned his back on. But the emphasis was elsewhere. What gave a story its interest was not the dramatic, sometimes violent action but the light it shed over the protagonist's inner self. With that outlook the novel's heroes and heroines could be regarded, seen through and exposed, but not glorified. The anti-hero of the present was already on the way, and Bellow became one of those who took care of him.

Dangling Man, the man without a foothold, was thus a significant watchword to Bellow's writing and has to no small extent remained so. He pursued the line in his next novel, *The Victim* (1947) and, years later, with mature mastery in *Seize the Day* (1956). With its exemplary command of subject and form the last-mentioned novel has received the accolade as one of the classic works of our time.

But with the third story in this stylistically coherent suite, it is as if Bellow had turned back in order at last to complete something which he himself had already passed. With his second stage, the decisive step, he had already left this school behind him, whose disciplined form and enclosed structure gave no play to the resources of exuberant ideas, flashing irony, hilarious comedy and discerning compassion which he also knew he possessed and whose scope he must try out. The result was something quite new, Bellow's own mixture of rich picaresque novel and subtle analysis of our culture, of entertaining adventure, drastic and tragic episodes in quick succession, interspersed with philosophic conversation with the reader—that too very entertaining—all developed by a commentator with a witty tongue and penetrating insight into the outer and inner complications that drive us to act or prevent us from acting and that can be called the dilemma of our age.

First in the new phase came *The Adventures of Augie March* (1953). The very wording of the title points straight to the picaresque, and the connexion is perhaps most strongly in evidence in this novel. But here Bellow had found his style, and the tone recurs in the following series of novels that form the bulk of his work: *Henderson the Rain King* (1959), *Herzog* (1964), *Mr. Sammler's Planet* (1970) and *Humboldt's Gift* (1975). The structure is apparently loose-jointed but for this very reason gives the author ample opportunity for descriptions of different societies; they have a rare vigour and stringency and a swarm of colourful, clearly defined characters against a background of carefully observed and depicted settings, whether it is the magnificent facades of Manhattan in front of the backyards of the slums and semi-slums, Chicago's impenetrable jungle of resourceful businessmen intimately intertwined with obliging criminal gangs, or the more literal jungle, in the depths of Africa, where the novel *Henderson the Rain King,* the writer's most imaginative expedition, takes place. In a nutshell they are all stories on the move and, like the first book, are about a man with no foothold, but (and it is important to add this) a man who keeps on *trying to find* a foothold during his wanderings in our tottering world.

Even a few minutes' sketch of Bellow's many-sided writings should indicate where that foothold lies. It cannot be pointed out, as none of his protagonists reaches it. But during their escapades they are all on the run, not *from* something but *towards* something, a goal somewhere which will give them what they lack—firm ground under their feet. "I want, I want, I want!" Henderson exclaims, and sets off for an unknown continent. What his demands are he does not know; what he demands is to find out, and his own desire is the unknown continent. "A worthwhile fate," Augie March calls his goal. And Herzog, the restless seeker after truth, for his part tries out one phrasing after the other of what he means by "a worthwhile fate." At one point he says confidently that "the realm of facts and that of value are not eternally separated." The words are uttered in passing but are worth dwelling on, and if we think of them as coming from Bellow himself they are essential. Giving value a place side by side with palpable facts is, as regards literature, a definite departure from realism. As a philosophy it is a protest against the determinism that must make man unaccountable for his actions as well as inert or hostile to life, since it prevents him from feeling, choosing and acting himself. The awareness of a value, on the other hand, gives man freedom, thereby responsibility, thereby a desire for action and a faith in the future. That is why Bellow, never one to look through rose-coloured spectacles, is at heart an optimist. It is the light of that conviction which makes the facets of his writing sparkle. His "anti-heroes" are victims of constant disappointment, born to defeat without end, and Bellow (it cannot be over-emphasized) loves and is able to transform the fate they find worthwhile into superb comedies. But they triumph nonetheless, they are heroes nonetheless, since they never give up the realm of values in which man becomes human. And, as Augie March says, anyone can become alive to this fact at any moment, however unfortunate he may be, "if he will be quiet and wait it out."

The realm of facts and that of value—the very combination of words is reminiscent of a work by the philosopher Wolfgang Köhler, professor first at Göttingen, then in Berlin, finally at Princeton, to which he fled from the Nazis. Köhler's book is called *The Place of Value in a World of Facts* and lent its name to an international Nobel symposium in Stockholm some years ago, at which a lecture was given by E. H. Gombrich, disciple and younger friend of Köhler. He told of the latter's last night in Berlin, before the flight could be carried out. Köhler spent the slow hours with like-minded friends, and while they waited, wondering if a patrol would clamp up the stairs at the last moment and pound on the door with rifle butts, they played chamber music. "Such is," Gombrich remarked, "the place of value in a world of facts."

The threatened position of value between obtrusive realities has not escaped Bellow; that is what he is always writing about. But he does not think that either mankind's conduct or the explosive development of the sciences betoken a world catastrophe. He is an optimist-in-spite-of-all, and thus also an opposition leader of human kindness. Truth must out, of course. But it is not always hostile. Facing the truth is not necessarily the same as braving death. "There may be truths on the side of life," he has said. "There may be some truths which are, after all, our friends in the universe."

In an interview once Bellow described something of what happens when he writes. Most of us, he supposed, have a primitive prompter or commentator within, who from earliest years has been telling us what the real world is. He himself has such a commentator in him; he has to prepare the ground for him and take notice of what he says. One is put in mind of another man who went out into the highways and byways with his questions, taking notice of his inner voice: Socrates and his daemon. This introspective listening demands seclusion. As Bellow himself puts it, "Art has something to do with the achievement of stillness in the midst of chaos. A stillness which characterizes prayer, too, and the eye of the storm." This was what prevailed when Köhler played chamber music on his last night in Berlin while, aware of imminent disaster, "being quiet and waiting it out." It is there that the value and dignity of life and mankind have their sole haven, ever storm-lashed, and it is from that stillness that Saul Bellow's work, borne on the whirlwind of disquiet, derives its inspiration and strength.

Dear Mr. Bellow, it is my task and my great pleasure to convey to you the warm congratulations of the Swedish Academy and to ask you to receive from the hands of His Majesty the King the Nobel Prize for Literature of the year 1976.

[© The Nobel Foundation, 1976.]

Bellow: Banquet Speech

Bellow's speech at the Nobel Banquet, 10 December 1976:

Your Majesties, Your Royal Highnesses, Ladies and Gentlemen,

There are not many things on which the world agrees but everyone I think acknowledges the importance of a Nobel Prize. I myself take most seriously the Nobel Committee's recognition of the highest excellence in several fields and I accept the honor of this award with profound gratitude.

I have no very distinct sense of personal achievement. I loved books and I wrote some. For some reason they were taken seriously. I am glad of that, of course. No one can bear to be ignored. I would, however, have been satisfied with a smaller measure of attention and praise. For when I am praised on all sides I worry a bit. I remember the scriptural warning, "Woe unto you when all men shall speak well of you." Universal agreement seems to open the door to dismissal. We know how often our contemporaries are mistaken. They are not invariably wrong, but it is not at all a bad idea to remember that they can't confer immortality on you. Immortality—a chilling thought. I feel that I have scarcely begun to master my trade.

But I need not worry too much that all men will speak well of me. The civilized community agrees that there is no higher distinction than the Nobel Prize but it agrees on little else, so I need not fear that the doom of universal approval is hanging over me. When I publish a book I am often soundly walloped by reviewers—a disagreeable but necessary corrective to self-inflation.

When the Committee's choice was announced and the press rushed at me (a terrifying phenomenon!) and asked how I felt about winning the Nobel Prize in literature, I said that the child in me (for despite appearances there is a child within) was delighted, the adult skeptical. Tonight is the child's night entirely. On Sunday I will have some earnest things to say from the pulpit. Sunday is the best day for dark reflections but the child's claim to this Friday night will not be disputed.

[© The Nobel Foundation, 1976. Saul Bellow is the sole author of his speech.]

Bellow: Nobel Lecture, 12 December 1976

I was a very contrary undergraduate more than 40 years ago. It was my habit to register for a course and then to do most of my reading in another field of study. So that when I should have been grinding away at "Money and Banking" I was reading the novels of Joseph Conrad. I have never had reason to regret this. Perhaps Conrad appealed to me because he was like an American—he was an uprooted Pole sailing exotic seas, speaking French and writing English with extraordinary power and beauty. Nothing could be more natural to me, the child of immigrants who grew up in one of Chicago's immigrant neighborhoods of course!—a Slav who was a British sea captain and knew his way around Marseilles and wrote an Oriental sort of English. But Conrad's *real* life had little oddity in it. His themes were straightforward—fidelity, command, the traditions of the sea, hierarchy, the fragile rules sailors follow when they are struck by a typhoon. He believed in the strength of these fragile-seeming rules, and in his art. His views on art were simply stated in the preface to *The Nigger of the Narcissus*. There he said that art was an attempt to render the highest justice to the visible universe: that it tried to find in that universe, in matter as well as in the facts of life, what was fundamental, enduring, essential. The writer's method of attaining the essential was different from that of the thinker or the scientist. These, said Conrad, knew the world by systematic examination. To begin with the artist had only himself; he descended within himself and in the lonely regions to which he descended, he found "the terms of his appeal." He appealed, said Conrad, "to that part of our being which is a gift, not an acquisition, to the capacity for delight and wonder . . . our sense of pity and pain, to the latent feeling of fellowship with all creation—and to the subtle but invincible conviction of solidarity that knits together the loneliness of innumerable hearts . . . which binds together all humanity—the dead to the living and the living to the unborn."

This fervent statement was written some 80 years ago and we may want to take it with a few grains of contemporary salt. I belong to a generation of readers that knew the long list of noble or noble-sounding words, words like "invincible conviction" or "humanity" rejected by writers like Ernest Hemingway. Hemingway spoke for the soldiers who fought in the First World War under the inspiration of Woodrow Wilson and other rotund statesmen whose big words had to be measured against the frozen corpses of young men paving the trenches. Hemingway's youthful readers were convinced that the horrors of the 20th century had sickened and killed humanistic beliefs with their deadly radiations. I told myself, therefore, that Conrad's rhetoric must be resisted. But I never thought him mistaken. He spoke directly to me. The feeling individual appeared weak—he felt nothing but his own weakness. But if he accepted his weakness and his separateness and descended into himself intensifying his loneliness, he discovered his solidarity with other isolated creatures.

I feel no need now to sprinkle Conrad's sentences with skeptical salt. But there are writers for whom the Conradian novel—all novels of that sort—are gone forever. Finished. There is, for instance, M. Alain Robbe-Grillet, one of the leaders of French literature, a spokesman for "thingism"—*choseisme*. He writes that in great contemporary works, Sartre's *Nausea*, Camus' *The Stranger*, or Kafka's *The Castle*, there are no characters; you find in such books not individuals but—well, entities. "The novel of characters," he says, "belongs entirely in the past. It describes a period: that which marked the apogee of the individual." This is not necessarily an improvement; that Robbe-Grillet admits. But it is the truth. Individuals have been wiped out. "The present period is rather one of administrative numbers. The world's destiny has ceased, for us, to be identified with the rise and fall of certain men of certain families." He goes on to say that in the days of Balzac's bourgeoisie it was important to have a name and a character; character was a weapon in the struggle for survival and success. In that time, "It was something to have a face in a universe where personality represented both the means and the end of all exploration." But our world, he concludes, is more modest. It has renounced the omnipotence of the person. But it is more ambitious as well, "since it looks beyond. The exclusive cult of the 'human' has given way to a larger consciousness, one that is less anthropocentric." However, he comforts us, a new course and the promise of new discoveries lie before us.

On an occasion like this I have no appetite for polemics. We all know what it is to be tired of "characters." Human types have become false and boring. D. H.

Lawrence put it early in this century that we human beings, our instincts damaged by Puritanism, no longer care for, were physically repulsive to one another. "The sympathetic heart is broken," he said. He went further, "We stink in each other's nostrils." Besides, in Europe the power of the classics has for centuries been so great that every country has its "identifiable personalities" derived from Molière, Ramne, Dickens or Balzac. An awful phenomenon. Perhaps this is connected with the wonderful French saying. *"S'il y a un caractère, il est mauvais."* It leads one to think that the unoriginal human race tends to borrow what it needs from convenient sources, much as new cities have often been made out of the rubble of old ones. Then, too, the psychoanalytic conception of character is that it is an ugly rigid formation—something we must resign ourselves to, not a thing we can embrace with joy. Totalitarian ideologies, too, have attacked bourgeois individualism, sometimes identifying character with property. There is a hint of this in M. Robbe-Grillet's argument. Dislike of personality, bad masks, false being have had political results.

But I am interested here in the question of the artist's priorities. Is it necessary, or good, that he should begin with historical analysis, with ideas or systems? Proust speaks in *Time Regained* of a growing preference among young and intelligent readers for works of an elevated analytical, moral or sociological tendency. He says that they prefer to Bergotte (the novelist in *Remembrance of Things Past*) writers who seem to them more profound. "But," says Proust, "from the moment that works of art are judged by reasoning, nothing is stable or certain, one can prove anything one likes."

The message of Robbe-Grillet is not new. It tells us that we must purge ourselves of bourgeois anthropocentricism and do the classy things that our advanced culture requires. Character? "Fifty years of disease, the death notice signed many times over by the serious essayists," says Robbe-Grillet, "yet nothing has managed to knock it off the pedestal on which the 19th century had placed it. It is a mummy now, but one still enthroned with the same phony majesty, among the values revered by traditional criticism."

The title of Robbe-Grillet's essay is *On Several Obsolete Notions*. I myself am tired of obsolete notions and of mummies of all kinds but I never tire of reading the master novelists. And what is one to do about the characters in their books? Is it necessary to discontinue the investigation of character? Can anything so vivid in them now be utterly dead? Can it be that human beings are at a dead end? Is individuality really so dependent on historical and cultural conditions? Can we accept the account of those conditions we are so "authoritatively" given? I suggest that it is not in the intrinsic interest of human beings but in these ideas and accounts that the problem lies. The staleness, the inadequacy of these repels us. To find the source of trouble we must look into our own heads.

The fact that the death notice of character "has been signed by the most serious essayists" means only that another group of mummies, the most respectable leaders of the intellectual community, has laid down the law. It amuses me that these serious essayists should be allowed to sign the death notices of literary forms. Should art follow culture? Something has gone wrong.

There is no reason why a novelist should not drop "character" if the strategy stimulates him. But it is nonsense to do it on the theoretical ground that the period which marked the apogee of the individual, and so on, has ended. We must not make bosses of our intellectuals. And we do them no good by letting them run the arts. Should they, when they read novels, find nothing in them but the endorsement of their own opinions? Are we here on earth to play such games?

Characters, Elizabeth Bowen once said, are not created by writers. They pre-exist and they have to be *found*. If we do not find them, if we fail to represent them, the fault is ours. It must be admitted, however, that finding them is not easy. The condition of human beings has perhaps never been more difficult to define. Those who tell us that we are in an early stage of universal history must be right. We are being lavishly poured together and seem to be experiencing the anguish of new states of consciousness. In America many millions of people have in the last forty years received a "higher education"—in many cases a dubious blessing. In the upheavals of the Sixties we felt for the first time the effects of up-to-date teachings, concepts, sensitivities, the pervasiveness of psychological, pedagogical, political ideas.

Every year we see scores of books and articles which tell the Americans what a state they are in—which make intelligent or simpleminded or extravagant or lurid or demented statements. All reflect the crises we are in while telling us what we must do about them; these analysts are produced by the very disorder and confusion they prescribe for. It is as a writer that I am considering their extreme moral sensitivity, their desire for perfection, their intolerance of the defects of society, the touching, the comical boundlessness of their demands, their anxiety, their irritability, their sensitivity, their tender-mindedness, their goodness, their convulsiveness, the recklessness with which they experiment with drugs and touch-therapies and bombs. The ex-Jesuit Malachi Martin in his book on the Church compares the modern American to Michelangelo's sculpture, *The Captive*. He sees "an unfinished struggle to emerge whole" from a block of matter. The American "captive" is beset in his struggle by "interpretations, admonitions, forewarnings and descriptions of himself by the self-appointed prophets, priests, judges and prefabricators of his travail," says Martin.

Let me take a little time to look more closely at this travail. In private life, disorder or near-panic. In families—for husbands, wives, parents, children—confusion; in civic behavior, in personal loyalties, in sexual practices (I will not recite the whole list; we are tired of hearing it)—further confusion. And with this private disorder goes public bewilderment. In the papers we read what used to amuse us in science fiction—*The New York Times* speaks of death rays and of Russian and American satellites at war in space. In the November *Encounter* so sober and responsible an economist as my colleague, Milton Friedman, declares that Great Britain by its public spending will soon go the way of poor countries like Chile. He is appalled by his own forecast. What—the source of that noble tradition of freedom and democratic rights that began with Magna Carta ending in dictatorship? "It is almost impossible for anyone brought up in that tradition to utter the word that Britain is in danger of losing freedom and democracy; and yet it is a fact!"

It is with these facts that knock us to the ground that we try to live. If I were debating with Professor Friedman I might ask him to take into account the resistance of institutions, the cultural differences between Great Britain and Chile, differences in national character and traditions, but my purpose is not to get into debates I can't win but to direct your attention to the terrible predictions we have to live with, the background of disorder, the visions of ruin.

You would think that one such article would be enough for a single number of a magazine but on another page of *Encounter* Professor Hugh Seton-Watson discusses George Kennan's recent survey of American degeneracy and its dire meaning for the world. Describing America's failure, Kennan speaks of crime, urban decay, drug-addiction, pornography, frivolity, deteriorated educational standards and concludes that our immense power counts for nothing. We cannot lead the world and, undermined by sinfulness, we may not be able to defend ourselves. Professor Seton-Watson writes, "Nothing can defend a society if its upper 100,000 men and women, both the decision-makers and those who help to mould the thinking of the decision-makers, are resolved to capitulate."

So much for the capitalist superpower. Now what about its ideological adversaries? I turn the pages of *Encounter* to a short study by Mr. George Watson, Lecturer in English at Cambridge, on the racialism of the Left. He tells us that Hyndman, the founder of the Social Democratic Federation, called the South African war the Jews' war; that the Webbs at times expressed racialist views (as did Ruskin, Carlyle and T. H. Huxley before them); he relates that Engels denounced the smaller Slav peoples of Eastern Europe as counter-revolutionary ethnic trash; and Mr. Watson in conclusion cites a public statement by Ulrike Meinhof of the West German "Red Army Faction" made at a judicial hearing in 1972 approving of "revolutionary extermination." For her, German anti-Semitism of the Hitler period was essentially anticapitalist. "Auschwitz," she is quoted as saying, "meant that six million Jews were killed and thrown on the waste heap of Europe for what they were: money Jews (Geldjuden)."

I mention these racialists of the Left to show that for us there is no simple choice between the children of light and the children of darkness. Good and evil are not symmetrically distributed along political lines. But I have made my point; we stand open to all anxieties. The decline and fall of everything is our daily dread, we are agitated in private life and tormented by public questions.

And art and literature—what of them? Well, there is a violent uproar but we are not absolutely dominated by it. We are still able to think, to discriminate, and to feel. The purer, subtler, higher activities have not succumbed to fury or to nonsense. Not yet. Books continue to be written and read. It may be more difficult to reach the whirling mind of a modern reader but it is possible to cut through the noise and reach the quiet zone. In the quiet zone we may find that he is devoutly waiting for us. When complications increase, the desire for essentials increases too. The unending cycle of crises that began with the First World War has formed a kind of person, one who has lived through terrible, strange things, and in whom there is an observable shrinkage of prejudices, a casting off of disappointing ideologies, an ability to live with many kinds of madness, an immense desire for certain durable human goods—truth, for instance, or freedom, or wisdom. I don't think I am exaggerating; there is plenty of evidence for this. Disintegration? Well, yes. Much is disintegrating but we are experiencing also an odd kind of refining process. And this has been going on for a long time. Looking into Proust's *Time Regained* I find that he was clearly aware of it. His novel, describing French society during the Great War, tests the strength of his art. Without art, he insists, shirking no personal or collective horrors, we do not know ourselves or anyone else. Only art penetrates what pride, passion, intelligence and habit erect on all sides—the seeming realities of this world. There is another reality, the genuine one, which we lose sight of. This other reality is always sending us hints, which, without art, we can't receive. Proust calls these hints our "true impressions." The true impressions, our persistent intuitions, will, without art, be hidden from us and we will be left with nothing but a "terminology for practical ends which we falsely call life." Tolstoy put the matter in much the same way. A book like his *Ivan Ilyitch* also describes these same "practical ends" which conceal both life and death from us. In his final sufferings *Ivan Ilyitch* becomes an individual, a "character," by tearing down the concealments, by seeing through the "practical ends."

Proust was still able to keep a balance between art and destruction, insisting that art was a necessity of life, a great independent reality, a magical power. But for a long time art has not been connected, as it was in the past, with the main enterprise. The historian Edgar Wind tells us in *Art and Anarchy* that Hegel long ago observed that art no longer engaged the central energies of man. These energies were now engaged by science–a "relentless spirit of rational inquiry." Art had moved to the margins. There it formed "a wide and splendidly varied horizon." In an age of science people still painted and wrote poetry but, said Hegel, however splendid the gods looked in modern works of art and whatever dignity and perfection we might find "in the images of God the Father and the Virgin Mary" it was of no use: we no longer bent our knees. It is a long time since the knees were bent in piety. Ingenuity, daring exploration, freshness of invention replaced the art of "direct relevance." The most significant achievement of this pure art, in Hegel's view, was that, freed from its former responsibilities, it was no longer "serious." Instead it raised the soul through the "serenity of form above any painful involvement in the limitations of reality." I don't know who would make such a claim today for an art that raises the soul above painful involvements with reality. Nor am I sure that at this moment, it is the spirit of rational inquiry in pure science that engages the central energies of man. The center seems (temporarily perhaps) to be filled up with the crises I have been describing.

There were European writers in the 19th century who would not give up the connection of literature with the main human enterprise. The very suggestion would have shocked Tolstoy and Dostoevski. But in the West a separation between great artists and the general public took place. They developed a marked contempt for the average reader and the bourgeois mass. The best of them saw clearly enough what sort of civilization Europe had produced, brilliant but unstable, vulnerable, fated to be overtaken by catastrophe, the historian Erich Auerbach tells us. Some of these writers, he says, produced "strange and vaguely terrifying works, or shocked the public by paradoxical and extreme opinions. Many of them took no trouble to facilitate the understanding of what they wrote–whether out of contempt for the public, the cult of their own inspiration, or a certain tragic weakness which prevented them from being at once simple and true."

In the 20th century, theirs is still the main influence, for despite a show of radicalism and innovation our contemporaries are really very conservative. They follow their 19th-century leaders and hold to the old standard, interpreting history and society much as they were interpreted in the last century. What would writers do today if it would occur to them that literature might once again engage those "central energies," if they were to recognize that an immense desire had arisen for a return from the periphery, for what was simple and true?

Of course we can't come back to the center simply because we want to; but the fact that we are wanted might matter to us and the force of the crisis is so great that it may summon us back to such a center. But prescriptions are futile. One can't tell writers what to do. The imagination must find its own path. But one can fervently wish that they–that we–would come back from the periphery. We do not, we writers, represent mankind adequately. What account do Americans give of themselves, what accounts of them are given by psychologists, sociologists, historians, journalists, and writers? In a kind of contractual daylight they see themselves in the ways with which we are so desperately familiar. These images of contractual daylight, so boring to Robbe-Grillet and to me, originate in the contemporary world view: We put into our books the consumer, civil servant, football fan, lover, television viewer. And in the contractual daylight version their life is a kind of death. There is another life coming from an insistent sense of what we are which denies these daylight formulations and the false life–the death in life–they make for us. For it is false, and we know it, and our secret and incoherent resistance to it cannot stop, for that resistance arises from persistent intuitions. Perhaps humankind cannot bear too much reality, but neither can it bear too much unreality, too much abuse of the truth.

We do not think well of ourselves; we do not think amply about what we are. Our collective achievements have so greatly "exceeded" us that we "justify" ourselves by pointing to them. It is the jet plane in which we commonplace human beings have crossed the Atlantic in four hours that embodies such value as we can claim. Then we hear that this is closing time in the gardens of the West, that the end of our capitalist civilization is at hand. Some years ago Cyril Connolly wrote that we were about to undergo "a complete mutation, not merely to be defined as the collapse of the capitalist system, but such a sea-change in the nature of reality as could not have been envisaged by Karl Marx or Sigmund Freud." This means that we are not yet sufficiently shrunken; we must prepare to be smaller still. I am not sure whether this should be called intellectual analysis or analysis by an intellectual. The disasters are disasters. It would be worse than stupid to call them victories as some statesmen have tried to do. But I am drawing attention to the fact that there is in the intellectual community a sizeable inventory of attitudes that have become respectable–notions about society, human nature, class, politics, sex, about mind, about the physical universe, the evolution of life. Few writers, even among the best, have taken the trouble to re-examine these attitudes or orthodoxies. Such attitudes only glow more powerfully in Joyce or D. H. Lawrence than in the books of lesser men; they are everywhere and no one challenges them seriously. Since the Twenties, how many novelists have taken a second look at D. H. Lawrence, or argued a different view of sexual potency or the effects of industrial civilization on the instincts? Literature has for nearly a century used the same stock of ideas, myths, strategies. "The most serious essayists of the last fifty years," says Robbe-Grillet. Yes, indeed. Essay after essay, book after book, confirm the most serious thoughts—Baudelairian, Nietzschean, Marxian, Psychoanalytic, etcetera, etcetera—of these most serious essayists. What Robbe-Grillet says about character can be said also about these ideas, maintaining all the usual things about mass society, dehumanization and the rest. How weary we are of them. How poorly they represent us. The pictures they offer no more resemble us than we resemble the reconstructed reptiles and other monsters in a museum of paleontology. We are much more limber, versatile, better articulated, there is much more to us, we all feel it.

What is at the center now? At the moment, neither art nor science but mankind determining, in confusion and obscurity, whether it will endure or go under. The whole species—everybody—has gotten into the act. At such a time it is essential to lighten ourselves, to dump encumbrances, including the encumbrances of education and all organized platitudes, to make judgments of our own, to perform acts of our own. Conrad was right to appeal to that part of our being which is a gift. We must hunt for that under the wreckage of many systems. The failure of those systems may bring a blessed and necessary release from formulations, from an over-defined and misleading consciousness. With increasing frequency I dismiss as merely respectable opinions I have long held—or thought I held—and try to discern what I have really lived by, and what others live by. As for Hegel's art freed from "seriousness" and glowing on the margins, raising the soul above painful involvement in the limitations of reality through the serenity of form, that can exist nowhere now, during this struggle for survival. However, it is not as though the people who engaged in this struggle had only a rudimentary humanity, without culture, and knew nothing of art. Our very vices, our mutilations, show how rich we are in thought and culture. How much we know. How much we even feel. The struggle that convulses us makes us want to simplify, to reconsider, to eliminate the tragic weakness which prevented writers—and readers—from being at once simple and true.

Writers are greatly respected. The intelligent public is wonderfully patient with them, continues to read them and endures disappointment after disappointment, waiting to hear from art what it does not hear from theology, philosophy, social theory, and what it cannot hear from pure science. Out of the struggle at the center has come an immense, painful longing for a broader, more flexible, fuller, more coherent, more comprehensive account of what we human beings are, who we are, and what this life is for. At the center humankind struggles with collective powers for its freedom, the individual struggles with dehumanization for the possession of his soul. If writers do not come again into the center it will not be because the center is pre-empted. It is not. They are free to enter. If they so wish.

The essence of our real condition, the complexity, the confusion, the pain of it is shown to us in glimpses, in what Proust and Tolstoy thought of as "true impressions." This essence reveals, and then conceals itself. When it goes away it leaves us again in doubt. But we never seem to lose our connection with the depths from which these glimpses come. The sense of our real powers, powers we seem to derive from the universe itself, also comes and goes. We are reluctant to talk about this because there is nothing we can prove, because our language is inadequate and because few people are willing to risk talking about it. They would have to say, "There is a spirit" and that is taboo. So almost everyone keeps quiet about it, although almost everyone is aware of it.

The value of literature lies in these intermittent "true impressions." A novel moves back and forth between the world of objects, of actions, of appearances, and that other world from which these "true impressions" come and which moves us to believe that the good we hang onto so tenaciously—in the face of evil, so obstinately—is no illusion.

No one who has spent years in the writing of novels can be unaware of this. The novel can't be compared to the epic, or to the monuments of poetic drama. But it is the best we can do just now. It is a sort of latter-day lean-to, a hovel in which the spirit takes shelter. A novel is balanced between a few true impressions and the multitude of false ones that make up most of what we call life. It tells us that for every human being there is a diversity of existences, that the single existence is itself an illusion in part, that these many existences signify something, tend to something, fulfill something; it promises us meaning, harmony and even justice. What Conrad said was true, art attempts to find in the universe, in matter as well as in the facts of life, what is fundamental, enduring, essential.

[© The Nobel Foundation, 1976. Saul Bellow is the sole author of the text.]

Jacinto Benavente
(12 August 1866 – 14 July 1954)

Montserrat Alás-Brun
University of Florida

BOOKS: *Teatro fantástico* (Madrid: Tipografía Franco-Española, 1892; revised, Madrid: Fortanet, 1905);

Vilanos (Madrid: Fortanet, 1893);

Versos (Madrid: Tipografía Franco-Española, 1893);

Cartas de mujeres: Colecionadas, first series (Madrid: Tipografía Franco-Española, 1893);

El nido ajeno: Comedia en tres actos, en prosa (Madrid: R. Velasco, 1894);

Gente conocida: Escenas de la vida moderna: Divididas en cuatro actos (Madrid: Imp. y lit. del Asilo de Huérfanos, 1896);

El marido de la Téllez: Boceto de comedia en un acto (Madrid: Administración Lírico-Dramática, 1897);

La comida de las fieras: Comedia en tres actos y un cuadro (Madrid: B. Rodríguez, 1898);

La farándula: Comedia en dos actos (Madrid: Fortanet, 1898);

Figulinas (Madrid: Fortanet, 1898);

Viaje de instrucción: Zarzuela en un acto y cuatro cuadros (Madrid: R. Velasco, 1900);

Despedida cruel: Comedia en un acto (Madrid: R. Velasco, 1901);

La gobernadora: Comedia en tres actos (Madrid: R. Velasco, 1901);

Modas: Sainete en un acto y en prosa (Madrid: R. Velasco, 1901);

Lo cursi: Comedia de tres actos (Madrid: R. Velasco, 1901);

Cartas de mujeres, 2 volumes, second and third series (Madrid: Mazo, 1901, 1902);

El tren de los maridos: Juguete cómico en dos actos y en prosa (Madrid: R. Velasco, 1902);

Amor de amar: Comedia en dos actos y en prosa (Madrid: R. Velasco, 1902);

El primo Román: Comedia en tres actos (Madrid: R. Velasco, 1902);

Sacrificios: Drama en tres actos (Madrid: Viuda de Tello, 1902);

Alma triunfante: Drama en tres actos (Madrid: R. Velasco, 1902);

El criado de Don Juan (Madrid: Centro Editorial Hispano-Americano, 1902);

*Jacinto Benavente, 2 December 1922
(AP World Wide)*

El automóvil: Comedia en dos actos y en prosa (Madrid: R. Velasco, 1903);

La noche del sábado: Novela escénica en cinco cuadros (Madrid: R. Velasco, 1903);

El hombrecito: Comedia en tres actos, original (Madrid: R. Velasco, 1903);

Al natural: Comedia en dos actos y en prosa (Madrid: R. Velasco, 1904);

Teatro, 38 volumes (Madrid: Fortanet, 1904–1931)– comprises volume 1, *El nido ajeno, Gente conocida, El marido de la Téllez,* and *De alivio;* volume 2, *Don Juan, La farándula, La comida de la fieras,* and *Teatro feminista;* volume 3, *Cuento de amor, Operación quirúrgica, Despedida cruel, La gata de Angora, Viaje de instrucción,* and *Por la herida;* volume 4, *Modas, Lo cursi, Sin querer,* and *Sacrificios;* volume 5, *La gobernadora* and *El primo Román;* volume 6, *Amor de amar* and *El tren de los maridos;* volume 7, *Alma triunfante, El automóvil,* and *La noche del sábado;* volume 8, *Los favoritos, El hombrecito, Mademoiselle de Belle-Isle,* and *Por qué se ama;* volume 9, *Al natural, La casa de la dicha,* and *El dragón de fuego;* volume 10, *Richelieu, La princesa Bebé,* and *No fumadores;* volume 11, *Rosas de otoño* and *Buena boda;* volume 12, *El susto de la condesa, Cuento inmoral, La sobresalienta,* and *Los malhechores del bien;* volume 13, *Las cigarras hormigas* and *Más fuerte que el amor;* volume 14, *Manon Lescaut, Los búhos,* and *Abuela y nieta;* volume 15, *La princesa sin corazón, El amor asusta, La copa encantada,* and *Los ojos de los muertos;* volume 16, *La historia de Otelo, La sonrisa de Gioconda, El último minué, Todos somos unos,* and *Los intereses creados;* volume 17, *Señora ama, El marido de su viuda,* and *La fuerza bruta;* volume 18, *De pequeñas causas, Hacia la verdad, Por las nubes, De cerca,* and *¡A ver qué hace un hombre!* volume 19, *La escuela de las princesas, La señorita se aburre, El príncipe que todo lo aprendió en los libros,* and *Ganarse la vida;* volume 20, *El nietecito, La losa de los sueños,* and *La malquerida;* volume 21, *El destino manda, El collar de estrellas,* and *La verdad;* volume 22, *La propia estimación* and *Campo de armiño* [second edition]; volume 23, *La túnica amarilla* and *La ciudad alegre y confiada* [second edition]; volume 24, *El mal que nos hacen, Los cachorros,* and *Caridad;* volume 25, *Mefistófela* and *La Inmaculada de los Dolores;* volume 26, *La ley de los hijos, Por ser con todos leal, ser para todos traidor,* and *La honra de los hombres;* volume 27, *La vestal de occidente, Una señora,* and *Una pobre mujer;* volume 28, *La cenicienta, Más allá de la muerte,* and *Por qué se quitó Juan de la bebida;* volume 29, *Lecciones de buen amor, Un par de botas,* and *La otra honra;* volume 30, *La virtud sospechosa, Nadie sabe lo que quiere o el bailarín y el trabajador,* and *¡Si creerás tú que es por mi gusto!* volume 31, *Alfilerazos, Los nuevos yernos,* and *El suicidio de Lucerito;* volume 32, *La mariposa que voló sobre el mar, El hijo de Polichinela,* and *A las puertas del cielo;* volume 33, *La noche iluminada* and *Y va de cuento;* volume 34, *¡El demonio fue antes ángel!* and *¡No quiero, no quiero!* volume 35, *Pepa Doncel* and *Para el cielo y los altares;* volume 36, *Vidas cruzadas* and *Los amigos del hombre;* volume 37, *Los andrajos de la púrpura* and *De muy buena familia;* and volume 38, *Literatura* and *La melodía del Jazz-Band;*

Rosas de otoño (Madrid: Fortanet, 1905);

Teatro rápido (Barcelona: A. López, 1906)–comprises *El criado de Don Juan, Comedia italiana, Los primeros, Maternidad, Paternidad, Confidencias, Modernismo, Flirt, La cartera, En la playa, Bodas reales, Entre artistas, El encanto de una hora,* and *La senda del amor;*

Los ojos de los muertos: Drama en tres actos y en prosa (Madrid: R. Velasco, 1907);

Más fuerte que el amor (Barcelona, 1907);

Todos somos unos: Sainete lírico en un acto y en prosa (Madrid: R. Velasco, 1907);

La copa encantada: Zarzuela en un acto (Madrid: R. Velasco, 1907);

Los intereses creados: Comedia de polichinelas en dos actos, un prólogo y tres cuadros (Madrid: R. Velasco, 1907);

El marido de su viuda: Comedia en un acto (Madrid: R. Velasco, 1908);

La fuerza bruta: Comedia en un acto y dos cuadros, en prosa (Madrid: R. Velasco, 1908);

Los buhos: Comedia en tres actos y en prosa (Madrid: Sucesores de Hernando, 1908);

El amor asusta: Comedia en un acto y en prosa (Madrid: Sucesores de Hernando, 1908);

El teatro del pueblo (Madrid: Fernando Fe, 1909);

La señorita se aburre: Comedia en un acto basada en una poesía de Tennyson (Madrid: R. Velasco, 1909);

El príncipe que todo lo aprendió en los libros: Cuento en dos actos y siete cuadros (Madrid: Artes Gráficas Mateu, 1910);

Obras escogidas (Madrid: Biblioteca Renacimiento, 1910);

La escuela de las princesas: Comedia en tres actos y en prosa (Madrid: R. Velasco, 1910);

El dragón de fuego: Drama en tres actos y un epílogo, divididos en nueve cuadros (Barcelona: E. Domenech, 1910);

De sobremesa: Crónicas, 6 volumes (Madrid: Imp. Española, 1910–1916);

Palabras, palabras (Madrid: F. Fé, 1911);

La losa de los sueños: Comedia en dos actos, en prosa (Madrid: Nuevo Mundo, 1911);

Acotaciones (Madrid: Gráficas Mateu, 1914);

La gata de Angora: Comedia en cuatro actos (Madrid: R. Velasco, 1914);

Operación quirúrgica: Comedia en un acto y en prosa (Madrid: R. Velasco, 1914);

La malquerida: Drama en tres actos y en prosa (Madrid: Nuevo Mundo, 1914);

El collar de estrellas: Comedia en cuatro actos, en prosa (Madrid: R. Velasco, 1915);

Campo de armiño: Comedia en tres actos (Madrid: R. Velasco, 1916);

La ciudad alegre y confiada: Comedia en tres cuadros y un prólogo considerados como tres actos, 2ª parte de "Los intereses creados" (Madrid: R. Velasco, 1916);

Crónicas y diálogos (Valencia: J. Pallarés, 1916);

La propia estimación: Comedia en tres actos y en prosa (Madrid: R. Velasco, 1916);

Mis mejores escenas (Madrid: Hesperia, 1916);

La sobrasalienta: Sainete lírico (Madrid, 1916);

El mal que nos hacen: Comedia en tres actos y en prosa (Madrid: Sanz Calleja, 1917);

Los niños (Madrid: Hesperia, 1917);

Las mejores páginas de Jacinto Benavente, 2 volumes, compiled by Alejandro Miquis (Madrid: Sáenz de Jubera, 1917–1918);

Los cachorros: Comedia en tres actos, en prosa (Madrid: Sanz Calleja, 1918);

Mefistófela: Comedia-opereta en tres actos, en prosa, text by Benavente, music by Prudencio Muñoz (Madrid: Sanz Calleja, 1918);

La Inmaculada de los Dolores: Novela escénica en cinco cuadros, considerados tres actos (Madrid: Sanz Calleja, 1918);

Páginas selectas (San José, Costa Rica: Falcó & Borrasé, 1918)–comprises *El cantor de la miseria, Leyes santuarias, La rebeldía, El pan nuestro, Cartas de mujeres, Paternidad, Los intereses creados, La escuela de las princesas, El nido ajeno, El príncipe que todo aprendió en los libros,* and *La losa de los sueños;*

La princesa sin corazón: Cuento de hadas (Madrid: Biblioteca Estrella, 1918);

Conferencias (Madrid: Sucesores de Hernando, 1924)–comprises "La moral en el teatro," "Influencia del escritor en la vida moderna," "Filosofía de la moda," "Psicología del autor dramático," "Algunas mujeres de Shakespeare," "La mujer y su mayor enemigo," and "Algunas particularidades del teatro antiguo español";

Lecciones de buen amor (Madrid: R. Velasco, 1924);

Cuando los hijos de Eva no son los hijos de Adán, based on Margaret Kennedy's novel *The Constant Nymph* (Madrid: Hernando, 1931);

Pensamientos (Madrid: Hernando, 1931);

La moral del divorcio: Conferencia dialogada, dividida en tres partes (Madrid: Helénica, 1932);

La duquesa gitana: Comedia de magia en cinco actos divididos en diez cuadros (Madrid: Helénica, 1932);

Santa Rusia: Primera parte de una trilogía (Madrid: Helénica, 1932);

La verdad inventada: Comedia en tres actos (Madrid: Artes gráficas, Sucesores de Rivadeneyra, 1933);

El rival de su mujer: Comedia en tres actos y en prosa (Madrid: Artes gráficas, Sucesores de Rivadeneyra, 1933);

La novia de nieve: Comedia en un prólogo y tres actos (Madrid: Artes gráficas, Sucesores de Rivadeneyra, 1934);

El pan comido en la mano: Comedia en tres actos (Madrid: Artes gráficas, Sucesores de Rivadeneyra, 1934);

Memorias de un madrileño, puestas en acción en cinco cuadros (Madrid: Artes gráficas, Sucesores de Rivadeneyra, 1934);

Ni al amor ni al mar: Drama en cuatro actos y un epílogo (Madrid: Artes gráficas, Sucesores de Rivadeneyra, 1934);

"No juguéis con esas cosas": Comedia en tres actos y en prosa (Madrid: Artes gráficas, Sucesores de Rivadeneyra, 1935);

Cualquiera lo sabe: Comedia en tres actos y en prosa (Madrid: Artes gráficas, Sucesores de Rivadeneyra, 1935);

Los intereses creados. Señora ama (Madrid: Espasa-Calpe, 1938);

La malquerida y La noche del sábado (Madrid: Espasa-Calpe, 1939);

Plan de estudios para una escuela de arte escénico (Madrid: Aguilar, 1940);

Obras completas, 11 volumes (Madrid: Aguilar, 1942–1958);

Así piensan los personajes de Benavente, edited by José María Viqueira (Madrid: Aguilar, 1958);

Recuerdos y olvidos: Memorias (Madrid: Aguilar, 1959);

Las terceras de ABC, edited by Adolfo Prego (Madrid: Prensa Española, 1976).

Editions and Collections: *Los intereses creados. La malquerida,* edited by José Montero Padilla (Madrid: Castalia, 1996);

Los intereses creados, edited by Francisco Javier Díaz de Castro and Almudena del Olmo Iturriarte (Madrid: Espasa-Calpe, 1998);

Los intereses creados. La ciudad alegre y confiada, edited by Eduardo Galán (Madrid: Biblioteca Nueva, 1998);

Teatro fantástico. La sonrisa de Gioconda, edited by Javier Huerta Calvo and Emilio Peral Vega (Madrid: Espasa-Calpe, 2001);

Señora ama. La malquerida, edited by Virtudes Serrano (Madrid: Cátedra, 2002).

Editions in English: *The Smile of Mona Lisa: A Play in One Act,* translated by John Armstrong Herman (Boston: R. G. Badger, 1915);

Plays, 4 volumes, edited and translated by John Garrett Underhill (New York: Scribners, 1917–1924)–comprises volume 1, *His Widow's Husband, The Bonds of Interest, The Evil Doers of Good,* and *La Malquerida;* volume 2, *No Smoking, Princess Bebé, The Governor's Wife,* and *Autumnal Roses;* volume 3, *The Prince Who Learned Everything out of Books, Saturday Night, In the Clouds,* and *The Truth;* and volume 4, *The School of Princesses, A Lady, The Magic of an Hour,* and *Field of Ermine;*

At Close Range: A Comedy in One Act, translated by Underhill (New York: S. French, 1936).

PLAY PRODUCTIONS: *El nido ajeno,* Madrid, Teatro de la Comedia, 6 October 1894;

Gente conocida, Madrid, Teatro de la Comedia, 21 October 1896;

El marido de la Téllez, Madrid, Teatro Lara, 13 February 1897;

De alivio, Madrid, Teatro de la Comedia, 27 February 1897;

Don Juan, translated from Molière's play, Madrid, Teatro de la Princesa, 31 October 1897;

La farándula, Madrid, Teatro Lara, 30 November 1897;

La comida de las fieras, Madrid, Teatro de la Comedia, 7 November 1898;

Teatro feminista, text by Benavente, music by Pablo Barbero, Madrid, Teatro de la Comedia, 28 December 1898;

Cuento de amor, translated from William Shakespeare's *Twelfth Night,* Madrid, Teatro de la Comedia, 11 March 1899;

Operación quirúrgica, Madrid, Teatro Lara, 4 May 1899;

Despedida cruel, Madrid, Teatro Lara, 7 December 1899;

La gata de Angora, Madrid, Teatro de la Comedia, 31 March 1900;

Viaje de instrucción, text by Benavente, music by Amadeo Vives, Madrid, Teatro Eslava, 6 April 1900;

Por la herida, Barcelona, Teatro de Novedades, 15 July 1900;

Modas, Madrid, Teatro Lara, 18 January 1901;

Lo cursi, Madrid, Teatro de la Comedia, 19 January 1901;

Sin querer, Madrid, Teatro de la Comedia, 3 March 1901;

Sacrificios, Barcelona, Teatro de Novedades, 19 July 1901;

La gobernadora, Madrid, Teatro de la Comedia, 8 October 1901;

El primo Román, Saragossa, Spain, Teatro Principal, 12 November 1901;

Amor de amar, Madrid, Teatro de la Comedia, 24 February 1902;

¡Libertad! based on Santiago Rusiñol y Prats's play, Madrid, Teatro de la Comedia, 17 March 1902;

El tren de los maridos, Madrid, Teatro Lara, 18 April 1902;

Alma triunfante, Madrid, Teatro de la Comedia, 2 December 1902;

El automóvil, Madrid, Teatro Lara, 19 December 1902;

La noche del sábado, Madrid, Teatro Español, 17 March 1903;

Los favoritos, adapted from Shakespeare's *Much Ado About Nothing,* Seville, Teatro de San Fernando de Sevilla, 20 March 1903;

El hombrecito, Madrid, Teatro de la Comedia, 23 March 1903;

Por qué se ama, Madrid, Teatro Español, 26 October 1903;

Mademoiselle de Belle-Isle, based on Alexandre Dumas père's play, Valladolid, Spain, El Gran Teatro Calderón de la Barca, 29 October 1903;

Al natural, Madrid, Teatro Lara, 20 November 1903;

La casa de la dicha, Barcelona, Teatro de las Artes, 9 December 1903;

No fumadores, Madrid, Teatro Lara, 3 March 1904;

Richelieu, based on Edward Bulwer-Lytton's play, Mexico City, 15 March 1904;

El dragón de fuego, Madrid, Teatro Español, 16 March 1904;

Buena boda, adapted from Emile Augier's *Un beau marriage,* Madrid, 1905;

Rosas de otoño, Madrid, Teatro Español, 13 April 1905;

El susto de la condesa, Barcelona, Teatro Novedades, 18 July 1905;

Cuento inmoral, Barcelona, Teatro Novedades, 22 July 1905;

Manon Lescaut, by Benavente and Alfonso Danvila, adapted from Abbe Prevost's novel, Madrid, Teatro Español, 30 November 1905;

Los malhechores del bien, Madrid, Teatro Lara, 1 December 1905;

La sobresalienta, text by Benavente, music by Ruperto Chapí, Madrid, Teatro Español, 23 December 1905;

Las cigarras hormigas, Madrid, Teatro de la Comedia, 24 December 1905;

El encanto de una hora, Madrid, 30 December 1905;

Más fuerte que el amor, Madrid, Teatro Español, 22 February 1906;

La princesa Bebé, Madrid, 31 March 1906;

El amor asusta, Madrid, Teatro Lara, 10 January 1907;

Los búhos, Madrid, Teatro Lara, 8 February 1907;

Abuela y nieta, Madrid, Teatro Lara, 21 February 1907;

La copa encantada, adapted from Ludovico Ariosto's story, text by Benavente, music by Vicente Lleó, Madrid, Teatro de la Zarzuela, 16 March 1907;

Todos somos unos, Madrid, Teatro Eslava, 21 September 1907;

La historia de Otelo, Madrid, Teatro Apolo, 11 October 1907;

Los ojos de los muertos, Madrid, Teatro de la Princesa, 7 November 1907;

Los intereses creados, Madrid, Teatro Lara, 9 December 1907;

Señora ama, Madrid, Teatro de la Princesa, 22 February 1908;

De pequeñas causas . . . , Madrid, Teatro de la Princesa, 14 March 1908;

El marido de su viuda, Madrid, Teatro Príncipe Alfonso, 19 October 1908;

La fuerza bruta, Madrid, Teatro Lara, 10 November 1908;

Hacia la verdad, Madrid, Teatro del Príncipe Alfonso, 23 December 1908;

Por las nubes, Madrid, Teatro Lara, 20 January 1909;

De cerca, Madrid, Teatro Lara, 10 April 1909;

La escuela de las princesas, Madrid, Teatro de la Comedia, 14 October 1909;

El último minué, Madrid, 23 October 1909;

La señorita se aburre, adapted from Alfred Tennyson's poem, Madrid, Teatro del Príncipe Alfonso, 1 December 1909;

El príncipe que todo lo aprendió en los libros, Madrid, Teatro del Príncipe Alfonso, 20 December 1909;

Ganarse la vida, Madrid, Teatro del Príncipe Alfonso, 20 December 1909;

El nietecito, adapted from a Brothers Grimm story, Madrid, Teatro del Príncipe Alfonso, 27 January 1910;

Caridad, Madrid, 1911;

El criado de Don Juan, Madrid, 29 March 1911;

La losa de los sueños, Madrid, Teatro Lara, 9 November 1911;

En este Madrid, Madrid, 2 April 1913;

La malquerida, Madrid, Teatro de la Princesa, 12 December 1913;

El destino manda, translated from Paul Hervieu's *Le destin est maître,* Madrid, Teatro de la Princesa, 25 March 1914;

El collar de estrellas, Madrid, Teatro de la Princesa, 4 March 1915;

La propia estimación, Madrid, Teatro de la Comedia, 22 December 1915;

Campo de armiño, Madrid, Teatro de la Princesa, 14 February 1916;

La túnica amarilla, translated from George C. Hazelton Jr. and Harry Benrimo's play, Madrid, Teatro de la Princesa, 22 April 1916;

La ciudad alegre y confiada, Madrid, Teatro Lara, 18 May 1916;

El mal que nos hacen, Madrid, Teatro de la Princesa, 23 March 1917;

Los cachorros, Madrid, Teatro de la Princesa, 8 March 1918;

La Mefistófela, text by Benavente, music by Prudencio Muñoz, Madrid, Teatro Reina Victoria, 29 April 1918;

La Inmaculada de los Dolores, Madrid, Teatro Lara, 30 April 1918;

La ley de los hijos, Madrid, Teatro de la Zarzuela, 23 December 1918;

La fuerza bruta, text by Benavente, music by Federico Chaves, Madrid, 1919;

La vestal de occidente, Madrid, Teatro de la Princesa, 2 March 1919;

Por ser con todos leal, ser para todos traidor, Madrid, Teatro del Centro, 5 March 1919;

La honra de los hombres, Madrid, Teatro Lara, 2 May 1919;

El audaz, adapted from Benito Pérez Galdós's novel, Madrid, Teatro Español, 6 December 1919;

La cenicienta, adaptation of *Cinderella,* Madrid, Teatro Español, 20 December 1919;

Y va de cuento, Madrid, Teatro de la Princesa, 22 December 1919;

Una señora, Madrid, Teatro del Centro, 2 January 1920;

Una pobre mujer, Madrid, Teatro de la Princesa, 3 April 1920;

Más allá de la muerte, Buenos Aires, 1920;

Por qué se quitó Juan de la bebida, Montevideo, Teatro Solís, 30 August 1922;

Lecciones de buen amor, Madrid, Teatro Español, 2 April 1924;

Un par de botas, Madrid, Teatro de la Princesa, 25 May 1924;

La otra honra, Madrid, Teatro Lara, 19 September 1924;

La virtud sospechosa, Madrid, Teatro Fontalba, 20 October 1924;

¡Si creerás tú que es por mi gusto! Madrid, 1925;

Nadie sabe lo que quiere, o El bailarín y el trabajador, Madrid, Teatro Cómico, 14 March 1925;

Alfilerazos, Buenos Aires, Teatro Avenida, 18 June 1925; Madrid, Teatro del Centro, 5 October 1925;

El suicidio de Lucerito, Madrid, Teatro Alcázar, 17 July 1925;

Los nuevos yernos, Madrid, Teatro Fontalba, 2 October 1925;

La mariposa que voló sobre el mar, Madrid, Teatro Fontalba, 22 December 1926;

El hijo de Polichinela, Madrid, 16 April 1927;

La noche iluminada, Madrid, Teatro Fontalba, 22 December 1927;

El demonio fue antes ángel, Madrid, Teatro Calderón, 18 February 1928;

¡No quiero, no quiero! Madrid, Teatro Fontalba, 10 March 1928;

Pepa Doncel, Madrid, Teatro Calderón, 21 November 1928;

Vidas cruzadas, Madrid, Teatro de Reina Victoria, 30 March 1929;

Los amigos del hombre, Madrid, Teatro Avenida, 27 October 1930;

Los andrajos de la púrpura, Madrid, Teatro Muñoz Seca, 6 November 1930;

De muy buena familia, Madrid, Teatro Muñoz Seca, 11 March 1931;

Literatura, Madrid, Teatro Alcázar, 14 April 1931;

La melodía del Jazz-Band, Madrid, Teatro Fontalba, 30 October 1931;

Cuando los hijos de Eva no son los hijos de Adán, based on Margaret Kennedy's novel *The Constant Nymph,* Madrid, Teatro Calderón, 5 November 1931;

Santa Rusia, Madrid, Teatro Beatriz, 6 October 1932;

La duquesa gitana, Madrid, Teatro Fontalba, 28 October 1932;

La moral del divorcio, Madrid, Teatro Avenida, 4 November 1932;

La verdad inventada, Madrid, Teatro Lara, 27 October 1933;

El rival de su mujer, Buenos Aires, Teatro Odeón, 1933;

El pan comido en la mano, Madrid, Teatro Fontalba, 12 January 1934;

Ni al amor ni al mar, Madrid, Teatro Español, 19 January 1934;

Memorias de un madrileño, Madrid, Teatro Lara, 8 November 1934;

La novia de nieve, Madrid, Teatro Español, 29 November 1934;

"No juguéis con esas cosas," Madrid, Teatro Eslava, 18 January 1935;

Cualquiera lo sabe, Madrid, Teatro de la Comedia, 13 February 1935;

Lo increíble, Madrid, Teatro de la Comedia, 25 October 1940;

Aves y pájaros, Madrid, Teatro Lara, 30 October 1940;

Abuelo y nieto, San Sebastián, Spain, Teatro del Príncipe, 29 August 1941;

Y amargaba, Madrid, Teatro de la Zarzuela, 19 November 1941;

La última carta, Madrid, Teatro Alcázar, 9 December 1941;

La honradez de la cerradura, Madrid, Teatro Español, April 1942;

Al fin, mujer, San Sebastián, Spain, Teatro del Príncipe, 13 September 1942;

¡Hija del alma! Madrid, Teatro Lara, 17 September 1942;

La enlutada, Saragossa, Spain, Teatro Principal, 6 October 1942;

El demonio del teatro, Madrid, Teatro Cómico, 28 October 1942;

La culpa es tuya, San Sebastián, Spain, Teatro de la Zarzuela, 16 December 1942;

Los niños perdidos en la selva, San Sebastián, Spain, Teatro Principal, 14 January 1944;

Don Magín, el de las magias, Barcelona, Teatro Barcelona, 16 March 1944;

Espejo de grandes, Teatro Escuela de Arte, Penal del Dueso, Cantabria, Spain, 12 October 1944; Madrid, Teatro Lara, 11 June 1946;

Nieve en mayo, Madrid, Teatro de la Comedia, 19 January 1945;

La ciudad doliente, Madrid, Teatro de la Comedia, 14 April 1945;

Titania, Buenos Aires, 25 September 1945;

La infanzona, Buenos Aires, 6 December 1945; Madrid, 10 January 1947;

Al servicio de su Majestad Imperial, Madrid, 1947;

Abdicación, Madrid, Teatro Lara, 27 March 1948;

Divorcio de almas, Madrid, Teatro Fontalba, 30 September 1948;

Adoración, Madrid, Teatro Cómico, 3 December 1948;

Al amor hay que mandarlo al colegio, Madrid, Teatro Lara, 29 September 1950;

Su amante esposa, Madrid, Teatro Infanta Isabel, 20 October 1950;

Tú una vez y el diablo diez, Valladolid, Spain, Teatro Lope de Vega, 23 October 1950;

Mater Imperatrix, Madrid, Teatro de la Comedia, 29 November 1950;

La vida en verso, Madrid, Teatro Infanta Isabel, 9 November 1951;

Ha llegado Don Juan, Barcelona, Teatro Comedia, 12 April 1952;

El lebrel del cielo, inspired by Francis Thompson's *The Hound of Heaven,* Madrid, Teatro Calderón, 25 April 1952;

Servir, Madrid, Teatro Nacional María Guerrero, 22 January 1953;

El alfiler en la boca, Madrid, Teatro Infanta Isabel, 13 February 1953;

Almas prisioneras, Madrid, Teatro Alvarez Quintero, 26 February 1953;

Caperucita asusta al lobo, Madrid, Teatro Infanta Isabel, 23 September 1953;

Hijos, padres de sus padres, Madrid, Teatro Lara, 11 February 1954;

El marido de bronce, Madrid, Teatro Infanta Isabel, 23 April 1954;

Por salvar su amor, Madrid, Teatro Calderón, 2 November 1954;

El bufón de Hamlet, Madrid, Teatro Goya, 1958.

OTHER: Lope de Vega, *Four Plays,* introduction by Benavente, translated by John Garrett Underhill (New York: Scribners, 1936).

TRANSLATIONS: William Shakespeare, *Cuento de amor: Comedia fantástica de Shakespeare* (Madrid: Revista Nueva, 1899);

Alexandre Dumas *père*, *Mademoiselle de Belle-Isle: Comedia en cinco actos y en prosa de Alejandro Dumas (padre)* (Madrid: R. Velasco, 1903);

Molière, *Don Juan: Comedia de Molière en cinco actos* (Madrid: Fortanet, 1904);

Paul Hervieu, *El destino manda: Drama en dos actos, original y en prosa* (Madrid: R. Velasco, 1914);

George C. Hazelton Jr. and Harry Benrimo, *La túnica amarilla: Leyenda china en tres actos, en prosa* (Madrid: Sanz Calleja, 1916).

Jacinto Benavente, the author of more than 170 plays, dominated the Spanish stage for half a century. He achieved fame and official recognition in his long career, but also had many detractors. After he received the Nobel Prize in Literature in 1922, his place in the literary canon was firmly established; but the decline of his creativity had already started by then and became more pronounced in the following decades. For a large part of the twentieth century, he was simultaneously the most revered and the most criticized playwright in Spain. He had great success with the Spanish public in commercial theaters and inspired many imitators; but despite his popularity and influence, a large group of respected intellectuals and critics maintained negative views about his plays and his impact on contemporary Spanish theater. These critics, including Ramón Pérez de Ayala, considered Benavente's work outdated and unworthy of praise. Pérez de Ayala later rectified his position, but other critics still blamed Benavente for the perceived crisis of Spanish theater. They believed that he was too self-complacent because of his success with the Spanish middle-class public. After being attacked by critics and almost forgotten by the theatergoing public since the 1970s, Benavente's disputed place in the canon has been seriously revised by scholars. Since the 1990s, his most important plays and his early works have reappeared in critical editions, and a younger generation of academics is evaluating his role in the renovation of the Spanish stage from new perspectives.

Jacinto Benavente y Martínez was born in Madrid on 12 August 1866. He was the youngest child of Venancia Martínez and Mariano Benavente, a respected doctor who is considered a pioneer in the field of pediatric medicine in Spain. The couple, who had two more sons, enjoyed a privileged place in Madrid society because of the doctor's reputation. Among his patients and friends were well-known actors and writers, including the first Spanish winner of the Nobel Prize in Literature, dramatist José Echegaray. The family had the opportunity to attend premieres and go to the theaters regularly.

Young Jacinto learned how to read at home and was ready to start his primary education at age five. Beginning in 1871, he attended Colegio San José, a municipal school affiliated with San Isidoro High School. During his childhood and early teenage years, he built several toy theaters and performed puppet shows for his friends and neighbors and the household maids. His first play was a fairy tale in one act, "El gato pardo" (The Leopard). He wrote and performed more plays for his puppet theater, such as the spectacle "Los cazadores de leones" (The Lion Hunters) and an adaptation of *Notre-Dame de Paris* (1831, translated as *The Hunchback of Notre Dame*, 1833) by Victor Hugo. He even wrote an ambitious full-length play, "Las mil y una noches" (Arabian Nights), in his last year in high school, but it was never produced and none of these adolescent works were ever published. Besides original plays, he memorized and recited for his admiring audience scenes from classic and contemporary authors, including William Shakespeare, Molière, Friedrich Schiller, and the Spanish playwrights Lope de Vega, Pedro Calderón de la Barca, and José Zorrilla.

Benavente started to go to the theaters with his family at an early age; later on he insisted that he could vividly remember all the plays and musicals he attended between ages four and twelve. He also read plays by both Spanish and foreign authors, especially Shakespeare, whom his father admired greatly. Because the young man studied French, English, Italian, and some Latin in his high-school years, he was able to read many plays in their original languages. He read *Hamlet* (circa 1600–1601) in translation at first, in Spanish and French, but was able to read it in English at age sixteen. He also attended the performances of Echegaray's plays, including his biggest success, *El gran Galeoto* (The Great Galeoto), produced in 1881, when Benavente was fifteen. He said in his memoirs (published in volume eleven of his *Obras completas* [Complete Works], 1942–1958) that he had always admired Echegaray, who later became unpopular with the young intellectuals of the early twentieth century because they considered him outdated.

Benavente's father was concerned that his youngest son spent too much time and energy rehearsing and performing plays instead of studying, so he told him to stop these activities. Benavente was disappointed, since he wanted to be an actor. He confessed in his memoirs that acting was "toda la ilusión de mi vida" (the big dream of my life). He was so affected by his father's decision that he became depressed, and he considered that moment the end of his childhood. His father, who wanted him to become an engineer, convinced him that he should attend college. He enrolled in the University of Madrid in 1882 but was not interested in academics. He often skipped class, was not a brilliant student, and switched from engineering to law after the first year because he disliked mathematics. When his father died in 1885, Benavente dropped out of college without hesitation and devoted himself to reading, writing, and traveling abroad between 1885 and 1892. His family's position allowed him to enjoy a comfortable life and avoid the precarious bohemian lifestyle that characterized other writers of the late nineteenth century.

Benavente attended the *tertulia literaria* (literary gatherings, with poetry readings and informal book discussions) at the Café Iberia, where he met established writers such as the poet Gaspar Núñez de Arce. He later joined a circle of young intellectuals who were highly critical of the status quo. He spent most of his time writing comedies and poems at home and reading the classics: Homer, Aeschylus, Virgil, Dante, Miguel de Cervantes, Alfred de Musset, and Giacomo Leopardi. He also read the works of contemporary Spanish writers such as the novelists Benito Pérez Galdós and Juan Valera, and the poets Ramón de Campoamor and Núñez de Arce. One of Benavente's older brothers, Mariano, encouraged him to continue writing.

Benavente had a close relationship with his mother, with whom he lived as an adult until her death in 1922. It appears that he never had a significant emotional relationship with anyone else. He prided himself on being a confirmed bachelor. Biographer Ángel Lázaro states that "Nadie le ha conocido novia en su juventud, y él niega que haya estado enamorado jamás" (No one knows of any sweetheart from his youth, and he denies that he has ever been in love). Lázaro goes on to assert that no one has ever been able to identify any woman as Benavente's lover, and no actress ever bragged of being the object of his affections.

Critics such as Eduardo Galán have wondered about the fact that there is so little available information about the private life of such a famous writer. Even in his memoirs, Benavente mostly tells anecdotes of the people he knew and the city where he lived, and only talks in detail about his childhood. There have always been persistent but unconfirmed rumors, mostly in theatrical circles, about his alleged homosexuality. When he was told about rumors regarding "ciertas anomalías fisiológicas" (certain physiological anomalies), the writer simply shrugged; he also ignored malicious whisperings about his sexual orientation. Lázaro wonders if Benavente is "el hombre despreocupado que quiere asustar a los moralistas o el escéptico que se considera más allá del Bien y del Mal" (the carefree man who wants to scare moralists or the skeptic who considers himself beyond Good and Evil). Homosexuality was taboo in Spanish society at that time and, for a large part of the twentieth century, was penalized as a crime.

Traditionally, Benavente's biographers have avoided the topic, for the most part, or addressed it in a rather indirect manner. Only late-twentieth-century studies approach the subject more openly, but they, with few exceptions, reach no definite conclusions. Since the late 1990s, there have been alternate readings of his work, uncovering homoerotic currents. Gérard Dufour was the first one to discuss the ambiguities in Leandro, one of the main characters in Benavente's most famous play, *Los intereses creados* (1907, The Bonds of Interest). Others have perceived homoerotic undertones in the friendship between Leandro and Crispín in that play. Echoing the opinion of the critics Francisco Javier Díaz de Castro and Almudena del Olmo Iturriarte in a 1998 edition of *Los intereses creados,* Javier Huerta Calvo and Emilio Peral Vega assert in a 2003 article that there are many references to homosexuality in Benavente's life as well as in his plays. They state that Benavente's short story from 1938, "Ganimedes" (included in *Obras completas*), a sensual retelling of the classic myth of Ganymede, the handsome ephebus who became Zeus's lover, offers a hidden confession of his alleged tendencies.

Huerta Calvo and Peral Vega also find manifestations of "ideales heterodoxos en materias de amor" (heterodox ideals regarding love) in other works by Benavente, mostly in his early plays, published in the volume *Teatro fantástico* (1892, Fantasy Theater). They see these ideals at work particularly in *Cuento de primavera* (Spring Story), an unproduced work that seems to follow the spirit of Shakespeare's comedies. Benavente was familiar with sixteenth- and seventeenth-century classic plays with cross-dressing roles from England and Spain, and they may have inspired him to portray characters of ambiguous sexual identity in his early works and beyond. In *Cuento de primavera,* one of the main characters is Ganimedes (Ganymede), a poet and page in the royal court who is described with androgynous characteristics but assumed to be male. After some ambiguous situations involving mistaken identities and cross-dressing, the ending of the play seems to reinforce traditional expectations about heterosexual attraction, but the plot twists are loaded with destabilizing ironies. Adding another layer to the ambiguities of the play, Ganimedes's role is supposed to be played by an actress, as revealed in the prologue.

Teatro fantástico was a compilation of unproduced short plays published in 1892 and again in 1905 in a revised, expanded edition. Besides *Cuento de primavera,* the 1892 edition also included three more plays: *El encanto de una hora* (The Magic of an Hour), *Amor de artista* (Artist's Love), and *Los favoritos* (The Favorites). The latter, based on Shakespeare's play *Much Ado About Nothing* (circa 1598–1599), was produced in Seville in 1903. *El encanto de una hora* was produced in Madrid in 1905, shortly after the second edition was published.

The other two plays from the first edition of *Teatro fantástico* have never been performed. All of them have one act only, except *Cuento de primavera*, which is a two-act comedy. The 1905 edition omitted *Los favoritos* and added two more one-act plays: *Comedia italiana* (Italian Comedy) and *El criado de Don Juan* (Don Juan's Servant). In addition, it included a puppet play, *La senda del amor* (The Path of Love); the plot for a mime's act, *La blancura de Pierrot* (The Whiteness of Pierrot); and a dialogue, *Modernismo* (Modernism). Of the new plays added in 1905, only *El criado de Don Juan* was ever produced; it was performed in Madrid in 1911.

Most critics tend to consider *El nido ajeno* (Another's Nest), produced in 1894, as the beginning of Benavente's career as a dramatist, while dismissing or ignoring his early plays entirely. One of the few exceptions among the critics of his time was the Nicaraguan poet Rubén Darío, who, in an article published in *España Contemporánea*, praised *Teatro fantástico* as an outstanding example of "la joven literatura" (the young literature) and even compared it to Shakespeare's *The Tempest* (1611) and *A Midsummer Night's Dream* (circa 1595–1596). Huerta Calvo and Peral Vega have paid close attention to Benavente's fantasy plays, which they consider highly innovative and an important part of modernist theater. They view *Teatro fantástico* as the foundation of symbolist theater in Spain, which had an important influence on the most innovative Spanish playwrights of the twentieth century, such as Federico García Lorca and Ramón del Valle-Inclán. In their view, Benavente anticipates avant-garde trends later developed in Europe by such writers as Gordon Craig. This anticipation is especially apparent in *El encanto de una hora,* with its antirealistic premise and its explicit reaction against a mimetic imitation of ordinary life.

In 1893 Benavente expanded his literary output and published three books: a collection of sketches, *Vilanos* (The Down of the Thistle), reprinted in 1905; *Versos* (Verses); and a series of fictional letters, *Cartas de mujeres* (Women's Letters), which became a commercial success and was also praised by critics; the second and third series followed in 1901 and 1902. His early poems from *Versos* have been consistently considered mediocre, even by the author himself. He never published another poetry book during his lifetime, although more than one hundred poems, found among his papers, appeared posthumously in the appendix to volume ten of *Obras completas*. Marcelino C. Peñuelas finds them similar to Benavente's early *Versos* in their themes, tone, and quality.

Benavente's first experiences with the stage were far more important for his future career as a respected writer than his early experiments in poetry, which he soon abandoned. In 1890 he finally realized his lifelong dream and joined the María Tubau theater company as an actor. There he met La Bella Geraldine (Geraldine the Beautiful), a strikingly attractive English actress and circus artist who was popular with Madrid audiences. He later toured several provincial towns in Spain as an impresario of her show. His fascination for the circus world is reflected in the settings of several plays, such as *La noche del sábado* (1903, Saturday Night), *Los cachorros* (1918, The Cubs), and *La fuerza bruta* (1919, Brute Force).

Benavente loved the backstage atmosphere. In an interview quoted by Lázaro, he confessed to a journalist that if he could not have been a playwright, he would have liked to have been a full-time actor, impresario, or stagehand. When he was a well-known playwright, he still enjoyed interpreting roles in his own plays; he liked to play Crispín's role in *Los intereses creados,* for instance. Occasionally, he also played parts in productions of other authors' plays, such as the leading role in a production of Zorrilla's *Don Juan Tenorio* (1844), a famous drama that was performed annually in Spain in early November. In 1899 he performed a role in the premiere of *Cenizas* (Ashes), the first play produced by Valle-Inclán, who eventually replaced Benavente as the major figure in the canon of the early-twentieth-century theater in Spain.

In the late years of the nineteenth century, Benavente participated actively in the intellectual life of Madrid and joined the writers who were associated with the modernist movement and the so-called Generation of 1898. He collaborated on the modernist journal *Helios* and attended the *tertulia literaria* of Café de Madrid, along with well-known writers such as Darío, Valle-Inclán, Gregorio Martínez Sierra, and the novelist Pío Baroja and his brother, the painter Ricardo Baroja. Because of differences in personalities and styles, the *tertulia* split into two groups in the early twentieth century, and Benavente, his friends and admirers started their own *tertulia* in the Cervecería Inglesa (English Brewery), while Valle-Inclán and his followers chose to go to the Horchatería Candela. (Benavente and Valle-Inclán nevertheless remained friends.) At the turn of the century, Benavente also traveled to France and Italy and acquired more cosmopolitan views, which are reflected in his first successful plays, especially in *La noche del sábado,* which is set in a summer resort for the European elite.

While he was establishing himself in the intellectual scene, Benavente tried to convince a family friend, Emilio Mario, who was the respected impresario of Teatro de la Comedia (Comedy Theater) in Madrid, to perform one of his early plays. For six or seven years, Benavente brought Mario about a dozen plays until Mario finally accepted one of them, *El nido ajeno*. It premiered on 6 October 1894 and was performed by a well-established company of actors, including Carmen Cobeña and Emilio Thuiller. Despite the impeccable credentials of the impresario and the lead actors, Benavente's first produced play was a resounding failure. It was poorly received by the public, and the majority of the critics wrote negative reviews. Most scholars attribute the failure of the play to the public's rejection of the thesis behind the plot, which offers a moral justification for a hypothetical case of adultery that is never consummated. There were loud complaints against the alleged immorality of the play. After the three performances stipulated by law as the minimum at that time, it was replaced by another play.

In appearance, the plot may have reminded the public of late-nineteenth-century dramas, including those by the popular Echegaray; but there are key differences that anticipate characteristics that are more fully developed in Benavente's later plays and that mark the advent of naturalist theater in Spain, as opposed to the post-Romantic melodramas to which the Spanish public had grown accustomed. Galán has pointed out the main innovative aspects of *El nido ajeno*: the use of prose instead of verse, the effective use of dialogue, the predominance of dramatic tension over action, the development of the characters' psychological complexity, the lack of violence and outbursts of passion, and the realistic tone that prevails in the play. In addition to its formal innovations, *El nido ajeno* also takes a subversive approach to the classic topic developed for centuries in Spanish "dramas de honor" (dramas in which the hero's loss of reputation results in crimes of passion to restore his honor). Benavente questions the conventions of the subgenre and denounces the oppressive situation of married women in Spanish society.

The public's and critics' adverse reactions to his first produced play undoubtedly affected young Benavente and forced him to be more cautious in his criticism of society's values. From then on, his theater is a balancing act: his subsequent plays offered social satire as long as it could be tolerated by the middle-class audience that filled the theaters at the time. He was fully aware of the limits imposed by the expectations of the theatergoing public and by the structure of commercial theater, and he did not cross that invisible line. He offered a type of criticism that was easy to agree with and condemned the vices of contemporary society such as excessive ambition or greed. Over time, his theater showed a marked tendency toward moralizing that the author himself regretted.

Benavente combined his early theatrical activities with the practice of journalism. He wrote his first article for *La Época* in 1895. Over his long career he wrote hundreds of newspaper articles that were collected later in *Obras completas* (volumes seven, nine, and eleven). In 1898 he edited the satirical magazine *Madrid Cómico* (Funny Madrid), whose chief editor was the prestigious novelist and critic Clarín (Leopoldo Alas). At the turn of the century he also contributed to *Germinal, Electra, Vida Nueva* (New Life), *Revista Nueva* (New Magazine), *Alma Española* (Spanish Soul), *La Lectura* (The Reading), *La Ilustración Española* (The Spanish Enlightment), and *El Arte del Teatro* (The Art of Theater). He contributed a regular column, "Notas de un lector" (A Reader's Notes), to the respected *Revista Contemporánea* (Contemporary Magazine). He eventually stopped this frantic pace, although he resumed his journalistic activities at the beginning of the twentieth century. He later confessed in an interview included in volume eleven of *Obras completas* that he was tired of meeting deadlines. In 1899 Benavente was the first editor of the journal *Vida literaria* (Literary Life), which was considered a platform for a new generation of writers. Benavente left his post the following year, stating that it distracted him from writing plays, a task that he never abandoned, despite the failure of his first play.

Two years after the disastrous and brief run of *El nido ajeno*, Benavente managed to convince the theater company of Cobeña and Thuiller to give him another chance with his comedy *Gente conocida* (People of Importance), which he had written before his first produced play. *Gente conocida* premiered in 1896, and the public liked the sharp, witty dialogue and the contemporary situations presented. It was his first success, to be followed by many more.

For his third produced play, performed in 1897, *El marido de la Téllez* (The Téllez Woman's Husband), Benavente took advantage of a recent society event that was much talked about in Madrid: the marriage of leading lady María Guerrero, who had been the impresario of Teatro Español (Spanish Theater) since 1895 and was adored by the Spanish public, and leading man Fernando Díaz Mendoza. The public enjoyed the exercise of decoding the possible parallels between the plot of the play and real life, and the comedy was successful. Guerrero later played the lead in many plays by Benavente. Her acting style was particularly well suited for the naturalistic tone that was the trademark of the author's early plays, in contrast with the old-fashioned declamatory style that prevailed in the nineteenth century. One of the most famous roles of her illustrious acting career was as Raimunda, the protagonist of Benavente's rural drama *La malquerida* (1913, The Passion Flower).

Critics agree that the talented Spanish actresses of the early twentieth century contributed greatly to the success of Benavente's plays. Benavente himself said that actress and director Rosario Pino was the ideal interpreter of many of his plays. It is also true that many actresses became popular because of their leading roles in his plays. Pino, for instance, was remembered in particular for her role as the protagonist of *Rosas de otoño* (1905, Autumnal Roses). Besides Pino and Guerrero, who dominated the Spanish stages in the early years of the twentieth century, a new generation of actresses displayed their acting talent in Benavente's plays in the 1920s and 1930s. Lola Membrives and Margarita Xirgu are among this distinguished group. Like Guerrero, they both directed their own theater companies and toured Spain and Latin America with other plays by Benavente in their repertoire, besides the ones that they premiered.

After Pino starred in *El marido de la Téllez* in 1897, Benavente's presence on the Spanish stage was almost constant for the next fifty-seven years. Until his death in 1954, he produced at least two or three new plays a year, and often four or five. Sometimes as many as seven or eight of his plays were performed in a single year, not including reruns. As early as 1901, he had six new plays produced in the same year: four premiered in Madrid, one in Barcelona, and one in Saragossa. Some of the critics who had attacked him so harshly in his first attempts as a playwright praised him enthusiastically a few years later.

Benavente reached his creative peak and also achieved his status as the most visible author on the Spanish stage in the first decade of the twentieth century, a position consolidated at the beginning of the next decade with the spectacular success of *La malquerida* in 1913. Several plays received uniform critical acclaim in the early 1900s. Among them, *La noche del sábado* marked the definite recognition of Benavente as the leading Spanish playwright of his time. It is considered one of the highlights in his career, and the author held it in great esteem. Others also consider *Rosas de otoño* one of Benavente's most memorable plays. He produced six other new plays and published four unproduced plays that same year. Another play that earned both popular success and the critics' praise was *Los malhechores del bien* (1905, The Evildoers of Good), despite the fact that the play was perceived as anti-Catholic in some conservative circles because of its denunciation of religious hypocrisy.

In the early years of the twentieth century, Benavente also devoted himself to journalism, a common activity for Spanish intellectuals at the time. From 1906 to 1908 and from 1914 to 1916, he published weekly articles in "Los Lunes del Imparcial" (Mondays of The Impartial), the literary section of *El Imparcial*, one of Madrid's leading newspapers. In 1912 and 1913 he wrote regularly for the popular magazine *Blanco y Negro* (Black and White). His column was titled "Sobremesa" (After-Dinner Conversations). In addition, he contributed to *ABC*, a well-known conservative newspaper from Madrid, in a regular column called "La tercera" (The Third One).

In this period, Benavente managed to combine his active career in journalism with resounding and undisputed success on the Spanish stage. He wrote and produced his most acclaimed plays between 1907 and 1913: *Los intereses creados*, *Señora ama* (1908, A Lady), and *La malquerida*. The first one, considered his masterpiece, remained popular through the entire twentieth century, as attested by the number of performances and editions of the play and the ample corpus of critical studies devoted to it. The other two, considered the best of his rural dramas, also achieved enduring success and have attracted considerable critical attention.

Los intereses creados, subtitled "comedia de polichinelas" (puppet show), premiered in Teatro Lara in Madrid on 9 December 1907. The setting is an imaginary country at the beginning of the seventeenth century. Some of the characters are inspired in the tradition of the Italian commedia dell'arte, as stated in the prologue. The main characters and the plot are inspired by the tradition of Spanish classic literature. Crispín, the central character, recalls the figure of the pícaro, the antihero in a subversive subgenre of the Spanish Golden Age novel. The archetypical friendship of the idealistic Leandro and the commonsensical Crispín also evokes that of Don Quixote and Sancho Panza and the relationship of masters and servants as represented in seventeenth-century Spanish theater. Leandro is a penniless youth who falls in love with beautiful Silvia, who also loves him, but her rich father, Polichinela, opposes the marriage. Crispín, a consummate trickster, poses as Leandro's servant and convinces everyone in town that Leandro is an important gentleman on a secret mission. Both of them are actually drifters who are fleeing from the law. When the truth is exposed and they are brought to trial by those they cheated, Crispín shows the other characters that it is in their best interest to drop all the charges and allow the wedding of Leandro and Silvia, so that Leandro can repay his debts. The father is forced by the others to accept the marriage, since the arrangement benefits everyone else. Thus, the story has a happy ending, proving Crispín's cynical point that "mejor que crear afectos es crear intereses" (it is better to create bonds of interest rather than bonds of love). Like a skilled puppeteer, Crispín masterfully manipulates all the threads of the plot. In the play, his determination to take advantage of others' foolishness, based on his knowledge of human nature, is far more convincing and engaging than Leandro's groundless idealistic attitude. At the end, although it may seem that love conquers all, the moral lesson conveys a deep skepticism and a pessimistic view of humankind.

Los intereses creados has received uniform praise, even by those critics who generally dislike Benavente's plays. Francisco Ruiz Ramón, one of the most influential historians of contemporary Spanish drama, considers *Los intereses creados* one of the masterpieces of twentieth-century Spanish theater. It is one of the few plays by Benavente that is still staged in Spain, and it has gone through many editions. The public and critics of the time reacted with enthusiasm when it was premiered, and theater scholars have always praised it highly. The Spanish Royal Academy awarded the Premio Piquer (Piquer Award) to this play in 1912. In a 1930 poll, fifty thousand people chose it as the best comedy by Benavente. In "Orientaciones para el montaje" (Suggestions for Staging the Play), included in the 1998 edition of *Los intereses creados. La ciudad alegre y confiada,* the playwright José Luis Alonso de Santos has placed *Los intereses creados* among the most important and significant Spanish plays of all time. Its sequel, *La ciudad alegre y confiada* (The Happy and Confident City), which premiered in 1916, is a lesser play that provoked scandal and achieved momentary success because of the political circumstances. Critics considered it a justification of Benavente's support of Germany in World War I, an uncommon position among Spanish intellectuals that earned the author many enemies and the scorn of fellow writers.

In February 1908, just two months after the triumphant premiere of *Los intereses creados,* Benavente temporarily set aside his trademark urban comedies to produce his first drama in a rural setting, *Señora ama*. By then he was the most sought-after playwright in Spain. He was still in his early forties and had already produced more than fifty plays. *Señora ama* was a striking departure from the cynical world of his "puppet show." The inspiration for the story and the main characters came to the author in one of his stays in Aldeancabo, a small village near Toledo, in Castile. In the early part of the twentieth century, he used to rest in his country house there and visit his godchild, Rosario, a little girl who lived in the village. There he met a woman who condoned the behavior of her notoriously philandering husband and even seemed to take pride in it. Benavente modeled Dominica, the protagonist of *Señora ama,* after her. In the play, the childless Dominica is proud of the attraction that her unfaithful husband, Feliciano, exerts over other women, and even concerns herself with the welfare of his former lovers and the illegitimate children that he has had with them. Once she discovers that she is pregnant, however, Dominica changes her attitude completely; she becomes consumed by jealousy and decides she will not tolerate her husband's infidelity anymore. Her sudden transformation almost leads to a tragedy when she suspects Feliciano may be having an affair with his brother's wife. Finally, the misunderstanding is cleared up, and Feliciano rejoices at the news that Dominica will give him a legitimate heir.

Most critics have praised *Señora ama* and tend to place it at the level of *La malquerida,* Benavente's best-known drama; the author himself said that it was his favorite among all the plays he wrote. Peñuelas, however, considers it "mediocre" and "second rate" because of the lack of dramatic action and the relative weakness of the main character. Benavente avoids the tragic ending that would have been the logical development of the conflict. Virtudes Serrano, by contrast, sets out to prove in her introduction to a 2002 edition of the play that Dominica is a great character and that there is true dramatic conflict in the play.

In 1909, one year after the premiere of *Señora ama,* Benavente founded the Teatro para Niños (Theater for Children) with the impresario Fernando Porredón. With this project he intended to promote quality plays for children, performed in the Teatro Príncipe Alfonso in Madrid. He wrote sketches for puppet shows, and in some cases he was also the puppeteer. He also wrote plays for this project such as *Ganarse la vida* (1909, Earning a Living). The best known of his children's plays is *El príncipe que todo lo aprendió en los libros* (The Prince Who Learned Everything from Books), which premiered in 1909. As part of the project, he produced plays written by Modernist playwrights such as Santiago Rusiñol, Eduardo Marquina, Martínez Sierra, and even Valle-Inclán, who contributed *Farsa infantil de la cabeza del dragón* (Children's Farce of the Dragon's Head) in 1910. This play was the last one performed for the Teatro para Niños. Benavente was enthusiastic about the project but soon encountered difficulties; he did not have all the necessary resources, and the public did not respond with much interest. He abandoned Teatro para Niños in 1910 but continued writing children's plays on occasion. In 1919 he wrote two children's plays: *La cenicienta* (Cinderella) and *Y va de cuento* (And Once Upon a Time). Years later, in 1934, he premiered *La novia de nieve* (The Snow Bride), his last experiment in that genre. For Linda S. Glaze, these three plays are "outstanding examples of the modern *comedia de magia*" or magic play, a subgenre that originated in the early eighteenth century and survived until the early twentieth century.

Benavente's interest in the renovation of the Spanish stage and the education of the public was not limited to his efforts to promote children's theater. As early as 1899, while he was building his reputation as a successful playwright, he was involved in another project, Teatro Artístico (Artistic Theater). It was an attempt to bring to the Spanish public alternative plays, productions different from those usually seen in the commercial theaters. He directed the plays and occasionally played roles in them, as he did in Valle-Inclán's *Cenizas*. He premiered one of his own plays, *Despedida cruel* (Cruel Farewell), in Teatro Lara for the first performance of Teatro Artístico in 1899. Subsequent productions included plays by classic and contemporary authors, such as Shakespeare's *The Taming of the Shrew* (1594) and Joaquín Dicenta's *Juan José* (1895).

Benavente's contributions to Spanish theater were awarded not only with immense popularity in his lifetime but also with public recognition and official honors. In 1912 he was elected to the Real Academia Española, or RAE (Spanish Royal Academy), to replace the respected scholar Marcelino Menéndez Pelayo, who had died.

In 1920, Benavente was named director of Teatro Español (the Spanish National Theater). In 1922, ten years after his nomination to the RAE, he received the Nobel Prize in Literature, becoming the second Spaniard to receive the honor. Benavente's reputation was enhanced among the public, but not necessarily among the critics. The hostile atmosphere against him among Spanish intellectuals and the negative criticism spurred by Pérez de Ayala's reviews did not disappear after Benavente received the Nobel Prize. Pérez de Ayala, however, did decide to participate in an homage to Benavente in the mid 1930s.

Benavente could not attend the Nobel award ceremony because he was in Argentina at that time participating in a theatrical tour with Membrives's company, an opportunity he had welcomed in order to cope with his grief over his mother's death earlier that year. It was his second trip to South America; he had gone with Guerrero's company to Argentina in 1906. After he was awarded the Nobel Prize, he visited Mexico, Cuba, and the United States, receiving more honors along the way. He was named an honorary citizen of New York City, for instance. It was really a victory tour for the author, who was then in the zenith of his career. Upon his return to Spain, he received the Great Cross of Alfonso el Sabio (King Alfonso the Wise), and the City Council of Madrid named him Favorite Son of the city in 1924.

Benavente's third and last transatlantic tour took place under different circumstances, more than twenty years later, in 1945, when he was in his late seventies. That year, he went to Argentina and premiered his last rural drama, *La infanzona* (The Noble Woman), in Buenos Aires. At that time, Argentina's capital was an important center for Spanish theater and also had a large community of Spanish refugees. Several famous actresses who had played leads in Benavente's plays, such as Membrives, Xirgu, and Catalina Bárcena, went to South America as exiles after the Spanish Civil War in the late 1930s. Benavente, however, chose to stay in Spain.

In 1947 Benavente resumed his contributions to Madrid's conservative newspaper *ABC*. In one of his first articles in this stage of his journalistic career, "Al dictado" (Taking Dictation), he defended Marshal Phillipe Pétain, the disgraced French military leader who had been imprisoned for treason in 1945 for cooperating with the Vichy government during World War II. The article had a considerable impact in Spain, then ruled by General Francisco Franco. In 1948 Benavente won the coveted Mariano de Cavia Prize in journalism for "Al dictado." Both the article and the award may have been politically motivated, considering that by the end of the Spanish Civil War, Benavente had moved from his defense of the loyalist cause in favor of the Spanish Republic to an apology for Franco's government, a former ally of the Axis powers.

Benavente's attempts to ingratiate himself with the Franco regime were nevertheless deemed insincere. Because of his reputation as a liberal and his initial endorsement of the Spanish Republic, he was blacklisted by Franco's government in the 1940s. His name could not appear in the Spanish press, which was controlled by rigid government censors. Instead, he had to be referred to in theatrical reviews as "the author of *La malquerida*." Even the ads and the playbills for his plays could not use his name.

Despite the problems with censorship, Benavente's plays were not banned, and the Spanish public continued to hold him in high esteem. When he died in Madrid on 14 July 1954, at age eighty-seven, he was still active on the Spanish stage. Two of his new plays were produced that year, and another one premiered posthumously in the same year. Ten years earlier, in 1944, tributes to Benavente had taken place in Spanish cities to commemorate the fiftieth anniversary of the premiere of *El nido ajeno,* and there were reruns of his most famous plays. Many intellectuals, however, had distanced themselves from him because of his defense of the German cause during World War I in his controversial play *La ciudad alegre y confiada* in 1916. Moreover, his apology for Franco's regime in lesser plays such as *Aves y pájaros* (1940, Birds and Fowl) or *Abuelo y nieto* (1941, Grandfather and Grandson) and in several newspaper articles did little to reconcile him with his peers. Even after his death, ideological biases have often tainted the appreciation of Jacinto Benavente's contributions to Spanish theater for half a century.

Biography:
Ángel Lázaro, *Vida y obra de Benavente* (Madrid: A. Aguado, 1964).

References:
Gerald G. Brown, *Historia de la literatura española. El siglo XX,* ninth edition (Barcelona: Ariel, 1981), pp. 176–182;

Gérard Dufour, "Note sur le personnage de Leandro dans *Los intereses creados* de Jacinto Benavente," *Cahier d'Etudes Romanes,* 7 (1982): 85–92;

Eduardo Galán, "Jacinto Benavente y el drama burgués," in Galán and others, *Teatro y pensamiento en la regeneración del 98* (Madrid: Fundación Pro-RESAD, 1998), pp. 149–206;

Linda S. Glaze, "The Tradition of the Comedia de Magia in Jacinto Benavente's Theater for Children," *Hispania,* 76, no. 2 (1993): 213–223;

Javier Huerta Calvo and Emilio Peral Vega, "Benavente y otros autores," in *Historia del teatro español. Del siglo XVIII a la época actual,* volume 2, edited by Fernando Doménech Rico and Peral Vega (Madrid: Gredos, 2003), pp. 2272–2310;

Ana Mariscal, *Cincuenta años de teatro en Madrid* (Madrid: El Avapiés, 1984);

Carmen Menéndez Onrubia, "Doña María la Brava," in *Autoras y actrices en la historia del teatro español,* edited by Luciano García Lorenzo (Murcia: Universidad de Murcia, 2000), pp. 155–177;

César Oliva, *Teatro español del siglo XX* (Madrid: Síntesis, 2004), pp. 33–37;

Marcelino C. Peñuelas, *Jacinto Benavente* (New York: Twayne, 1968);

Francisco Ruiz Ramón, *Historia del teatro español siglo XX,* fourth edition (Madrid: Cátedra, 1980), pp. 21–38.

1922 Nobel Prize in Literature Presentation Speech

by Per Hallström, Chairman of the Nobel Committee of the Swedish Academy, 10 December 1922

Jacinto Benavente has devoted his imaginative gifts mainly to the theatre, and it seems as if he has systematically guided the course of his development in this direction through many varieties of experience. But with this imaginative artist, system seems to be a free and direct expression of his whole being. It appears that no one could have reached his goal with less effort and brooding in comparison with the value of the achievement.

The feeling which has carried him on has also been of an unusually complete and harmonious nature: it is not only the dramatic art and the atmosphere of the theatre that he has loved; he has cherished an equally warm affection for life outside, for the world of realities which it was his task to bring to the stage. It is not a matter of mere uncritical and superficial worship of life. He has observed his world with extremely clear and keen eyes, and what he has seen he has measured and weighed with an alert and flexible intelligence. He has not allowed himself to be duped either by men or by ideas, not even by his own ideas or his own pathos. Nevertheless, he does not strike one as being in the least bitter, or even blasé.

His writing has thus obtained its most distinctive quality–grace. This is such a rare value, especially in our own times, that there is little demand for it on the market and it is not recognized by most people. Grace, however, is as precious as it is uncommon. It is the token of the balance of powers, of the self-discipline and assurance of art, especially when it is not an end in itself and a mere frivolity, but when, without apparent effort, it stamps its mark on the entire form-giving process. It does not, then, merely play on the surface, affecting the style; it also determines each proportion in the treatment of the subject and every line in its depiction.

This is precisely the case with Benavente. The effect he attains may vary greatly in strength, but it is based on unfailing tact and strict loyalty to the subject. He gives what the subject is able to give without effort and without bombast. The fare he provides may be more or less rich and interesting, but it is always unadulterated. This is a classic feature in Benavente.

Nevertheless, his bent is above all realistic, if we eliminate from that label all the customary flavour of social tendency, commonplace philosophy, or gross striving for effect. To reproduce the wealth and mobility of life, the play of characters, and the struggle between wills, in a way that comes as near truth as possible–that is his chief aim. When he aims at something beyond this–to stimulate thought, to solve problems, to demolish prejudices, to enlarge human sympathy–he does so with the most scrupulous care not to tamper with the objective accuracy of the literary description. He exercises this unusual discipline even when he is faced with the strongest temptation for a dramatist–dramatic and scenic effect. However easily a scene could be made more telling by increasing the tension of the conflict and plot, by putting on more flaring colours, by flogging up the emotions to their highest pitch, Benavente never does this at the expense of truth: he permits no blurring of the tone. He is a rare example of a born dramatist, one whose imagination, by itself, creates in accordance with the laws of the stage, but yet avoids anything theatrical as fully as all other false conventions.

His activity lies especially in comedy, but that term in Spanish is more inclusive than with us; it comprises what we may in general call middle-class plays without tragic conclusions. If there is such a conclusion, the pieces are called dramas, and Benavente has also written such plays, including the remarkable and moving play, *La malquerida* (1913) [The Wrongly Loved]. He has also composed many romantic and fantastic pieces, among which are exquisite achievements of poetic art, especially on a small scale.

But his central significance lies in his comedies, which, as we have seen, may well be as serious as they are gay; and in the short forms of comedy, which in Spanish literature have been developed into special species with old and glorious traditions. In the latter Benavente is an enchanting master because of his unlaboured wit and comic verve, his radiant good nature, and his grace, which combines all these qualities. I have time for only a few names: *De pequeñas causas* (1908) [For Small Reasons]; *El amor asusta* (1907) [Love Frightens]; *No fumadores* (1904) [Smoking Prohibited]. But there are many others, an entire treasury of merry jest, where the battle is waged so lightly and so elegantly that it is always good-tempered, however sharp the weapon itself may be.

In the larger works we encounter an amazing range of spheres of life and subject matter. They are taken from peasant life, from all circles of society in the town, from the artist's world down to the travelling circus people whom the poet embraces with a strong human sympathy and whom he values more highly than many other classes.

But it is mainly the life of the upper classes that he has treated in its two characteristic centres, Madrid and Moraleda, the latter a place not found on the map, but which in its sunny and alluring variety comprises the typical features of a provincial town in Castile. In *La farándula* (1897) [The Company of Comedians] the ambitious politician goes to this town in order to rally and to gain the support of the uncorrupted energies of the people for a somewhat vaguely defined ideal; in the play *La gobernadora* (1901) [The Governor's Wife], conceited ambition dreams of a larger stage for its greater talents. Moraleda is really a planetary world, which is attracted and illuminated by Madrid and does not reveal the full force of its comedy except in comparison with Madrid.

The capital and its spiritual content are made understandable much more fully through personal vicissitudes of fortune which are determined, as are its fashions and its culture, by the strata of its society. We see a distinct development in the art of Benavente. He begins by stressing the description of environment, with an abundant wealth of colour and life and features that reveal character. The dramatic element proper—unsought, like all the rest of the apparatus—exists for the most part merely to keep the action going. Its function is to arrange the whirl of life in a picture, composed in groups, with strong individual scenes. He has taken pains to create a faithful and artistic mirror of reality, which is then left to speak for itself.

Later his composition becomes more rigid. Although it is arranged firmly around a stronger, deeper, and more spiritual dramatic conflict, it is, nevertheless, almost as simple as when Benavente was merely writing episodes describing society. There is nothing artificial, nothing abstract and isolated, in the human fates which are represented. As before, they are still connected with the world around them, but the light is strictly limited, revealing only what is central from a dramatic point of view. The sharp characterization is carried just far enough to make the action clear; the psychology is merely a means, not an end. Nothing is laboriously prepared beforehand; nothing strikes one really as being prepared at all: every feature in the action comes, as it were, with the improvisation of life and may take one by surprise until one has reflected for a moment, just as happens in life itself. The technique, too, is purely realistic and has not searched for models in ancient tragedy. Summing up the past is not the main function of this kind of drama, nor is the dialogue a kind of cross-examination to discover the past. The required discoveries are made by life itself by means of the unforced course of the action.

Broadly speaking, Benavente does not seek to harrow the spectator; his object is a solution of conflicts that is harmonious even in melancholy and sorrow. This harmony is usually gained by resignation, not weary or aloof or pathetic, and without great gestures. The characters suffer, tear at their bonds, are attracted by fortune (the way to which is to pass over others' fortune), wrestle in conflicts, measure their world and themselves, and gain a clearer and wider vision through their constraint. That which has the last word is not passion, in fact not the ego at all, but the spiritual value that proves so great that, were it lost, the ego would be poor and fortune empty. The decision is made without capitulation, merely through the fact that the personality is face to face with the consequences of its choice of fate and chooses freely, on the basis of instinctive feeling rather than in accordance with theories.

I have time for only one or two titles of his strange, simple, and quiet dramas: *Alma triunfante* (1902) [Conquering Soul], *La propia estimación* (1915) [Self-Respect], and *Campo de armiño* (1916) [The White Scutcheon]. There are many others of equal value which are more or less like these. The distinctive mark of them all is a peculiarly pure humanity, which at first glance is surprising in the keen and flashing satirist, while the moderation and the freedom from all sentimentality in the mode of expression are in complete accordance with his schooling. As a matter of fact his qualities go well together: as his grace of form is a classic feature, so are his feeling and his insight classic, strictly schooled, well balanced, farsighted, and clear. His simplicity of expression and hushed tone come from the same source.

Nevertheless, Teutonic readers are often reminded, even when it comes to an art as good as this, that it has sprung from a national temperament other than ours and from other poetic traditions. The kind of lyric we desire, at least in the atmosphere of the world of drama, is on the whole probably unknown to the Romance nations. Half-light, both in nature and in the human soul, is lacking in them: all that human beings contain is expressed, or it seems that it *can* be expressed. Their thoughts may have brilliance, rapidity, and, of course, clarity; but they strike us as lacking in power, as belonging to a somewhat more vacant atmosphere, and as having less life in their inner being. What southerners say of our art may reveal equally great defects; but we must mutually accustom ourselves to admire what we understand and to leave outside our aesthetic judgments things which, for the reasons mentioned, fail to satisfy us.

In the works in which the Spaniard Benavente has abandoned his comedy descriptive of society and individuals, and instead has ranged over larger complexes of ideas and has sought to interpret all the unrest and yearning of our times, we cannot follow him with the admiration that has been bestowed upon him by his countrymen. This is true of *El collar de estrellas* (1915) [The Belt of Stars] and several other pieces.

I have not dwelt on the limitations of his art, but sought to indicate the central qualities of his craftsmanship in his country and in his time. I believe that scarcely any other contemporary dramatist has anywhere captured the life about him in such a many-sided and faithful manner and given it a form so immediate and, through its simple and noble art, so durable. The traditions of Spanish poetry comprise a strong, bold, and sound realism, a prolific power of growth, and an inimitable charm in the comic spirit which is merry and built on realities, not on conversational wit. Benavente has shown that he belongs to this school and, in a form peculiar to himself, has worked out a modern comedy of character containing much of the classic spirit. He has proved himself to be a worthy adherent of an ancient and elevated style of poetry; and that is to say a great deal.

[© The Nobel Foundation, 1922.]

Benavente: Banquet Speech

Introductory remarks by Professor H. G. Söderbaum at the Nobel Banquet at Grand Hôtel, Stockholm, 10 December 1922:

The art of poetry has this year donned the gleaming attire of drama and greets us from the far-reaching lands where the noble speech of Castile, the mother tongue of Lope de Vega and Calderón, forms the means of communicating thought for a considerable part of the population of our globe.

It has been said that "the business of the dramatist is to keep himself out of sight and to let nothing appear but his characters." We regret that circumstances have compelled the Prize winner in Literature to follow this rule so literally that on this occasion also he has kept out of sight; but we hope that the near future will give us the opportunity of forming a closer acquaintance with him and also with his work.

As Benavente was unable to be present, the speech was given by Count de Torata, Spanish Ambassador (Translation from the Spanish):

It is difficult to express the deep satisfaction I feel today. It would take Benavente's talent to come up to the level of my task and that of my audience. Also, I doubly regret the absence of the great author, for my sake as well as yours. The honour you have so rightfully bestowed on Jacinto Benavente you have also bestowed on Spain and all those countries in which our language is spoken, some of whose representatives I am happy to see among us. I hope that this Prize will contribute to a strengthening of the ties which unite us, to a mutual understanding between our countries, to reinforcing the cordiality of our friendship. Finally, permit me to express all the admiration and affection I feel for your country.

[© The Nobel Foundation, 1922.]

Henri Bergson
(18 October 1859 – 4 January 1941)

Philip B. Dematteis
Saint Leo University

BOOKS: *La spécialité* (Angers: Lachèse & Dolbeau, 1882):

Extraits de Lucrèce, avec un commentaire, des notes et une étudie sur la poésie, la philosophie, la physique, le texte et la langue de Lucrèce (Paris: Delagrave, 1884); edited and translated by Wade Baskin as *The Philosophy of Poetry: The Genius of Lucretius* (New York: Philosophical Library, 1959);

Essai sur les données immédiates de la conscience (Paris: Alcan, 1889) translated by F. L. Pogson as *Time and Free Will: An Essay on the Immediate Data of Consciousness* (London: Sonnenschein / New York: Macmillan, 1910)

Le bon sens et les études classiques: Discours prononcé a la distribution des prix du Concours général le 30 juillet 1895 (Paris: Delalain, 1895);

Matière et mémoire: Essai sur la relation du corps a l'ésprit (Paris: Alcan, 1896); translated by Nancy Margaret Paul and W. Scott Palmer as *Matter and Memory* (London: Allen & Unwin, 1911; New York: Holt, 1911);

Le rire: Essai sur la signification du comique (Paris: Alcan, 1901); translated by Cloudesley Brereton and Fred Rothwell as *Laughter: An Essay on the Meaning of the Comic* (New York: Macmillan, 1911);

Introduction à la métaphysique, Cahiers de la quinzaine, fourth series, no. 12 (Paris: Suresnes, 1903); translated by T. E. Hulme as *An Introduction to Metaphysics* (London: Macmillan, 1913; Indianapolis: Bobbs-Merrill, 1955);

Notice sur la vie et les oeuvres de M. Félix Ravaisson-Mollien (Paris: Firmin-Didot, 1904);

L'évolution créatrice (Paris: Alcan, 1907); translated by Arthur Mitchell as *Creative Evolution* (London & New York: Macmillan, 1911);

La Perception du changement: Conférences faites à l'Université d'Oxford les 26 et 27 mai 1911 (Oxford: Clarendon Press, 1911);

Dreams, translated by Edwin E. Slosson (New York: Huebsch, 1914);

La philosophie (Paris: Larousse, 1915);

Henri Bergson, circa 1920 (photograph by Hulton Archive/Getty Images)

La signification de la guerre, "Pages actuelles," 1914–1915, no. 18 (Paris: Bloud & Gay, 1915); translated as *The Meaning of the War: Life & Matter in Conflict* (London: Unwin, 1915);

L'énergie spirituelle: Essais et conférences (Paris: Alcan, 1919); translated by H. Wildon Carr as *Mind-Energy: Lectures and Essays* (New York: Holt, 1920; London: Macmillan, 1920);

Durée et simultanéité à propos de la théorie d'Einstein (Paris: Alcan, 1922; enlarged, 1923); translated by Leon Jacobson as *Duration and Simultaneity, with Reference to Einstein's Theory* (Indianapolis: Bobbs-Merrill, 1965);

L'intuition philosophique: Communication faite, au Congrès philosophique de Bologne le x avril M. CM. XI. (Paris: Helleu & Sergent, 1927);

Les deux sources de la morale et de la religion (Paris: Alcan, 1932); translated by Brereton, R. Ashley Audra, and W. Horsfall Carter as *The Two Sources of Morality and Religion* (New York: Holt, 1935; London: Macmillan, 1935);

La pensée et le mouvant: Essais et conférences (Paris: Alcan, 1934)–comprises "Croissance de la vérité: Mouvement rétrograde du vrai," "De la position des problèmes," "Le possible et le réel," "L'intuition philosophique," "La perception du changement," "Introduction à la métaphysique," "La philosophie de Claude Bernard," "Sur le pragmatisme de William James: Vérité et réalité," and "La vie et l'oeuvre de Ravaisson"; translated by Mabelle L. Andison as *The Creative Mind* (New York: Philosophical Library, 1946)–comprises "Growth of Truth: Retrograde Movement of the True," "Stating the Problems," "The Possible and the Real," "Philosophical Intuition," "The Perception of Change," "Introduction to Metaphysics," "The Philosophy of Claude Bernard," "On the Pragmatism of William James: Truth and Reality," and "The Life and Work of Ravaisson";

Mémoire et vie: Textes choisis, edited by Gilles Deleuze (Paris: Presses universitaires de France, 1957);

Ecrits et paroles: Textes, 3 volumes, edited by Rose-Marie Mossé-Bastide (Paris: Presses universitaires de France, 1957–1959);

Oeuvres, Edition du Centenaire, edited by André Robinet (Paris: Presses universitaires de France, 1959);

La nature de l'âme: Suivi de Le problème de la personalité, edited by André and Martine Robinet, Les Etudes bergsoniennes, no. 7 (Paris: Presses universitaires de France, 1966);

Mélanges: L'idée de lieu chez Aristote, Durée et simultanéité, correspondance, pièces diverses, documents (Paris: Presses universitaires de France, 1972); translated by Melissa McMahon, edited by Keith Ansell Pearson and John Mullarkey as *Key Writings* (New York & London: Continuum, 2002);

Cours I: Leçons de psychologie et de métaphysique (Paris: Presses universitaires de France, 1990);

Cours II: Leçons d'esthétique. Leçons de morale, psychologie et métaphysique (Paris: Presses universitaires de France, 1992);

Cours III: Leçons d'histoire de la philosophie moderne, théories de l'âme, edited by Henri Hude and Jean-Louis Dumas (Paris: Presses universitaires de France, 1995);

Bergson professeur: Au lycée Blaise Pascal de Clermont-Ferrand (1883–1888); cours 1885–1886; Essai sur la nature de l'enseignement philosophique initial, edited by Jean Bardy (Paris: L'Harmattan, 1998);

Cours de Bergson sur la philosophie grecque, edited by Hude and Françoise Vinel (Paris: Presses universitaires de France, 2000).

Editions in English: *Selections from Bergson*, edited by Harold A. Larrabee (New York: Appleton-Century-Crofts, 1949);

The World of Dreams, translated by Wade Baskin (New York: Philosophical Library, 1958);

Duration and Simultaneity, edited by Robin Durie (Manchester, U.K.: Clinamen Press, 1999).

Between the publication of his best-known work, *L'évolution créatrice* (translated as *Creative Evolution*, 1911), in 1907 and the outbreak of World War I in 1914, the French philosopher Henri Bergson developed a virtually cult-like international following among professional philosophers and laypersons alike. His colleague and disciple Edouard Le Roy could write with only slight exaggeration in 1913:

> There is a thinker whose name is today on everybody's lips, who is deemed by acknowledged philosophers worthy of comparison with the greatest, and who, with his pen as well as his brain, has overleapt all technical obstacles, and won himself a reading both outside and inside the schools. Beyond any doubt, and by common consent, Mr. Henri Bergson's work will appear to future eyes among the most characteristic, fertile, and glorious of our era. It marks a never-to-be-forgotten date in history; it opens up a phase of metaphysical thought; it lays down a principle of development the limits of which are indeterminable; and it is after cool consideration, with full consciousness of the exact value of words, that we are able to pronounce the revolution which it effects equal in importance to that effected by Kant, or even by Socrates. Everybody, indeed, has become aware of this more or less clearly.

Among his contemporaries, Bergson influenced not only other philosophers but also figures in literature, art, and music. His vitalistic, nonmechanistic concept of evolution appealed to many educated people who felt compelled to accept the scientific underpinnings of Darwinism but wanted to believe in a more exalted conception of humanity than descent from ape-like ancestors seemed to imply. His emphasis on intuition rather than intellect as providing an insight into ultimate reality seemed to many a welcome antidote to scientific rationalism. Furthermore,

Bergson's ideas were presented in an elegant and lucid style, rich in metaphor, image, and analogy, that won him the Nobel Prize in Literature in 1927. But his influence declined precipitously within a few years after his death in 1941, and he left no "Bergsonian" school or movement. As Leszek Kolakowski notes, "Bergson has survived only as a dead classic. Even in France interest in his work is only residual. To be sure, sometimes, somewhere, someone writes a doctoral thesis on 'Bergsonism,' yet it may fairly be said that today's philosophers, both in their research and in their teaching, are almost entirely indifferent to his legacy."

Bergson developed his philosophy in four major books: *Essai sur les données immédiates de la conscience* (1889; translated as *Time and Free Will: An Essay on the Immediate Data of Consciousness*, 1910), *Matière et mémoire: Essai sur la relation du corps a l'ésprit* (1896; translated as *Matter and Memory*, 1911), *L'évolution créatrice,* and *Les deux sources de la morale et de la religion* (1932; translated as *The Two Sources of Morality and Religion,* 1935). Although he deliberately eschewed the construction of a comprehensive philosophical system his ideas are consistent throughout as each successive work builds on the preceding ones by applying to new topics his fundamental distinction between the faculties of intuition and intelligence.

Henri-Louis Bergson was born in Paris on 18 October 1859—as many commentators have noted, the year in which Charles Darwin published *On the Evolution of Species by Means of Natural Selection.* He was the second of the seven children—four boys and three girls—of Jewish parents, Michel and Catherine Levison Bergson. Michel Bergson, a pianist and composer, was the son of a Polish trader named Berek Zbitkower; his adopted surname derives from *Berek-son* (the son of Berek). Catherine Bergson was from Doncaster in northern England; Henri Bergson learned English from her as a child and was later able to supervise the translations of his books. The family lived at 18 rue Lamartine, near the Opéra. In 1863 they moved to Switzerland when Michel Bergson took a position as a professor at the Geneva Conservatory; there they lived on the boulevard de Philosophes. They returned to Paris in 1866 and settled at 154 boulevard Magenta.

In 1868 Bergson enrolled at the Lycée Impérial Bonaparte (now the Lycée Condorcet) and boarded at the Jewish Springer Institution at 34 rue de La Tour d'Auvergne. In 1870 the rest of the family moved to London, where Bergson visited them during vacations from school. One of his brothers became a banker, another a businessman, and the third an actor; their sister Mina married the magician and occultist Samuel Liddell MacGregor Mathers, cofounder of the Hermetic Order of the Golden Dawn, and changed her name to Moina. Michel Bergson died in 1898; Catherine Bergson died in Folkestone, England, at age ninety-eight.

In 1875 Bergson won the first prize in rhetoric in the prestigious Concours Général, a national competition for the best students in each field taught in French colleges; in 1876 he won the first prize in philosophy; and in 1877 he won the prize in mathematics for his solution to the problem of the three circles, posed by the seventeenth-century French philosopher and mathematician Blaise Pascal. His solution appeared the following year in the *Annales de mathématiques*—his first published work, it has been collected in *Ecrits et paroles: Textes* (1957–1959, Writings and Speeches: Texts) and in *Mélanges: L'idée de lieu chez Aristote, Durée et simultanéité, correspondance, pièces diverses, documents* (1972, Mélanges: Aristotle's Concept of Place, Duration and Simultaneity, Correspondence, Diverse Pieces, Documents; translated as *Key Writings,* 2002). When he decided to enroll in the letters and humanities section of the Ecole Normale Supérieure, the institution at which university teachers were trained, his mathematics teacher complained to his parents that their son could have been a mathematician but would instead be a mere philosopher.

Bergson entered the Ecole Normale Supérieure in 1878, along with the future socialist politician Jean Jaurès and the future sociologist Emile Durkheim. He studied under the spiritualist philosophers Félix Ravaisson and Jules Lachelier and discovered the writings of the English philosopher of evolution, Herbert Spencer. He scored second highest in the *agrégation de philosophie,* a national competitive examination required of prospective teachers, in 1881 and took a teaching position at the *lycée* in Angers. Two years later he moved to Clermont-Ferrand, where he taught both at the Lycée Blaise-Pascal and at the university. In 1884 he published a volume of selections from the Roman Epicurean philosopher Lucretius's poem *De rerum natura* (On the Nature of Things), with a critical study of the texts, that went through several editions.

Bergson submitted *Essai sur les données immédiates de la conscience,* along with the required Latin thesis, "Quid Aristoteles de loco senserit" (Aristotle's Conception of Place), for the degree of docteur-ès-lettres from the University of Paris in 1889; the essay was published that same year by Félix Alcan in Paris in the series La bibliothèque de philosophie contemporaine (The Library of Contemporary Philosophy). Bergson argues that the traditional philosophical issue of the conflict of free will and determinism is a pseudoproblem that has arisen from misapprehending subjective experience as a succession of static mental states that follow one another as events in the external world do; accordingly, mental "states" are viewed in cause-and-effect terms just as external events are, and later states are taken to be determined by earlier ones. This mistake arises from viewing the mind through the faculty of the intelligence or intellect, which evolved to deal with and control external objects in space. The mind, however, is not spatial, and mental states do not exist. One's inner experience should instead be apprehended by means of intuition; in this case it will be seen correctly as *la durée* (duration), lived time as opposed to the time measured externally by clocks—a continuous, irreversible, unrepeatable flow. In duration there is no juxtaposition of events; therefore, there is no causation of one event by another. The deeper self thus reached is the seat of free will; in duration freedom is experienced directly:

> Il y aurait donc enfin deux moi différents, dont l'un serait comme la projection extérieure de l'autre, sa représentation spatiale et pour ainsi dire sociale. Nous atteignons le premier par une réflexion approfonie, qui nous fait saisir nos états internees comme des êtres vivants, sans cesse en voie de formation, comme des états réfractaires à la mesure, qui se pénètrent les uns les autres, et dont la succession dans la durée n'a rien de commun avec une juxtaposition dans l'espace homogène. Mais les moments où nous ressaisissons ainsi nous-mêmes sont rares, et c'est pourquoi nous sommes rarement libres. La plupart du temps, nous vivons extérieurement à nous-mêmes, nous n'apercevons de notre moi que son fantôme décoloré, ombre que la pure durée projette dans l'espace homogène. Notre existence se déroule donc dans l'espace plutôt que nous ne pensons; nous "sommes agis" plutôt que dans le temps: nous vivons pour le monde extérieur plutôt que pour nous; nous parlons plutôt que nous n'agissons nous-mêmes. Agir librement, c'est reprendre possession do soi, c'est se replacer dans la pure durée.

> (Hence there are finally two different selves, one of which is, as it were, the external projection of the other, its spatial and, so to speak, social representation. We reach the former by deep introspection, which leads us to grasp our inner states as living things, constantly *becoming*, as states not amenable to measure, which permeate one another and of which the succession in duration has nothing in common with juxtaposition in homogeneous space. But the moments at which we thus grasp ourselves are rare, and that is just why we are rarely free. The greater part of the time we live outside ourselves, hardly perceiving anything of ourselves but our own ghost, a colorless shadow which pure duration projects into homogeneous space. Hence our life unfolds in space rather than in time; we live for the external world rather than for ourselves; we speak rather than think; we "are acted" rather than act ourselves. To act freely is to recover possession of oneself, and to get back into pure duration [translated by F. L. Pogson.])

Essai sur les données immédiates de la conscience was widely reviewed in philosophy journals. Some reviewers suggested that the basic ideas came from the American Pragmatist philosopher William James's article "On Some Omissions of Introspective Psychology" (1884), which depicts thought as a stream of consciousness that the intellect distorts by dividing it into concepts. Bergson, however, denied having read or heard of James's article when he wrote *Essai sur les données immédiates de la conscience*.

In 1889 Bergson began teaching at the collège Rollin in Paris; he moved to the Lycée Henri V. the following year. In 1891 he married Louise Neuberger, a cousin of Marcel Proust; the future author served as best man at the wedding. The Bergsons' only child, Jeanne, was born the following year. Deaf from birth, she went on to study under the expressionist painter and sculptor Emile Antoine Bourdelle.

In 1896, after spending five years in a detailed study of recent research into pathological mental conditions—especially aphasia, the loss of the ability to use language—Bergson published *Matière et mémoire*, which is generally regarded as the most difficult of his works. In this volume he deals with another venerable philosophical issue: the relationship of mind and body, or, more specifically, of mind and the brain:

> D'une manière générale, l'état psychologique nous parait, dans la plupart des cas, déborder énormément l'état cérébral. Je veux dire que l'état cérébral n'en dessine qu'une petite partie, celle qui est capable de se traduire par des mouvements de locomotion. . . .
>
> . . . .
>
> Le cerveau ne doit donc pas être autre chose, à notre avis, qu'une espèce de bureau téléphonique central: son rôle est de "donner la communication," ou de la faire attendre. Il n'ajoute rien à ce qu'il reçoit. . . .

> (Speaking generally, the psychical state seems to us to be, in most cases, immensely wider than the cerebral state. I mean that the brain state indicates only a very small part of the mental state, the part which is capable of translating itself into movements of locomotion. . . .
>
> . . . .
>
> In our opinion, then, the brain is no more than a kind of central telephonic exchange: its office is to allow communication, or to delay it. It adds nothing to what it receives. . . . [translated by Nancy Margaret Paul and W. Scott Palmer])

Matter, according to Bergson, is just what it appears to be in perception and nothing else; there is no Kantian "thing-in-itself" that lies beyond the images one perceives. Therefore, matter has no occult or unknown powers; and the brain is material.

> La vérité est qu'il y aurait un moyen, et un seul, de réfuter le matérialisme: ce serait d'établir que la matière est absolument comme elle parait être. Par là on éliminerait de la matière tout virtualité, toute puissance

cachée, et les phénomènes de l'esprit auraient une réalité indépendante.

> (The truth is that there is one, and only one, method of refuting materialism: it is to show that matter is precisely that which it appears to be. Thereby we eliminate all virtuality, all hidden power from matter, and establish the phenomena of spirit as an independent reality [translated by Paul and Palmer].)

The occurrence of aphasia shows that memories are not stored in specific areas of the brain: a person with a lesion in the brain that causes aphasia understands what others say, knows what he or she wants to say, and does not suffer from paralysis of the speech organs, yet is unable to speak; also, in some forms of aphasia the parts of speech are forgotten in a semantic order, beginning with proper names, proceeding through common nouns, and ending with verbs, while in other forms some letters of the alphabet are forgotten but others are not. Thus, it is not memory that has been lost but the bodily mechanism that is needed to express it.

Bergson distinguishes two kinds of memory. One kind is a set of acquired bodily habits, dispositions to action such as walking or reciting a poem that one has learned; these habits can be put into effect without conscious thought, and they can be affected by lesions in the brain. The other is pure memory, which records everything that ever occurs during the course of one's life in every detail. Perception is permeated by this kind of memory; pure perception, unaccompanied by memory, does not exist. The brain filters out the vast amount of pure memory that is not needed for conscious action in the present. The mind is, thus, independent of the brain and uses the brain to carry out its purposes.

In 1898 Bergson became *maître de conférences*—roughly equivalent to a reader in a British university—at his alma mater, the Ecole normale supérieure. The following year he published an article in the *Revue de Paris* that is a departure from his metaphysical speculations but consistent with them; based on a lecture he had given during his early years in Auvergne, it appeared in book form in 1900 as *Le rire: Essai sur la signification du comique* (translated as *Laughter: An Essay on the Meaning of the Comic*, 1911). Bergson says that humor results from the incongruity between the essential freedom of the human spirit and situations in which someone acts in a mechanistic fashion similar to a marionette or a jack-in-the-box: clowns tumbling in the circus, someone slipping on a banana peel, or a person being made the victim of a practical joke that depends on people being creatures of habit. He analyzes verbal humor according to the same principles, saying that it depends applying to language, as if to a lifeless thing, the mechanical processes of repetition, reversal, transposition, and mutual interference. Each of these processes is the opposite of a living process: life is continually changing and never repeats itself or goes backward in time; and a living being is a system of interdependent elements so exclusively made for one another that none of them could belong to two different organisms and so could not interfere with elements in another system. Humor is disinterested: one cannot laugh if one cares too deeply about the butt of the joke. The comical situation is universal, where the tragic one is individual: thus, the titles of comedies tend to refer to character types, such as the miser, the misanthrope, or the shrew, whereas tragedies tend to be named for individuals, such as Oedipus, Antigone, King Lear, or Hamlet. Laughter is intrinsically social: one laughs as a member of a group, even if the other members of the group are only present in one's imagination. Laughter corrects the unsocial individual by punishment in the form of humiliation. Literary theorists influenced by Bergson's book on laughter include Arthur Koestler, who wrote *The Act of Creation* (1964).

In 1900 Bergson succeeded Charles Leveque as professor of Greek and Latin philosophy at the Collège de France, the most prestigious academic institution in the country. At the First International Congress of Philosophy, held in Paris in August 1900, Bergson presented the paper "Sur les origines psychologiques de notre croyance a la loi de causalite" (On the Psychological Origins of the Belief in the Law of Causality). In 1901 he was elected to the Academie des sciences morales et politiques.

In January 1903 Bergson contributed to the prestigious *Revue de metaphysique et de morale* the essay "Introduction à la métaphysique"; it was published in book form that same year (translated as *An Introduction to Metaphysics*, 1913). The method of intuitive introspection—the direct apprehension of process introduced in *Essai sur les données immédiates de la conscience*—is here applied to the cognition of ultimate reality: intuition provides truth about the world. The intellect is guided by the needs of the organism; the knowledge it acquires is not disinterested but is related to those needs. It gathers knowledge through analysis, dividing objects into the perspectives from which they are viewed and then reconstructing them by synthesizing the perspectives. This synthesis, while enabling the organism to satisfy its needs, never penetrates to the inner being of the objects. Intuition consists in entering into the object sympathetically, rather than looking at it from the outside, and provides absolute knowledge:

> les philosophes s'accordent, en dépit de leurs divergences apparentes, à distinguer deux manières profondément différentes de connaître une chose. La première implique qu'on tourne autour de cette chose; la seconde, qu'on entre en elle. La première dépend du point de vue où l'on se place et des symboles par lesquels on s'exprime. La seconde ne se prend d'aucun point de vue et ne s'appuie sur aucun symbole. De la

> première connaissance on dira qu'elle s'arrête au *relatif;* de la seconde, là où elle est possible, qu'elle atteint l'*absolu.*

> (philosophers, in spite of their apparent divergencies, agree in distinguishing two profoundly different ways of knowing a thing. The first implies that we move round the object; the second that we enter into it. The first depends on the point of view at which we are placed and on the symbols by which we express ourselves. The second neither depends on a point of view nor relies on any symbol. The first kind of knowledge may be said to stop at the *relative;* the second, in those cases where it is possible, to attain the *absolute* [translated by T. E. Hulme].)

In 1904 Bergson succeeded Gabriel Tarde in the chair of modern philosophy at the Collège de France. Three years later he published his best-known work, *L'évolution créatrice,* in which he introduces the concept of the *élan vital* (vital impulse) as the motive force in evolution. The *élan vital* is the living, enduring spirit with which one becomes acquainted in intuitive introspection. Life began in the form of simple unicellular organisms; if survival were all that counted, it could have remained at that level, since such organisms still exist and are, therefore, adapted to their environments. But the *élan vital* could not rest at that level; it wanted to break free of matter entirely, but this goal was unachievable. At first its effort took the form of increase in size, but matter is elastic only to a limited degree; therefore, the *élan vital* began to divide into various organs and organisms and ultimately into millions of individuals pursuing divergent paths of development, and it has striven ever upward into greater and greater complexity. The similar development of a complex organ such as the eye in such widely divergent organisms as mollusks and vertebrates shows that the basic impulse is the same in all of these organisms. It also shows the inadequacy both of a mechanistic theory of evolution, such as that advanced by Darwin, and of a teleological one that posits some final goal that the evolutionary process was designed to reach:

> La machine qu'est l'oeil est donc composée d'une infinité de machines, toutes d'une complexité extrême. Pourtant la vision est un fair simple. Dès que l'oeil s'oeuvre, la vision s'opère. Précisément parce que la fonctionnement est simple, la plus légère distraction de la nature dans la construction de la machine infiniment compliquée eût rendu la vision impossible. C'est ce contraste entre la complexité de l'organe et l'unité de la fonction qui déconcerte l'esprit.

> Une théorie mécanistique sera celle qui nous fera assister à la construction graduelle de la machine sous l'influence des circonstances extérieures, intervenant directement par une action sur les tissus ou indirectement par la sélection des mieux adaptés. Mais, quelque forme que prenne cette thèse, à supposer qu'elle vaille quelque chose pour le détail des parties, elle ne jette aucune lumière sur leur corrélation.

> Survient alors la doctrine de la finalité. Elle dit que les parties on été assemblées, sur un plan préconçu, en vue d'un but. En quoi elle assimile le travail de la nature à celui de l'ouvrier qui procède, lui aussi, par assemblage de parties en vue de la réalisation d'une idée ou de l'imitation d'un modèle. Le mécanisme reprochera donc avec raison au finalisme son caractère anthropomorphique. Mais il ne s'aperçoit pas qu'il procède lui-même selon cette méthode, en la tronquant simplement. Sans doute il a fail table rase de la fin poursuivie ou du modèle idéal. Mais il veut, lui aussi, que la nature ait travaillé comme l'ouvrier humain, en assemblant des parties. Un simple coup d'oeil jeté sur le développement d'un embryon lui eût pourtant montré que la vie s'y prend tout autrement. *Elle ne procède pas par association et addition d'éléments mais par dissociation et dédoublement.*

> (The mechanism of the eye is . . . composed of an infinity of mechanisms, all of extreme complexity. Yet vision is one simple fact. As soon as the eye opens, the visual act is effected. Just because the act is simple, the slightest negligence on the part of nature in the building of the infinitely complex machine would have made vision impossible. This contrast between the complexity of the organ and the unity of the function is what must give us pause.

> A mechanistic theory is one which means to show us the gradual building up of the machine under the influence of external circumstances intervening either directly by action on the tissue or indirectly by the selection of better-adapted ones. But, whatever form this theory may take, supposing it avails at all to explain the detail of the parts, it throws no light on their correlation.

> Then comes the doctrine of finality, which says that the parts have been brought together on a preconceived plan with a view to a certain end. In this it likens the labor of nature to that of the workman, who also proceeds by the assemblage of parts with a view to the realization of an idea or the imitation of a model. Mechanism, here, reproaches finalism with its anthropomorphic character, and rightly. But it fails to see that itself proceeds according to this method—somewhat mutilated! True, it has got rid of the end pursued or the ideal model. But it also holds that nature has worked like a human being by bringing parts together, while a mere glance at the development of an embryo shows that life goes to work in a very different way. *Life does not proceed by the association and addition of elements, but by dissociation and division* [translated by Arthur Mitchell].)

Evolution, then, is truly creative. It does not proceed by the rearrangement of preexisting parts; nor does it aim for an end that is already determined. In one of his best-known metaphors, Bergson compares the movement of evolution to "un obus qui a tout de suite éclaté en fragments, lesquels, étant eux-mêmes des espèces d'obus, ont éclaté à leur tour en fragments destinés à éclater encore, et ainsi de suite pendent fort longtemps" (a shell, which suddenly bursts into fragments, which fragments, being themselves shells, burst in their turn into fragments destined to burst again, and so on for a time incommensurably long). The *élan vital* has taken many paths as it cut its way through matter in its quest for freedom; it has had to adapt itself to its inorganic environment, just as a road has to follow the ups and downs of the hills through which it passes. The path that has led to the vegetable kingdom is a retrogression to torpor; the path that has led to the animal kingdom has continued the quest for freedom. Within the animal world two successful highways have been formed: that of the invertebrates and that of the vertebrates. On the side of consciousness or spirit, these orders have opposite and complementary means of acting on the world. In the invertebrates it is instinct, the faculty of using organized instruments—that is, instruments that form a part of the body of the organism that is using them, such as claws and teeth. In the vertebrates it is intelligence or intellect, the faculty of manufacturing and using unorganized instruments—that is, tools. Instinct culminates in the hymenoptera, the social insects such as bees and ants; intelligence culminates in the human species. Humanity, according to Bergson, should be designated not as *Homo sapiens* (man the wise) but as *Homo faber* (man the maker). The intellect has developed as a means of survival; it thinks in a "spatializing" manner that is useful in dealing with matter; it divides up the flow of reality, in which everything interpenetrates, into individual objects that exist beside one another. It applies the same procedure to time, dividing it into equal parts such as seconds, minutes, hours, and so on. Thus, intellect is inadequate for grasping the duration that characterizes ultimate reality.

But instinct and intelligence are not self-contained and mutually exclusive; both are manifestations of the *élan vital*. There is, therefore, some intelligence in all animals, including the insects, and some instinct in human beings. Instinct that is divorced from practical concerns and made disinterested and contemplative is intuition—which, as Bergson showed in his earlier works, is the means by which the philosopher can grasp duration, spirit, and life, which is the ultimate reality:

Une évolution autre eût pu conduire à une humanité ou plus intelligente encore, ou plus intuitive. En fait, dans l'humanité dont nous faisons partie, l'intuition est à peu près complètement sacrifiée à l'intelligence. Il semble qu'à conquérir la matière, et à se reconquérir de sa force. Cette conquête . . . exigeait que la conscience s'adaptât aux habitudes de la matière et concentrât toute son attention sur elles, enfin se déterminât plus spécialment en intelligence. L'intuition est là cependant, mais vague et surtout discontinue. C'est une lampe presque éteinte, qui ne se ranime que de loin en loin, pour quelques instants a peine. Mais elle se ranime, en somme, là où un intérêt vital est en jeu. Sur notre personnalité, sur notre liberté, sur la place que nous occupons dans l'ensemble de la nature, sur notre origine et peut-être aussi sur notre destinée, elle projette une lumière vacillante et faible, mais qui n'en perce pas moins l'obscurité de la nuit où nous laisse l'intelligence.

De ces intuitions évanouissantes, et qui n'éclairent leur objet que de distance en distance, la philosophie doit s'emparer, d'abord pour les soutenir, ensuite pour les dilater et les raccorder ainsi entre elles. Plus elle avance dans ce travail, plus elle s'aperçoit que l'intuition est l'esprit même et, en un certain sens, la vie même: l'intelligence s'y découpe par un processus imitateur de celui qui a engendré la matière.

(A different evolution might have led to a humanity either more intellectual still or more intuitive. In the humanity of which we are a part, intuition is, in fact, almost completely sacrificed to intellect. It seems that to conquer matter, and to reconquer its own self, consciousness has had to exhaust the best part of its power. This conquest . . . has required that consciousness should adapt itself to the habits of matter and concentrate all its attention on them, in fact determine itself more especially as intellect. Intuition is there, however, but vague and above all discontinuous. It is a lamp almost extinguished, which only glimmers now and then, for a few moments at most. But it glimmers wherever a vital interest is at stake. On our personality, on our liberty, on the place we occupy in the whole of nature, on our origin and perhaps also on our destiny, it throws a light feeble and vacillating, but which none the less pierces the darkness of the night in which the intellect leaves us.

These fleeting intuitions, which light up their object only at distant intervals, philosophy ought to seize, first to sustain them, then to expand them and so unite them together. The more it advances in this work, the more it will perceive that intuition is mind itself, and in a certain sense, life itself: the intellect has been cut out of it by a process resembling that which has generated matter [translated by Mitchell].)

The fourth and final chapter of *L'évolution créatrice*, "Le mécanisme cinématographique de la pensée et l'illusion mécanique" (The Cinematographical Mechanism of Thought and the Mechanistic Illusion), reviews the history of Western philosophy from Zeno of Elea to Herbert Spencer to show that by relying on the intellect, philosophers have failed to grasp the true nature of time and change and have falsified reality by imposing static and discrete concepts on experience. The book increased Bergson's popularity not only with professional philosophers but also with the general reading public; by 1918 it had gone through twenty-one editions.

In 1908 Bergson met William James in London. In a 4 October 1908 letter James wrote, "So modest and unpretending a man but such a genius intellectually! I have the strongest suspicions that the tendency which he has brought to a focus, will end by prevailing, and that the present epoch will be a sort of turning point in the history of philosophy." Shortly after their meeting, James presented the Hibbert Lectures at Manchester College of the University of Oxford, in which he said that Bergson had led him "to renounce the intellectualist method and the current notion that logic is an adequate measure of what can or cannot be" and "TO GIVE UP THE LOGIC, squarely and irrevocably" as a method, because "reality, life, experience, concreteness, immediacy, use what word you will, exceeds our logic, overflows, and surrounds it." The lectures were published in 1909 as *A Pluralistic Universe* and led many British and American readers to investigate Bergson's philosophy themselves. At that time James was assisting Arthur Mitchell in translating *L'évolution créatrice* into English and planned to write an introduction to the volume, but Mitchell died in August 1910. *Creative Evolution* appeared the following year and resulted in even more interest in Bergson in the English-speaking world. That same year Bergson wrote a preface titled "Sur le pragmatisme de William James: Vérité et réalité" (translated as "On the Pragmatism of William James: Truth and Reality," 1946) for the French translation of James's *Pragmatism*; in this preface he expressed both sympathy for and reservations about James's work.

From 5 to 11 April 1911 Bergson attended the Fourth International Congress of Philosophy in Bologna, Italy, where he gave the address "L'intuition philosophique" (translated as "Philosophical Intuition," 1946). In May he delivered two lectures at the University of Oxford; they were published that year in French by the Clarendon Press as *La perception du Changement* (translated as "The Perception of Change," 1946). Oxford conferred on him an honorary doctor of science degree. Two days later, he delivered the Huxley Memorial Lecture "La conscience et la vie" (translated as "Life and Consciousness," 1920) at Birmingham University; it appeared in *The Hibbert Journal* in October.

By 1911 students were calling the Collège de France "the house of Bergson." The following decade was the high point of the Bergson cult. His lectures were filled not only with students, including the future eminent philosophers Etienne Gilson and Jean Wahl, but also with other academics, society ladies and their escorts, tourists, and poets, including T. S. Eliot. Many of the attendees sat through lectures by other professors to be sure of hearing Bergson.

Even at the height of the "Bergson boom," however, dissenting voices were heard. Among them was the British philosopher Bertrand Russell, who published "The Philosophy of Bergson" in *The Monist* in 1912. Russell quotes from *Creative Evolution*:

> the great climax in which life is compared to a cavalry charge. "All organized beings, from the humblest to the highest, from the first origins of life to the time in which we are, and in all places as in all times, do but evidence a single impulsion, the inverse of the movement of matter, and in itself indivisible. All the living hold together, and all yield to the same tremendous push. The animal takes its stand on the plant, man bestrides animality, and the whole of humanity, in space and in time, is one immense army galloping beside and before and behind each of us in an overwhelming charge able to beat down every resistance and to clear many obstacles, perhaps even death."

Russell asks "whether there are any reasons for accepting such a restless view of the world" and answers that "there is no reason whatever for accepting this view, either in the universe or in the writings of M. Bergson." Russell says that the "two foundations of Bergson's philosophy, in so far as it is more than an imaginative and poetic view of the world, are his doctrines of space and time," and Russell goes on to argue in some detail that both doctrines are erroneous. Bergson was also criticized by the French philosopher Julien Benda, who attacked him from a Cartesian rationalist standpoint in many articles and two books: *Le Bergsonisme; ou, Philosophie de mobilité* (1912, Bergsonism; or, Philosophy of Mobility) and *Une philosophie pathétique* (1913, A Pathetic Philosophy). Benda held that Bergson wanted to replace logical thought with emotion, and philosophy with poetry; the supposed insight into absolute reality available through intuition is unverifiable and, therefore, unscientific. Bergsonism, he said, was a symptom of the cultural degradation of a democratic age in which science and philosophy were considered elitist.

In January 1913 Bergson made his first visit to the United States, at the invitation of Columbia University. In February he gave two lectures at the university; the first traffic jam in the history of Broadway is said to have occurred before the first lecture. Bergson went on to lecture before large audiences in several other American cities. In May he accepted the presidency of the British Society for Psychical Research and delivered the address "'Fantômes de vivants' et 'recherche psychique'" (translated as "'Phantasms of the Living' and 'Psychical

Research,'" 1920). Translations of his works appeared in English, German, Italian, Danish, Swedish, Hungarian, Polish, and Russian.

In 1914 Bergson was elected president of the Academie des sciences morales et politiques and named Officier de la Légion d'honneur and Officier de l'Instruction publique. That same year he was the first Jew elected to membership in the Academie française; he succeeded the historian Emile Ollivier, who had died in 1913. In May and June he delivered a course of eleven Gifford Lectures under the title "The Problem of Personality" at Edinburgh University.

Also in 1914, however, Bergson's work was attacked by Jacques Maritain from the standpoint of Thomism—the Christian Aristotelianism of St. Thomas Aquinas, which forms the official philosophy of the Roman Catholic Church—in his *La Philosophie bergsonienne: Etudes-critiques* (The Bergsonian Philosophy: Critical Studies; translated as *Bergsonian Philosophy and Thomism*, 1955). Maritain, who had been a disciple of Bergson before becoming a Thomist, charged that Bergson's metaphysics of pure becoming has no room for the concept of substance and, therefore, for the distinction between substance and accident, which is essential to the notion of transubstantiation that underlies the sacrament of the Eucharist. Also, Bergson's denial of fixed essences is incompatible with the notion that created beings have essences that reflect ideas in the mind of the Creator and, therefore, with the claim that the human essence was corrupted by Adam's sin and requires redemption through Christ. Furthermore, by making the *élan vital* immanent in the universe, Bergson's view eliminates the distinction between God and creation and, therefore, amounts to pantheism. On 1 June 1914 the Roman Catholic Church placed *Essai sur les données immédiates de la conscience, Matière et mémoire,* and *L'évolution créatrice* on the Index of Prohibited Books.

A second course of Gifford Lectures planned for the fall was canceled because of the outbreak of World War I in August. On 4 November 1914 Bergson published the article "La force qui s'use et celle qui ne s'use pas" (Wearing and Nonwearing Forces) in *Le Bulletin des Armées de la République Française*. In December he delivered the presidential address to the Academie des sciences morales et politiques; it was published in 1915 as *La signification de la guerre* and, along with the article "La force qui s'use et celle qui ne s'use pas," was translated that same year as *The Meaning of the War: Life & Matter in Conflict*. To concentrate on political and diplomatic activities related to the war, Bergson retired from all active duties at the Collège de France at the end of 1914 but did not resign from his professorship; his lectures were taken over by his assistant, Le Roy, who served as his "permanent substitute."

In 1915 Bergson was succeeded as president of the Academie des sciences morales et politiques by Alexandre Ribot. He also published a short summary of French philosophy at the request of the minister of public instruction. He began his diplomatic career with a trip to Spain in 1916, which was followed in 1917 by a mission to the United States as an emissary to President Woodrow Wilson. Bergson was officially inducted into the Academie française in January 1918.

In 1919 Bergson was made a commander of the Légion d'honneur. A collection of his shorter pieces appeared in 1919 as *L'énergie spirituelle: Essais et conférences* (Spiritual Energy: Essays and Lectures; translated as *Mind-Energy: Lectures and Essays,* 1920). It comprises "La conscience et la vie"; "L'âme et le corps" (translated as "The Soul and the Body"); "Fantômes de vivants' et 'recherche psychique'"; "Le rêve" (translated as "Dreams"); "Le souvenir du présent et la fausse reconnaissance" (translated as "Memory of the Present and False Recognition"); "L'effort intellectuel" (translated as "Intellectual Effort"); and "Le cerveau et la pensée: Une illusion philosophique" (translated as "Brain and Thought: A Philosophical Illusion"), a lecture he had given to the Congress of Philosophy in Geneva in 1904 under the title "Le paralogisme psycho-physiologique" (The Psycho-Physiological Paralogism).

In June 1920 Bergson received an honorary degree of doctor of letters from the University of Cambridge. He resigned his professorship at the Collège de France in 1921 and was appointed president of the International Commission for Intellectual Cooperation of the League of Nations, the forerunner of the United Nations Educational, Scientific, and Cultural Organization (UNESCO). At a meeting of the Societé de Philosophie in April 1922 he participated in a debate with Albert Einstein, who had won the Nobel Prize in physics the previous year, on Einstein's theory of relativity; Bergson published his views as *Durée et simultanéité à propos de la théorie d'Einstein* (1922; translated as *Duration and Simultaneity, with Reference to Einstein's Theory,* 1965). He criticizes the special theory of relativity on both mathematical and philosophical grounds. From a mathematical standpoint, he attacks the notion of multiplicity in Riemannian geometry that forms the basis of Einstein's theory. Philosophically, he holds that relativity depends on the notions of instants of time and simultaneity, which are spatialized abstractions that are incompatible with the real, irreversible, nonquantifiable time of duration. Bergson's views were attacked by the physicists Jean Becquerel and André Metz; he admitted in an appendix to the second edition of *Durée et simultanéité à propos de la théorie d'Einstein* that the mathematics he had used were inadequate, but he continued to uphold his philosophical critique of Einstein. He is generally—though not universally—regarded as having lost the debate with

Einstein, and some scholars contend that the dispute dealt a blow to his reputation from which it never recovered. He did not allow the book to be republished during his lifetime, and it was not included in the first edition of his *Oeuvres* (Works) in 1959.

Bergson suffered from crippling bouts of arthritis from 1925 until the end of his life. His term as president of the International Commission for Intellectual Cooperation ended in 1926. In 1927 he won the Nobel Prize in Literature "in recognition of his rich and vitalizing ideas and the brilliant skill with which they have been presented." Because of his illness, Bergson was unable to attend the Nobel banquet at the Grand Hotel in Stockholm on 10 December 1928; thus, instead of an address by the laureate, a letter from Bergson was read by the French minister, Armand Bernard. It was preceded by a brief comment by Professor Gösta Forssell: "Henri Bergson has given us a philosophical system which could have served Nobel's idea as a basis and support, the idea of acknowledging with his Prizes not human deeds but new ideas revealed through select personalities. Bergson's high-minded works strive to regain for man's consciousness the divine gift of intuition and to put reason in its proper place: serving and controlling ideas." While the literature prize is usually conferred on poets, playwrights, or fiction writers, Bergson's enormous contemporary importance and the gracefulness of his style made it impossible for the Nobel committee to ignore him. Also, since there is no Nobel Prize in philosophy, and philosophy is not a hard science like physics, chemistry, or medicine, the literature prize was the only available means of recognition at the committee's disposal. (In 1950 Bertrand Russell—who, like Bergson, was renowned for his writing style as well as for his accomplishments in philosophy—won the literature prize. Since 1993 the Schock Prize has been awarded every two years by the Royal Swedish Academy of Sciences in the fields of logic and philosophy and of mathematics; it is considered the equivalent of the Nobel Prize in those fields, although it is much less widely known.)

In 1932 Bergson published the last of his four major works, *Les deux sources de la morale et de la religion*. Certain species, Bergson says, have evolved in such a way that individuals of the species cannot exist in isolation but require the support of a community; bees and ants are the prime examples among the arthropods, and human beings are the prime example among the vertebrates. The communities, or societies, formed by the members of such species must be held together by some force that can overcome the selfish impulses of the individual members. In the insects, this role is played by instinct, which imposes precise and detailed obligations on each individual to assure the cohesion and orderly functioning of the group. In human societies, where more latitude is left to individual choice, it is played by habit:

Chacune de ces habitudes, qu'on pourra appeler "morales," sera contingente. Mais leur ensemble, je veux dire l'habitude de contracter ces habitudes, étant à la base même des sociétés et conditionnant leur existence, aura une force comparable à celle de l'instinct, et comme intensité et comme régularité. C'est là précisément ce que nous avons appelé "le tout de l'obligation." Il ne s'agira d'ailleurs que des sociétés humaines telles qu'elles sont au sortir des mains de la nature. Il s'agira de sociétés primitives et élémentaires. Mais la société humaine aura beau progresser, se compliquer et se spiritualiser: le statut de sa fondation demeurera, ou plutôt l'intention de la nature.

(Each of these habits, which may be called "moral," would be incidental. But the aggregate of them, I mean the habit of contracting these habits, being at the very basis of societies and a necessary condition of their existence, would have a force comparable to that of instinct in respect of both intensity and regularity. This is exactly what we have called the "totality of obligation." This, be it said, will apply only to human societies at the moment of emerging from the hands of nature. It will apply to primitive and to elementary societies. But, however much human society may progress, grow complicated and spiritualized, the original design, expressing the purpose of nature, will remain [translated by R. Ashley Audra, Cloudesley Brereton, and W. Horsfall Carter].)

In human beings, the habit of acquiring moral obligations is natural and instinctive, but the particular obligations are not; they vary from society to society, just as the capacity for language is instinctive but the syntax and grammar vary from language to language.

Both insect and human societies are "sociétés closes" (closed societies): each such society distinguishes itself from other societies formed by members of the same species, and the rules obeyed in each case are peculiar to the society in question; thus, in the case of the human society, the sum total of moral obligations is what Bergson calls a "morale close" (closed morality). Closed morality ensures the survival of the particular society and excludes other societies; thus, closed morality is necessarily concerned with war.

Bergson disagrees with the German philosopher Immanuel Kant that morality can be based on reason; morality is rooted in emotion, while reason, or what Bergson calls intelligence, can only rationalize and try to find support for the moral rules imposed by society. But intelligence allows the individual to question the norms of his or her society and is, therefore, a dangerous and potentially disruptive force. Nature, however, steps in and creates religion by means of "la fonction fabulatrice" (the mythmaking function) of the imagination. Deities are created who serve as the sources and enforcers of the moral rules. Religion also serves the vital function of providing an image of a life after death, since human beings, alone among the animals, are able to envision their own deaths and would, without the hope of an afterlife, become too depressed to act at all. Religion further allows people to believe that nature is controlled by friendly powers whose help may be invoked or even by unfriendly ones who might be propitiated, and thus it gives people a belief in their ability to exercise some control over their environment. This kind of religion, which serves to support the closed morality of a closed society, Bergson calls "religion statique" (static religion).

Closed morality and static religion are characteristic of primitive societies, but they continue to exist in more highly developed societies, which are still closed societies. In these more highly developed societies, however, the vision of another kind of society becomes possible: the "société ouverte" (open society), which would include all of humanity, and, corresponding to this society, a "morale ouverte" (open morality). Whereas closed morality is a morality of obligation and is felt as pressing on the individual from outside, the open morality is a morality of aspiration and attraction and is felt as pulling on the individual from within. It results from the contact, whether in person or by hearsay, with exceptional moral teachers—prophets, sages, and saints. These individuals, in turn, are inspired by their ability to perceive the *élan vital* in mystical experiences in which they feel at one with the universe as a whole and the source of all being. The religion that results from such experiences is "religion dynamique" (dynamic religion). It does not invoke personified deities who may be appeased through rituals but is a direct intuition of the creative life-force itself. It does not have doctrines; religion with rigid doctrines is static. Open morality and dynamic religion are concerned with creativity and progress, not with social cohesion; open morality is universal and aims at peace. Genuine, or complete, mystical experience must result in action; it cannot rest in contemplation of God.

Les deux sources de la morale et de la religion had a respectful reception from the philosophical community and the public, but Bergson's days as a philosophical luminary were past. The final book he published during his lifetime was *La pensée et le mouvant: Essais et conférences* (1934; translated as *The Creative Mind*, 1946), a collection of essays and lectures from earlier years.

By the time he wrote *Les deux sources de la morale et de la religion*, Bergson considered himself a Catholic in all but name. In his will, written on 8 February 1937, he said:

> Mes réflexions m'ont amené de plus en plus près du catholicisme où je vois l'achèvement complet du judaïsme. Je me serais converti, si je n'avais vu se préparer depuis des années la formidable vague d'antisémitisme qui va déferler sur le monde. J'ai voulu rester parmi ceux qui seront demain des persécutés.
>
> (My reflections have led me closer and closer to Catholicism, in which I see the complete fulfillment of Judaism. I would have become a convert, had I not foreseen for years a formidable wave of anti-Semitism about to break upon the world. I wanted to remain among those who tomorrow were to be persecuted.)

He went on to request that a priest pray at his funeral if the cardinal archbishop of Paris would authorize it; if not, he asked that a rabbi be invited to do so, without concealing from the clergyman or anyone else Bergson's moral adherence to Catholicism or his preference for a priest. After France fell to the Germans on 14 June 1940, he refused the Vichy government's offer to exempt him from its anti-Semitic laws and renounced all positions and honors he had received from the French government that could be construed as indicating his approval of the German puppet regime. In July, Bergson and his wife and daughter left Paris to spend the rest of the summer in Saint-Cyr-sur-Loire. They returned in November to the apartment at 47 boulevard Beauséjour where they had lived since 1929. At the end of the year, wearing a bathrobe and supported by a servant, Bergson stood in line to register as a Jew; some sources claim that he there contracted the bronchitis from which he died on 4 January 1941. A priest he had called to his deathbed arrived too late to administer last rites. He was buried in the small Garches Cemetery. After his death, Maritain's wife, Raïssa, claimed that Bergson had secretly been baptized a Catholic; but in a letter to Emmanuel Mounier that was published in the *Gazette de Lausanne* on 9 September 1941, Bergson's widow denied the allegation and quoted the passage from his will in which he gave his reason for not converting. She died in 1946; their daughter, Jeanne, died in 1961.

Bergson's popularity with the public and his prestige among philosophers had diminished well before his death. After World War II, they declined even further. The graceful, flowing style and vivid metaphors that had been admired in the early years of the twentieth century came to be regarded as rhetorical flourishes concealing thought that would not withstand close scrutiny. Furthermore, times had changed. As Harold A. Larrabee noted in the introduction to his edition of *Selections from Bergson*, published in 1949:

> Philosophers are still debating whether Bergson's philosophy as a whole deserves the epithets "irrational" or "anti-intellectual" which some have applied to it. But

the mere suspicion that those tags are not wholly inappropriate is enough to put us on our guard.

For we, unlike Bergson's earlier readers, are survivors of the Axis onslaught of 1939–45. In 1907, the enemy appeared to be what William James called "the beast, Intellectualism," and as against it, and all manner of nineteenth-century scientific and social rigidities, vitality and animal vigor had much in their favor. When Bergson attacked all the dead hands which close in upon the living, he spoke for the romantic rebel in all of us. But far worse beasts than intellectualism, overflowing, too, with savage vitality, have since come forth; and praise of blind instinct at the apparent expense of intelligent discrimination has a hollow ring indeed to those who have witnessed the abominations committed by the fanatics who boasted that they "thought with their blood."

This is not to accuse Bergson of the slightest sympathy with the instinct-trusting madmen who embittered his last years on earth.

Bergson left behind no "Bergsonian" school, but his work influenced philosophers such as James, George Santayana, Alfred North Whitehead, Arnold Hauser, Claude Simon, the political theorist Georges Sorel, and the existentialists Martin Heidegger, Maurice Merleau-Ponty, and Jean-Paul Sartre; Sartre said that *Essai sur les données immédiates de la conscience* was the text that first attracted him to philosophy. Like Bergson, the existentialists wanted to attain a pure view of phenomena that was not colored by concepts and categories borrowed from the physical sciences; they, however, preferred the more rigorous *epoché,* or "bracketing," method of the phenomenologist Edmund Husserl to Bergson's intuition. In literature, Bergson made an impact on Charles Péguy, Paul Valéry, George Bernard Shaw, John Dos Passos, Wallace Stevens, Willa Cather, and his wife's cousin Proust; in art, on the painter Claude Monet; and in music, on the composer Claude Debussy. Interest in Bergson was briefly reawakened in France by Gilles Deleuze's *Le Bergsonisme* (1966; translated as *Bergsonism,* 1988) and his use of Bergson's ideas in his analysis of the cinema. Deleuze himself died in 1995, and Bergson's philosophy is now primarily of historical interest.

Letters:

Correspondences, edited by André Robinet, Nelly Bruyère, Brigitte Sitbon-Peillon, and Suzanne Stern-Gillet (Paris: Presses universitaires de France, 2002);

Henri Bergson et Albert Kahn: Correspondances, edited by Sophie Coeuré and Frédéric Worms (Strasbourg: Desmaret / Boulogne: Musée départemental Albert-Kahn, 2003).

Bibliography:

P. A. Y. Gunter, *Henri Bergson: A Bibliography* (Bowling Green, Ohio: Philosophy Documentation Center, Bowling Green University, 1974; revised, 1986).

Biographies:

Jean Guitton, *La vocation de Bergson* (Paris: Gallimard, 1960);

Jean-Louis Vieillard-Baron, *Bergson* (Paris: Presses universitaires de France, 1991);

Philippe Soulez and Frédéric Worms, *Bergson: Biographie* (Paris: Flammarion, 1997).

References:

Lydie Adolphe, *La dialectique des images chez Bergson* (Paris: Presses universitaires de France, 1951);

Adolphe, *La philosophie religieuse de Bergson* (Paris: Presses universitaires de France, 1946);

Ian W. Alexander, *Bergson, Philosopher of Reflection* (London: Bowes & Bowes, 1957; New York: Hillary House, 1957);

Mark Antliff, ed., *Inventing Bergson: Cultural Politics and the Parisian Avant-Garde* (Princeton: Princeton University Press, 1993);

Roméo Arbour, *Henri Bergson et les lettres françaises* (Paris: Corti, 1955);

Randall E. Auxier, "A Dialogue on Bergson," *Process Studies,* 28 (Fall–Winter 1999): 339–345;

Gaston Bachelard, *The Dialectic of Duration,* translated by Mary McAllester Jones (Manchester, U.K.: Clinamen Press, 2000);

Michel Barlow, *Henri Bergson* (Paris: Editions universitaires, 1966);

Madeleine Barthélemy-Maudale, *Bergson* (Paris: Seuil, 1967);

Barthélemy-Maudale, *Bergson, adversaire du Kant* (Paris: Presses universitaires de France, 1964);

Barthélemy-Maudale, *Bergson et Teilhard de Chardin* (Paris: Seuil, 1963);

Albert Béguin and Pierre Thevenaz, eds., *Henri Bergson: Essais et témoignages* (Neuchâtel: La Baconnière, 1943);

Julien Benda, *Le bergsonisme; ou, Philosophie de la mobilité* (Paris: Mercure de France, 1912);

Benda, *Une philosophie pathétique* (Paris: J. Crémieu, 1913);

Benda, *Sur le succès du bergsonisme: Précédé d'une réponse aux défenseurs de la doctrine* (Paris: Mercure de France, 1914);

Richard Bilsker, *On Bergson* (Belmont, Cal.: Wadsworth, 2002);

Richard L. Brougham, "Reality and Appearance in Bergson and Whitehead," *Process Studies,* 24 (1995): 39–43;

Walter Brunting, "La filosofia irraciotialista de la historia en la actualidad," *Revista de Filosofia,* 5, no. 2 (1958): 3–17;

Frederick Burwick and Paul Douglass, eds., *The Crisis in Modernism: Bergson and the Vitalist Controversy* (Cambridge & New York: Cambridge University Press, 1992);

Milik Capec, *Bergson and Modern Physics: A Reinterpretation and Re-evaluation* (Dordrecht: Reidel, 1971);

Marie Cariou, *L'atomisme: Trois essais. Gassendi, Leibniz, Bergson et Lucrèce* (Paris: Montaigne, 1978);

Cariou, *Bergson et Bachelard* (Paris: Presses universitaires de France, 1995);

Cariou, *Bergson et le fait mystique* (Paris: Montaigne, 1976);

Cariou, *Lectures Bergsoniennes* (Paris: Presses universitaires de France, 1990);

Herbert Wildon Carr, *Henri Bergson: The Philosophy of Change* (London: Jack / New York: Dodge, 1912);

Jacques Chevalier, *Bergson* (Paris: Plon, 1926); translated by Lilian A. Clare as *Henri Bergson* (New York: Macmillan, 1928); French version revised and enlarged as *Bergson* (Paris: Plon, 1948);

Chevalier, *Entretiens avec Bergson* (Paris: Plon, 1955);

Frederick C. Copleston, *Bergson on Morality* (London: Oxford University Press, 1955);

André Cresson, *Bergson: Sa vie, son oeuvre, avec un exposé de sa philosophie* (Paris: Presses universitaires de France, 1941);

Gustavus Watts Cunningham, *A Study in the Philosophy of Bergson* (New York: Longmans, Green, 1916);

Victor Delbos, "Matière et Mémoire, essai sur la relation du corps a l'esprit," *Revue de métaphysique et de morale* (1897): 353–389;

Gilles Deleuze, "Bergson: 1859–1941," in *Les philosophes celebres,* edited by Maurice Merleau-Ponty (Paris: Mazenod, 1956), pp. 292–299;

Deleuze, *Le Bergsonisme* (Paris: Presses universitaires de France, 1966); translated by Hugh Tomlinson and Barbara Habberjam as *Bergsonism* (New York: Zone Books, 1988);

Deleuze, *Cinéma: L'image-mouvement* (Paris: Minuit, 1983); translated by Tomlinson and Habberjam as *Cinema 1: The Movement-Image* (Minneapolis: University of Minnesota Press, 1986);

Deleuze, *Cinéma: L'image-temps* (Paris: Minuit, 1985); translated by Tomlinson and Robert Galeta as *Cinema 2: The Time-Image* (Minneapolis: University of Minnesota Press, 1989);

Deleuze, *Différence et répétition* (Paris: Presses universitaires de France, 1968); translated by Paul Patton as *Difference and Repetition* (New York: Columbia University Press, 1994);

Jeanne Delhomme, "Nietzsche et Bergson: La représentation de la vérité," *Etudes bergsoniennes,* 5 (1960): 37–62;

Delhomme, *Vie et conscience de la vie: Essai sur Bergson* (Paris: Presses universitaires de France, 1954);

Matteo Fabris, *La filosofia sociale de Henri Bergson* (Bari: Resta, 1966);

Augustin Fressin, *La perception chez Bergson et chez Merleau-Ponty* (Paris: Société d'édition d'enseignement supérieur, 1967);

Bernard Gilson, *La révision Bergsonienne de l'esprit* (Paris: Vrin, 1996);

Lorenzo Giusso, *Bergson* (Milan: Bocca, 1949);

Jean-Christophe Goddard, *Mysticisme et folie: Essai sur la simplicité* (Paris: Desclée de Brouwer, 2002);

Henri Gaston Gouhier, *Bergson et le Christ des évangiles* (Paris: Fayard, 1961);

P. A. Y. Gunter, "Bergson, Mathematics, and Creativity," *Process Studies,* 28 (Fall–Winter 1999): 268–288;

Gunter, ed. and trans., *Bergson and the Evolution of Physics* (Knoxville: University of Tennessee Press, 1969);

Thomas Hanna, ed., *The Bergsonian Heritage* (New York: Columbia University Press, 1962);

François Heidsieck, *Henri Bergson et la notion d'espace* (Paris: Le Cercle du livre, 1957);

Harald Høffding, *La philosophie de Bergson: Exposé et critique,* translated by Jacques de Coussange (pseudonym of Barbe de Quirielle) (Paris: Alcan, 1916);

Léon Husson, *L'Intellectualisme de Bergson* (Paris: Presses universitaires de France, 1947);

Vladimir Jankélévitch, *Bergson* (Paris: Alcan, 1931);

Jankélévitch, *Henri Bergson* (Paris: Presses universitaires de France, 1959);

Robert Klawitter, "Henri Bergson and James Joyce's Fictional World," *Comparative Literature Studies,* 3, no. 4 (1966): 429–437;

Leszek Kolakowski, *Bergson* (Oxford & New York: Oxford University Press, 1985);

R. Lacey, *Bergson* (London & New York: Routledge, 1989);

Roger Etienne Lacombe, *La psychologie Bergsonienne* (Paris: Alcan, 1933);

Leonard Lawlor, *The Challenge of Bergsonism: Phenomenology, Ontology, Ethics* (London: Continuum, 2003);

Georges Lechalas, "Matière et mémoire, d'après un nouveau livre de M. Bergson," *Annales de philosophie chretienne* (May 1897): 147–164; (June 1897): 314–334;

Edouard Le Roy, *Une philosophie nouvelle: Henri Bergson* (Paris: Alcan, 1912); translated by Vincent Benson as *The New Philosophy of Henri Bergson* (London: Williams & Norgate / New York: Holt, 1913);

D. Lindsay, *The Philosophy of Bergson* (London: Dent, 1911);

Alfred Firmin Loisy, *Y a-t-il deux sources de la religion et la morale?* revised and enlarged edition (Paris: Nourry, 1934);

Jacques Maritain, *La Philosophie bergsonienne: Etudes critiques* (Paris: Rivière, 1914); translated by Mabelle L. Andison and J. Gordon Andison as *Bergsonian Philosophy and Thomism* (New York: Philosophical Library, 1955);

Vittorio Mathieu, *Bergson: Il profondo e la sua espressione* (Turin: Edizioni di "Filosofia," 1954);

André Metz, *Bergson et le bergsonisme* (Paris: Vrin, 1933);

François Meyer, *Pour connaître la pensée de Bergson* (Paris: Bordas, 1964);

F. C. T. Moore, *Bergson: Thinking Backwards* (Cambridge & New York: Cambridge University Press, 1996);

John Morrison Moore, *Theories of Religious Experience, with Special Reference to James, Otto and Bergson* (New York: Round Table Press, 1938);

Rose-Marie Mossé-Bastide, *Bergson, éducateur* (Paris: Presses universitaires de France, 1955);

Mossé-Bastide, *Bergson et Plotin* (Paris: Presses universitaires de France, 1960);

John Mullarkey, ed., *The New Bergson* (Manchester, U.K.: Manchester University Press, 1999);

Andrew C. Papanicolaou and P. A. Y. Gunter, eds., *Bergson and Modern Thought: Towards a Unified Science* (Chur, U.K. & New York: Harwood Academic, 1987);

Keith Ansell Pearson, *Philosophy and the Adventure of the Virtual: Bergson and the Time of Life* (London: Routledge, 2002);

Günther Pflug, *Henri Bergson: Quellen und Konsequenzen einer induktiven Metaphysik* (Berlin: De Gruyter, 1959);

Anthony Edward Pilkington, *Bergson and His Influence: A Reassessment* (Cambridge: Cambridge University Press, 1976);

Bento Prado, *Présence et champ transcendental: Conscience et négativité dans la philosophie de Bergson,* translated by Renaud Barbaras (Hildesheim: Olms, 2002);

Emile Rideau, *Les rapports de la matère et de l'esprit dans le bergsonisme* (Paris: Alcan, 1932);

André Robinet, *Bergson et les métamorphoses de la durée* (Paris: Seghers, 1965);

Robinet, "Le Passage à la conception biologique de la perception, de l'image et du souvenir chez Bergson," *Etudes philosophiques,* 15, no. 3 (1960): 375–388;

Algot Henrik Leonard Ruhe and Nancy Margaret Paul, *Henri Bergson: An Account of His Life and Philosophy* (London: Macmillan, 1914);

Bertrand Russell, "The Philosophy of Bergson," *Monist,* 22 (July 1912): 321–347; republished in *The Philosophy of Bergson, with a Reply by Mr. H. Wildon Carr and a Rejoinder by Mr. Russell* (Cambridge: Published for "The Heretics" by Bowes & Bowes, 1914; New York: Folcroft, 1971);

George Santayana, *Winds of Doctrine* (New York: Scribners, 1913), pp. 58–109;

Ben-Ami Scharfstein, *Roots of Bergson's Philosophy* (New York: Columbia University Press, 1943);

Joseph Louis Paul Segond, *L'intuition bergsonienne* (Paris: Alcan, 1913);

A. G. Sertillanges, *Henri Bergson et le Catholicisme* (Paris: Flammarion, 1941);

Joseph Solomon, *Bergson* (New York: Dodge, 1911; London: Constable, 1912);

Philippe Soulez, *Bergson politique* (Paris: Presses universitaires de France, 1989);

Newton Phelps Stallknecht, *Studies in the Philosophy of Creation, with Especial Reference to Bergson and Whitehead* (Princeton: Princeton University Press, 1934);

Karin Stephen, *The Misuse of Mind: A Study of Bergson's Attack on Intellectualism* (New York: Harcourt, Brace / London: Kegan Paul, Trench, Trübner, 1922);

John McKellar Stewart, *A Critical Exposition of Bergson's Philosophy* (London: Macmillan, 1911);

Albert Thibaudet, *Le bergsonisme,* 2 volumes (Paris: Editions de la nouvelle revue française, 1923);

Joseph de Tonquédec, *Dieu dans l'évolution créatice, avec deux lettres de M. Bergson* (Paris: Beauchesne, 1912);

Pierre Trotignon, *L'idée de vie chez Bergson et la critique de la métaphysique* (Paris: Presses universitaires de France, 1968);

Frédéric Worms, "Au-delà de l'histoire et du caractère: L'idée de philosophie Française, la Première Guerre mondiale et le moment 1900," *Revue de métaphysicque et de morale,* no. 3 (2001): 63–81;

Worms, "L'Intelligence gagnée par l'intuition? La relation entre Bergson et Kant," *Etudes philosophiques,* no. 4 (2001): 453–464;

Worms, *Introduction à Matière et mémoire: Suivie d'une brève introduction aux autres livres de Bergson* (Paris: Presses universitaires de France, 1998);

Worms, *Le Vocabulaire de Bergson* (Paris: Ellipses, 2000);

Worms, ed., *Bergson dans le siècle* (Paris: Presses universitaires de France, 2002).

Papers:

Henri Bergson's will directed that all of his papers be destroyed, and his widow burned them in the fireplace. Thus, the Bergson Archives at the Librairie Jacques Doucet in Paris contain only Bergson's personal library.

1927 Nobel Prize in Literature Presentation Speech

by Per Hallström, President of the Nobel Committee of the Swedish Academy, 10 December 1928

In his *L'évolution créatrice* (1907) *[Creative Evolution]*, Henri Bergson has declared that the most lasting and most fruitful of all philosophical systems are those which originate in intuition. If one believes these words, it appears immediately with regard to Bergson's system how he has made fruitful the intuitive discovery that opens the gate to the world of his thought. This discovery is set forth in his doctoral thesis, *Essai sur les données immédiates de la conscience* (1889) *[Time and Free Will]*, in which time is conceived not as something abstract or formal but as a reality, indissolubly connected with life and the human self. He gives it the name "duration," a concept that can be interpreted as "living time," by analogy with the life force. It is a dynamic stream, exposed to constant qualitative variations and perpetually increasing. It eludes reflection. It cannot be linked with any fixed point, for it would thereby be limited and no longer exist. It can be perceived and felt only by an introspective and concentrated consciousness that turns inward toward its origin.

What we usually call time, the time which is measured by the movement of a clock or the revolutions of the sun, is something quite different. It is only a form created by and for the mind and action. At the end of a most subtle analysis, Bergson concludes that it is nothing but an application of the form of space. Mathematical precision, certitude, and limitation prevail in its domain; cause is distinguished from effect and hence rises that edifice, a creation of the mind, whose intelligence has encircled the world, raising a wall around the most intimate aspirations of our minds toward freedom. These aspirations find satisfaction in "living time": cause and effect here are fused; nothing can be foreseen with certainty, for certainty resides in the act, simple in itself, and can be established only by this act. Living time is the realm of free choice and new creations, the realm in which something is produced only once and is never repeated in quite the same manner. The history of the personality originates in it. It is the realm where the mind, the soul, whatever one may call it, by casting off the forms and habits of intelligence becomes capable of perceiving in an inner vision the truth about its own essence and about the universal life which is a part of our self.

In his purely scientific account, the philosopher tells us nothing of the origin of this intuition, born perhaps of a personal experience skilfully seized upon and probed, or perhaps of a liberating crisis of the soul. One can only guess that this crisis was provoked by the heavy atmosphere of rationalistic biology that ruled toward the end of the last century. Bergson had been brought up and educated under the influence of this science, and when he decided to take up arms against it, he had a rare mastery of its own weapons and full knowledge of the necessity and grandeur it had in its own realm, the conceptual construction of the material world. Only when rationalism seeks to imprison life itself in its net does Bergson seek to prove that the dynamic and fluid nature of life passes without hindrance across its meshes.

Even if I were competent, it would still be impossible to give an account of the subtlety and scope of Bergson's thought in the few minutes at my disposal. The task is even more impossible for one who possesses only a very limited sense of philosophy and has never studied it.

At his starting point, the intuition of a living time, Bergson borrows in his analysis, in the development of his concepts, and in the sequence of his proofs, something of the dynamic, flowing, and almost irresistible essence of this intuition. One has to follow every movement; every moment introduces a new element. One has to follow the current, trying to breathe as best one can. There is scarcely time for reflection, for the moment one becomes static oneself, one loses all contact with the chain of reasoning.

In a singularly penetrating refutation of determinism our philosopher demonstrates that a universal intellect, which he calls Pierre, could not predict the life of another person, Paul, except in so far as he can follow Paul's experiences, sensations, and voluntary acts in all their manifestations, to the extent of becoming identical with him as completely as two equal triangles coincide. A reader who wants to understand Bergson completely must to a certain extent identify himself with the author and fulfil enormous requirements of power and flexibility of mind.

This is by no means to say that there is no point in following the author in his course, for good or ill. Imagination and intuition are sometimes capable of flights where intelligence lags behind. It is not always possible to decide whether the imagination is seduced or whether the intuition recognizes itself and lets itself be convinced. In any event, reading Bergson is always highly rewarding.

In the account, so far definitive, of his doctrine, *L'évolution créatrice*, the master has created a poem of striking grandeur, a cosmogony of great scope and unflagging power, without sacrificing a strictly scientific terminology.

It may be difficult at times to profit from its penetrating analysis or from the profundity of its thought; but one always derives from it, without any difficulty, a strong aesthetic impression.

The poem, if one looks at it in that way, presents a sort of drama. The world has been created by two conflicting tendencies. One of them represents matter which, in its own consciousness, tends downwards; the second is life with its innate sentiment of freedom and its perpetually creative force, which tends increasingly toward the light of knowledge and limitless horizons. These two elements are mingled, prisoners of each other, and the product of this union is ramified on different levels.

The first radical difference is found between the vegetable and the animal world, between immobile and mobile organic activity. With the help of the sun, the vegetable world stores up the energy it extracts from inert matter; the animal is exempt from this fundamental task because it can draw energy already stored up in the vegetables from which it frees the explosive force simultaneously and proportionately to its needs. At a higher level in the chain, the animal world lives at the expense of the animal world, being able, due to this concentration of energy, to accentuate its development. The evolutionary paths thus become more and more diverse and their choice is in no way blind: instinct is born at the same time as the organs that it utilizes. Intellect is also existent in an embryonic stage, but still mind is inferior to instinct.

At the top of the chain of being, in man, intelligence becomes predominant and instinct subsides, without however disappearing entirely; it remains latent in the consciousness that unites all life in the current of "living time"; it comes into play in the intuitive vision. The beginnings of intelligence are modest and manifestly timid. Intelligence is expressed only by the tendency and the ability to replace organic instruments instinctively by instruments sprung from inert matter, and to make use of them by a free act. Instinct was more conscious of its goal, but this goal was, on the other hand, greatly limited; intelligence engaged itself, on the contrary, in greater risks, but tended also toward infinitely vaster goals, toward goals realized by the material and social culture of the human race. Inevitably a risk existed, however: intelligence, created to act in the spatial world, might distort the image of the world by the modality thus acquired from its concept of life and might remain deaf to its innermost dynamic essence and to the freedom that presides over its eternal variation. Hence the mechanistic and deterministic conception of an external world created by the conquests of intelligence in the natural sciences.

We will find ourselves, then, irremediably cornered in an impasse, without any consciousness of freedom of mind and cut off from the sources of life we carry within us, unless we also possess the gift of intuition when we trace ourselves back to our origin. Perhaps one can apply to this intuition, the central point of the Bergsonian doctrine, the brilliant expression that he uses about intelligence and instinct: the perilous way toward vaster possibilities. Within the limits of its knowledge, intelligence possesses logical certainty, but intuition, dynamic like everything that belongs to living time, must without doubt content itself with the intensity of its certainty.

This is the drama: creative evolution is disclosed, and man finds himself thrust on stage by the *élan vital* of universal life which pushes him irresistibly to act, once he has come to the knowledge of his own freedom, capable of divining and glimpsing the endless route that has been travelled with the perspective of a boundless field opening onto other paths. Which of these paths is man going to follow?

In reality we are only at the beginning of the drama, and it can scarcely be otherwise, especially if one considers Bergson's concept that the future is born only at the moment in which it is lived. However, something is lacking in this beginning itself. The author tells us nothing of the will inherent in the free personality, of the will that determines action and that has the power to trace straight lines across the unforeseeable curves of this personality. Furthermore, he tells us nothing about the problem of life dominated by will power, about the existence or non-existence of absolute values.

What is the essence of the irresistible *élan vital,* that onslaught of life against the inertia of matter, which, according to Bergson's audacious and magnificent expression, will one day triumph perhaps over death itself? What will it make of us when it places at our feet all earthly power?

However complicated they may be, one cannot escape these questions. Is the philosopher perhaps at this very moment on his way to the solution, certainly as tentative and audacious as his previous work has been and richer still in possibilities?

There still remain some points to clarify. Does he perhaps seek to put an end to the dualism of the image he gives of the world in seeking out a kind of *élan vital* that applies to matter? We know nothing in this regard, but Bergson has himself presented his system as constituting, on many points, only an outline that must be completed in its details by the collaboration of other thinkers.

We are indebted to him, nevertheless, for one achievement of importance: by a passage he has forced through the gates of rationalism, he has released a creative impulse of inestimable value, opening a large access to the waters of living time, to that atmosphere in which the human mind will be able to rediscover its freedom and thus be born anew.

If the outlines of his thought prove sound enough to serve as guides to the human spirit, Bergson can be assured, in the future, of an influence even greater than the influence he is already enjoying. As stylist and as poet, he yields place to none of his contemporaries; in their strictly objective search for truth, all his aspirations are animated by a spirit of freedom which, breaking the servitude that matter imposes, makes room for idealism.

[© The Nobel Foundation, 1928.]

Bergson: Banquet Speech

Introductory remarks by Professor Gösta Forssell at the Nobel Banquet at Grand Hôtel, Stockholm, 10 December 1928:

Henri Bergson has given us a philosophical system which could have served Nobel's idea as a basis and support, the idea of acknowledging with his Prizes not human deeds but new ideas revealed through select personalities. Bergson's high-minded works strive to regain for man's consciousness the divine gift of intuition and to put reason in its proper place: serving and controlling ideas.

Bergson's speech (read by the French Minister, Armand Bernard, as Bergson could not attend) (Translation)

I wish I had been able to express my feelings in person. Permit me to do so through the French Minister, Mr. Armand Bernard, who has kindly consented to convey my message. I thank the Swedish Academy from the bottom of my heart. It has bestowed upon me an honour to which I should not have dared aspire. I recognize its value even more, and I am even more moved by it, when I consider that this distinction, given to a French writer, may be regarded as a sign of sympathy given to France.

The prestige of the Nobel Prize is due to many causes, but in particular to its twofold idealistic and international character: idealistic in that it has been designed for works of lofty inspiration; international in that it is awarded after the production of different countries has been minutely studied and the intellectual balance sheet of the whole world has been drawn up. Free from all other considerations and ignoring any but intellectual values, the judges have deliberately taken their place in what the philosophers have called a community of the mind. Thus they conform to the founder's explicit intention. Alfred Bernhard Nobel declared in his will that he wanted to serve the causes of idealism and the brotherhood of nations. By establishing a peace Prize alongside the high awards in arts and sciences, he marked his goal with precision.

It was a great idea. Its originator was an inventive genius and yet he apparently did not share an illusion widespread in his century. If the nineteenth century made tremendous progress in mechanical inventions, it too often assumed that these inventions, by the sheer accumulation of their material effects, would raise the moral level of mankind. Increasing experience has proved, on the contrary, that the technological development of a society does not automatically result in the moral perfection of the men living in it, and that an increase in the material means at the disposal of humanity may even present dangers unless it is accompanied by a corresponding spiritual effort. The machines we build, being artificial organs that are added to our natural organs, extend their scope, and thus enlarge the body of humanity. If that body is to be kept entire and its movements regulated, the soul must expand in turn; otherwise its equilibrium will be threatened and grave difficulties will arise, social as well as political, which will reflect on another level the disproportion between the soul of mankind, hardly changed from its original state, and its enormously enlarged body. To take only the most striking example: one might have expected that the use of steam and electricity, by diminishing distances, would by itself bring about a moral *rapprochement* between peoples. Today we know that this was not the case and that antagonisms, far from disappearing, will risk being aggravated if a spiritual progress, a greater effort toward brotherhood, is not accomplished. To move toward such a *rapprochement* of souls is the natural tendency of a foundation with an international character and an idealistic outlook which implies that the entire civilized world is envisaged from a purely intellectual point of view as constituting one single and identical republic of minds. Such is the Nobel Foundation.

It is not surprising that this idea was conceived and realized in a country as highly intellectual as Sweden, among a people who have given so much attention to moral questions and have recognized that all others follow from them, and who, to cite only one example, have been the first to grasp that the political problem par excellence is the problem of education.

Thus the scope of the Nobel Foundation seems to widen as its significance is more deeply realized, and to have benefited from it becomes an honour all the more deeply appreciated. No one is more fully aware of this than I am. I wished to say so before this illustrious audience, and I conclude, as I began, with the expression of my profound gratitude.

[© The Nobel Foundation, 1928. Henri Bergson is the sole author of his speech.]

Bjørnstjerne Bjørnson
(8 September 1832 – 26 April 1910)

Hans H. Skei
University of Oslo

BOOKS: *Synnøve Solbakken* (Christiania: Johan Dahls, 1857); translated by Augusta Bethell and Augusta Plesner as *Love and Life in Norway* (London: Cassell, Petter & Galpin, 1870);
Mellem slagene (Christiania: C. A. Dybwad, 1857);
Halte-Hulda (Bergen: H. J. Geelmuydens Enkes Officin og Forlag, 1858);
Arne (Bergen: H. J. Geelmuydens Enkes Officin og Forlag, 1859); translated as *Arne, or Peasant Life in Norway: A Norwegian Tale* (Bergen, 1860);
Småstykker (Christiania, 1860)—includes "Thrond," *En glad gut,* and "Faderen";
Kong Sverre (Copenhagen: Gyldendal, 1861);
Sigurd Slembe (Copenhagen: Gyldendal, 1862); translated by William Morton Payne as *Sigurd Slembe: A Dramatic Trilogy* (Boston: Houghton, Mifflin, 1888);
Maria Stuart i Skottland (Copenhagen: Gyldendal, 1864);
De Nygifte (Copenhagen: Gyldendal, 1865); translated by John Volk as *The Newly Married* (Chicago: Scandinavia, 1885);
Fiskerjenten (Copenhagen: Gyldendal, 1868); translated from the author's German edition by M. E. Niles as *The Fisher-Maiden: A Norwegian Tale* (New York: Leypoldt & Holt, 1869);
Arnljot Gelline (Copenhagen: Gyldendal, 1870); translated by Payne as *Arnljot Gelline* (New York: American-Scandinavian Foundation, 1917);
Digte og Sange (Copenhagen: Gyldendal, 1870; revised and enlarged editions, 1880, 1890, and 1914);
Fortællinger, 2 volumes (Copenhagen: Gyldendal, 1872)—comprises volume 1, *Arne, Synnøve Solbakken, Jærnbanen og Kirkegaarden,* and *Småstykker;* and volume 2, *En glad gut, Fiskerjenten,* and *Brudeslåtten;*
Sigurd Jorsalfar (Copenhagen: Gyldendal, 1872);
Brudeslåtten (Copenhagen: Gyldendal, 1873);
En fallit (Copenhagen: Gyldendal, 1875);
Redaktøren (Copenhagen: Gyldendal, 1874 [i.e., 1875]);
Kongen (Copenhagen: Gyldendal, 1877);
Magnhild (Copenhagen: Gyldendal, 1877);

Bjørnstjerne Bjørnson (from Plays, *translated by Edwin Bjørkman, 1913; Thomas Cooper Library, University of South Carolina)*

Vis-Knut (Chicago: Skandinavens boghandel, 1878); translated by Bernard Stahl as *Wise-Knut* (New York: Brandu's, 1909);
Det ny system (Copenhagen: Gyldendal, 1879);
Kaptein Mansana (Copenhagen: Gyldendal, 1879);
Leonarda (Copenhagen: Gyldendal, 1879);
En hanske (Copenhagen: Gyldendal, 1883); translated by Osman Edwards as *A Gauntlet* (London & New York: Longmans, Green, 1894);

Over ævne I (Copenhagen: Gyldendal, 1883); translated by William Wilson as *Pastor Sang* (London & New York: Longmans, Green, 1893);

Det flager i byen og på havnen (Copenhagen: Gyldendal, 1884); translated by Cecil Fairfax as *The Heritage of the Kurts* (London: Heinemann, 1892);

Geografi og kjærlighed (Copenhagen: Gyldendal, 1885);

Engifte og mangegifte: Et foredrag (Fagerstrand pr. Høvik: Bibliothek for de tusen hjem, 1888);

På Guds veje (Copenhagen: Gyldendal, 1889); translated by Elizabeth Carmichael as *In God's Way* (London: Heinemann, 1890; New York: Lovell, 1890);

Nye fortællinger (Copenhagen: Gyldendal, 1894)—comprises *Absalons hår, Et stygt barndomsminde, Mors hænder,* and *En dag;*

Over ævne II (Copenhagen: Gyldendal, 1895);

Paul Lange og Tora Parsberg (Copenhagen: Gyldendal, 1898); translated by H. L. Braekstad as *Paul Lange and Tora Parsberg* (London & New York: Harper, 1899);

Laboremus (Copenhagen: Gyldendal, 1901); translated as *Laboremus* (London: Chapman & Hall, 1901);

To fortællinger (Copenhagen: Gyldendal, 1901)—comprises *Støv* and *Ivar Bye;*

På Storhove (Copenhagen: Gyldendal, 1902);

Daglannet (Copenhagen & Christiania: Gyldendal, 1904);

Mary (Copenhagen & Christiania: Gyldendal, 1906);

To taler (Copenhagen: Gyldendal, 1906);

Når den ny vin blomstrer (Copenhagen & Christiania: Gyldendal, 1909).

Collection: *Samlede digterværker,* 9 volumes, edited by Francis Bull (Copenhagen & Christiania: Gyldendal, 1919–1920).

Editions in English: *Life by the Fells and Fiords: A Norwegian Sketch-Book* (London: Strahan, 1879)—includes *Arne* and *Brude-Slaatten;*

Works, 5 volumes, translated by Rasmus B. Anderson (New York: Doubleday, Page, 1882)—comprises volume 1, *Synnove Solbakken;* volume 2, *Magnild and Dust;* volume 3, *The Bridal March* and *Captain Mansana;* volume 4, *The Fisher Maiden;* and volume 5, *A Happy Boy, Blakken, Fidelity,* and *A Problem of Life;*

The Novels of Björnstjerne Björnson, 13 volumes, edited by Edmund Gosse (New York: Macmillan, 1895–1909)—comprises volume 1, *Synnövé Solbakken,* translated by Julie Sutter (1895); volume 2, *Arne,* translated by William Low (1895); volume 3, *A Happy Boy,* translated by Mrs. W. Archer (1896); volume 4, *The Fisher Lass* (1896); volume 5, *The Bridal March & One Day* (1896); volume 6, *Magnhild & Dust* (1897); volume 7, *Captain Mansana & Mother's Hands* (1897); volume 8, *Absalom's Hair &* *A Painful Memory* (1898); volumes 9–10, *In God's Way,* translated by Elizabeth Carmichael (1908); volumes 11–12, *The Heritage of the Kurts,* translated by Cecil Fairfax (1908); and volume 13, *Mary,* translated by Mary Morison (1909);

Three Comedies, translated by R. Farquharson Sharp (London: Dent, 1912)—comprises *The Newly-Married Couple, Leonarda,* and *The Gauntlet;*

Plays, translated by Edwin Bjørkman (New York: Scribners, 1913)—comprises *The Gauntlet, Beyond Our Power,* and *The New System;*

Plays, 2d Series, translated by Bjørkman (New York: Scribners, 1914)—comprises *Love and Geography, Beyond Human Might,* and *Laboremus;*

Three Dramas, translated by Sharp (London: Dent / New York: E. P. Dutton, 1914)—comprises *The Editor, The Bankrupt,* and *The King;*

Poems and Songs, translated by Arthur Hubbell Palmer (New York: American-Scandinavian Foundation, 1915).

PLAY PRODUCTIONS: *Mellem slagene,* Christiania [Oslo], Christiania Theater, 27 October 1857;

Kong Sverre, Christiania, Christiania Norske Teater, 9 October 1861;

Halte-Hulda, Christiania, Christiania Norske Teater, 25 April 1862;

Sigurd Slembe, parts 1 and 3, Trondheim, Trondhjems Teater, 30 September 1863;

De Nygifte, Copenhagen, Det Kongelige Theater, 23 November 1865;

Maria Stuart i Skottland, Christiania, Christiania Theater, 29 March 1867;

Sigurd Jorsalfar, Christiania, Christiania Theater, 10 April 1872;

En fallit, Stockholm, Nya Teatern, 19 January 1875;

Redaktøren, Stockholm, Nya Teatern, 17 February 1875;

Det ny system, Berlin, Residenz-Theater, 19 December 1878;

Leonarda, Christiania, Christiania Theater, 22 April 1879;

En hanske, Hamburg, Stadt-Theater, 11 October 1883;

Geografi og kjærlighed, Christiania, Christiania Theater, 21 October 1885;

Over ævne I, Stockholm, Nya Teatern, 3 January 1886;

Over ævne II, Paris, Théâtre de l'oeuvre, 1897;

Paul Lange og Tora Parsberg, Stuttgart, spring 1901;

Laboremus, Christiania, Nationaltheateret, 29 April 1901;

Kongen, Christiania, Nationaltheateret, 11 September 1902;

På Storhove, Christiania, Nationaltheateret, 4 November 1902;

Daglannet, Christiania, Nationaltheateret, 31 August 1905;

Når den ny vin blomstrer, Christiania, Nationaltheateret, 29 September 1909.

TRANSLATION: Victor Hugo, *Århundredenes legende* (Oslo, 1911).

Bjørnstjerne Bjørnson was awarded the Nobel Prize in Literature for 1903, as the third writer to receive this honor. He was an obvious choice for the Swedish Academy, especially since he, more than most writers, fulfilled the requirement that the recipient's literary works ought to be written in an "idealistic spirit." In addition to a lifelong career of writing poetry, stories, novels, and plays with high but shifting ideals, Bjørnson had used his position as an author of international renown to help persecuted individuals and oppressed nations. He was thus a more natural choice for the Swedish Academy than his contemporary and fellow Norwegian, Henrik Ibsen, although time has shown that Ibsen's work has more lasting value and appeal; Bjørnson's work is no longer read much, even in his native country, and his once so radically new and trendsetting plays are rarely performed. Yet, Bjørnson remains a significant author in Norwegian literary history, because he wrote in all genres and was the first author—before Ibsen—to produce historical dramas as well as realistic plays from the contemporary scene, with their implied discussions of social problems of many sorts.

Bjørnson was an important and decisive figure both as a writer and as a public voice in a nation that had obtained its freedom (from Denmark) and its own constitution only in 1814 and had had to accept a union with Sweden and a Swedish king who was also the king of Norway. Writers could, in the days when Bjørnson published his earliest work, really be "the trumpets that blow to battle, the unacknowledged legislators of the world," as Percy Bysshe Shelley maintained. Important changes in the Norwegian political system took place, after hard fights, in the 1880s; Bjørnson was actively involved on the left side of Norwegian politics. His role and influence were instrumental in the fight for secession from the union, which finally led to a peaceful solution and a free and independent Kingdom of Norway in 1905. Bjørnson was a great orator, and apparently nothing was too big or too small for him either to defend or to attack. Inevitably he made enemies on all sides, but he also earned respect and appreciation. A life of serious and varied literary production, much of which had been translated into many languages, had earned him this right. One literary historian, Francis Bull, sums up his long biographical study by stating that Bjørnson's life was the richest and fullest ever lived by a Norwegian.

Bjørnson was Norway's great national poet in the second half of the nineteenth century. Everything he did contributed to a feeling of national pride. He also wrote a series of historical plays that were, with one exception, rooted in the old and proud history from the days of the Viking kings and before Denmark came to rule Norway for more than four hundred years. Thus he proved, poetically, that Norwegians had a glorious past history, that they were an old people and had been a powerful kingdom. He championed a Norwegian flag and wanted Norwegians to celebrate their independence day (17 May), when they seceded from the union with Denmark, and later he advocated ending the union with Sweden. He was a devoted republican at that time, yet accepted the new king without hesitation, because peaceful solutions to national and international questions were also something he had worked for on the international scene for decades. A marvelous orator, he spoke to audiences of as many as fifty thousand people on many lecture tours in Norway and other Scandinavian countries. He was a liberal but could also be a pragmatist and often changed his views, and he was as strongly disliked as he was loved, which was perhaps inevitable since he used his popularity as a writer to participate in national politics. He was a personal Christian who for a period believed in "a joyful Christianity," on the model from the great Danish poet, historian, and theologian N. F. S. Grundtvig; yet, when he read the works of Charles Darwin and John Stuart Mill, he rejected the teachings of the church, although he may well have been a believer all his life. He even went as far as claiming that he was a socialist, but not with the utopian dreams in which some of their leaders believed. More than anything, he was a strong and stern moralist, who let his literary characters go through ordeals and struggles so that they might learn to control their natures and destructive powers in themselves that may seem to be beyond their control.

In many of his early works, his characters share traits that may well stem from the heroes in the Icelandic sagas—traits that Bjørnson thought he found among the peasants of his own time. He lived abroad for extended periods of his life and wrote some thirty thousand letters, always vibrant and enthusiastically involved in everything that happened in the nation and to the people whose foremost voice he wanted to be, even when Ibsen's star slowly rose above his and even when the great traveler, discoverer, and scientist Fridtjof Nansen became more of a national hero and symbol than Bjørnson. What he left behind is first and foremost his books, a few of which may have lasting value, although his literary reputation has been in decline for many decades. Among the old critics of the historical-biographical school he was the greatest of all Norwegian writers, but they wrote their literary histories with the same goal as Bjørnson had in most of his writing: to help in the building of a nation.

Bjørnstjern Martinius Bjørnson was born on 8 September 1832 in Kvikne in the Østerdalen valley in Norway. His father, Peder Bjørnson, came from southern Norway but was a clergyman at Kvikne. He had married Inger Elise Nordraak in 1831. She was the aunt of the composer Richard Nordraak, who wrote the music to Bjørnson's "Ja, vi elsker dette landet" (Norway thine is our devotion, written in 1859 and first sung publicly in 1864)–the country's national anthem. Bjørnstjern was named after his grandfather, Bjørn, and Martin Luther. He later added an "e" to the end of his first name (it translates literally as "bear-star"), and his parents must have had high hopes for their firstborn son to give him such a rare and pretentious name. His brothers and sisters, five in all, had common names.

When Bjørnson was five years old the family moved to Naesset vicarage in Romsdalen, in the west of the country. The area has some of the most impressive and dramatic landscapes in all of Norway, with high mountains and fjords that penetrate deep into the land. Bjørnson always claimed that his character was formed and molded by the natural beauty of Romsdalen's "wild land," where he later found himself to be really "at home." There he also became acquainted with the peasant population. He loved and admired them for their struggle and endurance and also for their silent acceptance of their lot, for their basic religious beliefs, and for their sense of tradition and for keeping up ways of life that had remained unchanged for hundreds of years. Bjørnson went to middle school in the small nearby town of Molde in 1844. He quickly became a leader among the schoolboys, and in the revolutionary year of 1848 he saw his first article in print in a newspaper and also tried to organize celebrations of independence day on 17 May. He moved to Christiania (which became Oslo in 1925) for his further education and entered what was known as a "student factory" to take courses toward *examen atrium* (high school exams). He later wrote a poem about his memories from these school years, "Gamle Heltberg" (1873, Old Heltberg), and boys who later became famous writers were in the same classroom: Ibsen, Jonas Lie, and Aasmund O. Vinje. Bjørnson may have been involved with too many interests to concentrate on his studies, and he only got passable grades after continuation exams in 1854. He planned to study theology at the university but quickly abandoned all such thoughts. His father refused to give him further financial support since the son had made up his mind to become a writer, which was an uncertain and not-too-profitable future career. Nothing could stop Bjørnson, however.

He did all sorts of work in his apprenticeship years and made a meager living by writing reviews of books and theater performances. The few and scattered poems that were published brought in little money, but he was in the midst of a group of students and intellectuals who knew that they represented the future of the nation, if they could only somehow take over the hegemony of the old, Romantic school of writers and artists. Bjørnson's ideal of a writer was Henrik Wergeland, who did not care for any of the rules or aesthetic laws for literature and accordingly wrote radically fresh and new poetry. Wergeland also tried to help people of the working classes and was always in the midst of some fight for human rights, always living at least as much as he was singing–as Bjørnson later said about himself. In an 1854 review of an anthology, Bjørnson attacked the Romantic poets, with Wergeland's nemesis Johan Sebastian Cammermeyer Welhaven as their leader. He was tired of all the Romantic dreaming and sick walks in moonlight, and he prophesied that new poets soon would replace the old ones and carry on the ideals from Wergeland.

Bjørnson obviously wanted to be the leader of this new generation of poets, but at this time he was primarily a journalist. He lived by his pen, but he did not write much literature. As a drama critic he advocated a long-standing dream of a Norwegian national theater, with actors who were allowed to speak Norwegian and not Danish. He even founded a magazine, *Illustreret Folkeblad* (Illustrated People's Magazine), with the goal of creating a Norwegian culture that was independent of Denmark. He had made a name for himself but had not really succeeded as a writer yet. He was impatient, but felt that the stories he wrote were not good enough.

The decisive experience that made him write his first successful play came in 1856 when he joined Scandinavian students in Uppsala–a movement known as "Scandinavianism" peaked about this time–and saw historical objects and relics. He became aware of Norway's long and glorious past, and he wanted to be the one who made this past come alive and become a potent force in the present, creating a new kind of national pride. In his essay "Hvorledes jeg blev Digter" (1857, How I Became a Writer), Bjørnson tells that he slept for three days after this visit, and then went to Søgne–where his father had moved in 1853–and wrote *Mellem slagene* (1857, Between the Battles) in three weeks. This one-act play takes as its subject the fight between royal pretenders in Norway in the twelfth century. The play had a moderate success when it was performed in Christiania in October 1857; but it was preceded in Bjørnson's career by several other works that were published before this play. He had prepared himself for many years; now he was ready to launch his first books.

Bjørnson made his debut when the first of his "peasant tales," *Synnøve Solbakken* (Sunny Hill), was serialized in *Illustreret Folkeblad* in the summer of 1857 and published as a book in the fall of the same year. The tale was written in Copenhagen, where Bjørnson spent almost a whole year (1856–1857). Throughout his career Bjørnson escaped to foreign countries to find peace and quiet from politics and other activities at home, and most of these periods abroad proved to be quite productive. In Copenhagen he not only wrote *Synnøve Solbakken* but also began writing the drama *Halte-Hulda* (Lame Hulda; published in 1858, performed in 1862) in addition to making notes for another peasant tale, *En glad gut* (A Happy Boy, included in *Småstykker* [1860, Short Pieces]), and one of his best historical plays, *Sigurd Slembe* (published in 1862, performed in 1863).

In 1857 Bjørnson had published a short story called "Thrond," which may be regarded as his first attempt at a peasant tale in the small format. It appeared originally in the Danish paper *Fædrelandet* (11 – 12 March 1857), then in the Norwegian magazine *Illustreret Nyhedsblad* (12 April 1857) before being included in *Småstykker*. He later changed this story considerably; but with *Synnøve Solbakken* he had reached full mastery and renewed a genre almost so that it became his own. *Synnøve Solbakken* has always been Bjørnson's most loved book. There were many tales from peasant life both in Denmark and Germany, but Bjørnson had learned from the Icelandic sagas and the Norwegian folktales, so that he now created a totally new narrative, written in a language that was Norwegian in rhythm, style, and syntax—quite different from the written Danish that was the official norm in Norway at this time. Literary historians Bull and Edvard Beyer have both claimed that Bjørnson here for the first time presented and defined one of the dominant themes in all his writing: the strong forces that can lead men astray if they are not put to the service of superior goals. Bjørnson's heroes—in his historical plays as well as in the peasant tales—must learn to control their emotions. Strong passions must be subdued; stubborn pride must yield to a more balanced understanding of oneself and a more generous acceptance of one's fellow men. The moral lessons are learned through loss and suffering, or from the examples of one's elders and superiors, always with the help of love and Christian faith.

After Bjørnson had championed the idea of a Norwegian theater in newspaper articles and reviews, others began to support it. The famous fiddle player Ole Bull, who had made a fortune playing all over the world (and who later created an "ideal" settlement in Pennsylvania, named Oleana), had his own theater in Bergen, on the west coast of Norway. In the fall of 1857 he hired Bjørnson to be the artistic director of his theater. Bjørnson did not return to Christiania until the summer of 1859, and the Bergen years were decisive in his career in many respects. There he learned the theater world from the inside; he became editor of a local newspaper; and he had his first opportunities to practice as an orator in front of large audiences. This experience in its turn seems to have influenced his lyrical poetry, which became broader and more general in its approach and outlook, as if he knew that he represented many and not only himself. And he met his future wife, Karoline Reimers, whom he married on 11 September 1858 and who stood by his side in good and bad times and survived her husband by twenty-four years. Bjørnson had been "engaged" to other girls before, and shortly after his marriage he fell in love with a Danish actress and even had thoughts of divorcing Karoline. But things calmed down little by little, with Bjørnson in Rome and his wife and son (Bjørn, born in 1859) in Copenhagen. They joined him in Rome in September 1861, and the family did not return to Norway until April 1863. This time Bjørnson stayed in Christiania for almost ten years, with the exception of a stay in Copenhagen in the winter of 1867–1868.

The years in Rome were productive, and when the thirty-one-year-old writer returned to Norway he was well established as a poet, a dramatist, and a writer of stories and tales. Only later did he write novels; in the early years of his career he alternated between saga plays and peasant tales, narratives set against a rural background. He called this alternation "crop rotation," and he carried on with this practice all through the 1860s and up to 1872. The government had awarded him a travel grant for his trip to Rome; now he was the first writer to receive a permanent annual grant from the same government.

The most significant books from these years are the peasant tales that followed *Synnøve Solbakken*: *Arne* (1859) and *En glad gut*. The latter is also among Bjørnson's most popular books, a well-structured story of aspirations and hopes, but also of love and happiness. The critics who found Bjørnson's peasants to be idealized versions of real people may also consider *En glad gut* too much of an idyll, but this point does not diminish the story. Several of the best known and most loved among Bjørnson's poems are also found as integral parts of these narratives.

Bjørnson finished *Halte-Hulda* in November 1857, but his best saga play is the powerful and dramatic three-part *Sigurd Slembe*. The theme of the drama is basically the same as in the peasant tales. Prince Sigurd is capable and the son of a king, but he is also a slave to his own violent nature and destructive forces with which he cannot cope. This violence in turn leads to his defeat in the struggle for the throne. Bjørnson had read and learned a great deal from the works of William Shakespeare and Friedrich Schiller, and their influence is clearly visible in another drama, *Maria Stuart i Skottland* (Mary Queen of Scots; published in 1864, performed in 1867), his only play with a subject outside Norwegian history.

From 1865 and for two and a half years Bjørnson was in charge of a theater in Christiania, where he had an excellent opportunity to create a Norwegian theater. Again, he was editor of a newspaper and was involved in politics, and it is more than likely that he needed to get away from political quarrels when he left for Copenhagen in 1867. During this stay Bjørnson came in contact with Grundtvig, and his basic attitudes and beliefs gradually changed, becoming firmly based in a personal, Christian faith. This shift is reflected in the first long narrative he wrote, *Fiskerjenten* (1868; translated as *The Fisher-Maiden*), an entertaining story about a girl who becomes an artist and who finally finds her "joyful beliefs" in a light and happy religion.

Bjørnson had written poetry all through his career, and in 1870 he published a great epic-lyrical cycle of poems, *Arnljot Gelline,* about a minor character from the saga of Olaf II Haraldsson, the king who became a saint after his death in 1030. Bjørnson also gathered most of the lyrical poems he had written so far in *Digte og sange* (1870, Poems and Songs), a collection that the author later revised and expanded several times. He included many political songs, commissioned or occasional poetry, commemorative works, and poems in which he saluted great contemporaries. The most powerful pieces may be his poems about the old Norwegian kings, such as "Olav Trygvasson" (first published in *Illustreret Folkeblad,* 1862), about the Viking king who fought all the smaller pretenders to make Norway one kingdom. Bjørnson included several poems from his early peasant tales, and they are light and joyful pieces. The poems he wrote after his encounter with antiquity in Rome have a heavier and more powerful rhythm. Contemporary composers often set Bjørnson's poems to music, and these songs are still part of Norwegian heritage.

When Grundtvig died in 1872, Bjørnson gave a speech at his funeral. Some people had thought that he might become the new leader of the movement Grundtvig had begun, but by this time Bjørnson had lost faith in the church and in Christianity as he saw it practiced. Also, he began appealing to his Danish friends to "change signals," that is, to seek reconciliation with the Germans; and he even believed in what one might call Pan-Germanism. The so-called signal feud caused Bjørnson much bitterness and led to a complete severing of ties with his Grundtvigian friends in Norway. This break was particularly awkward since he had bought a farm in Gausdal in 1874 and had begun to spend much time there, close to important figures in the Folk High School movement based on Grundtvig's ideas.

Bjørnson now came to rely on the discoveries of modern natural sciences, the work of Darwin included. In one of his best poems, "Salme" (1879, Psalm), he praises "the eternal spring of Life" and describes what is clearly the doctrine of evolution in a simplified, yet convincing and beautiful way.

Bjørnson included a new peasant tale, *Brudeslåtten* (The Bridal Dance), in the two-volume set of stories he published in 1872, the same year that his saga drama *Sigurd Jorsalfar* appeared, and he thus ended his "crop rotation." He then went to Rome, where he stayed from 1873 to 1875. A decisive change of direction in his career took place, and in 1875 he published *En fallit* (The Bankrupt) and *Redaktøren* (The Editor). These were contemporary plays, so-called problem dramas—the kind of literature the famous Danish critic Georg Brandes had strongly advocated. Literature, according to Brandes, should deal with problems of everyday life and treat them realistically. He was pleased with Bjørnson's work and claimed in a review that "two great powers, the present and reality, had at last come into their right." Later he would have good reason to be even more pleased with what Ibsen did. But Bjørnson was again first, opening new areas and new literary forms for others. Both plays were performed in Stockholm in 1875. Many felt that *Redaktøren* was a political statement from the left or liberal side, and it was not performed in Christiania for many years. *En fallit* was an immediate success and played not only in Scandinavia but on stages all over Europe—Bjørnson's first international success, even though many of his books had been translated into several languages. *En fallit* would probably have been an even more powerful play without the last act, where a kind of happy solution to all problems is spelled out. Ibsen said that he only asked questions; it was not his duty to provide the answers. Bjørnson, on the contrary, always wanted to teach a lesson and would not leave the reader or the theater audience with too many unanswered questions.

In 1877 Bjørnson published the prose narrative *Magnhild,* his first and perhaps his best realistic novel. Two years before Ibsen's *A Doll's House* (1879), Bjørnson was describing married life and giving a bleak picture of the conventional marriage to which divorce might indeed be the only reasonable solution. The novel is reminiscent of the peasant tales and of *Fiskerjenten*; it is the tale of a talented young woman who has a long and strenuous way to go before she can believe in her own artistic abilities. When she does, she leaves her elderly husband, but she does not do so because of a single, unequivocal "calling," in which Bjørnson so often had believed. Life and its demands had become more complex; the middle-aged writer had a wider if not deeper understanding of human life, although he remained willing to change former beliefs and opinions if he were able to convince himself that it would be the right and proper thing to do.

The new convictions set forth in *Magnhild* led to much criticism, as did the play *Kongen* (The King; published in 1877, performed in 1902). This drama is part realistic and part symbolistic, as Bjørnson challenges the monarchy, the state church, and the military establishment—in short, everything connected with the king and his powers. Bjørnson's opinions and attitudes had become radicalized in most respects; he even preferred republic to monarchy. And he always kept the public informed about his views in matters small and large.

The bitterness Bjørnson felt upon the reception of *Magnhild* and *Kongen* can be seen in his next play, *Det ny system* (1879, The New System). The conflict revolves around principles for railway construction but is really a conflict between the old and the new, between the conservatism of the old and the eagerness and the search for truth among the young. Likewise, in *Leonarda* (performed and published in 1879), Bjørnson gave dramatic form to a debate about marriage and divorce, finally "proving" that the divorced woman acted on the basis of a higher morality than the bishop himself.

In the years around 1880 Bjørnson was politically active, but now mainly in internal affairs in Norway. How influential he really was in the fight for parliamentarism in Norway in 1883 and 1884, or how much his lasting struggle to end the union with Sweden really mattered, is hard to say. Because he said and wrote so much, even publishing many of his political ideas in European newspapers, he certainly appears to be one of the central figures on the political scene, although some of the politicians grew weary of him when the conflict with Sweden took a dangerous turn in 1905. His ideas did not always find an enthusiastic public, as when he lectured on Nordic politics and Bible interpretations on a tour among Norwegian immigrants in the United States in 1880.

Bjørnson was so involved in everything around him—always willing to speak, lecture, teach, and make his opinions known by writing in papers and journals—that he produced almost no new literature in these years. His publisher in Copenhagen persuaded him to go abroad again, and beginning in the fall of 1882 he spent five years in Paris with his family. This sojourn helped him get back to creative work, and the first years in Paris were enormously productive. The first result was the play *En hanske* (A Gauntlet; performed and published in 1883), in which Bjørnson, through one of his characters, states that men should be held to the same standard of purity before marriage as women are. He came under fire from the clergy on the one side—because he demanded equality between the sexes—and the radicals and advocates of free love on the other. This work marked the beginning of a long and heated debate about sexuality and purity that split the members of the so-called modern breakthrough in Scandinavian literature. Bjørnson fell out with August Strindberg as well as with Brandes, and even if some old friendships could be repaired, Bjørnson was too much of a stern moralist for many of his contemporaries.

Bjørnson's new convictions, his belief in the doctrine of evolution, and his distrust in old inherited religious beliefs are clearly at work in the superb story *Støv* (Dust) from 1882. They are also present on all levels in *Over ævne I* (Beyond Our Power, published in 1883, performed in 1886; translated as *Pastor Sang,* 1893). This play is regarded as Bjørnson's most modern and perhaps also the best of all his works in the dramatic genre. The play was performed in Stockholm in 1886, but not in Norway and Denmark until 1899.

Even in this play Bjørnson is the didactic writer, but the tendentiousness of this text is less marked because he creates believable and strong characters and realistic action set in the middle of dramatic landscapes in northern Norway, which makes thoughts of God and his power plausible. The priest, Sang, awaits a miracle—here, if anywhere, is certainly the place for miracles, and Sang is such a pious and loving person that it might be reasonable if God proved his faith and convictions to be true by giving him a miracle. But the play shows that miracles are beyond human power, thus indicating that Christianity itself is out of reach.

Another play from this period, *Geografi og kjærlighed* (Geography and Love; performed and published in 1885), is in a much lighter register, almost a comedy about a busy and self-important husband. The exuberant humor of the play, which also has elements of a self-portrait, made this work one of the most popular of Bjørnson's plays, and it is still performed occasionally, more than a hundred years later.

In 1884 Bjørnson had completed a long and realistic novel, *Det flager i byen og på havnen* (translated as *The Heritage of the Kurts,* 1892). This book is also concerned with the problems of morality and has a clear didactic goal as it preaches celibacy for men before marriage. He had begun another novel in Paris, but *På Guds veje* (translated as *In God's Way*, 1890) did not appear till 1889. In this work, religious issues lead to a bitter conflict between two friends, a clergyman and a doctor, and only late and after much suffering do they realize that "where good people walk, there is God's Way."

Around 1890 Bjørnson was devoting much time and energy to politics, delivering speeches and writing newspaper articles almost on a daily basis. His audience had grown, and now he sent his articles to the big newspapers and magazines in Great Britain, France, Germany, and the United States. At home he carried on the fight to end the union with Sweden, even if he did not work for a political party any longer. He declared that he sympathized with practical socialism and became even more popular when he supported the female workers in a match factory when they went on a strike in 1889. He hoped for a peaceful resolution of the class conflicts but often created conflicts and oppositions himself in matters where he really had no reason to become involved. He was regarded with skepticism by many writers of a new generation, and he did of course oppose literary naturalism as well as the new Romanticism in Norwegian literature in the 1890s.

He had also found a new field of interest—international work for peace—and he believed strongly that wars could be avoided through serious arbitration. He even wrote an epic poem, "Fred" (Peace), in 1891, and in *Over ævne II* (Beyond Human Might; published in 1895, performed in 1897) he wrote what may well have been the first drama in world literature about the modern class struggle. The play depicts a strike in which the two sides are in absolute deadlock. Workers stand against factory owners; ideologies are totally opposed. Nothing but disaster can be the result, but the play ends on a dream of reconciliation and peace.

Bjørnson had a home at Aulestad, in Gausdal, Oppland county, outside Lillehammer, well away from city life and its demands. He spent more and more time abroad as he grew older, but when in Norway he could live outside of the conflicts in politics and cultural life in the capital. From 1893 the family spent their winters in Rome and their summers in Austria or Germany. Bjørnson also spent time in Paris but returned to Norway at least once a year, and then he often went on lecture and reading tours. His productivity was not as it had been in his best years, and only *Paul Lange og Tora Parsberg* (published in 1898, performed in 1901; translated as *Paul Lange and Tora Parsberg*, 1899) is on a par with his best political dramas. The chief male character has a sensitive nature and is thus almost defenseless in the tough political fights in which he has to participate. For years Bjørnson struggled to free himself from the suspicion that he had contributed to the suicide of Ole Richter, the real politician on whom his leading character obviously was based. Many considered the play to be an apology and a defense from Bjørnson's side.

Most of his time was spent writing articles. They brought him international fame, for instance when he supported Emile Zola with great vigor in the latter's 1898 defense of Alfred Dreyfus, the Jewish French army officer imprisoned for treason in 1894. Bjørnson made much money from his journalism, and most of it was spent on Aulestad and on his five surviving children (one had died shortly after being born). He had translated selected parts of Victor Hugo's *La Légende des siècles* (1859; translated as *The Legend of the Centuries*, 1874) into Norwegian, and he loved reading aloud from this work on his many tours around the country and in Denmark. The translation was not published until the year after Bjørnson's death. He was present when the new Nationaltheateret opened in 1899 with his son Bjørn as the first director, and he had the pleasure of directing his two *Over ævne* plays.

Bjørnson was awarded the Nobel Prize in Literature in 1903 "as a tribute to his noble, magnificent and versatile poetry, which has always been distinguished by both the freshness of its inspiration and the rare purity of its spirit." The permanent secretary of the Swedish Academy, C. D. af Wirsén, emphasized the same values in his presentation speech: "Your inspired and universally acknowledged poetic achievement, rooted in nature and in the life of the people as well as in strong personal convictions, combines morality and a healthy poetic freshness." At the Nobel banquet Bjørnson took the opportunity to express his views on moral fiction, which would invariably help mankind move along in a human progress toward better things. He defended literature in which "tendentiousness and art appear in the same proportion," but was also a strong advocate of the old ideas of right and wrong, since it is impossible for people to "shake off the ideas that have come down to them through the centuries of inherited morality."

For posterity it has been virtually impossible to understand why Ibsen (or, for that matter, Sweden's Strindberg) did not receive the prize. Even in 1903 it may have seemed surprising and brave of a Swedish institution to award this prestigious prize to one of the strongest and loudest opponents of the union, a person who at times one might think hated Swedes and everything Swedish. In a more general understanding of the literary scene and of the different Nordic candidates for the prize at this particular time, however, it should not be too much of a surprise that Bjørnson was the preferred choice, and certainly not if one keeps in mind "the idealistic spirit" that seemed to be a basic requirement, although the Academy could define this term in ways that served their own literary tastes.

The Nobel Prize came so late in Bjørnson's life that it did not change his attitudes or his writing at all. The money, however, came in handy, since upkeep on his Aulestad home was expensive.

Bjørnson suffered from an ear ailment beginning in 1899; he became deaf in one ear, and his health began to deteriorate considerably. He wrote a few plays of little importance, and the same is true for the novel *Mary* from 1906. He could still be a competent poet, however, and wrote several good poems, even if they were commissioned and written to celebrate something. In 1909 his last play appeared—*Når den ny vin blomstrer* (When the New Vine Blossoms), a light and easy comedy. Bjørnson was an old man by this time, and he had suffered from a serious stroke in 1909; yet, his faith and joy in life remained undiminished, as witnessed in his last play and in his last poems. He never recovered after the stroke, and he died in Paris on 26 April 1910.

Bjørnson was brought home on the warship *Norge* and buried with all the honors befitting a national poet and international celebrity. Knut Hamsun (himself a Nobel recipient in 1920) had written a poem in honor of Bjørnson's seventieth birthday in 1902; he was one of many writers who expressed their sorrow when Bjørnson died. Hamsun knew that everyone—including the nation itself—would pause for a moment of respect and silence when the great chronicler had passed away.

Bjørnson's significance lies perhaps foremost in the fact that he introduced new forms to Norwegian literature. He was a pioneer in lyrical poetry, in the writing of short stories and tales, in the saga plays, and in the modern realistic drama. Almost all writers of his own and the following generation were indebted to him in one way or other; many of them admitted as much, from Hamsun in Norway to Selma Lagerlöf in Sweden and Johannes V. Jensen in Denmark, all later recipients of the Nobel Prize.

Bjørnson was always a step ahead of Ibsen, who was four years his senior and a friend as well as rival. Bjørnson helped create the Nordic historical drama and the realistic contemporary problem play—yet, Ibsen definitely wrote the best plays in both these genres. Seen from a modern perspective, Ibsen is the greatest of all Norwegian writers of this period; but seen from the contemporary point of view, Bjørnson loomed so large that it was fitting to award him the Nobel Prize. His life and work were intimately linked to the political and cultural shifts in Norway during a period of strong growth and progress, and in many ways he embodies the changes, innovations, and development that the nation he helped create and define went through.

Bjørnstjerne Bjørnson's legacy is not only the books he left behind but the life he lived in the service of his country. He was always on the side of the weak and oppressed, demanding for all citizens the right to vote and complete equality for women. He brought new topics up for open and free discussion, and he was willing to debate everything, though his opinions and attitudes changed several times in questions of both politics and literature. Despite all his changes he remained a didactic writer with a moral lesson to give, which he often presented through exemplary narratives in which characters struggle to overcome their own natures and finally emerge victorious as good and decent people. He always believed in his own phrase, "Good deeds save the world," and he insisted that peace and prosperity and progress were possible and that it was the writer's task to contribute to a better future for everyone.

Letters:

Land of the Free: Bjørnstjerne Bjørnson's America Letters, 1880–1881, edited and translated by Eva Lund Haugen and Einar Haugen (Northfield, Minn.: Norwegian-American Historical Association, 1978).

Biographies:

Chr. Collin [Christen Christian Dreyer], *Bjørnstjerne Bjørnson: Hans barndom og ungdom,* 2 volumes (Christiania: Ascheoug, 1923; enlarged edition, Oslo: Gyldendal Norsk, 1932);

P. Amdam, *Bjørnstjerne Bjørnson 1832–1880* (Oslo: Gyldendal, 1993);

Aldo Keel, *Bjørnstjerne Bjørnson 1880–1910* (Oslo: Gyldendal, 1999).

References:

Edvard Beyer, "Bjørnstjerne Bjørnson," in *Norges litteraturhistorie,* volume 3, edited by Beyer (Oslo: Cappelen, 1975), pp. 93–225;

Francis Bull, "Bjørnstjerne Bjørnson," in *Norsk Litteraturhistorie,* volume 4, edited by Bull and others (Oslo: Ascheoug, 1963), pp. 467–705;

Christian Gierløff, *Bjørnstjerne Bjørnson* (Oslo: Gyldendal, 1932);

Gerhard Gran, *Bjørnstjerne Bjørnson* (Copenhagen: Schønbergske, 1916);

Harald Noreng, *Bjørnstjerne Bjørnsons dramatiske diktning* (Oslo: Gyldendal, 1954).

Papers:

Bjørnstjerne Bjørnson's papers, including manuscripts and correspondence, are housed at the National Library in Oslo.

1903 Nobel Prize in Literature Presentation Speech

by C. D. af Wirsén, Permanent Secretary of the Swedish Academy, 10 December 1903

Again this year the names of several candidates for the Nobel Prize in Literature have been submitted to the Swedish Academy for its approval; some of them are authors of European reputation. The Academy thinks that this year it should give priority to the poet Bjørnstjerne Bjørnson. Although we have the pleasure of seeing the illustrious laureate at this ceremony, custom requires that I speak of him in the third person as I give an account of the Academy's decision. But I reserve the right to address a few personal remarks to him at the end.

Bjørnstjerne Bjørnson is so generally known and his works are so familiar to educated Swedes that it is unnecessary to give a comprehensive appreciation of his universally and gladly acknowledged merits. Therefore I shall limit myself on this solemn occasion to the following remarks.

The poet to whom with true satisfaction the Swedish Academy has awarded the Nobel Prize in Literature was born at Kvikne, Norway, where his father was a minister and where as a child he could listen to the waters of the Orkla boiling at the bottom of a gorge. The last years of his childhood were, however, spent at Naesset in the beautiful valley of Romsdal where his father had been transferred. The vicarage of Naesset is situated between the two inlets of Langfjord, Eidsvaag and Eirisfjord. In that picturesque countryside of Norway, between these two fjords, the young boy often looked at the splendour of the sun setting behind the mountain or in the sea. There he learned to do farmwork. His love of the rustic nature of his country and his intimate knowledge of the life of the people date from that time. At the age of eleven he was sent to school at Molde. He did not do brilliantly, but the development of a great poet is not always measured by such standards. During his studies he came across one author who was to have a profound influence on his life: he began to read Sturleson. At this period, too, he became acquainted with the stories of Asbjørnson and the works of Oehlenschläger and Walter Scott. At the age of seventeen he went to Christiania (Oslo) to prepare for his baccalaureate, which he passed in 1852. Bjørnson has said that he knew of his poetic vocation after he took part in the First Student Assembly in Uppsala in 1856. In unforgettable words he has given us his impressions of the church of Riddarholm lit up by the rays of the setting sun, and of Stockholm in the splendour of the summer. Then he wrote *Mellem slagene* (1857) *[Between the Battles]* in a fortnight, to be followed by other works, among them the story *Synnøve Solbakken* (1857) *[Sunny Hill]*. Henceforth the reputation of Bjørnson was solidly established and an uninterrupted series of new works spread his name all over the world.

Bjørnson is a great epic and dramatic writer, but he is also a great lyric poet. *Synnøve Solbakken*, *Arne* (1858), and *En glad gut* (1860) *[A Happy Boy]* put him in the first rank of painters of contemporary life. In these sombre accounts he reveals himself as a man of the country and of the old saga; indeed it has been said, not without reason, that he describes the life of the peasant in the light of saga. But it should be added that the peasants whom he knew so well since his Romsdal days have—in the judgments of competent persons—preserved the laconic and reserved manner of talking which the poet has reproduced with such felicity. Although this reproduction is idealized and profoundly poetic, it is nonetheless faithful and true to nature.

As a dramatist Bjørnson has treated historical subjects, e.g. *Kong Sverre* (1861), *Sigurd Jorsalafar* (1872) *[Sigurd the Crusader]*, the masterly *Sigurd Slembe* (1862) *[Sigurd the Bad]*, in which the love of Audhild brings some light into a sombre situation and where the figure of Finnepigen stands in the splendour of an aurora borealis, the passionate drama *Maria Stuart i Skottland* (1864), and other creations of genius. But he has been equally successful in his choice of contemporary subjects, as in *Redaktøren* (1874) *[The Editor]*, *En fallit* (1874) *[The Bankrupt]*, etc. Even as an old man he has created a disinterested portrait of love in *Paul Lange og Tora Parsberg* (1898); in *Laboremus* (1901) he has extolled the right of the moral life against the natural forces of unrestrained passion. Finally, in *På Storhove* (1902) *[At Storhove]* he has paid dramatic homage to the guardian forces of the home as represented by Margareta, the faithful and constant support of her family. It should in fact be observed that Bjørnson's characters are of a rare purity, that his genius is always positive and in no way negative. His works are never adulterated; on the contrary they are pure metal, and whatever modifications the years and experience have imposed upon his point of view and that of others, he has never ceased to combat the claim of the senses to dominate man.

It is sometimes said that the Nobel Prize in Literature, designed for the best literary work, should preferably be awarded to young writers. That may be true, but even so the Academy believes it has met all reasonable demands.

The creative power of this man of seventy-one is so great that he published *På Storhove* in 1902, and the works published afterward bear witness to the youthful spirit that he has been able to preserve.

As a lyric poet Bjørnson is exemplary by his fresh simplicity and his profound sentiments. His poems are an inspirational source of inexhaustible wealth, and the melodious character of his verse has tempted many a composer to set it to music. . . . No country has a more beautiful anthem than "Ja, vi elsker dette Landet" [Yes, we love this country] by Bjørnson, and when one reads the sublime song of "Arnljot Gelline," in which the rhythms are like the majestic movements of waves, one likes to think that in future times the waves of memory will murmur "i store maaneskinsklare Naetter" [in clear moon-lit nights] as they play the name of the great national poet on the coasts of Norway.

Mr. Bjørnstjerne Bjørnson—Your genius has served the purest and most elevated ideas; it has put the highest demands on human life, in certain cases *(En hanske, 1883 [A Gauntlet])* even thought too high by many. But in their noble severity they are infinitely preferable to the laxness that is all too prevalent in the literature of our day. Your inspired and universally acknowledged poetic achievement, rooted in nature and in the life of the people as well as in strong personal convictions, combines morality and a healthy poetic freshness. Hence the Swedish Academy has seen fit to render homage to your illustrious genius by awarding you the Nobel Prize for this year, and it respectfully asks His Majesty the King to deign to give you this proof of its admiration.

[© The Nobel Foundation, 1903.]

Bjørnson: Banquet Speech

Bjørnson's speech at the Nobel Banquet at Grand Hôtel, Stockholm, 10 December 1903 (Translation):

I believe that the Prize I have received today will be regarded by the public as a gift from one nation to another. After the long struggle in which I have taken part to gain for Norway an equal place within the Union, a struggle which was often bitterly resented in Sweden, may I say that the decision is a credit to her name.

I am glad of this opportunity to express very briefly my views on the role of literature.

Let me, in the interest of brevity, evoke a picture I have had in my mind since my early youth, whenever I think of human progress. I see it as an endless procession in which men and women move steadily along. The line they follow is not invariably straight but it does take them forward. They are urged on by an irresistible force, purely instinctive at first but eventually more and more conscious. Not that human progress is ever entirely a matter of conscious effort, and no man has ever been able to make it so. It is in this no man's land between conscious progress and subconscious forging ahead that imagination is at work. In some of us, the gift of prescience is so great that it enables us to see far ahead to the new paths along which human progress will travel.

Nothing has ever moulded our conscience so strongly as our knowledge of what is good and what is evil. Therefore, our sense of good and evil is so much a part of our conscience that, to this day, no one can disregard it and feel at ease with himself. That is why I have always been so puzzled by the idea that we writers should lay down our sense of good and evil before we take up our pens. The effect of this reasoning would be to turn our minds into cameras indifferent to good and evil, to beauty and ugliness alike!

I do not want to dwell here on the extent to which modern man—always assuming he is a sane individual—can shake off a conscience that is the heritage of millions of years, and by which all the generations of mankind have been guided to the present day. I shall merely ask why those who subscribe to this theory choose certain images instead of others? Is their choice a purely mechanical one? Why are the pictures that present themselves to their imagination almost invariably shocking? Are they sure that it is not they, in fact, who have chosen them?

I do not think we need to wait for the answer. They can no more shake off the ideas that have come down to them through centuries of inherited morality than we can. The only difference between them and ourselves is that, whereas we serve these ideas, they try to rebel against them. I should quickly add here that not all is immoral that appears to be so. Many of today's guiding ideas were revolutionary ones in the past. What I do say is that the writers who reject tendentiousness and purpose in their work are the very ones who display it in every word they write. I could draw countless examples from the history of literature to show that the more a writer clamours for spiritual freedom, the more tendentious his work is liable to be. The great poets of Greece were equally at home with mortals and immortals. Shakespeare's plays were a great Teutonic Valhalla with brilliant sunshine at times and violent tempests at others. The world to him was a battlefield, but his sense of poetic justice, his sublime faith in life and its infinite resources guided the battles.

We may invoke from their graves, as often as we wish, the characters of Molière and Holberg, to see nothing but a procession of figures in frilly costumes and wigs who, with affected and grotesque gestures, fulfill their mission. They are as tendentious as they are verbose.

I spoke just now of our Teutonic Valhalla. Did not Goethe and Schiller bring something of the Elysian fields into it? The sky was loftier and warmer with them, life and art happier and more beautiful. We may perhaps say that those who have basked in this warmth, in this sunshine—young Tegnér, young Oehlenschläger, and young Wergeland, not forgetting Byron and Shelley—have all had something of the Greek gods in them.

This time and this trend are gone now, but I should like to mention two great men who belong to it. First, I think of my old friend in Norway who is now ill. He has lit many a beacon along our Norwegian coast to guide the mariner, to warn him of the danger that lies ahead. I think, too, of a grand old man in a neighbouring country to the east, whose light shines forth and gives happiness to many. Their spirit, their many years of work, were lit by a purpose that was ever brighter, like a flame in the evening wind.

I have said nothing here of the effect of tendentiousness on art, which it can make or mar. "Ich rieche die Absicht und werde verstimmt."

If tendentiousness and art appear in the same proportion, all is well. Of the two great writers I have mentioned, it may well be that the former's warnings are so severe as to be frightening. And the latter may lure us with the charms of an ideal that passes human understanding and therefore frightens, too. But what is necessary is that our courage to live is strengthened, not weakened. Fear should not turn us back from the paths which open before us. The procession must go on. We must be confident that life is fundamentally good, that even after frightening disasters and the most tragic events, the earth is bathed in a flood of strength whose sources are eternal. Our belief in it is its proof.

In more recent times, Victor Hugo has been my hero. At the bottom of his brilliant imagination lies the conviction that life is good and it is that which makes his work so colourful. There are those who talk of his shortcomings, of his theatrical mannerisms. Let them. For me, all his deficiencies are compensated by his *joie de vivre*. Our instinct of self-preservation insists on this, for if life did not have more good than evil to offer us, it would have come to an end long ago. Any picture of life that does not allow for this fact is a distorted picture. It is wrong to imagine, as some do, that it is the dark aspects of life which are bad for us. That is not true.

Weaklings and egotists cannot abide harsh facts but the rest of us can. If those who choose to make us tremble or blush were also able to hold out a promise that, for all that may befall us, life has happiness to offer us, we might say to ourselves: all right, we are faced in this plot and in these words with a mystery that is part of life, and we should be roused to fear or amusement according to the author's will. The trouble is that writers seldom achieve more than a sensation, and often not even that! We feel doubly dissatisfied, because the author's attitude to life is so negative and because he is not capable of leading us. Incompetence is always galling.

The greater the burden a man takes upon his shoulders, the stronger he must be to carry it. No words are unmentionable, no action or horror beyond powers of description, if one is equal to them.

A meaningful life—this is what we look for in art, in its smallest dewdrops as in its unleashing of the tempest. We are at peace when we have found it and uneasy when we have not.

The old ideas of right and wrong, so firmly established in our consciousness, have played their part in every field of our life; they are part of our search for knowledge and our thirst for life itself. It is the purpose of all art to disseminate these ideas and, for that, millions of copies would not be one too many.

This is the ideal I have tried to defend, as a respectful servant and enthusiast. I am not one of those who believe that an artist, a writer, is exempt from responsibility. On the contrary, his responsibility is greater than that of other men because he who is at the head of the procession must lead the way for those who follow.

I am deeply grateful to the Swedish Academy for recognizing my efforts in this direction and I now wish to raise my glass to the success of its work in promoting all that is sound and noble in literature.

[© The Nobel Foundation, 1903. Bjørnstjerne Bjørnson is the sole author of his speech.]

Heinrich Böll

(21 December 1917 – 16 July 1985)

Reinhard K. Zachau
University of the South

This entry was expanded by Zachau from his Böll entry in *DLB 69: Contemporary German Fiction Writers, First Series*. See also the Böll entry in *DLB Yearbook: 1985*.

BOOKS: *Der Zug war pünktlich: Erzählung* (Opladen: Middelhauve, 1949); translated by Richard Graves as *The Train Was on Time* (London: Arco, 1956; New York: Criterion Books, 1956);

Wanderer kommst du nach Spa . . . : Erzählungen (Opladen: Middlehauve, 1950); translated by Mervyn Savill as *Traveller, If You Come to Spa . . .* (London: Arco, 1956);

Die schwarzen Schafe: Erzählung (Opladen: Middelhauve, 1951);

Wo warst du, Adam? Roman (Opladen: Middelhauve, 1951); translated by Savill as *Adam, Where Art Thou?* (New York: Criterion Books, 1955); translated by Leila Vennewitz as "And Where Were You, Adam?" in *Adam and The Train: Two Novels* (New York: McGraw-Hill, 1970);

Nicht nur zur Weihnachtszeit: Eine humoristische Erzählung (Frankfurt am Main: Frankfurter Verlagsanstalt, 1952); published with *Der Mann mit den Messern*, edited by Dorothea Berger (New York: American Book Co., 1959);

Und sagte kein einziges Wort: Roman (Cologne & Berlin: Kiepenheuer & Witsch, 1953); translated by Graves as *Acquainted with the Night* (New York: Holt, 1954); translated by Vennewitz as *And Never Said a Word* (New York: McGraw-Hill, 1978);

Haus ohne Hüter: Roman (Cologne & Berlin: Kiepenheuer & Witsch, 1954); translated by Savill as *The Unguarded House* (London: Arco, 1957); translation republished as *Tomorrow and Yesterday* (New York: Criterion Books, 1957);

Das Brot der frühen Jahre: Erzählung (Cologne & Berlin: Kiepenheuer & Witsch, 1955); translated by Savill as *The Bread of Our Early Years* (London: Arco, 1957); translated by Vennewitz as *The Bread of Those Early Years* (New York: McGraw-Hill, 1976);

Heinrich Böll (right) receiving the 1972 Nobel Prize in Literature from Crown Prince Carl XVI Gustaf of Sweden (AP World Wide)

So ward Abend und Morgen: Erzählungen (Zurich: Arche, 1955);

Unberechenbare Gäste: Heitere Erzählungen (Zurich: Arche, 1956);

Irisches Tagebuch (Cologne & Berlin: Kiepenheuer & Witsch, 1957); translated by Vennewitz as *Irish Journal* (New York: McGraw-Hill, 1967; London: Secker & Warburg, 1983);

Im Tal der donnernden Hufe: Erzählung (Wiesbaden: Insel, 1957); edited by James Alldridge (London: Heinemann Educational, 1970);

Abenteuer eines Brotbeutels, und andere Geschichten, edited by Richard Plant (New York: Norton, 1957);

Die Spurlosen: Hörspiel (Hamburg: Hans-Bredow-Institut, 1957); published with Leopold Ahlsen, *Philemon und Baukis*, edited by Anna Otten (New York: Odyssey, 1967);

Doktor Murkes gesammeltes Schweigen und andere Satiren (Cologne & Berlin: Kiepenheuer & Witsch, 1958); edited by Gertrud Seidmann (London: Harrap, 1963);

Der Wegwerfer: Erzählung (Alfeld-Gronau: Hannoversche Papierfabriken, 1958);

Im Ruhrgebiet, text by Böll, illustrations by Karl Hargesheimer (Frankfurt am Main: Büchergilde Gutenberg, 1958);

Die ungezählte Geliebte (Zollikofen: Privately printed, 1958);

Erzählungen (Opladen: Middelhauve, 1958)–includes *Der Zug war pünktlich* and *Wanderer Kommst du nach Spa . . .*;

Die Waage der Baleks und andere Erzählungen (Berlin: Union, 1959);

Billard um halb zehn: Roman (Cologne & Berlin: Kiepenheuer & Witsch, 1959); translated by Patrick Bowles as *Billiards at Half-past Nine* (London: Weidenfeld & Nicolson, 1961; New York: McGraw-Hill, 1962);

Der Mann mit den Messern: Erzählungen (Stuttgart: Reclam, 1959); published with *Nicht nur zur Weihnachtszeit*, edited by Berger (New York: American Book Co., 1959);

Der Bahnhof von Zimpren: Erzählungen (Munich: List, 1959);

Aus unseren Tagen, edited by Gisela Stein (New York: Holt, Rinehart & Winston, 1960);

Menschen am Rhein, text by Böll, illustrations by Hargesheimer (Frankfurt am Main: Büchergilde Gutenberg, 1960);

Brief an einen jungen Katholiken (Cologne & Berlin: Kiepenheuer & Witsch, 1961);

Bilanz; Klopfzeichen; Zwei Hörspiele (Stuttgart: Reclam, 1961);

Erzählungen, Hörspiele, Aufsätze (Cologne & Berlin: Kiepenheuer & Witsch, 1961);

Als der Krieg ausbrach; Als der Krieg zu Ende war: Zwei Erzählungen (Frankfurt am Main: Insel, 1962); translated by Vennewitz as "Enter and Exit," in *Absent without Leave: Two Novellas* (New York: McGraw-Hill, 1965); translation republished in *Absent without Leave and Other Stories* (London: Weidenfeld & Nicolson, 1967);

Ein Schluck Erde: Drama (Cologne & Berlin: Kiepenheuer & Witsch, 1962);

Assisi (Munich: Knorr & Hirth, 1962);

Ansichten eines Clowns: Roman (Cologne & Berlin: Kiepenheuer & Witsch, 1963); translated by Vennewitz as *The Clown* (New York: McGraw-Hill, 1965);

Hierzulande: Aufsätze (Munich: Deutscher Taschenbuch, 1963);

1947 bis 1951: Erzählungen (Cologne & Opladen: Middelhauve, 1963); selections translated by Vennewitz as *Children Are Civilians, Too* (New York: McGraw-Hill, 1970; London: Secker & Warburg, 1973);

Die Essenholer und andere Erzählungen, edited by Fritz Bachmann (Frankfurt am Main: Hirschgraben-Verlag, 1963);

Zum Tee bei Dr. Borsig: Hörspiele (Munich: Deutscher Taschenbuch, 1964);

Entfernung von der Truppe: Erzählung (Cologne & Berlin: Kiepenheuer & Witsch, 1964); translated by Vennewitz as "Absent without Leave," in *Absent without Leave: Two Novellas* (New York: McGraw-Hill, 1965); translation republished in *Absent without Leave and Other Stories* (London: Weidenfeld & Nicolson, 1967);

Der Rat des Weltunweisen: Roman (Gütersloh: Mohn, 1965);

Frankfurter Vorlesungen (Cologne: Kiepenheuer & Witsch, 1966);

Ende einer Dienstfahrt: Erzählung (Cologne: Kiepenheuer & Witsch, 1966); translated by Vennewitz as *End of a Mission* (New York: McGraw-Hill, 1967); translation republished as *The End of a Mission* (London: Weidenfeld & Nicolson, 1968);

Die Spurlosen: Drei Hörspiele (Leipzig: Insel, 1966);

18 Stories, translated by Vennewitz (New York: McGraw-Hill, 1966);

Aufsätze, Kritiken, Reden (Cologne: Kiepenheuer & Witsch, 1967);

Georg Büchners Gegenwärtigkeit: Eine Rede (Berlin: Friedenauer Presse, 1967);

Hausfriedensbruch: Hörspiel; Aussatz: Schauspiel (Cologne: Kiepenheuer & Witsch, 1969);

Leben im Zustand des Frevels: Ansprache zur Verleihung des Kölner Literaturpreises (Berlin: Berliner Handpresse, 1969);

Geschichten aus zwölf Jahren (Frankfurt am Main: Suhrkamp, 1969);

Böll für Zeitgenossen: Ein kulturgeschichtliches Lesebuch, edited by Ralph Ley (New York: Harper & Row, 1970);

Gruppenbild mit Dame: Roman (Cologne: Kiepenheuer & Witsch, 1971); translated by Vennewitz as *Group Portrait with Lady* (New York: McGraw-Hill, 1973);

Erzählungen, 1950–1970 (Cologne: Kiepenheuer & Witsch, 1972);

Gedichte (Berlin: Literarisches Colloquium, 1972);

Versuch über die Vernunft der Poesie: Nobelvorlesung (Stockholm: Norstedt & Söner, 1973);

Neue politische und literarische Schriften (Cologne: Kiepenheuer & Witsch, 1973);

Die verlorene Ehre der Katharina Blum oder wie Gewalt entstehen und wohin sie führen kann: Erzählung (Cologne: Kiepenheuer & Witsch, 1974); translated by Vennewitz as *The Lost Honor of Katharina Blum: How Violence Develops and Where It Can Lead* (New York: McGraw-Hill, 1975);

Drei Tage im März: Ein Gespräch, by Böll and Christian Linder (Cologne: Kiepenheuer & Witsch, 1975);

Berichte zur Gesinnungslage der Nation (Cologne: Kiepenheuer & Witsch, 1975);

Gedichte: Mit Collagen von Klaus Staeck (Cologne: Labbe & Muta, 1975);

Wie kritisch darf engagierte Kunst sein? (Munich: Presseausschuß Demokratische Initiative, 1976);

Einmischung erwünscht: Schriften zur Zeit (Cologne: Kiepenheuer & Witsch, 1977);

Missing Persons and Other Essays, translated by Vennewitz (New York: McGraw-Hill, 1977; London: Secker & Warburg, 1977);

Querschnitte: aus Interviews, Aufsätzen und Reden, edited by Viktor Böll and Renate Matthaei (Cologne: Kiepenheuer & Witsch, 1977);

Werke: Romane und Erzählungen, 5 volumes, edited by Bernd Balzer (Cologne: Middelhauve/Kiepenheuer & Witsch, 1977);

Werke: Essayistische Schriften und Reden, 3 volumes, edited by Balzer (Cologne: Kiepenheuer & Witsch, 1977–1979);

Werke: Hörspiele, Theaterstücke, Drehbücher, Gedichte, edited by Balzer (Cologne: Kiepenheuer & Witsch, 1978);

Werke: Interviews, edited by Balzer (Cologne: Kiepenheuer & Witsch, 1978);

Mein Lesebuch (Frankfurt am Main: Fischer, 1978);

Eine deutsche Erinnerung: Interview mit René Wintzen (Cologne: Kiepenheuer & Witsch, 1979);

Du fährst zu oft nach Heidelberg und andere Erzählungen (Bornheim-Merten: Lamuv, 1979);

Fürsorgliche Belagerung: Roman (Cologne: Kiepenheuer & Witsch, 1979); translated by Vennewitz as *The Safety Net* (Franklin Center, Pa.: Franklin Library, 1981; London: Secker & Warburg, 1982);

Ein Tag wie sonst: Hörspiele (Munich: Deutsch Taschenbuch, 1980);

Was soll aus dem Jungen bloß werden? Oder: Irgendwas mit Büchern (Bornheim-Merten: Lamuv, 1981); translated by Vennewitz as *What's to Become of the Boy? or, Something to Do With Books* (New York: Knopf, 1984);

Warum haben wir aufeinander geschossen? by Böll and Lev Kopelev (Bornheim-Merten: Lamuv, 1981);

Der Autor ist immer noch versteckt, by Böll and Jürgen Wallmann (Hauzenberg: Pongratz, 1981);

Vermintes Gelände: Essayistische Schriften 1977–1981 (Cologne: Kiepenheuer & Witsch, 1982);

Verantwortlich für Polen? (Reinbek: Rowohlt, 1982);

Das Vermächtnis: Kurzroman (Bornheim-Merten: Lamuv, 1982); translated by Vennewitz as *A Soldier's Legacy* (New York: Knopf, 1985; London: Secker & Warburg, 1985);

Antikommunismus in Ost und West (Cologne: Bund-Verlag, 1982);

Die Verwundung und andere frühe Erzählungen (Bornheim-Merten: Lamuv, 1983); translated by Vennewitz as *The Casualty* (London: Chatto & Windus, 1986; New York: Farrar, Straus & Giroux, 1987);

Der Angriff (Cologne: Kiepenheuer & Witsch, 1983);

Bild, Bonn, Boenisch (Bornheim-Merten: Lamuv, 1984);

Katholisch und rebellisch: Ein Wegweiser durch, die andere Kirche (Reinbek: Rowohlt, 1984);

Veränderungen in Staech: Erzählungen 1962–1980 (Cologne: Kiepenheuer & Witsch, 1984);

Weil die Stadt so fremd geworden ist (Bornheim-Merten: Lamuv, 1985);

Heinrich Böll, on His Death (Bonn: Inter Nationes, 1985);

Frauen vor Flußlandschaft: Roman in Dialogen und Selbstgesprächen (Cologne: Kiepenheuer & Witsch, 1985); translated by David McLintock as *Women in a River Landscape: A Novel in Dialogues and Soliloquies* (New York: Knopf, 1988);

Die Juden von Drove (Berlin: Rütten & Loening, 1985);

Die Fähigkeit zu trauern. Reden und Schriften 1983–1985 (Bornheim-Merten: Lamuv, 1986);

The Stories of Heinrich Böll, translated by Vennewitz (New York: Knopf, 1986);

Feindbild und Frieden: Schriften und Reden, 1982–1983 (Munich: Deutscher Taschenbuch, 1987);

Rom auf den ersten Blick: Landschaften, Städte, Reisen (Bornheim-Merten: Lamuv, 1987);

Der Engel schwieg: Roman (Cologne: Kiepenheuer & Witsch, 1992); translated by Breon Mitchell as *The Silent Angel* (New York: St. Martin's Press, 1994; London: Deutsch, 1994);

Der General stand auf einem Hügel: Erzählungen aus dem Krieg (Cologne: Kiepenheuer & Witsch, 1995);

Der blasse Hund: Erzählungen (Cologne: Kiepenheuer & Witsch, 1995); translated by Mitchell as *The Mad Dog: Stories* (New York: St. Martin's Press, 1997);

Versuch über die Vernunft der Poesie, edited by Jochen Schubert (Berlin: Heinrich-Böll-Stiftung, 1999);

Kreuz ohne liebe (Cologne: Kiepenheuer & Witsch, 2003).

Editions and Collections: *18 Stories,* translated by Leila Vennewitz (Franklin Center, Pa.: Franklin Library, 1982);

Erzählungen, 1937–1983, 4 volumes, edited by Viktor Böll and Karl Heiner Busse (Cologne: Kiepenheuer & Witsch, 1997);

Brief aus dem Krieg 1939–1945, 2 volumes, edited by Jochen Schubert (Cologne: Kiepenheuer & Witsch, 2001).

TRANSLATIONS: Patrick White, *Zur Ruhe kam der Baum des Menschen nie,* translated by Böll and Annemarie Böll (Cologne: Kiepenheuer & Witsch, 1957);

Bernard Malamud, *Der Gehilfe,* translated by Böll and Annemarie Böll (Cologne: Kiepenheuer & Witsch, 1960);

John Millington Synge, *Ein wahrer Held,* translated by Böll and Annemarie Böll (Berlin: Kiepenheuer & Witsch, 1960);

J. D. Salinger, *Der Fänger im Roggen* (Cologne: Kiepenheuer & Witsch, 1962);

Salinger, *Franny und Zooey,* translated by Böll and Annemarie Böll (Cologne: Kiepenheuer & Witsch, 1963);

George Bernard Shaw, *Caesar und Cleopatra,* translated by Böll and Annemarie Böll (Frankfurt: Suhrkamp, 1965).

When in the summer of 1972 Heinrich Böll received the news that he had been awarded the Nobel Prize in Literature, he responded with the surprised question "Was, ich, und nicht Günter Grass?" (What, I, and not Günter Grass?). This response summarizes Böll's self-assessment of his place in West German postwar literature, sometimes referred to as "Grass-Böll literature," and it reflects Böll's competition with Grass, who is often regarded by critics as the better of the two. Böll's sales figures, however, reveal a different view. With thirty-one million books in print, having been translated into forty-five languages, he was the most popular post–World War II German writer. His unpretentious form and style helped him to become a chronologist of the first forty years of the Federal Republic of Germany. When a poll was conducted in the 1970s to name the ten most influential people in West Germany, Böll was mentioned in fourth place, after the politicians Helmut Schmidt, Willy Brandt, and Franz Joseph Strauß, as the man who "represents our conscience." Böll had become an important public figure in Germany—much against his will. The fascination he inspired both in Germany and abroad originated not only from his books but also from his personality. Many Germans believed that if they understood the essence of the man and what he stood for, they would be able to comprehend the political atmosphere of the Federal Republic better. Especially in the days of turmoil between 1969 and 1975, which to a large degree defined the "old" Federal Republic, where everybody followed political events with intense interest as a result of the dreadful recent political past, Böll helped shape that image, both with his books and with his public appearances.

Heinrich Theodor Böll was born in Cologne on 21 December 1917, the sixth child of Victor Böll and his second wife, Marie, neé Hermanns, during the worst famine year of World War I. Böll had two brothers and three sisters. His mother was an energetic, domineering woman from a long line of Catholic farmers and brewers. His father's family, as he wrote in "Über mich selbst" (About Myself, included in *Erzählungen, Hörspiele, Aufsätze,* 1961), "kamen vor Jahrhunderten von den britischen Inseln, Katholiken, die der Staatsreligion Henrich VIII. die Emigration vorzogen" (came centuries ago from the British Isles, Catholics, who preferred emigration to the state religion of Henry VIII). Victor Böll had come to Cologne from Essen in 1896, at the age of twenty-six, to advance socially and, together with an associate, to start his own business as carpenter and wood sculptor; he deliberately chose the southern city of Cologne, with its many Gothic churches. Victor Böll was a sensitive, nervous man, an artist who liked to tell stories to his sons. He created the kind of sculptures that were needed in the churches of the second German empire, which he supported enthusiastically. However, during the war, Victor Böll's enthusiasm for Kaiser Wilhelm II shifted to a cynical view of "der kaiserliche Narr" (the royal fool). Böll clearly inherited his anti-Prussian attitude from his father, who had always lived in the anti-Protestant Rhineland.

Böll's first childhood memory was of the returning and defeated Hindenburg army. His early years were happy ones for Böll's family, however. They had first lived in an apartment but soon acquired their own home in Cologne-Raderberg, Kreuznacher Straße 49. Some critics see Böll's writings as an attempt to reconstruct the happiness of childhood experiences, lost in the modern technological world. Böll's parents were liberal and understanding and never forced the children to join the Catholic Church, because of their own negative experiences in it. They also allowed Böll and his siblings to play with the socialists in their neighborhood, as he recalled in 'raderberg, Raderthal" (included in *Werke: Essayistische Schriften und Reden,* volume 2, 1977): "sie wären nie auf den Gedanken gekommen, zu tun, was die Professoren, Prokuristen, Architekten, Bankdirektoren taten: die verboten ihren Kindern, mit den 'Roten' zu spielen" (they never thought to do what the professors, attorneys, architects, and bank directors did: forbid their children to play with the "Reds"). But this idyll was interrupted when Böll went to a Catholic elementary school in 1924 while most of his friends went to public school; Böll later attended the Kaiser-Wilhelm-Gymnasium, which made him more aware of existing social distinctions. He could not understand why the "Reds" could not go with him.

In October 1930 Böll's father lost his business as a result of the world financial crisis of 1929. The family had to sell the house and their possessions; they were never assured of being able to pay their monthly apartment rent. This experience brought Böll even closer to his parents: he realized "daß meine Eltern völlig hilflos waren gegenüber diesen Umständen" (how my parents were totally helpless in the face of these conditions). In the following years the Bölls had to move several times and were forced to rent out rooms of their apartments to stay ahead of the money collectors. The family was sliding out of the *entbürgerlicht* (middle class) but were not really establishing themselves in a lower class. These experiences led Böll to describe himself sometimes as proletarian but later to use the term *kleinbürgerlich* (lower middle class). The term, usually seen as negative, has a more positive connotation in his work, for example in his essay "Zur Verteidigung der Waschküchen" (1959, In Defense of The Wash-House, included in *Erzählungen, Hörspiele, Aufsätze*).

Soon everyone got involved in the advance of the Nazis. Young Böll was in bed with the flu when Adolf Hitler became chancellor in 1933, and he remembered his mother saying: "That means war." During his last years at the gymnasium, Böll saw how the Nazis brought the unemployment caused by the 1929 depression under control: "wieder einige Jahre später waren die Arbeitslosen untergebracht, sie wurden Polizisten, Soldaten, Henker, Rüstungsarbeiter–der Rest zog in die Konzentrationslager" (the unemployed were given work as policemen, soldiers, executioners, and armament workers–and the rest went to concentration camps). His parents supported secret meetings of the now-illegal Catholic Youth in their apartment. The school, however, tried to remain neutral. Böll's main interest became literature: Leon Bloy, Georges Bernanos, Charles Dickens, Honoré de Balzac, and the German classic dramatists Heinrich von Kleist and Friedrich Hebbel later became his models. In Klaus Schröter's 1982 biography, Böll's brother recalls Böll's withdrawal into reading to the point of neglecting his studies and having to repeat a grade.

After graduating from the gymnasium in 1937, Böll worked for a bookstore in Bonn, where he catalogued collections of old books for a salary of ten marks a month. The job brought him into his first contact with banned books such as the works of Sigmund Freud and Karl Marx. He soon quit the job, considered becoming a librarian, began writing, and worked as a tutor, but essentially could not decide what to do. Every activity in those days, Böll later said in an interview with René Wintzen (1979), was overshadowed by the prospect of the war that everyone knew was coming, perhaps as early as 1938, but definitely by 1939.

In order to be admitted to a university, Böll first had to complete the compulsory labor service to which all *Abiturienten* (high-school graduates) were called. This labor service was the first Nazi organization with which he was associated, since he had avoided the Hitler Youth. In the winter of 1938–1939 he was called to work in Hesse, where he dug irrigation ditches and worked in the forest. After completion of his service, he enrolled at the University of Cologne to study German and classical philology and literature. Shortly after matriculation, in early 1939, he was called into military service for an eight-week training course, and when the war broke out in September, he had to continue his service until the end of the war in 1945. After his training as an infantryman, he served in France, Poland, and then again in France, where his right hand was injured when the train on which he was traveling struck a mine. In 1942 Böll married his girlfriend, Annemarie Cech, with whom he exchanged at least one letter a day, but he wrote nothing else in those six years. He was not ready to describe the war.

Also in 1942 his parents' apartment at Kreuznacher Straße 49 was destroyed in an air raid, and the family was evacuated to Ahrweiler, where his mother died during another air raid. The family was then evacuated to the rural Bergisches Land. Eventually, Böll was sent to the Eastern Front in the Crimea, where he was wounded in the leg. Shortly afterward, he was struck in the head by a shell fragment and was sent to a hospital in Odessa. The front, however, was rapidly approaching that city. Quickly released from the hospital, Böll was transferred to Jassy in Rumania, where eight days later he was seriously wounded in the back. He managed to stay in a hospital in Hungary until August 1944. By this time, he was trying to evade combat by faking illnesses and later by desertion. But in the confusion of the final war days, he was able to join the army again so that he could be taken prisoner by the Americans and thus could obtain a proper release from the army. He was captured on 9 April 1945 and was imprisoned in France and Belgium until the fall.

In November 1945 Böll, his wife, and other members of the family returned to Cologne. His first son, Christoph, who had been born earlier that year, died that winter. Cologne was an almost totally destroyed city in which only three hundred buildings were without damage; there was no transportation, no water, and no electricity. Böll helped with the reconstruction of the house in Bayenthal where his father lived, but he stayed away from public-works projects to express his reservations about the new system of government. He hoped this new system would become socialist but realized that the currency reform of 1948 destroyed this idea by introducing an economic system that favored the old ruling class in their retention of property. He enrolled at the University of Cologne in 1945, pro forma. He never really intended to study; he simply needed a ration card. Böll first worked in the family carpentry shop, but he soon found temporary employment with the statistical office of the city of Cologne. However, financially he was dependent on his wife's income as a middle-school teacher. During this time he wrote industriously, and in 1947 he published two short stories, "Die Botschaft" (Breaking the News) and "Kumpel mit dem langen Haar" (My Pal with the Long Hair), in the periodical *Karussell*.

Böll's stories also began to appear in 1947 in papers such as the *Rheinischer Merkur* and in Alfred Andersch's *Der Ruf*; they were published in 1950 in the volume *Wanderer kommst du nach Spa . . .* (translated as *Traveller, If You Come to Spa . . .* , 1956). These stories can be separated into two groups: war stories and stories dealing with the immediate postwar era. The war stories are told from the perspective of a first-person narrator, typically an unnamed German soldier who expresses Böll's own experiences and desire for a better world. His dreams are the normal dreams of an unpolitical *Bürger* (member of the German middle class): good books in a quiet home, family life, a wife, music, and art. The most significant element is the fatal outcome; the hero often does not survive. The mood of these stories is best characterized by a sentence from "Die Botschaft," in which the narrator has to report a soldier's death to the man's wife: "Da wußte ich, daß der Krieg niemals zu Ende sein würde, niemals, solange noch irgendwo eine Wunde blutete, die er geschlagen hat" (There I knew that the war would never be finished, never as long as somewhere a wound was bleeding that had been caused by the war). One of Böll's concerns in these stories was the honest representation of man's behavior in a war situation: completely falling apart under stress. He uses the term "ridiculous warrior." For that reason Böll was opposed to the influence on postwar German literature of Ernest Hemingway's ideas of male heroic superiority.

Many of the tales in the first collection deal with the postwar period. Typically, they describe returning veterans who do not participate in the *Wirtschaftswunder* (reconstruction period) after the currency reform of 1948. These recovering soldiers are looking for their private niche in the new society. One man works for a statistical office and counts people crossing a bridge; but he never counts his girlfriend, in order to maintain her humanity. It is an individual form of resistance—a theme that became Böll's central message in the next decades.

The stories did not provide enough income to support Böll's wife and sons (Raimund was born in 1947, René in 1948, and Vincent in 1950), and even the publication of two novels did not change Böll's financial situation significantly. His first publisher, Middelhauve, was mainly a publisher of science books and thus not interested in promoting literature. Middelhauve published Böll's first longer story, *Der Zug war pünktlich* (translated as *The Train Was on Time*, 1956), in 1949. A soldier, Andreas, boards an army train in the West (probably Cologne) to join a unit in the Ukraine. The story recounts his journey through Dresden, Kraków, and finally Lemberg, where two other soldiers take him to an expensive restaurant and to a bordello. There he meets the Polish resistance fighter Olina, for whom he develops a platonic love. Andreas, Olina, and the two other soldiers decide to flee in a general's car, and all four get killed by partisans.

The tension and atmosphere of the story is created by Andreas's premonition at the beginning of the trip that he "would never see Germany again." He knows he will die near Lemberg, because his mind goes blank when he thinks of the next town, Story. This unrealistic element of "fate" is important for Böll's style and gives it a special quality. The reader is convinced of Andreas's ability to see the future and thus anticipates his death. The novella takes on biblical dimensions: Andreas is seen as Jesus at the Last Supper and as having a Mary-Magdalene type of relationship with Olina, to whom he is a brother, not a lover. He persuades Olina to give up her political undercover war, which he considers immoral and insignificant. In the same way, Andreas is apolitical in his relationship to Nazi Germany, which was perhaps typical for the times.

Der Zug war pünktlich, with its religious and mystical treatment of the war, shows Böll's own limited understanding during this period (1945–1950) of the social aspects and causes of the war. The formal achievement of the novella, however, and its humanistic or antifascist spirit, drew praise. Gert Kalow calls it a *Geniewurf* (cast of genius), and Theodore Ziolkowski writes: "Never again has Böll written a story of such close perfection and inevitability . . . It is an artistic tour de force." Böll's success can also be seen in the fact that in 1949 he was invited for the first time to read at a meeting of the Gruppe 47, the major German literary circle of the 1950s and 1960s.

Der Zug war pünktlich was followed in 1951 by Böll's most famous war novel, *Wo warst du, Adam?* (translated as *Adam, Where Art Thou?* 1955). The novel is divided into episodic chapters, in which minor characters later become main characters. Except for this aspect, the episodes are not connected and can be seen as independent short stories. This individual quality is especially true of the chapters about the life and death of Lieutenant Greck and the building of the bridge at Berczaby. The episode about a woman named Ilona is an early treatment of concentration camps in German fiction. When Ilona sings the Litany of the Saints, the Nazi commander Filskeit realizes the amorality of the camps, and the beauty of music overcomes the horror of the SS. The main theme of the volume is the idea of the senselessness of man's existence: as the death of protagonist Feinhals in front of his parents' home shows, there is no escape from the senselessness of the war. *Wo warst du, Adam?* was praised by Richard Plant as succeeding in "conjuring up the agonies of WWII" as critics began using the word "compassionate" for Böll's fiction.

After publication of *Wo warst du, Adam?* Gruppe 47 again invited Böll to one of their meetings. He read his humorous story "Die Schwarzen Schafe" (1951, The Black Sheep), for which the group awarded him a prize of 1,000 marks and the invitation to become a permanent member. Without Gruppe 47, Böll would not have become as popular, especially in the 1950s. But the reputation of the group was enhanced reciprocally by the presence of Böll, who eventually became its most prestigious member.

Although *Der Zug war pünktlich* and *Wo warst du, Adam?* were for many years Böll's only two published novels dealing with World War II, it was known that a third manuscript existed, which Böll had always tried to disclaim. Finally, his son Rene Böll published this book in 1982 under the title *Das Vermächtnis* (translated as *A Soldier's Legacy*, 1985). Like *Der Zug war pünktlich,* it takes place in 1943. The book starts out in France and is told by a soldier, Wenk, who falls in love with a French girl. But soon his commander, Schelling, takes the girl away from him. Schelling is trying to find out why his soldiers' food ration is illegally kept away from them and discovers that Captain Schnecker is partly responsible for it. Schnecker kills Schelling; thus, the compassionate people die while the heartless ones survive the war, eventually to play a leading role in postwar society.

With the 1952 story "Die Waage der Baleks" (The Balek Scale, first published in *Frankfurter Allgemeine Zeitung,* 13 June 1953), Böll introduced the overriding concern in his writing: the criticism of postwar materialism. With this story, Böll's most popular, he approaches his subject historically, by setting it in a provincial Austrian town around 1900. It is a story of capitalist exploitation and a failed proletarian revolt, narrated in the classical style of Johann Peter Hebel or Kleist. Cesare Cases's Marxist interpretation of "Die Waage der Baleks" as social criticism hit a raw nerve for some readers at first. "Die Waage der Baleks" is now considered one of Böll's most important stories and the first in which he examined and condemned the economic conditions of society.

With the novel *Und sagte kein einziges Wort* (And Said Not a Single Word, 1953; translated as *Acquainted with the Night,* 1954), Böll changed to the publisher Kiepenheuer and Witsch and achieved an immediate breakthrough: this work is still one of his best-known books and made him financially independent. Poverty makes protagonist Fred Bogner sick and drives him away from the one room he shared with his wife and children. He drifts around the city and meets his wife, Käte, in cheap hotels on weekends. She is ready to separate from him, but in the final scene Fred recognizes his wife on the street and without her being aware of his presence, she touches his heart ("deren Anblick mein Herz berührte"). The novel is told in alternating first-person narratives by Fred and Käte. Fred is a drinker, has beaten his children, and is beginning to question the authority of the church. He is not ambitious and feels self-pity for being left out of society. He becomes antagonistic and wants no part of the new society (mirroring elements of Böll's own biography). The social criticism is explicit; the author especially criticizes the bigoted landlady, Frau Franke, who does not want to give the family another room, maintaining she needs it as a reception room for Catholic aid committees. There is also corruption in the church: the church officials fail to criticize the pharmaceutical industry for advertising contraceptives because the bishop's cousin is the chairman of the association of druggists. In the end, the pharmacy becomes the personification of modern-day society: cleanliness, contraception, and useless consumption. Neither Fred nor his wife goes along with these ideas, and the self-righteous Fred defends his own way of life. Eventually, he reconciles with Käte, who is expecting another child.

Und sagte kein einziges Wort demonstrates Böll's meticulously realistic style, which describes the world that surrounds the alienated Fred. Most critics agree that *Und sagte kein einziges Wort* is a preparatory stage to Böll's more political works, and they especially deplore its peaceful ending, which, according to Günter Wirth, contradicts the unsettling hostility Fred had shown to society. The novel is a good example to support Böll's claim that he was only interested in love and religion. Böll's novel is regarded more as a report than as fiction and is praised as the beginning of a literary renaissance in Western Germany.

In *Haus ohne Hüter* (1954; translated as *The Unguarded House,* 1957), Böll deliberately uses modern cinematic techniques. The story is told in consecutive chapters by two boys, Martin Bach and Heinrich Brielach. It is not a children's book, but the children's perspective adds an element of alienation, allowing readers to see the adult world in a different light. Both boys have lost their fathers in the war. Martin's mother, Nella, retreats into a dreamworld after the death of her husband, the poet Rai. A former friend, Albert Muchow, becomes Martin's "uncle" but cannot help him much. Heinrich, on the other hand, has to earn a living for his family on the black market while still attending school. His mother worked in a bakery and later moves in with the baker, the way she had with several other "uncles" before. Two themes stand out: the contrast of the poor and rich in postwar society and the relationship to the Nazi past. The Brielachs are stigmatized for their poverty and afraid to move their belongings in front of their scrutinizing neighbors. Martin, on the other hand, can live in luxury with his wealthy grandmother.

The novel gains momentum at the end when Gäseler, the murderer of Martin's father, is introduced. During the war, Gäseler had sent Rai on a reconnaissance mission, knowing that the poet was ill-equipped for it and probably would not survive. Since the war, Gäseler has become a conformist representative of the new capitalist system: vain and opportunistic, not unlike the devil in Nella's fantasies. In Gäseler's presence she can only feel "Sie langweilen nich" (cold, uncanny boredom). When she asks Gäseler to tell her about the war, he reveals himself as a representative of the new times: "Ich denke nicht oft daran. Ich versuche, es zu vergessen, und es gelingt mir . . . Man muß den Krieg vergessen" (I don't think about it any more. I try to forget it, and I can . . . People have to forget the war). But he has not forgotten the names of his Nazi heroes; only the death images have been erased from his mind. Nella replies, "Ohrfeigen an Leute verteilen, die den Krieg vergessen haben" (A slap in the face for all the people who have forgotten the war), and walks away without looking back. Hatred does not seem adequate to punish these Nazi conformers: they would not even understand it. Like Nella, Böll believed the Germans wanted to forget—the war, the Jews, the entire Nazi past—and had illusions about their popularity in the world.

Das Brot der frühen Jahre (1955; translated as *The Bread of Our Early Years,* 1957) covers the time span from about eight o'clock in the morning to about eight o'clock in the evening of a single day in the narrator's life in 1954 or 1955. Walter goes to the train station to meet Hedwig, who is the daughter of a friend of his father and who is coming to the city to study at the university. Walter has previously found her a room and is to take her there and go back to work. But when he sees Hedwig, his life changes:

Ich sah nur diesen grellgrünen Mantel, sah dieses Gesicht, und ich hatte plötzlich Angst, jene Angst, die Entdecker empfinden, wenn sie das neue Land betreten haben . . . Dieses Gesicht ging tief in mich hinein . . . es war, als würde ich durchbohrt ohne zu bluten.

(I saw only her dazzling green coat, her face, and I suddenly became fearful with that fear which explorers have when they enter upon a new land . . . Her face went deep into me . . . It was as if I had been pierced without bleeding.)

From that moment, Walter is a new person. He does not return to his old job, withdraws all his savings from the bank, breaks his engagement to his boss's daughter, and decides to live with Hedwig, without the sacrament of the church.

Böll continued the theme of love in the short story "So ward Abend und Morgen" (And It Became Night and Day, first published in *Westdeutsche Allgemeine Zeitung,* 24 December 1954). The relationship between man and woman is symbolized in a mythical sense as a cry of the man for company in his lonely life. The protagonist's wife has stopped talking to him; but on a Christmas evening he makes her say "no" twice and "yes" once—which saves his life. Böll's treatment of the relationship between the sexes also figured in a longer narrative, "Im Tal der Donnernden Hufe" (In the Valley of the Thundering Hooves, first published in *Frankfurter Allgemeine Zeitung,* 17 March 1954), about the sexual problems of two Catholic boys, Paul and Griff. An atheist girl, Mirzova, helps Paul overcome his anxiety by exposing her breasts. As a result, however, the girl has to leave town for a few years to avoid being labeled a prostitute by the narrow-minded townspeople. The story is constructed using traditional symbolism such as the pistol as a phallic object.

In the mid 1950s the Federal Republic under Chancellor Konrad Adenauer became stronger and chose a political course that Böll did not support. The turning point was the rearmament campaign. Until that time, he had been a supporter of the Christian Democratic Union (CDU). As a result of these developments, Böll "escaped" to Ireland for a few weeks in 1955. Later, when asked by Wintzen whether Ireland was his second home, Böll said that there was no such thing as a second homeland. Böll was a "Kölner" (a person from Cologne). His idea of "home" was centered in Cologne, as shown in his use of dialect; he could not represent Prussia or the eastern part of Germany. His definition of what is "German" concentrated on the use of language: he considered himself a German because he wrote in German.

Böll made a second trip to Ireland in 1956. His *Irisches Tagebuch* (1957; translated as *Irish Journal,* 1967) resulting from those trips is not a conventional travelogue. Rather, Böll gives travel impressions to show moral and historic realities and facts about Ireland and Germany. Despite his "flight," he continues his criticism of German society in a more subtle form in this book.

One of the reasons for Böll's retreat to Ireland had been the attacks on some of the satirical short stories he published in the 1950s, particularly *Nicht nur zur Weihnachtszeit* (1952; Not Only at Christmastime), which mocks the middle-class tendency to overcelebrate Christmas and use it as escape from reality. The mother of a family has saved Christmas decorations from before the war and protests whenever anybody tries to take the Christmas tree down. So the family celebrates Christmas every day of the year, at first in person, later with stand-in actors for the totally demoralized family members. Böll was attacked by the church as being inhuman and without love. He responded that he had not intended to denounce Christmas but rather the commercial aspects of it.

The title story of *Doktor Murkes gesammeltes Schweigen und andere Satiren* (1958; Doctor Murke's Collected Silences and Other Satires, first published in *Frankfurter Hefte*), is referred to by Cases as one of the finest works of European literature since World War II, and Walter Jens claims Böll's work culminates in this book. The "philosopher" Bur-Malottke wants to change the word *God* on a radio tape of one of his notorious talks to "jenes höhere Wesen, das wir verehren" (the higher being whom we revere); the word *God* gets cut out of the tape and spliced into another program, where an atheist's questions are now answered by Bur-Malottke's "God." What is left is cut-out "silence," and the journalist Murke takes the pieces home in a box. Murke shows the absurdity of the situation when he lets Bur-Malottke repeat the phrase "jenes höhere Wesen, das wir verehren" twenty-seven times. Murke hates the philosopher's opportunism. Böll wanted to show how poisoned was an intellectual climate that left religion out of the economic and political restoration of the 1950s; God got "cut" out of social considerations.

Böll's novel *Billard um halb zehn* (1959; translated as *Billiards at Half-past Nine*, 1961) is a family chronicle. But unlike Thomas Mann's novel *Buddenbrooks* (1901), which shows the downfall of a family, Böll shows the prosperity and rise of a middle-class family, the Fähmels, through whose perspective the novel presents fifty years of German history from 1907 to 1958. The novel, however, actually covers only a single day in 1958, the eightieth birthday of Heinrich Fähmel. Böll's symbolism divides people into two categories: "das Sakrament des Büffels" (the sacrament of the buffalo), comprising all militarists, Nazis, and the power-hungry, and "das Sakrament des Lamms" (the sacrament of the lamb), made up of the persecuted and émigrés, the sensitive people. Böll himself criticized this symbolism later as being too simplistic to comprehend the horrors and intricacies of German history. The formal juxtaposition also drew a lot of criticism. Some reviewers claimed that the experimental French *nouveau roman* (new novel) and the psychological novel were mutually exclusive forms and that Böll failed by trying to combine the two. Böll worked out this novel in a meticulous, almost mathematical way, by using a colored chart divided into three levels: the present, the reflective or memory level, and the level of motifs. But the resulting novel is too confusing; the lamb-buffalo symbolism does not convince. The St. Anton Abbey, however, stands out as the one effective symbol that ties the three generations together: the grandfather built it; the son blew it up; and the grandson does not know whether he wants to reconstruct or demolish it. Johanna Fähmel's attempt to shoot a high government official with a Nazi past fails to enhance the level of tension in the novel. Jens summarized the views of many critics when he observed that the novel form was too long for Böll, and that he should have stayed with the short story, which he could manage more easily. *Billard um halb zehn* is still one of Böll's best-known works, and it convinced critics that Böll could contribute "significant fiction." The most common praise for Böll's moderately experimental narrative technique was that he still retained more interest in story than in stylistic experimentation.

In the following years Böll's disenchantment with the course of German politics continued, especially with the role Catholicism played in it. In 1961, in one of his sharpest essays, "Hast Du was, dann bist Du was" (You Are What You Have, published in *Labyrinth*), he attacked Cologne's Cardinal Frings for what he considered Frings's hypocritical views, expressed in a pastoral letter in which Frings linked the idea of property for the general public *(Volksaktien)* with the principles of the Christian church; Böll commented caustically, "Die Heiligsprechung des Habenichts von Assisi war wohl ein Irrtum" (The canonization of the have-not Francis of Assisi probably was a mistake). Böll also attacked Chancellor Adenauer for too eagerly forgetting Germany's Nazi past and for his encouragement of the accumulation of property. In those years Böll also criticized the change by the Social Democratic Party (SPD) to a more capitalist ideology, as reflected in their Godesberg Program of 1959. As an advocate of socialism and even Marxism, Böll wanted two basic sociopolitical concepts expressed in the German party system, unlike the political system in the United States, in which both parties advocate capitalism. In his writings, Böll tried to change the course of the SPD.

In the early 1960s Böll, together with the artist HAP Grieshaber and others, founded the Christian socialist periodical *Labyrinth*. Here he published his first

Page from the manuscript for Böll's story "Als der Krieg ausbrach" (When the War Broke Out), published in 1962 (from Hermann Stresau, Heinrich Böll, *1964; Thomas Cooper Library, University of South Carolina)* play, *Ein Schluck Erde* (1962, A Piece of Earth), which depicts an old man who would like to combine Christianity and communism. Also in 1962, Böll completed the essay "Karl Marx," which praises the philosopher and presents him as a secular saint, as well as a study of St. Francis, titled *Assisi*). Both became models for Böll's further development. In an interview with Marcel Reich-Ranicki in 1967, Böll confessed his communist sympathies and wished communism as many years of power as capitalism had already had. He said that if he had not grown up in fascist Germany he would have certainly been a Communist by 1936. Böll also regretted that more Germans had not had the opportunity to become Communists in the 1930s, thereby purifying the political atmosphere. In spite of these statements, however, Böll is not a revolutionary writer.

Böll's 1961 work *Brief an einen jungen Katholiken* (Letter to a Young Catholic) makes clear that his development toward socialism was related to his disenchantment with the Catholic Church. In it he expresses his disapproval of what he considered the merger of church and government in the Federal Republic at that time. The *Brief an einen jungen Katholiken* started a process that ended with Böll's officially leaving the church in 1977 (in Germany, that meant he simply stopped paying "church taxes").

In 1962 Böll was invited on his first official trip to the Soviet Union, in connection with the new German-Soviet Cultural Exchange Program, a journey he resented at that time because he was busy working on a new book. This book, which became *Ansichten eines Clowns* (1963; translated as *The Clown*, 1965), is one of his most controversial novels. Hans Schnier, at twenty-seven, has left his wealthy parents' home to become a professional clown. The novel, which also became a play, takes place on one evening in Schnier's Bonn apartment after he has had a stage accident. Schnier feels sorry for himself since his girlfriend, Marie, left him to marry a *Berufskatholik* (administrator of the Catholic Church). Through several phone calls to relatives and friends, Hans discovers that Marie is now on her honeymoon trip, which will include a visit to the Pope. He decides to await her return by singing religious songs at the train station while wearing his clown costume. Hans advocates a form of marriage in which the church plays no role; only the mutual consent of the two partners matters. He has become a professional clown who, like a medieval court jester, criticizes society.

The entire novel shows Hans's isolated position: he can only live with one person, Marie, and she leaves him. Because of his artistic nature, Hans views the living and the dead differently than most people do. His sister Henriette, who died in World War II, is alive in his mind, while her "murderer," his mother, is dead for him, because she adjusts herself eagerly to the new social conditions and wants to forget. J. D. Salinger's *The Catcher in the Rye* (1951) was one model for *Ansichten eines Clowns;* Böll and his wife had just translated Salinger's novel into German in 1962. Holden Caulfield's character and his relationship to his sister clearly had an influence on Böll.

Ansichten eines Clowns was widely criticized for its anti-Catholic bias. Schröter admits that after reading this book he lost interest in Böll's work for a long time. According to Manfred Durzak, the novel was an aesthetic dead end for Böll, who had reached his satirical limits. Hans-Joachim Bernhard was of the opinion that the aesthetic balance was disrupted by Böll's subjectivity. But Frank Trommler saw in *Ansichten eines Clowns* a new phase in post–World War II German literary history, characterized by blunt political reasoning instead of formal artistic expression. Several reviewers rejected the book since Böll seemed no longer interested in prose experiments. They generally felt that by establishing himself as a writer more concerned with philosophical issues, with Weltanschauung than with narrative structure, Böll was moving away from Western traditions. The book displeased those critics who were used to innovative, intellectualized fiction. By 1975, however, academic scholarship took a kinder view of *Ansichten eines Clowns,* and Böll's novel became regarded more as a continuation of *Billard um halb zehn,* an imitation of the French *nouveau roman. Ansichten eines Clowns* turned out to be an important book for Böll's reputation since it divided the critics into two groups: those who saw a break in Böll's continuity and those who considered it his best and most straightforward book.

Subsequently, Böll became more interested in direct political writings. The *Frankfurter Vorlesungen* (1966, Frankfurt Lectures), given at the University of Frankfurt after a longer stay in Dugort, Ireland, where Böll had bought a home, is an example of this genre. Böll considered immigrating to Ireland, especially after the church attacks on *Ansichten eines Clowns.* The *Frankfurter Vorlesungen* present Böll's belief that home, love for the *Heimat* (homeland), memory, and language constitute the human being. The recent German rejection of provinciality is seen as negative, since more works of art have been created in remote places such as Dublin or Prague. Böll's intent is to analyze the "Abfall der Gesellschaft" (garbage of society) and to take the place of a political opposition that–according to Böll–no longer exists in West Germany. The Grand Coalition of the CDU and the SPD from 1965 to 1969 only confirmed Böll's political fears.

In the short novel *Entfernung von der Truppe* (1964; translated as "Absent without Leave," 1965), the author's detachment from German political life is noticeable. The narrator states that with his "desertion," a rejection of society, his life as a human being began. Despite its bleak plot, the story is told in a loose, humorous way, revealing the author's familiarity with the work of Laurence Sterne. Böll did not like to use the same form twice, but this work developed an experimental structure that is not completely successful.

Ende einer Dienstfahrt (1966; translated as *End of a Mission*, 1967) is really a novel about art and how to incorporate art into society. In its description of the military as a senseless machine, it is reminiscent of *Wo warst du, Adam?* It is presented in the Kleistean style (which Böll admired). The book describes a trial against the carpenters Gruhl, a father and son, who burned the son's army jeep as an act of antimilitary protest. The case is an embarrassment to the authorities, who want to play it down by keeping the press out and by giving the case to a mild judge. The Gruhls finally receive only six weeks' imprisonment. As he explains in "einführung in 'dienstfahrt'" (included in *Aufsätze, Kritiken, Reden*, 1967), Böll wants readers to understand his novella as a way of using art as a means to protest current trends in politics and society, a tendency that is romantic and can be traced to the dadaistic experiments of the 1920s:

> Um diese Zeit auch dachte ich besonders über die Tatsache nach, daß die komplette Nettigkeit der Gesellschaft der Kunst gegenüber ja nichts anderes als eine Art Gummizelle ist. Gleichzeitig las ich über die Provos in Amsterdam, las über Happenings, und die Erkenntnis, daß alle Kunst von dieser so fassunglosen wie unfaßbaren Gesellschaft ernst genommen wird, brachte mich auf die Idee, daß Kunst, also auch Happenings, eine, vielleicht die letzte Möglichkeit sei, die Gummizelle durch eine Zeitzünderbombe zu sprengen oder den Irrenhausdirektor durch eine vergiftete Praline außer Gefecht zu setzen; ich entschied mich zu einer Kombination von vergifteter Praline und Zeitzünderbombe.
>
> (I thought how the complete niceness of society toward art is nothing more than a kind of padded cell. At the same time, I was reading about the provos in Amsterdam and their antiestablishment Happenings. I recognized that all art is taken seriously by this bewildering and incomprehensible society. This recognition brought me to the idea that art, that is, a Happening, is perhaps the last chance to break out of this padded cell; it can become a time bomb or the way to take the director of this madhouse out of action with a poisoned chocolate sweet. I decided on a combination of poisoned chocolates and a time bomb.)

Most critics did not see the political time bomb, and did not want to see it. One reason is that art in the 1960s had removed itself from politics. The critics, as recorders of acceptable literary trends, could not see Böll's new and revolutionary element in the story. But art as a political "happening" became a program for the student revolts of the late 1960s. Böll wanted to show that the ruling class understood the danger of the Gruhls' political action and decided to cover it up. He also wanted to show the sympathy of the village people, who all understand and support the action. Jochen Vogt might be correct in asserting that this congenial understanding constitutes too much of a sense of idealized *Heimat*, as Böll had set out to write about in his *Frankfurter Vorlesungen*; it excludes readers from a different background.

In "Epilog zu Stifters *Nachsommer*" (1970, Epilogue to Stifter's *Indian Summer*; included in *Erzählungen, 1950–1970*, 1972), Böll imitates the language and plots of novelist Adalbert Stifter, who had been one of his nineteenth-century models. Böll, however, destroys the nineteenth-century middle-class world and shows in his story how that entire society was based on lies and deception. The story is an interesting variation on Böll's topic of language and morals.

During the following years Böll worked primarily on his next and longest novel, *Gruppenbild mit Dame* (translated as *Group Portrait with Lady*, 1973), which was published in 1971. But while doing this *Erinnerungsarbeit* (remembrance work), he also traveled more, and in August 1968 he happened to be in Czechoslovakia during the Soviet invasion. This situation provided an opportunity for him to protest Soviet policies, which in turn increased his political credibility with the Right. He considered the election of Brandt as chancellor in 1969 as an opportunity to overcome what he saw as the German authoritarian government that Adenauer's CDU had perpetuated; he welcomed the defeat of the CDU and former chancellor Kurt Georg Kiesinger, who was also a former member of the Nazi Party. In 1971 Böll was elected as the first German president of the International PEN Club and officially visited the New York PEN offices. Hans Werner Richter, the founder of the Gruppe 47, commented that "Böll can do things that we others cannot even dream of."

When *Gruppenbild mit Dame* appeared, the publishers called the book Böll's "most comprehensive, encompassing work," a "summation of his previous life and work." The heroine, Leni Pfeiffer, along with various other tenants, fights to save her apartment in a house her relatives want to tear down. Leni is a mixture of the Virgin Mary and Mary Magdalene, another one of Böll's attempts to mix his realism with Christian mythology. She is a "pure" soul, without any interest in the consumer- and achievement-driven society; she is helpful, sensual, possessing a natural instinct for the right thing to do, a "subversive madonna." She, together with her son, Lev, and the rest of her family—including her father and her brother, who were murdered by the Nazis because they refused to support the fascist war machine—introduces Böll's principle of *Leistungsverweigerung* (a rejection of the work ethic), a subversive concept attacking the dehumanization of life under capitalism. Because of their belief in *Leistungsverweigerung*, Lev and his mother become the center of a counterculture within the city—groups Böll believed are absolutely necessary as the only possibility to protect mankind from fascism and technology.

The novel struck a responsive chord when it appeared, during the years of student protests when people sought to create a utopia. Just as the students were attacked, Leni's behavior is criticized as unhealthy and destructive by her relatives, who see capitalistic profiteering as healthy and normal. The novel, however, offers another view, introduced by an inquiring journalist who collects information about Leni from the people around her and thereby discovers that she was the lover of a Russian prisoner of war during World War II. This excursion into the German past is honest, even though it is not always logically presented; Leni's friends and colleagues tell the journalist their reactions to her affair and the birth of her illegitimate son, Lev. The purity of the couple is contrasted with the petty reactions of her colleagues and friends. Although Boris, the wartime lover, remains indistinct as a character, Böll's intention to use Leni as a woman "die ganze Last dieser Geschichte . . . auf sich genommen hat" (who carried the burden of German history) is clear. The reader is invited to reflect on his or her own behavior during those years. Böll depicts what Karl Korn calls the "archaeology of Cologne's society," especially of the lower classes. Joachim Kaiser and other critics saw Böll's work as an experiment between "aesthetic and nonfictional reality" and as utopian construct of a better world through literature. If one follows those arguments, Böll is not immersed in the Romantic tradition, as is often assumed, but rather in Friedrich Schiller's tradition of classical education. Leni would then be a deliberate construct of an aesthetic human being well suited to solve West Germany's problems of the early 1970s.

Most of the criticism of the book concerns the structure. Rainer Nägele calls *Gruppenbild mit Dame* "a much more rambling novel than anything Böll had written previously." Böll never had a master plan for his books but rather developed them out of characters and minor details. Ziolkowski, however, calls the structure a "secular beatification" similar to medieval descriptions of saints. Reactions to *Gruppenbild mit Dame* are indicative of the criticism surrounding Böll from 1972 to 1974: conservatives used what they perceived as structural failures in his work to deduce his flawed logic. They were particularly annoyed by the Swedish Academy's decision to honor Böll (and the liberal trend in German political thinking) with the Nobel Prize; however, in view of the reputation of the prize, they did not dare to openly attack Böll's *Gesinnung* (ideology). The American reception of *Gruppenbild mit Dame* demonstrates the difficult standing Böll has had in the United States. The *Newsweek* reviewer (13 May 1973) wrote that he would rather read Grass but feels he ought to read Böll anyway out of "a guilty feeling" because Böll represented the accepted moral and political position of the time. And a critic for *Time* magazine (30 October 1972) implied that Böll received the Nobel Prize more for his "idealistic tendency" than for his literary qualities.

Böll's failure in the United States cannot be totally explained, especially since he is the most popular German author in Europe. An examination of secondary sources about Böll's work suggests that positive readings came only from those critics familiar with the socio-economic conditions of Germany, while others using more text-centered methods failed to understand the writer's message. The interdependence of critical methods and fictional text seems to preclude a positive reading of the foreign-language text, and it is apparent that a strictly text-centered reading does not capture its essence for an American audience.

Böll had often been a nominee for the Nobel Prize in Literature; but, had *Gruppenbild mit Dame* not appeared in 1971, Böll probably would not have received the 1972 award. *Gruppenbild mit Dame* is generally recognized as the single work that best represents the artistic summation of Böll's literary career. Leni is one of Germany's most remarkable literary personalities, with her generosity, compassion, and integrity, which gave Böll an effective vehicle to criticize the hypocrisy, commercialism, opportunism, and racism of postwar Germany. The work attempts both a reconciliation with the past and a condemnation of the pursuit of affluence in present-day Germany, while presenting a notion of a more compassionate society. In its Nobel nomination, the Swedish Academy singled out *Gruppenbild mit Dame* as Böll's "most grandly conceived work," one that addresses Germany's history with a critical and a constructive perspective.

After receiving the Nobel Prize (as the first German writer after Mann and Hermann Hesse to be so honored), Böll became an even more important public figure than before, praised by the Left as the "moral conscience of his age" and attacked from the Right as a writer without any real aesthetic value. Detractors claimed that the best writers never received the Nobel Prize. Böll responded that, as a German, he could not afford not to accept the Nobel Prize, since Germany had not had many good people whom the world could admire.

After the CDU viciously attacked Brandt's politics of negotiating treaties with Communist countries, his *Ostpolitik,* Böll got involved in Brandt's reelection campaign in 1972. When Böll realized the tendency of his adversaries to deliberately misunderstand his literary intentions, he decided to get involved more directly in the political arena—which, in hindsight, he saw as a mistake. By doing so Böll came down to the level of his political opponents, who usually were not trained in analyzing literature. In 1972 Böll published "Will Ulrike Meinhof Gnade oder fries Geleit?" a famous article in *Der Spiegel* defending Ulrike Meinhof and the terrorist Baader-Meinhof group against the guilty verdict prematurely anticipated by the tabloid *Bild Zeitung.* Böll looks at Meinhof as he had regarded his fictional character Leni: with a feeling that everybody in this society has the right to due process. Böll spoke against the slander in *Bild Zeitung* and maintained that Meinhof would find no mercy in a political climate in which former Nazis were being released without a trial—a correct description of the political practice at the time.

However, Böll's comparison of West German legal practices with those of the Nazis struck a raw nerve in most conservatives. In reaction to this article, the papers controlled by West German press mogul Axel Springer published a letter written by Prime Minister Filbinger of the State of Baden-Württemberg and others asking for Böll's resignation as president of the International PEN Club. On 1 June 1972 Böll's house was searched by the police, and on 7 June, in a debate in the West German Federal Parliament in Bonn, "fellow travelers" such as Böll were declared more dangerous than the Baader-Meinhofs themselves. The vicious reaction to the Meinhof article was Böll's first real experience with the political arena, if one considers earlier expressions of conservative indignation over Böll's novels as literary reactions. Böll was so antagonized by the conservative reaction to his plea for mercy that he decided never to comment about this matter again.

Böll's literary response to these events was his book *Die verlorene Ehre der Katharina Blum oder wie Gewalt entstehen und wohin sie führen kann* (1974; translated as *The Lost Honor of Katharina Blum: How Violence Develops and Where It Can Lead,* 1975), which initially appeared in July 1974 in *Der Spiegel.* It was the first work of fiction ever published by the periodical. The first edition of the book, published in August of 1974, sold one hundred thousand copies in a few weeks and two hundred thousand by the end of the year, which far surpassed the sales of his earlier books. The paperback edition sold more than one million copies and was translated into eighteen languages.

The heroine is Katharina, a housekeeper and a conformist, born in 1947, who has achieved some wealth. She loses her "honor" through the mudslinging of the periodical *Zeitung:* Böll wrote, "Sollten sich bei der Schilderung gewisser journalistischer Praktiken Ähnlichkeiten mit den Praktiken der 'Bild'-Zeitung ergeben haben, so sind diese Ähnlichkeiten weder beabsichtigt noch zufällig, sondern unvermeidlich" (If in describing certain journalistic practices there should be similarities with those of the *Bild-Zeitung,* these similarities are neither intentional nor accidental but unavoidable). The *Zeitung* finds out that Katharina fell in love with an army deserter and bank robber, kept him in her apartment overnight, and let him escape the following morning. Without any justification, the *Zeitung* dubs him a terrorist and Katharina his accomplice. Details about her love life are made up and published. Katharina is so enraged that she decides to kill the journalist Tötges, who is responsible. The story is based on Böll's belief that "daß Sprache, Liebe, Gebundenheit den Menschen zum Menschen machen" (language, love, and home constitute man), as he stated in the *Frankfurter Vorlesungen.* The book portrays other citizens as equally appalled by the *Zeitung* and ready for revenge against the slanderous press, which Böll describes as "öffentliche Gewalt" (public violence). This violence manifests itself in language when Kommissar Beizmenne asks Katharina "Hat er dich denn gefickt?" (Did he fuck you?) and she responds, "Nein, ich würde es nicht so nennen" (I would not say it that way). Katharina herself reveals the violence of language when Tötges approaches her with the words, "Ich schlage vor, daß wir jetzt bumsen" (I suggest that we have sex now), and she thinks "Gut, jetzt bumst's" (Bang, that's fine), and takes the pistol to shoot him (a pun on the German word *bumsen,* "bang" or "have sex").

Reviews of this book were generally more thorough than of *Gruppenbild mit Dame* and in their wide range show the high level German political culture had attained by the 1970s. One of the most quoted conservative opinions was that of Hans Habe, who in *Welt am Sonntag* (18 August 1974) of *Bild Zeitung's* Springer publishing house criticized Böll's use of language and the stylistic awkwardness of the book as evidence of the writer's personal flaws; the novel, he said, exposes Böll's "seine Unfähigkeit zu lieben, . . . die Schwäche seiner Logik und die Maßlosigkeit seines Urteils" (inability to love, . . . the weakness of his logic and his immaturity to judge). In America, Habe wrote in his review defending *Bild Zeitung's* practices, somebody with Tötges's ability would have received the Pulitzer Prize for his investigative reporting; in Germany, someone with these abilities gets killed. In comparing American investigative journalism to Tötges's activities he alludes to the provinciality of the Federal Republic, which, according to Habe, was largely the product of writers and intellectuals like Böll. *The New Yorker* (19 May 1975), on the other hand, characterized the institutional conflicts in *Die verlorene Ehre der Katharina Blum* as a manifestation of the psyche of the German people, asserting that the people and the institutions in the story are unmistakably German and that Böll's understanding of these German conditions makes the book worthwhile.

Mark W. Rectanus discussed the reasons for the problematic reception of Böll's work after *Die verlorene Ehre der Katharina Blum* in the United States. Rectanus felt that Germany was to a large extent still perceived in the United States within the context of the World War II experience and that no one understood Germany's current social problems. None of the reviewers of *Die verlorene Ehre der Katharina Blum* attempted to relate the book to an analysis of political, social, or economic institutions, or to the necessary analysis of the role of the media in the Federal Republic; instead they focused on the love story. But *Die verlorene Ehre der Katharina Blum* was able to engage the political Left in a discussion to define their own position, as no other German writer could at that time.

Böll's support for the weak and the helpless continued. In his function as International PEN president, he played host to Aleksandr Solzhenitsyn after the latter was exiled from the Soviet Union in 1974, and later to Wolf Biermann and Lev Kopelev, who were exiled from East Germany and the Soviet Union, respectively. Despite his support for Soviet dissidents, Böll continued to be one of the most popular German writers in the Soviet Union, probably even more popular than in West Germany.

In 1977, when German industrialist Hanns-Martin Schleyer was kidnapped and murdered by terrorists, and when several imprisoned terrorists committed suicide in the Stammheim prison, Böll was once again accused by conservatives of promoting terrorism. They criticized his 1975 satire *Berichte zur Gesinnungslage der Nation* (Reports on the Attitudinal State of the Nation), which attacks West German bureaucracy because of its supervision of so-called radicals. They also found fault with Böll's story "Du fährst zu oft nach Heidelberg" (You Go to Heidelberg Too Often, first published in *Frankfurter Allgemeine Zeitung*, 17 September 1977), an indictment of *Berufsverbote*—the law that kept suspected Communists out of government jobs.

In his novel *Fürsorgliche Belagerung* (1979; translated as *The Safety Net*, 1981), Böll summarizes his pessimistic experiences of the 1970s. The newspaper editor Fritz Tolm, a sensitive person, is ready to withdraw into private life because his house and family are constantly protected by police against a possible terrorist attack. In its recording of facts, the structure of the novel is similar to that of *Billard um halb zehn* but has its drawbacks as well. The story allows the reader to see the protection system from all sides—the family, the guards, and the terrorists. Family life has been destroyed through the complete safety net; there is no privacy for the protected. The critics agree that the novel fails, partly because Böll tries to use the family as a refuge, but this refuge has been destroyed by the safety measures.

Böll's involvement in political issues continued. He declared that Germany was the country he wanted to live in; it was worth improving. He participated in the 1981 Bonn peace demonstration. In 1983 Böll was recommended for an honorary citizenship in the city of Cologne. At first, the local CDU was opposed, not to recognizing Böll as a great writer but to honoring him as a social critic. In his acceptance speech, Böll discussed the common mistake of separating the two aspects and claimed that essays, reviews, and lectures are also literature. He said that they could not be separated from novels and short stories because they had been written with the same kind of moral consciousness, a combination unusual in German literature. Böll called his becoming the public moral conscience a sign of the corruption of German society: he felt that parliament and press should constitute the public moral conscience, not a single writer.

Böll's health had always been problematic. Diabetes and a liver disorder necessitated several hospital stays. His smoking habit worsened his circulatory problems. On 16 July 1985 he died at his son's estate in Langenbroich/Eiffel, one day after he had been released from the hospital. His last novel was finished before his death and published in August 1985 in an edition of one hundred thousand copies—another success added to his long list of best-sellers. It is a book about Bonn and its women, as the title suggests: *Frauen vor Flußlandschaft* (translated as *Women in a River Landscape*, 1988). Although this book was not intended as a roman à clef, it is easy to recognize certain politicians on the Bonn scene.

Böll's contribution to postwar German literature was significant. At a time when the political system was discredited to a point that most Germans, including writers, were ready to withdraw into a world of introspection, he set an example of an engagé writer. His Catholicism assisted him in his credibility as well as the fact that, although he was a regional writer for the lower Rhinelands, he was coincidentally writing in Cologne, the spiritual center of West German political power. His writing was at its best when he anticipated a political crisis; it became superior when he himself was drawn into the turmoil of a political power play. His ability to maintain his roots, his religion, and his moral character during his political involvement made him a model for the postwar West German writer.

Heinrich Böll set an example with his fervent political engagement for the reconstruction of a modest West German sense of identity. He redefined West Germans' upbringing and their *Heimat* as a modest place where civil engagement indeed makes a difference. The importance of Böll's influence became clear in Frank Schirrmacher's deliberate misunderstanding of Böll's intentions: Schirrmacher credits Böll with masterminding the German liberal conscience that had developed over the previous twenty-five years. Vogt refutes Schirrmacher's claim by stating that Böll's premise for writing originated in his experience of National Socialism, which younger people such as Schirrmacher lacked. Unlike the younger Schirrmacher, Böll had been directly affected by the Nazis; his redefinition of German nationhood would necessarily have to consider the Nazi past. Indeed, Böll's legacy to Germany's liberal political culture can be found in the Green Party's ecological redefinition of Germany as well as in the SPD's opposition to Germany's new international military role. Böll's most productive writing period coincided with the establishment of the social-liberal coalition in West Germany and with most Germans' desire to change their country's course to an essentially liberal position. Just as scholars are beginning to reexamine the values of the old Federal Republic, so too Böll's work will have to be reexamined.

Letters:

Die Hoffnung ist wie ein wildes Tier: Der Briefwechsel zwischen Heinrich Böll und Ernst-Adolf Kunz 1945–1953, edited by Herbert Hoven (Cologne: Kiepenheuer & Witsch, 1994).

Interviews:

Horst Bienek, *Werkstattgespräche mit Schriftstellern* (Munich: Deutscher Taschenbuch, 1965), pp. 168–184;

"Interview mit mir selbst," in Albrecht Beckel, *Mensch, Gesellschaft, Kirche bei Heinrich Böll* (Osnabrück: Fromm, 1966), pp. 7–12;

Im Gespräch: Heinrich Böll mit Heinz Ludwig Arnold (Munich: edition text + kritik/Richard Boorberg, 1971);

"Heinrich Böll and Dieter Wellershoff: *Gruppenbild mit Dame*: Ein Tonbandinterview," in *Die subversive Madonna: Ein Schlüssel zum Werk Heinrich Bölls,* edited by Renate Matthaei (Cologne: Kiepenheuer & Witsch, 1975), pp. 141–156;

"Ich tendiere nur zu dem scheinbar Unpolitischen: Gespräche mit Heinrich Böll," in Manfred Durzak, *Gespräche über den Roman* (Frankfurt: Suhrkamp, 1976), pp. 128–153.

Bibliographies:

Ferdinand Melius, ed., *Der Schriftsteller Heinrich Böll: Ein biographisch-bibliographischer Abriß* (Cologne: Kiepenheuer & Witsch, 1959);

Werner Lengning, ed., *Der Schriftsteller Heinrich Böll: Ein biographisch-bibliographischer Abriß* (Munich: Deutscher Taschenbuch, 1968);

Werner Martin, *Heinrich Böll: Eine Bibliographie seiner Werke* (Hildesheim: Olms, 1975);

Viktor Böll and Manfred Lange, "Auswahlbibliographie," in *Heinrich Böll,* edited by Heinz Ludwig Arnold (Munich: edition text + kritik, 1982), pp. 143–154.

Biographies:

Klaus Schröter, *Heinrich Böll: In Selbstzeugnissen und Bilddokumenten* (Reinbek: Rowohlt, 1982);

Heinrich Vormweg, *Der andere Deutsche: Heinrich Böll; eine Biographie* (Cologne: Kiepenheuer & Witsch, 2000).

References:

Charlotte Armster, "Katharina Blum: Violence and the Exploitation of Sexuality," *Women in German Yearbook: Feminist Studies and German Culture,* 4 (1988): 83–95;

Hans-Joachim Bernhard, *Die Romane Heinrich Bölls: Gesellschaftskritik und Gemeinschaftsutopie* (Berlin: Rütten & Loenig, 1970);

Hanno Beth, ed., *Eine Einführung in das Gesamtwerk in Einzelinterpretationen* (Kronberg: Scriptor, 1975);

Alfred Böll, *Bilder einer deutschen Familie: Die Bölls* (Bergisch-Gladbach: Lübbe, 1981);

Viktor Böll and Yvonne Jürgensen, *Heinrich Böll als Filmautor: Rezensionsmaterial aus dem Literaturarchiv der Stadtbücherei Köln* (Cologne: City of Cologne, 1982);

Keith Bullivant, "Heinrich Böll—A Tribute," *German Life & Letters,* 39 (1986): 245–251;

Robert A. Burns, *The Theme of Non-Conformism in the Works of Heinrich Böll* (Coventry: University of Warwick, 1973);

Michael Butler, ed., *The Narrative Fiction of Heinrich Böll: Social Conscience and Literary Achievement* (Cambridge: Cambridge University Press, 1994);

Cesare Cases, "'Die Waage der Baleks' dreimal gelesen," in Marcel Reich-Ranicki, *In Sachen Böll* (Cologne: Kiepenheuer & Witsch, 1971), pp. 224–232;

Robert C. Conard, *Heinrich Böll* (Boston: Twayne, 1978);

Mark E. Cory, "Some Observations on the Role of Violence in the Late Prose of Heinrich Böll," *University of Dayton Review*, 19 (1988-1989): 43-53;

Margareta Neovius Deschner, "Heinrich Böll's Utopian Feminism," *University of Dayton Review*, 2 (1985): 119-125;

Manfred Durzak, *Der deutsche Roman der Gegenwart* (Stuttgart: Kohlhammer, 1971), pp. 19-107;

Frank Finlay, *On the Rationality of Poetry: Heinrich Böll's Aesthetic Thinking* (Amsterdam & Atlanta: Rodopi, 1996);

Erhard Friedrichsmeyer, *Notes on the Major Works of Heinrich Böll* (New York: Monarch, 1975);

Frank Grützbach, ed., *Heinrich Böll: Freies Geleit für Ulrike Meinhof: Ein Artikel und seine Folgen* (Cologne: Kiepenheuer & Witsch, 1972);

Heinrich Böll und die DDR, eine Dokumentation (Berlin: Heinrich-Böll-Stiftung, 1997);

Heinrich Herlyn, *Heinrich Böll als utopischer Schriftsteller: Untersuchungen zum erzählerischen Werk* (Frankfurt: Lang, 1996);

Herlyn, *Heinrich Böll und Herbert Marcuse: Literatur als Utopie* (Lambertheim: Kübler, 1979);

Christine Gabriele Hoffman, *Heinrich Böll* (Hamburg: Dressler, 1977);

Joseph Hynes, "The Catcher on the Rhine: Heinrich Böll, 1917-1985," *Novel: A Forum on Fiction*, 3 (1990): 265-281;

Walter Jens, *Deutsche Literatur der Gegenwart: Themen, Stile, Tendenzen* (Munich: Piper, 1962);

Heinrich Jürgenbehring, *Liebe, Religion und Institution: Ethische und religiöse Themen bei Heinrich Böll* (Mainz: Matthias Grünewald, 1994);

Manfred Jurgensen, ed., *Böll: Untersuchungen zum Werk* (Bern: Francke, 1975);

Joachim Kaiser, *Erlebte Literatur: Vom 'Doktor Faustus' zum 'Fettfleck'* (Munich & Zurich: Piper, 1988);

Kaiser, "Leiden und Größe Heinrich Bölls. Zum Tod des bedeutenden Schriftstellers," *Süddeutsche Zeitung*, 17 July 1985;

Ingo Lehnick, *Der Erzähler Heinrich Böll: Änderungen seiner narrativen Strategie und ihre Hintergründe* (Frankfurt: Lang, 1997);

Christian Linder, *Heinrich Böll* (Reinbek: Rowohlt, 1978);

Enid MacPherson, *A Student's Guide to Böll* (London: Heinemann, 1972);

Materialien zur Interpretation von Heinrich Bölls "Fürsorgliche Belagerung" (Cologne: Kiepenheuer & Witsch, 1982);

Moray McGowan, "Pale Mother, Pale Daughter? Some Reflections on Böll's Leni Gruyten and Katharina Blum," *German Life & Letters*, 3 (1984): 218-228;

Aleidine Kramer Moeller, *The Woman as Survivor: The Evolution of the Female Figure in the Works of Heinrich Böll* (Frankfurt: Lang, 1991);

Rainer Nägele, *Heinrich Böll: Einführung in das Werk und in die Forschung* (Frankfurt am Main: Athenäum-Fischer, 1976);

Gerd Rademacher, ed., *Heinrich Böll als Lyriker. Eine Einführung in Aufsätzen, Rezensionen und Gedichtproben* (Frankfurt: Lang, 1985);

Mark W. Rectanus, "*The Lost Honor of Katharina Blum*: The Reception of a German Best-Seller in the USA," *German Quarterly*, 59 (1986): 252-269;

Marcel Reich-Ranicki, *In Sachen Böll: Ansichten und Einsichten* (Munich: Deutscher Taschenbuch, 1971);

Reich-Ranicki, *Mehr als ein Dichter: Über Heinrich Böll* (Cologne: Kiepenheuer & Witsch, 1986);

James Henderson Reid, *Heinrich Böll: A German for His Time* (Oxford: Wolff, 1988);

Reid, *Heinrich Böll: Withdrawal and Re-Emergence* (London: Wolff, 1973);

Wilhelm J. Schwarz, *Der Erzähler Heinrich Böll* (Bern: Francke, 1973); translated by Alexander Henderson and Elizabeth Henderson as *Heinrich Böll: Teller of Tales* (New York: Ungar, 1968);

Bernhard Sowinski, *Heinrich Böll: Kurzgeschichten* (Munich: Oldenbourg, 1988);

J. P. Stern, "An Honourable Man," in *Zu Heinrich Böll*, edited by Anna Maria Dell'Agli (Stuttgart: Klett, 1984), pp. 101-105;

Hermann Stresau, *Heinrich Böll* (Berlin: Colloquium, 1964);

Jochen Vogt, *Heinrich Böll* (Munich: C. H. Beck/edition text + kritik, 1978);

Günter Wirth, *Heinrich Böll: Essayistische Studie über religiöse und gesellschaftliche Motive im Prosawerk des Dichters* (Berlin: Union, 1967);

Reinhard K. Zachau, *Heinrich Böll: Forty Years of Criticism* (Columbia, S.C.: Camden House, 1994);

Theodore Ziolkowski, "Typologie und 'Einfache Form' in *Gruppenbild mit Dame*," in *Die subversive Madonna: Ein Schlüssel um Werk Bölls*, edited by Renate Matthaei (Cologne: Kiepenheuer & Witsch, 1975), pp. 123-140.

Papers:

The holdings of the former Böll-Archive of Kiepenheuer and Witsch and those of the Boston University Library were transferred to the Archives of the City of Cologne on 29 April 1983, when Heinrich Böll was awarded honorary citizenship of the city; they are administered by his nephew Viktor Böll (Literaturarchiv der Stadtbücherei: Köln, Zentralbibliothek, Josef-Hanbrich-Hof, 5000 Köln 1). The former Kiepenheuer and Witsch collection includes all of Böll's printed texts; the manuscripts and letters are in private possession. The former Boston University Library collection is described by Robert C. Conard in the *University of Dayton Review,* 10, no. 2 (Fall 1973): 11–14.

Böll: Autobiographical Statement

(Written at the time of the awarding of the Nobel Prize)

I was born December 21, 1917 in Cologne, on the Rhine, the son of the sculptor and cabinet-maker, Viktor Böll, and his wife, Maria, née Hermanns. Between 1924 and 1928 I attended elementary school in Köln Raderthal, and from 1928 to 1937, the state-run Kaiser-Wilhelm classical secondary school in Cologne. In spring 1937 I began as an apprentice bookseller (publishers, retail trade, antiquarian) for the Matth. Lempertz company in Bonn. I left this apprenticeship in spring 1938, started my first attempts to write, gave private lessons, read a great deal. During autumn 1938 I was conscripted into the national labour service, and released in spring 1939 after completing a six-month term of compulsory service. Because the completion of labour service was a precondition for permission to study at the university, I was able to begin my studies of Germanistics and Classical Philology during the summer term of 1939. Late in the summer of 1939 I was conscripted into the German Army shortly before the outbreak of the war. I took part in the Second World War; in autumn 1940, briefly in France, from 1941 to 1942 (after a severe case of typhus), in the replacement units in Germany, from early 1942 until summer 1943, along the English Channel coast in France, between summer 1943 and autumn 1944, in the Soviet Union, Romania and Hungary, from spring 1945 on, for a few weeks in western Germany, where I was taken prisoner by the Americans, and interned until October 1945 in a camp in France, and then for a few weeks in October/November 1945, in an English camp in Belgium.

As early as December 1945, I accompanied my wife and a few relatives in their return from evacuation in the countryside to Cologne, where over the years we settled down in a destroyed house. I started to write again, while simultaneously working on repairing the destroyed house, I started my studies again—merely formally, because proof of occupation was necessary to obtain a food rationing card. From 1946 to 1949 I published short stories, and in 1949 my first book, a novella, called *Der Zug war pünktlich,* was published. After a first invitation to a meeting of the Gruppe 47 in 1951, I met many German postwar writers with whom I afterwards became friends. I owe particular thanks, and hereby give them, to Hans Werner Richter, Alfred Andersch and many others that I cannot name in detail. Even if there occurred brief or permanent controversies during, or after, these meetings, the Gruppe 47 liberated many German authoresses and authors out of their isolation in a destroyed and fragmented postwar Germany. In 1942 I married Annemarie Cech, who has been irreplaceable, not only as my wife and companion, and not only as fellow experiencer and fellow sufferer in the fascist drama during the Nazi reign in Germany, but also for her critical awareness for language.

Our first child, Christoph, died in October 1945. Our sons Raimund, René and Vincent were born in 1947, 1948 and 1950 in the rubble of Cologne and grew up there.

Between 1950 and 1951 I worked as a temporary employee in the Cologne Bureau of Statistics. From summer 1951 on I have lived as a freelance writer with a fixed postal address in Cologne, but with a continually shifting place of work.

[© The Nobel Foundation, 1972.]

1972 Nobel Prize in Literature Presentation Speech

by Dr. Karl Ragnar Gierow, Permanent Secretary of the Swedish Academy (Translation from the Swedish)

Your Royal Highnesses, Ladies and Gentlemen,

He who attempts to seize in a single grasp the bountiful and very varied authorship of Heinrich Böll finds himself holding an abstraction. Through these writings—begun twenty years ago and culminating in last year's novel *Gruppenbild mit Dame*—there runs, however, a twin theme that might serve as such a synoptic abstraction. This could be phrased: The homeless and the aesthetics of the humane. But Böll's homeless are not ill-fated individuals or human wreckage cast up outside the bulwarks of society. He tells of a society without a roof over its head, a derailed, displaced epoch, standing on every street corner with hand outstretched, begging for the charity of a kindred spirit and human fellowship. This is the situation underlying Böll's *Ästhetik des Humanen.*

He writes about what every human being seeks in order to lead a human life, in little things as in great, about "das Wohnen, die Nachbarschaft und die Heimat, das Geld und die Liebe, Religion und Mahlzeiten," to quote his own enumeration. With its whole register from satire and high-spirited parody to deep suffering, this is a form of passionately engaged aesthetics and it also contains his literary program. He who sets out to portray the bare necessities of life keeps both feet on the ground.

Yet Böll has declared "Ich brauche wenig Wirklichkeit," a word to note, coming from one who is regarded and who perhaps regards himself as a realistic narrator. The reality he needs so little is that of the classic 19th century novel, the reality that after a meticulous study of detail is faithfully reproduced. Böll is highly proficient at the method but employs it ironically; there is no limit to the superfluity of detail.

But the jesting with this conscientious form of registration is itself a demonstration of how little Böll needs such a reality. His mastery includes the ability to bring his setting and its figures to life with scanty, sometimes barely suggested lines.

There is however another reality which Böll's writing continually requires: the background to his existence, the air his generation breathed, the heritage into which it came. That reality is the recurrent, intrusively observed subject of Heinrich Böll's writing, from the start up to the magnum opus already mentioned, *Gruppenbild mit Dame*, which so far crowns his work. Böll's real breakthrough came in the years 1953, 1954 and 1955 with three novels published one after the other—*Und sagte kein einziges Wort; Haus ohne Hüter;* and *Das Brot der frühen Jahre*. Although it was presumably not the author's intention, these three titles serve to indicate the reality which he so persistently and forcefully depicts. His background was Germany's years of famine, it was *Das Brot der frühen Jahre*, the bread that never sufficed and often was not there, the bread that had to be begged for or stolen if one was to survive, and that diet is an indelible memory. The heritage which he and his contemporaries had to administer was *Haus ohne Hüter*, house without caretaker, an existence in ruins, with time a widow and the future fatherless. The air he and his contemporaries breathed was inhaled with the heavy hand of dictatorship on their throats, *Und sagte kein einziges Wort,* because the hand smothered every sound.

It is not the smallest German miracle that after such years of destitution a new generation of writers, thinkers and researchers was ready so soon to shoulder their country's and their own essential task in the spiritual life of our time. The renewal of German literature, to which Heinrich Böll's achievements witness and of which they are a significant part, is not an experiment with form—a drowning man scorns the butterfly stroke. Instead it is a rebirth out of annihilation, a resurrection, a culture which, ravaged by icy nights and condemned to extinction, sends up new shoots, blossoms and matures to the joy and benefit of us all. Such was the kind of work Alfred Nobel wished his Prize to reward.

Dear Mr. Böll,

As a given consequence of the homelessness that is one of the main themes of your writing, comes the striving that you yourself have indicated with the words: "Die Suche nach einer bewohnbaren Sprache in einem bewohnbaren Land." This implies an antithesis of homelessness, a writing in which everyone can feel at home. You reject a literature for an initiated circle, you have declared, adding significantly: "Eine Kirche wird eingeweiht, aber durch diesen Akt der Einweihung nicht geschlossen, sondern geoffnet." It is this openness for the human aspect which gives space and raises the arches higher in your works. And it is works in that spirit which give us a certain right to set our hopes as well on a habitable world. With these words I express the congratulations of the Swedish Academy and ask you now to receive this year's Nobel Prize for Literature from the hands of His Royal Highness the Crown Prince.

[© The Nobel Foundation, 1972.]

Böll: Banquet Speech

Böll's speech at the Nobel Banquet in Stockholm, 10 December 1972 (in German)

Herr Ministerpräsident, meine Damen und Herren,

Anlässlich eines Besuchs in der Bundesrepublik Deutschland hat Seine Majestät der König von Schweden einen gelehrten Blick in die Schichten der Vergänglichkeit getan, aus der wir kommen und auf der wir wohnen. Vielleicht hat der eine oder andere von Ihnen auch gelegentlich einen Blick in diese Schichten getan. Jungfräulich oder gar unschuldig ist dieser Boden nicht, und nie ist er zur Ruhe gekommen. Das begehrte Land am Rhein, von Begehrlichen bewohnt, hat zahlreiche Herrscher gehabt, entsprechend viele Kriegen gesehen. Koloniale, nationale, regionale, lokale, konfessionelle Weltkriege. Progrome hat es gesehen, Vertreibung und immer kamen Vertriebene anderswoher und wurden andere anderswohin vertrieben. Und dass man dort deutsch sprach, war zu selbstverständlich, als dass mans nach innen oder aussen hätte demonstrieren müssen. Das taten andere, denen das weiche d nicht genügte, die nach einem harten t begehrten. Teutsche.

Gewalt, Zerstörung, Schmerz, Missverständnisse liegen auf dem Weg, den einer daherkommt, aus den Schichten vergangener Vergänglichkeit in eine vergängliche Gegenwart. Und es schufen Scherben, Geröll und Trümmer, schufen Ost- und Westverschiebungen nicht, was nach so viel, viel zu viel Geschichte zu erwarten gewesen wäre: Gelassenheit; wohl, weil man uns nie liess; den einen zu westlich, den anderen nicht westlich genug; den einen zu weltlich, den anderen nicht weltlich genug. Immer noch herrscht Misstrauen unter den Demonstrativ-Teutschen, als wäre die Kombination westlich und deutsch doch nur eine Täuschung der inzwischen unheilig gewordenen Nation. Wo doch gewiss sein müsste: wenn dieses Land je so etwas wie ein Herz gehabt haben sollte, lags da, wo der Rhein fliesst. Es war ein weiter Weg der deutschen Geschichte in die Bundesrepublik Deutschland.

Als Junge hörte auch ich in der Schule den sportlichen Spruch, dass der Krieg der Vater aller Dinge sei; gleichzeitig hörte ich in Schule und Kirche, dass die Friedfertigen, die Sanftmütigen, die Gewaltlosen also, das Land der Verheissung besitzen würden. Bis an sein Lebensende wohl wird einer den mörderischen Widerspruch nicht los, der den einen den Himmel *und* die Erde, den anderen nur den Himmel verheißt, und das in einer Landschaft, in der auch Kirche Herrschaft begehrte, erlangte und ausübte, bis auf den heutigen Tag.

Der Weg hierhin war ein weiter Weg für mich, der ich wie viele Millionen aus dem Krieg heimkehrte und nicht viel mehr besaß als die Hände in der Tasche, unterschieden von den anderen nur durch die Leidenschaft, schreiben und wieder schreiben zu wollen. Das Schreiben hat mich hierhergebracht. Gestatten Sie mir, die Tatsache, daß ich hier stehe, für nicht so ganz wahr zu halten, wenn ich zurückblicke auf den jungen Mann, der da nach langer Vertreibung und langem Umhergetriebensein in eine vertriebene Heimat zurückkehrte; nicht nur dem Tod, auch der Todessehnsucht entronnen; befreit, überlebend; Frieden–ich bin 1917 geboren–nur ein Wort, weder Gegenstand der Erinnerung noch Zustand; Republik kein Fremdwort, nur zerbrochene Erinnerung. Ich müßte hier sehr vielen danken, ausländischen Autoren, die zu Befreiern wurden, das Befremdende und das Fremde aus der Eingeschlossenheit befreiten, das sich selbst um seiner Materialität willen in die Eigenheit zurückverwies. Der Rest war Eroberung der Sprache in dieser Zurückverweisung an das Material, an diese Hand voll Staub, die vor der Tür zu liegen schien und doch so schwer zu greifen und zu begreifen war. Danken möchte ich auch für viel Ermutigung durch deutsche Freunde und deutsche Kritiker, danken auch für viele Versuche der Entmutigung, denn manches geschicht ohne Krieg, nichts aber, so scheint mir, ohne Widerstand.

Diese siebenundzwanzig Jahre waren ein langer Marsch, nicht nur für den Autor, auch für den Staatsbürger durch einen dichten Wald von Zeigefingern, die aus der vertrackten Dimension der Eigentlichkeit stammten, innerhalb derer verlorene Kriege zu eigentlich gewonnen werden. Gar mancher Zeigefinger war scharf geladen und hatte seinen Druckpunkt an und in sich selbst.

Mit Bangen denke ich an meine deutschen Vorgänger hier, die innerhalb dieser verfluchten Dimension Eigentlichkeit keine Deutschen mehr sein sollten. Nelly Sachs, von Selma Lagerlöf gerettet, nur knapp dem Tod entronnen. Thomas Mann, vertrieben und ausgebürgert. Hermann Hesse, aus der Eigentlichkeit ausgewandert, schon lange kein deutscher Staatsbürger mehr, als er hier geehrt wurde. Fünf Jahre vor meiner Geburt, vor sechzig Jahren, stand hier der letzte deutsche Preisträger für Literatur, der in Deutschland starb, Gerhart Hauptmann. Er hatte seine letzten Lebensjahre in einer Version Deutschland verlebt, in die er wohl trotz einiger Mißverständlichkeiten nicht hineingehörte. Ich bin weder ein Eigentlicher noch eigentlich keiner, ich bin ein Deutscher, mein einzig gültiger Ausweis, den mir niemand auszustellen oder zu verlängern braucht, ist die Sprache, in der ich schreibe. Als solcher, als Deutscher, freue ich mich über die große Ehre. Ich danke der Schwedischen Akademie und dem Land Schweden für diese Ehre, die wohl nicht nur mir gilt, auch der Sprache, in der ich mich ausdrücke und dem Land, dessen Bürger ich bin.

[© The Nobel Foundation, 1972. Heinrich Böll is the sole author of his speech.]

Translation by James Hardin and Philip B. Dematteis:

Mr. Prime Minister, Ladies and Gentlemen,

On the occasion of a visit to the Federal Republic of Germany His Majesty the King of Sweden took a scholarly look at the layers of transitoriness out of which we come and on which we live. Perhaps one or the other of you have also occasionally looked at these layers. This soil is not chaste or completely innocent and has never enjoyed peace and quiet. The coveted land along the Rhine, inhabited by covetous people, has had numerous rulers and, accordingly, has seen many wars. Colonial, national, regional, local, religious world wars. It has seen pogroms, banishment, and always the banished came from some other place and were banished elsewhere. And that German was spoken there was too obvious for it to be necessary to demonstrate that fact. Others did that, to whom the soft *d* [*Deutsche*] was not satisfactory, who desired a hard *t. Teutsche* [Teutons].

Violence, destruction, suffering, misunderstandings lie on the path on which one comes from the layers of past transitoriness into a transitory present. And it produced shards, rubble, and ruins but did not create shifts from East to West, which, after so much—far too much—history, would have been expected: composure; because we are never left alone; the one too Western, the other not Western enough; the one too worldly, the other not worldly enough. Still, mistrust prevails among the Teutonic types, as if the combination of western and German were only an illusion of the nation that has in the meantime become unholy. Yet, one thing is certain: if this land ever had something like a heart, it lay there, where the Rhine flows. It was a long way from German history to the Federal Republic of Germany.

As a boy I heard in school the sporting saying that war is the father of all things; simultaneously I heard in school and church that the peacemakers—that is, the meek, the powerless—would possess the Promised Land. To the very end of one's days, one cannot rid oneself of the murderous conclusion that, on the one hand, promises one heaven *and* earth and, on the other, only heaven; and this in a region in which the Church also desired power, achieved it, and exercised it, right up to the present day.

The road here was a long one for me, who like many millions returned home from the war with not much more than their hands in their pockets, different from the others only by the passion to want to write and again to write. Writing brought me here. Allow me to consider the fact that I stand here as not entirely true—when I look back at the young man who, after long banishment and long wandering, came back to a homeland driven apart; having escaped not only death but also the longing for death; liberated, surviving; peace—I was born in 1917—only a word, neither object of memory nor condition; republic no foreign word, only shattered memory. I would here have to thank very many foreign authors who became liberators, who freed that which had been considered strange and foreign from confinement, that for the sake of its materiality pointed back to one's own world. The rest was conquest of the language in this referring back to the material, to this hand full of dust, that seemed to lie before the door and yet was so hard to grasp and understand. I would also thank German friends and German critics for much encouragement; thanks also for many attempts at discouragement, because many a thing happens without war—not, however, it seems to me, without opposition.

These twenty-seven years were a long march for me as author and citizen through a dense forest of accusing fingers that pointed at me from that tortuous dimension of essential thinking within which lost wars are all too essentially won after all. Many of these fingers were fully loaded, ready to fire at random.

With trepidation I think about my German predecessors here, who inside this accursed dimension of reality were not supposed to be Germans. Nelly Sachs, rescued by Selma Lagerlöf, only narrowly escaped death. Thomas Mann, expelled and expatriated. Hermann Hesse, having emigrated from reality, already for a long time no longer a German citizen when he was honored here. Five years before I was born, sixty years ago, the last German prizewinner in literature who died in Germany stood here: Gerhart Hauptmann. He had spent the last years of his life in a version of Germany in which, in spite of sundry misunderstandings, he did not belong. I am neither a real one nor really none, I am a German; my only valid passport, which no one needs to issue or renew for me, is the language in which I write. As such, as a German, I rejoice at this great honor. I thank the Swedish Academy and the country of Sweden for this honor that, to be sure, applies not only to me but also to the language in which I express myself and the country whose citizen I am.

Böll: Nobel Lecture, 2 May 1973

An Essay on the Reason of Poetry
(Translation)

It is said by those who ought to know—and by others, who also ought to know, it is disputed—that in matters which to all appearances are rational, calculable and achieved by the combined efforts of architects, draughtsmen, engineers, workers—accomplishments such as a bridge—there remain a few millimetres or centimetres of incalculability. This incalculability (tiny with regard to the masses being treated and shaped) may stem from the difficulty of calculating with the nicest precision a mass of complicated interlocking chemical and technical details and materials in all their possible reactions, including the effects of the four classical elements (air, water, fire and earth). The problem here seems not merely to be the design, the repeatedly recalculated and checked technical/chemical/statistical composition, but—let me call it this—their incarnation, which can also be called their realisation. This remainder of incalculability, be it only fractions of millimetres, which correspond to unforeseen tiny differences in extension—what shall we call them? What lies hidden in this gap? Is it what we usually call irony, is it poetry, God, resistance, or (to use a popular phrase nowadays) fiction? Someone who ought to know, a painter who had previously been a baker, once told me that even baking breakfast rolls, which is done early in the morning, almost in the night, was extremely dicey business; you had to stick your nose and your backside out into the grey dawn in order more or less instinctively to find the right mixture of ingredients, temperature and baking time, since each and every day demanded its own freshly-baked rolls, an important, even holy element of the first morning meal for all those who shoulder the burden of the new day. Should we also call this almost incalculable element irony, poetry, God, resistance or fiction? How can we cope without it? Not to mention love. No one will ever know how many novels, poems, analyses, confessions, sufferings and joys have been piled up on this continent called Love, without it ever having turned out to be totally investigated.

When I am asked how or why I wrote this or that, I always find myself quite embarrassed. I would gladly furnish not merely the questioner, but myself as well, with an exhaustive answer, but can never do so. I cannot recreate the context in its entirety, yet I wish that I could, so that at least the literature I myself make might be made slightly less of a mysterious process than bridge-building and bread-baking.

And because literature in its incarnation as a whole, in its message and shape, can clearly have a liberating effect, it would after all be quite useful to tell people about the genesis of this incarnation, so that more people can share in this process. What is it that I myself, although I demonstrably produce it, cannot even approximately explain?—this something which from the first to the last line I myself set down on paper, vary repeatedly, rework, somewhat shift the emphasis of, yet which as it recedes in time grows alien to me, like something that is gone or past, retreating further and further from me, even as it is perhaps becoming important for others as a shaped message? Theoretically, the total reconstruction of the process would have to be possible, a form of parallel protocol created as the work progresses, and which, if done in detail, would probably be many times larger than the work itself. Not merely the intellectual and mental, but also the sensory and material dimensions would have to be satisfied, mental and physical nourishment and metabolism, the mood and flashes of wit *enlighteningly* provided, the function of one's environment not only in its incarnation as such, but also as backdrop. For example, I often watch sports shows with my mind almost completely blank, in order to practise contemplation with a blank mind, admittedly a rather mystical exercise—yet all these programmes would have to be included in their entirety in the protocol, since after all a kick or a leap might happen to spark some reaction or other in my thoughtless contemplation, or perhaps the movement of a hand, a smile, a commentator's word, a commercial. Every telephone call, the weather, letters, each individual cigarette would have to be included, a passing car, a pneumatic drill, the cackling of a hen that disturbs a context.

The table upon which I am writing this is 76.5 cm high, its top is 69.5 by 111 cm. It has turned legs, a drawer, seems to be seventy to eighty years old, was a possession of a great-aunt of my mother's, who, after her husband had died in a madhouse and she herself had moved into a smaller flat, sold it to her brother, my wife's grandfather. And so, after my wife's grandfather had died, it came into our possession, a despised and rather despicable piece of furniture of no value, knocking around somewhere, no one knows exactly where, until it surfaced during a move and proved to have been damaged by a bomb: somewhere, at some time or other, a piece of shrapnel had bored a hole through its top during the Second World War—already it would seem to be not merely of sentimental value, but an entry into a dimension of political and social history worth relating, using the table as an entrance vehicle, in which connection the deadly contempt of the furniture porters who nearly refused to bring it along would be more important than its present use, which is more of an accident than the stubbornness with which—and not for reasons of sentiment or memory, but rather for reasons of principle—we kept it from reaching the refuse dump, and as by now I have written a few things on this table, I might be permitted a passing attachment to it, with the emphasis on "passing." Not to mention the objects lying on this table; they are incidental and exchangeable, also accidental, with the possible exception of the Remington typewriter, model "Travel Writer de Luxe," produced in 1957, to which I am also attached, this means of production that has long since lost all interest for the tax authorities, although it has played a major part in their acquisition of such income, and still does so. On this instrument that any specialist would regard or touch only with disdain, I have written at a guess four novels and several hundred items, and even so I am attached to it not only for that reason, but again because of principles, as it still works and proves how small the writer's opportunities and ambitions for investment are. I mention the table and the typewriter in order to demonstrate to myself that not even these two necessary utensils are completely understandable to me, and were I to attempt to elucidate their origins with the necessary exact correctness, their precise material, industrial, social process of production and their origins, it would give rise to an almost endless compilation of British and West German industrial and social history. Not to mention the house, the space in which this table stands, the soil on which this house was built, especially not to mention the people who—probably for several centuries—lived in it, the living and the dead, not to mention those who bring the coal, wash the silverware, deliver the letters and newspapers—and especially not to mention those who are close, closer, closest to us. And yet mustn't *everything*, from the table to the pencils, that lie there in their history in its entirety, be brought in, including those close, closer, closest to us? Will there not be enough remainders, gaps, resistances, poetry, God, fiction left—even more than in building bridges and baking rolls?

It's true and it's easily said that language is material, and something does materialise as one writes. Yet how might one explain that—as is occasionally demonstrated—something like life appears, people, fates, actions; that this incarnation occurs on something so deathly pale as paper, where the imagination of the author is linked to that of the reader in a hitherto unexplained manner, a process that cannot be reconstructed in its entirety, where even the wisest, most sensitive interpretation remains only a more or less successful approximation; and how indeed might it be possible to describe, to register the transition from the conscious to the unconscious—in the person writing and the person reading, respectively—with the necessary total exactitude, and furthermore break it down into its national, continental, international, religious or ideological details, not neglecting the continually changing proportions of the two, in these two—the person writing and the person reading—and the sudden reversal where the one becomes the other; and that in this abrupt shift the one is no longer to be distinguished from the other? There will always be a remainder, whether you call it the inexplicable ("secret" would also be fine), there remains and will remain an area, however tiny, into which the reason of our origins will not penetrate, because it runs into the hitherto unexplained reason of poetry and of the art of the imagination, whose incarnation remains as elusive as the body of a woman, a man or even merely of an animal. Writing is—at least for me—movement forward, the conquest of a body that I do not know at all, away from something to something that I do not yet know; I never know what will happen—and here "happen" is not intended as plot resolution, in the sense of classical dramaturgy, but in the sense of a complicated and complex experiment that with given imaginary, spiritual, intellectual and sensual materials in interaction strives—on paper to boot!—towards incarnation. In this respect there can be no successful literature, nor would there be any successful music or painting, because no one can already have seen the object it is striving to become, and in this respect everything that is superficially called modern, but which is better named living art, is experiment and discovery—and transient, can be estimated and measured only in its historical relativity, and it appears to me irrelevant to speak of eternal values, or to seek them. How will we survive without this gap, this remainder, which can be called irony, be called poetry, be called God, fiction, or resistance?

Countries, too, are always only approaching what they claim to be, and there can be no state which does not leave this gap between the verbal expression of its constitution and its realisation, a space that remains, where poetry and resistance grow—and hopefully flourish. And there exists no form of literature which can succeed without this gap. Even the most precise account does without the atmosphere, without the imagination of the reader, even if the person writing it refuses to use it; and even the most precise account must omit—why, it must omit the exact and detailed description of circumstances that actually are required for the incarnation of the conditions of life . . . it must compose, transpose elements, and even its interpretation and its working protocol are not communicable, if only because the material called language cannot be reduced to a reliable and generally comprehensible communicative currency: so much history and invented history, national and social history, and historical relativity—which would have to be included—weighs down every word, as I have tried to suggest via the example of my work desk. And determining the range of the message is not only a problem of translation from one language to another, it is a much more weighty problem within languages, where definitions can entail world views, and world views can entail wars—I would merely remind you of the wars after the Reformation, which *although* explicable in terms of power politics and hegemony, *also* are wars about religious definitions. It is therefore, by the way, trivial to claim that after all, we do speak the same language, if we do not also demonstrate the load that each word can bear at the level of regional, and frequently even local history. For me, at least, much of the German I see and hear sounds stranger than Swedish, a language of which I unfortunately understand very little.

Politicians, ideologists, theologians and philosophers try time and again to provide solutions with nothing remaining, prefab solved problems. That is their duty—and it is ours, the writers'—since we know that we are not able to solve anything without remainders or resistance—to penetrate into the gaps. There are too many unexplained and inexplicable remainders, entire provinces of waste. Builders of bridges, bakers of rolls and writers of novels normally finish their jobs, and their remainders are not the most problematic areas. While we struggle over *littérature pure* and *littérature engagée*—one of the false dichotomies to which I shall return in a while—we are still not aware of—or are unawares diverted from—thoughts about *l'argent pur* and *l'argent engagé*. If one really observes and listens to politicians and economists talking about something as supposedly rational as money, then the mystical, or perhaps merely mysterious area within these three occupations already mentioned becomes less and less interesting and astonishingly harmless. Let us take, merely as an example, the amazingly bold recent attack on the dollar (which was modestly called a dollar crisis). Naive layman that I am, something occurred to me that no one called by name: two countries were deeply affected, and most emphatically found it necessary—if we assume that the word "freedom" is not merely a fiction—to do something so remarkable as to support the dollar, i.e., were asked to open their coffers; and these two countries had something historic in common, namely their defeat in the Second World War, and they are both spoken of as having something else in common: their industriousness and diligence. As for the person it concerns—the one who jingles his pocket money or flashes his tiny bankroll—can't it be made clear to him why, although he is by no means working less for his money, it fetches less bread, milk, coffee, miles in a taxi? How many gaps does the mysticism of money offer, and in which strongrooms is its poetry hidden away? Idealistic parents and educators have always tried to convince us that money is filthy. I have never understood that, because I only received money when I had worked (always excepting the large sum that I have been awarded by the Swedish Academy), and for anyone who has no choice other than to work, even the dirtiest job is clear. They provide a living for those close to him, and for him, too. Money is the incarnation of his work, and that is clean. Between work and what it brings in there admittedly is an unexplained remainder, which vague formulas such as to earn well or to earn poorly are far less successful at filling than the gap left by the interpretation of a novel or poem.

Compared to the unexplained gaps of money mysticism, the unexplained remainders of literature are strikingly harmless, and even so there are still people who with criminal frivolity let the word "freedom" roll off their tongue, where submission to a myth and its claims to power is unequivocally demanded and obtained. They then call for political insight, precisely when insight and perception about the problem are blocked. On the bottom line of my cheque I see four different groups of numbers, 32 characters in all, two of which resemble hieroglyphs. Five of these thirty-two characters are meaningful to me: three for my account number, two for the branch of the bank—what do the other twenty-seven represent, including quite a few zeroes? I am certain that all of these characters have a rational, meaningful, or as that lovely phrase would have it, an enlightening explanation. It's just that in my brain and my consciousness there is no room for this enlightening explanation, and what remains is the cipher mysticism of a secret science which I have more trouble penetrating, whose poetry and symbolism remains more alien to me than Marcel Proust's *Remem-*

brance of Things Past or the "Wessobrunn Prayer." What these 32 digits demand of me is trusting belief in the fact that everything is quite correct, that there remains no unclarity and, if I only were to make a slight effort, it all would be clear to me too; and yet for me something mysterious remains—or perhaps fear, much more fear than any realisation of poetry could produce in me. However, no successful currency policy is clear to those whose money is involved.

Thirteen digits on my telephone bill, too, and a few on each of my various insurance policies, not to mention my tax, car and telephone numbers—I won't take the trouble to count all these numbers that I ought to have in my head or at least written down, in order to be able to note my exact place in society at any time. If we quite happily multiply these 32 digits and the numbers on my cheque by six, or let's give a discount and multiply them by four, add in the numbers of one's birthday, a few contractions for religious affiliation, civil status—have we then at last grasped the Occident in the addition and the integration of its reason? Is this reason, as we perceive and accept it—and it is not only made enlightening for us, but actually enlightens us—perhaps merely an occidental arrogance that we have exported to the entire world, via colonialism or missions, or in a mixture of them both as an instrument of subjugation? And for those affected, aren't or wouldn't the differences between Christian, socialist, communist, capitalistic outlooks be small,—and even if the poetry of this reason does at times enlighten them, yet doesn't the reason of their poetry remain the victor? What did the greatest crime of the Indians consist of, when they were confronted with European reason exported to America? They didn't know the value of gold—of money! And they fought against something, against that which we even now are fighting as the most recent product of our reason, against the destruction of their world and environment, against the total subjugation of their earth by profit, which was more alien to them than their gods and spirits are to us. And what indeed could have revealed to them the Christian message—the new and joyous tidings—in this insane, hypocritical smugness with which on Sunday people served God, praising him as the Saviour, and on Monday once again opened the banks right on time, the places where they administered the only idea they truly believed in, that of money, possession and profit? For the poetry of water and wind, of buffalo and grass, in which their life found its form, there was only scorn—and now we civilised Westerners in our cities, the end product of our total rationality—for in all fairness it must be said: we have not spared ourselves—we are beginning to sense just how real the poetry of water and wind actually is, and what is incarnated therein. Did, or does, the tragedy of our churches perhaps indeed consist, not of what the Enlightenment might have designated as unreasonable matters, but in the despairing and desperately failed attempt to pursue or even overtake a reason that has never been and never can be merged with something so irrational as the incarnated God? Regulations, law texts, approval of experts, a figure-laden forest of numbered regulations, and the production of prejudices that have been hammered into us and set out along the tracks of history teaching, in order to make people ever more estranged from one another. Even in the extreme western reaches of Europe our rationality is in opposition to another, which we simply label irrational. The horrifying problem of Northern Ireland nevertheless consists of the fact that here two kinds of reason have been entangled and hopelessly attacked one another for centuries.

How many provinces of disparagement and disdain has history bequeathed to us? Continents are hidden under the victorious sign of our rationality. Entire populations remained strangers to one another, supposedly speaking the same language. Where marriage in the Western manner was prescribed as creating order, people ignored the fact that it was a privilege: unattainable, inachievable for those who worked the land, the people called farmhands and milkmaids, who simply didn't have the money even to buy a pair of sheets, and if they had saved up or stolen the money, wouldn't have had the bed to put the sheets on. And so they were left untouched in their illegitimacy; they produced kids anyway! From above and from the outside, everything seemed completely settled. Clear answers, clear questions, clear regulations, catechism as delusion. But please, no wonders, and poetry only as the sign of the supernatural, never the natural. And then people are surprised, even long for the old ways of life, when the disparaged and hidden provinces show signs of revolt, and then of course either the one party or the other must gain material and political profit from this revolt. Attempts have been made to bring order into the still unexplored continent called sexual love by means of regulations similar to those provided budding philatelists when they start their first album. Permitted and nonpermitted caresses are defined down to the most meticulous details, when suddenly, to their mutual horror, theo- and ideology confirm that on this continent which was regarded as determined, cooled and ordered, there yet remain a few unextinguished volcanoes—and volcanoes are simply not to be extinguished with tried and tested firefighting equipment. And just think of everything passed off, foisted off on God, this much-abused and pitiable authority: everything, yes, everything that was a problem: all the guides for inescapable misery in social, economic or sexual form pointed to him, everything despicable, contemptible, was palmed off on God, all the leftover & "remainders," and yet at the same time he was being preached about as the Incarnate, without considering that one cannot place the burden of man on God, nor the burden of God on man, if he is to be considered incarnate. And who then can be surprised if he has survived where godlessness was prescribed and where the misery of the world and one's own society was put off to an unfulfilled catechism of equally dogmatic form and a future that was ever further away, and ever further delayed, until it turned out to be a dismal present? And once again we can also only be reacting to it with insufferable arrogance if we here presume to denounce this course of events as reactionary; and similarly, it is arrogance of the same kind if the official custodians of God claim as their own this God who appears to have survived in the Soviet Union, without clearing away the refuse dump under which he is hidden here, and if they cite the appearance of God *there* as justification for a societal system *here*. Again and again, whether boasting of our convictions as Christians or atheists, we wish to capitalise on one pigheadedly represented system of ideas or another. This madness of ours, this arrogance "in itself" again and again buries both: the incarnate Deity, who is called God become Man, and the vision set in its place, that of the future of the entirety of mankind. We who so easily humiliate others, we are lacking in something: humility—which is not to be confused with subordination or obedience, let alone submission. This is what we have done to the colonised peoples: transformed their humility, the poetry of this humility transformed into their humiliation. We are always eager to subjugate and conquer, hardly a surprise in a civilisation whose first text in a foreign language has long been Julius Caesar's *De Bello Gallico,* and whose first exercise in self-satisfaction—unequivocal and clear answers and questions—was the catechism, one catechism or the other, a primer in infallibility and in complete, pre-fab, pre-explained problems.

I have got a bit away from the building of bridges, baking of rolls and writing of novels, and hinted at gaps, ironies, fictive areas, remnants, divinities, mystifications and resistance of other regions—they appeared to me worse, in greater need of illumination than the slight, unilluminated corners in which not our traditional reason, but the reason of poetry—as in for example a novel—lies hidden. The roughly two hundred figures, group by group (including a few codes), that I ought to have in exact sequences, in my head, or at least on a piece of paper, as a proof of my existence, without exactly knowing what they mean, incorporate little more than a pair of abstract claims and proofs of existence within a bureaucracy that not only claims to be, but actually is reasonable. People refer me to it and teach me to trust it blindly. May I not dare expect that people do not merely trust in, but strengthen the reason of poetry, not by leaving it in peace, but by absorbing a bit of its calmness and the pride of its humbleness, which can only be a humbleness towards those below, and never a humbleness towards those above. Regard for others, politeness and justice reside therein, and the wish to recognise and be recognised.

I do not wish to provide new missionary starting-points and vehicles, but I do believe that in the sense of poetic humbleness, politeness and justice I must say that I see considerable similarity, I see possibilities for rapprochement between the stranger a la Camus, the strangeness of the Kafkaesque official and the incarnated God, who after all remains a stranger and—if one neglects a few outbursts of temper—is polite and literal in a remarkable way. Why else has the Catholic church long—I don't know exactly how long—blocked direct access to the literal nature of the texts they declare holy, or else kept it hidden in Latin and Greek, available only to the initiated? I imagine it is in order to keep out the dangers they sensed in the poetry of the incarnated word, and to protect the reason of their power from the dangerous reason of poetry. And after all it is not accidental that the most important consequence of the Reformation was the discovery of languages and their corporeality. And what empire ever could do without language imperialism, i.e., the diffusion of their own language and suppression of the languages of those ruled? In this—but in no other—connexion I regard the for once not imperialistic, but supposedly anti-imperialistic attempts to denounce poetry, the sensuality of language, its incarnation and the power of the imagination (for language and the power of the imagination are one and the same), and to introduce the false dichotomy of information or poetry, as a new version of "divide et impera." It is the brand-new, but once again almost international arrogance of a New Reason, which may possibly permit the poetry of the Indians as an anti-ruling class force, but withholds its own poetry from the classes to be liberated in its own land. Poetry is not a class privilege, it has never been one. Again and again well-established feudal and bourgeois literatures have renewed themselves out of what they condescendingly called popular language, or, to use more modern phrases, jargon or slang. This process may readily be labeled linguistic exploitation, but nothing about this exploitation is changed by spreading propaganda about the false alternatives: information or poetry/literature. The nostalgia-flavoured disapproval perhaps to be found in the expressions' popular language, slang, jargon does not warrant sending poetry, as well, into the exile of the rubbish heap, nor all the forms and expressions of art.

Much about this is papal: withholding incarnation and sensuality from others while developing new catechisms which speak of the only correct and the truly false possibilities of expression. One cannot separate the power of the message from the power of the expression in which the message occurs; this paves the way for something that reminds me of the controversies about the communion in both forms, controversies that are theologically rather boring, but important as examples of rejected incarnations, and which in the Catholic part of the world became reduced to the pallor of the Host, which could not even be called a real piece of bread—not to mention the millions of hectolitres of wine withheld! Therein lay an arrogant misunderstanding, not merely of the substances involved, but even more of that which this substance was intended to incarnate.

No class can be liberated by first withholding something from them, and whether this new school of Manichaeism claims to be a- or antireligious, it thereby takes over the model of the Church as a ruling class, the model which could end with Hus being burned at the stake and Luther excommunicated. One may readily quarrel about the concept of beauty, develop new aesthetics—they are indeed overdue—but they must not begin by withholding matters, and they must not exclude one thing; the possibility of transferral that literature offers: it transfers us to South or North America, to Sweden, India, Africa. It can also transfer us to another class, another time, another religion and another race. It has—even in its bourgeois form—never been its goal to create strangeness, but to remove it. And although one may regard the class from which it is largely derived as overdue for replacement, yet as a product of this class it was in most cases also a hiding-place for resistance to that class. And the internationality of resistance must be preserved, that which keeps or makes one writer—Alexander Solzhenitsyn—a believer, and another—Arrabal—an embittered and bitter enemy of religion and the Church. Nor is this resistance to be comprehended as a mere mechanism or reflex which calls forth belief in God here, lack of belief in God there, but rather as the incarnation of the relationships of intellectual history as they are played out between various rubbish heaps and provinces of rebellion and apostasy . . . and also as recognition of their interconnections without arrogance and without claims of infallibility. To a political prisoner or perhaps only isolated dissidents in, e.g., the Soviet Union it may seem wrong or even insane when people in the Western world protest against the Vietnam War—psychologically, one can understand his situation in his cell or his social isolation—and yet he would have to realise that the guilt of the one cannot be ticked off against that of the other, and that when people demonstrate for Vietnam, they also demonstrate for him! I know that this sounds utopian, and yet this appears to me to be the only possibility of a new internationality, not neutrality. No author can take over alleged or specious divisions and judgements, and to me it appears almost suicidal that we are even and still discussing the division into committed literature and other kinds. Not only do we, precisely when we think that it is the one, have to intervene for the other with all our might; no, it is precisely through this falsified alternative that we accept a bourgeois principle of divisions, one which turns us into strangers. It is not only the division of our potential strength, but also of our potential—and I'll risk this without even blushing—incarnated beauty, since it too can liberate, just as the communicated thought can: it can be liberating in itself, or as the provocation that it may create. The strength of undivided literature is not the neutralisation of directions, but the internationality of resistance, and to this resistance belong poetry, incarnation, sensuality, imaginative power and beauty. The new Manichaean iconoclasticism which wants to take them away from us, which wants to take all art away from us, would rob not only us, but also those for whom it does what it believes it must do. No curse, no bitterness, not even the information about the desperate situation of a class is possible without poetry, and even to condemn it requires that it first must be recognised. Go and read Rosa Luxemburg carefully and note which statues Lenin ordered erected first: the first for Count Tolstoy, of whom he said that until this count began to write, Russian literature contained no peasants; the second for the "reactionary" Dostoevsky. If one wishes to choose an ascetic road to change, one might personally renounce art and literature, but one cannot do so for others until one has brought them to the knowledge or recognition of what they are to renounce. This renunciation must be voluntary, or else it becomes a papal decree, like a new catechism, and once again an entire continent, such as the continent of Love, would be doomed to a parched sterility. It is not merely for frivolity nor only to shock that art and literature have again and again transformed their forms, discovering new ones by experiment. In these forms they have also incarnated something, and that something was almost never the confirmation of what existed and was already available; and if it is extirpated, one gives up a further possibility: artifice. Art is always a good hiding-place, not for dynamite, but for intellectual explosives and social time bombs. Why would there otherwise have been the various Indices? And precisely in their despised and often even despicable beauty and lack of transparency lies the best hiding-place for the barb that brings about the sudden jerk or the sudden recognition.

Before concluding, I must state a necessary limitation. The weakness of my intimations and explanations unavoidably stems from the fact that although I question the tradition of reason in which—hopefully not completely successfully—I was brought up, I am nevertheless using the means of that very same reason, and it would be more than unfair to denounce this reason in all its dimensions. This reason has obviously succeeded in spreading doubt about its all-encompassing claim, about what I have called its arrogance, and in retaining experience in and memory of what I have called the reason of poetry, which I do not regard as a privileged, nor a bourgeois institution. It can be communicated, and precisely because its literalness and incarnation often appear strange, it can prevent or remove strangeness or alienation. After all, *befremdet zu sein* "being strange" can also involve being astounded, surprised, or merely moved. As for what I have said about humbleness—naturally only by way of suggestion—I say it is not thanks to my religious upbringing or memory, which always meant humiliating when it said humility, but from reading Dostoevsky early and late in life. And it is precisely because I consider as the most important literary shift the international movement for a classless, or no longer class-determined literature, the discovery of entire provinces of humbled people destined to be human waste, that I warn you about the destruction of poetry, about the arid sterility of Manichaeism, about the iconoclasticism of what appears to me to be a blind zeal which won't even tap up the bath water before it throws out the baby. It appears meaningless to me to denounce or to glorify the young or the old. It appears meaningless to me to dream of old ways of life that only can be reconstructed in museums; it appears meaningless to me to create dichotomies such as conservative/progressive. The new wave of nostalgia that clings to furniture, clothes, forms of expression and scales of feeling only serves to demonstrate that the new world grows ever stranger to us. That the reason upon which we have built and relied has not made the world more reliable or familiar; that the rational/irrational dichotomy also was a false one. Here I have had to avoid or abandon a great deal, because one thought always leads to another and we would get carried away if we were to survey every detail of these continents exhaustively. I have had to abandon humour, which also is not the privilege of any class, and yet is ignored in its poetry and as a hiding-place for resistance.

[© The Nobel Foundation, 1972. Heinrich Böll is the sole author of the text.]]

Joseph Brodsky
(Iosif Aleksandrovich Brodsky)
(24 May 1940 – 28 January 1996)

Alyssa Dinega Gillespie
University of Notre Dame

This entry was expanded by Gillespie from her Brodsky entry in *DLB 285: Russian Writers Since 1980*. See also the Brodsky entry in *DLB Yearbook: 1987*.

BOOKS: *Stikhotvoreniia i poemy,* compiled by Gleb Petrovich Struve and Boris Andreevich Filippov (Washington, D.C. & New York: Inter-Language Literary Associates, 1965)–includes "Bol'shaia elegiia Dzhonu Donnu," "Evreiskoe kladbishche," "Glagoly," "Ia obnial eti plechi . . . ," "Isaak i Avraam," "Kholmy," "Oboz," "Piligrimy," "Stansy," "Vorotish'sia na rodinu . . . ," and "Vot ia vnov' posetil . . .";

Ostanovka v pustyne (New York: Izdatel'stvo imeni Chekhova, 1970; revised edition, Ann Arbor, Mich.: Ardis, 1988)–includes "Bol'shaia elegiia Dzhonu Donnu," "Derev'ia v moem okne . . . ," "Dlia shkol'nogo vozrasta," "Einem Alten Architekten in Rom," "Enei i Didona," "Glagoly," "Gorbunov i Gorchakov." "Ia obnial eti plechi . . . ," "Isaak i Abraam," "Kholmy," "K Likomedu, na Skiros," "Lomtik medovogo mesiatsa," "Novye stansy k Avguste," "Oboz," "Ot okrainy k tsentru," "Pis'mo v butylke," "Sonet," "Stikhi na smert' T. S. Eliota," "Strofy," "Prorochestvo," "Ty vyporkhnesh', malinovka . . . ," and "Vorotish' sia rodinu . . .";

Chast' rechi: Stikhotvoreniia 1972–76 (Ann Arbor, Mich.: Ardis, 1977)–includes "1972 god," "Odissei–Telemaku," "Sreten'e," and "Tors";

Konets prekrasnoi epokhi: Stikhotvoreniia 1964–71 (Ann Arbor, Mich.: Ardis, 1977)–includes "Natiurmort," "Post Aetatem Nostram," "Rech' o prolitom moloke," and "Vremia goda–zima . . .";

V Anglii (Ann Arbor, Mich.: Ardis, 1977);

A Part of Speech (New York: Farrar, Straus & Giroux, 1980)–includes "1972," "Nunc Dimittis," "Odysseus to Telemachus," "Six Years Later," and "Torso";

Joseph Brodsky (left) receiving the 1987 Nobel Prize in Literature from King Carl XVI Gustaf of Sweden (AP Photo/Borje Thuresson)

Rimskie elegii (New York: Russica, 1982);

Novye stansy k Avguste: Stikhi k M.B., 1962–1982 (Ann Arbor, Mich.: Ardis, 1983);

Mramor (Ann Arbor, Mich.: Ardis, 1984); translated by Alan Myers with Brodsky as *Marbles: A Play in Three Acts* (New York: Farrar, Straus & Giroux, 1989);

Less Than One: Selected Essays (New York: Farrar, Straus & Giroux, 1986)–includes "Flight from Byzantium," "A Guide to a Renamed City," "In a Room and a Half," and "Less Than One"; Russian version published as *Men'she edinitsy: Izbrannye esse* (Moscow: Nezavisimaia gazeta, 1999);

Uraniia (Ann Arbor, Mich.: Ardis, 1987)–includes "Biust Tiberiia," "Ia vkhodil vmesto dikogo zveria . . . ," and "Osennii krik iastreba";

To Urania: Selected Poems 1965–1985 (New York: Farrar, Straus & Giroux, 1988)– includes "The Bust of Tiberius," "Gorbunov and Gorchakov," "The Hawk's Cry in Autumn," and "May 24, 1980";

Fondamenta degli Incurabili, translated by Gilberto Forti (Venice: Consorzio Venezia nuova, 1989); English version published as *Watermark* (New York: Farrar, Straus & Giroux, 1992);

Primechaniia paporotnika (Bromma, Sweden: Hylaea, 1990);

Ballada o malen'kom buksire (Leningrad: Detskaia literatura, 1991);

Naberezhnaia neistselimykh. Trinadtsat' essei (Moscow: Slovo, 1992)–includes "Naberezhnaia neistselimykh" [incomplete version]; complete version in *Venetsianskie tetradi: Iosif Brodskii i drugie,* by Brodsky and others, compiled by Ekaterina Margolis (Moscow: Ob"edinennoe gumanitarnoe izdatel'stvo, 2002);

Sochineniia, 4 volumes, edited by Gennadii F. Komarov (St. Petersburg: Pushkinskii fond / Paris, Moscow & New York: Tret'ia volna, 1992–1995; enlarged edition, 8 volumes, St. Petersburg: Pushkinskii fond, 1998–);

Vspominaia Akhmatovu, by Brodsky and Solomon Volkov (Moscow: Nezavisimaia gazeta, 1992);

Kappadokiia (St. Petersburg: Aleksandra, 1993);

Persian Arrow/Persidskaia strela, with etchings by Edik Steinberg (Verona: Edizione d'Arte Gibralfaro & ECM, 1994);

On Grief and Reason: Essays (New York: Farrar, Straus & Giroux, 1995)–includes "An Immodest Proposal";

V okrestnostiakh Atlantidy: Novye stikhotvoreniia (St. Petersburg: Pushkinskii fond, 1995);

Peizazh s navodneniem, compiled by Aleksandr Sumerkin (Dana Point, Cal.: Ardis, 1996)–includes "Dedal v Sitsilii," "Fin de Siècle," "Menia uprekali vo vsem . . . ," and "Peizazh s navodneniem";

So Forth: Poems (New York: Farrar, Straus & Giroux, 1996)–includes "Daedalus in Sicily," "Taps," "To My Daughter," "Fin de Siècle," and "View with a Flood";

Discovery, illustrated by Vladimir Radunsky (New York: Farrar, Straus & Giroux, 1999);

Collected Poems in English, 1972–1999, edited by Ann Kjellberg (New York: Farrar, Straus & Giroux, 2000);

Vtoroi vek posle nashei ery: Dramaturgiia Iosifa Brodskogo (St. Petersburg: Zvezda, 2001)–includes *Rosenkrants i Gil'denstern mertvy,* by Tom Stoppard, translated by Brodsky.

Editions and Collections: *Nazidanie: Stikhi 1962–1989,* compiled by Vladimir I. Ufliand (Leningrad: Smart, 1990);

Chast' rechi: Izbrannye stikhi 1962–1989 (Moscow: Khudozhestvennaia literatura, 1990);

Osennii krik iastreba: Stikhotvoreniia 1962–1989 (Leningrad: KTP LO IMA Press, 1990);

Kholmy: Bol'shie stikhotvoreniia i poemy, compiled by Iakov Gordin (St. Petersburg: LP VTPO "Kinotsentr," 1991);

Stikhotvoreniia, compiled by Gordin (Tallinn: Eesti Raamat, 1991);

Rozhdestvenskie stikhi (Moscow: Nezavisimaia gazeta, 1992; revised, 1996); translated by Melissa Green and others as *Nativity Poems* (New York: Farrar, Straus & Giroux, 2001);

Forma vremeni: Stikhotvoreniia, esse, p'esy, 2 volumes, compiled by Ufliand (Minsk: Eridan, 1992);

Peresechennaia mestnost': Puteshestviia s kommentariiami, edited by Petr L'vovich Vail' (Moscow: Nezavisimaia gazeta, 1995);

Brodskii o Tsvetaevoi (Moscow: Nezavisimaia gazeta, 1997);

Pis'mo Goratsiiu (Moscow: Nash dom, 1998);

Gorbunov i Gorchakov (St. Petersburg: Pushkinskii fond, 1999);

Ostanovka v pustyne (St. Petersburg: Pushkinskii fond, 2000);

Chast' rechi (St. Petersburg: Pushkinskii fond, 2000);

Konets prekrasnoi epokhi (St. Petersburg: Pushkinskii fond, 2000);

Novye stansy k Avguste (St. Petersburg: Pushkinskii fond, 2000);

Uraniia (St. Petersburg: Pushkinskii fond, 2000);

Peizazh s navodneniem (St. Petersburg: Pushkinskii fond, 2000);

Novaia Odisseia: Pamiati Iosifa Brodskogo (Moscow: Staroe literaturnoe obozrenie, 2001);

Peremena imperii: Stikhotvoreniia 1960–1996 (Moscow: Nezavisimaia gazeta, 2001).

Editions in English: *Elegy to John Donne and Other Poems,* translated by Nicholas William Bethell (London: Longmans, 1967)–includes "Farewell . . . ," "A Jewish Cemetery by Leningrad," "You've finally come home . . . ," "Pilgrims," "I can visit, once more . . . ," "I kissed those shoulders . . . ," "Hills," and "Elegy to John Donne";

The Living Mirror: Five Young Poets from Leningrad, with contributions by Brodsky, edited by Suzanne Massie, translated by Massie, Max Hayward, and George Kline (Garden City, N.Y.: Doubleday, 1972);

Selected Poems, translated by Kline (Harmondsworth, U.K.: Penguin, 1973; New York: Harper & Row, 1973)–

includes "Aeneas and Dido," "After Our Era," "Einem Alten Architekten in Rom," "Elegy to John Donne," "A Letter in a Bottle," "New Stanzas to Augusta," "Nunc Dimittis," "Odysseus to Telemachus," "A Prophecy," "A Slice of Honeymoon," "Stanzas," "Still Life," "To Lycomedes on Scyros," "The trees in my window, in my wooden-framed window . . . ," "You're coming home again. What does that mean?" "You'll flutter, robin redbreast, from those three . . . ," "Verses on the Death of T. S. Eliot," "Wagon Train," and "When I embraced these shoulders, I beheld";

Poems and Translations (Keele: University of Keele, 1977);

Verses on the Winter Campaign 1980, translated by Alan Myers (London: Anvil Poetry Press, 1981).

PLAY PRODUCTIONS: *Mramor,* New York, 1986; St. Petersburg, White Theater, 1996;

Demokratiia! [Act I], London, Gate Theatre, 16 October 1990; Hamburg, Deutsches Schauspielhaus, 28 October 1990.

RECORDINGS: *Joseph Brodsky Reading His Poems in Russian,* read by Brodsky and John Francis, Washington, D.C., Archive of Recorded Poetry and Literature (Library of Congress), 1979;

Joseph Brodsky, read by Brodsky and Mark Strand, New York, Academy of American Poets, 1980;

Joseph Brodsky Reading His Poems, read by Brodsky and Anthony Hecht, Washington, D.C., Gertrude Clarke Whittall Poetry and Literature Fund, 1984;

Winter, read by Brodsky, Watershed Media, 1987;

Joseph Brodsky Reads His Poetry, New York, Caedmon, 1988;

Joseph Brodsky Reading His Poetry, Washington, D.C., Gertrude Clarke Whittall Poetry and Literature Fund, 1992;

Rannie stikhotvoreniia, read by Brodsky, Moscow, Sintez, 1995;

A Maddening Space, read by Brodsky, New York, Mystic Fire, 1996.

OTHER: Vladislav Felitsianovich Khodasevich, *Izbrannaia proza,* 2 volumes, edited by Brodsky (New York: Serebriannyi vek, 1972);

Modern Russian Poets on Poetry, edited by Brodsky and Carl Proffer, introduction by Brodsky (Ann Arbor, Mich.: Ardis, 1976);

Streaked with Light and Shadow: Portraits of Former Soviet Jews in Utah, with an essay by Brodsky, text and interviews by Leslie G. Kelen, photographs by Kent M. Miles and Stacie Ann Smith (Salt Lake City: Oral History Institute, 2000).

TRANSLATIONS: *Bog sokhraniaet vse,* edited by Viktor Kulle (Moscow: MIF, 1992);

V ozhidanii varvarov: Mirovaia poeziia v perevodakh Iosifa Brodskogo, compiled by Aleksei Purin (St. Petersburg: Zvezda, 2001).

SELECTED PERIODICAL PUBLICATIONS–UNCOLLECTED: "Says poet Brodsky: 'A writer is a lonely traveler and no one is his helper,'" *New York Times Magazine* (1 October 1972): 11, 78–79, 82–85;

"Beyond Consolation," *New York Review of Books* (7 February 1974): 13–16;

"The Meaning of Meaning," *New Republic* (20 January 1986): 32–35;

"History of the Twentieth Century: A Roadshow," *Partisan Review,* 53 (1986): 327–343;

"Demokratiia!" *Kontinent,* 62 (1990): 14–42; Act I translated by Alan Myers as "Democracy!" *Granta,* 30 (Winter 1990): 199–233; Act II translated by Brodsky as "Democracy!" *Partisan Review* (Spring 1993): 184–194, 260–288; revised edition of Act II, *Performing Arts Journal,* 18 (September 1996): 92–123;

"Poeziia kak forma soprotivleniia real'nosti," *Russkaia mysl',* 3829 (25 May 1990); translated by Alexander Sumerkin and Jamey Gambrell as "Poetry as a Form of Resistance to Reality," *PMLA,* 107 (March 1992): 220–225.

Joseph Brodsky, the 1987 winner of the Nobel Prize in Literature, came of age in the Soviet Union during the "Thaw" period (late 1950s to early 1960s), and he has been widely recognized as the most gifted Russian poet of his generation. He is the direct successor to an illustrious quartet of modernist Russian poets who reached maturity during the pre-Soviet era and later suffered severely under Soviet rule: Marina Ivanovna Tsvetaeva, Osip Emil'evich Mandel'shtam, Anna Andreevna Akhmatova, and Boris Leonidovich Pasternak. The works and lives of these poets, among others, strongly influenced Brodsky's poetics and conditioned his fidelity to the Russian bardic tradition—of which he was, perhaps, the last true practitioner. Throughout his years living in emigration in the United States (since 1972), Brodsky measured his own poetic merit against the reflections of fellow Soviet émigré poets who also distanced themselves from the overbearing Soviet state machine. At the same time, he drew upon the Anglo-American poetic tradition to propel Russian verse well beyond the frontier of the hackneyed into new realms of form and meaning.

Brodsky's literary legacy includes multiple volumes of poetry, most written originally in Russian but some written in English, Brodsky's adopted tongue; Brodsky's own translations of his poems, sometimes undertaken jointly with professional Anglophone translators and poets; two plays that exist in divergent Russian and English variants; two hefty volumes of collected essays written in English; a prose reminiscence of Venice; several poems for children; and scores of book reviews, introductions, tributes to fellow poets, articles, and formal addresses published in a variety of books and periodicals. Many interviews with Brodsky have also been published in both English and Russian, although in some cases these pieces have been edited heavily, making their reliability uncertain. In the English-speaking world, Brodsky's reputation is primarily as an essayist and a quixotic, modern-day oracle; in the context of Russian letters, he is revered most of all for his poetry.

Brodsky was born Iosif Aleksandrovich Brodsky on 24 May 1940 in Leningrad, just one year before Nazi Germany invaded the Soviet Union and Leningrad came under siege, an event that inflicted widespread starvation and disease. The young Brodsky, together with his mother, survived the Siege of Leningrad intact; his father, meanwhile, was serving in the Soviet navy on the Finnish front. Apart from the fact that his mother taught him to read at the age of four, little is known about Brodsky's early childhood. He was the only child of Mariia Moiseevna Vol'pert and Aleksandr Ivanovich Brodsky. Mariia Moiseevna, the daughter of a Singer sewing-machine salesman, spent her childhood years in Latvia; Aleksandr Ivanovich, the son of a St. Petersburg print-shop owner, earned degrees in geography from the University of Leningrad and in journalism from the School of Red Journalists. Both were Jews, a circumstance that played no small role in their own—and, later, their son's—fates in the context of the official anti-Semitic hype that exploded in the Soviet Union in the postwar years.

In 1950, in response to a Politburo ruling that Jews should not hold high military rank, Aleksandr Ivanovich was dismissed from the navy. He eventually found a job as a freelance photojournalist, but the family's finances remained tight, and both of Brodsky's parents began to experience problems with their health. During the campaign against "rootless cosmopolites" of the early 1950s that led to the 1953 "Doctors' Plot" (a fabricated conspiracy in which nine doctors, most of them Jewish, were accused of plotting to murder top Soviet officials), Mariia Moiseevna and Aleksandr Ivanovich made preparations for the mass deportations of Jews to the Russian Far East that Joseph Stalin was rumored to be planning. However, Stalin's death in 1953 obviated this move.

Brodsky spent his childhood and adolescent years in a small communal apartment located in an elaborate, six-story building on the corner of Pestel' (Panteleimonovskaia) and Liteinyi Streets, an area that boasted a rich literary history. As Brodsky grew older, he barricaded off a small section of the family's forty-square-meter room with thick curtains and heavy chests and shelves heaped to the ceiling with suitcases. This cavernous hideout eventually become his private lair, which he stocked with forbidden books—including the novels of Charles Dickens, James Joyce, John Dos Passos, and Ernest Hemingway and the poetry of Robert Frost, Boris Abramovich Slutsky, John Donne, Konstanty Gałczyński, Tsvetaeva, and Mandel'shtam. In this space the young Brodsky listened to his beloved phonograph records—an eclectic mix of Dixieland jazz, Henry Purcell, and Joseph Haydn—and experienced his first romantic encounters; here, too, he kept his first typewriter and pounded out his first poems.

Brodsky was a wholly self-educated man. As a child, he attended several different public schools. Enamored of his father's navy uniform, he applied at age fourteen for admission to a submarine academy. Although he easily passed the admission examinations, he nonetheless was rejected because he was Jewish. A year later, Brodsky stood up one day during class at Middle School No. 196 on Mokhovaia Street and walked out the door, never to return. He later recalled this spontaneous moment as his first free act—an instinctive protest against the conformity and half-lies that the Soviet educational system inculcated in the youth of the nation. He rationalized his decision by the need to alleviate his family's dire financial situation, and he soon went to work as a milling-machine operator at the arsenal factory, which produced not military hardware but agricultural machinery and air compressors. This job was Brodsky's first contact with the true proletariat, and he relished the fresh range of linguistic expression to which he was exposed. A year later, however, nurturing a fleeting dream of becoming a neurosurgeon, he quit his factory job and went to work at the hospital morgue located next door to the arsenal. He did not stay long at this gruesome post. From 1957 onward he enlisted as a physical laborer in a series of geological expeditions that allowed him to travel all over the territory of the Soviet Union, from the White Sea in the north to the Tien Shan Mountains of Central Asia, and from Iakutsk in northeastern Siberia to Kazakhstan in the south. Between 1956 and 1962 he changed jobs no fewer than thirteen times.

While he was in Iakutsk in 1957, Brodsky stumbled upon a volume of verse by the early-nineteenth-century philosophical poet Evgenii Abramovich Baratynsky. The intellectual acuity of Baratynsky's poetry greatly attracted Brodsky, and he later claimed that he realized at this moment that poetry was his calling—the only thing he understood in life. Brodsky's own earliest poems date from 1957 and 1958. These years were a tumultuous period in Soviet history. The Hungarian uprising of 1956, crushed by the Soviet Army, had shocked the youth of Brodsky's generation into adulthood. Meanwhile, the Congress of Soviet Writers had been reconvened after a hiatus of twenty years, and Akhmatova was reinstated as a member; the unmasking of Joseph Stalin's cult of personality was in full swing; literary societies sprang up throughout Leningrad; and poetry, disseminated in samizdat (self-published) copies, displaced other forms of spiritual expression such as religion or philosophy. The unofficial literature of the late 1950s was devoted to bearing witness to evils of the past.

By the end of the decade, however, some of the younger authors took a turn away from social responsibility and toward aestheticism. For Brodsky, the work of the older poet Slutsky served as a kind of bridge between the two tendencies, moving as it did from bureaucratese and concrete historicism toward pure existentialism. Evgenii Borisovich Rein, a poet of Brodsky's own generation, was also influential; Brodsky and Rein, together with the young poets Anatolii Genrikhovich Naiman and Dmitrii Vasil'evich Bobyshev, first met at Leningrad poetry readings in 1959 and soon became close friends and associates. Brodsky's own public appearances at such evenings began in 1958, and in March 1959 his declamation of his poem "Evreiskoe kladbishche" (1965; translated as "A Jewish Cemetery by Leningrad," 1967) at a poetry competition held at the Gor'ky House of Books in Leningrad was a scandalous success, thanks to its taboo subject matter and daring new poetic idiom.

Brodsky's earliest works are characterized by metrical experimentation, musicality, and the presence of historical, mythological, and religious imagery. The poems are prone to overstatement, and at times their meanings do not quite match the force of the formal contortions to which the poet subjects his verse. This poetry, for the most part, is apolitical. In fact, the combination of the poet's studied social nonconformism with the location of his poems "on the border between song and . . . sacral hymns" has prompted the critic Viktor Sergeevich Kulle, in "Iosif Brodskii: Novaia Odisseia" (Joseph Brodsky: A New Odyssey, published in the 1998 edition of Brodsky's *Sochineniia* [Works]), to dub Brodsky's juvenilia his "Romantic" period. Common themes in the earliest poems include the cityscapes of Leningrad, the poet's alienation from surrounding Soviet society and the bombastic idiom it fosters, and an ironic recognition of the insistent materialism of the world in which the poet finds himself—a theme that is prominent in "Evreiskoe kladbishche." In another poem of 1958, "Piligrimy" (1965; translated as "Pilgrims," 1967), Brodsky charts a path out of this world and away from the false comforts it offers, including religious faith: "And this means, there is no point / In having faith in oneself or in God. / And this means that all that remains / Are Illusion and the Road."

The authorities at the time found Brodsky's apolitical poetry to be much more pernicious than works of overtly political dissent by other young writers such as the poet Evgenii Aleksandrovich Evtushenko. As David MacFadyen shows in his study *Joseph Brodsky and the Soviet Muse* (2000), Brodsky subverts Soviet sloganeering from within, thereby transcending the narrow political jargon that encapsulates Soviet reality, to speak instead in the expansive language of existential quest. At the same time, Brodsky signals, through biting irony and linguistic play, that he does not lose sight of the confining facts of his life. He goes outside the rules of the political game being played in the unofficial literature of the time as well as in the sanctioned, official literature; he dispenses with the rules entirely and simply talks about life, the soul, and longing. This psychological liberation from the mental grip of the system could not fail for long to attract the attention of the Komitet gosudarstvennoi bezopasnosti (KGB, State Security Committee).

Brodsky's first arrest came soon after the appearance of Aleksandr Ginzburg's samizdat publication *Sintaksis* (Syntax), a typewritten poetry journal put out in Moscow in the spring of 1960, which included both "Evreiskoe kladbishche" and "Piligrimy." Other poems by Brodsky had also been circulating in handwritten copies, and some were even being set to music. Brodsky was picked up by the KGB and taken for interrogation to the famous Kresty (Crosses) prison in Leningrad. He was kept in solitary confinement under the most austere conditions and was interrogated for twelve-hour stretches. No formal charges were filed, however, and he was soon released. A year or two later, a second arrest followed when Brodsky was implicated in the so-called Umansky affair, in which he was accused of planning to hijack a plane to Kabul, Afghanistan, and thereby escape the Soviet Union. Once again, he was released when no clear evidence was found against him.

The next several years were full of momentous events in Brodsky's life. In August 1961 Rein took Brodsky to meet Akhmatova at her dacha (summer cottage) in Komarovo. Together with Naiman and Bobyshev, the young poets began frequenting Akhmatova's home; their relationship to her was one of spiritual, more than literary, discipleship, while she herself dubbed the four the "magic chorus" and welcomed their company. Brodsky's poetic sensibilities were quite distant from Akhmatova's; indeed, he felt a direct poetic debt not to Akhmatova but to Tsvetaeva, whose fierce individualism and unflinching quest to go beyond all frontiers were much closer to Brodsky's own metaphysical drive than was Akhmatova's dignified restraint. Yet, Akhmatova was a powerful moral influence on the young Brodsky. Their friendship and mutual admiration—in 1963, Akhmatova autographed a copy of her latest book "To Iosif Brodsky, whose verses seem magical to me"—was immensely meaningful to Brodsky, as it seemed to sanction his position as the heir to the great poetic tradition of the Silver Age. At the same time Brodsky absorbed from Akhmatova a reverence for the poet as an interpreter of Christian culture (his first reading of an underground copy of the Old and New Testaments in 1963 affected him profoundly); he also learned the power of concrete detail and precise psychological motivations from her poetry.

A different kind of meeting occurred in February 1962, when the poet's friends introduced him to Marina Pavlovna Basmanova, a Leningrad artist and illustrator of children's books who was two years his senior. In accord with the bohemian mores of the period, the romance between Brodsky and Basmanova developed almost overnight. There was a strong physical attraction between the couple; yet, Basmanova was unwilling to commit to marriage (Brodsky's precarious political status, along with the fact that all he had to his name was his little corner of his parents' communal apartment, may have had something to do with her reluctance), while Brodsky insistently demanded her full and undying dedication to him. The result of this emotional mismatch was a long-lived, painful love-hate relationship punctuated by alternating fights, separations, and passionate reunions.

The poems that Brodsky wrote beginning in the early 1960s show him moving away from the sometimes clumsy experimentation and concrete settings of his juvenilia into a mature poetics, in which a metaphysical bent is already apparent. In the 1960 poem "Glagoly" (1965, Verbs), for instance, verbs become things with their own independent existence that seem to take the place of humans and, in so doing, satirize the automatization of Soviet life:

> Verbs, which live in cellars,
> speak—in cellars, are born—in cellars
> beneath several stories
> of general optimism.

> Every morning they go to work,
> mix chemicals and haul stones,
> but, in erecting a city, they erect not a city,
> but a monument to their own loneliness.

These verbs, as a stand-in for the poet, eventually are sacrificed to societal regimentation and "ascend Golgotha." The rhythmic driving-in of nails becomes the suffering, liberating rhythm of poetry, which will never desist in any of the three tenses of the verb—past, present, or future—and which ushers in the freedom of poetic imagination at the end of the poem: "The land of hyperboles lies beneath them, / as the heaven of metaphors soars above us!" No matter how brutally the state persecutes verbs (that is, poets and poetry), Brodsky seems to be saying, their subversive power will only increase with time.

In other poems of this period Brodsky abandons his earlier Romantic stance of protest against the insufficiencies of life and moves toward a cool alienation from human society and companionship. Not only metaphysical imaginings but also, strangely, his relationships to inanimate things and places begin to play a central role in his developing poetics. An example of this tendency can be found in the poem "Ia obnial eti plechi . . ." (1965; translated as "I kissed those shoulders . . . ," 1967), in which the poet, in bidding farewell to his lover, does not see or think of her at all (beyond the fragmented shoulders he embraces) but meditates instead on "what turned out to be behind her back": a table, a wall, a bright lamp, assorted shabby furniture, and a circling moth—all of which convey, tacitly, the poet's emotional detachment from the scene in which he himself participates. In "Vorotish'sia na rodinu . . ." (1965; translated as "You've finally come home . . . ," 1967) the poet, arriving home after a long absence, assesses the extent of his own aloneness—which is absolute: "How good it is that there is no one to blame, / how good it is that you are not tied to anyone, / how good it is that no one in the world / is obliged to love you until death." This proud declaration that "there is no one to blame" for the vicissitudes of his fate matured into an insistent eschewal of victimhood, a key ingredient of Brodsky's poetic self-definition.

In his poem "Ot okrainy k tsentru" (From the Suburbs toward the Center; published as "Vot ia vnov' posetil . . ." in 1965 in *Stikhotvoreniia i poemy;* translated as "I can visit, once more . . . ," 1967), Brodsky renders his alienation from the homeland in the form of a farewell jaunt through the suburbs of Leningrad in the company of his own "bednaia iunost'" (poor youth), which replaces any real human company to function as a kind of substitute muse. As in "Ia obnial eti plechi . . . ," the poet's attention is captured by the dilapidated objects that compose his physical surroundings–the bridges, industrial complexes, tramcars, cranes, silent storefronts, and black smoke that characterize the outskirts of contemporary Leningrad. These objects, rather than an emotional relationship to any other human being, propel him into a contemplation of soul, death, hell, heaven, and the uncertainty of life eternal. The statement of alienation from life that ends this poem is one of Brodsky's most potent: "Thank God, I'm an alien. / I don't blame anyone here. / There's nothing to learn. / I walk, hurry, overtake. / How easy it is for me now / since I have not parted with anyone. / Thank God that I am left on the earth without a fatherland." From then on, all the poet's efforts were directed toward chasing and "overtaking" his own potential, without regard for the proscriptions of the Soviet literary establishment.

In 1962 Brodsky discovered the work of the English metaphysical poets, primarily Donne, whose poetry–full of wit, coolly passionate, philosophically detached, highly intellectual, exquisitely crafted with intricate conceits and geometric figures–galvanized the young man. Both in its themes and in its foreignness to the dominant Russian poetic tradition, Donne's work corresponded perfectly to the feelings of alienation that Brodsky had already discovered in himself. At the same time Brodsky saw an equivalence between the English cultural vantage–an islander's perspective on the European continent–and his own Leningrad perch on the edge of the Soviet Empire. He located his feelings of cultural estrangement in the urban geography of Leningrad that had formed him as a child: the cruel winters, fantastic architectural styles, and endless, gray expanses of water–the element he always associated with the idea of freedom. These surroundings prompted him to believe more in the truth of the poetic word than in the inescapability of the daily grind, the necessity of political servitude, or the rectitude of conventional morality. Years later, he ended his essay "A Guide to a Renamed City" (written in 1979, published in 1986) with a tribute to the city of his birth: "Any dream will be inferior to this reality. Where a man doesn't cast a shadow, like water."

In 1962 and 1963, under the influence of Donne as well as of Tsvetaeva, whose powerful *poemy* (long narrative poems) he had recently discovered, Brodsky composed his own first *poemy*. This genre, distanced from the intimacy of the short lyric form, held the potential for the creation of a kind of "lyrico-philosophical" epic that remained attractive to Brodsky throughout the remainder of his creative life, becoming the hallmark of his poetic legacy. The characteristics of Brodsky's works in this genre are rhythmic and stanzaic inventiveness, extended complex metaphors, the mingling of wildly different linguistic registers, paradoxical thought patterns, a tight weaving together of intricate compositional and metaphysical strands, and an acidic sense of humor. Brodsky's earliest *poemy* all participated in the preservative or "neoclassical" mission of his verse with respect to the Russian poetic culture and language of previous ages; included among these works are "Kholmy" (1965; translated as "Hills," 1967), "Bol'shaia elegiia Dzhonu Donnu" (1965; translated as "Elegy to John Donne," 1967), and "Isaak i Avraam" (1965, Isaac and Abraham)–inspired, respectively, by Tsvetaeva, Donne, and the Old Testament.

On 4 May 1961 a decree announcing a struggle against so-called *tuneiadstvo* (social parasitism) was passed in the Soviet Union. Just two and a half years later, on 29 November 1963, a lengthy lampoon against Brodsky appeared in the newspaper *Vechernii Leningrad* (Evening Leningrad) under the heading "Okololiteraturnyi truten'" (A Semi-Literary Drone), signed by A. Ionin, M. Medvedev, and Iakov Lerner, a retired KGB agent. Lerner also convinced Aleksandr Andreevich Prokof'ev, the secretary of the Leningrad Writers' Union, to have a unanimous resolution drafted that stated that Brodsky was "incapable of contributing anything to literature" and that his works were "anti-Soviet and pornographic" and to recommend that Brodsky be expelled from Leningrad. Lerner's lampoon accused the poet of harboring plans to "betray the homeland" and dubbed Brodsky a "pigmy, self-assuredly clambering onto Parnassus." The article concluded with a call to the authorities to protect Leningrad and Leningraders from Brodsky's threat: "It's clear that we must cease coddling such semi-literary parasites . . . Not only Brodsky, but also all those who surround him, are walking along the same dangerous path . . . May semi-literary idlers like Joseph Brodsky receive the sternest rebuff. Let us teach them not to muddy the water!" During 1963 Brodsky had composed more than two thousand lines of poetry; he had also been translating the works of Cuban, Yugoslav, and Polish poets.

Lerner's lampoon portended trouble for Brodsky. In December 1963, at the urging of his friends, the poet fled Leningrad for Moscow. He voluntarily checked himself into the Kashchenko psychiatric hospital in Moscow, hoping to escape the authorities' notice there. Accounts of what followed are somewhat confused. Brodsky apparently soon learned that Basmanova had greeted the New Year in the company of Bobyshev at a dacha belonging to mutual friends in Zelenogorsk (outside Leningrad); Basmanova supposedly betrayed Brodsky with Bobyshev and then set the curtains of the house on fire, coolly commenting how beautiful the flames were. Brodsky, tormented by jealousy and anger, checked out of the psychiatric hospital on 5 January and returned to Leningrad in haste to sort matters out with Basmanova. During January and the first part of February he stayed constantly on the move, sleeping at various friends' dachas on the outskirts of the city. He seems to have spent some time with friends in the town of Tarusa, a writers' colony near Moscow, as well. In his 1967 poem "K Likomedu, na Skiros" (1970, To Lycomedes on Scyros), he reminisces obliquely about this chain of events when he identifies himself with Theseus, who escapes from the Minotaur (a stand-in for the KGB) and his hostile labyrinth (Leningrad) only to discover that Ariadne has taken up with Bacchus.

On the evening of 13 February 1964 Brodsky was unexpectedly arrested for the third time as he walked down a Leningrad street. Five days later he was brought to a closed trial on a charge of *tuneiadstvo*. The presiding judge ruled that Brodsky be sent for mandatory forensic psychiatric testing to determine whether he was suffering from any disorder that precluded a sentence of hard physical labor. On 19 February, Brodsky was sent for three weeks to the Priazhka psychiatric hospital. His *poema* "Gorbunov i Gorchakov" (Gorbunov and Gorchakov, written between 1965 and 1968, published in 1970), written in the form of an extended philosophical dialogue between two hospital inmates—who discuss their dreams, their meals, the view outside their window, and their musings about the soul and immortality—chronicles his experiences there. Brodsky was the only inmate in the hospital not allowed to have visits from his family. He claimed to find the ward environment maddening and to prefer solitary confinement in prison—his favorite formula for which was, as he wrote in his essay "Less Than One" (1986), "a lack of space counterbalanced by a surplus of time"—to this psychiatric torture. During his incarceration in the Priazhka hospital he was routinely injected with various substances and subjected to other "treatments" such as the "wrap," which consisted of being wrapped tightly in sheets and submerged in a tub of cold water and then left to dry, still confined in the wet linens. Ultimately, Brodsky was declared psychologically healthy and fit for work and was released.

Brodsky's second, open trial was held on 13 March 1964. He was defended by respected members of the Leningrad Writers' Union, including journalist and literary critic Frida Abramovna Vigdorova, editor Natal'ia Grudinina, and Herzen Institute professors Efim Grigor'evich Etkind and Vladimir Grigorevich Admoni, all of whom testified to Brodsky's immense talent as both a poet and a translator of poetry. Akhmatova also solicited the support of three Lenin Prize laureates in Brodsky's defense: composer Dmitrii Dmitrievich Shostakovich and writers Samuil Iakovlevich Marshak and Kornei Ivanovich Chukovsky addressed appeals for Brodsky's release to the Writers' Union, the Leningrad Party Committee, and Nikita Sergeevich Khrushchev himself. All these attempts proved ineffectual in the face of testimony by other witnesses, such as one worker who claimed that Brodsky's poetry was having a bad influence on his son by inciting him not to work. Throughout the trial Brodsky impressed his friends by his calm, unruffled mien; he claimed later that this ordeal was less important to him at the time than the recent catastrophe in his relationship with Basmanova, which had already sapped all his emotional energy.

Vigdorova made a stenographic record of a portion of the trial proceedings until she was forbidden by the judge to continue. She circulated these notes in samizdat, and they soon found their way abroad, where they were published in English translation in *The New Leader* and *Encounter* in August and September 1964, and in Russian in the émigré almanac *Vozdushnye puti* (Airy Paths) in 1965. This publication was the first time the internal workings of the Soviet legal system had been revealed to the outside world, and the transcript created an international sensation. Radio Free Europe made much of the story, and the British Broadcasting Corporation even produced a dramatization of the trial on radio. In the West, Brodsky's confused responses to Judge Savel'eva's relentless questions about his lack of professional qualifications to be a writer ("I didn't think—I didn't think this was a matter of education . . . I think that it is . . . from God") came to symbolize the clash between the evil Soviet bureaucracy and human truth and goodness, between unbridled state power and individual rights.

As a result of the publication of the court proceedings, Brodsky, who previously had been known only to a narrow circle of Leningrad writers and poets, became an international cause célèbre. Brodsky himself interpreted his trial as his necessary initiation into the grand tradition of Russian poets at odds with the state. Although in later years he usually refrained from discussing these painful events, he did maintain a sense of humor about them and once commented on the reasons for his persecution: "I combined in myself the most attractive features, in that I wrote poems and was a Jew" (quoted in Efim Grigor'evich Etkind's 1988 biographical notes on Brodsky). He also noted with macabre irony that, in contrast to the punishments meted out to other dissenting literary figures in the decade that followed, by Soviet standards his own treatment was "something absolutely homeopathic" (quoted in Valentina Polukhina, *Joseph Brodsky: A Poet for Our Time* [1989], from a 2 October 1986 interview by Ian Hamilton for BBC 2).

Brodsky was sentenced to five years of hard labor; the court explained that "Brodsky systematically fails to fulfill the obligation of a Soviet man with respect to material values and personal well-being as is evident from his frequent changes of jobs." He was again confined in the Kresty prison, and on 22 March he was shipped out on a prison train with other convicts (who, unlike Brodsky, had committed actual criminal acts) to the Konosha district in the region of Arkhangel'sk, in the far north of Russia; he settled in the village of Norinskaia, which consisted of just fourteen peasant families. The village was twenty miles from the nearest railroad station, surrounded by swampy northern forests. At first he was put up by a dairy farmer, Anisiia Pestereva; later he rented a tiny room in the hut of an old peasant couple, Konstantin and Afanasiia Pesterev. He paid for the room, furnished only with a table and sofa, with the small salary he earned for his work, which was seasonal and consisted variously of chopping wood, carting manure, shoveling grain stores, and laboring in the fields of the local state farm. His landlady later remembered him fondly and claimed that the villagers often took pity on him and assigned him comparatively easier tasks, such as pasturing the cows. On 14 August 1965 the village newspaper *Prizyv* (The Summons) published Brodsky's poem "Traktory na rassvete" (Tractors at Dawn, which appears in full in MacFadyen's *Joseph Brodsky and the Soviet Muse*), and on 4 September 1965 it published his poem "Oboz" (Wagon Train), for which he was paid two rubles and some change.

His grim surroundings and the hardships of daily life in Norinskaia notwithstanding, Brodsky remembered this period happily: "That was one of the best periods in my life. There have been no worse, but I don't think there have been better" (quoted in Solomon Volkov's *Conversations with Joseph Brodsky* [1998]). Vigdorova sent him her typewriter, and other friends sent him books, letters, and tins of instant coffee. Because the farmwork in the village was seasonal, Brodsky had long stretches of free time; because for the most part he spent his time in isolation, there were few distractions from his intellectual pursuits. During this period he perfected his knowledge of English, continued his translating work, and discovered to his great excitement the writings of T. S. Eliot and W. H. Auden. His own poetry was nourished by this reading and for the first time departed entirely from the Romantic idiom of his juvenilia and the pathetic idiom of official Soviet discourse. He achieved new spiritual and metaphysical heights in his writing that were, however, conditioned by a wry Romantic irony that remained characteristic of Brodsky's poetics and even of his conversational style for the remainder of his life. In his Norinskaia poems Brodsky makes use of the compositional possibilities of the baroque—the juxtaposition of the grotesque and the serious, the ephemeral and the eternal, the coarse and the eloquent—while at the same time distancing himself from pure lyricism and adopting, instead, a profoundly intellectual worldview. His language becomes saturated with subtextual references, sometimes preservative and sometimes parodic in function.

Exemplary of all these developments in Brodsky's poetics is his poignant elegy "Stikhi na smert' T. S. Eliota" (1970, translated as "Verses on the Death of T. S. Eliot," 1973), written upon Eliot's death on 4 January 1965. In this poem Eliot's magi (from his poem "The Journey of the Magi," 1927) are replaced by the androgynous figures of two mythic maidens, England and America, the two nations where Eliot made his home. Time is an overwhelming presence, and in fact time itself—not death or God—claims the poet's life. As Eliot departs the temporal world, "latching his door with a chain of years," Poetry, though orphaned by his death, still "breeds within the glass / of lonely days, each echoing each." Poetry, as Brodsky often wrote, is time reconfigured: "in the rhyme / of years the voice of poetry stands plain." Through the strength of his poetry Eliot has inscribed his being on the physical world. Brodsky's own poetic signature is now developed to the point at which he, too, etches himself into the consciousness of his physical surroundings—he knows now his own poetic strength. As Brodsky wrote in a letter to I. N. Tomashevskaia on 19 January 1965 (quoted by A. N. Krivomazov in his on-line biography of Brodsky): "I have accelerated too far now, and I will never stop until death itself. Everything somehow shimmers in the background, but that's not the main thing. Inside me is some sort of unheard-of infinity and indifference, and I will gather more and more speed all the time."

Many of Brodsky's best works were written during his exile in Norinskaia, including more than seventy lyric poems and several *poemy* (first published in book form in *Ostanovka v pustyne* [1970, A Halt in the Desert,]), including "Pis'mo v butylke" (1965, Letter in a Bottle), "Einem Alten Architekten in Rom" (1964, To an Old Architect in Rome), and "Novye stansy k Avguste" (1964, New Stanzas to Augusta). This last work is dedicated to Basmanova ("M.B."), who later visited him for a period of several months during his exile. He gladly welcomed other visitors as well—Rein and Naiman came, bringing an encouraging letter from Akhmatova on the occasion of Brodsky's twenty-fifth birthday—but the period he spent with Basmanova was the highlight of his exile, the happiest time in his long relationship with her. In "Novye stansy k Avguste" the absent Basmanova, like Augusta, the sister of George Gordon, Lord Byron, plays muse to Brodsky's exiled poet. Brodsky dedicated many other poems to Basmanova during his time in Norinskaia, including "Ty vyporkhnesh', malinovka . . ." (1964; translated as "You'll flutter, robin redbreast, from these three . . . ," 1973), "Dlia shkol'nogo vozrasta" (1964, For School Age, translated in David M. Bethea's *Joseph Brodsky and the Creation of Exile* [1994]), "Lomtik medovogo mesiatsa" (A Slice of Honeymoon, 1963), "Derev'ia v moem okne . . ." (The trees in my window, in my wooden-framed window . . . , 1964), and "Prorochestvo" (A Prophecy, 1965), all of which were first published in book form in *Ostanovka v pustyne*. Brodsky later collected his love poems to Basmanova in the volume *Novye stansy k Avguste* (New Stanzas to Augusta, 1983).

The furor that Brodsky's trial had raised abroad did not dissipate but rather escalated after his exile to Norinskaia. A collection of his works, titled *Stikhotvoreniia i poemy* (Lyric and Narrative Poems), compiled by Gleb Petrovich Struve and Boris Andreevich Filippov and financed by the Central Intelligence Agency, was published in New York in 1965. During the next few years, translations into English, German, French, Hebrew, Polish, and Czech followed. By contrast, only a handful of Brodsky's poems had been published by this time in Soviet periodicals—the first of these, "Proshchai . . ." (translated as "Farewell . . . ," 1967), in 1957. The authorities eventually bowed to international pressure and commuted Brodsky's sentence to one year and five months, and he was released in September 1965. Now world renowned, he was allowed to return to his native Leningrad and to earn a living as a translator; he translated Donne and Andrew Marvell into Russian and focused especially on the works of the Polish poets Cyprian Norwid, Zbigniew Herbert, Czesław Miłosz, and Gałczyński, from whom he learned to approach a serious subject indirectly, with a degree of jest, without losing sight of its deeper implications. He traveled freely, often visiting Lithuania and wintering in writers' colonies in the Crimea. He spent time in Moscow as well, where his friends Naiman and Rein had moved after the breakdown of their friendship with Bobyshev and Brodsky's subsequent exile. When Akhmatova died on 5 March 1966, Brodsky was a pallbearer at her funeral.

For two or three years after Brodsky's return to Leningrad, his relationship with Basmanova continued fitfully, and in 1968 she gave birth to his son, Andrei, whom, despite Brodsky's resistance, she registered under the maternal surname Basmanov. As before, she had no intention of marrying Brodsky, who was barely managing to make ends meet with the small income that his translations brought in, and who still lived in an alcove in his parents' share of the communal apartment on Liteinyi Street. By the time of Andrei's birth, Brodsky's relationship with Basmanova was decidedly over, although he continued wistfully addressing love poems to her during the next two decades of his life. Several passages in his 1967 *poema* "Rech' o prolitom moloke" (1977, A Speech about Spilled Milk) refer to the disintegration of his romantic hopes, as when he complains: "Knowing my status, my fiancée / for the fifth year hasn't budged to get married; / and where she is now, I have no idea: / the devil himself couldn't pry the truth out of her." This work is a self-deprecatory rant against Brodsky's disappointments in life—and, in particular, against the depraved political ideology that contaminates the society in which he lives. He voices his determination to continue his rebellion against the system and to fight for "democracy in the full sense of the word," claiming that "evil exists to be fought with, / and not to be hung like a yoke on one's shoulders."

In several poems written in the late 1960s and first published in book form in *Ostanovka v pustyne*, Brodsky sadly, or bitterly, bids good-bye to his affair with Basmanova. In "Sonet" (A Sonnet; translated as "Postscriptum" in *Selected Poems*, 1973), he begins, "What a pity that what your existence has come to mean for me, my existence did not come to mean for you." In "Strofy" (1968; translated as "Stanzas," 1973) he muses, "But my world will not end if / in future we share / only those jagged edges / where we've broken apart." In the wake of his breakup with Basmanova, Brodsky had several short-lived relationships with various women, among them Soviets and foreign Slavicists who came to meet him while traveling in the Soviet Union, but none of these connections ultimately endured.

After his release from northern exile in 1965, Brodsky's political troubles were far from over. Khrushchev had been forced from power in late 1964, and Leonid Il'ich Brezhnev took over, becoming the new general secretary of the Communist Party in 1966. The decade of the Thaw was coming to a close, and there began a wave of arrests and deportations of important writers and scholars—including, in 1974, Etkind, who had defended Brodsky at his 1964 trial, and the writer Vladimir Rafailovich Maramzin, who was in the process of compiling a samizdat collection of Brodsky's poetry. The availability today of much of Brodsky's early work results from Maramzin's efforts at collecting and organizing the poet's writings, given Brodsky's own carelessness with his archive, particularly in his youth. The literary critic Mikhail Kheifets, who had written an introduction to Maramzin's volume titled "Iosif Brodskii i nashe pokolenie" (Joseph Brodsky and Our Generation), was sentenced to four years in a labor camp and two years in exile.

Brodsky himself was one of the first casualties of the new cultural repression. Although immediately after his return to Leningrad he was offered the opportunity of publishing a selection of his poems in the journal *Iunost'* (Youth), the publication was canceled when Brodsky refused to acquiesce to Evtushenko's choice of his works, saying the selection made him emerge "looking like a shorn sheep" (cited in Volkov's *Conversations with Joseph Brodsky*). Several of Brodsky's poems were, however, published in Soviet periodicals and almanacs in 1966 and 1967. In addition, in 1966 he prepared a collection titled "Zimniaia pochta" (Winter Mail) for printing by the Leningrad branch of the publishing house Sovetskii pisatel' (Soviet Writer), but these plans apparently fell through when Brodsky was advised that the book would be published only if he agreed to become an informant for the KGB. In 1969 Robert Lowell invited Brodsky to take part in an international poetry festival in London; the same year, Brodsky was also asked to appear at the Festival of Two Worlds in Spoleto. He was refused a visa to attend either occasion; the bizarre response of the Soviet authorities to the latter invitation was that "There is no such poet. True, there was a Brodsky sent to prison a few years ago." Permission for Brodsky to attend a poetry festival in Czechoslovakia was also denied.

Events came to a head on the morning of 10 May 1972. Brodsky was urgently summoned to the Office of Visas and Registrations (OVIR), where he was asked whether he had received an invitation to immigrate to Israel. Brodsky replied that he had received two such invitations, although he had no idea who had sent them, and that he had not used them because, in the first place, he had not expected to be allowed to go and, in the second place, he had no interest in leaving home permanently. The official responded by setting before Brodsky a visa application accompanied by an invitation from a certain "Evrei Iakov" (Jacob the Jew), whom Brodsky was told to identify as his grandnephew; he was also assured that if he did not fill out the forms on the spot, he would be in for a "very hot time." Weary of his struggles and recognizing the inescapability of the situation, Brodsky complied. The following Monday he was ordered to turn in his passport, and he was given two weeks to leave the country. Brodsky told Volkov that he suspected that Evtushenko had been instrumental in urging this turn of events. Whatever the case, a bold open letter that Brodsky wrote to Brezhnev himself, asserting that "even if my nation does not need my body, my soul will come in handy," expressing his certainty that he would return some day to his native land "in the flesh or on paper," and urging Brezhnev to allow him at least to publish in the Soviet Union, had no effect. Brodsky at last was beyond the reach of the strong grasp of the state.

The theme of Empire—exemplified by Rome—is a common one in Brodsky's writings, beginning in the late 1960s. Earlier, the idea of Empire had naively signified for Brodsky the conflict between poet and society; in his mature poems, however, the disintegration of the Roman Empire became his way of describing the particular atmosphere of stagnation that was inaugurated under Brezhnev. For example, in Brodsky's poem "Vremia goda—zima . . ." (1977, The time of year is winter . . . ; translated in Bethea's *Joseph Brodsky and the Creation of Exile*), written between 1967 and 1970, the poet dwells on the edge of the empire, at the end of an era, and speaks through a state of stifling half-slumber about his feeling of entrapment. Caught like a fish on a hook, the poet attempts in vain to escape by exercising the powers of his magical language, which is a priori older than any state, and contents himself by observing stoically that "If we can't get the better of the evil power, then at least we can get the better of ourselves."

On 4 June 1972 Brodsky arrived in Vienna—ostensibly en route to Israel—where he was met by his friend Carl Proffer, founder of the American publishing house Ardis. Proffer soon led Brodsky to a meeting with Auden at that poet's summer residence, a farmhouse in the Austrian countryside, where Brodsky spent the next three weeks. In June and July, Brodsky and Auden appeared together at poetry readings in London and Oxford. Soon afterward, Brodsky accepted Proffer's invitation to the post of poet-in-residence with professorial status at the University of Michigan in Ann Arbor. Brodsky's way in the West had been paved by the appearance in New York in 1970 of his first authorized collection, *Ostanovka v pustyne*. This book encompassed a selection of his best lyrics written up to that point, along with several important *poemy*, including "Gorbunov i Gorchakov," and translations into Russian of four of Donne's poems. Anglophone readers were also able to become acquainted with his poetry through his first English-language collections *Elegy to John Donne and Other Poems* (1967) and *Selected Poems* (1973). The latter volume consisted of translations by George Kline that were overseen by Brodsky himself, and the book included a glowing preface written by Auden.

The history of Brodsky's life in emigration is far less eventful than that of his early years in the Soviet Union. Always a private man, he became more so as he grew older and settled into his hybrid identity as an American professor and man of letters and a Russian émigré poet. Brodsky remained at the University of Michigan for the next nine years. In 1981 he accepted a permanent position as Andrew Mellon Professor of Literature at Mount Holyoke College in South Hadley, Massachusetts. Over the years he also appeared as a guest lecturer and visiting professor at many other universities in both the United States and Britain, including Amherst College, Columbia University, New York University, Queens College, Smith College, and Cambridge University. During his early years in the United States, Brodsky confided in friends his fear of losing the pulse of Russian poetry and becoming alienated from the expressive possibilities of his native language. These fears proved, however, to be in vain; with time, the Russian language became the vessel for Brodsky's identity, the only defining reality in his life, and indeed the exact substance of sanctity and human meaning. "The holiest thing we have," Brodsky said in a 1983 interview with Natal'ia Gorbanevskaia (quoted in Valentina Polukhina's 2000 compilation), "is, perhaps, not our icons, not even our history–it is our language."

In Brodsky's cycle "Chast' rechi" (A Part of Speech), published in *Chast' rechi: Stikhotvoreniia 1972–76* (1977, A Part of Speech: Poems 1972–76), his language is jumbled and fragmented but does not lose its potency. The neologisms, grammatical impossibilities, and pure nonsense of the opening poem, for example, result in a surprisingly eloquent statement of loneliness and alienation:

> From nowhere with love, the umpteenth of Martober,
> dear respected mister sweetie, but it doesn't even matter
> who, since the features of the face, speaking
> frankly, I can no longer remember, neither yours, nor
> anyone's either true friend I greet you from one
> of the five continents, which is propped up by cowboys;
> I loved you more than the angels or god himself,
> and therefore I'm farther from you now, than from them both.

As the title of this cycle indicates, the poet himself is pared down, along with his utterances, to the elementary unit of meaning–the part of speech–and just as the splitting of the atom releases enormous stores of hidden energy, so too this fragmentation of linguistic matter gives rise to a corresponding intensification of meaning: "Of the entire person left to you is only a part / of speech. A part of speech in general. A part of speech."

Brodsky came to feel that (as he told Giovanni Buttafava in a 1987 interview, collected in Polukhina's 2000 compilation) "perhaps exile is the natural condition of a poet's existence, in contrast to the novelist, who must exist within the structures of the society he describes." Exile became the source of Brodsky's mature metaphysics in poems such as the 1975 "Osennii krik iastreba" (1987, The Hawk's Cry in Autumn), prompting him to formulate in his works a law of subtraction by which the process of living consists of the gradual shedding of every extraneous emotion, connection, and possession until the essential core of being is revealed through poetic truths, the primary instrument of which is rhyme. Bethea has traced this development in his *Joseph Brodsky and the Creation of Exile*. Perhaps the best illustration of the process is found in "1972 god" (1972), published in 1977, a wry self-portrait in verse written shortly after Brodsky's emigration, where unorthodox rhymes such as "trusosti / trudnosti / trupnosti" (cowardice / difficulty / corpseness) and "doverii / materii / poteri i" (trust / material / loss and) convey the inevitable, gradual decay of physical existence and of the poet's own body in particular. Brodsky's sense of humor, in this poem and throughout his poetry, was a saving power. His lifelong aversion to the stance of victimhood resulted, in his later years, in a trenchant command of language and its expressive possibilities. His stoicism is voiced most eloquently in his 1980 poem "Ia vkhodil vmesto dikogo zveria . . ." (1987, I entered in place of a wild beast . . . ; translated as "May 24, 1980," 1988), which ends with these well-known lines: "What should I say about life? / That it turned out to be long. / I feel solidarity with grief alone. / But as long as they haven't stuffed my mouth with clay, / only gratefulness will gush from it."

The strength of Brodsky's poetic voice and vision is demonstrated in the hundreds of poems published in his major collections of the American years: *Chast' rechi*; *Konets prekrasnoi epokhi* (1977, End of the Belle Epoque); *Novye stansy k Avguste*; *Uraniia* (1987, Urania); *Primechaniia paporotnika* (1990, Notes of a Fern); and *Peizazh s navodneniem* (1996, View with a Flood). Brodsky's refusal to relinquish either his command of the Russian language or his rightful position in the Russian poetic pantheon was not, however, the only factor that guaranteed his poetic survival in emigration. His adoption of the English language as his second mother tongue and of the United States as his second homeland undoubtedly played an important role in ensuring that he did not fade into nonexistence as the Soviet authorities had hoped. Instead, Brodsky remained an imposing literary presence. He gratefully received his United States citizenship in Detroit on 11 October 1977 (some sources incorrectly give the date as 1980); his posthumous children's book *Discovery* (1999) pays tribute to his love for his adoptive country. Brodsky's knowledge of the English language and love of English and American poetry prior to his emigration facilitated this turn of events. His love affair with English only deepened after he took up residency in the United States, and he often stressed his feeling of obligation toward the English language, as he observed in an essay for *The New York Times Magazine* (1 October 1972): "The measure of a writer's patriotism is how he writes in the language of the people among whom he lives." Despite the privacy of Brodsky's habits, his outsider's gaze upon his host culture, and his often critical view of American society, he remained always passionately engaged in dialogue with his adoptive country, and isolationism of the type practiced by another involuntary Russian exile, Aleksandr Isaevich Solzhenitsyn, was unimaginable for him.

Brodsky's first poem in English was "Elegy," dedicated to his mentor Auden. In 1972 Brodsky finally met the American poet Lowell, with whom he felt more comfortable than with Auden; in 1977 he wrote "Elegy: For Robert Lowell" in English and included it with the translations of his Russian lyrics in his 1980 collection *A Part of Speech*. This English collection was followed in 1988 by *To Urania* and, in 1996, by the posthumous collection *So Forth*. With each progressive collection in English, there is a visible acceleration of Brodsky's authorial control over the English versions of his poetry, demonstrating his increasing feeling of ease in the English language and his desire to exist as a full poetic presence in the Anglophone literary space. In *So Forth*, translations are not even marked as such, so that distinguishing between poems that exist in Russian-language versions and poems that do not is impossible at first glance. On many occasions Brodsky's authorized versions of works previously published in Russian depart significantly from the original versions, as he alters the semantic content of his lines to preserve a rhyme or metrical pattern or attempts to harness the different idiomatic potential of the English language, with varying degrees of success. Indeed, critical opinion on Brodsky's English-language poetry is strongly divided. Some commentators discern the same linguistic and philosophical brilliance in his English poems that marks his Russian works and find the oddities of his English appealing, revealing, even poetic. Other scholars contend that Brodsky never managed to develop a true understanding of the unique qualities of English verse or even a good grasp of English grammar, and that his English poems and translations suffer badly from his attempts to graft his extremely Russian sensibilities regarding rhyme, meter, and diction onto an unaccommodating medium; the unfortunate result, they claim, is often humor or vulgarity where, clearly, only a keen irony is intended.

Critical opinion on Brodsky's English-language prose, however, is essentially unanimous; in this genre, freed of the structural requirements of verse, Brodsky's expressive genius shines. His first collection of essays in English, *Less Than One*, was published in 1986, followed by *On Grief and Reason* in 1995; some of these essays first appeared as introductions to poetry collections. In addition, he published several articles and editorials in Anglophone periodicals over the years, including *The New York Times Magazine*, *TLS: The Times Literary Supplement*, *The New Yorker*, *The New York Review of Books*, *Newsweek*, *Vogue*, and *Mademoiselle*. Through these appearances in the mainstream press, he attained a powerful voice in the pressing intellectual debates of his time. The essays included in *Less Than One* and *On Grief and Reason* serve as a continuation of Brodsky's poetry and a kind of supplemental poetic autobiography, characterized by the same trenchant intellect and the same linguistic and metaphoric density that mark his poems.

Less Than One mostly looks backward—to Brodsky's parents and childhood, as well as to his cultural inheritance in his native city of Leningrad and in the Russian poetic tradition championed by his predecessors Akhmatova, Tsvetaeva, and Mandel'shtam. Brodsky dedicates the two essays that frame the collection, "Less Than One" and "In a Room and a Half," to reminiscences of his mother and father and of his early childhood in Soviet Leningrad. The young Brodsky as he depicts himself in his opening piece is disaffected and insecure, with an impaired sense of self—like the adult poet he later became, he feels he is "less than one." The title of the closing essay similarly expresses diminishment, inadequacy, and constraint, this time of the tiny physical space in which Brodsky and his parents once lived. These two essays are much more than straightforward memoirs of times past. Rather, they juxtapose Brodsky's memories of the Soviet past with his émigré present, sometimes evoking a jarring sense of incongruence and unreality ("The reality I face bears no relation and no correspondence to the room and a half and its two inhabitants, across the ocean and now nonexistent. . . . The only points in common are my own frame and a typewriter. Of a different make and with a different typeface"), while at other times creating a haunting illusion of echoes and uncanny correspondences, as when two crows perched on the poet's porch in Massachusetts remind him of his parents ("One is shorter than the other, the way my mother was up to my father's shoulder").

These essays are not so much about particular memories as about the nature of memory in general, the role that language plays in encoding and expressing memories, the relationship or lack thereof between material and intellectual existence, and the development of Brodsky's poetic consciousness through time. Brodsky challenges the Marxian dictum that "existence conditions consciousness," touting instead his discovery at a precociously young age of the "art of estrangement." This technique proved to be his salvation from the pervasive slavish mentality—adopted even by his parents—that was mandated by the totalitarian society in which he lived. His freedom from this mentality came in various forms: his commission of rebellious acts such as dropping out of school; his ability to filter his perceptions of the material world, for example, by ignoring the ubiquitous statues of Vladimir Lenin; and his development of an ethical sense that is based not on Soviet dogma, but on an instinctive perception of aesthetic beauty. Thus, the beautiful city of Leningrad, whose "left bank looked like the imprint of a giant mollusk called civilization. Which ceased to exist," serves as a receptacle of truth and, moreover, as the physical embodiment of Brodsky's concept of memory as it is delineated in these essays—a fossilized trace of time past. As he writes: "Memory, I think, is a substitute for the tail that we lost for good in the happy process of evolution. . . . There is something clearly atavistic in the very process of recollection, if only because such a process never is linear."

The autobiographical essays "Less Than One" and "In a Room and a Half" are anything but linear; they skip rapidly from topic to topic, sketching surprising correspondences with metaphysical accuracy, deadpan humor, and maximally condensed linguistic means. As a result, many lines of Brodsky's prose in these essays read like aphorisms (for example, "Prison is a lack of alternatives"; "The army is a peasant's idea of order"; "But then inhumanity is always easier to structure than anything else"). In Brodsky's other essays in *Less Than One*, he maintains this style as he ruminates on various topics, including the state of contemporary Russian prose, the nature of political tyranny, the legacy of poets such as Eugenio Montale and Constantine Cavafy, and the pernicious encroachment, in his view, of Eastern despotism on Russian cultural forms (including Christian Orthodoxy). Brodsky broaches the last topic in his essay "Flight from Byzantium." In the essays that make up *On Grief and Reason*, Brodsky mostly turns aside from his Russian background to address the works of American and European poets such as Frost, Thomas Hardy, and Rainer Maria Rilke, as well as his perceptions of the contemporary American society in which he lives.

Brodsky's prolific writings brought him many honors, and in the years following his emigration his literary success was considerable. In 1977 he received the John Simon Guggenheim Memorial Foundation Fellowship in poetry; in 1978 he was awarded an honorary degree of doctor of letters by Yale University; in 1979 an Italian translation of his works received both the Feltrinelli Prize for Poetry and the Mondello Literary Prize; on 23 May 1979 he was elected to the American Academy and Institute of Arts and Letters (in 1987 he resigned his membership in protest against the induction of Evtushenko as a foreign member of the Institute); in 1981 he was granted a "genius" award by the John D. and Catherine T. MacArthur Foundation; in 1986 he received the National Book Critics Circle Award for criticism for *Less Than One;* in 1987 he was awarded the Nobel Prize in Literature; in 1991 he was granted an honorary degree by Oxford University and received France's Order of the Legion of Honor; and also in 1991 he was chosen by the Library of Congress to serve as the poet laureate of the United States, which he did until 1992. Brodsky was frequently invited to give readings of his poetry, and he became famous for his powerful, sing-song declamatory style and his sardonic, witty, penetrating monologues in response to his audience's questions. He also cultivated friendships with other leading contemporary poets, including Lowell, Miłosz, Richard Wilbur, Mark Strand, Derek Walcott, Seamus Heaney, and Tomas Venclova, as well as with Western and Russian intellectuals such as Susan Sontag, Lev Vladimirovich Losev, and Aleksandr Sumerkin. Brodsky often traveled to England, and he made a habit of visiting Venice—the watery city that reminded him of his native Leningrad—almost every year during his winter break from teaching. These Venetian odysseys are memorialized in his book-length meditative essay *Watermark* (1992), published first in Italian translation as *Fondamenta degli Incurabili* (Fundamentals of the Incurable) in 1989, and translated into Russian as "Naberezhnaia neistselimykh" (Shores of the Incurable).

Brodsky was grateful for his relative good fortune; he once said, "I'm the happiest combination you can think of. I'm a Russian poet, an English essayist, and an American citizen!" (quoted in Cissie Dore Hill's "Remembering Joseph Brodsky," 2000). However, despite his professional successes in emigration, his life during these years was largely a solitary one, and his vocation as a university professor never became a true avocation. In addition to the keen feeling of cultural and linguistic alienation that was the norm of his new existence and shaped his writing so distinctively, he had another, more particular sorrow to bear: his parents, whom he had not seen since 1972, were repeatedly denied permission by the Soviet authorities to visit their son even for a short time, despite their ceaseless attempts over the years. Brodsky paid tribute to them in his essay "In a Room and a Half," hoping that by writing about them in the English language he would somehow manage to free them from their unwitting mental servitude to the Soviet regime, which had swallowed them alive: "I want English verbs of motion to describe their movements. This won't resurrect them, but English grammar may at least prove to be a better escape route from the chimneys of the state crematorium than the Russian." Brodsky's mother, ill with cancer, died in 1983, while his father passed away from a heart attack the following year.

Brodsky's own health suffered over the years. He had inherited his father's heart condition, and the emotional strain of his political persecution in the Soviet

Union and the physical strain of his eighteen months of hard labor in the far north had worsened matters. Moreover, heedless of doctors' orders, Brodsky all his life was an inveterate hard drinker and chain-smoker. He suffered his first heart attack on 13 December 1976, and during the last two decades of his life he underwent three separate heart-bypass operations.

Still, Brodsky's last years were eventful, busy, and largely peaceful. In South Hadley, Massachusetts, where he lived each spring, he owned a house built in the eighteenth century, the rustic decor and rough maple floors of which reminded him of his parents' room in the communal apartment of his youth. Brodsky was famous for his poetry courses at Mount Holyoke College, in which he required his students to memorize hundreds of lines of poetry during the course of the semester. He spent his autumns and winters in the bohemian environment of Greenwich Village in New York City, where he lived in an apartment on Morton Street with his cat. In New York, Brodsky had a wide circle of acquaintances within the Soviet émigré community, in particular the dancer Mikhail Nikolaevich Baryshnikov and the writer, translator, and dance aficionado Gennadii Smakov, a close friend of Brodsky's youth from Leningrad.

While he continued to write poetry and essays in both English and Russian, in 1984 Brodsky completed a drama, which he had begun in the Soviet Union in the 1960s, titled *Mramor* (Marbles). This play premiered on the New York stage in 1986, starring Wallace Shawn and Andre Gregory, and was subsequently performed in various locations in Europe and North America. The play, like "Gorbunov i Gorchakov," was inspired by Brodsky's nightmarish experiences in Soviet psychiatric hospitals, and it continues the dialogue that shapes the earlier *poema*; at the same time the play develops the picture of a post-Christian empire that Brodsky first put forth in his 1970 *poema* "Post Aetatem Nostram" (1977, After Our Era). In *Mramor*, Brodsky heightens both the terror and the humor of his poetic treatment of the subject, going beyond absurdism to portray a hilarious, horrible dystopia two hundred years in the future. A resurrected Roman Empire has established statistical norms for imprisonment, according to which three percent of the population, irrespective of any crimes committed, is shut up for life in a mile-high steel tower in the heart of the new Rome. The two characters of the play, Publius and Tullius, are unlikely cell mates in the prison tower, doomed to each other's company. Escape is unthinkable; when Tullius succeeds in an ingenious plan to exit briefly into the outside world, he nevertheless returns voluntarily to confinement, opting for the oblivion of sleeping pills over the liberation of real existence.

Brodsky's 1987 Nobel Prize address was an eloquent testament to his own refusal to submit to such oblivion; he declared the complete independence of the poet from any social or political norm, claimed that the only dictator to whom the poet must submit is language itself, and celebrated the continuity of culture according to aesthetic intuition—the source, according to Brodsky, of morality, rather than the other way around: "For a man with taste, particularly with literary taste, is less susceptible to the refrains and the rhythmical incantations peculiar to any version of political demagogy. The point is not so much that virtue does not constitute a guarantee for producing a masterpiece as that evil, especially political evil, is always a bad stylist." Despite the themes of Brodsky's address, the selection committee of the Swedish Academy denied that there was any political message for the Soviet government in their choice of the Russian émigré poet (who was, at age forty-seven, the second-youngest writer ever to be awarded the Nobel Prize). Instead, their press release cited Brodsky for the "luminous intensity of his writing," its "great breadth in time and space . . . and . . . the intellectual and sensitive side of this rich and intensely vital work." Initial reaction to Brodsky's Nobel Prize in his native Russia, nevertheless, was one of consternation and coverup; Gennadii Gerasimov, a Soviet Foreign Ministry spokesman, remarked at a press conference on the strange tastes of the Nobel Prize committee, and the prize was not announced publicly in the Soviet Union until news of it had leaked through from foreign shortwave radio broadcasts several weeks later. Still, even Gerasimov acknowledged that the prize would draw welcome attention to Russian poetry of the twentieth century; and reaction to Brodsky's prize among Western critics and intellectuals was uniformly ecstatic. His own initial response to the announcement of the honor was characteristically one of mixed pride and humor at his own expense: "A big step for me, a small one for mankind," he joked, adding, "It's Russian literature that got it."

After Brodsky became a Nobel laureate, his fame soared, and he was often distracted from his writing by the inevitable parade of journalists, letters from aspiring young poets, and other public obligations. His commitment to his compatriots did not wane, either; in 1979 he had been instrumental in the defection to the United States of the Bol'shoi Theater ballet star Aleksandr Godunov, and in later years he was active in assisting many Russian émigrés to the United States with letters of recommendation and well-placed telephone calls. He generously used portions of his Nobel Prize money to assist friends and prominent Russian émigrés in their times of need. In addition, he spent a good part of the money—against friends' advice—on expensive renovations on the apartment he rented in Greenwich Village; he also contributed a portion of the money toward propping up the Russian Samovar restaurant in Manhattan, which had struggled since its establishment in 1986 through a fire, flood, and other maintenance disasters.

Brodsky concerned himself with the state of American literary culture as well. In his October 1991 address to the Library of Congress as poet laureate he made what he termed, parodying Jonathan Swift, "An Immodest Proposal" (1995) that called for the dissemination of poetry in public places such as hotels and supermarkets in order to counteract what he saw as the degenerative effects of American popular culture. Ludicrous as the proposal might have sounded, it piqued the interest of Andrew Carroll, a young Columbia University graduate, and in 1993 he and Brodsky founded the American Poetry and Literacy Project, a nonprofit organization that, in the words of Brodsky's address, was devoted to making poetry a part of American culture "as ubiquitous as gas stations, if not as cars themselves," since poetry "is the only insurance available against the vulgarity of the human heart. Therefore, it should be available to everyone in this country and at a low cost." Carroll continued this project after Brodsky's death, and hundreds of thousands of free books of poetry were given away in hotel rooms and grocery stores, at truck stops and post offices.

Beginning in the early 1990s, Brodsky at last ceased addressing poems to the elusive "M.B." He was an intensely private person, and the few published accounts of events in his personal life are often of doubtful accuracy. What is clear, though, is that in his last years the poet's life changed dramatically. After an epistolary romance with a translator named Maria Sozzani and several joint sojourns with her in Venice, the couple were married in Stockholm on 1 September 1990. Maria Sozzani Brodsky was thirty years Brodsky's junior, the daughter of an Italian father and Russian mother. Some of Brodsky's friends observed that he was changed, softened, and seemed happy as never before. The couple's decision to leave his high-profile residence in Greenwich Village for the comparative tranquility of Brooklyn Heights also contributed significantly to his feeling of contentment. In June 1993 Sozzani Brodsky gave birth to the couple's only child, their daughter, Anna Alexandra Maria.

Brodsky's poems of the 1990s occasionally hint at the poet's emotional transformation when, at rare intervals, his tone of stoic forbearance and the landscape of psychic desolation give way to intonations of wonder, meekness, and tenderness. An example of this development is the 1994 poem "To My Daughter" (1996), written in English, in which Brodsky wistfully and a trifle ironically attempts to foresee himself reincarnated after his death—which, he rightly senses, is impending—as an item of "furniture in the corner." He thus tries to imagine away the impossibility of maintaining contact with the daughter whom he will never see grown. Ultimately, the metaphor of the stoic poet transformed into a chair is realized at the end of the poem in Brodsky's resorting to "somewhat wooden lines in our common language"; he intuits, sadly, that his feeble attempt to leave a poetic "message in a bottle" for his child is sure to fail. This intuition may have been prompted by Brodsky's disappointment after a long-awaited reunion with his son.

In 1972 Brodsky had addressed his tender poem "Odissei—Telemaku" (1977; translated as "Odysseus to Telemachus," 1973) to his then four-year-old son, Andrei Basmanov, as the poet faced expulsion from the Soviet Union. In this poem, a battle-weary Brodsky-Odysseus expresses his quiet grief at the insurmountable distances in space, time, and mind that are carrying him ever further away from his son: "I don't know where I am, / what lies ahead. . . . Grow big, my Telemachus, grow. Only the gods know whether we will see each other again." Yet, the reunion between father and son in the mid 1990s was a failure, as they discovered how little they had in common beyond their extreme physical similarity to each other.

With the advent of perestroika, Brodsky's reputation in his homeland began to change, perhaps also assisted by his winning of the Nobel Prize. For the first time since his exile, in 1987 and 1988 Brodsky's poems were published in the journals *Novyi mir* (New World) and *Neva;* the first Soviet editions of his collected works appeared in 1990, followed by many more such publications in Russia over the next several years. In March 1995 Anatolii Aleksandrovich Sobchak, the mayor of St. Petersburg, invited Brodsky to visit his native city the following summer. Brodsky politely declined, saying he had neither the emotional nor the physical resources available to weather such a public journey, although he planned a private one at some future date.

For the most part, the poems of Brodsky's final decade are dark, emotionally blank, intellectually acute, acridly humorous, and frankly self-deprecatory. He foresaw his own death clearly and linked it with the demise of his century, while taking stock of the achievements and failures of both. Such is the case, for example, in his 1989 poem "Fin de Siècle" (1996, Turn of the Century), which begins with the prediction that "The century soon will end, but I'll end sooner. / This is, I fear, not a matter of intuition. / Rather—the influence of nonbeing // on being: of the hunter, so to speak, on his prey, / whether it be the heart's muscle or a brick." In his 1993 poem "Dedal v Sitsilii" (1996; translated as "Daedalus in Sicily," 1996), Brodsky's portrait of the ancient inventor in old age is also a trenchant self-portrait: "All his life he was building something, inventing something. / All his life from these structures, from these inventions / he had to flee." Brodsky looks forward to his death in poem after poem in a matter-of-fact way, without a trace of sentimentality and often with a quiet, wry humor. So resigned to death is Brodsky in these poems that there is a sense that he has come to the end of his road and is ready—almost impatient—to die. He is tired of life and secure in the knowledge that he has imprinted himself as indelibly as possible on human letters. As in his 1993 poem "Peizazh s navodneniem," the flood of time rises to obliterate him, and he "wants to say something, sputtering with excitement, / but out of the multitude of words only one remains: *was*."

Brodsky died of massive heart failure on the night of 28 January 1996 at the age of fifty-five. Shortly afterward, his longtime friend Rein flew in from Moscow to speak at a memorial service in the Morse Auditorium of Boston University, where Brodsky had given his last public reading on 9 April 1995; friends and family remembered Brodsky at a service held at the Cathedral of St. John the Divine in New York City on 8 March 1996. Following a temporary interment at the cathedral, Brodsky's body was moved to its final resting place in the Cimitero di San Michele in Venice, where he had spent many of his happiest days.

Since his death, Brodsky's life and career have been commemorated many times, and two instances in particular stand out. The first occurred on what would have been his fifty-sixth birthday, 24 May 1996. A massive granite slab, inscribed "In this house from 1955 until 1972 lived the poet Iosif Aleksandrovich Brodsky," was unveiled outside the poet's childhood residence at 24 Liteinyi Street in St. Petersburg. Plans are under way for the establishment of a Brodsky literary museum to be housed in the same building. The other commemorative act was the creation, by the poet's widow, Sozzani Brodsky, of the Joseph Brodsky Memorial Fellowship Fund, which enables Russian writers, artists, and scholars to live and work in Italy. The idea for the fellowship had come from Brodsky himself. Shortly before he died, he had appealed to the mayor of Rome for the establishment of a Russian academy in that city. As Brodsky wrote to the mayor, "Italy was a revelation to the Russians; now it can become the source of their renaissance." The fund selected its first recipients, three Russian poets and scholars, in the spring of 2000 and awarded each a three-month fellowship at the American Academy or the French Academy in Rome.

Although the significance and worth of Joseph Brodsky's creative opus continues to be debated to this day, the fact that he challenged many preconceived political, aesthetic, and philosophical sensibilities of his time—in both his poetry and his prose works, in both English and Russian—is indisputable; indeed, precisely for this reason his writings still raise some hackles. Aware of his poetic calling at an early age, he firmly upheld the ideal of free poetic expression throughout his life, seemingly impervious to the potential damage of social pressure, political persecution, and cultural isolation. In his distinctive position as a citizen of two worlds, a master of two literary languages, and an inheritor of two poetic traditions, Brodsky devoted his talent to the creation of a hybrid poetry in which multiple literary tendencies were grafted together: baroque and avant-garde, ancient and metaphysical, English free verse and Russian metered and rhymed verse. The result was the literary rehabilitation of both languages. He freed Russian from the trite phrases of Soviet propaganda and the sentimentality of Russian émigré culture, injecting the language with intellectual heft, jolting rhythms, and disquieting—sometimes even crude—thematic content that was previously unthinkable. At the same time, he attempted to release contemporary American belles lettres from the trend he perceived toward amorphousness and irrelevance, and, by reintroducing the English language to the forgotten discipline of aesthetic form, to reconnect Anglophone poetry with its roots in Western high culture. Whether Brodsky will be judged by posterity to have been entirely successful in these endeavors still remains to be seen. What can be said with certainty, however, is that, thanks to his mastery of the art of detachment, Brodsky modeled an eloquent literary protest to both state-sponsored tyranny and the stifling banality of conformism that will not soon be forgotten.

Interviews:

Sven Birkerts, "The Art of Poetry XXVII: Joseph Brodsky," *Paris Review,* 83 (Spring 1982): 83–126;

Marianna Volkova and Solomon Volkov, *Iosif Brodskii v N'iu-Iorke: Fotoportrety i besedy s poetom* (New York: Slovo, 1990);

Volkov, *Conversations with Joseph Brodsky: A Poet's Journey through the Twentieth Century,* translated by Marian Schwartz (New York & London: Free Press, 1998); Russian version published as *Dialogi s Iosifom Brodskim* (Moscow: Nezavisimaia gazeta, 1998);

Valentina Polukhina, ed., *Bol'shaia kniga inter'viu* (Moscow: Zakharov, 1998; revised and enlarged, 2000);

"Form in Poetry: Joseph Brodsky and Derek Walcott in a Conversation with Bengt Jangfeldt," *Kenyon Review,* 23 (Spring 2001): 185–202;

Peter Vail, "A Conversation with Joseph Brodsky," in *Nativity Poems* (New York: Farrar, Straus & Giroux, 2001), pp. 103–112;

Cynthia L. Haven, *Joseph Brodsky: Conversations* (Jackson: University Press of Mississippi, 2003).

Bibliographies:

A. Ia. Lapidus and K. M. Azadovsky, *Iosif Brodskii: Ukazatel' literatury na russkom iazyke za 1962–1995 gg.* (St. Petersburg: Rossiiskaia natsional'naia biblioteka, 1997; enlarged, 1999);

Valentina Polukhina and Thomas Bigelow, "Selected Bibliography of Brodsky's Essays, Introductions, Reviews and Letters (in English and Russian Only)," *Russian, Croatian and Serbian, Czech and Slovak, Polish Literature,* 47, nos. 3–4 (2000): 409–416;

Viktor Sergeevich Kulle, "Bibliografiia Iosifa Brodskogo" <http://www.liter.net/=/Kulle/brodsky-biliograf.htm>;

Inez Ramsey, "Joseph Brodsky: Bibliography" <http://falcon.jmu.edu/~ramseyil/brodskybib.htm>.

Biographies:

Efim Grigor'evich Etkind, *Protsess Iosifa Brodskogo* (London: Overseas Publications Interchange, 1988);

Iakov Arkad'evich Gordin, comp., *Iosif Brodskii: Tvorchestvo, lichnost', sud'ba (Itogi trekh konferentsii)* (St. Petersburg: Zvezda, 1998);

A. N. Krivomazov, "Biografiia Iosifa Brodskogo" <http://br00.narod.ru>;

Lev Losev and Petr Vail', comps., *Iosif Brodskii: Trudy i dni* (Moscow: Nezavisimaia gazeta, 1998);

Liudmila Shtern, *Brodskii: Osia, Iosif, Joseph* (Moscow: Nezavisimaia gazeta, 2001); expanded and translated by Shtern as *Brodsky: A Personal Memoir* (Fort Worth, Tex.: Baskerville, 2004);

Vadim Semenov, *Iosif Brodskii v severnoi ssylke: Poetika avtobiografizma* (Tartu: Tartu University Press, 2004).

References:

David M. Bethea, *Joseph Brodsky and the Creation of Exile* (Princeton: Princeton University Press, 1994);

Chast' rechi: Al'manakh literatury i iskusstva, special Brodsky issue, no. 1 (1980);

Piotr Fast, "(Pseudo)-Autobiography in Brodsky's Lyrical Poetry," *Auto-Biography Studies,* 11 (Fall 1996): 125–139;

Iakov Arkad'evich Gordin, *Pereklichka vo mrake: Iosif Brodskii i ego sobesedniki* (St. Petersburg: Pushkinskii fond, 2000);

Gordin, comp., and Irina Anatol'evna Murav'eva, ed., *Mir Iosifa Brodskogo: Putevoditel'* (St. Petersburg: Zvezda, 2003);

Cissie Dore Hill, "Remembering Joseph Brodsky," *Hoover Digest,* 4 (2000);

Evgenii Kelebai, *Poet v dome rebenka: Prolegomeny k filosofii tvorchestva Iosifa Brodskogo* (Moscow: Universitet, 2000);

Elina Kolesnikova, *"Politicheskii tekst" Iosifa Brodskogo: Materialy k issledovaniiu* (Moscow: Maks, 2003);

Maija Könönen, *"Four Ways of Writing the City": St. Petersburg-Leningrad as a Metaphor in the Poetry of Joseph Brodsky* (Helsinki: Helsinki University Press, 2003);

D. L. Lakerbai, *Rannii Brodskii: Poetika i sud'ba* (Ivanovo: Ivanovskii gosudarstvennyi universitet, 2000);

R. C. Lamont, "Joseph Brodsky: A Poet's Classroom," *Massachusetts Review,* 15 (1974): 553–577;

Lev Losev, ed., *Poetika Brodskogo: Sbornik statei* (Tenafly, N.J.: Ermitazh, 1986);

Losev and Valentina Polukhina, eds., *Brodsky's Poetics and Aesthetics* (New York: St. Martin's Press, 1990);

Losev and Polukhina, eds., *Joseph Brodsky: The Art of a Poem* (New York: St. Martin's Press, 1998);

Losev and Polukhina, eds., *Kak rabotaet stikhotvorenie Brodskogo: Iz issledovanii slavistov na Zapade* (Moscow: Novoe literaturnoe obozrenie, 2002);

David MacFadyen, *Joseph Brodsky and the Baroque* (Montreal: McGill-Queen's University Press, 1998);

MacFadyen, *Joseph Brodsky and the Soviet Muse* (Montreal: McGill-Queen's University Press, 2000);

Michael Murphy, *Poetry in Exile: A Study of the Poetry of W. H. Auden, Joseph Brodsky and George Szirtes* (London: Greenwich Exchange, 2004);

Valentina Polukhina, *Brodsky through the Eyes of His Contemporaries* (New York: St. Martin's Press, 1992); republished in Russian as *Brodskii glazami sovremennikov* (St. Petersburg: Zvezda, 1997);

Polukhina, "Brodsky's Self-Portrait," in *Russian Literature Since 1917: New Directions,* edited by S. Grahem (London: Macmillan, 1992), pp. 122–135;

Polukhina, *Joseph Brodsky: A Poet for Our Time* (Cambridge & New York: Cambridge University Press, 1989);

Polukhina, "Poeticheskii avtoportret Brodskogo," *Russian, Croatian and Serbian, Czech and Slovak, Polish Literature,* 31 (1992): 375–392;

Polukhina, "The Prose of Joseph Brodsky: A Continuation of Poetry by Other Means," *Russian, Croatian and Serbian, Czech and Slovak, Polish Literature,* 41 (1997): 223–240;

Polukhina, Igor' Fomenko, and A. G. Stepanov, eds., *Poetika Iosifa Brodskogo: Sbornik nauchnykh trudov* (Tver: Tverskoi gosudarstvennyi universitet, 2003);

Andrew Reynolds, "Returning the Ticket: Joseph Brodsky's 'August' and the End of the Petersburg Text?" *Slavic Review,* 64, no. 2 (Summer 2005): 307–332;

David Rigsbee, *Styles of Ruin: Joseph Brodsky and the Postmodernist Elegy,* Contributions to the Study of World Literature, no. 93 (Westport, Conn.: Greenwood Press, 1999);

Russian, Croatian and Serbian, Czech and Slovak, Polish Literature, special Brodsky issues, 37, nos. 2–3 (1995); 47, nos. 3–4 (2000);

Bozena Shallcross, *Through the Poet's Eye: The Travels of Zagajewski, Herbert, and Brodsky* (Evanston, Ill.: Northwestern University Press, 2002);

Natal'ia Strizhevskaia, *Pis'mena, perspektivy: O poezii Iosifa Brodskogo* (Moscow: Graal', 1997);

Tomas Venclova, *Stat'i o Brodskom* (Moscow: Baltrus, Novoe izdatel'stvo, 2005).

Papers:

Joseph Brodsky's papers, representing all of his work up to the time he went into exile (June 1972), are located in the Russian National Library (RNB) in St. Petersburg. His papers from the émigré period are held in New York City by his widow, Maria Sozzani Brodsky, and the Brodsky Estate.

1987 Nobel Prize in Literature Presentation Speech

by Professor Sture Allén, of the Swedish Academy (Translation from the Swedish)

Your Majesties, Your Royal Highnesses, Ladies and Gentlemen,

A characteristic feature of the Nobel Prize winner Joseph Brodsky is a magnificent joy of discovery. He sees connections, words them pithily, sees new connections. Not seldom they are contradictory and ambiguous, often caught in a flash like this: "Memory, I think, is a substitute for the tail we lost for good in the happy process of evolution. It directs our movements. . . ."

In the remarkable writings to which the Swedish Academy has drawn attention this year, poetry as the highest manifestation of life is a theme throughout. It is developed with a poetic brilliance combined with both intellectual beauty and linguistic mastery.

Brodsky is nowadays an American citizen but he was born and grew up in Leningrad, or Peter as he calls the city after its old name of Petersburg. It is a setting in which Pushkin, Gogol and Dostoyevsky worked, and it is a setting whose architecture and ornaments—even in the war-damaged state of the 1940s and 1950s—relate an essential part of the history of our world.

The poet belongs to the classical Russian tradition with names such as Osip Mandelstam, Anna Akhmatova and the Nobel Prize winner Boris Pasternak. At the same time he is a virtuoso renewer of the poetical means of expression. Inspiration comes also from the West, especially the English-language poetry from the metaphysician John Donne to Robert Frost and Wystan Auden.

Latterly Brodsky has begun also to write in English. For him Russian and English are two attitudes to the world. Having both languages at one's disposal is like sitting on the top of an existential hill with a view over two slopes, over humanity's two tendencies of development, he has declared. The east-west background has given him an unusual thematic richness and a multitude of perspectives. Together with the writer's thorough insight into the culture of former epochs it has also conjured up a grand historical vision.

Brodsky has experienced what it means to live. "Life . . . / bares its teeth in a grin at each / encounter." Through all hardships—trial, internal banishment, exile—he has retained his integrity and his faith in literature and language. There are criteria for human behaviour, he says, which come not from society but from literature.

The poet plays a key part as examiner, tester and questioner. Poetry becomes the decisive counterweight against time, the principle of deformation. The poet also becomes the spokesman in the totalitarian society's apparent silence and the open society's stupefying flood of information.

Although Brodsky has defined his standpoint distinctly, political disputes are not prominent in him. The problem is raised to a more general level: man's duty is to live his own life, not a life determined by the categories and norms of others. "Freedom / is when you forget the spelling of the tyrant's name. . . ."

What could be more natural for a writer than to wrestle with the phenomenon of language? This struggle with his own tool is very intense in Brodsky's case. It marks his view of poetry and the poet: "Reading [Dostoyevsky] simply makes one realize that stream of consciousness springs not from consciousness but from a word which alters or redirects one's consciousness." The ultimate power, he maintains, is "the omnivorousness of his language which eventually comes to a point where it cannot be satisfied with God, man, reality, guilt, death, infinity, salvation . . . and then it takes on itself."

Brodsky's view of language also characterizes his view of states and societies: "For empires are held together by neither political nor military forces but by languages. Empires are, first and foremost, cultural entities; and it's language that does the job, not legions."

Language of course provides material for metaphors in poetry: "Late evening in Lithuania. / People drift home from mass, hiding the commas / of candles in parentheses of hands."

For Brodsky poetry stands out as a divine gift. The religious dimension that undeniably is to be found in his writings adheres, however, to no particular creed. Metaphysical and ethical questions are paramount, not doctrines.

Style and mood alternate in this richly orchestrated poetry. Here is the profound cultural analysis in the essays side by side with the rollicking ironies in the poem *History of the Twentieth Century*. Yet, for Joseph Brodsky poetry, even in its mirthful moments, is deadly earnest.

Dear Mr. Brodsky,

It has been my privilege and pleasure to introduce you to the audience in my native tongue. The gist of what I have said is contained, as it were, in a line from one of your recent poems: "Let me tell you: you are okay." In fact, you yourself belong to the history of the Twentieth Century alluded to. On behalf of the Swedish Academy I congratulate you on your remarkable achievements. May I ask you to step forward to receive, from the hands of His Majesty the King, the Nobel Prize for Literature 1987.

[© The Nobel Foundation, 1987.]

Brodsky: Banquet Speech

Brodsky's speech at the Nobel Banquet, 10 December 1987

Your Majesties, Ladies and Gentlemen,

I was born and grew up on the other shore of the Baltic, practically on its opposite grey rustling page. Sometimes on clear days, especially in autumn, standing on a beach somewhere in Kellomaki, a friend would poke his finger north-west across the sheet of water and say: See that blue strip of land? It's Sweden.

He would be joking, of course: because the angle was wrong, because according to the law of optics, a human eye can travel only for something like twenty miles in open space. The space, however, wasn't open.

Nonetheless, it pleases me to think, ladies and gentlemen, that we used to inhale the same air, eat the same fish, get soaked by the same—at times—radioactive rain, swim in the same sea, get bored by the same kind of conifers.

Depending on the wind, the clouds I saw from my window were already seen by you, or vice-versa. It pleases me to think that we have had something in common before we ended up in this room.

And as far as this room is concerned, I think it was empty just a couple of hours ago, and it will be empty again a couple of hours hence. Our presence in it, mine especially, is quite incidental from its walls' point of view. On the whole, from space's point of view, anyone's presence is incidental in it, unless one possesses a permanent—and usually inanimate—characteristic of landscape—of a moraine, say, of a hilltop, of a river bend. And it is the appearance of something or somebody unpredictable within a space well used to its contents that creates the sense of occasion.

So being grateful to you for your decision to award me the Nobel Prize for literature, I am essentially grateful for your imparting to my work an aspect of permanence, of a glacier's debris, let's say, in the vast landscape of literature.

I am fully aware of the danger hidden in this simile: coldness, uselessness, eventual or fast erosion. Yet if it contains a single vein of animated ore—as I, in my vanity, believe it does—then this simile is perhaps prudent.

As long as I am on the subject of prudence, I should like to add that through recorded history, the audience for poetry seldom amounted to more than 1 % of the entire population. That's why poets of antiquity or of the Renaissance gravitated to courts, the seats of power; that's why nowadays they flock to universities, the seats of knowledge. Your academy seems to be a cross between the two; and if in the future—in that time free of ourselves—that 1% ratio will be sustained, it will be, not to a small degree, due to your efforts. In case this strikes you as a dim vision of the future, I hope that the thought about the population explosion may lift your spirits somewhat. Even a quarter of that 1% will make a lot of readers, even today.

So my gratitude to you, ladies and gentlemen, is not entirely egoistical. I am grateful to you for those whom your decisions make and will make read poetry, today and tomorrow. I am not so sure that man will prevail, as the great man and my fellow American once said standing, I believe, in this very room; but I am quite positive that a man who reads poetry is harder to prevail upon than upon one who doesn't.

Of course, it's one hell of a way to get from Petersburg to Stockholm; but then for a man of my occupation the notion of a straight line being the shortest distance between two points has lost its attraction long time ago. So it pleases me to find out that geography in its own turn is also capable of poetic justice.

Thank you!

[© The Nobel Foundation, 1987. Joseph Brodsky is the sole author of the text.]

Press Release: The Nobel Prize in Literature 1987

from the Office of the Permanent Secretary of the Swedish Academy

This year's Nobel Prize winner in Literature was born in Leningrad and lives in New York. Aged only 47 he is one of the youngest ever to have been awarded a Nobel Prize in Literature. A sign of the luminous intensity of his writing is that he has already been translated into more than a dozen languages.

Brodsky is chiefly a poet and essayist. He belongs to the classical Russian tradition with predecessors such as Pushkin and the Nobel Prize winner Pasternak. At the same time he is a masterly renewer of poetical language and poetical forms of expression, inspired by Osip Mandelstam and Anna Achmatova among others.

Another of Brodsky's sources of inspiration is English poetry from the metaphysicist John Donne to W. H. Auden, he who wanted to be a lesser, atlantic Goethe. That language is the stuff that empires are made of is a vital thought with Brodsky as well.

For Brodsky, poetry is a divine gift. The religious dimension that one meets in his work is of a nature that adheres to no creed. Metaphysical and ethical questions are paramount.

The east-west background—literary, geographical, linguistic—has greatly influenced Brodsky's writing. It has given it an unusual wealth of themes and manifold perspectives. Together with the writer's profound insight into the literature of earlier epochs it has also conjured up a grand historical vision.

The change of environment and language after Brodsky had left the Soviet Union in 1972 naturally involved a severe nervous strain for the poet. In the poem "1972" (in the collection *A Part of Speech,* 1980) he depicts how he will gradually lose hair, teeth, consonants, verbs, and endings. Nevertheless he is now engaged on a prolific poetical work in Russian. Parallel with that he takes an active part in the translation of his works into English and sometimes writes directly in this language to great effect. *History of the Twentieth Century* (1986) is a series of poems in a tone of raillery and parody, written with a quite amazing mastery of the English idiom.

All literature really is about what time does to people, Brodsky has said, thus indicating a main theme in his writing. Parting, becoming deformed, growing old, dying are the work of time. Poetry helps us, gives us basically the only possibility of withstanding the pressure of existence.

Poetry's role in the world is another central theme. It may apply to totalitarian societies, in which the poet can become the mouthpiece for those who apparently are silent, or to open societies in which his voice threatens to be drowned in the flood of information. In the brilliant collection of essays *Less Than One* (1980) Brodsky feels his way in towards the core of the problem from various directions. The poet is a word craftsman, a master of language. Poetry is the highest form of language. Brodsky sees it also as the highest form of life. The poet becomes an instrument with a questioning sound.

The Swedish Academy's citation aims at the great breadth in time and space which characterizes Joseph Brodsky's writing and at both the intellectual and sensitive side of this rich and intensely vital work.

[© The Nobel Foundation, 1987.]

Brodsky: Nobel Lecture, 8 December 1987

(Translated from the Russian by Barry Rubin)

I

For someone rather private, for someone who all his life has preferred his private condition to any role of social significance, and who went in this preference rather far—far from his motherland to say the least, for it is better to be a total failure in democracy than a martyr or the crème de la crème in tyranny—for such a person to find himself all of a sudden on this rostrum is a somewhat uncomfortable and trying experience.

This sensation is aggravated not so much by the thought of those who stood here before me as by the memory of those who have been bypassed by this honor, who were not given this chance to address "urbi et orbi," as they say, from this rostrum and whose cumulative silence is sort of searching, to no avail, for release through this speaker.

The only thing that can reconcile one to this sort of situation is the simple realization that—for stylistic reasons, in the first place—one writer cannot speak for another writer, one poet for another poet especially; that had Osip Mandelstam, or Marina Tsvetaeva, or Robert Frost, or Anna Akhmatova, or Wystan Auden stood here, they couldn't have helped but speak precisely for themselves, and that they, too, might have felt somewhat uncomfortable.

These shades disturb me constantly; they are disturbing me today as well. In any case, they do not spur one to eloquence. In my better moments, I deem myself their sum total, though invariably inferior to any one of them individually. For it is not possible to better them on the page; nor is it possible to better them in actual life. And it is precisely their lives, no matter how tragic or bitter they were, that often move me—more often perhaps than the case should be—to regret the passage of time. If the next life exists—and I can no more deny them the possibility of eternal life than I can forget their existence in this one—if the next world does exist, they will, I hope, forgive me and the quality of what I am about to utter: after all, it is not one's conduct on the podium which dignity in our profession is measured by.

I have mentioned only five of them, those whose deeds and whose lot matter so much to me, if only because if it were not for them, I, both as a man and a writer, would amount to much less; in any case, I wouldn't be standing here today. There were more of them, those shades—better still, sources of light: lamps? stars?—more, of course, than just five. And each one of them is capable of rendering me absolutely mute. The number of those is substantial in the life of any conscious man of letters; in my case, it doubles, thanks to the two cultures to which fate has willed me to belong. Matters are not made easier by thoughts about contemporaries and fellow writers in both cultures, poets, and fiction writers whose gifts I rank above my own, and who, had they found themselves on this rostrum, would have come to the point long ago, for surely they have more to tell the world than I do.

I will allow myself, therefore, to make a number of remarks here—disjointed, perhaps stumbling, and perhaps even perplexing in their randomness. However, the amount of time allotted to me to collect my thoughts, as well as my very occupation, will, or may, I hope, shield me, at least partially, against charges of being chaotic. A man of my occupation seldom claims a systematic mode of thinking; at worst, he claims to have a system—but even that, in his case, is borrowing from a milieu, from a social order, or from the pursuit of philosophy at a tender age. Nothing convinces an artist more of the arbitrariness of the means to which he resorts to attain a goal—however permanent it may be—than the creative process itself, the process of composition. Verse really does, in Akhmatova's words, grow from rubbish; the roots of prose are no more honorable.

II

If art teaches anything (to the artist, in the first place), it is the privateness of the human condition. Being the most ancient as well as the most literal form of private enterprise, it fosters in a man, knowingly or unwittingly, a sense of his uniqueness, of individuality, of separateness—thus turning him from a social animal into an autonomous "I." Lots of things can be shared: a bed, a piece of bread, convictions, a mistress, but not a poem by, say, Rainer Maria Rilke. A work of art, of literature especially, and a poem in particular, addresses a man tete-a-tete, entering with him into direct—free of any go-betweens—relations.

It is for this reason that art in general, literature especially, and poetry in particular, is not exactly favored by the champions of the common good, masters of the masses, heralds of historical necessity. For there, where art has stepped, where a poem has been read, they discover, in place of the anticipated consent and unanimity, indifference and polyphony; in place of the resolve to act, inattention and fastidiousness. In other words, into the little zeros with which the champions of the common good and the rulers of the masses tend to operate, art introduces a "period, period, comma, and a minus," transforming each zero into a tiny human, albeit not always pretty, face.

The great Baratynsky, speaking of his Muse, characterized her as possessing an "uncommon visage." It's in acquiring this "uncommon visage" that the meaning of human existence seems to lie, since for this uncommonness we are, as it were, prepared genetically. Regardless of whether one is a writer or a reader, one's task consists first of all in mastering a life that is one's own, not imposed or prescribed from without, no matter how noble its appearance may be. For each of us is issued but one life, and we know full well how it all ends. It would be regrettable to squander this one chance on someone else's appearance, someone else's experience, on a tautology—regrettable all the more because the heralds of historical necessity, at whose urging a man may be prepared to agree to this tautology, will not go to the grave with him or give him so much as a thank-you.

Language and, presumably, literature are things that are more ancient and inevitable, more durable than any form of social organization. The revulsion, irony, or indifference often expressed by literature towards the state is essentially a reaction of the permanent—better yet, the infinite—against the temporary, against the finite. To say the least, as long as the state permits itself to interfere with the affairs of literature, literature has the right to interfere with the affairs of the state. A political system, a form of social organization, as any system in general, is by definition a form of the past tense that aspires to impose itself upon the present (and often on the future as well); and a man whose profession is language is the last one who can afford to forget this. The real danger for a writer is not so much the possibility (and often the certainty) of persecution on the part of the state, as it is the possibility of finding oneself mesmerized by the state's features, which, whether monstrous or undergoing changes for the better, are always temporary.

The philosophy of the state, its ethics—not to mention its aesthetics—are always "yesterday." Language and literature are always "today," and often—particularly in the case where a political system is orthodox—they may even constitute "tomorrow." One of literature's merits is precisely that it helps a person to make the time of his existence more specific, to distinguish himself from the crowd of his predecessors as well as his like numbers, to avoid tautology—that is, the fate otherwise known by the honorific term, "victim of history." What makes art in general, and literature in particular, remarkable, what distinguishes them from life, is precisely that they abhor repetition. In everyday life you can tell the same joke thrice and, thrice getting a laugh, become the life of the party. In art, though, this sort of conduct is called "cliché."

Art is a recoilless weapon, and its development is determined not by the individuality of the artist, but by the dynamics and the logic of the material itself, by the previous fate of the means that each time demand (or suggest) a qualitatively new aesthetic solution. Possessing its own genealogy, dynamics, logic, and future, art is not synonymous with, but at best parallel to history; and the manner by which it exists is by continually creating a new aesthetic reality. That is why it is often found "ahead of progress," ahead of history, whose main instrument is—should we not, once more, improve upon Marx—precisely the cliché.

Nowadays, there exists a rather widely held view, postulating that in his work a writer, in particular a poet, should make use of the language of the street, the language of the crowd. For all its democratic appearance, and its palpable advantages for a writer, this assertion is quite absurd and represents an attempt to subordinate art, in this case, literature, to history. It is only if we have resolved that it is time for Homo sapiens to come to a halt in his development that literature should speak the language of the people. Otherwise, it is the people who should speak the language of literature.

On the whole, every new aesthetic reality makes man's ethical reality more precise. For aesthetics is the mother of ethics; the categories of "good" and "bad" are, first and foremost, aesthetic ones, at least etymologically preceding the categories of "good" and "evil." If in ethics not "all is permitted," it is precisely because not "all is permitted" in aesthetics, because the number of colors in the spectrum is limited. The tender babe who cries and rejects the stranger or who, on the contrary, reaches out to him, does so instinctively, making an aesthetic choice, not a moral one.

Aesthetic choice is a highly individual matter, and aesthetic experience is always a private one. Every new aesthetic reality makes one's experience even more private; and this kind of privacy, assuming at times the guise of literary (or some other) taste, can in itself turn out to be, if not a guarantee, then a form of defense against enslavement. For a man with taste, particularly literary taste, is less susceptible to the refrains and the rhythmical incantations peculiar to any version of political demagogy. The point is not so much that virtue does not constitute a guarantee for producing a masterpiece, as that evil, especially political evil, is always a bad stylist. The more substantial an individual's aesthetic experience is, the sounder his taste, the sharper his moral focus, the freer—though not necessarily the happier—he is.

It is precisely in this applied, rather than Platonic, sense that we should understand Dostoevsky's remark that beauty will save the world, or Matthew Arnold's belief that we shall be saved by poetry. It is probably too late for the world, but for the individual man there always remains a chance. An aesthetic instinct develops in man rather rapidly, for, even without fully realizing who he is and what he actually requires, a person instinctively knows what he doesn't like and what doesn't suit him. In an anthropological respect, let me reiterate, a human being is an aesthetic creature before he is an ethical one. Therefore, it is not that art, particularly literature, is a by-product of our species' development, but just the reverse. If what distinguishes us from other members of the animal kingdom is speech, then literature—and poetry in particular, being the highest form of locution—is, to put it bluntly, the goal of our species.

I am far from suggesting the idea of compulsory training in verse composition; nevertheless, the subdivision of society into intelligentsia and "all the rest" seems to me unacceptable. In moral terms, this situation is comparable to the subdivision of society into the poor and the rich; but if it is still possible to find some purely physical or material grounds for the existence of social inequality, for intellectual inequality these are inconceivable. Equality in this respect, unlike in anything else, has been guaranteed to us by nature. I am speaking not of education, but of the education in speech, the slightest imprecision in which may trigger the intrusion of false choice into one's life. The existence of literature prefigures existence on literature's plane of regard—and not only in the moral sense, but lexically as well. If a piece of music still allows a person the possibility of choosing between the passive role of listener and the active one of performer, a work of literature—of the art which is, to use Montale's phrase, hopelessly semantic—dooms him to the role of performer only.

In this role, it would seem to me, a person should appear more often than in any other. Moreover, it seems to me that, as a result of the population explosion and the attendant, ever-increasing atomization of society (i.e., the ever-increasing isolation of the individual), this role becomes more and more inevitable for a person. I don't suppose that I know more about life than anyone of my age, but it seems to me that, in the capacity of an interlocutor, a book is more reliable than a friend or a beloved. A novel or a poem is not a monologue, but the conversation of a writer with a reader, a conversation, I repeat, that is very private, excluding all others—if you will, mutually misanthropic. And in the moment of this conversation a writer is equal to a reader, as well as the other way around, regardless of whether the writer is a great one or not. This equality is the equality of consciousness. It remains with a person for the rest of his life in the form of memory, foggy or distinct; and, sooner or later, appropriately or not, it conditions a person's conduct. It's precisely this that I have in mind in speaking of the role of the performer, all the more natural for one because a novel or a poem is the product of mutual loneliness—of a writer or a reader.

In the history of our species, in the history of Homo sapiens, the book is anthropological development, similar essentially to the invention of the wheel. Having emerged in order to give us some idea not so much of our origins as of what that sapiens is capable of, a book constitutes a means of transportation through the space of experience, at the speed of a turning page. This movement, like every movement, becomes a flight from the common denominator, from an attempt to elevate this denominator's line, previously never reaching higher than the groin, to our heart, to our consciousness, to our imagination. This flight is the flight in the direction of "uncommon visage," in the direction of the numerator, in the direction of autonomy, in the direction of privacy. Regardless of whose image we are created in, there are already five billion of us, and for a human being there is no other future save that outlined by art. Otherwise, what lies ahead is the past—the political one, first of all, with all its mass police entertainments.

In any event, the condition of society in which art in general, and literature in particular, are the property or prerogative of a minority appears to me unhealthy and dangerous. I am not appealing for the replacement of the state with a library, although this thought has visited me frequently; but there is no doubt in my mind that, had we been choosing our leaders on the basis of their reading experience and not their political programs, there would be much less grief on earth. It seems to me that a potential master of our fates should be asked, first of all, not about how he imagines the course of his foreign policy, but about his attitude toward Stendhal, Dickens, Dostoevsky. If only because the lock and stock of literature is indeed human diversity and perversity, it turns out to be a reliable antidote for any attempt—whether familiar or yet to be invented—toward a total mass solution to the problems of human existence. As a form of moral insurance, at least, literature is much more dependable than a system of beliefs or a philosophical doctrine.

Since there are no laws that can protect us from ourselves, no criminal code is capable of preventing a true crime against literature; though we can condemn the material suppression of literature—the persecution of writers, acts of censorship, the burning of books—we are powerless when it comes to its worst violation: that of not reading the books. For that crime, a person pays with his whole life; if the offender is a nation, it pays with its history. Living in the country I live in, I would be the first prepared to believe that there is a set dependency between a person's material well-being and his literary ignorance. What keeps me from doing so is the history of that country in which I was born and grew up. For, reduced to a cause-and-effect minimum, to a crude formula, the Russian tragedy is precisely the tragedy of a society in which literature turned out to be the prerogative of the minority: of the celebrated Russian intelligentsia.

I have no wish to enlarge upon the subject, no wish to darken this evening with thoughts of the tens of millions of human lives destroyed by other millions, since what occurred in Russia in the first half of the Twentieth Century occurred before the introduction of automatic weapons—in the name of the triumph of a political doctrine whose unsoundness is already manifested in the fact that it requires human sacrifice for its realization. I'll just say that I believe—not empirically, alas, but only theoretically—that, for someone who has read a lot of Dickens, to shoot his like in the name of some idea is more problematic than for someone who has read no Dickens. And I am speaking precisely about reading Dickens, Sterne, Stendhal, Dostoevsky, Flaubert, Balzac, Melville, Proust, Musil, and so forth; that is, about literature, not literacy or education. A literate, educated person, to be sure, is fully capable, after reading this or that political treatise or tract, of killing his like, and even of experiencing, in so doing, a rapture of conviction. Lenin was literate, Stalin was literate, so was Hitler; as for Mao Zedong, he even wrote verse. What all these men had in common, though, was that their hit list was longer than their reading list.

However, before I move on to poetry, I would like to add that it would make sense to regard the Russian experience as a warning, if for no other reason than that the social structure of the West up to now is, on the whole, analogous to what existed in Russia prior to 1917. (This, by the way, is what explains the popularity in the West of the Nineteenth-Century Russian psychological novel, and the relative lack of success of contemporary Russian prose. The social relations that emerged in Russia in the Twentieth Century presumably seem no less exotic to the reader than do the names of the characters, which prevent him from identifying with them.) For example, the number of political parties, on the eve of the October coup in 1917, was no fewer than what we find today in the United States or Britain. In other words, a dispassionate observer might remark that in a certain sense the Nineteenth Century is still going on in the West, while in Russia it came to an end; and if I say it ended in tragedy, this is, in the first place, because of the size of the human toll taken in course of that social—or chronological—change. For in a real tragedy, it is not the hero who perishes; it is the chorus.

III

Although for a man whose mother tongue is Russian to speak about political evil is as natural as digestion, I would here like to change the subject. What's wrong with discourses about the obvious is that they corrupt consciousness with their easiness, with the quickness with which they provide one with moral comfort, with the sensation of being right. Herein lies their temptation, similar in its nature to the temptation of a social reformer who begets this evil. The realization, or rather the comprehension, of this temptation, and rejection of it, are perhaps responsible to a certain extent for the destinies of many of my contemporaries, responsible for the literature that emerged from under their pens. It, that literature, was neither a flight from history nor a muffling of memory, as it may seem from the outside. "How can one write music after Auschwitz?" inquired Adorno; and one familiar with Russian history can repeat the same question by merely changing the name of the camp—and repeat it perhaps with even greater justification, since the number of people who perished in Stalin's camps far surpasses the number of German prison-camp victims. "And how can you eat lunch?" the American poet Mark Strand once retorted. In any case, the generation to which I belong has proven capable of writing that music.

That generation—the generation born precisely at the time when the Auschwitz crematoria were working full blast, when Stalin was at the zenith of his Godlike, absolute power, which seemed sponsored by Mother Nature herself—that generation came into the world, it appears, in order to continue what, theoretically, was supposed to be interrupted in those crematoria and in the anonymous common graves of Stalin's archipelago. The fact that not everything got interrupted, at least not in Russia, can be credited in no small degree to my generation, and I am no less proud of belonging to it than I am of standing here today. And the fact that I am standing here is a recognition of the services that generation has rendered to culture; recalling a phrase from Mandelstam, I would add, to world culture. Looking back, I can say again that we were beginning in an empty—indeed, a terrifyingly wasted—place, and that, intuitively rather than consciously, we aspired precisely to the recreation of the effect of culture's continuity, to the reconstruction of its forms and tropes, toward filling its few surviving, and often totally compromised, forms, with our own new, or appearing to us as new, contemporary content.

There existed, presumably, another path: the path of further deformation, the poetics of ruins and debris, of minimalism, of choked breath. If we rejected it, it was not at all because we thought that it was the path of self-dramatization, or because we were extremely animated by the idea of preserving the hereditary nobility of the forms of culture we knew, the forms that were equivalent, in our consciousness, to forms of human dignity. We rejected it because in reality the choice wasn't ours, but, in fact, culture's own—and this choice, again, was aesthetic rather than moral.

To be sure, it is natural for a person to perceive himself not as an instrument of culture, but, on the contrary, as its creator and custodian. But if today I assert the opposite, it's not because toward the close of the Twentieth Century there is a certain charm in paraphrasing Plotinus, Lord Shaftesbury, Schelling, or Novalis, but because, unlike anyone else, a poet always knows that what in the vernacular is called the voice of the Muse is, in reality, the dictate of the language; that it's not that the language happens to be his instrument, but that he is language's means toward the continuation of its existence. Language, however, even if one imagines it as a certain animate creature (which would only be just), is not capable of ethical choice.

A person sets out to write a poem for a variety of reasons: to win the heart of his beloved; to express his attitude toward the reality surrounding him, be it a landscape or a state; to capture his state of mind at a given instant; to leave—as he thinks at that moment—a trace on the earth. He resorts to this form—the poem—most likely for unconsciously mimetic reasons: the black vertical clot of words on the white sheet of paper presumably reminds him of his own situation in the world, of the balance between space and his body. But regardless of the reasons for which he takes up the pen, and regardless of the effect produced by what emerges from beneath that pen on his audience—however great or small it may be—the immediate consequence of this enterprise is the sensation of coming into direct contact with language or, more precisely, the sensation of immediately falling into dependence on it, on everything that has already been uttered, written, and accomplished in it.

This dependence is absolute, despotic; but it unshackles as well. For, while always older than the writer, language still possesses the colossal centrifugal energy imparted to it by its temporal potential—that is, by all time lying ahead. And this potential is determined not so much by the quantitative body of the nation that speaks it (though it is determined by that, too), as by the quality of the poem written in it. It will suffice to recall the authors of Greek or Roman antiquity; it will suffice to recall Dante. And that which is being created today in Russian or English, for example, secures the existence of these languages over the course of the next millennium also. The poet, I wish to repeat, is language's means for existence—or, as my beloved Auden said, he is the one by whom it lives. I who write these lines will cease to be; so will you who read them. But the language in which they are written and in which you read them will remain not merely because language is more lasting than man, but because it is more capable of mutation.

One who writes a poem, however, writes it not because he courts fame with posterity, although often he hopes that a poem will outlive him, at least briefly. One who writes a poem writes it because the language prompts, or simply dictates, the next line. Beginning a poem, the poet as a rule doesn't know the way it's going to come out, and at times he is very surprised by the way it turns out, since often it turns out better than he expected, often his thought carries further than he reckoned. And that is the moment when the future of language invades its present.

There are, as we know, three modes of cognition: analytical, intuitive, and the mode that was known to the Biblical prophets, revelation. What distinguishes poetry from other forms of literature is that it uses all three of them at once (gravitating primarily toward the second and the third). For all three of them are given in the language; and there are times when, by means of a single word, a single rhyme, the writer of a poem manages to find himself where no one has ever been before him, further, perhaps, than he himself would have wished for. The one who writes a poem writes it above all because verse writing is an extraordinary accelerator of conscience, of thinking, of comprehending the universe. Having experienced this acceleration once, one is no longer capable of abandoning the chance to repeat this experience; one falls into dependency on this process, the way others fall into dependency on drugs or on alcohol. One who finds himself in this sort of dependency on language is, I guess, what they call a poet.

[© The Nobel Foundation, 1987. Joseph Brodsky is the sole author of the text.]

Pearl S. Buck
(26 June 1892 – 6 March 1973)

Tracy Simmons Bitonti

See also the Buck entries in *DLB 9: American Novelists, 1910–1945* and *DLB 102: American Short-Story Writers, 1910–1945, Second Series*.

BOOKS: *East Wind: West Wind* (New York: John Day, 1930; London: Methuen, 1931);

The Good Earth (New York: John Day, 1931; London: Methuen, 1931);

Sons (New York: John Day, 1932; London: Methuen, 1932);

The Young Revolutionist (New York: Friendship, 1932; London: Methuen, 1932);

The First Wife and Other Stories (New York: John Day, 1933; London: Methuen, 1933);

The Mother (New York: John Day, 1934; London: Methuen, 1934);

A House Divided (New York: Reynal & Hitchcock, 1935; London: Methuen, 1935);

House of Earth (New York: Reynal & Hitchcock, 1935; London: Methuen, 1936)—comprises *The Good Earth, Sons,* and *A House Divided;*

The Exile (New York: Reynal & Hitchcock, 1936; London: Methuen, 1936);

Fighting Angel: Portrait of a Soul (New York: Reynal & Hitchcock, 1936; London: Methuen, 1937);

This Proud Heart (New York: Reynal & Hitchcock, 1938; London: Methuen, 1938);

The Chinese Novel (New York: John Day, 1939; London: Macmillan, 1939);

The Patriot (New York: John Day, 1939; London: Methuen, 1939);

Other Gods: An American Legend (New York: John Day, 1940; London: Macmillan, 1940);

Today and Forever: Stories of China (New York: John Day, 1941; London: Macmillan, 1941);

Of Men and Women (New York: John Day, 1941; London: Methuen, 1942);

American Unity and Asia (New York: John Day, 1942); republished as *Asia and Democracy* (London: Macmillan, 1943);

China Sky (New York: Triangle, 1942);

Pearl Buck receiving the 1938 Nobel Prize in Literature from King Gustav V of Sweden (photograph © Bettmann/CORBIS)

The Chinese Children Next Door (New York: John Day, 1942; London: Methuen, 1943);

Dragon Seed (New York: John Day, 1942; London: Macmillan, 1942);

What America Means to Me (New York: John Day, 1943; London: Methuen, 1944);

The Promise (New York: John Day, 1943; London: Methuen, 1944);

The Spirit and the Flesh (New York: John Day, 1944)—comprises *The Exile* and *Fighting Angel: Portrait of a Soul;*

The Dragon Fish (New York: John Day, 1944; London: Methuen, 1946);

China Flight (Philadelphia: Triangle/Blakiston, 1945);

The Townsman, as John Sedges (New York: John Day, 1945; London: Methuen, 1946);

Talk About Russia, by Buck and Masha Scott (New York: John Day, 1945);

Tell the People: Talks with James Yen about the Mass Education Movement (New York: International Mass Education Movement, 1945);

Portrait of a Marriage (New York: John Day, 1945; London: Methuen, 1946);

Pavilion of Women (New York: John Day, 1946; London: Methuen, 1947);

The Angry Wife, as Sedges (New York: John Day, 1947; London: Methuen, 1948);

Far and Near: Stories of Japan, China, and America (New York: John Day, 1947); republished as *Far and Near: Stories of East and West* (London: Methuen, 1949);

How It Happens: Talk About the German People, 1914–1933, by Buck and Erna von Pustau (New York: John Day, 1947);

Peony (New York: John Day, 1948); republished as *The Bondmaid* (London: Methuen, 1949);

The Big Wave (New York: John Day, 1948);

American Argument, by Buck and Eslanda Goode Robeson (New York: John Day, 1949; London: Methuen, 1950);

Kinfolk (New York: John Day, 1949; London: Methuen, 1950);

The Long Love, as Sedges (New York: John Day, 1949; London: Methuen, 1950);

The Child Who Never Grew (New York: John Day, 1950; London: Methuen, 1951; Rockville, Md.: Woodbine House, 1992);

One Bright Day (New York: John Day, 1950); enlarged as *One Bright Day and Other Stories for Children* (London: Methuen, 1952);

God's Men (New York: John Day, 1951; London: Methuen, 1951);

The Hidden Flower (New York: John Day, 1952; London: Methuen, 1952);

Bright Procession, as Sedges (New York: John Day, 1952; London: Methuen, 1952);

Come, My Beloved (New York: John Day, 1953; London: Methuen, 1953);

The Man Who Changed China: The Story of Sun Yat-sen (New York: Random House, 1953; London: Methuen, 1953);

Voices in the House, as Sedges (New York: John Day, 1953; London: Methuen, 1954);

My Several Worlds (New York: John Day, 1954; London: Methuen, 1955);

The Beech Tree (New York: John Day, 1954);

Imperial Woman (New York: John Day, 1956; London: Methuen, 1956);

Letter from Peking (New York: John Day, 1957; London: Methuen, 1957);

Friend to Friend, by Buck and Carlos Romulo (New York: John Day, 1958);

Command the Morning (New York: John Day, 1959; London: Methuen, 1959);

Fourteen Stories (New York: John Day, 1961); republished as *With a Delicate Air and Other Stories* (London: Methuen, 1962);

A Bridge for Passing (New York: John Day, 1962; London: Methuen, 1963);

Satan Never Sleeps (New York: Pocket Books, 1962);

The Living Reed (New York: John Day, 1963; London: Methuen, 1963);

The Joy of Children (New York: John Day, 1964);

Children for Adoption (New York: Random House, 1965);

Death in the Castle (New York: John Day, 1965; London: Methuen, 1966);

The Gifts They Bring: Our Debt to the Mentally Retarded, by Buck and Gweneth T. Zarfoss (New York: John Day, 1965);

For Spacious Skies: Journey in Dialogue, by Buck and Theodore F. Harris (New York: John Day, 1966);

Matthew, Mark, Luke, and John (New York: John Day, 1966);

The People of Japan (New York: Simon & Schuster, 1966; London: Hale, 1968);

The Time Is Noon (New York: John Day, 1967; London: Methuen, 1967);

To My Daughters, With Love (New York: John Day, 1967);

The New Year (New York: John Day, 1968; London: Methuen, 1968);

The Good Deed, and Other Stories of Asia, Past and Present (New York: John Day, 1969; London: Methuen, 1970);

The Three Daughters of Madame Liang (New York: John Day, 1969; London: Methuen, 1969);

Mandala (New York: John Day, 1970; London: Methuen, 1971);

The Kennedy Women (New York: Cowles, 1970; London: Methuen, 1970);

China as I See It, edited by Harris (New York: John Day, 1970; London: Methuen, 1971);

A Gift for the Children (New York: John Day, 1971);

Pearl Buck's America (New York: Bartholomew, 1971);

The Story Bible (New York: Bartholomew, 1971);

China Past and Present (New York: John Day, 1972);

The Goddess Abides (New York: John Day, 1972; London: Eyre Methuen, 1972);

Once Upon a Christmas (New York: John Day, 1972);

Pearl Buck's Oriental Cookbook (New York: Simon & Schuster, 1972);

All Under Heaven (New York: John Day, 1973; London: Eyre Methuen, 1973);

Mrs. Starling's Problem (New York: John Day, 1973);

The Rainbow (New York: John Day, 1974; London: Eyre Methuen, 1976);

Words of Love (New York: John Day, 1974);

East and West (New York: John Day, 1975);

Mrs. Stoner and the Sea, and Other Works (New York: Ace, 1976);

Secrets of the Heart (New York: John Day, 1976);

The Lovers and Other Stories (New York: John Day, 1977);

The Woman Who Was Changed, and Other Stories (New York: Crowell, 1979; London: Eyre Methuen, 1980);

Christmas Day in the Morning (New York: HarperCollins, 2002).

Collection: *Pearl Buck and Education: An Anthology of Her Writings,* edited by Peter J. Conn (Perkasie, Pa.: Pearl S. Buck Foundation, 1996).

TRANSLATION: *All Men Are Brothers [Shui Hu Chuan],* 2 volumes (New York: John Day, 1933).

When Pearl S. Buck won the Nobel Prize in Literature in 1938, she became the third American (and the first American woman) to do so. She also became a figure of controversy. The citation that accompanied the award praised the "rich and generous epic descriptions of Chinese peasant life" in Buck's novels and also singled out *The Exile* (1936) and *Fighting Angel: Portrait of A Soul* (1936), which were biographies of her parents, as "masterpieces." Her detractors, however, felt the Swedish Academy had shown poor judgment in selecting Buck over other writers, such as Theodore Dreiser, whose work they considered of superior literary quality. Despite the critics and the subsequent decline in her literary reputation, Buck enjoyed great popularity with readers during her lifetime, and her novels helped to introduce American readers to Asian culture; as biographer Peter J. Conn comments, "For two generations of Americans, Buck invented China."

Buck was born Pearl Comfort Sydenstricker on 26 June 1892 in Hillsboro, West Virginia. She was the fifth of seven children (but only the second to survive infancy) of Absalom Sydenstricker and Caroline (Carie) Stulting Sydenstricker, who were on furlough after ten years of Presbyterian missionary service in China. The family returned to China when Pearl was three months old, and in 1896 they settled in Chenchiang. Pearl spent much time with her Chinese *amah* (governess), Wang, a widow whom Carie Sydenstricker had rescued from a hard life in the streets. Pearl had a bilingual and bicultural upbringing, and throughout her life she retained the feeling that she did not quite belong in either American or Chinese culture.

In 1910 Pearl returned to the United States to enroll in Randolph-Macon Woman's College in Lynchburg, Virginia, where her older brother, Edgar, was a newspaper editor. She became president of her class and began writing and publishing poems and short stories. After graduation in 1914, she had accepted a job as a teaching assistant to her psychology professor, but a few months later she was called back to China to help care for her seriously ill mother.

On 30 May 1917 Pearl married John Lossing Buck, an agricultural economist who had come to China to work on methods of applying statistical analysis to improve Chinese farming. The couple settled first in Nanhsuchou and then moved to Nanking in 1919 when Lossing Buck was offered a position at Nanking University. On 4 March 1920 Buck gave birth to a daughter, Caroline Grace (Carol). The child suffered from the metabolic disease phenylketonuria (PKU), which had not at that time been diagnosed and which profoundly affected her mental development. Her daughter's condition was a lifelong source of grief, shame, and guilt for Buck. In addition, the discovery and removal of a uterine tumor in July 1920 necessitated a hysterectomy. Buck was also unhappy that Lossing Buck was absorbed in his work and distanced himself emotionally from her and from Carol, in a way that echoed her father's treatment of her mother. The marriage, which seemed to begin happily, soon disintegrated, though it lasted for seventeen years.

Buck's mother died in 1921. To comfort herself, Buck began writing her mother's biography as a private memorial to be shared with family members. Years later, this book became *The Exile.* By the time she had finished writing it, Buck had decided to become a writer. As Conn notes, "Writing offered Pearl an untraditional role and at least a chance of gaining the independence that an extra income might bring. At the same time, it was a career that could be adjusted to make room for her other obligations." Her first professionally published work was an essay titled "In China, Too," which appeared in the *Atlantic* in January 1924 and in which she examines the social changes wrought by modernity in Chinese life and culture, particularly the emerging liberation of Chinese women.

In 1924 the Bucks returned to America so that both of them could enter graduate school at Cornell University and so that they could have Carol's mental retardation properly assessed. At Christmastime they adopted a baby girl, Janice. Buck distinguished herself as she earned her master's degree in English, winning the Laura L. Messenger Memorial Prize for a 140-page essay on "China and the West," submitted under a male pseudonym, "David Barnes." In the spring of 1926, after the Bucks had returned to Nanking, her story "A Chinese Woman Speaks" appeared in two installments in *Asia* magazine.

"A Chinese Woman Speaks" is the story of Kwei-lan, who is betrothed at birth and is brought up well-schooled in the traditional female role of domestic, subservient wife, including endurance of the brutal practice of foot binding. To her amazement and initial dismay, however, she discovers that her Western-educated husband insists on treating her as an equal partner; he unbinds her feet and introduces her to modern Western ideas, which she learns to reconcile with her upbringing. Conn remarks that this story "celebrates tolerance and a version of cultural pluralism," a point of view Buck promoted throughout her life.

The political situation in China was extremely unstable. In March 1927 the Nanking Incident, a violent two days of bloodshed and looting aimed particularly at foreigners, forced the Bucks and other family members (her father and the family of her sister, Grace Yaukey) to flee Nanking after a terrifying day of hiding in the home of one of their servants. They retreated to the Japanese town of Unzen with little more than their lives and some clothing; the losses included the manuscript of Buck's first novel, though Lossing Buck managed to save the survey manuscript on which he was working. They were able to return to China in October 1927, settling in Shanghai; Lossing Buck then returned to Nanking, and Buck and the children joined him in July 1928.

Sometime during this period, Buck acquired a literary agent in America, David Lloyd. She had written to two potential agents, but as she recorded in her 1954 autobiography, *My Several Worlds,* the other agent told her "no one was interested in Chinese subjects." Buck was determined to be a professional writer primarily to improve her financial situation, in order to acquire more independence and especially to provide for the special needs of her daughter Carol, whom she had made the wrenching decision to institutionalize in the Vineland Training School in New Jersey on a trip to the United States in 1929.

During the restoration of her Nanking home, Buck uncovered the manuscript of her biography of her mother. She was also working on a novel titled "Wang Lung." She suggested to Lloyd that "A Chinese Woman Speaks" might constitute part of a novel, together with the story of Kwei-lan's brother, the whole to be titled "Winds of Heaven." During the 1929 trip to America, Buck received word from Lloyd that this book would be published by the John Day Company, under the title *East Wind: West Wind* (1930).

This novel was fairly well received. As Conn notes, "Several reviewers praised the book's authenticity, though the compliment was gratuitous, since few American readers knew enough about China to have any basis for judgment." The book was also the beginning of Buck's long and profitable relationship with the John Day Company and with its president, Richard Walsh, with whom Buck eventually fell in love. She writes in her autobiography that Lloyd had told her the manuscript of *East Wind: West Wind* had been rejected by every other publisher in New York and that he was about to withdraw it when the John Day Company accepted it. Walsh also told her that his editorial staff had been evenly divided in their opinions on the book, and he had cast the deciding vote in favor, "not, he told me quite frankly, because he thought it a very good book, since he did not, but because he believed that he saw evidence there of a writer who might continue to grow."

In May 1930 Buck finished the novel "Wang Lung," which was accepted by the John Day Company, though Walsh requested a title change. He also wanted to defer publication until summer or fall 1931, so that this second book would, as Conn writes, "profit from Pearl's growing reputation as a writer and interpreter of Asia." *East Wind: West Wind* was continuing to receive favorable reviews, and sales were increasing. When word came in January 1931 that the second novel had been chosen (in page proofs) as a selection of the Book-of-the-Month Club, however, guaranteeing a significant sales boost, Walsh revised its publication schedule, and it appeared on 2 March 1931 under his suggested title: *The Good Earth*.

Buck's second novel was a tremendous success and made her famous. As Conn summarizes:

> Every leading newspaper and magazine gave the book a major notice, and almost all the reviews were ecstatic. Sales were so strong that Richard [Walsh] had to borrow copies from the Book-of-the-Month Club inventory to meet bookstore demand. *The Good Earth* would eventually prove to be the best-selling book of both 1931 and 1932.

The Good Earth follows the shifting fortunes of Wang Lung, the son of a poor Chinese farmer, and his wife, O-lan, whom he buys as a slave but who becomes a dedicated helpmate. They have sons, a highly prized commodity in Chinese culture, but also daughters, considered a burden, one of whom is retarded and another whom O-lan deliberately smothers and whose body is left to be eaten by a starving dog during a terrible famine. Wang Lung initially acquires land and money through hard work, but the famine and drought drive his family, along with many others, to desperation. During the looting after a revolutionary uprising, O-lan uncovers a stash of jewels in a Nanking house, the profits from which enable Wang Lung to buy the house of the rich family from whom he had purchased O-lan. When his eldest son falls in love with a concubine Wang Lung had purchased for himself, the patriarch banishes him, and O-lan grows ill and dies. A flood, a revolutionary army, and the disdain of his educated, modernized sons further erode Wang Lung's world.

Critics have offered several reasons for the tremendous popularity of *The Good Earth*. Buck has been praised frequently for creating recognizable, even familiar characters with universal concerns, despite a setting and race that were previously alien to Western readers. Most Americans in 1931 knew little about China, and what they did know was clouded with clichés of the "heathen Chinee" whose cultural differences were regarded with disdain. Buck's depictions of Chinese life, drawn from her own experiences and observations, presented a vivid and sympathetic portrait. Conn also observes that "Underneath its alien details, the novel is a story of the land, a rather familiar American genre," and Depression-era audiences could especially relate to the struggles of farmers. In addition, the novel, like others of the period, "celebrated the traditional American virtue of simplicity."

Buck's next novel, *Sons* (1932), was a sequel to *The Good Earth*, focusing on Wang Lung's three sons, particularly Wang the Tiger, who becomes a fierce warrior. His story was influenced by Buck's translation of the Chinese novel *Shui Hu Chuan* (Water Margin), a text that dates back to at least the Ming dynasty and that chronicles the adventures of a group of twelfth-century bandits. Her translation appeared in 1933 under the title *All Men Are Brothers*. Buck received $30,000 for the rights to serialize *Sons* in *Cosmopolitan*. Lloyd also got Buck a $50,000 offer from M-G-M for movie rights to *The Good Earth*. The highly successful motion-picture version, which deviates in several ways from the novel, was released in 1937 and starred Paul Muni as Wang Lung and Luise Rainer as O-lan, a performance that earned her an Academy Award for best actress.

In 1932 Buck returned to the United States to accept a Pulitzer Prize for *The Good Earth*. She shied away from media attention, however, in part because she wished to keep Carol's existence private. Her newfound income, which was tremendous in the depths of the Depression, enabled her to set up an endowment at Vineland that would take care of Carol for life. *Sons* sold well and received positive reviews, with some commentators judging it even better than *The Good Earth*. Buck began to accept speaking engagements and became involved with causes including civil rights and family planning. In 1933 she received an honorary degree from Yale in the same week that her next book, *The First Wife and Other Stories*, appeared, again to excellent reviews.

Lossing Buck had completed a doctorate while the couple was in America, but he was eager to return to China. In 1933, during the journey, Buck told her husband that the marriage was over and that she wanted to separate. Her love for Walsh, with whom she was so much more compatible than Lossing Buck, had made her continued existence in the marriage unbearable, despite the social stigma that divorce still carried in those days. In 1934 she returned to the United States and a short time later purchased Green Hills Farm in Bucks County, Pennsylvania, which became her home for the rest of her life.

Although Buck was the John Day Company's most lucrative author, the business was struggling financially in the Depression years; she endeavored to help in other capacities by becoming a literary adviser (helping to sign up writers such as Chinese expatriate scholar Lin Yutang) and writing short stories to make money she could invest in the company. She also assisted with *Asia* magazine, of which Walsh had taken over editorship with the intention of turning it into a serious publication, not just a tourist magazine. The financial needs of the company also persuaded Buck to publish *The Mother* (1934), which she had drafted soon after *The Good Earth*. She was reluctant to release this novel, in part because she doubted its quality (she writes in *My Several Worlds* that when she finished it, she threw it in the wastebasket, and it only escaped permanent disposal because the houseboy was away from his duties, giving her the chance to retrieve it later) but also perhaps because she identified too closely with the frustrations of her protagonist. The unnamed heroine is deserted by her husband and left to care for her two sons and a daughter who is going blind. She enjoys sexual passion and desires more children, but remains celibate until one encounter that leaves her pregnant with a child she must abort. The afflicted daughter is married off to a poor family and soon dies from neglect and abuse, while the younger son is executed as a revolutionary; but the older son's wife gives birth to a boy, ending the novel on a somewhat more positive note. In his 1980 study of Buck's work, Paul A. Doyle comments: "The theme is worthy of a truly great work, and the material is there; but Buck has miscalculated the stylistic effects, and she has not thought out nor developed thoroughly enough the characterization of her central figure."

Good advance sales for *The Mother* and the sale of serial rights to *Cosmopolitan* for $35,000 gave the John Day Company a needed boost, though sales soon tapered off despite solid reviews. In the fall of 1934 the company underwent a reorganization and contracted with Reynal and Hitchcock to manufacture Day books. Reynal and Hitchcock published Buck's next novel, *A House Divided*, in January 1935. It is the third part of a trilogy with *The Good Earth* and *Sons*, focusing on Wang the Tiger's son Wang Yuan, who becomes a scholar. Despite his studies at an American university, he is still unsure how best to help China. Once again, reviews were generally positive, but when *A House Divided* was packaged together with *The Good Earth* and *Sons* as *House of Earth* (1935), sales were unimpressive. Buck suspected public interest in stories about China would begin to wane, and she felt she should start writing stories set in America.

In June 1935 Buck traveled to Reno to obtain a divorce; surprisingly, Walsh's wife, Ruby, went with her to give Walsh a divorce at the same time. Buck and Walsh were married the afternoon both divorces became final. Despite the personal scandal, her work continued to be honored: that same year, Buck received the William Dean Howells Medal from the American Academy of Arts and Letters for *The Good Earth* and was elected a member of the National Institute of Arts and Letters. She and Walsh adopted two baby boys, Richard and John, in the spring of 1936, and a year later adopted two more babies, Edgar and Jean.

Since Buck's father had died in 1931 and could no longer be harmed by the unflattering portrait of him in the work, Buck decided she could publish her biography of her mother. *The Exile* was released in 1936 and was such a success that she produced the sequel, *Fighting Angel*, soon afterward. Buck depicts her father's religious zeal, which caused him to neglect his wife and family, and his misogyny; she also chronicles the loneliness and disillusion of her mother, who was isolated from everything familiar and suffering the losses of her children, her own illnesses, and her husband's disdain. The books are not only a portrait of Buck's parents but also a depiction of Protestant missionary life in China at the end of the nineteenth century. Doyle praises these "decidedly superior biographies" and suggests that although they have been neglected as part of the decline of Buck's literary reputation, they deserve attention "not only as examples of excellent biographical writing but also as pictures of two completely rendered Americans and of a historical phenomenon characteristic of a particular time and place."

Buck's next novel, *This Proud Heart* (1938), continued her treatment of the struggles of women, this time in an American setting. The heroine, Susan Gaylord, is a sculptor who refuses to allow her incompatible husband to prevent her from pursuing her art. She studies with a mentor named David Barnes, who encourages her talent but also cautions her of the difficulties faced by women artists in gaining any respect from most male colleagues. After Susan's husband dies, she moves to Paris to study with a great master; she is sidetracked by a second marriage, to a wealthy painter named Blake Kinnaird, but eventually returns to her work on her "American Procession," a series of sculptures of women. When Blake is alienated by her resulting success, she moves out; he seeks reconciliation, but she decides to continue on her own. Reviewers commented that Susan's seemingly inexhaustible talents were too good to be true (or tolerable), and that Buck's prose style was rather awkward. Biographer Nora Stirling considers this novel "a downward step" in style from Buck's earlier books: "Studded with clichés and repetitions, lacking in variety and telling imagery, it remains curiously reminiscent of the radio serials, popular in the Thirties." Doyle comments, "Stylistically, *This Proud Heart* is a disaster; thematically, it has several rewarding moments."

News stories reported that when Buck heard she had won the Nobel Prize in 1938, she first said in Chinese, "wo pu hsiang" (I don't believe it), and then in English, "That's ridiculous. It should have gone to Dreiser." Many critics agreed. Although Buck writes in *My Several Worlds* that previous Nobel winner Sinclair Lewis told her not to let anyone minimize her winning of the prize, and others such as Carl Van Doren, Dorothy Canfield Fisher, and William Lyon Phelps defended her work, the prevailing attitude in literary circles was one of hostility. Doyle notes, "It was claimed that she was too youthful [at forty-six], that she had written too few important books to be considered of major stature, and that no woman writer deserved the award." Her immense popularity also counted against her; Conn points out that despite the enthusiastic reviews her works received in the daily and weekly press, Buck "was routinely ignored or belittled" by "the highbrow cultural gatekeepers who wrote for the serious quarterlies." In "Wang Lung's Children" (*New Republic*, 10 May 1939), Malcolm Cowley expressed his opinion that Buck's reputation suffered because of her popular success; the intellectuals felt that because she had been acclaimed first by the public and not by the literati, her work could not be of the same caliber as those whose reputations had begun first with the intellectuals. Among the charges leveled at Buck by her detractors was that her prose style was facile, clumsy, clichéd; but Conn offers a defense for this criticism: "She often said that she first composed her novels mentally in Chinese, and then translated them into English. Her stylized and often stilted prose originated in her effort to reproduce in English the altogether different cadences of Chinese speech."

Others felt, as the anonymous reviewer for *Time* (6 March 1939) did, that "The influence of her writing far transcends its importance as literature." Some critics believe that the awarding of the prize to Buck in 1938, amid the growing threats of fascism and war, was as much a political statement as an endorsement of her literary talent; as Conn writes,

> Pearl had established herself as a powerful voice against the rising tide of international violence and totalitarianism. In her novels, and also in literally scores of essays, reviews, and lectures, she had spoken out on behalf of liberal democracy, self-determination, and ideological and racial tolerance. . . . In a decade when writers on both the left and right insisted on the social responsibility of the artist, Pearl's exertions seemed exemplary.

Doyle, however, disagrees with the assumption that the prize was a political one: "The fact that Pearl Buck's writing exemplified a 'one-world' humanitarian sympathy, while it unquestionably increased Buck's reading audience, does not appear to have swayed the award committee to any appreciable extent." He does suggest, however, that another reason for her selection was that she was one of the most popular American writers read overseas: "The impact of an American writer on foreign countries is always a fundamental factor that influences the Nobel Committee's judgment—a fact often forgotten or deliberately ignored by American literary critics."

Buck's selection nevertheless tainted the reputation of the prize in some literary circles. Stirling quotes Robert Frost's remark that "If *she* can get it anybody can." In a 22 February 1950 letter to Joan Williams, William Faulkner (whose own Nobel Prize in Literature for 1949 was awarded in December 1950) wrote about the possibility of his own nomination: "I dont want it. I had rather be in the same pigeon hole with Dreiser and Sherwood Anderson, than with Sinclair Lewis and Mrs. Chinahand Buck." In *Intellectual America: Ideas on the March* (1941), Oscar Cargill countered this disdain:

> To reflective Americans outside the [literary] fraternity, to the "barbs" at least, the prize seemed well given as a reminder that pure aestheticism is not everything in letters. If the standard of her work was not so uniformly high as that of a few other craftsmen, what she wrote had universal appeal and a comprehensibility not too frequently matched.

In his presentation speech on 10 December 1938, Per Hallström, permanent secretary of the Swedish Academy, praised not only *The Good Earth*, the novel that had made Buck famous, but also the "vividly individualized" heroine of *The Mother*: "The mother is the most finished of Pearl Buck's Chinese female figures, and the book is one of her best." He added, however, that "in character descriptions and the storyteller's art she is at her best in the two biographies of her parents," which "should be called classics in the fullest sense of the word." Near the end of his speech, he said that the prize was awarded "for the notable works which pave the way to a human sympathy passing over widely separated racial boundaries and for the studies of human ideals which are a great and living art of portraiture."

At the Nobel Banquet at the City Hall in Stockholm that evening, Bertil Lindblad, director of the Stockholm Observatory at Saltsjöbaden, remarked to Buck, "you have in your literary works, which are of the highest artistic quality, advanced the understanding and the appreciation in the Western world of a great and important part of mankind, the people of China. You have taught us by your works to see the individuals in that great mass of people." He concluded, "it is of the greatest importance that the peoples of the earth learn to understand each other as individuals across distances and frontiers. When works of literature succeed in this respect they are certainly in a very direct way idealistic in the sense in which this word was meant by Alfred Nobel."

The topic of Buck's Nobel lecture, which was published in 1939, was *The Chinese Novel*. It was a revision of a talk she had given at Nanking years earlier, in which she endeavored to draw attention to a literary tradition as rich and significant as those of European and American cultures. In *My Several Worlds,* she expresses her initial misgivings about addressing the distinguished members of the Swedish Academy:

> What did I know to present to them? I had by then lived only long enough in the United States to realize that I knew too little of my own people, that it would take years of living and observation before in our patternless society I could discern the causes behind what we felt and said and did. It would be presumptuous to try to speak so soon. Moreover, I had been reminded often enough of my ignorance. Even when the Pulitzer Prize had been awarded *The Good Earth,* certain critics had objected to so American an award being given to a book about Chinese peasants, written by a woman, and worse than that, a woman who had never lived in her own country.

Sensitive to the potential criticism, Buck therefore chose "a subject I did know well, and about which very little is known by most westerners."

There is a lingering critical and popular misconception that Buck won the Nobel solely for *The Good Earth*. Even Buck's friend James A. Michener repeated this misinformation as late as 1992, in his introduction to a new edition of Buck's 1950 book *The Child Who Never Grew*. Buck reports in *My Several Worlds* that at a luncheon given by her Swedish publisher, she met Swedish novelist Selma Lagerlöf, a previous Nobel recipient who had served on the committee that selected Buck for the prize; Lagerlöf told Buck that she had cast her vote on the strength of *The Exile* and *Fighting Angel*. Buck also writes in her autobiography that when her publishers tried to emphasize that the award had been given for the body of her work, "orders began to come in from bookstore customers for a book, purportedly by me, entitled *The Body of Her Work*."

In *My Several Worlds*, Buck calls the four days she spent in Stockholm for the awarding of the prize "my most perfect single recollection." She comments on the reaction:

> The award came, as I have said before, at a time when I needed it most. I had met that difficult period of a writer's life, when the reaction, which the American public invariably bestows upon anyone whom it has discovered and praised, had set in. Since the praise is always too much and too indiscriminate the opposing criticism and contempt are also too much and too indiscriminate. My head had not been turned by the praise and its excess had only amused and touched me, but the rudeness of unjust criticism, a sort of stone-throwing which became merely imitative once it had begun, did temporarily destroy my confidence.

She adds, however, "The warmth of the Swedish people, combined with their dignity and their calm, restored my soul."

After receiving the prize, Buck was in even greater demand for speaking engagements, articles, and reviews. She maintained her writing schedule and reserved her mornings for regular writing time, producing some 2,500 words a day and rarely making major revisions. She also continued to read and respond to novel manuscripts for the John Day Company.

Her first novel after the Nobel Prize was *The Patriot* (1939). It follows the protagonist, Wu I-wan, son of a wealthy Shanghai banker, through many of the political and military events of the war between China and Japan in the 1930s, to such an extent that a reviewer for *The New Yorker* (4 March 1939) called the book a "documentary." Conn writes that "In a sense, the war came to Pearl's rescue as a writer, by authorizing her to return to the Chinese material she knew best."

She returned to an American subject, however, for her next novel, *Other Gods: An American Legend* (1940), a satire inspired in part by the fame of Charles Lindbergh. In the novel, Bert Holm, a handsome but fairly simple individual, succeeds in climbing one of the highest mountains in the world and is subsequently made a national idol by opportunistic image makers and the masses who are eager to have such a hero to follow. The main theme is the cult of celebrity in America. Reviews and sales were both mediocre at best.

From the late 1930s, Buck's priorities began to shift away from writing fiction and more toward humanitarian and philanthropic activities. Conn suggests that a main reason for this shift, besides her genuine desire to combat war and injustice in a more direct and "useful" fashion, was that "both her reputation and her self-confidence had been damaged beyond remedy by the Nobel Prize." Whereas before she had been "merely one of a large number of popular writers" such as Margaret Mitchell, "When the Swedish Academy abruptly elevated her to a supreme literary position, the decision represented a challenge, even an insult, to established highbrow opinion," and the resulting backlash reinforced her own doubts and insecurities about the quality of her work.

She did not, however, abandon fiction completely. In 1941 she published *Today and Forever,* a collection of short stories, many of which celebrate brave Chinese women warriors. A reviewer for *The Times Literary Supplement* (*TLS;* 8 February 1941) commented, "popular or too popular in manner though these stories are, they are at the same time very illuminating in their way." Buck's next novel, *Dragon Seed* (1942), appeared just after the attack on Pearl Harbor that brought the United States into World War II. Conn calls this timing "politically and commercially lucky," because "Americans were eager for encouraging stories about their new Asian allies." The book sold well, and M-G-M purchased movie rights. The novel traces the impact of the Japanese invasion of China on the family of farmer Ling Tan. It again documents historical events, particularly the December 1937 "rape of Nanking," in which Japanese troops burned most of the city, murdered Chinese soldiers and civilians alike, and raped some twenty thousand Chinese women. The story celebrates the courage of the townspeople and farmers who fight back. Reviews were good, though some critics complained about the didacticism and the awkward prose style. The reviewer for *Time* (26 January 1942) called the novel "the first sharp, fictional account of resistance in Occupied China." Her next novel, *The Promise* (1943), about the British betrayal of their Chinese allies in Burma, was, like its predecessor, intended as polemic.

Buck's political activism was such that the FBI had begun keeping a file on her in 1937, when she expressed her support for the Spanish Loyalists and for the Women's International League for Peace and Freedom. During World War II, her support for racial equality escalated, as did FBI interest in her. Conn notes, "As a prominent writer and an outspoken advocate for civil rights, Pearl met two of the main criteria [FBI director J. Edgar] Hoover used to identify suspicious persons." Buck was also one of the few white Americans who publicly

XV/10pt.

Today I am weary and spent, My Sister. In my heart it is as though a harp string had been too tightly drawn for many days and then suddenly relaxed, so that music is dead in it.

The hour have dreaded is over! No, I will not say how it went. I will tell you of the whole matter, and then you may judge of it for yourself. As for me — but I will not tell of the end before the beginning.

We sent the messenger to our parents, bearing our request that we be allowed to present ourselves the next day at noon. He returned saying that our father had left home for Tientsin as soon as he heard of my brother's arrival. Thus did he avoid the difficult moment — thus has he ever avoided decisions! But our mother signified her readiness to received my brother and me She made no mention of the foreign one, but after we had talked of this together, we decided to ignore the omission, although I doubted the wisdom of this. But my voice was but a feeble one in opposition, when my husband and my brother spoke together.

I went first, therefore, the next day, at the appointed hour, which was noon; a servant bore the gifts before me. My brother had chosen these gifts in

Page from a revised typescript for Buck's first novel, East Wind: West Wind *(1930), which depicts the experiences of a Chinese woman and her brother, who have been raised traditionally, and the woman's Western-educated husband (Harry Ransom Humanities Research Center, University of Texas at Austin)*

opposed the internment of Japanese Americans during the war.

Because she feared that she was becoming indelibly known as exclusively a writer about China, and because she felt that her gender as well as her subject matter contributed to her rejection by the literary establishment, Buck decided to begin publishing some of her novels under the male pseudonym "John Sedges." Her first novel as Sedges was *The Townsman,* which appeared in May 1945. It is a nineteenth-century frontier tale chronicling the settlement efforts of Jonathan Goodliffe in the small town of Median, Kansas. The novel also features a positively portrayed black family, the Parrys, to whom Jonathan is a friend. The novel was a moderate critical success, and her second Sedges novel, *The Angry Wife* (1947), also preached racial tolerance in a tale of two brothers who fought on opposite sides in the Civil War.

Her next novel under her own name was *Portrait of a Marriage* (1945), which depicts the relationship of William, a wealthy painter, and Ruth, a rural Pennsylvania farm woman, whose only common bond seems to be their unexplained mutual passion. Reviews and sales were, again, lackluster. When she went back to a Chinese subject with *Pavilion of Women* (1946), she fared better, at least in terms of sales; this novel, in which the upper-class Chinese wife Madame Wu declares her independence from her husband and befriends an excommunicated Catholic priest, was a Literary Guild selection. Reviews, while generally positive, were also patronizing in their emphasis on this book being "a woman's novel," by a woman, for women, about women's concerns, and therefore by implication incapable of possessing any real literary merit.

Besides the significance of women's experiences, another topic important to Buck was that of adoption, particularly of mixed-race and/or illegitimate children, who were particularly stigmatized and considered unadoptable. As she became more outspoken on the subject, people wanting to adopt and people seeking help finding homes for their "unadoptable" children began contacting her for assistance. In 1949 she established Welcome House, an international and interracial adoption agency. Buck is credited with coining the term "Amerasian" for children of Asian and American parentage, of whom there was a boom after World War II, mainly fathered by American servicemen. She also wrote several books for children, including *The Big Wave* (1948), for which she received the Children's Book Award of the Child Study Association of America. In 1952 Buck and Walsh adopted Henriette, born to an African American serviceman and a German woman, and in 1957 another daughter, Cheiko, child of an African American father and a Japanese mother.

In 1950 Buck finally broke her long silence about the existence and condition of her daughter Carol. Her article "The Child Who Never Grew" was published in *Ladies' Home Journal* in May of that year, and a longer version was published as a book, with all royalties going to the Vineland Training School. Buck wrote openly about the anguish she had experienced over her daughter's condition, while asserting the value of Carol's life. As Martha M. Jablow writes in an introduction to the 1992 edition of the book, Buck "was the first prominent person to acknowledge publicly a child with mental retardation," which at the time still carried tremendous social stigma. Such a revelation by a figure so famous "did not erase entirely" the stigma, but it was "a watershed." Jablow notes, "In the 1990s' tell-all atmosphere of celebrities baring their most private scars, it may be difficult to appreciate how much courage it took for Pearl Buck to speak out in 1950. But it was a painfully courageous act at that time." (An afterword by Janice Walsh in the 1992 edition records that Carol Buck lived comfortably at Vineland until her death from lung cancer at the age of seventy-two.)

Conn writes that Buck's later novels, which include *The Hidden Flower* (1952), about the doomed marriage of an American man and a Japanese woman, "were simply hastier, more lackluster versions of what she had written twenty years earlier." The magazine market for her stories also began to decline in the 1950s. In 1953 Walsh, her greatest supporter, suffered a stroke, and his health continued to worsen until his death in 1960. The publication of Buck's autobiography, *My Several Worlds,* in 1954 was, however, a needed lift; it sold well, was a main selection of the Reader's Digest Book Club, and earned positive reviews, several of which labeled it one of her best works.

Those commitments were expressed not only in Buck's novels but also in several nonfiction works. *Talk About Russia* (1945) was the story of Magnitogorsk, a successfully industrialized steelmaking city in the Soviet Union, as told through the experiences of Masha Scott, a Russian woman of peasant stock who had worked there. *Tell the People: Talks with James Yen about the Mass Education Movement* (1945) focused on Yen (Yan Yangchu), leader of the Mass Education Movement in China, an ambitious project to ameliorate poverty by reducing illiteracy among the peasantry. *American Argument* (1949) was a discussion with Eslanda Goode Robeson, wife of African American actor Paul Robeson, on a variety of social and political topics.

Except for the positive reception of *My Several Worlds,* in the early 1950s Buck's career was in decline. She began blaming her long-faithful agent, Lloyd, accusing him of neglecting his duties toward her, and she looked for new representation.

Buck's 1956 novel, *Imperial Woman,* is a fictionalized biography of one of the most powerful women in Chinese history: the Empress Dowager, Tz'u-hsi. Buck's portrayal was more sympathetic than that of the male writers and historians whose work had preceded hers. The novel *Command the Morning* (1959) focuses on the work of atomic scientists; nuclear disarmament was another of the public causes for which Buck was an activist.

In the fall of 1963 Buck wrote another novel in which, as Conn notes, a primary goal was once again "to educate American readers about a country and culture they did not know." This time the country was Korea, and her novel *The Living Reed* traces the experiences of four generations of the Kim family, from the first Korean–U.S. treaty in 1883 to the end of World War II. Conn reports that "reviews of the book indicated that her popularity remained highest among women readers."

Also in 1963, Buck met Theodore F. Harris and began a relationship that she subsequently spent much time defending. Harris, some forty years younger than Buck, was an Arthur Murray dance instructor she initially hired to teach her daughters to dance. He soon became her constant companion and a source of much scandal, alienating family and friends. In 1964 she installed Harris as president of the newly formed Pearl S. Buck Foundation, developed to further the work of Welcome House in assisting Amerasian children, particularly by providing sponsorship funding to children in Asia. In its early days the foundation struggled with financial mismanagement and accusations against Harris; aside from the widespread belief that he was an opportunist taking advantage of a rich and lonely old woman, there were allegations that he misappropriated funds, molested several Korean boys brought to the foundation, and used Buck's prestige as a cover to smuggle narcotics in her luggage on overseas trips. While Buck steadfastly refused to credit any of the accusations, matters came to a head when an exposé by associate editor Greg Walter titled "The Dancing Master" appeared in the July 1969 issue of *Philadelphia Magazine*. The ensuing publicity caused Harris to step down as president of the foundation, and Buck withdrew from its daily operations after it reorganized with new directors. She continued to defend and support Harris to the end of her life, cooperating with him on a two-volume biography of her (1969, 1971) and other works.

Buck continued to receive awards and honors, more for her philanthropic work than for her writing. In 1965, for example, she received four such honors: the Sojourner Truth Award from the Business and Professional Women of Philadelphia; induction into the Women's Hall of Fame at the New York World's Fair; the Humanitarian Award from the Jewish philanthropic organization Brith Shalom; and a special citation from the Women's International League for Peace and Freedom.

In 1967 Buck published what was perhaps her most personal novel, *The Time Is Noon*. It is a thinly veiled account of her life through the end of her first marriage: the heroine is unhappily married to a loutish farmer with whom she has a retarded daughter; she has witnessed the loveless marriage of her parents, a self-righteous preacher and his emotionally suffocated wife; and she falls in love with an aviator, with whom she has more in common than her husband. Buck had actually written this novel in the early 1930s, wanting to "get rid of all my life until that moment," as she wrote in *For Spacious Skies: Journey in Dialogue* (1966), but had set it aside on Walsh's advice that it might create too much controversy. Her decision to finally publish it was motivated in part by her desire to make money for the foundation.

Buck's 1968 novel, *The New Year,* is another example of her use of fiction to assist her humanitarian goals. Successful politician Chris Winters gives in to his conscience, acknowledging the son he fathered with a Korean woman when he was a serviceman during the Korean War. He and his wife, Laura, adopt the boy; not only does Laura manage to give her husband's illegitimate, biracial offspring a loving welcome, but their story actually improves Chris's chances in the gubernatorial race rather than harming them. Conn notes the "relentlessly optimistic tone" of this novel: "Rather than offering a realistic account of the sufferings of Amerasian children and the hazards of adoption, *The New Year* merely celebrates Pearl's dreams of justice and reconciliation."

Buck's last novel about China was *The Three Daughters of Madame Liang,* published in 1969. It was a Book-of-the-Month Club choice and a Reader's Digest "Condensed Book" selection. Madame Liang is a Shanghai restaurateur whose daughters—a doctor, a musician, and a painter—are recalled from the United States by the Chinese government and encounter the chaos of the Cultural Revolution.

Buck continued producing stories, children's books, and nonfiction until her death from lung cancer on 6 March 1973. She is buried at Green Hills Farm, and her tombstone bears the name "Pearl Sydenstricker" in Chinese characters. The work of the Pearl S. Buck Foundation continues, and critical and public interest in Buck's writing has been renewed somewhat by centennial celebrations in 1992, Conn's biography in 1996, and the re-emergence of *The Good Earth* as talk-show host Oprah Winfrey's book club selection for the fall of 2004. Jane M. Rabb, in her analysis of the reasons for Buck's critical neglect among literary and feminist scholars, notes that "The current academic enthusiasm for the multicultural and the interdisciplinary should revive interest in the best works of Buck, who is nothing if not multicultural and interdisciplinary." Conn concludes that Buck's "best work, by and large, was probably her nonfiction" and that her fiction was hobbled by the way she "used her novels as political and educational instruments, exchanging the challenges of novelistic art for the easier satisfactions of melodrama, propaganda, and protest." Nevertheless, he argues that "her achievements as a writer remain considerable—surely more notable than her virtually complete neglect by scholars and critics would imply."

Interview:

Bo Yu, "An Interview with Mrs. Buck," *Xiandai (Modern Times)*, 4, no. 5 (1934): 891–898.

Bibliography:

Lucille S. Zinn, "The Works of Pearl S. Buck: A Bibliography," *Bulletin of Bibliography*, 36 (October–December 1979): 194–208.

Biographies:

Cornelia Spencer [Grace Sydenstricker Yaukey], *The Exile's Daughter: A Biography of Pearl S. Buck* (New York: Coward-McCann, 1944);

Theodore F. Harris, *Pearl S. Buck: A Biography*, 2 volumes (New York: John Day, 1969, 1971);

Irvin Block, *The Lives of Pearl Buck: A Tale of China and America* (New York: Crowell, 1973);

Nora Stirling, *Pearl Buck: A Woman in Conflict* (Piscataway, N.J.: New Century, 1983);

Beverly Rizzon, *Pearl S. Buck: The Final Chapter* (Palm Springs: ETC, 1989);

Warren Sherk, *Pearl S. Buck: Good Earth Mother* (Philomath, Ore.: Drift Creek Press, 1992);

Peter J. Conn, *Pearl S. Buck: A Cultural Biography* (New York: Cambridge University Press, 1996).

References:

Phyllis Bentley, "The Art of Pearl S. Buck," *English Journal*, 24 (December 1935): 791–800;

Henry Seidel Canby, "*The Good Earth*: Pearl Buck and Nobel Prize," *Saturday Review of Literature* (19 November 1938): 8;

Oscar Cargill, *Intellectual America: Ideas on the March* (New York: Macmillan, 1941);

George A. Cevasco, "Pearl Buck and the Chinese Novel," *Asian Studies*, 5 (December 1967): 437–450;

Paul A. Doyle, *Pearl S. Buck* (New York: Twayne, 1965; revised, 1980);

Doyle, "Pearl S. Buck's Short Stories: A Survey," *English Journal*, 55 (January 1966): 62–68;

Xiongya Gao, *Pearl Buck's Chinese Women Characters* (Selinsgrove, Pa.: Susquehanna University Press / London & Cranbury, N.J.: Associated University Presses, 2000);

Ann LaFarge, *Pearl Buck* (New York: Chelsea House, 1988);

Karen J. Leong, *The China Mystique: Pearl S. Buck, Anna May Wong, Mayling Soong, and the Transformation of American Orientalism* (Berkeley: University of California Press, 2005);

Kang Liao, *Pearl S. Buck: A Cultural Bridge Across the Pacific* (Westport, Conn.: Greenwood Press, 1997);

"The Nobel Prize in Literature 1938," *Nobelprize.org* <http://nobelprize.org/literature/laureates/1938/index.html>;

Jane M. Rabb, "Who's Afraid of Pearl S. Buck?" in *The Several Worlds of Pearl S. Buck: Essays Presented at a Centennial Symposium, Randolph-Macon Woman's College, March 26–28, 1992*, edited by Elizabeth J. Lipscomb, Frances E. Webb, and Peter Conn (Westport, Conn.: Greenwood Press, 1994), pp. 103–110;

Mamoru Shimizu, "On Some Stylistic Features, Chiefly Biblical, of *The Good Earth*," *Studies in English Literature* (Tokyo), English Number (1964): 117–134;

Yüh-chao Yü, *Pearl S. Buck's Fiction: A Cross-Cultural Interpretation* (Nankang, Taipei: Institute of American Culture, Academia Sinica, 1981).

Papers:

Pearl S. Buck donated her manuscripts to the Pearl S. Buck Birthplace Foundation, the organization that maintains her Hillsboro home. They are housed in the Annie Merner Pfeiffer Library at West Virginia Wesleyan College. There are also Buck papers at the Lipscomb Library of Randolph-Macon Woman's College, Lynchburg, Virginia.

1938 Nobel Prize in Literature Presentation Speech

by Per Hallström, Permanent Secretary of the Swedish Academy

Pearl Buck once told how she had found her mission as interpreter to the West of the nature and being of China. She did not turn to it as a literary speciality at all; it came to her naturally.

"It is people that have always afforded me my greatest pleasure and interest," she said, "and as I live among the Chinese, it has been the Chinese people. When I am asked what sort of people they are, I cannot answer. They are not this or that, they are just people. I can no more define them than I can define my own relatives and kinsmen. I am too near to them and I have lived too intimately with them for that."

She has been among the people of China in all their vicissitudes, in good years and in famine years, in the bloody tumults of revolutions and in the delirium of Utopias. She has associated with the educated classes and with primordially primitive peasants, who had hardly seen a Western face before they saw hers. Often she has been in deadly peril, a stranger who never thought of herself as a stranger; on the whole, her outlook retained its profound and warm humanity. With pure objectivity she has breathed life into her knowledge and given us the peasant epic which has made her world-famous, *The Good Earth* (1931).

As her hero she took a man who led the same existence as his forefathers had during countless centuries, and who possessed the same primitive soul. His virtues spring from one single root: affinity with the earth, which yields its crops in return for a man's labours.

Wang Lung is created from the same stuff as the yellow-brown earth in the fields, and with a kind of pious joy he bestows upon it every ounce of his energy. The two belong to each other in origin, and they will become one again with the death he will meet with tranquility. His work is also a duty done, and thus his conscience is at rest. Since dishonesty avails nothing in his pursuits, he has become honest. This is the sum total of his moral conceptions, and equally few are his religious ones, which are almost entirely comprehended in the cult of ancestor-worship.

He knows that man's life is a gleam of light between two darknesses; from the one behind him runs the chain of forefathers from father to son, and the chain must not be broken by him, if he is not to lose his dim hope of survival in a surmised, unknown region. For then would expire a spark of the life-fire of the race, which each individual man has to care for.

And thus the story begins with Wang Lung's marriage and his dreams of sons in the house. Of his wife, O'Lan, he does not dream, for—as is proper and fitting—he has never seen her. She is a slave at the great house in the neighbouring town and cheap to buy, since she is said to be ugly. For that reason she has probably been left alone by the young sons of the house, and to this the bridegroom attaches great value.

Their life together is happy, for the wife proves to be an excellent helpmate, and the children soon make their appearance. She satisfies all the demands laid upon her, and she has no claims of her own. Behind her mute eyes is hidden a mute soul. She is all submission, but wise and prompt in action; a wife also in her paucity of words, springing from a philosophy of life learned in a hard school.

Success attends the two. They are able to set aside a little money, and Wang Lung's great passion, next to parenthood, his longing for more ground to cultivate, may now venture forth from subconsciousness. He is able to buy more fields, and everything promises happiness and increase.

Then comes a blow from the hand of fate; a drought descends upon the district. The good earth is changed into yellow, whirling dust. By selling land they could avert starvation, but that would be to bolt and lock the door to the future. Neither of them wishes to do that, so they set forth in company with the growing army of beggars to a city in the south, to live on the crumbs from the rich man's table.

O'Lan had made the journey once before in her childhood, when the end of it was that she was sold to save her parents and brothers.

Thanks to her experience, they accommodate themselves to the new life. Wang Lung toils as a beast of burden and the others beg with an acquired aptitude. Autumn and winter pass. With the spring, their yearning for their own land and its tilling becomes unendurable, but they have no money for the journey.

Then again fate intervenes—as natural a fate in China as drought and plague and flood. War, which is ever present somewhere in that great country, and the ways of which are as inscrutable as those of the powers of the air, stalks across the city and makes chaos of law and order. The poor plunder the homes of the rich.

Wang Lung goes with the mob without any definite motives, for his peasant soul revolts at deeds of violence, but by pure chance a handful of gold coins is almost forced into his hand. Now he can go home and begin the spring work on his rain-soaked soil. More than that, he can buy new fields; he is rich and happy.

He becomes still richer, though ultimately not happier, through the plunder acquired by O'Lan. From her days of slavery she knows something about hiding places in palaces, and she discovers a handful of precious stones. She takes them nearly as unpremeditatedly as a magpie steals glittering things, and hides them as instinctively. When her husband discovers them in her bosom, his whole world is transformed. He buys farm after farm. He becomes the leading man in the district, no longer peasant but lord, and his character changes colour. Simplicity and harmony with the earth vanish. In their place comes, slowly but surely, a curse for the desertion.

Wang Lung no longer has any real peace in his lordly leisure, with a young concubine in the house and O'Lan pushed into a dark corner, to die there when she has worn herself out.

The sons are not attractive figures. The eldest devotes himself to an empty life of indulgence, the second is swallowed up by greed for gold as a merchant and usurer. The youngest becomes one of the "war lords" who drain the unhappy country. Around them the Middle Empire is torn asunder in the tumult of new creation, which has become so agonizing in our days.

The trilogy does not carry us so far, however; it concludes with a sort of reconciliation between the third generation and the good earth. One of Wang Lung's grandsons, a man educated in the West, returns to the family estate and applies the knowledge he has acquired to the improvement of the conditions of work and life among the peasants.

The rest of the family live without roots in that conflict between old and new which Pearl Buck has described in other works—mostly in the tone of tragedy.

Of the many problems in this novel, the most serious and sombre one is the position of the Chinese woman. From the very beginning it is on this point that the writer's pathos emerges most strongly, and amid the calm of the epic work it constantly makes itself felt. An early episode in the work gives the most poignant expression of what a Chinese woman has been worth since time immemorial. It is given with impressive emphasis, and also with a touch of humour which is naturally rare in this book. In a moment of happiness, with his little first-born son dressed in fine clothes on his arm, and seeing the future bright before him, Wang Lung is on the point of breaking into boastful words but restrains himself in sudden terror. There, under the open sky, he had almost challenged the invisible spirits and drawn their evil glances upon himself. He tries to avert the menace by hiding his son under his coat and saying in a loud voice, "What a pity that our child is a girl, which no one wants, and is pitted with smallpox into the bargain! Let us pray that it may die!" And O'Lan joins in the comedy and acquiesces—probably without thinking at all.

In reality the spirits need not waste their glances on a girl child. Its lot is hard enough in any case. It is Pearl Buck's female characters which make the strongest impression. There is O'Lan with her scanty words, which carry all the more weight. Her whole life is portrayed in equally scanty but telling lines.

Quite a different figure is the chief character in the novel *The Mother* (1934). She is not referred to by any other designation, as if to indicate that her whole destiny is expressed in that word. She is, however, vividly individualized, a brave, energetic, strong character, of a more modern type than O'Lan's, perhaps, and without her slave temperament. The husband soon deserts his home, but she keeps it together for her children. The whole story ends in sorrow, but not in defeat. The mother cannot be crushed, not even when her younger son is beheaded as a revolutionary, and she has to seek a stranger's grave to weep by, for he has none. Just then a grandson is born, and she again has someone to love and sacrifice herself for.

The mother is the most finished of Pearl Buck's Chinese female figures, and the book is one of her best. But in character descriptions and the storyteller's art she is at her best in the two biographies of her parents, *The Exile* (1936) and *Fighting Angel* (1936). These should be called classics in the fullest sense of the word; they will endure, for they are full of life. In this respect the models from which the portraits are drawn are of great significance.

One seldom feels any great sense of gratitude for the company proffered in contemporary novels, and it is gladly forgotten. The characters have no great wealth of qualities, and the writer puts forth all his powers to lessen them, often by a persistent analysis with foregone results.

Here, however, one encounters two consummate characters, living unselfish lives of action, free from brooding and vacillation. They are profoundly unlike each other, and the fact that they are thrown together in a common struggle in a hard and strange world often leads to great tragedy—but not to defeat: they stand erect even to the very last. There is a spirit of heroism in both stories.

The mother, Carie, is richly gifted, brave and warm, of a genuine nature, harmonious amid ever-straining forces. She is tested to the utmost in sorrows and dangers; she loses many children because of the harshness of the conditions of life, and at times a terrible death threatens her in those troubled times. It is almost as hard for her to witness the never-ending suffering around her. She does what she can to mitigate it, and that is not a little, but no power is sufficient for such a task.

Even inwardly she passes through a hard and unceasing struggle. In her calling, and with her nature, she needs more than the conviction of faith. It is not enough for her that she has dedicated herself to God; she must also feel that the sacrifice has been accepted. But the sign of this, for which she begs and prays, never comes. She is compelled to persist in an untiring endeavour to find God and to content herself with trying to be good without divine help.

However, she preserves her spiritual health, her love for the life which has shown her so much that is terrible, and her eye for the beauty the world has to offer; she even retains her happiness and her humour. She resembles a fresh fountain springing from the heart of life.

The daughter tells her story with rare and lively perspicuity. The biography is precise in regard to the course of events, but creative imagination plays its part in the various episodes and in the description of the inner life of the character. Nothing is falsified, for this imagination is intuitive and true.

The language has vivid spontaneity; it is clear and suffused with a tender and soulful humour. There is, however, a flaw in the story. The daughter's devotion to her mother makes it impossible for her to do justice to her father. In his family life his limitations were obvious, limitations sharp and at times painful. As a preacher and soldier of Christ he was without blemish, in many respects even a great character; but he ought to have lived his life alone, free of the familial duties he hardly found time to notice, duties which in any case weighed lightly with him against his all-absorbing calling. Thus he was of little help to his wife, and in her biography he could not be fully understood.

This was accomplished, however, in another book, whose title is the key to his life and being: *Fighting Angel*. Andrew did not possess his wife's richly composite nature; his was narrow but deep, and as bright as a gleaming sword. He devoted every thought to his goal of opening the way to salvation for the heathens. Everything was insignificant compared to that. What Carie prayed for in vain, communion with God, he possessed wholly and unshakeably in the firm conceptions of his Biblical faith. With this faith he walked like a conqueror, further than any other in the immense heathen country, he endured all hardships without noticing them, and he encountered threats and dangers in the same manner. For the poor, blind, strange brown people he felt tenderness and love. Among them his stern nature broke into blossom. When he had won their souls to a confession of faith, he did not doubt the genuineness of the confession; with the naivete of a child, he accepted it as good. The door to God, always denied them before, had been opened to them, and to weigh them and judge them was now in the hands of Him who knows best. They had been given their possibility of salvation, and for Andrew it was urgent to give this possibility to all he could reach in that immense country, where thousands were dying every hour. His enthusiasm burned, and his work had something of genius in its magnitude and depth.

He strained his forces to the utmost in never-ending action, and the repose he allowed himself was the mystic's abandonment to the infinite amid ardent prayers. The whole of his life was a flame which rose straight and high, in spite of all storms; it could not be judged by ordinary conceptions. The daughter, whose portrait conceals none of his repellent features, maintained pure reverence before the nobility of the whole. One is profoundly thankful for both these perfectly executed pictures—each in its way so rare.

By awarding this year's Prize to Pearl Buck for the notable works which pave the way to a human sympathy passing over widely separated racial boundaries and for the studies of human ideals which are a great and living art of portraiture, the Swedish Academy feels that it acts in harmony and accord with the aim of Alfred Nobel's dreams for the future.

Mrs. Walsh, I have attempted a short survey of your work, indeed hardly necessary here, where the audience is so well acquainted with your remarkable books.

I hope, though, that I have been able to give some idea of their trend, toward opening a faraway and foreign world to deeper human insight and sympathy within our Western sphere—a grand and difficult task, requiring all your idealism and greatheartedness to fulfil as you have done.

May I now ask you to receive from the hands of His Majesty the King the Nobel Prize in Literature, conferred upon you by the Swedish Academy.

[© The Nobel Foundation, 1938.]

Buck: Banquet Speech

Introductory remarks by Bertil Lindblad, Director of the Stockholm Observatory at Saltsjöbaden, at the Nobel Banquet at the City Hall in Stockholm, 10 December 1938:

Mrs. Pearl Buck, you have in your literary works, which are of the highest artistic quality, advanced the understanding and the appreciation in the Western world of a great and important part of mankind, the people of China. You have taught us by your works to see the individuals in that great mass of people. You have shown us the rise and fall of families, and the land as the foundation upon which families are built. In this you have taught us to see those qualities of thought and feeling which bind us all together as human beings on this earth, and you have given us Westerners something of China's soul. When by the development of technical inventions the peoples of the earth are drawn closer to each other, the surface of the earth shrinks, so that East and West are no longer separated by almost insurmountable voids of distance, and when on the other hand, partly as a natural effect of this phenomenon, the differences of national character and ambitions clash to form dangerous discontinuities, it is of the greatest importance that the peoples of the earth learn to understand each other as individuals across distances and frontiers. When works of literature succeed in this respect they are certainly in a very direct way idealistic in the sense in which this word was meant by Alfred Nobel.

Buck's speech

It is not possible for me to express all that I feel of appreciation for what has been said and given to me. I accept, for myself, with the conviction of having received far beyond what I have been able to give in my books. I can only hope that the many books which I have yet to write will be in some measure a worthier acknowledgment than I can make tonight. And, indeed, I can accept only in the same spirit in which I think this gift was originally given—that it is a prize not so much for what has been done, as for the future. Whatever I write in the future must, I think, be always benefited and strengthened when I remember this day.

I accept, too, for my country, the United States of America. We are a people still young and we know that we have not yet come to the fullest of our powers. This award, given to an American, strengthens not only one, but the whole body of American writers, who are encouraged and heartened by such generous recognition. And I should like to say, too, that in my country it is important that this award has been given to a woman. You who have already so recognized your own Selma Lagerlöf, and have long recognized women in other fields, cannot perhaps wholly understand what it means in many countries that it is a woman who stands here at this moment. But I speak not only for writers and for women, but for all Americans, for we all share in this.

I should not be truly myself if I did not, in my own wholly unofficial way, speak also of the people of China, whose life has for so many years been my life also, whose life, indeed, must always be a part of my life. The minds of my own country and of China, my foster country, are alike in many ways, but above all, alike in our common love of freedom. And today more than ever, this is true, now when China's whole being is engaged in the greatest of all struggles, the struggle for freedom. I have never admired China more than I do now, when I see her uniting as she has never before, against the enemy who threatens her freedom. With this determination for freedom, which is in so profound a sense the essential quality in her nature, I know that she is *unconquerable*. Freedom—it is today more than ever the most precious human possession. We—Sweden and the United States—we have it still. My country is young—but it greets you with a peculiar fellowship, you whose earth is ancient and free.

[© The Nobel Foundation, 1938. Pearl S. Buck is the sole author of her speech.]

Buck: Nobel Lecture, 12 December 1938

The Chinese Novel

When I came to consider what I should say today it seemed that it would be wrong not to speak of China. And this is none the less true because I am an American by birth and by ancestry and though I live now in my own country and shall live there, since there I belong. But it is the Chinese and not the American novel which has shaped my own efforts in writing. My earliest knowledge of story, of how to tell and write stories, came to me in China. It would be ingratitude on my part not to recognize this today. And yet it would be presumptuous to speak before you on the subject of the Chinese novel for a reason wholly personal. There is another reason why I feel that I may properly do so. It is that I believe the Chinese novel has an illumination for the Western novel and for the Western novelist.

When I say Chinese novel, I mean the indigenous Chinese novel, and not that hybrid product, the novels of modern Chinese writers who have been too strongly under foreign influence while they were yet ignorant of the riches of their own country.

The novel in China was never an art and was never so considered, nor did any Chinese novelist think of himself as an artist. The Chinese novel, its history, its scope, its place in the life of the people, so vital a place, must be viewed in the strong light of this one fact. It is a fact no doubt strange to you, a company of modern Western scholars who today so generously recognize the novel.

But in China art and the novel have always been widely separated. There, literature as an art was the exclusive property of the scholars, an art they made and made for each other according to their own rules, and they found no place in it for the novel. And they held a powerful place, those Chinese scholars. Philosophy and religion and letters and literature, by arbitrary classical rules, they possessed them all, for they alone possessed the means of learning, since they alone knew how to read and write. They were powerful enough to be feared even by emperors, so that emperors devised a way of keeping them enslaved by their own learning, and made the official examinations the only means to political advancement, those incredibly difficult examinations which ate up a man's whole life and thought in preparing for them, and kept him too busy with memorizing and copying the dead and classical past to see the present and its wrongs. In that past the scholars found their rules of art. But the novel was not there, and they did not see it being created before their eyes, for the people created the novel, and what living people were doing did not interest those who thought of literature as an art. If scholars ignored the people, however, the people, in turn, laughed at the scholars. They made innumerable jokes about them, of which this is a fair sample: One day a company of wild beasts met on a hillside for a hunt. They bargained with each other to go out and hunt all day and meet again at the end of the day to share what they had killed. At the end of the day, only the tiger returned with nothing. When he was asked how this happened he replied very disconsolately, "At dawn I met a schoolboy, but he was, I feared, too callow for your tastes. I met no more until noon, when I found a priest. But I let him go, knowing him to be full of nothing but wind. The day went on and I grew desperate, for I passed no one. Then as dark came on I found a scholar. But I knew there was no use in bringing him back since he would be so dry and hard that he would break our teeth if we tried them on him."

The scholar as a class has long been a figure of fun for the Chinese people. He is frequently to be found in their novels, and always he is the same, as indeed he is in life, for a long study of the same dead classics and their formal composition has really made all Chinese scholars look alike, as well as think alike. We have no class to parallel him in the West—individuals, perhaps, only. But in China he was a class. Here he is, composite, as the people see him: a small shrunken figure with a bulging forehead, a pursed mouth, a nose at once snub and pointed, small inconspicuous eyes behind spectacles, a high pedantic voice, always announcing rules that do not matter to anyone but himself, a boundless self-conceit, a complete scorn not only of the common people but of all other scholars, a figure in long shabby robes, moving with a swaying haughty walk, when he moved at all. He was not to be seen except at literary gatherings, for most of the time he spent reading dead literature and trying to write more like it. He hated anything fresh or original, for he could not catalogue it into any of the styles he knew. If he could not catalogue it, he was sure it was not great, and he was confident that only he was right. If he said, "Here is art," he was convinced it was not to be found anywhere else, for what he did not recognize did not exist. And as he could never catalogue the novel into what he called literature, so for him it did not exist as literature.

Yao Hai, one of the greatest of Chinese literary critics, in 1776 enumerated the kinds of writing which comprise the whole of literature. They are essays, government commentaries, biographies, epitaphs, epigrams, poetry, funeral eulogies, and histories. No novels, you perceive, although by that date the Chinese novel had already reached its glorious height, after centuries of development among the common Chinese people. Nor does that vast compilation of Chinese literature, *Ssu Ku Chuen Shu,* made in 1772 by the order of the great Emperor Ch'ien Lung, contain the novel in the encyclopedia of its literature proper.

No, happily for the Chinese novel, it was not considered by the scholars as literature. Happily, too, for the novelist! Man and book, they were free from the criticisms of those scholars and their requirements of art, their techniques of expression and their talk of literary significances and all that discussion of what is and is not art, as if art were an absolute and not the changing thing it is, fluctuating even within decades! The Chinese novel was free. It grew as it liked out of its own soil, the common people, nurtured by that heartiest of sunshine, popular approval, and untouched by the cold and frosty winds of the scholar's art. Emily Dickinson, an American poet, once wrote, "Nature is a haunted house, but art is a house that tries to be haunted." "Nature," she said,

> Is what we see, Nature is what we know But have no art to say— So impatient our wisdom is, To her simplicity.

No, if the Chinese scholars ever knew of the growth of the novel, it was only to ignore it the more ostentatiously. Sometimes, unfortunately, they found themselves driven to take notice, because youthful emperors found novels pleasant to read. Then these poor scholars were hard put to it. But they discovered the phrase "social significance," and they wrote long literary treatises to prove that a novel was not a novel but a document of social significance. Social significance is a term recently discovered by the most modern of literary young men and women in the United States, but the old scholars of China knew it a thousand years ago, when they, too, demanded that the novel should have social significance, if it were to be recognized as an art.

But for the most part the old Chinese scholar reasoned thus about the novel:

> Literature is art. All art has social significance. This book has no social significance. Therefore it is not literature.

And so the novel in China was not literature.

In such a school was I trained. I grew up believing that the novel has nothing to do with pure literature. So I was taught by scholars. The art of literature, so I was taught, is something devised by men of learning. Out of the brains of scholars came rules to control the rush of genius, that wild fountain which has its source in deepest life. Genius, great or less, is the spring, and art is the sculptured shape, classical or modern, into which the waters must be forced, if scholars and critics were to be served. But the people of China did not so serve. The waters of the genius of story gushed out as they would, however the natural rocks allowed and the trees persuaded, and only common people came and drank and found rest and pleasure.

For the novel in China was the peculiar product of the common people. And it was solely their property. The very language of the novel was their own language, and not the classical Wen-li, which was the language of literature and the scholars. Wen-li bore somewhat the same resemblance to the language of the people as the ancient English of Chaucer does to the English of today, although ironically enough, at one time Wen-li, too, was a vernacular. But the scholars never kept pace with the living, changing speech of the people. They clung to an old vernacular until they had made it classic, while the running language of the people went on and left them far behind. Chinese novels, then, are in the "Pei Hua," or simple talk, of the people, and this in itself was offensive to the old scholars because it resulted in a style so full of easy flow and readability that it had no technique of expression in it, the scholars said.

I should pause to make an exception of certain scholars who came to China from India, bearing as their gift a new religion, Buddhism. In the West, Puritanism was for a long time the enemy of the novel. But in the Orient the Buddhists were wiser. When they came into China, they found literature already remote from the people and dying under the formalism of that period known in history as the Six Dynasties. The professional men of literature were even then absorbed not so much in what they had to say as in pairing into couplets the characters of their essays and their poems, and already they scorned all writing which did not conform to their own rules. Into this confined literary atmosphere came the Buddhist translators with their great treasures of the freed spirit. Some of them were Indian, but some were Chinese. They said frankly that their aim was not to conform to the ideas of style of the literary men, but to make clear and simple to common people what they had to teach. They put their religious teachings into the common language, the language which the novel used, and because the people loved story, they took story and made it a means of teaching. The preface of *Fah Shu Ching*, one of the most famous of Buddhist books, says, "When giving the words of gods, these words should be given forth simply." This might be taken as the sole literary creed of the Chinese novelist, to whom, indeed, gods were men and men were gods.

For the Chinese novel was written primarily to amuse the common people. And when I say amuse I do not mean only to make them laugh, though laughter is also one of the aims of the Chinese novel. I mean amusement in the sense of absorbing and occupying the whole attention of the mind. I mean enlightening that mind by pictures of life and what that life means. I mean encouraging the spirit not by rule-of-thumb talk about art, but by stories about the people in every age, and thus presenting to people simply themselves. Even the Buddhists who came to tell about gods found that people understood gods better if they saw them working through ordinary folk like themselves.

But the real reason why the Chinese novel was written in the vernacular was because the common people could not read and write and the novel had to be written so that when it was read aloud it could be understood by persons who could communicate only through spoken words. In a village of two hundred souls perhaps only one man could read. And on holidays or in the evening when the work was done he read aloud to the people from some story. The rise of the Chinese novel began in just this simple fashion. After a while people took up a collection of pennies in somebody's cap or in a farm wife's bowl because the reader needed tea to wet his throat, or perhaps to pay him for time he would otherwise have spent at his silk loom or his rush weaving. If the collections grew big enough he gave up some of his regular work and became a professional storyteller. And the stories he read were the beginnings of novels. There were not many such stories written down, not nearly enough to last year in and year out for people who had by nature, as the Chinese have, a strong love for dramatic story. So the storyteller began to increase his stock. He searched the dry annals of the history which the scholars had written, and with his fertile imagination, enriched by long acquaintance with common people, he clothed long-dead figures with new flesh and made them live again; he found stories of court life and intrigue and names of imperial favorites who had brought dynasties to ruin; he found, as he traveled from village to village, strange tales from his own times which he wrote down when he heard them. People told him of experiences they had had and he wrote these down, too, for other people. And he embellished them, but not with literary turns and phrases, for the people cared nothing for these. No, he kept his audiences always in mind and he found that the style which they loved best was one which flowed easily along, clearly and simply, in the short words which they themselves used every day, with no other technique than occasional bits of description, only enough to give vividness to a place or a person, and never enough to delay the story. Nothing must delay the story. Story was what they wanted.

And when I say story, I do not mean mere pointless activity, not crude action alone. The Chinese are too mature for that. They have always demanded of their novel character above all else. *Shui Hu Chuan* they have considered one of their three greatest novels, not primarily because it is full of the flash and fire of action, but because it portrays so distinctly one hundred and eight characters that each is to be seen separate from the others. Often I have heard it said of that novel in tones of delight, "When anyone of the hundred and eight begins to speak, we do not need to be told his name. By the way the words come from his mouth we know who he is." Vividness of character portrayal, then, is the first quality which the Chinese people have demanded of their novels, and after it, that such portrayal shall be by the character's own action and words rather than by the author's explanation.

Curiously enough, while the novel was beginning thus humbly in teahouses, in villages and lowly city streets out of stories told to the common people by a common and unlearned man among them, in imperial palaces it was beginning, too, and in much the same unlearned fashion. It was an old custom of emperors, particularly if the dynasty were a foreign one, to employ persons called "imperial ears," whose only duty was to come and go among the people in the streets of cities and villages and to sit among them in teahouses, disguised in common clothes, and listen to what was talked about there. The original purpose of this was, of course, to hear of any discontent among the emperor's subjects, and more especially to find out if discontents were rising to the shape of those rebellions which preceded the fall of every dynasty.

But emperors were very human and they were not often learned scholars. More often, indeed, they were only spoiled and willful men. The "imperial ears" had opportunity to hear all sorts of strange and interesting stories, and they found that their royal masters were more frequently interested in these stories than they were in politics. So when they came back to make their reports, they flattered the emperor and sought to gain favor by telling him what he liked to hear, shut up as he was in the Forbidden City, away from life. They told him the strange and interesting things which common people did, who were free, and after a while they took to writing down what they heard in order to save memory. And I do not doubt that if messengers between the emperor and the people carried stories in one direction, they carried them in the other, too, and to the people they told stories about the emperor and what he said and did, and how he quarrelled with the empress who bore him no sons, and how she intrigued with the chief eunuch to poison the favorite concubine, all of which delighted the Chinese because it proved to them, the most democratic of peoples, that their emperor was after all only a common fellow like themselves and that he, too, had his troubles, though he was the Son of Heaven. Thus there began another important source for the novel that was to develop with such form and force, though still always denied its right to exist by the professional man of letters.

From such humble and scattered beginnings, then, came the Chinese novel, written always in the vernacular, and dealing with all which interested the people, with legend and with myth, with love and intrigue, with brigands and wars, with everything, indeed, which went to make up the life of the people, high and low.

Nor was the novel in China shaped, as it was in the West, by a few great persons. In China the novel has always been more important than the novelist. There has been no Chinese Defoe, no Chinese Fielding or Smollett, no Austin or Brontë or Dickens or Thackeray, or Meredith or Hardy, any more than Balzac or Flaubert. But there were and are novels as great as the novels in any other country in the world, as great as any could have written, had he been born in China. Who then wrote these novels of China?

That is what the modern literary men of China now, centuries too late, are trying to discover. Within the last twenty-five years literary critics, trained in the universities of the West, have begun to discover their own neglected novels. But the novelists who wrote them they cannot discover. Did one man write *Shui Hu Chuan,* or did it grow to its present shape, added to, rearranged, deepened and developed by many minds and many a hand, in different centuries? Who can now tell? They are dead. They lived in their day and wrote what in their day they saw and heard, but of themselves they have told nothing. The author of *The Dream of the Red Chamber* in a far later century says in the preface to his book, "It is not necessary to know the times of Han and T'ang—it is necessary to tell only of my own times."

They told of their own times and they lived in a blessed obscurity. They read no reviews of their novels, no treatises as to whether or not what they did was well done according to the rules of scholarship. It did not occur to them that they must reach the high thin air which scholars breathed—nor did they consider the stuff of which greatness is made, according to the scholars. They wrote as it pleased them to write and as they were able. Sometimes they wrote unwittingly well and sometimes unwittingly they wrote not so well. They died in the same happy obscurity and now they are lost in it and not all the scholars of China, gathered too late to do them honor, can raise them up again. They are long past the possibility of literary post-mortems. But what they did remains after them because it is the common people of China who keep alive the great novels, illiterate people who have passed the novel, not so often from hand to hand as from mouth to mouth.

In the preface to one of the later editions of *Shui Hu Chuan,* Shih Nai An, an author who had much to do with the making of that novel, writes, "What I speak of I wish people to understand easily. Whether the reader is good or evil, learned or unlearned, anyone can read this book. Whether or not the book is well done is not important enough to cause anyone to worry. Alas, I am born to die. How can I know what those who come after me who read my book will think of it? I cannot even know what I myself, born into another incarnation, will think of it. I do not know if I myself then can even read. Why therefore should I care?"

Strangely enough, there were certain scholars who envied the freedom of obscurity, and who, burdened with certain private sorrows which they dared not tell anyone, or who perhaps wanting only a holiday from the weariness of the sort of art they had themselves created, wrote novels, too under assumed and humble names. And when they did so they put aside pedantry and wrote as simply and naturally as any common novelist.

For the novelist believed that he should not be conscious of techniques. He should write as his material demanded. If a novelist became known for a particular style or technique, to that extent he ceased to be a good novelist and became a literary technician.

A good novelist, or so I have been taught in China, should be above all else *tse ran,* that is, natural, unaffected, and so flexible and variable as to be wholly at the command of the material that flows through him. His whole duty is only to sort life as it flows through him, and in the vast fragmentariness of time and space and event to discover essential and inherent order and rhythm and shape. We should never be able, merely by reading pages, to know who wrote them, for when the style of a novelist becomes fixed, that style becomes his prison. The Chinese novelists varied their writing to accompany like music their chosen themes.

These Chinese novels are not perfect according to Western standards. They are not always planned from beginning to end, nor are they compact, any more than life is planned or compact. They are often too long, too full of incident, too crowded with character, a medley of fact and fiction as to material, and a medley of romance and realism as to method, so that an impossible event of magic or dream may be described with such exact semblance of detail that one is compelled to belief against all reason. The earliest novels are full of folklore, for the people of those times thought and dreamed in the ways of folklore. But no one can understand the mind of China today who has not read these novels, for the novels have shaped the present mind, too, and the folklore persists in spite of all that Chinese diplomats and Western-trained scholars would have us believe to the contrary. The essential mind of China is still that mind of which George Russell wrote when he said of the Irish mind, so strangely akin to the Chinese, "that mind which in its folk imagination believes anything. It creates ships of gold with masts of silver and white cities by the sea and rewards and faeries, and when that vast folk mind turns to politics it is ready to believe anything."

Out of this folk mind, turned into stories and crowded with thousands of years of life, grew, literally, the Chinese novel. For these novels changed as they grew. If, as I have said, there are no single names attached beyond question to the great novels of China, it is because no one hand wrote them. From beginning as a mere tale, a story grew through succeeding versions, into a structure built by many hands. I might mention as an example the well-known story, *The White Snake,* or *Pei She Chuan,* first written in the T'ang dynasty by an unknown author. It was then a tale of the simple supernatural whose hero was a great white snake. In the next version in the following century, the snake has become a vampire woman who is an evil force. But the third version contains a more gentle and human touch. The vampire becomes a faithful wife who aids her husband and gives him a son. The story thus adds not only new character but new quality, and ends not as the supernatural tale it began but as a novel of human beings.

So in early periods of Chinese history, many books must be called not so much novels as source books for novels, the sort of books into which Shakespeare, had they been open to him, might have dipped with both hands to bring up pebbles to make into jewels. Many of these books have been lost, since they were not considered valuable. But not all—early stories of Han, written so vigorously that to this day it is said they run like galloping horses, and tales of the troubled dynasties following—not all were lost. Some have persisted. In the Ming dynasty, in one way or another, many of them were represented in the great collection known as *T'ai P'ing Kuan Shi,* wherein are tales of superstition and religion, of mercy and goodness and reward for evil and well doing, tales of dreams and miracles, of dragons and gods and goddesses and priests, of tigers and foxes and transmigration and resurrection from the dead. Most of these early stories had to do with supernatural events, of gods born of virgins, of men walking as gods, as the Buddhist influence grew strong. There are miracles and allegories, such as the pens of poor scholars bursting into flower, dreams leading men and women into strange and fantastic lands of Gulliver, or the magic wand that floated an altar made of iron. But stories mirrored each age. The stories of Han were vigorous and dealt often with the affairs of the nation, and centered on some great man or hero. Humor was strong in this golden age, a racy, earthy, lusty humor, such as was to be found, for instance, in a book of tales entitled *Siao Ling,* presumed to have been collected, if not partly written, by Han Tang Suan. And then the scenes changed, as that golden age faded, though it was never to be forgotten, so that to this day the Chinese like to call themselves sons of Han. With the succeeding weak and corrupt centuries, the very way the stories were written became honeyed and weak, and their subjects slight, or as the Chinese say, "In the days of the Six Dynasties, they wrote of small things, of a woman, a waterfall, or a bird."

If the Han dynasty was golden, then the T'ang dynasty was silver, and silver were the love stories for which it was famous. It was an age of love, when a thousand stories clustered about the beautiful Yang Kuei Fei and her scarcely less beautiful predecessor in the emperor's favor, Mei Fei. These love stories of T'ang come very near sometimes to fulfilling in their unity and complexity the standards of the Western novel. There are rising action and crisis and dénouement, implicit if not expressed. The Chinese say, "We must read the stories of T'ang, because though they deal with small matters, yet they are written in so moving a manner that the tears come."

It is not surprising that most of these love stories deal not with love that ends in marriage or is contained in marriage, but with love outside the marriage relationship. Indeed, it is significant that when marriage is the theme the story nearly always ends in tragedy. Two famous stories, *Pei Li Shi* and *Chiao Fang Chi,* deal entirely with extramarital love, and are written apparently to show the superiority of the courtesans, who could read and write and sing and were clever and beautiful besides, beyond the ordinary wife who was, as the Chinese say even today, "a yellow-faced woman," and usually illiterate.

So strong did this tendency become that officialdom grew alarmed at the popularity of such stories among the common people, and they were denounced as revolutionary and dangerous because it was thought they attacked that foundation of Chinese civilization, the family system. A reactionary tendency was not lacking, such as is to be seen in *Hui Chen Chi,* one of the earlier forms of a famous later work, the story of the young scholar who loved the beautiful Ying Ying and who renounced her, saying prudently as he went away, "All extraordinary women are dangerous. They destroy themselves and others. They have ruined even emperors. I am not an emperor and I had better give her up"—which he did, to the admiration of all wise men. And to him the modest Ying Ying replied, "If you possess me and leave me, it is your right. I do not reproach you." But five hundred years later the sentimentality of the Chinese popular heart comes forth and sets the thwarted romance right again. In this last version of the story the author makes Chang and Ying Ying husband and wife and says in closing, "This is in the hope that all the lovers of the world may be united in happy marriage." And as time goes in China, five hundred years is not long to wait for a happy ending.

This story, by the way, is one of China's most famous. It was repeated in the Sung dynasty in a poetic form by Chao Teh Liang, under the title *The Reluctant Butterfly,* and again in the Yuan dynasty by Tung Chai-yuen as a drama to be sung, entitled *Suh Hsi Hsiang.* In the Ming dynasty, with two versions intervening, it appears as Li Reh Hua's *Nan Hsi Hsiang Chi,* written in the southern metrical form called "ts'e," and so to the last and most famous *Hsi Hsiang Chi.* Even children in China know the name of Chang Sen.

If I seem to emphasize the romances of the T'ang period, it is because romance between man and woman is the chief gift of T'ang to the novel, and not because there were no other stories. There were many novels of a humorous and satirical nature and one curious type of story which concerned itself with cockfighting, an important pastime of that age and particularly in favor at court. One of the best of these tales is *Tung Chen Lao Fu Chuan,* by Ch'en Hung, which tells how Chia Chang, a famous cockfighter, became so famous that he was loved by emperor and people alike.

But time and the stream pass on. The novel form really begins to be clear in the Sung dynasty, and in the Yuan dynasty it flowers into that height which was never again surpassed and only equalled, indeed, by the single novel *Hung Lou Meng,* or *The Dream of the Red Chamber,* in the Ts'ing dynasty. It is as though for centuries the novel had been developing unnoticed and from deep roots among the people, spreading into trunk and branch and twig and leaf to burst into this flowering in the Yuan dynasty, when the young Mongols brought into the old country they had conquered their vigorous, hungry, untutored minds and demanded to be fed. Such minds could not be fed with the husks of the old classical literature, and they turned therefore the more eagerly to the drama and the novel, and in this new life, in the sunshine of imperial favor, though still not with literary favor, there came two of China's three great novels, *Shui Hu Chuan* and *San Kuo—Hung Lou Meng* being the third.

I wish I could convey to you what these three novels mean and have meant to the Chinese people. But I can think of nothing comparable to them in Western literature. We have not in the history of our novel so clear a moment to which we can point and say, "There the novel is at its height." These three are the vindication of that literature of the common people, the Chinese novel. They stand as completed monuments of that popular literature, if not of letters. They, too, were ignored by men of letters and banned by censors and damned in succeeding dynasties as dangerous, revolutionary, decadent. But they lived on, because people read them and told them as stories and sang them as songs and ballads and acted them as dramas, until at last grudgingly even the scholars were compelled to notice them and to begin to say they were not novels at all but allegories, and if they were allegories perhaps then they could be looked upon as literature after all, though the people paid no heed to such theories and never read the long treatises which scholars wrote to prove them. They rejoiced in the novels they had made as novels and for no purpose except for joy in story and in story through which they could express themselves.

And indeed the people had made them. *Shui Hu Chuan,* though the modern versions carry the name of Shi Nai An as author, was written by no one man. Out of a handful of tales centering in the Sung dynasty about a band of robbers there grew this great, structured novel. Its beginnings were in history. The original lair which the robbers held still exists in Shantung, or did until very recent times. Those times of the thirteenth century of our Western era were, in China, sadly distorted. The dynasty under the emperor Huei Chung was falling into decadence and disorder. The rich grew richer and the poor poorer and when none other came forth to set this right, these righteous robbers came forth.

I cannot here tell you fully of the long growth of this novel, nor of its changes at many hands. Shih Nai An, it is said, found it in rude form in an old book shop and took it home and rewrote it. After him the story was still told and re-told. Five or six versions of it today have importance, one with a hundred chapters entitled *Chung I Shui Hu,* one of a hundred and twenty-seven chapters, and one of a hundred chapters. The original version attributed to Shih Nai An, had a hundred and twenty chapters, but the one most used today has only seventy. This is the version arranged in the Ming dynasty by the famous Ching Shen T'an, who said that it was idle to forbid his son to read the book and therefore presented the lad with a copy revised by himself, knowing that no boy could ever refrain from reading it. There is also a version written under official command, when officials found that nothing could keep the people from reading *Shui Hu*. This official version is entitled *Tung Kou Chi*, or, *Laying Waste the Robbers*, and it tells of the final defeat of the robbers by the state army and their destruction. But the common people of China are nothing if not independent. They have never adopted the official version, and their own form of the novel still stands. It is a struggle they know all too well, the struggle of everyday people against a corrupt officialdom.

I might add that *Shui Hu Chuan* is in partial translation in French under the title *Les Chevaliers Chinois*, and the seventy-chapter version is in complete English translation by myself under the title *All Men Are Brothers*. The original title, *Shui Hu Chuan*, in English is meaningless, denoting merely the watery margins of the famous marshy lake which was the robbers' lair. To Chinese the words invoke instant century-old memory, but not to us.

This novel has survived everything and in this new day in China has taken on an added significance. The Chinese Communists have printed their own edition of it with a preface by a famous Communist and have issued it anew as the first Communist literature of China. The proof of the novel's greatness is in this timelessness. It is as true today as it was dynasties ago. The people of China still march across its pages, priests and courtesans, merchants and scholars, women good and bad, old and young, and even naughty little boys. The only figure lacking is that of the modern scholar trained in the West, holding his Ph.D. diploma in his hand. But be sure that if he had been alive in China when the final hand laid down the brush upon the pages of that book, he, too, would have been there in all the pathos and humor of his new learning, so often useless and inadequate and laid like a patch too small upon an old robe.

The Chinese say "The young should not read *Shui Hu* and the old should not read *San Kuo*." This is because the young might be charmed into being robbers and the old might be led into deeds too vigorous for their years. For if *Shui Hu Chuan* is the great social document of Chinese life, *Sa Kuo* is the document of wars and statesmanship, and in its turn *Hung Lou Meng* is the document of family life and human love.

The history of the *San Kuo* or *Three Kingdoms* shows the same architectural structure and the same doubtful authorship as *Shui Hu*. The story begins with three friends swearing eternal brotherhood in the Han dynasty and ends ninety-seven years later in the succeeding period of the Six Dynasties. It is a novel rewritten in its final form by a man named Lo Kuan Chung, thought to be a pupil of Shih Nai An, and one who perhaps even shared with Shih Nai An in the writing, too, of *Shui Hu Chuan*. But this is a Chinese Bacon-and-Shakespeare controversy which has no end.

Lo Kuan Chung was born in the late Yuan dynasty and lived on into the Ming. He wrote many dramas, but he is more famous for his novels, of which *San Kuo* is easily the best. The version of this novel now most commonly used in China is the one revised in the time of K'ang Hsi by Mao Chen Kan, who revised as well as criticised the book. He changed, added and omitted material, as for example when he added the story of Suan Fu Ren, the wife of one of the chief characters. He altered even the style. If *Shui Hu Chuan* has importance today as a novel of the people in their struggle for liberty, *San Kuo* has importance because it gives in such detail the science and art of war as the Chinese conceive it, so differently, too, from our own. The guerillas, who are today China's most effective fighting units against Japan, are peasants who know *San Kuo* by heart, if not from their own reading, at least from hours spent in the idleness of winter days or long summer evenings when they sat listening to the storytellers describe how the warriors of the Three Kingdoms fought their battles. It is these ancient tactics of war which the guerillas trust today. What a warrior must be and how he must attack and retreat, how retreat when the enemy advances, how advance when the enemy retreats—all this had its source in this novel, so well known to every common man and boy of China.

Hung Lou Meng, or *The Dream of the Red Chamber*, the latest and most modern of these three greatest of Chinese novels, was written originally as an autobiographical novel by Ts'ao Hsüeh Ching, an official highly in favor during the Manchu regime and indeed considered by the Manchus as one of themselves. There were then eight military groups among the Manchus, and Ts'ao Hsüeh Ching belonged to them all. He never finished his novel, and the last forty chapters were added by another man, probably named Kao O. The thesis that Ts'ao Hsüeh Ching was telling the story of his own life has been in modern times elaborated by Hu Shih, and in earlier times by Yuan Mei. Be this as it may, the original title of the book was *Shih T'ou Chi*, and it came out of Peking about 1765 of the Western era, and in five or six years, an incredibly short time in China, it was famous everywhere. Printing was still expensive when it appeared, and the book became known by the method that is called in China, "You-lend-me-a-book-and-I-lend-you-a-book."

The story is simple in its theme but complex in implication, in character study and in its portrayal of human emotions. It is almost a pathological study, this story of a great house, once wealthy and high in imperial favor, so that indeed one of its members was an imperial concubine. But the great days are over when the book begins. The family is already declining. Its wealth is being dissipated and the last and only son, Chia Pao Yü, is being corrupted by the decadent influences within his own home, although the fact that he was a youth of exceptional quality at birth is established by the symbolism of a piece of jade found in his mouth. The preface begins, "Heaven was once broken and when it was mended, a bit was left unused, and this became the famous jade of Chia Pao Yü." Thus does the interest in the supernatural persist in the Chinese people; it persists even today as a part of Chinese life.

This novel seized hold of the people primarily because it portrayed the problems of their own family system, the absolute power of women in the home, the too great power of the matriarchy, the grandmother, the mother, and even the bondmaids, so often young and beautiful and fatally dependent, who became too frequently the playthings of the sons of the house and ruined them and were ruined by them. Women reigned supreme in the Chinese house, and because they were wholly confined in its walls and often illiterate, they ruled to the hurt of all. They kept men children, and protected them from hardship and effort when they should not have been so protected. Such a one was Chia Pao Yü, and we follow him to his tragic end in *Hung Lou Meng*.

I cannot tell you to what lengths of allegory scholars went to explain away this novel when they found that again even the emperor was reading it and that its influence was so great everywhere among the people. I do not doubt that they were probably reading it themselves in secret. A great many popular jokes in China have to do with scholars reading novels privately and publicly pretending never to have heard of them. At any rate, scholars wrote treatises to prove that *Hung Lou Meng* was not a novel but a political allegory depicting the decline of China under the foreign rule of the Manchus, the word Red in the title signifying Manchu, and Ling Tai Yü, the young girl who dies, although she was the one destined to marry Pao Yü, signifying China, and Pao Ts'ai, her successful rival, who secures the jade in her place, standing for the foreigner, and so forth. The very name Chia signified, they said, falseness. But this was a farfetched explanation of what was written as a novel and stands as a novel and as such a powerful delineation, in the characteristic Chinese mixture of realism and romance, of a proud and powerful family in decline. Crowded with men and women of the several generations accustomed to living under one roof in China, it stands alone as an intimate description of that life.

In so emphasizing these three novels, I have merely done what the Chinese themselves do. When you say "novel," the average Chinese replies, "*Shui Hu, San Kuo, Hung Lou Meng*." Yet this is not to say that there are not hundreds of other novels, for there are. I must mention *Hsi Yü Chi*, or *Record of Travels in the West*, almost as popular as these three. I might mention *Feng Shen Chuan*, the story of a deified warrior, the author unknown but said to be a writer in the time of Ming. I must mention *Ru Ling Wai Shi*, a satire upon the evils of the Tsing dynasty, particularly of the scholars, full of a double-edged though not malicious dialogue, rich with incident, pathetic and humorous. The fun here is made of the scholars who can do nothing practical, who are lost in the world of useful everyday things, who are so bound by convention that nothing original can come from them. The book, though long, has no central character. Each figure is linked to the next by the thread of incident, person and incident passing on together until, as Lu Hsün, the famous modern Chinese writer, has said, "they are like scraps of brilliant silk and satin sewed together."

And there is *Yea Shou Pei Yin*, or *An Old Hermit Talks in the Sun*, written by a famous man disappointed in official preferment, Shia of Kiang-yin, and there is that strangest of books, *Ching Hua Yuen*, a fantasy of women, whose ruler was an empress, whose scholars were all women. It is designed to show that the wisdom of women is equal to that of men, although I must acknowledge that the book ends with a war between men and women in which the men are triumphant and the empress is supplanted by an emperor.

But I can mention only a small fraction of the hundreds of novels which delight the common people of China. And if those people knew of what I was speaking to you today, they would after all say "tell of the great three, and let us stand or fall by *Shui Hu Chuan* and *San Kuo* and *Hung Lou Meng*." In these three novels are the lives which the Chinese people lead and have long led, here are the songs they sing and the things at which they laugh and the things which they love to do. Into these novels they have put the generations of their being and to refresh that being they return to these novels again and again, and out of them they have made new songs and plays and other novels. Some of them have come to be almost as famous as the great originals, as for example *Ching P'ing Mei*, that classic of romantic physical love, taken from a single incident in *Shui Hu Chuan*.

But the important thing for me today is not the listing of novels. The aspect which I wish to stress is that all this profound and indeed sublime development of the imagination of a great democratic people was never in its own time and country called literature. The very name for story was "hsiao shuo," denoting something slight and valueless, and even a novel was only a "ts'ang p'ien hsiao shuo," or a longer something which was still slight and useless. No, the people of China forged their own literature apart from letters. And today this is what lives, to be part of what is to come, and all the formal literature, which was called art, is dead. The plots of these novels are often incomplete, the love interest is often not brought to solution, heroines are often not beautiful and heroes often are not brave. Nor has the story always an end; sometimes it merely stops, in the way life does, in the middle of it when death is not expected.

In this tradition of the novel have I been born and reared as a writer. My ambition, therefore, has not been trained toward the beauty of letters or the grace of art. It is, I believe, a sound teaching and, as I have said, illuminating for the novels of the West.

For here is the essence of the attitude of Chinese novelists—perhaps the result of the contempt in which they were held by those who considered themselves the priests of art. I put it thus in my own words, for none of them has done so.

The instinct which creates *the arts* is not the same as that which produces art. The creative instinct is, in its final analysis and in its simplest terms, an enormous extra vitality, a super-energy, born inexplicably in an individual, a vitality great beyond all the needs of his own living—an energy which no single life can consume. This energy consumes itself then in creating more life, in the form of music, painting, writing, or whatever is its most natural medium of expression. Nor can the individual keep himself from this process, because only by its full function is he relieved of the burden of this extra and peculiar energy—an energy at once physical and mental, so that all his senses are more alert and more profound than another man's, and all his brain more sensitive and quickened to that which his senses reveal to him in such abundance that actuality overflows into imagination. It is a process proceeding from within. It is the heightened activity of every cell of his being, which sweeps not only himself, but all human life about him, or in him, in his dreams, into the circle of its activity.

From the product of this activity, art is deducted—but not by him. The process which creates is not the process which deduces the shapes of art. The defining of art, therefore, is a secondary and not a primary process. And when one born for the primary process of creation, as the novelist is, concerns himself with the secondary process, his activity becomes meaningless. When he begins to make shapes and styles and techniques and new schools, then he is like a ship stranded upon a reef whose propeller, whirl wildly as it will, cannot drive the ship onward. Not until the ship is in its element again can it regain its course.

And for the novelist the only element is human life as he finds it in himself or outside himself. The sole test of his work is whether or not his energy is producing more of that life. Are his creatures alive? That is the only question. And who can tell him? Who but those living human beings, the people? Those people are not absorbed in what art is or how it is made—are not, indeed, absorbed in anything very lofty, however good it is. No, they are absorbed only in themselves, in their own hungers and despairs and joys and above all, perhaps, in their own dreams. These are the ones who can really judge the work of the novelist, for they judge by that single test of reality. And the standard of the test is not to be made by the device of art, but by the simple comparison of the reality of what they read, to their own reality.

I have been taught, therefore, that though the novelist may see art as cool and perfect shapes, he may only admire them as he admires marble statues standing aloof in a quiet and remote gallery; for his place is not with them. His place is in the street. He is happiest there. The street is noisy and the men and women are not perfect in the technique of their expression as the statues are. They are ugly and imperfect, incomplete even as human beings, and where they come from and where they go cannot be known. But they are people and therefore infinitely to be preferred to those who stand upon the pedestals of art.

And like the Chinese novelist, I have been taught to want to write for these people. If they are reading their magazines by the million, then I want my stories there rather than in magazines read only by a few. For story belongs to the people. They are sounder judges of it than anyone else, for their senses are unspoiled and their emotions are free. No, a novelist must not think of pure literature as his goal. He must not even know this field too well, because people, who are his material, are not there. He is a storyteller in a village tent, and by his stories he entices people into his tent. He need not raise his voice when a scholar passes. But he must beat all his drums when a band of poor pilgrims pass on their way up the mountain in search of gods. To them he must cry, "I, too, tell of gods!" And to farmers he must talk of their land, and to old men he must speak of peace, and to old women he must tell of their children, and to young men and women he must speak of each other. He must be satisfied if the common people hear him gladly. At least, so I have been taught in China.

[© The Nobel Foundation, 1938. Pearl S. Buck is the sole author of the text.]

Ivan Bunin
(10 October 1870 – 8 November 1953)

Julian W. Connolly
University of Virginia

This entry was expanded by Connolly from his Bunin entry in *DLB 317: Twentieth-Century Russian Émigré Writers*.

BOOKS: *Stikhotvoreniia: 1887–1891 gg.* (Orel: Orlovskii vestnik, 1891);

"Na krai sveta" i drugie rasskazy (St. Petersburg: O. N. Popova, 1897);

Pod otkrytym nebom: Stikhotvoreniia (Moscow: Detskoe chtenie, 1898);

Stikhi i rasskazy (Moscow: Detskoe chtenie i Pedagogicheskii listok, 1900);

Listopad: Stikhotvoreniia (Moscow: Skorpion, 1901);

Novye stikhotvoreniia (Moscow: O. O. Gerbek, 1902);

Sobranie sochinenii, 5 volumes (St. Petersburg: Znanie, 1902–1909);

Stikhotvoreniia i rasskazy: 1907–1909 (St. Petersburg: Obshchestvennaia pol'za, 1910);

Derevnia (Moscow: Moskovskoe knigoizdatel'stvo, 1910); translated by Isabel F. Hapgood as *The Village* (New York: Knopf, 1923; London: Secker, 1923);

Pereval: Rasskazy 1892–1902 (Moscow: Moskovskoe knigoizdatel'stvo, 1912);

Rasskazy i stikhotvoreniia 1907–1910 gg. (Moscow: Knigoizdatel'stvo pisatelei, 1912);

Stikhotvoreniia (Moscow: Moskovskoe knigoizdatel'stvo, 1912);

Sukhodol: Povesti i rasskazy 1911–1912 gg. (Moscow: Knigoizdatel'stvo pisatelei, 1912);

Ioann Rydalets: Rasskazy i stikhi 1912–1913 gg. (Moscow: Knigoizdatel'stvo pisatelei v Moskve, 1913);

Zolotoe dno: Rasskazy 1903–1907 gg. (Moscow: Knigoizdatel'stvo pisatelei, 1913);

Polnoe sobranie sochinenii, 6 volumes (Petrograd: A. F. Marks, 1915);

Chasha zhizni: Rasskazy 1913–1914 gg. (Moscow: Knigoizdatel'stvo pisatelei v Moskve, 1915);

Gospodin iz San-Frantsisko: Proizvedeniia 1915–1916 gg. (Moscow: Knigoizdatel'stvo pisatelei v Moskve, 1916);

Ivan Bunin, 10 November 1933 (photograph © Bettmann/CORBIS)

Khram solntsa (Petrograd: Zhizn' i znanie, 1917);

Krik (Berlin: Slovo, 1921);

Nachal'naia liubov' (Prague: Slavianskoe izdatel'stvo, 1921);

Roza Ierikhona (Berlin: Slovo, 1924);

Mitina liubov' (Paris: Russkaia zemlia, 1925; Leningrad: Knizhnye novinki, 1925); translated from the French by Madelaine Boyd as *Mitya's Love* (New York: Holt, 1926);

Poslednee svidanie (Paris: N. P. Karbasnikov, 1926);

Delo korneta Elagina (Khar'kov: Kosmos, 1927);

Solnechnyi udar (Paris: Rodnik, 1927);

Khudaia trava (Moscow & Leningrad: Zemlia i fabrika, 1928);

Izbrannye stikhi (Paris: Sovremennye zapiski, 1929);

Grammatika liubvi: Izbrannye rasskazy (Belgrade: Russkaia biblioteka, 1929);

Zhizn' Arsen'eva: Istoki dnei (Paris: Sovremennye zapiski, 1930); translated by Gleb Struve and Hamish Miles as *The Well of Days* (London: Hogarth Press, 1933; New York: Knopf, 1934);

Bozh'e drevo (Paris: Sovremennye zapiski, 1931);

Ten' ptitsy (Paris: Sovremennye zapiski, 1931);

Sobranie sochinenii, 11 volumes (Berlin: Petropolis, 1934–1936);

Okaiannye dni (London, Ontario: Zaria, 1936); translated by Thomas Gaiton Marullo as *Cursed Days: A Diary of Revolution* (Chicago: Ivan R. Dee, 1998; London: Phoenix, 2000);

Osvobozhdenie Tolstogo (Paris: YMCA-Press, 1937); translated by Marullo and Vladimir T. Khmelkov as *The Liberation of Tolstoy* (Evanston, Ill.: Northwestern University Press, 2001);

Zhizn' Arsen'eva: II. Lika: Roman (Brussels: Petropolis, 1939);

Temnye allei (New York: Novaia zemlia, 1943; enlarged edition, Paris: La Press française et étrangère, 1946); translated by Richard Hare as *Dark Avenues and Other Stories* (London: Lehmann, 1949; Westport, Conn.: Hyperion, 1977);

Vospominaniia (Paris: Vozrozhdenie, 1950); translated by Vera Traill and Robin Chancellor as *Memories and Portraits* (Garden City, N.Y.: Doubleday, 1951; London: Lehmann, 1951);

Zhizn' Arsen'eva: Iunost' (New York: Chekhov, 1952); translated by Struve, Miles, Heidi Hillis, Susan McKean, and Sven A. Wolf as *The Life of Arseniev: Youth*, edited by Andrew Baruch (Evanston, Ill.: Northwestern University Press, 1994);

Vesnoi, v Iudee: Roza Ierikhona (New York: Chekhov, 1953);

Petlistye ushi i drugie rasskazy (New York: Chekhov, 1954);

O Chekhove: Nezakonchennaia rukopis' (New York: Chekhov, 1955);

Stikhotvoreniia (Leningrad: Sovetskii pisatel', 1956);

Ivan Bunin: Sbornik materialov, 2 volumes, Literaturnoe nasledstvo, volume 84 (Moscow: Nauka, 1973);

Publitsistika 1918–1953, edited by Oleg N. Mikhailov (Moscow: Nasledie, 1998).

Collections: *Sobranie sochinenii*, 5 volumes (Moscow: Pravda, 1956);

Sobranie sochinenii v deviati tomakh, 9 volumes, edited by A. S. Miasnikov, B. S. Riurikov, and A. T. Tvardovsky (Moscow: Khudozhestvennaia literatura, 1965–1967);

Sochineniia v trekh tomakh, 3 volumes (Moscow: Khudozhestvennaia literatura, 1982);

Sobranie sochinenii v shesti tomakh, 6 volumes, edited by IU. V. Bondarev, Oleg N. Mikhailov, and V. P. Rynkevich (Moscow: Khudozhestvennaia literatura, 1987–1988);

Sobranie sochinenii v chetyrekh tomakh, 4 volumes, edited by N. M. Liubimov (Moscow: Pravda, 1988);

Sobranie sochinenii v vos'mi tomakh, 8 volumes, edited by A. K. Baboreko (Moscow: Moskovskii rabochii, 1993–2000);

Sobranie sochinenii v shesti tomakh, 6 volumes (Moscow: Santaks, 1994);

Sobranie sochinenii v shesti tomakh, 6 volumes, edited by A. Farizova, I. Marev, G. Shitoeva, and V. Antonova (Moscow: Terra, 1997).

Editions in English: *Lazarus*, translated by Avrahm Yarmolinsky (Boston: Stratford, 1918)—comprises "Eleazar," by Leonid Andreyev, and "The Gentleman from San Francisco," by Bunin;

Reminiscences of Anton Chekhov, by Bunin, Maksim Gor'ky, and Aleksandr Kuprin, translated by S. S. Koteliansky and Leonard Woolf (New York: Huebsch, 1921);

The Gentleman from San Francisco and Other Stories, translated by Woolf, Koteliansky, and D. H. Lawrence (London: Hogarth Press, 1922; New York: Seltzer, 1923);

The Gentleman from San Francisco and Other Stories, translated by Bernard Guilbert Guerney (New York: Knopf, 1923);

The Dreams of Chang, and Other Stories, translated by Guerney (New York: Knopf, 1923; London: Secker); republished as *Fifteen Tales* (London: Secker, 1924; Great Neck, N.Y.: Core Collection Books, 1978);

Grammar of Love, translated by John Cournos (New York: Smith & Haas, 1934; London: Woolf, 1935);

The Elaghin Affair and Other Stories, translated by Guerney (New York: Knopf, 1935);

Shadowed Paths, translated by Ol'ga Shartse, edited by Philippa Hentges (Moscow: Foreign Languages Publishing House, 1944; Honolulu: University Press of the Pacific, 2001);

The Gentleman from San Francisco and Other Stories, translated by Shartse, introduction by Thompson Bradley (New York: Washington Square Press, 1963);

Velga, translated by Guy Daniels (New York: S. G. Phillips, 1970);

Stories and Poems, translated by Shartse and Irina Zheleznova (Moscow: Progress, 1979);

In a Far Distant Land: Selected Stories, translated by Robert Bowie (Ann Arbor, Mich.: Hermitage, 1983);

Long Ago: Fourteen Stories, translated by David Richards and Sophie Lund (London: Angel, 1984); enlarged as *The Gentleman from San Francisco and Other Stories* (London: Penguin / New York: Viking Penguin, 1987);

Light Breathing and Other Stories, translated by Shartse (Moscow: Raduga, 1988);

Wolves and Other Love Stories, translated by Mark C. Scott (San Bernardino, Cal.: Capra Press, 1989);

Sunstroke: Selected Stories, translated by Graham Hettlinger (Chicago: Ivan R. Dee, 2002);

The Elagin Affair and Other Stories, translated by Hettlinger (Chicago: Ivan R. Dee, 2005).

TRANSLATION: Henry Wadsworth Longfellow, *Pesn' o Gaiavate* (Moscow: Knizhnoe dielo, 1899).

The first Russian to be awarded the Nobel Prize in Literature, Ivan Bunin was the last of a prominent line of writers who belonged to the aristocracy—a line that includes Ivan Turgenev and Leo Tolstoy. Bunin lived well into the twentieth century, and he chronicled in haunting detail the slow decline and ultimate disappearance of a way of life taken for granted by the gentry writers of the nineteenth century. Throughout his long career he was moved by an acute awareness of the evanescence of human life, and his work records the full range of human emotion from ecstatic joy at the fulfillment of desire to inconsolable grief at the losses that frequently ensue.

Ivan Alekseevich Bunin was born on 10 (New Style, 22) October 1870 in Voronezh, a provincial capital three hundred miles southeast of Moscow. In later years he pointed out with pride that he could trace his lineage to a Lithuanian knight who had entered the service of Grand Prince of Moscow Vasilii II in the fifteenth century. His ancestors had served a series of Russian rulers, and in the nineteenth century two of his relatives achieved significant literary fame: Anna Bunina was the first professional woman writer in Russia, while Vasilii Zhukovsky, the illegitimate son of Afanasii Bunin and a captive Turkish woman, became a noted poet and translator and served as tutor to the future tsar Alexander II.

Despite the achievements of these forebears, Bunin's immediate family faced straitened circumstances at the time of his birth. Landowners throughout Russia were finding it increasingly difficult to maintain their prosperity; the emancipation of the serfs in 1861 and the rise of industry in the countryside in the second half of the nineteenth century contributed to the decline of the gentry estate. Bunin's father, Aleksei Nikolaevich Bunin, who had served as a volunteer in the Crimean War, preferred socializing with friends to managing his property, and while Bunin was still a child, his father was forced to sell off ancestral holdings until he was left with two small estates, Butyrki and Ozerki, in the province of Orel. According to Bunin's memoirs, *Vospominaniia* (1950; translated as *Memories and Portraits,* 1951), the personality of his mother, Liudmila Aleksandrovna, née Chubarova, was quite different from that of his father: she was deeply religious and inclined toward woeful premonitions and sadness. She was devoted to her children, but only four of the nine to whom she gave birth survived infancy. Bunin's second wife ascribed his wide mood swings to the contrasting dispositions of his parents.

A few years after Bunin's birth, his family found the cost of living in Voronezh beyond their means and moved to the Butyrki estate. Bunin recalled in an autobiographical note in 1915, "Here, in the deepest stillness of the fields, amidst crops that came right up to our doorstep in the summer, and amid snowdrifts in winter, passed my entire childhood, full of sad and original poetry." Bunin's immersion in nature left a lasting trace on his creative imagination: nuanced descriptions of natural phenomena became a hallmark of his mature writing. His brothers, Iulii and Evgenii, were much older than he, and his two sisters were infants during his early childhood. As a result, Bunin's playmates were the peasant children in the neighborhood, and his familiarity with peasant life also had a significant impact on his writing.

Bunin's early education was in the hands of an eccentric, impoverished nobleman, Nikolai Romashkov, who taught him to read from Russian translations of texts such as Homer's *Odyssey* and fed his imagination with vivid stories about chivalry. Romashkov wrote satirical poetry about topical issues; Bunin tried his hand at verse, as well, but noted in his memoirs that he did not write about contemporary concerns but about "some kind of spirits in a mountain valley on a moonlit night."

The death of his infant sister Aleksandra shocked Bunin and plunged him into months of tormented contemplation about what might lie beyond the grave. Wonderment about death and its implications for the living remained an element of his personality throughout his life.

In autumn 1881 Bunin enrolled in a gymnasium in Elets. He was not interested in disciplined education, and his academic success, especially in mathematics, steadily deteriorated. During the Christmas holidays of 1885 he told his parents that he did not wish to return to school, and they acceded to his desire. By this time they had sold the Butyrki estate to pay off their debts and had moved to the Ozerki estate, which had belonged to Bunin's mother's family. His brother Iulii, a political activist, had been arrested in 1884 and sentenced to house arrest for three years. With little else to do, Iulii took over his brother's education. Recognizing that Bunin had little affinity for mathematics, Iulii concentrated on history, political science, and literature. Under his brother's guidance Bunin read the works of such major Russian writers as Turgenev, Aleksandr Pushkin, Mikhail Lermontov, Fedor Tiutchev, Afanasii Fet, and Vsevolod Garshin. He also read the plays and sonnets of William Shakespeare and the poetry of the English Romantics in translation and tried to learn English so that he could read them in the original.

Stimulated by his reading, Bunin wrote a large quantity of poetry and a few prose sketches between 1886 and 1889. For the most part this early work reveals his reliance on the models of Pushkin, Lermontov, and Fet, but his notebooks also include translations of work by Johann Wolfgang von Goethe; Friedrich Schiller; George Gordon, Lord Byron; and Alphonse de Lamartine. A prominent literary figure of the day was Semen Nadson, a poet who expressed his longing to be of use to society and lamented his powerlessness to do so. Nadson's anguished idealism resonated powerfully among young Russians of Bunin's generation. When Nadson died of tuberculosis at twenty-five in January 1887, Bunin wrote a commemorative poem, "Nad mogiloi S. Ia. Nadsona" (At the Grave of S. Ia. Nadson). It was published in the journal *Rodina* (Homeland) on 22 February 1887, and Bunin's literary career was launched. Within a short time he published other poems in *Rodina* and in *Knizhki nedeli* (Books of the Week) and his first short stories, "Nefedka" and "Dva strannika" (Two Wanderers), in *Rodina*.

In August 1888 Iulii moved to Kharkov, and Bunin found himself increasingly bored with life in the country. On 20 January 1889 he was invited to join the staff of *Orlovsky vestnik* (Orel Messenger), a newspaper that covered social issues, literature, and trade. Before taking up the position he spent two months visiting Iulii in Kharkov, meeting his brother's radical friends and engaging in lengthy arguments about politics and ideology. After a trip to the Crimea, he began work at *Orlovsky vestnik* in autumn 1889. He used his position to publish his poems, stories, and literary articles in the paper. He fell in love with a coworker, Varvara Pashchenko, although she appears to have been ambivalent in her feelings for him. Bunin felt constrained by his lack of financial means, and Pashchenko's parents were opposed to her marrying an impecunious writer. The couple was forced to conceal their relationship, which placed additional stress on it; arguments and separations were followed by periods of renewed intimacy. Bunin incorporated many of the elements of his relationship with Pashchenko into his novel *Zhizn' Arsen'eva: Iunost'* (1952; translated as *The Life of Arseniev: Youth*, 1994).

In 1891 Bunin's *Stikhotvoreniia: 1887–1891 gg.* (Poems: 1887–1891) was published as a supplement to the *Orlovsky vestnik*. The following year he and Pashchenko moved to Poltava, where Bunin went to work with Iulii in the local zemstvo (provincial administrative organization) as a librarian. Later he became a statistician, which required him to travel throughout the region collecting data and observing the changing conditions of rural life. He distilled his observations into his fiction, and his work began appearing with more frequency in literary journals.

During this period Bunin became acquainted with followers of Tolstoy's philosophy of simplification, and for a time he was seized with enthusiasm for Tolstoyanism. He went to Moscow to meet Tolstoy in January 1894; although Tolstoy cautioned him against becoming a blind adherent of the simple life, the meeting made a powerful impression on him. Later that year Bunin began distributing literature put out by the Tolstoyan publishing house Posrednik (Mediator) and was arrested for selling books without a license. He was sentenced to three months' imprisonment but was saved from going to jail by the general amnesty ordered when Nicholas II succeeded Alexander III as tsar in October. Bunin's infatuation with the simple life soon passed, and he conveyed his reservations about the Tolstoyan ideal in the story "Na dache" (1897, At the Dacha). Tolstoy himself, however, remained one of Bunin's lifelong heroes, and decades later Bunin set down his views on Tolstoy and the meaning of Tolstoy's work in the treatise *Osvobozhdenie Tolstogo* (1937; translated as *The Liberation of Tolstoy*, 2001).

On 4 November 1894 Pashchenko wrote Bunin a note stating that she was leaving him. Her parents refused to give him any information as to her whereabouts. His despair was such that his parents feared that he would commit suicide. He was further devastated when he found out that Pashchenko had married their friend Arsenii Bibikov. Aware of his state of mind, Iulii urged him to travel to St. Petersburg and Moscow and immerse himself in the literary life in those cities. Following his brother's counsel, Bunin became acquainted with a broad spectrum of literary and intellectual figures ranging from members of the older generation, such as Dmitrii Grigorovich, to one of the rising stars of the nascent symbolist movement, Konstantin Bal'mont. He continued to feel isolated and unsettled, however. He was particularly troubled by a sense that he had received an inferior education and had not been properly prepared for a career.

Returning to the countryside for the spring and summer of 1895, Bunin worked on improving his English: he had begun translating Henry Wadsworth Longfellow's *The Song of Hiawatha* (1855). The translation was published in *Orlovsky vestnik* in 1896 and, with revisions, achieved great popularity and went through many editions. For the next several years periods of creative work in the countryside alternated with travel to the major cities or to the south and, ultimately, beyond Russia's borders. Bunin became acquainted with a growing circle of writers, including Anton Chekhov, Aleksandr Kuprin, Valerii Briusov, and Nikolai Teleshov.

Bunin's first major success came with the publication of his first collection of short stories, *"Na krai sveta" i drugie rasskazy* ("To the Edge of the World" and Other Tales), in 1897. Several of the stories display a populist orientation and expose the hardships faced by the common folk as their traditional mode of life is threatened by famine and relocation. These general themes are informed by Bunin's personal concern with issues such as growing old, the loss of cherished joys, and the mystery of death. Characteristic is the concluding section of the title story: having described the grief that attends the departure of a group of peasants from their native village in quest of a better life in a new territory, Bunin shifts focus from the sorrows of individuals to a broader reflection on the evanescence of human life. Referring to ancient burial mounds on the steppe, he asks: "But of what concern to them, these age-old, silent mounds, are the sorrows or joys of some kind of beings who will exist for a moment and then cede their place to others just like them, others who will again worry and rejoice and disappear just as completely without a trace from the face of the earth?" Repeatedly in these stories Bunin moves outward from the travails of his characters to the natural world, dissolving the tension of insoluble human dilemmas in nature's ceaseless flow.

Critics reacted positively to the collection. Commenting on "Na krai sveta" in the St. Petersburg paper *Novosti* (News) on 26 October 1895, Aleksandr Skabichevsky declared, "This is not genre painting, nor description of everyday life, nor ethnography . . . but poetry itself!" Skabichevsky's perception of a poetic quality to Bunin's prose was accurate: not only was Bunin's early prose lyrical and rhythmic, but he was also continuing to develop as a poet. In 1898 his verse collection *Pod otkrytym nebom* (Under the Open Sky) was published in Moscow, and it too met with critical acclaim.

In 1898 Bunin moved to Odessa to work for the newspaper *Iuzhnoe obozrenie* (Southern Review). He quickly became infatuated with Anna Tsakni, the daughter of the publisher of the paper, and they were married on 28 September. He soon regretted the hasty marriage. In a letter to his brother Iulii dated 14 December 1899 he described his wife as "foolish and immature as a puppy." In March 1900 Bunin left her and went to Moscow. Anna gave birth to a son, Nikolai, in August. Bunin returned to Odessa only to visit his son, who died in January 1905 of complications following scarlet fever and measles.

In 1901 Bunin published the poetry collection *Listopad* (Falling Leaves) and dedicated it to the writer Maksim Gor'ky (pseudonym of Aleksei Peshkov). Gor'ky had written Bunin to praise *Pod otkrytym nebom*, and the two had met in Yalta in 1899 and begun a friendship that lasted for nearly two decades. The long title poem is characteristic of Bunin's early verse. Personifying autumn as a "quiet widow" sorrowfully departing for the south as winter approaches, the poem highlights the beauty of nature's timeless changes. The collection garnered praise from notable figures across the literary spectrum. In early February 1901 Gor'ky wrote Briusov that he considered Bunin the foremost poet of the day, and a young poet from the symbolist camp, Aleksandr Blok, said that Bunin had won the right to one of the chief positions in contemporary Russian poetry. The collection, together with the translation of *The Song of Hiawatha,* earned Bunin his first major literary honor: the Imperial Academy of Sciences awarded him the coveted Pushkin Prize in October 1903.

While *Listopad* had been published by the symbolist house Skorpion, Bunin's artistic temperament had little in common with the excesses sometimes found in decadent literature; and when negotiations for Skorpion to publish additional volumes of his work collapsed, Bunin turned to the firm with which Gor'ky was closely identified: Znanie (Knowledge) published five volumes of his collected works from 1902 to 1909. The writers associated with Znanie were known as "realists" or "neorealists," but Bunin was never comfortable with labels, and his work defies ready categorization. The prose sketches he began writing at the turn of the twentieth century, for example, are nearly devoid of plot. Highly lyrical, they feature dense passages of description in which subtle gradations of color, smell, and sound are delicately woven together into a rich tapestry of sensation. Aptly characterized by Thomas Winner as "mood paintings," the sketches either convey a solitary narrator's reflections on the mysteries of human existence, as in "Sosny" (1901, Pines) and "Tuman" (1901, Mist), or paint an evocative picture of the slow decline of traditional forms of life in the countryside, as in "Epitafiia" (1901, Epitaph). Perhaps the best known of these sketches is "Antonovskie iabloki" (1900, Antonov Apples; translated as "Apple Fragrance," 1944), in which the rich and expansive estate life of past generations is contrasted with the more meager existence that survives on impoverished estates at the end of the nineteenth century. The writer's nostalgia for the vanishing beauty of the past is conveyed through a series of remembered scenes that anticipate Marcel Proust in their appreciation for the evocative power of sensual detail. But as exquisite as these mood paintings are, they represented a dead end for Bunin: having evoked the atmosphere of inevitable decline in the Russian countryside, he seemed to have gone as far as he could in this genre. Without a new perspective or a significant story to tell, he ran the risk of repeating himself.

In April 1903 Bunin departed for Constantinople (today Istanbul, Turkey). He had just read the entire Qur'an, and he wished to see the city that had played an important role in the history of Islam as well as in early Russian history. It was the first of many trips to Constantinople, Greece, and the Middle East, and he recorded his impressions in a series of travel sketches from 1907 to 1911. A reading of these sketches together with the poetry he wrote during the period reveals several underlying concerns. First, Bunin sought to identify the essence of a religion or culture by studying the environment in which it developed. Islam, he wrote in "Ten' ptitsy" (1908, The Shadow of a Bird), was born "in the wilderness," whereas the myths of ancient Greece were born from "sun, sea, and stone." Surveying the ruins of Egypt, Syria, Greece, and Palestine, Bunin became aware that every civilization seemed to undergo a cycle of birth, expansion, and annihilation. His appreciation of the inevitability of a civilization's decay took on topical significance when he returned to Russia and witnessed continuing dislocation and change at home. Strikes, demonstrations, and violent repression in 1905 convinced him that Russia was on an irreversible downward spiral.

Bunin's firsthand observations of the remains of earlier civilizations also deepened his preoccupation with death and loss. Annihilation was not merely a personal event; it affected civilizations, cultures, and religions alike. Nonetheless, Bunin always looked for signs of survival and renewal. Observing in "More bogov" (1908, The Sea of Gods) that "Vremia" (Time) has swallowed up the manifestations of solar worship practiced in ancient eras, Bunin exclaims: "But the Sun still exists!" Furthermore, by achieving an emotional or spiritual contact with relics of ancient life, the writer felt that his own life span had been expanded. As he put it in the poem "Mogila v skale" (1910, Cliff Tomb), the sight of a footprint left by a mourner in a grave five thousand years ago resurrected that moment of parting, and "The life given me by destiny was multiplied by five thousand years." Such moments of transcendence were immensely consoling to Bunin.

Bunin met his future wife, Vera Muromtseva, in November 1906. In 1909 he was awarded a second Pushkin Prize and elected an honorary member of the Imperial Academy. When he returned to fiction at the end of the decade he began chronicling the worrisome changes in the countryside with a depth and intensity that are not present in his earlier work. The first significant piece that reflected this new perspective was the novella *Derevnia* (1910; translated as *The Village*, 1923). The title suggests the breadth of Bunin's conception. *Derevnia* means both "village" and "countryside"; Bunin intended his depiction of one rural village to represent rural Russia at large. A character in the novella underscores this symbolism for the reader when he caustically declares about Russia: *"it is all a village."*

The two main characters in *Derevnia* are the brothers Tikhon and Kuzma Krasov. Bunin provides a capsule summary of the Krasov family background in the opening paragraphs: the brothers' great-grandfather was a serf who was killed by his master's dogs for stealing the affections of the master's lover. Their grandfather won his freedom and became a famous thief. Their father opened a shop in their native village, Durnovka (the name is derived from a word that means "bad" or "nasty"), but "went bankrupt, took up drinking . . . and died." Clearly, the Krasovs' emancipation from serfdom did not lead to prosperity and fulfillment. Nor does the present generation fare much better. Early in life Tikhon Krasov decided to devote himself to business, and after years of toil, he was able to buy the Durnovka estate from the family that had formerly been his family's masters. Yet, material gain has left him spiritually and emotionally impoverished. He has no heir; he is estranged from his wife; and he scarcely has any memories of the past to savor in his old age. At the end of the first part of the tale Tikhon is relieving himself outside his house as a train, a symbol of progress that has no meaning for him, roars by in the night. Kuzma initially seems to have a more ambitious agenda. Self-educated, he longs to make his mark on the world, leaves the village, and publishes a book of poetry. Yet, he too finds no significant outlet for his energies, and he returns to an empty life of idleness in Durnovka. Bunin now widens his focus to depict the lives of some of the Durnovka peasants; in particular, he follows the fate of a young woman who had been raped by Tikhon and is being readied for marriage to a crude, poorly educated man. Kuzma is horrified by the match but can do nothing to prevent it, and the marriage ceremony has more of the aura of a pagan orgy than a Christian ritual. Bunin concludes his narrative with a glimpse of one of the revelers wailing "with a wolf's voice" into the blizzard raging around her.

Bunin's readers reacted strongly to this somber image of Russia's destiny. His portrait of village life was a far cry from the idealized peasantry in Tolstoy's works, and some critics accused Bunin of being a bitter or fearful aristocrat slandering the people. Others, such as Gor'ky, welcomed the work as an unflinching diagnosis of the ills afflicting the countryside. Bunin thought that neither camp really understood his work and ascribed the uninformed nature of the criticism to the intelligentsia's ignorance of the true state of rural life.

Having exposed the moral bankruptcy of the lower classes, Bunin turned to the stratum of society that had long been viewed as the bastion of enlightenment and culture—the gentry. In a 1911 interview included in volume nine of his *Sobranie sochinenii v deviati tomakh* (1965–1967, Collected Works in Nine Volumes) Bunin pointed out that the landowners depicted in the works of Turgenev and Tolstoy were not typical representatives of the gentry but were "rare oases of culture." In his view, the life of the ordinary small landowner was much closer to that of the peasant than most people appreciated: "In no other country is the life of the gentry and peasantry so closely and intimately tied as among us. The soul of both, I think, is identically Russian."

A major work written at this time, the novella "Sukhodol" (1912; translated as "Dry Valley," 1935), illustrates Bunin's conviction. In this tale Bunin shows how the lives of a landowning family and their servants are intimately interwoven. The narrative structure of the tale supports this interweaving: the primary narrator is the last male descendent of the Khrushchev family, who presents the reader with the stories told by a servant, Natalia, who worked for the family. The saga of the Khrushchev clan, however, is not conveyed in a straightforward linear way: over the course of years Natalia retells her tales; with each telling new details emerge, until finally the reader has a full view of the extraordinary events that she witnessed. This lyrical structure underscores Bunin's belief in the importance of memory as a means of preserving the past, as well as in the power of a skillful narrative to make past events live again in the minds of an audience.

Natalia relates that the patriarch of the family was murdered by his illegitimate son, Gervaska; her mistress Tonia was driven mad by a failed love affair; and she herself was raped by a coarse peasant, Iushka. The events themselves, disturbing as they are, are not as striking as the fatalistic attitude that Natalia and the rest of the Dry Valley inhabitants adopt toward the misfortunes that befell them: deeply superstitious, they feel surrounded by uncanny primordial forces that they are unable to resist—indeed, they seem almost to thirst for chaos and destruction. The final stage of destruction will be the inevitable disappearance of the memories of Dry Valley. This sense of ultimate loss, in the opinion of Renato Poggioli, "gives *Dry Valley* a sense of tragic pathos which no work of Bunin . . . attained before or after."

In the early 1910s Bunin wrote a series of stories in which he strove to illuminate, as he put it in the 1911 interview, "the soul of the Russian man . . . the traits of the Slav's psyche." These works lay bare the dark, destructive forces lurking beneath the surface of everyday rural life. In "Nochnoi razgovor" (1912; translated as "A Night Conversation," 1923) he depicts the bitter disillusionment that overwhelms an idealistic young member of the gentry who spends an evening with some peasants and is horrified by the relish with which they swap tales of violence and slaughter. In "Ignat" (1912; translated as "A Simple Peasant," 1934) he describes the crude impulses that drive a peasant to a series of horrifying acts, including bestiality and murder. Yet, it is not just the peasants who come in for this kind of exposure. "Poslednii den'" (1913, The Last Day) portrays the senseless behavior of a landowner who has sold his estate to strangers and decides to give the new owners a grim welcome: he orders that his six dogs be hanged and their bodies left dangling from the tree.

In his quest to illuminate the "Slav's psyche" Bunin turned to folktale, epic, and religious literature as source material for his fiction and poetry of the early 1910s. The story "Zakhar Vorob'ev" (1912) indicates the fate of Russia's legendary warriors, the *bogatyr'*, in the modern era. Possessing enormous strength and desiring to impress those around him, the title character ends up drinking himself to death—a solitary victim of an insensitive world. Traditional spirituality too seems to have degenerated in the modern world, as Bunin shows in "Ia vse molchu" (1913; translated as "I Say Nothing," 1923). A young member of the gentry, Shasha Romanov, behaves in bizarre, self-destructive ways. Although his conduct evinces some traces of the ancient "holy fool" tradition, in which eccentric behavior and self-abnegation served to reproach those who had forgotten Christ's humility, his real motivations are a vile combination of masochism and exhibitionism. With characters such as these Bunin paints a stark picture of Russia's decline.

A journey to Ceylon (today Sri Lanka) in 1911, coupled with study of Buddhist philosophy, provided Bunin with a new perspective on the human condition. In Buddhism he found a persuasive explanation of the contradiction between life's capacity for providing moments of ecstatic happiness and the inevitable annihilation of that joy by loss and death. According to Buddhist doctrine, suffering results from desire; the only way to end suffering is to renounce desire—not only for love, passion, or material gain but for life itself. Over the next several years Bunin wrote stories that reflect these concepts. Some of these works, such as "Brat'ia" (1914; translated as "Brethren," 1923) and "Sny Changa" (1916; translated as "The Dreams of Chang," 1923), make overt reference to Buddhist thought.

"Brat'ia" is particularly rich in Buddhist aphorisms. The story juxtaposes the arduous life of a young ricksha puller in Colombo with the pleasure-sated existence of an Englishman who rides in his vehicle. The native is following the model of his father, who worked hard to provide for his family until he died from exhaustion. According to Buddhist teachings, the father must suffer reincarnation because of his immersion in earthly cares. The young man is fated to repeat his father's errors, for he began pulling the ricksha to earn money when he became infatuated with a woman. In doing so he became enmeshed in the chain of desire: his desire for love "is the desire for sons, just as the desire for sons is a desire for property, and a desire for property is a desire for well-being." Suffering is the inevitable result. They marry, but the bride disappears, and months later the youth discovers that she has become the chattel of rich Europeans in Colombo. He commits suicide but will return again and again "in a thousand incarnations." The Englishman departs on a ship; at sea he ruminates on the differences between the natives of Ceylon and the more "sophisticated" Europeans who have colonized the world. As he sees it, Europeans have lost their humility in the cosmos: "We elevate our Personality higher than the heavens; we wish to concentrate the entire world within it, no matter what we have said about universal brotherhood and equality."

With this story Bunin sets forth his understanding of a profound contradiction that underlies much of human life: the contradiction between the desire for self-gratification or self-aggrandizement and an awareness of the ultimate insignificance of any individual in the vast flow of cosmic processes. He goes on, in work after work, to depict characters who display their bondage to the ego either in love or in the accumulation of wealth and power. For the most part these works do not include overt references to Buddhism, and many of the protagonists are unaware that their desire will lead to unhappiness.

Perhaps the most compelling stories in which the drama of desire and suffering is enacted in Bunin's work of the early and mid 1910s are those that deal with the seductive power of love and passion. "Pri doroge" (1913; translated as "On the Great Road," 1934) and "Legkoe dykhanie" (1916; translated as "Gentle Breathing," 1922) focus, respectively, on a peasant girl and one of noble birth. "Legkoe dykhanie," which is just a few pages in length, offers a compressed view of a young woman's brief intoxication with the attractions of passion. It opens with a description of her portrait on her grave, then moves back in time to show what led to her early demise. Olia Meshcherskaia possessed an extraordinary zest for life; summoned to her high-school headmistress's office and reprimanded for forgetting that she is not yet a woman, Olia shocks the teacher by asserting that she *is* a woman because she has been seduced by an older man—the headmistress's brother. In the next sentence Bunin informs the reader that the following month Olia was shot and killed at a railway station by a Cossack officer "of plebeian appearance, who had absolutely nothing in common with the circle to which Olia Meshcherskaia belonged." Olia had had a sexual encounter with the officer and then told him that she had merely been toying with him; to prove it she had shown him the diary entry in which she described her seduction by her first lover, who was fifty-six. The officer then shot her in a jealous rage. Olia's early entrance into the realm of desire resulted in her untimely death, but her life did not flare up and burn out without a trace. In the final scene one of Olia's former teachers, who has become enchanted with the story of her tragic love, visits Olia's grave; her dreams will keep Olia's memory alive. In this story Bunin shows both the ecstatic and devastating effects of passion on the human soul. The conclusion suggests that the memory of such passion may endure long after the physical sensation has faded.

By this point in his career Bunin was regarded as one of the most distinguished writers of his generation; he was particularly hailed as an heir to the classical traditions of Russian literature. Russian art and literature were experiencing the throes of modernist experimentation in the 1910s, and Bunin took an active part in the debate over the proper models for writers and artists to follow. In a speech delivered during an anniversary celebration for the newspaper *Russkie vedomosti* (Russian Gazette) in October 1913 he declared that contemporary literature had departed from the standards set by Pushkin, Turgenev, and Tolstoy and was mired in vulgarity and falsehood. He perceived this development as emblematic of a general decline in the moral and spiritual values of society. The outbreak of World War I in August of the following year reinforced his dark view of societal trends. On 28 September 1914 he declared in the newspaper *Russkoe slovo* (Russian Word) that the violent acts carried out by the Germans served as a grim reminder that "the ancient beast is alive and strong in man." The dangerous assertion of the ego that Bunin evoked in "Brat'ia" seemed to him to have gained sway throughout Europe.

The fiction Bunin wrote at this time reflected his dismay over the current state of affairs. Especially disturbing is "Petlistye ushi" (1916; translated as "Noosiform Ears," 1983). The protagonist, Sokolovich, delivers a cynical tirade in a St. Petersburg tavern in which he argues that the lust for violence is more pronounced in modern times than in the age of Cain and Abel. He then goes out, picks up a prostitute, murders her in a hotel room, and coolly leaves the body to be discovered by the hotel staff. Bunin inserts several allusions to Fyodor Dostoevsky's *Prestuplenie i nakazanie* (1867; translated as *Crime and Punishment*, 1886), and the contrast that emerges between the two works is telling. The sensitive, self-doubting murderer of Dostoevsky's novel has been replaced by a cold-blooded, remorseless killer; and whereas a prostitute plays a redemptive role in Dostoevsky's murderer's life, in Bunin's tale the prostitute is not the killer's savior but his victim. Bunin seems to be saying that Dostoevsky's idealistic view of humanity's potential for redemption can be seen to be childishly naive at a time when the "ancient beast in man" has been unleashed.

Less horrifying, but perhaps even more effective in its indictment of modern egotism, is "Gospodin iz San-Frantsisko" (1916; translated as "The Gentleman from San Francisco," 1921), one of Bunin's best-known stories. An American businessman sets off with his family on a grand tour of Europe to reward himself for his years of relentless accumulation of wealth; the journey ends abruptly when he dies of a heart attack on the island of Capri. His riches are of no use to him now: his family is treated disrespectfully by the staff of the hotel in which he died, and since no coffin is available, his corpse is carted off in a crate that is normally used to transport bottled water. The ship that carries the gentleman's body back across the sea is the same one that had brought him to Europe with such great expectations. While the rich passengers stuff themselves at lavish dinners and dance the nights away in glittery ballrooms, many decks below them lies a makeshift coffin with its lifeless contents—a striking emblem of the ultimate fate of this vain and thoughtless world.

In February (New Style, March) 1917 a revolution resulted in the collapse of the Romanov dynasty. Bunin and Muromtseva spent the summer of 1917 with his relatives, the Pusheshnikovs, in the village of Glotovo, where they constantly worried that the peasants might come and burn the house down. They were in Moscow when the October (New Style, November) revolution brought the Bolsheviks to power. In May 1918 they went via Kiev to Odessa, where they stayed for nearly two years. In Moscow and Odessa, Bunin kept a journal that he published in 1936 as *Okaiannye dni* (translated as *Cursed Days: A Diary of Revolution*, 1998). The journal records scenes he witnessed, rumors and conversations he overheard, excerpts from newspapers and speeches, and his own impressions of events and conveys the sense of chaos and turmoil that Russia experienced during the revolutions and civil war. Bunin again castigates the debasement of cultural values that he finds in literature and the press. Labeling some contemporary writing "indecent trash," he says: "But almost all of Russia, almost all of Russian life, almost the entire Russian world is becoming this 'trash.'"

In January 1920 Bunin and Muromtseva were on one of the last boats to leave Odessa for Constantinople before the Red Army seized the city. From Constantinople they traveled through the Balkans to France. In 1922 Bunin finalized his divorce from his first wife and married Muromtseva. For most of the year the Bunins lived in a villa in the south of France, near Grasse, but they often spent the winter in Paris. They had many guests at the villa, including a young writer, Galina Kuznetsova, who lived with them for several years and engaged in a serious love affair with Bunin.

After a few years of writing sketches, Bunin began producing longer works of high quality in which he often returned to a favorite subject: the lure of passion, with its capacity to bring both ecstasy and pain. At one end of the spectrum in terms of length, *Mitina liubov'* (1925; translated as *Mitya's Love*, 1926) is a portrait of a young man's shattering discovery of the disparity between his idealized image of romantic love and the irresistible call of base sexual desire. At the other end, the brief "Solnechnyi udar" (1926; translated as "Sunstroke," 1934) is a masterpiece of concision and expressive vitality. Recalling Chekhov's "Dama s sobachkoi" (1899, Lady with a Lapdog) in showing how a casual affair can have lasting effects, "Solnechnyi udar" features a protagonist who lightheartedly spends the night with a woman he met on a riverboat; after she leaves he discovers that he desperately loves her but does not know her name. Bunin's descriptions of physical sensation and atmosphere provide a moving accompaniment to the emotional vicissitudes of the main character.

Another work written at this time sets the subject of desire in a more philosophical framework. In "Delo korneta Elagina" (1925; translated as "The Elaghin Affair," 1935) Aleksandr Elagin, a young military officer, is on trial for shooting Mariia Sosnovskaia, with whom he had been having an affair. Elagin testifies that Sosnovskaia wanted him to kill her, as well as himself, and her motivation becomes the focus of the story. She had many lovers and indulged in theatrical displays of emotion but seemed perpetually dissatisfied with her life. Some notes she made and her interest in the pessimistic writings of the German philosopher Arthur Schopenhauer indicate that she was seeking an escape from everyday life. Sosnovskaia's struggle reflects the dichotomy Bunin had identified in the mid 1910s between the impulse to assert one's ego by pursuing one's desires and a recognition of the futility of such striving.

In the same year in which Bunin created the enigmatic figure of Mariia Sosnovskaia he summarized his understanding of the fundamental bifurcation in human impulse in a philosophical sketch originally titled "Tsikady" (1925; translated as "Cicadas," 1935) and retitled "Noch'" (1925; translated as "Night," 1983). The narrator declares that he is one of a select group of artists and poets who have the capacity to feel not only their own time and place but also past times and other lands; such people have a heightened receptivity to life and are eager to enjoy all of its diverse richness, but their sensitivity makes them realize that all life ends in death and that immersion in its pleasures ultimately proves vain. The narrator identifies Solomon, Buddha, and Tolstoy as prime representatives of this group. He proclaims: "All the Solomons and Buddhas at first embrace the world with avidity; then, with great passion they curse its temptations"; they feel a dual torment, "the torment of withdrawal from the Chain, separation from it . . . and the torment of an intensified, terrible fascination with it." (Bunin expanded on this concept in relation to Tolstoy in *Osvobozhdenie Tolstogo*.) The narrator speaks for Bunin when he declares that while he too realizes the vanity of earthly striving, he feels that the time to turn his back on life has not yet come; the call of the world's beauty is stronger than all his philosophizing.

Another comment by the narrator hints at one of the driving forces behind Bunin's art. He says that the crown of every human life is the memory of that life, and he reveals his dream of leaving in the world "myself, my feelings, visions, and desires until the end of time." The vehicle by which this goal may be attained is art, and it appears that Bunin regarded his fiction and poetry as the path to whatever earthly immortality he might hope to attain. This impulse to fashion a permanent record of his feelings and visions perhaps fueled the major project he undertook in the late 1920s, a fictional autobiography comprising *Zhizn' Arsen'eva: Istoki dnei* (1930; translated as *The Well of Days*, 1933) and *Zhizn' Arsen'eva: Iunost'*.

In *Zhizn' Arsen'eva* Bunin depicts the evolution of an artistic soul. Drawing on events from his life, he traces the development of Aleksei Arsen'ev from impressionable child to young writer brimming over with the desire to observe and record the pageant of life. Throughout the novel he offers a dual perspective on events: the immediate sensations experienced by the hero at the time of their occurrence and the retrospective evaluation of those sensations by the mature Arsen'ev. The novel includes several of Bunin's most cherished themes: the youth's abiding sense of curiosity and wonder about the world, consciousness of the mystery of death, and eagerness to embrace the joys of this world, fleeting though they be. Death and passion are consistently juxtaposed, and one senses the writer's aspiration to transcend the constraints of individual mortality through union with another person, communion with nature, and ultimately through the creation of art. Although one of the last events in the novel is the death of Arsen'ev's first serious love, Lika (modeled both on Pashchenko and on Tsakni), the narrative ends with an evocation of Lika's reappearance in a dream. As long as the mind of the creative artist is capable of inspiration, survival after death remains possible.

The high quality of Bunin's literary output spurred efforts to promote him for the Nobel Prize in Literature during the 1920s, either on his own, or as part of a joint candidacy with other writers. These efforts began in earnest in 1922, when the Russian émigré literary community rallied around the idea that the Nobel Prize should go to a Russian émigré writer. Bunin's fellow émigré writer Mark Aldanov lobbied other literary luminaries such as Romain Rolland to support Bunin's candidacy. Rolland appeared willing to support Bunin, but he indicated that he believed that a joint candidacy of Bunin and Gor'ky would have a higher chance of success. Aldanov himself thought that a trio of candidates—Bunin, Dmitrii Merezhkovsky, and Kuprin—would make a better combination. Despite these early efforts and hopes, however, the Nobel Prize went to William Butler Yeats in 1923.

Over the course of the next decade, Aldanov and others made a renewed effort to promote Bunin's candidacy for the Nobel Prize. In 1930 Aldanov tried to enlist the support of Thomas Mann, but although the latter expressed admiration for Bunin's work, he held to the position that he would be bound to support a German candidate if one were put forth in competition with Bunin. Aldanov had high hopes for Bunin's success in 1932, but the prize went to John Galsworthy that year. Finally, on 9 November 1933, Bunin's cherished dream was realized: he became the first Russian writer to receive the Nobel Prize in Literature.

Bunin was of course overjoyed, but his way of life did not change significantly as a consequence of the award. After making a triumphal visit to the capitals of the Russian emigration–Berlin and Paris–he returned to his home in Grasse. For a brief period, foreign publishers showed an interest in his work, and new collections of his prose fiction in English appeared in the mid 1930s. This period of literary and financial success proved fleeting, however. After receiving the prize, Bunin was besieged with letters pleading for financial assistance, and he responded with as much generosity as he could. A series of financial missteps further eroded his savings, and thus, by the late 1930s, the relative comfort he had experienced earlier in the decade had dissipated.

With the outbreak of World War II, Bunin's fortunes took a serious turn. Stranded in their home near Grasse, the Bunins faced shortages of food and fuel, and Bunin was unable to write. By 1944 the tide of war had begun to turn, and Bunin went back to work on a project he had begun in the late 1930s: *Temnye allei* (translated as *Dark Avenues and Other Stories*, 1949), a collection of stories that first appeared in 1943 and in an enlarged version in 1946. Almost all of the stories deal with love and passion and follow a simple pattern: unexpectedly arriving in a person's life, passion flares up; reaches an ecstatic, incandescent peak; and then is snuffed out by a change of heart, violence, or death. The protagonists range from inexperienced adolescents to middle-aged couples finding love for the last time. Although some in the émigré community chided Bunin for the frankness of his depictions of sensuality, the works testify to his undying belief that moments of ecstatic union with another person can afford one a peak experience in an otherwise difficult or undistinguished life.

Although Bunin continued to write–revising old material, preparing new short prose pieces, and working on a book about his friendship with Chekhov that was published posthumously as *O Chekhove: Nezakonchennaia rukopis'* (1955, About Chekhov: An Unfinished Manuscript)–his health was failing, and he was in woeful financial straits. He died in his Paris apartment on 8 November 1953.

In an early note for *Zhizn' Arsen'eva*, Ivan Bunin wrote: "Life, perhaps, is given only for competition with death; man even struggles with it from the grave: it takes his name from him, but he writes it on a cross, on a stone; it seeks to cover with darkness all that he has experienced, while he strives to animate that experience in the word." Densely lyrical in structure and imbued with a striking intensity of feeling, the carefully crafted works that Bunin produced during his sixty years of literary creativity provide ample testimony to his own aspiration to resist the annihilating effects of time and death.

Biographies:

Vera Muromtseva-Bunina, *Zhizn' Bunina 1870–1906: Besedy s pamiat'iu* (Paris, 1958);

Aleksandr Baboreko, *I. A. Bunin: Materialy dlia biografii* (Moscow: Khudozhestvennaia literatura, 1967);

Thomas Gaiton Marullo, *Ivan Bunin: Russian Requiem, 1885–1920. A Portrait from Letters, Diaries, and Fiction* (Chicago: Ivan R. Dee, 1993);

Marullo, *Ivan Bunin: From the Other Shore, 1920–1933: A Portrait from Letters, Diaries, and Fiction* (Chicago: Ivan R. Dee, 1995);

Mikhail Roshchin, *Ivan Bunin* (Moscow: Molodaia gvardiia, 2000).

References:

Vladislav Afanas'ev, *I. A. Bunin: Ocherk tvorchestva* (Moscow: Prosveshchenie, 1996);

D. K. Burlaka, ed., *I. A. Bunin: Pro et contra* (St. Petersburg: Izdatel'stvo Russkogo Khristianskogo gumanitarnogo instituta, 2001);

Julian W. Connolly, *The Works of Ivan Bunin* (Boston: Twayne, 1982);

Militsa Grin, ed., *Ustami Buninykh*, 3 volumes (Frankfurt am Main: Posev, 1977–1982);

Serge Kryzytski, *The Works of Ivan Bunin* (The Hague: Mouton, 1971);

Iurii Mal'tsev, *Ivan Bunin: 1870–1953* (Moscow & Frankfurt am Main: Posev, 1994);

Thomas Gaiton Marullo, *If You See the Buddha: Studies in the Fiction of Ivan Bunin* (Evanston, Ill.: Northwestern University Press, 1998);

O. N. Mikhailov, *I. A. Bunin: Zhizn' i tvorchestvo* (Tula: Priokskoe knizhnoe izdatel'stvo, 1987);

Valerii Nefedov, *Chudesnyi prizrak: Bunin-khudozhnik* (Minsk: Polymia, 1990);

Renato Poggioli, "The Art of Ivan Bunin," *Harvard Slavic Studies*, 1 (1953): 249–277;

Thomas Winner, "Some Remarks about the Style of Bunin's Early Prose," in *American Contributions to the Sixth International Congress of Slavists*, volume 2: *Literary Contributions*, edited by W. E. Harkins (The Hague: Mouton, 1968), pp. 369–381;

James Woodward, *Ivan Bunin: A Study of His Fiction* (Chapel Hill: University of North Carolina Press, 1980);

Alexander F. Zweers, *The Narratology of the Autobiography: An Analysis of the Literary Devices Employed in Ivan Bunin's "The Life of Arsen'ev"* (New York: Peter Lang, 1997).

Papers:

Collections of Ivan Bunin's papers are in the Rossiskii gosudarstvennyi arkhiv literatury i iskusstva, Moscow; the Gosudarstvennyi muzei I. S. Turgeneva, Orel; the Institut mirovoi literatury, Moscow; the Rossiskaia gosudarstvennaia biblioteka, Moscow; and the Russian Archive of the Leeds University Library.

Bunin: Autobiographical Statement

(Written at the time of the awarding of the Nobel Prize)

I come from an old and noble house that has given to Russia a good many illustrious persons in politics as well as in the arts, among whom two poets of the early nineteenth century stand out in particular: Anna Búnina and Vasíly Zhukóvsky, one of the great names in Russian literature, the son of Athanase Bunin and the Turk Salma.

All my ancestors had close ties with the soil and the people: they were country gentlemen. My parents were no exception. They owned estates in Central Russia, in those fertile steppes in which the ancient Muscovite czars had settled colonists from all over the country for their protection against Tartar invasions from the South. That is why in that region there developed the richest of all Russian dialects, and almost all of our great writers from Turgenev to Leo Tolstoy have come from there.

I was born in Vorónezh in 1870; my childhood and youth were spent almost entirely in the country on my father's estates. During my adolescence the death of my little sister caused a violent religious crisis, but it left no permanent scars on my soul. I had a passion for painting, which, I think, shows in my writings. I wrote both poetry and prose fairly early and my works were also published from an early date.

Ever since I began to publish, my books have been both in prose and poetry, original writings as well as translations (from the English). If one divides my work by genre, one would find volumes of original poetry, two volumes of translations, and ten volumes of prose.

My works were soon recognized by the critics. They were subsequently honoured on several occasions, receiving in particular the Pushkin Prize, the highest prize awarded by the Russian Academy of Sciences. In 1909 that Academy elected me one of its twelve honorary members, a position that corresponds to the immortals of the French Academy. Among their number was Leo Tolstoy.

Nonetheless, there were several reasons why I was not widely known for a considerable time. I kept aloof from politics and in my writings did not touch upon questions concerning it. I did not belong to any literary school; I was neither decadent, nor symbolist, romantic, or naturalist. Moreover, I frequented few literary circles. I lived chiefly in the country; I travelled much in Russia as well as abroad; I visited Italy, Sicily, Turkey, the Balkans, Greece, Syria, Palestine, Egypt, Algeria, Tunisia, and the tropics. According to the words of Saadi I tried to "look at the world and leave upon it the imprint of my soul." I was interested in problems of philosophy, religion, morals, and history.

In 1910 I published my novel *Derévnya [The Village]*. It was the first of a series of works to give a picture of the Russian without make-up: his character and his soul, his original complexity, his foundations at once luminous and obscure, but almost always essentially tragic. These "ruthless" works caused passionate discussions among our Russian critics and intellectuals who, owing to numerous circumstances peculiar to Russian society and—in these latter days—to sheer ignorance or political advantage, have constantly idealized the people. In short, these works made me notorious; this success has been confirmed by more recent works.

I left Moscow because of the Bolshevik regime in May, 1918; until February, 1920, when I finally emigrated abroad, I lived in the south of Russia. Since then I have lived in France, dividing my time between Paris and the maritime Alps.

[© The Nobel Foundation, 1933. Ivan Bunin is the sole author of the text.]

1933 Nobel Prize in Literature Presentation Speech

by Per Hallström, Permanent Secretary of the Swedish Academy

Ivan Bunin's literary career has been clear and uncomplicated. He came from a family of country squires and grew up in the literary tradition of the times in which that social class dominated Russian culture, created a literature occupying a place of honour in contemporary Europe, and led to fatal political movements. "The lords of the scrupulous consciences" is what the following generation ironically called these men who, full of indignation and pity, set themselves up against the humiliation of the serfs. They deserved a better name, for they would soon have to pay with their own prosperity for the upheaval that they were going to cause.

Only the debris of the family possessions remained about the young Bunin; it was in the world of poetry that he could feel a strong rapport with the past generations. He lived in a world of illusions without any energy, rather than of national sentiment and hope for the future. Nonetheless he did not escape the influence of the reform movement; as a student, he was deeply struck by the appeal of Tolstoy's proclaiming fraternity with the humble and poor. Thus he learned like others to live by the toil of his hands, and for his part he chose the craft of cooper in the home of a co-religionist who greatly loved discussion. (He might well have tried a less difficult craft—the staves come apart easily, and it takes much skill to make a vessel that will hold its content.)

For a guide in more spiritual doctrines he had a man who fought with wavering energy against the temptations of the flesh in a very literal sense, and here vegetarianism entered his doctrine. During a voyage with him to Tolstoy's home to be presented to the master—Bunin was able to observe his victories and defeats. He was victorious over several refreshment stands in railroad stations but finally the temptation of the meat pâtés was too strong. Having finished chewing, he found ingenious excuses for his particular fall: "I know, however, that it is not the pâté that holds me in its power but I who hold it. I am not its slave; I eat when I want to; when I don't want to, I don't eat." It goes without saying that the young student did not want to stay long in this company.

Tolstoy himself did not attach great importance to Bunin's religious zeal. "You wish to live a simple and industrious life? That is good, but don't be priggish about it. One can be an excellent man in all kinds of lives." And of the profession of poet he said, "Oh well, write if you have a great fancy for it, but remember well that it can never be the goal of your life." This warning was lost on Bunin; he was already a poet with all his being.

He quickly attracted attention for verses that followed austere classical models; their subject was often descriptions of melancholic beauty of past life in the old manors. At the same time he developed in prose poems his power to render nature with all the fullness and richness of his impressions, having exercised his faculties with an extraordinary subtlety to reproduce them faithfully. Thus he continued the art of the great realists while his contemporaries devoted themselves to the adventures of literary programs: symbolism, neo-naturalism, Adamism, futurism, and other names of such passing phenomena. He remained an isolated man in an extremely agitated era.

When Bunin was forty, his novel *Derévnya* (1910) [*The Village*] made him famous and indeed notorious, for the book provoked a violent discussion. He attacked the essential point of the Russian faith in the future, the Slavophiles' dream of the virtuous and able peasant, through whom the nation must someday cover the world with its shadow. Bunin replied to this thesis with an objective description of the real nature of the peasants' virtues. The result was one of the most sombre and cruel works even in Russian literature, where such works are by no means rare.

The author gives no historical explanation of the decadence of the *muzhikí*, except for the brief information that the grandfather of the two principal characters in the novel was deliberately tracked to death by his master's greyhounds. This deed expresses well, in fact, the imprint borne by the spirit of the suppressed. But Bunin shows them just as they are without hesitating before any horror, and it was easy for him to prove the truthfulness of his severe judgment. Violence of the most cruel kind had recently swept the province in the wake of the first revolution—a foreshadowing of a later one.

For lack of another name, the book is called a novel in the translations but it really bears little resemblance to that genre. It consists of a series of immensely tumultuous episodes from lower life; truth of detail has meant everything to the author. The critic questioned not so much the details but their disinterested selection—the foreigner cannot judge the validity of the criticism. Now the book has had a strong revival because of events since then, and it remains a classic work, the model of a solid, concentrated, and sure art, in the eyes of the Russian émigrés as well as of those in the homeland. The descriptions of villages were continued in many shorter essays, sometimes devoted to the religious element which, in the eyes of the enthusiastic national generation, made the *muzhikí* the people of promise. In the writer's pitiless analysis the redemptive piety of the world is reduced to anarchic instincts and to the taste for self-humiliation, essential traits of the Russian spirit according to him. He was indeed far from his youthful Tolstoyan faith. But he had retained one thing from it: his love of the Russian land. He has hardly ever painted his marvellous countryside with such great art as in some of these novellas. It is as if he had done it to preserve himself, to be able to breathe freely once more after all he had seen of the ugly and the false.

In a quite different spirit *Sukhodól* (1911–1912) [*Dry Valley*], the short novel of a manor, was written as a counterpart to *Derévnya*. The book is not a portrayal of the present times, but of the heyday of the landed proprietors, as remembered by an old servant in the house where Bunin grew up. The author is not an optimist in this book, either; these masters have little vital force, they are as unworthy of being responsible for their own destinies and those of their subordinates as the severest accuser could have desired. In effect one finds here in large measure the materials for that defence of the people which Bunin silently passed over in *Derévnya*.

But nonetheless the picture appears now in a totally different light; it is filled with poetry. This is due in part to the kind of reconciliation that the past possesses, having paid its debt by death; but also to the sweet vision of the servant who gives charm to the confused and changing world in which, however, her youth was ruined. But the chief source of poetry is the author's imaginative power, his faculty for giving this book, with an intense concentration, the richness of life. *Sukhodól* is a literary work of *very* high order.

During the years which remained before the World War, Bunin made long trips through the Mediterranean countries and to the Far East. They provided him with the subjects of a series of exotic novellas, sometimes inspired by the world of Hindu ideas, with its peace in the abnegation of life, but more often by the strongly accentuated contrast between the dreaming Orient and the harsh and avid materialism of the West. When the war came, these studies in the spirit of the modern globe-trotters with the imprint created by the world tragedy were to result in the novella that came to be his most famous work: *Gospodín iz San Francisco* (1916) *[The Gentleman from San Francisco]*.

As often elsewhere, Bunin here simplifies the subject extremely by restricting himself to developing the principal idea with types rather than complex characters. Here he seems to have a special reason for this method: it is as if the author were afraid to come too close to his figures because they awaken his indignation and his hate. The American multi-millionaire, who after a life of ceaseless thirst for money, sets out as an old man into the world to refresh the dry consciousness of his power, his blindness of soul, and his avidity for senile pleasure, interests the author only in so far as he can show in what a pitiable manner he succumbs, like a bursting bubble. It is as if a judgment of the pitiless world were pronounced against his character. In place of a portrait of this pitifully insignificant man, the novella gives by its singularly resolute art a portrait of destiny, the enemy of this man, without any mysticism but only with strictly objective description of the game of the forces of nature with human vanity. The mystical feeling, however, is awakened in the reader and becomes stronger and greater through the perfect command of language and tone. *Gospodín iz San Francisco* was immediately accepted as a literary masterpiece; but it was also something else: the portent of an increasing world twilight; the condemnation of the essential guilt in the tragedy; the distortion of human culture which pushed the world to the same fate.

The consequences of the war expelled the author from his country, so dear to him despite everything, and it seemed a duty to remain silent under the severe pressure of what he had suffered. But his lost country lived again doubly dear in his memory, and regret gave him more pity for men. Still, he sometimes, with stronger reason, painted his particular enemy, the *muzhík*, with a sombre clear-sightedness of all his vices and faults; but sometimes he looked forward. Under all repellent things, he saw something of indestructible humanity, which he represented not with moral stress but as a force of nature, full of the immense possibilities of life. "A tree of God," one of them calls himself, "I see thus that God provides it; where the wind goes, there I follow." In this manner he has taken leave of them for the present.

From the inexhaustible treasures of his memories of the Russian nature, Bunin was later able to draw anew the joy and the desire to create. He gave colour and brilliance to new Russian destinies, conceived in the same austerity as in the era when he lived among them. In *Mítina lyubóv* (1924–1925) *[Mitya's Love]*, he analyzed young feelings with all the mastery of a psychology in which sense impressions and states of mind, marvellously rendered, are particularly essential. The book was very successful in his country, although it signalled the return to literary traditions which, with many other things, had seemed condemned to death. In what has been published of *Zhizn Arsénieva* (Part I, *Istóki dnéy*, 1930 *[The Well of Days]*), partially an autobiography, he has reproduced Russian life in a manner broader than ever before. His old superiority as the incomparable painter of the vast and rich beauty of the Russian land remains fully confirmed here.

In the literary history of his country, the place of Ivan Bunin has been clearly defined and his importance recognized for a long time and almost without divergence of opinions. He has followed the great tradition of the brilliant era of the nineteenth century in stressing the line of development which can be continued. He perfected concentration and richness of expression—of a description of real life based on an almost unique precision of observation. With the most rigorous art he has well resisted all temptations to forget things for the charm of words; although by nature a lyric poet, he has never embellished what he has seen but has rendered it with the most exact fidelity. To his simple language he has added a charm which, according to the testimonies of his compatriots, has made of it a precious drink that one can often sense even in the translations. This ability is his eminent and secret talent, and it gives the imprint of the masterpiece to his literary work.

Mr. Bunin—I have tried to present a picture of your work and of that austere art which characterizes it, a picture doubtlessly quite incomplete because of the little time at my disposal for a task so demanding. Please receive now, sir, from the hands of His Majesty the King, those marks of distinction which the Swedish Academy is conferring on you, together with its heartfelt congratulations.

[© The Nobel Foundation, 1933.]

Bunin: Banquet Speech

Introductory remarks by Professor Wilhelm Nordenson of the Caroline Institute at the Nobel Banquet at Grand Hôtel, Stockholm, 10 December 1933:

Not only the efforts to explore the subtleties of atoms and chromosomes have been rewarded today; also brilliant efforts to describe the subtleties of the human soul have been crowned with the golden laurel of the Nobel Prize. You have, Mr. Bunin, thoroughly explored the soul of vanished Russia, and in doing so, you have most meritoriously continued the glorious traditions of the great Russian literature. You have given us the most valuable picture of Russian society as it once was, and well do we understand the feelings with which you must have seen the destruction of the society with which you were so intimately connected. May our feelings of sympathy be of some comfort to you in the melancholy of exile.

Bunin's speech (Translation)

On November ninth, very far from here in a poor country house in an old Provençal town, I received the telephone call that informed me of the choice of the Swedish Academy. I would not be honest if I told you, as one does in such cases, that it was the profoundest emotional moment of my life. A great philosopher has said that even the most vehement feelings of joy hardly count in comparison with those which provoke sorrow. I do not wish to strike a note of sadness at this dinner, which I shall forever remember, but let me say nonetheless that in the course of the past fifteen years my sorrows have far exceeded my joys. And not all of those sorrows have been personal—far from it. But I can certainly say that in my entire literary life no other event has given me so much legitimate satisfaction as that little technical miracle, the telephone call from Stockholm to Grasse. The prize established by your great countryman, Alfred Nobel, is still the highest reward that can crown the work of a writer. Ambitious like most men and all writers, I was extremely proud to receive that reward at the hands of the most competent and impartial of juries, and be assured, gentlemen of the Academy, I was also extremely grateful. But I should have proved a paltry egotist if on that ninth of November I had thought only of myself. Overwhelmed by the congratulations and telegrams that began to flood me, I thought in the solitude and silence of night about the profound meaning in the choice of the Swedish Academy. For the first time since the founding of the Nobel Prize you have awarded it to an exile. Who am I in truth? An exile enjoying the hospitality of France, to whom I likewise owe an eternal debt of gratitude. But, gentlemen of the Academy, let me say that irrespective of my person and my work your choice in itself is a gesture of great beauty. It is necessary that there should be centres of absolute independence in the world. No doubt, all differences of opinion, of philosophical and religious creeds, are represented around this table. But we are united by one truth, the freedom of thought and conscience; to this freedom we owe civilization. For us writers, especially, freedom is a dogma and an axiom. Your choice, gentlemen of the Academy, has proved once more that in Sweden the love of liberty is truly a national cult.

Finally, a few words to end this short speech: my admiration for your royal family, your country, your people, your literature, does not date from this day alone. Love of letters and learning has been a tradition with the royal house of Sweden as with your entire noble nation. Founded by an illustrious soldier, the Swedish dynasty is one of the most glorious in the world. May His Majesty the King, the chivalrous King of a chivalrous people, permit a stranger, a free writer honoured by the Swedish Academy, to express to him these sentiments of profound respect and deep emotion.

[© The Nobel Foundation, 1933. Ivan Bunin is the sole author of his speech.]

Albert Camus
(7 November 1913 – 4 January 1960)

Catharine Savage Brosman
Tulane University

See also the Camus entries in *DLB 72: French Novelists, 1930–1960* and *DLB 321: Twentieth-Century French Dramatists.*

BOOKS: *Révolte dans les Asturies,* by Camus and others (Algiers: Charlot, 1936);

L'Envers et l'endroit (Algiers: Charlot, 1937);

Noces (Algiers: Charlot, 1939);

L'Etranger (Paris: Gallimard, 1942); translated by Stuart Gilbert as *The Outsider* (London: Hamilton, 1946); translation republished as *The Stranger* (New York: Knopf, 1946);

Le Mythe de Sisyphe (Paris: Gallimard, 1942); translated by Justin O'Brien as *The Myth of Sisyphus* (London: Hamilton, 1955);

Le Malentendu suivi de Caligula (Paris: Gallimard, 1944); translated by Gilbert as *Caligula and Cross Purpose* (New York: New Directions, 1947; London: Hamilton, 1947);

Lettres à un ami allemand (Paris: Gallimard, 1945);

La Peste (Paris: Gallimard, 1947); translated by Gilbert as *The Plague* (New York: Knopf, 1948; London: Hamilton, 1948);

L'Etat de siège (Paris: Gallimard, 1948);

Actuelles: Chroniques 1944–1948 (Paris: Gallimard, 1950);

Les Justes (Paris: Gallimard, 1950);

L'Homme révolté (Paris: Gallimard, 1951); translated by Anthony Bower as *The Rebel* (London: Hamilton, 1953; New York: Knopf, 1954);

Actuelles II: Chroniques 1948–1953 (Paris: Gallimard, 1953);

Les Esprits, adapted from Pierre de Larivey's play (Paris: Gallimard, 1953);

L'Eté (Paris: Gallimard, 1954);

Requiem pour une nonne, adapted from William Faulkner's novel (Paris: Gallimard, 1956);

La Chute (Paris: Gallimard, 1956); translated by O'Brien as *The Fall* (London: Hamilton, 1956; New York: Knopf, 1957);

Albert Camus with Helen Triber (left) and Torun Moberg at the 1957 Nobel Banquet in Stockholm (Getty Images)

L'Exil et le royaume (Paris: Gallimard, 1957); translated by O'Brien as *Exile and the Kingdom* (London: Hamilton, 1958; New York: Knopf, 1958);

Réflexions sur la peine capitale, by Camus and Arthur Koestler (Paris: Calmann-Lévy, 1957)—includes "Réflexions sur la guillotine," translated by Richard Howard as *Reflections on the Guillotine: An Essay on Capital Punishment* (Michigan City, Ind.: Fridtjof-Karla, 1959);

Actuelles III: Chroniques algériennes, 1939–1958 (Paris: Gallimard, 1958);

Discours de Suède (Paris: Gallimard, 1958); translated by O'Brien as *Speech of Acceptance upon the Award of the Nobel Prize for Literature, Delivered in Stockholm on the Tenth of December, Nineteen Hundred and Fifty-seven* (New York: Knopf, 1960);

Les Possédés, adapted from Fyodor Dostoevsky's novel (Paris: Gallimard, 1959); translated by O'Brien as *The Possessed* (London: Hamilton, 1960; New York: Knopf, 1960);

Carnets: mars 1935 – février 1942 (Paris: Gallimard, 1962); translated by Philip Thody as *Carnets* (London: Hamilton, 1963); translation republished as *Notebooks, 1935–1942* (New York: Knopf, 1963);

Théâtre, récits, nouvelles (Paris: Gallimard, 1962);

Carnets: janvier 1942 – mars 1951 (Paris: Gallimard, 1964); translated by O'Brien as *Notebooks, 1942–1951* (New York: Knopf, 1965); translated by Thody as *Carnets, 1942–1951* (London: Hamilton, 1966);

Essais (Paris: Gallimard, 1965);

Le Combat d'Albert Camus, edited by Norman Stokle (Quebec: Presses de l'Université Laval, 1970);

La Mort heureuse, Cahiers Albert Camus, no. 1 (Paris: Gallimard, 1971); translated by Howard as *A Happy Death* (London: Hamilton, 1972; New York: Knopf, 1972);

Le Premier Camus, suivi de Ecrits de jeunesse d'Albert Camus, Cahiers Albert Camus, no. 2 (Paris: Gallimard, 1973); translated by Ellen Conroy Kennedy as *Youthful Writings* (New York: Knopf, 1976; London: Hamilton, 1977);

Fragments d'un combat: 1938–1940, Alger Républicain, Le Soir Républicain, 2 volumes, edited by Jacqueline Lévi-Valensi and André Abbou (Paris: Gallimard, 1978);

Journaux de voyage (Paris: Gallimard, 1978); translated by Hugh Levick as *American Journals* (New York: Paragon House, 1987; London: Hamilton, 1988);

Caligula, version de 1941, suivi de La Poétique du premier Caligula, edited by A. James Arnold (Paris: Gallimard, 1984);

Albert Camus, éditorialiste à L'Express: mai 1955 – février 1956, edited by Paul-F. Smets (Paris: Gallimard, 1987);

Carnets: mars 1951 – décembre 1959 (Paris: Gallimard, 1989);

Le Premier Homme, edited by Catherine Camus (Paris: Gallimard, 1994); translated by David Hapgood as *The First Man* (London: Hamilton, 1995; New York: Knopf, 1995);

Camus à "Combat": éditoriaux et articles d'Albert Camus, 1944–1947, edited by Lévi-Valensi (Paris: Gallimard, 2002).

Collection: *Œuvres complètes d'Albert Camus*, 5 volumes (Paris: Club de l'Honnête Homme, 1983).

Editions in English: *The Myth of Sisyphus and Other Essays*, translated by Justin O'Brien (New York: Knopf, 1955);

Caligula and Three Other Plays, translated by Stuart Gilbert (New York: Knopf, 1958)—comprises *Caligula, Cross Purpose, State of Siege*, and *The Just Assassins*;

Resistance, Rebellion and Death, translated by O'Brien (London: Hamilton, 1961; New York: Knopf, 1961)—includes "Letters to a German Friend" and excerpts from *Actuelles: Chroniques 1944–1948, Actuelles II: Chroniques 1948–1953*, and *Actuelles III: Chroniques algériennes, 1939–1958*;

Lyrical and Critical, edited and translated by Philip Thody (London: Hamilton, 1967)—includes "Betwixt and Between" *[The Wrong Side and the Right Side]*, *Nuptials*, and *Summer*;

Lyrical and Critical Essays, edited by Thody, translated by Ellen Conroy Kennedy (New York: Knopf, 1968)—includes *The Wrong Side and the Right Side, Nuptials*, and *Summer*;

The Stranger, translated by Matthew Ward (New York: Knopf, 1988);

Between Hell and Reason: Essays from the Resistance Newspaper "Combat" 1944–1947, edited and translated by Alexandre de Gramont (Middletown, Conn.: Wesleyan University Press / Hanover, N.H.: University Press of New England, 1991);

The Plague; The Fall; Exile and the Kingdom; and Selected Essays, translated by Gilbert and O'Brien (New York: Everyman's Library, 2004).

PLAY PRODUCTIONS: *Le Malentendu*, Paris, Théâtre des Mathurins, 24 August 1944;

Caligula, Paris, Théâtre Hébertot, 26 September 1945;

L'Etat de siège, Paris, Théâtre Marigny, 27 October 1948;

Les Justes, Paris, Théâtre Hébertot, 15 December 1949;

Les Esprits, adapted from Pierre de Larivey's play, Angers, Festival d'Art Dramatique, 16 June 1953;

Requiem pour une nonne, adapted from William Faulkner's novel, Paris, Théâtre des Mathurins, 22 September 1956;

Les Possédés, adapted from Fyodor Dostoevsky's novel, Paris, Théâtre Antoine, 30 January 1959.

OTHER: Sébastien-Roch Nicolas [de] Chamfort, *Maximes et anecdotes*, preface by Camus (Monaco: Dac, 1944);

André Salvet, *Le Combat silencieux*, preface by Camus (Paris: Portulan, 1945);

Jean Camp and others, *L'Espagne libre*, preface by Camus (Paris: Calmann-Lévy, 1946);

Pierre-Eugène Clairin, *Dix estampes originales,* introduction by Camus (Paris: Rombaldi, 1946);

Jacques Méry, *Laissez passer mon peuple,* preface by Camus (Paris: Seuil, 1947);

Jeanne Héon-Canone, *Devant la mort,* preface by Camus (Angers: Siraudeau, 1951);

Daniel Mauroc, *Contre-Amour,* preface by Camus (Paris: Minuit, 1952);

"Herman Melville," in *Les Ecrivains célèbres,* edited by Raymond Queneau and others, volume 3 (Paris: Mazenod, 1953);

A. Rosmer, *Moscou sous Lénine–Les origines du communisme,* preface by Camus (Paris: Editions de Flore, 1953);

Désert vivant: Images et couleurs de Walt Disney, adapted by Camus, Marcel Aymé, Louis Bromfield, Julian Huxley, François Mauriac, André Maurois, and Henry de Montherlant (Paris: Société Française du Livre, 1954);

Konrad Bieber, *L'Allemagne vue par les écrivains de la Résistance française,* preface by Camus (Geneva: Droz, 1954);

"L'Enchantement de Cordes," in *Cordes-en-Albigeois,* edited by C. Targuebayre (Toulouse: Privat, 1954);

Oscar Wilde, *Ballade de la geôle de Reading,* preface by Camus (Paris: Falaize, 1954);

Roger Martin du Gard, *Œuvres complètes,* 2 volumes, preface by Camus (Paris: Gallimard, 1955);

La Vérité sur l'affaire Nagy, preface by Camus (Paris: Plon, 1958);

Henriette Grindat, *La Postérité du soleil,* text by Camus (Geneva: Engelberts, 1965).

TRANSLATIONS: James Thurber, *La Dernière Fleur* (Paris: Gallimard, 1952);

Pedro Calderón de la Barca, *La Dévotion à la croix* (Paris: Gallimard, 1953);

Dino Buzzati, *Un Cas intéressant, Avant-Scène,* no. 105 (1955): 1–25;

Félix Lope de Vega Carpio, *Le Chevalier d'Olmedo* (Paris: Gallimard, 1957).

When Albert Camus received the Nobel Prize in Literature in 1957, he was the ninth French writer so honored and (at not quite forty-four years of age) the youngest writer after Rudyard Kipling. The award projected the author to worldwide celebrity. He was already famous in France and elsewhere for works such as *L'Etranger* (1942; translated in England as *The Outsider* and in the United States as *The Stranger,* 1946), *Le Mythe de Sisyphe* (1942; translated as *The Myth of Sisyphus,* 1955), *La Peste* (1947; translated as *The Plague,* 1948), and *La Chute* (1956; translated as *The Fall,* 1956). In the highly charged political atmosphere of France during the 1950s, with opinion polarized over the Cold War and the Algerian colonial conflict, the award caused a furor; Camus's moderate positions and refusal to endorse revolutionary action infuriated many of his compatriots. Remarks he made in Stockholm concerning Algeria became notorious and added to the controversy. The result was, in the eyes of many, a severely compromised author and award, although thousands on both sides of the Atlantic commended the choice: "He is one of the few literary voices that has emerged from the chaos of the post-war world with the balanced, sober outlook of humanism," as a *New York Times* editorialist wrote.

Camus's popularity has endured, in France and abroad. He had two titles (*L'Etranger* and *La Peste*) on a 1970 top-ten list of twentieth-century French best-sellers; he was outranked only by Antoine de Saint-Exupéry, who had three. More than six million copies of *L'Etranger* had been sold by 2000; it has been translated into more than forty languages and is said to attract two hundred thousand new readers each year. Camus's work has drawn the attention not only of general readers and literary critics but also of intellectual historians, theologians, psychiatrists, and philosophers. His name occurs frequently in English-language publications, in a wide range of works, from mystery novels—*The Moth* (1993) and *The Black Hornet* (1994) by James Sallis—through journals of higher education such as *Academic Questions* to *The New Yorker* and *The Nation.*

It can even be suggested that Camus is too well known, cited carelessly and incorrectly for purposes and in senses foreign to the spirit of his work. To many people, the use of the words *stranger* and *absurd* in almost any contemporary literary context conveys, whether correctly or not, a Camusian note, even though other authors also have stressed the sense of alienation between man and the universe. Some are modern writers, such as André Malraux; some belong to earlier periods, such as Blaise Pascal. The ordeals of the Greek mythological hero Sisyphus are now known to many chiefly through their treatment by Camus, and mention of plague in a literary context often evokes Camus alone because readers overlook other works on the same subject. Few philosophies have been less well understood and yet more frequently mentioned than the existentialism with which he is persistently, if somewhat falsely, associated in the public mind.

Albert Camus was born on 7 November 1913 outside Mondovi, a village near Bône (now Annaba), in eastern Algeria, then a French territory. In his own eyes, his Algerian birth was the most important fact of his life. Acknowledging the Nobel Prize, he expressed gratitude to the committee "d'avoir voulu distinguer un écrivain français d'Algérie. Je n'ai jamais rien écrit qui ne se rattache, de près ou de loin, à la terre où je suis né" (for having wished to single out a French Algerian writer. I have never written anything that is not connected, closely or distantly, to the land where I was born). His attachment to his native territory sheds light on his entire life—not only his literary production but also his journalistic and political activities and particular unhappiness and public difficulties at the time of the Algerian war.

Camus's father, Lucien Auguste Camus, born in Algeria in 1885, was a supervisor on a vineyard. The author's mother, Catherine-Hélène Sintès Camus, born in Algeria in 1882, was, like many European Algerians, of Spanish blood; her ancestors came from Minorca. Camus had one brother, Lucien, born in 1910. Catherine-Hélène Camus was totally illiterate, doubtless in part because of family circumstances (she came from a large family that struggled to survive) but also because she was nearly deaf. Her hearing impairment created difficulties in the household and in her relationship with Albert; her illiteracy compounded the problem. She never read a word of his writings.

Being partly of Spanish blood presumably reinforced in Camus a tendency he shared with many Algerian compatriots: a powerful and obvious male pride. Commentators have viewed it as a Mediterranean trait, deriving from the large number of Algerian settlers of Mediterranean ancestry and from the native Arabs and Berbers, among whom the cult of the masculine is traditionally strong. Camus spoke of Algerians as "fiers de leur virilité, de leur capacité de boire ou de manger, de leur force et de leur courage" (proud of their virility, their capacity to drink or eat, their strength and courage). The term *un homme* (a man) was charged with meaning. During Meursault's trial in *L'Etranger*, Céleste, a man who runs a neighborhood restaurant, tells the court that Meursault is "un homme" (a man); when asked what "being a man" means, Céleste answers that everyone knows what it means. This notion of masculinity included a strong element of honor and responsibility, albeit exercised in a narrow range: "on ne manque pas à sa mère" (you don't let your mother down); "celui qui touche à mon frère, il est mort" (he who touches my brother is dead). It also involved vanity, a quick temper, and a passionate character. Men of this type saw or imagined insults easily and were quick to defend themselves, by their fists if necessary. Feminists have denounced this cult of male values and Camus's particular male chauvinism or *phallocratie*, since, they argue, machismo contributes to ethnic and national aggression, and the principle of defending not only one's mother but also women in general implies condescension and paternalism.

When World War I began in summer 1914, Camus's father was called into military service; he was wounded in the Battle of the Marne and died in a hospital in autumn 1914. Thus, Camus never knew him; moreover, he learned little about him, principally because his deaf mother, though not literally mute, spoke infrequently and may herself have known little of her husband's background. In Camus's works, fathers are often missing or shadowy; only in his unfinished autobiographical novel *Le Premier Homme* (1994; translated as *The First Man*, 1995) does a father appear directly and extensively. In contrast, a mother is a recurring figure throughout Camus's work. He wrote always of his own mother with respect and devotion, often connecting her to Algeria and the sense of home. In a letter to his friend Jules Roy, Camus commented, "Ce sont nos mères qui justifient la vie, c'est pourquoi je souhaite de mourir avant la mienne" (What justifies life is our mothers; that's why I wish to die before mine)—a wish that was, in fact, granted. Textual evidence can be marshaled to show that he was haunted by the maternal idea; the word *mother* bears considerable weight in his prose, as when it is paired with *truth*: "ma mère et ma vérité." There are suggestions, however, that the relationship was not an easy one; as Camus wrote in his *Carnets: janvier 1942 – mars 1951* (1964; translated as *Notebooks, 1942 – 1951*): "J'aimais ma mère avec désespoir. Je l'ai toujours aimée avec désespoir" (I loved my mother despairingly. I have always loved her despairingly).

Family circumstances obliged Catherine-Hélène Camus to resettle with her own widowed mother, Catherine Sintès, in Belcourt, an outlying district of Algiers, a city with more than 150,000 inhabitants, according to the 1906 census. Camus's mother first worked in a cartridge factory, then became a domestic, cleaning in houses and shops. As a war widow, she received only a small pension beginning late in the war and, later, extremely modest assistance for her sons, who also received scholarships and medical care. Though the income from Catherine-Hélène and her brother Etienne Sintès, who lived with them, was sometimes supplemented by another brother, the family lived on the edge of dire poverty. The small apartment had neither electricity nor running water, not even an oven—prepared dishes had to be taken to the baker's for cooking. The sanitary facilities consisted of a *toilette turque* (a hole).

Catherine Sintès, an unbending, perhaps jealous person, ruled the household with an iron hand and managed the money. Poverty dictated, to some degree, her tyrannical ways; but she also had a hard character.

Thus, discipline as well as poverty marked Camus's childhood. Characters in his fiction are frequently of modest means, and his early series of newspaper articles, "Misère de la Kabylie" (1939, Misery in Kabylia), concerned economic hardship among the Kabyles, a Berber tribal people living to the east of Algiers. When challenged by Jean-Paul Sartre for being and thinking like a bourgeois—an unpardonable sin to the bourgeois-baiting and often antagonistic Sartre—Camus observed that he had come from the humblest of backgrounds and had known genuine poverty, unlike Sartre, a son of the bourgeoisie. Yet, Camus said that his boyhood was not unhappy; he often depicted it as a time of joy, both "misérable et heureux" (poverty-stricken and happy). Upon learning he had won the Nobel Prize, he wrote in his *Carnets: mars 1951 – décembre 1959* (1989, Notebooks: March 1951 – December 1959): "A 20 ans, pauvre, et nu, j'ai connu la vraie gloire. Ma mère" (At age 20, poor and miserable, I knew real glory. My mother).

As a boy, Camus liked the streets, with their varied activities and faces, and the busy port of Algiers. He was fonder still of the beach, where, violating his grandmother's prohibition (she feared he would drown), he played on the sand and in the water. He learned to play European football (soccer), the street game of the period—though it was forbidden by his grandmother (shoes wear out quickly in rough play on pavement). Later, he was an enthusiastic team member, playing goalie for many years. He made friends easily, being of an open, cordial character. School, where he did well, was another counterworld that offset the silence, reprimands, and beatings at home.

Camus's school success earned him a scholarship to the Grand Lycée, one of two high schools in Algiers, the only one that included the uppermost grades. Against the opposition of his grandmother, who wanted him to go to work full-time, but with the support of an uncle by marriage, Gustave Acault, Camus enrolled. The curriculum, which was entirely secular, emphasized intellectual skills and the French cultural tradition. Literature and history occupied a significant place at all levels. One of his teachers was Jean Grenier, later his philosophy professor at the University of Algiers, an author of lyrical essays and a longtime mentor and friend. Under Grenier's guidance, Camus read the writings of the pre-Socratic philosophers, along with those of St. Augustine, Pascal, Søren Kierkegaard, and Friedrich Nietzsche. He had no religious belief: his family members were not practicing Catholics, and his first Communion was chiefly a symbolic step that left little mark on him.

Camus's work illustrated the appeal and powerful imprint of the French school system. In his last decade, he paid homage to what he called "la puissante poésie de l'école" (the powerful poetry [poetic effect] of school) and the role of the schoolmaster; he dedicated his Nobel speech to his elementary-school teacher Louis Germain. Hostile critics, however, accuse Camus of intellectual weakness in never having progressed beyond the limitations of the republican humanism of the Third Republic. His disagreement with Sartre and other neo-Marxist thinkers over the use of violence to achieve political ends, and his obstinate attachment to Algeria, may be attributed in part to the imprint of his schooling.

During the winter of 1930–1931, when Camus was seventeen, he was diagnosed with tuberculosis in his right lung. Perhaps because of inadequate diet—likely deficiencies of proteins and vitamins—or conceivably because of fatigue resulting from excessive activity, he did not have the strength to fight off the infection. He was obliged to drop out of the lycée, and thenceforth he lived with the disease, for which there was neither cure nor reliable and noninvasive treatment until 1945. In the 1930s, clinical use of the antimicrobial agent streptomycin became common, but its effectiveness was uncertain, and for Camus it never succeeded. He was also treated repeatedly by pneumothorax (lung collapse therapy). Such an illness was an enormous shock to a young man who had a promising career ahead of him. He often believed that the disease would kill him. The absurd meant for him first of all the disparity between a young consciousness hungry for experience and crying out for meaning, and a body condemned to illness and ultimately death. Camus was taken in by Acault, who assumed responsibility for him, fed him a diet heavy in meat (Acault was a butcher by trade), and provided other material assistance. Camus's uncle also lent him books.

Despite his illness, Camus, having returned to the lycée, retook his last year of courses, then spent a year in a university-preparatory class. He next enrolled (autumn 1933) in the University of Algiers. He attended lectures on Kierkegaard, Edmund Husserl, and Martin Heidegger and, in his third year, wrote a thesis on Christian metaphysics and Neoplatonism for the *diplôme d'études supérieures* (diploma of advanced studies) and received his degree (1936). For the rest of his life, the ancient Greeks, and Greece itself, constituted part of his thinking. Greek philosophy, along with his Mediterranean outlook, led him to consider both life and death without illusion.

In 1934 Camus married Simone Hié, a beautiful but unstable young woman addicted to morphine. Although they practiced a rather open union, it was not a happy one. By the autumn of 1936, the two had separated; the union ended officially with divorce in 1940.

In 1935 he joined the Algerian Communist Party, remaining a member until 1937, when the party itself excluded him on political grounds. The match had not been right from the start, since he was interested mainly in advancing the status of Algerian Muslims and improving workers' conditions, not in promoting the Stalinist platform for world revolution. While a party member, he worked at the Communist Maison de la Culture and, with friends, founded the Théâtre du Travail (Labor Theater), an amateur troupe that later, after it separated from party sponsorship, became the Théâtre de l'Equipe (Team Theater). Its repertory included a stage adaptation by Camus of Malraux's *Le Temps du mépris* (1935; translated as *Days of Wrath*, 1936) and an adaptation by Jacques Copeau of Fyodor Dostoevsky's *The Brothers Karamazov* (1879–1880). Camus acted, helped to write or adapt texts, and assisted with production. The group also wanted to produce a drama conceived collectively (but written mostly by Camus, it was said later) titled *Révolte dans les Asturies* (Revolt in Asturias); the production was forbidden by the Algiers city government for political reasons, but the text was published in 1936. Thereafter, Camus always considered the theater the prime artistic experience, involving text, performance, and collaboration.

Camus's first single-authored volume, *L'Envers et l'endroit* (translated as *The Wrong Side and the Right Side*, 1967), appeared in 1937 under the imprint of Edmond Charlot, an Algiers bookshop owner just launching a modest publishing venture. In these short sketches and narratives Camus treated such subjects as irony, love of life, "death in the soul" (inspired by his 1936 visit to Prague, where he had been unhappy), and a mother and child in Algiers. That same year he began a novel, reconstructed posthumously from manuscripts and published as *La Mort heureuse* (1971; translated as *A Happy Death*, 1972). Rather ill-formed and highly autobiographical, it deals with themes that recur in his later work and features a hero named Mersault (not Meursault, as in *L'Etranger*). There is considerable textual and organizational resemblance between the early novel and *L'Etranger*, although critics disagree on whether the latter should be considered a direct development or an offshoot or substitute. In 1939 Charlot published *Noces* (translated as *Nuptials*, 1967). This short collection of essays, praised by André Gide (by then an elder statesman of letters), includes some of Camus's most beautiful writing, treating in a poetic yet sober manner the sea, the desert, and death.

In July 1937 Camus sailed for Marseille, visited Paris for the first time, and spent a month in the mountains in the hope of strengthening his lungs. He found a position as a journalist for a liberal daily newspaper, *Alger Républicain*, in which his articles on Kabylia appeared. Shortly after World War II began (September 1939), the paper was forced by the censors to close. In 1940 Camus and the editor in chief, Pascal Pia, moved to Paris, where they worked for *France-Soir*, a daily; there, Camus established ties with literary figures and members of the Gallimard publishing firm.

In 1937 Camus had become romantically interested in Francine Faure, a student of mathematics. She came from a family long established in Oran and was one-quarter Jewish. She too had lost her father early in World War I. In the spring of 1939, unable to finish her university studies in Algiers, she took a job as a substitute teacher in Oran. Camus was simultaneously involved with Yvonne Ducailar, a graduate student and later a journalist, perhaps one of the great passions of his life. Although Faure's mother was not favorably impressed with Camus's credentials—ill with tuberculosis, without family money, and not yet divorced from his first wife—Faure was determined to pursue the relationship and demanded marriage. In December 1940, after his divorce was final, Camus, who was working in Lyon, where *Paris-Soir* had moved, and Faure, who had crossed with difficulty to France, were wed in the Free Zone, in Vichy (the town where the government was based after the fall of France the previous June). They then sailed back to Oran. Although work of any sort was scarce, Camus eventually found a position in a private school, and Faure resumed substitute teaching.

In January 1942 Camus fell gravely ill, spitting blood; tuberculosis was found in his left lung. In late summer he and his wife traveled to the mountains of south-central France in the Free Zone. She shortly sailed back to Oran, and he expected to follow; but when the Germans overran the zone demarcation line in November 1942 and occupied the entire country, no exit passes could be obtained, and Camus remained in a village called Le Panelier throughout the autumn and into the following year.

Camus first knew celebrity in 1942 with the publication by Gallimard of *L'Etranger* and *Le Mythe de Sisyphe*. The former, a short novel told in the first person, has been called, variously, a classical work in the mode of Voltaire's tales, an apologue, a symbolic narrative, and a bleak, Ernest Hemingway–like narrative. It attracted readers immediately by its style, its concision, and its themes of oppression and alienation. With few exceptions, its language is plain, characterized by parataxis (stringing sentence elements together sequentially without coordinating or subordinating connectives). In the first part, Meursault, an Algiers warehouse clerk, learns that his mother has died in a home for the elderly outside the city and travels there to attend her funeral. The day after returning, he goes swimming, picks up a girl, takes her to a comic movie, and invites her home. He shortly becomes involved with a neighborhood man of dubious character (apparently a pimp) named Raymond, who has had a dispute with his companion, an Arab woman. Meursault agrees to write for him a letter addressed to the woman, intended to lure her back. Some time later, Meursault joins Raymond and his friends at a beach party. During an encounter with a group of Arabs who seem to be the woman's relatives and are apparently looking for a fight, Raymond pummels one of them, who then slashes his arm and face with a knife. After being bandaged, Raymond returns to the spot with Meursault, finds his attacker, and proposes to shoot him. To forestall him, Meursault takes the gun. Later, he wanders out alone and ends up killing the Arab with the revolver when the man flashes a knife threateningly.

In the second part, Meursault, in prison, is tried on a capital charge of murder. The prosecutor interprets the crime as a cold-blooded, premeditated plot of revenge, although it really resulted from a series of chance events and thoughtless conduct. Meursault is portrayed as a sociopath who showed indifference to his mother's death by smoking and drinking coffee beside the coffin and later picking up the girl. His execution, the prosecutor argues, will rid the world of a dangerous man, both intelligent and morally monstrous. Meursault is condemned to death. While awaiting the outcome of his appeal, he receives a visit from the prison chaplain, who attempts to console him, on grounds that everyone dies eventually. Meursault, usually passive, loses his temper and shouts that such consolation is worthless and that the years of life he will lose are priceless—indeed, the only important thing. After this moment of illumination he discovers a kind of peace and feels at one with the world. At the end of the novel he anticipates his execution with a sense of exhilaration, wishing to be greeted with shouts of hatred; the crowd's hostility will affirm his being. Critics have noted that the imagined scene suggests scenes of Christ's judgment and death. While there is no clear-cut internal interpretation of the novel, in a foreword for a 1955 edition, Camus called Meursault "le seul Christ que nous méritons" (the only Christ we deserve).

Meursault's status as a stranger (that is, foreigner) is initially social: although utterly ordinary in many ways, he does not act and react to others and to social structures as one is supposed to, according to custom, religion, and law; he is thus viewed as alien, threatening. To deal with him, society calls on the elaborate mechanism called justice; he is convicted of a capital crime, whereas in fact he is culpable only of second-degree homicide or manslaughter. His situation can, or could in 1942, be read also as representing the oppression of France by the German occupiers (the true strangers) and the semicollaborationist Vichy government. The hero's alienation can, alternatively, be viewed as metaphysical: man is condemned to death in an incomprehensible and unforgiving universe. This quasi-existentialist interpretation is perhaps the most widespread. What is absent is any racial critique: postcolonial critics have noted that the Arabs and Berbers are nearly invisible, treated as "strangers," without their inferior status being questioned, whereas the Algerians of European descent are the genuine foreigners. The title cannot thus be interpreted to suggest colonial alienation except by the irony of missing meaning.

Among those who recognized the great merit of *L'Etranger* were Francis Ponge, Malraux, and Sartre. In a long article published in *Cahiers du Sud* in 1943, Sartre asserted that the topic was the absurdity of the human condition—at once a state and the lucid consciousness of that state. Yet, he noted, the book was not a *roman à thèse* (thesis novel); its burden is expressed in images, not in reasoning. Meursault's attitude toward his life—the present and a succession of presents—is, according to Sartre, the ideal of the absurd man. Sartre may have been the first critic to comment on the absence of causality in the book; paradoxically, once causality is limited, the smallest incident takes on weight, and everything contributes to the outcome. Gide expressed esteem for Camus's thought, but acknowledged aversion toward the book itself.

Le Mythe de Sisyphe, a short philosophical treatise, is close in spirit to the works of many existential writers, since it focuses on the human predicament as felt by a thinking subject who has no absolute grounds for choice or divine reassurance and faces death as the inevitable end. It begins with what Camus calls the only true philosophical question—suicide—and then develops the notion of the absurd. The absurd is neither in the world as such nor in man, but in the copresence of the two. Men's aspirations to immortality and the absolute are opposed by the world's indifference and the fact of mortality. Since the absurd is the very condition of human existence, it must be maintained, not denied; one must not give in to hope, belief in the invisible, or any other irrational position, including the "existentialist leap" seen in the writings of such authors as Kierkegaard and Karl Jaspers, by which they "leap over" the difficulty of existential isolation and meaninglessness. To maintain the absurd, one must remain conscious and in perpetual revolt. The essay ends with

Camus's version of the myth of Sisyphus pushing his rock: "La lutte elle-même vers les sommets suffit à remplir un coeur d'homme. Il faut imaginer Sisyphe heureux" (The struggle toward the summits is itself enough to fill a man's heart. One must imagine Sisyphus to be happy).

While many readers, especially undergraduates who first encounter *Le Mythe de Sisyphe,* are impressed by Camus as a thinker, his standing among professional philosophers and intellectuals was from the beginning much lower than his reputation among literary critics. Disparaging remarks made by Sartre and Simone de Beauvoir–the chief proponents of French existentialism–later contributed to the trend. Perhaps anticipating future criticism as well as defending himself against contemporary attacks, Camus often said that he was an artist or a *moraliste,* not a philosopher. Left-wing intellectuals have not ceased attacking *Le Mythe de Sisyphe*; in *The Content of the Form: Narrative Discourse and Historical Representation* (1987) Hayden White mocked Camus for "opposing 'totalitarianism' and holding up the prospect of an amiable anarchy as a desirable alternative." Handbooks and collections in modern philosophy often omit Camus, although selections from *Le Mythe de Sisyphe* were included in *Existentialism from Dostoevsky to Sartre* (1956), a major mid-century anthology edited by Walter Kaufmann.

In November 1943 Camus moved to Paris, where Pia had settled again after *France-Soir* had been obliged to close in Lyons. Camus found employment as a reader at Gallimard and also helped produce the underground Resistance paper *Combat,* then edited by Pia. Francine Camus was not able to join her husband until the autumn of 1944. Upon the liberation of Paris in August 1944, the paper, with Camus as editor in chief, appeared openly as the leading journal of opinion. He wrote many of the editorials, on such controversial issues as socialism, pacifist movements, punishment of Nazi collaborators, and Communist dictatorship. These pieces, many of which were collected in *Actuelles: Chroniques 1944–1948* (1950), were widely viewed as the conscience of France. For health reasons he withdrew temporarily from the paper in the winter of 1945; there were also periods when, in apparent disagreement with the policies of the newspaper, he ceased writing for it. He finally resigned in 1947 over ideological differences and financial difficulties.

During the *Combat* period, Camus was a highly visible figure in the neighborhood of Saint-Germain-des-Prés–the French existentialists' headquarters–and visited Sartre, Beauvoir, and some of their friends, including Arthur Koestler. Though she denied doing so, it is obvious that Beauvoir wrote him into her novel *Les Mandarins* (1954) as the character Henri Perron. In 1945 the Camus's twins, Jean and Catherine, were born. In 1946 he visited North America, principally New York but also Montreal and other cities; he lectured, met writers and intellectuals, and was received as a famous man.

In 1944 Gallimard brought out two plays by Camus in one volume: *Le Malentendu suivi de Caligula* (translated as *Caligula and Cross Purpose,* 1947). *Le Malentendu,* staged that year, received a cool reception; its somber quality helped strengthen the supposition that Camus was a nihilist. The play is based on the story Meursault reads on a scrap of newspaper in prison. Jan, having left home–an unidentified European country marked by gloom and dark skies–to live in North Africa, returns long afterward with his wife, Maria. Leaving her elsewhere, he goes to the inn run by his mother and sister, Martha, but does not identify himself. It is an existential test: Jan wants to share his wealth with them and bring them happiness, but first they must recognize him. Over the years they have murdered strangers for their money, hoping one day to escape their dreary circumstances. Jan, too, is murdered; they then discover his identity. The mother drowns herself; Martha joins her in death. It is not a question of remorse; they are amoral. Rather, the mother says she is too weary to continue, and Martha kills herself as an act of protest against the absurd, which turns acts against their agent and deprives life of meaning and happiness. In her last sentences, Martha tells Maria, who has found her husband dead, "Je ne puis mourir en vous laissant l'idée que . . . ceci est un accident. Car c'est maintenant que nous sommes dans l'ordre. . . . Priez votre Dieu qu'il vous fasse semblable à la pierre" (I cannot die leaving you with the idea . . . that this is an accident. For this is the normal order of things. . . . Ask your God to make you like stone). The title of the play, which translates literally as *misunderstanding,* refers not only to the crucial lack of recognition but also to the fundamental disparity between human aspirations toward fulfillment and the indifference of the world–that is, the absurd. Associated themes are exile, existential solitude, and the need for communication and its difficulty.

Caligula, staged in 1945, was received enthusiastically. Reworked more than any other text, it belongs, according to the author, along with *L'Etranger* and *Le Mythe de Sisyphe,* to the cluster of his absurd writings–constituting the first stage of his thought. The outline of the plot and many details come from the historian Suetonius, who reported how the Roman emperor Caligula was transformed by the death of his beloved sister Drusilla. In Camus's version, the emperor discovers, upon the death of one he loved, that life is imperfect. Although not a new revelation, as his courtiers point

Page from the manuscript for Camus's novel L'Etranger *(1942; translated as* The Stranger, *1946), in which an Algiers clerk is sentenced to death for killing an Arab in a moment of blind confusion (Archives du Fonds Albert Camus de l'Institut Mémoires de l'édition contemporaine)* out, to him it is dramatic: "Ce monde, tel qu'il est fait, n'est pas supportable.... Les hommes meurent et ils ne sont pas heureux" (This world, such as it is, is not bearable.... People die, and are not happy). Caligula wants to remedy this imperfection and achieve happiness by reaching the absolute and the impossible. He asks for the moon, an obvious symbol of the unattainable. Denied satisfaction, thenceforth he views all acts as morally equivalent, since neither heaven nor earth furnishes grounds for distinctions; he can pursue quantity and variety but not quality. He calls on the absolute political power that is his to turn his state upside down, confiscating the patricians' fortunes, putting people to death arbitrarily, demanding servile homage and adulation for his wildest caprice, and relishing the pleasure of destruction. Though at times he seems intoxicated with a strange happiness, he continually requires more stimulation, since even the sacrificial deaths of others leave him dissatisfied. His final act before he is assassinated by the patricians is to strangle his mistress, Caesonia. Viewed in terms of Camus's ideas in *Le Mythe de Sisyphe,* Caligula has not conquered the absurd but rather has given in to it.

Camus's second published novel, *La Peste,* appeared in 1947. He viewed it, along with *L'Homme révolté* (1951; translated as *The Rebel,* 1953), as constituting the second stage in his thought, sometimes called the humanist stage. It met with approval from many readers but with a cool reception from others, including Gide, who expressed disappointment, and Beauvoir, who in *La Force des choses* (1963) accused Camus of eluding true historical questions by fleeing into abstraction. Begun during the war, *La Peste* reflects Camus's separation from Algeria and his wife during those dark years. The action—in five acts, like a classical tragedy—takes place in Oran and is recounted by an anonymous first-person narrator. It concerns an outbreak of bubonic plague—its initial appearance, spread, and decline—and reactions to it. Dr. Rieux, whose wife is away at a sanitorium, combats the disease energetically by medical means. Rambert, a visiting journalist, wants to leave, despite the quarantine, to rejoin the woman he loves; the plague does not concern him, he argues. Paneloux, a Jesuit, preaches a sermon on collective guilt and divine punishment. Cottard, an unsavory character who is under suspicion and may be arrested for an unspecified crime, takes advantage of the crisis to remain at large and even indulges in profiteering through the black market.

Tarrou, a loner who befriends Rieux, has been concerned with how to achieve pure conduct in a world of violence, where every act has repercussions on others and where schemes to achieve social justice end in tyranny and terror. He joins the struggle against the plague by organizing effective paramedical teams. Tarrou's friendship means a great deal to Rieux; fraternity is a foundation on which to struggle. They are both present when a little boy dies. The child's suffering seems particularly scandalous, a brute denial of Paneloux's theology, founded on belief in a just God whose providential intervention in the world transforms evil into good. Paneloux himself is shaken by the death and moves toward a position of irrational submission to a divine power whose unfathomable will he must accept as the only possible explanation for the torture of children. Toward the end of the novel Tarrou falls ill; Rieux and his mother nurse him devotedly, but he too dies. Exhausted, Rieux, who has seen thousands die, learns also of his wife's death. Yet, he does not yield to despair. Affirming that there is more to admire in mankind than to despise, he identifies himself as the author of the chronicle.

The novel may be read on three levels. Literally, it recounts the outbreak of a fatal disease that is a fact of nature, the ways of confronting it, and the conclusions that can be drawn about natural evil and human response. Metaphorically, the plague stands for the German occupation of France and other European countries during World War II and the brutality exercised on the population. The various characters' responses illustrate the attitudes one can take toward tyranny. Allegorically, the plague represents moral and metaphysical evil viewed broadly. That is, it represents the human condition, in which—with the world and all its chances impinging upon them—people are born, suffer, make others suffer, and die, but in which the struggle with others against unhappiness, pain, and death provides a meaningful and authentic way of living.

In the late 1940s Camus's personal life and public life alike were complicated. Although admired by a wide reading public, he was in a difficult ideological situation resulting from Cold War political polarization. His disapproval of Soviet rhetoric and practice, and his humanism, agnostic but warm, provoked hostility among the pro-Communists; yet, as a man of the Left, basically, he did not embrace the pro-Western, capitalist faction either. During his three-month visit to South America in 1949, he was both ill and deeply depressed; he appears to have seriously contemplated suicide. His liaison with actress Maria Casarès, who had major roles in some of his plays, caused friction in his household; another woman, Patricia Blake, whom he met in America in 1946, also played a role in his life. Women were enormously important to him, although if sexual love was a source of his inspiration, as it may have been, its effects were subterranean, and his work lacks obvious erotic material. Both his political malaise and his personal difficulties persisted and even increased throughout his remaining years.

The first of two plays produced late in the 1940s was a complete stage failure. *L'Etat de siège* (1948; translated as *State of Siege* in *Caligula and Three Other Plays*, 1958), which he called a morality play (as in medieval drama), is an allegory on freedom, related to *La Peste*. The disaster in this case is not, however, expressed realistically, but symbolically, by Plague (a character), who arrives, strikes people down at random, and installs the New Order. The references are clear: Nazi Germany and its occupation of France; the Soviet Union and its rule over its satellites; Fascist Spain; and, as Camus said, any country without freedom. The scourge may also stand for the human condition in general. The young hero, Diego, discovers the secret to combating Plague: to revolt, to go beyond fear and use human freedom in the struggle, rather than abandoning freedom for the sake of comfort.

Les Justes (performed in 1949, published in 1950; translated as *The Just Assassins* in *Caligula and Three Other Plays*), based on events in Russia in 1905, is similarly connected to *L'Homme révolté* through its considerations of whether violence and oppression can justify counter-violence and under what conditions. The play concerns a group of five revolutionary terrorists in Moscow who plan to assassinate the grand duke as a protest against czarist tyranny. While they agree on their purpose, their motives and understanding of political good differ. One member, Dora, wonders whether their desired end—a world of justice—can be attained by cruel, unjust means. Yanek, whom she loves, is to throw a bomb at the grand duke's carriage. He does not, however, carry out the deed, because he sees two children in the carriage. He is told that sentimentality over children is foolish; only by spilling whatever blood is necessary, without concern for moral limits or consequences, can the revolution triumph. A second attempt is successful. After his arrest, Yanek is offered his life if he will furnish the names of his accomplices. He refuses, not only from loyalty but also because he believes justice requires him to pay for the life he took. When he is hanged, Dora asks to throw the next bomb; her desire to avenge her lover has overcome her political scruples. The play received mixed reviews.

The East-West confrontation in the Korean War (1950–1953) and the continuing French colonial war in Indochina, which ended in 1954, hardened Cold War positions and made the political middle ground almost untenable. Joseph Stalin's death in 1953 did not alter the situation materially. In France, an active Communist press, including the daily *L'Humanité,* attacked without respite the various governments of the Fourth Republic, Western policies, and all who did not subscribe to Communist party tenets. Sartre was one of many who, while not enrolled in the party and often critical of its positions, generally sided with it anyhow and violently condemned the United States. Camus's political predicament and malaise increased upon publication in 1951 of *L'Homme révolté*. The essay—which marked him in leftist radicals' eyes as ideologically simpleminded, utopistic, lacking in philosophical rigor, and essentially a traitor—takes as its point of departure the arguments on the absurd in *Le Mythe de Sisyphe* and reinforces the arguments of Rieux and Tarrou in *La Peste*. Camus's thesis is that the absurdist man must, by the logic of his position, rebel or protest. Since the eighteenth century, however, rebellion has had tragic consequences, including violent revolution, tyranny, and enslavement, all in the name of freedom: "La terreur, petite ou grande, vient alors couronner la révolution" (Terror, on a small or grand scale, then comes along to crown the revolution). Camus traces this phenomenon through the political and metaphysical protests of the eighteenth and nineteenth centuries, treating such thinkers and practitioners as Jean-Jacques Rousseau, Louis de Saint-Just, Georg Wilhelm Friedrich Hegel, and Nietzsche. The supreme agents of terror, beside the radicals of the French Revolution, were the Nazis and the Soviets, whose tyranny Camus condemns as a monstrous distortion of rebellion in the name of historical efficacy.

When a disciple of Sartre, Francis Jeanson, reviewed the essay unfavorably in a 1952 issue of Sartre's monthly *Les Temps Modernes,* attacking its faulty thinking, Camus replied by an open letter in the magazine. The letter occasioned a retort by Sartre, which set out their differences for all to see. The result was a permanent falling-out between the two former associates. Camus was not the only eminent figure formerly in Sartre's circle who broke with him. Maurice Merleau-Ponty, a philosopher of note, long a champion of Soviet policy, finally denounced it and gave his vocal support to the West; Raymond Aron, another philosopher and former friend of Sartre, had already left the Sartrean pale. These Cold War polarizations affected literary life throughout the decade.

Increasingly, Camus knew also the dilemma of fame, which, originating with the public, depends on continued public approval and often finds renewal difficult. Being lionized at a young age rarely helps a writer, even one who appears to prosper in it. One result of his predicament was recurring writer's paralysis; current theories about creative inhibition, or writer's block, identify great praise as a contributing factor. Camus's involvements in the theater in the 1950s, while reflecting a lifelong interest, may have been a way of deflecting the imperative to write and write well. During much of the decade he was engaged in attempts to find a theater of his own, where he could be the director. Despite friends' assistance and intervention with the French government (which subsidized theaters then as now) and his own persistence, the enterprise did not succeed. He did, however, take over one summer (1953) as director of the Festival d'Art Dramatique in Angers, where he staged two of his adaptations. Later, his highly successful 1956 adaptation of William Faulkner's *Requiem for a Nun* (1951) was followed in 1959 by his adaptation, which he also directed, of Dostoevsky's *The Possessed* (1871).

To the discomfort of working in a fractious, ideologically charged atmosphere, the burden of fame, and his theatrical involvements were added health problems and domestic tension throughout the 1950s. In 1953 Francine Camus, already depressed, fell into deeper mental difficulties, almost surely brought on by marital strife, itself resulting partly from having to share her husband with Casarès. The spouses lived apart for months; then, together, apparently without harmony; then again separately. Camus became involved with other women in addition to his wife and Casarès.

The greatest burden of all on Camus from the mid 1950s until his death was the Algerian war, which historians have generally agreed to date from 1 November 1954, when nationalist Algerian insurgents launched attacks against several police outposts and other government offices. The uprisings spread through the countryside and into the cities, where both police and army battled against the rebels. Official policy was that Algeria would remain French, and residents of French ancestry were assured repeatedly that the government would eliminate the guerrillas and terrorists and protect their lives and properties. Terrorism grew, however, frequently justified by the principle that Tunisian novelist and sociologist Albert Memmi later enunciated, that the violence of the oppressed merely reflects the violence of the oppressor. By 1957 French forces and rebels were engaged in a full-scale urban conflict called the Battle of Algiers. The army was able to destroy the terrorists' network in the city, but its brutal methods lost much public support for the idea of *Algérie française* (as the slogan went). Although the government denied it, there was ample evidence that torture was used to extract information from captured rebels. It was the Algerian crisis that brought down the Fourth Republic in May 1958, when Charles de Gaulle was called to power with a mandate to rule by decree for six months.

Before November 1954 Camus had written on the Algerian situation, and in the summer of 1955 he published an article on terrorism and repression. He subsequently contributed (to the weekly *L'Express* and other publications) articles proposing both immediate measures and long-term solutions for a reorganization of Algeria on a new footing, with improved status for Muslim residents. His vision of a society built on justice allowed him to have great understanding and sympathy for both Algerian communities (European and Muslim), even as tensions grew; it also dictated his stand against independence and especially the terrorist methods used eventually to achieve it, and it made him persona non grata among the many French intellectuals who pronounced colonialism an unconscionable evil. His 1956 visit to Algiers to speak on behalf of a civil truce was a total failure: his vision was dismissed as utopian, his sense of justice as warped, and "Camus le juste" was called a phony. Again, the tendency of absolute political thought toward extremism and totalitarianism—precisely what he had denounced in *L'Homme révolté*—made compromise impossible. His speech denouncing the 1956 Soviet invasion of Hungary provided further excuse for attacks from the left wing. Pressed to condemn not only French measures against the insurgents but also the very principle of *Algérie française,* he turned silent.

Notwithstanding his occasional writer's paralysis, Camus published in the 1950s a volume of lyrical essays, *L'Eté* (1954, Summer), which includes beautiful writings on Algeria, some composed earlier, and an essay on Prometheus, whose heroic sufferings in chains recall the punishment of Sisyphus. Two more collections of journalistic writings also appeared during the decade: *Actuelles II: Chroniques 1948–1953* in 1953 and *Actuelles III: Chroniques algériennes, 1939–1958* (including the civil truce speech) in 1958. *Réflexions sur la peine capitale* (1957, Reflections on Capital Punishment), by Camus and Koestler, includes Camus's essay "Réflexions sur la guillotine" (translated as *Reflections on the Guillotine: An Essay on Capital Punishment,* 1959). His position is that capital punishment is as morally revolting as the crime that supposedly warrants it, and that it should be abolished in France and elsewhere. He argues that supposed justifications for the death penalty (including its role as a deterrent) lack validity and that it is really vengeance taken by society.

Two works of fiction also date from the 1950s. *La Chute,* perhaps Camus's best novel, reflects his sense of alienation. The last of his novels published during his lifetime, it is an ironic masterpiece, analyzing the human heart and examining mid-twentieth-century attitudes and mores. Irony can be viewed as constituting a final stage in his thought, but the schema is approximate, and he never abandoned his earlier humanistic thinking. The novel is presented in the form of a first-person monologue spoken by a former lawyer from Paris who has renounced his profession and friends and gone into exile in Amsterdam. The monologue is directed toward an unnamed and unseen interlocutor who visits the bar where the former Parisian awaits his "clients." The theological suggestions of the title are reinforced by the concentric circles of the Amsterdam canals, suggesting the circles of hell in Dante's *The Divine Comedy;* by reminders of great evil in the form of Nazi persecution of the Jewish community; and especially by the name the protagonist has taken. He calls himself Jean-Baptiste Clamence, suggesting John the Baptist, who preached repentance, with his "voice . . . crying [vox clamantis] in the wilderness." Although the interlocutor is never heard directly, his comments can sometimes be guessed from Clamence's words, which also remind readers there is a listener and subtly involve them in the text. The *we* of the narrative (by which Clamence refers to himself and his listener) implicates, of course, the reader also.

Having personally practiced a wide variety of hypocrisies and seen much in others, having witnessed great crimes visited on Europe in the name of political ideals, and knowing, thanks to his profession, the human heart at its worst, Clamence is well placed to denounce the evils of his century and preach on the theme of culpability. He pronounces himself culpable first of all, of course. Marvelous little scenes evoked from the past illustrate the skill with which, by cultivating a false persona, he disguised his real character, filled with envy and will to power. But by acknowledging his failings, he raises himself above others; beating his breast, accusing himself, he becomes superior and can pass judgment. Thus, he explains his new profession, that of *juge-pénitent* (judge-penitent).

In the last section of the novel Clamence, suffering from a fever, speaks to the interlocutor from bed. It is—if not a pretext—at least a convenient way for Clamence to reveal his secret: a stolen fifteenth-century painting, Jan van Eyck's *Les Juges intègres* (The Honest Judges), kept in his cupboard. The thematic interconnections among the subject of the painting (an historic object, actually stolen in 1934 and never recovered), Clamence's earlier and present profession, and his judgments on others are enriched by his discovery that his visitor is also an attorney—perhaps a fellow spirit who will practice self-mortification with him. Awaiting his friend's confession, Clamence is a judge without mercy, a prophet without religion, and a confessor without God.

In 1957 Camus published his collection of short fiction, *L'Exil et le royaume* (translated as *Exile and the Kingdom,* 1958). The six stories, often anthologized, are among his best writing. The "exile" of the title is chiefly that of the human condition (as well as Camus's separation from his native land); the "kingdom" is the nearly unattainable happiness toward which all strive, or possibly some higher, spiritual dimension. Among major themes are alienation from others and inability to communicate. One story is called "Les Muets" (translated as "The Silent Men"); in "Le Renégat" (translated as "The Renegade"), a man's tongue is cut out; and in "La Pierre qui pousse" (translated as "The Growing Stone"), the hero, a French engineer, travels to a Brazilian jungle town, where he feels isolated and out of place until he undergoes what amounts to an initiation and becomes part of the community.

The same themes of separation and difficulty in communication recur in the other stories. In "La Femme adultère" (translated as "The Adulterous Woman"), however, Camus subtly brings out the emotional connections between human beings and the material world. The story deals not with physical adultery but with a spiritual communion established between Janine, the wife of a traveling salesman from coastal North Africa, and a severe but inviting landscape that she discovers on a visit to the south—a landscape with a strange appeal, reinforced by the presence of silent, solitary Arabs who seem mysteriously connected to the world. Looking over the desert at night, Janine feels a powerful sense of freedom and union with the world and experiences an illumination that contrasts with the pettiness and dullness of her life.

"L'Hôte" (translated as "The Guest") is set in a mountainous area of Algeria during the insurrection. The story illustrates the antagonisms between communities that nevertheless share a common land and love for it. Daru, a teacher in an isolated school, is told by a rural gendarme that he must hold overnight an Arab prisoner accused of killing a man and then deliver him to the authorities farther on. Reluctantly, Daru agrees to keep the prisoner for the night, but he is loath to turn him in, despite his brutishness. The next day Daru leads the Arab to a point where he may choose between two directions, one leading to nomads who will take him in without asking questions, the other to the French authorities in town. The prisoner is freed and allowed to choose; the teacher sees him walking toward the town. Later, on the blackboard, Daru finds a message telling him that he will pay for giving up the Arab. The story is both a political and an existential parable. It dramatizes the wartime dilemma of many Algerians—both colonials and indigenous residents—who did not want to get involved and yet were drawn into the conflict. Likewise, the story illustrates the impossibility of choosing satisfactorily—whatever Daru does will bring him trouble—and the solitude of the thinking and suffering subject.

"Jonas ou l'artiste au travail" (translated as "Jonas or The Artist at Work"), set in Paris, clearly reflects Camus's own dilemmas. After Jonas, a gifted painter, achieves great success, his life becomes contaminated by public recognition; he has become a commodity. People impinge so much on his time that work becomes difficult. Similarly, his personal life is complicated, in part by the awkward design of the apartment where he lives with his wife and children. Gradually, he withdraws from society and his family and spends all his time in a loft built into the apartment. At the end, he is found unconscious in the darkness, with a new canvas on which is visible only one unclear word, either *solidaire* or *solitaire*. Both words underline the ambiguity of the human condition and the position of the artist, who must feel solidarity with others and yet can create only in solitude.

Also in 1957 Camus was awarded the Nobel Prize in Literature. He had earlier received the Resistance Medal (1946) and the Prix des Critiques for *La Peste*, though he persistently rejected the Legion of Honor. Upon learning of the Nobel, he told a journalist that he felt rather young for the honor, and that he would himself have voted for Malraux. In his notebooks he expressed the hope that what he had said might be useful to others, but that it could not be so to himself, "livré maintenant à une sorte de folie" (given over now to a sort of insanity). His December Nobel speech in Stockholm included a moving statement of the artist's relationship to his audience:

> Je ne puis vivre personnellement sans mon art. Mais je n'ai jamais placé cet art au-dessus de tout. S'il m'est nécessaire au contraire, c'est qu'il ne se sépare de personne et me permet de vivre, tel que je suis, au niveau de tous. L'art n'est pas à mes yeux une réjouissance solitaire. Il est un moyen d'émouvoir le plus grand nombre d'hommes en leur offrant une image privilégiée des souffrances et des joies communes. Il oblige donc l'artiste à ne pas s'isoler; il le soumet à la vérité la plus humble et la plus universelle.

> (Personally, I cannot live without my art. But I have never placed this art above everything else. If it is necessary to me, indeed, it is because it is not separate from anyone and allows me to live, such as I am, on everyone's level. Art is not in my eyes a solitary enjoyment. It is a means of moving the greatest number of people by offering them a privileged picture of common sufferings and joys. It thus obliges the artist not to become isolated; it submits him to the most humble and most universal truth).

In Stockholm, Camus also made, during a question-and-answer session at the university, what became his most famous, or infamous, statement (reported by Dominique Birmann in *Le Monde*) on the Algerian war. Questioners raised various political issues, including freedom of speech and censorship in France. Then words from a Muslim militant concerning Camus's reluctance to intervene further in the Algerian conflict led to confused exchanges. After being subjected to a barrage of accusations and insults, Camus, visibly upset, finally retorted that he had always condemned terrorism—meaning terroristic repression of Algerian insurgents by French forces but also violence exercised by rebels against the French and fellow Muslims who would not cooperate with the rebellion. He denounced blind terrorism exercised in the streets and finally stated that while he believed in justice, he would also defend his mother (still alive in Algeria) before justice. This statement caused the greatest uproar and was seized upon by his political adversaries as evidence of his hypocrisy and incorrigible colonial attitudes.

Camus's last years were not tranquil. The prize itself contributed to his difficulties, since it created a tremendous stir around him, made him more of a public figure than before (thus reducing further his privacy), and caused unintentional alienation between him and old friends. He spoke of having "mal aux poumons" (being ill from Algeria as he was in the lungs). Yet, he worked on his dramatic adaptations and on *Le Premier Homme*, the manuscript of which was in his briefcase when he was killed in an automobile accident on 4 January 1960.

Camus feared speed, contrary to some reports. He had been with his family for the Christmas holiday in Lourmarin, in the south of France, at his vacation home, purchased with the Nobel money. There he had experienced some moments of morbidity worse than usual and had spoken of what sort of burial he wanted. Francine Camus and the twins took the train back to Paris. He also had planned to do so, but instead accepted the invitation of Michel Gallimard and his wife, who had spent New Year's with the Camus family, to drive back. On the second day of the journey, with Gallimard driving, the car swerved off the road and hit a plane tree, then another. Camus died instantly; Gallimard survived a few days; his wife and children were not gravely injured. Camus had written in his notebooks in 1951 that he sometimes wished to die a violent death. The event was widely treated as a supremely ironic manifestation of the absurd. Many newspapers and other publications devoted the whole or part of an issue to Camus and his place in French literature. In *France-Observateur* (7 January 1960), Sartre stressed the contradictions in Camus's position but praised him as the current heir of a long line of moralists whose works constituted perhaps the most original contribution of French letters. These memorial issues, produced with great haste, some as early as February, were the first stage in what became a tremendous Camus industry, still thriving.

Le Premier Homme was published from the manuscript left at his death. The title may be seen as having mythic suggestions; Algeria is viewed retrospectively as "la terre de l'oubli où chacun était le premier homme" (the land of forgetfulness, where each was the first man). There may be a reference to colonization, or to the Edenic quality, as Camus saw it, of the Mediterranean life, under "la lumière des premiers matins du monde" (the light of the world's first mornings). The title has contrasting connotations of Cain, the first biblical murderer, and, at the same time, of Camus's father, the first and only paternal ancestor whose life he imagines in detail. Finally, the title may refer to Everyman. As Camus observed in a notebook entry of 1954, "Tout homme est le premier homme, personne ne l'est" (Everyone is the first man; no one is). The work is dedicated to Camus's mother, portrayed as an extraordinary, Christ-like figure through her goodness and silent suffering.

The highly autobiographical narrative begins with the birth in Algeria of Jacques Cormery (J.C., like Jesus Christ). It then jumps ahead to a visit the adult Jacques pays to his father's grave in France, followed by a conversation with his former schoolmaster, who lives nearby. The narrative then returns to Jacques's childhood and young manhood, with flash-forwards to later periods. Certain passages clearly refer to the Algerian rebellion. Themes in the novel or announced in the accompanying notes include some of Camus's favorites: games and sports, school, exile, solitude, guilt, the natural world and its pleasures, and "un grand cri de joie et de gratitude envers l'adorable vie" (a great cry of joy and gratitude toward life, lovable life). One consequence of the publication of the novel was to invite critics to identify overlaps between it and other works, thus creating the image of a writer less distant from his fiction than had been assumed.

While Camus has remained widely read following his death, he has, nevertheless, lost some status among critics and in the academy. There has been a decline in his popularity on postgraduate reading lists, for instance, and, to judge by publications and sessions at scholarly meetings, a sharp fall in his prestige among professors, many theory-oriented. Camus-bashing persists, partly on philosophical grounds but chiefly on political and cultural grounds, including his machismo, Eurocentrism, and "humanism"—that is, holding the values of the Occident instead of supporting revolutionary socialism and Marxist realpolitik. Among critics who have noted the omission of native Algerians from most of his work and who have attacked him for feeling solidarity with the colonial French and thus refusing to espouse the cause of the rebels and independence are Conor Cruise O'Brien and Kateb Yacine (a Berber writer).

The latter charge illustrates two critical fallacies. One is judging by later standards a position adopted earlier: what appeared forward-looking when Camus first wrote about misery in Kabylia in the 1930s has generally been surpassed, while what looked practicable later in the century with respect to colonial territories may have appeared much less so when he was writing. The other fallacy is simply to ignore contrary evidence. True, until 1994 critics did not have access to *Le Premier Homme,* in which Camus depicts natives sympathetically and often shows great concern for them (for example, Arab women barricaded in their houses). But his articles on Kabylia were much more than a gesture: they were a call for wide-sweeping and comparatively radical changes. Critics also neglect Camus's behind-the-scenes efforts in the mid 1950s to find a political solution to the violence brought about by the Algerian uprising; moreover, the articles that constitute *Actuelles III: Chroniques algériennes, 1939-1958* were, as Peter Dunwoodie writes, "crushingly ignored." In an interview given in connection with the Nobel Prize, Camus stated that "c'est à elle [Algeria], et à son malheur, que vont toutes mes pensées" (all my thoughts go out to Algeria and its misfortune).

Despite criticisms coming from postcolonialists, feminists, and other radicals, including those who attack the idea of canonized authors, Camus's reputation as a major writer of his century is secure. Roger Martin du Gard, another Nobel laureate (1937), wrote in a 1948 letter to Gide that Camus was "celui de sa génération qui donne le plus grand espoir" (the one in his generation who inspires the greatest hope). Victor Brombert has explained how the French concept of the intellectual "remains bound up with the notion of a social, political and moral crisis" in which the writer, artist, or other intellectual considers himself obligated to intervene. Camus's writings in response to this duty may be flawed, though doubtless not so greatly as some have averred; but the moral gravity of his work is of lasting value, enduring past the particular conditions that gave rise to it. In the expression of Pierre-Henri Simon, a Catholic critic, Camus served as one of the high consciences of the nation. Even more, his achievement as an artist—one remembers his emphasis on art in his Nobel speech—puts him well above most of his contemporaries. Meursault, Caligula, and Clamence are among the most distinctive and yet characteristic creations of the literary imagination in twentieth-century literature. Camus's lucidity—that Mediterranean value, illustrated by the Greeks in their meditations on man and nature—produced keen, sensitive insights, couched in admirable, often lyrical prose. His enterprise was that identified by Paul Valéry as the poet's: not to feel but to make felt, "et bellement sensible" (and felt beautifully).

Letters:

Albert Camus, Jean Grenier: Correspondance: 1932–1960, edited by Marguerite Dobrenn (Paris: Gallimard, 1981); translated by Jan F. Rigaud as *Albert Camus, Jean Grenier: Correspondence, 1932–1960* (Lincoln: University of Nebraska Press, 2003);

Camus: De l'absurde à l'amour: Lettres inédites d'Albert Camus, edited by André Comte-Sponville (Vénissieux: Paroles d'Aube, 1995);

Correspondance 1939–1947 Albert Camus, Pascal Pia, edited by Yves Marc Ajchenbaum (Paris: Fayard/Gallimard, 2000);

Albert Camus – Jean Sénac: Correspondance 1947–1958, edited by Hamid Nacer-Khodja (Paris: Paris-Méditerranée, 2004).

Bibliographies:

Maurice Beebe, "Criticism of Albert Camus: A Selected Checklist of Studies in English," *Modern Fiction Studies,* 10 (Autumn 1964): 303–314;

Peter C. Hoy, *Camus in English* (Wymondham, U.K.: Brewhouse Press, 1968);

Robert F. Roeming, *Camus: A Bibliography* (Madison: University of Wisconsin Press, 1968);

Brian T. Fitch and Hoy, *Essai de bibliographie des études en langue française consacrées à Albert Camus (1937–1967)* (Paris: Minard, 1969);

Raymond Gay-Crosier, *Camus* (Darmstadt: Wissenschaftliche Buchgesellschaft, 1976);

Gay-Crosier, "Albert Camus," in *A Critical Bibliography of French Literature,* volume 6: *The Twentieth Century,* edited by Douglas W. Alden and Richard A. Brooks (Syracuse: Syracuse University Press, 1980), part 3, pp. 1573–1679.

Biographies:

Herbert R. Lottman, *Albert Camus: A Biography* (Garden City, N.Y.: Doubleday, 1979; revised edition, Corte Madera, Cal.: Gingko Press, 1997);

Patrick McCarthy, *Camus* (New York: Random House, 1982);

Roger Grenier, *Albert Camus soleil et ombre: Une biographie intellectuelle* (Paris: Gallimard, 1987);

José Lenzini, *L'Algérie de Camus* (Aix-en-Provence: Edisud, 1987);

Olivier Todd, *Albert Camus: Une vie* (Paris: Gallimard, 1996); translated by Benjamin Ivry as *Albert Camus: A Life* (New York: Random House, 1997).

References:

Richard H. Akeroyd, *The Spiritual Quest of Albert Camus* (Tuscaloosa, Ala.: Portals Press, 1976);

Alba Amoia, *Albert Camus* (New York: Continuum, 1989);

Alex Argyros, *Crimes of Narration: Camus' "La Chute"* (Toronto: Paratexte, 1985);

Ronald Aronson, *Camus & Sartre: The Story of a Friendship and the Quarrel that Ended It* (Chicago & London: University of Chicago Press, 2004);

G. V. Banks, *Camus: L'Etranger* (London: Edward Arnold, 1976; enlarged edition, Glasgow: University of Glasgow French and German Publications, 1992);

Michelle Beauclair, *Albert Camus, Marguerite Duras, and the Legacy of Mourning* (New York: Peter Lang, 1998);

Harold Bloom, ed., *Albert Camus* (New York & Philadelphia: Chelsea House, 1989);

Germaine Brée, *Camus and Sartre: Crisis and Commitment* (New York: Delta, 1972);

Brée, ed., *Camus: A Collection of Critical Essays* (Englewood Cliffs, N.J.: Prentice-Hall, 1962);

Victor Brombert, *The Intellectual Hero: Studies in the French Novel, 1880–1955* (Chicago & London: University of Chicago Press, 1960);

Stephen Eric Bronner, *Camus: Portrait of a Moralist* (Minneapolis & London: University of Minnesota Press, 1999);

Catharine Savage Brosman, *Albert Camus* (Detroit: Gale, 2000);

Brosman, *Existential Fiction* (Detroit: Gale, 2000);

James W. Brown, *'Sensing,' 'Seeing,' 'Saying' in Camus' 'Noces': A Meditative Essay* (Amsterdam & New York: Rodopi, 2004);

Michel-Antoine Burnier, *Choice of Action: The French Existentialists on the Political Front Line,* translated by Bernard Murchland (New York: Vintage, 1969);

Lionel Dubois, ed., *Albert Camus: La révolte* (Poitiers: Editions du Pont-Neuf, 2001);

Dubois, ed., *Albert Camus entre la misère et le soleil* (Poitiers: Editions du Pont-Neuf, 1997);

Dubois, ed., *Les Trois Guerres d'Albert Camus* (Poitiers: Editions du Pont-Neuf, 1995);

Peter Dunwoodie and Edward J. Hughes, *Constructing Memories: Camus, Algeria, and "Le Premier Homme"* (Stirling: Stirling French Publications, no. 6, 1998);

Bernard East, *Albert Camus ou l'homme à la recherche d'une morale* (Montreal: Bellarmin / Paris: Editions du Cerf, 1984);

David R. Ellison, *Understanding Albert Camus* (Columbia: University of South Carolina Press, 1990);

Franck Evrard, *Albert Camus* (Paris: Ellipses, 1998);

Eugene H. Falk, *Types of Thematic Structure: The Nature and Function of Motifs in Gide, Camus, and Sartre* (Chicago & London: University of Chicago Press, 1967);

Raymond Gay-Crosier, *L'Envers d'un échec: Etude sur le théâtre d'Albert Camus* (Paris: Lettres Modernes/Minard, 1967);

Gay-Crosier and Roger Quilliot, *La Réception de l'oeuvre de Camus en U.R.S.S. et en R.D.A.* (Paris: Lettres Modernes Minard, 1999);

Jacob Golomb, *In Search of Authenticity: From Kierkegaard to Camus* (London & New York: Routledge, 1995);

Jeanyves Guérin, ed., *Camus et la politique* (Paris: L'Harmattan, 1986);

Guérin, ed., *Camus et le premier "Combat" (1944–1947)* (La Garenne-Colombes: Editions de l'Espace Européen, 1990);

Patrick Henry, "Albert Camus, Panelier, and *La Peste*," *Literary Imagination,* 5 (Fall 2003): 383–404;

Histoires d'un livre: "L'Etranger" d'Albert Camus. Catalogue édité à l'occasion de l'exposition inaugurale présentée au Centre national des lettres à Paris, du 13 oct. au 9 nov. 1990 (Paris: IMEC, 1990);

Edward J. Hughes, *Camus: Le Premier Homme; La Peste* (Glasgow: University of Glasgow French and German Publications, 1995);

Tony Judt, *The Burden of Responsibility: Blum, Camus, Aron, and the French Twentieth Century* (Chicago: University of Chicago Press, 1998);

Walter Kaufmann, ed., *Existentialism from Dostoevsky to Sartre* (New York: Meridian Books, 1956);

Terry Keefe and Edmund Smyth, *Autobiography and the Existential Self: Studies in Modern French Writing* (New York: St. Martin's Press, 1995);

Steven G. Kellman, ed., *Approaches to Teaching Camus's "The Plague"* (New York: The Modern Language Association of America, 1995);

Adele King, ed., *Camus's "L'Etranger": Fifty Years On* (London: Macmillan, 1992);

Bettina L. Knapp, ed., *Critical Essays on Albert Camus* (Boston: G. K. Hall, 1988);

Morvan Lebesque, *Camus* (Paris: Seuil, 1963);

Richard Lehan, *A Dangerous Crossing: French Literary Existentialism and the Modern Novel* (Carbondale & Edwardsville: Southern Illinois University Press / London & Amsterdam: Feffer & Simons, 1973);

Jacqueline Lévi-Valensi, ed., *Camus et le théâtre* (Paris: IMEC Editions, 1992);

Lévi-Valensi and Agnès Spiquel, eds., *Camus et le lyrisme: Actes du Colloque de Beauvais 31 mai – 1er juin 1996* (Paris: SEDES, 1997);

James McBride, *Albert Camus: Philosopher and Littérateur* (New York: St. Martin's Press, 1992);

Geraldine F. Montgomery, *Noces pour femme seule: Le féminin et le sacré dans l'oeuvre d'Albert Camus* (Amsterdam: Rodopi, 2004);

Conor Cruise O'Brien, *Albert Camus of Europe and Africa* (New York: Viking, 1970);

Neal Oxenhandler, *Looking for Heroes in Postwar France: Albert Camus, Max Jacob, Simone Weil* (Hanover, N.H.: University Press of New England, 1996);

Roger Quilliot, *La Mer et les prisons: Essai sur Albert Camus* (Paris: Gallimard, 1956); revised by Quilliot and translated by Parker as *The Sea and Prisons: A Commentary on the Life and Thought of Albert Camus* (University: University of Alabama Press, 1970);

Phillip H. Rhein, *Albert Camus* (New York: Twayne, 1969; revised, 1989);

Anthony Rizzuto, *Camus: Love and Sexuality* (Gainesville: University Press of Florida, 1998);

Rizzuto, ed., *Albert Camus' "L'Exil et le Royaume": The Third Decade* (Toronto: Paratexte, 1988);

Emmanuel Roblès, *Albert Camus et la trêve civile* (Philadelphia: Celfan Edition Monographs, 1988);

Jacqueline Gabrielle Roston, *Camus's Récit "La Chute": A Rewriting Through Dante's "Commedia"* (New York: Peter Lang, 1985);

Peter Royle, *The Sartre-Camus Controversy: A Literary and Philosophical Critique* (Ottawa: University of Ottawa Press, 1982);

Jean-Paul Sartre, "Albert Camus," *France-Observateur,* no. 505 (7 January 1960);

Sartre, "Explication de *L'Etranger*," *Cahiers du Sud,* no. 253 (1943);

Sartre, "Réponse à Albert Camus," *Les Temps Modernes,* no. 82 (August 1952): 334–353;

Philip Thody, *Albert Camus* (London: Macmillan, 1989);

Ena C. Vulor, *Colonial and Anti-Colonial Discourses: Albert Camus and Algeria* (Lanham, Md. & Oxford: University Press of America, 2000);

David H. Walker, ed., *Albert Camus: Les extrêmes et l'équilibre* (Amsterdam & Atlanta: Rodopi, 1994);

Maurice Weyembergh, *Albert Camus ou la mémoire des origines* (Paris & Brussels: De Boeck Université, 1998);

James S. Williams, *Camus: La Peste* (London: Grant & Cutler, 2000);

Wolodymyr T. Zyla and Wendell M. Aycock, eds., *Albert Camus' Literary Milieu: Arid Lands* (Lubbock: Interdepartmental Committee on Comparative Literature, Texas Tech University, 1976).

Papers:

Although some of Albert Camus's papers are deposited at the Bibliothèque nationale de France in Paris, most remain in the Catherine and Jean Camus family archives. Camus's portion of his unpublished correspondence with Jules Roy is in the Bibliothèque Saint-Charles in Marseilles; Roy's portion is in the Fonds Camus of the Bibliothèque Méjane Aix-en-Provence. Two other correspondences are held (partly in originals, partly in photocopies) at the Special Collections division of the library at the University of Florida, Gainesville. See articles by Raymond Gay-Crosier summarizing their contents: "Une Correspondance inédite de l'époque du Théâtre de l'Equipe," *Albert Camus 14* (Paris: Lettres modernes, 1991), pp. 165–172 (letters to Françoise Maeurer), and "Encore une correspondance inédite: Albert Camus–Yvonne Ducailar, 1939–1946," *Albert Camus 15* (Paris: Lettres Modernes, 1993), pp. 183–196. A tapescript of Camus's unpublished handwritten corrections of 1939 and 1941 for *Caligula* is held in the same collection. Some papers are in the Harry Ransom Humanities Research Center at the University of Texas at Austin.

1957 Nobel Prize in Literature Presentation Speech

by Anders Österling, Permanent Secretary of the Swedish Academy

French literature is no longer linked geographically to the frontiers of France in Europe. In many respects it reminds one of a garden plant, noble and irreplaceable, which when cultivated outside its territory still retains its distinctive character, although tradition and variation alternately influence it. The Nobel Laureate for this year, Albert Camus, is an example of this evolution. Born in a small town in eastern Algeria, he has returned to this North African milieu to find the source of all the determining influences that have marked his childhood and youth. Even today, the man Camus is aware of this great French overseas territory, and the writer in him is often pleased to recall this fact.

From a quasi-proletarian origin, Camus found it necessary to get ahead in life on his own; a poverty-stricken student, he worked at all sorts of jobs to meet his needs. It was an arduous schooling, but one which, in the diversity of its teaching, was certainly not useless to the realist he was to become. In the course of his years of study, which he spent at the University of Algiers, he belonged to a circle of intellectuals who later came to play an important role in the North African Resistance. His first books were published by a local publishing house in Algiers, but at the age of twenty-five he reached France as a journalist and soon came to make his reputation in the metropolis as a writer of the first rank, prematurely tempered by the harsh, feverish atmosphere of the war years.

Even in his first writings Camus reveals a spiritual attitude that was born of the sharp contradictions within him between the awareness of earthly life and the gripping consciousness of the reality of death. This is more than the typical Mediterranean fatalism whose origin is the certainty that the sunny splendour of the world is only a fugitive moment bound to be blotted out by the shades. Camus represents also the philosophical movement called Existentialism, which characterizes man's situation in the universe by denying it all personal significance, seeing in it only absurdity. The term "absurd" occurs often in Camus's writings, so that one may call it a leitmotif in his work, developed in all its logical moral consequences on the levels of freedom, responsibility, and the anguish that derives from it. The Greek myth of Sisyphus, who eternally rolls his rock to the mountain top from which it perpetually rolls down again, becomes, in one of Camus's essays, a laconic symbol of human life. But Sisyphus, as Camus interprets him, is happy in the depth of his soul, for the attempt alone satisfies him. For Camus, the essential thing is no longer to know whether life is worth living but *how* one must live it, with the share of sufferings it entails.

This short presentation does not permit me to dwell longer on Camus's always fascinating intellectual development. It is more worthwhile to refer to the works in which, using an art with complete classical purity of style and intense concentration, he has embodied these problems in such fashion that characters and action make his ideas live before us, without commentary by the author. This is what makes *L'Etranger* (The Stranger), 1942, famous. The main character, an employee of a government department, kills an Arab following a chain of absurd events; then, indifferent to his fate, he hears himself condemned to death. At the last moment, however, he pulls himself together and emerges from a passivity bordering on torpor. In *La Peste* (The Plague), 1947, a symbolic novel of greater scope, the main characters are Doctor Rieux and his assistant, who heroically combat the plague that has descended on a North African town. In its calm and exact objectivity, this convincingly realistic narrative reflects experiences of life during the Resistance, and Camus extols the revolt which the conquering evil arouses in the heart of the intensely resigned and disillusioned man.

Quite recently Camus has given us the very remarkable story-monologue, *La Chute* (The Fall), 1956, a work exhibiting the same mastery of the art of storytelling. A French lawyer, who examines his conscience in a sailors' bar in Amsterdam, draws his own portrait, a mirror in which his contemporaries can equally recognize themselves. In these pages one can see Tartuffe shake hands with the Misanthrope in the name of that science of the human heart in which classical France excelled. The mordant irony, employed by an aggressive author obsessed with truth, becomes a weapon against universal hypocrisy. One may wonder, of course, where Camus is heading by his insistence on a Kierkegaardian sense of guilt whose bottomless abyss is omnipresent, for one always has the feeling that the author has reached a turning point in his development.

Personally Camus has moved far beyond nihilism. His serious, austere meditations on the duty of restoring without respite that which has been ravaged, and of making justice possible in an unjust world, rather make him a humanist who has not forgotten the worship of Greek proportion and beauty as they were once revealed to him in the dazzling summer light on the Mediterranean shore at Tipasa.

Active and highly creative, Camus is in the centre of interest in the literary world, even outside of France. Inspired by an authentic moral engagement, he devotes himself with all his being to the great fundamental questions of life, and certainly this aspiration corresponds to the idealistic end for which the Nobel Prize was established. Behind his incessant affirmation of the absurdity of the human condition is no sterile negativism. This view of things is supplemented in him by a powerful imperative, nevertheless, an appeal to the will which incites to revolt against absurdity and which, for that reason, creates a value.

[© The Nobel Foundation, 1957.]

Camus: Banquet Speech

Introductory remarks by B. Karlgren, Member of the Royal Academy of Sciences, at the Nobel Banquet at the City Hall in Stockholm, 10 December 1957:

Mr. Camus—As a student of history and literature, I address you first. I do not have the ambition and the boldness to pronounce judgment on the character or importance of your work—critics more competent than I have already thrown sufficient light on it. But let me assure you that we take profound satisfaction in the fact that we are witnessing the ninth awarding of a Nobel Prize in Literature to a Frenchman. Particularly in our time, with its tendency to direct intellectual attention, admiration, and imitation toward those nations who have—by virtue of their enormous material resources—become protagonists, there remains, nevertheless, in Sweden and elsewhere, a sufficiently large elite that does not forget, but is always conscious of the fact that in Western culture the French spirit has for centuries played a preponderant and leading role and continues to do so. In your writings we find manifested to a high degree the clarity and the lucidity, the penetration and the subtlety, the inimitable art inherent in your literary language, all of which we admire and warmly love. We salute you as a true representative of that wonderful French spirit.

Camus's speech (Translation)

In receiving the distinction with which your free Academy has so generously honoured me, my gratitude has been profound, particularly when I consider the extent to which this recompense has surpassed my personal merits. Every man, and for stronger reasons, every artist, wants to be recognized. So do I. But I have not been able to learn of your decision without comparing its repercussions to what I really am. A man almost young, rich only in his doubts and with his work still in progress, accustomed to living in the solitude of work or in the retreats of friendship: how would he not feel a kind of panic at hearing the decree that transports him all of a sudden, alone and reduced to himself, to the centre of a glaring light? And with what feelings could he accept this honour at a time when other writers in Europe, among them the very greatest, are condemned to silence, and even at a time when the country of his birth is going through unending misery?

I felt that shock and inner turmoil. In order to regain peace I have had, in short, to come to terms with a too generous fortune. And since I cannot live up to it by merely resting on my achievement, I have found nothing to support me but what has supported me through all my life, even in the most contrary circumstances: the idea that I have of my art and of the role of the writer. Let me only tell you, in a spirit of gratitude and friendship, as simply as I can, what this idea is.

For myself, I cannot live without my art. But I have never placed it above everything. If, on the other hand, I need it, it is because it cannot be separated from my fellow men, and it allows me to live, such as I am, on one level with them. It is a means of stirring the greatest number of people by offering them a privileged picture of common joys and sufferings. It obliges the artist not to keep himself apart; it subjects him to the most humble and the most universal truth. And often he who has chosen the fate of the artist because he felt himself to be different soon realizes that he can maintain neither his art nor his difference unless he admits that he is like the others. The artist forges himself to the others, midway between the beauty he cannot do without and the community he cannot tear himself away from. That is why true artists scorn nothing: they are obliged to understand rather than to judge. And if they have to take sides in this world, they can perhaps side only with that society in which, according to Nietzsche's great words, not the judge but the creator will rule, whether he be a worker or an intellectual.

By the same token, the writer's role is not free from difficult duties. By definition he cannot put himself today in the service of those who make history; he is at the service of those who suffer it. Otherwise, he will be alone and deprived of his art. Not all the armies of tyranny with their millions of men will free him from his isolation, even and particularly if he falls into step with them. But the silence of an unknown prisoner, abandoned to humiliations at the other end of the world, is enough to draw the writer out of his exile, at least whenever, in the midst of the privileges of freedom, he manages not to forget that silence, and to transmit it in order to make it resound by means of his art.

None of us is great enough for such a task. But in all circumstances of life, in obscurity or temporary fame, cast in the irons of tyranny or for a time free to express himself, the writer can win the heart of a living community that will justify him, on the one condition that he will accept to the limit of his abilities the two tasks that constitute the greatness of his craft: the service of truth and the service of liberty. Because his task is to unite the greatest possible number of people, his art must not compromise with lies and servitude which, wherever they rule, breed solitude. Whatever our personal weaknesses may be, the nobility of our craft will always be rooted in two commitments, difficult to maintain: the refusal to lie about what one knows and the resistance to oppression.

For more than twenty years of an insane history, hopelessly lost like all the men of my generation in the convulsions of time, I have been supported by one thing: by the hidden feeling that to write today was an honour because this activity was a commitment—and a commitment not only to write. Specifically, in view of my powers and my state of being, it was a commitment to bear, together with all those who were living through the same history, the misery and the hope we shared. These men, who were born at the beginning of the First World War, who were twenty when Hitler came to power and the first revolutionary trials were beginning, who were then confronted as a completion of their education with the Spanish Civil War, the Second World War, the world of concentration camps, a Europe of torture and prisons—these men must today rear their sons and create their works in a world threatened by nuclear destruction. Nobody, I think, can ask them to be optimists. And I even think that we should understand—without ceasing to fight it—the error of those who in an excess of despair have asserted their right to dishonour and have rushed into the nihilism of the era. But the fact remains that most of us, in my country and in Europe, have refused this nihilism and have engaged upon a quest for legitimacy. They have had to forge for themselves an art of living in times of catastrophe in order to be born a second time and to fight openly against the instinct of death at work in our history.

Each generation doubtless feels called upon to reform the world. Mine knows that it will not reform it, but its task is perhaps even greater. It consists in preventing the world from destroying itself. Heir to a corrupt history, in which are mingled fallen revolutions, technology gone mad, dead gods, and worn-out ideologies, where mediocre powers can destroy all yet no longer know how to convince, where intelligence has debased itself to become the servant of hatred and oppression, this generation starting from its own negations has had to re-establish, both within and without, a little of that which constitutes the dignity of life and death. In a world threatened by disintegration, in which our grand inquisitors run the risk of establishing forever the kingdom of death, it knows that it should, in an insane race against the clock, restore among the nations a peace that is not servitude, reconcile anew labour and culture, and remake with all men the Ark of the Covenant. It is not certain that this generation will ever be able to accomplish this immense task, but already it is rising everywhere in the world to the double challenge of truth and liberty and, if necessary, knows how to die for it without hate. Wherever it is found, it deserves to be saluted and encouraged, particularly where it is sacrificing itself. In any event, certain of your complete approval, it is to this generation that I should like to pass on the honour that you have just given me.

At the same time, after having outlined the nobility of the writer's craft, I should have put him in his proper place. He has no other claims but those which he shares with his comrades in arms: vulnerable but obstinate, unjust but impassioned for justice, doing his work without shame or pride in view of everybody, not ceasing to be divided between sorrow and beauty, and devoted finally to drawing from his double existence the creations that he obstinately tries to erect in the destructive movement of history. Who after all this can expect from him complete solutions and high morals? Truth is mysterious, elusive, always to be conquered. Liberty is dangerous, as hard to live with as it is elating. We must march toward these two goals, painfully but resolutely, certain in advance of our failings on so long a road. What writer would from now on in good conscience dare set himself up as a preacher of virtue? For myself, I must state once more that I am not of this kind. I have never been able to renounce the light, the pleasure of being, and the freedom in which I grew up. But although this nostalgia explains many of my errors and my faults, it has doubtless helped me toward a better understanding of my craft. It is helping me still to support unquestioningly all those silent men who sustain the life made for them in the world only through memory of the return of brief and free happiness.

Thus reduced to what I really am, to my limits and debts as well as to my difficult creed, I feel freer, in concluding, to comment upon the extent and the generosity of the honour you have just bestowed upon me, freer also to tell you that I would receive it as an homage rendered to all those who, sharing in the same fight, have not received any privilege, but have on the contrary known misery and persecution. It remains for me to thank you from the bottom of my heart and to make before you publicly, as a personal sign of my gratitude, the same and ancient promise of faithfulness which every true artist repeats to himself in silence every day.

[© The Nobel Foundation, 1957. Albert Camus is the sole author of his speech.]

Elias Canetti
(25 July 1905 – 14 August 1994)

Thomas H. Falk
Michigan State University

and

Dagmar C. G. Lorenz
University of Illinois at Chicago

This entry was expanded by Lorenz from Falk's Canetti entries in *DLB 85: Austrian Fiction Writers After 1914* and *DLB 124: Twentieth-Century German Dramatists, 1919–1992*.

BOOKS: *Die Blendung: Roman* (Vienna, Leipzig & Zurich: Reichner, 1936); translated by C. V. Wedgwood as *Auto-da-Fé* (London: Cape, 1946); translation republished as *The Tower of Babel* (New York: Knopf, 1947);

Komödie der Eitelkeit: Drama (Munich: Weismann, 1950); translated by Gitta Honegger as *Comedy of Vanity* (New York: Performing Arts Journal Publications, 1983);

Fritz Wotruba (Vienna: Rosenbaum, 1955);

Masse und Macht (Hamburg: Claassen, 1960); translated by Carol Stewart as *Crowds and Power* (London: Gollancz, 1962; New York: Viking, 1962);

Welt im Kopf, edited by Erich Fried (Graz & Vienna: Stiasny, 1962);

Hochzeit: Drama (Munich: Hanser, 1964); translated by Honegger as *The Wedding* (New York: Performing Arts Journal Publications, 1986);

Die Befristeten: Drama (Munich: Hanser, 1964); translated by Honegger as *Life-Terms* (New York: Performing Arts Journal Publications, 1983); translated by Stewart as *The Numbered* (London: Calder & Boyars, 1984);

Dramen (Munich: Hanser, 1964)—comprises *Hochzeit, Komödie der Eitelkeit,* and *Die Befristeten;*

Aufzeichnungen 1942–1948 (Munich: Hanser, 1965);

Die Stimmen von Marrakesch: Aufzeichnungen nach einer Reise (Munich: Hanser, 1967); translated by J. A. Underwood as *The Voices of Marrakesh: A Record of a Visit* (London: Calder & Boyars, 1978; New York: Seabury Press, 1978);

Elias Canetti (left) receiving the 1981 Nobel Prize in Literature from King Carl XVI Gustaf of Sweden (AP Photo/Reportagebild)

Der andere Prozeß: Kafkas Briefe an Felice (Munich: Hanser, 1969); translated by Christopher Middleton as *Kafka's Other Trial: The Letters to Felice* (London: Calder & Boyars, 1974; New York: Schocken, 1974);

Alle vergeudete Verehrung: Aufzeichnungen 1949–1960 (Munich: Hanser, 1970);

Die gespaltene Zukunft: Aufsätze und Gespräche (Munich: Hanser, 1972);

Macht und Überleben: Drei Essays (Berlin: Literarisches Colloquium, 1972);

Die Provinz des Menschen: Aufzeichnungen 1942–1972 (Munich: Hanser, 1973); translated by Joachim Neugroschel as *The Human Province* (New York: Seabury Press, 1978);

Der Ohrenzeuge: Fünfzig Charaktere (Munich: Hanser, 1974); translated by Neugroschel as *Earwitness: Fifty Characters* (New York: Seabury Press, 1979);

Das Gewissen der Worte (Munich: Hanser, 1975; enlarged, 1976); translated by Neugroschel as *The Conscience of Words* (New York: Seabury Press, 1979);

Der Überlebende (Frankfurt am Main: Suhrkamp, 1975);

Der Beruf des Dichters (Munich: Hanser, 1976);

Die gerettete Zunge: Geschichte einer Jugend (Munich: Hanser, 1977); translated by Neugroschel as *The Tongue Set Free: Remembrance of a European Childhood* (New York: Continuum, 1979);

Die Fackel im Ohr: Lebensgeschichte 1921–1931 (Munich: Hanser, 1980); translated by Neugroschel as *The Torch in My Ear* (New York: Farrar, Straus & Giroux, 1982);

Das Augenspiel: Lebensgeschichte 1931–1937 (Munich: Hanser, 1985); translated by Ralph Manheim as *The Play of the Eyes* (New York: Farrar, Straus & Giroux, 1986);

Das Geheimherz der Uhr: Aufzeichnungen 1973–1985 (Munich: Hanser, 1987); translated by Joel Agee as *The Secret Heart of the Clock: Notes, Aphorisms, Fragments 1973–1985* (New York: Farrar, Straus & Giroux, 1989);

Die Fliegenpein. Aufzeichnungen (Munich: Hanser, 1992); translated by H. F. Broch de Rothermann as *The Agony of Flies: Notes and Notations* (New York: Farrar, Straus & Giroux, 1994);

Aufzeichnungen 1942–1985. Die Provinz des Menschen. Das Geheimherz der Uhr (Munich: Hanser, 1993);

Werke, 10 volumes (Munich: Hanser, 1993–2005);

Nachträge aus Hampstead: Aus den Aufzeichnungen 1954–1971 (Zurich: Hanser, 1994); translated by John Hargraves as *Notes from Hampstead: The Writer's Notes, 1954–1971* (New York: Farrar, Straus & Giroux, 1998);

Wortmasken. Texte zu Leben und Werk von Elias Canetti, edited by Ortrun Huber (Munich: Hanser, 1995);

Aufzeichnungen 1992–1993 (Munich: Hanser, 1996);

Aufzeichnungen 1973–1984 (Munich: Hanser, 1999);

The Memoirs of Elias Canetti (New York : Farrar, Straus & Giroux, 1999)—comprises *The Tongue Set Free, The Torch in My Ear,* and *The Play of the Eyes;*

Party im Blitz: Die englischen Jahre, edited by Kristian Wachinger (Munich: Hanser, 2003); translated by Michael Hofmann as *Party in the Blitz* (London: Harvill, 2005);

Über den Tod, edited by Thomas Macho (Munich: Hanser, 2003);

Über die Dichter, edited by Peter von Matt (Munich: Hanser, 2004);

Aufzeichnungen für Marie-Louise, edited by Jeremy Adler (Munich: Hanser, 2005).

PLAY PRODUCTIONS: *The Numbered (Die Befristeten),* translated by Carol Stewart, Oxford, Playhouse Theatre, 5 November 1956;

Die Komödie der Eitelkeit, Brunswick, Germany, Staatstheater, 6 February 1965;

Hochzeit, Brunswick, Germany, Staatstheater, 3 November 1965;

Die Befristeten, Vienna, Theater in der Josefstadt, 17 November 1967.

OTHER: Veza Canetti, *Die gelbe Straße,* edited by Canetti (Munich: Hanser, 1990);

Veza Canetti, *Der Oger,* edited by Canetti (Munich: Hanser, 1991);

Veza Canetti, *Geduld bringt Rosen,* edited by Canetti (Munich: Hanser, 1992).

TRANSLATIONS: Upton Sinclair, *Leidweg der Liebe* (Berlin: Malik, 1930);

Sinclair, *Das Geld schreibt. Eine Studie über die amerikanische Literatur* (Berlin: Malik, 1930);

Sinclair, *Alkohol* (Berlin: Malik, 1932).

Bulgarian-born novelist and playwright Elias Canetti was awarded the Nobel Prize in Literature in 1981 for "writings marked by a broad outlook, a wealth of ideas and artistic power." Even prior to this turning point in his career, Canetti had attracted a small but loyal following among Austrian, British, German, and American intellectuals without, however, being a "popular" writer. His work includes outstanding writing in all major genres except poetry. Canetti was a polyglot and a voracious reader, a classical man of letters. Throughout his life he was an intellectual of independent means without an academic or professional position. He developed his ideas and a literary universe free from obligations to employers and research agencies, and his writings present a challenge to anthropologists, culture critics, philosophers, and scholars of social theory and psychology. Transcending traditional boundaries of genre and discipline, Canetti's literary and nonliterary texts are structurally and intellectually interconnected and function as a complex and idiosyncratic network of ideas that call into question "big" systems such as Marxism, capitalism, and fascism.

Canetti's achievements were honored throughout his career by coveted literary prizes indicating the high regard he enjoyed among critics and scholars worldwide. He received the Grand Prix International du Club Français du Livre in 1949, the Writer's Prize of the City of Vienna in 1966, the Great Austrian State Prize for Literature in 1967, the Georg Büchner Prize in 1972, the Franz Nabl Prize of the City of Graz in 1975, the Nelly Sachs Prize, and the Gottfried Keller Prize for

Die gerettete Zunge: Geschichte einer Jugend (1977; translated as *The Tongue Set Free: Remembrance of a European Childhood*, 1979). These distinctions were followed in 1980 by the Europa Prato Prize and the Johann Peter Hebel Prize; that same year he was also invited to the order Pour le Mérite. In 1981, in addition to the Nobel Prize, he was awarded the Franz Kafka Prize, and in 1983 he received the Great Service Cross of the Federal Republic of Germany. He received honorary doctoral degrees from the University of Manchester in 1975 and the University of Munich in 1976. Canetti was at home in several cultures and languages, but he chose German as his literary medium and emphasized his indebtedness to German culture even after World War II and the Holocaust.

Elias Jacques Canetti was born on 25 July 1905, the oldest of the three sons of Sephardic merchant Jacques Canetti and his wife, Mathilde, née Arditti, in Rustschuk, Bulgaria. The Canettis and the Ardittis were descendants of the Jews expelled from Spain in 1492. Canetti's father's ancestors had eventually settled in Adrianople, Turkey (now Edirne). His grandparents moved to Rustschuk, which developed into a prosperous trading center on the Danube River. Canetti's father retained his Turkish citizenship; consequently, his children were considered Turkish citizens. Canetti's mother came from one of Rustschuk's old and distinguished Sephardic families of scholars and intellectuals. In contrast to the Canettis, the Ardittis had an appreciation for progress, modern culture, and world literature.

Mathilde Arditti and Jacques Canetti had studied in Vienna, and their thinking and the cosmopolitan atmosphere of the imperial city influenced their lifestyle. Enamored of classical European drama and Vienna's outstanding theater tradition, they had dreamed of becoming actors at the Vienna Burgtheater. Only reluctantly did Jacques Canetti follow his father's wishes and enter the family's wholesale grocery business. Mathilde Canetti, the most influential person in her son's childhood and adolescence, used her enthusiasm for literature, notably dramas and novels, as a medium for Elias's education and inspired him to become an author and intellectual.

At home Canetti's family spoke Ladino, the language of the Sephardim in the Balkan states and around the Mediterranean, which had been derived from medieval Spanish and contained elements of Hebrew and non-Jewish languages. In addition, Canetti was exposed to Bulgarian, Hebrew, Turkish, Greek, Albanian, Armenian, Romanian, and Russian. His parents spoke German with one another as their intimate language and as a code when they did not want their children to understand what they were saying. The German language thus assumed a special fascination for the young Canetti. Being surrounded by so many languages early in life was undoubtedly a factor in his lifelong sensitivity to the spoken word and different linguistic registers. In his autobiographical writings Canetti reveals that many of his childhood experiences found their way into his mature writings, one example being his earliest memory: the fear of having his tongue cut off if he revealed his nanny's amorous activities. This episode, told in *Die gerettete Zunge,* connects language with the problem of truth and honesty, with sexuality, and with a sense of physical vulnerability.

When Canetti was six years old his father escaped the oppressive situation of working in a family business in a small Eastern European town by joining his brothers-in-law's business in Manchester, England. Mathilde Canetti welcomed the move. She was eager to remove her children from the influence of her orthodox in-laws, and she liked England because of its democratic tradition. Young Elias learned English without difficulty and was able to start school. In Manchester his father introduced him to literature and the life of the imagination, discussing what the boy read, including *The Arabian Nights,* Grimm's fairy tales, Daniel Defoe's *Robinson Crusoe* (1719–1722), Jonathan Swift's *Gulliver's Travels* (1726), tales from William Shakespeare, Miguel de Cervantes's *Don Quixote* (1605, 1615), the works of Dante, and Friedrich von Schiller's *Wilhelm Tell* (1804). He later said that he was grateful to his father for never telling him that fairy tales were untrue.

In October 1912 Jacques Canetti, a heavy smoker, died unexpectedly of a heart attack. Mathilde Canetti had just returned from a stay at the health resort of Bad Reichenhall, where she had sought help for her depression, a condition that became worse over the years. A romance with her physician caused her to postpone her date of return several times. Around the same time, the war on the Balkans began, which posed an increasing threat to the families in Bulgaria. After his father's death, Canetti, despite his inordinate attachment to his mother, harbored resentments and suspicions against her. Unable to tolerate life with her husband's brothers, Mathilde Canetti gave in to her nostalgia for Austria and moved to Vienna in May 1913. During an intermittent sojourn of three months in Lausanne, Switzerland, she subjected her son to a painful and humiliating crash course: she taught him German in record time so that he would be able to enter the third grade in elementary school. Through this troubling experience Canetti acquired the language he used for all of his major writings, the language that provided him with a tenuous sense of cultural identity.

Mathilde Canetti rented an apartment in the Leopoldstadt, a modest immigrant neighborhood near the Danube Canal and the Prater amusement park.

Canetti attended the Leopoldstadt elementary school and, on his way home from school, had his first encounter with anti-Semitism. In the first volume of his autobiography, *Die gerettete Zunge,* he recalls his mother's categorical rejection of the insults—she believed that her son, a Sephardic Jew, was not the intended target. Convinced that Elias was destined to become a foremost author, she encouraged him in his intellectual aspirations. She considered his Sephardic background an asset rather than a liability.

In 1916 the family moved to Zurich to avoid the ravages of World War I. The Swiss capital was a paradise for Canetti during his formative years. At age fourteen he completed his first literary work, an historical tragedy in five acts of 2,290 lines of blank verse titled "Junius Brutus." He dedicated the unpublished play to his principal and most exacting teacher, his mother. Decades later Canetti noted that his first play, for all its faults, was his earliest literary attempt in which he examined the horrors of the death penalty, which continued to be an issue of lifelong concern for him.

Much to Canetti's dismay, in 1921 Mathilde Canetti moved to Frankfurt am Main with her sons. If the previous five years had appeared like a dreamworld, the years in Frankfurt introduced Canetti to the harsh postwar reality in the defeated Germany. He was shocked by the effects of inflation when he saw an old woman die of hunger in the street. In 1922 another event, a mass demonstration against the murder of the Jewish politician and industrialist Walter Rathenau, revealed to Canetti the power of a crowd. In the following decades Canetti devoted his energy to studying and gaining an understanding of the phenomena of crowds and power in a variety of settings, modern and historical.

In 1924 Canetti enrolled at the University of Vienna as a student of chemistry to satisfy his mother's wish that he establish himself in a lucrative profession. His actual interest being literature, he immediately came under the influence of Karl Kraus, Vienna's great satirist and polemicist, editor and to a large extent sole author of the famous journal *Die Fackel* (The Torch). Canetti attended almost all of Kraus's public lectures and readings. He credited Kraus, a confirmed pacifist, with having him "gegen Krieg geimpft" (inoculated against war); moreover, Kraus's caricatures of political foes inspired Canetti's concept of the *akustische Maske* (acoustic mask), a detailed rendering of the linguistic idiosyncrasies associated with individual characters and using their speech patterns to encapsulate their emotional and mental makeup. This device became a crucial ingredient of Canetti's novel, *Die Blendung* (The Blinding, 1936; translated as *Auto-da-Fé,* 1946, and as *The Tower of Babel,* 1947), and his first two plays, *Komödie der Eitelkeit* (published in 1950, performed in 1965; translated as *Comedy of Vanity,* 1983) and *Hochzeit* (published in 1964, performed in 1965; translated as *The Wedding,* 1986).

At his first Kraus lecture Canetti met his future wife, Venetiana (Veza) Taubner-Calderon. Aged twenty-seven and known for her sophisticated literary taste and judgment, she became his second mentor and strongest supporter in Vienna and later, England. Mathilde Canetti strongly resented Taubner-Calderon's influence on her son and disapproved of the relationship. Canetti seems to have been drawn to Taubner-Calderon because of her literary interests and her active involvement in humanitarian and social causes. Most of all, her sense of fairness and independence impressed him. Having experienced abusive relationships within her immediate family and suffering from a physical disability (she was missing her left arm, whether as the result of an accident or a birth defect is unrecorded—the Canettis treated the subject as taboo), she had nonetheless succeeded in detaching from those who would oppress her and had established her own residence.

In 1928, frustrated by his studies and troubled by the 1927 riots in Vienna, which strengthened the political Right, Canetti went to Berlin with his friend Ibby Gordon, who introduced him to members of the avant garde. He stayed with Wieland Herzfelde, the head of the Malik publishing house, and met George Grosz, Bertolt Brecht, and Isaak Babel. He was both attracted to and repulsed by Berlin's gaudy bohemian scene. Some of the leading intellectuals, including Brecht, he disliked intensely. In 1929 Canetti completed his chemistry doctorate in Vienna, but he never worked as a chemist. That same year, he began writing *Die Blendung.* Originally, he had planned this work to be one in a series of eight novels, all of which were to make up a "Comédie Humaine an Irren" (Human Comedy of Madmen). According to his plans, each novel would have as its protagonist a character who dedicates his life to the pursuit of a single concept or ideal—the man of truth, the visionary who wants to live in outer space, the religious fanatic, the collector, the spendthrift, the enemy of death, the actor, and the bookman.

Dr. Peter Kien, the *Büchermensch* (bookman), is the protagonist of *Die Blendung.* Kien, at age forty, is the greatest living authority on sinology but has withdrawn to his personal library of twenty-five thousand volumes on the top floor of an apartment house at No. 24 Ehrlich Straße (Honest Street). (Even though it is never stated specifically, one can assume that the novel is set in Vienna.) Eight years earlier Kien had hired Therese Krumbholz (BentWood), who was then fifty-six, as a housekeeper. Each day she dusts one of the four rooms of the library from floor to ceiling and prepares Kien's meals, which he takes at his desk. Kien, having severed all contact with the world for the sake of his research, is leading the life of "Ein Kopf ohne Welt" (A Head without a World), as the first part of the novel is titled. Kien has a pathological relationship with books: he speaks to them, scolds them as one would a recalcitrant child, and on occasion suspects them of harboring ill will toward him. On other occasions Kien appears more rational: for example, his suggestion that a novel can help the reader to think himself into another person's place seems a reasonable account of what takes place in the reading process.

To assure the continued care of his library, Kien decides to marry his housekeeper, whose subservience he mistakes for loyalty; she agrees to the marriage because it will provide her with material security in her old age. Kien, far from seeking a relationship, allows Therese to speak to him for only a few minutes during lunch, and at that time he concentrates on not listening to her. While he remains completely devoted to his scholarly work, Therese sets about securing her future. She assumes that Kien must be rich because of the generous pay he gave her prior to their marriage, and even now he seems to pay no attention to money matters. When she asks for money to buy furniture, for instance, he gives her a large amount. What she does not understand is that he is trying to get rid of her so that he will not be bothered at his work. With this misunderstanding begins Therese's all-out search for Kien's bankbook and his will. Not finding either, she assumes that Kien deceived her about his finances. After a failed attempt at intimacy, which leaves both parties frustrated and disillusioned, Therese sets out to get revenge by invading Kien's space, making it impossible for him to work. Kien flees from the house.

Homeless and separated from his library, Kien becomes the easy prey of a ruthless exploiter, the dwarf Fischerle, in the section of the novel titled "Kopflose Welt" (Headless World). To continue his studies, Kien imagines that he is carrying his library in his head. Each day he adds more imaginary books to his head library, and each evening he imagines himself taking them out and stacking them on the floor of his hotel room. As he accumulates more and more imaginary books, he needs ever larger rooms. When the task becomes too great, he hires Fischerle, who introduces himself as the World Chess Champion Siegfried Fischer and plays along with the head-library game. Through a variety of tricks he swindles Kien out of most of his money.

One source Kien uses to build his head library is the municipal pawnshop, the Theresianum, which calls to mind the Vienna Dorotheum. Rather than buying books, he pays would-be customers not to pawn their books. Fischerle enlists four friends who pretend to want to pawn books in order to get their hands on Kien's money. One day as Kien is standing in the hallway of the Theresianum, his wife and the custodian of his apartment house come to pawn Kien's books. A row ensues; the police arrive; and Kien is accused of theft for preventing the sale of his own books. He sees Therese, but in his state of confusion believes that she did not throw him out of his apartment. Instead, he is convinced that he locked her in the apartment, causing her to die of starvation. When the police inform him that he is charged with a crime, he confesses to her "murder." The custodian, a retired policeman named Benedikt Pfaff, realizes that he can profit from the situation. He vouches for Kien at the police station and takes him to his own basement apartment. Forcing Kien to live in a dark room, Pfaff ensconces himself with Therese in Kien's top-floor apartment.

At this point Kien's brother Georg, a psychiatrist, arrives from Paris. In the third section of the novel, "Welt im Kopf" (World in the Head), Kien and Therese are divorced, and she is established as the owner of a dairy store on the other side of town. She and Pfaff will receive generous sums of money from Georg, provided that they stay away from the sinologist. Kien's apartment is refurbished and his library reclaimed from the pawnshop. By the time Georg returns to Paris he even seems to have cured his brother's psychosis. But suddenly Kien is once again overcome by his mania. He places his beloved books in a pile in the center of the room, sets them on fire, and perishes with them.

Although Canetti never wrote the seven other novels of the "Human Comedy of Madmen," some of the protagonists of those planned works appear in *Die Blendung* under slightly different guises. Kien's extreme pursuit of his scholarship calls to mind the man who would pursue one particular truth, or the visionary, or even the religious fanatic; likewise, Kien represents the collector and the spendthrift. The most fascinating aspect of the book is the meticulous development of the main characters' psychological imbalance. Kien, Therese, Fischerle, Pfaff, and even Georg each suffers from his or her own brand of madness, and the unveiling of each particular form of madness is carried out with great subtlety. In his only major work of fiction, a novel written at the age of twenty-five, Canetti exhibits an unusual mastery of storytelling.

It took Canetti a long time to convince himself that the book was worthy of publication. Finally, almost five years after Canetti completed the manuscript, his friend, the writer Stefan Zweig, found a publisher for it. The novel was well received by some critics and received praise from Hermann Broch, Alban Berg, Thomas

Mann, Robert Musil, and Hermann Hesse. However, since 1934 it had become increasingly difficult for Jewish authors to publish under Austro-Fascism, the so-called Ständestaat. After the Nazi takeover, the so-called Anschluss in March 1938, all publication venues in Austria were closed to oppositional and Jewish writers, and the Nuremberg racial laws took effect. Distributing *Die Blendung* on the German-speaking market was impossible. When the novel was translated into English after World War II, many critics and reviewers labeled the work "too difficult." Little effort was made to promote the translation, and it soon went out of print. After Canetti won the Nobel Prize he showed his bitterness for the years of neglect by withholding permission to have his works printed in England until 1985.

Two years before *Die Blendung* was published, in February 1934, Canetti had married Taubner-Calderon against his mother's wishes. His wife was an author in her own right. She had published a social-critical serial novel, *Die gelbe Straße* (1934; translated by Ian Mitchell as *The Yellow Street*, 1990), as well as short stories in the Socialist Vienna *Arbeiter-Zeitung* and elsewhere under a variety of pseudonyms. Like most Jewish authors, especially women authors, her works were rejected by Austrian publishers after the coup d'état in 1934. The couple took an apartment in the idyllic suburb of Grinzing, from where, as he writes in the third part of his autobiography, *Das Augenspiel* (1985; translated as *The Play of the Eyes*, 1986), he commuted every day to downtown Vienna to spend time in his favorite coffeehouse, the Café Museum, to observe the crowds. In 1937 Mathilde Canetti, who had lived in Paris since 1927, died. In November 1938 Elias and Veza Canetti left Vienna, fortunate to have been able to procure the necessary documents. They first went to Paris and from there to England, where they eventually took a modest apartment in the London suburb of Hampstead. For years the couple maintained separate residences, she in London, he in the suburbs. Canetti's notes and sketches in the posthumously published autobiographical volume *Party im Blitz: Die englischen Jahre* (2003; translated as *Party in the Blitz*, 2005) and Veza Canetti's *Der Fund* (2001, The Find) reveal the difficulty they faced as exiles in Britain. *Party im Blitz* also provides an impression of the author's need for independence as well as his affairs, including relationships with the writers Friedl Benedikt and Iris Murdoch and the painter Marie-Louise von Motesiczky.

In his London exile in the 1940s Canetti worked on his major work of nonfiction, *Masse und Macht* (1960; translated as *Crowds and Power*, 1962). The impetus for this ambitious study can be traced back to 15 July 1927, when Canetti observed the dynamics governing the crowd setting fire to the Palace of Justice in Vienna. Other experiences with crowd behavior, notably the seemingly inexplicable power of political leaders such as Adolf Hitler over the masses, compelled Canetti to examine the origins, makeup, and behavior of crowds in a vast array of social settings and cultures. Obviously familiar with the phenomenon of the authoritarian personality as discussed by Wilhelm Reich, the author of *Massenpsychologie des Faschismus* (1934; translated as *The Mass Psychology of Fascism*, 1946) and Theodor W. Adorno and others in *The Authoritarian Personality* (1950), Canetti steered clear of research informed by psychoanalysis and Marxist theory. He also avoided direct discussions of men associated with the war and the Holocaust such as Hitler or Adolf Eichmann. Instead, Canetti developed theses about the paranoid political leader by way of the classic case study of Daniel Paul Schreber, the Leipzig judge who chronicled his own schizophrenia in *Denkwürdigkeiten eines Nervenkranken* (1903, Memoirs of My Nervous Illness), and he took his examples for the dynamics of crowd behavior and domination from lesser-known, supposedly primitive cultures.

The fact that major players of the early to mid twentieth century are conspicuously absent while obscure figures are introduced to elucidate issues central to this epoch reveals that Canetti deliberately constructed an antihistory. He revised the most prominent models of history and society by way of his own perceptions and tried to "explain" his era through an anthropological model. His arguments are structured around concepts that he considered basic to the human condition: death, survival, dominance, submission, war, killing, and transformation, and he examined universal roles played by human beings throughout history.

To counterbalance the concentration required by his monumental project on crowds and power, Canetti took up writing his *Aufzeichnungen* (notebooks) in the 1940s. Following the tradition of Georg Christoph Lichtenberg, Heinrich Heine, and Friedrich Nietzsche, Canetti's aphorisms and diaristic entries include incisive observations and epiphanic insights on a broad range of topics including different cultural myths, languages, war and revolutions, Jewish history and experience, crowds and power, and individual authors and events. Some of the entries consist of miniature essays, which, according to some scholars, may someday be regarded as Canetti's most significant contribution to German literature. Eventually the *Aufzeichnungen* covered the years from 1942 to 1992 and were published in several volumes.

In writings and interviews Canetti repeatedly expressed his passion for the drama. Yet, only three plays by him were published and produced. In the winter of 1931–1932, shortly after completing *Die Blendung*, Canetti wrote his first play, *Hochzeit*, and followed it with a second play, *Komödie der Eitelkeit*, in 1933–1934. Both works were written in Vienna. His third play, *Die*

Befristeten (published in 1964, performed in 1967; translated as *Life-Terms*, 1983, and as *The Numbered*, 1984) was written in London during 1952 and 1953. *Die Befristeten* premiered in English, translated as *The Numbered*, on 5 November 1956 at the Playhouse Theatre in Oxford; its German premiere occurred on the Studiobühne (Studio Stage) of the Theater in der Josefstadt in Vienna on 17 November 1967. The other two plays premiered at the Staatstheater (State Theater) in Brunswick, Federal Republic of Germany: *Die Komödie der Eitelkeit* on 6 February 1965 and *Hochzeit* on 3 November 1965.

There are various reasons for the long delay between the writing and the publication and first performances of the plays. As with all his writings, Canetti insisted on reworking his plays with great care. Before leaving Vienna he gave several public readings of the first two plays; by the time he might have been ready to have them published and performed, Austria had been transformed into a fascist regime. It was difficult enough for a Jewish author to find a publisher, let alone for a Jewish playwright to find a producer and an audience. During the war Canetti concentrated on his scholarly project and his notebooks and diaries. Not until an edition of his three plays appeared with the Hanser publishing company in 1964 did Canetti become known in Germany as a playwright. Canetti believed that the proper moment for his plays to appear onstage was in the early 1960s, after German audiences had become familiar with the Theater of the Absurd.

Occasionally, Canetti indicated that he was planning a book on his theory of the drama. Although no such book emerged, three key concepts for his dramatic practice can be identified on the basis of interviews with the author, his notes, and his essays: the *akustische Maske*, the *Grundeinfall* (basic idea), and the *Verwandlung* (transformation). The acoustic mask, a character's linguistic structure, which is as unique as a fingerprint, reveals his or her emotional and intellectual makeup as well as his or her desires and goals in life.

According to Canetti, every drama has to proceed from a completely new *Grundeinfall*. The plot of the play must be so innovative that it transports the viewers into a world they have never before experienced; it must also introduce the audience to completely new and unexpected events. Based on the *Grundeinfall*, the author creates a world apart from everyday reality to appeal to the audience's critical faculties.

The notion of *Verwandlung* refers to Canetti's conviction that the theater is not only a place for entertainment but also an educational institution. The playwright's task is to challenge the audience with a shocking reality to induce a catharsis. Canetti does not seek to describe or interpret the world; he wants his grotesque and absurd dramatic antiworlds to bring about a transformation through confrontation and mental and emotional readjustment. Transformation—in contrast to rigidity, be it a lack of flexibility, an unwillingness to change, stubbornness, or stagnation—is also a central concept in Canetti's theory on crowds and power. The ability to become a different being, even across species boundaries, as in native myths and fairy tales, is the key to survival. It enables the weak and persecuted to escape from the power of tyrants, perhaps even from death.

Hochzeit has as its *Grundeinfall* the proximity of the desires for power, sex, and possession with self-destruction and, ultimately, death. The play depicts a merciless society void of a moral code and heading toward complete destruction. *Hochzeit* is divided into a prelude in five scenes and the main act. The prelude introduces the residents of an apartment house on Gütigkeitstraße (Kindness Street), all of whom are obsessed by the desire of owning the house in which they live. The landlady is a shrewd old woman who is visited every day by her granddaughter. Under the guise of concern the younger woman, who hopes that the old lady will soon die, plots to become the heiress and bring the house into her possession. Each time the landlady's parrot hears the word *Haus* (house), he repeats it three times, emphasizing the major theme of the play. Subsequent scenes within the prelude introduce the other residents, including a pompous schoolteacher and a young couple whose wedding is celebrated in the main act. They, too, are trying to cheat the old woman out of her house. The fifth scene takes place in the janitor's basement apartment, a setting that calls to mind the chapter "Der gute Vater" (The Good Father) in *Die Blendung*, a sinister farce on patriarchal patterns. In the play the janitor's wife is shown lying on her deathbed while her husband reads from the Book of Judges in the Bible. The episode in question tells how the blinded Samson pulls down the house upon the Philistines, thereby foreshadowing the events of the main act.

The wedding celebration in the main act introduces the audience to a depraved, bourgeois family. The bride's father, Oberbaurat Segenreich (Chief Construction Engineer Richly Blessed), insists in his vanity that everyone acknowledge that he has built a solid house and a fine family. However, it is obvious that the members of this family and the wedding party are driven by greed and the will to power: they want to acquire property and dominate other people. In addition, all of them are obsessed with sex. The sex-crazed mother of the bride can think of nothing but copulating with the groom; the bride lusts after three friends of the family; and—revealing the connection between sexuality, power, and domination—the eighty-year-old family physician, Dr. Bock (Stud), an erotomaniac and pedophile, brags that he has "had" all the women in the family and those present at the party. Into this macabre world Horch (Hark), an idealist, introduces a play within the play. He asks what each person would do if the one he or she loves were threatened by imminent danger. When a sudden earthquake changes the game into reality, and the characters could really save the person they love, they try to save themselves first. The play ends with cruel, hateful screams cutting through the silence. The parrot has the last word: "Haus! Haus! Haus!"

The premiere of *Hochzeit* caused a scandal. Spectators were offended by Canetti's explicit language, by the way the characters were portrayed, and by the message of the play. To make matters worse, the day before the premiere, a Brunswick newspaper had printed an anonymous article charging that the play was pornographic. Even though several writers and critics, including Günter Grass and Adorno, vouched for the high artistic quality of *Hochzeit,* the play closed after seven performances. Today *Hochzeit* is considered Canetti's most stageable play. It was successfully performed under the direction of Karl Paryla in 1970 in Cologne and had an enthusiastic reception when Canetti read it later that year at the Schauspielhaus (Playhouse) in Kiel. When the city of Vienna celebrated Canetti's eightieth birthday in October 1985, Hans Hollmann directed *Hochzeit* at the Akademietheater with a distinguished cast.

The *Grundeinfall* of *Komödie der Eitelkeit* is that the human race would waste away if individuals were deprived of the ability to see themselves in a mirror or through the eyes of others. A new government decree intended to eliminate vanity, interpreted in a narrow sense as the indulgence of selfishness, is imposed on the population. The ownership and use of mirrors are prohibited; photographing people is forbidden, and all photographs of human beings must be destroyed; and all movie houses must be closed and all movies destroyed. The punishment for violating the decree is long-term imprisonment or death. The play illustrates different reactions to the new social situation by way of some two dozen characters. The teacher Fritz Schakerl (Little Jackal) represents the strict disciplinarian. When he is not acting as an enforcer of conduct, he develops a severe stutter. He is the one who announces the decree; during the announcement he does not stammer a single time. S. Bleiss, a photographer, is in the business of perpetuating vanity. His favorite gimmick is to take pictures of poor newlyweds standing in front of his car, which the couple can pass off as their own when they show the picture. François Fant (Fop) steals all of his mother's mirrors and takes them to the carnival, where he smashes them with a ball while watching his reflection in them. Emilie Fant, François's mother, needs the mirrors for her brothel for ambience and to help her girls make themselves attractive for her customers. Heinrich Föhn (Hot Air) strolls across the stage, pontificating to his companion Leda Frisch (Fresh) that a self-image of good health provides the individual with a meaningful life.

The second half of the play, set ten years later, shows how the characters have come to terms with the decree. Schakerl has become the powerful chairman of a committee of crime fighters after he advocated the passage of a law under which the eyes of girls are torn out if they look into someone else's eyes to see themselves. Married to one such girl, Schakerl grows ill and despondent, a victim of the so-called mirror sickness, which can only be cured by looking into a mirror. When he obtains a mirror, his stammering returns. Bleiss is still dealing in vanity, going from door to door selling time in front of a mirror at ten schillings for two minutes. Although he is occasionally caught in this illegal venture, he survives. Emilie Fant has established a "Spiegelbordell" (mirror brothel) where almost all the characters of the play pay high prices to sit in front of mirrors and admire themselves. Föhn stands before a full-length mirror in a luxury cabin making pompous and trivial pronouncements. After each proclamation he pushes a button and hears applause; but each time, the applause grows weaker, until there is none. Becoming demented, he threatens in a thundering voice to destroy the establishment. The final scene shows the majority of the characters in Emilie's "Spiegelsaal" (Hall of Mirrors). Each is confronted by and recoils from a raging voice that summarizes his or her character traits, exposing the untruthfulness of the mask each had created. All raise high mirrors or pictures of themselves, but they never merge into a group; individual vanity prevails.

The reviews of opening night were so negative that *Komödie der Eitelkeit* closed after only eight performances. Yet, most reviewers thought highly of the play itself and placed the blame on the director, Helmut Matiasek. He had chosen the Nazi period as the setting, thereby transforming Canetti's drama into a commentary on National Socialism rather than leaving it more neutral as a general statement on totalitarian systems. The historically specific setting, appropriate to the author's own experience in the 1930s and 1940s, had supposedly prevented the catharsis Canetti intended. The most successful production of the play took place in Basel in February 1978 under the direction of Hollmann, who was familiar with Canetti's concepts of the *akustische Maske* and the *Grundeinfall.*

In *Die Befristeten* the *Grundeinfall* is a utopian society in which people are not tormented by the uncertainty of when they will die. At birth, people are given a locket containing their birth and death dates, along with a number that indicates the number of years they will live. Although everyone knows the information in his or her own locket, it is a crime to reveal it to others. An official called the Kapselan (locketeer) is the only one authorized to open the locket at the time of death to confirm the accuracy of the date recorded there. The play has three major and twenty minor characters, as well as a chorus. The minor characters have names such as Die Mutter 32 (The Mother 32), Der Junge 70 (The Boy 70), Zwei junge Herren, 28 und 88 (Two Young Men, 28 and 88), Der Mann, Dr. 46 (The Man, Dr. 46), and Der Junge zehn (The Boy 10). Each person's number determines his or her personality and behavior. The Mother 32, for example, is unable to persuade her son, the Boy 70, to be cautious while playing, because the son knows that he cannot be killed until he is seventy. The Boy 10 is a spoiled brat because he knows that his is only a short life. The dystopian character of this society is expressed in a woman's reminder to her granddaughter that the latter will live "bis zu deinem Augenblick" (only until your moment). Characters with high numbers assume a superior and arrogant attitude; those with low numbers obviously feel inferior and behave in an obsequious and downtrodden manner.

The major characters are Fünfzig (Fifty), Freund (Friend), and the Kapselan. Fünfzig resists the dictates of the Kapselan. For many years he has suspected that the lockets might be empty and that the Kapselan was a fraud. He reveals his suspicions to Freund and subsequently to the masses, who follow him merrily in precipitating the downfall of the deceptive system, driven by the idea that they will now live forever. However, the death of the first person puts an end to this dream. It turns out that the uncertainty of the time of one's death is worse than the certainty that death will occur at a predestined moment. Here, as elsewhere in Canetti's writing, the new system achieved through violent action is even less desirable than the previous one, despite the latter's imperfection.

Reviews of the premiere performance of *Die Befristeten* as *The Numbered* by the Meadow Players of the Oxford Playhouse Company, directed by Mionos Volanakis, were positive. The *Times* of London compared the play with works by Jean Giraudoux and Jean Cocteau: "Into this distinguished repertoire Mr. Elias Canetti's play erupts with a strangely mathematical absorption." *Oxford* magazine reported that "the writing is forceful and plain, as is the production. . . . In scene upon scene they build up the delicate web of tension, achieving with truth and economy effects which grip the mind." By contrast, the German-language premiere in Vienna under the direction of Friedrich Kallina on 17 November 1967 was not well received. The critic for *Die Welt* (The World) considered the drama a nice exercise for the mind but not a play for the stage. Other critics described Canetti's dramas as "difficult" or "uncomfortable." The frequent controversies occasioned by the performances suggest the public's unwillingness to take an honest, albeit pessimistic, look at itself. Canetti addressed such major issues as greed, power, lasciviousness, freedom, death, the depersonalization of the individual, and the creation of an inhumane mass society.

In 1952 Canetti had traveled to Morocco in the company of a movie team. The experience of a North African Arab society with a rich Sephardic history and subculture proved highly productive. It resulted in a manuscript initially titled "Moroccan Memoirs" and published under the title *Die Stimmen von Marrakesch: Aufzeichnungen nach einer Reise* (1967; translated as *The Voices of Marrakesh*, 1978). The volume successfully combines the genre of the travelogue and documentary with autobiographical writing.

Veza Canetti died on 1 May 1963. In her afterword to the 2001 edition of *Der Fund*, Angelika Schedel speculates that the death was a suicide; however, biographer Sven Hanuschek argues convincingly that Veza Canetti, in all likelihood suffering from cancer, died after weeks of hospitalization. In 1971 Canetti married Hera Buschor, an art restorer; their daughter, Johanna, was born in 1972. Canetti had met Buschor, daughter of classical archaeologist Ernst Buschor, in London in 1957. His relationship with the much younger woman (she was born in 1933) developed slowly over the years. Despite her background from parents supportive of the Nazi system, her common interests with Canetti in history, languages, and art prevailed. In the 1970s Canetti had acquired an apartment in Zurich and had begun living alternately in Hampstead and Zurich.

Another genre in which Canetti excelled was the essay. Some of his longer essays were collected in *Das Gewissen der Worte* (1975; enlarged, 1976; translated as *The Conscience of Words*, 1979). These essays explore figures who had a major impact on Canetti's writing and thinking during the decades he devoted to the study of crowds and power, among them Broch, Musil, Kraus, Stendhal, Leo Tolstoy, and Aristophanes. The essays also examine the human condition after the Holocaust and the atomic bomb—for the most part indirectly, without naming these specific reference points, but sometimes directly, as in "Dr. Hachiyas Tagebuch aus Hiroshima" (1975; translated as "Dr. Hachiya's Diary of Hiroshima," 1979), a sensitive and compassionate review of a Japanese survivor's account. Particularly revealing in the context of Canetti's theories on crowd management and his most direct commentary on Hitler's mentality is his review article "Hitler, nach Speer" (translated as "Hitler, According to Speer") in *Das Gewissen der Worte*.

The volumes of Canetti's autobiography not only serve as a chronicle of the author's life but also constitute an important contribution to historical and autobiographical writing. *Die gerettete Zunge* is devoted to

Canetti's experiences between 1904 and 1921 and discusses the formative experiences and social forces in the author's youth. These forces include his Sephardic background and important personalities such as his parents, his grandparents, and other people with whom he interacted as an adolescent in Bulgaria, Britain, Switzerland, Austria, and Germany. Of all the episodes, those set in interwar Germany are the bleakest and most pessimistic. The spontaneity and the easy flow of Canetti's narrative are deceptive. All of the key episodes are carefully chosen, and the characters are framed in such a way as to reveal aspects of the author's development and his creative processes. *Die Fackel im Ohr: Lebensgeschichte 1921–1931* (1980; translated as *The Torch in My Ear,* 1982) describes Canetti's experiences from the years 1921 to 1931, most notably his fascination and eventual disillusionment with Kraus, his courtship of Veza Canetti, and his increasing detachment from his mother. Rather than sketching a panoramic view of his life, Canetti focuses on central personalities. One of these figures is Broch, who provided him with insights concerning mass psychology; another is Abraham Sonne, a fellow patron of the Café Museum in Vienna and author of Hebrew poetry published under the pen name of Abraham ben Yitchak, who helped Canetti to overcome Kraus's overpowering influence. The third volume of Canetti's autobiography, *Das Augenspiel,* reviews experiences and events of the years 1931 to 1937.

In every part of his memoirs Canetti establishes connections between personal, social, historical, and political developments. For example, in the first volume he places his family's move from Vienna to Frankfurt into the larger context of the aftermath of World War I, and the second volume makes obvious the interplay between the author's intellectual development and the freewheeling revolutionary spirit of the times. Without addressing Austro-Fascism and National Socialism directly, as Veza Canetti did in her novel *Die Schildkröten* (1999; translated as *The Tortoises,* 2001), Canetti's memoirs indicate that the idyllic abode of the newlyweds in the Viennese suburb of Grinzing was a retreat from the increasingly threatening urban atmosphere. Interestingly, Canetti makes more of an issue about the proximity of his living quarters to the house of the publisher Ernst Benedikt (who because of the rising anti-Semitism had to relinquish his position as editor and his share in his paper *Die Neue Freie Presse* in 1934), than he does about the radicalization of the Austrian public and the Nazi threat. Although many of his interlocutors of those years chose exile, as did sculptor Anna Mahler in London and Sonne in Palestine, Canetti does not comment on their fates. The key figures in the autobiography reveal to what degree Canetti steered clear of the fashions of his time and refused to follow literary and ideological movements. He likewise treats with discretion his personal affairs, the waning passion in his marriage, his infatuation with Mahler, and his evolving relationship with Friedl Benedict, Ernst's daughter and a successful author in England.

During the war era Canetti was preoccupied with the killing, devastation, and suffering caused by the nation whose language he had adopted. He was greatly concerned about the consequences of the violence, the extent of which was not known at the time. Canetti, who was so closely identified with the culture of the aggressors, faced a double bind: an exile from Nazi-controlled Austria living in Great Britain, he felt that he owed a double loyalty, both to his country of exile and to the German culture to which he owed much of his creative impulse. Having learned German under almost traumatic circumstances, he noted in his *Aufzeichnungen* that the language of his spirit would forever be the German language, not despite the fact that he was a Jew but because of it. Canetti considered himself the protector of the unspoiled German language, whose task it was to return to the Germans their uncorrupted language to pay his debt of gratitude. Canetti continued to write in German, even though during the war and for several years afterward he was virtually unknown in German-speaking countries.

Unlike other exiles from Nazi-controlled territories, he did not publish during the war years or take part in the propaganda effort—doing so would have compromised his position as a neutral arbiter, which he wanted to establish. Even after Germany's defeat, when he had learned of the extent of the destruction and the devastation of the Holocaust, he refrained from taking sides. His *Aufzeichnungen* of the postwar years reveal the agony that resulted from his attempt to preserve his neutral stance. Canetti continued to examine the phenomenon of the masses and the paranoid leader in universal rather than specific terms, and he continued to state his compassion for all those who had suffered, including the Germans and the Japanese. Canetti avoided addressing the topics of Nazi anti-Semitism and the Holocaust directly, even though aspects of both are implied in his crowd studies and his *Aufzeichnungen,* which over the years sketch an increasingly pessimistic image of humanity.

Critics and the international media reacted with bewilderment to the announcement that Canetti, at the time still somewhat of a cult author lacking the international standing of his later years, was the recipient of the 1981 Nobel Prize in Literature. Because seven nations had supported Canetti's nomination for the Nobel Prize—Bulgaria, Germany, England, Austria, Israel, Spain, and Switzerland, countries where he had resided or been a visitor—Canetti's identity became an issue of debate. A similar stir had followed the 1966 nomination of Nelly Sachs, the German Holocaust poet living as a recluse in Sweden, and that of the Yiddish American novelist Isaac Bashevis Singer in 1978–both writers whose lives, like Canetti's, had been shaped by the exile experience. *The New York Times* noted that Canetti was "the first native of Bulgaria to win the prize." The *Times* of London identified Canetti as "the first British citizen to win the literature prize since Winston Churchill," observing that "most unusually of all for a British laureate, Dr. Canetti writes, and has always written, in German." A critic for the Austrian literary journal *Literatur und Kritik* wrote that Canetti, although not an Austrian citizen, could be counted among the representatives of Austrian literature on the basis of his views. The journal termed him the first author of Austrian spirit to receive the Nobel Prize.

In his presentation speech at the Nobel award ceremony, Johannes Edfelt of the Swedish Academy characterized Canetti as an exiled and cosmopolitan author and praised him for never having abandoned his true native land, the German language, and his love of classical German culture. Furthermore, Edfelt extolled the laureate's intellectual passion and his dedication to the cause of humanity. He interpreted Canetti's one novel, *Die Blendung,* as a metaphor of the dangers posed by hyperspecialization and the ensuing isolation of the individual on the one hand, and the rise of the internalized "massman" on the other. He observed structural and ideological affinities between *Die Blendung* and Canetti's critically acclaimed anthropological-philosophical study *Masse und Macht,* "a magisterial work" on "the origin, composition and reaction patterns of mass movements." Canetti's three plays, *Komödie der Eitelkeit, Hochzeit,* and *Die Befristeten,* were celebrated in the laudation for their portrayal of "extreme situations" and their insightful examination of a "unique world of ideas." Also recognized in the Nobel speech was Canetti's study of the tortured relationship of Franz Kafka and his fiancée Felice Bauer, as it emerges from the letters he sent her while writing *Der Prozeß* (1925; translated as *The Trial,* 1937). Canetti's essay on Kafka and Bauer had appeared separately in 1969 as *Der andere Prozeß* (translated as *Kafka's Other Trial,* 1974).

Edfelt gave his most heartfelt tribute to Canetti's autobiography, of which the first two volumes had appeared *(Die gerettete Zunge* and *Die Fackel im Ohr).* According to Edfelt, these highly personal texts represent "a peak in Canetti's writings" and reveal "his forceful epic power of description to its full extent" as they portray the political and cultural life in central Europe in the early 1900s. The laudation concluded on a note of highest acclaim: "with your versatile writings, which attack sick tendencies in our age, you wish to serve the cause of humanity. Intellectual passion is combined in you with the moral responsibility that . . . is nourished by mercy."

Confirming Edfelt's observations about his intellectual identity, Canetti presented his speech at the Nobel Banquet on 10 December 1981 in German. He credited three cities, Vienna, London, and Zurich, for having played a pivotal role in his intellectual development, because they represented to him peril, inspiration, and excess. Moreover, he also stated his indebtedness to three Jewish intellectuals and one non-Jewish author: the Viennese journalist and satirist Kraus, the Prague prose writer and lawyer Kafka, the Austrian novelist and mass psychologist Broch, and finally, the prose writer Musil, an observer and critic of Central European culture. Indeed, these four authors, foremost representatives of fin de siècle modernity, epitomize and transcend the multicultural legacy of the Habsburg Empire, the cultural realm that shaped Canetti. Citing these particular sites and names, Canetti placed himself within the larger European modernist tradition, the major achievement of which he characterized as the ethics of pacifism, most notably the distrust of power and authority and the institutions that administer them. Linking his own concerns with authors he admired, Canetti points in his speech to aspects of his own writing, which combines the personal and empirical with the philosophical and rational in an attempt to transcend conventional or fashionable concepts and thought patterns.

Even though Canetti did not mention his country and culture of origin, Bulgaria and Sephardic Jewry, the name of his native city, Rustschuk (now Ruse), was inscribed on the back of his chair in the hall of Nobel laureates, rather than the author's country of citizenship as is customary. Indeed, *Die gerettete Zunge* reveals Canetti's vivid memories of Rustschuk and the importance of his childhood place for his thought and creativity. Through his avoidance of Bulgaria in his writings Canetti seems to suggest his culture of origin perished as the result of the Holocaust and World War II. Susan Sontag, who quoted Canetti as saying that he set out to "grab this century by the throat," was impressed with his refusal to adopt a reductionist psychological approach, his opposition to historicism, and his rebellion against death. In his writings she recognized both his affinity with classical European authors and his fascination with Chinese, Buddhist, Muslim, and Christian thought. As was the case with many critics, she overlooked the significance of Jewish, especially Sephardic, tradition in Canetti's work and did not mention how profoundly the Holocaust, the war, and the atomic bomb affected the author.

Winning the Nobel Prize made Canetti financially independent for the first time in his life. The event also placed him at the forefront of literary debates and into the limelight, which he tried to avoid. Following the award, Canetti was in demand as an author, public lecturer, and reader, and aspiring scholars besieged him. Yet, he maintained his modest lifestyle, living in a nondescript modern apartment building in Zurich and remaining loyal to old friends. In 1988 Hera Canetti died of cancer, leaving her young daughter and her husband, who was now advanced in years, on their own.

In the late 1980s Canetti started to release new editions of Veza Canetti's novels and short stories with the Hanser publishing company. Aside from paying tribute to her creativity, his observations about his late wife's writings provide insights into his views on gender roles, femininity, and his and Veza Canetti's relationship.

Canetti died suddenly in Zurich on 14 August 1994. His grave site in the Fluntern Cemetery is close to that of James Joyce, whom he admired and who as a writer stood similarly apart from the crowds.

Since Canetti's death new publications by and about him have appeared from his extensive estate, which the author entrusted to the Zentralbibliothek Zürich. The posthumously published books include the fourth volume of his autobiography, *Party im Blitz*, impressions from Canetti's early years in England. Written in 1990, the work provides boldly stated observations about Canetti's personal aversions and predilections, his first impressions about British society, and astute insights into his own tenuous position as an exile. He also presents assessments of global events, politics, and society.

In light of the seemingly never-ending wars and conflicts in the late twentieth century involving nationality, ethnicity, and religion, Elias Canetti's increasingly critical, if not downright misanthropic, view of the human species deserves special attention. From the confrontation with inhumanity and brutality evolves Canetti's alternative anthropology that links human and nonhuman animal behavior in unexpected ways. Canetti's often misquoted and misinterpreted "opposition to death" is at the very core of his thinking, calling for a rigorous nonviolent ethic that rules out death—killing and suicide—as options, regardless what the circumstances may be. Canetti fiercely objected to the threat of death as a political tool (warfare), a means to discipline and punish (capital punishment), or a way of dealing with other species (hunting and slaughter). Indeed, his ethic calls for the elimination of killing or murder altogether, even in the realm of imagination, arts, and literature. Canetti's insistence that a fundamental reorientation and a global intellectual and educational effort be undertaken to delay the self-destruction of the human species constitutes his major contribution to the twentieth-century discourse on the human condition.

Biography:

Sven Hanuschek, *Elias Canetti: Biographie* (Munich: Carl Hanser, 2005).

References:

Heinz Ludwig Arnold, ed., *Literatur und Kritik,* special Canetti issue, no. 28, third edition (September 1982);

Friedbert Aspetsberger and Gerald Stieg, eds., *Elias Canetti: Blendung als Lebensform* (Königsberg: Athenäum, 1985);

Dagmar Barnouw, *Elias Canetti* (Stuttgart: Metzler, 1979);

Barnouw, *Elias Canetti zur Einführung* (Hamburg: Junius, 1996);

Kurt Bartsch and Gerhard Melzer, eds., *Elias Canetti: Experte der Macht* (Graz: Droschl, 1985);

Alfons-M. Bischoff, *Elias Canetti: Stationen zum Werk* (Bern & Frankfurt am Main: Lang, 1973);

Mechthild Curtius, *Kritik der Verdinglichung in Canettis Roman "Die Blendung" Eine Sozialpsychologische Literaturanalyse* (Bonn: Bouvier, 1973);

David Darby, ed., *Critical Essays on Elias Canetti* (New York: G. K. Hall, 2000);

William Collins Donahue, *The End of Modernism: Elias Canetti's Auto-da-Fé* (Chapel Hill: University of North Carolina Press, 2001);

Manfred Durzak, ed., *Zu Elias Canetti* (Stuttgart: Klett, 1983);

Friederike Eigler, *Das autobiographische Werk von Elias Canetti. Verwandlung, Identität, Machtausübung* (Tübingen: Stauffenburg, 1988);

Susanna Engelmann, *Babel – Bibel – Bibliothek. Canettis Aphorismen zur Sprache* (Würzburg: Königshausen & Neumann, 1997);

Thomas H. Falk, *Elias Canetti* (New York: Twayne, 1993);

Leslie Fiedler, "The Tower of Babel," *Partisan Review,* 3 (May/June 1947): 316–320;

Kristie A. Foell, *Blind Reflections: Gender in Elias Canetti's Die Blendung* (Riverside: Ariadne Press, 1994);

Helmut Göbel, *Elias Canetti* (Reinbek: Rowohlt, 2005);

Herbert G. Göpfert, ed., *Canetti lesen: Erfahrungen mit seinen Büchern* (Munich: Hanser, 1975);

Werner Hoffmann, ed., *Hüter der Verwandlung* (Munich: Hanser, 1985); translated by Michael Hulse as *Essays in Honor of Elias Canetti* (New York: Farrar, Straus & Giroux, 1987);

Walter Höllerer and Norbert Miller, eds., *Elias Canetti zu Ehren, Sprache im technischen Zeitalter,* 94 (1985);

Gitta Honegger, "Acoustic Masks: Strategies of Language in the Theater of Canetti, Bernhard, and Handke," *Modern Austrian Literature,* 18, no. 2 (1985): 57–66;

Heike Knoll, *Das System Canetti. Zur Rekonstruktion eines Wirklichkeitsentwurfes* (Stuttgart: M & P, 1993);

Michael Krüger, ed., *Einladung zur Verwandlung. Essays zu Elias Canettis "Macht und Macht"* (Munich: Hanser, 1995);

Detlef Krumme, *Lesemodelle: Canetti, Grass, Hölerer* (Munich: Hanser, 1983), pp. 31–84;

Richard H. Lawson, *Understanding Elias Canetti* (Columbia, S.C.: University of South Carolina Press, 1991);

Dagmar C. G. Lorenz, ed., *A Companion to the Works of Elias Canetti* (Columbia, S.C.: Camden House, 2004);

Michael Mack, *Anthropology as Memory: Elias Canetti's and Franz Baermann Steiner's Responses to the Shoah* (Tübingen: Niemeyer, 2001);

Modern Austrian Literature, special Canetti issue, 16, no. 3/4 (1983);

Edgar Piel, *Elias Canetti* (Munich: Beck, 1984);

David Roberts, *Kopf und Welt: Elias Canettis Roman "Die Blendung"* (Munich: Hanser, 1975);

Sidney Rosenfeld, "1981 Nobel Laureate Elias Canetti: A Writer Apart," *World Literature Today,* 56, no. 1 (1982): 5–9;

Angelika Schedel, "Nachwort," in Veza Canetti, *Der Fund* (Munich: Hanser, 2001), pp. 309–324;

Susan Sontag, "Mind as Passion," in her *Under the Sign of Saturn* (New York: Farrar, Straus & Giroux, 1980);

Adrian Stevens and Fred Wagner, eds., *Elias Canetti: Londoner Symposium* (Stuttgart: Verlag Hans-Dieter Heinz/Akademischer Verlag Stuttgart, 1991);

Kristian Wachinger, ed., *Elias Canetti: Bilder aus seinem Leben* (Munich: Carl Hanser, 2005).

Papers:
Elias Canetti left his papers to the Zentralbibliothek Zürich under the condition that his literary estate (120 boxes) be made available for research in 2004 and his personal papers (30 boxes) in 2024.

1981 Nobel Prize in Literature Presentation Speech

by Dr. Johannes Edfelt, of the Swedish Academy (Translation from the Swedish)

Your Majesties, Your Royal Highnesses, Ladies and Gentlemen,

The exiled and cosmopolitan author Canetti has one native land, and that is the German language. He has never abandoned it, and he has often avowed his love of the highest manifestations of the classical German culture.

In a speech in Vienna in 1936 Canetti praised Hermann Broch as one of the few contemporary representative writers. What irremissible demands, according to Canetti, must be made upon the truly representative man? He must be subject to his time as its "lowest slave" and yet be in opposition to it; in a wish for universality he must summarize his age, and he must possess the most distinct "conception of atmospheric impressions." Such criteria also mark Canetti's own writings. Pursued in different directions and comprising several genres, they are held together by a most original and vigorously profiled personality.

His foremost purely fictional achievement is the great novel *Die Blendung* ("Auto da Fé"), published in 1935 [1936] but attaining its full effect only during the last decades: against the background of National Socialism's brutal power politics, the novel acquires a deepened perspective.

Die Blendung was part of an originally planned series of novels which was to take the shape of a "*comédie humaine* of madmen." The book has such fantastic and demoniacal elements that associations with Russian 19th-Century writers like Gogol and Dostoevsky are apparent. It is an aspect of key importance when *Die Blendung* is regarded by several critics as a single fundamental metaphor for the threat exercised by the "mass man" within ourselves. Close at hand is the viewpoint from which the novel stands out as a study of a type of man who isolates himself in self-sufficient specialization, only to succumb helplessly in a world of ruthlessly harsh realities.

Die Blendung leads over to the big examination of the origin, composition and reaction patterns of the mass movements which Canetti, after decades of research and study, published with *Masse und Macht* ("Crowds and Power") in 1960. It is a magisterial work by a polyhistor who can disclose an overwhelmingly large number of viewpoints of men's behaviour as mass beings. In his basically a historical analysis what he wants to expose and attack by scrutinizing the origin and nature of the masses is, in the end, the religion of power. Survival becomes the nucleus of power. At last the mortal enemy is death itself: this is a principal theme, held to with a strangely pathetic strength, in Canetti's literary works.

Apart from the intensive work on *Masse und Macht* Canetti has written aphoristic notes, issued in several volumes. Abundant humour and a satirical bite in the observation of people's behaviour, a loathing of wars and devastation, bitterness at the thought of life's brevity are characteristic features here.

Canetti's three plays are all of a more or less absurd kind. In their portrayal of extreme situations, often depicting human vulgarity, these "acoustic masks," as he himself calls them, give an interesting glimpse into his unique world of ideas.

Among his many sharp-sighted portrait studies special mention can be made of *Der andere Prozeß* ("Kafka's Other Trial"), in which with intense involvement he examines Kafka's complicated relationship to Felice Bauer. The study resolves into a picture of a man whose life and work meant the relinquishing of power.

Finally, standing out as a peak in Canetti's writings, are his memoirs, so far in two large volumes. In these recollections of his childhood and youth he reveals his forceful epic power of description to its full extent. A great deal of the political and cultural life in central Europe in the early 1900's—especially the form it took in Vienna—is reflected in the memoirs. The peculiar environments, the many remarkable human destinies with which Canetti has been confronted and his unique educational path—always aiming at universal knowledge—are seen here in a style and with a lucidity that have very few qualitative equivalents in the memoirs written in the German language during this century.

Dear Mr. Canetti, with your versatile writings, which attack sick tendencies in our age, you wish to serve the cause of humanity. Intellectual passion is combined in you with the moral responsibility that—in your own words—"is nourished by mercy." I beg to convey to you the warm congratulations of the Swedish Academy, and ask you now to accept this year's Nobel Prize for Literature from the hands of His Majesty the King.

[© The Nobel Foundation, 1981.]

Canetti: Banquet Speech

Canetti's speech at the Nobel Banquet, 10 December 1981

Eure Majestäten, Eure Königlichen Hoheiten, meine Damen und Herren,

Einer Stadt, die man kennt, verdankt man viel und einer, die man kennen möchte, wenn man sich lange vergeblich nach ihr sehnt, vielleicht noch mehr. Aber es gibt, glaube ich, im Leben eines Menschen auch besondere Stadtgottheiten, durch Drohung, Unermesslichkeit oder Verklärung ausgezeichnete Gebilde. Die drei, die es für mich waren, sind Wien, London und Zürich.

Man mag es dem Zufall zuschreiben, dass es diese drei sind, aber dieser Zufall heisst noch Europa, und soviel Europa vorzuwerfen wäre,—denn was ist nicht alles von ihm ausgegangen!—heute, da der Atemschatten, unter dem wir leben, schwer auf Europa lastet, zittern wir zuerst um Europa. Denn dieser Kontinent, dem sich soviel verdankt, trägt auch eine grosse Schuld und er braucht Zeit, um seine Sünden wiedergutzumachen. Wir wünschen ihm leidenschaftlich diese Zeit, eine Zeit, in der sich eine Wohltat nach der anderen über die Erde verbreiten konnte, eine Zeit, die so segensreich wäre, dass niemand auf der ganzen Welt Grund mehr hätte, den Namen Europas zu verfluchen.

Zu diesem verspäteten, zum eigentlichen Europa haben in meinem Leben vier Männer gehört, von denen ich mich nicht zu trennen vermag. Ihnen verdanke ich es, dass ich heute vor Ihnen stehe und ich möchte ihre Namen vor Ihnen nennen. Der Erste ist Karl Kraus, der grösste Satiriker der deutschen Sprache. Er hat mich das Hören gelehrt, die unbeirrbare Hingabe an die Laute Wiens. Er hat mich, was noch wichtiger war, gegen Krieg geimpft, eine Impfung, die damals für Viele noch notwendig war. Heute, seit Hiroshima, weiss jeder, was Krieg ist, und dass jeder es weiss, ist unsere einzige Hoffnung.—Der Zweite ist Franz Kafka, dem es gegeben war, sich ins Kleine zu verwandeln und sich so der Macht zu entziehen. In diese lebenslange Lehre, die die notwendigste von allen war, bin ich bei ihm gegangen. Den Dritten wie den Vierten, Robert Musil und Hermann Broch, habe ich in meiner Wiener Zeit gekannt. Robert Musils Werk fasziniert mich bis zum heutigen Tage, vielleicht bin ich erst seit den späten Jahren imstande, es ganz zu erfassen. Damals in Wien war erst ein Teil davon bekannt und was ich von ihm lernte, war das Schwerste: dass man ein Werk auf Jahrzehnte hin unternehmen kann, ohne zu wissen, ob es sich vollenden lässt, eine Waghalsigkeit, die hauptsächlich aus Geduld besteht, die eine beinahe unmenschliche Hartnäckigkeit voraussetzt. Mit Hermann Broch war ich befreundet. Ich glaube nicht, dass sein Werk mich beeinflusst hat, wohl aber erfuhr ich im Umgang mit ihm von jener Gabe, die ihn zu diesem Werk befähigt hat: diese Gabe war sein Atem-Gedächtnis. Ich habe seither über Atmen viel nachgedacht und die Beschäftigung damit hat mich getragen.

Es wäre unmöglich für mich, heute nicht an diese vier Männer zu denken. Wären sie noch am Leben, so stünde wohl einer von ihnen an meiner Stelle da. Betrachten Sie es nicht als Anmassung, wenn ich etwas ausspreche, worüber mir keine Entscheidung zukommt. Aber ich möchte Ihnen von Herzen danken und ich glaube, ich darf das nur, wenn ich zuvor meine Schuld an diese vier vor Ihnen öffentlich bekannt habe.

[© The Nobel Foundation, 1981. Elias Canetti is the sole author of the text.]

Translation by James Hardin and Philip B. Dematteis:

Your Majesties, your Royal Highnesses, Ladies and Gentlemen:

One owes much to a city that one knows, and perhaps even more to one that one would like to know, if one has long yearned for it in vain. But I believe there are also in a person's life cities of a nigh divine nature, cities of peculiar distinction owing to their immeasurable richness, their transfigured state, or to outer threat. The three that were these things for me are Vienna, London, and Zurich.

One might attribute it to chance that these are the three, but this chance is called Europe, and there would be so much to criticize her for, because what all has not emanated from it! Today, since the shadow under which we live weighs heavily on Europe, we tremble especially for Europe. For this continent, to which so much is owed, bears also a great guilt and it needs time to make amends for its offenses. We passionately wish it this time, a time in which one blessing after another can spread over the earth, a time that would be so blessed that no one in the world would have more reason to curse the name of Europe.

In my lifetime have belonged to this latecomer, this real Europe, four men from whom I am unable to separate myself. To them I owe it that I stand before you today, and I would like to tell you their names. The first is Karl Kraus, the greatest satirist of the German language. He taught me how to listen, the unerring dedication to the sounds of Vienna. More important, he inoculated me against war, an inoculation that was still necessary for many at that time. Today, after Hiroshima, everyone knows what war is, and that everyone knows it is our only hope. The second is Franz Kafka, to whom it was given to transform himself into smallness, and so to evade authority. I followed him in this life-long apprenticeship, which was the most indispensable of all. The third, like the fourth, Robert Musil and Hermann Broch, I knew in my Vienna days. Robert Musil's work still fascinates me today; perhaps I have only been able to comprehend it entirely in recent years. At that time in Vienna only part of it was known, and what I learned from it was the most difficult: that one can undertake a work for decades without knowing whether one will be able to complete it, a foolhardiness that mainly consists of patience, that presupposes an almost inhuman obstinacy. I was a friend of Hermann Broch. I do not believe that his work influenced me, but I learned in the association with him of that gift that made him capable of accomplishing his work: this gift was his breath-memory. I have since then thought much about breathing, and this interest in it has sustained me.

It would be impossible for me not to think of these men today. If they were still alive, one of them would probably be standing in my place. I would like to thank you from my heart, and I believe I may be permitted to do so only if I first publicly acknowledge my debt to these four.

Giosuè Carducci
(27 July 1835 – 16 February 1907)

Thomas E. Peterson
University of Georgia

BOOKS: *Rime di Giosuè Carducci* (San Miniato: Tipografia Ristori, 1857);

Della scelta di curiosità letterarie inedite o rare (Bologna: G. Romagnoli, 1863);

Levia gravia, as Enotrio Romano (Pistoia: Tipografia Niccolai e Quarteroni, 1868); revised as *Levia gravia: 1861–1867,* as Carducci (Bologna: Zanichelli, 1881; revised, 1888);

Poesie di Giosuè Carducci (Enotrio Romano) (Florence: Barbèra, 1871; revised, 1875)—comprises *Decennali, Levia gravia,* and *Juvenilia;*

Primavere elleniche di Enotrio Romano (Florence: Barbèra, 1872);

Nuove poesie di Enotrio Romano (Imola: Galeati, 1873);

Studi letterari di Giosuè Carducci (Livorno: Vigo, 1874);

Delle poesie latine edite e inedite di Ludovico Ariosto (Bologna: Zanichelli, 1875); republished as *La gioventù di Ludovico Ariosto e le sue poesie latine* (Bologna: Zanichelli, 1881);

Intorno ad alcune rime dei secoli XIII e XIV ritrovate nei Memoriali dell'Archivio notarile di Bologna, studi di Giosuè Carducci (Imola: Galeati, 1876);

Bozzetti critici e discorsi letterari (Livorno: Vigo, 1876);

Odi barbare di Giosuè Carducci (Enotrio Romano) (Bologna: Zanichelli, 1877);

Satana e polemiche sataniche (Bologna: Zanichelli, 1879);

Juvenilia (Bologna: Zanichelli, 1880);

Tibullo, by Carducci and Rocco de Zerbi (Milan: Fratelli Treves, 1880);

Nuove odi barbare (Bologna: Zanichelli, 1882; revised and enlarged, 1886);

Giambi ed epodi di Giosuè Carducci (1867–1872), nuovamente raccolti e corretti con prefazione (Bologna: Zanichelli, 1882);

Confessioni e battaglie (Rome: Sommaruga, 1882); revised as *Confessioni e battaglie. Serie prima* (Rome: Sommaruga, 1883);

Confessioni e battaglie. Serie seconda (Rome: Sommaruga, 1883 [i.e., 1882]);

Ça ira. Settembre MDCCXCII [1792] (Rome: Sommaruga, 1883);

Giosuè Carducci (from Prose di Giosuè Carducci, *1905; Thomas Cooper Library, University of South Carolina)*

Confessioni e battaglie. Serie terza (Rome: Sommaruga, 1884);

Conversazioni critiche (Rome: Sommaruga, 1884);

Petrarca e Boccacci (Rome: Perino, 1884);

Rime nuove di Giosuè Carducci (Bologna: Zanichelli, 1887; revised, 1889);

Il libro delle prefazioni (Castello: Lapi, 1888);

Lo studio bolognese: Discorso di Giosuè Carducci per l'ottavo centenario (Bologna: Zanichelli, 1888);

Jaufré Rudel: Poesia antica e moderna (Bologna: Zanichelli, 1888);

Opere di Giosuè Carducci, 20 volumes in 10 (Bologna: Zanichelli, 1889–1909)—comprises volume 1, *Discorsi letterari e storici* (1889); volume 2, *Primi saggi* (1889); volume 3, *Bozzetti e scherme* (1889); volume 4, *Confessioni e battaglie* (1890); volume 5, *Ceneri e faville, serie prima, 1859–1870* (1891); volume 6, *Juvenilia e Levia gravia* (1891); volume 7, *Ceneri e faville, serie seconda, 1871–1876* (1893); volume 8, *Studi letterari* (1893); volume 9, *Giambi ed epodi e Rime nuove* (1894); volume 10, *Studi, saggi e discorsi* (1898); volume 11, *Ceneri e faville, serie terza e ultima, 1877–1901* (1902); volume 12, *Confessioni e battaglie, serie seconda* (1902); volume 13, *Studi su Giuseppe Parini: Il Parini minore* (1903); volume 14, *Studi su Giuseppe Parini: Il Parini maggiore, con un appendice inedita* (1907); volume 15, *Su Ludovico Ariosto e Torquato Tasso studi* (1905); volume 16, *Poesia e storia, con una fototipia* (1905); volume 17, *Odi barbare e Rime e ritmi. Con un' appendice* (1907); volume 18, *Archeologia poetica* (1908); volume 19, *Melica e lirica del settecento, con altri studi di varia letteratura* (1909); and volume 20, *Cavalleria e umanesimo* (1909);

Terze odi barbare (Bologna: Zanichelli, 1889);

Letture italiane, 3 volumes (Bologna: Zanichelli, 1890–1898);

Storia del «Giorno» di Giuseppe Parini (Bologna: Zanichelli, 1892);

Delle odi barbare di Giosuè Carducci, libri II ordinati e corretti (Bologna: Zanichelli, 1893);

Su l'Aminta di T. Tasso. Saggi tre di Giosuè Carducci, con una pastorale inedita di G. B. Giraldi Cinthio (Bologna: Zanichelli, 1896);

Degli spiriti e delle forme nella poesia di Giacomo Leopardi (Bologna: Zanichelli, 1898);

Rime e ritmi (Bologna: Zanichelli, 1899);

Poesie di Giosuè Carducci (Bologna: Zanichelli, 1901);

Prose di Giosuè Carducci (Bologna: Zanichelli, 1905);

Da un carteggio inedito di Giosuè Carducci, edited by Antonio Messeri (Bologna: Zanichelli, 1907).

Editions and Collections: *Opere. Edizione Nazionale*, 30 volumes (Bologna: Zanichelli, 1935–1940);

Giambi ed epodi, edited by Enzo Palmieri (Bologna: Zanichelli, 1959);

Odi barbare, edited by Manara Valgimigli (Bologna: Zanichelli, 1959);

Rime nuove, edited by Pietro Paolo Trompeo and Giambattista Salinari (Bologna: Zanichelli, 1961);

Rime e ritmi, edited by Valgimigli and Salinari (Bologna: Zanichelli, 1964);

Poesie e prose scelte, edited by Mario Fubini and Remo Ceserani (Florence: La Nuova Italia, 1968);

Poesie, edited by Giorgio Barberi Squarotti and Mario Rettori (Milan: Garzanti, 1982);

Prose, edited by Giovanni Falaschi (Milan: Garzanti, 1987);

Opere scelte, edited by Mario Saccenti (Turin: Unione Tipografico-Editrice Torinese, 1993).

Editions in English: *Poems of Italy: Selections from the Odes of Giosue Carducci*, translated by M. W. Arms (New York: Grafton Press, 1906);

Poems of Giosuè Carducci, translated by Maud Holland (New York: Scribners, 1907);

Selections from Carducci: Prose and Poetry, translated by Antonio Marinoni (New York: William R. Jenkins, 1913);

Carducci: A Selection of His Poems, translated by G. L. Bickersteth (London: Longmans, Green, 1913);

The Rime nuove of Giosuè Carducci, translated by Laura Fullerton Gilbert (Boston: R. G. Badger, 1916);

A Selection from the Poems of Giosuè Carducci, translated by Emily A. Tribe (London: Longmans, Green, 1921);

From the Poems of Giosuè Carducci, translated by Romilda Rendel (London, 1929);

The Barbarian Odes of Giosuè Carducci, translated by William Fletcher Smith (Menasha, Wis.: G. Banta, 1939);

The Lyrics and Rhythms of Giosue Carducci, translated by Smith (Colorado Springs, Colo.: Privately printed, 1942);

Twenty-Four Sonnets of Giosue Carducci, translated by Arthur Burkhard (Yarmouth Port, Mass.: Register Press, 1947);

Giosue Carducci: Selected Verse, translated by David H. Higgins (Warminster, U.K.: Aris & Phillips, 1994).

OTHER: *L'arpa del popolo. Scelta di poesie religiose, morali e patriottiche cavate dai nostri autori e accomodate all'intelligenza del popolo,* edited by Carducci (Florence: Galileiana, 1855);

Antologia latina e saggi di studi sopra la lingua e letteratura latina, edited by Carducci (Florence: Galileiana, 1855);

Vittorio Alfieri, *Satire e poesie minori di Vittorio Alfieri,* edited by Carducci (Florence: Barbèra, 1858);

Alessandro Tassoni, *La Secchia rapita e l'Oceano di Alessandro Tassoni, con note,* edited by Carducci (Florence:

Barbèra, 1858); republished as *La Secchia rapita e altre poesie* (Florence: Barbèra, 1861);

Giuseppe Parini, *Poesie di Giuseppe Parini,* edited by Carducci (Florence: Barbèra, 1858);

Vincenzo Monti, *Le poesie liriche di Vincenzo Monti,* edited by Carducci (Florence: Barbèra, 1858; revised and enlarged, 1862);

Alfieri, *Del principe e delle lettere, con altre prose di Vittorio Alfieri,* edited by Carducci (Florence: Barbèra, 1859);

Lorenzo de' Medici, *Poesie di Lorenzo de' Medici,* edited by Carducci (Florence: Barbèra, 1859);

Giuseppe Giusti, *Le poesie di Giuseppe Giusti, con un discorso sulla vita e sulle opere dell'autore,* edited by Carducci (Florence: Barbèra, 1859; revised and enlarged, 1861 and 1862);

Salvator Rosa, *Satire, odi e lettere di Salvator Rosa,* edited by Carducci (Florence: Barbèra, 1860);

Gabriele Rossetti, *Poesie di Gabriele Rossetti,* edited by Carducci (Florence: Barbèra, 1861);

Cino da Pistoia, *Rime di m. Cino da Pistoia e d'altri del secolo XIV,* edited by Carducci (Florence: Barbèra, 1862);

Monti, *Canti e poemi di Vincenzo Monti,* 2 volumes, edited by Carducci (Florence: Barbèra, 1862);

Angelo Ambrogini Poliziano, *Le Stanze, l'Orfeo e le Rime di messer Angelo Ambrogini Poliziano, rivedute su i codici e su le antiche stampe e illustrate con annotazioni di varii e nuove da G. Carducci* (Florence: Barbèra, 1863);

Lucretius, *Di T. Lucrezio Caro Della natura delle cose, libri VI,* edited by Carducci and Alessandro Marchetti (Florence: Barbèra, 1864);

Monti, *Tragedie, drammi e cantate di Vincenzo Monti, con appendice di versi inediti o rari,* edited by Carducci (Florence: Barbèra, 1865);

Dino Frescobaldi, *Rime di Matteo di Dino Frescobaldi,* edited by Carducci (Pistoia: Società Tipografica Pistoiese, 1866);

Poeti erotici del secolo XVIII, edited by Carducci (Florence: Barbèra, 1868);

Cantilene e ballate, strambotti e madrigali nei secoli XIII e XIV, edited by Carducci (Pisa: Nistri, 1871);

Lirici del secolo XVIII, edited by Carducci (Florence: Barbèra, 1871);

Benedetto Menzini, *Satire, rime e lettere scelte di Benedetto Menzini,* edited by Carducci (Florence: Barbèra, 1874);

Petrarch, *Rime di Francesco Petrarca sopra argomenti storici, morali e diversi,* edited by Carducci (Livorno: Vigo, 1876);

Strambotti e rispetti dei secoli XIV, XV, XVI raccolti da G. Carducci, per nozze Teza-Perlasca (Bologna: Zanichelli, 1877);

Francesco Domenico Guerrazzi, *Lettere di F. D. Guerrazzi a cura di Giosuè Carducci,* 2 volumes, edited by Carducci (Livorno: Vigo, 1880, 1882);

La poesia barbara nei secoli XV e XVI, edited by Carducci (Bologna: Zanichelli, 1881);

Pietro Metastasio, *Lettere disperse e inedite di Pietro Metastasio,* edited by Carducci (Bologna: Zanichelli, 1883);

Alberto Mario, *Scritti di Alberto Mario,* edited by Carducci (Bologna: Zanichelli, 1884); enlarged by Carducci and Jessie White Mario as *Scritti letterari e artistici di Alberto Mario* (Bologna: Zanichelli, 1901);

Letture italiane scelte e ordinate a uso del ginnasio superiore, edited by Carducci and Ugo Brilli (Bologna: Zanichelli, 1885);

Monti, *Scelte poesie di Vincenzo Monti,* edited by Carducci (Livorno: Vigo, 1885);

Antiche laudi cadorine, edited by Carducci (Pieve di Cadore: Tipografia Berengan, 1892);

Letture del Risorgimento italiano, edited by Carducci (Bologna: Zanichelli, 1895; enlarged, 2 volumes, 1896, 1897);

Torquato Tasso, *Teatro di Torquato Tasso,* edited by Carducci and Angelo Solerti (Bologna: Zanichelli, 1895);

Cacce in rima dei secoli XIV e XV raccolte da G. Carducci per nozze Morpurgo-Franchetti (Bologna: Zanichelli, 1896);

Petrarch, *Le Rime di Francesco Petrarca di su gli originali commentate da G. Carducci e S. Ferrari* (Florence: Sansoni, 1899);

Mario, *Scritti politici di Alberto Mario,* edited by Carducci (Bologna: Zanichelli, 1901);

Primavera e fiore della lirica italiana, 2 volumes, edited by Carducci (Florence: Sansoni, 1903);

Antica lirica italiana (canzonette, canzoni, sonetti dei secoli XIII–XV), edited by Carducci (Florence: Sansoni, 1907).

Giosuè Carducci's poetry glorifies the era of the Italian Risorgimento–the lengthy struggle leading up to national unification in 1861. The "age of Carducci" coincides with a vigorous public commitment to the sacred ideal of the homeland and to the role of literature in advancing that civic ideal by defending human dignity. When Carducci was awarded the Nobel Prize in Literature on 10 December 1906 (less than three months before his death), C. D. af Wirsén, the secretary of the Swedish Academy, described him as "a poet who is always moved by patriotism and a love of liberty, who never sacrifices his opinions to gain favour, and who never indulges in base sensualism . . . a soul inspired by the highest ideals." As the major Italian poet of his age, Carducci represented in literature the national destiny of Italy over the final third of the nineteenth century. A robust and passionate man, he advocated a restoration of the classical heritage and a return to the civic and natural virtues it represents. Working in several literary forms, he exhorted the Italians to revitalize themselves and to honor the greatness of their ancient, medieval, and Renaissance civilizations. Carducci was commonly referred to as "l'ultimo scudiero dei classici" (the last shield bearer of the classics), and his focus on history spans the centuries and engages Italy's heroes, from those of the newly formed state to those of antiquity. He embodied the classical figure of the *vate,* or poet-prophet, who sang of the glory of the civilization and natural landscape of Italy.

Carducci produced several highly structured and technically accomplished volumes of poetry, beginning with the 1857 *Rime di Giosuè Carducci* (Lyrics of Giosuè Carducci) and ending with the 1901 *Poesie di Giosuè* (Poetry of Giosuè Carducci). The bibliographical history of the works is complex, given the poet's ongoing involvement in different collections at the same time and his habit of reworking poems over a period of many years. The years of composition of his major collections are: *Juvenilia* (1871), 1850–1860; *Levia gravia* (1868, Light and Serious Poems), 1861–1871; *Giambi ed epodi* (1882, Iambics and Epodes), 1867–1879; *Rime nuove* (1887, The New Lyrics), 1861–1887; *Odi barbare* (1877, Barbarian Odes), 1877–1889; and *Rime e ritmi* (1899, Lyrics and Rhythms), 1887–1899. Thus, Carducci organized his overlapping collections on a thematic and formal basis, not a chronological one. Aided by the poet's copious self-documentation, scholars can date with confidence almost all of Carducci's major poems; while each of the separate collections has its own character, they have in common the subject matter of poetry itself. Carducci is a radical stylistic innovator whose formal deviation from established meters and verse forms set a pattern for the poets of the twentieth century. During his forty-four-year career at the University of Bologna, Carducci gained fame as a lecturer and scholar, as the one genuine heir of Italian classicism as well as the major patriotic poet of the nation. At the same time, his career was full of contradictions and reversals as well as personal tragedy.

Born in Val di Castello (Pietrasanta) in northwest Tuscany on 27 July 1835, Giosuè Alessandro Giuseppe Carducci resided from 1838 to 1849 in Bólgheri, in the Tuscan Maremma near the Tyrrhenian Sea. Carducci's mother, Ildegonda Celli, was a well-educated and liberal woman; his father, Michele Carducci, was a provincial physician who taught his son Latin and encouraged him to study the works of Virgil, Homer, Torquato Tasso, and Alessandro Manzoni. Giosuè had two younger brothers, Dante and Valfredo. Michele Carducci, also a member of the Carbonaria (Charcoal-burners), a secret society committed to ending the Austrian occupation, was imprisoned for his republican beliefs. Giosuè inherited his parents' cosmopolitanism and his father's political passion. He wrote his first satiric poem in 1846, and by 1850 he had expressed his anti-Romantic, proclassical sympathies in verse. When the family moved to Florence in 1849, his literary education expanded to include Giacomo Leopardi, Friedrich von Schiller, and George Gordon, Lord Byron.

From 1849 to 1852 he attended the school of the Scolopi friars in Florence, specializing in rhetoric and classical and Italian literature. In 1852 Carducci founded with a group of classmates the Academy of the Filomusi (Muse Lovers), a literary group that provided the forum for his delivery of two early speeches, "Su lo stato attuale della letteratura italiana" (On the Current State of Italian Literature) and "Della Italia" (On Italy). On 16 June 1855 he graduated from the Scuola Normale Superiore of Pisa after writing a thesis on chivalric poetry. In the same year, he and some of his classmates founded a literary society, the Società degli Amici Pedanti (Society of Friendly Pedants), whose declared adversary was Romanticism, which they saw as an enervating and listless cultural tendency that had sapped the will of the Italians with its mysticism, dream states, and evasions of the political problems confronting the country.

Shortly after starting a teaching job in the small Tuscan town of San Miniato in 1857, Carducci was twice warned by the archducal authorities that he might lose the job because of his strident prorepublican positions. Also in 1857 Carducci's brother Dante committed suicide after a bitter argument with their father. Less than a year later, in 1858, their father also died. Carducci was then working in Arezzo as an instructor of Italian literature, rhetoric, and Greek. In 1859 he married his cousin Elvira Menicucci, and their first child, Beatrice, was born. The couple went on to have a son, Dante, and two more daughters, Laura and Libertà.

Carducci supported the annexation of Tuscany to Piedmont and publicly exalted the Savoy monarch, Victor Emmanuel II, for that reason. (With the Italian unification, Carducci began a decade-long distancing from the monarchy, based on what he saw as its denial of the patriotic ideals of the republican Giuseppe Mazzini and an unsavory alliance with the Catholic Church, which sought to impede the annexation of Rome and its territories to the new nation.) When Giuseppe Garibaldi liberated Sicily in 1860 and crossed over to the mainland with his expeditionary force of one thousand red-shirted soldiers, a jubilant Carducci wrote the ode "Sicilia e la rivoluzione" (Sicily and the Revolution), published in the poetry review *Viola del pensiero* in 1863. On 26 September

1860 Carducci was appointed to the chair of Italian literature at the University of Bologna, a position he held for forty-four years. His appointment was a defining moment in his life and career. In his inaugural lecture at this oldest of universities, he announced the renewal of Italian letters under the sign of the now unified Italian nation and the classical literary tradition. A consummate reader of the classic works of Latin, Greek, and Italian literature, Carducci saw the new state as the fulfillment of the promise of the republic of ancient Rome; this concept presupposed a classical ideal of humanity in harmony with nature.

Carducci's early poetry is anti-Romantic and anti-clerical in nature; it possesses a strongly classical and patriotic tone. The poems of the first book, *Rime di Giosuè Carducci*, were eventually reworked and given a definitive form in the 1880 edition of *Juvenilia*. Enrico Thovez refers to the *Juvenilia* as an "archaeological exhumation of Greek mythology and Roman rhetoric." While this assessment is a fair one, it concerns the earliest work, when the poet was still experimenting with a variety of academic forms and maturing; in a more positive light, it suggests the extent of Carducci's knowledge of philology, rhetoric, and Italian and Roman literary and political history. Carducci remained an inveterate experimenter and imitator of sources. His poems displayed a mastery of various metric and stanzaic solutions. Thus, the reader is rarely afforded the experience of a pure lyric. On a linguistic plane, the reader of Carducci's poetry must gloss references from the historical matrices of ancient Rome, the medieval Italy of the communes, and the Risorgimento; the reader must also consider the poetic traditions of the classical period in Rome and Greece, the lyrical vocabulary of the *dolce stil nuovo* (sweet new style, designating courtly love lyrics) tradition, the language of the chivalric epics of the Renaissance, the moral odes of Giuseppe Parini and Vincenzo Monti, and the transition from neoclassicism into Romanticism.

Fiercely anticlerical in a country in which the Catholic Church long exercised considerable political power, Carducci combined his erudition with the secular progressive thrust of the Enlightenment. But rather than drawing on the political thinkers of the eighteenth century, he drew on its literary examples, especially the neoclassical poets Parini, Monti, Vittorio Alfieri, and Ugo Foscolo, and sought his political models in the distant past of republican and imperial Rome. The poetic results can be bookish, since the idealistic fervor the poet imputes to the past and its ability to inspire change in the present is unrealistic. His nostalgic dream and his desire that the future Italian state will overcome the crises that beset it after unification are charged with a monumental sense of gravity, which strikes the reader as somehow false. Yet, there is another Carducci, the poet of melancholy landscapes and the pastoral rhythms of the countryside, the exquisite love poet and the author of parodies and satires.

Carducci had many complaints about the new state, with its capital in Turin. He was skeptical of the monarchy of Victor Emmanuel and the ruling elite of the Liberal Party, which effectively dismissed the republicanism of Mazzini and marginalized Garibaldi. Carducci praises Garibaldi in "Dopo Aspromonte" (1864, After Aspromonte), an ode that recounts the Sicilian's heroism, his being wounded at the battle of Aspromonte on 29 August 1862, and his subsequent arrest, all as part of the struggle against the absolutism of the reactionary governments of Europe. Carducci saves his most biting sarcasm for Pope Pius IX, who continued to resist the territorial unification of Italy by blocking the resolution of the Institutional Question (the annexation of papal Rome to the Italian state, which finally occurred in 1870).

In the two-hundred-line hymn "A Satana" (1865, To Satan), published under the pen name Enotrio Romano (a pseudonym he used frequently to denote his polemical side as a defender of the Roman heritage), Carducci exalts a life principle that is not Christian or otherwise dependent on religious dogma. The title of this tour de force should not be misunderstood: by "Satan" he intends the regenerative, creative forces of Nature and human Reason. Not only was Carducci unfazed about offending the clerics or the bourgeoisie, but he seemed to invite controversy, especially when he republished the poem on 8 December 1869 in the Bolognese newspaper *Indipendente* as a political protest against the Church on the occasion of the meeting of the Twentieth Vatican Council. In these lines he defends the moral validity of the temples torn down by the early Christians:

> Che val se barbaro
> Il nazareno
> Furor de l'agapi
> Dal rito osceno
>
> Con sacra fiaccola
> O templi t'arse
> E i segni argolici
> A terra sparse?
>
> (To what avail did
> the barbarous Christian
> fury of *agape*,
> in obscene ritual,
>
> With holy torch
> burn down your temples,
> scattering their
> Greek statuary? [translated by David H. Higgins])

This Satan, "bello e orribile / Mostro si sferra" (beautiful and awful / a monster is unleashed), is at once a destructive, devouring force that roams over the earth, and a figure of reason and the native human ability to achieve harmony in nature and construct a noble, just, and free civilization. Poetry is a primary means toward this end, and Carducci seeks to expand the number of its practical applications. On the one hand, he does so in order to evoke the majesty, equilibrium, and serenity of nature; on the other, he chastizes the indolent and corrupt, making of poetry a political vehicle.

Carducci's *Levia gravia* includes poems "light and heavy," as the title indicates. As Carducci wrote in a letter to Felice Tribolati on 24 September 1868, "*Levia gravia* vuol dire: fantasie di gioventù, e dolori ed esperimenti della vita: cose leggere per sentimento e per istile, mescolate ad altre gravi per le stesse ragioni" (*Levia gravia* means: the fantasies of youth, and the sorrows and experiments of life: things that are light in their feelings and style, mixed with others that are heavy for the same reasons). The poet understands the dichotomy of light and heavy as one of ease and difficulty, both of composition and comprehension. He is aware that the cult of the past that he proposes, which embraces the great figures of antiquity and the Italian tradition, goes against the grain of a certain literary taste and will seem ponderous and burdensome to many; he also knows that his incessant formal experimentation may be seen as frivolous or lacking in substance. From his perspective, the light and heavy are natural features of youth and memory; the memory of youth that comes forward in the collection includes the youth of the new country, remembered through the icons of its past poetical and historical greatness. In the opening lines to the sonnet "L'antica poesia toscana" (1866, Ancient Tuscan Poetry), the speaker is, in fact, the old Tuscan poetry:

> Su le piazze pe' campi e ne' verzieri
> d'amor tra i ludi e le tenzon civili
> crebbi' e adulta cercai templi e misteri,
> scuole pensose ed agitati esili.
>
> Or dove son le donne alte e gentili,
> i franchi cittadini e' cavalieri?
> dove le rose de' giocondi aprili?
> dove le querce de' castelli neri?
>
> (On the piazzas, in the fields and meadows
> of love among the delights and civic battles
> I grew up and as an adult sought temples and mysteries,
> pensive schools and agitated exiles.
>
> Oh but now where are the noble and graceful ladies,
> the stalwart citizens and knights?
> Where the roses of joyous Aprils?
> Where the oaks of black castles?)

In *Giambi ed epodi,* the most satirical of Carducci's poetic collections, aspects of his personal style emerge, in particular the penchant for polemic and melancholy. As the self-proclaimed spokesman of the "Third Italy," he was disappointed when the new country did not prove to be the glorious thing he had hoped for; thus, he became a serious critic of the present. His political enemies at this time were the Italian monarchy, the Vatican, the feudalist aristocracy, the Historic Right of the Liberal Party, and the Romantics. His inspiration came from Mazzini and Garibaldi, the French Revolution, and the historical example of the age of the Italian communes (thirteenth-century city-states). The epode is a moral-satirical form made up of distichs (or couplets) in which the second line–the *epòdo*–is shorter. Carducci's main literary model in this regard is Horace, whose iambic epodes are largely satires inspired by Archilochus. Carducci believed that this type of acerbic poetry belongs justly to a limited period in one's life–for him, it was a three-year period, 1867 to 1869 (though some works included in this collection, notably "Il canto dell'amore" [1878, Love Song], were written much later).

The thirty-one poems of *Giambi ed epodi* include evocations of Italy's past as mirrored in the geography; the poet frequently wrote poems based on visits to specific sites. For example, after an 1867 trip to the origins of the Tiber River in the Tuscan Appenines, Carducci wrote an ode to those new friends who had hosted him. In "Agli amici della valle Tiberina" (To Friends in the Tiber Valley), the Tiber River possesses the transcendent virtues of the Roman people, and nature is viewed as healthy and virtuous, so that the landscape itself takes on a metahistorical significance.

Giambi ed epodi is dominated by satires and invectives, appropriate subjects in the poet's view for those classical verse forms; the targets are predominately the Italian middle classes, whose mediocrity Carducci denounces, comparing them (and their institutions, first among them the Catholic Church) negatively to the glories of republican Rome, as recounted by Livy and embodied by Mazzini, the subject of the 1872 sonnet "Giuseppe Mazzini":

> Qual da gli aridi scogli erma su 'l mare
> Genova sta, marmorëo gigante,
> Tal, surto in bassi dí, su 'l fluttuante
> Secolo, ei grande, austero, immoto appare.
>
> (Like Genoa, a marble giant standing
> solitary above the sea on its barren reefs, so he too appears,
> tall, severe, motionless, rising above the stormy
> century in a time barren of greatness. [translated by Higgins])

Giambi ed epodi includes homages in the form of imitations of such poets as Victor Hugo and Heinrich Heine, whose work had helped Carducci grow as a poet. The structure of the book suggests an ascensional path, beginning with the "Prologue," which announces the poet's great sorrow over his deceased family members and his desire to endure this time of darkness, not simply in grief but in protest against "the false world" and the cowardice and fraud that that world adores. He concludes the book with "Il canto dell'amore," a hymn to universal love and a celebration of the Italian nation (seen in lofty panoramic views with its landscape figured as a woman cherished by her lover, the sun) as it moves forward in progress and under the sign of Libertà (Freedom).

Also in *Giambi ed epodi* are poems centered on civic virtues and vices, lofty patriotic ideals, and the highly personal emotions of regret, melancholy, and nostalgia. One example of Carducci's satirical bent is the ironic epode "Canto dell'Italia che va in Campidoglio" (1872, Song of Italy on Its Way to the Capitoline), which documents the historic moment when Rome and its territories have finally been annexed by the Italian state and Rome has been named the capital, though the king has yet to pay a visit. The poem is an account of the king's first visit to the capital.

With the *Rime nuove,* Carducci's polemical voice is diminished, though not eliminated. On a personal level he is more introspective; on an historical level he is more retrospective. From the start, as a poet, he tended to control the overly subjective impulses with classical forms and derivations; but some things are genuinely beyond one's control. Carducci was stricken by the death of his mother on 3 February 1870, and on 9 November 1870 his son, Dante, died at age two and a half. This event is recalled in several poems, primarily in the *Rime nuove.* In the first of these, "Funere mersit acerbo" (Plunged into Bitter Death), written on the day of the boy's death, Carducci addresses the spirit of his brother who died thirteen years earlier, asking if he has heard the voice of little Dante, who has just now passed on. The title is a Virgilian hemistich (half a line of verse) from when Aeneas descends to the underworld and hears the weeping of the souls of dead children.

In the *Rime nuove,* the poet repudiates the contentiousness of his earlier persona, instead looking inward. Still, the historical passion remains strong. The sonnet form is revitalized by Carducci, who, in "Il sonetto" (1870, The Sonnet), inserts himself in the secular tradition among the greatest Italian lyric poets:

Sesto io no, ma postremo, estasi e pianto
E profumo, ira ed arte, a' miei dí soli
Memore innovo ed a i sepolcri canto.

(Not sixth, but last, I bring to it new gifts of ecstasy
and grief and scent, of anger and of art,
as mindful of my solitary days and of our dead, I sing.
 [translated by Higgins])

The poets alluded to in the final tercet are Dante (ecstasy), Petrarch (grief), Tasso (scent), Alfieri (anger), and Foscolo (art). Much of the Carduccian style concerns his cultivation and imitation of the poetic models of the past. Good taste and decorum are essential components of these models and are found lacking in the modern poetry of symbolism and decadence. The moderns, like the Romantics, eschew the old categories of distinction of levels; Carducci recovers them. The moderns, he claims, do not recognize the oratorical, rhetorical purpose of the division of form and content, or the value of imitation. Carducci maintains the division and engages in imitation as the one proper means to discover his own authentic voice. Carducci sees Romanticism and the poets of the nineteenth-century avant-garde *scapigliatura* (bohemianism) movement as mired in dream-like mysteries and uncertainties; if such poets sing of illness and physical degradation, he presents himself as a picture of emotional and intellectual virtue and health. He tends to ignore those aspects of Romanticism that represent a continuation of the neo-classical tradition, including the cult of beauty and the preference for the idyll, the hymn, and the elegy.

In "Classicismo e Romanticismo" (1869, Classicism and Romanticism), Carducci presents the opposition of these two currents in Italian culture as much more than a clash of aesthetics; rather it is a choice between the dignified and solar force of reason and heroism, of classical strength and virtue, versus the vainly spiritualistic, sentimental, weak, lunar, and enervated Romanticism:

Ma tu, luna, abbellir godi co 'l raggio
Le ruine ed i lutti;
Maturar nel fantastico vïaggio
Non sai né fior né frutti.

(But thy delight, O moon, is adorning ruins
and tombs with thy rays;
yet in thy fabled voyage thou art helpless
to ripen either flower or fruit. [translated by Higgins])

Carducci was viewed as a wholesome bulwark against the Romantic decadence. His reputation and influence grew considerably in the 1870s and 1880s; his reputation as a scholar and orator contributed to his prestige as a poetic authority, and the acclaim with which his nuanced and technically accomplished books of verse were received added to his fame as a public figure.

Carducci's hostility to the current of *verismo* (regionalist realism) that arose in the 1880s reflected his increasingly aristocratic and elitist political ideology. He sang the praises of the Risorgimento, recasting its political and military leaders as heroic patriots. He composed celebratory verses on the anniversaries of battles and conquests, creating in the process a gap between the heraldic and idealized version of events and the often mediocre reality. While the actual unification that resulted in the "Third Italy" was accomplished by a distinct minority and through feats more diplomatic than military, the poet preferred to mythologize and glorify the new nation, endowing it with the aura of the earlier two imperial Italys, that of the ancient Roman Republic and that of the Renaissance popes. As Carducci came to recognize the severity of this gap between the ideal and the real, his emotional distress began to mount.

In the gap between the ideal and real there emerges another Carducci: the melancholic whose intimate strains of amorous passion and nostalgic evocations of the desolate landscape of the Maremma result in a newly modern form of the idyll. In "Idillio maremmano" (1872, Maremman Idyll), the poet evokes the distant memory of a ladylove from the Maremma. Written as a *capitolo*–an amorous or satirical poem written in Dantean terza rima–the melancholy idyll is tinged with regret:

> Oh come fredda indi la vita mia,
> Come oscura e incresciosa è trapassata!
> Meglio era sposar te, bionda Maria!
>
> Meglio ir tracciando per la sconsolata
> Boscaglia al piano il bufolo disperso,
> Che salta fra la macchia e sosta e guata,
> Che sudar dietro al piccioletto verso!
> Meglio oprando obliar, senza indagarlo;
> Questo enorme mister de l'universo!
>
> (Oh how cold has my life been since,
> how dark and tedious has it sped away!
> To marry you would have been the better course, my fair-haired Maria!
>
> Better far to range through the desolate
> thickets of our plains, tracking down some lost steer,
> which leaps amongst the scrub, pauses and watches,
> Than to sweat after puny poetry!
> Better far to labour, and forget this vast mystery of the universe,
> than to question it! [translated by Higgins])

In 1874 Carducci declared an end to the writing of epodes and began working on more objective odes, and with them returned to a purer and more serene art. In the ode "Davanti San Guido" (1874, completed in 1886, Outside San Guido), the poet travels back to his childhood home in the town of Bólgheri near Pisa. It is a confessional poem that alternates between dream and reality, youth and adulthood. Its dominant motifs are the figure of Carducci's grandmother and a double row of cypress trees who recognize the poet and speak to him. The poem is a prime example of Carducci's ability to include a broad variety of themes and emotional tonalities within a still coherent overall structure. As translator David H. Higgins writes, "These are the trees which, in the poem, vainly invite Carducci to stay and pick up the threads of his happy childhood and adolescence. The offer is debated at length by Carducci, but declined: it is too late." The poet addresses himself to the trees, which represent a purer time and way of thinking than the poet now enjoys in his late middle age.

In response to the crises in his own life and that of the nation, and in harmony with his readings of Charles Baudelaire, Carducci's poetry grew less nominal and more verb-centered. The increased motion and movement in his verse occurs in an imaginary space that is remote from the historical situation he had invoked with such optimism in his earlier patriotic poems. As he recognizes the inertia and stasis of the Italian nation, he enters into that situation of crisis on a wholly personal plane, providing a new dynamic variously described as sentimental, nostalgic, and melancholy. "Davanti San Guido" serves as an example of this fundamental stylistic change, as does the poem "Pianto antico" (1871, Grief of Ages), written on the death of his son. The sonnet contrasts the perennial life cycle of a budding pomegranate tree in the household garden to the abrupt and absolute cessation of the innocent life on which the poet had placed so much hope:

> Sei ne la terra fredda,
> Sei ne la terra negra;
> Né il sol piú ti rallegra
> Né ti risveglia amor.
>
> (Thou art in the cold earth,
> thou art in the darkling earth;
> nor doth the sun cheer thee,
> nor love awake thee more. [translated by Higgins])

Carducci strikes a new depth in brief elegies and laments such as "Pianto antico." Walter Binni labels Carducci a "poet of the contrast of earthly existence," as one who deals with the feelings of vitality and of death translated into light and darkness, sound and silence, the green earth in its springtime fertility and the black tomb-like earth of winter. The rhyme scheme of "Pianto antico" is also found in the celebrated "Tedio invernale" (1875, Winter Tedium) and "San Martino" (1883, Saint Martin's Day).

In 1872 daughter Libertà was born to the poet and his wife. Also that year, Carducci wrote the sonnet "Il bove" (The Ox). This best known of Carducci's poems concerns the virtue and piety of the ox, a simple beast of burden. It is reminiscent of the sonnet to Mazzini, in which the central figure was also a giant, alone. Though modern critics have belittled the humanization of the ox, "Il bove" lays down a simple and irrefutable truth in a distinctive manner reminiscent of the realistic Italian landscape painters of the late nineteenth century. The impact of the final tercet concerning the ox's dignified gaze is heightened by the use of hypallage, the rhetorical figure of radically altering the natural word order: "E del grave occhio glauco entro l'austera / Dolcezza si rispecchia ampio e qüieto / Il divino del pian silenzio verde" (Whilst in the sweet severity of your solemn, glaucous eye / is reflected, broad and calm, / the divine silence of the green plain [translated by Higgins]).

In July 1871 Carducci received a letter of admiration from the Milanese socialite Carolina Cristofari Piva, the wife of an army officer and mother of seven children. Her connection to the writer was through a common friend, the poet Maria Antonietta Torriani. Carducci quickly responded to Cristofari Piva's letter, and the two began a poetically amorous correspondence even before their first meeting, in April 1872. The relationship grew into an intense love affair that provided the inspiration for some of Carducci's most remarkable love poetry. Piva is referred to as Lina (and sometimes Lidia) in these poems. In "Primavere elleniche (II. Dorica)" (1872, Hellenic Springtimes [II. Dorian Mode]), she is praised in the ideal landscape of an imagined and archaic Sicily, saturated with the figures of Greek myth. This divine beauty is able to administer a draft of nepenthe and other sacred balms to her hero—the poet—just as Helen of Troy was empowered in classic times. She is endowed by oreads and dryads with bouquets of flowers and the ability to understand the glorious and woeful tales they tell.

The love affair with Piva lasted for several years and provided the sentimental material for many powerful poems. In a farewell letter to Piva (who died in 1881), Carducci wrote on 15 July 1878:

Amami dunque ancora; e ricòrdati, con benevolenza, del bene; e oblia, con pia indulgenza, i miei torti. Io ricordo e amo e desidero con molta mestizia, ma non senza una speranza di conforto e di gioia. Addio, dolce amore. Io ti amo ancora come nei primi giorni che mi ti desti. E non voglio avere altri ricordi tristi e affannosi.

(So love me still; and remember, with benevolence, the good; and forget, with pious indulgence, my faults. I remember and I love and I desire with much sadness, but not without a hope of comfort and joy. Farewell, my sweet love. I still love you as I did in the first days when you gave yourself to me. And I do not wish to have any other sad and troubled memories.)

Carducci had other dalliances—including Annie Vivante, Adele Bergamini, Dafne Gargiolli—who, in addition to Piva, played an important part in the history of his poetry.

Before their affair ended, Piva accompanied Carducci on an 1878 visit to Trieste and the former seaside retreat of the Austrian archduke Maximillian, Miramare. The sapphic ode "Miramar" (1889) is an homage to that leader, whom Napoleon III had named emperor of Mexico in 1864 and who was slain by rebels loyal to Benito Juarez on an 1867 mission to Mexico with his wife, the Empress Charlotte. After the slaying, Charlotte went insane. In Carducci's view, these events are a manifestation of *Nemesis,* the paying of an historical debt incurred by one's ancestors. The poem is remarkable for its setting and for the generous attitude of the poet toward a man who had been the resident leader (in Lombardy and Venetia) of Italy's occupier and its primary enemy during the Risorgimento. Also in 1878, Carducci wrote an ode to the queen of Italy and was named the official poet of the House of Savoy.

From the 1880s forward, Carducci's poetry was extolled by academic and nonacademic critics alike as the embodiment of a fresh neoclassicism, elevated in its mythic virtues above the baseness of daily life, combined in its essence with the spiritual reclamation of the Italian countryside and its agriculturally based virtues. The countryside is viewed as a primitive landscape compatible with the myth of infancy—both the infancy of the individual (as in Carducci's memorialistic evocations of his childhood) and that of the Italian culture. While the critic Thovez in 1926 accused Carducci of a false and brittle archaism based on outdated rhetorical models, far more important was the earlier praise by Benedetto Croce, who extolled Carducci in 1920 as the "poet of history," a vital and wholesome voice of civic and heroic inspiration to his countrymen.

In the *Rime nuove,* Carducci's historical and anthropological research emerges in a way reminiscent of the Romanticists' exploration of popular folklore, legends, and verse forms. In fact, the poet who had polemically opposed Romanticism now dedicated a celebratory ode to Shelley: "Presso l'urna di Percy Bysshe Shelley" (1884, By the Funeral Urn of Percy Bysshe Shelley). Preoccupied with death, Carducci writes of an Elysium shared only by the great poets: "la bella / isola risplendente di fantasia" (that blessed / island of the imagination), and of his final doubts about immortality.

In his celebrated sonnet "Traversando la Maremma toscana" (1885, Crossing the Tuscan Maremma), Carducci evokes a by-now-familiar sentimental landscape, but with irony toward himself and toward the code of courtly love. Stricken by melancholy upon seeing the landscape of his youth, acknowledging the vanity of his efforts, he finds solace in the landscape:

> E dimani cadrò. Ma di lontano
> Pace dicono al cuor le tue colline
> Con le nebbie sfumanti e il verde piano
> Ridente ne le pioggie mattutine.
>
> (And tomorrow I shall fall. But from afar
> Your hills speak peace to my heart,
> as the mists rise and sunlight plays upon your green plain
> amongst the morning showers. [translated by Higgins])

"San Martino" is another Anacreontic ode in four quatrains like "Pianto antico." In it, a hunter stands at the threshold of a stone house, turning a spit and watching in the sunset the migration of birds. The landscape is depicted with the minimalist techniques of the impressionists or the Italian *macchiaioli* (blotch-painters), the equivalent being a swift application of colors and sounds to reflect passing climatic phenomena and other sensory impressions.

Among the forty-seven sonnets in *Rime nuove* are the twelve of *Ça ira* (1883, It Will Pass), a sequence initially published as a pamphlet in praise of the spirit of the French Revolution. Inspired by his reading of Jules Michelet's *Histoire de la Révolution française* (1847–1853), Carducci proposed the French Revolution as a heroic model to his countrymen; and when several legislators, journalists, and educators objected to his sonnet series, accusing him of Jacobin tendencies, he responded with *Ça ira (Prosa)*, a lengthy polemic divided into ten chapters, in the third series of *Confessioni e battaglie* (1884, Confessions and Battles). When the final sonnet closes, the French have defeated the Prussians at Valmy, and Johann Wolfgang von Goethe has the final word, as he attests to the monumental import of the current events: "Al mondo oggi da questo / luogo incomincia la novella storia" (Events you witness here today / Chart new horizons for the human race [translated by Arthur Burkhard]). Here and throughout his poetic production Carducci writes of man in history, not of man in the cosmos. His frequent recourse to irony is necessary because of the persistent force of *Nemesis,* or the reality of vendettas and retributive justice in human history: "Ahimè, tutta la storia umana è un orribile marea di sangue" (Alas, all of human history is a horrible tide of blood). Herein lies the progressivist and ultimately positivist orientation of the poet. In *Ça ira* the notion of *Nemesis* is the revenge of the French populace against centuries of monarchical abuse. While such a blind force works for the good in this instance, in others it does not; what Carducci dreams of is a final victory over *Nemesis* by Reason.

Plutarch was a major inspiration for Carducci, representing the ability to isolate the particular human essence within a given historical context, and to mirror the national glory. In this spirit, the final poem of the *Rime nuove,* "Congedo" (1873, completed in 1887, Envoi), presents the figure of the poet as a blacksmith whose arduous work is centered on the forge: investing all his skills and memories, his artistry and intellect, into the poem, the craftsman yields up the final product of "uno strale / D'oro" (a golden shaft) that he casts to the sun, desiring no more.

The first edition of *Odi barbare* was followed by editions in 1882 and 1889. In this ambitious project Carducci aims to re-create in Italian verse the quantitative verse forms of classical Greek and Latin poetry. He seeks modern versions of the hexameter and pentameter line forms set into imitations of the classic elegy and such strophic forms as the Alchaic, the Archilochean, and the sapphic. At the same time he does not impose the metric stresses those forms would dictate, but allows for their natural, grammatical accenting in Italian. The "barbaric" verse is not a scientific re-creation on Carducci's part but an intuitive one; his knowledge of classical Greek meter was mediocre, so he was free to approximate and not get bogged down in unnecessary philological details. Even those scholars who are expert in the classical verse forms he adopts will not necessarily recognize them because of the impracticality of adapting a language in which rhythms are generated by tonic accents to a language in which rhythms are determined by the length of vowel sounds.

Odi barbare begins in light and moves toward darkness, the inverse of the ascensional pattern of *Levia gravia.* Carducci designated these works as "barbaric" or "pagan" in order to indicate the foreignness of their sound to the classical poets, should they hear the adaptation of their strophic poetic forms into Italian. One of the effects of this ongoing experiment is a novel sense of the beauty of words, and by extension of the calm and repose that is generated by their use in this highly skilled and anachronistic compositional format. The themes are those of separation from the world of struggle and harking back to the landscapes of one's childhood and youth.

By creating an alternative to the qualitative "parisyllabic" verse of the Italian lyric and epic tradition, Carducci created an opening for the entry of free verse in the poetry of coming generations. Since parisyllabic verse tends to be rhythmic and repetitive, by going against it and suppressing rhyme, one creates a less melodic, more severe, and more elevated metrical space. If traditional Italian verse lends itself too easily to musical harmonies and facile sentimentality, Carducci's pursuit of a neutral ground with precedents in the dignity and sobriety of the classical past suggested new, more modern, tonalities to his poetic successors.

One of Carducci's best-known barbaric odes, "Alle fonti del Clitunno" (1876, At the Springs of the Clitunno), maps the historical-mythic itinerary of the Clitunno (Clitumnus) River from its source near Spoleto in Umbria as it proceeds downstream. The thirty-nine sapphic quatrains are mostly unrhymed, though the poet is free to rhyme if he wishes. By invoking the tutelary river god of the Umbrians, Etruscans, and Romans and referring to Virgil's evocation in the *Georgics* of this site and the bleaching in the sacred water of the coats of livestock intended for rituals, the poet imagines a living historical record that might again serve as a model for cultural prosperity. The conceit of the river's mythic correspondence to ancient history allows the poet to evoke the various distant cultures (in contrast to what he saw as the mystical fanaticism of Christianity) in order to praise the fertility and abundance associated with the god Pan and the pagan religions of the indigenous pre-Roman cultures. The poem ends with the poet's praise of Italy in its natural beauty as it renews itself. Carducci's positivistic conviction that secular civilization is progressing is complicated by the evocation of ancient religions, beliefs, and the expression of piety found in classical and earlier indigenous myths. In the final stanza, "il vapore" (the steam engine) is depicted as a symbol of Italy moving forward to meet the challenge of industrial civilization, together with the ancient virtues and fecundity symbolized by the river.

In December 1876 Carducci wrote "Alla stazione in una mattina d'autunno" (At the Station, One Autumn Morning), a poem that characterizes the strength of his more melancholy later poems. Carducci's later poetry grows pessimistic and anticipates, with a proliferation of autumnal and wintery images, his own decline. In response to the crisis of this perceived twilight, the poet seeks an escape into dream and memory. The vision of autumn alludes to the autumn of his own life, when literature and myth no longer offer solace and consolation: metaphors of death abound, the primary one being that of the monstrous train whose arrival marks the final separation between the poet and his beloved. With the lover's departure, the dream of love itself departs. The image of the train has a wholly different resonance from the steam engine in "Alle fonti del Clitumno":

Già il mostro, conscio di sua metallica
anima, sbuffa, crolla, ansa, i fiammei
   occhi sbarra; immane pe 'l buio
   gitta il fischio che sfida lo spazio.
Va l'empio mostro; con traino orribile
sbattendo l'ale gli amor miei portasi.

(Already the monster, aware of its metallic soul,
puffs, shudders, pants, glaring flames;
   huge in the darkness it whistles
   challenging the empty air.
The monster departs, pitiless;
   with flapping wings it bears off my beloved in its awful train. [translated by Higgins])

A nostalgia for the classical world now permeates Carducci's poetics, a vision born from books and a disdain for the mediocrity of the current day. "Dinanzi alle Terme di Caracalla" (1877, By the Baths of Caracalla) is a pastoral symphony in various movements; in it Carducci deplores the touristic indulgence in monuments and ruins. If Italy had become a musty museum for the arid and self-involved perusal of curiosity seekers, Carducci exhorts his countrymen to reinhabit the greatness of the past and to be satisfied with nothing less in the present.

The *Canzone di Legnano* (1879, Song of Legnano) is an epic song projected in three parts, of which only the first, "Il parlamento" (The Parliament), is complete. It first appeared in the periodical *Rassegna settimanale* (30 March 1879) and was subsequently included in *Rime nuove*. It is concerned with the truthful evocation of the free commune of Milan in the Middle Ages and the resistance against the German emperor Frederick Barbarossa, who devastated Milan in 1162, a fact that led to the formation of the Lombard League, an armed coalition of cities that defeated Barbarossa at the Battle of Legnano in 1176, thus regaining the cities' autonomy. Such an historical theme is intended to praise the current nation and glorify its struggles. Despite Carducci's dedication to civic poetry, the lower class is conspicuously absent from his treatments of Italian society, and the middle class is the target of much criticism. Rather than addressing the urgent economic and educational needs of the nation, as had been done by Mazzini or the Federalist Carlo Cattaneo, Carducci looked to literature for his model of the nation, to the classic Roman republic. Unimpressed by the recent discoveries of classical philology and archaeology, he preferred to filter his classicism through the eighteenth-century Enlightenment myths, in particular the idealism of serenity and beauty, and the view of poetry as a heroic act. In the early 1890s his scholarship focused on Parini, culminating in the publication of *Storia del «Giorno» di Giuseppe Parini* (1892, History of the "Day" of Giuseppe Parini).

In the poems of *Rime e ritmi* it is clear that Carducci's days of poetic genius are past; yet, some remarkable poems are produced nonetheless, such as the twelve-line elegy "Ad Annie" (1890, To Annie). Carducci met the twenty-year-old Annie Vivante, then an aspiring writer and opera singer, in 1889; she became the amorous presence in this final book of poems. In "Ad Annie" the poet adopts the form of the Horatian *paraclausithyron,* the song before the woman's closed door:

Batto a la chiusa imposta con un ramicello di fiori
glauchi ed azzurri, come i tuoi occhi, o Annie.
Vedi: il sole co 'l riso d'un tremulo raggio ha baciato
la nube, e ha detto–Nuvola bianca, t'apri.

(I knock at the closed shutter with a branch of flowers
sea-green and blue, like your eyes, oh Annie.
See: the sun with its tremulous smiling ray has kissed
the cloud, and said: "Open up, white cloud.")

Good taste and decorum are essential components of classical poetry, and thus of Carducci's. These elements are absent from modern poetry, which, starting with Romanticism, tends to dismiss the oratorical, rhetorical purpose of poetry and the classical division of form and content. Two stylistic registers in particular are prevalent throughout Carducci's work: the noble and dignified classical diction, and the day-to-day language of satire, journalism, and populist polemics. While Carducci believed in the function and specific properties of genres—the ode to celebrate, the iambic to polemicize, the sonnet to lyricize, the ballad for romantic narration, and the elegy to solemnize—he knew that this faith in fixed genres belongs to an earlier time. He knew that, in the modern era, any reliance on them would be a reminiscence, and to that extent ironic. While Carducci tended to ignore the poetry of Symbolism, which focuses on the unconscious motivations and mysteries of the poet's psyche, ultimately his exploration of the self leaves the greatest imprint on the modern reader, more than the heraldic verse.

Luigi Baldacci has stated that Carducci is "il piú centrifugo dei poeti italiani" (the most centrifugal of Italian poets), resistant to categorization. One does not find abrupt transitions in the work but rather a slow evolution in response to changes in the outside world and the poet's personal life. There are many internal references within the poems, and also a self-referential tendency that includes the occasional lament of the poet's inability to truly master his medium, or of the inability of poetry to measure up to the demands of a tragic and disordered reality.

The first great critic of Carducci's poetic opus was Croce, the authoritative founder of the journal *La critica.* According to Croce, Carducci's "historical reconstructions" in verse are successful because "the sentiment of the poet doesn't gloss the event, but permeates it." Moreover, Carducci's love is "*voluptas* in the elevated meaning of the word, the joy of one's entire being, of one's eyes and one's imagination." Writing in 1920, Croce contrasted Carducci's "pure and sober poetry . . . in which the fundamental and essential lines are always drawn with confidence" to the other literature that had dominated Europe over the previous fifty years, "the nausea of all that impressionism, symbolism, sensualism, verism, vaunted as superrefined art."

Later generations were less impressed by Carducci's "religion of letters" and his wholesome and heroic "human dignity." In the aftermath of World War II, Natalino Sapegno labeled Carducci a "minor" poet, reflecting the taste of the era; but this judgment itself has waned as Carducci's critical fortunes have risen once again, in particular regarding the derivations of twentieth-century poets from the stylistic novelty of his work. Sapegno also writes that Carducci exhibits "an ingenuous ability to ignite and give himself over to the sung rhythms of his fantasies, in the bursting energy of his plastic imagination." This strength of imagination and willingness to venture into the unknown distinguished Carducci's writings during his own lifetime—an historical period when Italians had few things to celebrate and much to be disappointed about—and guarantees his continued relevance.

In addition to his work as a poet, Carducci's gifts as a public speaker were considerable. On 4 June 1882 he gave an extemporaneous speech on the death of Garibaldi two days earlier. He spoke publicly at Arqua to memorialize Petrarch and at Certaldo on Boccaccio. When the monument to Dante Alighieri was dedicated in Trent on 13 September 1896, Carducci delivered a celebratory poem for the occasion. In 1890 he was named a senator just as the first of two terms of Prime Minister Francesco Crispi (1887–1891, 1893–1896) was about to end. When the Italian Socialist Party was formed in 1892, Italy was facing the growing phenomenon of class struggle, including strikes by newly formed labor unions and peasant uprisings. Carducci, a member of the Liberal Party, opposed the Socialists and defended the imperialistic politics of Crispi, whose government was unresponsive to the problems of the Italian laborer and farmer, particularly in the south, where the problems of ignorance, poverty, and a subsistence-level agricultural economy were aggravated. Carducci ultimately came to believe that his own role as *vate,* or prophetic bard, was best served by his embrace of the existing monarchy. Under his guidance, the Facoltà di Lettere (Department of Italian Literature) at Bologna grew from a small to a large program; his regular lectures were heavily attended by students from around the university and by the general public, especially women. Carducci's fame was such that after 1880 he was generally considered as the national authority on matters of Italian literary scholarship.

There is in Carducci the scholar a positivistic use of the historical method. His critical thought endures in two major areas. One is the literary history he assiduously pursued from his adolescent years forward with major studies of Dante, Parini, Tasso, Ludovico Ariosto, and especially Petrarch, in the form of his commentary in an 1899 edition of Petrarch's *Rime*. As a literary historian his work is distinguished by the clarity and equanimity of his judgments, even as regards a figure such as Manzoni, whom he criticized in verse. The second area is represented by the three volumes (or "series") of *Confessioni e battaglie*, texts of a more cultural flavor. This prose has a familiar character, including many colorful polemics and personal reminiscences. The quintessentially Tuscan character of the man and his language forms a link between the region and the nation as between the entire range of the social classes, from the popular to the aristocratic.

While Croce valued the poetry highly, he undervalued Carducci's prose. This oversight is significant, given Croce's enormous influence during the first half of the twentieth century. In fact, Carducci is the greatest nineteenth-century Italian critic after Francesco De Sanctis. As his critical prose matured, Carducci's best essays were not the highly synthetic ones—typically celebratory, nationalistic, and moralizing—but rather the analytic, keenly insightful, and technical examinations of texts, such as his studies of Politian, Petrarch, and Leopardi. In this area of literary analysis he surpasses De Sanctis. Carducci provides as close to an exhaustive representation of the Italian literary patrimony that one can find; there are few periods or masters in the Italian literary canon he did not treat. He has also incorporated into his readings the contributions of the major literary historians of the previous two centuries. The technique of this "poor laborer of literature," as he called himself, was to reconstruct the historical times and context of an author by a close textual and linguistic analysis of individual works. Thus he provides in the composite a rigorous history of the literary institutions and of Italian literary forms.

Carducci suffered a paralytic attack to his right arm and hand on 25 September 1899; a debilitating hemiplegia was the long-term result. In 1901 he lost most of his ability to write because of increased weakening from the attack two years earlier. He was forced to dictate most of his works.

In 1904 he was awarded a pension for life by the Italian Parliament, as had been done only for Alessandro Manzoni. In December 1904 he retired from teaching and soon afterward hired a personal nurse who assisted him until the end of his life. His temperament grew even more restless and melancholy. While he received many homages and honors, he avoided public gatherings and preferred whenever possible (even against doctors' orders) to travel to his favorite spot in the Lombard Alps, Madesimo.

When on 10 December 1906 the Swedish Academy awarded the Nobel Prize in Literature to Carducci, he was too frail to travel, but a celebratory event was held at his home in Bologna at the same hour. (Earlier in 1906, Carducci's home had been purchased for the nation by the queen.) Vittorio Puntoni, the rector of the University of Bologna, had been nominating Carducci for the prize since 1902; but these efforts were unsuccessful until a member of the Academy, Baron De Bildt, made the nomination. The baron was present in Bologna for the personal conferral; Carducci mustered the strength to gesture positively to the small group in attendance—including his wife and three daughters—and then, after the baron's speech, which extolled the poet's exaltation of the ideals of country, freedom, and justice, managed to utter a few words: "Salutatemi il popolo svedese, nobile nei pensieri e negli atti" (Please send my greetings to the Swedish people, noble in their thoughts and their actions).

Carducci did not have much opportunity to enjoy the prize or to spend the money; he died on 16 February 1907. Certainly the fact that Carducci was the first Italian to win the Nobel Prize in Literature enhanced his reputation; but in Italy, Carducci's fame was already considerable. The effect of the award was perhaps more important internationally, as it informed the world that the first poet laureate of the relatively new Italian nation had been conferred with this high honor.

The general tendency of twentieth-century criticism has been to ignore Carducci's philological novelty and rigor and to consider the challenge of his poetry as a fact of the past. Yet, this view is a misreading of the Tuscan poet's insistence on historical and practical matters in combination with an archaic lexicon and anachronistic reliance on classical forms. In the seeming incongruities lies his true contemporaneity to later poets and scholars. Carducci unknowingly set the benchmark for free verse; he also perfected a form of secular contemplation in verse that seeks to confront death honestly in the sphere of the immanent. In his oratory and prose he emerged as the most dignified and respected spokesman of his age; he was called on to memorialize and eulogize, to make sense of the changing tides of the modern world. In addition, he gave an increasingly literate Italian public a dignified vision of its national narrative, which combined past, present, and future. As he wrote in "Il canto dell'amore," from *Giambi ed epodi*: "Il mondo è bello e santo l'avvenir" (The world is beautiful and holy is the future).

Letters:
Lettere. Edizione Nazionale, 22 volumes (Bologna: Zanichelli, 1938–1968).

Biographies:
Giovanni Papini, *L'uomo Carducci* (Bologna: Zanichelli, 1913);

Mario Biagini, *Giosuè Carducci* (Milan: Mursia, 1976).

References:
Luigi Baldacci, "Carducci," in his *Secondo Ottocento* (Bologna: Zanichelli, 1969), pp. 55–73;

Walter Binni, *Carducci e altri saggi* (Turin: Einaudi, 1973), pp. 3–83;

Benedetto Croce, *Giosuè Carducci. Studio critico* (Bari: Laterza, 1920);

Cesare De Lollis, *Appunti sulla lingua poetica del Carducci (1912)*, in his *Scrittori d'Italia* (Milan & Naples: Ricciardi, 1968), pp. 539–570;

Mario Praz, *Il classicismo di Giosuè Carducci (1935)*, in his *Gusto neoclassico* (Milan: Rizzoli, 1974), pp. 359–374;

Luigi Russo, *Carducci senza retorica* (Bari: Laterza, 1957);

Giambattista Salinari, "Giosuè Carducci," in *Storia della letteratura italiana, VIII: Dall'Ottocento al Novecento* (Milan: Garzanti, 1968), pp. 627–729;

Mario Santoro, *Introduzione al Carducci critico* (Naples: Liguori, 1968);

Natalino Sapegno, *Storia di Carducci (1949)*, in his *Ritratto del Manzoni e altri saggi* (Bari: Laterza, 1961), pp. 205–225;

Renato Serra, *Per un catalogo (1910)*, in his *Scritti*, I, edited by G. De Robertis and A. Grilli (Florence: Le Monnier, 1938), pp. 71–100;

Raffaele Sirri, *Retorica e realtà nella poesia giambica del Carducci* (Naples: Il Tripode, 1965);

Enrico Thovez, *Il pastore, il gregge e la zampogna: dall'Inno a Satana alla Laus vitae* (Naples: Ricciardi, 1926).

Papers:
The "Casa Carducci" in Bologna is the center of Giosuè Carducci studies; it houses an archive of the poet's books and manuscripts and maintains a comprehensive catalogue of studies of his work.

1906 Nobel Prize in Literature Presentation Speech

by C. D. af Wirsén, Permanent Secretary of the Swedish Academy, 10 December 1906

From the unusually large number of poets and authors proposed for the Nobel Prize this year, the Swedish Academy has chosen a great Italian poet who for a long time has attracted the attention both of the Academy and of the entire civilized world.

Since antiquity, Northern men have been drawn to Italy by her history and her artistic treasures as well as by her sweet and gentle climate. The Northerner does not stop until he has arrived in the eternal city of Rome, just as the war for Italian unity could not stop before Rome was conquered. But before arriving in Rome the visitor is fascinated by the beauty of so many other places. Among these, in the Appenines, is the Etruscan city of Bologna, which is known to us through the *Songs of Enzo* by Carl August Nicander.

Since the Middle Ages, when a famous university gave it the title of learned, Bologna has been of great importance in the cultural history of Italy. Although in ancient times it was renowned as an authority on jurisprudence, it has now become especially famous for its poetic marvels. Thus, it is today still worthy of the expression "Bononia docet" (Bologna teaches). For its greatest poetic attainments of the present, it is indebted to the man to whom the Nobel Prize has been awarded this year—Giosuè Carducci.

Carducci was born on July 27, 1835, in Val di Castello. He himself has given an interesting account of his impressions from his childhood and youth, and he has been the subject of several good biographies.

In order to judge properly the development of his mind and his talents, it is important to know that his father, Dr. Michele Carducci, was a member of the Carboneria (a secret political society working for Italian unity) and was active in the political movements for Italian liberty, and that his mother was an intelligent and liberal woman.

Michele obtained a position as a doctor in Castagneto. The young poet thus spent his earliest years in the Tuscan Maremma. He learned Latin from his father, and Latin literature was to become very familiar to him. Although Carducci later opposed Manzoni's ideas with great fervour, he was also strongly influenced for a long time by his father's admiration for the poet. At this time he also studied the *Iliad* and the *Aeneid*,

Tasso's *Gerusalemme,* Rollin's Roman history, and Thier's work on the French Revolution.

It was a time of great political tension, and one can well believe that in those days of discord and oppression the young poet's fiery imagination absorbed everything which had to do with ancient liberty and the impending unification.

The boy soon turned into a little revolutionary. As he himself recounts, in his games with his brothers and friends he organized little republics which were governed by archons or consuls or tribunes. Vigorous brawls frequently broke out. Revolution was considered a normal state of affairs; civil war was always the order of the day. The young Carducci stoned a make-believe Caesar who was about to cross the Rubicon. Caesar had to flee and the republic was saved. But the next day the little patriotic hero got a sound trouncing from the conquering Caesar.

Not too much stress need be laid on these games, since they are frequent among young boys. But Carducci did, in fact, embrace strong republican sympathies in later life.

In 1849 the family moved to Florence, where Carducci was enrolled in a new school. Here, in addition to his required studies, he first read the poetry of Leopardi, Schiller, and Byron. And soon he started writing poetry—satiric sonnets. He later studied at the Scuola Normale Superiore in Pisa, where he seems to have shown a great deal of energy in his work. After finishing his studies he became a teacher of rhetoric in San Miniato. Because of his expressions of radical ideas, the grand-ducal government annulled his later election to a post at the Arezzo elementary school. Afterward, however, he taught Greek at the lyceum in Pistoia. Finally he obtained a chair at the University of Bologna, where he has had a long and highly successful career.

These in brief are the general lines of his external life. There has been no lack of struggle in his career. He was, for example, even suspended for some time from teaching in Bologna, and on several occasions he was involved in lively polemics with several Italian authors. He suffered great personal tragedies, of which his brother Dante's suicide was undoubtedly the most painful. But his family life and his love for his wife and children have offered him great consolation.

The fight for Italian liberty was extremely important to the development of his sensibility. Carducci was a passionate patriot; he followed the war with all the fire of his soul. And no matter how much he may have been embittered by the defeats at Aspromonte and Mentana, and no matter how much he was disillusioned by the new parliamentary government, which was not being organized in accordance with his desires, he was, nevertheless, overjoyed at the triumph of his sacred patriotic cause.

His ardent nature was tormented by anything which in his opinion interfered with the fulfilment of the work for Italian unity. He was not one to wait patiently; he continuously demanded immediate results and felt a strong aversion to diplomatic delays and the diplomatic *festina lente.*

In the meantime his poetry blossomed abundantly. Although he is also the author of excellent historical and literary criticism, we should be concerned above all with his poetry, for it is through his poetry that he has won his greatest fame.

The volume *Juvenilia* (1863) contains, as the title indicates, his youthful work of the 1850's. Two qualities characterize this collection: on the one hand, its classical cast and intonation, sometimes carried to the point where Carducci salutes Phoebus Apollo and Diana Trivia; and on the other, its profoundly patriotic tone, accompanied by a violent hatred of the Catholic Church and of the Pope's power, the strongest obstacles to Italian unity.

In strong opposition to ultramontanism, Carducci in his songs evokes the memories of ancient Rome, the images of the great French Revolution, and the figures of Garibaldi and Mazzini. At times, when he believes Italy's state hopeless and fears that all of its ancient virtues and valiant deeds have been vitiated, he plunges into the profoundest despair.

This bitterness helps to explain Carducci's numerous attacks on various authors and on other people; Carducci was generally violent in his polemics. But in *Juvenilia* there are also poems with a more positive content, like the song to Victor Emanuel, written in 1859 at the moment when it became obvious that a war with Austria would soon break out. In this song he jubilantly celebrates the monarch who bore the banner of Italian unity.

True patriotism is expressed in the sonnet "Magenta" and in the poem "Il Plebiscito," in which he renews his enthusiastic praise of Victor Emanuel. . . . The most beautiful of the poems in *Juvenilia* is probably the poem to the Savoy cross. . . .

The later collection called *Levia gravia* (1868) [*Light and Heavy*] contains the poems of the sixties. A certain sadness can be heard in many of these poems. The long delay of the conquest of Rome contributed much to Carducci's bitter feelings, but there were a great many other things which Carducci passionately regretted in the prevailing politics of the day. Carducci had expected more from the new political conditions than they could offer. Yet we encounter some very beautiful poems in this collection. Carducci was familiar with fourteenth-century poetry, and a great many echoes of this epoch are heard, for instance, in "Poeti di Parte Bianca" [Poets of the White Party] and in his poem on the proclamation of the Italian kingdom.

Only in the *Rime nuove* (1877) [New Rhymes] and in the three collections of the *Odi barbare* (1877–1889) [The Barbarian Odes] do Carducci's full lyrical maturity and accomplished stylistic beauty appear. Here we no longer find the same disdainful poet who fought with sword and fire under the pseudonym of Enotrio Romano. Instead, the character of the poet seems wholly transformed; sweeter, softer melodies are to be heard. The introductory poem "Alla Rima" [To Rhyme] is extremely musical, a true hymn to the beauty of rhyme. Its ending excellently characterizes Carducci himself. . . . Evidently Carducci understood his own temperament, which he compares with the Tyrrhenian Sea. But his uneasiness is not continuous, and notes of real joy resound in the enchanting poem "Idillio di Maggio" [A May Eclogue]. "Mattinata" [Morning], which clearly recalls Hugo, is also lovely, as are the songs entitled "Primavere Elleniche" [Hellenic Springtimes]. . . .

"Ca Ira" [The Rebellion], a section of the *Rime nuove,* is composed of a series of sonnets. Although it is not of great poetic value, it does represent Carducci's more or less unreserved apotheosis of the French Revolution.

The poet's greatness is more fully revealed in his *Odi barbare,* the first collection of which came out in 1877, the second in 1882, and the third in 1889. There is some justification, however, for criticism of the work's form.

Although Carducci adopted ancient meters, he transformed them so entirely that an ear accustomed to ancient poetry will not hear the classical rhythms. Many of these poems attain the pinnacle of perfection in their poetic content. Carducci's genius has never reached greater heights than in some of his *Odi barbare*. One need only name the fascinating "Miramar" and the melodious and melancholy poem "Alla Stazione in una Mattinata d'Autunno" [To the Station On an Autumn Morning], products of the most noble inspiration. The song "Miramar" is about the unfortunate emperor Maximilian and his brief Mexican adventure. It excels as much in its moving tragic tone as it does in its vivid nature imagery. The Adriatic shore is depicted with perfect mastery. This song exhales a certain feeling of compassion which is rare in Carducci's treatment of Austrian subject matter, but which he expressed yet another time in the beautiful song on the Empress Elizabeth's sad fate in *Rime e Ritmi* (1898) [Rhymes and Rhythms]. . . .

Many contrasts clearly are to be found in a violent and rich poetic nature like Carducci's. Disapproval from many sides has thus been mixed with the just admiration for this poet. Yet Carducci is without doubt one of the most powerful geniuses of world literature, and such disapproval, voiced also by his compatriots, has not been spared even the greatest poets. No one is without defect.

The blame is not, however, directed at his sometimes passionate republican tendencies. Let his opinions remain his own possession. No one will contest his independent political position. In any case, his hostility toward the monarchy has subsided with the years. He has come more and more to consider the Italian dynasty as the protector of Italian independence. In fact, Carducci has even dedicated poems to the queen mother of Italy, Margherita. A venerable woman revered by almost all factions, her poetic soul has been celebrated by Carducci's grandiose art. He has paid her beautiful and affectionate homage in the magnificent song "Alla Regina d'Italia" [To the Queen of Italy] and in the immortal poem "Il Liuto e la Lira" [Lute and Lyre], in which, through the Provençal sirventes and the pastoral, he expresses his admiration of the noble princess. . . . The petty, obstinate republicans, because of these and other tributes, have looked upon Carducci as a deserter of their cause. He justly responded, however, that a song of admiration dedicated to a magnanimous and good woman has nothing whatever to do with politics, and that he reserved the right to think and write whatever he pleased about the reigning Italian family and its members.

The reasons for the antagonism of his friends and political partisans toward him are of a completely different origin. This antagonism is occasioned less by his ferocious assaults on persons of differing political opinions than by his overenthusiastic paganism, which often assumes a biting tone toward Christianity itself. His anti-Christian sentiments have above all produced his much discussed hymn to Satan.

There is a good deal of justice in many of the attacks on Carducci's anti-Christianity. Although one cannot perfectly approve of the way in which he has tried to defend himself in *Confessioni e battaglie* [Confessions and Battles] and in other writings, a knowledge of the attendant circumstances helps to explain, if not to justify, Carducci's attitudes.

Carducci's paganism is understandable to a Protestant, at least. As an ardent patriot who saw the Catholic Church as in many ways a misguided and corrupt force opposed to the freedom of his adored Italy, Carducci was quite likely to confuse Catholicism with Christianity, extending to Christianity the severe judgments with which he sometimes attacked the Church.

Still we must not forget the genuine religious sentiments expressed in some of his poems. It is helpful to remember the end of "La Chiesa di Polenta" [The Church of Polenta], which stands in healthy contrast to "In una Chiesa Gotica" [In a Gothic Church].

And as to the impetuous *Inno a Satana* (1865) [*Hymn to Satan*], it would be a great wrong to Carducci to identify him, for example, with Baudelaire and to accuse Carducci of poisonous and unhealthy "Satanism." In fact, Carducci's Satan has an ill-chosen name. The poet clearly means to imply a Lucifer in the literal sense of the word—the carrier of light, the herald of free thought and culture, and the enemy of that ascetic discipline which rejects or disparages natural rights. Yet it seems strange to hear Savonarola praised in a poem in which asceticism is condemned. The whole of the hymn abounds with such contradictions. Carducci himself in recent times has rejected the entire poem and has called it a "vulgar sing-song." Thus, there is no reason to dwell any longer on a poem which the poet himself has disavowed.

Carducci is a learned literary historian who has been nurtured by ancient literature and by Dante and Petrarch. But he cannot be easily classified. He is not devoted to romanticism, but rather to the classical ideal and Petrarchan humanism. Regardless of the criticism which can justly be launched against him, the irrefutable truth remains that a poet who is always moved by patriotism and a love of liberty, who never sacrifices his opinions to gain favour, and who never indulges in base sensualism, is a soul inspired by the highest ideals.

And insofar as his poetry in the aesthetic sense attains a rare force, Carducci can be considered worthy in the highest degree of the Nobel Prize in Literature.

The Swedish Academy thus pays respect to a poet who already enjoys a world-wide reputation, and adds its homage of admiration to the many praises already given him by his country. Italy has elected Carducci senator and repaid the honour he has brought her by assigning him a life-long pension amounting to a considerable sum.

At the banquet, C. D. af Wirsén spoke in Italian about the poet whom illness had prevented from coming to Stockholm. Subsequently he addressed himself to the Italian chargé d'affaires, Count Caprara, and recalled that through the Nobel Prize Sweden had wanted to honour his country and one of her greatest sons at the same time. Mr. Caprara expressed his gratitude in French and, after a speech addressed to the country of Alfred Nobel, promised to convey the homage to the poet.

[© The Nobel Foundation, 1906.]

Camilo José Cela
(11 May 1916 – 17 January 2002)

Lucile C. Charlebois
University of South Carolina

This entry was expanded by Charlebois from her Cela entry in *DLB 322: Twentieth-Century Spanish Fiction Writers*. See also the Cela entry in *DLB Yearbook: 1989*.

BOOKS: *La familia de Pascual Duarte* (Madrid & Burgos: Aldecoa, 1942); translated by John Marks as *Pascual Duarte's Family* (London: Eyre & Spottiswoode, 1946); translated by Anthony Kerrigan as *The Family of Pascual Duarte* (Boston: Little, Brown, 1964);

Nuevas andanzas y desventuras de Lazarillo de Tormes (Madrid: La Nave, 1944); revised as *Nuevas andanzas y desventuras de Lazarillo de Tormes, y siete apuntes carpetovetónicos* (Madrid: Airon, 1952);

Pabellón de reposo (Madrid: Afrodisio Aguado, 1944); bilingual edition, with English translation by Herma Briffault as *Rest Home* (New York: Las Américas, 1961);

Pisando la dudosa luz del día: Poemas de una adolescencia cruel (Barcelona: Zodíaco, 1945; revised and enlarged edition, Palma de Mallorca: Papeles de Son Armadans, 1963);

Esas nubes que pasan (Madrid: Afrodisio Aguado, 1945);

Mesa revuelta (Madrid: Ediciones de los Estudiantes Españoles, 1945; enlarged edition, Madrid: Taurus, 1957);

El bonito crimen del carabinero, y otras invenciones (Barcelona: José Janés, 1947); republished in part as *El bonito crimen del carabinero* (Barcelona: Picazo, 1972);

Las botas de siete leguas: Viaje a la Alcarria, con los versos de su cancionero, cada uno en su debido lugar (Madrid: Revista de Occidente, 1948); translated by Frances M. López-Morillas as *Journey to the Alcarria* (Madison: University of Wisconsin Press, 1964); revised as *Nuevo viaje a la Alcarria* (Barcelona: Plaza y Janés, 1986);

San Juan de la Cruz, as Matilde Verdú (Madrid: Hernando, 1948);

El gallego y su cuadrilla y otros apuntes carpetovetónicos (Madrid: Ricardo Aguilera, 1949; revised and enlarged edition, Barcelona: Destino, 1967);

Camilo José Cela (left) receiving the 1989 Nobel Prize in Literature from King Carl XVI Gustaf of Sweden (AP World Wide)

La colmena (Buenos Aires: Emecé, 1951; Barcelona: Noguer, 1955); translated by J. M. Cohen and Arturo Barea as *The Hive* (London: Gollancz, 1953; New York: Farrar, Straus & Young, 1953);

Avila (Barcelona: Noguer, 1952); translated by John Forrester as *Avila* (Barcelona: Noguer, 1952);

Santa Balbina, 37, gas en cada piso (Melilla: Mirto y Laurel, 1952);

Del Miño al Bidasoa: Notas de un vagabundaje (Barcelona: Noguer, 1952);

Timoteo el incomprendido (Madrid: Rollán, 1952);

Baraja de invenciones (Valencia: Castalia, 1953);

Café de artistas (Madrid: Tecnos, 1953);

Mrs. Caldwell habla con su hijo (Barcelona: Destino, 1953); translated by J. S. Bernstein as *Mrs. Caldwell Speaks to Her Son* (Ithaca, N.Y.: Cornell University Press, 1968);

Ensueños y figuraciones (Barcelona: G. P., 1954);

Historias de Venezuela: La catira (Barcelona: Noguer, 1955);

Vagabundo por Castilla (Barcelona: Seix Barral, 1955);

Judíos, moros y cristianos: Notas de un vagabundaje por Avila, Segovia y sus tierras (Barcelona: Destino, 1956);

El molino de viento y otras novelas cortas (Barcelona: Noguer, 1956);

Mis páginas preferidas (Madrid: Gredos, 1956);
Cajón de sastre (Madrid: Cid, 1957);
Nuevo retablo de don Cristobita; invenciones, figuraciones y alucinaciones (Barcelona: Destino, 1957);
La rueda de los ocios (Barcelona: Mateu, 1957);
Historias de España: Los ciegos, los tontos (Madrid: Arión, 1957); enlarged as volume 1 of *A la pata de palo* (Barcelona: Noguer, 1965);
La obra literaria del pintor Solana (Madrid: Papeles de Son Armadans, 1957);
Recuerdo de don Pío Baroja (Mexico City: De Andrea, 1958);
La cucaña: Memorias (Barcelona: Destino, 1959); republished as *La rosa* (Barcelona: Destino, 1979; revised edition, Madrid: Espasa-Calpe, 2001);
Primer viaje andaluz: Notas de un vagabundaje por Jaén, Córdoba, Sevilla, Segovia, Huelva y sus tierras (Barcelona: Noguer, 1959);
Cuadernos del Guadarrama (Madrid: Arión, 1960);
Los viejos amigos, 2 volumes (Barcelona: Noguer, 1960, 1961);
Cuatro figuras del 98: Unamuno, Valle-Inclán, Baroja, Azorín, y otros retratos y ensayos españoles (Barcelona: Aedos, 1961);
Tobogán de hambrientos (Barcelona: Noguer, 1962);
Gavilla de fábulas sin amor (Palma de Mallorca: Papeles de Son Armadans, 1962);
Obra completa, 25 volumes (Barcelona: Destino, 1962–1990);
Garito de hospicianos; o, Guirigay de imposturas y bambollas (Barcelona: Noguer, 1963);
El solitario, published with Rafael Zabaleta, *Los sueños de Quesada* (Palma de Mallorca: Papeles de Son Armadans, 1963);
Toreo de salón: Farsa con acompañamiento de clamor y murga (Barcelona: Lumen, 1963);
Once cuentos de fútbol (Madrid: Nacional, 1963);
Las compañías convenientes y otros fingimientos y cegueras (Barcelona: Destino, 1963);
Izas, rabizas y colipoterras: Drama con acompañamiento de cachondeo y dolor de corazón, text by Cela, photographs by Juan Colom (Barcelona: Lumen, 1964);
Páginas de geografía errabunda (Madrid: Alfaguara, 1965);
Viaje al Pirineo de Lérida: Notas de un paseo a pie por el Pallars, Sobirá, el Valle de Arán y el Condado de Ribagorza (Madrid: Alfaguara, 1965);
Nuevas escenas matritenses, 7 volumes (Madrid: Alfaguara, 1965–1966); republished in one volume as *Fotografías al minuto* (Madrid: Sala, 1972);
A la pata de palo, 4 volumes (Madrid: Alfaguara, 1965–1967)—comprises volume 1, *Historias de España;* volume 2, *La familia del héroe; o, Discurso histórico de los últimos restos (ejercicios para una sola mano);* volume 3, *El ciudadano Iscariote Reclús;* and volume 4, *Viaje a U.S.A.; o, El que la sigue la mata;* republished in one volume as *El tacatá oxidado: Florilegio de carpetovetonismos y otras lindezas* (Barcelona: Noguer, 1973);
Madrid (Madrid: Alfaguara, 1966);
Calidoscopio callejero, marítimo y campestre (Madrid: Alfaguara, 1966);
María Sabina (Madrid: Papeles de Son Armadans, 1967); republished with *El carro de heno; o, El inventor de la guillotina* (Madrid: Alfaguara, 1970);
Diccionario secreto, 2 volumes (Madrid: Alfaguara, 1968, 1972);
La bandada de palomas (Barcelona: Labor, 1969);
Víspera, festividad y octava de San Camilo del año 1936 en Madrid (Madrid: Alfaguara, 1969); translated by John H. R. Polt as *San Camilo, 1936* (Durham, N.C.: Duke University Press, 1991);
Homenaje al Bosco, I: El carro de heno; o, El inventor de la guillotina (Madrid: Papeles de Son Armadans, 1969);
Al servicio de algo (Madrid: Alfaguara, 1969);
Barcelona (Barcelona: Alfaguara, 1970);
La Mancha en el corazón y en los ojos (Barcelona: EDISVEN, 1971);
Obras selectas (Madrid: Alfaguara, 1971);
La bola del mundo: Escenas cotidianas (Madrid: Sala, 1972);
oficio de tinieblas 5; o, novela de tesis escrita para ser cantada por un coro de enfermos (Barcelona: Noguer, 1973);
A vueltas con España (Madrid: Semanarios y Ediciones, 1973);
Balada del vagabundo sin suerte y otros papeles volanderos (Madrid: Espasa-Calpe, 1973);
Cuentos para leer después del baño (Barcelona: La Gaya Ciencia, 1974);
Prosa, edited by Jacinto Luis Guereña (Madrid: Narcea, 1974);
Rol de cornudos (Barcelona: Noguer, 1976);
Enciclopedia del erotismo (Madrid: Sedmay, 1977); expanded as *Diccionario del erotismo*, 2 volumes (Barcelona: Grijalbo, 1988);
La insólita y gloriosa hazaña del cipote de Archidona (Barcelona: Tusquets, 1977);
Los sueños vanos, los ángeles curiosos (Barcelona: Argos Vergara, 1979);
Album de taller (Barcelona: Ambit, 1981);
El espejo y otros cuentos (Madrid: Espasa-Calpe, 1981);
Los vasos comunicantes (Barcelona: Bruguera, 1981);
Vuelta de hoja (Barcelona: Destino, 1981);
Mazurca para dos muertos (Barcelona: Seix Barral, 1983); translated by Patricia Haugaard as *Mazurka for Two Dead Men* (New York: New Directions, 1992);
El juego de los tres madroños (Barcelona: Destino, 1983);
El asno de Buridán (Madrid: El País, 1986);

Las orejas del niño Raúl (Madrid: Debate Literatura Infantil, 1986);
Dedicatorias (Madrid: Observatorio, 1986);
Conversaciones españolas (Barcelona: Plaza y Janés, 1987);
Cristo versus Arizona (Barcelona: Seix Barral, 1988);
Los caprichos de Francisco de Goya y Lucientes (Spain: Silex, 1989);
El hombre y el mar (Barcelona: Plaza y Janés, 1990);
Galicia, text by Cela, illustrations by Laxeiro, photographs by Víctor Vaqueiro (Vigo, Spain: Ir Indo, 1990);
Discurso para unha xove dama amante dos libros (Vigo, Spain: Ir Indo, 1991);
Cachondeos, escarceos y otros meneos (Madrid: Temas de Hoy, 1991);
Desde el palomar de Hita (Barcelona: Plaza y Janés, 1991);
Páginas escogidas, edited by Darío Villanueva (Madrid: Espasa-Calpe, 1991);
Torerías: El gallego y su cuadrilla, Madrid, Toreo de salón y otras páginas taurinas, edited by Andrés Amorós (Madrid: Espasa-Calpe, 1991);
El camaleón soltero (Madrid: Grupo Libro 88, 1992);
El huevo del juicio (Barcelona: Seix Barral, 1993);
Memorias, entendimientos y voluntades (Barcelona: Plaza y Janés/Cambio 16, 1993);
El asesinato del perdedor (Barcelona: Seix Barral, 1994);
La cruz de San Andrés (Barcelona: Planeta, 1994);
La dama pájara y otros cuentos (Madrid: Espasa-Calpe, 1994);
A bote pronto (Barcelona: Seix Barral, 1994);
El color de la mañana (Madrid: Espasa-Calpe, 1996);
Poesía completa (Spain: Galaxia Gutenberg / Barcelona: Círculo de lectores, 1996);
Diccionario geográfico popular de España (Madrid: Comunidad de Madrid/Fundación de Camilo José Cela, Marqués de Iria Flavia/Noésis, 1998);
Historias familiares (Barcelona: Macia & Nubiola, 1998);
Madera de boj (Madrid: Espasa-Calpe, 1999); translated by Haugaard as *Boxwood* (New York: New Directions, 2002);
Homenaje al Bosco, II: La extracción de la piedra de la locura; o, El inventor del garrote (Barcelona: Seix Barral, 1999);
Cuadernos de El Espinar: Doce mujeres con flores en la cabeza (N.p.: L. Estal de Lletres, 2002).

PLAY PRODUCTIONS: *María Sabina,* libretto by Cela, translated by Luz Castaños and Theodore S. Beardsley, score by Leonardo Balada, New York, Carnegie Hall, 17 April 1970;

La sima de las penúltimas inocencias, by Cela and José María Subirachs Barcelona, Palacio de Pedralbes, 30 November 1993; Madrid, Hotel Ritz, 14 December 1993.

OTHER: *Homaneje y recuerdo a Gregorio Marañón (1887–1960),* edited by Cela (Madrid: Papeles de Son Armadans, 1961);
Fernando de Rojas, *La Celestina puesta respetuosamente en castellano moderno por Camilo José Cela quien añadió muy poco y quitó aun menos,* adapted by Cela (Barcelona: Destino, 1979);
Miguel de Cervantes Saavedra, *El Quijote,* edited by Cela (Alicante: Rembrandt, 1981).

TRANSLATION: Bertolt Brecht, *La resistible ascensión de Arturo Ui* (Madrid: Júcar, 1975).

In 1942 Camilo José Cela published his first major work of narrative fiction, the novel *La familia de Pascual Duarte* (translated as *Pascual Duarte's Family,* 1946), which signaled the reemergence of Spain's tradition of excellence relative to the modern European novel. This book secured for him a place alongside other young Spanish novelists whose works were indicators of Spain's gradual recovery from the civil war their country had endured from 18 July 1936 through 1 April 1939. Cela's reputation grew rapidly, and because he remained in Spain instead of going into exile, his works give testimony to his country's struggle through the thirty-six years of Francisco Franco's rule and the eventual emergence in 1975 of Spain as a democracy. Despite the controversies that have always surrounded his chosen themes and stylistic devices and his opinions about such matters as democracy, homosexuality, prostitution, technology, and younger Spanish writers, Cela's unwavering dedication to the profession of writing was recognized toward the end of his career when he was awarded important Spanish literary prizes, such as the Premio Nacional (1984), the Príncipe de Asturias (1987), the Planeta Prize (1994), and the Cervantes Prize (1995). In 1989 he was awarded the Nobel Prize in Literature. He received the Pluma de Oro (Golden Pen) in 1995 and the Premio Gallegos del Mundo de las Letras (Galicians of the World of Arts Prize) in 2001 for his lifetime literary achievements.

Cela wrote short stories, essays, poetry, drama, travel books, and newspaper columns, but his novels in particular pay tribute to the strength of the Spanish spirit. They also attest to Cela's self-imposed goal of renewed experimentation with narrative style. Cela's works confirm his dissatisfaction with conformity. Decades of repression and censorship, which had become a way of life for Spaniards since 1936, were catalysts for Cela's literary audacity, his penchant for scandal, and a purposeful disregard for historical accuracy, as well as a rejection of in-depth psychological character portrayals. In light of the public scrutiny to which he had been subjected when censors deemed *La familia de Pascual Duarte* the product of a depraved mind, Cela intentionally fashioned the offensive public persona to which his only son, Camilo José Cela Conde, attests in *Cela, mi padre* (1989, Cela, My Father). Such acrimony culminated in Cela's chosen epitaph: "El que resiste, gana" (He who withstands, wins).

Cela was born Camilo José Manuel Juan Ramón Cela y Trulock in Iria Flavia (O Coruña), Spain, on 11 May 1916, of Italian, British, Welsh, and Spanish ancestry. His parents were Camila Emmanuela Trulock y Bertorini and Camilo Cela y Fernández. He had four siblings: Jorge, Rafael, Juan-Carlos, and Teresa María. Cela often boasted of his lineage, believing that it gave him a special objectivity with which to understand his country, its history, and traditions. His father worked as a customs official, and in 1933 the family established permanent residence in Madrid. In his autobiographical volume *La cucaña: Memorias* (1959, The Greasy Pole: Memoirs; republished as *La rosa* [1979], The Rose), Cela depicts himself as a difficult child, and his eccentricities began to take root in his university years (1934–1935 and 1939), during which he began and abandoned studies of medicine and law at the Central University of Madrid. In 1934 the first of two bouts with tuberculosis changed his life: his convalescence afforded him the opportunity to read the seventy-one-volume collection of the Biblioteca de Autores Españoles (Library of Spanish Authors), thereby fostering his budding literary aspirations. Cela did not take a university degree. Instead, his friendship with Pedro Salinas, a leading Spanish poet and critic, inspired him to start writing poetry.

Cela's first work was *Pisando la dudosa luz del día: Poemas de una adolescencia cruel* (Treading the Dubious Light of Day: Poems of a Cruel Adolescence), written in 1936 but not published until 1945 because of his feelings of insecurity as an inexperienced writer and because of wartime hardships that limited publication of works by unknown authors. It is a collection of virulently expressive poems written at the height of the aerial bombings of Madrid in the first phase of the civil war. From 1940 on, when Cela began to frequent the prestigious Café Gijón *tertulia* (literary discussion group) in Madrid, the way was paved for the unflagging literary output of the six decades of his life as a writer.

In 1937 he was drafted into the Nationalist army and was discharged two years later for wounds received in the line of duty. Those of his critics who have been less than favorable have made a practice of emphasizing the fact that Cela fought on the side of the insurgents in addition to having worked for a brief period as a censor for various publications in the early days of the Francoist regime.

Cela's first novel, *La familia de Pascual Duarte,* is about a disadvantaged man who was born to a violent, alcoholic father and an unschooled, promiscuous, and loveless mother in the early part of the twentieth century in Extremadura, one of the poorest regions of Spain. Pascual is a criminal who, while imprisoned, writes a first-person account of the events of his life. He continually assures the anonymous *señor* (sir) to whom his discourse is directed of his repentance, but ultimately the reader must make the final judgment concerning Pascual's sincerity and the cause of his murderous acts and the matricide with which his narration ends. Playing right into the predetermined innocence of his symbolic name (the Paschal lamb sacrificed at the first Passover), he casts himself in the role of victim, all the while narrating his crimes in distorted chronological fashion. His inherited bad blood is underscored by the first lines of his written confession: "Yo, señor, no soy malo aunque no me faltarían motivos para serlo. Los mismos cueros tenemos todos los mortales al nacer y sin embargo, cuando vamos creciendo, el destino se complace en variarnos como si fuésemos de cera" (I am not, sir, a bad person, though in all truth I am not lacking in reasons for being one. We are all born naked, and yet, as we begin to grow up, it pleases Destiny to vary us, as if we were made of wax [translated by Anthony Kerrigan]). As he begins to recount the events of his life (and the lives of his parents, sister Rosario, retarded brother Mario, and wives Lola and Esperanza), contradictions, gaps, and enigmas surface. His recollection is spotty and replete with an accompanying rationale that is meant to condone his repeated acts of violence.

As John Kronik has pointed out, Pascual re-creates himself through his memoirs and thus permits his narrative to vacillate between the points of view of one who is sentenced to death and of the young man from Extremadura whose manhood was constantly brought into question. Five of his chapters are self-proclaimed moments of poetic and existential insight more befitting a poet than a murderer. On the other hand, his memory is tainted with colloquialisms, folk sayings, and a crudely scatological depiction of those events he selected to include in the episodic plotting of his story. In the same breath with which he excuses his bad memory, he nevertheless provides ample descriptions that can only be credited to fabrication and/or outright self-contradiction. In sum, his retrospection is lucid and graphic, as are his well-phrased jailhouse meditations on life and its meaning.

Cela frames Pascual's words in a context of subversion, beginning with a "Preliminary Note by the Transcriber," who claims to have "found the pages here transcribed in the middle of 1939 in a pharmacy at Almendralejo (God knows who put them there in the first place!). And from that day to this I have . . . brought some order into them, transcribed them, and made them make sense." The note is followed by other quasi-official documents: "Duarte's letter to the First Recipient of His Manuscript" (don Joaquín Barrera López, who was a good friend of the Count of Torremejía, don Jesús González de la Riva, whom Pascual murdered); an "Extract from the Last Will and [Handwritten] Testament of don Joaquín Barrera López"; and lastly, Pascual's own tongue-in-cheek dedication to his victim, "don Jesús . . . who, at the moment when the author of this chronicle came to kill him, called him Pascualillo, and smiled." As Pascual ends his confession with the words he uttered after having killed his mother ("I could breathe"), more documents are appended by the Transcriber, including a further explanation about the perplexing chronology of Pascual's life after the matricide and the murder of don Jesús, the lack of information concerning the crime for which Pascual received the death sentence, and the fate of the manuscript of his confession. Included are also two letters, dated 9 and 12 January 1942, from eyewitnesses, both of which are at odds regarding Pascual's demeanor at the time of his death by garrotte. These materials further confound Pascual's veracity while purposefully exacerbating the ambiguities that plague the discourse.

The shocking and sordid details in *La familia de Pascual Duarte* were condemned by censors and critics alike on the first publication of the novel. The second edition was seized by government censors in 1943 and held for two years until it could be published again in Spain. Since then, however, *La familia de Pascual Duarte* has gone through more than 250 editions, second only to Miguel de Cervantes's *Don Quixote*. It has been translated into thirty-three languages and continues to generate much debate, particularly concerning the pathology of criminality. The novel launched a series of works, such as *Nada* (1944, Nothing) by Carmen Laforet, that shared in Pascual's graphic depiction of the conditions of life in Spain in the time preceding and following 1939. Studies in historiography have made it possible to view Cela's Paschal lamb as the first of many disavowals of the Francoist regime's sanitization of Spanish history.

In "Algunas palabras al que leyere" (A Few Words to Whoever Might Read This), his prologue to *Mrs. Caldwell habla con su hijo* (1953; translated as *Mrs. Caldwell Speaks to Her Son,* 1968), Cela classifies his second novel, *Pabellón de reposo* (1944; translated as *Rest Home,* 1961), as the antithesis of *La familia de Pascual Duarte.* Even those harsh critics of Cela's first novel praised *Pabellón de reposo* for its lyrically sensitive treatment of seven patients who are dying of tuberculosis as well as for its use of their narrating voices in what constitutes a new beginning for them in the face of death. The work is admittedly tied to Cela's firsthand experience with the same illness, itself the invisible protagonist to whom reverence is paid by way of the diary entries, letters, and other modes of narrative discourse in which these ailing men and women express their innermost fears and longings.

Except for one character named Felisa, all of the patients are identified by numbers (52, 37, 14, 40, 11, 73, and 103 [Felisa]). An authorial voice is heard sparingly over the course of the otherwise fragmented narrative discourse, breaking forth only to inform readers of a letter received from a "well-known physician and specialist in tuberculosis, Dr. A. M. S.," who begged its recipient to stop publishing the novel in weekly newspaper installments. Overall, the commentaries of the sanatorium residents are what provide the details of their profiles: for example, number 37 says that her "friend in 52" is "a dreamer and a romantic"; and number 40 says of number 14 that "His eyes are more burning than ever, his smile more bitter, his nose more pinched in his face that is whiter. He looks like an amorous romantic poet, triumphant and suicidal, and scarcely twenty-five years old." Their lives give poignancy to their illness as they attempt to find happiness, plan for the future, attend to business, and mend broken family relationships from within their confinement. A masterpiece of structural symmetry, the novel is divided into two equal parts, each one subdivided into seven chapters that in turn correspond to their respective patient-narrators. The refrain-like appearance of a red-headed gardener, pulling his rusted green wheelbarrow, marks the end of each chapter in the second part of the novel, thereby signaling the objective correlative of death carting away its victims one by one with unrelenting predictability.

This symmetry substantiates Cela's preference for aesthetics over stylistics in dealing with the topic of tuberculosis. William David Foster comments that *Pabellón de reposo* represents "the first . . . of Cela's many attempts to order the chaos of the universe into a meaningful pattern." Other critics, such as J. M. Castellet, point to the determinism and sustained *tremendista* modality as indicative of Cela's commitment to technical innovation. This work, which appears milder than *La familia de Pascual Duarte,* is in reality shockingly intimate, however lyrical, regarding the insidious power of death over the characters, whose blood-spattered bedclothes are a constant reminder of their impending fate.

Interspersed with the publication of Cela's first two novels are the picaresque adventures he created for Spain's archetypal rogue, Lazarillo de Tormes (*Nuevas andanzas y desventuras de Lazarillo de Tormes* [1944, New Adventures and Misfortunes of Lazarillo de Tormes]), and the first of many short stories that are an important segment of his work. Among these collections of short works of prose fiction are *Esas nubes que pasan* (1945, Those Clouds that Go Past and Disappear), *El bonito crimen del carabinero, y otras invenciones* (1947, The Tidy Crime of the Armed Policeman and Other Tales), and *Las botas de siete leguas: Viaje a la Alcarria, con los versos de su cancionero, cada uno en su debido lugar* (1948, The Boots of Seven Leagues: Journey to the Alcarria, with Verses from Its Songbook of Poems, Each One in Its Due Place; translated as *Journey to the Alcarria*, 1964). The latter was one of the products of Cela's ardent desire to fathom the essence of Iberian Spain through a series of walking tours. In 1949 he published more short prose works under the heading of *El gallego y su cuadrilla y otros apuntes carpetovetónicos* (The Galician and His Troupe and Other Thoroughly Spanish Notes). These tales led to the creation of a subgenre known as the *apunte carpetovetónico*, which, in a fashion similar to the hybrid prose works of his literary forebears of the "Generation of 1898" and José Ortega y Gasset (in his "walking and seeing" essays), is likened by Cela to a slice-of-life sketch, in either narration or drawing, of a character type or way of life that is specific to a certain time and place in Spain and whose particular pathos is derived from its own bittersweet quality.

Cela's *apuntes* flourished throughout the 1950s and 1960s, as evidenced in *Del Miño al Bidasoa* (1952, From The Miño to the Bidassoa Rivers), *Judíos, moros y cristianos* (1956, Jews, Moors and Christians), *Cuadernos del Guadarrama* (1960, Guadarrama Notebooks), and *Páginas de geografía errabunda* (1965, Pages about Wandering). Within this same time frame he also published the novellas *Timoteo el incomprendido* (1952, Timoko the Misunderstood), *Santa Balbina, 37, gas en cada piso* (1952, Santa Balbina Street, or Gas in Every Apartment), *El molino de viento y otras novelas cortas* (1956, The Windmill and Other Short Novels), and *Café de artistas* (1953, Artists' Café), as well as more collections of short stories: *Baraja de invenciones* (1953, Pack of Tales), *Nuevo retablo de don Cristobita* (1957, Don Cristobita's New Tableau), *La rueda de los ocios* (1957, The Chorus of Those who Possess Leisure Time), *Cajón de sastre* (1957, Hodgepodge), and *Historias de España: Los ciegos, las tontos* (1957, Stories about Spain: The Blind Ones, the Foolish Ones). His literary fecundity of the 1950s was enhanced by three new novels: *La colmena* (1951; translated as *The Hive*, 1953), *Mrs. Caldwell habla con su hijo*, and *Historias de Venezuela: La catira* (1955, Stories of Venezuela: The Blonde).

La colmena was first published in Buenos Aires, because the Spanish censors objected to its themes of hunger, depravity, promiscuity, violence, and repression. The novel takes up the desperation and sense of hopelessness felt by the sickly characters in *Pabellón de reposo*. This time, the emotions are seen through the quasi-objective style of a roving journalist who injects his narration with slice-of-life conversations among more than 350 characters who live in Madrid in early 1940, during a time of severe shortages as the Spanish capital struggled through the aftermath of its civil war. Characterized technically by qualities of simultaneity, cinematography, fragmentation, and deconstruction, *La colmena* is one of its author's most accomplished works. In writing about the novel as literary genre in "Algunas palabras al que leyere," Cela refers to *La colmena* as a "clock novel . . . made of multiple wheels and tiny pieces which work together in harmony so that it [the clock] works." The novel moves around the actions of a two-day period. Of the six parts of the novel, chapters 1, 2, and 4 constitute the first day, with the second day being spread out over chapters 3, 5, and 6. Everything occurs from afternoon through late night, with only the "Finale" taking place in the morning three or four days later.

Readers are plunged midstream into the mundane conversations of Madrid's teeming masses, with particular emphasis on doña Rosa's café "La Delicia," don Celestino's bar "Aurora," brothels, and the apartments of married couples, as well as the open space of streets and the empty lot outside Madrid's bullring. The novel opens with a timely reminder from doña Rosa: "Don't let's lose our sense of proportion," an admonition that is immediately muted by the swell of the buzzing voices of the "hive." Against the backdrop of incessant coughing (implying tuberculosis) and music, one soon gets the impression of overhearing private matters (clandestine sexual encounters, financial problems, and illicit propositions of various kinds) amid the nervousness of a society just getting used to a regime in which suspicious behavior or criticism of the new government warranted prosecution. Little of what is presented makes sense (in any true narrative fashion) until the dead body of doña Margot is found in the early evening hours of the first day (chapter 2). From that point on, various individuals' names begin to provide direction, as characters such as her son, his homosexual partner, and the itinerant Martín Marco subtly are connected with other characters, incidents, and bits of information, thus forming story lines that hold the promise of solving the murder.

The descriptions of people and places are pointedly realistic, and all-encompassing abject poverty is depicted with genuine pathos evoked for children and young women such as Elvira, who is lucky to have a stale orange and a fistful of roasted chestnuts for supper. Much of the action involves liaisons between relatively affluent married men and less-fortunate women, such as Merceditas (sold into bondage at the age of thirteen), Purita (in charge of five younger siblings), or Victorita (who will go to any lengths to get money for the medicine that her boyfriend needs if he is to survive the tuberculosis from which he suffers). Among the more helpless is a six-year-old gypsy boy who lives under a bridge and eats sporadically, depending upon how many coins he collects from people who like to hear him sing. Just when tensions converge concerning doña Margot's murder (and other illicit activities), the action is brought to an irregularly open-ended conclusion, as friends and family of Martín Marco read in the morning newspaper that he is being sought for questioning, at the same time that he, happier than ever before, is on his way to the cemetery to pay his respects at his mother's grave.

La colmena received resounding praise from such respected critics as Ricardo Gullón, Gonzalo Torrente Ballester, Dámaso Alonso, Gregorio Marañón, and González Ruano; yet, many of the more conservative literary critics of the time condemned its radical departure from the prevailing literary realism of the 1950s. Eugenio de Nora, for example, whose seminal *La novela contemporánea* (1968, The Contemporary [Spanish] Novel) assured his place as a voice of authority, branded Cela a rebellious author whose works, like *La familia de Pascual Duarte,* were hyperrealistic, crudely offensive, and unacceptable for the literary and moral sensibilities of Franco's conservative Catholic Spain. Even present-day Hispanists, such as biographer Ian Gibson, persist in denigrating Cela's achievement in *La colmena* by underscoring the precedent set by John Dos Passos's novel *Manhattan Transfer* (1925) and hence casting aspersions on the originality of *La colmena* and the revolutionary point of departure it heralded for the Spanish novel.

Mrs. Caldwell habla con su hijo shocked the Spanish reading public of its day by way of its taboo-driven theme of incest. The implied dialogue of the title is embedded in a narrative discourse of bawdy double entendres and heightened fragmentation. In a foreword to the novel, Mrs. Caldwell is identified by a friend and the editor of her papers as someone who has "died in the Royal Insane Asylum" of London; the 213 segments of her written tribute to her son, Eliacim (who died a sailor while on a training mission in the Aegean Sea), are irregular in length and coherence, matching perfectly the grieving mother's self-centered, schizophrenic discourse. Because this mother-son relationship could only have been handled indirectly by way of the surrealistic images that break forth from Mrs. Caldwell's writings, their conversation had to be equally evasive. Her narrative consciousness aside, Eliacim's mother is fully aware that she is treading new ground and provides a cleverly veiled rationale for her statements: "It's a long and strange story, Eliacim darling, that I don't think ought to be told entirely." In addition, a chapter titled "The Devil's Presence" proffers strong evidence that Mrs. Caldwell was probably sexually abused as a child by her father, hence transferring her sexual deviance to her only child.

Mrs. Caldwell follows Pascual Duarte's need to bare her soul in writing, while at the same time sharing with the reporter-narrator of *La colmena* an understanding of the tragedy of the human condition: "The people who pass in the street, my son, are . . . boring, resigned, monotonous . . . With their debts, their stomach ulcers, their family problems, their insane, miraculous plans, etc., walk with their spirits cowed, in no particular direction, with the secret hope that death will catch them by surprise, like the ax murderer who waits in ambush at the doors of schools." She also resembles her predecessors in *Pabellón de reposo,* for she too awakes with increasing regularity to a blood-stained pillow. Her fragmentary messages are encoded in contradiction and ambiguity, at times sworn to her son to be truthful yet at the same time outrightly "lying." Mrs. Caldwell creates her own and her son's characters, together with episodes related to their friends, habits, and lives, all of which are based solely on her distorted perception of reality. What makes good sense to her comes across as absurd, as in the titles of her scribbles ("In the Swimming Pool" [chapter 13], "Lord Macaulay" [chapter 42], and "China and Crystal" [chapter 114]). Contrary to Cela's previous novels, *Mrs. Caldwell habla con su hijo* offers no sustained editorial interference except the "Letters from the Royal Insane Asylum" and a concluding "Editor's Note" that provides a keen tongue-in-cheek exegesis of her final statement: "In Mrs. Caldwell's original, there follow two blurred, and completely undecipherable pages with obvious signs of moisture, showing unmistakable signs of having spent hours and hours under water, like a drowned sailor."

By allowing a mentally and physically ill character such freedom of expression, Cela introduced the way for a repertoire of subjects that had, for the most part, been off-limits for Spanish readers. Mrs. Caldwell attests to marital infidelity, suicide, vice, fetishism, sexual abuse, violence, and hatred. In keeping with the prudence that was still required of Spanish writers in the early 1950s, Cela purposefully conferred upon his female narrator a name that was obviously not Spanish, bestowing her with autonomy but at the same time offering pointed, stylized commentary about Spanish mothers: "In far-off Spain, mothers bite their sons on the neck, drawing blood, to demonstrate their tenacious, unchanging love." Such public national self-scrutiny, in turn, facilitated more criticism relative to such sacred institutions as "Family Life" (chapter 110) and marriage (in chapter 199, "The Well-Matched Married Couple"), all of which served as metaphors for the hypocrisy of the rules of etiquette and social decorum. It is not surprising that overall the novel has generated scant critical attention.

Similar outrage among critics was expressed when Cela was promised a sizable amount of money in 1953 by the Venezuelan government to spend time in that country in order to write a novel (*La catira*) that would accurately depict the nation's spirit. Like *Nuevas andanzas y desventuras de Lazarillo de Tormes* of 1944, *La catira* has never been considered one of Cela's major works; yet, it earned him the Critics' Prize and the Andrés Bello Medal of Honor, which was conferred upon him by Venezuelan president Ramón José Velásquez. Also at this juncture in his career, Cela was inducted into the Royal Spanish Academy of the Language (1957); since then, he has been looked on as a leading literary figure and pioneer in post–Spanish Civil War prose fiction.

Cela moved to Majorca in 1956. He named the journal he founded that same year *Papeles de Son Armadans* (Papers from Son Armadans), after the neighborhood in Palma where he lived with his wife, María del Rosario Conde Picavea, whom he had married in 1944, and their son, born in 1946. *Papeles de Son Armadans* grew to be one of the only viable publishing outlets available to international writers and artists whose works would be otherwise banned by the regime on the Iberian Peninsula. With his brother Jorge, Cela also established the Alfaguara publishing house, which became one of the leading presses in Spain for the contemporary Spanish novel. Until 1989, when he returned to Spain to live (outside of Madrid in Guadalajara), he spent what were perhaps the most productive years of his career in his beloved Balearic house in La Bonanova. There he was instrumental in starting the Conversaciones Poéticas de Formentor, a colloquium for artists and writers such as Joan Miró and Robert Graves. There he also became friends with Pablo Picasso, who contributed various drawings to illustrate *Papeles de Son Armadans* that were later incorporated into Cela's *Gavilla de fábulas sin amor* (1962, Bundle of Loveless Fables). In his 1964 pictorial essay *Izas, rabizas y colipoterras: Drama con acompañamiento de cachondeo y dolor de corazón* (the title words are neologisms without a suitable translation; the subtitle is Drama Accompanied by Joking and Heartache), Cela collaborated with the photographer Juan Colom, whose striking images of streetwalkers and other destitute Spanish women of the time boldly raised public consciousness about prostitution.

Cela continued to write such varied works as *La cucaña*, the first part of his autobiography; *La obra literaria del pintor Solana* (1957, The Literary Works of the Painter [José Gutiérrez] Solana), which originated as his acceptance speech for membership in the Royal Spanish Academy of the Language; tributes to Spanish intellectuals such as Pío Baroja and Gregorio Marañón; and more travel journals, such as *Primer viaje andaluz: Notas de un vagabundaje por Jaén, Córdoba, Sevilla, Segovia, Huelva y sus tierras* (1959, First Andalusian Trip: Notes of a Traveler through Jaén, Córdoba, Sevilla, Segovia, Huelva and Their Lands), *Viaje al Pirineo de Lérida: Notas de un paseo a pie por el Pallars, Sobirá, el Valle de Arán y el Condado de Ribagorza* (1965, Journey to the Pyrenees of Lérida: Notes of a Passage on Foot through Pallars, Sobirá, the Valle de Arán and the Condado de Ribagorza), *Madrid* (1966), and *Barcelona* (1970). His repertoire of short stories also expanded with *Garito de hospicianos* (1963, Gambling Den of Hospiced People), *El solitario* (1963, The Recluse), *Toreo de salón* (1963, Armchair Bullfighting), and *La bandada de palomas* (1969, The Flock of Pigeons).

During the 1960s Cela's propensity for innovation resulted in increasing diversity and critical acclaim. In 1961 he wrote *Cuatro figuras del 98* (Four Important People of the Generation of 1898) in tribute to his literary and spiritual mentors. This volume was followed by short works including *Nuevas escenas matritenses* (1965–1966, New Scenes from Madrid) and *Tobogán de hambrientos* (1962, Toboggan of Starving People), which critics such as Jorge A. Marbán consider to mark the apex of his excellence as an *apuntes* writer. Cela's iconoclasm advanced his radical departure from literary conventions, as evidenced in such titles as *Cuentos para leer después del baño* (1974, Stories to Read after One's Bath) and *Enciclopedia del erotismo* (1977, Encyclopedia of Eroticism). His works became markedly layered with scatology and sexual innuendos, as, for example, in *Diccionario secreto* (1968, 1972; Secret Dictionary) and *Rol de cornudos* (1976, Catalogue of Cuckolds). This period of experimentation also yielded Cela's debut as a playwright with *María Sabina* (1967) and *Homenaje al Bosco, I: El carro de heno; o, El inventor de la guillotina* (1969, Homage to Bosch, I: The Haywain; or, The Inventor of the Guillotine).

Spanish readers became familiar with Cela's thoughtful yet unflinchingly provocative side when his essays about the state of affairs in Spain as the Franco dictatorship waned began appearing in Spanish dailies such as *El País, El Independiente,* and *ABC.* These essays were later republished in such collections as *Al servicio de algo* (1969, In the Service of Something), *A vueltas con España* (1973, Again Talking about Spain), *Vuelta de hoja* (1981, Next Page), *Los vasos comunicantes* (1981, Communicating Vessels), *El camaleón soltero* (1992, The Unmarried Chameleon), *El huevo del juicio* (1993, The Egg of Judgment), and *El color de la mañana* (1996, The Color of the Morning).

In Cela's widely misunderstood Spanish Civil War novel, *Víspera, festividad y octava de San Camilo del año 1936 en Madrid* (1969, Eve, Feast and Octave of St. Camillus's Day 1936 in Madrid; translated and commonly referred to as *San Camilo, 1936,* 1991), an anonymous narrator attempts to appease his guilt and sense of cowardice for not having participated in the events of the outbreak of the civil war and in particular in the siege of the Montaña Barracks in Madrid, which took the lives of many of his friends. He feels obliged to keep a written account of the events, and his most useful writing tool is a looking glass that fuels his introspection and serves as a metaphor for the stream-of-consciousness mode of storytelling in the novel. Maryse Bertrand de Muñoz speaks of the "river-paragraphs" that overtake a fluctuating second- and third-person narration of fact and fiction surrounding 18 July 1936, as the narrator "write[s] and write[s] telling God what's happening on earth" while also pleading for an explanation concerning why "in Spain only the dead are important." Cela's concern for symmetry is again manifested in the subtitles and pertinent epigraphs that emphasize the upheavals of a country on the brink of civil war. *San Camilo, 1936* is divided into three parts: structured around "The Eve of St. Camillus's Day," "St. Camillus's Day," and "The Octave of St. Camillus." Also included is a somewhat dissonant epilogue in which the young narrator and his mentor-uncle, Jerónimo, discuss how to survive the impending catastrophe. The narrator's hallucinatory verbal odyssey is meticulously punctuated by a numerical ordering of things in twos and threes and a carefully orchestrated progression of events in harmony with precise clock time, radio news bulletins, and conversations in bars throughout Madrid. The urban landscape is similar to that of *La colmena,* but the sustained focus on the city brothels gives the impression that the Spanish capital has nothing else with which to provide refuge for its politicians and ordinary citizens.

San Camilo, 1936 is also propelled by the constant movement set in motion in part 1 as a result of the deaths of the prostitute Magdalena and two important political figures from opposing sides: Lieutenant Colonel José Castillo and Joaquín Calvo Sotelo. As the syncopated narration of their funeral corteges fuels the action, other characters emerge and posit a future of further destruction, such as the young woman Virtudes, who dies in childbirth, and the frightened homosexual Matiítas, who commits suicide in a spectacularly grotesque manner once the war begins. The horror of the war notwithstanding, the narrator finds solace in his uncle Jerónimo's words of wisdom: "don't squander your twenty years in the service of anybody. . . . look out for the Spaniard you carry inside you . . . even though you think this is the end of the world it's not . . . it's only a purgation of the world, a preventive and bloody purgation but not an apocalyptic one."

As with much of Cela's work after *La colmena,* criticism of *San Camilo, 1936* has been varied. Those who view it positively, such as David Herzberger, Pierre Ullman, and Bertrand de Muñoz, share a postmodern orientation. Paul Ilie, on the other hand, exemplifies less-favorable commentaries in his assessment of "the politics of obscenity" that underscore the novel. Still others fail to discern that the kernels of Cela's life that are integrated into the novel disparage Cela by attributing to him the narrator's cowardice. The stridency of this response, however, culminated with the publication in 1973 of Cela's outlandish novel *oficio de tinieblas 5* (office of darkness 5), which is written entirely in lowercase letters, with minimal punctuation. It borrows from Gottfried Wilhelm Leibniz in its division of the narration into 1,194 "monads" (short text fragments) that confirm the first of three epigraphs to the work: "naturally, this is not a novel but rather the purge of my heart."

The irregular structure of *oficio de tinieblas 5* is clarified by a long subtitle: *novela de tesis escrita para ser cantada por un coro de enfermos* (thesis novel written to be sung by a choir of sickly people). It is intended to take place on the first of April, when ecclesiastical homage is rendered to those people who have successfully passed through the process of canonization on their way to official sainthood. Sarcasm and parody of church rituals and belief aside, the date is significant because it marks the official proclamation in 1939 of the end of the Spanish Civil War and the beginning of Franco's rule. In addition, the thematics of the novel and the criticism it levels on modern society signal the pinnacle of Cela's career in terms of breaking with tradition. Taboos are unleashed in an unceasing litany of sexual freedom and deviance. The characters (more than 120 of them), whether real (Napoleon Bonaparte, the Roman emperor Trajan, Picasso) or fictitious, are spared no mercy as the stylized sketches of their lives are converted into deconstructed stories that are grouped together as fiction, sometimes in sequenced monads, for example, numbers 939–941 (El Cid and Charlemagne).

As with Cela's use of the titular number 5 to indicate an absence of logic, a poetics of deceit governs every absurdity coming from the narrator-author as he is reminded that people love to be entertained with lies (monad 372). He understands that his existence, like that of the narrator of *San Camilo, 1936,* is one of negation and self-destruction facing emotional and spiritual bankruptcy (monad 449). For him, his "office of darkness" facilitates searching for what holds humankind hostage: "it is magic in the service of evil struggling against mankind" (monad 1097).

The narration, in the first and second persons, flows from introspection about "defeat . . . at twenty-five years of age" to the certainty of death. The narrator's anonymity is carried over to those family members whose antics and bizarre relationships become an integral part of his written testimony: they are referred to as "yourcousin" (written as one word), "your father don't mention his name," "your little grandmother," and "your mother." Because "yourcousin" bears on his forehead a signature wrinkle in the shape of an inverted question mark (unique to Spanish orthography), it is clear that the family is of Spanish-speaking lineage. Such nonsensical practices as the grandfather's obsession with making tape recordings of chirping dead birds confound every aspect of the narration and any semblance of a story. In contrast to the anonymity within the narrator's family, however, is a panoply of invented and real names, such as "monseñor metrófanes david peloponesiano" (monad 1186), "sir joshua nehemit" (monad 1189), James Meredith, Fred Hampton, and Martin Luther King Jr., all of which lift the narrative from its Spanish origins and catapult it into a universal realm where it is not uncommon to hear references to the Holocaust, Vietnam, or Bosnia.

In sum, the story in *oficio de tinieblas 5* is about the life and death of humankind as it is refracted in characters such as Napoleon, El Cid, "yourcousin," or "your father don't mention his name," whose endeavors respond to a dynamics of negation and annihilation. For that reason the narrative axis (beginning with monad 794) follows along the lines of fourteen death notices (of some of the more cohesively sustained characters) and ends with the minute-by-minute account of the narrator's own demise at "23h, 59' 59" yes, it would have been more convenient to be defeated on time 0h 0' 0'"" (monad 1194).

The broadened scope and increasingly uninhibited tenor of Cela's literary undertakings during the 1970s prompted even critics and enthusiasts who had praised *La familia de Pascual Duarte* and *La colmena* as premier examples of post–Spanish Civil War fiction to proclaim that his career as a novelist had come to an end.

Cela continued nonetheless to write short fiction (collected in *Balada del vagabundo sin suerte y otros papeles volanderos* [1973, The Luckless Vagabond's Ballad and Other Loose Papers], *El espejo y otros cuentos* [1981, The Mirror and Other Short Stories], and *Las orejas del niño Raúl* [1986, Young Raul's Ears]), essays, and *Nuevo viaje a la Alcarria* (1986, New Journey to Alcarria), a revised version of his acclaimed 1948 travel book. Two years after Franco's death in 1975, Cela was named by King Juan Carlos I as a senator to the Spanish parliament, a service that prompted him to write a series of essays about Spain's transition to democratic rule. In 1980 he was inducted into the Galician Academy, and, much to his critics' surprise, in 1984 he was awarded the country's Premio Nacional (National Prize) for his novel *Mazurca para dos muertos* (1983; translated as *Mazurka for Two Dead Men,* 1992), which was a resounding success, selling more than 180,000 copies in 1984 and another 235,000 in 1990.

Mazurca para dos muertos marks a return to more traditional storytelling while also implementing a new discursive model. With perhaps the exception of *La colmena* and *oficio de tinieblas 5,* the fictive truths around which Cela's novels revolve are disclosed at the outset: Pascual is a criminal; the patients in *Pabellón de reposo* know they are going to die; Mrs. Caldwell's son has already died; and the Spanish Civil War is an historical fact. The same unveiling applies in *Mazurca para dos muertos* despite its protracted account of the full details of the story. Someone with obvious narrative omniscience begins by explaining that "In that whorehouse where he earned his living, Gaudencio would play a fairly wide repertoire of tunes but there is one mazurka, Ma Petite Marianne, that he played only twice: in November 1936 when Lionheart [Afouto] was killed, and in January 1940 when Moucho was killed. He never would play it again." Because nobody understands much about what is taking the lives of so many of their men, the narration is dismissive of the significance of the war, and it is overshadowed by what remains foremost in the minds of the Gamuzo family: avenging the untimely deaths of two of their kinsmen, Afouto and Lázaro Codesal. Afouto was murdered by Fabián Minguela Abrogán (Moucho), while Lázaro Codesal died on military assignment "at the Tizzi-Azza post in Morocco," where he "was treacherously killed by a Moor [from the Tafersit tribe]." The events pertaining to both are told to don Camilo on a visit to his family after years of having been away, with narrative and chronological time blending into "the prudent onward march of the world spinning and turning as the drizzle falls with neither beginning nor end."

The typically lush landscape and bountiful legends and superstitions of Galicia support an atmosphere in which death and annihilation, vengeance, murder, violence, and family honor are the principle coordinates of a narrative grid of incidents that have made widows of most of the women. The voices of matriarchs such as Ramona and Adega are crucial to the discourse that expands with each retelling of basically the same events. Everything don Camilo hears centers around what happened before and after either the Spanish Civil War or Afouto's murder.

The oscillating rhythm of past memory and present narration emphasizes the oral transmission of information, while references to the mazurka mark the musical substructure of circularity, repetition, and refrain in the novel: "I play whatever I like. . . . That piece of music isn't for any Tom, Dick, or Harry and I'm the only one that knows when to play it and what it means." The alternating voices that carry on the oral tradition offer brief conversational vignettes that clarify previous utterances, introduce new characters, or explain linguistic peculiarities that are a part of the Galician lexicon that is intrinsic to the novel (Cela included in the Spanish edition a map of the area and a vocabulary of Galician terms). The discourse unfolds in ritualistic fashion as pieces of information are disseminated relative to the family's plans for avenging Afouto's murder. Moucho is eventually killed by Tanis Gamuzo's two dogs, Sultan and Moor, and poetic justice is inversely conferred upon Lázaro Codesal, whose life was ended by a Moorish assassin.

The move away from Madrid as chosen fictive space for Cela's later novels is most evident in *Cristo versus Arizona* (1988, Christ versus Arizona), which takes place in Tombstone, Arizona, and covers the years from 1895 through 1988 amid the desert flora and fauna of the southwestern United States, where Spain left an indelible mark on the diverse indigenous cultures. The narrator, Wendell Espana, offers what he repeatedly states to be a true report of the events he witnessed during his life in the "Sodom and Gomorrah" of Tombstone, where "law and order are worthless." In contrast to his sworn truthfulness, his testimony is dotted with tongue-in-cheek insistence on the inaccuracies of the episodes included in his chronicle, primarily because he writes down what has been told him by word of mouth, thus following *Mazurca para dos muertos* in preferring oral over written transmission. Aware of the licentious and graphic quality of the stories, Wendell is insistent upon not publishing his chronicle until all of his sources are dead, a narrative strategy that calls to mind the confusing paratextual documents that frame Pascual's confession-driven manuscript.

Unlike Pascual, however, Wendell is merely the chronicler of the hybridized time and place into which he was born and of which his identity bears all the signs (including the mark his father made on him with a branding iron to commemorate the beginning of the twentieth century). Wendell, at twenty-two years of age, haphazardly made his mother's acquaintance in the brothel where she worked, after he had paid for her services. Whereas matricide forever seals Pascual's fate, Wendell (like Eliacim in *Mrs. Caldwell habla con su hijo*) is plagued with the consequences of his implied incest. Perhaps for that reason he insists upon clarifying repeatedly that his name is "Wendell Espana, Wendell Liverpool Espana, maybe it is Span or Aspen instead of Espana, I never really found out," despite the fact that "many people keep thinking that my name is Wendell Liverpool Lochiel, that was before knowing who my parents had been."

He never reveals the real motive for keeping his written record, but at the same time he fills it with information, dates of events, and names of characters, such as the well-known prostitutes Big Nose Kate, Pumice Stone, Big Minnie, and Betty Pink Casey; the Earp and Clanton families; Sheriff Sam W. Lindo; Sitting Bull; and Cochise. His account models "the litany to Our Lady who is the armor that preserves us from sin," which echoes rhythmically throughout the narration. In addition, the litany to the Mother of God also parallels a registry that the prostitute Cyndy keeps of her regular clients. Interspersed with the sordid background of barroom and brothel scenes, lynchings, and gunfights are legends (about snakes, desert plants, and elixirs) and indigenous mythologies (including the invocation of a litany to St. Joseph in order to stave off poisonous vipers). Once again, a chain of character-driven incidents holds the narration together.

Wendell's story is made up of one hyperbolically long sentence. His is the prose of an unschooled individual, but it is, nevertheless, pointedly critical of the malevolence visited upon native America by the colonizing Spaniards (and, by extension, Europeans), and also remindful of certain themes that are in the forefront of Cela's later novels, among them the depiction of twentieth-century life as a division between "winners and losers" whose actions square them off with a legal system in which poorly trained judges and executioners purportedly strive to achieve justice. Most visible in *Cristo versus Arizona* are the criminals and foreigners who make their way to Tombstone, where "more than half of the hanged were foreigners"; equally striking are the large numbers of Chinese and African Americans. The same applies to the Native American population: "the Sioux were defeated by the White Man at Wounded Knee, the heroic adventures of Chief Little Big Man had nothing to do with the movie." For all of the incriminatory words about how "everything Yankee is bad," no one bears the brunt of Cela's chastisement more than the Spaniards themselves, as Wendell calls to mind his own ethnic background by naively explaining his use of Spanish: "one has to perpetrate the savage act in the same language and with the same tongue as the one with which one curses and blesses." In full recognition and public admission of the many sins covering a "heart-shaped stone" that is a symbolic gathering point in the nearby Arizona desert as well as a metaphor for Europe's expansion into the Americas by way of Tombstone, a serious "examination of conscience" precedes Wendell's parting plea for mercy in the Agnus Dei litany with which he ends his chronicle. Luis Blanco Vila is correct in his assertion that *Cristo versus Arizona* enjoyed little popularity in Spain because its readers were unable to grasp the meaning of the Wild West and were therefore unwilling to accept Wendell's invitation for self-scrutiny.

Cela received the Nobel Prize in Literature in 1989. That same year his divorce from his wife of forty-four years fueled a wave of public criticism, which intensified in 1991 when he wed Marina Castaño, a journalist several decades his junior. The fifth Spanish Nobel laureate since Vicente Aleixandre in 1973, Cela was overjoyed at having won this prize, which he admitted (in a 6 November 1989 *El País* interview) that he had sought since having written *La familia de Pascual Duarte*. In a 1996 *Paris Review* interview he pointedly stated that he "was one of the least awarded Spanish writers." His candidacy had first been proposed to the Nobel committee in 1959, and again in 1975 (by Marcel Bataillon, a well-known French Hispanist), in 1982, and in 1987. *The New York Times* (20 October 1989) was quick to report that "Some scholars today question . . . the academy's choice of Mr. Cela," citing noted Hispanist Julio Ortega's tepid acknowledgment that "Mr. Cela is a conventional, safe choice." Notwithstanding diverse reactions to the selection of Cela over the 150 candidates presented for the award that year, the prize appeared to give tacit recognition to Spain's peaceful transition to democracy and full partnership in Europe's emerging profile as a united world power. On a more personal level, Cela's friend and fellow writer Francisco Umbral summed it up best: "his triumph coincided with the separation from his wife, an illness, meeting Marina, and a change in city and home, the return to the Alcarria of his younger days, and his final move to [the fashionable] Puerta de Hierro" district in Madrid. Additionally, Umbral's opinion about "the hard part of winning the Nobel being not so much winning as knowing how to cope with it" provides a veiled assessment of the effects such fame had on Cela.

There is general agreement that 1989 marked the diminution of Cela's creativity. Until the time of his death in 2001, Cela's private life and characteristic public gaffes, rather than his literary output, became the rallying points for commentary about him. When the long-awaited novel *Madera de boj* (translated as *Boxwood*, 2002), which he had been promising since at least 1994, finally appeared in October 1999, Jesús Ruiz Mantilla reported that Cela had said winning the Nobel Prize had so overwhelmed him that he threw away all of his previous notes for the novel and only began working on it in earnest years later. *Madera de boj* and other novels took second place to public appearances, interviews, and endorsements, which he claimed the Nobel legitimized. A few years before his death, a caustic public remark about homosexuality and the Spanish poet Federico García Lorca's legacy led to a vociferous outcry from critics demanding that the Nobel commission consider rescinding its 1989 decision. While nothing ever came of it, the incident did little to bolster public or critical acceptance of Cela's last three novels. When he won Spain's most prestigious literary award, the Cervantes Prize, in 1995, there was little jubilation. From 1990 through 1991 and from 1993 to 1995, Cela wrote (almost) daily articles for the *El Independiente* and *ABC* newspapers, respectively. He also devoted an inordinate amount of time to such public venues as presiding over the panel of judges for the Príncipe de Asturias Prize in 1991 and giving lectures for the opening of the "Jornadas Semana del Seguro" in May 1991 and the International Congress on the Spanish Language (although the press criticized him for reading the same speeches).

For Cela the Nobel Prize was curiously misaligned with other events in his life that distorted his lifelong goal of nurturing the creative process through writing. According to a 2004 memoir by Cela's last assistant and secretary, Gaspar Sánchez Salas, Cela had often said that "money in literature, if it comes along, is always icing on the cake"; but as Umbral points out, he will also be remembered as the Nobel recipient whose financial worries prevented him from writing. His lavish expenses included a Bentley automobile and a large house in Puerta de Hierro. Financial concerns were behind his entering his novel *La cruz de San Andrés* (1994, St. Andrew's Cross) in the competition for the commercialized Planeta Prize, worth fifty million pesetas, which he won in 1994. Spanish newspapers frequently gave accounts of the corporate network that he and Castaño created in order to shield his personal assets. Both his son and his brother Jorge, in expressing regret that Cela had allowed himself to become fodder for the tabloid press, echoed Umbral's comment concerning the utter loneliness that shrouded the Nobel laureate's last years in Puerta de Hierro. For Cela, however, no reward was greater than the Nobel's symbolic public repudiation of the scorn of his harshest and most unrelenting critics.

Despite his waning career, he composed the second part of his long-awaited autobiography: *Memorias, entendimientos y voluntades* (1993, Memories, Understandings and Wishes). In addition, he developed more *apuntes*-type works, such as *Cachondeos, escarceos y otros meneos* (1991, Jokes, Dabblings and Other Fidgeting), the play *La sima de las penúltimas inocencias* (1993, The Sinkhole of Penultimate Innocence), the play *La dama pájara y otros cuentos* (1994, Lady Bird and Other Tales), and *Historias familiares* (1998, Familiar Stories). Also among these works is a return (as with prior works devoted to Solana and Picasso) to the world of art: *Los caprichos de Francisco de Goya y Lucientes* (1989, Francisco de Goya's Caprices). In 1999 *Homenaje al Bosco, II: La extracción de la piedra de la locura; o, El inventor del garrote* (Homage to Bosch, II: The Origins of the Source of Insanity; or, The Inventor of the Garrote), the second part of his 1969 play *El carro de heno,* was published but, despite having been commissioned for the celebration of the quincentennial discovery of the Americas, never staged because of its projected length (almost six hours) and proposed budget (millions of pesetas). He also wrote three novels of considerable length: *El asesinato del perdedor* (1994, The Murder of the Loser), *La cruz de San Andrés,* and *Madera de boj,* which all share the same themes as Cela's fiction over the years: social deviance and rejection of authority and fanaticism.

In *El asesinato del perdedor,* Mateo Ruecas is jailed for having shown public affection to his girlfriend Soledad in a Spanish town called N.N. His case is emblematic of the many others in the novel whose "errors" form the mismatched episodic vignettes that destabilize an already dizzying, fragmented text for which several narrator-authors claim responsibility. It is made clear at the onset that any "concession to the collective good taste, to cunning and uneducated public good taste" is out of order. The novel opens with a soliloquy of sorts by Michael Percival, "el Agachadizo" (the Stooped-Over), who lived some two hundred years ago. He mumbles about how to deal with enemies, addressing some invisible listeners: "make every effort to infect them with some humiliating illness . . . AIDS or leprosy or nostalgia." Even though Percival's enigmatic figure resurfaces rarely over the course of the novel, he functions as a marker in an otherwise aimless narration of disconnected characters and events. He also becomes loosely associated with Mateo, a metaphor for those whom society has labeled as "losers." Unlike Pascual, Mateo feels an overwhelming sense of shame for having spent time in jail, which causes him to take his own life. His "error" is juxtaposed with lascivious and scatological stories that mirror and at the same time minimize greatly his own. An array of silly characters (including Mrs. Belushi, Juan Grujidora, Estefanía Yellowbird, Zaqueo Nicomediano, Professor Maurus Waldawj, M.D., and Pamela Pleshette of Restricted Beach, Florida) underscores the ridiculousness of Mateo's faux pas, again attesting to Cela's use of parody and sarcasm as a means of cutting down to size all societally sanctioned pretensions of greatness. In this way, Cela undermines even his own narratorial authority and, therefore, favors literary invention over historical accuracy. The masses, however, continue to be entertained by the misfortunes of such "losers" (prostitutes, beggars, people with physical impediments and little formal education), who end up in public executions for which people clamor to get tickets.

The discourse amounts to a catalogue of utterances and antics replete with gymnastics, pantomime, and Chaplinesque mimicry. The gossip that spreads in everyday life about people's misfortunes runs current with the spontaneity of the text; short snippets of conversations parody the narration and allow the discourse to proceed along the same chatty lines. Periodic references are made to a "choir of beggars" who provide the music for the public executions. Also distinguishable is a constrained theatrical subtext that transforms *El asesinato del perdedor* into a linguistic, narrative, thematic, philosophical, and fictive spectacle, not the least of which is the metamorphosis of Pascual Duarte into Esteban Ojeda, who confirms the transformation by claiming that he "was pretty famous years ago, when I wrote a few pages which began like this: I am not, sir, a bad person, though in all truth I am not lacking in reasons for being one, etc." Later, Ojeda says that he "would like to write in the first person, it is always easier. It's as if I were Mateo Ruecas, I close my eyes and I feel like I am Mateo Ruecas, the loser about whom they speak in this true story. My girlfriend is called Soledad." Continuing Cela's fondness for accompanying documents, readers are also presented with a letter written by Juana Olmedo, coordinator of the Mateo Ruecas Effort, to Mr. Sebastián Cardeñosa López of O Coruña (Galicia), reminding him of the harm that was done to Mateo because of his modest social status and the "errors" of the Spanish judicial system; she cites a need to change "article 431 of the Penal Code, referring to public scandals" and asks that he write a formal condemnation of the matter so that, as petitioned her by Mateo's mother, no other poor Spanish family ever again has to suffer the abuses of a legal system that is rife with poorly trained judges.

El asesinato del perdedor provoked ire, frustration, and disillusionment among readers accustomed to the more traditional storytelling format to which Spanish novels had returned in the 1980s, and it has been given little critical attention. Nevertheless, Pascual Duarte's late-twentieth-century reincarnation is evidence of

Cela's lifelong commitment to artistic invention. The same can be said of *La cruz de San Andrés,* which intertwines elements of theater and narrative in keeping with its author's goal of constant renewal. This novel deals with multiple themes ranging from metafiction to philosophy, feminism, religious fanaticism, historiography, literary invention, and life at the end of the millennium. It chronicles the collapse of the López Santana family, which is celebrated as a "black Mass of confusion" and is unabashedly thrown, like "rotten entrails," to its readers as transcribed from the original "manuscript" of sorts, which was boastfully written by narrator Matilde Verdú (under whose name Cela published the book) on rolls of toilet paper.

The structure of the novel, like that of *Mazurca para dos muertos,* echoes a more traditional manner of writing; yet, the chapters are given subtitles that are befitting of plays: "Dramatis personae," "Plot," "Exposition," "Complication," and "Denouement/Ending, Final Coda, and Internment of the Last Puppets." The dramatic vicissitudes of the López Santana family are highlighted by myriad references to icons of pop culture (Betty Boop, Ava Gardner, Marilyn Monroe, Robert Taylor, and L. Ron Hubbard). There is one prevailing third-person voice that comments on the other narrators. Additionally, recognition is given to the source document that was written by the character Pilar Seixón, but Matilde Verdú, who sometimes also refers to herself as Matilde Lens and Matilde Meizoso, remains the primary chronicler.

Matilde tells her story based on cues from her own conversational interludes with an unnamed interrogating voice who occasionally says things such as "Take a short break and continue," or "Do you believe that history has to be told in detail and stopping for minutiae and nuisances?" Matilde also embellishes her tale with parts of her own life, principally claiming that she and her husband, because of their political affiliation with the Republican faction of the Spanish Civil War, were crucified on St. Andrew's crosses. When, however, it is revealed that Matilde is simply satisfying the editorial demands of her literary agent, Paula Fields, in order to earn the $600,000 she has been promised for her manuscript, the noble undertaking of her chronicle turns as farcical as the toilet paper on which it is written. As Fran, the last of the López Santana family members, slits his wrists in obedience to the leader of the secret cult of the "Community of the Daybreak of Jesus Christ," so too disintegrates the family and, by extension, the ignoble chronicle.

Madera de boj is both a tribute to those who drowned in the waters off the coast of Spain's northwestern promontory and a narrative elegy to that portion of the Atlantic Ocean that bathes Galicia's "Coast of Death" and *finisterre* (land's end). The litany-like narration is intentionally mired in sentences that go on for pages, interrupted by casual conversational exchanges, a Galician register of terms and expressions, recipes, legends and superstitions, aphorisms, punctilious references to the area's maritime topography, flora and fauna, and a blend of foreign names (Knut Skien, Juanito Jorick, James and Hans E. Allen, and Marco Polo). The endless tossing of the discourse is a metaphor for a sea that is an "open book in which everything was written and could be read with ease" and also the source of a "never-ending list of shipwrecks" that populate a virtual world of dead people. Both narrator and reader assume the role of "sailors" and, as such, have scant assurance that the compass that the narrating voice inherited will be of use because of the disquieting, yet alluring, submerged gold from the teeth of all the sailors who drowned there—which, seafarers say, throws reliable navigational instruments wildly off course.

The anonymous narrator shows extensive knowledge of the maritime and the English-speaking worlds. Having developed a successful whaling industry (which ended up dividing them), his ancestors were also tied to water: his Norwegian uncle, Knut Skien, hunted whales and the mythical Marco Polo ram; his cousin, Vitiño Leis Agulleiro, was the captain of the shipwrecked *Arada;* and his grandfather founded the Royal Regatta Club of Galicia in 1902. Their favorite pastimes included playing rugby, tennis, and cricket, and reciting Edgar Allan Poe's poetry in Galician while facing the sea. The most wealthy among them, Uncle Dick, spent an entire lifetime aimlessly pursuing his dream of building a house out of boxwood, a shrub that is used decoratively in gardens but unsuitable for the construction of large structures. Given the clearly enunciated premise that legend and fantasy are "more powerful than the truth," *Madera de boj* constitutes an allegorical superstructure about struggling to attain what is beyond reach.

In 2000 Camilo José Cela University was founded on the outskirts of Madrid. It is a small, private institution that offers computer-based instruction with an emphasis on research and critical inquiry.

Cela died on 17 January 2002. He bequeathed his small forest resort along the coast of Sant Elm in Majorca to the Grup d'Ornitologia Balear (Balearic Ornithology Group). He also left several unfinished projects, among them a novel to be called "Dry sicuta" (Dry Hemlock). In November 2002 his widow appeared at the Reina Sofía Museum in Madrid to unveil *Cuadernos de El Espinar: Doce mujeres con flores en la cabeza* (Notebooks from The Espinar Residence: Twelve Women with Flowers on Their Heads), facsimiles of twelve etchings by Cela. Public scrutiny of his work continued, focusing on an accusation of plagiarism in *La cruz de San Andrés,* of which he was posthumously found not guilty, and an alleged prior agreement with the Planeta publishing house to submit the novel for the 1994 Planeta Prize, which Cela had won. Sánchez Salas has asserted that the Nobel laureate is innocent of these charges, as well as of using ghostwriters toward the end of his career. Cela's death also drew attention because of questions of inheritance, the legal rights to his literary legacy, and the future direction of the Cela Foundation, which he had established some years before in Iria Flavia, Galicia, as the repository for his manuscripts and relevant papers. The degree to which Cela's life and works have generated both praise and criticism is brought home by several biographical accounts of his life: *Cela: Un cadáver exquisito* (2002, Cela, an Exquisite Corpse) by Umbral; *Desmontando a Cela* (2002, Dismantling Cela) by journalist Tomás García Yebra; *Cela, el hombre que quiso ganar* (2003, Cela, the Man Who Wanted to Win) by Gibson; and the two published works of Sánchez Salas, *Cela: El hombre a quien ví llorar* (2002, Cela: The Man I Saw Cry) and *Cela: Mi derecho a contar la verdad* (2004, Cela: My Right to Tell the Truth).

As has often been stated, Camilo José Cela's works of prose fiction do not placate the painful soul-searching of the human condition. To quote the Nobel committee, his is a "rich and intensive prose, which with restrained compassion forms a challenging vision of man's vulnerability." Cela's novels far surpass capturing the spirit of Spain in the twentieth century; they lay bare the workings of the human species over the course of time. Cela's disjointed language parallels the truncated bond between people of all places and walks of life. The shocking imperfections and personal failings of his characters are exponentially equivalent to Cela's disdain for the entrapment of politically constrained social and literary correctness. In the words of the anonymous narrator of *Madera de boj,* "the model is Emile Zola or doña Emilia Pardo Bazán, now it's not anymore like before, now people have discovered that the novel is a reflection of life and life has no ending other than death, that pirouette that is never the same."

Interviews:

"Un escritor sin miedo," *El País,* Suplemento Mensual de las Letras, 6 November 1989, International Edition, 1–3;

Valerie Miles, "Camilo José Cela: The Art of Fiction CXLV," *Paris Review,* 139 (Summer 1996): 124–163.

Biographies:

Camilo José Cela Conde, *Cela, mi padre* (Madrid: Temas de Hoy, 1989);

Francisco Umbral, *Cela: Un cadáver exquisito* (Barcelona: Planeta, 2002);

Gaspar Sánchez Salas, *Cela: El hombre a quien ví llorar* (Barcelona: Carena, 2002);

Tomás García Yebra, *Desmontando a Cela* (Madrid: Libertarias, 2002);

Ian Gibson, *Cela, el hombre que quiso ganar* (Madrid: Aguilar, 2003);

Sánchez Salas, *Cela: Mi derecho a contar la verdad* (Barcelona: Belacqva, 2004).

References:

Maryse Bertrand de Muñoz, "El estatuto del narrador en San Camilo, 1936," in *Crítica semiológica de textos literarios hispánicos,* edited by Miguel Angel Garrido Gallardo (Madrid: Consejo Superior de Investigaciones Científicas, 1986), pp. 579–589;

Luis Blanco Vila, *Para leer a Camilo José Cela* (Madrid: Palas Atenea, 1991);

Silvia Burunat, "El monólogo interior en Camilo José Cela," in her *El monólogo como forma narrativa en la novela española* (Madrid: José Porrúa Turanzas, 1980), pp. 57–82;

"Camilo José Cela, a Spanish Novelist, Wins Nobel Prize," *New York Times,* 20 October 1989;

J. M. Castellet, "Iniciación a la obra narrativa de Camilo José Cela," *Revista Hispánica Moderna,* 28 (1962): 107–150;

"Cela creó con Marina Castaño una red de sociedades para blindar su patrimonio," *El País,* 5 February 2002;

"Cela repitió su discurso de Zacatecas de 1997, que era igual a otro de 1992," *El País,* 19 October 2001;

Lucile C. Charlebois, *Understanding Camilo José Cela* (Columbia: University of South Carolina Press, 1998);

Javier Cuartas, "El pueblo de Puerto Rico recibe el Premio Príncipe de Asturias de las Letras," *El País,* 22 April 1991, p. 19;

William David Foster, *Forms of the Novel in the Work of Camilo José Cela* (Columbia: University of Missouri Press, 1967);

Paul Ilie, *La novelística de Camilo José Cela* (Madrid: Gredos, 1961);

Ilie, "The Politics of Obscenity in San Camilo, 1936," *Anales de la Novela de Posguerra,* 1 (1976): 25–63;

ínsula, special Cela/Nobel Prize in Literature issue, 518–519 (February–March 1990);

Robert Kirsner, *The Novels and Travels of Camilo José Cela* (Chapel Hill: University of North Carolina Press, 1964);

John Kronik, "Pascual's Parole," *Review of Contemporary Fiction,* 4, no. 3 (1984): 111–118;

Jorge A. Marbán, "Fases y alcance del humorism en los apuntes carpetovetónicos de Cela," *Hispanic Journal*, 2 (Spring 1981): 71–79;

Eloy E. Merino, *El nuevo Lazarillo de Camilo J. Cela: Política y cultura en su palimpsesto* (Lewiston, N.Y.: Edwin Mellen Press, 2000);

Janet Pérez, *Camilo José Cela Revisited* (New York: Twayne, 2000);

José Luis S. Ponce de León, *La novela española de la Guerra Civil* (Madrid: ênsula, 1971);

Olga Prjevalinsky, *El sistema estético de Camilo José Cela* (Valencia: Castalia, 1960);

Review of Contemporary Fiction, special Cela issue, 4, no. 3 (1984);

Jesús Ruiz Mantilla, "Con el Nobel cogí miedo a *Madera de boj*," *El País*, 28 September 1999;

Darío Villanueva, "La intencionalidad de lo sexual en Cela," *Los Cuadernos del Norte*, 51 (October–November 1988): 54–57.

Papers:
Camilo José Cela's papers are at the Cela Foundation in Iria Flavia, Galicia, Spain.

1989 Nobel Prize in Literature Presentation Speech

by Professor Knut Ahnlund, of the Swedish Academy (Translation from the Swedish)

Your Majesties, Your Royal Highnesses, Ladies and Gentlemen,

Camilo José Cela has written upwards of a hundred books, a veritable library in itself, filled with the most astounding contrasts, popular, crudely humorous tales side by side with some of the darkest and most desolate works in European literature.

Once Cela was a young poet in a Madrid on the verge of civil war. More than almost any writer he was at the center of those agonizing events, both as one of those responsible for them and as a resistance fighter. It was after serving in the trenches, being wounded and lying awhile in field hospitals, after the war was over and he had come home and Spain had embarked on her many dreary years under the new regime, that he made his debut–as a prose writer. In high quarters there was a desire to see edifying books, preferably cheerful and sunny ones. Cela's first novel was about a multiple murderer who relates his life history before his execution. *La familia de Pascual Duarte, Pascual Duarte's Family*, was printed secretly in a garage in Burgos in 1942, and by the time it had come to the authorities' notice the edition was almost sold out. Gradually the censors became resigned; next to *Don Quixote* it must be the most widely read of all Spanish novels. This story of a matricide can be read as an allegory, a fairy tale about Spain's monstrous sufferings and furious internal strife.

It opened the sluice-gates. Cela's works grew in range and splendor. If they had anything in common it was the swarms of characters appearing in them; it was hardly a matter of the hierarchy of main characters and secondary ones that is customary in novels. On the stage where the author lets dramas of life and of Spain play themselves out under grim starlight, one could argue, with only slight exaggeration, that there were only secondary characters.

La Colmena or *The Beehive*, with more than 300 characters, depicts Madrid life during the first sad years of the Franco era. It was Cela's boldest challenge hitherto to the authorities' repression of free expression. Although it was translated into many languages, the Spaniards themselves were long denied access to it.

Eighteen years later, in 1969, when Cela published his novel *San Camilo 1936*, the mesh of censorship had numerous gaps and tears in it, so this book was at last published where it was written. To some extent, the Madrid of *The Beehive* still exists in *San Camilo 1936*, but illuminated by streaks of visionary light, and swathed in an apocalyptic glow. The action takes place in Madrid during the week immediately on the eve of the Civil War. Here we encounter the young man with the sad burning eyes, see him mingling with the city's crowds or staring into the mirror of his own bitter reflections. To a great extent the narrative is an incantation, an exorcization, an invocation, and so it points forward to the work which must be Cela's most obscure, *Oficio de Tinieblas 5*–a poetic apocalypse, a major poem eleven hundred and ninety-four verses long, an overall vision of life's dark absurd anti-logic, arranged in a form similar to the Mass.

In *Mazurca para dos muertos*, Cela, after his forays into the border lands where language and existence meet chaos, came back to the realities of Spanish life which he had depicted in so many facets. It is an account of the lives of ordinary people in the green and damp Galicia where he lived as a child. But most of all, perhaps, it is a tale about Death, an imagistic fresco depicting the tumult, insanities, comedy and tragedy of human life, always against the background of death, which in the end gathers everything and everyone to itself. Its great, crude humor is part of a tradition that goes back to Aristophanes, Rabelais and Shakespeare, yet it resembles nothing we have ever read in that line.

In his classical travel books from the forties and fifties, redolent with a quieter humor, we meet a more gentle, pliant Cela; Cela the vagabond, looking for milieux and cultures that at the time were in the process of disappearing.

As a whole, what we have before us is an extraordinarily rich, weighty and substantial body of writings that possess great wildness, license and violence, but which nonetheless in no way lack sympathy or common human feeling, unless we demand that those sentiments should be expressed in the simplest possible way. Cela has renewed and revitalized the Spanish language as few others have done in our modern age. As a creator of language he is in the tradition of Cervantes, Góngora, Quevedo, Valle-Inclán and Garcia Lorca; Spanish has not really been quite the same language since those writers have put their marks in its great book.

Dear Camilo José Cela,

I have devoted a few brief minutes to describing a body of work so great and varied as to defy any summary. Your contribution to the rights of creative imagination spans nearly half a century, including long periods under difficult conditions, but in the end it won out. In recent years the wealth of Latin American literature has been widely discussed everywhere. Perhaps too little attention has been paid, however, to its counterpart in the country where Spanish was first spoken. Personally, and on behalf of the Swedish Academy, may I congratulate you most cordially, and may I ask you to receive from the hands of His Majesty the King this year's Nobel Prize in Literature.

[© The Nobel Foundation, 1989.]

Cela: Banquet Speech

Cela's speech at the Nobel Banquet, 10 December 1989

Your Majesties, Your Royal Highness, Your Excellencies, Ladies and Gentlemen,

The Swedish Academy is honouring me by inscribing my name in the margins of the roll of illustrious personages of contemporary world literature. It is an honour which is out of all proportion to my skill and ability. Apart from showing my gratitude with all my heart, I would like to be permitted to make clear that, if I have dared to arrive where I am now, it is only because I understand that the Prize is not just being awarded to me, but also to my contemporaries who write in the glorious language which is our tool: Spanish. I do not wish to dwell on this very sincere confession, for, since my teacher has been Miguel de Cervantes, I know full well that an argument, however good, does not seem so successful when propounded at length.

When on my way to Stockholm, in response to your benevolence, I asked myself about the reasons which brought me here. I surmised that your purpose was to reward the occupation rather than the person. If so, you have not erred, for, according to Cervantes—Cervantes once and for ever—the goal of literature is to give justice its rightful place by rendering to everyone what is his, and by understanding and upholding good laws. Literature is hazardously and irreversibly, my life, my death and my suffering, my vocation and my servitude, my constant yearning and my well-merited consolation. How peaceful my conscience becomes after I have said this!

Amongst the names honoured by the Nobel Prize, there are illustrious scientific personages, both global and contemporary, who are guided by the same praiseworthy aims which distinguish and characterize all of us: peace in our heads and our hearts, and solidarity between human beings and between peoples. I am aware that we have not reached the goal that we are aiming at, and that there are still many steps to be taken in serenity and good sense, with constancy, no doubt, but also with luck. I propose that we never wander off this salubrious road.

I raise a toast to the King and Queen of Sweden, who reign over a nation at peace; to the people of Sweden, who love peace; to the Swedish Academy and other Nobel Institutions, who sponsor peace; and to all those in the entire world who defend and proclaim peace. I raise a toast to peace.

[© The Nobel Foundation, 1989. Camilo José Cela is the sole author of his speech.]

Press Release: The Nobel Prize in Literature 1989

from the Office of the Permanent Secretary of the Swedish Academy

This year's Nobel Prize for literature goes to the Spanish writer Camilo José Cela. With him is rewarded the leading figure in Spain's literary renewal during the postwar era.

The background of Cela's experience is the cruel Spanish civil war, which divided the country into two factions whose borders could cut right through ties of family and friendship. He himself was drawn into the fighting and was badly wounded.

Cela is a restless spirit. In him is united a marked fondness for experiment with a provocative attitude. At the same time he can be included in an old Spanish tradition of hilarious grotesqueness—which is often the other side of despair. Compassion for man's hopeless suffering is there, but tightly controlled.

The basic features of his attitude are evident already in the book which made his name—*The Family of Pascual Duarte* (1942). It is a powerful, in parts gruesome novel, which in spite of being censored and banned had an almost unparalleled impact. After *Don Quixote* it is probably the most read novel in Spanish literature.

We seldom meet any characters in his books which are drawn in any detail. Instead, often like Mahfouz in *Midaq Alley,* Cela captures the crowd, the buzzing, as in *The Hive* (1951). The effect is attained by means of a feverish montage, which is reflected in other authors.

A sensation was caused in 1969 by *San Camilo,* which tells of the week before the outbreak of the civil war. The decisive factor was that the mighty flow of words with its pictures of violence and sexual obsession within the small sphere seemed to reflect happenings on the national plane.

In *Oficio de Tinieblas 5* (Requiem of Darkness 5), 1973, and *Mazurca para dos muertos* (Mazurca for Two Dead), 1983, the experiments with form of language and content—in different ways—have been carried very far. The books are at once challenging and defiantly dark but also secretly enticing. The latter is a macabre but cheerfully obscene dance of death that is valid far beyond the depiction of Galician everyday life.

Especially noteworthy is what Cela has done as publisher of the literary magazine *Papeles de Son Armadans*. Many is the writer who has found an open forum here during years of hardship. In search of the Spain that Cela saw disappear in those years, he roamed far and wide. Perhaps the most enjoyable of all the accounts of his travels—at the same time humorous masterpieces—are *Journey to the Alcarria* (1948) and *Del Mino al Bidasoa* (From Mino to Bidasoa), 1952.

[© The Nobel Foundation, 1989.]

Cela: Nobel Lecture, 8 December 1989

Eulogy to the Fable
Translated from the Spanish by Mary Penney

Distinguished Academicians,

My old friend and mentor Pío Baroja—who did not receive the Nobel Prize because the bright light of success does not always fall on the righteous—had a clock on his wall. Around the face of that clock there were words of enlightenment, a saying that made you tremble as the hands of the clock moved round. It said "Each hour wounds; the last hour kills." In my case, many chimes have been rung in my heart and soul by the hands of that clock—which never goes back—and today, with one foot in the long life behind me and the other in hope for the future, I come before you to say a few words about the spoken word and to reflect in a spirit of goodwill and hopefully to good avail on liberty and literature. I do not rightly know at what point one crosses the threshold into old age but to be on the safe side I take refuge in the words of Don Francisco de Quevedo who said: "We all wish to reach a ripe old age, but none of us are prepared to admit that we are already there."

However one cannot ignore the obvious. I also know that time marches inexorably onwards. So I will say what I have to say here and now without resorting to either inspiration or improvisation, since I dislike both.

Finding myself here today, addressing you from this dais which is so difficult to reach, I begin to wonder whether the glitter of words—my words in this case—has not dazzled you as to my real merit which I feel is a poor thing compared to the high honour you have conferred upon me. It is not difficult to write in Spanish; the Spanish language is a gift from the gods which we Spaniards take for granted. I take comfort therefore in the belief that you wished to pay tribute to a glorious language and not to the humble writer who uses it for everything it can express: the joy and the wisdom of Mankind, since literature is an art form of all and for all, although written without deference, heeding only the voiceless, anonymous murmur of a given place and time.

I write from solitude and I speak from solitude. Mateo Alemán in his *Cuzmán de Alfarache* and Francis Bacon in his essay *Of Solitude*,—both writing more or less at the same period—said that the man who seeks solitude has much of the divine and much of the beast in him. However I did not seek solitude. I found it. And from my solitude I think, work, and live—and I believe that I write and speak with almost infinite composure and resignation. In my solitude I constantly keep in mind the principle expounded by Picasso, another old friend and mentor, that no lasting work of art can be achieved without great solitude. As I go through life giving the impression that I am belligerent, I can speak of solitude without embarrassment and even with a certain degree of thankful, if painful, acceptance.

The greatest reward is to know that one can speak and emit articulate sounds and utter words that describe things, events and emotions.

When defining man, philosophers have traditionally used the standard medium of close genus and specific difference that is to say reference to our animal status and the origin of differences. From Aristotle's *zoón politikón* to Descartes' *res cogitans* such reference has been an essential means of distinguishing man from beast. But however much moral philosophers may challenge what I'm going to say, I maintain that it would not be difficult to find abundant evidence identifying language as the definitive source of human nature which, for better or worse, sets us apart from all other animals.

We are different from other animals, although since Darwin we know that we have evolved from them. The evolution of language is thus a fundamental fact which we cannot ignore.

The phylogenesis of the human species covers a process of evolution in which the organs that produce and identify sounds and the brain which makes sense of those sounds develop over a long period of time which includes the birth of Mankind. No subsequent phenomena, neither *El Cantar de Mío Cid* nor *El Quijote*, nor quantum theory, can compare in importance to the first time that the most basic things were given a name. However for obvious reasons I am not going to dwell here on the evolution of language in its primeval and fundamental sense. Rather I will deal with its secondary and accidental but relatively more important meaning for those of us who were born into a society whose tradition is more literary than secular.

Ethnologists such as the distinguished A. S. Diamond believe that the history of language, of all languages, follows a pattern in which at the very beginning sentences are simple and primitive but go on to become more complicated in terms of syntactic and semantic variations. By extrapolating from this historically verifiable trend, it can be deduced that this increasing complexity evolves from the initial stage where communication relies mainly on the verb, building up to the present situation where it is nouns, adjectives and adverbs that give flavour and depth to the sentence. If this theory is correct and if we apply a little imagination, we might conclude that the first word to be used was a verb in its most immediate and urgent tense, namely the imperative.

And indeed the imperative still retains considerable importance in communication. It is a difficult tense to use. It must be handled with care since it requires a highly detailed knowledge of the rules of the game which are not always straightforward. A badly-placed imperative can bring about the exact opposite of the desired objective. John Langshaw Austin's famous triple distinction (locutionary, illocutionary and perlocutionary language) is an erudite demonstration of the thesis that perlocutionary language tends to provoke specific behaviour on the part of the interlocutor. It is useless to issue an order if the person to whom it is addressed dissembles and ends up doing whatever he likes.

Thus from *zoón politikón* to *res cogitans* sufficient distinctions have been drawn between the beast that grazes and the man that sings albeit not always in well-measured tones.

In Plato's *Dialogue* which bears his name, Cratylus hides Heraclitus among the folds of his tunic. The philosopher Democritus through his interlocutor Hermogenes speaks of the concepts of fullness and emptiness. The same can be said of Protagoras the anti-geometrician who irreverently maintained that "Man is the measure of all things": what they are and how they are, what they are not and how they are not.

Cratylus was concerned with language—what it is and what it is not—and developed those ideas at some length in his discourse with Hermogenes. Cratylus believes that what things are called is naturally related to what they are. Things are born or created or are discovered or invented. From their very beginning they contain essentially the exact term which identifies them and distinguishes them from everything else. He seems to be trying to tell us that this distinction is unique and comes from the same ovum as the thing itself. Except in the reasoned world of the etymologist, a dog has always been a dog in all the ancient languages and love has been love since first it was felt. The boundaries of paradox in the thoughts of Cratylus in contrast to Heraclitus' hypotheses are hidden in the dovetailed indivisibility or unity of opposites, their harmony (day and night), the constant movement and reaffirmation of their substance. The same is true of words as things in their own right (there is no dog without the cat and no love without hate).

Conversely Hermogenes thought that words were mere conventions established by humans for the reasonable purpose of understanding one another. Man is confronted with things or they are presented to him. Faced with something new, man gives it a name. The significance of things is not the spring in the woods but the well dug by man. The parabolic frontier of the senses, and of expression, as expounded by Hermogenes and concealed by Democritus and at times by Protagoras, comes up time and again: is man who measures and designates all things generic or individual? Is the measurement of those things a mere epistemological concept? Are things only physical matter or are they also feelings and concepts? By reducing being to illusion, Hermogenes kills off truth in the cradle; the contradictory conclusion that the only possible propositions are those which man formulates by himself and to himself, renders real what is true and what is not true. You will recall that according to Victor Henry's famous aporia man can give a name to things but he cannot take them over; he can change the language but he cannot change it any way he wishes. Referring in perhaps overcautious terms to the exactitude of names Plato seems to sympathise obliquely with Cratylus' position: things are called what they have to be called (an organic and valid theory that is on the verge of being acknowledged in pure reason as a principle) and not what man decides they should be called according to which way the wind is blowing at any given time (this being a changing or even fluctuating corollary, dependent on the changing suppositions present at the same time as, or prior to, a given thing).

This attitude, originally romantic and consequently demagogical, was the starting point for the Latin poets, headed by Horace. It gave rise to all the ills which have afflicted us in this field since that time and which we have not been able to remedy. *Ars Poetica*, verses 70 to 72, sings of the prevalence of usage in the evolution of language (not always a welcome development):

Multa renascentur quae iam cecidere cadentque quae nunc sunt in honore vocabula, si volet usus, quem penes arbitrium est et ius et norma loquendi.

This time-bomb, however pleasing in its charity, had several complex consequences leading finally to the supposition that language is made by the people—and inevitably by the people alone—and that it is futile to try and subject language to the precise and reasonable rules of logic. This dangerous assertion by Horace that usage determines what is right and acceptable in language created a rubbish-dump clogged with overgrown efforts in which the shortcut became the highway along which man progressed bearing the banner of language blowing freely and trembling in the breeze, obstinately continuing to confuse victory with the subservience inherent in its very image.

While Horace was partly right (and we should not deny that), he was also wrong in a number of ways and we should not try to hide that either. But we should also acknowledge the contribution of Cratylus and Hermogenes by refining their principles. Cratylus' position falls within what is referred to as natural or ordinary or spoken language, which is the product of the constant use of a historical and psychological path, while Hermogenes' proposition fits into what we understand as artificial or specialized language or jargon, deriving from a more or less formal arrangement or from some formal method based on logic but with no historical or psychological tradition behind it—at least at the time it is conceived. The first Wittgenstein, the author of the *Tractatus,* is a celebrated modern exponent of Hermogenes' proposition. Thus in that sense it would not be illogical to talk of Cratylian or natural or human language and of Hermogenean or artificial or parahuman language. Like Horace my point of reference is obviously the former, the language of life and literature, without technical or defensive obstacles. Max Scheler—and indeed phenomenologists generally—is also referring to what I will now call Cratylian language when he talks about language as an indication or announcement or expression, as is Karl Bühler when he classifies the three functions of language as symptom, signal and symbol.

It goes without saying that Hermogenean language naturally accommodates its original artificiality. On the other hand Cratylian language does not adapt to extraneous territory where there are often hidden pitfalls alien to its essential transparency.

It is dangerous to admit that in the final analysis natural, Cratylian language is the offspring of a magical marriage between the people and chance. Because people do not create language they determine its development. We can say, albeit with considerable res-ervations, that people solve to a certain extent the puzzle of language by giving names to things; but they also adulterate and hybridize it. If people were not subject to those hidden pitfalls referred to earlier this issue would be much more urgent and linear. What is not put forward but which nevertheless lies hidden within the true heart of the matter is one and the same and already determined; and neither I nor anyone else can change that.

The Cratylian language, the structure or system described by Ferdinand de Saussure as "langue," is the common language of a community (or rather more *in* than *of* a community), is formed and authenticated by writers and regulated and generally orientated by Academies. These three estates—the community, the writer and the Academies—do not always fulfil their respective duties. Very often they invade and interfere in other areas. It would appear that neither the Academies, nor the writers nor the community are happy with their own roles. While not competent to do so they prefer to define the role of others which, perhaps even rightly in principle, will always be unclear and ill-defined and, even worse, end up dissipating and obscuring the subject of their attention, namely the language and the verb which should be essentially transparent. The algebraic and mere instrument with no value other than its usefulness, in the final analysis as in Unamuno's *Love and Pedagogy.*

The final determining factor, the State, which is neither the community nor the writers nor the Academies, conditions and constrains everything, intervenes in a thousand different ways (administrative jargon, government pronouncements, television, etc.) compounding, more by bad example than by inhibition, disorder and disarray, chaos and confusion.

But no one says anything about popular, literary, academic, state and other excesses. Language evolves not in its own way which in principle would be appropriate, but is rather pushed around by the opposing forces surrounding it.

The community to whom Horace's lines are recited eventually believe that this is how a language should evolve and tries to incorporate phrases, styles and expressions that are neither intuitive nor the product of their subconscious—which at least might produce something valid or plausible—but rather deliberately and consciously invented, or, even worse, imported (at the wrong time and against sound common sense).

Writers, obviously with some exceptions, follow the often defective usage in their own environment and introduce and sanction expressions that are cumbersome and, worse still, divorced from the essential spirit of the language.

The Academies' problems stem from the basis on which they operate: as institutions they tend to be conservative and afraid of being challenged.

The erosion of the Cratylian language by Hermogenean influences is becoming more pronounced and there is a danger that it will desiccate that living language and render the natural language artificial. As I have already said, this threat is caused by invented, gratuitously incorporated or inopportunely resurrected or revitalised language.

There seems to be some political reason behind the impetus that now leads, as it has in the past, gaily to abandon the principles of a language in the face of a blunt attack by those besieging it. In my view the risks outweigh the possible benefits—which are somewhat Utopian—that might accrue at some future unspecified date. While I am far from being a purist, I would like to call on writers in the first instance and then on Academies and on States to a lesser degree to put an end to the chaos. There is undoubtedly a continuity in language that supersedes any classifications we wish to establish but that does not constitute grounds for tearing down the natural frontiers of language. If we allow that we would be admitting to a defeat that has not yet taken place.

Let us rally our genius in defence of language, all languages, and let us never forget that confusing procedure with the rule of Law, just as observing the letter rather than the spirit of the Law, always leads to injustice which is both the source and consequence of disorder.

Thought is intrinsically linked to language. Moreover, freedom is also probably linked to certain linguistic and conceptual patterns. Together they provide the broad framework for all human endeavour; those that seek to explore and expand human frontiers, also those that seek to undermine the status of man. Thought and liberty are found in the minds of heroes and villains alike.

But this generalisation obscures the need for greater precision if we are to arrive at an understanding of the real meaning of what it is to think and to be free. Insofar as we are able to identify the phenomena that take place in the mind, thinking for man means thinking about being free. There has been much argument regarding the extent to which this freedom or liberty is something concrete or whether it is just another slick phenomenon produced by the human mind. But such argument is probably futile. A wise Spanish philosopher has pointed out that the illusion and the real image of freedom are one and the same thing. If man is not free, if he is bound by chains that psychology, biology, sociology and history seek to identify, as a human being he also carries within himself the idea, which may be an illusion but which is absolutely universal, that he is free. And if we wish to be free we will organise our world in much the same way as we would if we were free.

The architectural design on which we have tried to build successfully or otherwise the complex framework of our societies, contains the basic principle of human freedom and it is in the light of that principle that we value, exalt, denigrate, castigate and suffer: the aura of liberty is the spirit enshrined in our moral codes, political principles and legal systems.

We know that we think. We think because we are free. The link between thought and freedom is like a fish biting its own tail or rather a fish that wants to get hold of its own tail; because being free is both a direct consequence of and an essential condition for thought. Through thought man can detach himself as much as he wants from the laws of nature; he can accept and submit to those laws, for example like the chemist who has gone beyond the boundaries of phlogiston theory will base his success and prestige on such acceptance and submission. In thought however, the realms of the absurd lie side by side with the empire of logic because man does not think only in terms of the real and the possible. The mind can shatter its own machinations into a thousand pieces and rearrange them into a totally different image.

Thus one can have as many rational interpretations of the world based on empirical principles as the thinker wishes primarily on the basis of the promise of freedom. Free thinking in this narrow sense is that antithesis of the empirical world and finds expression in the fable. Thus the capacity to create fables would appear to be the third element in the human status—the others being thought and freedom—and this capacity can turn things round in such a way that things which before they became the subject of a fable were not even untruths become truths.

Through the process of thought man begins to discover hidden truth in the world, he can aim to create his own different world in whatever terms he wishes through the medium of the fable. Thus truth, thought, freedom and fable are interlinked in a complicated and on occasion suspect relationship. It is like a dark passageway with several side-turnings going off in the wrong direction; a labyrinth with no way out. But the element of risk has always been the best justification for embarking on an adventure.

The fable and scientific truth are not forms of thought. They are rather heterogeneous entities which cannot possibly be compared with one another since they are subject to completely different rules and techniques. Consequently, it is not appropriate to brandish the standard of literature in the struggle to free men's minds. Literature should rather be regarded as a counterweight to the newfound slavish submission to science. I would go further and say that I believe that a prudent and careful distinction must be drawn between those forms of science and literature which join together to confine man within rigid limits which deny all ideas of freedom, and that we must be daring and offset those forms by other scientific and literary experiences aimed at engendering hope. By unreservedly trusting in the superiority of human freedom and dignity, rather than suspect truths which dissolve in a sea of presumption, would be an indication that we have progressed. However in itself it is not enough. If we have learned anything it is that science is incapable of justifying aspirations to freedom and that on the contrary it rests on crutches that tilt it in exactly the opposite direction. Science should be based solely on the most profound exigencies of human freedom and will. That is the only means of enabling science to break away from utilitarianism which cannot withstand the pitfalls of quantity and measurement. This leads us to the need to recognise that literature and science although heterogeneous cannot remain isolated in a prophylactic endeavour to define areas of influence and this for two reasons, namely the status of language (that basic instrument of thought) as well as the need to define the limits of and distinguish between that which is commendable and laudable and that which must be denounced by all committed individuals.

I believe that literature as an instrument for creating fables is founded on two basic pillars which provide it with strength to ensure that literary endeavour is worthwhile. Firstly aesthetics, which impose a requirement on an essay, poem, drama or comedy to maintain certain minimum standards which distinguish it from the sub-literary world in which creativity cannot keep pace with the readers' emotions. From socialist reality to the innumerable inconstancies of would-be experimentalists, wherever aesthetic talent is lacking the resulting sub-literature becomes a monotonous litany of words incapable of creating a genuine worthwhile fable.

The second pillar on which literary endeavour rests is ethics which complements aesthetics and which has a lot to do with all that has been said up to now regarding thought and freedom. Of course ethics and aesthetics are in no way synonymous nor do they have the same value. Literature can balance itself precariously on aesthetics alone—art for art's sake—and it could be that aesthetics in the long run may be a more comprehensive concept than ethical commitment. We can still appreciate Homer's verses and medieval epic canticles although we may have forgotten or at least no longer automatically link them with ethical behaviour in ancient Greek cities or in feudal Europe. However art for art's sake is by definition an extremely difficult undertaking and one which always runs the risk of being used for purposes which distort its real meaning.

I do believe that ethical principle is the element which makes a work of literature worthy of playing the noble role of creating a fable. But I must explain clearly what I mean because the literary fable as a means of expressing the links between man's capacity to think and the perhaps Utopian idea of being free cannot be based on just any kind of ethical commitment. My understanding is that a work of literature can only be subject to the ethical commitment of the person, the author, to his own idea of freedom. Of course no-one, not even the cleverest and most balanced literary author, can ever (or rather cannot always) overcome his humanity; anyone can have a blind spot and freedom is a sufficiently ambiguous concept and many blinding errors can be committed in its name. Nor can an aesthetic sense be acquired from a textbook. Thus, the literary fable must be based on both a sense of ethics and a commitment to aesthetics. That is the only way it can acquire a significance that will transcend ephemeral fashions or confused appreciation that can quickly change. The history of man is changing and tortuous. Consequently, it is difficult to anticipate ethical or aesthetic sensibilities. There are writers who are so tuned in to the feeling of their time that they become magnificent exponents of the prevailing collective trend and whose work is a conditional reflex. Others take on the thankless and not sufficiently applauded task of carrying freedom and human creativity further along the road, even if in the end that too may lead nowhere.

This is the only way in which literature can fulfil its role of closely identifying its commitment to the human status and, if we wish to be absolutely precise in this thesis, the only endeavour that can unreservedly be called true literature. However, human society cannot be linked to geniuses, saints and heroes alone.

In this task of seeking out freedom, the fable has the benefit of the well-known characteristic of the intrinsic malleability of the literary story. The fable does not need to subject itself to anything that might restrict its scope, novelty and element of surprise. Thus, unlike any other form of thought it can wave the Utopian banner high. Perhaps that is why the most avid authors of treatises of political philosophy have opted to use the literary story to convey Utopian propositions that would not have found ready acceptance outside the realms of fiction at the time they were written. There are no limits to the Utopianism that the fable can express since by its very nature the fable itself is based on Utopianism.

However, the advantages of literary expression are not confined to the ease with which it can convey Utopian propositions. The intrinsic plasticity of the story, the malleability of the situations, personalities and events it creates provide a superb foundry from which one can, without undue risk, set up an entire factory, or, to put it another way, a laboratory in which men conduct experiments on human behaviour in optimum conditions. But the fable does not restrict itself to expressing the Utopian. It can also analyse carefully what it means and what its consequences are in the myriad different alternative situations ranging from learned prediction to the absurd that creative thought can produce.

The role of literature as an experimental laboratory has been often highlighted in science fiction; speculation about the future that has subsequently been realised. Critics have heaped praise on novelists who have a talent for predicting in their fables the basic coordinates which subsequently have been substantiated. But the real usefulness of the fable as a test-tube lies not in its anecdotal capacity for accurately predicting something technical but as a means of conveying in a timely, direct or negative fashion all possible facets of a world that may be possible now or in the future. It is the search for human commitment, for tragic experiences, that can shed light on the ambiguity of blindly choosing options in the face of the demands placed upon us by our world, now or in the future, that turns the fresco of literature into an experimental laboratory. The value of literature as a means of carrying out experiments on behaviour has little to do with prediction since human behaviour only has a past, present and future in a very specific, narrow sense. There are, however, basic aspects of our nature which have an impressive permanency about them and which cause us to be deeply moved by an emotional story from a completely different age to the one we live in. It is this "universal man" that is the most prized figure in literary fable, an experimental workshop in which there are no frontiers and no ages. It is the Quixotes, the Othellos, the Don Juans that illustrate to us that the fable is a game of chess played over and over again, a thousand times with whatever pieces destiny throws up at any given time.

In absolute terms it might appear that this detracts from the so-called freedom I am advocating and indeed that would be the case if one did not take account of the role of that imperfect, voluble and confused personality, the author, the man. The magic of Shylock would never have emerged without the genius of the Bard, whose unreliable memory was of course far more inconsistent than that of the characters to whom he gave life and to whom in the end he denied death. And what of those anonymous scholars and jugglers whom we remember only for the result produced by their talents. There is undoubtedly something that must be remembered over whatever sociology or history tries to impose upon us and that is that thus far and insofar we can conceive of the future of mankind, works of literature are very much subject to the needs of the author; that is to say to a single source of those ethical and aesthetic insights I referred to earlier, an author who acts as a filter for the current which undoubtedly emanates from the whole surrounding society. It is perhaps this link between Man and Society that best expresses the very paradox of being a human being proud of his individuality, and at the same time tied to the community that surrounds him and from which he cannot disengage himself without risking madness. There is a moral here; the limitations of literature are precisely those of human nature and they show us that there is another status, identical in other ways, which is that of gods and demons. Our mind can imagine demiurges and the ease with which human beings invent religions clearly demonstrates that this is so. Our capacity to create fables provides a useful literary means of illustrating those demiurges, as indeed we have done constantly since Homer wrote his verses. But even that cannot lead us to mistake our nature or put out once and for all the tenuous flame of freedom that burns in the innermost being of the slave who can be forced to obey but not to love, to suffer and die but not to change his most profound thoughts.

When the proud, blind rationalist renewed in enlightened minds the biblical temptation, the last maxim of which promised "You will be as gods" he did not take account of the fact that Man had already gone much further down that road. The misery and the pride that for centuries had marked Man's efforts to be like the gods had already taught Man a better reason; that through effort and imagination they could become Men. For my part, I must say proudly that in this latter task, much of which still remains to be accomplished, the literary fable has always been, and in all circumstances proved to be, a decisive tool; a weapon that can cleave the way forward in the endless march to freedom.

[© The Nobel Foundation, 1989. Camilo José Cela is the sole author of the text.]

Sir Winston Churchill

(30 November 1874 – 24 January 1965)

Laurence Kitzan

This entry was expanded by Kitzan from his Churchill entry in *DLB 100: Modern British Essayists, Second Series.*

BOOKS: *The Story of the Malakand Field Force: An Episode of Frontier War* (London & New York: Longmans, Green, 1898);

The River War: An Historical Account of the Reconquest of the Soudan, edited by Francis William Rhodes (2 volumes, London & New York: Longmans, Green, 1899; revised, 1 volume, 1902);

Savrola: A Tale of the Revolution in Lauranian (New York: Longmans, Green, 1900; London: Longmans, Green, 1900);

London to Ladysmith via Pretoria (London & New York: Longmans, Green, 1900);

Ian Hamilton's March: Together with Extracts from the Diary of Lieutenant H. Frankland, a Prisoner of War at Pretoria (London & New York: Longmans, Green, 1900);

Mr. Broderick's Army (London: Humphreys, 1903; Sacramento, Cal.: Churchilliana, 1977);

Why I Am a Free Trader (London: Stead, 1905);

Lord Randolph Churchill, 2 volumes (London & New York: Macmillan, 1906);

For Free Trade: A Collection of Speeches Delivered at Manchester or in the House of Commons during the Fiscal Controversy Preceding the Late General Election (London: Humphreys, 1906; Sacramento, Cal.: Churchilliana, 1977);

My African Journey (London: Hodder & Stoughton, 1908; New York: Doubleday, Doran, 1909);

Liberalism and the Social Problem (London: Hodder & Stoughton, 1909; Doubleday, Doran, 1910);

The People's Rights (London: Hodder & Stoughton, 1909; New York: Taplinger, 1971);

Prison and Prisoners: A Speech Delivered in the House of Commons, 20th July, 1910 (London & New York: Cassell, 1910);

The World Crisis, 6 volumes (London: Butterworth, 1923–1931; New York: Scribners, 1923–1931);

Sir Winston Churchill (right) receiving the 1953 Nobel Prize in Literature from King Gustav VI Adolf of Sweden at the Swedish Embassy in London (AP World Wide)

abridged and revised, 1 volume (London: Butterworth, 1931; New York: Scribners, 1931);

Parliamentary Government and the Economic Problem: The Romanes Lecture Delivered in the Sheldonian Theatre, 19 June 1930 (Oxford: Clarendon Press, 1930);

My Early Life: A Roving Commission (London: Butterworth, 1930); republished as *A Roving Commission: My Early Life* (New York: Scribners, 1930);

India: Speeches and an Introduction (London: Butterworth, 1931);

Thoughts and Adventures (London: Butterworth, 1932); republished as *Amid These Storms: Thoughts and Adventures* (New York: Scribners, 1932);

Marlborough: His Life and Times, 4 volumes (London: Harrap, 1933–1938; New York: Scribners, 1933–1938);

Great Contemporaries (London: Butterworth, 1937; New York: Putnam, 1937); revised and enlarged (London: Butterworth, 1938); revised edition (London: Macmillan, 1943); revised edition (London: Odhams, 1958);

Arms and the Covenant: Speeches, edited by Randolph S. Churchill (London: Harrap, 1938); republished as *While England Slept: A Survey of World Affairs, 1932–1938* (New York: Putnam, 1938);

Step by Step: 1936–1939 (London: Butterworth, 1939; New York: Putnam, 1939);

Addresses Delivered in the Year Nineteen Hundred and Forty to the People of Great Britain, of France, and to the Members of the English House of Commons (San Francisco: Ransohoffs, 1940);

Broadcast Addresses to the People of Great Britain, Italy, Poland, Russia and the United States (San Francisco: Ransohoffs, 1941);

Into Battle: Speeches, edited by Randolph S. Churchill (London: Cassell, 1941); republished as *Blood, Sweat and Tears* (New York: Putnam, 1941);

The Unrelenting Struggle: War Speeches, edited by Charles Eade (London: Cassell, 1942; Boston: Little, Brown, 1942);

The End of the Beginning: War Speeches, edited by Eade (London: Cassell, 1943; Boston: Little, Brown, 1943);

Winston Churchill, Prime Minister: A Selection from Speeches Made by Winston Churchill During the Four Years That Britain Has Been at War (New York: British Information Services, 1943);

Onwards to Victory: War Speeches, edited by Eade (London: Cassell, 1944; Boston: Little, Brown, 1944);

The Dawn of Liberation: War Speeches, edited by Eade (London: Cassell, 1945; Boston: Little, Brown, 1945);

Victory: War Speeches, edited by Eade (London: Cassell, 1946; Boston: Little, Brown, 1946);

War Speeches: 1940–1945 (London: Cassell, 1946);

Secret Session Speeches, edited by Eade (London: Cassell, 1946); republished as *Winston Churchill's Secret Session Speeches* (New York: Simon & Schuster, 1946);

The Sinews of Peace: Post-War Speeches, edited by Randolph S. Churchill (London: Cassell, 1948; Boston: Houghton Mifflin, 1949);

Maxims and Reflections, edited by Colin Coote and Denzil Batchelor (London: Eyre & Spottiswoode, 1948; Boston: Houghton Mifflin, 1949);

The Second World War, 6 volumes (Boston: Houghton Mifflin, 1948–1953; London: Cassell, 1948–1954)—comprises volume 1, *The Gathering Storm;* volume 2, *Their Finest Hour;* volume 3, *The Grand Alliance;* volume 4, *The Hinge of Fate;* volume 5, *Closing the Ring;* and volume 6, *Triumph and Tragedy;* abridged by Denis Kelly as *The Second World War,* by Churchill and the editors of *Life,* 2 volumes (New York: Time, 1959); abridged by Kelly, with a new epilogue by Churchill, as *Memoirs of the Second World War* (Boston: Houghton Mifflin, 1959);

Painting as a Pastime (London: Odhams Benn, 1948; New York: Whittlesey House, 1950);

Europe Unite: Speeches 1947 and 1948, edited by Randolph S. Churchill (London: Cassell, 1950; Boston: Houghton Mifflin, 1950);

In the Balance: Speeches 1949 and 1950, edited by Randolph S. Churchill (London: Cassell, 1951; Boston: Houghton Mifflin, 1952);

The War Speeches of the Rt. Hon. Winston S. Churchill, O.M., C.H., P.C., M.P., 3 volumes, edited by Eade (London: Cassell, 1952; Boston: Houghton Mifflin, 1953);

Stemming the Tide: Speeches 1951 and 1952, edited by Randolph S. Churchill (London: Cassell, 1953; Boston: Houghton Mifflin, 1954);

Sir Winston Churchill, a Self-Portrait, edited by Coote and P. D. Bunyan (London: Eyre & Spottiswoode, 1954); expanded as *A Churchill Reader: The Wit and Wisdom of Sir Winston Churchill,* edited by Coote and and Bunyan (Boston: Houghton Mifflin, 1954);

The Wisdom of Winston Churchill: Being a Selection of Aphorisms, Reflections, Precepts, Maxims, Epigrams, Paradoxes, and Opinions from His Parliamentary and Public Speeches, 1900–1955, edited by F. B. Czarnomski (London: Allen & Unwin, 1956); abridged as *The Eloquence of Winston Churchill,* edited by Czarnomski (New York: New American Library, 1957);

A History of the English-Speaking Peoples, 4 volumes (London: Cassell, 1956–1958; New York: Dodd, Mead, 1956–1958)—comprises volume 1, *The Birth of Britain;* volume 2, *The New World;* volume 3, *The Age of Revolution;* and volume 4, *The Great Democracies;*

Catalogue of an Exhibition of Paintings by the Rt. Hon. Sir Winston Churchill, edited by Alfred M. Frankfurter (Kansas City, Mo., 1958);

Paintings by the Rt. Hon. Sir Winston S. Churchill, Exhibited at the Royal Academy of Arts, London, 1959 (London: The Academy, 1959);

The American Civil War (London: Cassell, 1961; New York: Dodd, Mead, 1961);

The Unwritten Alliance: Speeches 1953 to 1959, edited by Randolph S. Churchill (London: Cassell, 1961);

Frontiers and Wars [selections from Churchill's early nonfiction] (New York: Harcourt, Brace & World, 1962);

The Island Race (New York: Dodd, Mead, 1964);

Churchill: His Paintings: A Catalog, compiled by David Coombs (London: Hamilton, 1967; Cleveland: World, 1967);

Young Winston's Wars: The Original Despatches of Winston S. Churchill, War Correspondent, 1897–1900, edited by Frederick Woods (London: Cooper, 1972; New York: Viking, 1973); revised as *Winston S. Churchill, War Correspondent, 1895–1900* (London & Washington, D.C.: Brassey's, 1992).

Editions and Collections: *A Churchill Anthology: Selections from the Writings and Speeches of Sir Winston Churchill,* edited by F. W. Heath (London: Odhams, 1965);

Churchill's History of the English-Speaking Peoples, abridged by Henry Steele Commager (New York: Dodd, Mead, 1965);

Marlborough: His Life and Times, abridged by Commager (New York: Scribners, 1968);

The Collected Works of Sir Winston Churchill: Centenary Limited Edition, 34 volumes (London: Library of Imperial History, 1973–1976);

Winston S. Churchill: His Complete Speeches, 1897–1963, 8 volumes, edited by Robert Rhodes James (New York: Chelsea House, 1974);

The Collected Essays of Sir Winston Churchill, 4 volumes, edited by Michael Wolff (London: Library of Imperial History, 1976);

The Great Republic: A History of America [from *A History of the English-Speaking Peoples*], edited by Winston S. Churchill (New York: Random House, 1999).

Preeminent British statesman Sir Winston Churchill was awarded the Nobel Prize in Literature in 1953. In his presentation speech, Sigfrid Siwertz, a member of the Swedish Academy, noted that "Churchill's political and literary achievements are of such magnitude that one is tempted to resort to portray him as a Caesar who also has the gift of Cicero's pen. Never before has one of history's leading figures been so close to us by virtue of such an outstanding combination." Churchill was not at the presentation, and at the Nobel Banquet his wife, Lady Clementine Churchill, read his speech; but he probably was pleased at the reference to Cicero, a master writer and orator, as well as the reference to Julius Caesar. Like Caesar's, his first career was in the army, and he always showed a special interest in the military as well as in developing his political skills. Politics was Churchill's enduring passion, and it was as a politician and statesman that his primary reputation stands; however, Churchill's political career must also be seen in conjunction with his outstanding literary achievements. From an early age his writings underpinned his political career, but his histories and other writings were also significant contributions to literature.

Winston Leonard Spencer Churchill, born at Blenheim Palace on 30 November 1874, was the first of two children of Lord Randolph Churchill, the younger son of the seventh duke of Marlborough, and the former Jennie Jerome, the daughter of a wealthy American businessman. All of these factors played significant roles in his life. He had a romanticized view of his Marlborough background and became an avid defender of the reputation of the first duke, whom he perceived as having been unjustly attacked as a traitor by historians; he was also a strong defender of the reputation of his father, Lord Randolph, who at the time of Winston's birth was just beginning what could have been a brilliant political career but ended in disaster. Late in his life Churchill strongly emphasized his American heritage.

Churchill began his precarious and sometimes unhappy experience in the academic side of his education at private schools, and then at Harrow, where, as he notes in *My Early Life: A Roving Commission* (1930), examiners "almost invariably" set questions "to which I was unable to suggest a satisfactory answer." Since young Churchill did not excel at curricula with strong emphases on the classical languages, and because he had from an early age enjoyed marshalling his battalions of toy soldiers, Lord Randolph decided that his son was destined for a military career. After two failed attempts at the entrance exams to the Royal Military Academy at Sandhurst, Churchill entered Sandhurst in 1893, where he found a curriculum much more suited to his tastes; he was able to cultivate his interest in history, the subject in which he had shown the most ability at Harrow. To his great satisfaction he passed eighth out of a class of 150 students. He received his commission as second lieutenant in the Fourth Hussars in February 1895, shortly after the death of his father. The regiment was posted to India in the following year, where Churchill began his writing career—a financial necessity brought on by being an officer in a fashionable cavalry regiment in which a lieutenant's salary met less than half of his needs. His widowed mother also chronically exceeded her own limited income and found it difficult to meet the financial demands of two sons.

Roy Jenkins, in *Churchill: A Biography* (2001), notes that Churchill responded to his shortfall in income by evolving "two firm rules which he followed faithfully for the rest of his life. The first was that expenditure should be determined by needs (generously interpreted) rather than by resources. . . . Second, he decided that when the gap between income and expenditure became uncomfortably wide the spirited solution must always be to increase income rather than to reduce expenditure." His mother was pressed to use her social connections to get him posted to scenes of military activity, where he not only would see military service but also would be able to act as a paid newspaper correspondent. In 1895, even before going to India, he had fulfilled both desires by receiving permission to be an observer among the Spanish forces attempting to subdue an insurrection in Cuba, where, to his immense satisfaction, he had for the first time in his life come under fire; his letters from Cuba were published by the *Daily Graphic*.

Once in India, Churchill was able to obtain permission to accompany Sir Bindon Blood's punitive expedition to the Swat Valley on the northwest frontier, again as a correspondent, for two newspapers, *The Pioneer* and the *Daily Telegraph*. He quickly found himself actively immersed in a dangerous frontier campaign, where he plunged eagerly into active combat and learned about both the thrill of battle and the human dimensions of war. Churchill's 15 October 1897 letter to his newspapers described a skirmish in which he was involved:

> Now, suddenly, grim tragedy burst upon the scene. As the soldiers rose from the shelter of the rocks behind which they had been firing, an officer turned quickly round, his face covered with blood. He put his hands to his head and fell on the ground. Two of the men ran to help him away. One fell shot through the leg. A sepoy who was still firing sprang into the air and, falling, began to bleed terribly. Another fell close to him. Everyone began to pull these men along, dragging them roughly over the rocky ground in spite of their groans. Another officer was immediately shot. Several Sikhs ran forward to his help. Thirty yards away was the crest of the spur. From this a score of tribesmen were now firing with deadly effect. Over it ran a crowd of swordsmen, throwing pieces of rock and yelling. It became impossible to remain an impassive spectator. The two officers who were left [one of them was Churchill] used their revolvers. The men fired wildly. One officer and two wounded sepoys were dropped on the ground. The officer lay on his back. A tall man in dirty-white linen pounced on him with a sword. It was a horrible sight.

Churchill was already developing the style, which he used so effectively in his later books, of using short, breathless sentences to suggest the feeling of combat.

He used this experience to publish his first book, *The Story of the Malakand Field Force* (1898), a reworking of his newspaper columns. The introductory chapters of this book give the background to the conflict and describe the progress of the campaign before he arrived. It was Churchill's first excursion into the research and writing of history.

An aspect of Churchill's relatively short stay in India (about nineteen months) was his determination to in some way make up for his lack of a university education. He read steadily through the books sent to him by his mother. First came the volumes of Edward Gibbon and Thomas Babington Macaulay, which had an impact on his speeches and his writing, followed by Adam Smith's *Wealth of Nations* (1776), Charles Darwin's *Origin of Species* (1859), and Plato's *Republic* (in translation). He also read through twenty-seven volumes of the *Annual Register,* starting with the year of his birth (1874), and he pasted in his own summaries and commentaries on the politics of this period. Already he was preparing for a career beyond the military.

The Story of the Malakand Field Force brought Churchill considerable notice in England and some critical and financial success. The vigorous and colorful descriptions of military actions and the emphasis on the courage of British troops, a quality that he himself shared, became the hallmark of his military books. Also evident was his willingness to comment critically on government policies, a trait that garnered him his share of enemies in the future and almost immediately caused him difficulty in the achievement of the next adventure he had planned.

Early in 1898 it was evident that the British government was prepared to launch the final push against the government of the Khalifa in the Sudan, where, in 1885, the British general Charles Gordon had been killed at Khartoum. The expedition against Omdurman, now the capital of the Sudan, was led by Sir Herbert Kitchener, the commander of the Egyptian army, and included a sizable contingent of British troops. Churchill was determined to be part of that expedition. Kitchener, aware of the inconvenience of having as part of his forces an officer/newspaper correspondent who could be critical of the actions of his superiors, strongly resisted, and it took considerable lobbying by Jennie Churchill and various other allies to get Churchill attached to the Twenty-first Lancers. The literary result of this adventure was *The River War: An Historical Account of the Reconquest of the Soudan* (1899), a book that fulfilled Kitchener's misgivings about having Churchill accompany the expedition. Criticisms published in the book, even though he omitted or modified most of them in later editions, laid the groundwork for the coolness between the two men when they were colleagues in the Liberal cabinet at the beginning of World War I–Churchill as First Lord of the Admiralty and Kitchener as Secretary for War–a coolness that was exacerbated by differences of opinion on the Dardanelles Campaign of 1915.

The River War begins with four chapters of background to the conflict in the Sudan and several more on the initial campaigns before Churchill's arrival on the scene. There are detailed descriptions of the battles, including those that did not go well for the British. Describing the scene when the Mahdist forces overwhelmed the defensive lines of General Gordon in Khartoum in 1885, Churchill wrote: "Mad with the joy of victory and religious frenzy, they rushed upon him [Gordon] and, while he disdained even to fire his revolver, stabbed him in many places. The body fell down the steps and lay—a twisted heap—at the foot. There it was decapitated." But the most memorable and colorful description of battle came when Churchill himself was part of the cavalry charge of the Twenty-first Lancers at the Battle of Omdurman:

> Stubborn and unshaken infantry hardly ever meet stubborn and unshaken cavalry. Either the infantry run away and are cut down in flight, or they keep their head and destroy nearly all the horsemen by their musketry. On this occasion two living walls had actually crashed together. The Dervishes fought manfully. They tried to hamstring the horses. They fired their rifles, pressing the muzzles into the very bodies of their opponents. They cut reins and stirrup-leathers. They flung their throwing spears with great dexterity. They tried every device of cool, determined men practiced in war and familiar with cavalry; and, besides, they swung sharp, heavy swords which bit deep.

The charge, like the more famous Charge of the Light Brigade in the Crimean War, might have been, militarily, a mistake; but it was, like its predecessor, a glorious exploit, and Churchill, in the middle of it, shared in the glory.

This glory was already made known to the public through his columns in the *Morning Post,* which enabled Churchill not only to dine with the political elite in England but also to aspire, not yet twenty-five years old, to a political career. He ran as a Conservative candidate in a by-election and lost but did well enough to give himself some encouragement for the future. His potential, however, still needed some more development, and his opportunity came with the beginning of the Boer War in South Africa in 1899.

Fourth Churchill had resigned his commission in the Hussars before the byelection in 1899, but he sailed for South Africa both as a well-paid correspondent for the *Morning Post* and with a promise of a commission in the Lancashire Hussars. This dual position certainly made ambiguous his later claim to be a noncombatant, and there is some doubt whether his activities after the armored train that he was accompanying was wrecked could be viewed as strictly noncombatant, though he was unarmed (his pistol having been lost in the confusion of the wreck) when he was captured by the Boers. Shortly before he was to be released as a noncombatant from the prison camp in Pretoria, he escaped and made his way down the railway to the Portuguese port of Lourenço Marques, an adventure he described in detail in his *London to Ladysmith via Pretoria* (1900) and repeated with relish in *My Early Life*. The publicity of both his capture and his escape gained him a great deal of attention in England, as did his account of the Boer War campaigns in *London to Ladysmith via Pretoria* and *Ian Hamilton's March: Together with Extracts from the Diary of Lieutenant H. Frankland, a Prisoner of War at Pretoria* (1900).

Upon Churchill's return to England in 1900, he ran again as a Conservative candidate in the election of that year, and this time was elected as part of the Conservative victory in an election much of which was fought on the imperial issues of war in South Africa. Almost immediately he began a lucrative lecture tour in Britain recounting his South African adventures, and a somewhat less lucrative tour in the United States. The income from his public lectures gave him the financial resources to sit in Parliament, necessary because members of Parliament were not paid. Back in London he began working out a speaking style in Parliament that was most effective for him. He quickly learned that it was best to have a major speech fully prepared and largely written out, and then memorized, and soon he was speaking with some impact. Meanwhile he began a serious questioning of his political opinions and allegiances.

While he was in India, Churchill began his one and only novel, *Savrola: A Tale of the Revolution in Laurania,* serialized in 1899 and published in 1900. It included something of a political statement that could be attributed to Churchill himself. The heroine, Lucille, modeled idealistically on Churchill's mother, is married to Molara, the dictator of Laurania, but is attracted to Savrola, a patrician with democratic tendencies, modeled on Churchill himself, or perhaps his father. Savrola is ambitious but desirous to bring liberty, fairness, peace, and prosperity to the people. He is also a man of great courage and manages, despite violence, bombardment, betrayal, and exile, to establish a more just state for his people. The book is idealistic and romantic and continues to be reprinted.

While serving his apprenticeship in Parliament, Churchill was busy working on a biography of his father, *Lord Randolph Churchill,* published in two volumes in 1906 and still recognized, despite some shortcomings, as one of his best works. The book was an act of homage to a father whom he admired but to whom he never had been able to get close. In this biography, Churchill concentrated on the more successful aspects of Lord Randolph's political career and presented him in the best light possible. He saw his father's Fourth Party and his championing of Tory democracy as an embodiment of Savrola's patrician concern for the working class, and he gave this policy more consistency than Lord Randolph, essentially an opportunist in politics, ever had. Churchill decided that his father's liberal principles would be his own, and this decision was the catalyst for the first big switch in his political career.

The occasion for Churchill's growing dissatisfaction with the Conservative Party was the emerging split within the party over Joseph Chamberlain's tariff reform campaign and Prime Minister Alfred Balfour's attempt to shut down divisive debate by party members instead of coming out clearly, as Churchill wanted, in favor of continuing the Free Trade policy that had dominated political economic theory in Britain for at least a half century. Churchill saw himself as standing for cheap food for the working class. This conviction, and the feeling that the Conservative Party lacked any commitment to social reform, as well as a sense of frustration over the lack of any apparent movement in his own political career, led Churchill to defect to the Liberal Party in 1904. His victory in the election of 1906 was part of a Liberal landslide majority.

Though the switch in party allegiance earned Churchill the enduring hostility of many Conservatives and did not overcome the suspicions of many of his new Liberal colleagues, his political ambitions certainly were realized. From 1905 to 1915 he was continuously in office. He started out as Under Secretary for the Colonies, a position in which he was a constant trial to the Colonial Secretary Lord Elgin, who was continually faced with the task of keeping his subordinate's enthusiasm in some sort of check. Together they tried to deal with the constitutional aftereffects of the Boer War and the annexation of the two Boer republics. While in this office, Churchill went on a four-month tour of East Africa in 1907–1908, partially for some sport, and partially because of his interest in colonial problems, which he proceeded to analyze in detail. The product of this tour was a slim volume, *My African Journey* (1908).

Shortly after Churchill's return from South Africa in 1908, he was promoted to the cabinet as president of the Board of Trade. He also met Clementine Ogilvy Hozier, a twenty-two-year-old woman of "flawless beauty" (as Violet Bonham Carter recalled in a 1965 memoir), and they were married in September. Theirs was a long and affectionate relationship in which her only real rival was politics—even on their honeymoon Churchill carried on an extensive political correspondence. As much as it was within her power, she was often a moderating influence on some of his more extreme enthusiasms. They had five children: a son, Randolph, and four daughters, Diana, Sarah, Marigold (who died in 1921, aged two years and nine months), and Mary.

In 1910 Churchill succeeded David Lloyd George as Home Secretary. While at the Board of Trade and as Home Secretary, he worked with Lloyd George on the social legislation that began Britain's journey to becoming a social welfare state. Labor exchanges, old-age pensions, unemployment insurance, and a national health-insurance scheme helped Churchill to fulfill, as he saw it, his duty to the working classes. On the other hand, as his duties as Home Secretary called for the maintenance of order in the increasingly volatile labor unrest between 1910 and 1914 and led to his dispatch of police and military units to strikebound areas, such actions gave him a reputation for being antilabor.

In 1911 Churchill became First Lord of the Admiralty and was immediately transported from the more mundane duties of looking after the welfare of the people to the exciting international arena of enhancing national defense in the increasingly tense era preceding the outbreak of World War I. He was now working in the same milieu as had his illustrious ancestor, the first duke of Marlborough, and circumstances placed him in a situation that could win him a considerable amount of glory. In the meantime, he was thrust into the middle of the emotional debates of the naval race with Germany and the battle over appropriations for the construction of more dreadnoughts.

Churchill consistently supported a dreadnought construction program designed to keep Britain well ahead of any German construction, and naval estimates increased substantially. As the international crisis deepened in 1913 and 1914, he was one of the first cabinet ministers to see the necessity of supporting Foreign Minister Lord Grey's policy of backing France in the event of war. When the fighting did break out in August 1914, he plunged with enthusiasm into the organization of war, though naval disasters at the beginning somewhat dimmed his luster. Still, he was willing to undertake such adventures as personally organizing the evacuation of Antwerp and pressing on his colleagues plans for ending the stalemate on the Western Front. That last endeavor landed him in a project that spelled temporary disaster to his career.

With the French and the British bogged down facing the Germans in trenches across Belgium and France, from the English Channel to Switzerland, and with their Russian allies having serious difficulties keeping their armies adequately equipped to prevail against the Germans, Austrians, and Turks, Churchill proposed a flank attack, first of all in the north, with an invasion of Schleswig-Holstein from the sea. When this plan met with opposition, he picked up a scheme for a naval attack through the Dardanelles to Constantinople, to drive the Turks out of the war, to encourage the Greeks, the Bulgarians, and the Romanians to ally against the Germans, and to open up a direct channel of supply to and from Russia. The attack could be by ships alone or with a coordinated land campaign on the Gallipoli Peninsula. Churchill quickly became a convert to the Dardanelles scheme and in December 1914 began planning for a naval attack alone, barely noticing growing opposition from his colleagues, most ominously from Lord Fisher, Churchill's own choice as First Sea Lord. When the naval attack failed, possibly because it had not been pushed vigorously enough, and a land operation was now added to the plan, Lord Kitchener was distinctly not enthusiastic about diversions of troops from the Western Front. British and Imperial troops began arriving at Gallipoli piecemeal, allowing the Turks to rally their defenses, and several months of murderous battle followed, with the allies pinned to the beaches, until the expedition was withdrawn in December 1915. By this time Churchill was no longer First Lord of the Admiralty.

Churchill had fallen from his exalted position as one of the architects of the British war effort as a result of several factors. His "impetuousness," a term often used about Churchill by his colleagues, had led him to attempt to interfere in areas outside of his own specific responsibility, which created tension even with old allies, such as Lord Grey at the Foreign Office and Lloyd George, Chancellor of the Exchequer. The enthusiasm of his support for the Dardanelles project, often frustrated by the timidity and incompetence of field commanders at the local level, made Churchill an obvious and convenient scapegoat for the fiasco. Most importantly, the prime minister, Herbert Asquith, who had tolerated Churchill's eccentricities, had come to the reluctant conclusion that a coalition with the Conservatives was essential to pursue the war, but the price of their leader, Bonar Law, was the dismissal of Churchill from the Admiralty.

The loss of the Admiralty and the revelation of how little support he had in the Liberal Party was a severe blow to Churchill and threw him into a period of the depression that hounded him throughout his life—"black dog" as he called it. His wife came to his rescue with a diversion. Churchill, who had never been interested in art, was persuaded to try experiments with his children's paint boxes, and these efforts captured his interest. He quickly abandoned the pastels of watercolors in favor of the boldness of oils; his skill improved, and painting became his hobby and passion for the rest of his life. In "Painting as a Pastime," included in his book of essays *Thoughts and Adventures* (1932), Churchill wrote about the time when he was dismissed from the Admiralty: "Like a sea-beast fished up from the depths, or a diver too suddenly hoisted, my veins threatened to burst from the fall in pressure. I had great anxiety and no means of relieving it; I had vehement convictions and small power to give effect to them." From this dilemma painting rescued him, and he found that he could distract his mind even from politics for long periods of time.

By July 1917 Churchill's political fortunes had revived, and he appeared to have been forgiven the Dardanelles debacle, if not by everyone, at least by his prime minister. Lloyd George wanted Churchill in the critical Munitions Ministry because, like Lloyd George himself, he could stir things up, push people, get things done, and could keep crucial munitions production at the level that Lloyd George's control of that ministry had already achieved. Churchill, who was as usual constantly coming up with ideas and could not help trespassing on the territories of other ministries, did provide plenty of shells for the endless artillery barrages of the Western Front and also began producing large numbers of tanks for what he believed would be the final offensive in 1919, after the Americans had arrived in strength.

The downfall of the Lloyd George coalition, precipitated by a Conservative backbench revolt against continuing the wartime alliance and the defeat of the Lloyd George Liberals in the election of 1922, included Churchill's losing decisively in his own constituency. He lost again, running as a Liberal, in the general election of 1923, and as an Independent Anti-Socialist in a 1924 by-election, before winning in the 1924 general election as a Constitutionalist. With no Conservative opponent in this last election, the victory marked a way station on his migration back to the Conservative Party. It also provided him with a safe House of Commons seat, in Epping, for the rest of his life. Meanwhile, he had on his mind the vindication of his disgrace over the Dardanelles, and he had begun work on *The World Crisis: 1911–1918,* published in six volumes (1923–1931).

The volumes of *The World Crisis* sold well. Here was the story of a tremendous conflict, told by an insider. It was full of maps, statistical tables, and extracts from the letters of the participants of the great drama, all set in the vivid if sometimes overblown style of a master storyteller, speaking of bloody battles in the military sphere and tense struggles in the political. It established, at least to Churchill's own satisfaction, how he could have won the war years earlier if he had had full control and support in the Dardanelles Campaign from the beginning. Arthur Balfour, his sometimes friend and sometimes enemy, lightly mocked *The World*

Crisis as "Winston's brilliant autobiography, disguised as world history." John Maynard Keynes, the prominent economist who was no friend of Churchill's economic policies in the 1920s, nevertheless wrote an admiring review in the *Nation* (9 March 1929):

> The chronicle is finished. With what feelings does one lay down Mr. Churchill's two-thousandth page? Gratitude to one who can write with so much eloquence and feeling of things which are part of the lives of all of us of the war generation, but which he saw and knew much closer and clearer. Admiration for his energies of mind and his intense absorption of intellectual interest and elemental emotion on what is for the moment the matter in hand–which is his best quality. A little envy, perhaps, for his undoubting conviction that frontiers, races, patriotisms, even wars if need be, are ultimate verities for mankind, which lends for him a kind of dignity and even nobility to events, which for others are only a nightmare interlude, something to be permanently avoided.

Having moved practically to the doorstep of the Conservative Party in the election of 1924, Churchill was invited the rest of the way when Prime Minister Stanley Baldwin offered him the cabinet post of Chancellor of the Exchequer, a post he held until the defeat of the Conservatives in the election of 1929. He approached his new ministry with his usual vigor, and at the same time he contributed a stream of advice to Baldwin on all matters political.

The Labour Party formed the government in 1929, and in the aftermath a growing rift developed between Churchill and most of the Conservative leadership over the issue of constitutional advances in India. When the Labour government, unable to cope with enormous problems because of the Depression, yielded to the formation of a coalition national government with Labour leader Ramsay MacDonald as prime minister–a coalition that, after the election of 1931, was massively supported by the Conservative Party–Churchill was not asked to be in the cabinet. Even more revealing of his isolation, when Baldwin succeeded MacDonald as prime minister in 1935, Baldwin felt no need to offer a cabinet office to his former Chancellor of the Exchequer. Churchill's political career appeared to be effectively over.

Churchill had a congenial distraction while he was pursuing his ultimately futile opposition to Indian reform. He became involved in the rehabilitation of the political reputation of the first duke of Marlborough, who, Churchill felt, had been unjustly maligned by the nineteenth-century historian Thomas Babington Macaulay in his multivolume *History of England from the Accession of James II* (1848–1861). Macaulay had depicted the duke as lacking sexual, political, and financial morality and had labeled him a traitor. The research for Churchill's four-volume *Marlborough: His Life and Times* (1933–1938) probably began in 1931 or 1932; Churchill employed several researchers and visited the battlefields. The writing of these lengthy volumes proceeded briskly, and there were respectable sales in both Britain and the United States. In the same period he finished *Thoughts and Adventures* and *Great Contemporaries,* the latter not published until 1937 and revised in 1938, 1943, and 1958. In 1932 he also received from a publisher a considerable advance for the four volumes of *A History of the English-Speaking Peoples,* finished in 1939 but not published until the 1950s, after extensive revisions. In addition to all these works, Churchill contributed well-paying articles to journals and newspapers. Since he could no longer rely on the salary of a cabinet minister, he counted on his writings to maintain an income large enough to keep his family in the lifestyle that Churchill expected.

Churchill's war against the leadership of the Conservative Party over the issue of Indian constitutional reform, during which he had fought fruitlessly to alert the British public to the dangers being posed both to India and to the British Empire, had serious consequences for the other great crusade upon which he embarked in the 1930s. Churchill had badgered so persistently and had made claims about the consequences of ignoring the warnings that were essentially incapable of proof until a considerable period of time had passed, if at all, that he had undermined his credibility when he began to warn the leadership and the country of the dangers posed by Adolf Hitler's Germany.

In *The Gathering Storm,* the first of his six volumes on *The Second World War* (1948–1953), Churchill outlines how his growing apprehension over the Nazi threat had become acute in 1936 when German troops marched into the Rhineland, which had been demilitarized by the Treaty of Versailles in 1919. His speeches in Parliament and in public at times were followed with close attention and at other times were disregarded because they ran counter to the prevailing desire not only for keeping estimates for the armed forces low, but also for disarmament and the avoidance of armed conflict. Churchill desperately wanted to be in the cabinet, where he could exert greater pressure on his colleagues to heed his warnings. But if MacDonald, whom he despised, had ignored him, as did Baldwin, with whom his friendly relations of the 1920s had suffered because of the India quarrel, Churchill did not get any more consideration from Neville Chamberlain, who became prime minister in 1937, a move Churchill had supported. Chamberlain feared bringing Churchill into his cabinet because, as he explained, "If I take him into the Cabinet he will dominate it. He won't give others a

MEMORANDUM OF AGREEMENT, made this twenty-ninth day of July 1930, between WINSTON S. CHURCHILL, of London, England, hereinafter called "the Author", and CHARLES SCRIBNER'S SONS, of New York City, U.S.A., hereinafter called "the Publishers", their successors and assigns, WHEREBY it is mutually agreed as follows respecting a work by said Author tentatively entitled MEMOIRS:

1. The Publishers shall, during the legal term of copyright and renewals thereof, have the sole and exclusive right of publishing the said work in volume form in the English language throughout the United States of America ~~and the Dominion of Canada~~. It is understood that the Author retains the right of serial publication.

2. The Author guarantees to the Publishers that the said work is in no way whatever a violation of any existing copyright and that it contains nothing of a libellous or scandalous character, and that he will indemnify the Publishers from all suits, claims, and proceedings, damages and costs, which may be made, taken or incurred by or against them on the ground that the said work is an infringement of copyright or contains anything libellous or scandalous.

3. Said Publishers, in consideration of the right herein granted and of the guarantees aforesaid, agree to publish said work at their own expense, in such style and manner as they shall deem most expedient, and to pay said Author the following royalties and moneys:

(a) A royalty of FIFTEEN (15) per cent. of the published price on the first ~~ten thousand (10,000)~~ copies of said work sold by them in the United States of America and TWENTY (20) per cent. for all copies sold thereafter.

~~(b) A royalty of TEN (10) per cent. of the published price on all copies of said work sold by them in the Dominion of Canada.~~

(c) Ten (10) per cent. of the sum received from the sale of any copies of said work as a remainder. The Author shall first be given the option for sixty days of purchasing such copies at the price the Publishers reasonably expect to get in the open market.

No royalties shall be payable upon any copies given away for the purpose of review or in the interests of the sale, or for the purpose of securing publicity for the said work.

~~(d) A total sum in advance and on account of said royalties of Twenty-five Hundred Dollars ($2,500.00), payable on the date of publication of said work.~~

4. The sum of Two Hundred Dollars ($200.00) shall be allowed by the Publishers for author's alterations, to be remitted to said Author if no author's alterations are made in the American edition of said work.

5. The first statement shall not be rendered until six months after date of publication; and thereafter statements shall be rendered semi-annually, in the months of February and August, settlements to be made in cash four months after date of statement.

If the Publishers give notice at any time that, in their opinion, the demand for said work has ceased, or if the said work be allowed to go out of print and they neglect to issue a new edition within six months of having received written notice thereof, then in any of these cases all rights conveyed under this agreement shall revert to the Author without further notice.

Said Publishers shall have the right, when the sales of the full-priced editions shall render it advisable, to publish a cheaper edition of said work and shall pay a royalty of TEN (10) per cent. of the published price of such cheaper edition or editions, on every copy sold.

The Author shall receive on publication six presentation copies of said work, and shall be entitled to purchase further copies for personal use at the lowest Trade price.

In consideration of the mutuality of this contract, the aforesaid parties agree to all its provisions, and in testimony thereof affix their signatures and seals.

Witness to signature of
Winston S. Churchill

Witness to signature of
Charles Scribner's Sons

Pages from the publishing contract, annotated by Churchill, for Churchill's volume of recollections, published in the United States by Scribners in 1930 as A Roving Commission: My Early Life *(Rare Books and Special Collections, Princeton University Libraries)* chance of even talking." Chamberlain preferred to be the dominant force in his cabinet.

Churchill developed many sources of information, even in the Foreign Office, and used the statistical information fed to him on the extent of German rearmament to reveal the growing strength of Germany and the momentum that would soon enable the Germans to undermine the security of even Britain and France. When Chamberlain flew to Munich to meet Hitler and returned home with the agreement that destroyed Czechoslovakia's barriers against German attack (and shortly destroyed the independence of that state), Duff Cooper resigned from the cabinet, following the earlier resignation of Anthony Eden. Churchill was building allies among the younger leaders of the Conservatives. He commented in Parliament on what had happened in the negotiations on the Czech state: "£1 was demanded at the pistol's point. When it was given, £2 were demanded at the pistol's point. Finally the dictator consented to take £1.17s6d. and the rest in promises of goodwill for the future." He continued that this concession was not the end of the problem but rather the beginning of a process that would compel Britain to fight for freedom. If Churchill's stand against the Nazi threat was not as consistent as he later maintained in *The Gathering Storm,* it was still intensive enough in speeches and newspaper articles to ensure that when his dire predictions were vindicated, and Chamberlain led Britain into war with Germany in 1939 upon the German invasion of Poland, Churchill was brought into the cabinet, once again in the Admiralty.

The war for Churchill at the Admiralty, as well as for the nation, did not begin well. Churchill busied himself organizing the safety of the sea-lanes for the merchant fleet and launching a vigorous campaign against the German U-boats that were claiming casualties even in what had been considered protected areas. This campaign was a major concern throughout the war; protecting Britain's vital supply lines extended eventually from the hunting of the submarines at sea to air attacks on their bases and manufacturing facilities. The British navy was also unable to prevent what became a successful German attack on and occupation of Norway.

Though the main brunt of the fighting had to this point been borne by the navy, the blame for the lack of success was pinned not on Churchill, who had the advantage of being only recently on the job, but on Chamberlain. Discontent within the country was matched by growing restlessness within Parliament, and the Labour opposition was soon joined in criticism by an increasing number of Conservatives. Chamberlain's attempt to create a national coalition was effectively stymied by Labour's refusal to serve in a Chamberlain cabinet, and soon pressure mounted from senior members of his own supporters within the Conservatives to make way for a new prime minister. When Chamberlain reluctantly bent to this pressure, the question of a successor became paramount. Public opinion polls placed Churchill narrowly in second place to Eden, but Chamberlain's own preference was his Foreign Secretary, Lord Halifax. It was a preference shared by many leaders of all parties, on the grounds that Churchill was too impetuous. However, this preference was not shared by Halifax, who correctly realized that with Churchill in the cabinet, an essential, Churchill would soon be running the entire war effort—he was already up to his old habits at the Admiralty of poaching on the responsibilities of other ministers—and he might as well have the entire responsibility. Since Halifax would not budge, Chamberlain gave way, and on 10 May 1940, King George VI requested that Churchill form a new administration.

Churchill quickly formed a small war cabinet, consisting of himself, the two leading members of the Labour Party—Clement Attlee and Arthur Greenwood—and Halifax and Chamberlain, who efficiently and loyally served in this cabinet until cancer forced him to resign a few months later. For Churchill, a coalition forced him to maintain a careful balancing act, with representatives in the larger cabinet from Labour and the Liberals, as well as from various factions of the Conservatives. In addition, he from time to time brought in individuals from outside the parliamentary ranks to make use of their talents and influence. To Parliament in his opening speech he offered an example of his talent for coining memorable phrases: "I have nothing to offer but blood, toil, tears and sweat." Even discounting his immediate invigoration of the war effort in the administration, and the ceaseless monitoring of events and possibilities that could bring Britain to victory, Churchill's speeches in Parliament and on the radio offered the inspiration that Britain stood in great need of in the many dark years of warfare to follow.

The life of Churchill to the end of the war was the history of the British participation in World War II; he almost literally lived at his office for most of the week, to be in close contact with events. When he felt it necessary, he attempted direct diplomacy and flew to Paris after Germany invaded France in an effort to prop up the quickly fading French war effort. When Hitler invaded Russia in 1941, Churchill put on hold his long-standing opposition to the Soviet state to offer aid: "If Hitler invaded Hell, I would at least make a favorable reference to the Devil in the House of Commons." Following up, in 1942 he flew to Moscow to meet Joseph Stalin and explain why Britain was not yet in a position to open a second front on the European continent.

Almost ceaselessly he worked to get the moral and material support of the United States.

Churchill had spent considerable periods of time after 1929 touring in the United States, and his books were almost as well known there as in Britain. He did not hesitate to claim kinship to the Americans because of his mother. He found a sympathetic audience in President Franklin Delano Roosevelt, who worked hard to overcome the isolationism that had dominated American opinion and politics since 1919. In 1941 this sympathy bore fruit when Britain and its dominions stood virtually alone facing imminent invasion by the victorious Germans. The American Congress passed a Lend-Lease Bill, which provided Britain with material and financial resources. When the Americans entered the war after the Japanese attack on Pearl Harbor on 7 December 1941, the relationship and cooperation between Churchill and Roosevelt grew even closer as they met in Casablanca in 1943 to discuss war strategy after the elimination of the Germans from North Africa. The two allies also met twice in Quebec, in 1943 and 1944.

It was good to have allies as powerful as the Americans and the Russians. The Russians had hung on, stubbornly bringing the German juggernaut to a halt and then, in return, began destroying the German armies on their road to Berlin. The Americans and the British in 1943 opened up a "second front," invaded Italy, and in a series of hard-fought battles, pushed their way up the peninsula, and drove Italy out of the war. In June 1944, D-Day landings in Normandy began the process of clearing the Netherlands, Belgium, and France of German forces, and early in 1945 a Canadian army including British forces crossed the Rhine River with an American army, opening a campaign that led to the final disintegration of the German armies. While the British military were now on the winning end of the war, Churchill was at times less than happy with his powerful allies, as his fertile ideas on the conduct of the war and the postwar settlement met with frequent defeat.

When Germany finally collapsed and surrendered in May 1945, Churchill's pleasure in the victory was marred by his premonition of a Soviet-dominated Europe. He was tired and unwell, but performed his duties. He lunched with the king, made a victory speech on the radio and one in Parliament, spoke to vast crowds celebrating victory in the streets, attended a thanksgiving service, and dined with members of his family. He then faced the prospect of the continuation of the war with Japan, and the collapse of the coalition in the House of Commons, which had seen Britain through all the difficulties of the European campaign. Partisan politics reemerged.

Having just fought a war with the help of the leaders of the Labour Party, whom he was to praise as valuable and loyal colleagues, Churchill in the election campaign in the summer of 1945 apparently rediscovered all his old antipathies to socialism. He proceeded to state openly that a Labour government would institute programs that would bring in the initial stages of a totalitarian state. If this claim was designed as a scare tactic, it did not work with the majority of the voters. It was soon clear that while Churchill was popular, the party he led, perceived as having left Britain in poor shape to face Hitler, was not yet forgiven by the British electorate. Churchill was disappointed when Labour won a landslide victory.

Out of office, and merely a spectator as the war against Japan came to an end in August with the dropping of the atomic bombs on Hiroshima and Nagasaki, Churchill turned once again to the portion of his life's work that he had set aside for the six years of war. He began to write, working on what became a best-seller both in Britain and the United States, his six volumes of *The Second World War*. Though his publishers had initially feared that the volumes were overdocumented for the public taste, these fears did not appear to be justified. The book-buying public warmed to the authentic voice of one of the major and best-known participants in that great event; readers felt that they were being let in on the great affairs of state that had remained hidden to them. Though a work of history, it was also a memoir of a remarkable period of Churchill's life, and Churchill was now a public figure of such dimension that a memoir appealed to people who in their various ways had shared in the events that he described.

While Churchill was busy writing, the Labour government was having its difficulties trying to run a state with resources that had been seriously depleted during the war. Its program of reforms had to give way too often to the need for austerity, and not unnaturally many people were disenchanted with the slow pace of Britain's economic recovery. When the election of 1950 was held, the landslide majority melted away to a slim majority of fewer than twenty seats over the combined total of the opposition, most of whom were Conservatives. The Labour cabinet ministers still failed to find answers to the problems that faced the nation, and, discouraged by a fractious opposition and a dwindling majority, Attlee wearily called another election in the autumn of 1951. Labour polled more votes than the Conservatives, but the Conservatives had achieved a majority, though a smaller one than Churchill predicted. It was enough. Churchill was once again prime minister and had won his first election as leader of a political party.

While in opposition Churchill had assumed the role of European elder statesman, and in a major speech delivered in Zurich in 1946 he put his case for a united Europe that would feature a partnership between France and a revived Germany. This unity was a theme he promoted over the next few years; but Churchill was vague about just what Britain's role in such a union would be. Clearly Britain was an integral part of the core of Europe, and France would need its help to balance Germany in the future. On the other hand, Churchill could not envision Britain without its empire or the Commonwealth that was continuing to emerge from the empire. Just as clearly, the Commonwealth could not fit within the framework of a united Europe. His great idea of a united Europe did not appeal to the Labour government that was still busy trying to find the resources for its own great ideas. Now, as prime minister, Churchill bent his efforts to achieve another one of his plans.

Churchill, who had never been comfortable with the high casualty rates in the war and had second-guessed himself about the appropriateness of the bombing that destroyed the German city of Dresden, was appalled when nuclear advances had led to the creation of the hydrogen bomb. While he somewhat favored the bomb as a deterrent, he knew his history well enough to believe that a weapon once created had every chance of being used, as the atomic bomb had been in Japan. The impact of a hydrogen bomb explosion detonated in anger would be horrendous, and Churchill tried to persuade President Dwight Eisenhower and Stalin to hold a summit conference that would solve the outstanding problems of the Cold War and end the specter of a devastating war between the superpowers. To Churchill's great disappointment, Stalin and Eisenhower and their advisers were not interested, and international rivalries and tensions continued unabated.

Churchill's health appeared to be holding up. He was careful to get medical attention as soon as anything troubled him, and occasionally he traveled with his doctor in tow for added security. But in June 1953 he suffered a minor stroke, which incapacitated him for a period of time. From that point there was increasing talk of his retiring to allow Eden to succeed him, and to a certain extent Churchill fed the speculation. Finally, on 5 April 1955, he succumbed to increasing pressure and resigned, but kept his seat in Parliament.

In October 1953 Churchill learned he had won the Nobel Prize in Literature, "for his mastery of historical and biographical description as well as for brilliant oratory in defending exalted human values," as the citation read. He could not attend the ceremonies in Stockholm in December, but King Gustav VI Adolf of Sweden presented him with the award at the Swedish Embassy in London on 12 November. The award pleased Churchill, especially the monetary prize; he wrote to his wife, "£12,100 free of tax. Not so bad." Biographer Roy Jenkins reports that Churchill later said he would rather have been given the Nobel Peace Prize; but that award might have been controversial, because many people considered Churchill a warmonger. The Nobel Prize had little effect on his career, because of his age and fragile health.

For the last ten years of his life, Churchill went into gradual but obvious decline. He suffered a series of small strokes, a broken leg, and a reduction in his indulgent lifestyle. He had to cut down on his brandy and his trademark cigars; he had to resist his wife's pressuring him to go on a diet; and he had to have a male nurse to watch over him in case of further falls. He took vacations in the Mediterranean and grieved as many of his old friends died. He suffered through the suicide of his daughter Diana in 1963. While he could, he undertook the revisions of *A History of the English-Speaking Peoples,* published in four volumes.

Churchill was made an honorary citizen of the United States in 1963. Even though he was not able to attend the ceremony, and was represented by his son Randolph, he appreciated the honor granted him by the American Congress, as he had appreciated the honor of being allowed to address Congress on three occasions, in 1941, 1942, and 1952. Churchill felt his inheritance from his mother had stood him well, and though often frustrated with American policy, he clearly recognized the importance for Britain of American friendship.

Churchill suffered another stroke early in 1965, and on 24 January he died. He was given a state funeral, a rare honor for one not of royal blood. His body lay in state in Westminster Hall, and the funeral was held in St. Paul's Cathedral. A special train carried him to his burial place in the churchyard at Bladon, next to the Blenheim Palace estate where he had been born more than ninety years earlier.

Churchill ended his life as perhaps the best-known British statesman of all time. A partial explanation for his good fortune appears to be that Churchill arrived on the political scene not simply as a Churchill, or the son of a noted father, but as a known author whose works were reasonably well read. He was a capable writer who had a penchant for heroics and the ability and opportunity to highlight his actions. He therefore entered the House of Commons in 1900 as a star, a relatively minor one perhaps, but still a star. Once he moved to the Liberal Party and was given political office, he was able to translate the experience and skills he had developed as an author into the ability to organize the departments that he was placed in charge of, a skill that was appreciated by his superiors in the party.

Churchill also could expound and defend his actions in government both vocally, in the House of Commons, or in writing, usually effectively. With Churchill, speechwriting was an aspect of his literary pursuits, and the two processes gradually intertwined. He also continued writing specifically for publication, and the publications kept his name before the public even when he was not in office. Newspapers and book publishers often competed for the privilege of publishing his work and were willing to pay handsomely, because his writing was popular enough with the public to be profitable. Churchill made his living through his writings and maintained a lifestyle at a comfortable, even indulgent, level.

Included in the scope of Churchill's histories are his biographies of his father and the duke of Marlborough as well as the fragments of his autobiography, *My African Journey* and *My Early Life*. His books of essays, *Thoughts and Adventures* and *Great Contemporaries,* are about his adventures and the great men he has known who had made an impact upon him. The novel *Savrola* is his heroic and romantic dream. Even *A History of the English-Speaking Peoples,* published after he had received the Nobel Prize, represents Churchill's definition of who he really was and reflected his strong patriotism. His type of history, based on the personal element of his life, in the hands of a skilled writer, automatically creates with it an interested readership, carried along by emotion and pointed relevance. They were histories that used the past to illuminate the present.

Churchill was mainly a storyteller, and the storyteller must deal with the specific, the individual whose actions must be described and to some extent understood and explained. One of the hardest tasks of a master storyteller is to create an atmosphere that catches the readers immediately. One example in Churchill's work is his description in *The World Crisis* of Britain's entry into World War I:

> It was 11 o'clock at night—12 by German time—when the ultimatum expired. The windows of the Admiralty were thrown wide open in the warm night air. Under the roof from which Nelson had received his orders were gathered a small group of Admirals and Captains and a cluster of clerks, pencil in hand, waiting. Along the Mall from the direction of the Palace the sound of an immense concourse singing "God save the King" floated in. On this deep wave there broke the chimes of Big Ben; and, as the first stroke of the hour boomed out, a rustle of movement swept across the room. The war telegram, which meant "Commence hostilities against Germany," was flashed to the ships and establishments under the White Ensign all over the world.

> I walked across the Horse Guards Parade to the Cabinet room and reported to the Prime Minister and the Ministers who were assembled there that the deed was done.

It is simple and direct, not the kind of prose that would have the ordinary reader reaching for a dictionary, and it brought the reader immediately into the event. In the same way, in his excellent descriptions of battle scenes, the narrative flows with an elegance that speaks of elevated heroism, and Churchill once more brings the reader directly into the center of the conflict. Some of the best examples come from *Marlborough: His Life and Times*. Churchill took great pains to present a balanced account of Marlborough's campaigns and battles and to give due credit to both his allies' contributions and the strategies and tactics of his opponents. Churchill tried to convey the sense of the deadly confrontations of the battles, as he did in his description of Marlborough's final great victory, Malplaquet, in 1709. One of Marlborough's allies, the young Prince of Orange, led his forces repeatedly against the French trenches:

> Here, in line with the Highlanders fought the redoubtable Dutch Blue Guards, the flower of their army. The Prince of Orange had most of his staff shot around him. General Oxenstiern fell dead at his side. The Prince's own horse collapsed, and he advanced on foot. . . . Concealed . . . was a nest of French batteries mounting twenty cannon. From these there now burst a horrible flanking fire of cannon-balls and grapeshot which tore through the Dutch and Scottish ranks, killing or wounding thousands of men as they moved in faultless discipline towards their goal. The ground was soon heaped with blue uniforms and Highlanders, over whom the rear attack moved forward steadily, paying their toll. Nevertheless the young Prince, his surviving generals, and Deputy Goslinga arrived, with the mass of the Dutch and the Scots, before the French entrenchments, endured their volleys at close quarters, tore away the abattis, stormed the parapets, and captured the works. But they were now too few.

Churchill's histories have not been without their critics, both immediately after they were published and up to the present. He was an amateur historian, not a trained professional. He wrote his histories too quickly, not giving himself sufficient time for reflection or checking. There were occasional errors of fact and, in the view of the critics, many errors of interpretation. Because the books were so centered on Churchill and his family, he was attacked for being self-serving, out to justify his policies during World War I, for example, or, in the case of his biographies, to whitewash the reputations of his father and of the duke of Marlborough. His coverage of what critics considered to be important topics was flawed; cultural, intellectual, social, and economic analyses were seldom present, if at all. Early in his writing career he had developed the habit of extensive quotations of documents in the belief (erroneous belief, said the critics) that the documents told the complete story better than the historian. This practice made some of his works much longer than they needed to be. And the justification for the quotation was further vitiated by the fact that Churchill was selective in his choice of documents. In *The Second World War,* critics pointed out, he constantly quoted his own letters and memoranda, seldom giving the replies. Documents in some of his histories were edited in such ways as to make them untrustworthy. Despite all these criticisms, Robin Prior, himself a critic of Churchill's *The World Crisis,* pointed out in a 1983 study that Churchill's histories have lived on when "more accurate works have been long forgotten."

Churchill's histories emphasized mainly politics and wars because these were subjects about which he felt most comfortable writing; he could use his own experiences to interpret the politics and wars of his time and of the past. He believed that an historian could and should judge people and events, though he was more likely to fully express his views on the distant past rather than on the periods when the people concerned were still living. An extensive portion of volume four of *A History of the English-Speaking Peoples* is given to a description of the American Civil War, in which he did not hesitate to judge the generals. He was clearly hostile to Ulysses S. Grant and his policy of attrition but was favorable to Robert E. Lee. Even with Lee, though, he could be critical if he felt criticism was merited; after the Battle of Gettysburg, Lee carried out a successful retreat: "He carried with him his wounded and his prisoners. He had lost only two guns, and the war."

For most of his histories, Churchill sought help. When writing the biography of his father, he made use of the information available from his father's still living contemporaries. For *The World Crisis* he received documents and other help from his own contemporaries. There were always friends to read his manuscripts and suggest corrections in grammar and punctuation and even advice on substance. In his last three lengthy works, *Marlborough: His Life and Times, The Second World War,* and *A History of the English-Speaking Peoples,* he employed research assistants to search out documents and to check facts. As he rewrote his manuscript for *A History of the English-Speaking Peoples* in the 1950s, he sought the advice of eminent scholars in the various periods of history he was covering. Some were even asked for papers on aspects of their specialties. Churchill, however, did not always take advice and would absorb the research and papers and rework them to fit his own interpretations and interests. The books he produced, no matter how much help he had along the way, were his own work, his own judgments, and written in his own style.

If Churchill had critics of his work as an historian, he also had critics of his style of writing and speaking. Manfred Weidhorn, an English professor and author of many works on Churchill, summarized many of these assessments in his 1979 study. Churchill was often redundant, sentimental, melodramatic, and portentous; he too frequently could not resist purple passages such as "I turn from the pink and ochre panorama of Athens and Piraeus, scintillating with delicious life and plumed by the classic glories and endless miseries and triumphs of its history" (from *Victory: War Speeches,* 1946). His style and language could be archaic, too closely suggestive of his early models, Gibbon and Macaulay. He was also prone to overuse of superlatives and exaggeration; too many events that he was involved in were presented as being vital or great moments in history.

On the other hand, Churchill's style of writing and speaking had many strengths. He was a master of creating memorable sentences and phrases such as those in his wartime speeches, recorded in *The Second World War:* "Never in the field of human conflict was so much owed by so many to so few," and "we shall defend our island, whatever the cost may be, we shall fight on the beaches, we shall fight on the landing-grounds, we shall fight in the fields and in the streets, we shall fight in the hills; we shall never surrender." Churchill's sense of humor is constantly present in all his works, but most notably in *My Early Life,* where much of the fun is at his own expense. Often his sense of involvement and emotion shines through.

Two passages from *The Second World War* are excellent examples of Churchill's style at its best. Near the end of the first volume, Churchill summarizes the impact of becoming prime minister:

> Thus, then, on the night of the tenth of May, at the outset of this mighty battle, I acquired the chief power in the State, which henceforth I wielded in ever-growing measure for five years and three months of world war, at the end of which time, all our enemies having surrendered unconditionally or being about to do so, I was immediately dismissed by the British electorate from all further conduct of their affairs.

This passage is succinct and powerful in its emotion. More exuberant was Churchill's reaction when he heard about the Japanese attack on Pearl Harbor:

> So we had won after all! Yes, after Dunkirk; after the fall of France; after the horrible episode of Oran; after the threat of invasion, when, apart from the Air and the

Navy, we were an almost unarmed people; after the deadly struggle of the U-boat war—the first Battle of the Atlantic, gained by a hands-breadth; after seventeen months of lonely fighting and nineteen months of my responsibility in dire stress, we had won the war. England would live; Britain would live; the Commonwealth of Nations and the Empire would live. How long the war would last or in what fashion it would end, no man could tell, nor did I at this moment care. Once again in our long Island history we should emerge, however mauled or mutilated, safe and victorious. We should not be wiped out. Our history would not come to an end.

Perceptions of style vary with the individual. Some people prefer the ornate, others stark simplicity. Most people can tolerate varying combinations of both. It is unlikely that many of the readers of Churchill's works have been or are bothered by the shortcomings of his style as perceived by his critics. Churchill's prose often reveals its power and attraction if read aloud. Churchill created the impression that he was talking to the reader, often because that was exactly what he was doing. He had fallen into the habit of dictating his works, whether they were books, speeches, newspaper articles, or memos to the civil servants of the departments he controlled. Maurice Ashley, the historian who was one of the researchers for Churchill's biography of the duke of Marlborough, described Churchill's system as it had evolved by 1930: "He would walk up and down the room (when I worked for him it was usually his bedroom) puffing at a cigar while a secretary patiently took it all down as best she could in Pitman. Occasionally he would say, 'Scrub that and start again.' At times he would stop . . .; at others he would be entirely swept on by the stimulus of his imagination." Churchill, with his writings, talked to people and took them into his confidence.

Siwertz, in his presentation speech for the awarding of the Nobel Prize in Literature in 1953, noted that "Churchill's eloquence in the fateful hours of freedom and human dignity was heart-stirring." Siwertz was referring to Churchill's speeches during World War II; but elements of this eloquence were always present in his written work and made him a fitting candidate for the Nobel Prize.

Letters:

Roosevelt and Churchill, Their Secret Wartime Correspondence, edited by Francis L. Loewenheim, Harold D. Langley, and Manfred Jonas (New York: Saturday Review Press, 1975);

Churchill & Roosevelt: The Complete Correspondence, 3 volumes, edited by Warren F. Kimball (Princeton: Princeton University Press, 1984);

The Secret History of World War II: The Ultra-Secret Wartime Letters and Cables of Roosevelt, Stalin and Churchill, edited by Stewart Richardson (New York: Richardson & Steirman, 1986);

The Churchill–Eisenhower Correspondence, 1953–1955, edited by Peter G. Boyle (Chapel Hill: University of North Carolina Press, 1990);

Winston Churchill and Emery Reves: Correspondence, 1937–1964, edited by Martin Gilbert (Austin: University of Texas Press, 1997);

Speaking for Themselves: The Personal Letters of Winston and Clementine Churchill, edited by Mary Soames (London & New York: Doubleday, 1998); republished as *Winston and Clementine: The Personal Letters of the Churchills* (Boston: Houghton Mifflin, 1999);

The Duce's Dossier: The Secret Mussolini–Churchill Wartime Correspondence, edited by Anthony J. Pansini (Waco, Tex.: Greenvale, 2001);

Defending the West: The Truman–Churchill Correspondence, 1945–1960, edited by G. W. Sand (Westport, Conn.: Praeger, 2004).

Bibliographies:

Frederick Woods, *A Bibliography of the Works of Sir Winston Churchill, KG, OM, CH* (London: Vane, 1963; revised edition, London: Kaye & Ward, 1969);

Curt J. Zoller, *Annotated Bibliography of Works About Sir Winston S. Churchill* (Armonk, N.Y. & London: M. E. Sharpe, 2004).

Biographies:

Randolph S. Churchill and Martin Gilbert, *Winston S. Churchill,* 24 volumes (London: Heinemann, 1966–2000; Boston: Houghton Mifflin, 1966–2000)—includes *The Churchill War Papers,* edited by Gilbert;

Henry Pelling, *Winston Churchill* (London: Macmillan, 1974);

William Manchester, *The Last Lion: Winston Spencer Churchill, Visions of Glory 1874–1932* (Boston & Toronto: Little, Brown, 1983);

Mary Soames, *Winston Churchill: His Life as a Painter: A Memoir by His Daughter* (London: Collins, 1990; Boston: Houghton Mifflin, 1990);

Gilbert, *Churchill: A Life* (New York: Holt, 1991);

John Charmley, *Churchill: The End of Glory: A Political Biography* (London: Hodder & Stoughton, 1993);

Norman Rose, *Churchill: An Unruly Life* (London & New York: Simon & Schuster, 1994);

Geoffrey Best, *Churchill: A Study in Greatness* (London: Hambledon & London, 2001);

Roy Jenkins, *Churchill: A Biography* (New York: Farrar, Straus & Giroux, 2001);

David Coombs and Minnie Churchill, *Sir Winston Churchill's Life Through His Paintings* (London:

Chaucer, 2003; Delray Beach, Fla.: Levenger, 2003).

References:

Maurice Ashley, *Churchill as Historian* (London: Secker & Warburg, 1968);

Violet Bonham Carter, *Winston Churchill as I Knew Him* (London: Eyre & Spottiswoode/Collins, 1965);

Robert Rhodes James, *Churchill: A Study in Failure 1900–1939* (London: Weidenfield & Nicolson, 1970);

John Lukacs, *Churchill: Visionary. Statesman. Historian.* (New Haven & London: Yale University Press, 2002);

Robin Prior, *Churchill's "World Crisis" as History* (London & Canberra: Croom Helm, 1983);

Mary Soames, *A Churchill Family Album: A Personal Anthology* (London: A. Lane, 1982);

Soames, *Clementine Churchill: The Biography of a Marriage* (Boston: Houghton Mifflin, 1979; revised and updated, 2003);

A. J. P. Taylor and others, *Churchill Revised: A Critical Assessment* (New York: Dial, 1969);

Algis Valiunas, *Churchill's Military Histories: A Rhetorical Study* (Lanham, Boulder, New York & Oxford: Rowman & Littlefield, 2002);

Manfred Weidhorn, *Sir Winston Churchill* (Boston: Twayne, 1979);

Chris Wrigley, *Winston Churchill: A Biographical Companion* (Santa Barbara, Denver & Oxford: ABC-CLIO, 2002).

Papers:

The papers of Sir Winston Churchill are located in the Churchill Archives Centre, Churchill College, Cambridge, United Kingdom. Information is available online at <http://www.chu.cam.ac.uk/churchill_papers/the_papers/>.

1953 Nobel Prize in Literature Presentation Speech

by Sigfrid Siwertz, Member of the Swedish Academy

Very seldom have great statesmen and warriors also been great writers. One thinks of Julius Caesar, Marcus Aurelius, and even Napoleon, whose letters to Josephine during the first Italian campaign certainly have passion and splendour. But the man who can most readily be compared with Sir Winston Churchill is Disraeli, who also was a versatile author. It can be said of Disraeli as Churchill says of Rosebery, that "he flourished in an age of great men and small events." He was never subjected to any really dreadful ordeals. His writing was partly a political springboard, partly an emotional safety valve. Through a series of romantic and self-revealing novels, at times rather difficult to read, he avenged himself for the humiliation and setbacks that he, the Jewish stranger in an England ruled by aristocrats, suffered despite his fantastic career. He was not a great writer but a great actor, who played his leading part dazzlingly. He could very well repeat Augustus' words of farewell: "Applaud, my friends, the comedy is over!"

Churchill's John Bull profile stands out effectively against the elder statesman's chalk-white, exotic mask with the black lock of hair on the forehead. The conservative Disraeli revered the English way of life and tradition which Churchill, radical in many respects, has in his blood, including steadfastness in the midst of the storm and the resolute impetus which marks both word and deed. He wears no mask, shows no sign of cleavage, has no complex, enigmatic nature. The analytical *morbidezza,* without which the modern generation finds it hard to imagine an author, is foreign to him. He is a man for whom reality's block has not fallen apart. There, simply, lies the world with its roads and goals under the sun, the stars, and the banners. His prose is just as conscious of the goal and the glory as a runner in the stadium. His every word is half a deed. He is heart and soul a late Victorian who has been buffeted by the gale, or rather one who chose of his own accord to breast the storm.

Churchill's political and literary achievements are of such magnitude that one is tempted to resort to portray him as a Caesar who also has the gift of Cicero's pen. Never before has one of history's leading figures been so close to us by virtue of such an outstanding combination. In his great work about his ancestor, Marlborough, Churchill writes, "Words are easy and many, while great deeds are difficult and rare." Yes, but great, living, and persuasive words are also difficult and rare. And Churchill has shown that they too can take on the character of great deeds.

It is the exciting and colourful side of Churchill's writing which perhaps first strikes the reader. Besides much else, *My Early Life* (1930) is also one of the world's most entertaining adventure stories. Even a very youthful mind can follow with the keenest pleasure the hero's spirited start in life as a problem child in school, as a polo-playing lieutenant in the cavalry (he was considered too dense for the infantry), and as a war correspondent in Cuba, in the Indian border districts, in the Sudan, and in South Africa during the Boer War. Rapid movement, undaunted judgments, and a lively perception distinguish him even here. As a word-painter the young Churchill has not only verve but visual acuteness. Later he took up painting as a hobby, and in

Thoughts and Adventures (1932) discourses charmingly on the joy it has given him. He loves brilliant colours and feels sorry for the poor brown ones. Nevertheless, Churchill paints better with words. His battle scenes have a matchless colouring. Danger is man's oldest mistress and in the heat of action the young officer was fired to an almost visionary clear-sightedness. On a visit to Omdurman many years ago I discovered how the final struggle in the crushing of the Mahdi's rebellion, as it is depicted in *The River War* (1899), was branded on my memory. I could see in front of me the dervish hordes brandishing their spears and guns, the ochre-yellow sand ramparts shot to pieces, the Anglo-Egyptian troops' methodical advance, and the cavalry charge which nearly cost Churchill his life.

Even old battles which must be dug out of dusty archives are described by Churchill with awesome clarity. Trevelyan masterfully depicts Marlborough's campaigns, but in illusory power it is doubtful that Churchill's historic battle scenes can be surpassed. Take, for instance, the Battle of Blenheim. One follows in fascination the moves of the bloody chess game, one sees the cannon balls plough their furrows through the compact squares, one is carried away by the thundering charge and fierce hand-to-hand fighting of the cavalry; and after putting the book down one can waken in the night in a cold sweat, imagining he is right in the front rank of English redcoats who, without wavering, stand among the piles of dead and wounded loading their rifles and firing their flashing salvoes.

But Churchill became far more than a soldier and a delineator of war. Even in the strict but brilliant school of the parliamentary gamble for power he was, perhaps from the outset, something of a problem child. The young Hotspur learned, however, to bridle his impetuosity, and he quickly developed into an eminent political orator with the same gift of repartee as Lloyd George. His sallies, often severe, excluded neither warmth nor chivalry. In his alternation between Toryism and radicalism, he followed in the footsteps of his father, Lord Randolph Churchill. He has also portrayed the latter's short, uneasy, tragically interrupted political and personal life in a work which has an undisputed place of honour in England's profuse biographical literature.

Even the First World War, despite all setbacks, meant a vast expansion for Churchill as both politician and writer. In his historical works the personal and the factual elements have been intimately blended. He knows what he is talking about. In gauging the dynamics of events, his profound experience is unmistakable. He is the man who has himself been through the fire, taken risks, and withstood extreme pressure. This gives his words a vibrating power. Occasionally, perhaps, the personal side gets the upper hand. Balfour called *The World Crisis* (1923–29) "Winston's brilliant autobiography, disguised as world history." With all due respect to archives and documents, there is something special about history written by a man who has himself helped to make it.

In his great book on the Duke of Marlborough (1933–38), whose life's work is so similar to Churchill's own, he makes an intrepid attack on his ancestor's detractors. I do not know what professional historians say of his polemic against Macaulay, but these diatribes against the great general's persistent haters and revilers are certainly diverting and temperamental.

The Marlborough book is not only a series of vivid battle scenes and a skillful defence of the statesman and warrior. It is also a penetrating study of an enigmatic and unique personality; it shows that Churchill, in addition to all else, is capable of real character-drawing. He returns again and again to the confusing mixture in Marlborough of methodical niggardliness and dazzling virtuosity: "His private fortune was amassed," he says,

> upon the same principles as marked the staff-work of his campaigns, and was a part of the same design. It was only in love or on the battlefield that he took all risks. In these supreme exaltations he was swept from his system and rule of living, and blazed resplendent with the heroic virtues. In his marriage and in his victories the worldly prudence, the calculation, the reinsurance, which regulated his ordinary life and sustained his strategy, fell from him like a too heavily embroidered cloak, and the genius within sprang forth in sure and triumphant command.

In his military enthusiasm Churchill forgets for a moment that Marlborough's famous and dearly loved Sarah was by no means one to let herself be ordered about. But it is a wonderful passage.

Churchill regretted that he had never been able to study at Oxford. He had to devote his leisure hours to educating himself. But there are certainly no educational gaps noticeable in his mature prose. Take, for example, *Great Contemporaries* (1937), one of his most charming books. He is said to have moulded his style on Gibbon, Burke, and Macaulay, but here he is supremely himself. What a deft touch and at the same time what a fund of human knowledge, generosity, and gay malice are in this portrait gallery!

Churchill's reaction to Bernard Shaw is very amusing, a piquant meeting between two of England's greatest literary personalities. Churchill cannot resist poking fun at Shaw's blithely irresponsible talk and flippancy, which contrasted with the latter's fundamental gravity. Half amused, half appalled, he winces at the way in which the incorrigibly clowning genius was forever tripping himself up and turning somersaults between the most extreme antitheses. It is the contrast between the writer, who must at all costs create surprises, and the statesman, whose task it is to meet and master them.

It is not easy to sum up briefly the greatness of Churchill's style. He says of his old friend, the Liberal statesman, John Morley, "Though in conversation he paraded and manœuvred nimbly and elegantly around his own convictions, offering his salutations and the gay compliments of old-time war to the other side, [he] always returned to his fortified camp to sleep." As a stylist Churchill himself, despite his mettlesome chivalry, is not prone to such amiable arabesques. He does not beat about the bush, but is a man of plain speaking. His fervour is realistic, his striking-power is tempered only by broad-mindedness and humour. He knows that a good story tells itself. He scorns unnecessary frills and his metaphors are rare but expressive.

Behind Churchill the writer is Churchill the orator—hence the resilience and pungency of his phrases. We often characterize ourselves unconsciously through the praise we give others. Churchill, for instance, says of another of his friends, Lord Birkenhead, "As he warmed to his subject, there grew that glow of conviction and appeal, instinctive and priceless, which constitutes true eloquence." The words might with greater justification have been said of Churchill himself.

The famous desert warrior, Lawrence of Arabia, the author of *The Seven Pillars of Wisdom,* is another who has both made and written history. Of him Churchill says, "Just as an aeroplane only flies by its speed and pressure against the air, so he flew best and easiest in the hurricane." It is again striking how Churchill here too speaks of the same genius that carried his own words through the storm of events.

Churchill's mature oratory is swift, unerring in its aim, and moving in its grandeur. There is the power which forges the links of history. Napoleon's proclamations were often effective in their lapidary style. But Churchill's eloquence in the fateful hours of freedom and human dignity was heart-stirring in quite another way. With his great speeches he has, perhaps, himself erected his most enduring monument.

Lady Churchill—The Swedish Academy expresses its joy at your presence and asks you to convey to Sir Winston a greeting of deep respect. A literary prize is intended to cast lustre over the author, but here it is the author who gives lustre to the prize. I ask you now to accept, on behalf of your husband, the 1953 Nobel Prize in Literature from the hands of His Majesty the King.

[© The Nobel Foundation, 1953.]

Churchill: Banquet Speech

Introductory remarks by G. Liljestrand, Member of the Royal Academy of Sciences, at the Nobel Banquet at the City Hall in Stockholm, 10 December 1953:

In the past, several prime ministers and ministers of foreign affairs and even two Presidents of the United States have been awarded the Nobel Peace Prize. Now, for the first time, a great statesman has received the Prize in Literature. But Sir Winston Churchill is a recognized master of the English language, that wonderful and flexible instrument of human thought. His monumental biographies are already classics, and his works on contemporary history are an outflow of deep and intimate first-hand knowledge, of lucidity of style as well as of humour and generosity. But to Sir Winston the English language has also provided an important tool, with the aid of which part of his job has been finished. His words, accompanied by corresponding deeds, have inspired hope and confidence in millions from all parts of the world during times of darkness. With a slight alteration we might use his own words: Never in the field of human conflict was so much owed by so many to one man. We would like to ask Lady Churchill to convey to her husband our respectful and sincere admiration and reverence for what he has given us in his writings and his speeches.

As Churchill was unable to be present, the speech was read by Lady Churchill:

The Nobel Prize in Literature is an honour for me alike unique and unexpected and I grieve that my duties have not allowed me to receive it myself here in Stockholm from the hands of His Majesty your beloved and justly respected Sovereign. I am grateful that I am allowed to confide this task to my wife.

The roll on which my name has been inscribed represents much that is outstanding in the world's literature of the twentieth century. The judgment of the Swedish Academy is accepted as impartial, authoritative, and sincere throughout the civilized world. I am proud but also, I must admit, awestruck at your decision to include me. I do hope you are right. I feel we are both running a considerable risk and that I do not deserve it. But I shall have no misgivings if you have none.

Since Alfred Nobel died in 1896 we have entered an age of storm and tragedy. The power of man has grown in every sphere except over himself. Never in the field of action have events seemed so harshly to dwarf personalities. Rarely in history have brutal facts so dominated thought or has such a widespread, individual virtue found so dim a collective focus. The fearful question confronts us; have our problems got beyond our control? Undoubtedly we are passing through a phase where this may be so. Well may we humble ourselves, and seek for guidance and mercy.

We in Europe and the Western world, who have planned for health and social security, who have marvelled at the triumphs of medicine and science, and who have aimed at justice and freedom for all, have nevertheless been witnesses of famine, misery, cruelty, and destruction before which pale the deeds of Attila and Genghis Khan. And we who, first in the League of Nations, and now in the United Nations, have attempted to give an abiding foundation to the peace of which men have dreamed so long, have lived to see a world marred by cleavages and threatened by discords even graver and more violent than those which convulsed Europe after the fall of the Roman Empire.

It is upon this dark background that we can appreciate the majesty and hope which inspired the conception of Alfred Nobel. He has left behind him a bright and enduring beam of culture, of purpose, and of inspiration to a generation which stands in sore need. This world-famous institution points a true path for us to follow. Let us therefore confront the clatter and rigidity we see around us with tolerance, variety, and calm.

The world looks with admiration and indeed with comfort to Scandinavia, where three countries, without sacrificing their sovereignty, live united in their thought, in their economic practice, and in their healthy way of life. From such fountains new and brighter opportunities may come to all mankind. These are, I believe, the sentiments which may animate those whom the Nobel Foundation elects to honour, in the sure knowledge that they will thus be respecting the ideals and wishes of its illustrious founder.

[© The Nobel Foundation, 1953. Sir Winston Churchill is the sole author of his speech.]

J. M. Coetzee
(9 February 1940 –)

Michael Marais
Rand Afrikaans University

and

Merritt Moseley
University of North Carolina at Asheville

This entry was expanded by Moseley from Marais's Coetzee entry in *DLB 225: South African Writers*. See also the Coetzee entry in *DLB 326: Booker Prize Novels, 1969–2005*

BOOKS: *Dusklands* (Johannesburg: Ravan, 1974; London: Secker & Warburg, 1982; New York: Penguin, 1985);

In the Heart of the Country (London: Secker & Warburg, 1977; bilingual edition, Johannesburg: Ravan, 1978); republished as *From the Heart of the Country* (New York: Harper & Row, 1977);

Waiting for the Barbarians (London: Secker & Warburg, 1980; Johannesburg: Ravan, 1981; Harmondsworth, U.K. & New York: Penguin, 1982);

Life & Times of Michael K (London: Secker & Warburg, 1983; Johannesburg: Ravan, 1983; New York: Viking, 1984);

Foe (London: Secker & Warburg, 1986; Johannesburg: Ravan, 1986; New York: Viking, 1987);

White Writing: On the Culture of Letters in South Africa (New Haven: Yale University Press, 1988; Sandton, South Africa: Radix in association with Yale University Press, 1988);

Age of Iron (London: Secker & Warburg, 1990; New York: Random House, 1990);

Doubling the Point: Essays and Interviews, edited by David Attwell (Cambridge, Mass.: Harvard University Press, 1992);

The Master of Petersburg (London: Secker & Warburg, 1994; New York: Viking, 1994);

Giving Offense: Essays on Censorship (Chicago: University of Chicago Press, 1996);

Boyhood: Scenes from Provincial Life (London: Secker & Warburg, 1997; New York: Viking, 1997);

J. M. Coetzee (left) receiving the 2003 Nobel Prize in Literature from King Carl XVI Gustaf of Sweden (AP Photo/Jonas Ekstromer, Pool)

The Lives of Animals, by Coetzee and others, edited by Amy Gutmann (Princeton, N.J.: Princeton University Press, 1999);

Disgrace (London: Secker & Warburg, 1999; New York: Viking, 1999);

The Novel in Africa, Doreen B. Townsend Center Occasional Papers, no. 17 (Berkeley, Cal.: Doreen B. Townsend Center for the Humanities, 1999);

The Humanities in Africa/Die Geisteswissenschaften in Afrika (Munich: Siemens Stiftung, 2001);

Stranger Shores: Literary Essays, 1986–1999 (London: Secker & Warburg, 2001; New York: Viking, 2001);

Youth: Scenes from Provincial Life II (London: Secker & Warburg, 2002; New York: Viking, 2002);

Letter of Elizabeth, Lady Chandos, to Francis Bacon (Austin, Texas: Intermezzo, 2002);

Elizabeth Costello: Eight Lessons (London: Secker & Warburg, 2003); published as *Elizabeth Costello* (New York: Viking, 2003);

His Man and He: Nobel Lecture, December 7, 2003 (London: Rees & O'Neill, 2004); published as *Lecture and Speech of Acceptance, Upon the Award of the Nobel Prize, Delivered in Stockholm in December 2003* (New York: Penguin, 2004);

Slow Man (London: Secker & Warburg, 2005; New York: Viking, 2005).

OTHER: Marcellus Emants, *A Posthumous Confession*, translated by Coetzee, Library of Netherlandic Literature, volume 7 (Boston: Twayne, 1975; London: Quartet, 1986);

Wilma Stockenström, *The Expedition to the Baobab Tree*, translated by Coetzee (Johannesburg: Jonathan Ball, 1983; London: Faber & Faber, 1983);

A Land Apart: A South African Reader, edited by Coetzee and André P. Brink (London & Boston: Faber & Faber, 1986); republished as *A Land Apart: A Contemporary South African Reader* (New York: Viking, 1987);

Daniel Defoe, *Robinson Crusoe*, introduction by Coetzee (Oxford: Oxford University Press, 1999);

Rutger Kopland, *Memories of the Unknown*, translated by James Brockway, introduction by Coetzee (London: Harvill, 2001);

Robert Musil, *The Confusions of Young Törless*, translated by Shaun Whiteside, introduction by Coetzee (London & New York: Penguin, 2001);

Landscape with Rowers: Poetry from the Netherlands, translated and introduced by Coetzee (Princeton, N.J.: Princeton University Press, 2003);

Graham Greene, *Brighton Rock*, introduction by Coetzee (London: Vintage, 2004; New York: Penguin, 2004).

SELECTED PERIODICAL PUBLICATIONS–UNCOLLECTED: "The Great South African Novel," *Leadership SA*, 2 (1983): 74, 77, 79;

"The Novel Today," *Upstream: A Magazine of the Arts*, 6 (1988): 2–5.

J. M. Coetzee published his first novel, *Dusklands*, in 1974. Since that time he has become one of South Africa's leading writers; and increasingly, he has achieved a position at the forefront of contemporary writers in English. He was the first novelist to be twice awarded the London-based Booker Prize, given for the best novel of the year (for *Life & Times of Michael K*, 1983, and *Disgrace*, 1999). His international reputation was marked by the announcement in 2003 that he was that year's Nobel Prize winner in Literature.

John Maxwell Coetzee was born in Cape Town on 9 February 1940 to an attorney father and a schoolteacher mother. He spent most of his childhood in Cape Town and Worcester—a period of his life that he recalls in his autobiographical work *Boyhood: Scenes from Provincial Life* (1997). A section of *Boyhood* is devoted to the holidays that Coetzee spent as a child on his uncle's farm in the Karoo, the semidesert region of the Cape Province. In all probability his perennial fascination with the primeval aspect of the South African landscape stems from his boyhood visits to this region, which forms the main setting of his novel *Life & Times of Michael K*.

Coetzee's parents were *bloedsappe*, Afrikaners who supported General Jan Smuts and dissociated themselves from the Afrikaner nationalist movement that eventually came to power in South Africa in 1948. Although Coetzee came from an Afrikaans-speaking background, he attended various English middle schools and, after graduating from a Roman Catholic boys' school in 1956, went on to study English literature and mathematics at the University of Cape Town, receiving his B.A. in 1960 and M.A. in 1963. This bilingual upbringing has enabled Coetzee to depict English- and Afrikaans-speaking characters in his fiction with equal facility—an uncommon occurrence in South African literature, which, as part of the legacy of a divided society, usually is riddled with ethnic stereotypes.

Having found his studies at the University of Cape Town, particularly in English, tedious, Coetzee left South Africa for England in 1962 to pursue a career as a computer programmer, working for International Business Machines (IBM) for two years and then for International Computers from 1964 to 1965. In his 2002 memoir/novel *Youth: Scenes from Provincial Life II*, the main character, John, enacts this same history, though the move to London is motivated by revulsion from South Africa and by artistic aspirations, and the career in computer programming is chosen almost inadvertently. Coetzee completed his master's thesis in 1963 and married Philippa Jubber the same year; the couple has two children, Nicolas, born in 1966, and Gisela, born in 1968. Evidently, computer programming did not prove rewarding; John, in *Youth*, explains to an uncomprehending human resources officer, "I don't find working for

IBM very satisfying at a human level. I don't find it fulfilling." Under a Fulbright exchange program, Coetzee, after only four years in England, left for the United States and commenced work on a doctoral thesis in English at the University of Texas at Austin.

The time Coetzee spent at the University of Texas crucially influenced his development as a novelist. His doctoral research on the fiction of Samuel Beckett, for example, made a definite impression on his subsequent novelistic practice, as is evident in his use of minimalist scenarios and a limited number of characters. Moreover, in Texas, Coetzee first encountered reports and accounts of the Khoi people, written by early European explorers, travelers, and missionaries in South Africa; these documents provided the germ for his first work, *Dusklands,* specifically for "The Narrative of Jacobus Coetzee." Another important influence from this period on his writing was the Vietnam War, which reached its height during his stay in the United States. The war affected Coetzee deeply, and, besides prompting him to take part in an antiwar demonstration (for which he was arrested), it impelled him to a comparison of U.S. colonialism with South African colonialism. As David Attwell contends in his essay "The Problem of History in the Fiction of J. M. Coetzee" (1990), Coetzee "could scarcely avoid associating the spectacle of the bombing of Vietnam with the legacy he was trying to shake off as a South African." This association led directly to the creation of *Dusklands*.

Coetzee stayed in the United States while writing his dissertation, which he completed in 1969; as an assistant professor he taught at the State University of New York at Buffalo from 1968 to 1971. *Dusklands* was published two years after Coetzee's return to South Africa to take up a lecturing position in English at the University of Cape Town in 1972. Written partly in America and partly in South Africa, it consists of two novellas, "The Vietnam Project" and "The Narrative of Jacobus Coetzee," set in America and South Africa, respectively. "The Vietnam Project" takes place during the Vietnam War and deals with the endeavors of Eugene Dawn, an expert in psychological warfare, to design a propaganda policy that will undermine the foundations of Vietnamese culture and render the North Vietnamese subservient to the United States. By contrast, the second novella is set in eighteenth-century South Africa and centers on the exploration of the South African interior and subsequent extermination of an aboriginal tribe by Jacobus Coetzee, an historically verifiable personage and distant forebear of the author himself.

Geographically separate and at a temporal remove of two centuries, these two novellas initially appear to be completely independent. The title of the combined text, however, by implication classifies both the United States and South Africa as "dusklands" and thus suggests that they have something in common—a shared history of colonialism. Coetzee, in a 1978 interview with Stephen Watson, describes the South African colonial condition as "only one manifestation of a wider historical situation to do with colonialism, late colonialism, neo-colonialism." Moreover, apart from the commonality of theme and analogous historical situations hinted at by the title, the name "Coetzee" is used in both novellas in *Dusklands;* Eugene Dawn's immediate superior is named Coetzee, and the second sentence of the novella is "Coetzee has asked me to revise my essay." This further evidence of the links between them confirms the intimation that they operate contrapuntally in their exploration of the metaphysics of colonialism. In terms of its structure, however, the U.S. invasion of Vietnam in "The Vietnam Project" precedes the European invasion of southern Africa in "The Narrative of Jacobus Coetzee." This inversion of the actual temporal sequence of these historical occurrences suggests that history, rather than manifesting a linear progression through time, statically repeats itself.

In its depiction of two self-doubting and egocentric protagonists who seek to affirm their reality by positing themselves in opposition to an "other," *Dusklands* describes Western colonialism as an epiphenomenon of the divided consciousness of Western humanity. It is depicted as a symptom of a specific epistemological and ontological condition: in order to constitute itself, the self has to attempt to "know" the other. Being grounded in Western consciousness, this "mental aberration" is not confined to a particular period, place, or economic structure. As long as the struggle for recognition that it activates continues, history is bound to repeat itself. Furthermore, as the novel makes clear, this struggle manifests itself on both individual and national planes in the rampant desire to affirm a vestigial sense of identity.

International critical response to *Dusklands* was slow in coming but generally favorable. Reviewing the novel in *Africa Today* (1980), Peter LaSalle detected in the work "a fullness that is utterly real, without the extremes of one-dimensional, deadpan moralizing or equally one-dimensional, comic caricaturing that have marked, and marred, so much fiction about Africa by both blacks and whites." Locally, *Dusklands* elicited immediate attention. Described as the advent of "the modern novel in English" in South Africa by Jonathan Crewe in *Contrast* (1974) and as a welcome departure from "South African liberal realism" by Watson in *Research in African Literatures* (1986), its appearance on what was perceived to be a literary scene in serious danger of stagnation was welcomed. Although admired by many critics for its aesthetic innovations, this work has been persistently criticized on political grounds for neglecting the material factors of oppression in its portrayal of colonialism. Peter Knox-Shaw, for example, concludes a perceptive reading of the text with the reservation that "It is regrettable that a writer of such considerable and varied talents should play down the political and economic aspects of history in favor of a psychopathology of Western life." This criticism of the oblique relation to history of *Dusklands* has, in various permutations, become the basis of a growing local critique of all of Coetzee's novels.

By the time of the publication of his second novel, *In the Heart of the Country* (1977), Coetzee had spent twelve years teaching and was well established in his academic post at the University of Cape Town. As an unpublished address he gave to the Aquarius Workshop, a student group, on 22 April 1975 shows, however, he had not fallen prey to the complacency and self-deception of what he termed the academic who "thinks of himself as a member of a critical intelligentsia that is in the political community but not of it." On the contrary, he was acutely aware of the ideological implications of a career as a writer-academic. In this address, "The Writer and the University: Notes on the Economics of Writing," he touches on the ambivalence inherent in being paid by the State but simultaneously "protected by the tradition of academic free speech," a tradition he skeptically defines as "the union rule of academics that an academic may say what he wishes, under certain circumstances, provided that he does not go beyond the bounds of the liberal ideology." Two years later these intimations of self-censorship in the liberal academic milieu were thrown into relief by the more concrete hazards of writing in a country where political repression extends tangibly to the cultural domain: before being cleared for general circulation, a consignment of the first edition of *In the Heart of the Country* was impounded for a brief period by South African customs officials.

In addition to having been embargoed, *In the Heart of the Country* had an interesting publication history. The original manuscript combined English text with Afrikaans dialogue. To facilitate acceptance by a British publisher for distribution on the international market, however, Coetzee translated the dialogue into English. Thus, the novel exists in two editions: a wholly English edition, first published in Great Britain by Secker and Warburg in 1977, and a South African edition that appeared under the Ravan Press imprint in 1978 and presents the text in its original bilingual form.

In the Heart of the Country is similar to *Dusklands* in that it is presented in epistolary form as the interior monologue of a deranged narrator. The protagonist of the later novel is Magda, a woman who lives with her father and their servants, Klein-Anna and Hendrik, on a remote and lonely sheep farm somewhere in South Africa, probably the Karoo. The exact geographical location of this setting is not stipulated, and neither is the historical period in which the action occurs—the first of many indeterminacies in this highly ambivalent novel. Such ambiguities are immediately apparent from the opening paragraph, in which Magda recalls watching her remarried father returning home: "Today my father brought home his new bride. They came clip-clop across the flats in a dog-cart drawn by a horse with an ostrich-plume waving on its forehead, dusty after the long haul. Or perhaps they were drawn by two plumed donkeys, that is also possible." The final result of this obfuscatory technique is that the novel defies any coherent reconstruction of its plot. So, for example, it is not clear whether Magda, who is jealous of the sexual relationship that her father may or may not have contrived with Klein-Anna, does or does not murder him. In fact, the text undermines all certainty by providing the reader with two accounts of the putative murder; yet, after each account the father reappears later in the story. What follows the purported murder is equally ambivalent: Magda attempts to regain her position of mastery over Hendrik and Klein-Anna but, upon failing, tries to form an egalitarian relationship with them. Hendrik, however, seemingly rapes her and then, together with Klein-Anna, deserts the farm.

Among all this indeterminacy, however, there are several concerns in this novel that the reader familiar with *Dusklands* will readily be able to identify, such as the relationship of dominance and subservience that underpins the father-child and master-slave relations. Furthermore, Magda's apparent murder of her father, which brings about a change in the relationships of dominance and subservience in *In the Heart of the Country,* is reminiscent of the transposable relationships in *Dusklands*—for instance, Jacobus Coetzee's forfeiture of his position of mastery and selfhood in the course of his encounter with the Khoi. Moreover, the mythical archetype of patricide can be found in Eugene Dawn's "New Life for Vietnam" report in "The Vietnam Project." Part of Eugene Dawn's study involves the formulation of a strategy to counter the Vietnamese myth of the demise of the father, a myth described as "a justification of the rebellion of sons against a father who uses them as hinds. The sons come of age, rebel, mutilate the father and divide the patrimony."

The political significance of the patricidal myth, together with Magda's depiction of her "masterful father" as an authoritarian, retributive patriarch, suggests a reading of *In the Heart of the Country* in which the hierarchy on the farm forms a microcosm of the South African political situation, with the farm representing South Africa itself; the father the Afrikaner *baas,* or the

Afrikaner government; and Klein-Anna and Hendrik the oppressed black race. If the novel is read in this way, then the killing of the father could be construed as the end of the old apartheid order, which is premised upon the traditional roles of master and servant or dominance and subservience. Magda's attempts to forge a new and equal relationship with Hendrik and Klein-Anna could be seen as an attempt, in the interregnum following the death of the old order, to establish a new order that is not premised on power relations. Such a reading, however, runs the serious risk of simplifying, to the point of absurdity, an extraordinarily complex text. It fails, for example, to account for the enigmatic ending of the novel and its exploration of the part played by language, as a political weapon, in reinforcing the hierarchical roles that maintain the established order. In this respect Lloyd Spencer rightly singles out language as the "new obsession" that distinguishes this novel from its predecessor.

The political role of language is directly referred to by Magda when she observes that she "was born in a language of hierarchy, of distance and perspective." It is the "antique feudal language" that inscribes the division between subject and object, self and other, and master and servant that dictates Magda's relationship with her servants. It is not the contravention of the color bar that annoys her about her father's liaison with Klein-Anna but his "violation" of the old language of division: "I am a conserver rather than a destroyer, perhaps my rage at my father is simply rage at the violations of the old language, the correct language, that take place when he exchanges kisses and pronouns of intimacy with a girl who yesterday scrubbed the floors and today ought to be cleaning the windows." The "pronouns of intimacy" referred to are, of course, the first-person-plural pronouns "we" and "us" that bridge the division between subject and object, "I" and "you," which underpins the language of separation or apartheid. This underpinning emerges in another extraordinary linguistic description by Magda of her father's relationship with Klein-Anna: "My father is exchanging forbidden words with Klein-Anna. . . . *Ons* [We], he is saying to her, *ons twee* [we two]; and the word reverberates in the air between them. . . . How can I speak to Hendrik as before when they corrupt my speech? How do I speak to them?" For the old order to conserve itself, language must function as a medium of separation rather than a means of intercourse. As such, social intercourse between self and other is more to be feared than sexual intercourse.

Following her father's death, which symbolizes the collapse of the old order, Magda attempts to reassert the relationship of dominance and subservience on the farm. She fails, however, owing to the disintegration of what she calls the "father-tongue": "The language that should pass between myself and these people has been subverted by my father and cannot be recovered." She then attempts to realize her fantasy of an egalitarian new order. And, as her words to Klein-Anna indicate, she is acutely aware that the institution of anarchic relationships requires the creation of a new language of equality: "I have never learned the speech of men, ek wou slegs praat, ek het nooit geleer hoe 'n mens met 'n ander mens praat nie [I only wanted to talk, I never learned how a person talks to another person]. . . . I have never known words of true exchange, wisselbare woorde [exchangeable words], Anna. Woorde wat ek aan jou kan gee kan jy nie teruggee nie [Words that I can give you, you cannot return]. Hulle is woorde sonder waarde [They are words without value]. Verstaan jy [Do you understand]? No value." It is her desire to replace this language of division with a language of exchange that leads her to establish a sexual relationship with Hendrik. By means of this relationship she clearly wishes to replicate her father's affair with Klein-Anna, one that she suspects was conducted through "forbidden words" and "pronouns of intimacy." Rather than being equal, however, her relationship with Hendrik is characterized by the will to power and the language of alienation, as is made clear by Hendrik's rape of her: "He has forced his way into me. I toss from side to side and weep, but he is relentless. . . . 'Almal kry lekker [everyone enjoys it],' he says harshly. Are those his words?" Thus she comes to realize that "There has been no transfiguration" of the roles of dominance and subservience, that they have simply been reversed, not changed.

The novel ends with Magda, now alone on the farm, pleading with "sky-creatures" whom she believes are sending her messages. Significantly, one of her main pleas is for a language that entrenches anarchic rather than power relations: "Why will no one speak to me in the true language of the heart? The medium, the median—that is what I wanted to be! Neither master nor slave, neither parent nor child, but the bridge between, so that in me the contraries should be reconciled!" And in her abortive attempt to converse with these creatures she devises a language that can only be described as a composite of the Indo-European group of languages. The suggestion seems to be that Magda's failure to create a language of exchange is not to be seen as a personal failure but should instead be attributed to the fact that the languages that have formed her consciousness of self and other inscribe subject positions of dominance. In this regard, Michael Vaughan contends that "The whole of Western civilization is implicated in the drive towards subjugation and mastery."

As with *Dusklands,* then, this novel ultimately emerges as an exploration of the cognitive structures that govern the West's imperial will to power. And, once again, this concern with the epistemological dimension of power, rather than its material conditions, dissatisfied some South African critics, such as Vaughan, who believe that endeavors of this kind do not constitute effective political protest. Such criticism, of course, ignores the materiality of language and discourse. It fails to see that discourse and material situations are closely interrelated, that the former may generate the latter.

Detractors of the novel also contend that characters such as Magda, enthralled as they are by a Western colonial consciousness, represent the impotence of the individual, his/her inability to change the political status quo. Thus, Vaughan, for example, considers Coetzee's novels to be a response to the "patent ineffectuality of liberal ideas and strategies" that are premised on "an ontology of individual freedom." As far as Vaughan is concerned, then, protest, which presupposes a theory of individual agency, is simply "not available to Coetzee as a strategy." Apart from this line of criticism, the novel has been praised for its artistry and intellectuality. Spencer, for example, regards it as the "most brilliant" and also the "most forbidding" of Coetzee's novels, one that pushes "the novel of ideas to the borders of impenetrability."

In South Africa *In the Heart of the Country* received both the Central News Agency (CNA) Prize, the country's premier literary award, and the Mofolo-Plomer Literary Prize. A 1985 Franco-Belgian motion-picture adaptation of the novel, *Dust,* starred Jane Birkin as Magda and Trevor Howard as her father. Marion Hänsel, who directed and wrote the screenplay, won the Silver Lion for Best First Work at the Venice Film Festival.

With the publication of *Waiting for the Barbarians* (1980), Coetzee's third novel, it became evident that the politics of colonization constituted a recurrent theme in his fiction. Set in the frontier settlement of a state referred to simply as the Third Empire, the novel opens with the arrival from the capital of Colonel Joll to crush a rumored barbarian rebellion on the frontier. This opening sets the stage for another encounter between colonizer and colonized. Yet, by the end of the novel, Joll has failed to engage with the phantom barbarians, upon which he and his demoralized troops retreat to the capital, leaving the fortress town once more in the control of its magistrate, the unnamed protagonist of the novel. In the interview with Watson in 1978, a period during which he, in all probability, was writing *Waiting for the Barbarians,* Coetzee commented that "in a way it's easier and more difficult being a writer in South Africa than in Western European countries; because there are such gigantic subjects of such unassailable importance facing a writer in South Africa." For Coetzee, one of these "gigantic subjects" is obviously the colonial dialectic, a subject of such "unassailable importance" that writing about it is not so much a matter of choice as a matter of necessity. This compulsion constitutes a form of determinism that limits the writer's freedom of choice, and this, in turn, is one of the difficulties that Coetzee perceives of being a writer in South Africa.

As with its geography, the historical period in which *Waiting for the Barbarians* is set is not specified. Leon Whiteson, among others, considers this lack of specificity a technical failing, arguing: "The geography is garbled: there is desert and snow, lizards and bears." However, as Lance Olsen points out, this indeterminacy is calculated to "jam our notions of where and when." The writer himself, in an interview with Dick Penner, makes the same point: "I just put together a variety of locales and left a lot of things vague with a very definite intention that it shouldn't be pinned down to some specific place." By refraining from establishing the setting and period, Coetzee signals his intention to explore the epistemology and ontology of colonialism. In other words, he refuses to posit history as an a priori fact and, instead, attempts to represent that which generates it. The emphasis is therefore again on the cognitive structures that create material realities.

The nebulous aspect of the setting of the novel—evident, for example, in its "jumbled" geography that is diffusely described at one point as a "haze of desert"—also emphasizes the unreality of Empire. Like the United States and South Africa in Coetzee's first novel, the frontier here is a "duskland" whose inhabitants have to assert their reality by defining themselves in contradistinction to another cultural group. This group's identity as "barbarians" is thus largely a creation of Empire, an ideological construct that validates Empire's sense of its own significance by affirming its status as a superior, civilized culture. In the absence of this construct, Empire cannot exist. As the novel proceeds, however, it becomes increasingly evident that the native inhabitants of the area do not fit the role of "barbarian" and "foe" that Empire has created for them. In fact, the title of the novel, by alluding to Constantine Cavafy's 1904 poem of the same title in which the barbarians never arrive, suggests that the "barbarians" will never attack the settlement. By not doing so, they fail to conform to Empire's expectations with regard to the manner in which "barbarians" behave and thus fail to endorse the identity that has been thrust upon them. By consistently refusing to adopt an oppositional position in relation to Empire, the colonial other resists all imposed identities and consequently remains an absence in the colonial record.

During the first year of publication, *Waiting for the Barbarians* received the James Tait Black Memorial Prize, the Geoffrey Faber Award, and the CNA Literary Prize for 1980. It was, as Penner contended, "Coetzee's most highly praised and probably his most widely read work" to that point. Despite this overwhelmingly favorable response, however, there has been critical discontent with Coetzee's refusal to specify historical place and time. In addition to Whiteson's critique, Irving Howe has complained that this lack of specificity leads to a loss of "urgency," a lack of "bite and pain." This criticism resurfaces in Paul Rich's argument that Coetzee's "vision of empire" lacks "any understanding of the historical forces that produce actual imperial systems at particular phases of history." Vaughan takes issue with Coetzee for not providing any "material logic" for the oppression of the barbarians and for not offering a solution to the problems of colonialism.

Coetzee continued his demythologizing project in *Life & Times of Michael K,* a novel in which Michael K, a member of the oppressed majority in a futuristic South Africa embroiled in civil war, retreats from Cape Town to a farm in the Karoo, where he lives in a burrow and tends a vegetable patch. On the surface this novel, with its memoir-title reminiscent of the early novel of the seventeenth and eighteenth centuries and its loose episodic structure, seems to be an eccentric reworking of the picaresque novel. Upon closer inspection, though, it becomes evident that this episodic design is informed by a recurring pattern of events in which Michael K is first colonized and then escapes. Starting with the opening scene of the novel, in which Anna K, with the assistance of a midwife, gives birth to her son, Michael K, each of these sequences is depicted as a birth of sorts. In each of these cases, however, Michael K's otherness palimpsestically reasserts itself after the linguistic colonization of being named and possessed—as becomes evident, for example, in his literal escape from the concentration camps.

This pattern of linguistic appropriation followed by escape includes not only Michael K but also the South African landscape. In the course of the novel, for example, the reader finds that the homestead, a sign of settlement in the Prince Albert district, is erased by explosives and that the Karoo farm reverts to veld. In other words, the space that the colonial enterprise attempted to domesticate, by, in the words of Jacobus Coetzee, "turning it into orchard and farm," reasserts its original identity. Moreover, the fact that this novel is set in a future South Africa engaged in a revolutionary war suggests that the European culture that was inscribed on the subcontinent of Africa during the colonial era is in the process of being erased. In both the case of Michael K and the South African landscape, then, "the thing possessed," to cite Coetzee's observation on the representation of the South African landscape in Sidney Clouts's poetry, "begins to mutate and shed its old name almost as soon as it is taken over by language."

The analogy, verging on identity, between Michael K and the South African landscape is one of the most noteworthy features of the novel. It provides movement to what is otherwise a remarkably static and deliberately reiterative rather than progressive text, a narrative in which the protagonist undergoes no discernible psychological development—despite the clear allusion in the title to the subgenre of the bildungsroman. Indeed, Michael K is described as a "hard little stone, barely aware of its surroundings, enveloped in itself and its interior life," and remarks of himself: "I was mute and stupid in the beginning, I will be mute and stupid at the end." In the course of the novel, however, Michael K does gravitate from a "botanical" to a "geological" perspective in terms of his attitude toward the South African landscape, a terrain that Coetzee describes elsewhere as being "of rock, not of foliage." This development is brought about by his move from the exotic, Europeanized landscape of Cape Town—that is, an initially alien landscape that has been legitimized or rewritten with imperial labels—to the more indigenous landscape of the Karoo, a region that gains its name from the Khoi word meaning "dry."

By the end of the novel Michael K is able to liken himself to an earthworm and a mole—comparisons that suggest his fusion with the earth and echo his decision, on the Karoo farm, to live in a burrow rather than in the homestead, that is, to settle for, in Coetzee's words in a different context, "an unsettled habitation *in* the landscape." The suggestion is that Michael K is now able to recognize and identify with the "true" South Africa underlying the European labels, the South Africa that continually escapes the "frenzied application of European metaphor." Significantly, the reader is told that Michael K "could not imagine himself spending his life driving stakes into the ground, erecting fences, dividing up the land."

Michael K's fusion with the landscape also suggests the bridging of the Cartesian split between self and world, a split that has characterized the consciousness of all Coetzee's protagonists thus far. The reason for the significant change in consciousness introduced by this novel is that it, unlike Coetzee's previous texts, is told, for the most part, from the perspective of the colonized rather than the colonizer, a technical change that culminates in a shift in emphasis from the colonizing impulse itself to the escape from such attempts. Apart from the matter of Cartesian consciousness, some remarkable effects are achieved by this shift in point of view. For instance, it accounts for the fact that, in a novel set in a country that is obsessed with racial classification, Michael K's racial identity is never mentioned. As Coetzee said in a 6 March 1984 interview from which Dick Penner quotes in his *Countries of the Mind: The Fiction of J. M. Coetzee* (1989), "Other people in the book can think of him what they want. The important thing is that he doesn't." The significant silence about race in the novel can therefore be construed as an analogue of the ultimate failure of the colonizer to confine the other in racial categories.

The response elicited by *Life & Times of Michael K* does not differ significantly from the pattern established by the reception of Coetzee's earlier novels. On the one hand, it was widely acclaimed and awarded the prestigious Booker-McConnell Prize in Britain, the CNA Literary Award in South Africa, and the Prix Femina Etranger in France; on the other hand, the advocates of a form of historical realism responded in what by then had become predictable terms. Thus, fellow South African novelist Nadine Gordimer, in her review of the novel for the *New York Review of Books* (2 February 1994), praised Coetzee's artistry but criticized the passivity of his "hero" and what she saw as an attempt to depict the realization of "an idea of survival . . . outside a political doctrine."

Although these prescriptive criticisms have been widely debated, the most intriguing response to them thus far has been from Coetzee himself. Over the years he has consistently refused to discuss his work in any but the most general terms, let alone react to formal criticism of it. It is therefore remarkable that in an interview with Attwell, published in the volume edited by Attwell, *Doubling the Point: Essays and Interviews* (1992), Coetzee responded directly and in detail to this line of criticism with its implicit charge that he should have written a different book, one in which Michael K joins the band of guerrillas that visits the Karoo farm:

> One writes the books one wants to write. One doesn't write the books one doesn't want to write. The emphasis falls not on *one* but on the word *want* in all its own resistance to being known. The book about going off with the guerillas, the book in the heroic tradition, is not a book I *wanted-to-write,* wanted enough to be able to bring off, however much I might have wanted to have written it–that is to say, wanted to be the person who had successfully brought off the writing of it.

Instead of responding to Gordimer's criticism on its own terms, that is, by clarifying his position on the relation of *Life & Times of Michael K* to the public, political arena, Coetzee responded in terms of the assumed privacy of the experience of writing, an experience that, he stated earlier in the interview, places him in a realm that is governed by forces and prescriptions other than those prevalent in the public arena: "The novel becomes less a *thing* than a *place* where one goes every day for several hours a day for years on end. What happens in that place has less and less discernible relation to the daily life one lives or the lives people are living around one. Other forces, another dynamic, take [*sic*] over."

In 1986 Coetzee taught at Johns Hopkins University in Baltimore, Maryland, as Hinkley Professor of English, a one-semester appointment he received again in 1989. In his next novel, *Foe* (1986), Coetzee departed altogether from the South African geopolitical context. The first section of the novel is set on a deserted island and constitutes a retelling of Daniel Defoe's *Robinson Crusoe* (1719) by Susan Barton, the castaway narrator of *Foe*. It deals with her stay on the island and focuses primarily on the relationship of Cruso (Coetzee's spelling) with Friday. In the second section the island is replaced by Defoe's house in England, and the focus falls on Susan Barton's relationship with Friday. Although on the surface the settings of this novel appear to constitute a departure from those encountered in Coetzee's previous novels, they actually duplicate scenarios with which the reader is familiar from these works: typically, a man or woman in a deserted landscape or house. In all these cases, with the exception of Michael K, the protagonist adopts a position of mastery in relation to that which is beyond him or her. It could therefore be argued that *Foe* lays bare the fact that the minimalist scenarios sketched out in Coetzee's various narratives are all, in Allan Gardiner's phrase, "encounters of the Robinsonian kind."

Given his fascination with the colonization process, it is not surprising that so many of Coetzee's novels reenact the Robinson Crusoe paradigm with its classic encounter between colonizer and colonized and the dialectic of self and other that informs this relationship. After all, *Robinson Crusoe,* as a literary reflection of the expansive imperialist thrust of Europeans that started in the seventeenth century, has over the centuries gained the status of a folktale of white empire. One could even go as far as to say that this fable forms a paradigm of the conventional Western mode of thinking about the cultural other. This reason seems to be behind Coetzee's decision to rework Defoe's novel, for which he wrote the introduction to the 1999 Oxford World's Classics edition.

Many of Coetzee's changes to the story affect the racial dimension of the relationship of master to servant that pertains between Cruso and Friday and that forms the subject of part 1 of the novel. Rather than the "comely, handsome" European-looking Carib with skin that is "not quite black, but very tawny . . . of a bright kind of dun olive colour that had in it something very agreeable" of Defoe's story, Friday, in Coetzee's hands, becomes an African whose features and complexion are described by Susan Barton as: "the small dull eyes, the broad nose, the thick lips, the skin not black but a dark grey, dry as if coated with dust." Clearly this change is calculated to emphasize the racial aspect of the relationship between Cruso and Friday. Another significant change that Coetzee introduces to the Robinson Crusoe story is his reduction of Defoe's highly loquacious Robinson Crusoe to a laconic hater of words. Furthermore, Friday, who in the original develops into a fairly adept user of pidgin English, in Coetzee's text becomes a mute whose tongue has been cut out. The effect of this change is to highlight the strictly utilitarian use to which language is put on the island. Thus, Susan Barton ascertains that Friday's vocabulary is limited to words of command—that while he, for example, understands the functional word *firewood,* which denotes a commodity that he fetches when ordered to do so, he does not understand the generic word *wood*. And, when she asks Cruso how many "words of English" Friday knows, he responds by saying: "As many as he needs. . . . This is not England, we have no need of a great stock of words." Language on Coetzee's island emerges as a tool of empire that is used to dominate the other. In fact, this emphasis on language as an instrument of power gains a metafictional dimension when Susan Barton refers to "the new Friday whom Cruso created." Like the author of a character, Cruso through language creates an identity for his mute slave by naming him Friday.

Part 2 of the novel marks a shift from the silence of the island to the social world of England, referred to by Susan Barton as the "world of words." On the surface this change of setting initially appears to juxtapose the malignant use of language as an instrument of domination with a more benign use of language as a means to freedom, that is, Susan Barton's attempt through language to free Friday—to, in her words, "educate him out of darkness and silence" and "to build a bridge of words over which, when one day it is grown sturdy enough, he may cross to the time before Cruso." As the novel progresses, however, it becomes increasingly evident that this well-intentioned attempt at voicing the other is, in fact, no different from attempts at silencing it. Thus, Susan Barton eventually comes to realize that, like Cruso, she, too, has through language become the author and determiner of Friday's existence: "Friday has no command of words and therefore no defence against being re-shaped day by day in conformity with the desires of others. I say he is a cannibal and he becomes a cannibal. . . . What he is to the world is what I make of him." As Gayatri Spivak has suggested, "*Foe,* in history, is the site where the line between friend and foe is undone."

Like Michael K, however, Friday resists such attempts at linguistic appropriation. Although his silence initially appears to render him vulnerable to linguistic reification, it is in fact the means through which he resists the languages of imperialism. By virtue of his inaccessible silence, Friday preserves his difference, his status as other, and avoids assimilation by the West.

In South Africa *Foe* has been harshly dealt with by critics who insist that fiction writing should supplement history. Instead of engaging with a recognizable South African social and political context (or so their argument goes), this novel perversely escapes (or retreats) into postmodernist theorizing and games playing—a mode of writing and theoretical discourse that such readers consider inappropriate in the South African political context. Michael Chapman's attack on *Foe* is the most extreme of the responses elicited by this novel in South Africa: "In our knowledge of the human suffering on our own doorstep of thousands of detainees who are denied recourse to the rule of law, *Foe* does not so much speak to Africa as provide a kind of masturbatory release, in this country, for the Europeanising dreams of an intellectual coterie."

In what has been interpreted as a response to such negative critiques, Coetzee, in a talk given at the 1987 *Weekly Mail* Book Week in Johannesburg, outlined his views on the relation of his novels to history. After commenting on the tendency of South African critics "to subsume the novel under history, to read novels as . . . imaginative investigations of . . . real historical circumstances; and conversely, to treat novels that do not perform this investigation . . . as lacking in seriousness," he argued for the legitimacy of a novelistic practice that, in the process of evolving "its own paradigms and myths," demythologizes history. Equally telling, in this regard, is Coetzee's response to a question in a 1987 interview with Tony Morphet on whether *Foe* could be seen as "a retreat from the South African situation": "*Foe* is a retreat from the South African situation in a narrow temporal perspective. It is not a retreat from the subject of colonialism or from questions of power."

In 1987 Coetzee was awarded the Jerusalem Prize for the Freedom of the Individual in Society for *Life & Times of Michael K*. In his acceptance speech he remarked on the manner in which the South African state's structures of power have created "deformed and stunted relations between human beings" and on the extent to which literary representations of life in this country "no matter how intense . . . suffer from the same stuntedness and deformity." He then commented that South African literature "is a literature of bondage. . . . a less than fully human literature." A few years later he published *Age of Iron* (1990), a novel that focuses on the deforming impact of apartheid structures on life and art in South Africa.

Age of Iron differs from its predecessors in that it deals quite explicitly with contemporary political realities in South Africa. The setting is specified as Cape Town, and, although the date is not provided, various details situate the novel temporally in the winter of 1986, a period in South African history that, as the title of the novel suggests, was characterized by unmitigated violence, bloodshed, and political intransigence. It was a time of death not only for the country as a whole but also for Coetzee personally, who, during the writing of the novel, lost four relatives—his former wife (the couple had divorced in 1980), both parents, and his son, Nicolas. Not surprisingly, then, the novel is, as Malvern Van Wyk Smith claims, "a meditation on death, on many levels."

Its protagonist, Mrs. Curren, is an elderly woman suffering from terminal cancer who, on the day she is informed of the incurability of her condition, encounters in her backyard a mysterious tramp named Vercueil. The latter, she thus infers, is an angel of death. The other relationships in the novel are also marked by death: Mrs. Curren's domestic servant, Florence, harbors two teenage "comrades" (activists for the African National Congress [ANC]) in her quarters, one of whom is her son and both of whom die violently in the course of the novel. Even the settings are tainted by death: Mrs. Curren's house is in an advanced state of decay, and so is the country as a whole. Moreover, Mrs. Curren's visit to the township while assisting Florence in her search for her missing son is metaphorically depicted as a visit to Hades, and the township is physically described as a "zone of killing and degradation." It comes as no surprise that this bleak novel ends with the implied death of Mrs. Curren herself—a conclusion that is conveyed in the form of a letter that itself is defunct since, as Van Wyk Smith points out, it is addressed to Mrs. Curren's daughter in Canada "who is, to all intents and purposes, 'dead.'"

In terms of its depiction of relationships of power, *Age of Iron* follows a similar pattern to Coetzee's earlier novels. The by now familiar scenario in which one character attempts to re-create another is repeated in this novel in Mrs. Curren's relationship with Vercueil. Although their interaction is realistically portrayed and set in a specified urban setting, a network of allusions and references to the Circe myth from Homer's *The Odyssey* make it clear that this relationship constitutes yet another island encounter "of the Robinsonian kind." Whereas Circe attempts to turn Odysseus into a pig, Mrs. Curren endeavors to turn Vercueil into a manservant and angel of death. Both, however, fail in these attempts at re-creation. Odysseus receives from Hermes the mythical herb moly, which renders him immune to Circe's spells, while Vercueil's silence and addiction to alcohol protect him from Mrs. Curren's authorial endeavors.

Although Coetzee's treatment of this relationship follows a clearly recognizable course, the same cannot be said of Mrs. Curren's relationship to Florence and her children, which eventually forms the subject of a metafictional meditation on the status of art in South Africa. In developing this relationship, Coetzee sets up an opposition between white suburbia and black township life in South Africa, an opposition that is emphasized by Mrs. Curren's visit to Guguletu township, during which she is confronted with a "looming world of rage and violence" where people are "revealed in their true names." The indubitable reality of this "otherworld" questions the reality of her own white bourgeois environment, which occludes it in media representations of South Africa as "a land of smiling neighbours." Thus, as Mrs. Curren comes to realize following her visit to the township, the very fabric of her society is baseless, a fiction manufactured by the social engineers of apartheid.

In protest, Mrs. Curren contemplates burning herself outside the House of Parliament, which she refers to as the "House of Lies." She hopes, by immolating herself in this way, to "redeem" herself and "rise above my times." But, as she eventually realizes, such an act would be "deeply false," not the innocent self-effacing gesture of protest it purports to be, but a self-affirming "spectacle," calculated both to rid her of the strong sense of unreality that plagues her following her visit to the township and to gain her recognition from the "otherworld." Hence her obsession with Florence's imagined reaction to the "spectacle," were she to see it. Significantly, her speculations in this regard culminate with the dream in which "Florence does not stop to watch. Gaze fixed ahead, she passes as if through a congregation of wraiths." Like the representations of the cultural other in Coetzee's earlier novels, Florence refuses to acknowledge the doubting self's existence and thereby enable it to affirm its reality.

There is a strong indication in these passages that Mrs. Curren's "spectacle" should be seen as an analogue for white literature in South Africa. Not only is it compared to a literary work open to multiple interpretations, but Mrs. Curren likens herself to "a juggler, a clown, an entertainer," that is, to an artist of sorts. The suggestion seems to be that, like Mrs. Curren's "spectacle," literature by white South African writers constitutes a trivial gesture whose function is narcissistic rather than interventionist, that is, calculated to allay an endemic sense of guilt and to affirm a precarious sense of self. Indeed, the novel implies that the white South African writer's order of experience is so different from that of the black South African as to render it impossible for him/her to represent black life. The point is that even language—the very condition of possibility for the novel and for protest—has been contaminated by the politics of violence in South Africa. Thus, *Age of Iron* questions the possibility of effective literary protest from within the prison house of a deformed language.

Despite its trenchant criticism of white writing, however, this novel does not advocate silence as the only authentic avenue open to the white writer. After all, as a linguistic artifact, the novel itself is a product of white South African writing. Moreover, Mrs. Curren, significantly enough, keeps on writing until she dies. After echoing Hamlet with the words, "The rest should be silence," she goes on to say: "But with this—whatever it is—this voice that is no voice, I go on. On and on." And she does so in order to preserve that which "is condemned unheard," which is "everything indefinite, everything that gives when you press it." This category encompasses everything that has become obsolete in the age of iron in which "only blows are real, blows and bullets": people such as Vercueil, concepts such as Mrs. Curren's liberal humanist values, and words and "devious discourse" such as the novel form itself. The point behind the notion of the "unheard" seems to be that the function of literature in a society that has been dehumanized by an iniquitous political system should be to preserve the idea of humanity. This concept of the function of literature explains the constant allusions to the Circe myth in the novel. Just as the herb moly that Hermes gave Odysseus protected him from being transformed into a pig by Circe, so too art could protect South Africans from the dehumanizing influence of the cycle of violence in their society.

Age of Iron is ultimately a meditation on the role of literature in an "age of iron," that is, in a political climate that is hostile not only to the idea of humanity but also to the literary form that, over the centuries, has served as a vehicle for this idea. As such it is also a response of sorts to attempts to dictate the form that the novel should follow in South Africa, attempts that inevitably relegate that which deviates from the prescribed pattern to the status of the "unheard." Van Wyk Smith touches on this metafictional debate in *Age of Iron* when he argues that Mrs. Curren's "intimate quest for a validating narrative, a story that attempts to write her back into a meaningful history even while recognising its own inability to do so, is precisely Coetzee's response to those who demand an actualised text commensurate with sociopolitical events."

Apart from Van Wyk Smith's article, the response from the South African critical establishment to the provocative metafictional polemic of this novel was surprisingly sparse. The general responses to the novel, however, have been positive on the whole. Lionel Abrahams found that "the articulate passion with which the novel's protagonist and its author respond to the historical horror. . . . is vastly different from the usual, more or less excited, gestures of solidarity or provocation, cheek or subscription that pass as protest." Benita Parry saw it as an "elegy to liberal humanism," and Riaan Malan described it similarly as "the death rattle of the white liberal tradition in South African writing, and perhaps in South African society, too." Such responses hint at Coetzee's concern with the deforming effect apartheid structures have had on South African life and art.

In 1991 Coetzee spent a semester as visiting professor of English at Harvard University. His next novel, *The Master of Petersburg,* was published in 1994 and was therefore written during the period in which the apartheid government finally collapsed. Far from dealing with this momentous transition, though, *The Master of Petersburg* is set in late-nineteenth-century Russia. So, while *Age of Iron* seemed to suggest a desire on Coetzee's part to engage more directly with the overt politics of the day in South Africa, the later novel appears to indicate a return to the strategy of temporal and geographical displacement that characterizes his earlier work. Apart from this difference, these two novels are remarkably similar.

As in the earlier text, in *The Master of Petersburg* Coetzee deals with the deforming impact of societal structures of power and the role that literature plays in either reinforcing or resisting these structures. Set in St. Petersburg, this novel focuses on the murder of a young student, Ivanov, by a group of nihilists led by Sergei Nechaev. This incident is probably best remembered as the historical event that prompted Fyodor Dostoevsky to write *The Devils* (1871), a work in which he tried to link moral evil and political nihilism. Dostoevsky achieved this identification by means of the biblical story of the Gadarene swine, a tale in which unclean devils, having been exorcised from two possessed men by Jesus Christ, enter a herd of swine. This story generates in the novel a series of analogies that suggest Russia is a "sick man" possessed by devils and that the swine that the devils enter when exorcised are the revolutionaries.

In *The Master of Petersburg* Coetzee employs the same parallels—as becomes apparent when his own character, Dostoevsky, argues that it is futile to imprison revolutionaries such as Sergei Nechaev since nihilism is a "spirit" for which the individual is merely a "vehicle," a "host." This parallelism does not mean, however, that Coetzee shares the actual Dostoevsky's conviction that the nihilists are possessed by the devil. It is significant in this regard that Coetzee applies the story of the Gadarene swine not only to Russia and the phenomenon of revolutionary nihilism but also to Dostoevsky himself and his literary response to this phenomenon. Thus, in *The Master of Petersburg,* Dostoevsky is depicted as a "sick man" possessed by devils. And, while engaging in sexual intercourse with him, Anna Sergeyevna, at the onset of climax, utters the word "devil." Importantly, in this scene the sexual act is depicted as both an inspiration and an exorcism, with Anna Sergeyevna occupying the dual role of muse and exorcist. As the novel ends shortly afterward with Dostoevsky commencing work on *The Devils,* the implication is, therefore, that this text is also to be equated with the exorcised spirits in the story of the Gadarene swine. The further inference is that the readers within whom copies of the novel can be said to take up residence correspond to the swine in the biblical story.

Coetzee's reworking of the story of the Gadarene swine in *The Master of Petersburg* appears to be a comment on the implication of writer and literature in the power dynamics or "sickness" of the social context in which they are located. Through applying the story to the artist and the artistic process itself, Coetzee suggests that Dostoevsky and his work are not immune to the "sickness" of Russia. Both are a part of Russia and are therefore also "sick."

The point Coetzee makes in this text is, therefore, similar to that which emerges from his previous novel: that the literature produced in an "age of iron," that is, a society and a period that have been "defined" and thus debased by "unnatural structures of power," is "a less than fully human literature." In its inevitable preoccupation with "power and the torsions of power," such literature is as "stunted" and "deformed" as the life that it seeks to represent. Accordingly, it colludes with the networks of power that have dehumanized the society. In this regard, it is significant that the imagery Coetzee uses in *The Master of Petersburg* to indicate the ability of literature to brutalize is similar to that which he uses in *Age of Iron* to suggest the dehumanizing impact of the state's power relations.

In 1999 Coetzee published three books. The pamphlet *The Novel in Africa* is the text of a lecture delivered in Berkeley, California, on 11 November 1998. *The Lives of Animals* is also based on a lecture: Coetzee delivered the central text as a Tanner Lecture in the Humanities at Princeton University, but it is actually more of a postmodernist fiction. At the heart of the book is a story that Coetzee read at Princeton; the story purports to be a lecture on animal rights delivered by an elderly novelist, Elizabeth Costello, with interpolations by other characters, who are responding to the lecture. The rest of the book is composed of responses to Coetzee/Costello's lecture by various real-world academics in disciplines such as anthropology and bioethics.

The third book published in 1999 was Coetzee's eighth novel, *Disgrace,* which is set in South Africa in the late 1990s. The protagonist, David Lurie, is a fifty-two-year-old professor at the Technical University of Cape Town. The novel opens with a consideration of the fate of an aging scholar, a specialist in the Romantic poets who is reduced to teaching introductory courses in "communications," which he despises, as the university has changed its emphasis from liberal arts to that of "technical education." Lurie has a brief affair with Melanie, one of his female students, who is oddly passive and ambivalent about the relationship. When the affair comes to the attention of the university authorities—Lurie suspects that Melanie's boyfriend has informed on him—Lurie is told by the school administration to apologize and enter into counseling if he wishes to save his career. Seeing himself as being scapegoated by the forces of political correctness, he pleads guilty to the charge of sexual harassment but refuses to apologize or be repentant.

Leaving the university in disgrace, Lurie goes to visit his lesbian daughter, Lucy, who lives alone on a smallholding in the Eastern Cape. She is eking out a meager existence managing dog kennels and raising flowers and vegetables for market in cooperation with her black neighbor, Petrus. For a time Lurie finds a sort of peace on the farm as he helps Lucy, though the two have had an uneasy relationship since he and Lucy's mother divorced some years earlier. The fragile peace is shattered, however, when the farm is invaded by three men who at first pretend to need help and then attack Lurie and his daughter, setting him on fire and locking him in the bathroom while they sexually assault Lucy.

The remainder of the novel concerns Lurie's and his daughter's attempts to come to terms with what has happened to them. The three attackers were black, and Lucy comes to see the rape as a sort of retribution for historical racial injustice. She is pregnant as a result of the rape and is determined to keep the child. Lurie is horrified by her response, but he too sees the assault in terms of historical inevitability, as the result of a sort of inherited guilt.

Sales for *Disgrace* far exceeded those for *Waiting for the Barbarians*. In a review of *Disgrace* for *The New York Times* (11 November 1999), Christopher Lehmann-Haupt noted that the book reflects the uncertainty of postapartheid South Africa, where "all values are shifting"; he also noted that "The effect of the novel's plot is deeply disturbing, in part because of what happens to David and Lucy, but equally because of the disintegrating context of their experiences." Reviewing the book for the 27 July 1999 *Mail & Guardian* (Johannesburg), Jane Taylor called the novel "remarkable in its gauging of the contemporary dilemmas arising from our circumstances in a society obsessed by our own violent context." Noting that central to the work is "the failure of the imagination," she pointed out that in this aspect *Disgrace* is linked to *The Lives of Animals*: "these two works in conjunction explore the sealing off of imaginative identification that has been a necessary precondition for us to engage in the long-term and sustained business of slaughter."

Writing in *The New Republic* (20 December 1999), James Wood argued that "a significant weakness" in the novel is the "formal parallel of disgrace": as a result of what happened to Lucy, and her reaction to it, Lurie comes to accept the necessity of being penitent for his actions, but the "formal parallel" equates his disgrace with Lucy's, and hers is, Wood argued, "not one that she earned or deserved." Wood also noted that the "rather shocking notion of rape as historical reparation. . . . has earned Coetzee a certain amount of covert condemnation." *Disgrace* was generally critically well received, however, and earned Coetzee a second Booker Prize—he thus became the first novelist in the thirty-one-year history of the award to win twice.

This singular distinction may have helped to draw an unusual amount of attention to *Disgrace,* which has attracted a large body of critical commentary, some of it focused on the apparently pessimistic picture of life, for at least some people, in a new majority-ruled South Africa. Moreover, because Lucy's attackers are black, the novel led to a "bruising clash" with the ANC, the ruling party of South Africa. Denouncing the book as the work of a racist who believed blacks were "savage, violent and incapable of refinement through education," the party referred Coetzee's novel to the South African Human Rights Commission as a work promoting racial hatred.

Coetzee's relationship with South Africa had always been complex, and the events depicted in *Disgrace* suggest that the choice of whites in the new society was, like Lucy, to accept harsh conditions or to leave. He has chosen to leave. In 2002 he moved to Australia with his companion, literary critic Dorothy Driver, where he accepted an honorary research fellowship at the University of Adelaide. Always reticent, he has refused to confirm the widespread interpretation that he was shaken by the reaction to *Disgrace*. Malan, by contrast, suggests that the book itself was "clearly a valedictory to South Africa" and if that is so, then the reaction by the ANC or anyone else would have nothing to do with his departure. However, his new residence in Australia (combined with his frequent temporary residencies elsewhere, including the University of Chicago, where he spent one semester per year from 1996 to 2003, and where he remains a member of the Committee on Social Thought), and the subject matter of his work since 2002 complicate one's understanding of how Coetzee is still a South African novelist.

In *Stranger Shores: Literary Essays, 1986–1999* (2001) he reflects on South African life and letters (in a volume that demonstrates the breadth of his interests and knowledge by also commenting on English, Dutch, Russian, Egyptian, Indian, Israeli, Czech, and Argentine authors). Reviewing the work of Breyten Breytenbach, he reflects on the "gruesome reports . . . of attacks on whites in the countryside of the new South Africa"—the most sensational feature of *Disgrace*—and concludes that "the circulation of horror stories is the very mechanism that drives white paranoia about being chased off the land and ultimately into the sea." In an essay on Gordimer, Coetzee reveals, if only by indirection, his own disagreements with Gordimer's politically committed, sometimes polemical, writing:

> she has been concerned to give her work a social justification, and thus to support her claim to a place inside history, a history which she herself has to some extent been successful in shaping, as, in her fictional oeuvre, she has written the struggle of Africa against Europe upon the consciousness of the West.

Coetzee is a different kind of writer, as his next book made clear.

Youth is in one way obviously a second volume of Coetzee's memoirs, following on from *Boyhood*. Like that earlier book, it tells the story of a South African living in Cape Town and suffering from a range of miseries. The laconic narrator calls the main character "he," though from the discourse of other characters he is identified as "John." The story is told in the third person and present tense. Many details of John's life accord with those of Coetzee's: youth in Worcester, undergraduate studies at the University of Cape Town, expatriation to London, work as a computer programmer at IBM and International Computers.

But in Britain at least, *Youth* was marketed as fiction. The proof copy distributed to reviewers called it Coetzee's first novel since *Disgrace*. Eileen Battersby in the *Irish Times* (6 April 2002) welcomed it as a "taut new novel," and it is true that nothing in the book acknowledges that John is Coetzee. Nor, despite John's longing to be an artist, is there anything in the book (which ends with its protagonist, age twenty-four, still at loose ends in London) to show that its main character possesses the seeds of future worldwide literary success. An interview with Coetzee (conducted by e-mail) referred to *Youth* as "your most recent novel in the form of a memoir," and in his responses Coetzee consistently referred to John as "he." John Updike refers to *Youth* as "the second installment of what seems to be an ongoing memoirist project."

It is certainly the portrait of an artist as a young man, and like James Joyce's semi-autobiographical novel about his alter ego Stephen Dedalus, it mixes bitter recollection with a generous dose of irony (though the irony is easy to miss because of the austere language, and has been missed by some reviewers). John is by no means an admirable or even likable protagonist; nor does he admire or like himself. He is indolent, usually nearly friendless, and self-absorbed; self-conscious about his outsider status, he knows his artistic ambitions set him apart from his fellows as do his unimpressive appearance, wrong clothes, and, in London, provincial accent. He is good at mathematics and, without particularly wanting it, achieves success as a computer programmer in early-1960s London. More surprisingly, he is a successful seducer of women. This achievement is tainted by the fact that he never seems to enjoy sex or bring joy to his sex partners, and he behaves badly toward women. Disapproving reviewers called John "a model of romantic gloom and willed turmoil . . . a monster of self-absorption" (Jason Cowley, *The Observer*, 21 April 2002), and Mark Shechner (*Buffalo News*, 15 September 2002), reading John autobiographically, summed up Coetzee as "a summa cum laude in stylish depression and the South African master of the blues." But the picture is redeemed by the irony with which John is sometimes handled, as when the narrator reveals that "As for his own writing, he would hope to leave behind, were he to die tomorrow, a handful of poems that, edited by some selfless scholar and privately printed in a neat little duodecimo pamphlet, would make people shake their heads and murmur beneath their breath, 'Such promise! Such a waste!' That is his hope."

John is a proxy for Coetzee if he is not Coetzee, and some of the things he thinks and the positions he takes shed light on Coetzee's later career. When he writes his first story (he is mostly a poet at this point) he is disquieted that, though living in England, he is still writing about South Africa:

> He would prefer to leave his South African self behind as he has left South Africa itself behind. South Africa was a bad start, a handicap. An undistinguished, rural family, bad schooling, the Afrikaans language: from each of these component handicaps he has, more or less, escaped. He is in the great world earning his own living and not doing too badly, or at least not failing, not obviously.

Those last modifications exemplify the careful tone and the ironic distance between narrator and John that characterize *Youth*. Near the end of the book comes the diagnosis: "If he were a warmer person he would no doubt find it all easier: life, love, poetry. But warmth is not in his nature." The chill is emotional and finds its symbolic counterpart in the cold London to which the African John has exiled himself. John has flown past the nets—language, upbringing—and it is typical of the subdued representation of the artist in embryo that the book ends, not with some artistic advance, but with a rueful acknowledgment of deficiency and a readiness to die.

In the autumn of 2003 Coetzee published his next novel and, within weeks, received word that he was the 2003 Nobel laureate for Literature. The novel, *Elizabeth Costello*, like *Youth*, challenged genre expectations. The subtitle of the British edition is *Eight Lessons*, and the U.S. edition identifies the chapters as "lessons" in the table of contents. Moreover, the contents of the book have an unusual publishing history. Lessons 1 and 6, called "Realism" and "Eros," were published in slightly different form in *Salmagundi*, a literary quarterly, in 1997 and 2003. The postscript, "Letter of Elizabeth, Lady Chandos, to Francis Bacon," was published as a pamphlet by Intermezzo Press in 2002. Earlier versions of Lesson 2, "The Novel in Africa," and Lesson 5, "The Humanities in Africa," had also been separately published, in Berkeley, California, and in Munich. And the central portion of *Elizabeth Costello*, Lessons 3 and 4, which are titled "The Lives of Animals: The Philosophers and the Animals" and "The Lives of Animals: The Poets and the Animals," were the 1997–1998 Tanner Lectures at Princeton University published as *The Lives of Animals*.

The invitation to Coetzee to deliver the Tanner Lectures parallels the situation of his fictional Elizabeth Costello. A famous and aging Australian novelist, Elizabeth is invited to lecture at Appleton College in Massachusetts. Expected to speak about literature, she surprises her hosts by giving two powerful, intransigent lectures on the mistreatment of animals, giving offense by insisting on the equivalence between that treatment and the Holocaust. Similarly, Coetzee, invited to deliver the Tanner Lectures, read what amounted to two stories: the accounts of how Elizabeth delivered her animal-rights lectures at Appleton College, complete with the audience reaction, her son's sad and her daughter-in-law's furious responses, and Elizabeth's own hesitancies. She is not a good lecturer; her son even remembers that, though a fiction writer, she read stories badly to her children. The second lecture ends with Elizabeth's frustration: as her son is driving her to the airport, she speaks through tears. "Calm down, I tell myself, you are making a mountain out of a molehill. This is life. Everyone else comes to terms with it, why can't you? *Why can't you?*" John consoles her, after a fashion, with a reminder of her age and mortality: "There, there. It will soon be over."

In one of the responses printed in *The Lives of Animals,* literary critic Marjorie Garber says that "the genre of these lectures, then, is metafiction, and together they constitute a version of the academic novel, though critically this one is suffused with pathos rather than comedy." Invited lectures comprising, or approximating, an academic novel were thus followed by a novel consisting of lectures.

There is a further metafictional move when the two lectures of *The Lives of Animals* are incorporated into *Elizabeth Costello,* which begins with some metafictional placing gestures. The first sentence is "There is first of all the problem of the opening, namely, how to get us from where we are, which is, as yet, nowhere, to the far bank." Elizabeth is put before the reader (at yet another lecturing engagement at a college): "The blue costume, the greasy hair, are details, signs of a moderate realism. Supply the particulars, allow the significations to emerge of themselves. A procedure pioneered by Daniel Defoe." The self-conscious commentary continues:

> The presentation scene itself we skip. It is not a good idea to interrupt the narrative too often, since storytelling works by lulling the reader or listener into a dream-like state in which the time and space of the real world fade away, superseded by the time and space of the fiction. Breaking into the dream draws attention to the constructedness of the story, and plays havoc with the realist illusion. However, unless certain scenes are skipped over we will be here all afternoon. The skips are not part of the text, they are part of the performance.

Coetzee has carefully emphasized several of the features of *Elizabeth Costello* that led reviewers to deny that it is a novel. One is that, though it is quite "realistic" in one sense—it is much like a series of lectures and arguments about art and morality and belief, which is what it purports to be—in others it completely fails any "realistic" aim. It lacks particulars, of the Defoe sort; it never lulls the reader into a dream-like state. And this lack is related to the claim that it is dangerous to interrupt the narrative; a low proportion of *Elizabeth Costello* is narrative at all. There are narrative framings: each lesson places Elizabeth in a setting and provides her with a challenge for the exposition of her ideas. Besides American colleges, these include a conference in Amsterdam, an African university where her sister is receiving an honorary degree, an ocean liner where she is providing intellectual stimulation for the passengers, and a "place" that seems to be purgatory, while reminiscent of Franz Kafka's "Vor dem Gesetz" (Before the Law) segment of *Der Prozeß* (1925; translated as *The Trial,* 1937) as well as the camps of the Holocaust. But the heart of each lesson is Elizabeth's expatiating. She is not always consistent, and presumably is not always speaking for the author (this claim is hard to be sure about); she is provided with able and intelligent people who disagree with her and challenge her beliefs.

Critical reaction to *Elizabeth Costello* varied widely. The genre question was common: Tony Freemantle in the *Houston Chronicle* (23 November 2003) asked if it was "a pseudo-biographical, quasi-philosophical work of nonfiction masquerading as a novel? Or is it a novel simply not dressed up to look like one?" In the *Guardian* (30 August 2003) Hermione Lee called it a "fragmentary and inconclusive book, more like a collection of propositions about belief, writing and humanity than a novel." She did identify a unifying thematic core, noting that "Costello (and presumably Coetzee) opposes 'embodiment'—fullness, the sensation of being—against mechanical, abstract, rational cogitation. . . . Every episode in the novel acts out this opposition between 'embodiment' and 'reason.' Coetzee puts Costello in the almost untenable position of mounting a reasoned attack on reason." And Andrew Marr of *The Daily Telegraph* (6 September 2003) concurred: "The evil that Costello identifies is based on the triumph of reason and the downgrading of imagination." Many reviewers judged that the issue that had received the most attention—kindness to animals—functioned as one instance, but not the only one, of the human defect of failure of imagination. By contrast, Jonathan Yardley, writing for the *Washington Post* (16 November 2003), dismissed the book as "an exercise in the higher self-indulgence: a succession of almost unimaginably tiresome ruminations, cast in the form of formal academic addresses, about big-ticket issues in which Coetzee himself is interested, ranging from storytelling to cruelty to animals (this one gets two full chapters all to itself) to the mystery of artistic genius to evil pure and simple."

In December 2003 Coetzee delivered his Nobel Prize lecture. His address, called "He and His Man," is a speculation on Robinson Crusoe. He considers Crusoe as a writer, losing his fertility, and ends with some reflections on the relationship between Crusoe (who is writer, but is also written) and Defoe:

> How are they to be figured, this man and he? As master and slave? As brothers, twin brothers? As comrades in arms? Or as enemies, foes? What shall he give this nameless fellow with whom he shares his evenings and

sometimes his nights too, who is absent only in the daytime, when he, Robin, walks the quays inspecting the new arrivals and his man gallops about the kingdom making his inspections?

"He and His Man" was also published in *Queen's Quarterly* (identified as a short story) and (as an essay) in *World Literature Today*.

When asked in an 8 December 2003 interview with Attwell about the significance of the Nobel Prize to him personally and in general terms, Coetzee replied:

> In its conception the literature prize belongs to days when a writer could still be thought of as, by virtue of his or her occupation, a sage, someone with no institutional affiliations who could offer an authoritative word on our times as well as on our moral life. . . . The idea of writer as sage is pretty much dead today. I would certainly feel very uncomfortable in the role.

He also commented that he was already "being peppered with invitations to travel far and wide to give lectures," which he considered "one of the stranger aspects of literary fame: you prove your competence as a writer and an inventor of stories, and then people clamour for you to make speeches and tell them what you think about the world."

The awarding of the Nobel Prize has probably changed Coetzee less than would have been the case for another writer. His inwardness and resistance to the publicity dimension of being a writer in the twenty-first century ensure that. The prize may have raised the stakes in his critical reception: for example, Yardley's negative review of *Elizabeth Costello*, published in the *Chicago Sun-Times* (14 December 2003), was headlined "An Overrated Nobelist?" Reviewing Coetzee's next novel, *Slow Man* (2005), for *The Independent (London)* (2 September 2005), D. J. Taylor wrote, "As with many a writer of this degree of celebrity—a Nobel Prize back in 2003, two Booker garlands—the novel's chief distinction is that it resembles other works by J M Coetzee only more so." Rosemary Sorenson, writing for *The Courier Mail* (10 September 2005) in Coetzee's adopted Australia, said the "Nobel prize-winner's arrogant pursuit of his own writerly interest is part of his attraction. You like it or you lump it, and it's so dashing it's easy to like it for what it is." Whether receiving the prize has changed what Coetzee writes, or just the mental map of those who read him, is unclear, but "Nobel-Prize-winning" has henceforth been enrolled among the modifiers—"challenging," "uncompromising," "brilliant," perhaps even "exasperating"—that attach themselves to the name J. M. Coetzee.

Coetzee's first post–Nobel novel, *Slow Man*, appeared in fall 2005. This book is set in Australia and focuses on retired photographer Paul Rayment, who is forced to reevaluate his life when his leg is amputated after a bicycle accident. His new situation becomes more difficult when he falls in love with his day nurse, a married Croatian woman named Marijana. Then Elizabeth Costello appears, visiting Paul to challenge and encourage him. Brad Hooper of *Booklist* called Elizabeth's presence an "exasperating contrivance," while the reviewer for *Publishers Weekly*, noting that "Some readers will object to this cleverness," went on to say that "the story of how Paul will take charge of his life and love continues to engage, while Elizabeth Costello the device softens into a real character, one facing frailties of her own."

In 1986, in his article "Into the Dark Chamber: The Writer and the South African State" (collected in *Doubling the Point*), Coetzee articulates the South African novelist's desire for the freedom that true change would bring: "When the choice is no longer limited to *either* looking on in horrified fascination as the blow falls *or* turning one's eyes away, then the novel can once again take as its province the whole of life, and even the torture chamber can be accorded a place in the design." Elsewhere, he has argued that such freedom is a precondition for the writing of novels that are truly great. Coetzee has freed himself from the expectation that his works will intervene in history; from the "handicaps" of South African residency; from the "public" expectations of the famous writer; and from some of the superfluities of fiction. The announcement of his Nobel Prize praised not only the "well-crafted composition, pregnant dialogue and analytical brilliance" of his novels but also the fact that Coetzee is "a scrupulous doubter, ruthless in his criticism of the cruel rationalism and cosmetic morality of western civilisation." The intellectual honesty and the scrupulous doubting recognized by the Swedish Academy are the real wellspring of Coetzee's freedom.

Interviews:

Stephen Watson, "Speaking: J. M. Coetzee," *Speak*, 1, no. 3 (1978): 21–24;

Avril Herber, "John Coetzee," in *Conversations: Some People, Some Place, Some Time–South Africa*, edited by Herber (Johannesburg: Bateleur, 1979), pp. 174–178;

Sophie Mayoux, "J.-M. Coetzee: 'Il n'est pas de texte qui ne soit politique,'" *La Quinzaine Littéraire*, 357 (1981): 6;

Folke Rhedin, "Exilen i hemlandet tre vita sydafrikanska föfattare intervjuas av Folke Rhedin," *Bonniers Litterära Magasin*, 53, no. 1 (1984): 14–20;

Tony Morphet, "An Interview with J. M. Coetzee," *Social Dynamics,* 10, no. 1 (1984): 62–65; reprinted in *TriQuarterly,* 69 (Spring/Summer 1987): 454–462;

Rhedin, "Interview," *Kunapipi,* 6, no. 1 (1984): 6–11;

J. D. Sévry, "Interview de J. M. Coetzee," in *J. M. Coetzee: Dossier for Société des Anglicistes de l'Enseignment Supérieur–Colloque de Brest, 9–11 Mai 1985,* edited by Sévry (Montpellier: Université Paul Valéry, 1985), pp. 43–53;

Claude Wauthier, "Jean-Marie Coetzee contra la répression," in *J. M. Coetzee: Dossier for Société des Anglicistes de l'Enseignment Supérieur–Colloque de Brest, 9–11 Mai 1985,* p. 54;

Tony Morphet, "Two Interviews with J. M. Coetzee, 1983 and 1987," *TriQuarterly,* 69 (Spring/Summer 1987): 454–464;

Richard Begam, "An Interview with J. M. Coetzee," *Contemporary Literature,* 33 (Fall 1992): 419–431;

"An Interview with J. M. Coetzee," *World Literature Today,* 70 (Winter 1996): 107–110;

David Attwell, "An Exclusive Interview with J M Coetzee," *DN Kultur* (8 December 2003) <http://www.dn.se/DNet/jsp/polopoly.jsp?d=1058&a=212382>.

Bibliography:

Kevin Goddard and John Read, *J. M. Coetzee: A Bibliography* (Grahamstown: National English Literary Museum, 1990).

References:

Derek Attridge, "Ethical Modernism: Servants as Others in J. M. Coetzee's Early Fiction," *Poetics Today,* 25, no. 4 (Winter 2004): 653–671;

Attridge, "Literary Form and the Demands of Politics: Otherness in J. M. Coetzee's *Age of Iron,*" in *Aesthetics and Ideology,* edited by George Levine (New Brunswick, N.J.: Rutgers University Press, 1994), pp. 243–263;

David Attwell, "The Problem of History in the Fiction of J. M. Coetzee," in *Rendering Things Visible: Essays on South African Literary Culture of the 1970s and 1980s,* edited by Martin Trump (Johannesburg: Ravan, 1990), pp. 94–133;

Rita Barnard, "J. M. Coetzee's *Disgrace* and the South African Pastoral," *Contemporary Literature,* 44, no. 2 (Summer 2003): 199–224;

Colin Bower, "J. M. Coetzee: Literary Con Artist and Poseur," *scrutiny2: issues in English studies in southern africa,* 8, no. 2 (2003): 3–23;

André P. Brink, "Writing against Big Brother: Notes on Apocalyptic Fiction in South Africa," *World Literature Today,* 58, no. 2 (1984): 189–194;

Annamaria Carusi, "*Foe:* The Narrative and Power," *Journal of Literary Studies,* 5, no. 2 (1989): 134–144;

Michael Chapman, "The Writing of Politics and the Politics of Writing: On Reading Dovey on Reading Lacan on Reading Coetzee on Reading . . . (?)," *Journal of Literary Studies,* 4, no. 3 (1988): 327–341;

Leon De Kock, "Symposium on *Disgrace,*" *scrutiny2: issues in English studies in southern africa,* 7, no. 1 (2002): 1–46;

Isidore Diala, "Nadine Gordimer, J. M. Coetzee, and André Brink: Guilt, Expiation, and the Reconciliation Process in Post-Apartheid South Africa," *Journal of Modern Literature,* 25, no. 2 (Winter 2001): 50–68;

John Douthwaite, "Melanie: Voice and Its Suppression in J. M. Coetzee's *Disgrace,*" *Current Writing: Text and Reception in Southern Africa,* 13, no. 1 (2001): 130–162;

Teresa Dovey, "Coetzee and His Critics: The Case of *Dusklands,*" *English in Africa,* 14, no. 2 (1987): 15–30;

Dovey, "The Intersection of Postmodern, Postcolonial and Feminist Discourse in J. M. Coetzee's *Foe,*" *Journal of Literary Studies,* 5, no. 2 (1989): 119–133;

Dovey, *The Novels of J. M. Coetzee: Lacanian Allegories* (Johannesburg: Ad. Donker, 1988);

Susan VanZanten Gallagher, *A Story of South Africa: J. M. Coetzee's Fiction in Context* (Cambridge, Mass.: Harvard University Press, 1991);

Allan Gardiner, "J. M. Coetzee's *Dusklands:* Colonial Encounters of the Robinsonian Kind," *World Literature Written in English,* 27, no. 2 (1987): 174–184;

Graham Huggan and Stephen Watson, eds., *Critical Perspectives on J. M. Coetzee* (London: Macmillan, 1996);

Rosemary Jane Jolly, *Colonization, Violence and Narration in White South African Writing: André Brink, Breyten Breytenbach and J. M. Coetzee* (Athens: Ohio University Press, 1996);

Peter Knox-Shaw, "*Dusklands:* A Metaphysics of Violence," *Commonwealth Novel in English,* 2, no. 1 (1983): 65–81;

Sue Kossew, "The Anxiety of Authorship: J. M. Coetzee's *The Master of Petersburg* (1994) and André Brink's *On the Contrary* (1993)," *English in Africa,* 23, no. 1 (1986): 67–88;

Kossew, ed., *Critical Essays on J. M. Coetzee* (New York: G. K. Hall, 1998);

Margaret Lenta, "Autrebiography: J. M. Coetzee's *Boyhood* and *Youth,*" *English in Africa,* 30, no. 1 (May 2003): 157–169;

Lenta, "Fictions of the Future," *English Academy Review,* 5 (1988): 133–145;

Michael Marais, "Languages of Power: A Story of Reading *Michael K*/Michael K," *English in Africa,* 16, no. 2 (1989): 31–48;

Marais, "Places of Pigs: The Tension between Implication and Transcendence in J. M. Coetzee's *Age of Iron* and *The Master of Petersburg*," *Journal of Commonwealth Literature,* 31, no. 1 (1996): 83–96;

Brian May, "J. M. Coetzee and the Question of the Body," *MFS: Modern Fiction Studies,* 47, no. 2 (Summer 2001): 391–420;

Tony Morphet, "Reading Coetzee in South Africa," *World Literature Today,* 78, no. 1 (January–April 2004): 14–16;

Lance Olsen, "The Presence of Absence: Coetzee's *Waiting for the Barbarians*," *Ariel,* 16, no. 2 (1985): 47–56;

Dick Penner, *Countries of the Mind: The Fiction of J. M. Coetzee* (New York: Greenwood Press, 1989);

Paul Rich, "Apartheid and the Decline of Civilization Idea: An Essay on Nadine Gordimer's *July's People* and J. M. Coetzee's *Waiting for the Barbarians*," *Research in African Literature,* 15 (1984): 365–393;

Rich, "Tradition and Revolt in South African Fiction: The Novels of André Brink, Nadine Gordimer and J. M. Coetzee," *Journal of Southern African Studies,* 9, no. 1 (1982): 54–73;

Gayatri Chakravorty Spivak, "Theory in the Margin: Coetzee's *Foe* Reading Defoe's *Crusoe/Roxana*," *English in Africa,* 17, no. 2 (1990): 1–23;

Paola Splendora, "'No More Mothers and Fathers': The Family Sub-Text in J. M. Coetzee's Novels," *Journal of Commonwealth Literature,* 38, no. 3 (July 2003): 148–161;

Louis Tremaine, "The Embodied Soul: Animal Being in the Work of J. M. Coetzee," *Contemporary Literature,* 44, no. 4 (Winter 2003): 587–612;

Malvern Van Wyk Smith, "Waiting for Silence; or, The Autobiography of Metafiction in Some Recent South African Novels," *Current Writing,* 3, no. 1 (1991): 91–104;

Michael Vaughan, "Literature and Politics: Currents in South African Writing in the Seventies," *Journal of Southern African Studies,* 9, no. 1 (1982): 118–138;

Stephen Watson, "Colonialism and the Novels of J. M. Coetzee," *Research in African Literatures,* 17, no. 3 (1986): 370–392;

Paul Williams, "*Foe*: The Story of Silence," *English Studies in Africa,* 31, no. 1 (1988): 33–39;

Gilbert Yeoh, "J. M. Coetzee and Samuel Beckett: Ethics, Truth-Telling, and Self-Deception," *Critique: Studies in Contemporary Fiction,* 44, no. 4 (Summer 2003): 331–348;

Lois Parkinson Zamora, "Allegories of Power in the Fiction of J. M. Coetzee," *Journal of Literary Studies,* 2, no. 1 (1986): 1–14.

2003 Nobel Prize in Literature Presentation Speech

by Per Wästberg of the Swedish Academy, 10 December 2003 (Translation from the Swedish)

Your Majesties, Your Royal Highnesses, Esteemed Nobel Laureates, Ladies and Gentlemen,

To write is to awaken counter-voices within oneself, and to dare enter into dialogue with them. The dangerous attraction of the inner self is John Coetzee's theme: the senses and bodies of people, the interiority of Africa. "To imagine the unimaginable" is the writer's duty. As a post-modern allegorist, Coetzee knows that novels that do not seek to mimic reality best convince us that reality exists.

Coetzee sees through the obscene poses and false pomp of history, lending voice to the silenced and the despised. Restrained but stubborn, he defends the ethical value of poetry, literature and imagination. Without them, we blinker ourselves and become bureaucrats of the soul.

John Coetzee's characters seek refuge beyond the zones of power. *Life and Times of Michael K.* gives form to the dream of an individual outside the fabric of human coexistence. Michael K. is a virgin being, viewing the world from an infinite remove. Although exposed to the violence of racist tyranny, he achieves through passivity a freedom that confounds both the apartheid regime and the guerrilla forces simply because he wants nothing: neither war nor revolution, neither power nor money.

Waiting for the Barbarians is a disturbing love story about wanting to possess another person and to turn that person inside out as though she were a riddle to be solved. Everyone who has recognised the threat of totalitarianism and felt the desire to own another person can learn from Coetzee's dark fables. With intense concreteness and verbally disciplined desperation, he tackles one of the great problems of the ages: understanding the driving forces of brutality, torture and injustice.

Who does the writing, who seizes power by taking pen in hand? Can black experience be depicted by a white person? In *Foe,* Friday is an African, already dehumanised by Defoe. To give speech to Friday would be to colonise him and deny him what remains of his integrity. The girl in *Waiting for the Barbarians* speaks an unintelligible language and has been blinded by torture; Michael K. has a harelip and Friday has had his tongue cut out. His life is recounted by Susan Barton: that is, through "white writing," the title of one of Coetzee's books.

However hard we attempt to grasp Michael and Friday, they have been made, by Coetzee, unsullied by interpretation. They remain silent. But between the lines, in what is unspoken, there is a distillation of feelings uncommon in contemporary literature.

The myth of the survivor on a desert island is the only story there is, Coetzee once said. Several of his books treat similar solitudes. Is it possible to stand outside history? Does freedom from the diktat of authority exist? "I don't like accomplices. God, let me be alone," says Jacobus Coetzee in the first novel, *Dusklands,* rejoicing in being abandoned. But he remains the tool of history, and what compels the natives to take him seriously is his victorious violence. He does, however, ask himself whether the blacks populate a wonderful world closed to his own senses: "Perhaps I have killed something of inestimable value."

Coetzee's work runs like a high-tension cable across an inhospitable South African landscape. Mrs. Curran in *Age of Iron* has witnessed monstrous actions but is unable to condemn them using the words of others. Neither will Coetzee himself sign petitions or join in political rallies.

In the dystopian novel *Disgrace,* David Lurie does not achieve creativity and freedom until, stripped of all dignity, he is afflicted by his own shame and history's disgrace. In this work, Coetzee summarises his themes: race and gender, ownership and violence, and the moral and political complicity of everyone in that borderland where the languages of liberation and reconciliation carry no meaning.

Every new book by Coetzee is astonishingly unlike his others. He intrudes into the uninhabited spaces of his readers. In his autobiographies, he pitilessly ransacks his former selves. In his essay-novel *Elizabeth Costello* he combines, with uninhibited humour and irony, contemporary narrative and myth, philosophy and gossip.

Dear John Coetzee,

Your work is limited in pages, limitless in scope. What I have said in Swedish to those present here is merely in so many words: "Don't listen to me, just go home and read, and some images will stay with you forever."

In your own life, you have recently moved along the very latitude that unites Cape Town and Adelaide. You may have left South Africa; it will hardly leave you. For the Swedish Academy, national roots are irrelevant and we do not recognize what in Europe is often called the literary periphery.

You are a Truth and Reconciliation Commission on your own, starting with the basic words for our deepest concerns. Unsettling and surprising us, you have dug deeply into the ground of the human condition with its cruelty and loneliness. You have given a voice to those outside the hierarchies of the mighty. With intellectual honesty and density of feeling, in a prose of icy precision, you have unveiled the masks of our civilization and uncovered the topography of evil.

I would like to express the warmest congratulations of the Swedish Academy as I now request you to receive this year's Nobel Prize for Literature from the hands of His Majesty the King.

[© The Nobel Foundation, 2003.]

Coetzee: Banquet Speech

Coetzee's speech at the Nobel Banquet, 10 December 2003

Your Majesties, Your Royal Highnesses, Ladies and Gentlemen; Distinguished Guests, Friends

The other day, suddenly, out of the blue, while we were talking about something completely different, my partner Dorothy burst out as follows: "On the other hand," she said, "*on the other hand,* how proud your mother would have been! What a pity she isn't still alive! And your father too! How proud they would have been of you!"

"Even prouder than of my son the doctor?" I said. "Even prouder than of my son the professor?"

"Even prouder."

"If my mother were still alive," I said, "she would be ninety-nine and a half. She would probably have senile dementia. She would not know what was going on around her."

But of course I missed the point. Dorothy was right. My mother would have been bursting with pride. *My son the Nobel Prize winner.* And for whom, anyway, do we do the things that lead to Nobel Prizes if not for our mothers?

"*Mommy, Mommy, I won a prize!*"

"*That's wonderful, my dear. Now eat your carrots before they get cold.*"

Why must our mothers be ninety-nine and long in the grave before we can come running home with the prize that will make up for all the trouble we have been to them?

To Alfred Nobel, 107 years in the grave, and to the Foundation that so faithfully administers his will and that has created this magnificent evening for us, my heartfelt gratitude. To my parents, how sorry I am that you cannot be here.

Thank you.

[© The Nobel Foundation, 2003. J. M. Coetzee is the sole author of the text.]

Press Release: The Nobel Prize in Literature 2003

from the Office of the Permanent Secretary of the Swedish Academy

The Nobel Prize in Literature for 2003 is awarded to the South African writer John Maxwell Coetzee, "who in innumerable guises portrays the surprising involvement of the outsider."

J. M. Coetzee's novels are characterised by their well-crafted composition, pregnant dialogue and analytical brilliance. But at the same time he is a scrupulous doubter, ruthless in his criticism of the cruel rationalism and cosmetic morality of western civilisation. His intellectual honesty erodes all basis of consolation and distances itself from the tawdry drama of remorse and confession. Even when his own convictions emerge to view, as in his defence of the rights of animals, he elucidates the premises on which they are based rather than he argues for them.

Coetzee's interest is directed mainly at situations where the distinction between right and wrong, while crystal clear, can be seen to serve no end. Like the man in the famous Magritte painting who is studying his neck in a mirror, at the decisive moment Coetzee's characters stand behind themselves, motionless, incapable of taking part in their own actions. But passivity is not merely the dark haze that devours personality, it is also the last resort open to human beings as they defy an oppressive order by rendering themselves inaccessible to its intentions. It is in exploring weakness and defeat that Coetzee captures the divine spark in man.

His earliest novel, *Dusklands*, was the first example of the capacity for empathy that has enabled Coetzee time and again to creep beneath the skin of the alien and the abhorrent. A man working for the American administration during the Vietnam war dreams of devising an unbeatable system of psychological warfare, while at the same time his private life disintegrates around him. His reflections are juxtaposed with a report on an expedition to explore the country of the native Africans, which purports to have been written by one of the 18th-century Boer pioneers. Two forms of misanthropy, one of them intellectual and megalomaniac, the other vital and barbaric, reflect each other.

One element in his next novel, *In the Heart of the Country*, is the portrayal of psychosis. A careworn spinster living with her father observes with distaste his love affair with a young coloured woman. She has fantasies of murdering both of them, but everything seems to indicate that she decides rather to immure herself in a perverse pact with the house servant. The actual sequence of events cannot be determined, as the reader's only sources are her notes, where lies and truths, crudeness and refinement alternate capriciously line by line. The high-flown Edwardian literary style of the woman's monologue harmonises strangely with the surrounding African landscape.

Waiting for the Barbarians is a political thriller in the tradition of Joseph Conrad, in which the idealist's naivety opens the gates to horror. The playful metanovel *Foe* spins a yarn about the incompatibility and inseparability of literature and life, told by a woman who yearns to be part of a major narrative when in reality only one of minor importance is offered.

With *Life and Times of Michael K,* which has its roots in Defoe as well as in Kafka and Beckett, the impression that Coetzee is a writer of solitude becomes clearer. The novel deals with the flight of an insignificant citizen from growing disorder and impending war to a state of indifference to all needs and speechlessness that negates the logic of power.

The Master of Petersburg is a paraphrase of Dostoevsky's life and fictional world. To die in one's heart away from the world, the temptation that Coetzee's imagined characters face, turns out to be the principle of the unconscionable liberty of terrorism. Here, the writer's struggle with the problem of evil is tinged with demonology, an element that recurs in his most recently published work, *Elizabeth Costello*.

In *Disgrace* Coetzee involves us in the struggle of a discredited university teacher to defend his own and his daughter's honour in the new circumstances that have arisen in South Africa after the collapse of white supremacy. The novel deals with a question that is central to his works: Is it possible to evade history?

His autobiographical *Boyhood* circles mainly around his father's humiliation and the psychological cleavage it has caused the son, but the book also conveys a magic impression of life in the old-fashioned South African countryside with its eternal conflicts between the Boers and the English and between white and black. In its sequel, *Youth,* the writer dissects himself as a young man with a cruelty that is oddly consoling for anyone able to identify with him.

There is a great wealth of variety in Coetzee's works. No two books ever follow the same recipe. Extensive reading reveals a recurring pattern, the downward spiralling journeys he considers necessary for the salvation of his characters. His protagonists are overwhelmed by the urge to sink but paradoxically derive strength from being stripped of all external dignity.

[©The Nobel Foundation, 2003].

Coetzee: Nobel Lecture, 7 December 2003

He and His Man

> But to return to my new companion. I was greatly delighted with him, and made it my business to teach him everything that was proper to make him useful, handy, and helpful; but especially to make him speak, and understand me when I spoke; and he was the aptest scholar there ever was.
>
> –Daniel Defoe, *Robinson Crusoe*

Boston, on the coast of Lincolnshire, is a handsome town, writes his man. The tallest church steeple in all of England is to be found there; sea-pilots use it to navigate by. Around Boston is fen country. Bitterns abound, ominous birds who give a heavy, groaning call loud enough to be heard two miles away, like the report of a gun.

The fens are home to many other kinds of birds too, writes his man, duck and mallard, teal and widgeon, to capture which the men of the fens, the fen-men, raise tame ducks, which they call decoy ducks or duckoys.

Fens are tracts of wetland. There are tracts of wetland all over Europe, all over the world, but they are not named fens, *fen* is an English word, it will not migrate.

These Lincolnshire duckoys, writes his man, are bred up in decoy ponds, and kept tame by being fed by hand. Then when the season comes they are sent abroad to Holland and Germany. In Holland and Germany they meet with others of their kind, and, seeing how miserably these Dutch and German ducks live, how their rivers freeze in winter and their lands are covered in snow, fail not to let them know, in a form of language which they make them understand, that in England from where they come the case is quite otherwise: English ducks have sea shores full of nourishing food, tides that flow freely up the creeks; they have lakes, springs, open ponds and sheltered ponds; also lands full of corn left behind by the gleaners; and no frost or snow, or very light.

By these representations, he writes, which are made all in duck language, they, the decoy ducks or duckoys, draw together vast numbers of fowl and, so to say, kidnap them. They guide them back across the seas from Holland and Germany and settle them down in their decoy ponds on the fens of Lincolnshire, chattering and gabbling to them all the time in their own language, telling them these are the ponds they told them of, where they shall live safely and securely.

And while they are so occupied the decoy-men, the masters of the decoy-ducks, creep into covers or coverts they have built of reeds upon the fens, and all unseen toss handfuls of corn upon the water; and the decoy ducks or duckoys follow them, bringing their foreign guests behind. And so over two or three days they lead their guests up narrower and narrower waterways, calling to them all the time to see how well we live in England, to a place where nets have been spanned.

Then the decoy-men send out their decoy dog, which has been perfectly trained to swim after fowl, barking as he swims. Being alarmed to the last degree by this terrible creature, the ducks take to the wing, but are forced down again into the water by the arched nets above, and so must swim or perish, under the net. But the net grows narrower and narrower, like a purse, and at the end stand the decoy-men, who take their captives out one by one. The decoy-ducks are stroked and made much of, but as for their guests, these are clubbed on the spot and plucked and sold by the hundred and by the thousand.

All of this news of Lincolnshire his man writes in a neat, quick hand, with quills that he sharpens with his little pen-knife each day before a new bout with the page.

In Halifax, writes his man, there stood, until it was removed in the reign of King James the First, an engine of execution, which worked thus. The condemned man was laid with his head on the cross-base or cup of the scaffold; then the executioner knocked out a pin which held up the heavy blade. The blade descended down a frame as tall as a church door and beheaded the man as clean as a butcher's knife.

Custom had it in Halifax, though, that if between the knocking out of the pin and the descent of the blade the condemned man could leap to his feet, run down the hill, and swim across the river without being seized again by the executioner, he would be let free. But in all the years the engine stood in Halifax this never happened.

He (not his man now but he) sits in his room by the waterside in Bristol and reads this. He is getting on in years, almost it might be said he is an old man by now. The skin of his face, that had been almost blackened by the tropic sun before he made a parasol out of palm or palmetto leaves to shade himself, is paler now, but still leathery like parchment; on his nose is a sore from the sun that will not heal.

The parasol he has still with him in his room, standing in a corner, but the parrot that came back with him has passed away. *Poor Robin!* the parrot would squawk from its perch on his shoulder, *Poor Robin Crusoe! Who shall save poor Robin?* His wife could not abide the lamenting of the parrot, *Poor Robin* day in, day out. *I shall wring its neck,* said she, but she had not the courage to do so.

When he came back to England from his island with his parrot and his parasol and his chest full of treasure, he lived for a while tranquilly enough with his old wife on the estate he bought in Huntingdon, for he had become a wealthy man, and wealthier still after the printing of the book of his adventures. But the years in the island, and then the years traveling with his servingman Friday (poor Friday, he laments to himself, squawk-squawk, for the parrot would never speak Friday's name, only his), had made the life of a landed gentleman dull for him. And, if the truth be told, married life was a sore disappointment too. He found himself retreating more and more to the stables, to his horses, which blessedly did not chatter, but whinnied softly when he came, to show that they knew who he was, and then held their peace.

It seemed to him, coming from his island, where until Friday arrived he lived a silent life, that there was too much speech in the world. In bed beside his wife he felt as if a shower of pebbles were being poured upon his head, in an unending rustle and clatter, when all he desired was to sleep.

So when his old wife gave up the ghost he mourned but was not sorry. He buried her and after a decent while took this room in *The Jolly Tar* on the Bristol waterfront, leaving the direction of the estate in Huntingdon to his son, bringing with him only the parasol from the island that made him famous and the dead parrot fixed to its perch and a few necessaries, and has lived here alone ever since, strolling by day about the wharves and quays, staring out west over the sea, for his sight is still keen, smoking his pipes. As to his meals, he has these brought up to his room; for he finds no joy in society, having grown used to solitude on the island.

He does not read, he has lost the taste for it; but the writing of his adventures has put him in the habit of writing, it is a pleasant enough recreation. In the evening by candlelight he will take out his papers and sharpen his quills and write a page or two of his man, the man who sends report of the duckoys of Lincolnshire, and of the great engine of death in Halifax, that one can escape if before the awful blade can descend one can leap to one's feet and dash down the hill, and of numbers of other things. Every place he goes he sends report of, that is his first business, this busy man of his.

Strolling along the harbour wall, reflecting upon the engine from Halifax, he, Robin, whom the parrot used to call poor Robin, drops a pebble and listens. A second, less than a second, before it strikes the water. God's grace is swift, but might not the great blade of tempered steel, being heavier than a pebble and being greased with tallow, be swifter? How will we ever escape it? And what species of man can it be who will dash so busily hither and thither across the kingdom, from one spectacle of death to another (clubbings, beheadings), sending in report after report?

A man of business, he thinks to himself. Let him be a man of business, a grain merchant or a leather merchant, let us say; or a manufacturer and purveyor of roof tiles somewhere where clay is plentiful, Wapping let us say, who must travel much in the interest of his trade. Make him prosperous, give him a wife who loves him and does not chatter too much and bears him children, daughters mainly; give him a reasonable happiness; then bring his happiness suddenly to an end. The Thames rises one winter, the kilns in which the tiles are baked are washed away, or the grain stores, or the leather works; he is ruined, this man of his, debtors descend upon him like flies or like crows, he has to flee his home, his wife, his children, and seek hiding in the most wretched of quarters in Beggars Lane under a false name and in disguise. And all of this—the wave of water, the ruin, the flight, the pennilessness, the tatters, the solitude—let all of this be a figure of the shipwreck and the island where he, poor Robin, was secluded from the world for twenty-six years, till he almost went mad (and indeed, who is to say he did not, in some measure?).

Or else let the man be a saddler with a home and a shop and a warehouse in Whitechapel and a mole on his chin and a wife who loves him and does not chatter and bears him children, daughters mainly, and gives him much happiness, until the plague descends upon the city, it is the year 1665, the great fire of London has not yet come. The plague descends upon London: daily, parish by parish, the count of the dead mounts, rich and poor, for the plague makes no distinction among stations, all this saddler's worldly wealth will not save him. He sends his wife and daughters into the countryside and makes plans to flee himself, but then does not. *Thou shalt not be afraid for the terror at night,* he reads, opening the Bible at hazard, *not for the arrow that flieth by day; not for the pestilence that walketh in darkness; nor for the destruction that wasteth at noon-day. A thousand shall fall at thy side, and ten thousand at thy right hand, but it shall not come nigh thee.*

Taking heart from this sign, a sign of safe passage, he remains in afflicted London and sets about writing reports. I came upon a crowd in the street, he writes, and a woman in their midst pointing to the heavens. *See,* she cries, *an angel in white brandishing a flaming sword!* And the crowd all nod among themselves, *Indeed it is so,* they say: *an angel with a sword!* But he, the saddler, can see no angel, no sword. All he can see is a strange-shaped cloud brighter on the one side than the other, from the shining of the sun.

It is an allegory! cries the woman in the street; but he can see no allegory for the life of him. Thus in his report.

On another day, walking by the riverside in Wapping, his man that used to be a saddler but now has no occupation observes how a woman from the door of her house calls out to a man rowing in a dory: *Robert! Robert!* she calls; and how the man then rows ashore, and from the dory takes up a sack which he lays upon a stone by the riverside, and rows away again; and how the woman comes down to the riverside and picks up the sack and bears it home, very sorrowful-looking.

He accosts the man Robert and speaks to him. Robert informs him that the woman is his wife and the sack holds a week's supplies for her and their children, meat and meal and butter; but that he dare not approach nearer, for all of them, wife and children, have the plague upon them; and that it breaks his heart. And all of this— the man Robert and wife keeping communion through calls across the water, the sack left by the waterside— stands for itself certainly, but stands also as a figure of his, Robinson's, solitude on his island, where in his hour of darkest despair he called out across the waves to his loved ones in England to save him, and at other times swam out to the wreck in search of supplies.

Further report from that time of woe. Able no longer to bear the pain from the swellings in the groin and armpit that are the signs of the plague, a man runs out howling, stark naked, into the street, into Harrow Alley in Whitechapel, where his man the saddler witnesses him as he leaps and prances and makes a thousand strange gestures, his wife and children running after him crying out, calling to him to come back. And this leaping and prancing is allegoric of his own leaping and prancing when, after the calamity of the shipwreck and after he had scoured the strand for sign of his shipboard companions and found none, save a pair of shoes that were not mates, he had understood he was cast up all alone on a savage island, likely to perish and with no hope of salvation.

(But of what else does he secretly sing, he wonders to himself, this poor afflicted man of whom he reads, besides his desolation? What is he calling, across the waters and across the years, out of his private fire?)

A year ago he, Robinson, paid two guineas to a sailor for a parrot the sailor had brought back from, he said, Brazil—a bird not so magnificent as his own well-beloved creature but splendid nonetheless, with green feathers and a scarlet crest and a great talker too, if the sailor was to be believed. And indeed the bird would sit on its perch in his room in the inn, with a little chain on its leg in case it should try to fly away, and say the words *Poor Poll! Poor Poll!* over and over till he was forced to hood it; but could not be taught to say any other word, *Poor Robin!* for instance, being perhaps too old for that.

Poor Poll, gazing out through the narrow window over the mast-tops and, beyond the mast-tops, over the grey Atlantic swell: *What island is this,* asks Poor Poll, *that I am cast up on, so cold, so dreary? Where were you, my Saviour, in my hour of great need?*

A man, being drunk and it being late at night (another of his man's reports), falls asleep in a doorway in Cripplegate. The dead-cart comes on its way (we are still in the year of the plague), and the neighbours, thinking the man dead, place him on the dead-cart among the corpses. By and by the cart comes to the dead pit at Mountmill and the carter, his face all muffled against the effluvium, lays hold of him to throw him in; and he wakes up and struggles in his bewilderment. *Where am I?* he says. *You are about to be buried among the dead,* says the carter. *But am I dead then?* says the man. And this too is a figure of him on his island.

Some London-folk continue to go about their business, thinking they are healthy and will be passed over. But secretly they have the plague in their blood: when the infection reaches their heart they fall dead upon the spot, so reports his man, as if struck by lightning. And this is a figure for life itself, the whole of life. Due preparation. We should make due preparation for death, or else be struck down where we stand. As he, Robinson, was made to see when of a sudden, on his island, he came one day upon the footprint of a man in the sand. It was a print, and therefore a sign: of a foot, of a man. But it was a sign of much else too. *You are not alone,* said the sign; and also, *No matter how far you sail, no matter where you hide, you will be searched out.*

In the year of the plague, writes his man, others, out of terror, abandoned all, their homes, their wives and children, and fled as far from London as they could. When the plague had passed, their flight was condemned as cowardice on all sides. But, writes his man, we forget what kind of courage was called on to confront the plague. It was not a mere soldier's courage, like gripping a weapon and charging the foe: it was like charging Death itself on his pale horse.

Even at his best, his island parrot, the better loved of the two, spoke no word he was not taught to speak by his master. How then has it come about that this man of his, who is a kind of parrot and not much loved, writes as well as or better than his master? For he wields an able pen, this man of his, no doubt of that. *Like charging Death himself on his pale horse*. His own skill, learned in the counting house, was in making tallies and accounts, not in turning phrases. *Death himself on his pale horse*: those are words he would not think of. Only when he yields himself up to this man of his do such words come.

And decoy ducks, or duckoys: What did he, Robinson, know of decoy ducks? Nothing at all, until this man of his began sending in reports.

The duckoys of the Lincolnshire fens, the great engine of execution in Halifax: reports from a great tour this man of his seems to be making of the island of Britain, which is a figure of the tour he made of his own island in the skiff he built, the tour that showed there was a farther side to the island, craggy and dark and inhospitable, which he ever afterwards avoided, though if in the future colonists shall arrive upon the island they will perhaps explore it and settle it; that too being a figure, of the dark side of the soul and the light.

When the first bands of plagiarists and imitators descended upon his island history and foisted on the public their own feigned stories of the castaway life, they seemed to him no more or less than a horde of cannibals falling upon his own flesh, that is to say, his life; and he did not scruple to say so. *When I defended myself against the cannibals, who sought to strike me down and roast me and devour me,* he wrote, *I thought I defended myself against the thing itself. Little did I guess,* he wrote, *that these cannibals were but figures of a more devilish voracity, that would gnaw at the very substance of truth.*

But now, reflecting further, there begins to creep into his breast a touch of fellow-feeling for his imitators. For it seems to him now that there are but a handful of stories in the world; and if the young are to be forbidden to prey upon the old then they must sit for ever in silence.

Thus in the narrative of his island adventures he tells of how he awoke in terror one night convinced the devil lay upon him in his bed in the shape of a huge dog. So he leapt to his feet and grasped a cutlass and slashed left and right to defend himself while the poor parrot that slept by his bedside shrieked in alarm. Only many days later did he understand that neither dog nor devil had lain upon him, but rather that he had suffered a palsy of a passing kind, and being unable to move his leg had concluded there was some creature stretched out upon it. Of which event the lesson would seem to be that all afflictions, including the palsy, come from the devil and are the very devil; that a visitation by illness may be figured as a visitation by the devil, or by a dog figuring the devil, and vice versa, the visitation figured as an illness, as in the saddler's history of the plague; and therefore that no one who writes stories of either, the devil or the plague, should forthwith be dismissed as a forger or a thief.

When, years ago, he resolved to set down on paper the story of his island, he found that the words would not come, the pen would not flow, his very fingers were stiff and reluctant. But day by day, step by step, he mastered the writing business, until by the time of his adventures with Friday in the frozen north the pages were rolling off easily, even thoughtlessly.

That old ease of composition has, alas, deserted him. When he seats himself at the little writing-desk before the window looking over Bristol harbour, his hand feels as clumsy and the pen as foreign an instrument as ever before.

Does he, the other one, that man of his, find the writing business easier? The stories he writes of ducks and machines of death and London under the plague flow prettily enough; but then so did his own stories once. Perhaps he misjudges him, that dapper little man with the quick step and the mole upon his chin. Perhaps at this very moment he sits alone in a hired room somewhere in this wide kingdom dipping the pen and dipping it again, full of doubts and hesitations and second thoughts.

How are they to be figured, this man and he? As master and slave? As brothers, twin brothers? As comrades in arms? Or as enemies, foes? What name shall he give this nameless fellow with whom he shares his evenings and sometimes his nights too, who is absent only in the daytime, when he, Robin, walks the quays inspecting the new arrivals and his man gallops about the kingdom making his inspections?

Will this man, in the course of his travels, ever come to Bristol? He yearns to meet the fellow in the flesh, shake his hand, take a stroll with him along the quayside and hearken as he tells of his visit to the dark north of the island, or of his adventures in the writing business. But he fears there will be no meeting, not in this life. If he must settle on a likeness for the pair of them, his man and he, he would write that they are like two ships sailing in contrary directions, one west, the other east. Or better, that they are deckhands toiling in the rigging, the one on a ship sailing west, the other on a ship sailing east. Their ships pass close, close enough to hail. But the seas are rough, the weather is stormy: their eyes lashed by the spray, their hands burned by the cordage, they pass each other by, too busy even to wave.

[© The Nobel Foundation, 2003. J. M. Coetzee is the sole author of the text.]

Grazia Deledda

(21 September 1871 – 15 August 1936)

Stefania Lucamante
Catholic University of America

and

E. Ann Matter
University of Pennsylvania

This entry has been expanded by Matter from Lucamante's Deledda entry in *DLB 264: Italian Prose Writers, 1900–1945*.

BOOKS: *Nell'azzurro* (Milan: Trevisani, 1890);
Stella d'Oriente, as Ilia di Saint-Ismael (Cagliari: Avvenire di Sardegna, 1891);
Fior di Sardegna (Rome: Perino, 1891);
Amore regale (Rome: Perino, 1892);
La regina delle tenebre (Turin: Orsiglia, 1892);
Anime oneste (Milan: Cogliati, 1893);
Racconti sardi (Sassari: Dessí, 1894);
Tradizioni popolari di Nuoro in Sardegna (Roma: Forzani & Senato, 1894);
La via del male (Turin: Speirani, 1896);
Il tesoro (Turin: Speirani, 1897);
L'ospite (Rocca San Casciano: Cappelli, 1897);
Paesaggi sardi (Turin: Speirani, 1897);
I tre talismani (Palermo: Sandron, 1899);
N.S. del buon consiglio: Leggenda sarda (Palermo: Sandron, 1899);
La giustizia (Turin: Speirani, 1899);
Giaffah (Palermo: Sandron, 1899);
Le disgrazie che può cagionare il denaro (Palermo: Sandron, 1899);
Le tentazioni (Milan: Cogliati, 1899);
Il vecchio della montagna (Turin: Roux & Viarengo, 1900);
Dopo il divorzio (Turin: Roux & Viarengo, 1902); republished as *Naufraghi in porto* (Milan: Treves, 1920); translated by Maria Hornor Lansdale as *After the Divorce: A Romance* (New York: Holt, 1905);
La regina delle tenebre (Milan: Agnelli, 1902);
Elias Portolu (Turin & Rome: Roux & Viarengo, 1903); translated by Martha King (London: Quartet, 1992);

*Grazia Deledda, 25 November 1927
(photograph © Bettmann/CORBIS)*

Cenere (Rome: Ripamonti & Colombo, 1904); translated by Helen Hester Colvill as *Ashes (Cenere): A Sardinian Story* (London & New York: John Lane, 1908);
I giuochi della vita (Milan: Treves, 1905);
Nostalgie (Rome: Nuova Antologia, 1905);
Amori moderni (Rome: Voghera, 1907);
L'ombra del passato (Rome: Nuova Antologia, 1907?);
L'edera (Rome: Nuova Antologia, 1908);
Il nonno (Rome: Nuova Antologia, 1908);
Il nostro padrone (Milan: Treves, 1910);
Sino al confine (Milan: Treves, 1910);
Nel deserto (Milan: Treves, 1911);
Chiaroscuro (Milan: Treves, 1912);
Colombi e sparvieri (Milan: Treves, 1912);

L'edera: Dramma in tre atti, by Deledda and Camillo Antona-Traversi (Milan: Treves, 1912);

Canne al vento (Milan: Treves, 1913); translated by King as *Reeds in the Wind* (New York: Italica, 1999);

Le colpe altrui (Milan: Treves, 1914);

Marianna Sirca (Milan: Treves, 1915);

Il fanciullo nascosto (Milan: Treves, 1916);

L'incendio nell'uliveto (Milan: Treves, 1918);

Il ritorno del figlio e La bambina rubata (Milan: Treves, 1919);

La madre (Milan: Treves, 1920); translated by Mary G. Steegman as *The Woman and the Priest* (London: Cape, 1922); translation republished as *The Mother* (New York: Macmillan, 1923; London: Cape, 1928);

La grazia: Dramma pastorale in tre atti, by Deledda, Claudio Guastallo, and Vicentino Michetti (Milan: Ricordi, 1921);

Cattive compagnie (Milan: Treves, 1921);

Il segreto dell'uomo solitario (Milan: Treves, 1921);

Il Dio dei viventi (Milan: Treves, 1922);

Il flauto nel bosco (Milan: Treves, 1923);

La danza della collana: Romanzo, seguito dal bozzetto drammatico "A sinistra" (Milan: Treves, 1924);

La fuga in Egitto (Milan: Treves, 1925);

Cani, gatti, pulcini ed altri animali: Scene rustiche (Palermo & Rome, 1926);

Il sigillo d'amore (Milan: Treves, 1926);

Il cieco di Gerico (Rome: Nuova Antologia, 1927);

Annalena Bilsini (Milan: Treves, 1927);

Il vecchio e i fanciulli (Milan: Treves, 1928);

Il dono di Natale (Milan: Treves, 1930);

La casa del poeta (Milan: Treves, 1930);

Il paese del vento (Milan: Treves, 1931);

La vigna sul mare (Milan: Treves, 1932);

Sole d'estate (Milan: Treves, 1933);

L'argine (Milan: Treves, 1934);

La chiesa della solitudine (Milan: Treves, 1936); translated by E. Ann Matter as *The Church of Solitude* (Albany: State University of New York Press, 2002);

Cosima (Milan: Treves, 1937); translated by King (New York: Italica, 1988);

Versi e prose giovanili, edited by Antonio Scano (Milan: Treves, 1938);

Il cedro del Libano (Milan: Garzanti, 1939).

Collections: *Romanzi e novelle,* Omnibus, 5 volumes, edited by Emilio Cecchi (Milan: Mondadori, 1941–1969);

Scritti scelti (Milan: Mondadori, 1959)—comprises *Canne al vento, Un dramma, La festa del Cristo, Chiaroscuro, La palma,* and *Contratto;*

Opere scelte, 2 volumes, edited by Eurialo De Michelis, I classici contemporanei italiani (Milan: Mondadori, 1964);

Romanzi e novelle, edited by Natalino Sapegno, I meridiani (Milan: Mondadori, 1971);

I grandi romanzi, edited by Marta Savini (Rome: Newton, 1993)—comprises *Il vecchio della montagna, Elias Portolu, Cenere, L'edera, Colombi e sparvieri, Canne al vento, Marianna Sirca, La madre, Annalena Bilsini,* and *Cosima.*

Editions in English: *Chiaroscuro and Other Stories,* translated by Martha King (London: Quartet, 1994);

After the Divorce, translated by Susan Ashe (Evanston, Ill.: Northwestern University Press, 1995);

Elias Portolu, translated by King (Evanston, Ill.: Northwestern University Press, 1995);

Ashes, translated by Janice M. Kozma (Madison, N.J.: Fairleigh Dickinson University Press, 2004).

OTHER: Adalgiso Lanfranchi, *Mirandolina: Romanzo per giovinette,* preface by Deledda (Rocca San Casciano: Cappelli, 1912);

Nicola Pascazio, *Dalla trincea alla reggia (combattendo con la Brigata Sassari): impressioni di un ferito,* preface by Deledda (Milan: Società Editoriale Italiana, 1916);

Le piú belle pagine di Silvio Pellico, selected by Deledda (Milan: Treves, 1923);

Il libro della terza elementare: letture, religione, storia, geografia, aritmetica, compiled by Deledda (Rome: La libreria dello Stato, 1930).

SELECTED PERIODICAL PUBLICATIONS–UNCOLLECTED: "Sangue sardo," *Ultima moda* (1888);

"Remigia Helder," *Ultima moda* (1888);

"Memorie di Fernanda," *Ultima moda* (1888);

"La pesca miracolosa," *La Sardegna* (1889);

"Il castello di San Loor," *La Sardegna* (1889).

Grazia Deledda was the only Italian woman–and, after Selma Lagërlof of Sweden, the second of only nine women writers in the twentieth century–to receive the Nobel Prize in Literature, which she was awarded in 1926. Her name thus stands out in the Italian canon as a significant example for all the female writers who have succeeded her. Her fiction is profoundly rooted in Sardinian ethics and history and expands on the universal themes of love, money, death, and family relationships.

She was born Grazia Maria Cosima Deledda on 21 September 1871 in Nuoro on the island of Sardinia. The daughter of wealthy landowners Giovanni Antonio and Francesca Cambosu Deledda, she was, as she described herself in the autobiographical work *Cosima* (1937; translated, 1988), "una bambina bruna, con gli occhi castanei, limpidi e grandi, le mani e i piedi minuscoli, vestita di un grembiale grigiastro con le tasche, con le calze di grosso cotone grezzo e le scarpe rustiche a lacci, più paesana che borghese" (a dark-haired child, serious, with big, bright brown eyes, with minuscule hands and feet, dressed in a gray smock with pockets, with heavy cotton socks and rustic lace shoes, more peasant than bourgeois). Giovanni Deledda–a good, gentle, and understanding man, as well as a dialectal poet with great faith in the good nature of people–died in November 1892, after which the family faced financial problems. Neither of Grazia's two brothers, one mentally ill and the other a spendthrift, was able to restore the original wealth accumulated by their astute father. Yet, from Nuoro, which was known for its literary associations and even called the "Athens of Sardinia," Deledda managed to establish connections with writers and editors in Rome, even "A costo di rubare un litro d'olio per poter comprare spedire le sue novelle a Roma" (at the cost of stealing a liter of oil in order to mail her novellas to the Continent), as she wrote in *Cosima*.

Considering the time in which the author lived and, more specifically, the intense isolation of Nuoro from the mainland, Deledda had an adequate if somewhat atypical education; she attended a conventional school until the fourth grade and also received private tutoring in Italian, French, Latin, and readings of her choice. Her early output reflects ample influence from the most popular and readily available feuilletons and popular novels. The young Deledda read the works of the most famous Italian writers of the day, including Gabriele D'Annunzio, Edmondo De Amicis, Antonio Fogazzaro, Giovanni Verga, and Ada Negri. Later she read the writings of Alessandro Manzoni, Sir Walter Scott, Silvio Pellico, and Carlo Goldoni, as well as of Russian authors such as Leo Tolstoy, Nikolai Vasil'evich Gogol, Maksim Gor'ky, and Fyodor Dostoevsky. She had great admiration particularly for Dostoevsky and often remarked on his ability to portray human passions in their most contradictory and unexpected moments.

Deledda was writing and publishing by her early twenties. She contributed to several newspapers and periodicals–namely *La Sardegna* and *Vita Sarda*–and her short stories were collected in *Nell'azzurro* (1890, Into the Blue), *Racconti sardi* (1894, Sardinian Short Stories), *L'ospite* (1897, The Guest), and *Le tentazioni* (1899, The Temptations). Like the works of Luigi Pirandello, these short stories introduced themes that she resumed in her subsequent, longer narratives. Expanding on subjects first presented in short-story form, her novels focus on the torment of passion, a deterministic view of life, a much-stressed morality, the representation of crimes or transgressions for which one must be held accountable, and emotions such as remorse, desperation, and hope for redemption. But, as Natalino Sapegno has argued, as quoted by Giuliana Sanguinetti Katz in "Immagini e strutture in un racconto della Deledda" (1994), a superstition–that the condition of being is related to magic and nature–renders Deledda's sense of morality for her characters quite opaque. For Mario Massaiu, on the other hand, in "Il folklore sardo nell'opera di Grazia Deledda" in *Sardegna in prospettiva euromediterranea* (1977), the writer's ideological involvement in the archaic situation of her fellow Sardinians is expressed in her works of fiction through her skillful juxtaposition of folkloric material. Sapegno also diverges from the interpretation of Angelo Pellegrino, as presented in "Deledda Grazia" in *Dizionario Biografico degli Italiani*, volume 36 (1988), who maintains the thesis of Deledda's systematic disengagement from the current events of the war–that during wartime she conceived of her stories in a sort of "historical vacuum." As Sanguinetti Katz points out again in "Immagini e strutture in un racconto della Deledda," Sapegno was always convinced of Deledda's ability to interpret the relics of the past history of her region, in which folklore and mythology play a great role, as well as her ability to look toward a twentieth century of progress and inventions.

In 1894 *Tradizioni popolari di Nuoro in Sardegna* (Popular Traditions of Nuoro in Sardinia) was published, and from then on Deledda's research on popular culture and folklore accentuated her fascination with her regional background; with few exceptions, Sardinia and the everyday life of Sardinians served as the topics of her works. Though confined in her small Sardinian town, Deledda was, from an early age, profoundly conscious of the particular way that she perceived her life in Nuoro and interpreted it in fiction. In the fall of 1899 Deledda accepted an invitation to visit Cagliari, the capital of Sardinia, and for the first time left the microcosm of Nuoro. As she recalled later in *Cosima*, she was impressed by the different landscape that met her eyes at the exit of the Cagliari train station. The palm trees, the sea, and the openness of the city imbued Cagliari with an almost exotic atmosphere, especially in comparison with the austere, enclosed, and still primitive world of Nuoro.

In 1900, after a brief engagement, Deledda married Palmiro Madesani, a government employee whom she had met in Cagliari, and they moved soon afterward to Rome, where he was reassigned. Her encounter with Madesani marked a defining moment in her life, for the marriage fulfilled certain of her needs at the time. It satisfied a social necessity for a woman of her age (twenty-nine); marriage saved her the "embarrassment" of becoming a *zitella* (spinster) who, even worse, nourished artistic ambitions. It also met her ambition to leave Nuoro and its suffocating environment. In the context of her fiction, a relocation to Rome–the city of Deledda's dreams–often occasions for her characters a psychological rebirth or the onset of a new, artistic life. Her characters almost always perceive a move to Rome as a turning point in their lives, although the city represents more often than not the corruption and temptations of the modern world, versus the patriarchal nature of Sardinian society. As a husband, Madesani was a faithful companion and became even more so in his eventual role as her literary agent, taking care of her communications with publishers and with the press.

From 1895 onward, Deledda published novels of myth, archaic destinies, and tragic misfortunes. The births of her two sons with Madesani–Sardus in 1900 and Franz in 1903–did not interfere with her prolific production, which continued steadily with the publication of one novel a year until her death. In her works she describes a world dictated mainly by passions and almost pagan in its outlook. As in the fiction of Giovanni Verga, considered the most significant writer of verismo in Italian literature, in Deledda's novels and short stories the opening pages usually project an unhappy scenario and almost immediately display the predestined victim and the setting in which the story will develop. The wild and relatively unexplored Sardinian inland frequently provides the background of her narratives; in the short stories she constructs her characters, both male and female, according to a pattern of repetition, and they recur later in the novels in what is best described as a set categorization. For example, the characters and the settings from her first short story, "Vita silvana" (1884, Life in the Woods), appear in subsequent works such as *Elias Portolu* (1903; translated, 1992), *L'edera* (1908, The Ivy), *Canne al vento* (1913; translated as *Reeds in the Wind,* 1999), *Marianna Sirca* (1915), and *La madre* (1920, The Mother; translated as *The Woman and the Priest,* 1922).

Although descriptions of Sardinian society infuse her narratives, Deledda does not provide the reader with historical details of any sort. Yet, no worthwhile discussion of her major works can commence without an understanding of the geopolitical and historical context in which she wrote them. In defining the physical borders of "her" Sardinia–that is, not the island as a whole or even as the spatial expanse of her fiction but, rather, the Sardinia that lies close to her heart–she enables the reader to visualize the inner core of this captivating isle located in the center of the Mediterranean Sea. Sardinia is the land of the *Nuraghes,* the prehistoric agglomerates where life began and prospered thousands of years before the Moors and the Catalans colonized them. Deledda faithfully, if evocatively, renders in both short and long narrative works the harsh landscape of the Nuorese region–the pinnacled mountains of the Gennargentu, the little villages that lie at their base, and the pieces of land, typically cultivated with olive trees, known in the Logudorese dialect as *tancas.* She writes of a setting in which life unfolds according to passion; in terms of their nature and way of life, Sardinians reflected an ancestral, pre-Christian culture that was obviously remote from the modernization already in process in the coastal parts of the island and in the "upwardly mobile" towns of Sassari and Cagliari. In Deledda's day Nuoro had scarcely more than six thousand inhabitants, and in her fiction Sardinia remains–along with its peripheral areas–an island "within" an island, where passions, social divisions, and inequities interfere with progress and modern civilization.

She viewed the process of assimilation attempted on the island by the Piedmontese regime, based in Turin, in terms that parallel those expressed by Antonio Gramsci regarding the question of Southern Italy. As Gramsci wrote in his *Il Risorgimento* (1949), the role of Piedmont was similar to that of a political party directing the efforts of previously segregated classes throughout Italy, thus exercising a form of "dittatura senza egemonia" (dictatorship without hegemony). For Deledda, the rule of the island by the government of Turin marked a heavy imposition, both political and economic, upon Sardinians; they faced a continual battle against the external power of Piedmont that reminded them incessantly of their oppression by the Moors and the Catalans in previous eras. Given this context, the *banditi* in Deledda's fiction are outlaws, not surprisingly, who are forced to find refuge in the caves of the Supramonte and Gennargentu (located in central Sardinia) by an outsider's judicial system, that of Turin, which does not understand the unspoken laws of the island and its system of justice. Moreover, the *banditi* are not only enslaved men but also *padroni,* landowners who–in order to sustain their code of honor and, paradoxically, their family's feuds–kill an adversary and are then forced to leave the village for fear of an "iniquitous" trial, which commonly brings about starvation and dishonor for their whole family.

These *banditi* in Deledda's fiction become symbolic and typified characters that reify the perennial struggle between obedience to power and the desire to oppose wrongful laws with inner strength–laws resulting from the rational decisions of the invader. The *banditi* are considered outlaws, because their own "primitive" culture does not correspond to the laws of the colonizers. According to the dictates of Sardinian society, however, they are not outlaws. In Deledda's novels the *banditi* continue visiting friends and relatives in their home villages despite public displays of ostracism against them. Adhering to a code of honor, these men generally refrain from robbing churches, but when they commit such a crime, they are perceived as outlaws in the eyes of their own community as well.

The clash between Sardinian culture and the cultural hegemony of the Piedmontese produced acutely oppressive financial sanctions and laws for the islanders—as exemplified by the *ademprivi,* a tax imposed by the Turin government of 1865, which ignited the *su connottu* (back to tradition) riots of 1868, protesting the end of traditional communal land use. The Piedmontese failed to understand both the Sardinian economy, which was based largely on stock raising and extensive agriculture, and the millenary cooperation between the landowners and the shepherds, who raised their stock on these lands; this inability to grasp the central features of Sardinian livelihood only escalated as a result of an 1869 law on ground wheat. Unable to transform the laws of the community into laws relating to property, the Sardinian economy began to falter, as Neria De Giovanni describes in her book *Come leggere "Canne al vento" di Grazia Deledda* (1993, How to Read Grazia Deledda's Reeds of the Wind). Deledda accurately portrays the decline of the wealthy *pastori* (shepherds) in her novels of Sardinia and shows how the rising number of *pastori* forced to become *banditi* was related to the heavy land taxes imposed by the central government—which expropriated the landowners' property when they failed to pay.

Deledda's stories take place in an immemorial time, where the flocks and the harvest still determine the spatial and temporal "coordinates" of a people. Details of the customs of cheesemaking and of the roasting of *porchetto* (baby pig), for example, evoke a primordial existence that spatially and temporally departs from the industrialization and progress elsewhere, particularly on the mainland. The inner feelings of the characters, such as their economic and moral anguish in being *perdenti* (losers), in Verga's sense of the word, denote some of the emotional repercussions of the contrast between their simple way of life on the island and life on the mainland. Deledda hints that only nature—through its positive as well as negative effects on humans and with its sense of pity and remission—can regulate island life. Initially, she followed the deterministic theses of Alberto Niceforo's *La delinquenza in Sardegna* (1897, Delinquency in Sardinia), which gave a genetic reason for criminality in Sardinian culture; Niceforo asserted that Sardinian fathers passed the gene for crime on to their sons.

Deledda's works are also intensely grounded in the superstitions that infuse regional folktales and in certain local myths, such as the ones that surround the tombs of giants, the *janas* (witches), and the houses of fairies; these myths are also connected to actual geographic sites—especially to those hills, mountains, and rivers on the island that are closely linked to the *Nuraghes* era. Massaiu has long analyzed the folkloric component in Deledda's work, stating again in "Il folklore sardo nell'opera di Grazia Deledda" that

> la curiosità erudita, il dato etnografico sono ancora presenti, anzi sono presenti con frequenza e forse con intensità maggiore che nell'opera giovanile, ma nell'opera d'arte matura (approssimativamente a partire da Elias Portolu) sono assunti nella vitale materia d'arte, in quanto perennità di valori.

> (the erudite curiosity, the ethnographic data are still present, are indeed present with great frequency and, perhaps, with greater intensity in her adult work than in her earlier years, but in the works of her maturity [starting approximately with *Elias Portolu*] they are assumed within the artistic material, so as to show the perennial meaning of their values.)

In addition, features of verismo, the literary movement that influenced Deledda's first period of Sardinian narratives, surface in several ways in her fiction. The characters speak in Deledda's Logudorese dialect, and much of their speech, upon closer reading, in fact reveals a syntax that is preeminently Sardinian rather than Italian. The frequent use of dialectal terms and Sardinian surnames emphasizes the authenticity of the characters in the stories. The importance of land as the sole form of possession is another theme that relates Deledda's work to verismo. Quarrels about the land and its passage to the next generation in the family often set a plot in motion. The regional settings of Deledda's fiction can actually still be found on a current map of Sardinia and depict the travels of characters such as Felix of *Canne al vento.*

The private homes of the *Nuoresi,* the inhabitants of Nuoro, and the *tancas,* denoting the lands that they own, are segregated; they are unconnected to any kind of urban environment, such as the piazzas, the city halls, and the markets that are usually found in nineteenth- and twentieth-century Italian fiction. According to Luca Pinna in *La famiglia esclusiva* (1971), the only social structure remaining in Sardinia is the family: "il nucleo familiare in Sardegna . . . essere considerato come l'unica struttura sociale entro la quale le persone soddisfano tutte le loro attese economiche di collaborazione e di cooperazione, oltre che affettive" (the nuclear family in Sardinia . . . may be considered the only social structure within which people satisfy their needs for cooperation and collaboration, along with sentimental ones). Members of such tight family nuclei attach a higher value to their goods than to other people's things. Consequently, the house of the family is a space the force of which is exclusively centripetal and prevents the members of the family therein from reaching out for help, since no one from the outside is better than those who live within the walls of the house. The shut windows of a house, to which she alludes in her novels of Sardinia, prevent people from gazing into and thus invading the privacy of a family's home. They in effect stand for the Sardinians' innate sense of privacy and fear of interference in one's life. This space is where Deledda's characters err in their often tragic lives. Only late in her career does she turn the tragic natural setting of the island into a bucolic and serene backdrop, as seen in the works that take place in her husband's region, the Padania.

Elias Portolu, which was first serialized in *Nuova Antologia* from August to October 1900 before publication as a book, firmly anchors Deledda's creative and poetic world in her homeland of Sardinia and was the first of her novels to do so. The novel relates the story of the Portolu family from the day Elias, the youngest son of Zia Annedda (Aunt Annedda) and Zio Berte (Uncle Berte) Portolu, returns from the *Continente*, the mainland of Italy; Elias is newly released after several years in prison for theft, a sentence that he feels was unjust. On the first page of the book Deledda compares his long absence from the island to a frequent reason for travel among Sardinian men—the pursuit of a proper education on the mainland. In her view, these absences create a sense of displacement and alienation in such men, for departure from the motherland means a temporary deracination, even in the case of young Sardinians who leave for the purpose of studying in Rome. She describes Elias as a man whose skin has been made so fair and delicate from his imposed inertia in the prison that one of Zio Annedda's friends comments: "è bianco come una ragazza" (he is as white as a girl). This comment lends the character a sexual ambiguity at an early stage of the novel—an ambiguity that Deledda enhances a few pages later through Elias's own retelling of the simple work that the prisoners were given in jail: he calls his labor "lavoretti manuali da calzolaio, o da donnicciuola!" (little manual jobs for a cobbler, or a little woman). In her fiction she typically associates infantile and feminine traits with the transgressor. As Ada Testaferri states in her contribution to *Donna: Women in Italian Culture* (1989), "questa debolezza iniziale lo predisporrebbe dunque a un comportamento diverso . . . rivela da parte del soggetto un rapporto di dipendenza dalla famiglia, e di immaturità. . . . Il destino del soggetto dipende dalla soluzione data al problema etico; attraverso esso, il soggetto aspira alla maturazione" (the initial weakness would predispose him to a different behavior . . . also showing lack of maturity in his relationship with the family. . . . The subject's destiny depends on the solution given to the ethical problem; and it is only this way that he can aspire to maturation).

Deledda sharply contrasts Elias's feminine traits with the speech of Zio Berte. Zio Berte's way of talking stresses the significance and influence of men in a house because of the continuity they bestow on the family. His speech also emphasizes the necessity for these individuals to show submission and reverence to paternal figures, thus confirming their role as economic providers for the family. The relationship between father and son is always perceived in hierarchical terms, with the father intended also as the master of his children. A mother is, instead, a mere housekeeper who, at the moment of her death—as in *L'incendio nell'uliveto* (1918, The Fire in the Olive Grove)—passes on her keys to the prospective wife of her son as a symbol of domestic legacy and sole power in a patriarchal society.

Scandal is the ostracizing factor that the tight family unit in *Elias Portolu* cannot abide. It disrupts the source of serenity and balance that the family's own inner energy as a whole provides to each member. After his return, Elias must take another journey, albeit a psychological one, of internal growth and suffering, removing him from the scandal of loving Maddalena, the young woman already promised to his brother Pietro. *Elias Portolu* was well received as a novel that explored issues of morality.

Deledda's first great novel, *Cenere* (1904; translated as *Ashes (Cenere): A Sardinian Story*, 1908), is an oedipal narrative that starts with the seduction of Olí, a young and beautiful girl. After Olí gives birth out of wedlock to a son, Anania, she leaves without revealing her destination, and the child is raised by his natural father, a well-to-do landowner, and by the father's wife, a good-hearted woman. Together they take care of Anania, who, like many young men in Deledda's Sardinia, goes to Rome to pursue his studies, thanks to his parents' benevolence and financial assistance. Yet, the trauma of his abandonment by Olí constantly jeopardizes Anania's chances for success: his attempt at finding his mother, which signals that he wishes to discover his heritage, ultimately ends in his ruin. Deledda suggests that passion leads to Olí's own ruin; commencing her youth with the betrayal of Anania's father, she ends her life violently. The last scene of the novel depicts her suicide: as a scapegoat, or a sacrificial lamb, Olí cuts her throat to purify her son from the guilt of illegitimacy that binds them together. Afterward, Anania finds ashes in the charm he has worn since the time of his birth. That his life is forever marred by the initial, original mistake of his mother plays out Deledda's conviction that the world—Sardinian society in particular—does not allow for forgiveness.

The unconsciously incestuous desire of Anania to find his natural mother is expressed, according to Vittorio Spinazzola in his article for *Problemi* (1973), in the young man's will to submit her to his own protective supremacy. Yet, Anania feels hate against his mother, and he renounces—rather than experiences—in a morbidly destructive way, the typical rites of sexual initiation. As Anna Dolfi writes in her book *Grazia Deledda* (1979), the incest taboo as a perennial longing for childhood constitutes, in the context of class conflict, the main theme of the novel. Anania is aware of his actual provenance, and though trying with his law studies to reach a better status, he also realizes that he will never be able to speak or behave as a person of a class different from the one of his biological origins. Marilyn Migiel asserts in her contribution to the *Stanford Italian Review* (1985) that "Education as any force leading to upward social mobility is associated in *Cenere* with the diabolical"; that is, education spoils the human resources in the individual, who is only concerned with the social aspects of his studies. Anania finds some salvation and liberation only in death—his mother's death. The devilish, tormented side of him, at which Deledda hints all along in the novel, jibes with the tragedy of Olí's suicide.

The end of *Cenere* suggests an uncertain future for Anania. On the one hand, the ability of man to control his destiny is limited by hereditary characteristics, implying that Anania is condemned to remain in the immobile waters of primitive Sardinian society. On the other, Deledda's characterization of Olí manifests the everlasting ability of women to put their children before anything else, even themselves, thereby hinting at hopes for Anania's future. The lack of a resolute ending gives *Cenere*, like *Colombi e sparvieri* (1912, Doves and Falcons) and *Elias Portolu*, an open structure that is further accentuated by the travel motif. As Giorgio Bárberi Squarotti asserts in his article "La tecnica e la struttura del romanzo deleddiano" (1975, The Technique and Structure of the Deleddian Novel), Deledda is one of a handful of Italian writers who convey travel, or the journey, whether physical or psychological, as an experience of expiation for a character: in an act of self-punishment, Olí gives up her child in Sardinia and departs, wandering the island with itinerant beggars until Anania finds her again; Elias's first trip away from the island takes him to prison, while the scandal of desiring Maddalena evolves into a psychological journey that results in his joining the priesthood; and in *Canne al vento,* Efix goes on a pilgrimage through the mountains. According to Bárberi Squarotti, Deledda translates expiation into the kind of journey that occurs in fairy tales. In the novel, however, all that the reader sees of such travels is the return—the reappearance of a character who, typically, has derived a sense of solitude from the experience of isolated meditation. Indeed, her novels recount few details regarding the geography of travels beyond Sardinia, even in her later novels, which thus disprove the notion that sheer geographic ignorance impelled her to refrain from writing about places other than Sardinia.

The exception to the lack of outside description is *Dopo il divorzio* (1902; translated as *After the Divorce: A Romance,* 1905), in which Costantino's jail time on the mainland for a false murder conviction is described in some detail, but only to emphasize his misery when he learns that his wife, Giovanna, has taken advantage of a new law and divorced him. The description of Costantino's prison environment serves to emphasize the domestic prison in which Giovanna is cast. Left alone with a child when her husband is sent away, she allows herself to be courted by the rich and brutal Brontu, and eventually she marries him. When Costantino returns, he finds her in greater misery than when he had left her. *Dopo il divorzio* ends with Giovanna and Costantino falling into each other's arms. This ending was amended for the English translation of 1905, to which Deledda added an "Epilogue" in which Brontu dies and Costantino and Giovanna are reunited as a happy family. In 1920 Deledda recast the novel with a new title, *Naufraghi in porto* (Shipwrecks in Port); in this version, Costantino actually commits the crime for which he had been falsely accused: he murders the wicked old woman who had encouraged Giovanna to leave him for Brontu. As Carla Locatelli has pointed out, this change does not just give the novel a new ending but makes it another novel altogether. Unlike the earlier version, *Naufraghi in porto* hints darkly that Costantino was not an innocent victim but was predetermined to be a murderer. This point is something that has not been fully appreciated by the secondary literature.

Deledda's next most significant novel, *L'edera,* also concerns the issue of predestination. The plot pivots on the murder of Ziu Zua (Uncle Zua), an old relative of the Decherchi family; Annesa, a girl whom the Decherchis took into their household when she was quite young, kills Ziu Zua in order that the family's debts would be paid and they would retain the only properties they have left—their house and one *tanca.* As events unfold, the novel shows how her crime need not have been committed; yet, the authorities will not catch Annesa, thus reconfirming their extraneous existence beside Sardinian inner laws and rules. The idea of expiation and penitence for the murder she carried out, however, will persist in her soul. The decadence of the Sardinian aristocrats lies at the center of *L'edera;* still more preoccupied by societal position within their small village and ancient fiefdom than with actual economic concerns, they are unable to progress with the times. The poor, who have always lived at the side of the *padroni*, both physically and psychologically, will also be ruined; humble people with no possessions, they remain, at all costs, traditionally faithful to their masters.

Annesa commits a crime to save the honor and family name of her benefactors. From the moment they gave her shelter, after discovering her abandoned on the side of the road in Barunei, with no family name of her own, she has devoted herself to the Decherchis. She now stays close to the family, "come l'edera che si attacca al muro" (like ivy sticks to a wall) until the wall falls, as her longtime secret lover, Paulu, says bitterly after an outburst from the heroine. Following her murderous act, a moment in which Annesa somehow loses her ability to understand the path to follow for her future and irreversibly taints her life, the village priest, Prete Virdis, visits her in the hope of helping her retrieve a sense of morals and ethics. Yet, insistently projecting herself as a member of the family by using the possessive *nostra*, Annesa says to Prete Virdis:

> Non so . . . È vero; da molti e molti anni non credevo più in Dio, perché troppe sventure cadevano sulla nostra famiglia, come fulmini sullo stesso albero. . . . In questi giorni, però, ho pensato a Dio, qualche volta: e ora penso che ella ha ragione, prete Virdis, ma io non sono malvagia come lei crede; io ho fatto male a me stessa, è vero, ma l'ho fatto per far del bene agli altri. E sono pronta ancora, le ripeto: mi dica che cosa devo fare.
>
> (I do not know . . . It is true; I have not believed in God for many, many years, because too many disgraces were falling upon our family, like lightning bolts on the same tree. . . . These days my thoughts have sometimes addressed God: and now I think you were right, Prete Virdis, but I am not as wicked as you think; I have hurt myself, it's true, but I have done it to do some good to others. And I am ready: tell me what to do.)

On the last page of the novel, the message of the author is clear: Annesa will eventually marry Paulu, but the old tree to which she alludes in her talk with Prete Virdis—a metaphor for the Decherchi family, who are now stained by the crime—will no longer bear any fruit. Her life will continue to be one of repentance and sacrifice, not unlike her life before she unnecessarily murdered Ziu Zua.

Approximately five years after *L'edera* came out, *Canne al vento* was published—one of the few novels that Deledda counted as a favorite. It tells of the three Pintor sisters, who once owned all the land surrounding their village but are now left with a tiny plot and their servant, Efix, to take care of it. Signor Predu, their cousin, is a rich and powerful landowner who hovers as a constant threat to the sisters. Resembling a Greek tragedy, *Canne al vento* focuses on both Efix, who believes himself guilty of killing his master, Don Zame, the father of the young women, and on Lia, the fourth Pintor sister, who is physically absent from the narrative but whom other characters—subsequently including Giacinto, the son she left behind—frequently discuss. Lia left the family and the island some time ago for the Continent. For Efix, she represented true love; though an act of self-defense, his murder of Lia's father occurred because the oppressive Don Zame was trying to prevent his dissatisfied daughter from running away. Haunted by his master's death and Lia's departure, Efix feels he must expiate all his life for the crime he has committed. When he takes walks in the forest and in the fields to calm himself, Efix hears the noise of the *panas* (women who died giving birth), and he sees the *ammattadore* (little elf) and the *janas;* all three of these phenomena are tropes of the ancestral and mythical heritage of Sardinia that Deledda studied years before. Efix's world is limited to the care of the Pintor sisters' poor possessions, until the day a letter announces Giacinto's arrival; Efix and the sisters harbor hopes that Lia's son will help return the family to their former affluence. Yet, as they all eventually learn, Giacinto arrives on the island to escape the law on the other side of the sea for a crime he has committed. After several misunderstood incidents, and because one of the sisters, Noemi, reacts hysterically to what she believes is her servant's wrongdoing, Efix leaves the house and takes up the life of a wandering beggar, dying in the end only after he has suffered for his terrible crime.

Marianna Sirca, one of Deledda's most accomplished works, embodies an analysis of one year in the lives of the two main characters, Marianna Sirca and Simone Sole—particularly of the development of their impossible love. As many critics have noted, this simple story resembles Verga's "L'amante di Gramigna" (The Mistress of Gramigna, first published in *Vita dei Campi* [1897, Country Life]) through its treatment of the motif of passion and of the character of the *bandito*. The love between Marianna, a wealthy young woman, and her former servant turned bandit, Simone, is forbidden because of their vastly disparate social backgrounds. Although she was born into poor circumstances, Marianna lives according to the path laid out by her family—particularly by her uncle, a rich priest who adopted her when she was a child. He treats her like a prison inmate: under lock and key, she lives constantly under his control and is incapable of any independent action. She thus follows an existence that strikingly parallels the life of Simone, but as a servant he can scarcely conceive of falling in love with Marianna. Only after her uncle dies and she becomes the sole heir to his fortune, and after Simone adopts the ways of a bandit in order to feed his family, do the two meet again and fall in love.

The reasons for the love between Marianna and Simone are not purely sentimental; in essence, they have plainly tired of pursuing the lives that others had planned for them. Marianna experiences serenity and peace only in the countryside, in the pure simplicity of her father, Berte's, company, and—while she cannot help but blame her father for the awful life she led with her uncle—she nonetheless wants to return to her roots as a shepherd's daughter. Simone, on the other hand, turns out not to be the great bandit she believed he was, and she feels deceived by her own desperate longing for love. Simone falls in love with Marianna because he hopes that her presence and wealth will end his undesirable existence as an outlaw, much in the same way that she sees in him the possibility of a more lively and satisfying life than the one she has lived until then: "E Marianna aveva obbedito. Aveva obbedito sempre fin da quando bambina era stata messa come un uccellino in una gabbia nella casa dello zio, a spandere la gioia e la luce della sua fanciullezza, attorno al melanconico sacerdote, in cambio della possibile eredità di lui" (And Marianna had obeyed. Had always obeyed, since as a girl she had been put like a bird in a cage in her uncle's house, to irradiate the joy and the light of her youth around the melancholic priest, in exchange for his future inheritance).

A figure of fascination in Sardinian lore, the bandit is a masculine figure who lives on the periphery of society in order to keep his name and his dignity; by not robbing from priests or churches and by visiting his family regularly, the bandit does display a certain code of honor. Simone, however, is not a true *bandito* because he is tired of living like an outlaw and wants finally to rest. By loving Simone, Marianna challenges the societal taboos that protect the honor of a woman, but she cannot forgive him his ambivalence about ceding, for her, his "freedom" as a bandit and taking responsibility for his own actions—as she herself has done by associating her name with Simone's. As Deledda's novels show, Sardinian women follow their passions and the weight of their decisions until the end, even at the risk of great losses to themselves. Whereas men appear weak and act indecisively until their own ends, women such as Marianna in *Marianna Sirca*, Annesa in *L'edera*, and Olí in *Cenere* exhibit enduring strength. In "Woman as Outlaw: Grazia Deledda and the Politics of Gender," published in *Modern Language Notes* (1995), Susan Briziarelli wrote that

Deledda's positioning of her female characters alongside the marginalized and rebel group of outlaws illustrates and gives voice to her vision of a society constructed along a class and power axis. It is clear that she aligns her strong women ideologically with the socially outcast group, finding in them the common denominator not only of courage and rebellion, but of transgression against society. As sheltered women with little formal education and few positive roles, Deledda's female characters cannot visualize their own struggle within a consciously ideological framework, but tend rather to associate it with that of the *banditi,* as metaphor for society's outcasts.

The famed Italian critic Attilio Momigliano noted in 1948 that *La madre*, Deledda's next significant work, and *Elias Portolu* are quite similar, especially in terms of their main characters: reflecting a feminine beauty and delicate manners, Paulo in *La madre* recalls Elias both physically and psychologically. A novel that explores erotic themes, *La madre* relates the story of Paulo, a young priest, who is assigned the parish of his mother's old village. Apparently, the village has fallen under a strange curse that brings ruin upon the priests who serve there, as if affirming the independence of a religion that dates prior to Christianity. Paulo's predecessor smoked, went out with women, and drank excessively, and Paulo himself is on the verge of treading the same path. His mother, Maria Maddalena, who silently toiled as a maid in the seminary for years to support her son's aspirations for the priesthood, keeps a watch on him and his weaknesses; she is prepared to compensate for them in case of danger. From the window she observes Paulo in the dark of night as he departs for the house of a lonely and wealthy woman, Agnese. The mother immediately senses the risky nature of this relationship; yet, when Paulo asks her to deliver a letter to Agnese, she does so, albeit with some hesitation.

The weight of her son's guilt and the terror of losing all that she has long worked and fought for is paramount to Maria Maddalena, and she suddenly drops dead in the modest church of Aar as her son says Sunday mass. As Testaferri asserts in *Donna: Women in Italian Culture*, the Jungian archetypes of the moon and the night in the novel are key. Together they enhance the repressive, occluded atmosphere surrounding Paulo, who feels at once the necessity of both his mother's and Agnese's presence, yet becomes suffocated by them. When Paulo's mother closes a door with large bars in one of the first sequences of the novel, she represents—according to Testaferri—the repressive primary archetype of the Great Mother, whereas Agnese in her "castle" stands for the Terrible Mother. A figure of seduction, Agnese lures the poor young priest toward deception and the corruption of the sacred vows. Paulo's eventual victory over Agnese is, in Testaferri's words, "un'ovvia vittoria in senso cristiano, cioè è superamento della carne e trionfo della luminosità, trionfo cioè dell'archetipo del Maschile" (the victory in a Christian sense, the one surpassing the flesh with the triumph of luminosity, that is the triumph of the Masculine archetype). This victory may also be viewed as Deledda's final manifestation of sympathy and understanding for a mother who sacrificed herself entirely on her son's behalf.

Six years after the appearance of *La madre*, Grazia Deledda received the Nobel Prize in Literature; her only travel away from Sardinia and Italy occurred when she went to Stockholm to accept the award. Deledda received the prize with little personal fanfare; being a Nobel laureate did not materially change her quiet life. The reception in Italy of the honor given her was cool, almost skeptical, especially since several other authors, notably Luigi Pirandello, were thought to be much better candidates. Pirandello, who did win the Nobel Prize in Literature in 1934, had already expressed his frustration with Deledda's fame and literary success in his novel *Suo marito* (1911, Her Husband), a satire of the Deledda-Madesani partnership. Perhaps because of this ridicule, perhaps just because of her reclusive nature, Deledda did not in any way vaunt her status as a Nobel winner. For the next decade, until her death in 1936, she continued to live surrounded by family and to write a novel a year.

She published ten more novels before her death, and one more was published posthumously. In this last period Deledda allowed herself to be more autobiographical. *Cosima,* published the year after her death, tells the story of her own childhood in Nuoro. Two less cheerful novels, *Il paese del vento* (1931) and *La chiesa della solitudine* (1936; translated as *The Church of Solitude,* 2002), focus on themes of physical and spiritual health. In the first, the protagonist, Nina, who has gone to live by the seaside with her new husband, finds her old love, Gabriele, dying of tuberculosis. Gabriele is, even in his illness, a romantic figure, but Nina's decision to turn away from her childhood obsessions and toward a new life with her practical and rather stolid husband echoes Deledda's own life with Madesani. *La chiesa della solitudine* portrays Maria Concezione, a young woman who is introduced as she leaves the hospital after having a cancerous breast removed. Maria Concezione's struggle with mortality is mirrored in the sufferings of several other characters, but her self-imposed silence about her own illness becomes desperate when her inability to speak almost causes the death of the man she loves. The autobiographical element in this work is strong, since Deledda had been diagnosed with breast cancer several years earlier and was dying as she wrote this novel, the last to be published in her lifetime.

The author of more than four hundred short stories and more than forty novels, Grazia Deledda died on 15 August 1936 in Rome. Her talent resided notably in her microscopic analysis of the people, the feelings, and the nature of Sardinia—which she made known to a wide readership through her extensive writings. Traces of the motifs and themes she employed in her fiction and plays continue to appear in the works of Sardinian writers such as Salvatore Mannussu, Salvatore Salta, and Giuseppe Dessì. She also influenced many Italian women writers, especially in the ways they address the role of women in patriarchal societies such as that of Southern Italy. Deledda's voice was distinctive and highly original, a product of her compelling Sardinian heritage. As the third-person narrator in *Cosima* states, in veiled allusion to the writer: "Tutto del resto, è straordinario per lei: pare venuta da un mondo diverso da quello dove vive, e la sua fantasia è piena di ricordi confusi di quel mondo di sogno, mentre la realtà di questo non le dispiace, se la guarda a modo suo, cioè anch'esso coi colori della sua fantasia" (Everything is extraordinary for her: she seems to have come from a world entirely different from the one in which she lives, and her fantasy is crowded with dazed memories of that dreamworld, while she does not mind the reality of this, if she looks at it in her own way, that is, with the colors of her imagination).

Letters:

Lettere di Grazia Deledda a Marino Moretti (1913–1923) (Padova: Rebellato, 1959);

Lettere inedite (Milan: Fabbri, 1966).

Bibliography:

Remo Branca, *Bibliografia deleddiana* (Milan: L'Eroica, 1938).

Biographies:

Carolyn Balducci, *A Self-Made Woman: Biography of Nobel-Prize-Winner Grazia Deledda* (Boston: Houghton Mifflin, 1975);

Marilyn Migiel, "Grazia Deledda (1871–1936)," in *Italian Women Writers: A Bio-Bibliographical Sourcebook,* edited by Rinaldina Russell (Westport, Conn.: Greenwood Press, 1994), pp. 111–118.

References:

Francesco Alziator, "Grazia Deledda e le tradizioni popolari," in *Convegno Nazionale di studi deleddiani, Nuoro, 30 settembre 1972: Atti* (Cagliari: Fossataro, 1975), pp. 175–189;

Mario Aste, "Echoes of 'Verismo' in Deledda's *La chiesa della solitudine,*" in *The Flight of Ulysses: Studies in Memory of Emmanuel Hatzantonis,* edited by Augustus Mastri (Chapel Hill, N.C.: Annali d'italianistica, 1997), pp. 257–266;

Giorgio Bárberi Squarotti, "La tecnica e la struttura del romanzo deleddiano," in *Convegno Nazionale di studi deleddiani, Nuoro, 30 settembre 1972: Atti* (Cagliari: Fossataro, 1975), pp. 127–159;

Paola Blelloch, "Grazia Deledda's and Gavino Ledda's Writing on Sardinia: Two Sides of the Same Reality," *Italian Quarterly,* 18 (1995): 47–58;

Remo Branca, *Il segreto di Grazia Deledda* (Cagliari: Fossataro, 1971);

Susan Briziarelli, "Woman as Outlaw: Grazia Deledda and the Politics of Gender," *Modern Language Notes,* 110 (1995): 20–31;

Carol Burton, "Deledda's Purgatorio," *Italica,* 57 (1980): 96–106;

Antonio Cara, *"Cenere" di Grazia Deledda nelle figurazioni di Eleonora Duse* (Nuoro: Istituto Superiore Regionale Etnografico, 1984);

Daniela Cavallero, "Io e Lei: *Una donna* e *Cosima*: Due esempi di autobiografia al femminile," *Romance Languages Annual,* 5 (1993): 174–179;

Alberto Maria Cirese, "Grazia Deledda e il mondo tradizionale sardo," *Problemi,* 36–37 (1973): 328–331;

Cirese, *Intellettuali, folklore, istinto di classe: Note su Verga, Deledda, Scotellaro, Gramsci* (Turin: Einaudi, 1976);

Rosario Contarino, "Il mito della Sardegna nel Lawrence viaggiatore e critico della Deledda," *Campi Immaginabili,* 3 (1991): 119–126;

Bice De Chiara, *Picologismo deleddiano in "Elias Portulu" e "Canne al vento"* (Naples: Loffredo, 1975);

Neria De Giovanni, *Come leggere "Canne al vento" di Grazia Deledda* (Milan: Mursia, 1993);

Eurialo De Michelis, "Riassunto sulla Deledda," *Arcadia,* 5 (1972): 35–79;

Giuseppe Dessí, "Grazia Deledda cent'anni dopo," *Nuova Antologia,* 513 (1971): 307–311;

Floro Di Zenzo, *Vocazione narrativa di Grazia Deledda* (Naples: Glaux, 1967);

Maria Luisa Dodero Costa, "I. S. Turgenev e Grazia Deledda," in *Mondo slavo e cultura italiana: Contributi italiani al IX congresso internazionale degli slavisti, Kiev 1983,* edited by Jitka Kresalkova (Rome: Veltro, 1983), pp. 110–121;

Anna Dolfi, *Grazia Deledda* (Milan: Mursia, 1979);

Carlo Ferrucci, "Grazia Cosima Deledda," *Nuovi-Argomenti,* 53–54 (1977): 304–315;

Jill Franks, "The Regionalist Community: Indigenous versus Outsider Consciousness in Deledda's *La madre* and Lawrence's Sea and Sardinia," in *Regionalism Reconsidered: New Approaches to the Field,* edited by David Jordan (New York: Garland, 1994), pp. 87–103;

Giuseppe Giacalone, *Ritratto critico di Grazia Deledda* (Rome: Ciranna, 1965);

Lorenzo Greco, "Amore fra cugini: Letteratura e contesto antropologico nella Deledda," *Il Ponte,* 38, nos. 1–2 (1982): 109–122;

D. B. Gregor, "Polychrome in Grazia Deledda," *Modern Languages,* 51 (1970): 160–166;

Lynn Gunzberg, "Ruralism, Folklore, and Grazia Deledda's Novels," *Modern Language Studies,* 13, no. 3 (1983): 112–122;

Giulio Herczeg, "La struttura della frase di Grazia Deledda," in *Italia linguistica nuova ed antica: Studi linguistici in memoria di Oronzo Parlangeli,* edited by Vittore Pisani, Ciro Santoro, Giovan Battista, and P. Mancarella, Collana di saggi e testi, nos. 6–7 (Galatina: Congedo, 1976–1978), pp. 19–55;

Margherita Heyer-Caput, "Per svelare Il segreto dell'uomo solitario di Grazia Deledda," *Quaderni d'Italianistica: Official Journal of the Canadian Society for Italian Studies,* 22 (2001): 121–138;

Rebecca Hopkins, "Re-examining Female Desire: Inheritance Law, Colonialism, and Folklore in Grazia Deledda's *La volpe*," *Quaderni d'Italianistica: Official Journal of the Canadian Society for Italian Studies,* 23 (2002): 59–86;

Janice M. Kozma, *Grazia Deledda's Eternal Adolescents: The Pathology of Arrested Maturation* (Madison, N.J.: Fairleigh Dickinson University Press, 2002);

Giuseppe Leone, "La narrativa di Grazia Deledda tra verismo e decadentismo," *Cristallo,* 38, no. 3 (1996): 96–99;

Carla Locatelli, "Le morali del desiderio deleddiano: *Dopo il divorzio*," in Deledda, *Dopo il divorzio,* La Biblioteca dell'identità 25 (Cagliari: Società Editrice L'Unione Sarda, 2004), pp. vii–xxxiii;

Olga Lombardi, *Invito alla lettura di Grazia Deledda* (Milan: Mursia, 1979);

Alessandro Madesani, Gino Pilandri, and Umberto Foschi, eds., *Nel paese del vento: Grazia Deledda, Lina Sacchetti, Isotta Gervasi a Cervia* (Ravenna: Longo, 1998);

Mario Massaiu, "Il folklore sardo nell'opera di Grazia Deledda," in his *Sardegna in prospettiva euromediterranea. Le 'nuove nazioni' esemplificate con una cultura insulare* (Florence: Olschki, 1977), pp. 323–333;

Massaiu, *La Sardegna di Grazia Deledda* (Milan: CELUC, 1972);

Allen E. McCormick, "Grazia Deledda's *La madre* and the Problems of Tragedy," *Symposium,* 22 (1968): 62–67;

Mario Miccinesi, *Grazia Deledda* (Florence: Nuova Italia, 1975);

Marilyn Migiel, "The Devil and the Phoenix: A Reading of Grazia Deledda's *Cenere*," *Stanford Italian Review*, 5, no. 1 (1985): 55–73;

Attilio Momigliano, *Storia della letterature italiana* (Milan-Messina: Principato, 1948);

Bice Mortara Garavelli, "La lingua di Grazia Deledda," *Strumenti Critici*, 65 (1991): 145–163;

Anco Marzio Mutterle, "I colori dell'idillio," *Studi novecenteschi*, 14 (1987): 197–208;

Giuseppe Petronio, "Grazia Deledda e i suoi critici," *Problemi*, 79 (1987): 124–137;

Antonio Piromalli, "Durata e disfacimento della realtà nelle trame narrative di Grazia Deledda," *Italianistica*, 3 (1974): 118–122;

Piromalli, *Grazia Deledda* (Florence, 1968);

Dino Provenzal, "Grazia Deledda e il Premio Nobel," *Anima e Pensiero*, 2 (1966): 17–19;

Ada Ruschioni, *Dalla Deledda a Pavese* (Milan: Vita & Pensiero, 1977);

Giuliana Sanguinetti Katz, "Grazia Deledda vista attraverso il suo epistolario," *Campi Immaginabili: Rivista Quadrimestrale di Cultura*, 16–18 (1996): 29–40;

Sanguinetti Katz, "Immagini e strutture in un racconto della Deledda," *Quaderni d'Italianistica*, 15 (1994): 205–215;

Sanguinetti Katz, "La scoperta dell'identità femminile nel romanzo *Cosima* di Grazia Deledda," *Rivista di Studi Italiani*, 12, no. 1 (1994): 55–73;

Antonio Scano, *Grazia Deledda* (Milan: Virgilio, 1972);

Ines Scaramucci, *Studi del Novecento: Prospettive e itinerari* (Milan: IPL, 1968);

Vittorio Spinazzola, "Grazia Deledda e il pubblico," *Problemi*, 35 (1973): 269–277;

Ada Testaferri, "Infrazione all'Eros proibito come processo d'individuazione in *La madre* di Grazia Deledda," in *Donna: Women in Italian Culture,* edited by Testaferri (Ottawa: Dovehouse, 1989), pp. 109–120;

Maria Tettamanzi, *Grazia Deledda* (Brescia: La scuola, 1969);

Antonio Tobia, *Grazia Deledda* (Rome: Ciranna, 1971);

Simona Wright, "Elementi narrativi nell'opera deleddiana con particolare attenzione all'*Incendio nell'oliveto*," *Nemla Italian Studies*, 18 (1994): 83–103;

Patrizia Zambon and Pier Luigi Renai, "Preliminare di indagine sulle novelle di Grazia Deledda per il *Corriere della Sera* (1909–1914)," *Problemi*, 79 (1987): 138–157.

Papers:
An important archive of Grazia Deledda's letters and other papers is held privately by her family.

Deledda: Autobiographical Statement

(Written at the time of the awarding of the Nobel Prize)

I was born in the little town of Nuoro in Sardinia in 1871 [according to other sources, 1875]. My father was a fairly well-to-do landowner who farmed his own land. He was also a hospitable man and had friends in all of the towns surrounding Nuoro. When these friends and their families had to come to Nuoro on business or for religious holidays, they usually stayed at our house. Thus I began to know the various characters of my novels. I went only to elementary school in Nuoro. After this, I took private lessons in Italian from an elementary school teacher. He gave me themes to write about, and some of them turned out so well that he told me to publish them in a newspaper. I was thirteen and I didn't know to whom I should go to have my stories published. But I came across a fashion magazine. I took the address and sent off a short story. It was immediately published. Then I wrote my first novel, *Fior di Sardegna* (1892) [Flower of Sardinia], which I sent to an editor in Rome. He published it, and it was quite successful. But my first real success was *Elias Portolú* (1903), which was first translated by the *Revue des deux mondes,* and then into all of the European languages. I have written a great deal:

Novels: Anime oneste, romanzo famigliare (1895) [Honest Souls], with preface by Ruggero Bonghi; *Il vecchio della montagna* (1900) [The Old Man of the Mountain] followed by a dramatic sketch, *Odio vince* (1904) [Hate Wins]; *Elias Portolú* (1903); *Cenere* (1904) [Ashes]; *Nostalgie* (1905); *La via del male* (1896) [The Evil Way]; *Naufraghi in porto* [originally *Dopo il divorzio,* 1902] (1920) [After the Divorce]; *L'edera* (1908) [The Ivy]; *Il nostro padrone* (1910) [Our Master]; *Sino al confine* (1910) [Up to the Limit]; *Nel deserto* (1911) [In the Desert]; *Colombi e sparvieri* (1912) [Doves and Falcons]; *Canne al vento* (1913) [Canes in the Wind]; *Le colpe altrui* (1914) [The Others' Faults]; *Marianna Sirca* (1915); *L'incendio nell'oliveto* (1918) [The Fire in the Olive Grove]; *La Madre* (1920) [The Mother]; *Il segreto dell'uomo solitario* (1921) [The Secret of the Solitary Man]; *Il Dio dei viventi* (1922) [The God of the Living]; *La danza della collana* (1924) [The Dance of the Necklace], followed by the dramatic sketch *A sinistra* (1924) [To the Left]; *La fuga in Egitto* (1925) [The Flight into Egypt]; *Annalena Bilsini* (1927).

Short Stories: "Il giuochi della vita" (1905) [The Gambles in Life]; "Chiaroscuro" (1912) [Light and Dark]; "Il fanciullo nascosto" (1915) [The Hidden Boy]; "Il ritorno del figlio" (1919) [The Son's Return]; "La bambina rubata" (1919) [The Stolen Child]; "Cattive compagnie" (1921) [Evil Company]; "Il flauto nel bosco" (1923) [The Flute in the Wood]; "Il sigillo d'amore" (1926) [The Seal of Love].

L'edera (1912) [The Ivy], a play in three acts, with the collaboration of Camillo Antona-Traversi.

In 1900 I took my first trip. It was to Cagliari, the beautiful Sardinian capital. There I met my husband. We later moved to Rome, where I am presently living. I have also written some poems which have not been collected in a volume.

Biographical note on Grazia Deledda:

Grazia Deledda (1875–1936) continued to write extensively after she received the Nobel Prize. *La casa del poeta* (1930) [The Poet's House] and *Sole d'estate* (1933) [Summer Sun], both collections of short stories, reflect her optimistic vision of life even during the most painful years of her incurable illness. Life remains beautiful and serene, unaltered by personal suffering; man and nature are reconciled in order to overcome physical and spiritual hardship.

In many of her later works, Grazia Deledda combined the imaginary and the autobiographical; this blend is readily apparent in her novel, *Il paese del vento* (1931) [Land of the Wind]. In another novel, *L'argine* (1934) [*The Barrier*], the renunciation of worldly things, including love, mirrors the life of the author who, accepting self-sacrifice as a higher manner of living, is reconciled with God. The common trait of all her later writings is a constant faith in mankind and in God.

Two of Grazia Deledda's novels were published posthumously: *Cosima* (1937) and *Il cedro di Libano* (1939) [The Cedar of Lebanon].

[© The Nobel Foundation, 1926.]

1926 Nobel Prize in Literature Presentation Speech

by Henrik Schück, President of the Nobel Foundation, 10 December 1927

The Swedish Academy has awarded the Nobel Prize of 1926 to the Italian author Grazia Deledda.

Grazia Deledda was born in Nuoro, a small town in Sardinia. There she spent her childhood and her youth, and from the natural surroundings and the life of the people she drew the impressions which later became the inspiration and the soul of her literary work.

From the window of her house she could see the nearby mountains of Orthobene with their dark forests and jagged grey peaks. Farther off was a chain of limestone mountains which sometimes appeared violet, sometimes lemon-coloured, sometimes dark blue, depending on the variations of the light. And in the distance, the snowy peaks of Gennargentù emerged.

Nuoro was isolated from the rest of the world. The few visitors to the town usually arrived on horseback, with the women mounted behind the men. The monotony of daily life was interrupted only by traditional religious or popular holidays and by the songs and dances in the main street at carnival time.

In this environment, Grazia Deledda's view of life developed into something uniquely ingenuous and primitive. In Nuoro it was not considered shameful to be a bandit. "Do you think," says an old peasant woman in one of Deledda's novels, "that bandits are bad people? Well, you're wrong. They are only men who need to display their skill, that's all. In the old days men went to war. Now there aren't any more wars, but men still need to fight. And so they commit their hold-ups, their thefts, and their cattle stealing, not to do evil but only to display somehow their ability and their strength." Thus the bandit rather enjoys the sympathy of the people. If he is caught and put in prison, the peasants have an expressive phrase which means that he has "run into trouble." And when he is freed no stigma is attached to him. In fact, when he returns to his home town, he is greeted with the words, "More such trouble a hundred years from now!"

The vendetta is still the custom in Sardinia, and a person is respected if he takes blood revenge on the killer of a kinsman. Indeed, it is considered a crime to betray the avenger. One author writes, "Even if the reward on his head were three times its size, not a single man in the whole district of Nuoro could be found to betray him. Only one law reigns there: respect for a man's strength and scorn of society's justice."

In this town, so little influenced by the Italian mainland, Grazia Deledda grew up surrounded by a savagely beautiful natural setting and by people who possessed a certain primitive grandeur, in a house that had a sort of biblical simplicity about it. "We girls," Grazia Deledda writes, "were never allowed to go out except to go to Mass or to take an occasional walk in the countryside." She had no chance to get an advanced education, and like the other middle-class children in the area, she went only to the local school. Later she took a few private lessons in French and Italian because her family spoke only the Sardinian dialect at home. Her education, then, was not extensive. However, she was thoroughly acquainted with and delighted in the folk songs of her town with its hymns to the saints, its ballads, and its lullabies. She was also familiar with the legends and traditions of Nuoro. Furthermore, she had an opportunity at home to read a few works of Italian literature and a few novels in translation, since by Sardinian standards her family was relatively well-to-do. But this was all. Yet the young girl took a great liking to her studies, and at only thirteen she wrote a whimsical but tragic short story, "Sangue Sardo" (1888) [Sardinian Blood], which she succeeded in publishing in a Roman newspaper. The people at Nuoro did not at all like this display of audacity, since women were not supposed to concern themselves with anything but domestic duties. But Grazia Deledda did not conform; instead she devoted herself to writing novels: first, *Fior di Sardegna* [Flower of Sardinia], published in 1892; then *La via del male* (1896) [The Evil Way], *Il vecchio della montagna* (1900) [The Old Man of the Mountain], *Elias Portolú* (1903), and others with which she made a name for herself. She came to be recognized as one of the best young female writers in Italy.

She had, in fact, made a great discovery—she had discovered Sardinia. In the middle of the eighteenth century a new movement had arisen in European literature. Writers at that time were tired of the models constantly drawn from Greek and Roman literature. They wanted something new. Their movement quickly joined forces with another which had begun in the same epoch with Rousseau's adoration of man in his natural state, untouched by civilization. The new school formed from these two movements advanced and gained force, particularly in the great days of Romanticism. The school's most recent trophies have been won by the work of Grazia Deledda. It is true that in descriptions of local colour and peasant life she had predecessors even in her own country. The so-called "regionalist" school in Italian literature had had such notable representatives as Verga, in his descriptions of Sicily, and Fogazzaro, in his descriptions of the Lombardo-Veneto region. But the discovery of Sardinia decidedly belongs to Grazia Deledda. She knew intimately every corner of her native land. She stayed in Nuoro until she was twenty-five; only then did she find the courage to go to Cagliari, the capital of Sardinia. Here she met Madesani, the man whom she married in 1900. After her marriage she and her husband moved to Rome, where she divided her time between her work as a writer and her family duties. In the novels written after she moved to Rome, she continued to deal with Sardinian subjects as in the work entitled *L'Edera* (1908) [The Ivy]. But in the novels written after *L'Edera,* the action frequently takes place in a less localized atmosphere, as, for example, in her most recent novel *La Fuga in Egitto* (1925) [The Flight into Egypt], which the Academy has examined and appreciated. However, her conception of man and nature is, as always, fundamentally Sardinian in character. Although she is now artistically more mature, she remains the same serious, eloquent, but unpretentious writer who wrote *La via del male* and *Elias Portolú.*

It is rather difficult for a foreigner to judge the artistic merit of her style. I shall therefore quote one of the most famous Italian critics on this matter. "Her style," he writes, "is that of the great masters of the narrative; it has the characteristic marks of all great novelists. No one in Italy today writes novels which have the vigour of style, the power of craftsmanship, the structure, or the social relevance which I found in some, even the latest, works of Grazia Deledda such as *La Madre* (1920) [The Mother] and *Il Segreto dell'uomo solitario* (1921) [The Secret of the Solitary Man]." One might note only that her composition does not have the strong consistency which might be desired; unexpected passages often give the impression of hasty transitions. But this defect is more than generously compensated for by her many virtues. As a painter of nature she has few equals in European literature. She does not uselessly waste her vivid colours; but even then, the nature which she describes has the simple, broad lines of ancient landscapes, as it has their chaste purity and majesty. It is a marvellously lively nature in perfect harmony with the psychological life of her characters. Like a truly great artist, she succeeds in incorporating her representation of people's sentiments and customs into her descriptions of nature. Indeed, one need only recall the classic description of the pilgrim's sojourn on Mount Lula in *Elias Portolú.* They depart on a May morning. Family after family ascends toward the ancient votive church, some on horseback, some in old wagons. They carry along enough provisions to last a week. The wealthier families lodge in the great shelter standing next to the church. These families are descended from the church's founders, and each has a spike in the wall and a hearth to indicate the area which belongs to it. No one else can set foot in this area. Each evening the families gather in their respective areas for as long as the feast lasts. They cook their food over the fireplace and tell legends, play music, and sing during the long summer night. In the novel *La via del male,* Grazia Deledda describes equally vividly the strange Sardinian marriage and funeral customs. When a funeral is to take place, all of the doors are shut, all of the shutters are closed, every fire is put out, no one is permitted to prepare food, and hired mourners wail their improvised dirges. The descriptions of such primitive customs are so lifelike and so simple and natural that we are almost moved to call them Homeric. In Grazia Deledda's novels more than in most other novels, man and nature form a single unity. One might almost say that the men are plants which germinate in the Sardinian soil itself. The majority of them are simple peasants with primitive sensibilities and modes of thought, but with something in them of the grandeur of the Sardinian natural setting. Some of them almost attain the stature of the monumental figures of the Old Testament. And no matter how different they may seem from the men we know, they give us the impression of being incontestably real, of belonging to real life. They in no way resemble theatrical puppets. Grazia Deledda is a master of the art of fusing realism with idealism.

She does not belong to that band of writers who work on a thesis and discuss problems. She has always kept herself far removed from the battles of the day. When Ellen Key once tried to interest her in such discussions, she answered, "I belong to the past." Perhaps this confession of attitude is not completely just. Certainly Grazia Deledda feels tied by strong bonds to the past, to the history of her people. But she also knows how to live in and respond to her own times. Although she lacks interest in theories, she has a great deal of interest in every aspect of human life. She writes in a letter, "Our great anguish is life's slow death. This is why we must try to slow life down, to intensify it, thus giving it the richest possible meaning. One must try to live above one's life, as a cloud above the sea." Precisely because life seems so rich and admirable to her, she has never taken sides in the political, social, or literary controversies of the day. She has loved man more than theories and has lived her own quiet life far from the world's uproar. "Destiny," she writes in another letter, "caused me to be born in the heart of lonely Sardinia. But even if I had been born in Rome or Stockholm, I should not have been different. I should have always been what I am—a soul which becomes impassioned about life's problems and which lucidly perceives men as they are, while still believing that they could be better and that no one else but themselves prevents them from achieving God's reign on earth. Everything is hatred, blood, and pain; but, perhaps, everything will be conquered one day by means of love and good will."

These last words express her vision of life, a serious and profound vision with a religious cast. It is frequently sad, but never pessimistic. She believes that the forces of good ultimately will triumph in the life struggle. The principle which dominates all her work as a writer is represented clearly and concisely at the end of her novel *Cenere* (1904) [Ashes]. Anania's mother is ruined. In order not to be an obstacle to her son's happiness, she has taken her own life and now lies dead before him. When he was only a baby, she had given him an amulet. He opens it and finds that it contains only ashes. "Yes, all was ashes: life, death, man; the very destiny which produced her. And still in the last hour, as he stood before the body of the most miserable of human creatures, who after doing and suffering evil in all of its manifestations had died for someone else's good, he remembered that among the ashes there often lurks the spark of a luminous and purifying flame. And he hoped. And he still loved life."

Alfred Nobel wanted the Prize in Literature to be given to someone who, in his writings, had given humanity that nectar which infuses the health and the energy of a moral life. In conformity with his wishes, the Swedish Academy has awarded the Prize to Grazia Deledda, "for her idealistically inspired writings which with plastic clarity picture the life on her native island and with depth and sympathy deal with human problems in general."

At the banquet, Archbishop Nathan Söderblom, Member of the Swedish Academy, addressed the laureate:

Dear Madame—The proverb says, "All roads lead to Rome." In your literary work, all roads lead to the human heart. You never tire of listening affectionately to its legends, its mysteries, conflicts, anxieties, and eternal longings. Customs as well as civil and social institutions vary according to the times, the national character and history, faith and tradition, and should be respected religiously. To do otherwise and reduce everything to a uniformity would be a crime against art and truth. But the human heart and its problems are everywhere the same. The author who knows how to describe human nature and its vicissitudes in the most vivid colours and, more important, who knows how to investigate and unveil the world of the heart—such an author is universal, even in his local confinement.

You, Madame, do not limit yourself to man; you reveal, first of all, the struggle between man's bestiality and the high destiny of his soul. For you the road is extended. You have seen the road sign which many travellers pass by without noticing. For you the road leads to God. For this reason you believe in rebirth in spite of the degradation and frailty of man. You know that it is possible to reclaim the swamp so that it becomes firm and fertile land. Therefore, a bright ray gleams in your books. Through darkness and human misery you let shine the solace of eternal light.

[© The Nobel Foundation, 1926.]

José Echegaray
(19 April 1832 – 4 September 1916)

Judy B. McInnis
University of Delaware

BOOKS: *Cálculo de variaciones: Lecciones explicadas en la Escuela de Ingenieros de Caminos, Canales y Puertas* (Madrid: José C. de la Peña, 1858);

Memoria sobre los trabajos de perforación del tunel, de los Alpes escrita en el año 1860 durante las prácticas de la Escuela especial de Ingenieros de Caminos, Canales y Puertos, by Echegaray, Manuel Pardo, and Luis Vasconi (Madrid: Viuda de D. J. C. de la Peña, 1863);

Problemas de geometría (Madrid: T. Fortanet, 1865);

Discursos leídos ante la Real Academia de Ciencias Exactas, Físicas y Naturales en la recepción pública de Sr. D. José Echegaray: Historia de las matemáticas puras en España (Madrid: Eusebio Aguado, 1866);

Introducción a la geometría superior (Madrid: Eusebio Aguado, 1867);

Teorías modernas de la física: Unidad de las fuerzas materiales: Colección de artículos (Madrid: Francisco Roig, 1867; expanded edition, Madrid: M. Rivadeneyra, 1873);

Discurso pronunciado por el Sr. D. José Echegaray en la sesión celebrada en las Cortes Constituyentes el día 5 de mayo de 1869 en poco de los artículos 20 y 21 del proyecto de Constitución (Madrid: M. Rivadeneyra, 1869);

Influencia del estudio de las ciencias en la educación de la mujer (Madrid: M. Rivadeneyra, 1869);

Teoría matemática de la luz (Madrid: Viuda de Aguado e Hijo, 1871);

El libro talonario, as Jorge Hayaseca y Eizaguirre (Madrid: José Rodríguez/Alonso Gullón, 1874);

La esposa del vengador (Madrid: José Rodríguez, 1874);

La última noche (Madrid: José Rodríguez, 1875);

En el puño de la espada (Madrid: José Rodríguez, 1875);

Un sol que nace y un sol que muere (Madrid: José Rodríguez, 1876);

Cómo empieza y cómo acaba (Madrid: R. Velasco, 1876);

Discursos y rectificación del Señor Don José de Echegaray pronunciados en las sesiones de los días 7, 9 y 11 de Julio de 1877, con motivo del dictamen de la comisión de Información parlamentaria referente a las operaciones del Tesoro (Madrid: Viuda e Hijos de G. Antonio García, 1877);

José Echegaray, circa 1900 (photograph © Bettmann/CORBIS)

El gladiador de Rávena: Imitación de las últimas escenas de la tragedia alemana de Frederico Halm (Munch de Bellinghaussen), based on a work by Frederich Halm (Madrid: José Rodríguez, 1877);

O locura o santidad (Madrid: José M. Ducazcal, 1877); translated by Hannah Lynch as *Folly or Saintliness,* in *The Great Galeoto [and] Folly or Saintliness: Two Plays Done from the Verse of José Echegaray into English Prose* (London: John Lane / Boston: Lamson Wolffe, 1895);

Iris de paz (Madrid: T. Fortanet, 1877);

Para tal culpa tal pena (Madrid: José Rodríguez, 1877);

Lo que no puede decirse (Madrid: T. Fortanet, 1877);

En el pilar y en la cruz (Madrid: José Rodríguez, 1878);

Correr en pos de un ideal (Madrid: José Rodríguez, 1878);

Algunas veces aquí (Madrid: José Rodríguez, 1878);

Morir por no despertar (Madrid: Tip. Yagües, 1879);

En el seno de la muerte (Madrid: José Rodríguez, 1879);

Bodas trágicas (Madrid: José Rodríguez, 1879);

Mar sin orillas (Madrid: José Rodríguez, 1879);

Ni la paciencia de Job (Madrid: José Rodríguez, 1879);

La muerte en los labios (Madrid: José Rodríguez, 1880);

El gran Galeoto (Madrid: José Rodríguez, 1881); translated by Lynch as *The Great Galeoto* in *The Great Galeoto, [and] Folly or Saintliness: Two Plays Done from the Verse of José Echegaray into English Prose* (London: John Lane / Boston: Lamson Wolffe, 1895);

Haroldo el Normando (Madrid: José Rodríguez, 1881);

Los dos curiosos impertinentes (Madrid: José Rodríguez, 1882);

Conflicto entre dos deberes (Madrid: Cosme Rodríguez, 1882);

Un milagro en Egipto (Madrid: Cosme Rodríguez, 1883);

Anales de teatro y de la música con un estudio sobre el realismo (Madrid: Ricardo Fé, 1884);

Piensa mal . . . y acertarás? (Madrid: Cosme Rodríguez, 1884);

La peste de Otranto (Madrid: José Rodríguez, 1884);

Teatro, 10 volumes (Madrid: Cosme Rodríguez, 1884);

Obras dramáticas escogidas, 2 volumes (Madrid: Tello, 1884);

Vida alegre y muerte triste (Madrid: José Rodríguez, 1885);

El bandido Lisandro (Madrid: José Rodríguez, 1886);

De mala raza (Madrid: José Rodríguez, 1886);

Dos fanatismos (Madrid: José Rodríguez, 1887);

El conde Lotario (Madrid: José Rodríguez, 1887);

La realidad y el delirio (Madrid: José Rodríguez, 1887);

El hijo de carne y el hijo de hierro (Madrid: José Rodríguez, 1888);

Lo sublime en lo vulgar (Madrid: José Rodríguez, 1888);

Manantial que no se agota (Madrid: José Rodríguez, 1889);

Los rígidos (Madrid: José Rodríguez, 1889);

Siempre en ridículo (Madrid: Tip. Yagües, 1890); translated by T. Walter Gilkyson as *Always Ridiculous* (Boston: R. G. Badger, 1916);

Examen de varios submarinos comparados con "El Peral": Colección de artículos publicados en "El Heraldo de Madrid" (Madrid: José M. Ducazcal, 1891);

El prólogo de un drama (Madrid: José Rodríguez, 1891);

Irene de Otranto (Madrid: José Rodríguez, 1891);

Un crítico incipiente (Madrid: José Rodríguez, 1891);

Comedia sin desenlace (Madrid: José Rodríguez, 1892);

El hijo de Don Juan (Madrid: José Rodríguez, 1892); translated by James Graham as *The Son of Don Juan* (London: Unwin, 1895; Boston: Roberts, 1895);

Sic vos non vobis; o La última limosna (Madrid: José Rodríguez, 1892);

Mariana (Madrid: José Rodríguez, 1892); translated by Graham as *Mariana* (New York: Roberts, 1895);

El poder de la impotencia (Madrid: José Rodríguez, 1893);

A la orilla del mar (Madrid: José Rodríguez, 1893);

Informe sobre la producción y distribución de electricidad de la Compañía Madrileña, by Echegaray, Ricardo Becerro de Bengoa, and Francisco de P. Rojas (Madrid: F. Rodríguez, 1894);

La rencorosa (Madrid: José Rodríguez, 1894);

Mancha que limpia (Madrid: José Rodríguez, 1895);

El primer acto de un drama (Madrid: José Rodríguez, 1895);

El estigma (Madrid: José Rodríguez, 1895);

De la legalidad común en materias literarias (Madrid: Hijos de F. A. García, 1896);

La cantante callejera (Madrid: Evaristo Odriózola, 1896);

Amor salvaje (Madrid: Evaristo Odriózola, 1896);

Semíramis, o, La hija del aire, adapted from Pedro Calderón de la Barca's play (Madrid: Evaristo Odriózola, 1896);

La calumnia por castigo (Madrid: Sucesores de Rodríguez y Odriózola, 1897);

Resolucion de ecuaciones y teoria de Galois: Lecciones explicadas en el Ateneo de Madrid (Madrid: J. A. García, 1897);

Discurso leído por el Excmo. Sr. D. José Echegaray el día 10 de noviembre de 1898 en el Ateneo científico, literario y artístico de Madrid con motivo de la apertura de su cátedra: ¿Qué es lo que contribuye la fuerza de las naciones? (Madrid: Sucesores de Rivadeneyra, 1898);

La duda (Madrid: R. Velasco, 1898);

El hombre negro (Madrid: R. Velasco, 1898); translated by Ellen Watson as *The Man in Black* (N.p., 1899);

Silencio de muerte (Madrid: R. Velasco, 1899);

Dramas (Madrid: La Novela Ilustrada, 1900);

Lances entre caballeros: Este libro contiene una reseña histórica del duelo y un proyecto de bases para la redacción de un código del honor en España (Madrid: Sucesores de Rivadeneyra, 1900);

Páginas escogidas: Estudios literarios de E. Gómez Carrillo, Conrado Solsona, José Echegaray, by Echegaray and others, edited by Juan Navarro Reverter (Paris: Garnier Hermanos, 1900);

El loco Dios (Madrid: R. Velasco, 1900); translated by Elizabeth Howard West as *The Mad Man Divine* (Boston: Gorham Press, 1908);

Congresos internacionales de ferrocarriles, tranvías y electricidad, celebrados en Paris en el año 1900: Memorias de los ingenieros de caminos, canales y puertos, by Echegaray and others (Madrid: Hijos de J. A. García, 1901);

Malas herencias (Madrid: R. Velasco, 1902);

Observaciones y teorías sobre la afinidad química (Madrid: Antonio Marzo, 1902);

La escalinata de un trono (Madrid: R. Velasco, 1903);

La desequilibrada (Madrid: R. Velasco, 1904);

Discurso leído en la Universidad Central en la solemne inauguración del curso académico de 1905 a 1906 por D. José Echegaray y Eizaguirre: La Ciencia y la Crítica

(Madrid: Imprenta Colonial [Estrada Hermanos], 1905);

Ciencia popular: Colección de artículos publicados en los periódicos "El Imparcial" y "El Liberal" (Madrid: Hijos de J. A. García, 1905);

A fuerza de arrastrarse (Madrid: R. Velasco, 1905);

Los tres sueños de Colilla (Madrid: Viuda de Rodriguez Serra, 1905?);

Monólogos en verso: "Entre dolora y cuento," "El moderno Endimión," "El canto de la Sirena" (Madrid: R. Velasco, 1906);

Conferencias sobre física matemática, 5 volumes (Madrid: Imprenta de la "Gaceta de Madrid," 1906–1910);

El preferido y los cenicientos, as Librado Ezguieura (Madrid: R. Velasco, 1908);

Muestras (Madrid: Editorial Ibero Americana, 1908);

Vulgarización científica (Madrid: Rafael Gutiérrez Jiménez, 1910);

Recuerdos, 3 volumes (Madrid: Ruiz Hermanos, 1917).

Editions and Collections: *José Echegaray: Teatro escogido*, edited by Amando Lázaro Ros (Madrid: Aguilar, 1955)—includes *El libro talonario, La última noche, En el puño de la espada, O locura o santidad, En el seno de la muerte, La muerte en los labios, El gran Galeoto, Piensa mal . . . y acertarás?, De mala raza, Sic vos non vobis o la última limosna, Mancha que limpia, La duda*, and *A fuerza de arrastrarse;*

Echegaray, edited by Julio Mathías (Madrid: Espasa, 1970)—includes selections from *El libro talonario, En el puño de la espada, El gran Galeoto, Mancha que limpia*, and *A fuerza de arrastrarse.*

Editions in English: *Mariana*, translated by Frederico Sarda and Carlos D. S. Wuppermann (New York: Moods, 1909);

The Atonement of Helen: A Drama in Four Acts by Franklin Winter from the Spanish of José Echegaray (New York: Manuscripts Universal, 1915).

PLAY PRODUCTIONS: *El libro talonario*, Madrid, Teatro Apolo, 18 February 1874;

La esposa del vengador, Madrid, Teatro Español, 14 November 1874;

La última noche, Madrid, Teatro Español, 2 March 1875;

En el puño de la espada, Madrid, Teatro Apolo, 12 October 1875;

Un sol que nace y un sol que muere and *Cómo empieza y cómo acaba*, Madrid, Teatro Español, 9 November 1876;

El gladiador de Ravena, Madrid, Teatro Novedades, 10 November 1876;

O locura o santidad, Madrid, Teatro Español, 22 January 1877;

Iris de paz, Madrid, Teatro Español, 10 February 1877;

Para tal culpa tal pena, Madrid, Teatro Español, 27 April 1877;

Lo que no puede decirse, Madrid, Teatro Español, 14 October 1877;

En el pilar y en la cruz, Madrid, Teatro Español, 26 February 1878;

Correr en pos de un ideal, Madrid, Teatro Español, 15 October 1878;

Algunas veces aquí, Madrid, Teatro Apolo, 15 October 1878;

Morir por no despertar, Madrid, Teatro Apolo, 10 February 1879;

En el seno de la muerte, Madrid, Teatro Español, 12 April 1879;

Bodas trágicas, Madrid, Teatro Apolo, 24 May 1879;

Mar sin orillas, Madrid, Teatro Español, 20 December 1879;

La muerte en los labios, Madrid, Teatro Español, 30 November 1880;

El gran Galeoto, Madrid, Teatro Español, 19 March 1881;

Los dos curiosos impertinentes, Madrid, Teatro Español, 8 April 1881;

Haroldo el Normando, Madrid, Teatro Español, 3 December 1881;

Conflicto entre dos deberes, Madrid, Teatro Español, 14 December 1882;

Piensa mal ... ¿y acertarás? Madrid, Teatro Español, 5 February 1884;

Un milagro en Egipto, Madrid, Teatro Español, 24 March 1884;

La peste de Otranto, Madrid, Teatro Español, 12 December 1884;

Vida alegre y muerte triste, Madrid, Teatro Español, 7 March 1885;

El bandido Lisandro, Madrid, Teatro Español, 13 February 1886;

De mala raza, Barcelona, then Madrid, Teatro Español, 4 March 1886;

El conde Lotario, Valencia, 2 June 1886;

Los dos fanatismos, Madrid, Teatro Español, 15 January 1887;

La realidad y el delirio, Madrid, Teatro Español, 12 April 1887;

El hijo de carne y el hijo de hierro, Madrid, Teatro de la Princesa, 14 January 1888;

Lo sublime en lo vulgar, Barcelona, 4 July 1888;

Manantial que no se agota, Madrid, Teatro Español, 9 March 1889;

Los rígidos, Madrid, Teatro Español, 19 November 1889;

Siempre en ridículo, Madrid, Teatro Español, 21 December 1890;

El prólogo de un drama, Valladolid, 27 December 1890;

Irene de Otranto, Madrid, Teatro Real, 12 February 1891;

Un crítico incipiente, Madrid, Teatro de la Comedia, 27 February 1891;

Comedia sin desenlace, Madrid, Teatro de la Comedia, 17 December 1891;

El hijo de Don Juan, Madrid, Teatro Español, 29 March 1892;

Sic vos non vobis, o la última limosna, Madrid, Teatro de la Comedia, 1892;

Mariana, Madrid, Teatro de la Comedia, 5 December 1892;

El poder de la impotencia, Madrid, Teatro de la Comedia, 4 March 1893;

A la orilla del mar, Madrid: Teatro de la Comedia, 12 December 1893;

La rencorosa, Madrid, Teatro de la Comedia, 13 March 1894;

María Rosa, translated from Angel Guimerá's play, Madrid, Teatro de la Princesa, 24 November 1894;

Mancha que limpia, Madrid, Teatro Español, 9 February 1895;

El primer acto de un drama, Madrid, Teatro Novedades, 25 February 1895;

El estigma, Madrid, Teatro Español, 15 November 1895;

La cantante callejera, Madrid, Teatro Español, 26 March 1896;

Tierra baja, translated from Guimerá's play, Madrid, Teatro Español, 1896;

Amor salvaje, Madrid, Teatro de la Comedia, 1896;

Semíramis o la hija del aire, translated from Pedro Calderón de la Barca's play, Madrid, 1896;

La calumnia por castigo, Madrid, Teatro Español, 22 January 1897;

La duda, Madrid, Teatro Español, 11 February 1898;

El hombre negro, Madrid, Teatro Español, 22 April 1898;

Silencio de muerte, Madrid, Teatro Español, 9 December 1898;

El loco Dios, Madrid, Teatro Español, 8 November 1900;

Malas herencias, Madrid, Teatro Español, 20 November 1902;

La escalinata de un trono, Madrid, Teatro Español, 19 February 1903;

La desequilibrada, Madrid, Teatro Español, 14 December 1903;

A fuerza de arrastrarse, Madrid, Teatro Español, 7 February 1905;

El preferido y los cenicientos, as Librado Ezguieura, Madrid, Teatro Español, 1908;

El moderno Endimión, Entre dolora y cuento, and *El canto de la sirena,* Madrid, 1908.

TRANSLATIONS: Angel Guimerá, *María-Rosa* (Madrid: José Rodríguez, 1894);

Guimerá, *Tierra baja* (Madrid: Florencio Fiscowich, 1896).

SELECTED PERIODICAL PUBLICATIONS–UNCOLLECTED: "El tiempo y su medida," *Almanaque de la Ilustración Española y Americana* (1897);

"El reloj maravilloso," *Almanaque de la Ilustración Española y Americana* (1898);

"El tiempo al revés," *Almanaque de la Ilustración Española y Americana* (1900);

"El conflicto de los siglos," *Almanaque de la Ilustración Española y Americana* (1901);

"El loco de los relojes," *Almanaque de la Ilustración Española y Americana* (1903).

José Echegaray became Spain's first Nobel Prize in Literature winner in 1904, sharing the prize with French poet Frédéric Mistral. He had distinguished himself previously as a politician and a scientist; but his literary fame came from his plays. For some thirty years he was one of Spain's leading popular dramatists, and although the value of his work was disputed by critics, it earned him a place in the history of modern Spanish drama.

José Echegaray y Eizaguirre was born on Holy Thursday, 19 April 1832, the year preceding the commencement of the first Carlist War in Madrid. He was the eighth child born to José Echegaray Lacosta, of Aragonese descent, and Manuela Eizaguirre Chaler, of Basque origin. His father, who worked as both a medical doctor and a professor of botany, moved the family to Murcia in 1837. An industrious and gifted student, José had completed preparatory school at age fourteen and convinced his father to enroll him in the School of Civil Engineering, then considered the most difficult and prestigious profession. Upon graduation in 1853, he became second engineer on a road project in Almería, a post with so few duties that he had time to read voraciously in his favorite field of drama.

Seven months later he returned to Madrid, was appointed secretary of the School of Civil Engineering, and was assigned to teach the courses of hydraulics, differential and integral calculus, and applied mathematics, courses for which he produced several textbooks. Through the publication of various scientific and mathematical papers, he soon became Spain's foremost mathematician. He devoted his speech upon induction into the Academy of Exact Sciences in 1865 to the dearth of skilled mathematicians in his country. Spain, he declared, had never produced even a third-rate mathematician because of the Inquisition and its legacy of fear and prejudice. Echegaray endeavored to correct this situation with an enormous production of scientific textbooks, papers, and articles, written for both specialists and laypersons. The journal of the Office of Public Works and the periodical *El Economista,* which he founded with Gabriel Rodríguez, published scientific papers and monographs by Echegaray in the early years of his career. In addition to reading his own papers at the Academy of Science, he introduced and responded to those of others; he undertook the same task after his induction into the Royal Academy. Among the authors he presented to the Spanish public were Fernanflor (Isidoro Fernández Flórez), Luis Soles Eguilaz, Enrique Segovia Rocaberti, Clarín (Leopoldo Alas), Arístides Sáenz de Urraca, Manuel Wertheimer, Fernando Soldevilla, and Mario Méndez Bejarano.

Avidly devoted to the theater, he attended opening nights and wrote his first play, "La cortesana" (The Courtesan), treating a woman's rehabilitation in the style of Alexandre Dumas *fils*'s *La Dame aux camélias* (1852, The Lady of the Camellias). The actor/producer Joaquín Arjona softened his rejection of the play with praise of its energy but criticism of its impracticality for the stage. Echegaray tore it up and, turning his attention to economics, contributed many articles to *El Economista,* in which he argued for free trade, as he did also in discourses delivered at El Ateneo, a prestigious debating society. Meanwhile he continued reading French, German, and Spanish contemporary fiction and drama, and his attendance at the theater never faltered. He dabbled in poetry, writing a poem of 150 lines for his literary brother Miguel Echegaray in 1854. The latter's success in having his drama *Cara o cruz* (Heads or Tails) staged in Madrid at the Teatro Circo prompted Echegaray to try his hand at dramaturgy once again. He completed a verse drama in three acts and a prologue but regarded it as an apprenticeship and did not seek its staging or publication. In the late 1850s he brought his third attempt in the dramatic genre, "La hija natural" (The Illegitimate Daughter), to the attention of the actress Teodora Lamadrid. She praised the play but did nothing to encourage its production, which did not occur until 1877 under the title *Para tal culpa tal pena* (The Punishment Fits the Crime).

At the age of twenty-five, on 16 November 1857, Echegaray married Ana Perfecta Estrada, a young woman so exquisite that King Amadeus (Amadeo de Saboya) later declared that the surpassing beauties of Spain were the Cathedral of Burgos and the wife of José Echegaray. The happy marriage produced two children: daughter Ana, who went on to have three children of her own before her early death, and son Manuel, who never married and remained in the parental home throughout his father's life. While Echegaray enjoyed considerable prestige in his scientific career, his salary did not adequately support a comfortable middle-class standard. To augment his income, he established a preparatory academy but soon had to yield to his School of Civil Engineering boss's protests against moonlighting, an activity in which most professionals of the time engaged. The same boss prevented him from accepting a lucrative position as adviser to the building of a network of railroads and bridges throughout Italy. However, his employer did finance a journey to view the solar eclipse from Las Palmas and to visit major cities in England, France, and Italy, then to study the tunnel built through the Alps.

Meanwhile, between 1860 and 1862, Echegaray found time to write two one-act plays, *Un sol que nace y un sol que muere* (Sun Rising and Sun Setting) and *Morir por no despertar* (To Die Not To Awake), that were eventually staged successfully in 1876 and 1879, respectively. "El banquero" (The Banker), a play in three acts that Echegaray wrote in 1864, was staged in 1875 under the title *La última noche* (The Last Night). Its cold reception confirmed Echegaray's belief that a dramatic author had best not attempt direct representation of his own philosophy and experience. The play dealt with the financial world the playwright knew well, but his ruthless, conniving principal character did not appeal to the Spanish audience.

Echegaray shaped and was shaped by a period of great political upheaval. During the nineteenth century there were revisions of the Spanish Constitution in 1808, 1812, 1834, 1837, 1845, 1856, 1869, 1873, and 1876, primarily because of the unresolved issue of the throne. Fernando VII had suppressed the Salic Law to make his daughter Isabella, rather than his brother Carlos, heir to the throne. Carlist supporters enveloped Spain in civil war three times in the nineteenth century, and their descendants still cavil over the diversion of the throne to Isabella's line. The economy suffered while the country depleted its resources on efforts to maintain the remnants of empire in Cuba and the Philippine Islands, lost finally in war against the United States in 1898.

The deaths of the exiled soldier-politician Leopoldo O'Donnell in 1867 and the dictator General Ramón María Narváez in 1868 weakened the government of the Liberal Luis González Bravo. Generals Juan Prim and Francisco Serrano y Domínguez marched on Madrid, and Queen Isabella II was forced to seek refuge with Napoleon III in Biarritz. Echegaray was pleasantly surprised to be named director of public works, since he had not sought the appointment by actively engaging in politics. He held the post only until 1869, when he replaced his superior Serrano as minister of development. Echegaray was handily elected representative from Asturias. He endorsed the Liberals' platform and championed both religious and economic freedom while instituting reforms in engineering schools and the mining industry.

Echegaray headed the commission to welcome Amadeus as king of Spain upon his arrival in the southeastern city of Cartagena on 30 December 1870. Receiving word that General Prim had been assassinated and that revolutionaries also planned to assassinate Amadeus, Echegaray, speaking for the king (who had not yet learned Spanish), calmed the crowds with a brilliant discourse. He resigned as minister of development in that year but was reappointed again in the summer of 1872. During this chaotic period, with uprisings of the separatists in the colonies and of the Carlists on the peninsula, Amadeus abdicated on 11 February 1873, and the Senate declared Spain a republic. Military forces dissolved the government ministers' emergency meeting, and Echegaray narrowly escaped death on his way home through the street mobs to pack his bags and seek refuge in Paris.

He used the six months he resided in France with his family to write the one-act play *El libro talonario* (1874, The Account Book). Upon his return to Madrid, he presented the play to the actress Matilde Díez as the work of his fictitious friend Jorge Hayaseca. Díez saw through the ruse and perceived that the play could be a success, especially if the public knew it was written by such a highly placed person as Echegaray, who had since been appointed as minister of finance, following General Manuel Pavía y Rodríguez's coup d'état on 3 January 1874. In that position Echegaray saved Spain from bankruptcy by creating the Bank of Spain, which could lend money to the state, thus freeing the country from the usurious interest rates of foreign banks. Borrowing 500 million pesetas at 5 percent, the state was able to repay its debts incurred in the Carlist civil wars. Then, to the amazement of his friends, Echegaray decided to resign from political life and from his scientific career to dedicate himself exclusively to drama. The success of *En el puño de la espada* (On the Hilt of the Sword), performed at the Teatro Apolo in 1875, and the dissolution that same year of the Democratic Party, his political affiliation, precipitated this career change, one he stuck to except for a brief period in 1905 when he was again recruited to serve as minister of finance and again managed to balance the budget.

A man of prodigious energy throughout his life, Echegaray kept abreast of developments in science, politics, and literature, the three careers in which he distinguished himself. The degree of his success in literature was corroborated by his election in 1882 to the Royal Academy of the Language, a seat he had to wait twelve years to occupy because Ramón Mesoneros Romanos, the man selected to give the induction speech, was too busy to devote time to a task that he felt merited a superlative effort. Echegaray remained an active member of the organization until his death in 1916. His production of stage successes ceased with the Nobel Prize in 1904; his last success was *A fuerza de arrastrarse* (By Dint of Crawling), produced in February 1905. *El preferido y los cenicientos* (The Chosen One and the Disregarded Someones), which the playwright presented in 1908 under the pseudonym Librado Ezguieura to avoid the protests that had swamped his most recent works, flopped. He devoted the last years of his life to quiet home life, writing his memoirs, and editing his collected works.

Echegaray accurately gauged the taste and temper of the Spanish public and ruled the stage from 1876 to 1905. He worked closely with the major actors and actresses of the period, often tailoring his plays to their strengths. He approached his writing like carpentry, constructing the taut development of plot and action to reach a surprising climax coinciding with the fall of the curtain. In this choice he diverged from the newer literary trends of realism and naturalism, whose authors focused upon character and often presented works with little plot development, concentrating instead on the setting and ambience, which often fatalistically determined the characters' choices. Echegaray rejected determinism and frequently chose to present characters who challenge theories of inherited weakness or defect. The playwright favored Romantic free form over the neoclassical rules in drama as much as he favored free trade in the economic sphere. His decision to limit scene changes and concentrate dramatic action within a relatively circumscribed time frame stemmed more from economies of production than from respect for the neoclassical unities of time, place, and action.

No single factor has complicated the evaluation of Echegaray's work more than the Nobel Prize he shared with Mistral in 1904. The strong protest of a group of young writers and critics against the Nobel committee's choice of Echegaray, whom they regarded as an outmoded dramatist catering to the bad taste of the Spanish public, has made all subsequent critics of his plays take a stand upon the literary merit of his works and to defend or deplore the committee's selection. The Nobel award sparked a furor in Spain comparable to igniting the dynamite whose discovery had enabled Alfred Nobel to fund the prize.

In one of his sonnets, Echegaray used the metaphor of a scientist constructing and igniting a dynamite stick to describe his creative procedure in the writing of a play:

Escojo una pasion, tomo una idea,
Un problema, un carácter . . . y lo infundo,
Cual densa dinamita, en lo profundo
De un personaje que mi mente crea.

....
La mecha enciendo. El fuego se propaga,
El cartucho revienta sin remedio,
Y el astro principal es quien lo paga.

(I choose a passion. I take an idea,
A problem, a character . . . and I infuse it
With powerful dynamite, in the depths
Of a character that my mind creates.
....
I ignite the fuse. Fire breaks out.
The cartridge explodes necessarily and inevitably.
And the principal star is the one who pays for it.)

The plays produced under this impulse are today generally classified as melodramas depicting tragic conflicts between love and honor, "*drama ripio*" (potboilers) in which the primary marks of punctuation are the exclamation point and the ellipsis, the first to indicate high emotion and the second to indicate emotion so extreme that the speaker is reduced to silence as he or she stands in a *tableau vivant* with the other actors. Of the sixty-eight dramas that Echegaray presented on the Madrid stage, only a handful receive accolades from modern literary critics and historians, and even these plays are sometimes criticized for their bombastic expression of hackneyed sentiments and their pedestrian versification. That Echegaray wrote nearly half of his plays in verse indicates the extent to which he still adhered to Romantic theories of dramatic construction, even at the end of the nineteenth century and the early years of the twentieth, when the realist preference for prose dialogue had become the norm in the theater.

The virulent reaction to the Nobel Prize, in the form of a manifesto published in a major newspaper and signed by fifty intellectuals, among them the foremost drama critics and several members of the "Generation of 1898" (including Azorín, Miguel de Unamuno, Rubén Darío, Ramiro de Maeztu, Manuel Machado, Antonio Machado, Jacinto Grau, Francisco Villaespesa, Ramón del Valle Inclán, and Pío Baroja), has predisposed modern critics to concentrate upon the defects of his plays and consign them, often unread, to the dustbin of the vagaries of public taste. Absorbed with the issue of his meriting or not meriting the Nobel Prize, critics only in the late twentieth century have gone beyond addressing the negative judgments of his plays to evaluate their form and content in the contexts of their specific period and of the history of Western drama. Several of the protesting contemporaries later recanted their condemnation, and not one ever achieved Echegaray's success on the stage.

The dramatist's health did not permit him to travel to Stockholm to receive the prize. In lieu of that ceremony, his Spanish champions organized a national homage of four major events: Alfonso XIII's conferring of the prize upon the playwright in the Senate palace before an impressive array of Spanish writers and intellectuals and the Swedish ambassador; an impromptu parade on the following day in which the Madrid populace, led by bands of students, filed past the Biblioteca Nacional, where Echegaray received their ovation; a ceremony in the Ateneo attended by Alfonso XIII and government officials, in which the renowned writers Benito Pérez Galdós, Santiago Ramón y Cajal, Juan Valera, and Marcelino Menéndez y Pelayo participated; and a production of *El gran Galeoto* (1881; translated as *The Great Galeoto,* 1895) in the Real Theater.

Most modern scholars would concede that—within Spain—Galdós, Clarín, and Emilia Pardo Bazán produced works of more lasting import and aesthetic merit than Echegaray's and would therefore have been more fitting recipients of the Nobel Prize, just as outside Spain and in the genre of drama, Henrik Ibsen was clearly the most influential writer of the period. A similar controversy was sparked when Bjørnstjerne Bjørnson, an author today known outside Norway no more than Echegaray is known outside Spain, received the Nobel Prize in 1903, in what some critics consider a direct insult to Ibsen. In the first years of the Nobel Prize in Literature, members of the committee put a narrow construction upon Nobel's instruction to select a "person who shall have produced . . . the most distinguished work of an idealistic tendency." In the committee's view, this description precluded giving the prize to naturalistic or even realistic writers: neither Emile Zola nor Thomas Hardy ever received the prize. C. D. af Wirsén, secretary of the Swedish Academy, despised both Ibsen and August Strindberg, and he spoke for the committee in praising Echegaray not for signaling the future but for resurrecting the past glory of Lope de Vega and Pedro Calderón de la Barca. Echegaray, in Wirsén's view, purified the Golden Age concepts of honor and devotion to duty by rejecting intolerance and fanaticism. He continued the Spanish tradition of "luxurious flowering of fantasy" combined with "subtle and at times conventional casuistry," "brilliant coloring," "affection for rhetorical antithesis," "emphatic language," and "tangled intrigue." Along with praise for Echegaray's intense lyricism, sharp disharmonies, tragic resolutions, and vigorous dialectic, Wirsén cited Echegaray's sometimes violent "striking effects" as especially laudable: the spectacular conflict combined with high-flown passion and rhetoric that today most repels critics and amuses spectators rather than purging them of pity and fear, the Aristotelian tragic imperative that Wirsén credited the Spanish dramatist with achieving.

Echegaray's neo-Romantic dramas polarize good and evil: the audience never vacillates about which character they should identify with, and even if a good character meets a tragic end, he or she always emerges as the moral victor. The mixture of good and evil within a single character, which distinguishes realistic and naturalistic drama, was a "confusing" mixture Bjørnson condemned in his acceptance speech for the Nobel Prize in 1903. Echegaray sometimes makes the villain the principal character of a drama, but he never "confuses" the public about the good or evil in a character for more than a few scenes—just enough to maintain interest and mystery. Echegaray lays a road map of his villains' descent into evil; such persons may retain a high position, but the dramatist depicts them as utterly alienated from society. Having abandoned the ideal of fostering love for their fellow human beings and instead concentrating entirely upon the acquisition of power and material wealth, they enjoy an empty triumph. In Echegaray's dramas, vice must be punished, either directly upon the perpetrator or indirectly upon his or her offspring and/or his or her accomplices.

Echegaray's *A fuerza de arrastrarse* anticipated Jacinto Benavente's *Los intereses creados* (1907, Bonds of Interest) in the portrayal of the cynical Plácido, who joins astuteness with sycophantic flattery to marry his employer's physically and spiritually ugly daughter. To achieve power Plácido manipulates the press and court gossip, while making a joke of the honor code. Echegaray contrasts Plácido with his friend Javier who, relying only on his talent and industry, rises not so high and more slowly, but with his self-respect intact and his happiness unsullied. Plácido loses not only his self-respect but also the respect of Blanca, the one good woman whom he truly loved. His self-loathing is so extreme that he asks Blanca to keep the portrait of his mother, which he had sold to finance his initial foray into the capital, because he believes it will be contaminated by the ambience of the palace where he lives with his vapid, unfaithful wife and his cowardly and pompous father-in-law. Throughout *A fuerza de arrastrarse*, Echegaray emphasizes the metaphor of life as theater, specifically a farce. Throughout his career Echegaray depicted a corrupt society dominated by ruthless, materialistic, and self-seeking opportunists.

Benavente found in Echegaray a cynical view of the world stage, but in contrast to his mentor the later playwright would leave the spectator with a rueful shrug, while the earlier would prompt the audience to recall the Christian ideal. In *La última noche,* Don Carlos abandons Ernesto, the son of his friend Don Juan, to his death after having persuaded him to conspire against the government. Don Carlos switches sides to his profit, then tries to woo the boy's sister, Elena, away from his own son, Alfredo, with the offer of a diamond necklace. Teresa, Don Carlos's long-suffering Catholic wife, reminds Alfredo that however great are his passions (love of Elena and hatred of his father), the soul has the power to choose for good or ill:

Es libre la humana grey,
y al que tiene libertad
nunca la fatalidad
se impone, Alfredo, por ley.
Esto me dijiste. . . .

(The human flock is free,
And upon one who has liberty
Never can fate
Impose itself, Alfredo, as a law.
This you told me. . . .)

Don Carlos denounces his family for following Christ's teachings—teachings that led to crucifixion. His friend Ramón agrees that Christ rules in few hearts in the modern world:

¡Conversiones!
Eres por Cristo bien cándido.
En el siglo en que vivimos,
y en el globo en que habitamos,
sólo verás conversiones . . .
militares, o en los altos
círculos de la política,
o en la deuda del Estado;
pero en las conciencias nunca,
pero en las almas . . . ¡ay, Carlos!
no busques ya conversiones
cual la conversión de Pablo.

(Conversions!
You are through Christ very innocent.
In the age in which we live,
And on the globe that we inhabit,
You will only see such conversions as
Military ones, or those in the highest
Reaches of politics
Or in the State's debt level;
But never in peoples' consciences,
But in their souls . . . Oh, Carlos!
Don't look now for conversions
Like Paul's conversion.)

Although Echegaray does not often enunciate the Christian ethic so clearly, it is always implicit; his own doubts about its impact upon society determined his preference for tragedy.

Even in the second half of his career, while sometimes adopting realistic and naturalistic topics, Echegaray clung to the Catholic doctrine of free will, refusing to show the determination of character by heredity or environment. Thus, in *De mala raza* (1886, Bad Roots), Adelina, whose mother and grandmother were rather free with their favors, guards her virtue, while Paquita, a woman with impeccable background, takes a lover. In *El hijo de Don Juan* (1892; translated as *The Son of Don Juan*, 1895), Echegaray follows Ibsen's *Ghosts* (1881) in the presentation of the son who suffers from syphilis because of his father's promiscuity; but he does not allow the physical infirmity to taint the son's moral or spiritual character. While Ibsen's Oswald planned to marry Regina because he knew she would terminate his existence once sickness destroyed his mind, Echegaray's Lázaro renounces his fiancée to spare her seeing his descent. Echegaray underscores the sinful life and egotistical lack of concern for anything but pleasure, the flaws that produced disease, by presenting Don Juan and his cronies onstage and insisting that they freely chose their evil life. Lázaro's name recalls the biblical Lazarus, whom Christ resurrected from death; thus, Echegaray returns to Catholic doctrine to suggest that Lázaro will be rewarded in heaven, if punished on Earth. Modern critics tend to perceive such moralizing as facile, puerile idealism, clichés, and superficiality in art, attributes that masked what Roberto G. Sánchez calls the "fundamental insecurity" of both the playwright and his contemporary bourgeois public.

To appreciate Echegaray's immense popularity at the height of his career, not only in Spain but also in Mexico, Germany, Italy, France, and England, one needs to consider his milieu. Like Echegaray, most of the popular dramatists of the nineteenth century exploited sensationalism and spectacle and continued to write their plays in verse; dramatists were slow to adopt the prose medium favored by the realist and naturalist writers. This period was the age of great actors and actresses who cultivated a high-blown style best shown off in melodramatic vehicles such as those triumphing then in Paris, London, and New York as well as Madrid. Echegaray deliberately catered to public taste, and he gave lessons to such "highbrow" authors as Galdós in how to do so—lessons that Galdós took to heart, although the latter tended to show the triumph of the good character, while his mentor showed that character's defeat. Echegaray's formulaic art held the stage for thirty years and was succeeded by the "School of Echegaray," made up of Eugenio Sellés Marqués de Gerona, Leopoldo Cano y Masas, José Feliú y Codina, and Joaquín Dicenta, dramatists who, as Wanda C. Ríos-Font points out, rewrote the "melodramatic paradigm."

Echegaray shifted from plays featuring a male protagonist to works featuring a female lead, less from concern for women's liberation than from the decline of Antonio Vico and the death of Rafael Calvo, two outstanding actors whose companies presented his works, and from the emergence of María Guerrero as the most talented performer of the period. In Echegaray's dedication of *Mariana* (1892; translated, 1895) to the acting company of the Comedia Theater, he singled out Guerrero for her skill in displaying the wide range of emotions of the lead role, "from the insubstantial coquetry of the salon, from deep and painful feeling to the ultimate screams of passion and tragic outbursts." From his description the reader easily perceives the grandiloquent style of acting that Echegaray characterized as "inspired" and "sublime." For this style and for his clear division of good and evil, modern critics classify Echegaray's plays as melodrama.

Ríos-Font points out that Echegaray never used the term "melodrama" to describe his plays but instead coupled them with tragedy, or if they had a happy ending, comedy or farce. The word "melodrama" in his time referred primarily to monologues or dialogues incorporating song to express a character's high emotion. The basically conservative genre affirmed the triumph of society in a happy ending in which the good hero or heroine emerges victorious over the evil villain and is reintegrated into society. The genre had been imported from France; there it enjoyed great success with a bourgeois audience, whose tastes were beginning to dictate what would be presented onstage. It demanded spectacle, and the melodramas soon incorporated lavish sets and sound effects with such elements as storms at sea, battles, and horses onstage. From the melodrama Echegaray adopted the polarization of good and evil in distinct characters; from Romanticism he borrowed the alienated hero and the theme of tragic love. In his first period, from 1874 to 1885, he continued under the spell of Romanticism, writing primarily in verse, often setting his plays in the distant past, and frequently reworking Spanish legend or showcasing figures such as physician and theologian Michael Servetus in *La muerte en los labios* (1880, Death Upon His Lips) or the title character of *Haroldo el Normando* (1881, Harold the Norman). From 1885 to 1888 he wrote mostly in prose, returning to verse in 1888 and 1889 and then continuing in prose as he shifted to more realistic and naturalistic drama.

Ríos-Font demonstrates that Echegaray's drama, like melodrama in general, always affirms society's conservative values. Sensitive, good heroes or heroines may find themselves on the wrong side of society's and their own values, but they do not pose fundamental questions about those values even when their lives are at stake. *En el puño de la espada* features Don Fernando's killing himself upon discovering that he is the illegitimate offspring of Don Juan Albornoz's rape of Violante. His respect for patriarchal law is such that he cannot commit patricide; yet, his mother's stain, though incurred against her will, must be washed out with blood. Since she failed in her suicide attempt immediately following the rape and lived to marry Don Rodrigo while bearing Albornoz's child, Fernando must assume the burden of excising the bastardized bloodline and preventing the public from ever learning of the rape. In *Mancha que limpia* (1895, The Cleansing Stain) Matilde, falsely accused of an illicit affair with Julio, kills Enriqueta (the seeming innocent who, in fact, is Julio's mistress) immediately after the latter has exchanged wedding vows with Matilde's beloved Fernando. The falsely maligned Matilde cleanses not her own stain but that which has spread over Fernando through his alliance with an impure woman, one who would have borne children of questionable paternity. Fernando then claims the deed as his own, for the old code accorded immunity for men avenging their honor. He protects Matilde, who would have been subject to a life sentence or death for committing murder. Thus, Echegaray varied the resolution of honor-code conflict in his contemporary plays, while still upholding the basic tenets of that code; he expected the audience to applaud Matilde's deed, not condemn it.

In *Cómo empieza y cómo acaba* (1876, How It Begins and How It Ends) Magdalena attempts to cleanse the stain of adultery by murdering her blackmailing lover Don Enrique de Torrente, but in the darkness she mistakenly stabs her gentle husband, Don Pablo de Aguilar, instead. This twist was perceived as a revolutionary revision of the denouement the seventeenth-century Calderón de la Barca imposed upon his famous honor plays—a denouement in which the woman always paid with her life for adultery, real or imagined, and society endorsed the husband's vengeful murder. In Echegaray's play, the dying Don Pablo forgives Magdalena and conceals her murderous act from their child, María, by claiming that he inflicted the wound by his own hand.

In *Mariana* the stain upon a woman's honor awaits cleansing until the next generation. Discovering that Daniel Montoya, the man she loves, is the son of the lover who had ruined her mother, Mariana rejects Daniel's marriage proposal and instead marries a military man twice her age. On her wedding day Daniel appears at her home and entreats her to escape with him. Prostrate from her conflicting emotions (passion for Daniel, vengeance for her mother, duty to her husband), Mariana throws herself into Daniel's arms, all the while screaming for the General to come and take vengeance upon his unfaithful wife. He does, and she dies at his hand. The play ends with the promise of a duel between Daniel and the General, a duel in which Daniel will receive the death he longs for.

In some plays Echegaray returns to the ancient association of bastardy with a flawed moral character. The prime example is the evil, lascivious Manfredo of *En el seno de la muerte* (1879, In Death's Bosom), who seduces his brother Jaime's wife, Beatriz. Besieged by the French, Jaime chooses not to open the floodgates over the route Manfredo and Beatriz are traveling, even though doing so would save the lives of many Spanish soldiers and give great support to the king of Aragón. When his crime is discovered, Manfredo takes his own life after offering the knife to Jaime; the latter, brokenhearted upon discovering the infidelity of the persons he loved most in the world, also kills himself for having betrayed his country to save the unworthy lovers. At the conclusion of the play, Echegaray indicates that the repentant Beatriz will join her husband in death. Echegaray depicts the illegitimate Child Snow in *Piensa mal . . . y acertarás?* (1884, Impose an Evil Construction . . . and Be Right?) much as Nathaniel Hawthorne portrayed Pearl in *The Scarlet Letter* (1850): precocious, imaginative, but strange. Child Snow's undefined status within the patriarchy disturbs the adults, all of whom invent genealogies for her. Her mother, Forgetfulness, loves the child but treats her coldly and in the end gives her up to Hope and her newly discovered biological father, Valentine. It is not surprising that Echegaray would resort to the honor code and its ancillary themes of adultery and bastardy in his period plays taking place in earlier centuries (*En el seno de la muerte* takes place in 1285, *En el puño de la espada* in the early sixteenth century), but he develops it as well in dramas set in contemporary times. Of course, adultery is a piquant problem in every age, and its bloody resolution in terms of the honor code was less anachronistic in late-nineteenth-century Spain than it would be today. The theme permitted Echegaray to do what he did best: portray characters driven to the edge of madness or beyond through conflict of emotions, sometimes brought about by conflict of duties.

If one is willing to suspend disbelief and to accept the rather improbable situations into which Echegaray thrusts his characters, one must concede that few playwrights could better depict the various shades of emotion. His masterpiece, *El gran Galeoto,* provides occasion for myriad emotions: Julián's indulgent love for his young wife, Teodora; her veneration and love for her husband and her affection for his protégée, Ernesto; and the malice that motivates Julián's brother Severo and the latter's wife, Mercedes, and son, Pepito. The members of Severo's family initiate the slander that envelops the family, slander that has no cause other than Julián's allowing Ernesto to escort Teodora to the theater and to promenades in the park. The playwright slowly reveals how the power of suggestion takes hold of Ernesto and Teodora, first to make them uncomfortable in each other's presence, then to modulate their fraternal affection into a wistful romantic longing, a longing they never admit until others judge them guilty of having consummated an adulterous love affair. When Count Nebreda insults Teodora, Julián challenges him to a duel and is carried, dying, from the field to Ernesto's nearby apartment. There, he discovers Teodora, who had come to persuade Ernesto to prevent the duel; Julián dies believing that the two young people were guilty. In the end Ernesto embraces Teodora and with that embrace accepts society's false construction of their history. Alluding to the story of Guinevere and Lancelot, between whom Galahad served as intermediary, Ernesto declares that gossip has been the intermediary between himself and Teodora. He also alludes to the fifth canto of Dante's *Inferno,* in which Paolo and Francesca recall falling into an adulterous affair upon reading about the love of Lancelot and Guinevere; the book itself served as their intermediary. Frederick A. De Armas has pointed out that Echegaray also relies upon this story to depict the guilty passion of Magdalena and Don Enrique in *Cómo empieza y cómo acaba.* This kind of intertextuality is a device Echegaray often uses in his plays.

While Echegaray frequently portrayed adulterous women, he could not, as Ibsen and George Bernard Shaw did, present reformed prostitutes or respectable women rejecting marriage or abandoning home and hearth simply from intellectual conviction. The women Echegaray put onstage abandon the home only if driven to do so by evil, tyrannical, and unfaithful husbands. In *La desequilibrada* (1904, The Unbalanced Woman), Teresina turns her son over to the man she truly loves. She judges herself an unfit mother because she precipitated her evil husband's drowning and refused to save him. Again, unlike Ibsen and Shaw, Echegaray focused his female characters' discontent upon love. If she could just find her one true love, even the wealthiest woman would sign over her fortune and become his voluntary slave. Teresina rejects her fiancé, Mauricio, when she discovers he has refrained from exposing her father's criminal business deals—not to protect her but rather his mother. Scarcely touching upon the damage Mauricio himself would have suffered from the just or unjust tarnishing of the reputation of his own father (who was implicated since he was Teresina's father's steward), Echegaray maintains the rejected fiancé as a paragon of virtue throughout the play. Mauricio incarnates the good in contrast to the nefarious Roberto, who wins Teresina only to torment and betray her sexually and economically. In this play, as was his wont, Echegaray brought the curtain down with a surprising and highly dramatic finale.

Echegaray, while treating the topic of woman's dependency and sometimes enslavement, never showed her establishing her economic independence as did Ibsen, Shaw, and Oscar Wilde. He presents wealthy women, but never women who have earned that wealth; it has always been earned by a male figure, father or husband. He did deal with the subject of men's unprincipled economic exploitation of the poor and/or the gullible, as in *La última noche,* and with the issue of the tainted sources of wealth, as in *La desequilibrada* and *O locura o santidad* (1877; translated as *Folly or Saintliness,* 1895). His veneration for Miguel de Cervantes's *Don Quixote* (1605, 1615) as well as the opportunity to fashion scenes of heartrending pathos or frightening violence led him to deal with the topic of madness in several plays, not only showing how male and female characters lose their hold on reality but also how family and society treat the insane, specifically how a person may be certified as mad and institutionalized. In several dramas Echegaray treated realistically the abuses this procedure might involve, especially when greedy family members wished to gain control of a reputedly unstable person's fortune. In these plays, including *La desequilibrada* and *O locura o santidad,* Echegaray depicted most realistically the economic as well as the affective bases of marriage.

Critics today recognize that Echegaray deliberately developed a hybrid dramatic formula not from ignorance of the realistic and naturalistic dramas of Ibsen, Strindberg, Zola, Shaw, and other European dramatists, but from an accurate assessment of the Spanish audience's thirst for action and involved plot development. After several abortive efforts in the more realistic vein, Echegaray hit upon the formula that appealed to the Spanish public. The object of drama was to produce aesthetic emotions or pleasure, and this goal depended upon the aesthetic energy released in the well-made plot crafted by a playwright who could legitimately present the probable, the improbable, and even the impossible. In the prologue to *El gran Galeoto,* Ernesto struggles to write a play in which the villain is gossip—not a specific person but the accumulation of veiled innuendo and barbs leveled against the protagonist by everyone he meets. Julián informs him that his play must have love and jealousy, sensation and explosion, and characters interacting in ways readily perceptible to the audience. Echegaray then proceeds to give his audience this play, using Ernesto's idea and Julián's devices: a play with victims and villains, characters who embody the abstract concept and engage first in duels of words, then in duels of swords and pistols, to the delight and edification of the audience. Julio Mathías, in his notes for a 1970 volume of selections from Echegaray's plays, describes *El gran Galeoto* and Echegaray's other neo-Romantic dramas as made up of "40% traditional Romanticism: violent, exalted and anarchic, 25% Realism, then very much in vogue as heir to the Romantic movement, 20% melodrama in the exaggerated striving for effect in the depiction of situations and sentiments, and 15% a mixture of equal parts of local color and social satire."

Echegaray proved the victim of his own successful formula: it stood him in good stead through the year following his reception of the Nobel Prize but then fell out of fashion. The prize focused attention upon Echegaray and fanned the flame of youthful critical disdain. The younger generation perceived him as an embodiment of the old guard's conservative values in both form and content, when in fact he had been the standard-bearer of new liberal ideas throughout his lifetime; but his notable success in the fields of science and politics before he became Spain's most popular playwright made him an easy target for discontented youth. One century later, José Echegaray's readers and critics evaluate his works more dispassionately, both within the specific context of his national literature and within the larger context of world literature. They agree that he incorporated many new elements into his dramas, including a sophisticated use of intertextuality, symbolism, and metatheater.

Letters:

El neorromanticismo español y su época: Epistolario de José Echegaray a María Guerrero, edited by Carmen Menéndez Onrubia and Julián Ávila Arellano, Anejos de la revista Segismundo, 12 (Madrid: Consejo Superior de Investigaciones Científicas, 1987).

Interview:

Luis Antón del Olmet and Arturo García Carraffa, *Los Grandes Españoles: Echegaray* (Madrid: Imprenta de Alrededor del Mundo, 1912).

Biographies:

Augusto Martínez Olmedilla, *José Echegaray (El madrileño tres veces famoso): Su vida–su obra–su ambiente* (Madrid: Imprenta Sáez, 1949);

Francisco Sánchez Maba, *Don José Echegaray: Vida y pensamiento* (Madrid: Instituto Nacional de Enseñanza Media "Cervantes," 1966);

Javier Fornieles Alcaraz, *Trayectoria de un intelectual de la Restauración: José Echegaray* (Almería: Confederación Española de Cajas de Ahorro, 1989).

References:

Rafael Bosch, "La influencia de Echegaray sobre *Torquemada en el purgatorio* de Galdós," *Revista de Estudios Hispánicos,* 1 (1967): 243–253;

José Manuel Cabrales Arteaga, "El teatro neorromántico de Echegaray," *Revista de Literatura,* 101 (1989): 77–94;

Vicente Cabrera, "Valle-Inclán y la escuela de Echegaray: Un caso de parodia literaria," *Revista de Estudios Hispánicos,* 7 (1973): 193–213;

Alberto Castilla, "Una parodia de *El gran Galeoto,*" *Hispanófila,* 26 (May 1983): 33–40;

Frederick A. De Armas, "José Echegaray (Premio Nóbel 1904)," in *Premio Nóbel: Once Grandes escritores del mundo hispánico,* edited by Bárbara Mujica (Washington, D.C.: Georgetown University Press, 1997), pp. 1–60;

Dru Dougherty, "El otro teatro noventayochista," in *Studies in Honor of Sumner M. Greenfield,* edited by H. L. Boudreau and Luis González del Valle (Lincoln, Neb.: Society of Spanish and Spanish-American Studies, 1985), pp. 81–93;

John Dowling, "La recepción del teatro de Echegaray en México, 1875–1878," *Crítica hispánica,* 17 (Spring 1995): 36–51;

C. Eguía Ruiz, "Echegaray dramaturgo. El ocaso de su estrella," *Razón y Fe,* 47 (1917): 26–37;

Halfdan Gregersen, "Ibsen and Echegaray," *Hispanic Review,* 1 (October 1933): 338–340;

Gregersen, *Ibsen and Spain* (Cambridge, Mass.: Harvard University Press, 1936);

Librada Hernández, "El teatro de José Echegaray: Un enigma crítico," dissertation, University of California, Los Angeles, 1987;

James H. Hoddie, "Echegaray and Gladós: Ties Between *El gran Galeoto* and *Tormento,*" *Romanistisches Jahrbuch,* 50 (1999): 401–411;

Fernando Ibarra, "La aventura parisiense de *El gran Galeoto,*" *Revue de Littérature Comparée,* 46 (1972): 428–437;

Lawrence LaJohn, "Azorín's Criticism of José Echegaray," *Occasional Papers in Language, Literature and Linguistics* [Ohio University Modern Language Department], series A, 7 (April 1968): 1–6;

George P. Mansour, "Time in the Prose of José Echegaray," *Kentucky Romance Quarterly,* 13 Supp. (1967): 17–24;

Judy B. McInnis, "Echegaray, Ibsen y la generación del 98," in her *El 98 se pasea por el Callejón del Gato: Proceso a una generación* (Alicante: Ayuntamiento de Murcia, 1999), pp. 164–175;

Wilma Newberry, "Echegaray and Pirandello," *PMLA: Publications of the Modern Language Association of America,* 81 (March 1966): 123–129;

Newberry, *The Pirandellian Mode in Spanish Literature from Cervantes to Sastre* (Albany: State University of New York Press at Albany, 1973);

Gilbert Paolini, "Un acercamiento a la obra de Echegaray," in *Saggi in onore di Giovanni Allegra* (Perugia: Univ. degli Studi Perugia, 1995), pp. 479–491;

Paolini, "Noctis imago en *El hijo de don Juan* de Echegaray y *Los espectros* de Ibsen," *Letras Peninsulares*, 5 (Winter 1992–1993): 337–345;

Wanda C. Ríos-Font, "The Impersonation of the Feminine: Gender and Melodramatic Discourse in the Theater of José Echegaray," *Hispanófila*, 36, no. 1 (1992): 21–30;

Ríos-Font, *Rewriting Melodrama: The Hidden Paradigm in Modern Spanish Theater* (Lewisburg, Pa.: Bucknell University Press, 1997);

Edgard Samper, "José Echegaray ou la souveraineté de l'individu," in *Logique des traverses: De l'influence*, edited by Frédéric Regard (Saint-Etienne, France: Université de Saint-Etienne, 1992), pp. 75–97;

Roberto G. Sánchez, "Mancha que no se limpia o el dilemma Echegaray," *Cuadernos hispanoamericanos: Revista mensual de cultura hispánica*, 297 (1975): 601–612;

Gonzalo Sobejano, "Echegaray: Temas y modos," in *Historia y crítica de la literatura española*, volume 5, edited by Iris M. Závala (Barcelona: Editorial Crítica, 1982), pp. 656–662;

Sobejano, "Echegaray, Galdós y el melodrama," *Anales Galdosianos* (1978): 94–115;

"Spain's Homage to Echegaray," *American Monthly Review of Reviews*, 31 (May 1905): 613–614;

Amy J. Sparks, "La refundición por Echegaray de *La hija del aire (segunda parte)* de Calderón," in *Calderón: Actas del Congreso internacional sobre Calderón y el teatro español del Siglo de Oro*, edited by Luciano García Lorenzo (Madrid: Consejo Superior de Investigaciones Científicas, 1983), pp. 1463–1469;

Elizabeth Wallace, "The Spanish Drama of To-Day," *Atlantic Monthly*, 102 (1908): 357–366.

1904 Nobel Prize in Literature Presentation Speech

by C. D. af Wirsén, Permanent Secretary of the Swedish Academy, 10 December 1904

One sometimes hears it said that the Nobel Prizes should be awarded to authors still in the prime of life and consequently at the height of their development, in order to shelter them from material difficulties and assure them a wholly independent situation.

The institutions charged with awarding these Prizes should like to bear such striking witness to the value of a young genius; but the statutes of the Nobel Foundation stipulate that the works eligible for such a reward must be of exceptional importance and confirmed by experience. Thus there cannot be any hesitation in choosing between a talent in process of formation and a proven genius at the end of his development. The jury does not have the right to ignore a still active author of European fame, merely because he is old. The works of an old writer are often proof of a unique and youthful energy. The Swedish Academy therefore was right to render homage to Mommsen and Bjørnson in awarding them Nobel Prizes even at a time when both were past their prime. In making its choice among the candidates proposed this year for the Nobel Prize, the Academy has again given its attention to several literary veterans of recognized fame, and it has wished to renew its pledge to genius held in high esteem in the literary world.

The Academy has thought particularly of two authors who would both have been worthy of the whole Nobel Prize. Both have attained the final limits not only of the poetic art, but even of human life; one is seventy-four years old, the other two years younger. Therefore the Academy believes it should not wait longer to confer on them a distinction they both equally merit, although from different points of view, and it has awarded half the annual Prize to each. If the material value of the award is thus diminished for each of the laureates, the Academy nonetheless wishes to state publicly that, in this particular case, it considers each of these two Prizes as the equivalent of the whole Prize.

I

The Academy has given one of the awards to the poet Frédéric Mistral. In the freshness of his poetic inspiration this venerable old man is younger than most of the poets of our time. One of his principal works, *Lou pouèmo dóu Rose* [The Song of the Rhone], was published not long ago, in 1897, and when the Provençal poets celebrated their fiftieth anniversary on May 31, 1904, Mistral tuned his lyre for a poetry that in verve and vigour does not yield to any of his previous works.

Mistral was born on September 8, 1830, in the village of Maiano (in French, Maillane), which is situated midway between Avignon and Arles in the Rhone Valley. He grew up in this magnificent natural setting among the countryfolk and soon became familiar with their work. His father, François Mistral, was a well-to-do farmer, devoted to the customs of his faith and of his ancestors. His mother nursed the soul of the child with the songs and traditions of his birthplace.

During his studies at the College of Avignon, the young boy learned the works of Homer and Virgil, which made a profound impression on him, and one of his professors, the poet Roumanille, inspired in him a deep love for his maternal language, Provençal.

According to the wish of his father, Frédéric Mistral took a law degree at Aix-en-Provence; after that he was left free to choose his career as he pleased. His choice was soon made. He devoted himself to poetry and painted the beauties of Provence in the idiom of the country, an idiom which he was the first to raise to the rank of a literary language.

His first attempt was a long poem about rustic life; then he published poems in a collection entitled *Li Prouvençalo* (1852). After that he spent seven consecutive years on the work that established his universal fame, *Mirèio* (1859).

The action of this poem is very simple. A good and attractive peasant girl cannot marry a poor young man whom she loves because her father refuses his consent. In despair she flees from the paternal home and goes to seek succour at the church on the site of the pilgrimage of the Three Saint Marys on the island of Camargue in the Rhone delta. The author recounts in charming fashion the youthful love of the young people and retraces with masterly hand how Mirèio rushes across the rocky plains of the Crau. Smitten by a sunstroke in the torrid Camargue, the unfortunate young girl crawls to the chapel of the pilgrimage site to die. There, in a vision, the three Marys appear to her at the very instant in which she breathes her last.

The value of this work is not in the subject nor in the imagination displayed in it, no matter how interesting the figure of Mirèio may be. It lies in the art of linking together the episodes of the story and of unreeling before our eyes all Provence with its scenery, its memories, its ancient customs, and the daily life of its inhabitants. Mistral says that he sings only for the shepherds and the country people; he does so with Homeric simplicity. He is, indeed, by his own admission, a student of the great Homer. But far from imitating him slavishly, he gives proof of a very personal originality in his descriptive technique. A breath of the Golden Age animates a number of his descriptions. How can one forget his paintings of the white horses of the Camargue? Galloping, with manes flying in the wind, they seem to have been touched by Neptune's trident and set free from the sea god's chariot. If you remove them from their beloved pastures at the edge of the sea, they always escape in the end. Even after long years of absence, they return to the well-known plains which they salute with their joyous neighing as they hear again the breaking of the waves on the shore.

The rhythm of this poem has beauty and harmony, and its artistic composition succeeds on all counts. The source from which Mistral has drawn is not psychology; it is nature. Man himself is treated purely as a child of nature. Let other poets sound the depths of the human soul! Mirèio is a half-opened rose, still all shining from the rosy light of dawn. This is the spontaneous work of an original spirit and not the fruit of purely reflective labour.

The poem was greeted with enthusiasm from its first appearance. Lamartine, worn out with personal cares but always smitten by beautiful poetic works, wrote "A great poet is born!" He compared Mistral's poem to one of the islands of an archipelago, to a floating Delos which must have detached itself from its group in order to join, in silence, the fragrant Provence. He applied to Mistral these words of Virgil: "Tu Marcellus eris!"

Seven years after the publication of *Mirèio*, Mistral published a second work of equal dimensions, *Calendau* (1867). It has been said that the action of this poem is too fantastic and improbable. But it matches its predecessor in the charm of its descriptions. How could one question the grandeur of its ideas about the ennoblement of man through trial? While *Mirèio* celebrates peasant life, *Calendau* presents a gripping picture of the sea and the forests. It is like a brilliant glistening of water in several remarkably precise scenes about the life of the fisherman.

Mistral is not only an epic poet; he is also a great lyricist. His collection, *Lis Isclo d'or* (1876) [Islands of Gold], contains some poems of an immortal beauty. Suffice it to recall the stanzas on the drum of Arcole, on the dying mower, on the chateau of Roumanin with its memories of the times of the troubadours that seem to evoke the splendour of the sunsets, or, again, the beautiful mystic chant that should be spoken in the veiled twilight of the evening, "la coumunioun di sant."

In other lyric poems Mistral insists with fervour on the rights of neo-Provençal to an independent existence and seeks to protect it against all attempts to neglect or discredit it.

The poem in the form of a short story, "Nerto" (1884), offers many beautiful pages for the reader's admiration. But the epic narrative, *Lou pouèmo dóu Rose*, is more profound. Composed by a poet of sixty-seven years, it is still full of life, and its numerous vignettes of the regions washed by the Rhone are most engaging. What a superb type is that proud and devout captain of the ship *Aprau*, who thinks that one must be a sailor to know how to pray! Another ravishing little scene shows us the pilot's daughter, Anglora, whose imagination has been fed on old legends. One night she imagines that she has seen Lou Dra, the god of the river, in the moonlit waves of the Rhone and that she has been touched by him. The very verses here seem to stream and sparkle in the moonlight.

In short, Mistral's works are all lofty monuments to the glory of his beloved Provence.

This year is a year of celebration for him. Fifty years ago on St. Estelle's day he founded, together with six literary friends, the Association of Provençal Poets, whose goal was to purify and give a definitive form to the Provençal language. The language which is spoken from St. Remy to Arles and, without significant differences, in all the Rhone Valley from Orange to Martigues, served as a basis for a new literary language, as earlier the Florentine dialect had served to form Italian. Experts such as Gaston Paris and Koschwitz tell us that this movement was not at all retrograde. It did not seek to restore to life the old Provençal, but on the basis of dialects in use among the people, it attempted to create a national language understood by all. The efforts of the Provençal poets have not been slow to be crowned with success. In his great neo-Provençal dictionary, *Tresor dóu Félibrige* (1879–1886), a giant work on which he has worked for more than twenty years, Mistral has recorded the wealth of the Provençal dialects and built an imperishable monument to the *lengo d'Or*.

It goes without saying that a man like Mistral has received all kinds of honours. The French Academy has awarded him a prize four times. The Institute of France gave him the Reynaud prize of 10,000 francs for his dictionary. The universities of Halle and Bonn have conferred honorary doctorates on him. Several of his poems have been translated into various foreign languages. *Mirèio* has been set to music by Gounod, and *Calendau* by the composer Maréchal.

One knows the motto given by Mistral to the Association of Provençal Poets: "Lou soulèu me fai canta" ("The sun makes me sing"). His poems have, in effect, spread the light of the Provençal sun in many countries, even in Northern regions where they have made many hearts rejoice.

Alfred Nobel demanded idealism from an author to be judged worthy of the Prize he established. Is it not amply found in a poet whose work, like that of Mistral, is distinguished by a healthy and flourishing artistic idealism; in a man who has devoted his entire life to an ideal, the restoration and development of the spiritual interests of his native country, its language and its literature?

II

After the splendour of the Greek theatre, it is principally among the English and the Spanish that a national dramatic art has developed. To understand modern Spanish drama, it is necessary to know what conditions in the life of past periods lie behind it. For a long time Spanish drama has displayed sharp contrasts. On the one hand, there is the most luxurious flowering of fantasy; on the other, an extremely subtle and at times conventional casuistry. In one place, there is brilliant colouring, and in another, a great affection for rhetorical antithesis. Emphatic language is coupled with tangled intrigue. Striking effects are violent, the lyric order intense. Disharmonies are sharp, and conflicts almost always have a tragic resolution. Dialectic is vigorous. However, interior life is very rich, and the severe, inflexibly applied dictates of honour do not exclude the luxury of sudden expressions of fantasy. In Spanish drama the artificial has managed to become fused with a genuine originality.

The heir and continuator of these glorious and characteristic traditions is the writer who has been awarded half of the Nobel Prize this year. A son of the modern age and perfectly independent in his judgments, he has not the same conception of the world Calderón had. Loving liberty and having fought often for tolerance, he is no friend of despotism or of hierarchy, but still there is in him the same exotic ardour and the same dignity which from oldest times have been the distinctive marks of Spanish dramatists. This writer is José de Echegaray. Like his forebears, he knows how to present conflict, is extremely moving and vitally interested in different temperaments and ideals, and like them he enjoys studying the most complicated cases of conscience. He is complete master of the art of producing in the audience pity and fear, the well-known fundamental effects of tragedy. Just as in the masters of the old Spanish drama, there is in him a striking union of the most lively imagination and the most refined artistic sense. For this it can be said of him—as a critic otherwise unsympathetic to him declared—"that he is of pure Spanish breed." However, his conception of the world is vast. His sense of duty has been purified, his fundamental conceptions are benevolent, and his moral heroism, while retaining a peculiar national character, has the features of a universal humanity.

José de Echegaray was born in Madrid in 1833 [1832] but spent his childhood years in Murcia, where his father held the chair of Greek Studies at the Institute. Receiving his bachelor's degree at fourteen, he soon entered the School of Civil Engineering, where he distinguished himself by his zealous application and his penetrating skill. Five years later, in 1853, he completed his engineering career after having compiled a most brilliant record. Mathematics and mechanics had been his favourite studies, and his singular understanding of these branches of learning enabled him, after one year, to be appointed a professor in the very school which he had so recently attended as a student. It appears that for some years his struggle for existence was quite hard, and he had to give private lessons in order to sustain the most modest way of life. In spite of everything, he soon became an eminent professor, distinguishing himself both in pure and applied mathematics, and became an outstanding engineer. At the same time he energetically studied political economy, embracing the ideas of free trade. Soon, that great talent, that vivacious engineer, was called to the highest and greatest tasks. Three times he has been a minister of his country's government. According to those who know him, whether they were adversaries or friends, he has always shown a singular skill in the administration of public finance and public works.

We can easily understand the general astonishment when this scholar, who had published treatises on analytic geometry, physics, and electricity, dedicated his indefatigable energy to writing for the theatre. It has been said that his creations for the stage had the form of equations and problems. If the new manifestation of his genius was enthusiastically acclaimed by numerous admirers, it also found severe critics. Nevertheless, no one could deny that his works were distinguished by a deep moral sense. In a way, the critics were not mistaken who maintained that in his dramas, following the example of some surgeons, he rarely used any other method than that of "urere et secare"; still, however, there is something to admire in this Muse of romantic exaltation and austere severity which condemns any compromise with duty.

Despising the transient approval of fashion and listening only to the inspirations of his genius, Echegaray pursued his triumphal career, demonstrating a dramatic fecundity which makes us think of Lope de Vega and Calderón.

Even in his youth, when he was attending the School of Civil Engineering, he was enthusiastic about drama and used his savings to obtain theatre tickets. In 1865 he wrote a play entitled *La hija natural* [The Illegitimate Daughter], which was followed by *El libro talonario* [Book of Accounts] in 1874. The playbill carried a pseudonym instead of the author's name, but it did not take the public long to guess that the acclaimed dramatist was Echegaray, then Spain's Minister of Finance. Some months later *La última noche* [The Last Night] was staged, and since then his fertile imagination has not stopped engendering ever-new creations. He works with such speed that in one year he has published three or four works. Since lack of time prohibits a complete review here of all of his productions, suffice it to make brief mention of some which have won general attention. Echegaray scored his first triumph in November, 1874, with the drama *La esposa del vengador* [The Avenger's Wife], in which his true genius was revealed and in which, side by side with certain exaggerations, the greatest beauties can be admired. The public could imagine that it had been taken back to the Golden Age of Spanish drama, and it saluted Echegaray as the regenerator of the most brilliant era of the nation's dramatic poetry. *En el puño de la espada* [The Sword's Handle], presented the following year, was received with the same applause. The sublime power that is manifest in this noble conception so moved the many spectators that the applause did not stop with the performance, and, after the last act, Echegaray had to appear on stage seven times to receive the acclaim of the audience. But great controversies arose in 1878 when, in *En el pilar y en la cruz* [The Stake and the Cross], the poet showed himself the defender of free thought against intolerance, of humanity against fanaticism. Typical of Echegaray, as he himself has observed, is his *Conflicto entre dos deberes* [Conflict of Duties], which was presented in 1882. A conflict of duties is found in almost all of his dramas, but rarely has the conflict been pushed to such an extreme as in this piece. Two other dramas have made his name famous. These two inspired, excellent plays are *O locura ó santidad* [Madman or Saint] and *El gran Galeoto* [Great Galeoto], the former presented in January, 1877, and the latter in March, 1881. In *O locura ó santidad* there is a great wealth of ideas and profound genius. It shows a man who, moved by his righteousness to sacrifice his prosperity and worldly goods, is considered crazy and treated as such by his friends and by the world at large. Lorenzo de Avendano renounces a name and a fortune when he learns unexpectedly but undeniably that they do not legally belong to him, and he persists in his resolution when the one indisputable proof of his illegitimacy has disappeared. Such idealism is judged madness by his family, and Lorenzo is looked upon by everybody as a Don Quixote, stubborn and simple-minded. The structure of the drama is firm and solid, demonstrating that it is the work of an engineer who calculates precisely all the elements that have gone into it, but it shows us to a still greater degree the poet of mature creative genius. More than an external collision, it treats the internal conflict of an extremely sad figure. It consists of a struggle between duty and opportunism, and Lorenzo in following the dictate of his conscience reaches martyrdom. Experience has always shown that very frequently he who faithfully obeys his conscience must be prepared to bear the fate of a martyr.

El gran Galeoto made an even greater impression. In the first month after it opened, it went through no fewer than five editions and inspired a national subscription to honour its author. Because of the masterful portrayal of the psychology of the characters the play has a lasting value. It shows the power of slander. The most innocent trait is disfigured and scandalously deformed by the gossip of people. Ernesto and Teodora have nothing for which to reproach themselves, but the world believes them guilty, and at last, abandoned by everyone, they end by throwing themselves into one another's arms. Subtlety of psychological analysis is revealed with such masterly detail of observation that those two noble spirits, in no way desirous of stealing the right of their neighbour, become mutually enamoured without suspecting it. They discover the fact of their love only by means of the persecution to which they see themselves exposed. Romanticism triumphs in this drama whose poetic beauty is clearly perceptible, whose lyric details possess a dazzling colouring, and whose structure is without a flaw.

Echegaray goes on working as a dramatist. This year (1904) he has published a new play, *La desequilibrada* [The Disturbed Woman], whose first act is a genuine masterpiece of exposition and individualization, and which in its entirety reveals no weakening of poetic inspiration. In this play, we are shown Don Mauricio de Vargas, a clear type of that chivalry so dear to Echegaray, that chivalry which does not want to buy even its own happiness at the cost of compromising duty.

Thus it is just that the Nobel Prize be awarded to this great poet, whose production is distinguished by its virile energy and whose mode of seeing is impregnated with such high ideals that with abundant reason an eminent German critic has been able to say of him: "Er verlangt Recht und Pflichterfüllung unter allen Umständen."

Echegaray has put in the mouth of one of the characters of *El gran Galeoto* the most pessimistic words about the world, which "never recognizes the subtleties of the genius until three centuries after his death."

No doubt this can happen. But against the general application of the above thesis we can offer the justified admiration which the work of Echegaray has aroused. To those tributes of appreciation the Swedish Academy has agreed to add still one more, awarding the Nobel Prize in homage to the celebrated poet, the honour and glory of the Spanish Academy, José de Echegaray.

At the banquet, C. D. af Wirsén pointed out that sharing in the Prize did not diminish in any way the value of the laureates. He recalled to mind the works—pure, limpid, and fresh—of Frédéric Mistral, naming the principal ones and asking the Minister of France, Mr. Marchand, to convey to the famous Provençal poet the homage which the Swedish Academy and all those assembled took pleasure in rendering him. The speaker then reviewed the imposing work of Echegaray and expressed regrets for his state of health and explained that the Minister of Spain had been prevented from attending this banquet and from receiving the congratulations for his famous countryman.

The Minister of France, Mr. Marchand, replied to the Secretary of the Swedish Academy and recalled that in the preceding year he had thanked them for the Prize awarded to Mr. and Mrs. Curie; this time he spoke for the great poet of whom Provence is justly proud. He told of a most touching event. Forty-five years ago the French Academy, which did not have at its disposal resources as great as those with which the great Nobel had endowed the Swedish Academy, decided, at the suggestion of Lamartine, who was enthusiastic about Mirèio, to award the prize of 3 000 francs to Mistral. When they asked the author, who had been leading a simple life in the country, what he would do with the Prize, he answered, "It is a prize for poetry; it is not to be touched!" The modest poet shared his "overabundance" with others.

Mr. Marchand also acted as spokesman for his colleague, the Minister of Spain, to express Mr. Echegaray's gratitude.

[©The Nobel Foundation, 1904.]

T. S. Eliot
(26 September 1888 – 4 January 1965)

Jewel Spears Brooker
Eckerd College

This entry was expanded by Brooker from her Eliot entry in *DLB 45: American Poets, 1880–1945, First Series*. See also the Eliot entries in *DLB 7: Twentieth-Century American Dramatists; DLB 10: Modern British Dramatists, 1900–1945; DLB 63: Modern American Critics, 1920–1955;* and *DLB 245: British and Irish Dramatists Since World War II, Third Series*.

BOOKS: *Prufrock and Other Observations* (London: Egoist, 1917);

Ezra Pound: His Metric and Poetry (New York: Knopf, 1918);

Poems (Richmond, Surrey: Leonard & Virginia Woolf at The Hogarth Press, 1919);

Ara Vos Prec (London: Ovid Press, 1920); revised as *Poems* (New York: Knopf, 1920);

The Sacred Wood: Essays on Poetry and Criticism (London: Methuen, 1920; New York: Knopf, 1921);

The Waste Land (New York: Boni & Liveright, 1922; Richmond, Surrey: Leonard & Virginia Woolf at The Hogarth Press, 1923);

Homage to John Dryden: Three Essays on Poetry of the Seventeenth Century (London: Leonard & Virginia Woolf at The Hogarth Press, 1924);

Poems 1909–1925 (London: Faber & Gwyer, 1925; New York & Chicago: Harcourt, Brace, 1932);

Journey of the Magi (London: Faber & Gwyer, 1927; New York: Rudge, 1927);

Shakespeare and the Stoicism of Seneca (London: Oxford University Press, 1927);

A Song for Simeon (London: Faber & Gwyer, 1928);

For Lancelot Andrewes: Essays on Style and Order (London: Faber & Gwyer, 1928; Garden City, N.Y.: Doubleday, Doran, 1929);

Dante (London: Faber & Faber, 1929);

Animula (London: Faber & Faber, 1929);

Ash-Wednesday (New York: Fountain Press / London: Faber & Faber, 1930);

Marina (London: Faber & Faber, 1930);

Thoughts After Lambeth (London: Faber & Faber, 1931);

Triumphal March (London: Faber & Faber, 1931);

T. S. Eliot, right, being applauded by Swedish royalty after receiving the 1948 Nobel Prize in Literature (AP Photo)

Charles Whibley: A Memoir (London: Oxford University Press, 1931);

Selected Essays 1917–1932 (London: Faber & Faber, 1932; New York: Harcourt, Brace, 1932);

John Dryden: The Poet, The Dramatist, The Critic (New York: Terence & Elsa Holliday, 1932);

Sweeney Agonistes: Fragments of an Aristophanic Melodrama (London: Faber & Faber, 1932);

The Use of Poetry and The Use of Criticism: Studies in the Relation of Criticism to Poetry in England (London: Faber & Faber, 1933; Cambridge, Mass.: Harvard University Press, 1933);

After Strange Gods: A Primer of Modern Heresy (London: Faber & Faber, 1934; New York: Harcourt, Brace, 1934);

The Rock: A Pageant Play (London: Faber & Faber, 1934; New York: Harcourt, Brace, 1934);

Elizabethan Essays (London: Faber & Faber, 1934); revised as *Essays on Elizabethan Drama* (New York: Harcourt, Brace, 1956); republished as *Elizabethan Dramatists* (London: Faber & Faber, 1963);

Words for Music (Bryn Mawr, Pa.: Privately printed, 1934);

Murder in the Cathedral, acting edition (Canterbury: H. J. Goulden, 1935); complete edition (London: Faber & Faber, 1935; New York: Harcourt, Brace, 1935);

Essays Ancient & Modern (London: Faber & Faber, 1936; New York: Harcourt, Brace, 1936);

Collected Poems 1909–1935 (London: Faber & Faber, 1936; New York: Harcourt, Brace, 1936);

The Family Reunion (London: Faber & Faber, 1939; New York: Harcourt, Brace, 1939);

Old Possum's Book of Practical Cats (London: Faber & Faber, 1939; New York: Harcourt, Brace, 1939);

The Idea of a Christian Society (London: Faber & Faber, 1939; New York: Harcourt, Brace, 1940);

East Coker (London: Faber & Faber, 1940);

Burnt Norton (London: Faber & Faber, 1941);

Points of View, edited by John Hayward (London: Faber & Faber, 1941);

The Dry Salvages (London: Faber & Faber, 1941);

The Classics and the Man of Letters (London, New York & Toronto: Oxford University Press, 1942);

The Music of Poetry (Glasgow: Jackson, Son, Publishers to the University, 1942);

Little Gidding (London: Faber & Faber, 1942);

Four Quartets (New York: Harcourt, Brace, 1943; London: Faber & Faber, 1944);

Reunion by Destruction (London: Pax House, 1943);

What Is a Classic? (London: Faber & Faber, 1945);

Die Einheit der Europäischen Kultur (Berlin: Carl Habel, 1946);

A Practical Possum (Cambridge, Mass.: Harvard Printing Office & Department of Graphic Arts, 1947);

On Poetry (Concord, Mass.: Concord Academy, 1947);

Milton (London: Geoffrey Cumberlege, 1947);

A Sermon (Cambridge: Cambridge University Press, 1948);

Selected Poems (Harmondsworth, U.K.: Penguin/Faber & Faber, 1948; New York: Harcourt, Brace & World, 1967);

Notes Towards the Definition of Culture (London: Faber & Faber, 1948; New York: Harcourt, Brace, 1949);

From Poe to Valéry (New York: Harcourt, Brace, 1948);

The Undergraduate Poems of T. S. Eliot, unauthorized publication (Cambridge, Mass., 1949);

The Aims of Poetic Drama (London: Poets' Theatre Guild, 1949);

The Cocktail Party (London: Faber & Faber, 1950; New York: Harcourt, Brace, 1950; revised edition, London: Faber & Faber, 1950);

Poems Written in Early Youth (Stockholm: Privately printed, 1950; London: Faber & Faber, 1967; New York: Farrar, Straus & Giroux, 1967);

Poetry and Drama (Cambridge, Mass.: Harvard University Press, 1951; London: Faber & Faber, 1951);

The Film of Murder in the Cathedral, by Eliot and George Hoellering (London: Faber & Faber, 1952; New York: Harcourt, Brace, 1952);

The Value and Use of Cathedrals in England Today (Chichester: Friends of Chichester Cathedral, 1952);

An Address to Members of the London Library (London: London Library, 1952; Providence, R.I.: Providence Athenaeum, 1953);

The Complete Poems and Plays (New York: Harcourt, Brace, 1952);

Selected Prose, edited by Hayward (Melbourne, London & Baltimore: Penguin, 1953);

American Literature and the American Language (St. Louis: Department of English, Washington University, 1953);

The Three Voices of Poetry (Cambridge: Cambridge University Press, 1953; New York: Cambridge University Press, 1954);

The Confidential Clerk (London: Faber & Faber, 1954; New York: Harcourt, Brace, 1954);

Religious Drama: Mediaeval and Modern (New York: House of Books, 1954);

The Cultivation of Christmas Trees (London: Faber & Faber, 1954; New York: Farrar, Straus & Cudahy, 1956);

The Literature of Politics (London: Conservative Political Centre, 1955);

The Frontiers of Criticism (Minneapolis: University of Minnesota Press, 1956);

On Poetry and Poets (London: Faber & Faber, 1957; New York: Farrar, Straus & Cudahy, 1957);

The Elder Statesman (London: Faber & Faber, 1959; New York: Farrar, Straus & Cudahy, 1959);

Geoffrey Faber 1889–1961 (London: Faber & Faber, 1961);

Collected Plays (London: Faber & Faber, 1962);

George Herbert (London: Longmans, 1962);

Collected Poems 1909–1962 (London: Faber & Faber, 1963; New York: Harcourt, Brace & World, 1963);

Knowledge and Experience in the Philosophy of F. H. Bradley (London: Faber & Faber, 1964; New York: Farrar, Straus, 1964);

To Criticize the Critic and Other Writings (London: Faber & Faber, 1965; New York: Farrar, Straus & Giroux, 1965);

The Waste Land: A Facsimile and Transcript of the Original Drafts Including the Annotations of Ezra Pound, edited by Valerie Eliot (London: Faber & Faber, 1971; New York: Harcourt Brace Jovanovich, 1971);

Selected Prose of T. S. Eliot, edited by Frank Kermode (London: Faber & Faber, 1975; New York: Harcourt Brace Jovanovich, 1975);

*The Varieties of Metaphysical Poetry: The Clark Lectures at Trinity College, Cambridge, 1926, and the Turnbull Lectures at the Johns Hopkins University, 1933, edited by Ronald Schuchard (London: Faber & Faber, 1993; New York: Harcourt Brace, 1994);

Inventions of the March Hare: Poems, 1909–1917, edited by Christopher Ricks (London: Faber & Faber, 1996; New York: Harcourt Brace, 1996).

Editions: *The Waste Land: Authoritative Text, Contexts, Criticism,* edited by Michael North, Norton Critical Edition (New York: Norton, 2001);

The Annotated Waste Land, with T.S. Eliot's Contemporary Prose, edited by Lawrence Rainey (New Haven: Yale University Press, 2005).

PLAY PRODUCTIONS: *Sweeney Agonistes,* Poughkeepsie, N.Y., Vassar Experimental Theatre, 6 May 1933; London, Group Theatre Rooms, 11 November 1934;

The Rock, London, Sadler's Wells Theatre, 28 May 1934;

Murder in the Cathedral, Canterbury Chapter House, 15 June 1935; London, Mercury Theatre, 1 November 1935; New Haven, Yale University Theatre, 20 December 1935; New York, Manhattan Theater, 20 March 1936;

The Family Reunion, London, Westminster Theatre, 21 March 1939; Aurora, N.Y., Wells College, 8 June 1940; New York, Cherry Lane Theatre, 1947;

The Cocktail Party, Edinburgh, Royal Lyceum Theatre, 22 August 1949; New York, Henry Miller's Theater, 21 January 1950; London, New Theatre, 3 May 1950;

The Confidential Clerk, Edinburgh, Royal Lyceum Theatre, 25 August 1953; London, Lyric Theatre, 16 September 1953; New York, Morosco Theatre, 11 February 1954;

The Elder Statesman, Edinburgh, Royal Lyceum Theatre, 24 August 1958; London, Cambridge Theatre, 25 September 1958; Milwaukee, Fred Miller Theatre, 27 February 1963.

PRODUCED SCRIPT: *Murder in the Cathedral,* by Eliot and George Hoellering, motion picture, Classic, 1952.

OTHER: Edgar Ansel Mowrer, *This American World,* preface by Eliot (London: Faber & Gwyer, 1928);

Ezra Pound, *Selected Poems,* edited by Eliot (London: Faber & Gwyer, 1928);

"Address by T. S. Eliot, '06, to the Class of '33, June 17, 1933," *Milton Graduates Bulletin,* 3 (November 1933): 5–9;

Harvard College Class of 1910. Seventh Report, includes an autobiographical note by Eliot (June 1935): 219–221;

Marianne Moore, *Selected Poems,* edited by Eliot (New York: Macmillan, 1935; London: Faber & Faber, 1935);

Djuna Barnes, *Nightwood,* introduction by Eliot (New York: Harcourt, Brace, 1937); introduction and preface by Eliot (London: Faber & Faber, 1950);

Pound, *Literary Essays,* edited by Eliot (London: Faber & Faber, 1954; Norfolk, Conn.: New Directions, 1954);

From Mary to You, includes an address by Eliot (St. Louis: Mary Institute, 1959), pp. 133–136;

The Criterion, 1922–1939, 18 volumes, edited by Eliot (London: Faber & Faber, 1967).

T. S. Eliot, the 1948 winner of the Nobel Prize in Literature, is one of the giants of modern literature, highly distinguished as a poet, literary critic, dramatist, and editor/publisher. In 1910 and 1911, while still a student, he wrote "The Love Song of J. Alfred Prufrock" (1915) and other poems that are landmarks in the history of literature. In these college poems, Eliot articulated distinctly modern themes in forms that were both a striking development of and a marked departure from those of nineteenth-century poetry. Within a few years he had composed another landmark poem, "Gerontion" (1920), and within a decade, one of the most famous and influential poems of the century, *The Waste Land* (1922). While the origins of *The Waste Land* are in part personal, the voices projected are universal. Eliot later denied that he had large cultural problems in mind, but, nevertheless, in *The Waste Land* he diagnosed the malaise of his generation and indeed of Western civilization in the twentieth century. In 1930 he published his next major poem, *Ash-Wednesday,* written after his conversion to Anglo-Catholicism. Conspicuously different in style and tone from his earlier work, this confessional sequence charts his continued search for order in his personal life and in history. The culmination of this search as well as of Eliot's poetic writing is his meditation on time and history, the works known collectively as *Four Quartets* (1943): *Burnt Norton* (1941), *East Coker* (1940), *The Dry Salvages* (1941), and *Little Gidding* (1942).

Eliot was almost as renowned a literary critic as he was a poet. From 1916 through 1921 he contributed approximately one hundred reviews and articles to various periodicals. This early criticism was produced at night under the pressure of supplementing his meager salary—first as a teacher, then as a bank clerk—and not, as is sometimes suggested, under the compulsion to rewrite literary history. A product of his critical intelligence and superb training in philosophy and literature, his essays, however hastily written and for whatever motive, had an immediate impact. His ideas quickly solidified into doctrine and became, with the early essays of I. A. Richards, the basis of the New Criticism, one of the most influential schools of literary study in the twentieth century. Through half a century of critical writing, Eliot's concerns remained more or less constant; his position regarding those concerns, however, was frequently refined, revised, or, occasionally, reversed. Beginning in the late 1920s, Eliot's literary criticism was supplemented by religious and social criticism. In these writings, such as *The Idea of a Christian Society* (1939), he can be seen as a deeply involved and thoughtful Christian poet in the process of making sense of the world between the two World Wars. These writings, sympathetically read, suggest the dilemma of the serious observer of Western culture in the 1930s, and rightly understood, they complement his poetry, plays, and literary journalism.

Eliot is also an important figure in twentieth-century drama. He was inclined from the first toward the theater—his early poems are essentially dramatic, and many of his early essays and reviews are on drama or dramatists. By the mid 1920s he was writing a play, *Sweeney Agonistes* (published in 1932, performed in 1933); in the 1930s he wrote an ecclesiastical pageant, *The Rock* (performed and published in 1934), and two full-blown plays, *Murder in the Cathedral* (performed and published in 1935) and *The Family Reunion* (performed and published in 1939); and in the late 1940s and the 1950s he devoted himself almost exclusively to plays, of which *The Cocktail Party* (performed in 1949, published in 1950) has been the most popular. His goal, realized only in part, was the revitalization of poetic drama in terms that would be consistent with the modern age. He experimented with language that, though close to contemporary speech, is essentially poetic and thus capable of spiritual, emotional, and intellectual resonance. His work has influenced several important twentieth-century playwrights, including W. H. Auden and Harold Pinter. Eliot also made significant contributions as an editor and publisher. From 1922 to 1939 he was the editor of a major intellectual journal, *The Criterion*, and from 1925 to 1965 he was an editor/director in the publishing house of Faber and Faber. In both capacities he worked behind the scenes to nurture the intellectual and spiritual life of his times.

Thomas Stearns Eliot was born on 26 September 1888 in St. Louis, Missouri; he was the second son and seventh child of Charlotte Champe Stearns and Henry Ware Eliot, members of a distinguished Massachusetts family recently transplanted to Missouri. Eliot's family tree includes settlers of the Massachusetts Bay Colony, prominent clergymen and educators, a president of Harvard University (Charles William Eliot), and three presidents of the United States (John Adams, John Quincy Adams, and Rutherford B. Hayes). In 1834 the poet's grandfather, William Greenleaf Eliot, a graduate of Harvard Divinity School, moved to St. Louis to establish a Unitarian mission. He quickly became a leader in civic development, founding the first Unitarian Church, Washington University (which he served as president), Smith Academy, and Mary Institute.

The Eliot family lived in downtown St. Louis, not far from the Mississippi River, and the poet spent his formative years in a large house (no longer standing) at 2635 Locust Street. His family summered in New England, and in 1897 Henry Ware Eliot built a house near the sea at Gloucester, Massachusetts. The summers in this spacious house on Cape Ann provided the poet with his happiest memories, which he tapped through the years for poems such as "Marina" (1930) and *The Dry Salvages*.

From these few facts, several points emerge as relevant to Eliot's mind and art. First, feeling that "the U.S.A. up to a hundred years ago was a family extension" (as he wrote in a 1928 letter to Herbert Read), Eliot became acutely conscious of history—his own, that of his family, his country, his civilization, his race—and of the ways in which the past constantly impinges on the present and the present on the future. Second, despite the fact that Eliot was blessed with a happy childhood in a loving family, he was early possessed by a sense of homelessness. In 1928, just after he had changed his religion from Unitarian to Anglican and his citizenship from American to British, he summed up the result of these formative years in Missouri and Massachusetts, describing himself in a letter to Read as "an American who . . . was born in the South and went to school in New England as a small boy with a nigger drawl, but who wasn't a southerner in the South because his people were northerners in a border state . . . and who so was never anything anywhere." As he had written to his brother, Henry, in 1919, a few years after settling in London, "one remains always a foreigner." Third, Eliot had an urban imagination, the shape and content of which came from his childhood experience in St. Louis. In a 1930 letter quoted in an appendix to *American Literature and the American Language* (1953), he said that "St. Louis affected me more deeply than any other environment has done." Several of his signature images—city streets and city slums, city rivers and city skies—were etched on his mind in St. Louis. City scenes, even sordid ones, as he suggested in a 1914 letter to Conrad Aiken, helped him to feel alive, alert, and self-conscious.

Eliot was educated at Smith Academy in St. Louis (1898–1905), Milton Academy in Massachusetts (1905–1906), Harvard University (B.A., June 1909; M.A., February 1911; Ph.D. courses, October 1911 –

May 1914), University of Paris-Sorbonne (October 1910 – June 1911), and Merton College, Oxford University (October 1914 – May 1915). He devoted a further year (1915–1916) to a doctoral dissertation on the philosophy of F. H. Bradley, eventually published in 1964.

As an undergraduate at Harvard, Eliot emphasized language and literature—Latin, Greek, German, and French. Perhaps the most far-reaching consequence of his undergraduate career was his accidental discovery in December 1908 of Arthur Symons's *Symbolist Movement in Literature* (1899), a book that he claimed had changed the course of his life. First, Symons introduced him to the poetry of Jules Laforgue and Charles Baudelaire. From Laforgue, Eliot learned how to handle emotion in poetry, through irony and a quality of detachment that enabled him to see himself and his own emotions essentially as objects for analysis. From Baudelaire, he learned how to use the sordid images of the modern city, the material "at hand," in poetry, and of even greater consequence, he learned something of the nature of good and evil in modern life. Second, Symons stimulated Eliot to take a course in French literary criticism from Irving Babbitt in 1910. Babbitt nurtured Eliot's budding Francophilia, his dislike of Romanticism, and his appreciation of tradition. These tastes are evident in most of Eliot's early literary criticism.

During the year he spent at the Sorbonne in Paris, Eliot came to know the work of the Roman Catholic philosopher Charles Maurras through the *Nouvelle Revue Française* and, perhaps of greater significance, attended the lectures of Henri Bergson, in the process deepening the reflections on time and consciousness that are explored in the early poetry and receive their most explicit treatment in *Four Quartets*. Paris was also important in the development of Eliot's urban imagination. He took advantage of the popular arts, of opera and ballet, and of museums, but most of all he absorbed the images of urban life seen on the back streets along the river Seine. Near the end of his year in Paris, Eliot visited London for the first time, and before returning home, he also visited northern Italy and Munich.

During his time at Harvard, he studied with some of the most distinguished philosophers of the century, including George Santayana, Josiah Royce, and Bertrand Russell. He focused on Indic religion and idealist philosophy (especially Immanuel Kant), with further work in ethics and psychology. The Indic studies (two years of Sanskrit and Indian philosophy) abetted his innate asceticism and provided a more comprehensive context for his understanding of culture. Inevitably, these Eastern materials entered his poetry. The Indian myth of the thunder god, for example, provides the context for section 5 ("What the Thunder Said") of *The Waste Land,* and Buddha's fire sermon the context for section 3 ("The Fire Sermon"). Eliot's most fruitful extracurricular activity at Harvard was his association with the college literary magazine, the *Harvard Advocate*. Several of his earliest poems were published first in this periodical, and at least one of his lifelong friendships, that with fellow poet Aiken, was formed in this nursery of writers and poets.

One of the special pleasures of Eliot's years in Boston was the close relationship that developed with his cousin Eleanor Hinkley, three years his junior. As a student at Radcliffe College, she had taken George Pierce Baker's famous "47 Workshop" in theater. In 1912, through amateur theatricals at her house, Eliot met Emily Hale, with whom he fell in love and at one time intended to marry. Eliot's letters to Hinkley are among his most high-spirited, preserving intact his youthful wit and urbanity. His letters to Hale will probably be among his most revealing, but until the year 2020, they remain under seal at Princeton University. Evidently, he never ceased loving her, and in the late 1920s he resumed contact. Their relationship, which seems to have been decorous in all senses of the word, continued for two decades or more, ending before his second marriage in 1957.

Arriving at Oxford in October 1914, Eliot found that most of the British students had left for the Western Front. He had hoped to meet Bradley, a member of Merton, but the old don was by this time a recluse, and they never met. At the end of the academic year, he moved to London and continued working on his dissertation, which he finished a year later. Eliot's immersion in contemporary philosophy, particularly in Bradley's idealism, had many effects, of which two proved especially important. Positively, these materials suggested methods of structure that he was able to put to immediate use in his postwar poems. Negatively, his work in philosophy convinced him that the most sophisticated answers to the cultural and spiritual crisis of his time were inadequate. This conclusion contributed to his decision to abandon the professorial career for which his excellent education had prepared him and instead to continue literary pursuits.

Eliot's career as a poet can be divided into three periods—the first coinciding with his studies in Boston and Paris and culminating in "The Love Song of J. Alfred Prufrock" in 1911; the second coinciding with World War I and with the financial and marital stress of his early years in London, and culminating in *The Waste Land* in 1922; and the third coinciding with his angst at the economic depression and the rise of Nazism and culminating in the wartime *Four Quartets* in 1943. The poems of the first period were preceded only by a few exercises, published in school magazines, but in 1910 and 1911 he wrote four poems—"Portrait of a Lady," "Preludes," "Rhapsody on a Windy Night," and "The Love Song of J. Alfred Prufrock"—that introduce themes to which, with variation and development, Eliot returned time and again. One of the most significant is the problem of isolation, with attention to its causes and consequences in the contemporary world. In "Portrait of a Lady" a man and woman meet, but the man is inarticulate, imprisoned in thought. In this ironic dramatization of a "conversation galante," the woman speaks without thinking and the man thinks without speaking (a structure to be repeated in "A Game of Chess" in *The Waste Land*).

The profound isolation of the characters in "Portrait of a Lady" becomes in "The Love Song of J. Alfred Prufrock" an isolation that is absolute. The specific lady is succeeded by generalized women; the supercilious youth by the middle-aged intellectual he will become, for whom women and indeed the entire universe exist as abstractions. The poignance of this poem derives in part from a tension between Prufrock's self-generated isolation and his obsession with language. Although he is afraid to speak, he can think only in the language of dialogue. This dialogue with himself, moreover, consistently turns on the infinite possibilities (or impossibilities) of dialogue with others. In "Rhapsody on a Windy Night" the female Other, similarly isolated and isolating, is a young prostitute in a stained dress hesitating in a doorway, desired and despised at once, overshadowed by an old prostitute, the pockmarked moon, smiling feebly on the midnight walker.

In these early poems, the progression from a feeble attempt to communicate in "Portrait of a Lady" to a total failure in "The Love Song of J. Alfred Prufrock" is paralleled on other levels. The isolation is sexual, social, religious, and (because Eliot is a poet) vocational. In "Portrait of a Lady," other people and perhaps God exist, but they are unreachable; in "The Love Song of J. Alfred Prufrock" and "Rhapsody on a Windy Night" they exist only as aspects of the thinker's mind; in "Preludes," the Other, whether human or divine, has been so thoroughly assimilated that he/she can no longer be defined. This situation is explicitly aesthetic. The drawing-room protagonist of "Portrait of a Lady" is paralleled by an artist in the concert room, and both the suitor and the pianist fail to reach their listeners. In both cases, the failure is described in ceremonial terms that superimpose the religious on the sexual and aesthetic. J. Alfred Prufrock—as lover, prophet, poet—also fails to reach his audience. These failures are skillfully layered by the use of imagery that defines Prufrock's problem as sexual (how to relate to women), religious (how to raise himself from the dead, how to cope with his own flesh on a platter), and rhetorical (how to sing, how to say, how to revise). And as "The Love Song of J. Alfred Prufrock" shows most clearly, the horizontal and vertical gaps mirror a gap within, a gap between thought and feeling, a partition of the self.

Between the poems of 1910–1911 and *The Waste Land*, Eliot lived through several experiences that are crucial in understanding his development as a poet. His decision to put down roots, or to discover roots, in Europe stands, together with his first marriage and his conversion, as the most important of his entire life. Eliot had been preceded in London by his Harvard friend Aiken, who had met Ezra Pound and showed him a copy of "The Love Song of J. Alfred Prufrock." Eliot called on Pound on 22 September 1914, and Pound immediately adopted him as a cause, promoting his poetry and introducing him to William Butler Yeats and other artists. In 1915, at a time when Eliot was close to giving up on poetry, Pound arranged for the publication of "The Love Song of J. Alfred Prufrock" in *Poetry* magazine, and in 1917 he facilitated the publication of *Prufrock and Other Observations*. Pound continued to play a central role in Eliot's life and work through the early 1920s. He influenced the form and content of Eliot's next group of poems, the quatrains in *Poems* (1919), and more famously, he changed the shape of *The Waste Land* by urging Eliot to cut several long passages.

The impact of Pound, however, pales beside that of Vivienne (or Vivien) Haigh-Wood, the pretty English governess Eliot married in 1915. In a 24 April letter to Hinkley describing his social life at Oxford, Eliot mentioned that he had met an English girl named Vivien. Pound, as part of his strategy for keeping Eliot in England, encouraged him to marry her, and on 26 June, without notifying his parents, he did so at the Hampstead Registry Office. However lovingly begun, the marriage was in most respects a disaster. In the 1960s, in a private paper, Eliot admitted that it was doomed from the start: "I think that all I wanted of Vivienne was a flirtation or a mild affair: I was too shy and unpractised to achieve either . . . I came to persuade myself that I was in love with her simply because I wanted to burn my boats and commit myself to staying in England. And she persuaded herself (also under the influence of Pound) that she would save the poet by keeping him in England." The odd nature of this misalliance was immediately evident to Eliot's friends, including Russell, Mary Hutchinson, and Virginia Woolf. Vivienne Eliot, who had suffered from "nerves" for years, became irrecoverably ill after the marriage, and Eliot, himself in fragile health, felt partially responsible for her deterioration. This burden is the biographical shadow behind a motif recurrent in the poems and plays—the motif of "doing a girl in." The struggle to cope emotionally and financially with his wife's escalating illness exhausted Eliot and led, in 1921, to his collapse. His failed attempt between 1915 and 1922 to build a bridge across the gulf that separated them, reflected most conspicuously in part 2 of *The Waste Land*, is a lived experience behind all of his subsequent work.

Eliot had arrived in England the month that World War I began. Like his European friends, he was deeply disturbed by unfolding events and desperately worried about acquaintances on the battlefield. In May 1915 his close friend Jean Verdenal was killed. On 31 May the first German bomb hit London, killing twenty-eight people and wounding sixty. Within a week or two of this watershed event, Eliot moved to the City (the financial district), where he remained throughout the war. In 1916 he wrote to his brother that "The present year has been . . . the most awful nightmare of anxiety that the mind of man could conceive." Eliot, who loved both France and England, tried to enlist, but his application was complicated by his failure to pass the medical exam. By the time the war ended in November 1918, an influenza epidemic was sweeping over the world, claiming nearly three times as many lives as had been lost in the war. By then both Eliots were gravely ill, and it took them years to recover completely.

The events of these years were formative in Eliot's life and art. First, the precipitous marriage complicated his attitude toward sexuality and human love. Some of the poems written during and immediately after the war ("Sweeney Erect," for example, and *The Waste Land*) connect sexuality with violence in troubling ways. Second, the marriage, the war, and the change of vocation generated estrangement from America in general and from his family in particular. His family disapproved of the marriage and the decision to drop philosophy as a career, and because the family lived in America, far from the bloodshed, they had a superficial idea of the suffering in Europe. Eliot continued to brood over the fact that his dying father believed that his son had made a mess of his life. Third, the events of these years led to severe financial distress. To support himself and his chronically ill wife, Eliot took a job as a teacher–in the fall of 1915 at High Wycombe Grammar School, and throughout 1916 at Highgate Junior School. Finding the teaching of young boys draining work, he gave it up at the end of 1916, and in March 1917 he began work in the Colonial and Foreign Department of Lloyds Bank. Although he stayed with Lloyds for the next nine years, he discovered that banking, like teaching, did not produce nearly enough income to cover his expenses and Vivienne Eliot's medical bills. He was thus forced to supplement his duties as teacher, banker, and nurse to his wife with night work as lecturer, reviewer, and essayist. Working from 1916 to 1920 under great pressure (a fifteen-hour workday was common for him), he wrote essays, published in 1920 as *The Sacred Wood*, that reshaped literary history.

Eliot's early essays can be seen as a discursive variation on the subjects underlying the early poems; his awareness, for example, of the problem of isolation, its causes and its consequences, is evident in the essays. In the poems, the emphasis is on isolation of individuals and classes from one another and on the human isolation from God. In the literary criticism, the emphasis is on the artist in isolation, cut off from his audience and from great artists and thinkers of both the present and the past. In "Tradition and the Individual Talent" (1919), Eliot attempts to cope with the isolation of the artist resulting from the early twentieth century's massive repudiation of the past, a repudiation that severed man's intellectual and spiritual roots. Eliot deals with the implications of this disaster by defining "tradition" as an ideal structure in which the "whole of the literature of Europe from Homer and within it the whole of the literature of his [the artist's] own country has a simultaneous existence and composes a simultaneous order." To put it more simply, he defines tradition not as a canon but as an ongoing and fluid relationship of writers, living and dead, within the mind and bones of the contemporary poet. Eliot's reaction against Romanticism, similarly, is related to the fact that Romanticism celebrates the artist in isolation. Eliot's notion that modern poetry should be complex derives in part from his attempt to overcome his isolation from his readers by forcing them to become involved as collaborators in his poetry. He suggests that a text is a self-sufficient object and at the same time a construct collaboratively achieved by a reader. His account of the way a poet's mind works by unifying disparate phenomena is consistent with his dialectical imagination, as is his account of literary history.

In regard to his poetry, the period between 1911 and 1918 is for the most part a long dry stretch. He included in the Prufrock volume a few short pieces written in London and Oxford in 1914 and 1915, and he copied others not ready for publication into his notebook (published in 1996 as *Inventions of the March Hare: Poems, 1909–1917*). By 1916 he was afraid that "The Love Song of J. Alfred Prufrock" had been his swan song. And by 1917 he had become, by his own testimony, quite desperate. To get going again, Eliot wrote a handful of poems in French, one of which, "*Dans le Restaurant*," in a truncated English version, ended up in *The Waste Land*. Eliot and Pound were at their closest during these years, and some of the impetus for Eliot's revival as a poet came from his flamboyant friend. Both felt that the freedom achieved in the previous decade of revolution in the arts had degenerated to license, and they decided to move back toward more precise forms. For Eliot, the result was the quatrain poems, so called because they were modeled, at Pound's suggestion, on the quatrains of Theophile Gautier's *Emaux et Camees* (1852). These Gautier-inspired poems, all highly polished satires, include "The Hippopotamus," "Sweeney Erect," "Sweeney among the Nightingales," "Burbank with a Baedeker," "Mr. Eliot's Sunday Morning Service," "Whispers of Immortality," and "A Cooking Egg." The themes of the French poems and the quatrain poems overlap with those of the earlier poems—social and metaphysical loneliness, the absence of love, personal and cultural sterility, death—but the tone is even darker, with violence just beneath the surface. The focus—international, cultural, institutional—is broader than in the earlier poems. Prufrock is primarily an individual; Burbank and Sweeney are primarily types. Eliot's miserable marriage and the experience of World War I seem to be the two most important events behind this shift in his work.

Eliot's most significant single poem between 1911 and 1922 was "Gerontion." Important in itself, it also serves as a transition to *The Waste Land,* to which, for thematic reasons, Eliot considered it an appropriate prelude, and to which, until dissuaded by Pound, he considered prefixing it. Formally, "Gerontion," like "The Love Song of J. Alfred Prufrock," descends from the dramatic monologue, but it is bolder and more comprehensive. The earlier poem is a portrait of an individual mind, but "Gerontion" is a portrait of the Mind of Europe, a container for fragments of history from the Battle of Thermopylae in 480 B.C.E. to the Treaty of Versailles in 1919. The title character, as his name indicates, is old; born in ancient Greece, he survives as a desiccated Socrates "waiting for rain" on the doorstep of modern Europe. Like Prufrock, Gerontion is an intellectual, and the poem consists of his thoughts. To order these thoughts, Eliot uses the structural metaphor of houses within houses.

One of the most significant houses in this Chinese box-like poem is war-ravaged Europe, a house of horrors with "many cunning passages, contrived corridors." Eliot began writing the poem in 1917, with the war still raging, and finished it in early 1919, a few months after the Armistice. Europe's great dynastic and political houses lay in ruins, and nine million of her young had been slain for Western civilization. Different people analyzed the crisis in different ways; for Eliot, the violence was inseparable from a collapse of common ground in culture, the loss of the mythic substructure that enables the individual to understand his relatedness to anyone or anything. The collapse of shared assumptions in many fields—religion, physics, philosophy, art—produced a crisis in epistemology, in knowing, and this crisis is basic to all of Eliot's work.

Eliot's early years as a literary man bore tangible fruit in 1920 with the publication of his recent poems (as *Ara Vos Prec* in England, *Poems* in America) and the best of his literary criticism *(The Sacred Wood).* As he wrapped up the details surrounding these projects, he moved on to what became a watershed in the history of European poetry. In December 1919 Eliot wrote to his mother that his New Year's resolution was "to write a long poem I have had on my mind for a long time." That long poem, *The Waste Land,* continues his exploration of what he saw as the decay of European civilization; but whereas "Gerontion" is his most impersonal poem, *The Waste Land* is to some extent quite personal, for it is strongly colored by a breakdown in his own life. In the years following his marriage, Eliot had suffered continuously from overwork and financial strain. The death of his father in 1919 also took a heavy toll, as did the loss of friends in the war. His most severe distress, however, was that associated with the breakdown of his marriage. It had become increasingly clear that he and Vivienne Eliot were not good for each other. His comments about her in the letters are kind (they reflect, mainly, concern for her health and respect for her resourcefulness), but as the poems "Hysteria" (1915) and "Ode" (1918) suggest, his feelings were more negative than he could ever have admitted to his family or friends, or even to himself. In the 1960s, in a private paper (quoted in *The Letters of T. S. Eliot,* 1988), he finally acknowledged what had long been evident: "To her the marriage brought no happiness . . . to me, it brought the state of mind out of which came *The Waste Land.*"

These years of unmitigated anxiety culminated, finally, in serious illness. In 1921, on the verge of a nervous breakdown, Eliot was forced to take a rest leave from the bank. In October he went for a month to Margate; and then, leaving Vivienne Eliot in Paris, he went to a sanatorium in Switzerland. In this protected environment, he devoted himself to completing the "long poem" that had been on his mind for years, a work in which his illness is included as part of the material. In January 1922 Eliot returned to London, stopping briefly in Paris, where he left the typescript of the poem, then called "He Do the Police in Different Voices," with Pound. The latter immediately recognized it as a work of genius but thought it needed to be reduced in length. Eliot accepted most of Pound's suggestions and later testified that Pound was "a marvelous critic because he . . . tried to see what you were trying to do." In October 1922 *The Waste Land* appeared in England in the first issue of the *Criterion,* the journal Eliot edited for most of the next two decades; in November it appeared in America in the *Dial,* with Eliot receiving the *Dial* Award of $2,000.

The Waste Land was taken by some critics as a tasteless joke, by others as a masterpiece expressing the disillusionment of a generation. As far as Eliot was concerned, it was neither. He needed, he explained in a 1959 *Paris Review* interview, to get something off his chest, adding, "one doesn't know quite what it is that one needs to get off the chest until one's got it off." In a lecture at Harvard, quoted in *The Waste Land* facsimile (published in 1971), he responded to those who considered the poem to be a cultural statement: "To me it was only the relief of a personal and wholly insignificant grouse against life; it is just a piece of rhythmical grumbling." The grumbling is personal, of course, which is why he calls it insignificant, but its causes are inseparable from those that set a generation or more of intelligent Westerners to grumbling. Eliot's grouse against life is part of a larger and shared discontent about postwar civilization and the conditions of modern life. Another aspect of Eliot's grumbling that is more than personal is his anxiety about possibility in art. A major theme in his poetry and prose from the beginning had been the situation of the artist who is isolated from his audience by a collapse of common ground in culture. Deprived of a shared mythic or religious frame, the modern artist was forced to come up with other means of unity. He had to find, as Eliot put it in his review of James Joyce's *Ulysses* (1922), "a way of controlling, of ordering, of giving a shape and a significance to the immense panorama of futility and anarchy which is contemporary history." The "narrative method," rooted in sequence, in an orderly flow of life (and of stories) from beginning to end, had been rendered obsolete by modern science and by conditions of history.

In *The Waste Land,* consequently, Eliot experimented with a method that he hoped would be "a step towards making the modern world possible for art." He called it the "mythical method" and defined it as the manipulation of a continuous parallel between an ordered world of myth (an abstraction) and a chaotic world of history, contemporary or otherwise. In keeping the chaos of his own time on the surface, the artist is being true to history; in referring this chaos to a timeless order, he is being true to art. The mythical method enabled Eliot in *The Waste Land* to deal simultaneously with such issues as his illness and failed marriage and larger issues such as the upheavals in politics, philosophy, and science that surrounded World War I. The title and much of the symbolism were taken from Sir James Frazer's *The Golden Bough* (1890-1915) and Jessie Weston's Arthurian studies, collected in *From Ritual to Romance* (1920). Frazer argued that all myths descended from a single ancestor (a monomyth) that in his reconstruction describes a land in which a king and his people are so interrelated that impotence in the ruler leads to sterility in the people and devastation in the land. Weston, a disciple of Frazer's, argued that the Grail stories were part of this larger myth. The monomyth had special relevance to early-twentieth-century culture: God had been declared dead; the earth had been devastated by war; political leaders had proven impotent; an entire generation of young men had been slaughtered in France and Belgium; and survivors resembled ghosts on the streets of the city. The ancestor myth is not present in its entirety in *The Waste Land* but is generated in the reader's mind by juxtaposition of fragments of its many variants and, as in *Ulysses,* by a complex web of references. The poem features many voices from many times and places, and together they reveal shifting perspectives on situations in which failures of leadership, community, and love have produced a wasteland. The use of slivers of myth to generate structure and the use of shifting perspectives are hallmarks of the radical form of *The Waste Land.*

Another aspect of form in the poem is parataxis, that is, the juxtaposition without transition of fragments, some no more than a single word. Bits of myth, literature, religion, and philosophy from many times and cultures are combined with snatches of music and conversation so contemporary they could have come from yesterday's newspaper. Meaningless in themselves, the fragments in this literary collage become powerfully suggestive in their juxtaposition and in the way they echo and explain one another as they generate larger wholes.

The Waste Land consists of five parts in which Eliot's own verse is mixed with fragments of the verse of others. The primary subject of the first section, "Burial of the Dead," is death: death as a problem in waste disposal, death as part of a natural cycle, death as part of life, death as an end, death as a beginning. Eliot's montage includes the death of the year, of individuals, of cities, of civilizations. All of these deaths go back in Frazer's genealogy to primitive rituals in which death is followed by a ritualistic "planting" intended to insure a rich harvest. Eliot refers specifically to such rituals in the lines, "That corpse you planted last year in your garden, / Has it begun to sprout?" The planting, in April, of a male corpse (or part of one, usually the genitals) in mother earth is at the center of many ancient fertility ceremonies. But Eliot's lines refer also to the contemporary world, where planting the corpse ensures harvest by acting as organic fertilizer, and where April is cruel because, in "breeding / Lilacs out of the dead land," it promises what it does not deliver—new life.

The underlying subject of the second section, "A Game of Chess," is sex, in myth part of an interest in life. In history, though, as Eliot shows, sex is often not associated with life at all. He juxtaposes two "love" scenes—minidramas from opposite ends of the social scale, both displaying sterile and meaningless relationships. The relationship of an upper-middle-class couple is structured by a game of chess, and that of a Cockney couple by visits to the pub. Through allusion, other sterile sexual situations—Ophelia's, Cleopatra's, Philomela's—are superimposed. The underlying subject of section three, "The Fire Sermon," is again the sexual wound behind the decay of civilization. As in "A Game of Chess," there are two contemporary sexual situations—one, a homosexual proposition; the other, a mechanical sexual transaction between a typist and a clerk. Both situations issue from boredom; both, obviously, are loveless and fruitless. The underlying subject in the short fourth section, "Death by Water," is again death. The drowning of a sailor, followed by dissolution, is juxtaposed, through allusion, to the "death" by water of Christian baptism and of Frazer's vegetation myths, both of which are ritualistic preludes to rebirth. The ritualistic death by water involves purification; the contemporary death by water is also, ironically, a purification, a literal cleansing of bones.

The underlying subject of the last section of *The Waste Land*, "What the Thunder Said," is restoration, not as a fact, but as a remote possibility. The previous images of drought and sterility reappear, but now accompanied by images suggesting the possibility of revitalization. Thunder sounds in the distance; Christ, the slain and resurrected hero whose death effects restoration, walks the land; the mythic hero whose personal trials can secure communal blessing approaches the Chapel Perilous. The title of this section refers to an Indian legend in which men, gods, and devils listen to the thunder and then construct from that sound the positive message that can restore the wasteland and make its inhabitants fruitful again. The poem ends, however, not with restoration but with an avalanche of fragments, the most concentrated in the entire poem. The last fragment ("Shantih Shantih Shantih"), by chance a benediction, is the cruelest in that, like April, and perhaps like thunder, it awakens expectations that it does not satisfy.

Restoration, then, is present only as a whisper; it all hinges, finally, on one's willingness to take the given and to construct something that will enable the retrieval of structure and meaning. The last lines suggest a distinction that became crucial in Eliot's own life: while it may not be possible to reclaim Western civilization, it may be possible to restore order in one's personal life.

In 1926 Eliot was invited to give the Clark Lectures at Cambridge (published in 1993 as *The Varieties of Metaphysical Poetry*), and in 1932, by this time a world-renowned poet and critic, he was invited to Harvard as the Charles Eliot Norton Professor of Poetry. Three events of the intervening decade are important in following the shape of his life and art. First, his financial and in a sense his vocational situation was settled when, in 1925, he left Lloyds Bank for the publishing house of Faber and Gwyer (later Faber and Faber). Second, his marital situation continued to deteriorate, ending with his permanent separation from Vivienne Eliot in 1932; and third, in 1927, his spiritual odyssey culminated in baptism into the Anglican Church and naturalization as a British subject. The financial nightmare had begun to fade in 1922 when he launched *The Criterion*. When Eliot announced on the eve of World War II that he was bringing *The Criterion* to a close, he was able to look back with considerable pride on the quality and range of his accomplishments. By publishing the work of such distinguished writers as Paul Valéry, Marcel Proust, Joyce, Woolf, D. H. Lawrence, Auden, Jacques Maritain, Maurras, and Wilhelm Worringer, he had greatly enhanced intellectual fellowship in Europe. At Faber and Faber, Eliot found a congenial and enduring group of associates, and through the publishing house, he was able to be a mentor and friend to younger writers.

The community of intellectuals and artists of which Eliot became a part assuaged somewhat the sense of fragmentation that had always haunted him. The sexual and the religious aspects of his isolation, however, proved resistant to improvement. He and Vivienne Eliot were unable to forge any sort of unity, and as their relationship and her health continued to worsen, he suffered in ways that surfaced in his poetry. Inseparable from his realization that human love, and in particular, sexual love, had failed was his turn toward God and the church. The emptiness and desolation of this period are perfectly caught in "The Hollow Men," composed in fragments over a two- or three-year period and first appearing as a single poem in *Poems 1909–1925* (1925).

Written in the style of what Eliot once said was the best part of *The Waste Land*—the water-dripping song in "What the Thunder Said"—"The Hollow Men" is based on four main allusions: Dante's *Divine Comedy* (circa 1310–1314), William Shakespeare's *Julius Caesar* (1599), Joseph Conrad's *Heart of Darkness* (1902), and an event in English history, the Gunpowder Plot of 1605. Dante, Shakespeare, and Conrad are arguably the most important writers in the background of Eliot's art, and *Heart of Darkness* is probably second only to *The Divine Comedy* as an intellectual/

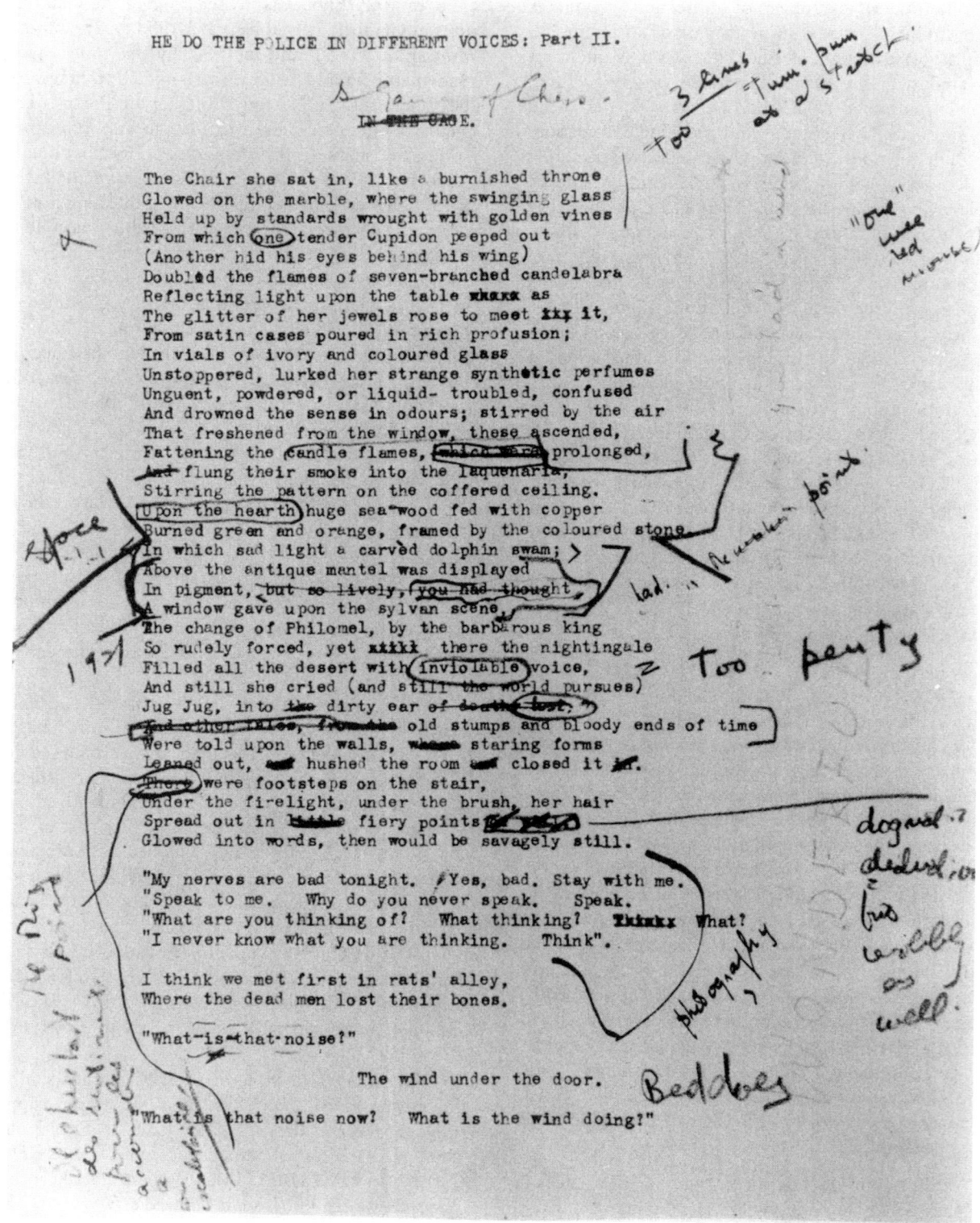

Page from the revised typescript for Eliot's poem *The Waste Land* (1922), with comments and revisions by Ezra Pound and remarks by Vivienne Eliot (by permission of Valerie Eliot; Henry W. and Albert A. Berg Collection, New York Public Library, Astor, Lenox and Tilden Foundation)

spiritual resource. Conrad's Mr. Kurtz, a cultivated European idealist and carrier of civilization to dark places, glimpses as he dies a vision that he expresses as "The horror! The horror!" These words, included in Eliot's original epigraph for *The Waste Land,* describe the vision both Conrad and Eliot saw beneath the veneer of European civilization. And they describe what Conrad probably and Eliot certainly saw beneath the surface of modern idealism.

In "The Hollow Men," Eliot focuses on the idealism shared by such figures as Brutus, Guy Fawkes, and (as in *The Waste Land*) Kurtz, and in an epigraph that is also a conclusion, he quotes from *Heart of Darkness* the simple announcement by a jungle boy: "Mistah Kurtz— he dead." The death of Kurtz and all that he stands for is at the center of the meaning of this poem. The "Old Guy" of the epigraph is not only Guy Fawkes but also "the old man" whose death, according to Saint Paul, is the condition of new life. Many figures in Eliot's early poems, including all the gods and semigods from Frazer, have to die or be put to death as the condition for the continuation of life. Those who cannot die cannot really live. The most striking of these death-in-life figures is the Sibyl of Cumae who presides over *The Waste Land.* In "The Hollow Men," Eliot does not go beyond a presentation of emptiness, but in the act of presenting that, he seems to accept the death that is the essential step toward his own *vita nuova.* In "Gerontion" and *The Waste Land,* Eliot had seen the death-in-life figures as primarily other than himself. But in "The Hollow Men," in trying to voice his own inarticulate emptiness, he numbers himself among the living dead. His idealism, like that of Brutus, Fawkes, and Kurtz, has led him to the cactus land.

The way out of the cactus land led Eliot to his baptism on 29 June 1927 into the Anglican Communion. In November, in what seemed to him part of the same ritual, he was naturalized as a British citizen. Many of Eliot's contemporaries, having adopted him as a sort of spokesman, felt that in embracing traditional Christianity he had abandoned them. He explained in "Thoughts After Lambeth" (1931) that he had never intended to be the spokesman for a generation; that he had been trying all along to work out his own salvation; and that, for "powerful and concurrent reasons," he had been drawn inexorably toward Christianity. In March 1932, in a brief article in the *Listener,* he explained, "In my own case, I believe that one of the reasons was that the Christian scheme seemed to me the only one which would work . . . the only possible scheme which found a place for values which I must maintain or perish." Like Blaise Pascal, Eliot had proceeded to the Christian position by a careful process of rejection and elimination. He had considered Buddhism and tried schemes from philosophy and anthropology, and he concluded that these options failed to account for the world as he saw it and were an inadequate basis for order in life and in art. In a striking revision of his early aesthetic of impersonality, Eliot used his own spiritual struggle as material in his next major poem, *Ash-Wednesday.*

Ash-Wednesday is composed of six lyrics, three of which had been published separately before the 1930 publication of all six under one title. The title refers to the first day of Lent, a day of repentance and fasting in which Christians acknowledge their mortality and begin the forty-day period of self-examination leading to the new life promised by Easter. The structure of this sequence comes from Eliot's new principle of order, the Christian scheme that for him had subsumed both Bradley and Frazer. In place of the monomyth as a reference point, Eliot now uses the Incarnation of Christ— not only in *Ash-Wednesday* but also in *Four Quartets* and the plays. The Incarnation represents an intersection of the human and the divine, of time and the timeless, of movement and stillness. Eliot's earlier schemes had been a means of making art possible in the chaos of contemporary history; his new scheme, however, is a means of making life, of which art is only a part, possible. The integration of life and art can be seen in the fact that *Ash-Wednesday* is at once more personal, confessional even, and at the same time more formal and stylized than the earlier work.

For all its brightness, *Ash-Wednesday* remains a poem about twilight, about "the time of tension between dying and birth." The tension is resolved in *Marina* (published as a Christmas pamphlet in 1930), frequently regarded as Eliot's most beautiful short poem. It consists of an interior monologue spoken by Pericles, Prince of Tyre, who in Shakespeare's play sails the seas in search of his beloved wife, lost after giving birth at sea to an infant daughter, also lost and presumably dead. Eliot's monologue, inspired by Shakespeare's recognition scene, conveys the wonder and awe the old prince experiences in realizing that the beautiful girl standing before him is Marina, a recognition that not only restores a daughter but also leads to the restoration of his wife.

The decade inaugurated with *Ash-Wednesday* was an eventful one for Eliot. In 1932 he published *Selected Essays 1917–1932,* a collection of his literary criticism through the 1920s. The same year, in September, he returned to America to deliver the prestigious Charles Eliot Norton lectures at Harvard. Vivienne Eliot remained in England. In this critical moment, Eliot decided that they could no longer live together. For several reasons, he did not want to divorce her, and so he asked his London solicitor to prepare a "Deed of Separation." After he returned to England, they lived apart and rarely saw each other. Her health declined even more, and in 1939 she was institutionalized by her brother Maurice.

The most rewarding part of Eliot's year in America, his first visit home in eighteen years, was that it enabled him to renew his relationship with surviving members of his family. In December he traveled to California, ostensibly to give a lecture at Scripps College, but actually to spend time with Hale, who was a professor there. Except for the distress caused by the situation with his wife, Eliot enjoyed his homecoming. His Harvard lectures, a survey of high points in English criticism from the Renaissance to the 1920s, were published in 1933 as *The Use of Poetry and the Use of Criticism*. In January 1933 he delivered the Turnbull Lectures at Johns Hopkins University, and in May the Page-Barbour Lectures at the University of Virginia. The Virginia lectures, published as *After Strange Gods* in 1934, constituted an attempt to fine-tune his old concept of tradition, rechristening it "orthodoxy." Back in England, he lectured at Edinburgh and Cambridge, the Cambridge lectures later printed as *The Idea of a Christian Society*. Also in the 1930s, Eliot realized his longstanding ambition of becoming a dramatist, finishing both *Murder in the Cathedral* and *The Family Reunion*. He also published *Old Possum's Book of Practical Cats* (1939), light poems composed for his godchildren.

Eliot's major poetic achievement during the 1930s was *Burnt Norton*, composed in 1935, initially considered as an independent work—and included as such in *Collected Poems 1909-1935* (1936)—but becoming during the war the first of four comparable works that together are known as *Four Quartets*. This sequence—*Burnt Norton, East Coker, The Dry Salvages,* and *Little Gidding*—is widely regarded as Eliot's masterpiece. He himself thought *Four Quartets* his greatest achievement and *Little Gidding* his best poem.

Whereas his early poems had been centered on the isolated individual, *Four Quartets* is centered on the isolated moment, the fragment of time that takes its meaning from and gives its meaning to a pattern, a pattern at once in time, continuously changing until the supreme moment of death completes it, and also out of time. Since the individual lives and exists only in fragments, he can never quite know the whole pattern; but in certain moments, he can experience the pattern in miniature. These timeless moments—"the moment in the rose-garden, / The moment in the arbour where the rain beat, / The moment in the draughty church at smokefall"—provide for Eliot the means of conquering time. This moment of sudden illumination, in and out of time, Eliot associates with the Word-made-flesh, the Incarnation; and also with the word-made-art, poetry.

The part/pattern configuration, especially in these three dimensions, is both the main subject and the main principle of form in *Four Quartets*.

The fact that *Four Quartets* is a meditation on time and a celebration of pattern points to a secondary principle of form, albeit the one usually mentioned first by critics. From the collective title and from a lecture called *The Music of Poetry* (1942), delivered early in the year he finished *Little Gidding*, it is clear that Eliot was working with a musical analogy throughout *Four Quartets*, especially in regard to structure. The most conspicuous analogies to music include statement and counterstatement, theme and variation, tempo variation, and mood variation. By using the musical analogy, Eliot was able to avoid monotony, the plague of long and complex philosophical poems. The analogy with music is useful in clarifying the nondiscursive nature of *Four Quartets*, but as Eliot warns in *The Music of Poetry* and in essays on the French symbolists, it should not be pushed too far.

The title of each meditation refers to a specific place important to the poet. Burnt Norton is the name of a country house in Gloucestershire that Eliot visited in the summer of 1934 in the company of Hale. Pending the availability of Eliot's many letters to this friend of more than half a century, the exact nature of their relationship cannot be known. But it seems likely that on this summer day in the rose garden, Eliot, guilt-torn and exhausted from his disastrous marriage and recent separation, experienced a temptation to deny the present by returning to the road not taken in 1914. This temptation seems to have generated the lines that now open *Burnt Norton*.

The title of *East Coker* refers to the village in Somersetshire from which, in the seventeenth century, Eliot's family had immigrated to America, and to which, after his death, Eliot's own ashes were to be returned. The mystery of beginnings and ends—"In my beginning is my end," "In my end is my beginning"—in and out of history is explored in this work. The third of the *Four Quartets* takes its title from a small but enormously treacherous group of rocks, the Dry Salvages, located off the coast of Cape Ann, Massachusetts, where Eliot had passed his childhood summers. These rocks, the cold and seemingly limitless ocean in which they are anchored, and the great Mississippi River of his childhood are the major symbols in this meditation.

The last of the *Four Quartets* takes its title from a tiny village in Huntingdonshire, Little Gidding, which in the seventeenth century had been a community of dedicated Christians under the leadership of Nicholas Ferrar. Eliot, who visited Little Gidding in 1936, admired the example of this small group that had renounced position and wealth for a life of work and prayer. Each of these four places is associated with Eliot's part/pattern, stillness/movement theme. He insists on the importance of specific places, just as he does on the importance of specific moments. The timeless moment, in fact, can only occur in a specific place–a rose garden, a draughty church, a rain-washed arbor. The places are only fragments of the pattern; they constitute, nevertheless, the only way to transcendence.

The *Four Quartets* all have the same general form. The first part of each consists of a meditation on time and consciousness, arranged as a statement/counter-statement/recapitulation. The second consists of a highly structured poetical passage followed by a relatively prosaic passage, both on the general subject of being trapped in time. The third explores implications of the first two in terms of a journey metaphor, some concept of the movement of the self in and out of time. The fourth is a brief lyric treating of death and rebirth. The fifth begins with a colloquial passage and then ends with a lyric that secures closure by returning to the beginning and collecting major images. The fifth section in each work incorporates a meditation on the problem of the artist who must still move in stillness, keep time in time (both continuously move in step, and continuously be still).

Eliot's career as a poet virtually ended with *Four Quartets*. His long-standing despair over Western civilization, at the heart of "Gerontion" and *The Waste Land* and still conspicuous in 1939 in his farewell editorial for *The Criterion*, was somewhat displaced by the onset of World War II. He realized anew that there were traditions and principles worth dying for, and he did what he could to help preserve them–for example, serving as a fire watcher on the roof of Faber and Faber during the bombing of London in 1940, an experience represented in the "compound ghost" section of *Little Gidding*. This period was marked by the loss of friends, including Yeats in 1939 and Joyce and Woolf in 1941. In January 1947, the most painful chapter in his personal history came to an end when, after years of illness, Vivienne Eliot died of a heart attack. Pound was by this time confined in a mental hospital, St. Elizabeth's in Washington, D.C., charged with treason for radio speeches made during the war. With other concerned friends, Eliot did what he could to improve the situation of his old benefactor. Against these lengthening shadows, Eliot must have experienced some pleasure in his growing reputation as one of the greatest living poets and distinguished men of letters.

What remained of Eliot's creative energy was put into his comedies–*The Cocktail Party, The Confidential Clerk* (performed in 1953, published in 1954), and *The Elder Statesman* (performed in 1958, published in 1959). The first was a popular success, winning international prizes and, when it opened on Broadway, attracting an audience that included Ethel Barrymore and the duke and duchess of Windsor. In the late 1940s and 1950s Eliot returned to America for several appearances at universities, including Princeton, the University of Chicago, and Washington University. He continued with his work at Faber and Faber during the 1950s, and he accepted invitations to lecture in South Africa, Edinburgh, and other places.

Beginning in the late 1940s, Eliot received almost every accolade the West had to offer a poet. Several universities, including his alma mater, bestowed honorary doctorates. In 1948 he received England's most exclusive and prestigious civilian prize, the Order of Merit, and, in the same year, the Nobel Prize in Literature. He responded to the Nobel with a mixture of gratitude and humor. Biographer Peter Ackroyd records that when asked what he received the prize for, Eliot said that he assumed it was for "the entire corpus." The reporter responded, "When did you write that?" In *The New York Times* (21 November 1948) a reporter asked how it felt to win the Nobel Prize, and Eliot replied, "One does not feel any different. It isn't that you get any bigger to fit the world, the world gets smaller to fit you." The biggest difference made by the Nobel, perhaps, was that it increased Eliot's anxiety regarding his future work. Knowing his best work was in the past, he feared that the prize would create expectations he could no longer satisfy. In the decade that followed, nevertheless, he continued to receive international awards. The status of this most private and difficult poet is indicated by his coverage in popular magazines (in March 1950 he appeared on the cover of *Time*) and by the size of his audiences (he attracted a crowd of nearly fifteen thousand for a 1956 lecture in Minneapolis). Eliot accepted all of this attention with characteristic grace and good humor. As his obituary in the London *Times* (6 January 1965) noted, "He was, above all, a humble man; firm, even stubborn at times, but with no self-importance; quite unspoilt by fame; free from spiritual or intellectual pride." This quotation is substantiated by the testimony of those who knew him as a person rather than as a monument.

The most important event in Eliot's later life was his second marriage. In his sixty-ninth year (1957), he married Esme Valerie Fletcher, his devoted secretary at Faber and Faber since 1950, and almost forty years his junior. By all accounts, this happy marriage rejuvenated the poet. His obvious contentment may seem to contradict most of his earlier references to sexual love, but in fact his belated marital bliss reveals with special clarity a larger pattern in his life and art. That pattern involves a continuous quest for wholeness. His early obsession with brokenness and isolation can easily be seen in retrospect as the negative expression of a quest for wholeness and communion. The second marriage is important because it is the complement in his personal life of the religious unity he found through commitment to the Incarnation, and of the aesthetic unity he achieved in *Four Quartets*. The personal unity, the "new person / Who is you and me together," is celebrated in his swan song, *The Elder Statesman*, most explicitly in its dedicatory poem, "A Dedication to My Wife."

T. S. Eliot's last years, though happy, were darkened by illness. He died of emphysema in London on 4 January 1965. The London *Times* obituary was titled "The Most Influential English Poet of His Time," and the long obituary in *Life* magazine concluded with "Our age beyond any doubt has been, and will continue to be, the Age of Eliot." Such claims inevitably provoke reaction and reevaluation. In Eliot's case, the reevaluation, well under way even before his death, has reaffirmed his stature as a great poet and a central figure in the European tradition.

Letters:

The Letters of T. S. Eliot, volume 1 *[1898–1922],* edited by Valerie Eliot (San Diego: Harcourt Brace Jovanovich, 1988; London: Faber & Faber, 1988).

Interviews:

Henry Hewes, "T. S. Eliot at Seventy" and "Eliot on Eliot," *Saturday Review,* 41 (13 September 1958): 30–32;

Helen Gardner, "The 'Aged Eagle' Spreads His Wings: A 70th Birthday Talk with T. S. Eliot," *Sunday Times,* 21 September 1958, p. 8;

Donald Hall, "The Art of Poetry, I: T. S. Eliot," *Paris Review,* 21 (Spring/Summer 1959): 47–70; reprinted in *Writers at Work,* Second Series (New York: Viking, 1963), pp. 91–110;

Leslie Paul, "A Conversation with T. S. Eliot," *Kenyon Review,* 27 (Winter 1964/1965): 11–21.

Bibliographies:

Donald C. Gallup, *T. S. Eliot: A Bibliography,* revised and extended edition (New York: Harcourt, Brace & World, 1969);

Mildred Martin, *A Half-Century of Eliot Criticism: An Annotated Bibliography of Books and Articles in English, 1916–1965* (Lewisburg, Pa.: Bucknell University Press, 1972);

Beatrice Ricks, *T. S. Eliot: A Bibliography of Secondary Works* (Metuchen, N.J.: Scarecrow Press, 1980);

Robert Canary, *T. S. Eliot: The Poet and His Critics* (Chicago: American Library Association, 1982);

Stuart Y. McDougal, "T. S. Eliot," in *Sixteen Modern American Authors: A Survey of Research and Criticism Since 1972,* edited by Jackson R. Bryer (Durham, N.C.: Duke University Press, 1989), pp. 154–209;

Sebastian D. G. Knowles and Scott A. Leonard, *An Annotated Bibliography of a Decade of T. S. Eliot Criticism: 1977–1986* (Orono, Me.: National Poetry Foundation, 1992).

Biographies:

Peter Ackroyd, *T. S. Eliot: A Life* (London: Hamilton, 1984; New York: Simon & Schuster, 1984);

Tony Sharpe, *T. S. Eliot: A Literary Life* (Basingstoke, U.K.: Macmillan, 1991; New York: St. Martin's Press, 1991);

Lyndall Gordon, *T. S. Eliot: An Imperfect Life* (London: Vintage, 1998; New York: Norton, 1999).

References:

Richard Badenhausen, *T. S. Eliot and the Art of Collaboration* (Cambridge: Cambridge University Press, 2005);

Calvin Bedient, *He Do the Police in Different Voices: "The Waste Land" and Its Protagonist* (Chicago: University of Chicago Press, 1986);

Caroline Behr, *T. S. Eliot: A Chronology of His Life and Works* (London: Macmillan, 1983);

Jewel Spears Brooker, *Mastery and Escape: T. S. Eliot and the Dialectic of Modernism* (Amherst: University of Massachusetts Press, 1994);

Brooker, ed., *Approaches to Teaching Eliot's Poetry and Plays* (New York: Modern Language Association, 1988);

Brooker, ed., *The Placing of T. S. Eliot* (Columbia: University of Missouri Press, 1991);

Brooker, ed., *T. S. Eliot: The Contemporary Reviews* (Cambridge: Cambridge University Press, 2004);

Brooker, ed., *T. S. Eliot and Our Turning World* (London: Macmillan, 2001);

Brooker and Joseph Bentley, *Reading The Waste Land: Modernism and the Limits of Interpretation* (Amherst: University of Massachusetts Press, 1990);

Ronald Bush, *T. S. Eliot: A Study in Character and Style* (New York: Oxford University Press, 1984);

Bush, ed., *T. S. Eliot: The Modernist in History* (Cambridge: Cambridge University Press, 1991);

Donald J. Childs, *T. S. Eliot: Mystic, Son & Lover* (New York: St. Martin's Press, 1997);

David Chinitz, *T. S. Eliot and the Cultural Divide* (Chicago: University of Chicago Press, 2003);

John Xiros Cooper, *T. S. Eliot and the Ideology of "Four Quartets"* (Cambridge: Cambridge University Press, 1995);

Lois Cuddy and David H. Hirsch, eds., *Critical Essays on T. S. Eliot's "The Waste Land"* (Boston: G. K. Hall, 1989);

J. L. Dawson, P. D. Holland, and D. J. McKitterick, eds., *A Concordance to The Complete Poems and Plays of T. S. Eliot* (Ithaca, N.Y.: Cornell University Press, 1995);

Denis Donoghue, *Words Alone: The Poet T. S. Eliot* (New Haven: Yale University Press, 2000);

Helen Gardner, *The Composition of Four Quartets* (New York: Oxford University Press, 1978);

Piers Gray, *T. S. Eliot's Intellectual and Poetic Development, 1909–1922* (Atlantic Highlands, N.J.: Humanities Press, 1982);

M. A. R. Habid, *The Early T. S. Eliot and Western Philosophy* (Cambridge: Cambridge University Press, 1999);

Jason Harding, *The Criterion: Cultural Politics and Periodical Networks in Inter-War Britain* (Oxford: Oxford University Press, 2002);

Eloise Knapp Hay, *T. S. Eliot's Negative Way* (Cambridge, Mass.: Harvard University Press, 1982);

Ted Hughes, *A Dancer to God: Tributes to T. S. Eliot* (New York: Farrar, Straus & Giroux, 1992);

Manju Jain, *A Critical Reading of The Selected Poems of T. S. Eliot* (Oxford: Oxford University Press, 1991);

Jain, *T. S. Eliot and American Philosophy* (Cambridge: Cambridge University Press, 1992);

Russell Kirk, *Eliot and His Age: T. S. Eliot's Moral Imagination in the Twentieth Century,* revised edition (Peru, Ill.: Sherwood Sugden, 1984);

Roger Kojecký, *T. S. Eliot's Social Criticism* (New York: Farrar, Straus & Giroux, 1972);

Cassandra Laity and Nancy K. Gish, eds., *Gender, Desire, and Sexuality in T. S. Eliot* (Cambridge: Cambridge University Press, 2004);

Edward Lobb, ed., *Words in Time: New Essays on Eliot's "Four Quartets"* (London: Athlone Press, 1993);

Benjamin G. Lockerd Jr., *Aethereal Rumours: T. S. Eliot's Physics & Poetics* (Lewisburg, Pa.: Bucknell University Press, 1998);

James Longenbach, *Modernist Poetics of History: Pound, Eliot, and the Sense of the Past* (Princeton: Princeton University Press, 1987);

Randy Malamud, *T. S. Eliot's Drama: A Research and Production Sourcebook* (Westport, Conn.: Greenwood Press, 1992);

Malamud, *Where the Words are Valid: T. S. Eliot's Communities of Drama* (Westport, Conn.: Greenwood Press, 1994);

Dominic Manganiello, *T. S. Eliot & Dante* (New York: St. Martin's Press, 1989);

John T. Mayer, *T. S. Eliot's Silent Voices* (Oxford: Oxford University Press, 1989);

Louis Menand, *Discovering Modernism: T. S. Eliot and His Context* (New York: Oxford University Press, 1987);

A. David Moody, *Thomas Stearns Eliot: Poet* (Cambridge: Cambridge University Press, 1994);

Moody, ed., *Cambridge Companion to T. S. Eliot* (Cambridge: Cambridge University Press, 1994);

Michael North, *The Political Aesthetic of Yeats, Eliot, and Pound* (Cambridge: Cambridge University Press, 1991);

North, *Reading 1922: A Return to the Scene of the Modern* (Oxford: Oxford University Press, 1999);

Jeffrey Perl, *Skepticism and Modern Enmity: Before and After Eliot* (Baltimore: Johns Hopkins University Press, 1989);

Lawrence Rainey, *Revisiting "The Waste Land"* (New Haven: Yale University Press, 2005);

Christopher Ricks, *Eliot and Prejudice* (Berkeley: University of California Press, 1988);

John Paul Riquelme, *Harmony of Dissonances: T. S. Eliot, Romanticism, and Imagination* (Baltimore: Johns Hopkins University Press, 1991);

Ronald Schuchard, *Eliot's Dark Angel: Intersections of Life and Art* (Oxford: Oxford University Press, 1999);

Sanford Schwartz, *The Matrix of Modernism: Pound, Eliot, & Early 20th-Century Thought* (Princeton: Princeton University Press, 1985);

Martin Scofield, *T. S. Eliot: The Poems* (Cambridge: Cambridge University Press, 1988);

Richard Shusterman, *T. S. Eliot and the Philosophy of Criticism* (New York: Columbia University Press, 1988);

Eric Sigg, *The American T. S. Eliot* (Cambridge: Cambridge University Press, 1989);

William Skaff, *The Philosophy of T. S. Eliot: From Skepticism to a Surrealist Poetic, 1909–1927* (Philadelphia: University of Pennsylvania Press, 1986);

B. C. Southam, *A Guide to the Selected Poems of T. S. Eliot*, sixth edition (San Diego: Harcourt Brace, 1994);

David Spurr, *Conflicts in Consciousness: T. S. Eliot's Poetry and Criticism* (Urbana: University of Illinois Press, 1984);

Stanley Sultan, *Eliot, Joyce & Company* (Oxford: Oxford University Press, 1987);

John Timmerman, *T. S. Eliot's Ariel Poems* (Lewisburg, Pa.: Bucknell University Press, 1994).

Papers:

The most valuable collections of T. S. Eliot's papers are located in the Eliot Collection, Houghton Library, Harvard University; the Henry W. and Albert A. Berg Collection, New York Public Library; the Hayward Collection, King's College at Cambridge University; the Donald Gallup papers, Beinecke Library, Yale University; and the Princeton University Library. Many of these papers are restricted, and one major collection (the Emily Hale papers at Princeton) is sealed until the year 2020. Smaller collections are located in several universities around the world. Some individuals—Valerie Eliot and several of the poet's surviving correspondents—also own valuable collections.

1948 Nobel Prize in Literature Presentation Speech

by Anders Österling, Permanent Secretary of the Swedish Academy

In the impressive succession of Nobel Prize winners in Literature, T. S. Eliot marks a departure from the type of writer that has most frequently gained that distinction. The majority have been representatives of a literature which seeks its natural contacts in the public consciousness, and which, to attain this goal, avails itself of the media lying more or less ready at hand. This year's Prize winner has chosen to take another path. His career is remarkable in that, from an extremely exclusive and consciously isolated position, he has gradually come to exercise a very far-reaching influence. At the outset he appeared to address himself to but a small circle of initiates, but this circle slowly widened, without his appearing to will it himself. Thus in Eliot's verse and prose there was quite a special accent, which compelled attention just in our own time, a capacity to cut into the consciousness of our generation with the sharpness of a diamond.

In one of his essays Eliot himself has advanced, as a purely objective and quite uncategorical assumption, that poets in our present civilization have to be difficult to approach. "Our civilization," he says, "comprehends great variety and complexity, and this variety and complexity, playing upon a refined sensibility, must produce various and complex results. The poet must become more and more comprehensive, more allusive, more indirect, in order to force, to dislocate if necessary, language into his meaning."

Against the background of such a pronouncement, we may test his results and learn to understand the importance of his contribution. The effort is worth-while. Eliot first gained his reputation as the result of his magnificent experiment in poetry, *The Waste Land,* which appeared in 1922 and then seemed bewildering in several ways, due to its complicated symbolic language, its mosaic-like technique, and its apparatus of erudite allusion. It may be recalled that this work appeared in the same year as another pioneer work, which had a still more sensational effect on modern literature, the much discussed *Ulysses,* from the hand of an Irishman, James Joyce. The parallel is by no means fortuitous, for these products of the nineteen-twenties are closely akin to one another, in both spirit and mode of composition.

The Waste Land—a title whose terrifying import no one can help feeling, when the difficult and masterly word-pattern has finally yielded up its secrets. The melancholy and sombre rhapsody aims at describing the aridity and impotence of modern civilization, in a series of sometimes realistic and sometimes mythological episodes, whose perspectives impinge on each other with an indescribable total effect. The cycle of poems consists of 436 lines, but actually it contains more than a packed novel of as many pages. *The Waste Land* now lies a quarter of a century back in time, but unfortunately it has proved that its catastrophic visions still have undiminished actuality in the shadow of the atomic age.

Since then Eliot has passed on to a series of poetic creations of the same brilliant concentration, in pursuance of the agonized, salvation-seeking main theme. The *horror vacui* of modern man in a secularized world, without order, meaning, or beauty, here stands out with poignant sincerity. In his latest work, *Four Quartets* (1943), Eliot has arrived at a meditative music of words, with almost liturgical refrains and fine, exact expressions of his spiritual experiences. The transcendental superstructure rises ever clearer in his world picture. At the same time a manifest striving after a positive, guiding message emerges in his dramatic art, especially in the mighty historical play about Thomas of Canterbury, *Murder in the Cathedral* (1935), but also in *The Family Reunion* (1939), which is a bold attempt to combine such different conceptions as the Christian dogma of original sin and the classical Greek myths of fate, in an entirely modern environment, with the scene laid in a country house in northern England.

The purely poetical part of Eliot's work is not quantitatively great, but as it now stands out against the horizon, it rises from the ocean like a rocky peak and indisputably forms a landmark, sometimes assuming the mystic contours of a cathedral. It is poetry impressed with the stamp of strict responsibility and extraordinary self-discipline, remote from all emotional clichés, concentrated entirely on essential things, stark, granitic, and unadorned, but from time to time illuminated by a sudden ray from the timeless space of miracles and revelations.

Insight into Eliot must always present certain problems to be overcome, obstacles which are at the same time stimulating. It may appear to be contradictory to say that this radical pioneer of form, the initiator of a whole revolution in style within present-day poetry, is at the same time a coldly reasoning, logically subtle theorist, who never wearies of defending historical perspectives and the necessity of fixed norms for our existence. As early as the 1940's, he had become a convinced supporter of the Anglican Church in religion and of classicism in literature. In view of this philosophy of life, which implies a consistent return to ideals standardized by age, it might seem that his modernistic practice would clash with his traditional theory. But this is hardly the case. Rather, in his capacity as an author, he has uninterruptedly and with varying success worked to bridge this chasm, the existence of which he must be fully and perhaps painfully conscious. His earliest poetry, so convulsively disintegrated, so studiously aggressive in its whole technical form, can finally also be apprehended as a negative expression of a mentality which aims at higher and purer realities and must first free itself of abhorrence and cynicism. In other words, his revolt is that of the Christian poet. It should also be observed in this connection that, on the whole, Eliot is careful not to magnify the power of poetry in relation to that of religion. In one place, where he wishes to point out what poetry can really accomplish for our inner life, he does so with great caution and reserve: "It may make us from time to time a little more aware of the deeper, unnamed feelings which form the substratum of our being, to which we rarely penetrate; for our lives are mostly a constant evasion of ourselves."

Thus, if it can be said with some justification that Eliot's philosophical position is based on nothing but tradition, it ought nevertheless to be borne in mind that he constantly points out how generally that word has been misused in today's debates. The word "tradition" itself implies movement, something which cannot be static, something which is constantly handed on and assimilated. In the poetic tradition, too, this living principle prevails. The existing monuments of literature form an idealistic order, but this is slightly modified every time a new work is added to the series. Proportions and values are unceasingly changing. Just as the old directs the new, this in its turn directs the old, and the poet who realizes this must also realize the scope of his difficulties and his responsibility.

Externally, too, the now sixty-year-old Eliot has also returned to Europe, the ancient and storm-tossed, but still venerable, home of cultural traditions. Born an American, he comes from one of the Puritan families who emigrated from England at the end of the seventeenth century. His years of study as a young man at the Sorbonne, at Marburg, and at Oxford, clearly revealed to him that at bottom he felt akin to the historical milieu of the Old World, and since 1927 Mr. Eliot has been a British subject.

It is not possible in this presentation to indicate more than the most immediate fascinating features in the complicated multiplicity of Eliot's characteristics as a writer. The predominating one is the high, philosophically schooled intelligence, which has succeeded in enlisting in its service both imagination and learning, both sensitivity and the analysis of ideas. His capacity for stimulating a reconsideration of pressing questions within intellectual and aesthetic opinion is also extraordinary, and however much the appraisement may vary, it can never be denied that in his period he has been an eminent poser of questions, with a masterly gift for finding the apt wording, both in the language of poetry and in the defence of ideas in essay form.

Nor is it due only to chance that he has written one of the finest studies of Dante's work and personality. In his bitter moral pathos, in his metaphysical line of thought, and in his burning longing for a world order inspired by religion, a *civitas dei,* Eliot has indeed certain points of contact with the great Florentine poet. It redounds to his honour that, amidst the varied conditions of his milieu, he can be justly characterized as one of Dante's latest-born successors. In his message we hear solemn echoes from other times, but that message does not by any means therefore become less real when it is given to our own time and to us who are now living.

Mr. Eliot—According to the diploma, the award is made chiefly in appreciation of your remarkable achievements as a pioneer within modern poetry. I have here tried to give a brief survey of this very important work of yours, which is admired by many ardent readers in this country.

Exactly twenty-five years ago, there stood where you are now standing another famous poet who wrote in the English tongue, William Butler Yeats. The honour now passes to you as being a leader and a champion of a new period in the long history of the world's poetry.

With the felicitations of the Swedish Academy, I now ask you to receive your Prize from the hands of His Royal Highness the Crown Prince.

[© The Nobel Foundation, 1948.]

Eliot: Banquet Speech

Introductory remarks by Gustaf Hellström of the Swedish Academy at the Nobel Banquet at the City Hall in Stockholm, 10 December 1948:

Humility is also the characteristic which you, Mr. Eliot, have come to regard as man's virtue. "The only wisdom we can hope to acquire is the wisdom of humility." At first it did not appear that this would be the final result of your visions and your acuity of thought. Born in the Middle West, where the pioneer mentality was still alive, brought up in Boston, the stronghold of Puritan tradition, you came to Europe in your youth and were there confronted with the prewar type of civilization in the Old World: the Europe of Edward VII, Kaiser Wilhelm, the Third Republic, and *The Merry Widow*. This contact was a shock to you, the expression of which you brought to perfection in *The Waste Land,* in which the confusion and vulgarity of the civilization became the object of your scathing criticism. But beneath that criticism there lay profound and painful disillusionment, and out of this disillusionment there grew forth a feeling of sympathy, and out of that sympathy was born a growing urge to rescue from the ruins of the confusion the fragments from which order and stability might be restored. The position you have long held in modern literature provokes a comparison with that occupied by Sigmund Freud, a quarter of a century earlier, within the field of psychic medicine. If a comparison might be permitted, the novelty of the therapy which he introduced with psychoanalysis would match the revolutionary form in which you have clothed your message. But the path of comparison could be followed still further. For Freud the most profound cause of the confusion lay in the *Unbehagen in der Kultur* of modern man. In his opinion there must be sought a collective and individual balance, which should constantly take into account man's primitive instincts. You, Mr. Eliot, are of the opposite opinion. For you the salvation of man lies in the preservation of the cultural tradition, which, in our more mature years, lives with greater vigour within us than does primitiveness, and which we must preserve if chaos is to be avoided. Tradition is not a dead load which we drag along with us, and which in our youthful desire for freedom we seek to throw off. It is the soil in which the seeds of coming harvests are to be sown, and from which future harvests will be garnered. As a poet you have, Mr. Eliot, for decades, exercised a greater influence on your contemporaries and younger fellow writers than perhaps anyone else of our time.

Eliot's speech

When I began to think of what I should say to you this evening, I wished only to express very simply my appreciation of the high honour which the Swedish Academy has thought fit to confer upon me. But to do this adequately proved no simple task: my business is with words, yet the words were beyond my command. Merely to indicate that I was aware of having received the highest international honour that can be bestowed upon a man of letters, would be only to say what everyone knows already. To profess my own unworthiness would be to cast doubt upon the wisdom of the Academy; to praise the Academy might suggest that I, as a literary critic, approved the recognition given to myself as a poet. May I therefore ask that it be taken for granted, that I experienced, on learning of this award to myself, all the normal emotions of exaltation and vanity that any human being might be expected to feel at such a moment, with enjoyment of the flattery, and exasperation at the inconvenience, of being turned overnight into a public figure? Were the Nobel Award similar in kind to any other award, and merely higher in degree, I might still try to find words of appreciation: but since it is different in kind from any other, the expression of one's feelings calls for resources which language cannot supply.

I must therefore try to express myself in an indirect way, by putting before you my own interpretation of the significance of the Nobel Prize in Literature. If this were simply the recognition of merit, or of the fact that an author's reputation has passed the boundaries of his own country and his own language, we could say that hardly any one of us at any time is, more than others, worthy of being so distinguished. But I find in the Nobel Award something more and something different from such recognition. It seems to me more the election of an individual, chosen from time to time from one nation or another, and selected by something like an act of grace, to fill a peculiar role and to become a peculiar symbol. A ceremony takes place, by which a man is suddenly endowed with some function which he did not fill before. So the question is not whether he was worthy to be so singled out, but whether he can perform the function which you have assigned to him: the function of serving as a representative, so far as any man can be, of a thing of far greater importance than the value of what he himself has written.

Poetry is usually considered the most local of all the arts. Painting, sculpture, architecture, music, can be enjoyed by all who see or hear. But language, especially the language of poetry, is a different matter. Poetry, it might seem, separates peoples instead of uniting them.

But on the other hand we must remember, that while language constitutes a barrier, poetry itself gives us a reason for trying to overcome the barrier. To enjoy poetry belonging to another language, is to enjoy an understanding of the people to whom that language belongs, an understanding we can get in no other way. We may think also of the history of poetry in Europe, and of the great influence that the poetry of one language can exert on another; we must remember the immense debt of every considerable poet to poets of other languages than his own; we may reflect that the poetry of every country and every language would decline and perish, were it not nourished by poetry in foreign tongues. When a poet speaks to his own people, the voices of all the poets of other languages who have influenced him are speaking also. And at the same time he himself is speaking to younger poets of other languages, and these poets will convey something of his vision of life and something of the spirit of his people, to their own. Partly through his influence on other poets, partly through translation, which must be also a kind of recreation of his poems by other poets, partly through readers of his language who are not themselves poets, the poet can contribute toward understanding between peoples.

In the work of every poet there will certainly be much that can only appeal to those who inhabit the same region, or speak the same language, as the poet. But nevertheless there is a meaning to the phrase "the poetry of Europe," and even to the word "poetry" the world over. I think that in poetry people of different countries and different languages—though it be apparently only through a small minority in any one country—acquire an understanding of each other which, however partial, is still essential. And I take the award of the Nobel Prize in Literature, when it is given to a poet, to be primarily an assertion of the supra-national value of poetry. To make that affirmation, it is necessary from time to time to designate a poet: and I stand before you, not on my own merits, but as a symbol, for a time, of the significance of poetry.

[© The Nobel Foundation, 1948. T. S. Eliot is the sole author of his speech.]

Odysseus Elytis
(2 November 1911 – 18 March 1996)

Marinos Pourgouris
Brown University

BOOKS: *Prosanatolismoi* (Athens: Pyrsos, 1939);

Ílios o Prôtos (Athens: Glaros, 1943);

Asma Îrôiko kai Penthimo gia ton chameno Anthypolochago tîs Alvanias (Athens: Ikaros, 1946);

To Axion Esti (Athens: Ikaros, 1959); translated by Edmund Keeley and George Savidis as *The Axion Esti* (Pittsburgh: University of Pittsburgh Press, 1974; London: Anvil Press Poetry, 1980);

Exî kai mia Typseis gia ton Oyrano (Athens: Ikaros, 1960);

O Ílios o Íliatora (Athens: Ikaros, 1971);

To Fôtodentro kai î Dekatî Tetartî Omorfia (Athens: Ikaros, 1971);

Ta Rô tou Erôta (Athens: Asterias, 1972; expanded edition, Athens: Ypsilon, 1986);

To Monogramma (Athens: Ikaros, 1972);

O Zôgrafos Theofilos (Athens: Ermeias, 1973);

Ta Eterothalî (Athens: Ikaros, 1974);

Anoichta Chartia (Athens: Ikaros, 1974); translated by Olga Broumas as *Open Papers* (Townsend, Wash.: Copper Canyon Press, 1995);

Î Mageia tou Papadiamantî (Athens: Ermeias, 1976);

Sîmatologeion (Athens: Ermeias, 1977);

Anaphora ston Andrea Empeiriko (Athens: Ikaros, 1978);

Maria Nefelî (Athens: Ikaros, 1978); translated by Athan Anagnostopoulos as *Maria Nephele: A Poem in Two Voices* (Boston: Houghton Mifflin, 1981);

Odysseas Elytis: Eklogî, 1935–1977, edited by Renas Chatzidaki (Athens: Akmon, 1979);

Tria Poiîmata me sîmaia Eykairias (Athens: Ikaros, 1982);

Îmerologio enos Atheatou Apriliou (Athens: Ypsilon, 1984); translated by David Connolly as *Journal of an Unseen April* (Athens: Ypsilon, 1998);

O Mikros Nautilos (Athens: Ikaros, 1986); translated by Broumas as *The Little Mariner* (Townsend, Wash.: Copper Canyon Press, 1999);

To Dômatio me tis Eikones, by Elytis and Eugenios Aranitsis (Athens: Ikaros, 1986);

Ta Dîmósia kaí ta Idiôtikî (Athens: Ikaros, 1990);

Idiôtikî Odos (Athens: Ypsilon, 1990);

Odysseus Elytis (left) receiving the 1979 Nobel Prize in Literature from King Carl XVI Gustaf of Sweden (AP Photo)

Ta Elegeia tîs Oxôpetras (Athens: Ikaros, 1991); translated by Connolly as *The Oxopetra Elegies* (Amsterdam: Harwood, 1996);

En Leukô (Athens: Ikaros, 1992); translated by Connolly as *Carte Blanche: Selected Writings* (Amsterdam: Harwood, 1999);

Dytika tîs Lypîs (Athens: Ikaros, 1995);

O Kîpos me tis Aytapates (Athens: Ypsilon, 1995);

2 X 7 E. (Athens: Ikaros, 1996);

Ek tou Plîsion, edited by Ioulita Iliopoulou (Athens: Ikaros, 1998);

Aytoprosôpografia se Logo Proforiko (Athens: Ypsilon, 2000).

Collection: *Poïisî* (Athens: Ikaros, 2002).

Editions in English: *The Sovereign Sun: Selected Poems*, translated by Kimon Friar (Philadelphia: Temple University Press, 1974; Newcastle upon Tyne: Bloodaxe, 1990);

Odysseus Elytis: Selected Poems, edited by Edmund Keeley and Philip Sherrard (New York: Viking, 1981; London: Anvil Press Poetry, 1981);

Six and One Remorses for the Sky: And Other Poems, translated by Jeffrey Carson (Helsinki: Eurographica, 1985);

What I Love: Selected Poems of Odysseas Elytis, translated by Olga Broumas (Townsend, Wash.: Copper Canyon Press, 1986);

The Collected Poems of Odysseus Elytis, translated by Carson and Nikos Sarris (Baltimore: Johns Hopkins University Press, 1997);

Eros, Eros, Eros: Selected and Last Poems, translated by Broumas (Townsend, Wash.: Copper Canyon Press, 1998).

TRANSLATIONS: *Deuterî Grafî* [anthology] (Athens: Ikaros, 1976);
Sappho, *Sapfô* (Athens: Ikaros, 1984);
Î Apokalypsî tou Iôannî (Athens: Ypsilon, 1985);
Krinagoras, *Krinagoras* (Athens: Ypsilon, 1987).

Odysseus Elytis is one of Greece's most celebrated writers, and in 1979 he became the second Greek poet (after George Seferis in 1963) to receive a Nobel Prize in Literature. He is generally credited, along with other poets of the 1930s generation, with redefining modern Greek identity in his poetry. His 1959 collection *To Axion Esti* (Worthy It Is; translated as *The Axion Esti,* 1974) exemplifies this redefinition of "Greekness." In his early career, Elytis was a fervent supporter of Surrealism and Freudian theory. Apart from his prolific poetic career, Elytis is known as a theorist and a painter. Influenced by Max Ernst's technique of collage, his paintings are often visual depictions of his poetic images, combining Byzantine iconography with sexuality, geographical loci with aesthetic symbolism, or abstract colorful representations with sensuality. Many of Elytis's poems have become relatively popular through having been set to music by such composers as Mikis Theodorakis, Manos Hadjidakis, Dimitris Lagios, and Linos Kokotos.

Elytis was born Odysseus Alepoudellis on 2 November 1911 in Heracleion, Crete. He was the sixth and last child of Maria and Panayiotis Alepoudellis, both from the island of Lesbos, who had moved to Crete and established, in 1895, a successful soap factory. In 1914 the Alepoudellis family business moved to the suburb of Piraeus in Athens, and young Odysseus and his family spent their summer vacations on Lesbos, a place often visited by the prominent Greek politician Eleftherios Venizelos, who became a close friend of the family. Elytis's childhood memories of the Aegean landscape and seascape later significantly influenced his poetry.

In 1916 he enrolled in the Makris Private School, which he attended for seven years. In the years that followed, the Alepoudellis family traveled extensively in Italy, Switzerland, Yugoslavia, and Germany and spent some summers on the island of Spetses. In 1918 the family suffered the loss of Elytis's eldest sister, Myrsini, who died on 31 December. In 1925, while vacationing on Spetses, Elytis's father died of pneumonia. Elytis later recounted the impact of these emotional wounds in "The Chronicle of a Decade," published in *Anoichta Charta* (1974; translated as *Open Papers,* 1995). He was deeply affected by these losses; less than two years after his father's death, Elytis suffered a nervous breakdown and was forced to spend two months in bed. His aspirations of becoming a track athlete were ended. While recovering in bed he fervently read Greek and foreign literature. The most profound influence on him was the work of Alexandrian poet Constantine Cavafy, which introduced him to poetry. "Cavafy was needed for me to be shaken," he later wrote in *Anoichta Chartia;* "A deep curiosity got hold of me, that was later destined to turn into a deep interest, and later on, a deep admiration."

In 1928 Elytis graduated from high school. That year the poet Kostas Karyotakis, whose pessimistic poetry explored the miserable state of society in the aftermath of industrialization and capitalism, committed suicide, and in subsequent years he became more popular among the youth than any other poet of the time. Strongly influenced by both Cavafy and Karyotakis, Elytis attempted to write his first poems in imitation of them. When, however, he discovered in Kaufmann's bookstore, in Athens, the Surrealist poetry of Paul Eluard, he came to the realization that the poetry of Cavafy and Karyotakis did not correspond to the way he experienced life as a young man. The discovery of Eluard's poetry is, perhaps, the most significant event in his early poetic orientation.

In 1930 Elytis entered the Law School of Athens University, where he met the young poet George Sarandaris, who ushered him even further into Surrealism. By 1934 Elytis destroyed all the poems he had written previously and wrote a new, short collection titled "Prota Poiîmata (First Poems). These poems were published in 1939 in the volume *Prosanatolismoi* (Orientations), in an edition of 310 copies. The first lines of the first poem of the collection read: "Eros / The archipelago," and these words became the most frequently repeated and explored concepts in his poetry. As the poet later confided in an interview on National Greek Television (included in *Aytoprosôpografia se Logo Proforiko* [2000, Self Portrait]), "It is characteristic that the first two verses of my book *[Prosanatolismoi]* are: 'Eros, the Archipelago.' In a way this foreshadows the entire evolution, in terms of content, of my poetry.'

The most important year in Elytis's poetic development was 1935, the year he met and befriended the poet Andreas Empeirikos. Together they attempted to promote the movement of Surrealism in Greece. Empeirikos had recently returned from France and was close to the French Surrealist circle. Along with Empeirikos and the painter Stratis Eleftheriadis-Teriade—the publisher of the well-known French Surrealist periodical *Minotaure*—Elytis traveled to Lesbos, where he was involved in the discovery and promotion of the art of folk painter Theophilos Hadjimichael (known by his first name), who died in 1934. Their efforts eventually culminated in the opening of a Theophilos Museum in Lesbos (in 1964) and the recognition of Theophilos by European artistic circles. Elytis's experiences in this regard are recounted in a 1973 long essay titled *O Zôgrafos Theofilos* (The Painter Theophilos).

Also in 1935, mobilizing around the literary magazine *Nea Grammata*, which presented his first poems, Elytis met the renowned poets Giorgos Katsimbalis and Seferis—a close friend of T. S. Eliot and Ezra Pound. In 1936 he also met the poet Nikos Gatsos, of whom he became a lifelong friend. In the next few years, this generation of mostly young writers and artists established Greece's first literary cafés and produced some of the most profound poetry in modern Greek literature. They became known as "The Generation of the Thirties."

In 1940 Benito Mussolini's army invaded Greece, and Elytis was recalled to serve as a second lieutenant on the Albanian front. He had already joined the army in December 1936 and had trained at the School of Reserve Officers in Corfu from January to September 1937, completing his service in March 1938. During Mussolini's invasion, Elytis's unit served under fire, and after a long and tiring campaign, he contracted typhus and was admitted, severely ill, to a hospital in Ioannina. He recovered and returned to an Athens that was, by then, occupied by German forces. During the Nazi occupation of Greece (1941–1944), Elytis worked on two collections of poetry: *Ílios o Prôtos* (1943, Sun the First, published in an edition of 600 copies) and *Asma Îrôiko kai Penthimo gia ton chameno Anthypolochago tîs Alvanias* (Song Heroic and Mourning for the Lost Second Lieutenant of the Albanian Campaign, first published in 1945 in the periodical *Tetradio*, then as a book in 1946).

Ílios o Prôtos is filled with images of beautiful naked bodies, sunny Greek landscapes, and blooming orchards. It clearly states the refusal of the poet to succumb to the weight of oppression and presents his resistance to whatever violates the free expression of the human spirit. The first poem of the collection—all the poems are numbered and usually bear no titles—expresses precisely this resistance to the "darkness" that is often imposed on people: "I no more know the night death's fearful anonymity / In an inlet of my soul moors a fleet of stars." This refusal to compromise and adjust to an oppressive force does not simply refer to the particular historical period of Greece's occupation by the Germans. The suggestions are clearly universal, referring to a wider definition of oppression. In some poems, resistance to the historically dark times is suggested in images of natural regeneration:

> It's a long time since the last rain was heard
> Above the ants and lizards
> Now the sky burns boundless
> Fruits paint their mouths
> Earth's pores slowly open
> And by water dripping in syllables
> A huge plant looks the sun in the eye!

Sanguine messages of both personal and collective regeneration are scattered throughout the collection: "What I love is born incessantly," and "we build and dream and sing."

The second collection that draws from Elytis's wartime experience is *Asma Îrôiko kai Penthimo gia ton chameno Anthypolochago tîs Alvanias*. Elytis described the principal concept behind the collection to his translator Kimon Friar:

> The virtues I found embodied and living in my comrades formed in synthesis a brave young man of heroic stature, one whom I saw in every period of our history. They had killed him a thousand times, and a thousand times he had sprung up again, breathing and alive. He was no doubt the measure of our civilization, compounded of his love not of death but of life. It was with his love of Freedom he recreated life out of the stuff of death.

As in *Ílios o Prôtos,* Elytis constructs an alternative reality that transubstantiates the enslaving conditions of war and death into a song for freedom. The heroic stature of the second lieutenant is juxtaposed to those forces that violate human freedom: "Those who committed the evil—a black cloud took them / But he who confronted it in the sky's roads / Ascends now alone and resplendent!" The mood of the collection is slowly uplifted with each poem: whereas the collection begins with a mournful lament over the passing of the sun and the coming of darkness, it ends with a hope of regeneration made possible because of the second lieutenant's sacrifice: "Now the dream beats faster in the blood / The world's rightest moment rings out: / Freedom, / Greeks show the way in the darkness: / FREEDOM / For you the sun will weep with joy."

Following the conclusion of World War II and the departure of the German occupying forces from Greece, a civil war broke out between leftist guerillas and the national government. Like many other Greeks who were suspected of leftist sympathies, Elytis was denied a passport and remained confined in Greece until 1948, when he was finally given permission to travel outside the country. Leaving Greece, he went to Paris, where he met most of the poets he had been admiring from a distance, including André Breton, Pierre Reverdy, Pierre-Jean Jouve, Giuseppe Ungaretti, Eliot, and Eluard (Elytis had already met Eluard during the latter's visit to Greece in 1946). The painter Eleftheriadis-Teriade also put him in contact with Pablo Picasso. Still in Paris in 1949, he met the painters Henri Matisse, Fernand Léger, and Alberto Giacometti. Though the Greek government refused to renew his passport, he stayed in Paris, and in 1950 he met Jean-Paul Sartre and Albert Camus. His encounters and friendships with these writers, painters, and thinkers are described in "The Chronicle of a Decade." He returned to Athens in 1951.

During the 1950s Elytis worked on and published two major collections: *To Axion Esti* (1959, Worthy It Is, translated as *The Axion Esti*, 1980) and *Exî kai mia Typseis gia ton Oyrano* (1960, Six and One Remorses for the Sky, published in an edition of 550 copies). *To Axion Esti* is, without a doubt, Elytis's most popular collection both in Greece and abroad. He began working on it around 1954 and sent it to his publisher in 1959; the first edition was 815 copies. It is a monumental and long work divided into three sections that bear hymnological titles: "The Genesis," "The Passion," and "The Gloria." In "The Genesis" seven free-verse hymns are presented, each describing stages in the creation of the Greek landscape (by the poet/seer) and the aesthetic principles that accompany it. The first line of the section is "In the beginning the light," bringing to mind the Book of Genesis ("Let there be light," 1.3) as well as the first sentence of John's Gospel ("In the beginning was the Word," 1.1). The poet continues to literarily re-create the Greek landscape (the intense light of the sun, the archipelago, the islands) until his psyche begins to resemble the world he has created: "This then am I / and the world the Small the Great." The second section, "The Passion," is the most architecturally complex part. Translators Jeffrey Carson and Nikos Sarris, in *The Collected Poems of Odysseus Elytis* (1997), describe the structural division of this section ("sequence"):

> Three forms are represented in this sequence: free verse psalms (P), odes of complex metrical responsion (O), and prose readings (R). There are three sections, identically structured: PPOROPPOROPP. In the first, consciousness confronts tradition (Greeks resist in Albania in World War II); in the second it confronts danger (occupation of Greece in WWII); in the third, it overcomes danger (civil war, post WWII).

"The Gloria" is a celebration of Greek landscape, poetic creation, and the feminine body. It celebrates the triumph of the eternal creative forces (both natural and human) over ephemeral human concerns: "Now the Gods' humiliation Now the ashes of Man / Now Now the zero / and Forever the world the small the great!" Though *To Axion Esti* was highly praised in academic and artistic circles, it remained largely unknown to the Greek public until the composer Theodorakis set it to music in 1964. The success that followed the first performance of the work was unprecedented.

Like *To Axion Esti*, *Exî kai mia Typseis gia ton Oyrano* was sent to the publisher in 1959. This collection, however, does not present a unified theme but rather consists of seven poems with different topics. In one of the most powerful poems of the collection, "The Autopsy," the body of a young man is dissected; but instead of flesh and blood, what is revealed is emotional or imagistic experiences, always connected to Nature: "the olive root's gold" in his heart, "the intense cyan-blue horizon line" beneath his skin, and "glaucous traces in the blood." In what became a recurring technique in Elytis's poetry, landscape is infused with sentiment and becomes a projection and celebration of the human body.

In the 1960s, translators abroad began to take notice of Elytis's poetry, and translations of his poems appeared in German, English, Italian, and French. During this period, Elytis traveled extensively. In 1961 he journeyed to the United States as a guest of the State Department; he visited New York, Washington, New Orleans, Santa Fe, Los Angeles, San Francisco, Buffalo, and Boston, and he met Yves Bonnefoy and Allen Ginsberg. In 1962, invited by the Soviet government, he visited the Soviet Union along with Empeirikos and Giorgos Theotokas; the three traveled to Odessa, Moscow, and Leningrad, and met Yevgeny Yevtuchenko. In 1965, invited by the Union of Bulgarian Writers, he visited Bulgaria and toured the country accompanied by the local poet Elisaveta Bagriana. In 1967, just before the military coup, he visited Egypt (Alexandria, Cairo, Luxor, and Aswan), and in 1969, unable to work under the fascist regime in Greece, he moved to Paris, where he stayed for about a year. In 1971, still in self-exile, he stayed in Cyprus for four months.

In 1961, while aboard the ship bringing him to the United States, Elytis composed the song cycle "Little Cyclades," included in his 1972 collection *Ta Ró tou Erôta* (The Rhos of Eros), which was later set to music, like *To Axion Esti,* by various Greek composers. The songs of "Little Cyclades" praise the luminous beauty of the Cycladic landscape, as presented through emotionally charged moments in life: love (as in the song "Marina"), separation (as in "The Little Northern Wind"), or simply joy (as in "The Poulia"). Elytis's interest in lyric poetry and music also led to the composition in 1970 (during his stay in Cyprus) of a libretto, *O Ílios o Íliatora* (1971, The Sovereign Sun), which was put to music by Lagios. These songs return to the ever-present (in Elytis's poetry) symbol of the sun and the emotional values it comes to represent in the Greek landscape. As in *Ílios o Prôtos,* Elytis evokes natural elements of the Greek landscape (sun, winds, mountains, sea) and man-made elements that harmoniously coexist with this landscape (fishing boats, orchards, beautiful young bodies) in order to confront the historical darkness of political oppression and social stagnation.

In 1972 the Greek fascist government offered him the Grand Prize for Literature, which he refused. Around the same time he was awarded a grant by the Ford Foundation, which enabled him to survive the economic hardships of the early 1970s. Meanwhile, he continued to compose poetry but refused to publish anything in Athens (because of the dictatorial regime). His two collections of poetry composed during the Junta rule were published in Cyprus instead. *To Fôtodentro kai î Dekatî Tetartî Omorfia* (The Light-Tree and the Fourteenth Beauty) was written between 1969 and 1970 and was published in 1971. In these poems, as he explained in a 1979 interview with Andonis Decavalles (quoted in *The Collected Poems of Odysseus Elytis*), Elytis returns to the use of light: "I give Greece again through the analogy of light upon the senses. . . . I express in them [the poems] my poetic understanding of the quintessence of the Greek realm." The twenty-one poems of the collection are united not only in their use of light but also, as the critic Mario Vitti notes, in their attitude toward death:

> In the *Light-Tree* death is something immanent in humans, a natural, unavoidable, and unknown episode. Fear towards it remains in the boundaries of stoicism. The poet does not attempt a mood of rebellion against it; neither does he try to justify it by turning it into a power tending towards light. . . .

The second collection of poetry published by Elytis in Cyprus during the Junta years was *To Monogramma* (The Monogram), which appeared in 1972. It is one of his most erotic collections, consisting of seven poems, all addressed to an unknown and absent beloved. One of its astounding characteristics is its strict architectural structure. Each poem has a specific number of lines (all multiples of seven), and the lines within each poem are visually symmetric. The first poem (seven lines) has a 3-1-3 line structure; the second poem (twenty-one lines) has a 3-4-7-4-3 line structure; the third poem (thirty-five lines) has a 1-7-5-9-5-7-1 line structure; the fourth and longest poem (forty-nine lines) has an 11-1-7-11-7-1-11 line structure; the fifth poem is symmetrical to the third; the sixth to the second; and the seventh to the first. This volume was not the first time Elytis used symmetry and architecture in his poetry. In fact, all of his collections are related to the number seven (usually including seven poems or multiples of seven). In addition to *To Monogramma,* the number appears continually in his poetry: *Prosanatolismoi* includes "Seven Nocturnal Heptastichs" (seven poems of seven lines each), "Windows toward the Fifth Season" (seven poems), "Orion" (seven poems of seven lines each), "Dionysos" (seven poems), "Clepsydras of the Unknown" (seven poems), "Clear Skies" (twenty-one poems), and "The Concert of the Hyacinths" (twenty-one poems); *Ílios o Prôtos* includes twenty-one poems; and *Asma Îrôiko kai Penthimo gia ton chameno Anthypolochago tîs Alvanias* includes fourteen poems. Many of his collections are also symmetrical, as, for example, the poems of *Prosanatolismoi.*

In 1974 Elytis published *Ta Eterothalî* (The Stepchildren), two units of seven poems each. All the poems of this collection are dated and placed in chronological sequence: the first, "Psalm and Mosaic for Spring in Athens," is dated 1939, and the last, "Mystic Versicles," is dated 1972. Apart from the abundant references to ancient Greek sources, this collection includes odes or poems referring to particular individuals that Elytis befriended: Picasso ("Ode to Pablo Picasso"), the poet Sarandaris ("George Sarandaris"), the painter Nikos Hadjikyriakos Ghikas ("Small Analogon"), and Eleftheriadis-Teriade ("Villa Natacha").

After the fall of the Junta, Elytis began working on two poetry collections and various essays. In 1974 he published *Anoichta Chartia,* a volume of essays dating from the mid 1930s to the 1970s. This volume includes the lengthy "Chronicle of a Decade," one of the most important accounts of the reception of the Surrealist movement in Greece and one of the first attempts to establish a specifically Hellenic modernist literary tradition. He also worked extensively on a series of essays that were eventually published, in 1992, under the title *En Leukô* (translated as *Carte Blanche: Selected Writings,* 1999). This publication includes *Anaphora ston Andrea Empeiriko* (Report to Andreas Empeirikos, first published in 1978)—a moving eulogy of his good friend, who passed away in 1975. Around 1974 Elytis also began working on one of his most powerful collections, which was published in 1978 under the title *Maria Nefeli* (translated as *Maria Nephele*, 1981).

Maria Nefeli is divided into three parts, each representing a "dialogue," or simultaneous monologues, between two voices: Maria Nephele, a girl of the city, and the Antiphonist, the voice of the poet. Etymologically, "Nephele" in ancient Greek means "cloud," giving a mood of inapproachable melancholy to the character; apart from its literal meaning as "the other voice," the word "Antiphonist" designates, in the Orthodox tradition, the chanter who sings responsively to, or reciprocates, the main chant. Elytis also returns to a strict architectural structure and the use of the number seven. Each of the three parts is divided into fourteen poems: seven are narrated by the Antiphonist and seven by Maria Nephele. Visually, each poem narrated by the Antiphonist is placed next to a poem narrated by Maria Nephele (or vice versa), forcing an exchange between the two characters. When Maria Nephele is distressed (as in "Bonjour Tristesse"), the Antiphonist transforms sadness into a playful song (as in "Morning Exercises"); Maria Nephele talks about the tourist-filled modern island of Mykonos as the island of her choice, whereas the Antiphonist prefers the more isolated and unpopular island of Patmos; she speaks of her "Twenty-Four-Hour Life," while he speaks of "The Lifelong Moment"; she argues that every age has its Trojan War, and he responds that every age has its Helen.

In 1975 Elytis was offered an honorary doctorate from the Philosophical School of the University of Thessaloníki, and he was proclaimed an honorary citizen of Lesbos. In 1979 he was proclaimed an honorary citizen of Heracleion, Crete. In 1975 *Books Abroad* dedicated an entire issue to his poetry; in 1976 *Exî kai mia Typseis gia ton Oyrano* was translated into French; and in 1978 Ingemar Rhedin began translating *To Axion Esti* into Swedish. The greatest surprise for the poet, however, came in October 1979, when the secretary of the Swedish Academy announced the awarding of the 1979 Nobel Prize in Literature to Elytis "for his poetry, which, against the background of Greek tradition, depicts with sensuous strength and intellectual clear-sightedness modern man's struggle for freedom and creativeness." Other candidates for the 1979 Nobel Prize in Literature included Graham Greene, Jorge Luis Borges, Gabriel García Márquez, and Simone de Beauvoir. The announcement was understandably received with tremendous enthusiasm in Greece.

Elytis went to Stockholm to receive the prize. His lecture was delivered in French rather than Greek, not simply because he was fluent in that language but because, as evident throughout his essays, he wished to emphasize direct communication rather than translation, which (as he stressed in his lecture) is always bound to fail. On 8 December, in the Stockholm Concert Hall, Elytis began his lecture by setting the general mood of his poetic ideology:

> May I be permitted, I ask you, to speak in the name of luminosity and transparency? The space I have lived in and where I have been able to fulfill myself is defined by these two states. States that I have also perceived as being identified in me with the need to express myself.

The connection between poetical expression and life as well as the association of life with "luminosity and transparency"—inevitably linked with the Greek landscape—are indeed characteristics that underline the conceptualization of his entire poetic creation. To put it simply, he links ethical values to physical values. In *Anoichta Chartia* the concept is further elaborated: "In Greece light and history are one and the same thing—meaning that in the final analysis the one reproduces the other, the one interprets and justifies the other, even the void which is blackness; for this country, by offering equality of ethical and physical values, does not happen to know any other chiaroscuro."

The awarding of the Nobel Prize increased media attention to Elytis's work, and for the first time public interest was also drawn to his artwork, which he had engaged in as far back as 1935. Stockholm's Thyelska Galeriet exhibited many of his collages in 1979, and the Zoumboulakis Gallery exhibited them in Athens the following year. His first artistic attempts had been greatly influenced by Surrealism and particularly by the paintings of Ernst, Yves Tanguy, and Oscar Domínguez. Elytis turned to the art of collage more seriously in the 1960s, and he continued to create collages, inexhaustibly, until his death. His conceptions are sometimes purely based on color and shape (as in the work of Piet Mondrian, Georges Braque, or Matisse), or they represent images that are often found in his poetry. Some of these collages were published in his collections: his early collages are included in *Ta Rô tou Erôta* and in Ilias Petropoulou's *Elytís, Moralís, Tsarouchís* (1974), while the collages of the 1980s and 1990s are mainly collected in the 1986 publication *To Dômatio me tis Eikones* (The Room with the Icons, with text by Eugenios Aranitsis) and Elytis's 1995 book of prose titled *O Kípos me tis Aytapates* (The Garden with the Self-Deceptions).

Elytis lived and continued to create for seventeen years after receiving the Nobel Prize in Literature. His post-Nobel popularity kept him busy. The few years that immediately followed the Nobel presentation were spent almost entirely on award receptions, presentations, and speeches around the globe. In 1980 he was presented with an honorary doctorate from the Sorbonne in France, and in 1981 he received an honorary doctorate from the University of London. He was also declared an honorary citizen of Larnaca and Paphos (Cyprus), and he was invited by the Spanish prime minister Adolfo Suárez González to visit Spain, where he was declared an honorary citizen of Toledo (in the fall of 1980). The Royal Society of Literature (United Kingdom) presented him with the Benson Medal in 1981, an award given as lifetime recognition in poetry, fiction, history, and belles lettres. Also in 1981, Rutgers University, in the United States, established the Elytis Chair of Modern Greek Studies in honor of the poet, and in March 1982 he was presented, by Mayor D. Beis of Athens, with the Gold Medal of Honor of the City of Athens.

During the 1980s Elytis published three collections of poetry: *Tria Poiïmata me sîmaia Eykairias* (1982, Three Poems Under a Flag of Convenience), *Ïmerologio enos Atheatou Apriliou* (1984; translated as *Journal of an Unseen April*, 1998), and *O Mikros Nautilos* (1986; translated as *The Little Mariner*, 1999). He also published three books of translations: *Sapfô* (1984, Sappho), *Î Apokalypsî tou Iôannî* (1985, St. John's Revelation), and *Krinagoras* (1987). Along with *Deuterî Grafî* (Second Writing), published in 1976, these translations are testimony to the wide spectrum of poetic interests and influences in Elytis's work. His translations include the poetry of Jouve, Eluard, Ungaretti, Arthur Rimbaud, Comte de Lautréamont, Vladimir Mayakovsky, Federico García Lorca, Bertolt Brecht, and Isidore Lucien Ducasse.

Tria Poiïmata me sîmaia Eykairias presents three long poems ("The Garden Sees," "The Almond of the World," and "Ad Libitum"), each divided into seven subsections. In "The Garden Sees," the poet reaffirms his conviction that art is a force that creates life:

> Whether Plotinus was right
> or not will one day become clear
> the great eye with its transparency
> and a sea behind it like Helen
> binding the sun
> together with other flowers in her hair
> a million signs
> omega zeta eta.

(A rearrangement of the three Greek letters "omega zeta eta" reveals the word "Zoe," which means Life.) The Garden "sees": it is not merely a decorative realm but also a creative force that looks back at the viewer, much like art does. Life is also celebrated in "The Almond of the World," where the poet playfully views it as "One more cigarette / which lasts until we expire," but "with really superb moments." The last section, "Ad Libitum," ends with a revealing postscript: "the more I age the less I understand / experience untaught me the world." Old age brings the poet to a wise silence, where "the omega leans to alpha" and "disunites time."

Elytis returns to the beginning of his youthful interests with *Ïmerologio enos Atheatou Apriliou*. It is a dated diary of forty-nine entries, spanning from 1 April to 7 May 1981, and it is reminiscent of his early experiments with Surrealism. Although, as he often repeated, he was never an orthodox Surrealist, the entries in this collection appear to be more personal; the images are dreamlike, often reaching deep into the poet's childhood memories.

Elytis's greatest poetic achievement of the 1980s is undoubtedly *O Mikros Nautilos*. Like *To Axion Esti* and *Maria Nephele,* it is a highly structured collection composed of four sections in prose, titled "To Anoint the Repast" (each section is divided into seven short narratives), alternating with three sections in verse, titled "With Both Light and Death" (each section is divided into seven poems). Each prose section is preceded by a separate part, titled "Spotlight," and each verse section is followed by a section titled "What One Loves." The entire collection is introduced with an "Entrance" and concluded with an "Exit."

The "Entrance" introduces "journeying" as the underlining theme of the collection. The seven scenes of each "Spotlight" describe horrible moments in the history of Greece and specific moments of betrayal from ancient to modern Greece, such as Miltiades's condemnation and Phidias's imprisonment in the fifth century B.C.; Emperor Constantine's arrest of his own son Crispus in the Byzantine years; and the imprisonment of Kolokotronis, a celebrated Greek hero of the 1821 revolution. "What One Loves" is a compilation of "snapshots," or moments, that the poet collects in his metaphorical travel bag: lines of poetry (from Sappho, Sophocles, Cavafy, William Blake, Friedrich Hölderlin, Novalis, and Pound), references to concerts, symphonies, and songs (by Antonio Vivaldi, Wolfgang Amadeus Mozart, Ludwig von Beethoven, Theodorakis, and Hadjidakis), paintings (by Paul Klee, Matisse, Picasso, Braque, Juan Gris, and Jean Arp), or simply words that the poet finds interesting (such as Alexandra, anemone, bergamot, and bougainvillea) and geographical places with which he has some emotional connection (Corfu, Lesbos, Aegina, Cyprus, Chios, and Cairo). "Anoint the Repast" and "With Both Light and Death" are the most elaborate sections of *O Mikros Nautilos,* as the poet expresses himself in lucid philosophical concepts or emotionally charged images. The "Exit" ends in a surprisingly pensive tone with the poet speculating whether his personal creations are able to influence the public sphere (and as a consequence provide a sense of justice), or whether they simply remain "small happinesses" relevant only to himself.

Elytis further continues to explore the relationship between the public and the private spheres in two works published in 1990: *Ta Dîmósia kaí ta Idiôtikî* (The Public and the Private) and *Idiôtikî Odos* (The Private Road). In the last five years of his life he also wrote two poetic collections, *Ta Elegeia tîs Oxôpetras* (1991, The Elegies of the Jutting Rock, translated as *The Oxopetra Elegies*, 1996) and *Dytika tîs Lypîs* (1995, West of Sorrow). Publication of *Ta Elegeia tîs Oxôpetras* coincided with the celebration of Elytis's eightieth birthday. It is a book of fourteen poems that, as Carson suggests, are modeled after the elegies of Hölderlin. Like *O Mikros Nautilos*, this collection also begins with the announcement of a journey: "Now, I look forward to the boat that, even if you get in it, / Will arrive empty at a long sea Kerameikos / With stone Korai holding flowers." The poems that follow take the reader to a fixed time where the actions of poets are "elegized." The poet remembers Hölderlin's mad love for Susette Gontard (in "Cupid and Psyche"), Novalis's beloved, twelve-year-old Sophie von Kühn (in "Elegy of Grüningen"), and one of his favorite nineteenth-century Greek poets, Dionysios Solomos (in "Awe and Whelming of Solomos"). One of the most personal elegies of the collection is "La Pallida Morte" (Pale Death), which, as Elytis's translators suggest, was composed after he "spent part of the winter of 1989–90 in the Evangelismos Hospital in Athens, suffering from anemia." The poem announces this "near-death" experience from its opening line ("Scentless is death yet / The nostrils catch it like / A flower . . ."), and it gradually moves to declaring Death's inability to kill the poet: "But of these men, death, nobody knows anything to say / Except the poet. Jesus of the sun. Who then rises every Saturday / He. The Is, the Was, and the Coming."

Elytis's final collection, *Dytika tîs Lypîs,* was written in the summer of 1995 in Porto Rafti, Greece, where the poet was vacationing with fellow poet Ioulita Iliopoulou, who had been his partner for about a decade (he had never married nor had children). The seven poems of the collection are "more dense," as Elytis wrote to Carson, "and for this reason more difficult, but closer to my ideal." The title of the collection signals its mood: on one hand, the life of the eighty-three-year-old poet is moving westward toward its setting; but on the other hand, it also moves "west of sorrow," that is, beyond where sorrow itself sets. The biographical events in the poet's life are insignificant: "what remains," the collection concludes, "is poetry alone."

Elytis died of a stroke in his apartment in Athens (23 Skoufa Street) on 18 March 1996. A posthumous collection titled *Ek tou Plîsion* (From Nearby) was put together by his heir, Iliopoulou, and was published in 1998.

Odysseus Elytis's popularity in Greece remains astounding. He became a national commodity after the Nobel Prize, as evident in a continuous inclusion of his name in cultural and national symbolism: more than a dozen streets in Greece and Cyprus are named after him; a life-sized statue sculpted by Yiannis Papas was placed in one of Kolonaki's most central squares (Plateia Dexamenis); and a cruise ship, a theater on the island of Ios, and a hotel in Thessaly have all been given his name. Biographical information and scattered lines from his poetry adorn tourist pamphlets enticing visitors to travel to the Greek islands. Such cultural incorporation comes as a stark contrast not only in relation to the deeper essence of his poetry but also to the ascetic life he had led in his small apartment. Elytis's poetry clearly resists superficial classifications. His multifaceted style of writing, along with his lucid theoretical formulations, earned him an enduring place in modern Greek literature.

References:

Roderick Beaton, *Eisagôgî stî Neoellînikî Logotechnia* (Athens: Ekdoseis Nefelî, 1996);

Books Abroad, special Elytis issue, 49, no. 4 (1975);

Andonis Decavalles, *O Elytîs: Ap? to Chryso ôs to Asîmenio Poiîma* (Athens: Kedros, 1988);

Decavalles, *Odysseus Elytis: From the Golden to the Silver Poem* (New York: Pella, 1994);

Nikos Demou, *Odysseus Elytis* (Athens: Ekdoseis Nefelî, 1992);

Daniil Iakov, *Î Archaiognôsia tou Odyssea Elytîs* (Athens: Ekdoseis Zîtros, 2000);

Ivar Ivask, *Odysseus Elytis: Analogies of Light* (Norman: University of Oklahoma Press, 1981);

Andreas Karantonis, *Gia ton Odyssea Elytîs* (Athens: Ekdoseis Papadîma, 1992);

M. G. Meraklis, *Dekapente Ermîneutikes Dokimes gia ton Odyssea Elytîs* (Athens: Ekdoseis Patakî, 1984);

Andreas Mpelezinis, *O Opsimos Elytîs* (Athens: Ikaros, 1999);

Ilias Petropoulou, *Elytîs, Moralîs, Tsarouchîs* (Athens: Pleias, 1974);

Mario Vitti, *Gia ton Odyssea Elytîs* (Athens: Ekdoseis Kastaniôtî, 1998);

Vitti, *Î Genia tou Trianta: Ideologia kai Morfî* (Athens: Ermîs, 2000);

Vitti, *Odysseas Elytîs* (Athens: Ermîs, 1991).

1979 Nobel Prize in Literature Presentation Speech

*by Dr. Karl Ragnar Gierow, of the Swedish Academy
(Translation from the Swedish)*

Your Majesties, Your Royal Highnesses, Ladies and Gentlemen,

When Giorgos Seferis, compatriot of this year's Nobel Prize winner in literature, came here in 1963 to receive the same award, he presented at the airport a bunch of hyacinths each to the then Secretary of the Swedish Academy and to its officiating director that winter as a greeting to their respective wives. He had picked them himself on Hymettus, the mountain a few miles east of Athens where Aphrodite had her miraculous spring and where, ever since antiquity, hyacinths grow wild in a profusion which makes the whole mountain smell of honey.

The episode comes naturally to mind now that we have the pleasure of welcoming Odysseus Elytis, the Greek writer who in his youth made his name with the collection *The Concert of Hyacinths,* in which he calls to his beloved: "Take with you the light of hyacinths and baptize it in the wellspring of day" and assures her that "when you glitter in the sun that on you glides waterdrops, and deathless hyacinths, and silences, I proclaim you the only reality."

But there is a more immediate reason today to think of the chivalrous gesture in the inhospitable sleet of the airport. The hyacinths Seferis gave us were not at all like those we are accustomed to see. And, freshly picked as they were, they became symbols not only of the climatic difference between the giver's sunny south and our snowy north. If Odysseus Elytis, the author of *The Concert of Hyacinths,* had wished to use that flower as one of the analogies between environment and perception that are an essential part of his cultural outlook, he could have said that our potplants are a west-European rationalization of something which in his country grows wild, thereby acquiring its everlasting beauty. To this beauty he has devoted most of what he has written, and a recurrent theme is the prevalent west-European misconception of all that goes to make up the distinctive world of ideas whose legitimate heir he is.

He has arrived at his critical view of our all too rationalistic picture of Greece, which he traces back to the Renaissance's ideal of antiquity, by his own familiarity with western Europe's poetry, art and way of thinking. It may seem like a paradox—one which he himself has pointed out—that it was this western Europe, branded by him for its sterile rationalism, which gave Elytis the impulse that all at once set free his own writing: surrealism, which cannot be said to exaggerate reason.

The paradox is, if not apparent, at any rate not entirely unusual. Like a rebellious pulse of exuberant life surrealism broke through the hardened arteries of calcified forms. Outside France too poetry was dominated by a school which called itself "Les Parnassiens" but which never reached even the foot of Parnassus, if we share Elytis's view of what Greece has been and still is. But also on the Greek Parnassus of that time sat the same connoisseurs of degeneration who, in ornate words, declared their pessimistic conviction that nothing in this world was worth anything except their ability to express perfectly this very thought. If such an atmosphere is to be called captivating, surrealism came as a liberation, a religious revival, even if the sign of the saved here and there was a mere speaking with tongues.

But much of the best that happens when an art form is rejuvenated is not the result of a definite program but the fruit of an unforeseen cross. For Greek poetry the contact with surrealism meant a flowering which allows us to call the last fifty years Hellas's second highwater mark. In none of the numerous important poets who have created this age of greatness can we see more clearly than in Elytis what this vigorous cross signified: the exciting meeting between epoch-making modernism and inherited myth.

A cursory presentation of a poet hard to understand should, then, first establish his relationship to these two components—surrealism and myth. The task is not as easy as it looks. We have his own word for it: "I considered surrealism," he says on the one hand, "as the last available oxygen in a dying world, dying, at least, in Europe." On the other hand he states definitely: "I never was a disciple of the surrealist school." Nor was he. Elytis will have nothing to do with its fundamental poetry, the automatic writing with its unchecked torrent of chance associations. His explorations in poetry's means of expression lead him to surrealism's antipodes. Even if its violent display of unproven combinations released his own writing, he is a man of strict form, the master of deliberate creation.

Read his *To Axion Estí,* by many regarded as his most representative work. With its painstaking composition and stately rhetoric it leaves not one syllable to chance. Or take his love poem *Monogram,* with its ingenious mathematical basis; it has few counterparts in the literature we know. It comprises seven songs, each with seven lines or multiples of seven in a rising scale 7-2 1-35 up to the middle song's culmination of 49, where the poem turns round and descends the staircase with exactly the same number of lines, 35-21—down to the final song's 7, the starting point. This is nothing that need worry the poem's readers; it has its beauty without our having to count its steps. But poetry with this structure like an Euclidean linear drawing does not take after surrealism's *écriture automatique*.

Elytis's relationship to the other component, to Greek myth, also calls for clarification. We are used to seeing Greece's treasure of myths melted down and remoulded to contemporary west-European patterns. We have an Antigone à la Racine, an Antigone à la Anouilh and we shall have more. For Elytis such treatment is odious, a rationalistic pot-cultivation of wildflowers. He himself writes no Antigone à la Breton. He imitates no myths at all and attacks those compatriots who do. In this world of ideas he also has his share of responsibility, though his writing is a repetition not of ancient tales from the Greek past but of the way in which myths are produced.

He sees his Greece with its glorious traditions, its mountains whose peaks with their very names remind us how high the human spirit has attained, and its waters the Aegean Sea, Elytis's home, whose waves for thousands of years have washed ashore the riches that the West has been able to gather in and pride itself on. For him this Greece is still a living, ever-active myth, and he depicts it just as the old mythmakers did, by personifying it and giving it human form. It lends a sensuous nearness to his visions, and the myth that is the creed of his poetry is incarnated by beautiful young people in an enchanting landscape who love life and each other in dazzling sunshine where the waves break on the shore.

We can call this an optimistic idealization and, despite the concreteness, a flight from the present moment and reality. Elytis's very language, ritually solemn, is constantly striving to get away from everyday life with its pettiness. The idealization explains both the rapture and the criticism that his poetry has aroused. Elytis himself has given his view of the matter, point by point. Greek as a language, he says, opposes a pessimistic description of life, and for *la poésie maudite* it has no expressions. For west-Europeans all mysticism is associated with the darkness and the night, but for the Greeks light is the great mystery and every radiant day its recurrent miracle. The sun, the sea and love are the basic and purifying elements.

Those who maintain that all true poetry must be a reflection of its age and a political act he can refer to his harrowing poem about the second lieutenant who fell in the Albanian war. Elytis, himself a second lieutenant, chanced to be one of the two officers who opened the secret order of general mobilization. He took part at the front in the passionate and hopeless fight against Mussolini's crushing superiority, and his lament over the fallen brother-in-arms, who personifies Greece's never-completed struggle for existence, is committed poetry in a much more literal and harsher sense than that familiar to those who usually clamour for literature's commitment.

Elytis's conclusions from his participation were of a different nature. The poet, he says, does not necessarily have to express his time. He can also heroically defy it. His calling is not to jot down items about our daily life with its social and political situations and private griefs. On the contrary, his only way leads "from what is to what may be." In its essence, therefore, Elytis's poetry is not logically clear as we see it but derives its light from the limpidity of the present moment against a perspective behind it. His myth has its roots by the Aegean Sea, which was his cradle, but the myth is about humanity, drawing its nourishment not from a vanished golden age but from one which can never be realized. It is pointless to call this either optimism or pessimism. For, if I have understood him aright, only our future is worth bearing in mind and the unattainable alone is worth striving for.

Cher Maitre,

Malheureusement, mais sans doute au soulagement de l'auditoire, je ne parle pas votre langue. Pour employer la locution anglaise spécifique à quelque chose d'etrange: "It's Greek to me." Mais votre poésie n'est certainement pas étrangère, portée par la mer, qui est en même temps la mere de la civilisation européenne. Dans cette descendance nous mettons notre gloire, et, par consequent, il faut que je contredise votre diagnostic de notre état deplorable. Ce dont nous sommes atteints, ce n'est pas du tout d'un excès de rationalisme. Au contraire, la maladie de l'Europe occidentale c'est justement que le rationalisme est rationné. Et le peu que nous en détenons encore, ce ne sont pas les devoirs que nous ont donnés à apprendre nos philosophes de la renaissance. La sagesse claire et la logique pure de Platon et d'Aristote, peut-être aussi de Protagoras, de Gorgias et de Socrate lui-même, voilà les racines du rationalisme, dont nous ne voyons aujourd'hui que les épaves pitoyables.

Néanmoins Socrate, quand la raison ne lui donnait pas de gouverne, a écouté la voix de son daimon, et, cher maître, c'est avec une admiration très profonde que nous avons écouté se faire entendre en votre poésie la même voix de mystère, le daimonde votre pays.

J'ai grand plaisir à vous transmettre les felicitations les plus cordiales de l'Académie suédoise et à vous demander de recevoir des mains de Sa Majesté le Roi le Prix Nobel de litérature de cette année.

[© The Nobel Foundation, 1979.]

Translation of French paragraphs by Michael L. Lazare:

Dear Master,

Unfortunately—but without a doubt to the relief of the audience—I do not speak your tongue. To use the English phrase referring to something foreign, "It's Greek to me." But your poetry is certainly not foreign, having been borne by the sea of whom European civilization was also born. We glory in this ancestry, and therefore I must contradict your appraisal of our sad state. What troubles us is not at all an excess of rationalism. To the contrary, the ailment of Western Europe is in fact a lack of sufficient rationalism. And the little we still possess does not consist of the imperatives which our Renaissance philosophers gave us to learn. The clear wisdom and pure logic of Plato and Aristotle, perhaps also of Protagoras, Gorgias and Socrates himself: here are the roots of rationalism, of which today we see only the pitiful remnants.

Nonetheless Socrates, when his thoughts were not guided by reason, listened to the inner voice of his genius, and, dear master, we have listened with deep admiration as the same voice of mystery, the guiding spirit of your country, has made itself heard in your poetry.

It gives me great pleasure to offer you the most heartfelt congratulations of the Swedish Academy, and to ask you to receive, from the hands of His Majesty the King, this year's Nobel Prize in Literature.

Elytis: Banquet Speech

Elytis's speech at the Nobel Banquet, 10 December 1979

Sire, Madame, Altesses Royales, Mesdames, Messieurs,

Le voyage d'Odysseus, dont il m'a été donné de porter le nom, semble ne devoir jamais s'achever. Et c'est heureux.

Comme l'observait un de nos grands poètes contemporains, l'essentiel n'est pas dans le retour à Ithaque, qui met un terme à presque tout, mais dans l'errance qui est connaissance et aventure. Ce besoin de l'homme de découvrir, de connaître, de s'initier à ce qui le dépasse, est irrépressible. Nous sommes tous captifs de cette soif de connaître "le miracle," de croire que le miracle se produit, pourvu que nous y soyons préparés et que nous l'attendions.

En me consacrant, à mon tour, pendant plus de quarante ans, à la poésie, je n'ai rien fait d'autre. Je parcours des mers fabuleuses, je m'instruis en diverses haltes. Et me voici, aujourd'hui, à l'escale de Stockholm avec pour seul capital, dans mes mains, quelques mots helléniques. Ils sont modestes, mais vivants puisqu'ils se trouvent sur les lèvres de tout un peuple.

Ils sont âgés de trois mille ans, mais aussi frais que si l'on venait de les tirer de la mer. Parmi les galets et les algues des rives de l'Egée. Dans les bleus vifs et l'absolue transparence de l'éther. C'est le mot "ciel," c'est le mot "mer," c'est le mot "soleil," c'est le mot "liberté." Je les dépose respectueusement à vos pieds. Pour vous remercier. Pour remercier le noble peuple de Suède et ses maîtres à penser qui, en s'opposant à l'estimation quantitative des valeurs, conservent le secret de renouveler chaque année le miracle. Je vous remercie.

[© The Nobel Foundation, 1979. Odysseus Elytis is the sole author of his speech.]

Translation by Michael L. Lazare:

Sire, Madam, Your Royal Highnesses, Ladies and Gentlemen:

The voyages of Odysseus, whose name it has been given to me to bear, seem to never be completed. And this is a good thing.

One of our great contemporary poets observed that the value is not in the return to Ithaca, which brings an end to almost everything, but rather in the wandering, which is knowledge and adventure. Man's desire to discover, to know, to enter in that which surpasses him, is irrepressible. We are all captives of this thirst to know "the miracle," to believe that the miracle will happen as long as we are ready for it and await it.

In devoting myself to poetry for more than forty years, I have done nothing else. I travel seas full of marvels, I learn in varied stopping places. And here I am today, in the Stockholm port of call, with a few words of Greek the only currency in my hands. These words are modest but full of life, since they are spoken by an entire people.

They are three thousand years old, but as fresh as if they had just been pulled from the sea. Among the pebbles and the algae of the Aegean coast. In the vibrant blues and absolute transparency of the air. They are the word "sky"; the word "sea"; the word "sun"; the word "liberty." I lay them respectfully at your feet. To give thanks to you. To give thanks to the noble people of Sweden and its best thinkers who, in opposing a quantitative valuation of worth, conserve the secret of renewing the miracle each year. I thank you.

Press Release: The Nobel Prize in Literature 1979

from the Office of the Permanent Secretary of the Swedish Academy

Odysseus Elytis's name tells us a great deal about him as a person and a writer.

Odysseus—the seafarer, the Homeric poem's hero, alive with the spirit of freedom, with defiant intrepidity, enterprise, and an insatiable appetite for all the adventures and sensuous experiences that the seas and isles of Greece can offer. Odysseus is the name given to the poet by his parents. It testifies to the feeling for the past and to the links with the myths and distinctive character of Greek tradition. The family comes from the Aegean islands. The poet was born in Crete just before the liberation from Turkish rule.

Elytis is the name he adopted at the very beginning of his career as a writer. The name is a composite one, with allusion to several concepts dear to the poet's heart—it could be called a much abridged manifesto. The components in the name are to serve as a reminder of the Greek words for Greece (Ellas), hope (elpídha), freedom (eleftheria) and the mythical woman who is the personification of beauty, erotic sensuality and female allure, Helena (Eléni). Eros and Heros are closely connected in Elytis's world of poetry or myth.

The sea and the islands, their fauna and flora, the smooth pebbles on the beaches, the surge of the waves, the prickly black sea-urchins, the tang of salt, and the light over the water are constantly recurring elements in his writing—like the bright flood of sunlight which baptizes this world with its all-pervading lustre, at once fertile and purifying. Sensuality and light irradiate Elytis's poetry. The perceptible world is vividly present and overwhelming in its wealth of freshness and astonishing experiences.

But through Elytis's evocative verbal art, this world is also elevated to a symbolic reality. It becomes an ideal for the world that is not always so bright and true and wonderful, but which should be, and could be. We should always praise and worship this world for what it ought to be, and for what it, thereby, can be to us: a life-giving source of strength. Elytis's extolling of existence, of man and his potentialities, and life in communion with the rest of creation, is no idealizing or illusory escapism. It is a moral act of invocation of the kind to be found so many times in Greek history, from the present-day struggles for freedom against fascist or other oppression far back through the centuries to the heroic phase of the classical era. What matters is not to submit. What matters is constantly to bear in mind what life should be, and what man can shape for himself in defiance of all that threatens to destroy him and violate him.

This is not political writing in the narrow sense of the word. It is a writing of preparedness, which aims at defending the moral integrity or pride that is essential if we are to be able to resist at all, and to endure hardships and dangers, outrage and adversity. These sides of Elytis's poetry emerged strongly during the first years of the 1940s when he took part in the campaign in Albania against the fascist invasion. He passed through what he himself calls a crisis. Everything had to be tried out afresh—how to live, what the use of poetry was, how the beauty of poetry and art could serve in the fight for human dignity and resistance, yet preserve its freedom as art.

The poem *Heroic and Elegiac Song for the Lost Second Lieutenent of the Albanian Campaign* was written during this war, most of it based on personal experience. It immediately evoked response and became a kind of generation document for the young. It has kept its position as an expression of the Greeks' indomitable spirit of resistance. The fallen soldier is a representative of the Greeks who were killed in this war, but also of all those who have fallen during Greece's long history of struggle for national liberty and individuality. Here, as so often in Elytis's writing, realistic and mythical depiction are combined.

The Albanian campaign and the "heroic and elegiac song" about it were, in a way, a turning point for Elytis as a poet. His first verses had been published in the middle of the 1930s in a magazine which was then a forum for young writers, *Nea Ghrámmata*—in fact, a school for budding poets. The impulses from French surrealism, in particular, made themselves felt—in Elytis's case, chiefly from Paul Éluard. Surrealism became a liberator. It helped the young writers to find themselves, not least, in relation to the great Greek classical tradition, which might threaten to become oppressive and to stagnate in stereotyped and rhetorical formulae. Elytis's first poems, before *Heroic and Elegiac Song,* are youthfully sensual, full of light, brilliant, and very evocative in their visual and charming freshness. They quickly established him as one of the leading new Greek poets.

With *Herioc and Elegiac Song,* however, other sides of the writer emerged and insisted on becoming part of his creative world—sides which had been there from the outset but which now demanded more room: the tragic and the heroic. In the poetic cycle which many regard as Elytis's foremost work, *To Axion Estí* (Worthy It Is), these very complex experiences and programs have been given a form which makes this work one of 20th century literature's most concentrated and richly-faceted poems. The cycle is a kind of lyric drama or myth with strains from Hesiod, the Bible and Byzantine hymns. In its severe and polyphonic structure it is also linked to the avant-gardism of modern western writing. The cycle begins almost as drama of creation, concerning not only the poet himself, but, through him, us all. For, Elytis says, "I do not speak about myself. I speak for anyone who feels like myself but does not have enough naiveté to confess it." But it is also about the origin of Greece, in fact of the world. Then follows an architecturally complicated section with descriptions of the war and other scourges that have afflicted Greece and modern man. After this section, which represents a crisis or path of suffering, comes a concluding part, the actual song of praise; mature man is tempered and strengthened through his experiences but also fortified in his indomitable and defiant will to defend life and its sensuous abundance.

In one of his short essays, Elytis sums up his intentions: "I consider poetry a source of innocence full of revolutionary forces. It is my mission to direct these forces against a world my conscience cannot accept, precisely so as to bring that world through continual metamorphoses more in harmony with my dreams. I am referring here to a contemporary kind of magic whose mechanism leads to the discovery of our true reality. It is for this reason that I believe to the point of idealism, that I am moving in a direction which has never been attempted until now. In the hope of obtaining a freedom from all constraints, and the justice which could be identified with absolute light. . . ."

In its combination of fresh, sensuous flexibility and strictly disciplined implacability in the face of all compulsion, Elytis's poetry give a shape to its distinctiveness, which is not only very personal but also represents the traditions of the Greek people.

[© The Nobel Foundation, 1979.]

Elytis: Nobel Lecture, 8 December 1979
(Translation)

May I be permitted, I ask you, to speak in the name of luminosity and transparency? The space I have lived in and where I have been able to fulfill myself is defined by these two states. States that I have also perceived as being identified in me with the need to express myself.

It is good, it is right that a contribution be made to art, from that which is assigned to each individual by his personal experience and the virtues of his language. Even more so, since the times are dismal and we should have the widest possible view of things.

I am not speaking of the common and natural capacity of perceiving objects in all their detail, but of the power of the metaphor to only retain their essence, and to bring them to such a state of purity that their metaphysical significance appears like a revelation.

I am thinking here of the manner in which the sculptors of the Cycladic period used their material, to the point of carrying it beyond itself. I am also thinking of the Byzantine icon painters, who succeeded, only by using pure color, to suggest the "divine."

It is just such an intervention in the real, both penetrating and metamorphosing, which has always been, it seems to me, the lofty vocation of poetry. Not limiting itself to what is, but stretching itself to what can be. It is true that this step has not always been received with respect. Perhaps the collective neuroses did not permit it. Or perhaps because utilitarianism did not authorize men to keep their eyes open as much as was necessary.

Beauty, Light, it happens that people regard them as obsolete, as insignificant. And yet! The inner step required by the approach of the Angel's form is, in my opinion, infinitely more painful than the other, which gives birth to Demons of all kinds.

Certainly, there is an enigma. Certainly, there is a mystery. But the mystery is not a stage piece turning to account the play of light and shadow only to impress us.

It is what continues to be a mystery, even in bright light. It is only then that it acquires that refulgence that captivates and which we call Beauty. Beauty that is an open path—the only one perhaps—towards that unknown part of ourselves, towards that which surpasses us. There, this could be yet another definition of poetry: the art of approaching that which surpasses us.

Innumerable secret signs, with which the universe is studded and which constitute so many syllables of an unknown language, urge us to compose words, and with words, phrases whose deciphering puts us at the threshold of the deepest truth.

In the final analysis, where is truth? In the erosion and death we see around us, or in this propensity to believe that the world is indestructible and eternal? I know, it is wise to avoid redundancies. The cosmogonic theories that have succeeded each other through the years have not missed using and abusing them. They have clashed among themselves, they have had their moment of glory, then they have been erased.

But the essential has remained. It remains.

The poetry that raises itself when rationalism has laid down its arms, takes its relieving troops to advance into the forbidden zone, thus proving that it is still the less consumed by erosion. It assures, in the purity of its form, the safeguard of those given facts through which life becomes a viable task. Without it and its vigilance, these given facts would be lost in the obscurity of consciousness, just as algae become indistinct in the ocean depths.

That is why we have a great need of transparency. To clearly perceive the knots of this thread running throughout the centuries and aiding us to remain upright on this earth.

These knots, these ties, we see them distinctly, from Heraclitus to Plato and from Plato to Jesus. Having reached us in various forms they tell us the same thing: that it is in the inside of this world that the other world is contained, that it is with the elements of this world that the other world is recombined, the hereafter, that second reality situated above the one where we live unnaturally. It is a question of a reality to which we have a total right, and only our incapacity makes us unworthy of it.

It is not a coincidence that in healthy times, Beauty is identified with Good, and Good with the

Sun. To the extent that consciousness purifies itself and is filled with light, its dark portions retract and disappear, leaving empty spaces—just as in the laws of physics—filled by the elements of the opposite import. Thus what results of this rests on the two aspects, I mean the "here" and the "hereafter." Did not Heraclitus speak of a harmony of opposed tensions?

It is of no importance whether it is Apollo or Venus, Christ or the Virgin who incarnate and personalize the need we have to see materialized what we experience as an intuition. What is important is the breath of immortality that penetrates us at that moment. In my humble opinion, Poetry should, beyond all doctrinal argumentation, permit this breath.

Here I must refer to Hölderlin, that great poet who looked at the gods of Olympus and Christ in the same manner. The stability he gave a kind of vision continues to be inestimable. And the extent of what he has revealed for us is immense. I would even say it is terrifying. It is what incites us to cry out—at a time when the pain now submerging us was just beginning—: "What good are poets in a time of poverty?" *Wozu Dichter in dürftiger Zeit?*

For mankind, times were always *dürftig*, unfortunately. But poetry has never, on the other hand, missed its vocation. These are two facts that will never cease to accompany our earthly destiny, the first serving as the counter-weight to the other. How could it be otherwise? It is through the Sun that the night and the stars are perceptible to us. Yet let us note, with the ancient sage, that if it passes its bounds the Sun becomes "hubris." For life to be possible, we have to keep a correct distance to the allegorical Sun, just as our planet does from the natural Sun. We formerly erred through ignorance. We go wrong today through the extent of our knowledge. In saying this I do not wish to join the long list of censors of our technological civilization. Wisdom as old as the country from which I come has taught me to accept evolution, to digest progress "with its bark and its pits."

But then, what becomes of Poetry? What does it represent in such a society? This is what I reply: poetry is the only place where the power of numbers proves to be nothing. Your decision this year to honor, in my person, the poetry of a small country, reveals the relationship of harmony linking it to the concept of gratuitous art, the only concept that opposes nowadays the all-powerful position acquired by the quantitative esteem of values.

Referring to personal circumstances would be a breach of good manners. Praising my home, still more unsuitable. Nevertheless it is sometimes indispensable, to the extent that such interferences assist in seeing a certain state of things more clearly. This is the case today.

Dear friends, it has been granted to me to write in a language that is spoken only by a few million people. But a language spoken without interruption, with very few differences, throughout more than two thousand five hundred years. This apparently surprising spatial-temporal distance is found in the cultural dimensions of my country. Its spatial area is one of the smallest; but its temporal extension is infinite. If I remind you of this, it is certainly not to derive some kind of pride from it, but to show the difficulties a poet faces when he must make use, to name the things dearest to him, of the same words as did Sappho, for example, or Pindar, while being deprived of the audience they had and which then extended to all of human civilization.

If language were not such a simple means of communication there would not be any problem. But it happens, at times, that it is also an instrument of "magic." In addition, in the course of centuries, language acquires a certain way of being. It becomes a lofty speech. And this way of being entails obligations.

Let us not forget either that in each of these twenty-five centuries and without any interruption, poetry has been written in Greek. It is this collection of given facts which makes the great weight of tradition that this instrument lifts. Modern Greek poetry gives an expressive image of this.

The sphere formed by this poetry shows, one could say, two poles: at one of these poles is Dionysios Solomos, who, before Mallarmé appeared in European literature, managed to formulate, with the greatest rigor and coherency, the concept of pure poetry: to submit sentiment to intelligence, ennoble expression, mobilize all the possibilities of the linguistic instrument by orienting oneself to the miracle. At the other pole is Cavafy, who like T. S. Eliot reaches, by eliminating all form of turgidity, the extreme limit of concision and the most rigorously exact expression.

Between these two poles, and more or less close to one or the other, our other great poets move: Kostis Palamas, Angelos Sikelianos, Nikos Kazantzakis, George Seferis.

Such is, rapidly and schematically drawn, the picture of neo-Hellenic poetic discourse.

We who have followed have had to take over the lofty precept which has been bequeathed to us and adapt it to contemporary sensibility. Beyond the limits of technique, we have had to reach a synthesis, which, on the one hand, assimilated the elements of

Greek tradition and, on the other, the social and psychological requirements of our time.

In other words, we had to grasp today's European-Greek in all its truth and turn that truth to account. I do not speak of successes, I speak of intentions, efforts. Orientations have their significance in the investigation of literary history.

But how can creation develop freely in these directions when the conditions of life, in our time, annihilate the creator? And how can a cultural community be created when the diversity of languages raises an unsurpassable obstacle? We know you and you know us through the 20 or 30 per cent that remains of a work after translation. This holds even more true for all those of us who, prolonging the furrow traced by Solomos, expect a miracle from discourse and that a spark flies from between two words with the right sound and in the right position.

No. We remain mute, incommunicable.

We are suffering from the absence of a common language. And the consequences of this absence can be seen—I do not believe I am exaggerating—even in the political and social reality of our common homeland, Europe.

We say—and make the observation each day—that we live in a moral chaos. And this at a moment when—as never before—the allocation of that which concerns our material existence is done in the most systematic manner, in an almost military order, with implacable controls. This contradiction is significant. Of two parts of the body, when one is hypertrophic, the other atrophies. A praiseworthy tendency, encouraging the peoples of Europe to unite, is confronted today with the impossibility of harmonization of the atrophied and hypertrophic parts of our civilization. Our values do not constitute a common language.

For the poet—this may appear paradoxical but it is true—the only common language he still can use is his sensations. The manner in which two bodies are attracted to each other and unite has not changed for millennia. In addition, it has not given rise to any conflict, contrary to the scores of ideologies that have bloodied our societies and have left us with empty hands.

When I speak of sensations, I do not mean those, immediately perceptible, on the first or second level. I mean those which carry us to the extreme edge of ourselves. I also mean the "analogies of sensations" that are formed in our spirits.

For all art speaks through analogy. A line, straight or curved, a sound, sharp or low-pitched, translate a certain optical or acoustic contact. We all write good or bad poems to the extent that we live or reason according to the good or bad meaning of the term. An image of the sea, as we find it in Homer, comes to us intact. Rimbaud will say "a sea mixed with sun." Except he will add: "that is eternity." A young girl holding a myrtle branch in Archilochus survives in a painting by Matisse. And thus the Mediterranean idea of purity is made more tangible to us. In any case, is the image of a virgin in Byzantine iconography so different from that of her secular sisters? Very little is needed for the light of this world to be transformed into supernatural clarity, and inversely. One sensation inherited from the Ancients and another bequeathed by the Middle Ages give birth to a third, one that resembles them both, as a child does its parents. Can poetry survive such a path? Can sensations, at the end of this incessant purification process, reach a state of sanctity? They will return then, as analogies, to graft themselves on the material world and to act on it.

It is not enough to put our dreams into verse. It is too little. It is not enough to politicize our speech. It is too much. The material world is really only an accumulation of materials. It is for us to show ourselves to be good or bad architects, to build Paradise or Hell. This is what poetry never ceases affirming to us—and particularly in these *dürftiger* times—just this: that in spite of everything our destiny lies in our hands.

I have often tried to speak of solar metaphysics. I will not try today to analyse how art is implicated in such a conception. I will keep to one single and simple fact: the language of the Greeks, like a magic instrument, has—as a reality or a symbol—intimate relations with the Sun. And that Sun does not only inspire a certain attitude of life, and hence the primeval sense to the poem. It penetrates the composition, the structure, and—to use a current terminology—the nucleus from which is composed the cell we call the poem.

It would be a mistake to believe that it is a question of a return to the notion of pure form. The sense of form, as the West has bequeathed it to us, is a constant attainment, represented by three or four models. Three or four moulds, one could say, where it was suitable to pour the most anomalous material at any price. Today that is no longer conceivable. I was one of the first in Greece to break those ties.

What interested me, obscurely at the beginning, then more and more consciously, was the edification of that material according to an architectural model that varied each time. To understand this there is no need to refer to the wisdom of the Ancients who conceived the Parthenons. It is enough to evoke the humble builders of our houses and of our chapels in the Cyclades, finding on each occasion the best solution.

Their solutions. Practical and beautiful at the same time, so that in seeing them Le Corbusier could only admire and bow.

Perhaps it is this instinct that woke in me when, for the first time, I had to face a great composition like "Axion Esti." I understood then that without giving the work the proportions and perspective of an edifice, it would never reach the solidity I wished.

I followed the example of Pindar or of the Byzantine Romanos Melodos who, in each of their odes or canticles, invented a new mode for each occasion. I saw that the determined repetition, at intervals, of certain elements of versification effectively gave to my work that multifaceted and symmetrical substance which was my plan.

But then is it not true that the poem, thus surrounded by elements that gravitate around it, is transformed into a little Sun? This perfect correspondence, which I thus find obtained with the intended contents, is, I believe, the poet's most lofty ideal.

To hold the Sun in one's hands without being burned, to transmit it like a torch to those following, is a painful act but, I believe, a blessed one. We have need of it. One day the dogmas that hold men in chains will be dissolved before a consciousness so inundated with light that it will be one with the Sun, and it will arrive on those ideal shores of human dignity and liberty.

[© The Nobel Foundation, 1979. Odysseus Elytis is the sole author of the text.]

Rudolf Eucken

(5 January 1846 – 15 September 1926)

Uwe Dathe
University of Kiev, Ukraine

BOOKS: *De Aristotelis dicendi ratione: Pars prima, Observationes de particularum usu* (Göttingen: Hofer, 1866);

Über den Sprachgebrauch des Aristoteles: Beobachtungen über die Praepositionen (Berlin: Weidemann, 1868);

Über die Methode und die Grundlagen der Aristotelischen Ethik, Separatabdruck aus dem Programm des Frankfurter Gymnasiums (Berlin: Weidemann, 1870);

Über die Bedeutung der Aristotelischen Philosophie für die Gegenwart: Akademische Antrittsrede (Berlin: Weidemann, 1872);

Die Methode der Aristotelischen Forschung in ihrem Zusammenhang mit den philosophischen Grundprincipien des Aristoteles dargestellt (Berlin: Weidemann, 1872);

Über den Werth der Geschichte der Philosophie: Akademische Antrittsrede (Jena: Mauke, 1874);

Geschichte und Kritik der Grundbegriffe der Gegenwart (Leipzig: Veit, 1878); translated by M. Stuart Phelps as *The Fundamental Concepts of Modern Philosophic Thought, Critically and Historically Considered* (New York: Appleton, 1880); original German revised as *Die Grundbegriffe der Gegenwart: Historisch und kritisch entwickelt* (Leipzig: Veit, 1893); revised as *Geistige Strömungen der Gegenwart* (Leipzig: Veit, 1904; revised, 1909, 1916; revised edition, Berlin & Leipzig: Vereinigung wissenschaftlicher Verleger, 1920); translated by Meyrick Booth as *Main Currents of Modern Thought: A Study of the Spiritual and Intellectual Movements of the Present Day* (London: Unwin / New York: Scribners, 1912);

Geschichte der philosophischen Terminologie: Im Umriss dargestellt (Leipzig: Veit, 1879);

Über Bilder und Gleichnisse in der Philosophie (Leipzig: Veit, 1880);

Zur Erinnerung an K. Ch. F. Krause: Festrede gehalten zu Eisenberg am 100. Geburtstage des Philosophen (Leipzig: Veit, 1881);

Aristoteles' Anschauung von Freundschaft und von Lebensgütern (Berlin: Habel, 1884);

Prolegomena zu Forschungen über die Einheit des Geisteslebens in Bewusstsein und Tat der Menschheit (Leipzig: Veit, 1885);

Rudolf Eucken (from William Tudor Jones, An Interpretation of Rudolf Eucken's Philosophy, 1912; Thomas Cooper Library, University of South Carolina)

Beiträge zur Geschichte der neuern Philosophie vornehmlich der deutschen: Gesammelte Abhandlungen (Heidelberg: Georg Weiss, 1886); revised and enlarged as *Beiträge zur Einführung in die Geschichte der Philosophie* (Leipzig: Dürr, 1906);

Die Philosophie des Thomas von Aquino und die Kultur der Neuzeit (Halle: Pfeffer, 1886; revised edition, Sachsa: Haacke, 1910);

Die Einheit des Geisteslebens in Bewusstsein und Tat der Menschheit: Untersuchungen (Leipzig: Veit, 1888; revised edition, Berlin: De Gruyter, 1925);

Die Lebensanschauungen der grossen Denker: Eine Entwicklungsgeschichte des Lebensproblems der Menschheit von Plato bis zur Gegenwart (Leipzig: Veit, 1890; revised, 1896, 1899, 1902, 1904, 1905, 1907, 1909, 1911, 1912, 1917, 1918; revised edition, Berlin & Leipzig: Vereinigung wissenschaftlicher Verleger, 1919; revised, 1921, 1922; revised edition, Berlin: De Gruyter, 1928); translated by Williston S. Hough and W. R. Boyce Gibson as *The Problem of Human Life as Viewed By the Great Thinkers from Plato to the Present Time* (New York: Scribners, 1909; London: Unwin, 1909; revised, 1914, 1916);

Der Kampf um das Gymnasium: Gesichtspunkte und Anregungen (Stuttgart: J. G. Cotta, 1891);

Der Kampf um einen geistigen Lebensinhalt: Neue Grundlegung einer Weltanschauung (Leipzig: Veit, 1896; revised, 1907, 1918; revised edition, Berlin & Leipzig: Vereinigung wissenschaftlicher Verleger, 1921; revised edition, Berlin: De Gruyter, 1924);

Der Wahrheitsgehalt der Religion (Leipzig: Veit, 1901; revised, 1905, 1912; revised edition, Berlin: De Gruyter, 1920); translated by W. Tudor Jones as *The Truth of Religion* (London: Williams & Norgate / New York: Putnam, 1911); excerpt of translation published as *The Transient and the Permanent in Christianity* (London: Lindsey Press, 1914);

Das Wesen der Religion, philosophisch betrachtet: Vortrag auf der Sächsischen kirchlichen Konferenz zu Chemnitz am 17. April 1901 (Leipzig: Georg Wigand, 1901); translated by Jones as "The Nature of Religion, Philosophically Considered: An Address Delivered Before the Curch Conference of Saxony, Held at Chemnitz," in *The Point of View in Theology and Religion: The Monthly Magazine of the Unitarian Church, Swansea,* 1, no. 4;

Thomas von Aquino und Kant: Ein Kampf zweier Welten (Berlin: Reuther & Reichard, 1901);

Gesammelte Aufsätze zur Philosophie und Lebensanschauung (Leipzig: Dürr, 1903); edited and translated by Booth as *Collected Essays of Rudolf Eucken* (London: Unwin, 1914; New York: Scribners, 1914);

Grundlinien einer neuen Lebensanschauung (Leipzig: Veit, 1907; revised, 1913); translated by Alban G. Widgery as *Life's Basis and Life's Ideal: The Fundamentals of a New Philosophy of Life* (London: Black, 1911; revised, 1912);

Hauptprobleme der Religionsphilosophie der Gegenwart (Berlin: Reuther & Reichard, 1907; revised, 1907, 1909, 1912); translated by Lucy Judge Gibson and W. R. Boyce Gibson as *Christianity and the New Idealism: A Study in the Religious Philosophy of To-day* (London & New York: Harper, 1909);

Der Sinn und Wert des Lebens (Leipzig: Quelle & Meyer, 1908; revised, 1910, 1911, 1914, 1917, 1918, 1920, 1921, 1922); translated by Lucy Judge Gibson and W. R. Boyce Gibson as *The Meaning and Value of Life* (London: Black, 1909);

Einführung in eine Philosophie des Geisteslebens (Leipzig: Quelle & Meyer, 1908); translated by F. L. Pogson as *The Life of the Spirit: An Introduction to Philosophy* (London: Williams & Norgate / New York: Putnam, 1909); original German edition revised as *Einführung in die Hauptfragen der Philosophie* (Leipzig: Quelle & Meyer, 1919; revised, 1921); revised as *Einführung in die Philosophie* (Leipzig: Quelle & Meyer, 1925);

Naturalismus oder Idealismus: Nobelrede (Stockholm: Imprimerie Royale/Norstedt & Fils, 1909); republished by the Euckenbund (Jena: Neuenhahn, 1922); translated by Widgery as *Naturalism or Idealism? The Nobel Lecture* (Cambridge: W. Heffer, 1912);

Können wir noch Christen sein? (Leipzig: Veit, 1911); translated by Lucy Judge Gibson as *Can We Still Be Christians?* (New York: Macmillan, 1914; London: Black, 1914);

Religion and Life: Lecture Delivered at Essex Hall London, translated by Gustav F. Beckh (London: British and Foreign Unitarian Association, 1911);

Back to Religion (Boston: Pilgrim Press, 1912);

Erkennen und Leben (Leipzig: Quelle & Meyer, 1912; revised edition, Berlin: De Gruyter, 1923); translated by Jones as *Knowledge and Life* (London: Williams & Norgate / New York: Putnam, 1913);

Zur Sammlung der Geister (Leipzig: Quelle & Meyer, 1913; revised, 1914);

Ethics and Modern Thought: A Theory of Their Relations: The Deems Lectures, Delivered in 1913 at New York University, translated by Margaret von Seydewitz (New York & London: Putnam, 1913); published as *Present-Day Ethics in Their Relations to the Spiritual Life: Being the Deems Lectures Delivered in 1913 at New York University,* edited by Jones (London: Williams & Norgate, 1913);

Die weltgeschichtliche Bedeutung des deutschen Geistes (Stuttgart & Berlin: Deutsche Verlags-Anstalt, 1914);

Die sittlichen Kräfte des Krieges (Leipzig: Gräfe, 1914);

Die Träger des deutschen Idealismus (Berlin: Ullstein, 1915; revised, 1919, 1924);

Ethische und hygienische Aufgaben der Gegenwart: Zwei Vorträge, by Eucken and Max von Gruber (Berlin: Mässigkeits-Verlag, 1916);

Die geistesgeschichtliche Bedeutung der Bibel: Rede zur Feier des 100 jährigen Bestehens der Hamburg-Altonaischen Bibelgesellschaft (Leipzig: Kröner, 1917);

Die geistigen Forderungen der Gegenwart (Berlin: Otto Reichl, 1917);

Bilder aus dem Welt- und Menschenleben: Feldpostausgabe aus "Gesammelte Aufsätze" (Leipzig: Meiner, 1917);

Moral und Lebensanschauung: Feldpostausgabe aus "Gesammelte Aufsätze" (Leipzig: Meiner, 1917);

Was bleibt unser Halt? Ein Wort an ernste Seelen (Leipzig: Quelle & Meyer, 1918);

Mensch und Welt: Eine Philosophie des Lebens (Leipzig: Quelle & Meyer, 1918; revised, 1920, 1923);

Geistesprobleme und Lebensfragen: Ausgewählte Abschnitte aus den Werken, edited by Otto Braun (Leipzig: Reclam, 1918; revised, 1921);

Deutsche Freiheit: Ein Weckruf (Leipzig: Quelle & Meyer, 1919);

Unsere Forderung an das Leben: Mit einem Anhang: Aufruf zur Gründung eines Euckenbundes (Leipzig: Reclam, 1920);

Der Sozialismus und seine Lebensgestaltung (Leipzig: Reclam, 1920; revised, 1926); translated by Joseph McCabe as *Socialism: An Analysis* (London: Unwin, 1921; New York: Scribners, 1922);

Lebenserinnerungen: Ein Stück deutschen Lebens (Leipzig: Koehler, 1921; revised, 1922); translated by McCabe as *Rudolf Eucken: His Life, Work, and Travels, by Himself* (London: Unwin, 1921; New York: Scribners, 1922);

Prolegomena und Epilog zu einer Philosophie des Geisteslebens (Berlin & Leipzig: Vereinigung wissenschaftlicher Verleger/De Gruyter, 1922);

Das Lebensproblem in China und Europa, by Eucken and Carson Chang (Leipzig: Quelle & Meyer, 1922);

Der Kampf um die Religion in der Gegenwart (Langensalza: H. Beyer, 1922; revised, 1923);

The Spiritual Outlook of Europe To-Day, translated by W. R. V. Brade (London: Faith Press, 1922);

The Individual and Society, translated by Brade (London: Faith Press, 1923);

Ethik als Grundlage des staatsbürgerlichen Lebens (Langensalza: H. Beyer, 1924).

Editions and Collections: *Einführung in die Hauptfragen der Philosophie und der Sinn und Wert des Lebens* (Zürich: Coron, 1967);

Gesammelte Werke in elf Bänden, 11 volumes, edited by Rainer A. Bast (Hildesheim: Olms, 2005–)—comprises volume 1, *Die Einheit des Geisteslebens in Bewusstsein und That der Menschheit;* volume 2, *Gesammelte Aufsätze zur Philosophie und Lebensanschauung* and *Beiträge zur Einführung in die Geschichte der Philosophie;* volume 3, *Grundlinien einer neuen Lebensanschauung;* volume 4, *Geistige Strömungen der Gegenwart;* volume 5, *Der Wahrheitsgehalt der Religion;* volume 6, *Der Sinn und Wert des Lebens* and *Erkennen und Leben;* volume 7, *Mensch und Welt: Eine Philosophie des Lebens;* volume 8, *Der Kampf um einen geistigen Lebensinhalt: Neue Grundlegung einer Weltanschauung;* volume 9, *Einführung in die Philosophie* and *Geschichte der philosophischen Terminologie;* volume 10, *Kleinere Arbeiten;* volume 11, *Prolegomena und Epilog zu einer Philosophie des Geisteslebens* and *Lebenserinnerungen.*

OTHER: "Zur Würdigung Comtes und des Positivismus," in *Philosophische Aufsätze: Eduard Zeller zu seinem fünfzigjährigen Doctor-Jubiläum gewidmet* (Leipzig: Fues, 1887), pp. 53–82;

"Wissenschaft und Religion," in *Beiträge zur Weiterentwicklung der christlichen Religion* (Munich: J. F. Lehmann, 1905), pp. 241–281;

"Philosophie und Geschichte," in *Systematische Philosophie: Die Kultur der Gegenwart: Teil I, Abteilung VI,* edited by Paul Hinneberg (Berlin & Leipzig: Teubner, 1907), pp. 247–281;

"What Does a Free Christianity Require in Order to Become Victorious?" in *Freedom and Fellowship in Religion: Proceedings and Papers of the Fourth International Congress of Religious Liberals,* edited by Charles W. Wendte (Boston: International Council, 1907), pp. 379–389;

"Zur Einführung," in Johann Gottlieb Fichtes, *Reden an die deutsche Nation* (Leipzig: Insel, 1909), pp. i–xvi;

"Die Bedeutung der Religion in Geschichte und Gegenwart," in *Die XIV. Christliche Studenten-Konferenz Aarau 1910* (Bern: Francke, 1910), pp. 63–81;

"Die deutsche Philosophie und die religiöse Reformbewegung der Gegenwart," in *Fünfter Weltkongreß für Freies Christentum und Religiösen Fortschritt: Berlin 5. bis 10. August 1910: Protokoll der Verhandlungen,* edited by Max Fischer and Friedrich Michael Schiele (Berlin: Protestantischer Schriftenvertrieb, Schöneberg, 1910), pp. 748–754; translated as *German Philosophy and the Religious Reform-Movement of To-day* (London: Williams & Norgate, 1910);

"The Work of Borden Parker Bowne," translated by M. L. Perrin, in Ralph Tyler Flewelling, *Personalism and the Problem of Philosophy: An Appreciation of the Work of Borden Parker Bowne* (New York & Cincinnati: Methodist Book Concern, 1915), pp. 17–31;

"Der Geist im Lande," in *Deutsche Volkskraft nach zwei Kriegsjahren: Vier Vorträge* (Berlin & Leipzig: Teubner, 1916), pp. 35–41;

"Krieg und Kultur," in *Meyers Großes Konservations-Lexikon: Kriegsnachtrag: Erster Teil* (Leipzig & Wien: Bibliographisches Institut, 1916), pp. 317–322;

"Die Einheit der deutschen Weltanschauung," in *Vom inneren Frieden des deutschen Volkes: Ein Buch gegenseitigen Verstehens und Vertrauens,* edited by Friedrich Thimme (Leipzig: Hirzel, 1916), pp. 11–23;

"Meine persönlichen Erinnerungen an Nietzsche," in *Den Manen Friedrich Nietzsches,* edited by Max Oehler (Munich: Musarion, 1921), pp. 51–55;

"The Ethical Basis of Immortality," in *Immortality,* edited by James Marchand (London & New York: Putnam, 1924), pp. 124–144.

SELECTED PERIODICAL PUBLICATIONS–UNCOLLECTED: "Beiträge zum Verständnis des Aristoteles," *Neue Jahrbücher für Philologie und Pädagogik,* 99 (1869): 243–252, 817–820;

"Fortlage als Religionsphilosoph," *Zeitschrift für Philosophie und philosophische Kritik,* 82 (1883): 180–196;

"Leibniz und Geulinx: Eine Studie zur Geschichte der Philosophie," *Philosophische Monatshefte,* 19 (1883): 525–542;

"Parteien und Parteinamen in der Philosophie," *Philosophische Monatshefte,* 20 (1884): 1–32;

"Moritz Seebeck: Ein Lebensbild aus dem neunzehnten Jahrhundert," *Deutsche Rundschau,* 50 (1887): 224–237;

"Der Neuthomismus und die neue Wissenschaft," *Philosophische Monatshefte,* 24 (1888): 575–581;

"Zur philosophischen Terminologie: Ein Vorschlag und eine Aufforderung," *Archiv für Geschichte der Philosophie,* 1 (1888): 309–313;

"Aristoteles' *Urteil über die Menschen,*" *Archiv für Geschichte der Philosophie,* 3 (1890): 541–558;

"Philosophical Terminology and Its History: Expository and Appelatory," *Monist,* 6 (1895–1896): 497–515;

"Hegel To-Day," translated by Thomas J. McCormack, *Monist,* 7 (April 1897): 321–339;

"Liberty in Teaching in the German Universities," *Forum,* 27 (1897): 476–486;

"Die Stellung der Philosophie zur religiösen Bewegung der Gegenwart," *Zeitschrift für Philosophie und philosophische Kritik,* 112 (1898): 161–178;

"Die weltgeschichtliche Krise der Religion," *Deutsche Rundschau,* 107 (1901): 197–209;

"The Status of Religion in Germany," *Forum,* 31 (1901): 387–397;

"Der moderne Mensch und die Religion," *Neue Deutsche Rundschau,* 13 (1902): 673–682;

"Zur Erinnerung an Kant," *Der Türmer: Monatsschrift für Gemüt und Geist,* 6 (1903–1904), volume 1, pp. 513–520;

"Was können wir heute aus Schiller gewinnen?," *Kant-Studien,* 10 (1905): 253–260;

"Religion und Kultur," *Religion und Geisteskultur,* 1 (1907): 7–12;

"Alter und neuer Idealismus," *Zeitschrift für Philosophie und philosophische Kritik,* 132 (1908): 1–4;

"Die päpstliche Enzyklika wider die Modernisten," *Internationale Wochenschrift für Wissenschaft, Kunst und Technik,* 2 (1908): 97–110;

"The Problem of Immortality," *Hibbert Journal,* 6 (1908): 836–851;

"Gedanken über das Ideal der Volksbildung," *Volksbildungsarchiv,* 1 (1910): 217–226;

"What Is Driving Men Today Back to Religion?" *Harvard Theological Review,* 5 (1912): 273–282;

"Knowledge and Life," *Philosophical Review,* 22, no. 1 (1913): 1–16;

"Aufruf zur Gründung einer Luthergesellschaft," *Deutscher Wille: Des Kunstwarts 31. Jahr,* 31 (1917): 182–184;

"Luther und die geistige Erneuerung des deutschen Volkes," *Luther-Jahrbuch,* 1 (1919): 27–34;

"Luther und wir," *Luther,* 1 (1919): 3–12.

In 1908 Rudolf Eucken became the first philosopher to win the Nobel Prize in Literature. The decision of the Swedish Academy surprised not only the German and international public but also the winner himself. At the beginning of the twentieth century, Eucken had a broad German and international readership; his views on the truth of religion, in particular, were absorbed by many readers, including clergymen and educated people interested in religious problems. In addition to his books, Eucken wrote more than 400 papers and articles in journals, magazines, newspapers, and anthologies, as well as about 150 reviews, 30 forewords, and many contributions for philosophical and theological dictionaries. According to the citation from the Swedish Academy, Eucken was awarded the Nobel Prize "in recognition of his earnest search for truth, his penetrating power of thought, his wide range of vision, and the warmth and strength of presentation with which in his numerous works he has vindicated and developed an idealistic philosophy of life."

In contrast to this emphatic recognition for Eucken's idealism, the philosopher is virtually forgotten by both the public and academics at the end of the twentieth century. Only Eucken's early academic writings continue to attract the attention of some philosophers. His later work, the articles, papers, pamphlets, and books in which Eucken developed a neo-idealistic philosophy of life, is philosophically uninteresting, because in his late writings he did not argue to open a dialogue about philosophical questions but rather to appeal to his growing following. But as Eucken's philosophical Weltanschauung was an important part of the German and international criticism of modern Western civilization, historians and scholars in cultural studies are still interested in it.

Rudolf Christoph Eucken was born on 5 January 1846 in Aurich (East Frisia, Germany) to Protestant, middle-class parents. His father, Ammo Becker Eucken, worked for the postal service and died when Rudolf was five. His mother, Ida Maria Gittermann, was a deeply religious woman. His only brother died in 1850. Eucken attended school until 1863 and then studied philosophy, philology, and history at the University of Göttingen until 1866. Eucken's most important philosophical teachers were Rudolf Hermann Lotze and Gustav Teichmüller. He attended Teichmüller's lectures and seminars on Aristotle and the history of concepts and wrote a dissertation on the language of Aristotle. Teichmüller put Eucken in contact with the philosopher Friedrich Adolf Trendelenburg, who taught at Berlin University. In 1866 Eucken went to Berlin to meet Trendelenburg. He attended lectures and became a member of Trendelenburg's private circle, where he met other influential scholars.

In the 1860s Trendelenburg held a special place among academic philosophers in Germany. He criticized Georg Wilhelm Friedrich Hegel, Immanuel Kant, and almost all contemporary philosophical movements, especially the neo-Kantians, and tried to revive philosophical thinking by a neo-Aristotelian system. Until 1871 Eucken shared Trendelenburg's neo-Aristotelian views and wrote at that time some valuable philological-philosophical papers on the language of Aristotle.

From 1866 to 1871 Eucken worked as a teacher of Greek, Latin, and philosophy at several high schools in Berlin, Husum, and Frankfurt am Main. When he became professor of philosophy and pedagogic at Basel in 1871, he was considered among almost all contemporary philosophers to be Trendelenburg's most faithful disciple and a talented historian of philosophy. At Basel, Eucken met Friedrich Nietzsche and Jacob Burckhardt, studied Plato and the early Fathers of the Church, and began to distance himself from Trendelenburg's neo-Aristotelian ideas. Eucken's book *Die Methode der Aristotelischen Forschung in ihrem Zusammenhang mit den philosophischen Grundprincipien des Aristoteles dargestellt* (1872, Aristotle's Philosophical Method in Its Connection with His Main Principles) uncovers the methodological faults of Aristotle's system and shows that any modern revival of Aristotle is not capable of solving the philosophical problems of the present.

In 1874 Eucken moved to Jena, where he held a professorship in philosophy until 1920. Prior to his appointment at Jena, Eucken stopped researching Aristotle and began to analyze the cultural and spiritual problems of his time. From that period there is an informative document on Eucken's general philosophical point of view. In a letter dated 31 December 1873, Eucken explained to the chancellor of Jena University his own philosophical program:

> It is my fervent hope, that I am able to teach philosophy in such a way that the students do not get only a simple increase of knowledge, but above all a general engrossment in the spiritual life. Just in the fragmentation of interests and opinions, predominant and inevitable in our time, it should be the task of philosophy to point to the homogeneity of human being and to defend the unity of all higher culture [Bildung]. The marvellous progress of all sciences and the tremendous perfection of modern technology will not be enough for the last desires of the whole man without such a philosophical center.

Eucken noticed differences in thinking and in contemporary life that seriously threatened the homogeneous human sense of being. Throughout his life Eucken tried by philosophical means to get over the permanent crisis of the life and culture of the modern world.

When Eucken arrived at Jena, he had a clear philosophical concern, but he did not have any conceptual means to implement his programmatic vision. He only knew that the demands of the present could not be fulfilled by falling back on ancient philosophical systems. Eucken wrote in his autobiography *Lebenserinnerungen: Ein Stück deutschen Lebens* (1921; translated as *Rudolf Eucken: His Life, Work, and Travels, by Himself*, 1921) that during the late 1870s he primarily looked for answers, but at the same time he also wanted to publish productive philosophical ideas. At the end of the 1870s Eucken therefore published books closely related to the essential philosophical problems but without any fixed systematic opinion. These books are Eucken's great contributions to the history of philosophical concepts and technical terms, as well as to the theory of metaphors.

In his studies *Geschichte und Kritik der Grundbegriffe der Gegenwart* (1878; translated as *The Fundamental Concepts of Modern Philosophic Thought, Critically and Historically Considered*, 1880) and *Geschichte der philosophischen Terminologie* (1879, History of Philosophical Terminology), Eucken developed original views on the interdependence of language and thinking and on the meaning of concepts and technical terms. He was one of the most astute critics of philosophical language for his time and advanced important ideas for the reform of philosophical terminology. Eucken's small book *Über Bilder und Gleichnisse in der Philosophie* (1880, On Images and Similes in Philosophy) is the most interesting publication from the nineteenth century on metaphors. According to Eucken, figurative expressions and metaphors provide more than mere aesthetic ornamentation or expository illustration in philosophical arguments; they serve an essential heuristic function. Metaphors, Eucken argued, should not usurp the place of concepts but should instead pave the way for thoughts and help wherever concepts are missing.

Eucken's philosophical and semiotic reflections influenced Georg Runze, Gottlob Frege, Ferdinand Tönnies, and Karl Jaspers and have been appreciated by Theodor W. Adorno. Nevertheless, Eucken's proposal to found an academy or at least an editorial group to collect historical material and to edit a comprehensive historical dictionary of philosophical concepts and terms remained unsuccessful. Disappointed by this failure, Eucken changed his field of research and published in the 1880s many important papers (not only in philosophical journals but also in widespread German newspapers) on several problems of the history of philosophy. But Eucken was primarily interested in a systematic treatment of the problem of human life. Both his weighty books of the 1880s—*Prolegomena zu Forschungen über die Einheit des Geisteslebens in Bewusstsein und Tat der Menschheit* (1885, Prolegomena to Research on the Unity of the Spiritual Life in Consciousness and Action of Mankind) and *Die Einheit des Geisteslebens in Bewusstsein und Tat der Menschheit* (1888, Research on the Unity of the Spiritual Life in Consciousness and Action of Mankind)—had one main idea, as Eucken later summarized in his book *Prolegomena und Epilog zu einer Philosophie des Geisteslebens* (1922, Prolegomena and Epilogue to a Philosophy of Spiritual Life). Both studies struggled against the tremendous spiritual fragmentation that jeopardized the internal connection of modern human life and hindered all creative urge. To argue for this idea Eucken criticized the spiritual movements ("syntagmas" in Eucken's word) dominating at that time—naturalism and intellectualism. Neither of them helped to resolve the problem of human life because they separated the spiritual life from the individual, whereas Eucken tried to mediate both. Thus, he inferred from the detailed criticism of both syntagmas his own system of a personal world.

Eucken developed the characteristics of his system along complicated lines of thought and used an extremely individual, unusual, and sophisticated terminology. Most of Eucken's academic colleagues at German universities did not know what to do with both books. But those who followed Eucken's strict arguments carefully were convinced of their importance. The neo-Kantian philosopher Paul Natorp wrote comprehensive reviews, and Frege, Eucken's colleague at Jena University and the founder of modern mathematical logic, took over some methodological and gnoseological stimulations. Later, both works were held in high esteem by such important thinkers as Max Scheler, Edmund Husserl, José Ortega y Gasset, Ernst Troeltsch, and Heinrich Rickert. The people whom Eucken did not reach with these scholarly books, however, were the main addressees of his philosophical program. Like a professor of philosophy, Eucken wanted to stimulate the academic discussion, but above all he hoped to convince the multipliers of philosophical-ideological thoughts (*weltanschauliche*)—teachers, journalists, editors, priests, and writers—of the importance of his philosophical Weltanschauung. Eucken had little popular success with these books because both were too academic for a general audience.

In Jena, Eucken visited private circles of scholars, delivered public lectures, and took part in the academic and local cultural life. At Moritz Seebeck's house he met Irene Passow, who belonged to the famous German families Passow, Ulrichs, Gildemeister, and Smidt. The couple became engaged in 1881 and were married in 1882. Irene Eucken was a talented fashion designer and painter who occasionally worked with such artists as Ernst Ludwig Kirchner, Emil Nolde, and Henry van der Velde. Both husband and wife played an important role in the cultural life of Jena. They supported local artists and art societies; organized concerts, poetry readings, and discussions; and ran an international salon of philosophy. Irene and Rudolf Eucken had three children. Their daughter, Ida Maria Eucken, studied voice, and both sons were successful scholars: Arnold Eucken taught chemistry at the universities of Breslau (now Wrocław, Poland) and Göttingen, while Walter Eucken held professorships in economics at Tübingen and Freiburg and belonged to the founders of the Freiburg school of ordoliberalism.

Because of the disappointing receptions of his books in the late 1880s, Eucken changed both his strategies of argumentation and publication. After 1890 he published increasingly in general magazines, pedagogical and theological journals, church papers, and influential newspapers. In order to react to new spiritual, social, and political challenges and changes, Eucken revised his books and brought them up to date over a period of several decades, so that some of his works went through more than eight editions. In these revised and enlarged editions Eucken modified some of his arguments, but he did not change any major idea of his philosophical system. This new strategy to attract a wider readership for his philosophical opinions was connected with a fundamental change in

Eucken's style. His conceptual and linguistic precision degenerated as he turned much of his philosophical terminology into more common expressions. From that time his thinking stressed personal ethical effort more than intellectual idealism. Eucken spoke now with the temper and tone of a prophet burdened with a divine message of awakening and inspiration and help for the present perplexity. Even in his most soaring speculations, he had an eye for the problems of the man in the street. He was prophetic and practical. Eucken's readers did not expect austere arguments. They studied his writings because they hoped to get the feeling of being invited by their philosophical leader to share a common experience of hidden spiritual connections.

The first step toward the new philosophical strategy was the book *Die Lebensanschauungen der grossen Denker: Eine Entwicklungsgeschichte des Lebensproblems der Menschheit von Plato bis zur Gegenwart* (1890, translated as *The Problem of Human Life as Viewed by the Great Thinkers from Plato to the Present Time*, 1909), his most successful book. Among its readers were scholars and educated people looking for the meaning of life. It went through some twenty editions. As the title indicates, in this work Eucken showed in a semischolarly way that the problem of human life was one of the central issues of all great thinkers since Plato.

With the books *Der Kampf um einen geistigen Lebensinhalt: Neue Grundlegung einer Weltanschauung* (1896, The Struggle for a Spiritual Content of Life), *Der Wahrheitsgehalt der Religion* (1901; translated as *The Truth of Religion*, 1911), *Grundlinien einer neuen Lebensanschauung* (1907; translated as *Life's Basis and Life's Ideal: The Fundamentals of a New Philosophy of Life*, 1911), and *Der Sinn und Wert des Lebens* (1908; translated as *The Meaning and Value of Life*, 1909), and also with his pamphlets, articles, and public lectures, Eucken aimed at creating a *Lebensanschauung* or Weltanschauung for the modern man. He promised all loyal adherents *(Gesinnungsgenossen)* in the struggle for the recovery of an eternal spiritual world amid the darkness of the present world a Weltanschauung that would give them moral stability and reliable orientation. In the first edition of *Die Lebensanschauungen der grossen Denker* he wrote that the enormous changes of the last decades and centuries had shaken the spiritual condition of mankind despite the progress in social life, politics, and technology. These changes had provoked gigantic problems and glaring contradictions, which on no account could be accepted. The tremendous expansion and division of external human work had replaced attention to the inner unity of human being; the impetuous pursuit of external success had suppressed the concern about spiritual equilibrium. On the basis of this general stocktaking Eucken appealed for a radical turning back. He did not request a withdrawal from politics and economy, nor did his philosophical program intend any kind of escapism. Eucken argued that politics and economy would rule the external life, but since they cannot solve the problems of inner man, everyone should fight for a spiritual purpose in life besides external work.

Eucken attacked academic philosophers for forgetting the problem of human life. While most people sought the meaning of life, most professors of philosophy discussed only methodological and gnoseological questions. Because of his preaching the virtues of his Weltanschauung to those who looked seriously for spiritual profundity, Eucken had hardly any effect within academic philosophical circles in Germany or in other countries. A typical academic reaction to Eucken's prophetic activism is Bernard Bosanquet's remark: "There is in Eucken's immense literary output no really precise and serious contribution to philosophical science. Free cognition has been submerged by moralistic rhetoric."

Eucken was a productive author but a boring writer. His books were written in a ponderous style full of clichés, repetitions, and vague philosophical terms, making him a philosopher of questionable literary merit, which is why the awarding of the Nobel Prize in Literature came as such a surprise. Among the nominees in 1908, the top candidates initially were the Swedish novelist Selma Lagerlöf (who did receive the prize the following year) and the English poet A. C. Swinburne, but the Nobel committee could not make a decision between these two. Eucken was suggested as a compromise solution by Vitalis Norström, professor of philosophy at Gothenburg University, who admired Eucken's philosophical writings. Eucken's output was seen as consistent with the terms of Alfred Nobel's will directing that the literature prize should go to a work or works written with an idealistic tendency.

Swedish documents and letters of some members of the Nobel committee show that Eucken's nomination had a Swedish background. These supporters felt the philosopher was needed as a counterweight to the demonstration in support of his Jena colleague and leading materialist Ernst Haeckel, whose lecture during Uppsala's 1907 bicentennial celebration for Carolus Linnaeus had been enthusiastically received. With Eucken's Nobel Prize, Scandinavia's reading public rediscovered the idealistic, religious tradition in philosophy. After Eucken's Nobel lecture, Swedish, Danish, and Finnish idealistic thinkers renewed their campaign against materialistic, antireligious movements.

In Germany, Eucken's Nobel award received only a muted response. Of course, all German newspapers published short articles about the decision of the Swedish Academy, but most of these articles paid tribute to both German Nobel Prize winners of 1908, Eucken and the chemist Paul Ehrlich. Eucken's prize did not start an academic debate about his philosophy in his own country. Eucken's academic colleagues remained unresponsive to his greatest international public success, because for them, the Nobel Prize was only further evidence that Eucken was more a popular philosophical author than a serious scholar. Eucken did receive many congratulations from German teachers and clergymen. About this group of followers, Eucken wrote in an unpublished letter to the Polish philosopher Marian Zdziechowski from 16 January 1909: "They are my most loyal friends."

Contrary to the muted academic response in Germany, leading French thinkers sent heartfelt greetings to Eucken. After 1908 a wave of interest in Eucken began among French-speaking intellectuals. Henri Bergson, Emile Boutroux, and Desire Mercier wrote commentaries on Eucken's philosophy.

Immediately prior to the decision of the Nobel committee, two of Eucken's most influential, most popular, but also most unscholarly books appeared: *Hauptprobleme der Religionsphilosophie der Gegenwart* (1907; translated as *Christianity and the New Idealism: A Study in the Religious Philosophy of To-day,* 1909) and *Der Sinn und Wert des Lebens*. When the Nobel Prize was announced, there was a run on Eucken's latest books among German readers. Above all, *Der Sinn und Wert des Lebens,* a simple summary of Eucken's main ideas, became a best-seller. It could not be printed fast enough to meet the swelling demand. Many unpublished letters to Eucken, collected in his literary estate, show the incredible influence of *Der Sinn und Wert des Lebens*. From 1908 until the end of World War I it was a highly popular gift for Christmas and other religious occasions. Thus, as Eucken's academic influence decreased, his success outside of philosophy departments increased accordingly, as the German educated classes absorbed his philosophy of life.

Eucken found his disciples not only in Germany but also in Japan, China, India, England, Italy, Spain, Scandinavia, the Baltic Nations, and in the United States, where the first Eucken Clubs were founded at theological schools. He won many prizes and received honorary doctorates. He delivered academic and public lectures in more than one hundred German cities, as well as in Austria, Hungary, the Netherlands, Norway, Denmark, Sweden, Finland, Great Britain, and Latvia. During the fall semester of 1912–1913 Eucken taught as a German exchange professor at Harvard and visited several American universities to deliver lectures and to collect honors. After the turn of the century he started to assemble his disciples in informal groups and more formal associations in order to institutionalize his Weltanschauung. Prior to World War I he took the first concrete steps toward a society based on his own philosophy of life.

During World War I Eucken was convinced of his moral obligation both to encourage the Germans and to defend German policy. Therefore, he traveled throughout the country to give talks in universities, schools, adult evening classes, city halls, theaters, and clubs. He wrote pamphlets and articles, signed open letters, communiqués, and appeals, and joined several patriotic committees, clubs, and organizations. Like many other German scholars, writers, and clergymen, Eucken believed that the common wartime experience could reunify the fragmented German population. Although Eucken supported the German war propaganda, he never shared anti-Semitic or chauvinistic opinions. Toward the end of the war, when the general situation both in Europe and Germany became worse, Eucken strengthened his efforts to prevent the threatening collapse of morality and religion in Germany. His most far-reaching action was the foundation of the Luther Society in 1918. With the help of Martin Luther's religious idealism, the members of the society hoped both to reunify the divided German people and to create a new moral basis for the postwar era.

Eucken believed that only a new, modern spiritual leader could solve the deep social and mental crisis of Weimar Germany. To organize all idealistic-minded people, some of Eucken's adherents wrote an *Aufruf zur Gründung eines Euckenbundes* (Appeal to Found an Eucken League) and explained that, above all, Eucken had recognized not only the confused state of life and the threatening collapse of all moral values but also the only possible way to rescue people from the spiritual crisis of that time. In autumn 1919, friends, students, and disciples of the philosopher founded the Euckenbund (Eucken League), which was one of many German associations based on a particular Weltanschauung. The educated classes in Germany responded with such associations to their decreasing influence in almost all spheres of the postwar society. To lead the Euckenbund, Eucken retired as professor and resigned from the chair of the Luther Society in 1920. As long as Eucken lived, the Euckenbund did not tend to take part in political decisions, to reform institutions, or to develop a democratic attitude toward the Weimar Republic; it was just interested in awakening a new consciousness for the crisis of the modern world and in the redemption of all endangered souls.

Eucken was a popular university lecturer who attracted thousands of students from all over the world. One of his most famous students, Gerhart Hauptmann, winner of the Nobel Prize in Literature in 1912, described him as a fascinating, prophetic teacher, who had conducted almost all Jena students to the absolute spiritual life. Eucken's Nobel lecture, *Naturalismus oder Idealismus* (translated as *Naturalism or Idealism?* 1912) had been published in 1909; Irene Eucken and the Euckenbund republished this work in 1922, when Germany was in physical and spiritual shambles. Because of the rising inflation, however, only a relatively small number of enthusiasts could buy the reprinted lecture.

Toward the end of his life Eucken was only one of many spiritual leaders in Weimar Germany—prophets who wanted to deliver their simple moral philosophy within a society looking for eternal spiritual values behind everyday life. When Rudolf Eucken died on 15 September 1926, he went down in history as one of the last academic scholars who believed in the possibility of influencing and even changing both society and the common spiritual life by idealistic philosophical systems and appeals.

Letters:

"Die deutsche Sprache in Ungarn. Briefwechsel zwischen Maurus Révai und Rudolf Eucken," *Nord und Süd: Deutsche Monatsschrift,* 40 (1916);

"Aus Briefen von Rudolf Eucken, William James, Henri Bergson an Julius Goldstein," *Der Morgen,* 5 (1929–1930): 411–415;

"Abdruck eines unveröffentlichten Briefes von Rudolf Eucken an Herrn Privatdozenten Ernst Bratuschek," *Mitteilungen des Euckenbundes,* no. 1/3 (1931): 1–4;

Wladimir Szylkarski, "Aus Euckens Briefwechsel mit Teichmüller," *Archiv für spiritualistische Philosophie und ihre Geschichte,* 1 (1940): 412–438;

Hans Meyer, "Unbekannte Briefe Rudolf Euckens an Jakob Froschhammer," *Philosophisches Jahrbuch,* 55 (1942): 245–250;

"Correspondence between Prof. Rudolf Eucken and Rabindranath Tagore," in *Rabindranath Tagore in Germany: A Cross-Section of Contemporary Reports,* edited and translated by Dietmar Rothermund (New Delhi: Max Mueller Bhavan, 1962), pp. 54–56;

Hans-Ulrich Lessing, "Briefe an Dilthey anlässlich der Veröffentlichung seiner Ideen über eine beschreibende und zergliedernde Psychologie," *Dilthey-Jahrbuch,* 3 (1985): 204–205, 223–225;

Edmund Husserl, *Briefwechsel: Husserliana Dokumente III,* volume 6: *Philosophenbriefe,* edited by Karl Schumann (Dordrecht, Boston & London: Kluver, 1993), pp. 85–94.

References:

Gunnar Ahlström, "Kleine Geschichte der Zuerkennung des Nobelpreises an Rudolf Eucken," *Nobelpreis für Literatur 1908: Rudolf Eucken, Philosophische Schriften* (Zürich: Coron, 1967), pp. 9–17;

Barbara Beßlich, "Epigone des Idealismus oder moderner Philosoph? Rudolf Eucken zwischen wissenschaftlicher Nostalgie und literarischem Prophetentum," in her *Wege in den "Kulturkrieg": Zivilisationskritik in Deutschland 1890–1914* (Darmstadt: Wissenschaftliche Buchgesellschaft, 2000), pp. 45–118;

Bernard Bosanquet, "W. R. B. Gibson–The Philosophy of Eucken," *Quarterly Review* (London), no. 22 (1914): 365–389;

Uwe Dathe, "Begriffsgeschichte und Philosophie: Zur Philosophie Rudolf Euckens," in *Philosophiegeschichte und Hermeneutik,* edited by Volker Caysa and Klaus-Dieter Eichler (Leipzig: Universitätsverlag, 1996), pp. 85–96;

Dathe, "Der Eucken-Nachlaß und die Geschichte seiner Bearbeitung," *Mitteilungen: Thüringer Universitäts- und Landesbibliothek Jena,* 8, no. 1 (1998): 17–27;

Dathe, "Jena, 12. Januar 1900: Rudolf Euckens Rede zur Jahrhundertfeier," in *Angst vor der Moderne: Philosophische Antworten auf Krisenerfahrungen: Der Mikrokosmos Jena 1900–1940,* edited by Klaus M. Kodalle (Würzburg: Königshausen & Neumann, 2000), pp. 45–61;

Dathe, "Der Nachlaß Rudolf Euckens: Eine Bestandsübersicht," *Zeitschrift für neuere Theologiegeschichte,* 9 (2002): 268–301;

Dathe, "Der Philosoph bestreitet den Krieg: Rudolf Euckens politische Publizistik während des Ersten Weltkrieges," in *Zwischen Wissenschaft und Politik: Studien zur Jenaer Universität im 20. Jahrhundert,* edited by Herbert Gottwald and Matthias Steinbach (Jena & Quedlinburg: Bussert & Stadeler, 2000), pp. 47–64;

Dathe, "Rudolf Eucken–ein Gegner des Monismus und Freund des Monisten," in *Monismus um 1900–Wissenschaftskultur und Weltanschauung,* edited by Paul Ziche (Berlin: Verlag für Wissenschaft und Bildung, 2000), pp. 41–59;

Dathe, "Rudolf Eucken als Sprachkritiker und Zeichenphilosoph," *Zeitschrift für Semiotik,* 23 (2001): 27–38;

Dathe and Nils Goldschmidt, "Wie der Vater, so der Sohn? Neuere Erkenntnisse zu Walter Euckens Leben und Werk anhand des Nachlasses von Rudolf Eucken in Jena," *ORDO. Jahrbuch für die*

Ordnung von Wirtschaft und Gesellschaft, 54 (2003): 49–74;

Hans Düfel, "Voraussetzungen, Gründung und Anfang der Luther-Gesellschaft. Lutherrezeption zwischen Aufklärung und Idealismus," *Lutherjahrbuch,* 60 (1993): 72–117;

Walter Eucken, "Vorwort," in Rudolf Eucken, *Die Lebensanschauungen der großen Denker: Eine Entwicklungsgeschichte des Lebensproblems der Menschheit von Plato bis zur Gegenwart* (Berlin: De Gruyter, 1950);

Ferdinand Fellmann, *Phänomenologie als ästhetische Theorie* (Freiburg & Munich: Alber, 1989), pp. 140–158, 160–162, 167–171;

Othmar Feyl, "Briefe aus dem Nachlaß des Jenaer Philosophen Rudolf Eucken (1900–1926): Zeitüberlegenheit und historisch-politische Wirklichkeit eines idealistischen Philosophen," *Wissenschaftliche Zeitschrift der Friedrich-Schiller-Universität Jena,* 10, no. 2 (1960–1961): 249–294;

Kurt Flasch, "Rudolf Eucken spricht vor ausrückenden Kriegern," in his *Die geistige Mobilmachung: Die deutschen Intellektuellen und der Erste Weltkrieg: Ein Versuch* (Berlin: Alexander Fest, 2000), pp. 15–35;

W. R. Boyce Gibson, *Rudolf Eucken's Philosophy of Life* (London: Black, 1912);

Nils Goldschmidt, *Entstehung und Vermächtnis ordoliberalen Denkens: Walter Eucken und die Notwendigkeit einer kulturellen Ökonomik* (Münster: LIT, 2002);

Friedrich Wilhelm Graf, "George Tyrrell über seinen Ausschluß aus dem Jesuitenorden: Vier unveröffentlichte Briefe George Tyrrells an Rudolf Eucken," *Zeitschrift für neuere Theologiegeschichte,* 5 (1998): 228–247;

Graf, "Die gescheiterte Berufung Husserls nach Jena. Drei unbekannte Briefe," *Dilthey-Jahrbuch,* 10 (1996): 135–142;

Graf, "Die Positivität des Geistigen: Rudolf Euckens Programm neoidealistischer Universalintegration," in *Kultur und Kulturwissenschaften um 1900. Volume II: Idealismus und Positivismus,* edited by Rüdiger vom Bruch, Graf, and Gangolf Hübinger (Stuttgart: Steiner, 1997), pp. 53–85;

Reinhold J. Haskamp, *Spekulativer und phänomenologischer Personalismus. Einflüsse J. G. Fichtes und Rudolf Euckens auf Max Schelers Philosophie der Person* (Freiburg & Munich: Alber, 1966);

Max Horkheimer, "Rudolf Eucken: Ein Epigone des Idealismus," *Frankfurter Zeitung,* 4 November 1926;

Uwe Hossfeld, Rosemarie Nöthlich, and Lennart Olsson, "Wissenschaftspolitik international: Ernst Haeckel und der Nobelpreis für Literatur 1908," in *Klassische Universität und akademische Provinz—Studien zur Universität Jena von der Mitte des 19. bis in die dreißiger Jahre des 20. Jahrhunderts,* edited by Matthias Steinbach and Stefan Gerber (Jena & Quedlinburg: Bussert & Stadeler, 2005), pp. 97–102;

Friedrich von Hügel, "The Religious Philosophy of Rudolf Eucken," *Hibbert Journal,* 10 (1912): 660–677;

Edmund Husserl, "Die Phaenomenologie und Rudolf Eucken," *Die Tatwelt,* 3 (1927): 10–11;

William Tudor Jones, *An Interpretation of Rudolf Eucken's Philosophy* (New York: Putnam, 1912);

Hermann Lübbe, *Politische Philosophie in Deutschland. Studien zu ihrer Geschichte* (Basel & Stuttgart: Schwabe, 1962), pp. 178–188;

Lübbe, "Rudolf Eucken," in *Biographisches Lexikon für Ostfriesland,* edited by Martin Tielke (Aurich: Ostfriesische Landschaft, 1993), pp. 134–137;

Fritz Medicus, "Rudolf Eucken zum Gedächtnis," *Kant-Studien,* 31 (1926): 445–454;

Brunhild Neuland, "Irene Eucken: Vom Salon zum Eucken-Haus," in *Entwurf und Wirklichkeit: Frauen in Jena 1900 bis 1933,* edited by Gisela Horn (Rudolstadt & Jena: Hain, 2001), pp. 219–233;

Peter Neuner, *Religiöse Erfahrung und geschichtliche Offenbarung: Friedrich von Hügels Grundlegung der Theologie* (Munich, Paderborn, & Wien: Schöningh, 1977);

Max Scheler, "Die deutsche Philosophie der Gegenwart," in his *Gesammelte Werke 7* (Bern & Munich: Francke, 1973), pp. 273–275;

Edwin E. Slosson, "Rudolf Eucken (Twelve Major Prophets of Today VII)," *Independent: A Weekly Magazine,* 74 (27 February 1913): 445–456;

Ferdinand Tönnies, "Rudolf Euckens Grundbegriffe der Gegenwart in neuer Fassung," *Deutsche Literaturzeitung,* 32 (1911): col. 69–75;

Ernst Troeltsch, *Der Historismus und seine Probleme: Erstes (einziges) Buch: Das logische Problem der Geschichtsphilosophie* (Tübingen: Mohr, 1922), pp. 134–136, 485–493;

Max Vollert, "Die Berufung Rudolf Euckens nach Jena, 1873," in *Beiträge zur thüringischen und sächsischen Geschichte. Festschrift für Otto Dobenecker* (Jena: Gustav Fischer, 1929), pp. 505–522;

Max Wundt, *Die Philosophie an der Universität Jena in ihrem geschichtlichen Verlaufe dargestellt* (Jena: Gustav Fischer, 1932), pp. 429–484;

Wundt, *Rudolf Eucken: Rede, gehalten bei der Eucken-Gedächtnisfeier der Universität Jena am 9. Januar 1927* (Langensalza: Beyer & Söhne, 1927).

Papers:

Rudolf Eucken's extensive literary estate (correspondence, working manuscripts, personal and professional papers, collections of material, the literary estate of Irene and Ida Eucken, and material on the Euckenbund) is at the Thüringer Universitäts-und Landesbibliothek Jena, Abteilung Handschriften und Sondersammlungen, 07740 Jena, Postfach, Germany.

1908 Nobel Prize in Literature Presentation Speech

by Harald Hjärne, Director of the Swedish Academy, on 10 December 1908

Alfred Nobel was a man of action who, during his successful business career in the competing markets of many countries and in the international trade centres, had developed an awareness of the inner contradictions and dangers of modern developments. Mankind still seemed to him to need help, and therefore he thought that the best investment for his own fortune would be to use this interest to support those of whom the future would reveal that—in the words of his will—"mankind profited most from them."

The ambiguity of all human work and its tools or weapons challenged him to a personal deed in behalf of human progress. He knew the enormous usefulness of his own technical inventions for military purposes; therefore, he wanted to support any promising efforts toward international peace. How could his worldly mind have overlooked that all our civilization is full of strife, that it invites abuse as well as proper use, and that it can be turned toward evil as well as good?

His chief interest, however, was the intellectual sphere, despite its inherent contradictions. It appeared to him, the cosmopolitan familiar with the languages and civilizations of France and England, as a complex of arts and sciences, of exact natural science and humanistic belles-lettres. The former he sought to stimulate by supporting discoveries and inventions for the benefit of mankind. Turning to literature with the same philanthropic concern, he established a prize for what he called "excellence in works of an idealistic tendency."

Alfred Nobel was deeply influenced by the outlook of Victor Rydberg's poetry and philosophy. He knew what ideals mean to the human mind, to the will that creates and maintains civilization, cultivates and reaps its fruits, and through the struggle and darkness of life breaks a path toward a new dawn of light and peace. Wherever such ideals are manifested in their infinite variety and strengthen the willingness of men to serve each other—whether in the poet's inspiration, the philosopher's attempt to solve the riddle of life, the historian's biographies, or the work of any scholar or writer that looks toward those ideals as models in his freedom and independence—there one finds the literature that Alfred Nobel had in mind. This literature makes use of whatever art and science can offer, and from it mankind "profits the most" precisely because it mirrors the ideal truth without any regard for the useful. The creations and forms of this literature are as manifold as the ideals, and they are forever new and free.

The Swedish Academy has therefore felt that it acted with the sanction of Alfred Nobel when it decided this year to award the literary prize founded by Nobel to one of the most prominent thinkers of our age, Professor Rudolf Eucken, "in recognition of his earnest search for truth, his penetrating power of thought, his wide range of vision, and the warmth and strength of presentation with which in his numerous works he has vindicated and developed an idealistic philosophy of life."

For over thirty years Professor Eucken has been publishing profound contributions in several areas of philosophy. His activity as a writer has yielded increasingly many and important books as his basic philosophy has become both more coherent and more comprehensive. Particularly in recent years he has published the works that afford us the most thorough introduction to his thought; moreover, the wider public has received from him uncommonly lucid and powerful expositions of his attempts to resolve the most urgent problems of contemporary civilization. Thus he is in the midst of giving the final shape to his mature thought, and everywhere one can see new ideas which we hope he will be able to develop fully in the near future.

I cannot here give a detailed account of Eucken's long and versatile career as a philosopher, because time is short and the subject difficult for one with little knowledge of most of his special fields. I can only make some generalizations and dwell in particular on the historical foundations of his *Weltanschauung* and his views on the meaning of historical processes. Professor Eucken considers history a decisive influence on his philosophy, and it was philological and historical studies that led him toward philosophy. Ever since his early days the actual life of man and society has meant much more to him than the abstractions of mere thought analysis. Unfortunately we shall have to omit many interesting ramifications of his thought in order to get a clear picture at least of its main results.

The confident and rising idealism today in the intellectual life not only of Germany but everywhere on the higher and freer levels of civilized life is very different from those proud constructions which bore that name and which went bankrupt half a century ago with Hegel's magnificent system. It was an attempt to derive the inexhaustible wealth of life and the world from abstract categories and concepts by means of a daring dialectic, and to force all human research, all civilization, under the yoke of a complete system of thought. But closer analysis revealed this attempt to be beyond the competence of the philosophical search for truth, and in fact it accelerated the change to an equally dogmatic materialism.

We Swedes know that even at the zenith of dialectic absolutism Boström directed his logical criticisms toward its basic attitudes. By going back to earlier views both here and abroad, he developed a different outlook which has had its adherents in this country up to the present. There is an indisputable resemblance between his views and those developed by Professor Eucken in his writings. This is not surprising, for they both represent a basic type that since the earliest days of civilization—notwithstanding temporary eclipses—has preserved its vitality in the face of pantheistic abstractions as well as materialistic fear of thought. But this characteristic agreement in their basic views does not exclude independent and personal development; on the contrary it rather promotes it, and no branch of philosophy has produced so many marked profiles as realistic idealism. Socrates and Plato were led by this idealism to hold that philosophy is a search for truth rather than a fixed dogma, and this tireless search, by whatever means, has characterized philosophy throughout the ages. Thus Eucken and Boström reached their common goal by quite different means.

Since his youth Eucken has carefully observed the busy and steady philosophical attempts to reassess external and inner experience and to gain firm ground again after the collapse of the bold philosophical systems. Philosophy turned in different directions with varying expectations and success. Sometimes the motto was "Back to Kant," and the great metaphysical iconoclast served as a model for thorough studies of the limits of human knowledge, or else one listened hesitantly to his declaration of an eternal realm of reason based on unassailable moral postulates. Again there were attempts to give philosophy a safe position by tying it to the victorious advances of modern science or, more successfully, by independently questioning its presuppositions and methods. There were attempts to discover the secrets of the human soul in its manifestations, whether by observation or experiment, and there was hope that such research would lead toward the discovery of the proper relation of physical and psychological existence.

Eucken has been familiar with all these schools, but his main field has been historical and critical research on the emergence and development of mainstreams of thought in connection with the evolution and change of general culture. Like so many pioneers in his field, he has always been convinced that there can be no true progress without a proper regard for tradition and that there is more to the annals of philosophy than a kaleidoscope of systems rising and falling with equal suddenness. As Eucken has often emphasized, there can be no continuity in philosophy unless it grows like the other sciences and continually treats and develops the same problems, lest every mind should believe that he could start all over from the beginning only to be replaced by someone else in the same manner.

Apart from collections of monographs and essays in this field, Eucken as early as 1878 published the first comprehensive results of his method. In *Grundbegriffe der Gegenwart* [Basic Concepts of Modern Thought] he discusses the origin, formulation, and development of common modern concepts since the days of ancient philosophy and scholasticism. Such terms are "subjective and objective," "experience and evolution," "monism and dualism," "mechanistic and organic," "law and individuality," "personality and character," "theoretical and practical," "immanence and transcendence." But he is not interested merely in definition of terms; he wants to describe the leading goals and attitudes of a period by elucidating, in his own words, "concepts as a mirror of their time." With each dissection the object becomes more clearly delineated. In the fourth edition, which appeared this year, the scope of the book has widened; it has become a thorough critique of the conflicts in modern civilization; accordingly, the title of the book has been changed to *Geistige Strömungen der Gegenwart* (1908) [Main Currents of Modern Thought]. Indeed, the author has developed his own basic ideas in it, and it is a rewarding labour to study them in their wealth and complexity.

A thinker who considers the perennial questions of human civilization from this point of view will soon learn that he cannot solve them either by ignoring their close interrelation or by limiting himself to epistemological questions. Undoubtedly these problems constantly impinge upon each other; they cover the whole of human existence, influence individuals that are particularly susceptible to their importance, and thereby exercise a reforming power over entire communities and ages. The attempt to trace them in their vital and seminal role amounts to giving a comprehensive survey of human intellectual history. At the same time such a project is more conducive to arousing and widening philosophical interest than a mere analysis of conflicting dogmas, schools, and sects. Eucken undertook such a task in *Die Lebensanschauungen der grosser Denker: Eine Entwicklungsgeschichte des Lebensproblems der Menschheit von Plato his zur Gegenwart* (1890) [The Problem of Human Life as Viewed by the Great Thinkers from Plato to the Present Time]. This work, revised and expanded through seven editions, bears witness not only to the depth and scope of Eucken's research but to his mastery of marshalling his thoughts and to the maturity of his style.

Eucken has developed his own philosophy in several works such as *Der Kampf um einen geistigen Lebensinhalt: Neue Grundlegung einer Weltanschauung* (1896) [The Struggle for a Spiritual Content of Life: New Principles of a Philosophy] and *Grundlinien einer neuen Lebensanschauung* (1907) [Life's Basis and Life's Ideal: The Fundamentals of a New Philosophy of Life] as well as the more popular *Der Sinn und Wert des Lebens* (1908) [The Meaning and Value of Life] and *Einführung in eine Philosophie des Geisteslebens* (1908) [Introduction to a Philosophy of the Mind]. The last mentioned work in particular is a masterly and lucid exposition of his views.

In recent years Eucken has also turned his attention to religious questions, in *Der Wahrheitsgehalt der Religion* (1901) [The Truth of Religion] and *Hauptprobleme der Religionsphilosophie der Gegenwart* (1907) [Main Problems of Contemporary Philosophy of Religion], the latter based on three lectures delivered during a theological summer institute at the University of Jena. This year he has developed his ideas about the philosophy of history at some length in a treatise that forms part of the great encyclopaedic work *Die Kultur der Gegenwart* [Contemporary Civilization]. According to hints in recent works he is now planning a thorough re-examination of ethical problems.

His deep insights into history and his significant attempts to relate his own thoughts on the forces of life to the evidence of history place Eucken far above the superficial attitudes that exaggerate and misinterpret the inner meaning of history. These attitudes, at the cost of an unprejudiced love of truth, have become all too common in this century of history.

Furthermore, Eucken sees a threat to civilization in the caricature of historicism, which partly intends to drag all firm goals and higher aims into the whirlpool of a misunderstood relativity and partly supports the frequent attempts to limit and paralyze the human will by fitting all human developments and achievements into a supposed naturalistic and fatalistic causal nexus. But in contrast to Nietzsche, for instance, he does not believe in the right or ability of the overweening individual to maintain his own will to power in the face of the obligations to the eternal majesty of moral laws. It is not the individual or the superman in his separate existence, but the strong character formed in the consciousness of free harmony with the intellectual forces of the cosmos, and therefore profoundly independent, that in Eucken's view is called upon to liberate us from the superficial compulsion of nature and the never completely inescapable pressure of the historical chain of cause and effect.

In history as well as in his personal existence man has life of a higher nature, a life originating not in nature but existing in itself and through itself, a life of the mind, which is in reality beyond time but which is revealed to us only in temporal manifestations. All true development presupposes some basis of existence. To the extent to which man comes to participate in the intellectual life, he acquires a power that is eternal and above the vicissitudes of time. This eternal life is a realm of truth, for truths with a limited existence are unthinkable. At the same time it is an infinite whole of living power, far above the world as it appears to us but exercising its influence in the world for us and through us. It is not an abstract castle in the air to which we can escape on the wings of a mystical and supposedly logical imagination, but as a wholly living power it confronts our entire personality with an either-or, a choice of the will that makes the evolution of man and mankind a ceaseless struggle between the higher and the lower life.

History is the mirror of mankind's victories and defeats in this struggle, the vicissitudes of which have been due to the self-determination of the free personality. Hence no philosophy of history can predict the future of this struggle. Even the civilization handed to us as a heritage does not survive by itself but demands our persistent and personal struggle for the true and genuine life of the mind. Nothing else can justify and support our endeavours for morality and art and our political and social work.

"Utilitarianism," Eucken says, "which ever form it assumes, is irreconcilably opposed to true intellectual culture. Any intellectual activity degenerates unless it is treated for its own sake." Although a great admirer and lover of art, Eucken has turned with equal severity against the aestheticism which is preached so loudly in our days and which "infects only reflective and pleasure-loving hedonists." "No art that values itself and its task can afford to condemn morality. A creative artist of the highest order has hardly ever been a follower of an aesthetic view of life." Our Runeberg is a poet after his heart, for such an outlook "with its indifference to moral values and its arrogant exclusiveness is quite foreign to him." And only those nations, whether great or small, that have created and maintained a civilization full of genuine intellectual life have a contribution to make to mankind. A contribution may be made only by those nations whose future consists not in a vain endeavour to use material force and weapons to "transform quantity into quality," but in the ever growing revelation of eternal life within the limits of temporal existence.

Eucken does not reject a metaphysics that tries to express conceptually those things that are accessible to us in the infinite realm of truth and life. But he has not constructed an everlasting system, nor did he want to do so. His philosophy, which he himself calls a philosophy of action, operates primarily with the forces of human evolution and is therefore more dynamic than static. We may regard him as a *Kulturphilosoph* who fully meets the standards and needs of our age.

Professor Eucken—The lofty and scholarly idealism of your *Weltanschauung*, which has found such vigorous expression in your many and widely read works, has justified the Swedish Academy in awarding to you the Nobel Prize in Literature for this year.

The Academy greets you with sincere and respectful admiration and hopes that your future works, too, will bear ample fruit for the benefit of culture and humanity.

At the banquet, Hjärne addressed, in German, his personal congratulations to Professor Eucken. He recalled Thuringia and, in particular, the University of Jena, the heart of German humanism, and the relations of that university with the history of the Swedish Reformation. In his reply, Mr. Eucken spoke enthusiastically about the idealism for which he had struggled and expressed his gratitude toward Sweden and the Swedish Academy.

[© The Nobel Foundation, 1908.]

Eucken: Nobel Lecture, 27 March 1909

Naturalism or Idealism?

The history of mankind knows of certain questions that are at once very old and always new: they are very old because any way of life contains an answer to them, and always new because the conditions on which those ways of life depend are constantly shifting and may at critical stages change so much that truths safely accepted for generations may become open problems causing conflict and bewilderment.

Such a question is the contrast between naturalism and idealism with which we are dealing today. The meaning of these words has been blunted by usage; they cause many a misunderstanding, and only through laziness do we put up with such catchwords. But their inadequacy cannot conceal the great contrast which lies behind them and which sharply divides men. This contrast concerns our attitude to the whole of reality and the resulting task that dominates our life; it concerns the question whether man is entirely determined by nature or whether he can somehow—or indeed essentially—rise above it. We are all agreed on the very close ties between man and nature which he should not abandon. But it has been argued and is still being argued vehemently whether his whole being, his actions and sufferings, are determined by these ties or whether he possesses life of another kind which introduces a new stage of reality. The one attitude characterizes naturalism, the other idealism, and these two creeds differ fundamentally both in their goals and in their pursuits of them. For if the additional life of man exists only in his imagination, we should eradicate all traces of it from human opinions and institutions. Instead, we should aim at the closest ties with nature and develop to a pure state the natural character of human life; for thus life would restore the ties with its true origins which it severed unjustly and to its lasting damage. But if one recognizes in man a new element beyond nature, the task will consist in giving it the strongest possible support and contrasting it clearly with nature. In this case life will take up its main position in the new element and look at nature from that point of view. This contrast in attitudes emerges nowhere as clearly as in the place of the soul in the two systems. Nature, of course, has its share in the life of the soul and in numerous manifestations deeply influences human life. But this natural life of the soul is peripheral, mere appendix to the material phenomena of nature. Its only purpose is the preservation of physical life, for man's higher psychological development, his cleverness and resourcefulness, compensate for the brute strength, swiftness of movement, or sharpness of the senses in which animals excel. But even in its extreme form this life has neither purpose nor content in itself; it remains a conglomeration of disparate points. It does not coalesce in an inner community of life, nor does it constitute an inner world peculiar to itself. Thus action is never directed toward an inner purpose but toward the utilitarian purpose of preserving life. Naturalism, if it remains true to its purpose, reduces human life to that norm. Idealism, on the other hand, maintains the emancipation of inwardness; according to it the disparate phenomena of life coalesce in an all-embracing inner world. At the same time, idealism demands that human life should be governed by its peculiar values and goals, the true, the good, and the beautiful. In its view the subordination of all human aspiration to the goal of usefulness appears an intolerable humiliation and a complete betrayal of the greatness and dignity of man. Such divergent and even contradictory attitudes seem to be irreconcilable: we have to choose between harsh alternatives.

With regard to this choice the present time is undeniably divided against itself, particularly since profound changes in the setup of life have brought new aspects of the problem to light. Centuries of tradition had accustomed us to striving primarily for an invisible world and to valuing the visible world only to the degree of its relation to the invisible world. To the medieval mind man's home is a transcendental world; in this world we are merely travellers abroad. We cannot penetrate it, nor does it give us any scope for achievements or hold us by any roots. In such a conception nature easily appears as a lower sphere which one approaches at one's own peril. When Petrarch had climbed Mount Ventoux and was enraptured by the splendour of the Alps, he had serious doubts whether such delight at the creation was not an injustice to the Creator and did not deprive Him of the worship due to Him alone. Thus he took refuge with St. Augustine to regain the security of a religious mood.

These things have changed. We set greater store by the world of immediate experience and many things have helped to make it completely our home. Science has been the leader in this movement, for it has brought about a closer relationship with nature, resulting in many new impulses that have not only enriched parts of our life but have deeply affected its totality. The speculative and subjective thought of former ages was unable to analyze sensual perceptions and did not penetrate to the essence of things. Moreover, its recognition of certain regularities in nature lagged far behind the discovery of mathematical laws of nature first formulated by the genius of Kepler. And not only did it fail to penetrate nature, it failed equally to turn its powers to the use of man and to the advancement of his welfare. Occasional technical inventions were the result of chance rather than superior insight; on the whole, man remained defenceless against nature. Only a century ago men were still awkward and powerless in this regard. In that age of great poets and thinkers, how much time was wasted with overcoming natural obstacles, how inconvenient was travelling, and how cumbersome postal services. In all these respects our age has seen changes never dreamed of by history before. The accumulation of scientific knowledge since the seventeenth century was brought to a triumphant conclusion in the nineteenth. By unravelling the separate strands of natural processes and tracing them back to their ultimate elements, by formulating the effects of these elements in simple formulas, and finally by using the idea of evolution to combine what had been separated, scientific research has given us a closer and more direct experience of nature in all its aspects. At the same time the theory of evolution has shown man's dependence on nature: understanding himself in nature, his own essence appeared to become clearer to him.

The change of concepts was accompanied by a change of the realities of life. Technology seized upon the results of science and caused a revolution in man's relationship with his environment. Former ages had held that his position in the world was essentially determined and not subject to change; man had to suffer whatever dark fate or the will of God had decreed. Even if he could—and was expected to—alleviate suffering in individual instances, he was no match for the totality of suffering and there was no hope of either tearing up evil by the root or making life richer and more joyous. In our age, however, we are translating into action the conviction that by common effort mankind can raise the level of life, that a rule of reason can gradually replace the tyranny of irrational forces. Man may again feel victorious and creative. Even if his powers are limited at any given moment, that moment is only one in a long chain. The impossibilities of a former age have been realized in ours. We have witnessed surprising breakthroughs in our own age and can see no limit to this progressive movement. Man's existence has been immeasurably enriched; it has become an attraction and a challenge for him.

Technological progress becomes even more exciting when it enters into the service of the social idea which demands that not only a small élite but humanity at large should profit by it. This demand creates an entirely new challenge, requiring tremendous energy but also giving rise to new complications and harsh contrasts which, in turn, intensify the passion of man's work in this world and enrich its meaning. The transformation of environment has become the purpose of human life; life seems real only insofar as it deals with things. Man no longer needs the escape to an invisible world in order to find and realize exalted goals.

These facts are indisputable. Our material environment and our relation to it have assumed tremendous importance. Any philosophy and any course of action based on it must reckon with this fact. But naturalism goes beyond this fact, for it maintains that man is completely defined by his relationship with the world, that he is only a piece of the natural process. That is a different contention which requires careful examination. For history has taught us that our judgment is easily confused and exaggerated when revolutionary changes upset the old balance of things. Facts and opinions are confused by man, who is helpless against error and passion. At such a time, it becomes an urgent task to separate the facts from the interpretations given to them. Naturalism, too, is subject to such a scrutiny when it turns a fact into a principle, sees the totality of human life determined by man's closer relation to nature, and adjusts all values accordingly.

The chief argument against such a limitation of human life is the result not of subjective reflection but of an analysis of the modern movement itself. The emergence and the progress of that movement reveal an intellectual capacity which, whether it manifests itself as intellectual and technical mastery of nature or as practical social work, proves the existence of a way of life that cannot be accounted for, if man is understood as a mere natural being. For in coming closer to nature man shows himself superior to it. As a mere part of nature, man's existence would be a series of isolated phenomena. All life would proceed from and depend on contact with the outside world. There would be no way of transcending the limitation of the senses. There would be no place at all for any activity governed by a totality or superior unity, nor for any inner coherence of life. All values and goals would disappear and reality would be reduced to mere actuality. But the experience of human work shows a very different picture.

Modern science has not been the result of a gradual accumulation of sensual perceptions but a deliberate break with the entire stock of traditional knowledge. Such a break was deemed necessary because the old concepts had been too anthropomorphic, whereas a scientific understanding of nature presupposed an acknowledgment of its complete independence from man. But our concepts could not have formulated the independence of nature unless thought had emancipated itself from sensual impressions, and through analysis and new synthesis created a new view of nature. This re-creation was caused by the search for truth and the desire to identify with things as they are and thus to bring about an inner expansion of life. But how could nature be conceived in such a manner without the element of chance and distortion, inherent in the perspective of the individual, unless thought could operate independently of sensual perception? Logical thought, striving for a unified conception of the universe, transformed the immediate sensual perception; it provided the sensual existence with the foundation of a world of thought. Man's tremendous intellectual achievement of a conception of nature in its totality proves his superiority over the natural world and the existence of another level of reality. Thus we may say that naturalism with its emphasis on nature is refuted nowhere with more cogency than in modern science as it transformed nature into an intellectual conception. The more we recognize the intellectual achievement and inner structure of modern science, the clearer becomes the distance from naturalism.

The superiority of man to mere nature is also proved by modern technology, for it demands and proves imaginative anticipation and planning, the tracing of new possibilities, exact calculations, and bold ventures. How could a mere natural being be capable of such achievements?

The social movement, too, reveals man as not entirely limited by a given order, but as a being that perceives and judges a given situation and is confident that it can change it essentially by its own efforts. We have come to set greater store by material things, but we value them not because of their sensual characteristics but because they serve us to enhance life and to dominate the world completely. We do not aim at an increase in sensual pleasures but at a situation in which any man and all men together can develop their full strength. The mere mention of a social idea implies common interests beyond the egotism of the individual, and this idea would never have reached the power it has had it not been conceived of both as a duty and as a privilege. The ethical element inherent in it gave it the power to win over minds, to attract enthusiastic disciples, and to prevail even over reluctance. But there is no place at all for such an ethical element in the realm of mere nature; thus the mere existence of a social movement refutes naturalism.

These considerations lead to the conclusion that naturalism is by no means an adequate expression of the modern way of life. On the contrary, that way of life has outgrown its origins and has revealed far greater spiritual independence than naturalism could acknowledge. Life itself has contradicted that interpretation of life. The fact that environment means more to us does not mean that we are a mere part of it. Naturalism makes the mistake of ascribing to nature itself the changes the mind effected in it. The mistake resulted from concentrating on the effects and ignoring the power which alone could produce them.

Still the fact remains that mind needs environment as an object to work on, and to that extent it is dependent on it. But does not such a situation confront life with an intolerable conflict? The transformation of the environment has released vast intellectual energies which fortify the claim of life for happiness and satisfaction. Will life not feel intolerably confined if man must deal only with the outside world, if he may never return to himself and use the results of his stupendous labours for his own welfare? The achievement itself is limited narrowly if its object is invariably outside ourselves and can never be taken into our own life. Scientific research in an external object can never lead to true, complete, and inner knowledge. As long as we regard man simply as a being next to us, there can be no inner community of mutual love. Energy that is not dominated by, and does not return to, a centre, will never constitute the content of life; it leaves us empty in the midst of bustling excitement. This is a common and painful modern experience. But is not such a sensation of emptiness itself proof that there are more profound depths within us which demand satisfaction? Thus we are faced with the question whether life does not somehow go beyond the position reached so far, whether it could not return from an occupation with outside objects to an occupation with itself and to the experience and shaping of itself. Only life's own movement can give such an answer; let us see whether it is in the affirmative.

I think we can say confidently that it is. We need only regard clear and indisputable individual phenomena as a whole and appreciate that whole in its full significance in order to recognize that there is indeed a great movement within us which generates an essentially new way of life. Hitherto our discussion had seen life as something between subject and object, between man and world, between energy and thing. However, the thing was touched only from the outside; it remained inwardly foreign to us. But now intellectual activity takes a turn to the effect that the object is taken into the process of life, is incorporated into the soul and excites and moves us as part of our own life. The artist's creative activity, for instance in Goethe, is an example of this. We call such creativity objective, but that is not to say that the outside world is pictured in its sensual being without any addition of the soul; rather, the external object becomes part of the soul. There is a fruitful relation of energy and object; they combine, enhance one another, and create a new complete living entity. In such life a soul is breathed into the object, or the soul that is in it is made to sound, and in effecting the object, energy loses its initial indeterminate character and assumes full definition. The poet appears as a magician who gives to things a language in which they proclaim their own being, but they come alive only in the soul of the poet, only in an inner world. Something similar to this artistic process occurs in practical life, in the relationship of men as it finds its expression in law and morality. The other man who at first seems a complete outsider is taken into the circle of our own life when we become capable of identifying ourselves with him. Nowhere is the process of making the seemingly strange your own as marked as in love, the highest relationship of two individuals. For here the gap between oneself and the other is completely bridged; what was strange becomes an integral part of one's own life. Nor can we love our people, our country, or the whole of mankind unless we find in them our own life and being. In another direction the search for truth leads to a broadening of our inner life. For how could we desire so powerfully to recognize the object unless it did not somehow exist within our own life, unless the toil spent on it did not contribute to the perfection of our own being?

Thus the beautiful, the good, and the true agree in that the object becomes part of the inner process of life, but this cannot possibly happen without deep changes in the structure and meaning of that process. For now life is dealing primarily with itself; energy and object meet in it and demand a balance. However, there can be no balance unless both are comprehended in one whole, which finds its life and perfection in them. Thus life enters into a relationship with itself, it is structured in itself in different degrees and begets within itself a new depth, a comprehensive and persistent energy. If this happens, the whole can be present and effective in each detail. It is only in this way that convictions and attitudes are possible, and character and personality can manifest themselves in their manifold activities. The integration into the process of life gives to the object a new and higher form, and so life is not merely the representation or appropriation of a given reality; it enhances and creates; it does not find a world, but must make a world for itself.

Thus life faces not only the outside world, but itself. It creates its own realm of the mind. By combining with each other, the different movements produce an inner world, and this inner world, through a complete reversal of the initial situation, becomes the point of departure for all intellectual activity. This world is not a private world; the good, true, and beautiful are not peculiar to each individual. We live in a common world and the individual achievement is valid for all and becomes their possession. In this consists the greatness of that new world. The new life in the individual has a universal character, and in the quest for this life the individual more and more finds his true self and abandons his limited point of departure. Mere self-preservation becomes increasingly less satisfying.

If we look more closely at this development of life and consider its energies and forms, the complete reversal it caused and the new tasks it created, we cannot really doubt any more that it is not a mere figment of man's imagination designed for his pleasure and comfort. It is obviously a new level of reality which creates new tasks for man. The movement toward the new goals, the development of a more intimate basic relationship with reality, and the grafting of an infinite life onto human existence cannot possibly be mere human creations. Man could not even imagine such things. There must be an impulse of life from the universe that embraces and carries us and gives us the strength to fight for the new reality, to introduce it into the world of natural reality, and to participate in the movement of the universe. Without being rooted in the actuality of the universe, our aspirations could never gain a firm foothold and direction. Life on our level could not exist within itself and enhance itself unless the totality of reality exists within itself and is in an inward motion.

The importance of man and the tension of his life increase immeasurably in this process of change. Belonging at first to the level of nature, he rises to a new level of reality in which he is active with the energy of the whole, and so he does not remain a mere part of a given order but becomes a stage on which worlds meet and search for their further development. And he is more than a stage. For although that movement of the world cannot arise out of him, it cannot be activated on this stage without his decision and action. He cooperates in the totality of worlds so that limitation and freedom, finiteness and infinity, meet in him. The world ceases to be foreign to him, and with the whole of its life it becomes his own and inmost essence.

It is this development of life to its full self-realization which idealism seizes upon and on which it models its goals and concentrates its efforts, even though the level of nature remains and man's intellectual life can develop only in constant intercourse with it. But this does not dispose of the fundamental contrast that idealism, unlike naturalism, understands not mind by nature but nature by mind.

The ever-renewed conflict between the two convictions is due to the fact that the new world, however much it must be effective from the bottom of our souls, can be gained only in a constant struggle that always creates new complications. It is not only the individual who has to make this world his own; mankind at large has to fight for its more definite form, which is not given to us but has to be discovered and realized by ourselves. History knows of many approaches to this goal, but none has proved perfect in the end. We experience the world of the mind at first only separately and vaguely; it is our task to achieve a comprehensive form to give it a fully definite character and make it a complete and safe possession. Now at high points of history, humanity has made the attempt at such a synthesis of life that would embrace and give form to the whole of being. Success may seem to attend such an effort in its first surge, but soon obstacles arise, and as they grow it becomes clear that life does not in its entirety fit the measure prescribed for it. Individual movements free themselves from the projected structure, and the period of positive creation and coalescence of the elements is followed by a period of criticism and disintegration, so that the search for the unity of life leads to a new synthesis. Thus, epochs of concentration and expansion follow upon each other, and both serve man's aspiration for a spiritual content of life. Past achievements will always appear too small, and the need for spiritual preservation of life will always lead to a new effort. In such tenacity of purpose, such continuous progress, and such struggle with infinity the tremendous greatness of mankind is realized.

The experience of European civilization since the Greek era has revealed this process with particular forcefulness. Greek life has its lasting importance in the cheerful energy with which it engaged upon an original synthesis of the entire range of our existence. It did so by means of art, in particular fine arts, and this synthesis served as a point of departure for the manifold ramifications of civilization. Science tried to determine the permanent artifice of the cosmos behind the chaos of shifting phenomena. Action was to turn the human commonwealth into a strictly measured and well-constructed work of art, and the individual was to combine in perfect harmony all the manifold energies and desires of his soul. These endeavours resulted in a thorough patterning of life. Activity was aroused everywhere, a balance of conflicting sides was achieved together with stability and an inner cheerfulness. All these achievements have become a permanent gain. But mankind could not stop at this. The experience of life created greater tasks, greater contrasts and conflicts than could be solved by it. It became apparent that an end had been set abruptly and prematurely, and that the soul had depths not fully sounded by it. The whole had rested on the assumption of the immediate presence and irresistible power of the intellect in human life, and a weaker age came to doubt this presence. A period of disintegration followed. The manifold elements separated, but despite all its negative aspects, this period prepared for a new synthesis. Such a synthesis appeared in original Christianity, where the whole of reality was subordinated to the moral idea, and the variety of life was made subject to the moral obligation. But considering man's moral frailty and the lack of reason in the human world, the strength for the solution of such a task had to be derived from a superhuman order. Thus, the moral synthesis had at the same time a religious character and together with it affected the entire range of life. This concentration led to an enormous deepening of life; it created a pure inner world and first established the absolute supremacy of mind over nature.

But though this life remains valid in our world, its original form has encountered increasingly strong opposition ever since the beginning of the modern period. A new humanity full of high spirits found in it too little for the development of its power. At the same time, a desire for a universal culture that would embrace all branches of life with equal love, felt confined by that moral-religious synthesis. Hence a new synthesis arose, in which the basic idea is the unlimited development of all energies and in which the enhancement of life has become its purpose. This urge has set in motion whatever appeared to be at rest. Constant progress has affected not only nature, but man himself. Nothing seems to be more characteristic of man than his ability to rise toward the infinite by the powers of his mind despite his natural limitations. This life is still flooding about us from all sides and is penetrating ever more deeply into the ramifications of being. However, at the bottom of our souls and at the height of intellectual effort, new doubts are beginning to arise about this solution. First we have begun to doubt whether the entire range of being can really be turned into an upward movement, and whether this movement itself does not create new problems and complications that it could not cope with; whether the release of all energies has not conjured up contrasts and passions that are threatening the sanity of our existence. And even if we could suppress these doubts, other and greater ones arise from the question whether the transformation into incessant activity really exhausts life and satisfies the soul. For if motion does not find its balance in a state of rest superior to it from which it can be comprehended, the possibility of life's existence within itself disappears. We can no longer assign any content to life; it is a constant and impatient longing for the remote which never returns to itself and forms itself. Nor can we defend ourselves against a boundless relativism, if the truth of today is superseded tomorrow. The restlessness and haste of such progressive activity cannot prevent a growing emptiness and the consciousness of it. Despite the greatness of technical achievements in particular fields, man in the entirety of his existence is doomed to decline: the powerful and individual personality will gradually disappear.

But as soon as we realize the limitations and defects of this modern synthesis of life, we cease to believe in it. The old order will disintegrate and the contrasts will again emerge in full power. Self-assured activity once more will give way to brooding reflection; we shall once more enter from a positive into a critical period.

If life thus lacks a dominating unity and a centre, while at the same time the transformation of the outside world achieves splendid triumphs, it is understandable if the balance of life is lost, and external successes gradually come to dominate the picture. The achievement makes us forget the power that produced it. Education works from the outside to the inside, and in the end man appears completely a product of his environment because the central energy could no longer cope with the affluence of the outside world. In such an atmosphere naturalism wields power over souls, and we fully understand how it gains ground as the expression of a peculiar situation. But it is precisely through our understanding of it that we are more firmly convinced that it is not the whole truth of human experience.

Its attempt to reduce man entirely to the level of nature can succeed only so long as human existence does not bring forth new energies and goals. But since we have recognized that man represents a new degree of reality which makes intellectual activity possible, we can no longer simply return to nature. The new reality may temporarily be lost in the consciousness of man, but the results of history are embedded in his soul, in the midst of all struggles, doubts, and errors. Even in the midst of negation they have put him far above the level of mere nature, and naturalism appears to be sufficient only because it borrows widely and unscrupulously from idealism. If these borrowings disappear and naturalism has to rely on its own resources, its inadequacies become glaring. There will be a decisive rebellion against an intolerably shallow view of life, accompanied by a strong movement toward idealism and the search for a new synthesis of life.

For certainly the new and strong desire for life's existence within itself and for a rich inner world cannot be satisfied by a return to an earlier stage. There may be imperishable truths in the older syntheses of life, but how can we explain the tremendous shocks and the feeling of uncertainty about the whole of life if those truths, as they have been historically transmitted, contained the final truth? We have considered the deep changes that the modern age has brought about, and we have recognized the closer concatenation of man with his environment and the greater importance of that environment. At the same time, we have seen the harsh obstacles met by the striving for a complete intellectualization of existence, we feel the deep gap between the immediate being of man and the demands of intellectual life, and we realize that we must revise our image of man in order to reach the point of intellectual creativity. We can no longer hope to set the whole of existence in motion at one stroke. First of all we must try to form a nucleus of life and to fortify that position; then we shall have to cope with environment and gradually encroach upon it. The new insights and tasks of the modern age will be fully utilized in this endeavour, especially the tremendous progress made in human welfare which we owe to science. Only we must not assimilate these new elements in their immediate sensual form. We shall have to extract the nucleus of truth, and this can be done only in the context of our entire historical experience. Any conviction that is to carry mankind needs an open mind for the movements of the time, but such open-mindedness should not lead to helpless drifting in their wake.

A revival of idealism may well face many difficulties and obstacles, but the task is imperative and we cannot shirk it. Once mankind has attained an existence of life within itself it cannot resign it again; it has to use all its power and ingenuity to carry out that imperative demand. Once man has escaped from the fetters of natural life, he cannot possibly agree to them again; once risen to independent activity, he cannot again be the plaything of inscrutable powers; having penetrated to the universe and its infinity, he cannot again return to the limitations of a natural being; once the desire for an inner relationship to the world has stirred within him, external relationships will no longer satisfy him. Thus, there is an urge beyond naturalism in all directions.

The peculiar experiences and needs of our own time most strongly demand the revival of the movement toward idealism. The steady increase of work and the rush of the struggle for existence have obscured the meaning of life and deprived our life of a dominating goal. Can we hope to regain such a goal without a powerful concentration and elevation in the soul of man? There are senile features in the colorful picture of modern life, and there is a great urge for rejuvenation, for a production of pure and original beginnings. Would not such an urge be folly if man were wholly determined by the necessity of a natural process? The creativity of the mind has at all times been surrounded and often covered by petty interests, but it makes a considerable difference whether we can check such obscurantism or not. If we can, we need a goal that unites and elevates men; otherwise we are at the mercy of human pettiness, and there is far too much of it in our world today. In the confusion of everyday life little distinction is made between what is high and low, true or seeming, genuine or spurious. There is no sense of the substantial, no acknowledgement of the great either-or pervading human life. We shall have to separate the wheat from the chaff and in an act of concentration gather whatever the time contains in good and important things, the wealth of good will and readiness to sacrifice, so that these things will unite for a common effort and give to life a content worth living for. But how can we carry out such a separation and such a collection unless there is an inner synthesis of life that lifts mankind above the insecurity of individual reflection?

The contrast expressed in the struggle of naturalism and idealism is not confined to the general outline of life; it is found in any particular realm which represents a totality of conviction. It makes a tremendous difference whether man submits to a given existence and tries to improve it only in spots or whether, inspired by the belief in an ascending movement of the universe, he is able to contribute independently to that movement, to discover new goals, and to release new energies. Literature is a case in point, as I shall indicate in a few words. Naturalism cannot give to literature an inner independence or allow it an initiative of its own; for if literature is only a hand of life on the dial of time, it can only imitate and register events as they happen. By means of impressive descriptions it may help the time to understand its own desires better; but since creative power is denied to it, it cannot contribute to the inner liberation and elevation of man. At the same time it necessarily lacks dramatic power, which cannot exist without the possibility of an inner change and elevation. But the perspective and the task change completely if literature acknowledges the possibility of a decisive turn in human life, of the ascension to another level, and if it feels called upon to help bring about that ascension. In that case it can help to shape life and to lead the time, by representing and simultaneously guiding what is rising in man's soul. Literature can clarify and confirm by drawing certain simple outlines in the bewildering chaos of the time and by confronting us with the chief problems of our intellectual existence and persuading us of their importance. It can raise our life to greatness above the hubbub of everyday life by the representation of eternal truths, and in the midst of our dark situation it can strengthen our belief in the reason of life. It can act in the way envisaged by Alfred Nobel when he gave to literature a place of honour in his foundation.

Thus there are strong reasons for our continued belief in idealism and for our attempt to give it a form that corresponds to the sum of our historical experiences. But such an attempt will never truly succeed unless it is considered a personal necessity and is carried out as a matter of intellectual self-preservation. Exhilaration, courage, and firm belief can arise only from such an acknowledgement of a binding necessity, not from a hankering after remote and alien goals, but from a belief in life as it is active within us and makes us participate inwardly in the large context of reality. Only such faith can enable us to cope with the enormous obstacles and fill us with the confidence of success.

Du musst glauben, du musst wagen
Denn die Götter leitn kein Pfand;
Nur ein Wunder kann dich tragen
In das schöne Wunderland.

[© The Nobel Foundation, 1909. Rudolf Eucken is the sole author of the text.]

Nobel Prize Laureates in Literature, 1901–2005

1901: Sully Prudhomme (France)
1902: Theodor Mommsen (Germany; born Denmark)
1903: Bjørnstjerne Bjørnson (Norway)
1904: Frédéric Mistral (France) and José Echegaray (Spain)
1905: Henryk Sienkiewicz (Poland)
1906: Giosuè Carducci (Italy)
1907: Rudyard Kipling (United Kingdom; born Bombay, British India)
1908: Rudolf Eucken (Germany)
1909: Selma Lagerlöf (Sweden)
1910: Paul Heyse (Germany)
1911: Maurice Maeterlinck (Belgium)
1912: Gerhart Hauptmann (Germany)
1913: Rabindranath Tagore (India)
1914: No prize was awarded
1915: Romain Rolland (France)
1916: Verner von Heidenstam (Sweden)
1917: Karl Gjellerup (Denmark) and Henrik Pontoppidan (Denmark)
1918: No prize was awarded
1919: Carl Spitteler (Switzerland)
1920: Knut Hamsun (Norway)
1921: Anatole France (France)
1922: Jacinto Benavente (Spain)
1923: William Butler Yeats (Ireland)
1924: Władysław Reymont (Poland)
1925: George Bernard Shaw (United Kingdom; born Ireland)
1926: Grazia Deledda (Italy; born Sardinia)
1927: Henri Bergson (France)
1928: Sigrid Undset (Norway; born Denmark)
1929: Thomas Mann (Germany)
1930: Sinclair Lewis (United States)
1931: Erik Axel Karlfeldt (Sweden)
1932: John Galsworthy (United Kingdom)
1933: Ivan Bunin (stateless; domicile in France; born Russia)
1934: Luigi Pirandello (Italy)
1935: No prize was awarded
1936: Eugene O'Neill (United States)
1937: Roger Martin du Gard (France)
1938: Pearl S. Buck (United States)
1939: Frans Eemil Sillanpää (Finland)
1940: No prize was awarded
1941: No prize was awarded
1942: No prize was awarded
1943: No prize was awarded
1944: Johannes V. Jensen (Denmark)
1945: Gabriela Mistral (Chile)
1946: Hermann Hesse (Switzerland; born Germany)
1947: André Gide (France)
1948: T. S. Eliot (United Kingdom; born United States)
1949: William Faulkner (United States)
1950: Bertrand Russell (United Kingdom)
1951: Pär Lagerkvist (Sweden)
1952: François Mauriac (France)
1953: Sir Winston Churchill (United Kingdom)
1954: Ernest Hemingway (United States)
1955: Halldór Laxness (Iceland)
1956: Juan Ramón Jiménez (Spain)
1957: Albert Camus (France; born Algeria)
1958: Boris Pasternak (USSR)
1959: Salvatore Quasimodo (Italy)
1960: Saint-John Perse (France; born Guadeloupe Island)
1961: Ivo Andrić (Yugoslavia; born Bosnia)
1962: John Steinbeck (United States)
1963: Giorgos Seferis (Greece; born Turkey)
1964: Jean-Paul Sartre (France)
1965: Mikhail Sholokhov (USSR)
1966: Shmuel Yosef Agnon (Israel) and Nelly Sachs (Sweden; born Germany)
1967: Miguel Ángel Asturias (Guatemala)
1968: Yasunari Kawabata (Japan)
1969: Samuel Beckett (Ireland)
1970: Aleksandr Solzhenitsyn (USSR)
1971: Pablo Neruda (Chile)
1972: Heinrich Böll (Federal Republic of Germany)
1973: Patrick White (Australia; born United Kingdom)
1974: Eyvind Johnson (Sweden) and Harry Martinson (Sweden)
1975: Eugenio Montale (Italy)
1976: Saul Bellow (United States; born Canada)
1977: Vicente Aleixandre (Spain)
1978: Isaac Bashevis Singer (United States; born Poland)

1979: Odysseus Elytis (Greece)
1980: Czesław Miłosz (Poland/United States)
1981: Elias Canetti (United Kingdom; born Bulgaria)
1982: Gabriel García Márquez (Colombia)
1983: William Golding (United Kingdom)
1984: Jaroslav Seifert (Czechoslovakia)
1985: Claude Simon (France)
1986: Wole Soyinka (Nigeria)
1987: Joseph Brodsky (United States; born USSR)
1988: Najīb Mahfūz (Egypt)
1989: Camilo José Cela (Spain)
1990: Octavio Paz (Mexico)
1991: Nadine Gordimer (South Africa)
1992: Derek Walcott (Saint Lucia)
1993: Toni Morrison (United States)
1994: Kenzaburō Ōe (Japan)
1995: Seamus Heaney (Ireland)
1996: Wisława Szymborska (Poland)
1997: Dario Fo (Italy)
1998: José Saramago (Portugal)
1999: Günter Grass (Federal Republic of Germany)
2000: Gao Xingjian (France; born China)
2001: V. S. Naipaul (United Kingdom; born Trinidad)
2002: Imre Kertész (Hungary)
2003: J. M. Coetzee (South Africa)
2004: Elfriede Jelinek (Austria)
2005: Harold Pinter (United Kingdom)

Contributors

Dvir Abramovich . . . . *University of Melbourne*
Montserrat Alás-Brun . . . . *University of Florida*
Tracy Simmons Bitonti . . . . *Rock Hill, South Carolina*
Jewel Spears Brooker. . . . . *Eckerd College*
Catharine Savage Brosman . . . . *Tulane University*
Park Bucker. . . . . *University of South Carolina Sumter*
Lucile C. Charlebois . . . . *University of South Carolina*
Julian W. Connolly . . . . *University of Virginia*
Uwe Dathe . . . . *University of Kiev, Ukraine*
Santiago Daydí-Tolson . . . . *University of Texas at San Antonio*
Philip B. Dematteis . . . . *Saint Leo University*
Thomas H. Falk . . . . *Michigan State University*
Julian A. Garforth . . . . *Beckett International Foundation, University of Reading*
Alyssa Dinega Gillespie. . . . . *University of Notre Dame*
Laurence Kitzan . . . . *Saskatcon, Saskatchewan*
Dagmar C. G. Lorenz . . . . *University of Illinois at Chicago*
Stefania Lucamante . . . . *Catholic University of America*
Michael Marais . . . . *Rand Afrikaans University*
Judy B. McInnis. . . . . *University of Delaware*
E. Ann Matter . . . . *University of Pennsylvania*
Vasa D. Mihailovich . . . . *University of North Carolina*
Merritt Moseley. . . . . *Univeristy of North Carolina at Asheville*
Keith M. Opdahl . . . . *Greencastle, Indiana*
Thomas E. Peterson . . . . *University of Georgia*
Marinos Pourgouris . . . . *Brown University*
Oralia Preble-Niemi. . . . . *University of Tennessee at Chattanooga*
Hans H. Skei. . . . . *University of Oslo*
Reinhard K. Zachau . . . . *University of the South*

Cumulative Index

Dictionary of Literary Biography, Volumes 1-329
Dictionary of Literary Biography Yearbook, 1980-2002
Dictionary of Literary Biography Documentary Series, Volumes 1-19
Concise Dictionary of American Literary Biography, Volumes 1-7
Concise Dictionary of British Literary Biography, Volumes 1-8
Concise Dictionary of World Literary Biography, Volumes 1-4

Cumulative Index

DLB before number: *Dictionary of Literary Biography*, Volumes 1-329
Y before number: *Dictionary of Literary Biography Yearbook*, 1980-2002
DS before number: *Dictionary of Literary Biography Documentary Series*, Volumes 1-19
CDALB before number: *Concise Dictionary of American Literary Biography*, Volumes 1-7
CDBLB before number: *Concise Dictionary of British Literary Biography*, Volumes 1-8
CDWLB before number: *Concise Dictionary of World Literary Biography*, Volumes 1-4

A

Aakjær, Jeppe 1866-1930 .... DLB-214
Aarestrup, Emil 1800-1856 .... DLB-300
Abbey, Edward 1927-1989 .... DLB-256, 275
Abbey, Edwin Austin 1852-1911 .... DLB-188
Abbey, Maj. J. R. 1894-1969 .... DLB-201
Abbey Press DLB-49
The Abbey Theatre and Irish Drama, 1900-1945 .... DLB-10
Abbot, Willis J. 1863-1934 .... DLB-29
Abbott, Edwin A. 1838-1926 .... DLB-178
Abbott, Jacob 1803-1879 .... DLB-1, 42, 243
Abbott, Lee K. 1947- DLB-130
Abbott, Lyman 1835-1922 .... DLB-79
Abbott, Robert S. 1868-1940 .... DLB-29, 91
'Abd al-Hamid al-Katib circa 689-750 .... DLB-311
Abe Kōbō 1924-1993 .... DLB-182
Abelaira, Augusto 1926- DLB-287
Abelard, Peter circa 1079-1142? DLB-115, 208
Abelard-Schuman DLB-46
Abell, Arunah S. 1806-1888 .... DLB-43
Abell, Kjeld 1901-1961 .... DLB-214
Abercrombie, Lascelles 1881-1938 .... DLB-19
    The Friends of the Dymock Poets Y-00
Aberdeen University Press Limited DLB-106
Abish, Walter 1931- DLB-130, 227
Ablesimov, Aleksandr Onisimovich 1742-1783 .... DLB-150
Abraham à Sancta Clara 1644-1709 ..... DLB-168
Abrahams, Peter 1919- DLB-117, 225; CDWLB-3
Abramov, Fedor Aleksandrovich 1920-1983 .... DLB-302
Abrams, M. H. 1912- DLB-67
Abramson, Jesse 1904-1979 .... DLB-241
Abrogans circa 790-800 .... DLB-148
Abschatz, Hans Aßmann von 1646-1699 .... DLB-168

Abse, Dannie 1923- DLB-27, 245
Abu al-'Atahiyah 748-825? DLB-311
Abu Nuwas circa 757-814 or 815 .... DLB-311
Abu Tammam circa 805-845 .... DLB-311
Abutsu-ni 1221-1283 .... DLB-203
Academy Chicago Publishers DLB-46
Accius circa 170 B.C.-circa 80 B.C. DLB-211
"An account of the death of the Chevalier de La Barre," Voltaire DLB-314
Accrocca, Elio Filippo 1923-1996 ...... DLB-128
Ace Books DLB-46
Achebe, Chinua 1930- DLB-117; CDWLB-3
Achtenberg, Herbert 1938- DLB-124
Ackerman, Diane 1948- DLB-120
Ackroyd, Peter 1949- DLB-155, 231
Acorn, Milton 1923-1986 .... DLB-53
Acosta, José de 1540-1600 .... DLB-318
Acosta, Oscar Zeta 1935?-1974? DLB-82
Acosta Torres, José 1925- DLB-209
Actors Theatre of Louisville DLB-7
Adair, Gilbert 1944- DLB-194
Adair, James 1709?-1783? DLB-30
Aðalsteinn Kristmundsson (see Steinn Steinarr)
Adam, Graeme Mercer 1839-1912 .... DLB-99
Adam, Robert Borthwick, II 1863-1940 .... DLB-187
Adame, Leonard 1947- DLB-82
Adameşteanu, Gabriel 1942- DLB-232
Adamic, Louis 1898-1951 .... DLB-9
Adamov, Arthur Surenovitch 1908-1970 .... DLB-321
Adamovich, Georgii 1894-1972 .... DLB-317
Adams, Abigail 1744-1818 .... DLB-183, 200
Adams, Alice 1926-1999 .... DLB-234; Y-86
Adams, Bertha Leith (Mrs. Leith Adams, Mrs. R. S. de Courcy Laffan) 1837?-1912 .... DLB-240
Adams, Brooks 1848-1927 .... DLB-47
Adams, Charles Francis, Jr. 1835-1915 .... DLB-47

Adams, Douglas 1952-2001 .... DLB-261; Y-83
Adams, Franklin P. 1881-1960 .... DLB-29
Adams, Glenda 1939- DLB-325
Adams, Hannah 1755-1832 .... DLB-200
Adams, Henry 1838-1918 .... DLB-12, 47, 189
Adams, Herbert Baxter 1850-1901 .... DLB-47
Adams, James Truslow 1878-1949 .... DLB-17; DS-17
Adams, John 1735-1826 .... DLB-31, 183
Adams, John Quincy 1767-1848 .... DLB-37
Adams, Léonie 1899-1988 .... DLB-48
Adams, Levi 1802-1832 .... DLB-99
Adams, Richard 1920- DLB-261
Adams, Samuel 1722-1803 .... DLB-31, 43
Adams, Sarah Fuller Flower 1805-1848 .... DLB-199
Adams, Thomas 1582/1583-1652 .... DLB-151
Adams, William Taylor 1822-1897 ...... DLB-42
J. S. and C. Adams [publishing house] DLB-49
Adamson, Harold 1906-1980 .... DLB-265
Adamson, Sir John 1867-1950 .... DLB-98
Adamson, Robert 1943- DLB-289
Adcock, Arthur St. John 1864-1930 .... DLB-135
Adcock, Betty 1938- DLB-105
    "Certain Gifts" DLB-105
    Tribute to James Dickey Y-97
Adcock, Fleur 1934- DLB-40
Addams, Jane 1860-1935 .... DLB-303
Addison, Joseph 1672-1719 .... DLB-101; CDBLB-2
Ade, George 1866-1944 .... DLB-11, 25
Adeler, Max (see Clark, Charles Heber)
Adlard, Mark 1932- DLB-261
Adler, Richard 1921- DLB-265
Adonias Filho (Adonias Aguiar Filho) 1915-1990 .... DLB-145, 307
Adorno, Theodor W. 1903-1969 .... DLB-242
Adoum, Jorge Enrique 1926- DLB-283

Cumulative Index

Advance Publishing Company DLB-49

Ady, Endre 1877-1919. . . . . . DLB-215; CDWLB-4

AE 1867-1935 . . . . DLB-19; CDBLB-5

Ælfric circa 955-circa 1010 . . . . DLB-146

Aeschines circa 390 B.C.-circa 320 B.C. DLB-176

Aeschylus 525-524 B.C.-456-455 B.C.
. . . . .DLB-176; CDWLB-1

Aesthetic Papers DLB-1

Aesthetics
  Eighteenth-Century Aesthetic
    Theories DLB-31

African Literature
  Letter from Khartoum Y-90

African American
  Afro-American Literary Critics:
    An Introduction DLB-33
  The Black Aesthetic: Background DS-8
  The Black Arts Movement,
    by Larry Neal DLB-38
  Black Theaters and Theater Organizations
    in America, 1961-1982:
    A Research List DLB-38
  Black Theatre: A Forum [excerpts] . . . DLB-38
  Callaloo [journal] Y-87
  Community and Commentators:
    Black Theatre and Its Critics DLB-38
  The Emergence of Black
    Women Writers DS-8
  The Hatch-Billops Collection DLB-76
  A Look at the Contemporary Black
    Theatre Movement DLB-38
  The Moorland-Spingarn Research
    Center DLB-76
  "The Negro as a Writer," by
    G. M. McClellan DLB-50
  "Negro Poets and Their Poetry," by
    Wallace Thurman DLB-50
  Olaudah Equiano and Unfinished Journeys:
    The Slave-Narrative Tradition and
    Twentieth-Century Continuities, by
    Paul Edwards and Pauline T.
    Wangman DLB-117
  PHYLON (Fourth Quarter, 1950),
    The Negro in Literature:
    The Current Scene DLB-76
  The Schomburg Center for Research
    in Black Culture DLB-76
  Three Documents [poets], by John
    Edward Bruce DLB-50

After Dinner Opera Company Y-92

Agassiz, Elizabeth Cary 1822-1907 . . . . . . DLB-189

Agassiz, Louis 1807-1873 . . . . DLB-1, 235

Agee, James
  1909-1955 . . . . DLB-2, 26, 152; CDALB-1
  The Agee Legacy: A Conference at
    the University of Tennessee
    at Knoxville Y-89

Agnon, Shmuel Yosef 1887-1970 . . . . DLB-329

Aguilera Malta, Demetrio 1909-1981 . . . . DLB-145

Aguirre, Isidora 1919- DLB-305

Agustini, Delmira 1886-1914 . . . . DLB-290

Ahlin, Lars 1915-1997 . . . . DLB-257

Ai 1947- DLB-120

Ai Wu 1904-1992 . . . . DLB-328

Aichinger, Ilse 1921- DLB-85, 299

Aickman, Robert 1914-1981 . . . . DLB-261

Aidoo, Ama Ata 1942- DLB-117; CDWLB-3

Aiken, Conrad
  1889-1973 . . . . DLB-9, 45, 102; CDALB-5

Aiken, Joan 1924-2004 . . . . DLB-161

Aikin, Lucy 1781-1864 . . . . DLB-144, 163

Ainsworth, William Harrison
  1805-1882 . . . . DLB-21

Aïssé, Charlotte-Elizabeth 1694?-1733 . . . DLB-313

Aistis, Jonas 1904-1973 . . . . . DLB-220; CDWLB-4

Aitken, Adam 1960- DLB-325

Aitken, George A. 1860-1917 . . . . DLB-149

Robert Aitken [publishing house] DLB-49

Aitmatov, Chingiz 1928- DLB-302

Akenside, Mark 1721-1770 . . . . DLB-109

Akhmatova, Anna Andreevna
  1889-1966 . . . . DLB-295

Akins, Zoë 1886-1958 . . . . DLB-26

Aksakov, Ivan Sergeevich 1823-1826 . . . . .DLB-277

Aksakov, Sergei Timofeevich
  1791-1859 . . . . DLB-198

Aksyonov, Vassily 1932- DLB-302

Akunin, Boris (Grigorii Shalvovich
  Chkhartishvili) 1956- DLB-285

Akutagawa Ryūnsuke 1892-1927 . . . . DLB-180

Alabaster, William 1568-1640 . . . . DLB-132

Alain de Lille circa 1116-1202/1203 . . . . . DLB-208

Alain-Fournier 1886-1914 . . . . DLB-65

Alanus de Insulis (see Alain de Lille)

Alarcón, Francisco X. 1954- DLB-122

Alarcón, Justo S. 1930- DLB-209

Alba, Nanina 1915-1968 . . . . DLB-41

Albee, Edward 1928- . . . DLB-7, 266; CDALB-1

Albert, Octavia 1853-ca. 1889 . . . . DLB-221

Albert the Great circa 1200-1280 . . . . . . DLB-115

Alberti, Rafael 1902-1999 . . . . DLB-108

Albertinus, Aegidius circa 1560-1620 . . . . DLB-164

Alcaeus born circa 620 B.C. DLB-176

Alcoforado, Mariana, the Portuguese Nun
  1640-1723 . . . . DLB-287

Alcott, Amos Bronson
  1799-1888 . . . . DLB-1, 223; DS-5

Alcott, Louisa May 1832-1888
  . . . DLB-1, 42, 79, 223, 239; DS-14; CDALB-3

Alcott, William Andrus 1798-1859 . . . . DLB-1, 243

Alcuin circa 732-804 . . . . DLB-148

Aldana, Francisco de 1537-1578 . . . . DLB-318

Aldanov, Mark (Mark Landau)
  1886-1957 . . . . DLB-317

Alden, Henry Mills 1836-1919 . . . . DLB-79

Alden, Isabella 1841-1930 . . . . DLB-42

John B. Alden [publishing house] DLB-49

Alden, Beardsley, and Company DLB-49

Aldington, Richard
  1892-1962 . . . . .DLB-20, 36, 100, 149

Aldis, Dorothy 1896-1966 . . . . DLB-22

Aldis, H. G. 1863-1919 . . . . DLB-184

Aldiss, Brian W. 1925- DLB-14, 261, 271

Aldrich, Thomas Bailey
  1836-1907 . . . . .DLB-42, 71, 74, 79

Alegría, Ciro 1909-1967 . . . . DLB-113

Alegría, Claribel 1924- DLB-145, 283

Aleixandre, Vicente 1898-1984 . . . . . DLB-108, 329

Aleksandravičius, Jonas (see Aistis, Jonas)

Aleksandrov, Aleksandr Andreevich
  (see Durova, Nadezhda Andreevna)

Alekseeva, Marina Anatol'evna
  (see Marinina, Aleksandra)

d'Alembert, Jean Le Rond 1717-1783 . . . . DLB-313

Alencar, José de 1829-1877 . . . . DLB-307

Aleramo, Sibilla (Rena Pierangeli Faccio)
  1876-1960 . . . . DLB-114, 264

Aleshkovsky, Petr Markovich 1957- . . . DLB-285

Aleshkovsky, Yuz 1929- DLB-317

Alexander, Cecil Frances 1818-1895 . . . . . DLB-199

Alexander, Charles 1868-1923 . . . . DLB-91

Charles Wesley Alexander
  [publishing house] DLB-49

Alexander, James 1691-1756 . . . . DLB-24

Alexander, Lloyd 1924- DLB-52

Alexander, Meena 1951- DLB-323

Alexander, Sir William, Earl of Stirling
  1577?-1640 . . . . DLB-121

Alexie, Sherman 1966- DLB-175, 206, 278

Alexis, Willibald 1798-1871 . . . . DLB-133

Alf laylah wa laylah
  ninth century onward DLB-311

Alfred, King 849-899 . . . . DLB-146

Alger, Horatio, Jr. 1832-1899 . . . . DLB-42

Algonquin Books of Chapel Hill DLB-46

Algren, Nelson
  1909-1981 . . . . .DLB-9; Y-81, 82; CDALB-1
  Nelson Algren: An International
    Symposium Y-00

Ali, Agha Shahid 1949-2001 . . . . DLB-323

Ali, Ahmed 1908-1994 . . . . DLB-323

Ali, Monica 1967- DLB-323

'Ali ibn Abi Talib circa 600-661 . . . . DLB-311

Aljamiado Literature DLB-286

Allan, Andrew 1907-1974 . . . . DLB-88

Allan, Ted 1916-1995 . . . . DLB-68

Allbeury, Ted 1917- DLB-87

Alldritt, Keith 1935- DLB-14

Allen, Dick 1939- DLB-282

Allen, Ethan 1738-1789 ....DLB-31

Allen, Frederick Lewis 1890-1954 ....DLB-137

Allen, Gay Wilson 1903-1995 ..... DLB-103; Y-95

Allen, George 1808-1876 ....DLB-59

Allen, Grant 1848-1899 .... DLB-70, 92, 178

Allen, Henry W. 1912-1991................Y-85

Allen, Hervey 1889-1949......... DLB-9, 45, 316

Allen, James 1739-1808 ....DLB-31

Allen, James Lane 1849-1925............DLB-71

Allen, Jay Presson 1922- DLB-26

John Allen and Company DLB-49

Allen, Paula Gunn 1939- DLB-175

Allen, Samuel W. 1917- DLB-41

Allen, Woody 1935- DLB-44

George Allen [publishing house] DLB-106

George Allen and Unwin Limited DLB-112

Allende, Isabel 1942- DLB-145; CDWLB-3

Alline, Henry 1748-1784 ....DLB-99

Allingham, Margery 1904-1966..........DLB-77

  The Margery Allingham Society.........Y-98

Allingham, William 1824-1889 ....DLB-35

W. L. Allison [publishing house] DLB-49

The *Alliterative Morte Arthure and the Stanzaic Morte Arthur* circa 1350-1400 ....DLB-146

Allott, Kenneth 1912-1973 ....DLB-20

Allston, Washington 1779-1843 .....DLB-1, 235

Almeida, Manuel Antônio de 1831-1861 ....DLB-307

John Almon [publishing house] DLB-154

Alonzo, Dámaso 1898-1990............DLB-108

Alsop, George 1636-post 1673 ....DLB-24

Alsop, Richard 1761-1815 ....DLB-37

Henry Altemus and Company..........DLB-49

Altenberg, Peter 1885-1919 ....DLB-81

Althusser, Louis 1918-1990 ....DLB-242

Altolaguirre, Manuel 1905-1959 ....DLB-108

Aluko, T. M. 1918- DLB-117

Alurista 1947- DLB-82

Alvarez, A. 1929- DLB-14, 40

Alvarez, Julia 1950- DLB-282

Alvaro, Corrado 1895-1956............DLB-264

Alver, Betti 1906-1989......DLB-220; CDWLB-4

Amadi, Elechi 1934- DLB-117

Amado, Jorge 1912-2001 ....DLB-113

Amalrik, Andrei 1938-1980 ....DLB-302

Ambler, Eric 1909-1998.................DLB-77

The Library of America................DLB-46

The Library of America: An Assessment After Two Decades Y-02

America: or, A Poem on the Settlement of the British Colonies, by Timothy Dwight DLB-37

American Bible Society
  Department of Library, Archives, and Institutional Research Y-97

American Conservatory Theatre DLB-7

American Culture
  American Proletarian Culture: The Twenties and Thirties DS-11

Studies in American Jewish Literature........Y-02

The American Library in Paris Y-93

American Literature
  The Literary Scene and Situation and . . . (Who Besides Oprah) Really Runs American Literature? Y-99

  Who Owns American Literature, by Henry Taylor Y-94

  Who Runs American Literature? Y-94

American News Company..............DLB-49

A Century of Poetry, a Lifetime of Collecting: J. M. Edelstein's Collection of Twentieth-Century American Poetry Y-02

The American Poets' Corner: The First Three Years (1983-1986) Y-86

American Publishing Company..........DLB-49

American Spectator
  [Editorial] Rationale From the Initial Issue of the American Spectator (November 1932)................DLB-137

American Stationers' Company DLB-49

The American Studies Association of Norway..........................Y-00

American Sunday-School Union DLB-49

American Temperance Union DLB-49

American Tract Society................DLB-49

The American Trust for the British Library ...Y-96

American Writers' Congress 25-27 April 1935 ....DLB-303

American Writers Congress
  The American Writers Congress (9-12 October 1981) Y-81

  The American Writers Congress: A Report on Continuing Business Y-81

Ames, Fisher 1758-1808................DLB-37

Ames, Mary Clemmer 1831-1884 ....DLB-23

Ames, William 1576-1633 ....DLB-281

Amfiteatrov, Aleksandr 1862-1938 ......DLB-317

Amiel, Henri-Frédéric 1821-1881........DLB-217

Amini, Johari M. 1935- DLB-41

Amis, Kingsley 1922-1995
  ...DLB-15, 27, 100, 139, 326; Y-96; CDBLB-7

Amis, Martin 1949- DLB-14, 194

Ammianus Marcellinus circa A.D. 330-A.D. 395 ....DLB-211

Ammons, A. R. 1926-2001 ....DLB-5, 165

Amory, Thomas 1691?-1788 ....DLB-39

Amsterdam, 1998 Booker Prize winner, Ian McEwan DLB-326

Amyot, Jacques 1513-1593.............DLB-327

Anand, Mulk Raj 1905-2004..........DLB-323

Anania, Michael 1939- DLB-193

Anaya, Rudolfo A. 1937- DLB-82, 206, 278

Ancrene Riwle circa 1200-1225...........DLB-146

Andersch, Alfred 1914-1980 ....DLB-69

Andersen, Benny 1929- DLB-214

Andersen, Hans Christian 1805-1875 ....DLB-300

Anderson, Alexander 1775-1870 ....DLB-188

Anderson, David 1929- DLB-241

Anderson, Frederick Irving 1877-1947....DLB-202

Anderson, Jessica 1916- DLB-325

Anderson, Margaret 1886-1973 ....DLB-4, 91

Anderson, Maxwell 1888-1959 .... DLB-7, 228

Anderson, Patrick 1915-1979............DLB-68

Anderson, Paul Y. 1893-1938 ....DLB-29

Anderson, Poul 1926-2001 ....DLB-8

  Tribute to Isaac Asimov Y-92

Anderson, Robert 1750-1830...........DLB-142

Anderson, Robert 1917- DLB-7

Anderson, Sherwood 1876-1941
  ....DLB-4, 9, 86; DS-1; CDALB-4

Andrade, Jorge (Aluísio Jorge Andrade Franco) 1922-1984 ....DLB-307

Andrade, Mario de 1893-1945..........DLB-307

Andrade, Oswald de (José Oswald de Sousa Andrade) 1890-1954 ....DLB-307

Andreae, Johann Valentin 1586-1654 ....DLB-164

Andreas Capellanus fl. circa 1185 ....DLB-208

Andreas-Salomé, Lou 1861-1937 ....DLB-66

Andreev, Leonid Nikolaevich 1871-1919 ....DLB-295

Andres, Stefan 1906-1970 ....DLB-69

Andresen, Sophia de Mello Breyner 1919- DLB-287

Andreu, Blanca 1959- DLB-134

Andrewes, Lancelot 1555-1626 ..... DLB-151, 172

Andrews, Charles M. 1863-1943.........DLB-17

Andrews, Miles Peter ?-1814 ....DLB-89

Andrews, Stephen Pearl 1812-1886 ......DLB-250

Andrian, Leopold von 1875-1951 ....DLB-81

Andrić, Ivo 1892-1975 .... DLB-147, 329; CDWLB-4

Andrieux, Louis (see Aragon, Louis)

Andrus, Silas, and Son.................DLB-49

Andrzejewski, Jerzy 1909-1983 ....DLB-215

Angell, James Burrill 1829-1916 ....DLB-64

Angell, Roger 1920- DLB-171, 185

Angelou, Maya 1928- DLB-38; CDALB-7

  Tribute to Julian Mayfield..............Y-84

Anger, Jane fl. 1589 ....DLB-136

Angers, Félicité (see Conan, Laure)

Cumulative Index

The Anglo-Saxon Chronicle
circa 890-1154 .... DLB-146

Angus and Robertson (UK) Limited DLB-112

Anhalt, Edward 1914-2000............. DLB-26

Anissimov, Myriam 1943- DLB-299

Anker, Nini Roll 1873-1942 .... DLB-297

Annenkov, Pavel Vasil'evich
1813?-1887..................DLB-277

Annensky, Innokentii Fedorovich
1855-1909 .... DLB-295

Henry F. Anners [publishing house]...... DLB-49

Annolied between 1077 and 1081 .... DLB-148

Anouilh, Jean 1910-1987.............. DLB-321

Anscombe, G. E. M. 1919-2001 .... DLB-262

Anselm of Canterbury 1033-1109....... DLB-115

Anstey, F. 1856-1934 ....DLB-141, 178

'Antarah ('Antar ibn Shaddad al-'Absi)
?-early seventh century?........... DLB-311

Anthologizing New Formalism DLB-282

Anthony, Michael 1932- DLB-125

Anthony, Piers 1934- DLB-8

Anthony, Susanna 1726-1791 .... DLB-200

Antin, David 1932- DLB-169

Antin, Mary 1881-1949 ....DLB-221; Y-84

Anton Ulrich, Duke of Brunswick-Lüneburg
1633-1714..................... DLB-168

Antschel, Paul (see Celan, Paul)

Antunes, António Lobo 1942- DLB-287

Anyidoho, Kofi 1947- DLB-157

Anzaldúa, Gloria 1942- DLB-122

Anzengruber, Ludwig 1839-1889 .... DLB-129

Apess, William 1798-1839.........DLB-175, 243

Apodaca, Rudy S. 1939- DLB-82

Apollinaire, Guillaume 1880-1918 .. DLB-258, 321

Apollonius Rhodius third century B.C..... DLB-176

Apple, Max 1941- DLB-130

Appelfeld, Aharon 1932- DLB-299

D. Appleton and Company DLB-49

Appleton-Century-Crofts DLB-46

Applewhite, James 1935- DLB-105

Tribute to James Dickey................ Y-97

Apple-wood Books DLB-46

April, Jean-Pierre 1948- DLB-251

Apukhtin, Aleksei Nikolaevich
1840-1893 ....DLB-277

Apuleius circa A.D. 125-post A.D. 164
.... DLB-211; CDWLB-1

Aquin, Hubert 1929-1977.............. DLB-53

Aquinas, Thomas 1224/1225-1274 ...... DLB-115

Aragon, Louis 1897-1982 .... DLB-72, 258

Aragon, Vernacular Translations in the
Crowns of Castile and 1352-1515 ... DLB-286

Aralica, Ivan 1930- DLB-181

Aratus of Soli
circa 315 B.C.-circa 239 B.C. DLB-176

Arbasino, Alberto 1930- DLB-196

Arbor House Publishing Company DLB-46

Arbuthnot, John 1667-1735............ DLB-101

Arcadia House DLB-46

Arce, Julio G. (see Ulica, Jorge)

Archer, William 1856-1924............. DLB-10

Archilochhus
mid seventh century B.C.E.........DLB-176

The Archpoet circa 1130?-? DLB-148

Archpriest Avvakum (Petrovich)
1620?-1682.................... DLB-150

Arden, John 1930- DLB-13, 245

Arden of Faversham DLB-62

Ardis Publishers Y-89

Ardizzone, Edward 1900-1979 .... DLB-160

Arellano, Juan Estevan 1947- DLB-122

The Arena Publishing Company DLB-49

Arena Stage......................... DLB-7

Arenas, Reinaldo 1943-1990........... DLB-145

Arendt, Hannah 1906-1975 .... DLB-242

Arensberg, Ann 1937- Y-82

Arghezi, Tudor 1880-1967 ... DLB-220; CDWLB-4

Arguedas, José María 1911-1969 .... DLB-113

Argüelles, Hugo 1932-2003 .... DLB-305

Argueta, Manlio 1936- DLB-145

'Arib al-Ma'muniyah 797-890 .... DLB-311

Arias, Ron 1941- DLB-82

Arishima Takeo 1878-1923............ DLB-180

Aristophanes circa 446 B.C.-circa 386 B.C.
...................DLB-176; CDWLB-1

Aristotle 384 B.C.-322 B.C.
...................DLB-176; CDWLB-1

Ariyoshi Sawako 1931-1984........... DLB-182

Arland, Marcel 1899-1986 .... DLB-72

Arlen, Michael 1895-1956 ....DLB-36, 77, 162

Arlt, Roberto 1900-1942.............. DLB-305

Armah, Ayi Kwei 1939- ...DLB-117; CDWLB-3

Armantrout, Rae 1947- DLB-193

Der arme Hartmann ?-after 1150 .... DLB-148

Armed Services Editions............. DLB-46

Armitage, G. E. (Robert Edric) 1956- .. DLB-267

Armstrong, Martin Donisthorpe
1882-1974..................... DLB-197

Armstrong, Richard 1903-1986 .... DLB-160

Armstrong, Terence Ian Fytton (see Gawsworth, John)

Arnauld, Antoine 1612-1694........... DLB-268

Arndt, Ernst Moritz 1769-1860 .... DLB-90

Arnim, Achim von 1781-1831........... DLB-90

Arnim, Bettina von 1785-1859 .... DLB-90

Arnim, Elizabeth von (Countess Mary Annette
Beauchamp Russell) 1866-1941 .... DLB-197

Arno Press DLB-46

Arnold, Edwin 1832-1904 .... DLB-35

Arnold, Edwin L. 1857-1935 ....DLB-178

Arnold, Matthew
1822-1888 .... DLB-32, 57; CDBLB-4

Preface to *Poems* (1853) DLB-32

Arnold, Thomas 1795-1842 .... DLB-55

Edward Arnold [publishing house]...... DLB-112

Arnott, Peter 1962- DLB-233

Arnow, Harriette Simpson 1908-1986 ..... DLB-6

Arp, Bill (see Smith, Charles Henry)

Arpino, Giovanni 1927-1987...........DLB-177

Arrabal, Fernando 1932- DLB-321

Arrebo, Anders 1587-1637 .... DLB-300

Arreola, Juan José 1918-2001 .... DLB-113

Arrian circa 89-circa 155................DLB-176

J. W. Arrowsmith [publishing house] DLB-106

Arrufat, Antón 1935- DLB-305

Art
John Dos Passos: Artist Y-99

The First Post-Impressionist
Exhibition.....................DS-5

The Omega Workshops............DS-10

The Second Post-Impressionist
Exhibition DS-5

Artaud, Antonin 1896-1948 .... DLB-258, 321

Artel, Jorge 1909-1994 .... DLB-283

Arthur, Timothy Shay
1809-1885 ....DLB-3, 42, 79, 250; DS-13

Artmann, H. C. 1921-2000............. DLB-85

Artsybashev, Mikhail Petrovich
1878-1927..................... DLB-295

Arvin, Newton 1900-1963 .... DLB-103

Asch, Nathan 1902-1964 .... DLB-4, 28

Nathan Asch Remembers Ford Madox
Ford, Sam Roth, and Hart Crane Y-02

Ascham, Roger 1515/1516-1568........ DLB-236

Aseev, Nikolai Nikolaevich
1889-1963 .... DLB-295

Ash, John 1948- DLB-40

Ashbery, John 1927- DLB-5, 165; Y-81

Ashbridge, Elizabeth 1713-1755 .... DLB-200

Ashburnham, Bertram Lord
1797-1878 .... DLB-184

Ashendene Press.................... DLB-112

Asher, Sandy 1942- Y-83

Ashton, Winifred (see Dane, Clemence)

Asimov, Isaac 1920-1992 ....DLB-8; Y-92

Tribute to John Ciardi Y-86

Askew, Anne circa 1521-1546.......... DLB-136

Aspazija 1865-1943........ DLB-220; CDWLB-4

Asselin, Olivar 1874-1937.............. DLB-92

The Association of American Publishers Y-99

The Association for Documentary Editing.... Y-00

The Association for the Study of
   Literature and Environment (ASLE)......Y-99
Astell, Mary 1666-1731...............DLB-252
Astley, Thea 1925- DLB-289
Astley, William (see Warung, Price)
Asturias, Miguel Ángel
   1899-1974 .... DLB-113, 290, 329; CDWLB-3
Atava, S. (see Terpigorev, Sergei Nikolaevich)
Atheneum Publishers..................DLB-46
Atherton, Gertrude 1857-1948.....DLB-9, 78, 186
Athlone Press........................DLB-112
Atkins, Josiah circa 1755-1781........DLB-31
Atkins, Russell 1926- DLB-41
Atkinson, Kate 1951- DLB-267
Atkinson, Louisa 1834-1872...........DLB-230
The Atlantic Monthly Press............DLB-46
Attaway, William 1911-1986............DLB-76
Atwood, Margaret 1939- DLB-53, 251, 326
Aubert, Alvin 1930- DLB-41
Aub, Max 1903-1972..................DLB-322
Aubert de Gaspé, Phillipe-Ignace-François
   1814-1841.......................DLB-99
Aubert de Gaspé, Phillipe-Joseph
   1786-1871.......................DLB-99
Aubigné, Théodore Agrippa d'
   1552-1630......................DLB-327
Aubin, Napoléon 1812-1890 ....DLB-99
Aubin, Penelope
   1685-circa 1731 ....DLB-39
   Preface to *The Life of Charlotta
      du Pont* (1723) DLB-39
Aubrey-Fletcher, Henry Lancelot (see Wade, Henry)
Auchincloss, Louis 1917- DLB-2, 244; Y-80
Auden, W. H.
   1907-1973...........DLB-10, 20; CDBLB-6
Audiberti, Jacques 1899-1965 ....DLB-321
Audio Art in America: A Personal Memoir....Y-85
Audubon, John James 1785-1851........DLB-248
Audubon, John Woodhouse
   1812-1862......................DLB-183
Auerbach, Berthold 1812-1882 ....DLB-133
Auernheimer, Raoul 1876-1948 ....DLB-81
Augier, Emile 1820-1889 ....DLB-192
Augustine 354-430....................DLB-115
Aulnoy, Marie-Catherine Le Jumel
   de Barneville, comtesse d'
   1650/1651-1705..................DLB-268
Aulus Gellius
   circa A.D. 125-circa A.D. 180? DLB-211
Austen, Jane 1775-1817 ......DLB-116; CDBLB-3
Auster, Paul 1947- DLB-227
Austin, Alfred 1835-1913..............DLB-35
Austin, J. L. 1911-1960................DLB-262
Austin, Jane Goodwin 1831-1894 ....DLB-202
Austin, John 1790-1859 ....DLB-262

Austin, Mary Hunter
   1868-1934 .... DLB-9, 78, 206, 221, 275
Austin, William 1778-1841..............DLB-74
Australie (Emily Manning)
   1845-1890 ....DLB-230
Authors and Newspapers Association DLB-46
Authors' Publishing Company...........DLB-49
Avallone, Michael 1924-1999 ..... DLB-306; Y-99
   Tribute to John D. MacDonald..........Y-86
   Tribute to Kenneth Millar.............Y-83
   Tribute to Raymond Chandler Y-88
Avalon Books DLB-46
Avancini, Nicolaus 1611-1686..........DLB-164
Avendaño, Fausto 1941- DLB-82
Averroës 1126-1198...................DLB-115
Avery, Gillian 1926- DLB-161
Avicenna 980-1037 ....DLB-115
Ávila Jiménez, Antonio 1898-1965 ......DLB-283
Avison, Margaret 1918-1987 ....DLB-53
Avon Books DLB-46
Avyžius, Jonas 1922-1999 ....DLB-220
Awdry, Wilbert Vere 1911-1997 ....DLB-160
Awoonor, Kofi 1935- DLB-117
Ayala, Francisco 1906- DLB-322
Ayckbourn, Alan 1939- DLB-13, 245
Ayer, A. J. 1910-1989.................DLB-262
Aymé, Marcel 1902-1967................DLB-72
Aytoun, Sir Robert 1570-1638..........DLB-121
Aytoun, William Edmondstoune
   1813-1865 ....DLB-32, 159
Azevedo, Aluísio 1857-1913............DLB-307
Azevedo, Manuel Antônio Álvares de
   1831-1852......................DLB-307
Azorín (José Martínez Ruiz)
   1873-1967......................DLB-322

B

B.V. (see Thomson, James)
Ba Jin 1904-2005 ....DLB-328
Babbitt, Irving 1865-1933 ....DLB-63
Babbitt, Natalie 1932- DLB-52
John Babcock [publishing house]........DLB-49
Babel, Isaak Emmanuilovich
   1894-1940......................DLB-272
Babits, Mihály 1883-1941 ... DLB-215; CDWLB-4
Babrius circa 150-200.................DLB-176
Babson, Marian 1929- DLB-276
Baca, Jimmy Santiago 1952- DLB-122
Bacchelli, Riccardo 1891-1985..........DLB-264
Bache, Benjamin Franklin 1769-1798.....DLB-43
Bachelard, Gaston 1884-1962 ....DLB-296
Bacheller, Irving 1859-1950 ....DLB-202
Bachmann, Ingeborg 1926-1973 ....DLB-85

Bačinskaitė-Bučienė, Salomėja (see Nėris, Salomėja)
Bacon, Delia 1811-1859.............DLB-1, 243
Bacon, Francis
   1561-1626 .....DLB-151, 236, 252; CDBLB-1
Bacon, Sir Nicholas circa 1510-1579 .....DLB-132
Bacon, Roger circa 1214/1220-1292 .....DLB-115
Bacon, Thomas circa 1700-1768.........DLB-31
Bacovia, George
   1881-1957 ....DLB-220; CDWLB-4
Richard G. Badger and Company........DLB-49
Bagaduce Music Lending Library Y-00
Bage, Robert 1728-1801................DLB-39
Bagehot, Walter 1826-1877 ....DLB-55
Baggesen, Jens 1764-1826 ....DLB-300
Bagley, Desmond 1923-1983 ....DLB-87
Bagley, Sarah G. 1806-1848?...........DLB-239
Bagnold, Enid
   1889-1981 ....DLB-13, 160, 191, 245
Bagryana, Elisaveta
   1893-1991 ....DLB-147; CDWLB-4
Bahr, Hermann 1863-1934 ....DLB-81, 118
Baïf, Jean-Antoine de 1532-1589 ....DLB-327
Bail, Murray 1941- DLB-325
Bailey, Abigail Abbot
   1746-1815 ....DLB-200
Bailey, Alfred Goldsworthy 1905-1997 ....DLB-68
Bailey, H. C. 1878-1961................DLB-77
Bailey, Jacob 1731-1808 ....DLB-99
Bailey, Paul 1937- DLB-14, 271
Bailey, Philip James 1816-1902 ....DLB-32
Francis Bailey [publishing house].......DLB-49
Baillargeon, Pierre 1916-1967 ....DLB-88
Baillie, Hugh 1890-1966 ....DLB-29
Baillie, Joanna 1762-1851..............DLB-93
Bailyn, Bernard 1922- DLB-17
Bain, Alexander
   English Composition and Rhetoric (1866)
   [excerpt] DLB-57
Bainbridge, Beryl 1933- DLB-14, 231
Baird, Irene 1901-1981 ....DLB-68
Baker, Augustine 1575-1641............DLB-151
Baker, Carlos 1909-1987 ....DLB-103
Baker, David 1954- DLB-120
Baker, George Pierce 1866-1935 ....DLB-266
Baker, Herschel C. 1914-1990..........DLB-111
Baker, Houston A., Jr. 1943- DLB-67
Baker, Howard
   Tribute to Caroline Gordon Y-81
   Tribute to Katherine Anne Porter Y-80
Baker, Nicholson 1957- DLB-227; Y-00
   Review of Nicholson Baker's *Double Fold:
      Libraries and the Assault on Paper* Y-00
Baker, Samuel White 1821-1893 ....DLB-166
Baker, Thomas 1656-1740 ....DLB-213

Walter H. Baker Company
("Baker's Plays") DLB-49

The Baker and Taylor Company DLB-49

Bakhtin, Mikhail Mikhailovich
1895-1975 .... DLB-242

Bakunin, Mikhail Aleksandrovich
1814-1876 .... DLB-277

Balaban, John 1943- DLB-120

Bald, Wambly 1902-1990 .... DLB-4

Balde, Jacob 1604-1668 .... DLB-164

Balderston, John 1889-1954 .... DLB-26

Baldwin, James 1924-1987
...... DLB-2, 7, 33, 249, 278; Y-87; CDALB-1

Baldwin, Joseph Glover
1815-1864. .... DLB-3, 11, 248

Baldwin, Louisa (Mrs. Alfred Baldwin)
1845-1925 .... DLB-240

Baldwin, William circa 1515-1563 ...... DLB-132

Richard and Anne Baldwin
[publishing house] DLB-170

Bale, John 1495-1563 .... DLB-132

Balestrini, Nanni 1935- DLB-128, 196

Balfour, Sir Andrew 1630-1694 .... DLB-213

Balfour, Arthur James 1848-1930 .... DLB-190

Balfour, Sir James 1600-1657 .... DLB-213

Ballantine Books DLB-46

Ballantyne, R. M. 1825-1894 .... DLB-163

Ballard, J. G. 1930- DLB-14, 207, 261, 319

Ballard, Martha Moore 1735-1812 ...... DLB-200

Ballerini, Luigi 1940- DLB-128

Ballou, Maturin Murray (Lieutenant Murray)
1820-1895 .... DLB-79, 189

Robert O. Ballou [publishing house] DLB-46

Bal'mont, Konstantin Dmitrievich
1867-1942 .... DLB-295

Balzac, Guez de 1597?-1654 .... DLB-268

Balzac, Honoré de 1799-1855 .... DLB-119

Bambara, Toni Cade
1939-1995 .... DLB-38, 218; CDALB-7

Bamford, Samuel 1788-1872 .... DLB-190

A. L. Bancroft and Company DLB-49

Bancroft, George 1800-1891 ... DLB-1, 30, 59, 243

Bancroft, Hubert Howe 1832-1918 .... DLB-47, 140

Bandeira, Manuel 1886-1968 .... DLB-307

Bandelier, Adolph F. 1840-1914 .... DLB-186

Bang, Herman 1857-1912 .... DLB-300

Bangs, John Kendrick 1862-1922 ..... DLB-11, 79

Banim, John 1798-1842 .... DLB-116, 158, 159

Banim, Michael 1796-1874 .... DLB-158, 159

Banks, Iain (M.) 1954- DLB-194, 261

Banks, John circa 1653-1706 .... DLB-80

Banks, Russell 1940- DLB-130, 278

Bannerman, Helen 1862-1946 .... DLB-141

Bantam Books DLB-46

Banti, Anna 1895-1985 .... DLB-177

Banville, John 1945- DLB-14, 271, 326

Banville, Théodore de 1823-1891 .... DLB-217

Bao Tianxiao 1876-1973 .... DLB-328

Baraka, Amiri
1934- DLB-5, 7, 16, 38; DS-8; CDALB-1

Barańczak, Stanisław 1946- DLB-232

Baranskaia, Natal'ia Vladimirovna
1908- DLB-302

Baratynsky, Evgenii Abramovich
1800-1844 .... DLB-205

Barba-Jacob, Porfirio 1883-1942 .... DLB-283

Barbauld, Anna Laetitia
1743-1825 .... DLB-107, 109, 142, 158

Barbeau, Marius 1883-1969 .... DLB-92

Barber, John Warner 1798-1885 .... DLB-30

Bàrberi Squarotti, Giorgio 1929- DLB-128

Barbey d'Aurevilly, Jules-Amédée
1808-1889 .... DLB-119

Barbier, Auguste 1805-1882 .... DLB-217

Barbilian, Dan (see Barbu, Ion)

Barbour, John circa 1316-1395 .... DLB-146

Barbour, Ralph Henry 1870-1944 .... DLB-22

Barbu, Ion 1895-1961 ...... DLB-220; CDWLB-4

Barbusse, Henri 1873-1935 .... DLB-65

Barclay, Alexander circa 1475-1552 ..... DLB-132

E. E. Barclay and Company DLB-49

C. W. Bardeen [publishing house] DLB-49

Barham, Richard Harris 1788-1845 ..... DLB-159

Barich, Bill 1943- DLB-185

Baring, Maurice 1874-1945 .... DLB-34

Baring-Gould, Sabine 1834-1924 ... DLB-156, 190

Barker, A. L. 1918-2002 .... DLB-14, 139

Barker, Clive 1952- DLB-261

Barker, Dudley (see Black, Lionel)

Barker, George 1913-1991 .... DLB-20

Barker, Harley Granville 1877-1946 ...... DLB-10

Barker, Howard 1946- DLB-13, 233

Barker, James Nelson 1784-1858 .... DLB-37

Barker, Jane 1652-1727 .... DLB-39, 131

Barker, Lady Mary Anne 1831-1911 .... DLB-166

Barker, Pat 1943- DLB-271, 326

Barker, William circa 1520-after 1576 .... DLB-132

Arthur Barker Limited DLB-112

Barkov, Ivan Semenovich 1732-1768 ..... DLB-150

Barks, Coleman 1937- DLB-5

Barlach, Ernst 1870-1938 .... DLB-56, 118

Barlow, Joel 1754-1812 .... DLB-37

The Prospect of Peace (1778) DLB-37

Barnard, John 1681-1770 .... DLB-24

Barnard, Marjorie (M. Barnard Eldershaw)
1897-1987 .... DLB-260

Barnard, Robert 1936- DLB-276

Barne, Kitty (Mary Catherine Barne)
1883-1957 .... DLB-160

Barnes, Barnabe 1571-1609 .... DLB-132

Barnes, Djuna 1892-1982 .... DLB-4, 9, 45; DS-15

Barnes, Jim 1933- DLB-175

Barnes, Julian 1946- DLB-194; Y-93

Notes for a Checklist of Publications Y-01

Barnes, Margaret Ayer 1886-1967 .... DLB-9

Barnes, Peter 1931- DLB-13, 233

Barnes, William 1801-1886 .... DLB-32

A. S. Barnes and Company DLB-49

Barnes and Noble Books DLB-46

Barnet, Miguel 1940- DLB-145

Barney, Natalie 1876-1972 .... DLB-4; DS-15

Barnfield, Richard 1574-1627 ....DLB-172

Baroja, Pío 1872-1956. .... DLB-322

Richard W. Baron [publishing house] DLB-46

Barr, Amelia Edith Huddleston
1831-1919 .... DLB-202, 221

Barr, Robert 1850-1912 ....DLB-70, 92

Barral, Carlos 1928-1989 .... DLB-134

Barrax, Gerald William 1933- DLB-41, 120

Barrès, Maurice 1862-1923 .... DLB-123

Barreno, Maria Isabel (see The Three Marias:
A Landmark Case in Portuguese
Literary History)

Barrett, Eaton Stannard 1786-1820...... DLB-116

Barrie, J. M.
1860-1937 ..... DLB-10, 141, 156; CDBLB-5

Barrie and Jenkins DLB-112

Barrio, Raymond 1921- DLB-82

Barrios, Gregg 1945- DLB-122

Barry, Philip 1896-1949 ....DLB-7, 228

Barry, Robertine (see Françoise)

Barry, Sebastian 1955- DLB-245

Barse and Hopkins DLB-46

Barstow, Stan 1928- DLB-14, 139, 207

Tribute to John Braine Y-86

Barth, John 1930- DLB-2, 227

Barthelme, Donald
1931-1989 ....DLB-2, 234; Y-80, 89

Barthelme, Frederick 1943- DLB-244; Y-85

Barthes, Roland 1915-1980 .... DLB-296

Bartholomew, Frank 1898-1985 ....DLB-127

Bartlett, John 1820-1905 .... DLB-1, 235

Bartol, Cyrus Augustus 1813-1900.... DLB-1, 235

Barton, Bernard 1784-1849............. DLB-96

Barton, John ca. 1610-1675 .... DLB-236

Barton, Thomas Pennant 1803-1869 .... DLB-140

Bartram, John 1699-1777 .... DLB-31

Bartram, William 1739-1823 .... DLB-37

Barykova, Anna Pavlovna 1839-1893 . . . . DLB-277

Bashshar ibn Burd circa 714-circa 784 . . . . DLB-311

Basic Books DLB-46

Basille, Theodore (see Becon, Thomas)

Bass, Rick 1958- DLB-212, 275

Bass, T. J. 1932- Y-81

Bassani, Giorgio 1916-2000 . . . . DLB-128, 177, 299

Basse, William circa 1583-1653 . . . . DLB-121

Bassett, John Spencer 1867-1928 . . . . DLB-17

Bassler, Thomas Joseph (see Bass, T. J.)

Bate, Walter Jackson 1918-1999 . . . . . . DLB-67, 103

Bateman, Stephen circa 1510-1584 . . . . DLB-136

Christopher Bateman
  [publishing house] DLB-170

Bates, H. E. 1905-1974 . . . . DLB-162, 191

Bates, Katharine Lee 1859-1929 . . . . DLB-71

Batiushkov, Konstantin Nikolaevich
  1787-1855 . . . . DLB-205

B. T. Batsford [publishing house] DLB-106

Batteux, Charles 1713-1780 . . . . DLB-313

Battiscombe, Georgina 1905- DLB-155

The Battle of Maldon circa 1000 . . . . DLB-146

Baudelaire, Charles 1821-1867 . . . . DLB-217

Baudrillard, Jean 1929- DLB-296

Bauer, Bruno 1809-1882 . . . . DLB-133

Bauer, Wolfgang 1941- DLB-124

Baum, L. Frank 1856-1919 . . . . DLB-22

Baum, Vicki 1888-1960 . . . . DLB-85

Baumbach, Jonathan 1933- Y-80

Bausch, Richard 1945- DLB-130

  Tribute to James Dickey Y-97

  Tribute to Peter Taylor Y-94

Bausch, Robert 1945- DLB-218

Bawden, Nina 1925- DLB-14, 161, 207

Bax, Clifford 1886-1962 . . . . DLB-10, 100

Baxter, Charles 1947- DLB-130

Bayer, Eleanor (see Perry, Eleanor)

Bayer, Konrad 1932-1964 . . . . DLB-85

Bayle, Pierre 1647-1706 . . . . DLB-268, 313

Bayley, Barrington J. 1937- DLB-261

Baynes, Pauline 1922- DLB-160

Baynton, Barbara 1857-1929 . . . . DLB-230

Bazin, Hervé (Jean Pierre Marie Hervé-Bazin)
  1911-1996 . . . . DLB-83

The BBC Four Samuel Johnson Prize
  for Non-fiction Y-02

Beach, Sylvia 1887-1962 . . . . DLB-4; DS-15

Beacon Press DLB-49

Beadle and Adams DLB-49

Beagle, Peter S. 1939- Y-80

Beal, M. F. 1937- Y-81

Beale, Howard K. 1899-1959 . . . . DLB-17

Beard, Charles A. 1874-1948 . . . . DLB-17

Beat Generation (Beats)
  As I See It, by Carolyn Cassady DLB-16

  A Beat Chronology: The First Twenty-five
    Years, 1944-1969 . . . . DLB-16

  The Commercialization of the Image
    of Revolt, by Kenneth Rexroth DLB-16

  Four Essays on the Beat Generation . . . DLB-16

  in New York City DLB-237

  in the West DLB-237

  Outlaw Days DLB-16

  Periodicals of DLB-16

Beattie, Ann 1947- DLB-218, 278; Y-82

Beattie, James 1735-1803 . . . . DLB-109

Beatty, Chester 1875-1968 . . . . DLB-201

Beauchemin, Nérée 1850-1931 . . . . DLB-92

Beauchemin, Yves 1941- DLB-60

Beaugrand, Honoré 1848-1906 . . . . DLB-99

Beaulieu, Victor-Lévy 1945- DLB-53

Beaumarchais, Pierre-Augustin Caron de
  1732-1799 . . . . DLB-313

Beaumer, Mme de ?-1766 . . . . DLB-313

Beaumont, Francis circa 1584-1616
  and Fletcher, John
  1579-1625 . . . . DLB-58; CDBLB-1

Beaumont, Sir John 1583?-1627 . . . . DLB-121

Beaumont, Joseph 1616-1699 . . . . DLB-126

Beauvoir, Simone de 1908-1986 . . . . . DLB-72; Y-86

  Personal Tribute to Simone de Beauvoir Y-86

Beaver, Bruce 1928- DLB-289

Becher, Ulrich 1910-1990 . . . . DLB-69

Becker, Carl 1873-1945 . . . . DLB-17

Becker, Jurek 1937-1997 . . . . DLB-75, 299

Becker, Jurgen 1932- DLB-75

Beckett, Mary 1926- DLB-319

Beckett, Samuel
  1906-1989 . . . . DLB-13, 15, 233, 319,
                                    321, 329; Y-90; CDBLB-7

Beckford, William 1760-1844 . . . . DLB-39, 213

Beckham, Barry 1944- DLB-33

Bećković, Matija 1939- DLB-181

Becon, Thomas circa 1512-1567 . . . . DLB-136

Becque, Henry 1837-1899 . . . . DLB-192

Beddoes, Thomas 1760-1808 . . . . DLB-158

Beddoes, Thomas Lovell 1803-1849 . . . . . . DLB-96

Bede circa 673-735 . . . . DLB-146

Bedford-Jones, H. 1887-1949 . . . . DLB-251

Bedregal, Yolanda 1913-1999 . . . . DLB-283

Beebe, William 1877-1962 . . . . DLB-275

Beecher, Catharine Esther
  1800-1878 . . . . DLB-1, 243

Beecher, Henry Ward
  1813-1887 . . . . DLB-3, 43, 250

Beer, George L. 1872-1920 . . . . DLB-47

Beer, Johann 1655-1700 . . . . DLB-168

Beer, Patricia 1919-1999 . . . . DLB-40

Beerbohm, Max 1872-1956 . . . . DLB-34, 100

Beer-Hofmann, Richard 1866-1945 . . . . DLB-81

Beers, Henry A. 1847-1926 . . . . DLB-71

S. O. Beeton [publishing house] DLB-106

Begley, Louis 1933- DLB-299

Bégon, Elisabeth 1696-1755 . . . . DLB-99

Behan, Brendan
  1923-1964 . . . . DLB-13, 233; CDBLB-7

Behn, Aphra 1640?-1689 . . . . DLB-39, 80, 131

Behn, Harry 1898-1973 . . . . DLB-61

Behrman, S. N. 1893-1973 . . . . DLB-7, 44

Beklemishev, Iurii Solomonvich
  (see Krymov, Iurii Solomonovich)

Belaney, Archibald Stansfeld (see Grey Owl)

Belasco, David 1853-1931 . . . . DLB-7

Clarke Belford and Company DLB-49

Belgian Luxembourg American Studies
  Association Y-01

Belinsky, Vissarion Grigor'evich
  1811-1848 . . . . DLB-198

Belitt, Ben 1911-2003 . . . . DLB-5

Belknap, Jeremy 1744-1798 . . . . DLB-30, 37

Bell, Adrian 1901-1980 . . . . DLB-191

Bell, Clive 1881-1964 . . . . DS-10

Bell, Daniel 1919- DLB-246

Bell, Gertrude Margaret Lowthian
  1868-1926 . . . . DLB-174

Bell, James Madison 1826-1902 . . . . DLB-50

Bell, Madison Smartt 1957- DLB-218, 278

  Tribute to Andrew Nelson Lytle Y-95

  Tribute to Peter Taylor Y-94

Bell, Marvin 1937- DLB-5

Bell, Millicent 1919- DLB-111

Bell, Quentin 1910-1996 . . . . DLB-155

Bell, Vanessa 1879-1961 . . . . DS-10

George Bell and Sons DLB-106

Robert Bell [publishing house] DLB-49

Bellamy, Edward 1850-1898 . . . . DLB-12

Bellamy, Joseph 1719-1790 . . . . DLB-31

John Bellamy [publishing house] DLB-170

La Belle Assemblée 1806-1837 . . . . DLB-110

Bellezza, Dario 1944-1996 . . . . DLB-128

Belli, Carlos Germán 1927- DLB-290

Belli, Gioconda 1948- DLB-290

Belloc, Hilaire 1870-1953 . . . . DLB-19, 100, 141, 174

Belloc, Madame (see Parkes, Bessie Rayner)

Bellonci, Maria 1902-1986 . . . . DLB-196

Bellow, Saul 1915-2005
  . . . . DLB-2, 28, 299, 329; Y-82;
                                              DS-3; CDALB-1

  Tribute to Isaac Bashevis Singer Y-91

Belmont Productions DLB-46	The Tilling Society. Y-98	Bernardin de Saint-Pierre 1737-1814. . . . . DLB-313
Belov, Vasilii Ivanovich 1932- DLB-302	Benson, Jackson J. 1930- DLB-111	Bernari, Carlo 1909-1992. . . . . .DLB-177
Bels, Alberts 1938- DLB-232	Benson, Robert Hugh 1871-1914 . . . . . . DLB-153	Bernhard, Thomas 1931-1989 . . . . .DLB-85, 124; CDWLB-2
Belševica, Vizma 1931- . . . DLB-232; CDWLB-4	Benson, Stella 1892-1933 . . . . DLB-36, 162	Berniéres, Louis de 1954- DLB-271
Bely, Andrei 1880-1934 . . . . DLB-295	Bent, James Theodore 1852-1897. . . . . . .DLB-174	Bernstein, Charles 1950- DLB-169
Bemelmans, Ludwig 1898-1962 . . . . DLB-22	Bent, Mabel Virginia Anna ?-? DLB-174	Béroalde de Verville, François 1556-1626 . . . . DLB-327
Bemis, Samuel Flagg 1891-1973 . . . . DLB-17	Bentham, Jeremy 1748-1832. . . . DLB-107, 158, 252	Berriault, Gina 1926-1999 . . . . DLB-130
William Bemrose [publishing house] DLB-106	Bentley, E. C. 1875-1956. . . . . DLB-70	Berrigan, Daniel 1921- DLB-5
Ben no Naishi 1228?-1271?. DLB-203	Bentley, Phyllis 1894-1977 . . . . DLB-191	Berrigan, Ted 1934-1983 . . . . DLB-5, 169
Benavente, Jacinto 1866-1954. . . . . DLB-329	Bentley, Richard 1662-1742 . . . . DLB-252	Berry, Wendell 1934- DLB-5, 6, 234, 275
Benchley, Robert 1889-1945. . . . . DLB-11	Richard Bentley [publishing house] DLB-106	Berryman, John 1914-1972. . . . DLB-48; CDALB-1
Bencúr, Matej (see Kukučin, Martin)	Benton, Robert 1932- DLB-44	Bersianik, Louky 1930- DLB-60
Benedetti, Mario 1920- DLB-113	Benziger Brothers DLB-49	Berssenbrugge, Mei-mei 1947- DLB-312
Benedict, Pinckney 1964- DLB-244	Beowulf circa 900-1000 or 790-825 . . . . DLB-146; CDBLB-1	Thomas Berthelet [publishing house]. DLB-170
Benedict, Ruth 1887-1948 . . . . DLB-246	Berberova, Nina 1901-1993 . . . . DLB-317	Berto, Giuseppe 1914-1978. . . . . .DLB-177
Benedictus, David 1938- DLB-14	Berent, Wacław 1873-1940 . . . . DLB-215	Bertocci, Peter Anthony 1910-1989 . . . . .DLB-279
Benedikt Gröndal 1826-1907 . . . . DLB-293	Beresford, Anne 1929- DLB-40	Bertolucci, Attilio 1911-2000 . . . . DLB-128
Benedikt, Michael 1935- DLB-5	Beresford, John Davys 1873-1947. . . . . DLB-162, 178, 197	Berton, Pierre 1920-2004 . . . . DLB-68
Benediktov, Vladimir Grigor'evich 1807-1873. . . . . DLB-205	"Experiment in the Novel" (1929) [excerpt]. DLB-36	Bertrand, Louis "Aloysius" 1807-1841 . . . .DLB-217
Benét, Stephen Vincent 1898-1943 . . . . DLB-4, 48, 102, 249	Beresford-Howe, Constance 1922- DLB-88	Besant, Sir Walter 1836-1901 . . . . . . DLB-135, 190
Stephen Vincent Benét Centenary Y-97	R. G. Berford Company. DLB-49	Bessa-Luís, Agustina 1922- DLB-287
Benét, William Rose 1886-1950 . . . . DLB-45	Berg, Elizabeth 1948- DLB-292	Bessette, Gerard 1920- DLB-53
Benford, Gregory 1941- Y-82	Berg, Stephen 1934- DLB-5	Bessie, Alvah 1904-1985. . . . . DLB-26
Benítez, Sandra 1941- DLB-292	Bergengruen, Werner 1892-1964 . . . . . . DLB-56	Bester, Alfred 1913-1987. . . . . DLB-8
Benjamin, Park 1809-1864 . . . . DLB-3, 59, 73, 250	Berger, John 1926- DLB-14, 207, 319, 326	Besterman, Theodore 1904-1976 . . . . . . DLB-201
Benjamin, Peter (see Cunningham, Peter)	Berger, Meyer 1898-1959 . . . . DLB-29	Beston, Henry (Henry Beston Sheahan) 1888-1968 . . . . .DLB-275
Benjamin, S. G. W. 1837-1914 . . . . DLB-189	Berger, Thomas 1924- DLB-2; Y-80	Best-Seller Lists An Assessment. Y-84
Benjamin, Walter 1892-1940 . . . . DLB-242	A Statement by Thomas Berger. Y-80	What's Really Wrong With Bestseller Lists. Y-84
Benlowes, Edward 1602-1676 . . . . DLB-126	Bergman, Hjalmar 1883-1931. . . . . DLB-259	Bestuzhev, Aleksandr Aleksandrovich (Marlinsky) 1797-1837 . . . . DLB-198
Benn, Gottfried 1886-1956 . . . . DLB-56	Bergman, Ingmar 1918- DLB-257	Bestuzhev, Nikolai Aleksandrovich 1791-1855. . . . . DLB-198
Benn Brothers Limited DLB-106	Bergson, Henri 1859-1941 . . . . DLB-329	Betham-Edwards, Matilda Barbara (see Edwards, Matilda Barbara Betham-)
Bennett, Alan 1934- DLB-310	Berkeley, Anthony 1893-1971. . . . . DLB-77	Betjeman, John 1906-1984 . . . . .DLB-20; Y-84; CDBLB-7
Bennett, Arnold 1867-1931. . . . DLB-10, 34, 98, 135; CDBLB-5	Berkeley, George 1685-1753 . . . . DLB-31, 101, 252	Betocchi, Carlo 1899-1986. . . . . DLB-128
The Arnold Bennett Society. Y-98	The Berkley Publishing Corporation DLB-46	Bettarini, Mariella 1942- DLB-128
Bennett, Charles 1899-1995 . . . . DLB-44	Berkman, Alexander 1870-1936 . . . . DLB-303	Betts, Doris 1932- DLB-218; Y-82
Bennett, Emerson 1822-1905 . . . . DLB-202	Berlin, Irving 1888-1989. . . . . DLB-265	Beveridge, Albert J. 1862-1927. . . . . .DLB-17
Bennett, Gwendolyn 1902-1981 . . . . DLB-51	Berlin, Lucia 1936- DLB-130	Beveridge, Judith 1956- DLB-325
Bennett, Hal 1930- DLB-33	Berman, Marshall 1940- DLB-246	Beverley, Robert circa 1673-1722 . . . . . DLB-24, 30
Bennett, James Gordon 1795-1872 . . . . . . DLB-43	Berman, Sabina 1955- DLB-305	Bevilacqua, Alberto 1934- DLB-196
Bennett, James Gordon, Jr. 1841-1918 . . . . DLB-23	Bernal, Vicente J. 1888-1915. . . . . DLB-82	Bevington, Louisa Sarah 1845-1895. . . . . DLB-199
Bennett, John 1865-1956 . . . . DLB-42	Bernanos, Georges 1888-1948 . . . . DLB-72	Beyle, Marie-Henri (see Stendhal)
Bennett, Louise 1919- DLB-117; CDWLB-3	Bernard, Catherine 1663?-1712 . . . . .DLB-268	Bèze, Théodore de (Theodore Beza) 1519-1605 . . . . DLB-327
Benni, Stefano 1947- DLB-196	Bernard, Harry 1898-1979 . . . . DLB-92	Bhatt, Sujata 1956- DLB-323
Benoist, Françoise-Albine Puzin de La Martinière 1731-1809 . . . . DLB-313	Bernard, John 1756-1828 . . . . DLB-37	
Benoit, Jacques 1941- DLB-60	Bernard of Chartres circa 1060-1124? . . . DLB-115	
Benson, A. C. 1862-1925 . . . . DLB-98	Bernard of Clairvaux 1090-1153 . . . . DLB-208	
Benson, E. F. 1867-1940 . . . . DLB-135, 153	Bernard, Richard 1568-1641/1642 . . . . . . DLB-281	
The E. F. Benson Society Y-98	Bernard Silvestris fl. circa 1130-1160 . . . . DLB-208	Białoszewski, Miron 1922-1983 . . . . DLB-232

Bianco, Margery Williams 1881-1944 . . . . DLB-160

Bibaud, Adèle 1854-1941 . . . . DLB-92

Bibaud, Michel 1782-1857 . . . . DLB-99

Bibliography
   Bibliographical and Textual Scholarship
     Since World War II Y-89

   Center for Bibliographical Studies and
     Research at the University of
     California, Riverside Y-91

   The Great Bibliographers Series Y-93

   Primary Bibliography: A Retrospective Y-95

Bichsel, Peter 1935- DLB-75

Bickerstaff, Isaac John 1733-circa 1808 . . . . DLB-89

Drexel Biddle [publishing house] DLB-49

Bidermann, Jacob
   1577 or 1578-1639 . . . . DLB-164

Bidwell, Walter Hilliard 1798-1881 . . . . DLB-79

Biehl, Charlotta Dorothea 1731-1788 . . . . . DLB-300

Bienek, Horst 1930-1990 . . . . DLB-75

Bierbaum, Otto Julius 1865-1910 . . . . DLB-66

Bierce, Ambrose 1842-1914?
     . . . . . . DLB-11, 12, 23, 71, 74, 186; CDALB-3

Bigelow, William F. 1879-1966 . . . . DLB-91

Biggers, Earl Derr 1884-1933 . . . . DLB-306

Biggle, Lloyd, Jr. 1923-2002 . . . . DLB-8

Bigiaretti, Libero 1905-1993 . . . . DLB-177

Bigland, Eileen 1898-1970 . . . . DLB-195

Biglow, Hosea (see Lowell, James Russell)

Bigongiari, Piero 1914-1997 . . . . DLB-128

Bilac, Olavo 1865-1918 . . . . DLB-307

Bilenchi, Romano 1909-1989 . . . . DLB-264

Billinger, Richard 1890-1965 . . . . DLB-124

Billings, Hammatt 1818-1874 . . . . DLB-188

Billings, John Shaw 1898-1975 . . . . DLB-137

Billings, Josh (see Shaw, Henry Wheeler)

Binchy, Maeve 1940- DLB-319

Binding, Rudolf G. 1867-1938 . . . . DLB-66

Bing Xin 1900-1999 . . . . DLB-328

Bingay, Malcolm 1884-1953 . . . . DLB-241

Bingham, Caleb 1757-1817 . . . . DLB-42

Bingham, George Barry 1906-1988 . . . . . . DLB-127

Bingham, Sallie 1937- DLB-234

William Bingley [publishing house] DLB-154

Binyon, Laurence 1869-1943 . . . . DLB-19

Biographia Brittanica DLB-142

Biography
   Biographical Documents Y-84, 85

   A Celebration of Literary Biography Y-98

   Conference on Modern Biography Y-85

   The Cult of Biography
     Excerpts from the Second Folio Debate:
     "Biographies are generally a disease of
     English Literature" Y-86

   New Approaches to Biography: Challenges
     from Critical Theory, USC Conference
     on Literary Studies, 1990 . . . . Y-90

   "The New Biography," by Virginia Woolf,
     New York Herald Tribune,
     30 October 1927 . . . . DLB-149

   "The Practice of Biography," in *The English
     Sense of Humour and Other Essays*, by
     Harold Nicolson DLB-149

   "Principles of Biography," in *Elizabethan
     and Other Essays*, by Sidney Lee . . . DLB-149

   Remarks at the Opening of "The Biographical
     Part of Literature" Exhibition, by
     William R. Cagle Y-98

   Survey of Literary Biographies Y-00

   A Transit of Poets and Others: American
     Biography in 1982 . . . . Y-82

   The Year in Literary
     Biography Y-83–01

Biography, The Practice of:
   An Interview with B. L. Reid Y-83

   An Interview with David Herbert Donald . . . Y-87

   An Interview with Humphrey Carpenter Y-84

   An Interview with Joan Mellen Y-94

   An Interview with John Caldwell Guilds Y-92

   An Interview with William Manchester . . . Y-85

John Bioren [publishing house] DLB-49

Bioy Casares, Adolfo 1914-1999 . . . . DLB-113

Bird, Isabella Lucy 1831-1904 . . . . DLB-166

Bird, Robert Montgomery 1806-1854 . . . . DLB-202

Bird, William 1888-1963 . . . . DLB-4; DS-15

   The Cost of the *Cantos*: William Bird
     to Ezra Pound Y-01

Birken, Sigmund von 1626-1681 . . . . DLB-164

Birney, Earle 1904-1995 . . . . DLB-88

Birrell, Augustine 1850-1933 . . . . DLB-98

Bisher, Furman 1918- DLB-171

Bishop, Elizabeth
   1911-1979 . . . . DLB-5, 169; CDALB-6

   The Elizabeth Bishop Society Y-01

Bishop, John Peale 1892-1944 . . . . . DLB-4, 9, 45

Bismarck, Otto von 1815-1898 . . . . DLB-129

Bisset, Robert 1759-1805 . . . . DLB-142

Bissett, Bill 1939- DLB-53

Bitov, Andrei Georgievich 1937- DLB-302

Bitzius, Albert (see Gotthelf, Jeremias)

Bjørnboe, Jens 1920-1976 . . . . DLB-297

Bjørnson, Bjørnstjerne 1832-1910 . . . . DLB-329

Bjørnvig, Thorkild 1918- DLB-214

Black, David (D. M.) 1941- DLB-40

Black, Gavin (Oswald Morris Wynd)
   1913-1998 . . . . DLB-276

Black, Lionel (Dudley Barker)
   1910-1980 . . . . DLB-276

Black, Winifred 1863-1936 . . . . DLB-25

Walter J. Black [publishing house] DLB-46

Blackamore, Arthur 1679-? DLB-24, 39

Blackburn, Alexander L. 1929- Y-85

Blackburn, John 1923-1993 . . . . DLB-261

Blackburn, Paul 1926-1971 . . . . DLB-16; Y-81

Blackburn, Thomas 1916-1977 . . . . DLB-27

Blacker, Terence 1948- DLB-271

Blackmore, R. D. 1825-1900 . . . . DLB-18

Blackmore, Sir Richard 1654-1729 . . . . . . DLB-131

Blackmur, R. P. 1904-1965 . . . . DLB-63

Blackwell, Alice Stone 1857-1950 . . . . DLB-303

Basil Blackwell, Publisher DLB-106

Blackwood, Algernon Henry
   1869-1951 . . . . DLB-153, 156, 178

Blackwood, Caroline 1931-1996 . . . . . DLB-14, 207

William Blackwood and Sons, Ltd. DLB-154

Blackwood's Edinburgh Magazine
   1817-1980 . . . . DLB-110

Blades, William 1824-1890 . . . . DLB-184

Blaga, Lucian 1895-1961 . . . . DLB-220

Blagden, Isabella 1817?-1873 . . . . DLB-199

Blair, Eric Arthur (see Orwell, George)

Blair, Francis Preston 1791-1876 . . . . DLB-43

Blair, Hugh
   Lectures on Rhetoric and Belles Lettres (1783),
     [excerpts] DLB-31

Blair, James circa 1655-1743 . . . . DLB-24

Blair, John Durburrow 1759-1823 . . . . DLB-37

Blais, Marie-Claire 1939- DLB-53

Blaise, Clark 1940- DLB-53

Blake, George 1893-1961 . . . . DLB-191

Blake, Lillie Devereux 1833-1913 . . . . DLB-202, 221

Blake, Nicholas (C. Day Lewis)
   1904-1972 . . . . DLB-77

Blake, William
   1757-1827 . . . . DLB-93, 154, 163; CDBLB-3

The Blakiston Company DLB-49

Blanchard, Stephen 1950- DLB-267

Blanchot, Maurice 1907-2003 . . . . DLB-72, 296

Blanckenburg, Christian Friedrich von
   1744-1796 . . . . DLB-94

Blandiana, Ana 1942- DLB-232; CDWLB-4

Blanshard, Brand 1892-1987 . . . . DLB-279

Blasco Ibáñez, Vicente 1867-1928 . . . . DLB-322

Blaser, Robin 1925- DLB-165

Blaumanis, Rūdolfs 1863-1908 . . . . DLB-220

Bleasdale, Alan 1946- DLB-245

Bledsoe, Albert Taylor
   1809-1877 . . . . DLB-3, 79, 248

Bleecker, Ann Eliza 1752-1783 . . . . DLB-200

Blelock and Company DLB-49

Blennerhassett, Margaret Agnew
   1773-1842 . . . . DLB-99

Geoffrey Bles [publishing house] DLB-112

Blessington, Marguerite, Countess of
   1789-1849 . . . . DLB-166

Blew, Mary Clearman 1939- DLB-256

Blicher, Steen Steensen 1782-1848 ...... DLB-300

The Blickling Homilies circa 971 .... DLB-146

Blind, Mathilde 1841-1896 .... DLB-199

The Blind Assassin, 2000 Booker Prize winner,
Margaret Atwood. DLB-326

Blish, James 1921-1975 .... DLB-8

E. Bliss and E. White
[publishing house] DLB-49

Bliven, Bruce 1889-1977 .... DLB-137

Blixen, Karen 1885-1962 .... DLB-214

Bloch, Ernst 1885-1977 .... DLB-296

Bloch, Robert 1917-1994. .... DLB-44

    Tribute to John D. MacDonald Y-86

Block, Lawrence 1938- DLB-226

Block, Rudolph (see Lessing, Bruno)

Blok, Aleksandr Aleksandrovich
1880-1921 .... DLB-295

Blondal, Patricia 1926-1959 .... DLB-88

Bloom, Harold 1930- DLB-67

Bloomer, Amelia 1818-1894 .... DLB-79

Bloomfield, Robert 1766-1823 .... DLB-93

Bloomsbury Group. DS-10

    The *Dreannought* Hoax DS-10

Bloor, Ella Reeve 1862-1951. .... DLB-303

Blotner, Joseph 1923- DLB-111

Blount, Thomas 1618?-1679. .... DLB-236

Bloy, Léon 1846-1917. .... DLB-123

Blume, Judy 1938- DLB-52

    Tribute to Theodor Seuss Geisel Y-91

Blunck, Hans Friedrich 1888-1961 .... DLB-66

Blunden, Edmund 1896-1974 ....DLB-20, 100, 155

Blundeville, Thomas 1522?-1606 .... DLB-236

Blunt, Lady Anne Isabella Noel
1837-1917 .... DLB-174

Blunt, Wilfrid Scawen 1840-1922 .....DLB-19, 174

Bly, Nellie (see Cochrane, Elizabeth)

Bly, Robert 1926- DLB-5

Blyton, Enid 1897-1968. .... DLB-160

Boaden, James 1762-1839 .... DLB-89

Boal, Augusto 1931- DLB-307

Boas, Frederick S. 1862-1957 .... DLB-149

The Bobbs-Merrill Company DLB-46, 291

    The Bobbs-Merrill Archive at the
Lilly Library, Indiana University..... Y-90

Boborykin, Petr Dmitrievich
1836-1921 .... DLB-238

Bobrov, Semen Sergeevich
1763?-1810 .... DLB-150

Bobrowski, Johannes 1917-1965 .... DLB-75

Bocage, Manuel Maria Barbosa du
1765-1805...................... DLB-287

Bodenheim, Maxwell 1892-1954 ...... DLB-9, 45

Bodenstedt, Friedrich von 1819-1892.... DLB-129

Bodini, Vittorio 1914-1970 .... DLB-128

Bodkin, M. McDonnell 1850-1933........ DLB-70

Bodley, Sir Thomas 1545-1613......... DLB-213

Bodley Head...................... DLB-112

Bodmer, Johann Jakob 1698-1783........ DLB-97

Bodmershof, Imma von 1895-1982 ...... DLB-85

Bodsworth, Fred 1918- DLB-68

Böðvar Guðmundsson 1939- DLB-293

Boehm, Sydney 1908-1990............. DLB-44

Boer, Charles 1939- DLB-5

Boethius circa 480-circa 524 .... DLB-115

Boethius of Dacia circa 1240-? DLB-115

Bogan, Louise 1897-1970 .... DLB-45, 169

Bogarde, Dirk 1921-1999 .... DLB-14

Bogdanov, Aleksandr Aleksandrovich
1873-1928..................... DLB-295

Bogdanovich, Ippolit Fedorovich
circa 1743-1803 .... DLB-150

David Bogue [publishing house]........ DLB-106

Bohjalian, Chris 1960- DLB-292

Böhme, Jakob 1575-1624 .... DLB-164

H. G. Bohn [publishing house] DLB-106

Bohse, August 1661-1742 .... DLB-168

Boie, Heinrich Christian 1744-1806 ...... DLB-94

Boileau-Despréaux, Nicolas 1636-1711....DLB-268

Bojunga, Lygia 1932- DLB-307

Bok, Edward W. 1863-1930 ..... DLB-91; DS-16

Boland, Eavan 1944- DLB-40

Boldrewood, Rolf (Thomas Alexander Browne)
1826?-1915..................... DLB-230

Bolingbroke, Henry St. John, Viscount
1678-1751 .... DLB-101

Böll, Heinrich
1917-1985.....DLB-69, 329; Y-85; CDWLB-2

Bolling, Robert 1738-1775............. DLB-31

Bolotov, Andrei Timofeevich
1738-1833..................... DLB-150

Bolt, Carol 1941- DLB-60

Bolt, Robert 1924-1995 .... DLB-13, 233

Bolton, Herbert E. 1870-1953........... DLB-17

Bonaventura..................... DLB-90

Bonaventure circa 1217-1274........... DLB-115

Bonaviri, Giuseppe 1924- DLB-177

Bond, Edward 1934- DLB-13, 310

Bond, Michael 1926- DLB-161

Bondarev, Iurii Vasil'evich 1924- DLB-302

The Bone People, 1985 Booker Prize winner,
Keri Hulme DLB-326

Albert and Charles Boni
[publishing house] DLB-46

Boni and Liveright DLB-46

Bonnefoy, Yves 1923- DLB-258

Bonner, Marita 1899-1971 .... DLB-228

Bonner, Paul Hyde 1893-1968 ....DS-17

Bonner, Sherwood (see McDowell, Katharine
Sherwood Bonner)

Robert Bonner's Sons.................. DLB-49

Bonnin, Gertrude Simmons (see Zitkala-Ša)

Bonsanti, Alessandro 1904-1984 ....DLB-177

Bontempelli, Massimo 1878-1960....... DLB-264

Bontemps, Arna 1902-1973 .... DLB-48, 51

The Book Buyer (1867-1880, 1884-1918,
1935-1938.....................DS-13

The Book League of America........... DLB-46

Book Reviewing

    The American Book Review: A Sketch ... Y-92

    Book Reviewing and the
Literary Scene Y-96, 97

    Book Reviewing in America Y-87–94

    Book Reviewing in America and the
Literary Scene Y-95

    Book Reviewing in Texas............. Y-94

    Book Reviews in Glossy Magazines. Y-95

    Do They or Don't They?
Writers Reading Book Reviews...... Y-01

    The Most Powerful Book Review
in America [*New York Times
Book Review*] Y-82

    Some Surprises and Universal Truths Y-92

    The Year in Book Reviewing and the
Literary Situation Y-98

Book Supply Company DLB-49

The Book Trade History Group. Y-93

The Booker Prize Y-96–98

    Address by Anthony Thwaite,
Chairman of the Booker Prize Judges
Comments from Former Booker
Prize Winners Y-86

Boorde, Andrew circa 1490-1549....... DLB-136

Boorstin, Daniel J. 1914- DLB-17

    Tribute to Archibald MacLeish Y-82

    Tribute to Charles Scribner Jr. Y-95

Booth, Franklin 1874-1948 .... DLB-188

Booth, Mary L. 1831-1889 .... DLB-79

Booth, Philip 1925- Y-82

Booth, Wayne C. 1921- DLB-67

Booth, William 1829-1912 .... DLB-190

Bor, Josef 1906-1979 .... DLB-299

Borchardt, Rudolf 1877-1945 .... DLB-66

Borchert, Wolfgang 1921-1947 ...... DLB-69, 124

Bording, Anders 1619-1677 .... DLB-300

Borel, Pétrus 1809-1859 .... DLB-119

Borgen, Johan 1902-1979 .... DLB-297

Borges, Jorge Luis
1899-1986 ... DLB-113, 283; Y-86; CDWLB-3

    The Poetry of Jorge Luis Borges Y-86

    A Personal Tribute.................. Y-86

Borgese, Giuseppe Antonio 1882-1952... DLB-264

Börne, Ludwig 1786-1837 ....DLB-90
Bornstein, Miriam 1950- DLB-209
Borowski, Tadeusz
    1922-1951 ....DLB-215; CDWLB-4
Borrow, George 1803-1881 ......DLB-21, 55, 166
Bosanquet, Bernard 1848-1923 ....DLB-262
Boscán, Juan circa 1490-1542 ....DLB-318
Bosch, Juan 1909-2001................DLB-145
Bosco, Henri 1888-1976................DLB-72
Bosco, Monique 1927- DLB-53
Bosman, Herman Charles 1905-1951 ...DLB-225
Bossuet, Jacques-Bénigne 1627-1704 ......DLB-268
Bostic, Joe 1908-1988................DLB-241
Boston, Lucy M. 1892-1990 ....DLB-161
Boston Quarterly Review...................DLB-1
Boston University
    Editorial Institute at Boston University....Y-00
    Special Collections at Boston University...Y-99
Boswell, James
    1740-1795..........DLB-104, 142; CDBLB-2
Boswell, Robert 1953- DLB-234
Bosworth, David Y-82
    Excerpt from "Excerpts from a Report
    of the Commission," in *The Death
    of Descartes*......................Y-82
Bote, Hermann circa 1460-circa 1520....DLB-179
Botev, Khristo 1847-1876 ....DLB-147
Botkin, Vasilii Petrovich 1811-1869 .....DLB-277
Botta, Anne C. Lynch 1815-1891 .....DLB-3, 250
Botto, Ján (see Krasko, Ivan)
Bottome, Phyllis 1882-1963............DLB-197
Bottomley, Gordon 1874-1948..........DLB-10
Bottoms, David 1949- DLB-120; Y-83
    Tribute to James Dickey Y-97
Bottrall, Ronald 1906-1959 ....DLB-20
Bouchardy, Joseph 1810-1870 ....DLB-192
Boucher, Anthony 1911-1968 ....DLB-8
Boucher, Jonathan 1738-1804..........DLB-31
Boucher de Boucherville, Georges
    1814-1894 ....DLB-99
Boudreau, Daniel (see Coste, Donat)
Bouhours, Dominique 1628-1702 ....DLB-268
Bourassa, Napoléon 1827-1916 ....DLB-99
Bourget, Paul 1852-1935 ....DLB-123
Bourinot, John George 1837-1902 ......DLB-99
Bourjaily, Vance 1922- DLB-2, 143
Bourne, Edward Gaylord 1860-1908......DLB-47
Bourne, Randolph 1886-1918 ....DLB-63
Bousoño, Carlos 1923- DLB-108
Bousquet, Joë 1897-1950 ....DLB-72
Bova, Ben 1932- Y-81
Bovard, Oliver K. 1872-1945..........DLB-25

Bove, Emmanuel 1898-1945 ....DLB-72
Bowen, Elizabeth
    1899-1973 ....DLB-15, 162; CDBLB-7
Bowen, Francis 1811-1890........DLB-1, 59, 235
Bowen, John 1924- DLB-13
Bowen, Marjorie 1886-1952...........DLB-153
Bowen-Merrill Company..............DLB-49
Bowering, George 1935- DLB-53
Bowers, Bathsheba 1671-1718 ....DLB-200
Bowers, Claude G. 1878-1958 ....DLB-17
Bowers, Edgar 1924-2000 ....DLB-5
Bowers, Fredson Thayer
    1905-1991 ....DLB-140; Y-91
    The Editorial Style of Fredson Bowers Y-91
    Fredson Bowers and
    Studies in Bibliography............Y-91
    Fredson Bowers and the Cambridge
    Beaumont and Fletcher.............Y-91
    Fredson Bowers as Critic of Renaissance
    Dramatic Literature Y-91
    Fredson Bowers as Music Critic Y-91
    Fredson Bowers, Master Teacher Y-91
    An Interview [on Nabokov] Y-80
    Working with Fredson Bowers Y-91
Bowles, Paul 1910-1999...... DLB-5, 6, 218; Y-99
Bowles, Samuel, III 1826-1878...........DLB-43
Bowles, William Lisle 1762-1850 ....DLB-93
Bowman, Louise Morey 1882-1944.......DLB-68
Bowne, Borden Parker 1847-1919 ......DLB-270
Boyd, James 1888-1944 ....DLB-9; DS-16
Boyd, John 1912-2002 ....DLB-310
Boyd, John 1919- DLB-8
Boyd, Martin 1893-1972 ....DLB-260
Boyd, Thomas 1898-1935 .....DLB-9, 316; DS-16
Boyd, William 1952- DLB-231
Boye, Karin 1900-1941 ....DLB-259
Boyesen, Hjalmar Hjorth
    1848-1895.............DLB-12, 71; DS-13
Boylan, Clare 1948- DLB-267
Boyle, Kay 1902-1992   DLB-4, 9, 48, 86; DS-15;
    ....Y-93
Boyle, Roger, Earl of Orrery 1621-1679 ...DLB-80
Boyle, T. Coraghessan
    1948- DLB-218, 278; Y-86
Božić, Mirko 1919- DLB-181
Brackenbury, Alison 1953- DLB-40
Brackenridge, Hugh Henry
    1748-1816 ....DLB-11, 37
    The Rising Glory of America DLB-37
Brackett, Charles 1892-1969 ....DLB-26
Brackett, Leigh 1915-1978 ....DLB-8, 26
John Bradburn [publishing house]........DLB-49
Bradbury, Malcolm 1932-2000 .....DLB-14, 207
Bradbury, Ray 1920- DLB-2, 8; CDALB-6

Bradbury and Evans DLB-106
Braddon, Mary Elizabeth
    1835-1915 ....DLB-18, 70, 156
Bradford, Andrew 1686-1742.........DLB-43, 73
Bradford, Gamaliel 1863-1932.........DLB-17
Bradford, John 1749-1830 ....DLB-43
Bradford, Roark 1896-1948...........DLB-86
Bradford, William 1590-1657 ....DLB-24, 30
Bradford, William, III 1719-1791......DLB-43, 73
Bradlaugh, Charles 1833-1891 ....DLB-57
Bradley, David 1950- DLB-33
Bradley, F. H. 1846-1924...............DLB-262
Bradley, Katherine Harris (see Field, Michael)
Bradley, Marion Zimmer 1930-1999.......DLB-8
Bradley, William Aspenwall 1878-1939 .....DLB-4
Ira Bradley and Company DLB-49
J. W. Bradley and Company DLB-49
Bradshaw, Henry 1831-1886...........DLB-184
Bradstreet, Anne
    1612 or 1613-1672........DLB-24; CDALB-2
Bradūnas, Kazys 1917- DLB-220
Bradwardine, Thomas circa 1295-1349 ...DLB-115
Brady, Frank 1924-1986 ....DLB-111
Frederic A. Brady [publishing house]......DLB-49
Braga, Rubem 1913-1990 ....DLB-307
Bragg, Melvyn 1939- DLB-14, 271
Brahe, Tycho 1546-1601 ....DLB-300
Charles H. Brainard [publishing house]....DLB-49
Braine, John
    1922-1986 ....DLB-15; Y-86; CDBLB-7
Braithwait, Richard 1588-1673 ....DLB-151
Braithwaite, William Stanley
    1878-1962 ....DLB-50, 54
Bräker, Ulrich 1735-1798 ....DLB-94
Bramah, Ernest 1868-1942 ....DLB-70
Branagan, Thomas 1774-1843 ....DLB-37
Brancati, Vitaliano 1907-1954 ....DLB-264
Branch, William Blackwell 1927- DLB-76
Brand, Christianna 1907-1988 .... DLB-276
Brand, Max (see Faust, Frederick Schiller)
Brandão, Raul 1867-1930..............DLB-287
Branden Press DLB-46
Brandes, Georg 1842-1927 ....DLB-300
Branner, H.C. 1903-1966..............DLB-214
Brant, Sebastian 1457-1521 ....DLB-179
Brantôme (Pierre de Bourdeille)
    1540?-1614 ....DLB-327
Brassey, Lady Annie (Allnutt)
    1839-1887 ....DLB-166
Brathwaite, Edward Kamau
    1930- DLB-125; CDWLB-3
Brault, Jacques 1933- DLB-53
Braun, Matt 1932- DLB-212

Cumulative Index

Braun, Volker 1939- DLB-75, 124

Brautigan, Richard 1935-1984 .... DLB-2, 5, 206; Y-80, 84

Braxton, Joanne M. 1950- DLB-41

Bray, Anne Eliza 1790-1883 .... DLB-116

Bray, Thomas 1656-1730 .... DLB-24

Brazdžionis, Bernardas 1907-2002 .... DLB-220

George Braziller [publishing house] DLB-46

The Bread Loaf Writers' Conference 1983 .... Y-84

Breasted, James Henry 1865-1935 .... DLB-47

Brecht, Bertolt 1898-1956 .... DLB-56, 124; CDWLB-2

Bredel, Willi 1901-1964 .... DLB-56

Bregendahl, Marie 1867-1940 .... DLB-214

Breitinger, Johann Jakob 1701-1776 .... DLB-97

Brekke, Paal 1923-1993 .... DLB-297

Bremser, Bonnie 1939- DLB-16

Bremser, Ray 1934-1998 .... DLB-16

Brennan, Christopher 1870-1932 .... DLB-230

Brentano, Bernard von 1901-1964 .... DLB-56

Brentano, Clemens 1778-1842 .... DLB-90

Brentano, Franz 1838-1917 .... DLB-296

Brentano's DLB-49

Brenton, Howard 1942- DLB-13

Breslin, Jimmy 1929-1996 .... DLB-185

Breton, André 1896-1966 .... DLB-65, 258

Breton, Nicholas circa 1555-circa 1626 .... DLB-136

The Breton Lays 1300-early fifteenth century DLB-146

Brett, Lily 1946- DLB-325

Brett, Simon 1945- DLB-276

Brewer, Gil 1922-1983 .... DLB-306

Brewer, Luther A. 1858-1933 .... DLB-187

Brewer, Warren and Putnam DLB-46

Brewster, Elizabeth 1922- DLB-60

Breytenbach, Breyten 1939- DLB-225

Bridge, Ann (Lady Mary Dolling Sanders O'Malley) 1889-1974 .... DLB-191

Bridge, Horatio 1806-1893 .... DLB-183

Bridgers, Sue Ellen 1942- DLB-52

Bridges, Robert 1844-1930 .... DLB-19, 98; CDBLB-5

The Bridgewater Library DLB-213

Bridie, James 1888-1951 .... DLB-10

Brieux, Eugene 1858-1932 .... DLB-192

Brigadere, Anna 1861-1933 .... DLB-220; CDWLB-4

Briggs, Charles Frederick 1804-1877 .... DLB-3, 250

Brighouse, Harold 1882-1958 .... DLB-10

Bright, Mary Chavelita Dunne (see Egerton, George)

Brightman, Edgar Sheffield 1884-1953 .... DLB-270

B. J. Brimmer Company DLB-46

Brines, Francisco 1932- DLB-134

Brink, André 1935- DLB-225

Brinley, George, Jr. 1817-1875 .... DLB-140

Brinnin, John Malcolm 1916-1998 .... DLB-48

Brisbane, Albert 1809-1890 .... DLB-3, 250

Brisbane, Arthur 1864-1936 .... DLB-25

British Academy DLB-112

The British Critic 1793-1843 .... DLB-110

British Library
   The American Trust for the British Library Y-96
   The British Library and the Regular Readers' Group Y-91
   Building the New British Library at St Pancras Y-94

British Literary Prizes DLB-207; Y-98

British Literature
   The "Angry Young Men" DLB-15
   Author-Printers, 1476-1599 .... DLB-167
   The Comic Tradition Continued DLB-15
   Documents on Sixteenth-Century Literature DLB-167, 172
   Eikon Basilike 1649 .... DLB-151
   Letter from London Y-96
   A Mirror for Magistrates DLB-167
   "Modern English Prose" (1876), by George Saintsbury DLB-57
   Sex, Class, Politics, and Religion [in the British Novel, 1930-1959] DLB-15
   Victorians on Rhetoric and Prose Style DLB-57
   The Year in British Fiction Y-99–01
   "You've Never Had It So Good," Gusted by "Winds of Change": British Fiction in the 1950s, 1960s, and After DLB-14

British Literature, Old and Middle English
   Anglo-Norman Literature in the Development of Middle English Literature DLB-146
   The *Alliterative Morte Arthure and the Stanzaic Morte Arthur* circa 1350-1400 .... DLB-146
   Ancrene Riwle circa 1200-1225 .... DLB-146
   The *Anglo-Saxon Chronicle* circa 890-1154 .... DLB-146
   The Battle of Maldon circa 1000 .... DLB-146
   Beowulf circa 900-1000 or 790-825 .... DLB-146; CDBLB-1
   The Blickling Homilies circa 971 .... DLB-146
   The Breton Lays 1300-early fifteenth century DLB-146
   The Castle of Perseverance circa 1400-1425 .... DLB-146
   The Celtic Background to Medieval English Literature DLB-146
   The Chester Plays circa 1505-1532; revisions until 1575 .... DLB-146
   Cursor Mundi circa 1300 .... DLB-146

   The English Language: 410 to 1500 .... DLB-146
   The Germanic Epic and Old English Heroic Poetry: *Widsith, Waldere,* and *The Fight at Finnsburg* DLB-146
   Judith circa 930 .... DLB-146
   The Matter of England 1240-1400 .... DLB-146
   The Matter of Rome early twelfth to late fifteenth centuries DLB-146
   Middle English Literature: An Introduction DLB-146
   The Middle English Lyric DLB-146
   Morality Plays: *Mankind* circa 1450-1500 and *Everyman* circa 1500 .... DLB-146
   N-Town Plays circa 1468 to early sixteenth century DLB-146
   Old English Literature: An Introduction DLB-146
   Old English Riddles eighth to tenth centuries DLB-146
   The Owl and the Nightingale circa 1189-1199 .... DLB-146
   The Paston Letters 1422-1509 .... DLB-146
   The Seafarer circa 970 .... DLB-146
   The *South English Legendary* circa thirteenth to fifteenth centuries DLB-146

The British Review and London Critical Journal 1811-1825 .... DLB-110

Brito, Aristeo 1942- DLB-122

Brittain, Vera 1893-1970 .... DLB-191

Briusov, Valerii Iakovlevich 1873-1924 .... DLB-295

Brizeux, Auguste 1803-1858 .... DLB-217

Broadway Publishing Company DLB-46

Broch, Hermann 1886-1951 .... DLB-85, 124; CDWLB-2

Brochu, André 1942- DLB-53

Brock, Edwin 1927-1997 .... DLB-40

Brockes, Barthold Heinrich 1680-1747 .... DLB-168

Brod, Max 1884-1968 .... DLB-81

Brodber, Erna 1940- DLB-157

Brodhead, John R. 1814-1873 .... DLB-30

Brodkey, Harold 1930-1996 .... DLB-130

Brodsky, Joseph (Iosif Aleksandrovich Brodsky) 1940-1996 .... DLB-285, 329; Y-87
   Nobel Lecture 1987 .... Y-87

Brodsky, Michael 1948- DLB-244

Broeg, Bob 1918- DLB-171

Brøgger, Suzanne 1944- DLB-214

Brome, Richard circa 1590-1652 .... DLB-58

Brome, Vincent 1910-2004 .... DLB-155

Bromfield, Louis 1896-1956 .... DLB-4, 9, 86

Bromige, David 1933- DLB-193

Broner, E. M. 1930- DLB-28
   Tribute to Bernard Malamud Y-86

Bronk, William 1918-1999 .... DLB-165

Bronnen, Arnolt 1895-1959 .... DLB-124

Brontë, Anne 1820-1849 . . . . .DLB-21, 199

Brontë, Charlotte
1816-1855 . . . . . .DLB-21, 159, 199; CDBLB-4

Brontë, Emily
1818-1848 . . . . . . DLB-21, 32, 199; CDBLB-4

The Brontë Society Y-98

Brook, Stephen 1947- DLB-204

Brook Farm 1841-1847 . . . . .DLB-1; 223; DS-5

Brooke, Frances 1724-1789. . . . . .DLB-39, 99

Brooke, Henry 1703?-1783. . . . . .DLB-39

Brooke, L. Leslie 1862-1940 . . . . .DLB-141

Brooke, Margaret, Ranee of Sarawak
1849-1936 . . . . DLB-174

Brooke, Rupert
1887-1915 . . . . .DLB-19, 216; CDBLB-6

The Friends of the Dymock Poets. Y-00

Brooker, Bertram 1888-1955 . . . . .DLB-88

Brooke-Rose, Christine 1923- DLB-14, 231

Brookner, Anita 1928- DLB-194, 326; Y-87

Brooks, Charles Timothy 1813-1883. . .DLB-1, 243

Brooks, Cleanth 1906-1994 . . . . DLB-63; Y-94

Tribute to Katherine Anne Porter Y-80

Tribute to Walker Percy Y-90

Brooks, Gwendolyn
1917-2000 . . . . .DLB-5, 76, 165; CDALB-1

Tribute to Julian Mayfield Y-84

Brooks, Jeremy 1926-1994. . . . . .DLB-14

Brooks, Mel 1926- DLB-26

Brooks, Noah 1830-1903. . . . . DLB-42; DS-13

Brooks, Richard 1912-1992 . . . . .DLB-44

Brooks, Van Wyck 1886-1963 . . . . DLB-45, 63, 103

Brophy, Brigid 1929-1995 . . . . DLB-14, 70, 271

Brophy, John 1899-1965 . . . . .DLB-191

Brorson, Hans Adolph 1694-1764 . . . . . . .DLB-300

Brossard, Chandler 1922-1993 . . . . .DLB-16

Brossard, Nicole 1943- DLB-53

Broster, Dorothy Kathleen 1877-1950 . . . .DLB-160

Brother Antoninus (see Everson, William)

Brotherton, Lord 1856-1930 . . . . .DLB-184

Brougham, John 1810-1880 . . . . .DLB-11

Brougham and Vaux, Henry Peter
Brougham, Baron 1778-1868. . . .DLB-110, 158

Broughton, James 1913-1999 . . . . .DLB-5

Broughton, Rhoda 1840-1920 . . . . .DLB-18

Broun, Heywood 1888-1939 . . . . DLB-29, 171

Browder, Earl 1891-1973 . . . . .DLB-303

Brown, Alice 1856-1948. . . . . .DLB-78

Brown, Bob 1886-1959 . . . . . . .DLB-4, 45; DS-15

Brown, Cecil 1943- DLB-33

Brown, Charles Brockden
1771-1810 . . . . DLB-37, 59, 73; CDALB-2

Brown, Christy 1932-1981. . . . . .DLB-14

Brown, Dee 1908-2002 . . . . .Y-80

Brown, Frank London 1927-1962 . . . . .DLB-76

Brown, Fredric 1906-1972 . . . . .DLB-8

Brown, George Mackay
1921-1996. . . . . .DLB-14, 27, 139, 271

Brown, Harry 1917-1986 . . . . .DLB-26

Brown, Ian 1945- DLB-310

Brown, Larry 1951- DLB-234, 292

Brown, Lew 1893-1958 . . . . .DLB-265

Brown, Marcia 1918- DLB-61

Brown, Margaret Wise 1910-1952. . . . . .DLB-22

Brown, Morna Doris (see Ferrars, Elizabeth)

Brown, Oliver Madox 1855-1874. . . . . .DLB-21

Brown, Sterling 1901-1989. . . . . . .DLB-48, 51, 63

Brown, T. E. 1830-1897. . . . . .DLB-35

Brown, Thomas Alexander (see Boldrewood, Rolf)

Brown, Warren 1894-1978. . . . . .DLB-241

Brown, William Hill 1765-1793 . . . . .DLB-37

Brown, William Wells
1815-1884 . . . . .DLB-3, 50, 183, 248

Brown University
The Festival of Vanguard Narrative. Y-93

Browne, Charles Farrar 1834-1867 . . . . . . .DLB-11

Browne, Frances 1816-1879 . . . . .DLB-199

Browne, Francis Fisher 1843-1913. . . . . . . .DLB-79

Browne, Howard 1908-1999 . . . . .DLB-226

Browne, J. Ross 1821-1875. . . . . .DLB-202

Browne, Michael Dennis 1940- DLB-40

Browne, Sir Thomas 1605-1682 . . . . .DLB-151

Browne, William, of Tavistock
1590-1645 . . . . .DLB-121

Browne, Wynyard 1911-1964 . . . . . . .DLB-13, 233

Browne and Nolan. DLB-106

Brownell, W. C. 1851-1928 . . . . .DLB-71

Browning, Elizabeth Barrett
1806-1861 . . . . .DLB-32, 199; CDBLB-4

Browning, Robert
1812-1889 . . . . .DLB-32, 163; CDBLB-4

Essay on Chatterton DLB-32

Introductory Essay: Letters of Percy
Bysshe Shelley (1852). DLB-32

"The Novel in [Robert Browning's]
'The Ring and the Book'" (1912),
by Henry James DLB-32

Brownjohn, Allan 1931- DLB-40

Tribute to John Betjeman Y-84

Brownson, Orestes Augustus
1803-1876 . . . . .DLB-1, 59, 73, 243; DS-5

Bruccoli, Matthew J. 1931- DLB-103

Joseph [Heller] and George [V. Higgins] Y-99

Response [to Busch on Fitzgerald]. Y-96

Tribute to Albert Erskine Y-93

Tribute to Charles E. Feinberg Y-88

Working with Fredson Bowers Y-91

Bruce, Charles 1906-1971 . . . . .DLB-68

Bruce, John Edward 1856-1924

Three Documents [African American
poets] DLB-50

Bruce, Leo 1903-1979 . . . . .DLB-77

Bruce, Mary Grant 1878-1958. . . . . .DLB-230

Bruce, Philip Alexander 1856-1933. . . . . . .DLB-47

Bruce-Novoa, Juan 1944- DLB-82

Bruckman, Clyde 1894-1955. . . . . .DLB-26

Bruckner, Ferdinand 1891-1958. . . . . .DLB-118

Brundage, John Herbert (see Herbert, John)

Brunner, John 1934-1995. . . . . .DLB-261

Tribute to Theodore Sturgeon Y-85

Brutus, Dennis
1924- DLB-117, 225; CDWLB-3

Bryan, C. D. B. 1936- DLB-185

Bryan, William Jennings 1860-1925 . . . . .DLB-303

Bryant, Arthur 1899-1985 . . . . .DLB-149

Bryant, William Cullen 1794-1878
. . . . .DLB-3, 43, 59, 189, 250; CDALB-2

Bryce, James 1838-1922. . . . . .DLB-166, 190

Bryce Echenique, Alfredo
1939- DLB-145; CDWLB-3

Bryden, Bill 1942- DLB-233

Brydges, Sir Samuel Egerton
1762-1837 . . . . DLB-107, 142

Bryskett, Lodowick 1546?-1612 . . . . .DLB-167

Buchan, John 1875-1940 . . . . .DLB-34, 70, 156

Buchanan, George 1506-1582 . . . . .DLB-132

Buchanan, Robert 1841-1901 . . . . .DLB-18, 35

"The Fleshly School of Poetry and
Other Phenomena of the Day"
(1872) DLB-35

"The Fleshly School of Poetry:
Mr. D. G. Rossetti" (1871),
by Thomas Maitland DLB-35

Buchler, Justus 1914-1991 . . . . .DLB-279

Buchman, Sidney 1902-1975 . . . . .DLB-26

Buchner, Augustus 1591-1661 . . . . .DLB-164

Büchner, Georg
1813-1837 . . . . .DLB-133; CDWLB-2

Bucholtz, Andreas Heinrich 1607-1671. . . .DLB-168

Buck, Pearl S.
1892-1973 . . . . . . .DLB-9, 102, 329; CDALB-7

Bucke, Charles 1781-1846 . . . . .DLB-110

Bucke, Richard Maurice 1837-1902. . . . . . .DLB-99

Buckingham, Edwin 1810-1833. . . . . .DLB-73

Buckingham, Joseph Tinker 1779-1861 . . . .DLB-73

Buckler, Ernest 1908-1984. . . . . .DLB-68

Buckley, Vincent 1925-1988 . . . . .DLB-289

Buckley, William F., Jr. 1925- DLB-137; Y-80

Publisher's Statement From the
Initial Issue of National Review
(19 November 1955). DLB-137

Buckminster, Joseph Stevens
1784-1812 . . . . .DLB-37

Buckner, Robert 1906-1989. . . . . .DLB-26

Budd, Thomas ?-1698 . . . . DLB-24

Budé, Guillaume 1468-1540 . . . . DLB-327

Budrys, A. J. 1931- DLB-8

Buechner, Frederick 1926- Y-80

Buell, John 1927- DLB-53

Buenaventura, Enrique 1925-2003 . . . . . . DLB-305

Bufalino, Gesualdo 1920-1996 . . . . DLB-196

Buffon, Georges-Louis Leclerc de
1707-1788 . . . . DLB-313

"Le Discours sur le style" DLB-314

Job Buffum [publishing house] DLB-49

Bugnet, Georges 1879-1981 . . . . DLB-92

al-Buhturi 821-897 . . . . DLB-311

Buies, Arthur 1840-1901 . . . . DLB-99

Bukiet, Melvin Jules 1953- DLB-299

Bukowski, Charles 1920-1994 . . . DLB-5, 130, 169

Bulatović, Miodrag
1930-1991 . . . . DLB-181; CDWLB-4

Bulgakov, Mikhail Afanas'evich
1891-1940 . . . . DLB-272

Bulgarin, Faddei Venediktovich
1789-1859 . . . . DLB-198

Bulger, Bozeman 1877-1932 . . . . DLB-171

Bull, Olaf 1883-1933 . . . . DLB-297

Bullein, William
between 1520 and 1530-1576 . . . . . . DLB-167

Bullins, Ed 1935- DLB-7, 38, 249

Bulosan, Carlos 1911-1956 . . . . DLB-312

Bulwer, John 1606-1656 . . . . DLB-236

Bulwer-Lytton, Edward (also Edward
Bulwer) 1803-1873 . . . . DLB-21

"On Art in Fiction" (1838) DLB-21

Bumpus, Jerry 1937- Y-81

Bunce and Brother DLB-49

Bunin, Ivan 1870-1953 . . . . DLB-317, 329

Bunner, H. C. 1855-1896 . . . . DLB-78, 79

Bunting, Basil 1900-1985 . . . . DLB-20

Buntline, Ned (Edward Zane Carroll
Judson) 1821-1886 . . . . DLB-186

Bunyan, John 1628-1688 . . . . . DLB-39; CDBLB-2

The Author's Apology for
His Book DLB-39

Burch, Robert 1925- DLB-52

Burciaga, José Antonio 1940- DLB-82

Burdekin, Katharine (Murray Constantine)
1896-1963 . . . . DLB-255

Bürger, Gottfried August 1747-1794 . . . . . . DLB-94

Burgess, Anthony (John Anthony Burgess Wilson)
1917-1993 . . . . . . DLB-14, 194, 261; CDBLB-8

The Anthony Burgess Archive at
the Harry Ransom Humanities
Research Center Y-98

Anthony Burgess's 99 Novels:
An Opinion Poll Y-84

Burgess, Gelett 1866-1951 . . . . DLB-11

Burgess, John W. 1844-1931 . . . . DLB-47

Burgess, Thornton W. 1874-1965 . . . . DLB-22

Burgess, Stringer and Company DLB-49

Burgos, Julia de 1914-1953 . . . . DLB-290

Burick, Si 1909-1986 . . . . DLB-171

Burk, John Daly circa 1772-1808 . . . . DLB-37

Burk, Ronnie 1955- DLB-209

Burke, Edmund 1729?-1797 . . . . . DLB-104, 252

Burke, James Lee 1936- DLB-226

Burke, Johnny 1908-1964 . . . . DLB-265

Burke, Kenneth 1897-1993 . . . . DLB-45, 63

Burke, Thomas 1886-1945 . . . . DLB-197

Burley, Dan 1907-1962 . . . . DLB-241

Burley, W. J. 1914- DLB-276

Burlingame, Edward Livermore
1848-1922 . . . . DLB-79

Burliuk, David 1882-1967 . . . . DLB-317

Burman, Carina 1960- DLB-257

Burnet, Gilbert 1643-1715 . . . . DLB-101

Burnett, Frances Hodgson
1849-1924 . . . . DLB-42, 141; DS-13, 14

Burnett, W. R. 1899-1982 . . . . DLB-9, 226

Burnett, Whit 1899-1973 . . . . DLB-137

Burney, Fanny 1752-1840 . . . . DLB-39

Dedication, The Wanderer (1814) DLB-39

Preface to Evelina (1778) DLB-39

Burns, Alan 1929- DLB-14, 194

Burns, Joanne 1945- DLB-289

Burns, John Horne 1916-1953 . . . . Y-85

Burns, Robert 1759-1796 . . . . DLB-109; CDBLB-3

Burns and Oates DLB-106

Burnshaw, Stanley 1906- DLB-48; Y-97

James Dickey and Stanley Burnshaw
Correspondence Y-02

Review of Stanley Burnshaw: The
Collected Poems and Selected
Prose Y-02

Tribute to Robert Penn Warren Y-89

Burr, C. Chauncey 1815?-1883 . . . . DLB-79

Burr, Esther Edwards 1732-1758 . . . . DLB-200

Burroughs, Edgar Rice 1875-1950 . . . . DLB-8

The Burroughs Bibliophiles Y-98

Burroughs, John 1837-1921 . . . . DLB-64, 275

Burroughs, Margaret T. G. 1917- DLB-41

Burroughs, William S., Jr. 1947-1981 . . . . . DLB-16

Burroughs, William Seward 1914-1997
. . . . DLB-2, 8, 16, 152, 237; Y-81, 97

Burroway, Janet 1936- DLB-6

Burt, Maxwell Struthers
1882-1954 . . . . DLB-86; DS-16

A. L. Burt and Company DLB-49

Burton, Hester 1913-2000 . . . . DLB-161

Burton, Isabel Arundell 1831-1896 . . . . . . DLB-166

Burton, Miles (see Rhode, John)

Burton, Richard Francis
1821-1890 . . . . DLB-55, 166, 184

Burton, Robert 1577-1640 . . . . DLB-151

Burton, Virginia Lee 1909-1968 . . . . DLB-22

Burton, William Evans 1804-1860 . . . . . . DLB-73

Burwell, Adam Hood 1790-1849 . . . . DLB-99

Bury, Lady Charlotte 1775-1861 . . . . DLB-116

Busch, Frederick 1941-2006 . . . . DLB-6, 218

Excerpts from Frederick Busch's USC
Remarks [on F. Scott Fitzgerald] Y-96

Tribute to James Laughlin Y-97

Tribute to Raymond Carver Y-88

Busch, Niven 1903-1991 . . . . DLB-44

Bushnell, Horace 1802-1876 . . . . DS-13

Business & Literature
The Claims of Business and Literature:
An Undergraduate Essay by
Maxwell Perkins Y-01

Bussières, Arthur de 1877-1913 . . . . DLB-92

Butler, Charles circa 1560-1647 . . . . DLB-236

Butler, Guy 1918- DLB-225

Butler, Joseph 1692-1752 . . . . DLB-252

Butler, Josephine Elizabeth 1828-1906 . . . DLB-190

Butler, Juan 1942-1981 . . . . DLB-53

Butler, Judith 1956- DLB-246

Butler, Octavia E. 1947-2006 . . . . DLB-33

Butler, Pierce 1884-1953 . . . . DLB-187

Butler, Robert Olen 1945- DLB-173

Butler, Samuel 1613-1680 . . . . DLB-101, 126

Butler, Samuel
1835-1902 . . . . DLB-18, 57, 174; CDBLB-5

Butler, William Francis 1838-1910 . . . . . . DLB-166

E. H. Butler and Company DLB-49

Butor, Michel 1926- DLB-83

Nathaniel Butter
[publishing house] DLB-170

Butterworth, Hezekiah 1839-1905 . . . . DLB-42

Buttitta, Ignazio 1899-1997 . . . . DLB-114

Butts, Mary 1890-1937 . . . . DLB-240

Buzo, Alex 1944- DLB-289

Buzzati, Dino 1906-1972 . . . . DLB-177

Byars, Betsy 1928- DLB-52

Byatt, A. S. 1936- DLB-14, 194, 319, 326

Byles, Mather 1707-1788 . . . . DLB-24

Henry Bynneman
[publishing house] DLB-170

Bynner, Witter 1881-1968 . . . . DLB-54

Byrd, William circa 1543-1623 . . . . DLB-172

Byrd, William, II 1674-1744 . . . . DLB-24, 140

Byrne, John Keyes (see Leonard, Hugh)

Byron, George Gordon, Lord
1788-1824 . . . . DLB-96, 110; CDBLB-3

The Byron Society of America Y-00

Byron, Robert 1905-1941 . . . . DLB-195

Byzantine Novel, The Spanish DLB-318

C

Caballero Bonald, José Manuel
1926- DLB-108

Cabañero, Eladio 1930- DLB-134

Cabell, James Branch 1879-1958 . . . . DLB-9, 78

Cabeza de Baca, Manuel 1853-1915 . . . . . DLB-122

Cabeza de Baca Gilbert, Fabiola
1898-1993 . . . . DLB-122

Cable, George Washington
1844-1925 . . . . DLB-12, 74; DS-13

Cable, Mildred 1878-1952 . . . . DLB-195

Cabral, Manuel del 1907-1999 . . . . DLB-283

Cabral de Melo Neto, João
1920-1999 . . . . DLB-307

Cabrera, Lydia 1900-1991 . . . . DLB-145

Cabrera Infante, Guillermo
1929- DLB-113; CDWLB-3

Cabrujas, José Ignacio 1937-1995 . . . . DLB-305

Cadell [publishing house] DLB-154

Cady, Edwin H. 1917- DLB-103

Caedmon fl. 658-680 . . . . DLB-146

Caedmon School circa 660-899 . . . . DLB-146

Caesar, Irving 1895-1996 . . . . DLB-265

Cafés, Brasseries, and Bistros DS-15

Cage, John 1912-1992 . . . . DLB-193

Cahan, Abraham 1860-1951 . . . . DLB-9, 25, 28

Cahn, Sammy 1913-1993 . . . . DLB-265

Cain, George 1943- DLB-33

Cain, James M. 1892-1977 . . . . DLB-226

Cain, Paul (Peter Ruric, George Sims)
1902-1966 . . . . DLB-306

Caird, Edward 1835-1908 . . . . DLB-262

Caird, Mona 1854-1932 . . . . DLB-197

Čaks, Aleksandrs
1901-1950 . . . . DLB-220; CDWLB-4

Caldecott, Randolph 1846-1886 . . . . DLB-163

John Calder Limited
[Publishing house] DLB-112

Calderón de la Barca, Fanny
1804-1882 . . . . DLB-183

Caldwell, Ben 1937- DLB-38

Caldwell, Erskine 1903-1987 . . . . DLB-9, 86

H. M. Caldwell Company DLB-49

Caldwell, Taylor 1900-1985 . . . . DS-17

Calhoun, John C. 1782-1850 . . . . DLB-3, 248

Călinescu, George 1899-1965 . . . . DLB-220

Calisher, Hortense 1911- DLB-2, 218

Calkins, Mary Whiton 1863-1930 . . . . DLB-270

Callaghan, Mary Rose 1944- DLB-207

Callaghan, Morley 1903-1990 . . . . . DLB-68; DS-15

Callahan, S. Alice 1868-1894 . . . . DLB-175, 221

Callaloo [journal] Y-87

Callimachus circa 305 B.C.-240 B.C. DLB-176

Calmer, Edgar 1907-1986 . . . . DLB-4

Calverley, C. S. 1831-1884 . . . . DLB-35

Calvert, George Henry
1803-1889 . . . . DLB-1, 64, 248

Calverton, V. F. (George Goetz)
1900-1940 . . . . DLB-303

Calvin, Jean 1509-1564 . . . . DLB-327

Calvino, Italo 1923-1985 . . . . DLB-196

Cambridge, Ada 1844-1926 . . . . DLB-230

Cambridge Press DLB-49

Cambridge Songs (Carmina Cantabrigensia)
circa 1050 . . . . DLB-148

Cambridge University
Cambridge and the Apostles DS-5

Cambridge University Press DLB-170

Camden, William 1551-1623 . . . . DLB-172

Camden House: An Interview with
James Hardin Y-92

Cameron, Eleanor 1912-2000 . . . . DLB-52

Cameron, George Frederick
1854-1885 . . . . DLB-99

Cameron, Lucy Lyttelton 1781-1858 . . . . . DLB-163

Cameron, Peter 1959- DLB-234

Cameron, William Bleasdell 1862-1951 . . . . DLB-99

Camm, John 1718-1778 . . . . DLB-31

Camões, Luís de 1524-1580 . . . . DLB-287

Camon, Ferdinando 1935- DLB-196

Camp, Walter 1859-1925 . . . . DLB-241

Campana, Dino 1885-1932 . . . . DLB-114

Campbell, Bebe Moore 1950- DLB-227

Campbell, David 1915-1979 . . . . DLB-260

Campbell, Gabrielle Margaret Vere
(see Shearing, Joseph, and Bowen, Marjorie)

Campbell, James Dykes 1838-1895 . . . . . . DLB-144

Campbell, James Edwin 1867-1896 . . . . . . DLB-50

Campbell, John 1653-1728 . . . . DLB-43

Campbell, John W., Jr. 1910-1971 . . . . DLB-8

Campbell, Ramsey 1946- DLB-261

Campbell, Robert 1927-2000 . . . . DLB-306

Campbell, Roy 1901-1957 . . . . DLB-20, 225

Campbell, Thomas 1777-1844 . . . . DLB-93, 144

Campbell, William Edward (see March, William)

Campbell, William Wilfred 1858-1918 . . . . DLB-92

Campion, Edmund 1539-1581 . . . . DLB-167

Campion, Thomas
1567-1620 . . . . DLB-58, 172; CDBLB-1

Campo, Rafael 1964- DLB-282

Campton, David 1924- DLB-245

Camus, Albert 1913-1960 . . . . . . DLB-72, 321, 329

Camus, Jean-Pierre 1584-1652 . . . . DLB-268

The Canadian Publishers' Records Database . . . Y-96

Canby, Henry Seidel 1878-1961 . . . . DLB-91

Cancioneros DLB-286

Candelaria, Cordelia 1943- DLB-82

Candelaria, Nash 1928- DLB-82

Candide, Voltaire DLB-314

Canetti, Elias
1905-1994 . . . . . DLB-85, 124, 329; CDWLB-2

Canham, Erwin Dain 1904-1982 . . . . DLB-127

Canitz, Friedrich Rudolph Ludwig von
1654-1699 . . . . DLB-168

Cankar, Ivan 1876-1918 . . . . . DLB-147; CDWLB-4

Cannan, Gilbert 1884-1955 . . . . DLB-10, 197

Cannan, Joanna 1896-1961 . . . . DLB-191

Cannell, Kathleen 1891-1974 . . . . DLB-4

Cannell, Skipwith 1887-1957 . . . . DLB-45

Canning, George 1770-1827 . . . . DLB-158

Cannon, Jimmy 1910-1973 . . . . DLB-171

Cano, Daniel 1947- DLB-209

Old Dogs / New Tricks? New
Technologies, the Canon, and the
Structure of the Profession Y-02

Cantú, Norma Elia 1947- DLB-209

Cantwell, Robert 1908-1978 . . . . DLB-9

Jonathan Cape and Harrison Smith
[publishing house] DLB-46

Jonathan Cape Limited DLB-112

Čapek, Karel 1890-1938 . . . . DLB-215; CDWLB-4

Capen, Joseph 1658-1725 . . . . DLB-24

Capes, Bernard 1854-1918 . . . . DLB-156

Capote, Truman 1924-1984
. . . . DLB-2, 185, 227; Y-80, 84; CDALB-1

Capps, Benjamin 1922- DLB-256

Caproni, Giorgio 1912-1990 . . . . DLB-128

Caragiale, Mateiu Ioan 1885-1936 . . . . DLB-220

Carballido, Emilio 1925- DLB-305

Cardarelli, Vincenzo 1887-1959 . . . . DLB-114

Cardenal, Ernesto 1925- DLB-290

Cárdenas, Reyes 1948- DLB-122

Cardinal, Marie 1929-2001 . . . . DLB-83

Cardoza y Aragón, Luis 1901-1992 . . . . . . DLB-290

Carducci, Giosuè 1835-1907 . . . . DLB-329

Carew, Jan 1920- DLB-157

Carew, Thomas 1594 or 1595-1640 . . . . . . DLB-126

Carey, Henry circa 1687-1689-1743 . . . . DLB-84

Carey, Mathew 1760-1839 . . . . DLB-37, 73

M. Carey and Company DLB-49

Carey, Peter 1943- DLB-289, 326

Carey and Hart DLB-49

Carlell, Lodowick 1602-1675 . . . . DLB-58

Carleton, William 1794-1869 . . . . DLB-159

G. W. Carleton [publishing house] DLB-49

Carlile, Richard 1790-1843 . . . . DLB-110, 158

Carlson, Ron 1947- DLB-244

Carlyle, Jane Welsh 1801-1866 .... DLB-55

Carlyle, Thomas
1795-1881 .... DLB-55, 144; CDBLB-3

"The Hero as Man of Letters:
Johnson, Rousseau, Burns"
(1841) [excerpt] DLB-57

The Hero as Poet. Dante; Shakspeare
(1841) DLB-32

Carman, Bliss 1861-1929 .... DLB-92

Carmina Burana circa 1230 .... DLB-138

Carnap, Rudolf 1891-1970 .... DLB-270

Carnero, Guillermo 1947- DLB-108

Carossa, Hans 1878-1956 .... DLB-66

Carpenter, Humphrey
1946-2005 .... DLB-155; Y-84, 99

Carpenter, Stephen Cullen ?-1820? DLB-73

Carpentier, Alejo
1904-1980 .... DLB-113; CDWLB-3

Carr, Emily 1871-1945 .... DLB-68

Carr, John Dickson 1906-1977 .... DLB-306

Carr, Marina 1964- DLB-245

Carr, Virginia Spencer 1929- DLB-111; Y-00

Carrera Andrade, Jorge 1903-1978 ...... DLB-283

Carrier, Roch 1937- DLB-53

Carrillo, Adolfo 1855-1926 .... DLB-122

Carroll, Gladys Hasty 1904-1999 .... DLB-9

Carroll, John 1735-1815 .... DLB-37

Carroll, John 1809-1884 .... DLB-99

Carroll, Lewis
1832-1898 ..... DLB-18, 163, 178; CDBLB-4

The Lewis Carroll Centenary Y-98

The Lewis Carroll Society
of North America Y-00

Carroll, Paul 1927-1996 .... DLB-16

Carroll, Paul Vincent 1900-1968 .... DLB-10

Carroll and Graf Publishers DLB-46

Carruth, Hayden 1921- DLB-5, 165

Tribute to James Dickey................ Y-97

Tribute to Raymond Carver............. Y-88

Carryl, Charles E. 1841-1920 .... DLB-42

Carson, Anne 1950- DLB-193

Carson, Rachel 1907-1964 .... DLB-275

Carswell, Catherine 1879-1946 .... DLB-36

Cartagena, Alfonso de circa 1384-1456 .. DLB-286

Cartagena, Teresa de 1425?-? DLB-286

Cărtărescu, Mirea 1956- DLB-232

Carter, Angela
1940-1992 .... DLB-14, 207, 261, 319

Carter, Elizabeth 1717-1806 .... DLB-109

Carter, Henry (see Leslie, Frank)

Carter, Hodding, Jr. 1907-1972 .... DLB-127

Carter, Jared 1939- DLB-282

Carter, John 1905-1975 .... DLB-201

Carter, Landon 1710-1778 .... DLB-31

Carter, Lin 1930-1988 .... Y-81

Carter, Martin 1927-1997 .... DLB-117; CDWLB-3

Carter, Robert, and Brothers DLB-49

Carter and Hendee DLB-49

Cartwright, Jim 1958- DLB-245

Cartwright, John 1740-1824 .... DLB-158

Cartwright, William circa 1611-1643 .... DLB-126

Caruthers, William Alexander
1802-1846 .... DLB-3, 248

Carver, Jonathan 1710-1780 .... DLB-31

Carver, Raymond 1938-1988 ... DLB-130; Y-83,88

First Strauss "Livings" Awarded to Cynthia
Ozick and Raymond Carver
An Interview with Raymond Carver..... Y-83

Carvic, Heron 1917?-1980 .... DLB-276

Cary, Alice 1820-1871 .... DLB-202

Cary, Joyce 1888-1957 ... DLB-15, 100; CDBLB-6

Cary, Patrick 1623?-1657 .... DLB-131

Casal, Julián del 1863-1893 .... DLB-283

Case, John 1540-1600 .... DLB-281

Casey, Gavin 1907-1964 .... DLB-260

Casey, Juanita 1925- DLB-14

Casey, Michael 1947- DLB-5

Cassady, Carolyn 1923- DLB-16

"As I See It" DLB-16

Cassady, Neal 1926-1968 .... DLB-16, 237

Cassell and Company................ DLB-106

Cassell Publishing Company DLB-49

Cassill, R. V. 1919-2002 .... DLB-6, 218; Y-02

Tribute to James Dickey............... Y-97

Cassity, Turner 1929- DLB-105; Y-02

Cassius Dio circa 155/164-post 229 ..... DLB-176

Cassola, Carlo 1917-1987 .... DLB-177

Castellano, Olivia 1944- DLB-122

Castellanos, Rosario
1925-1974 .... DLB-113, 290; CDWLB-3

Castelo Branco, Camilo 1825-1890 ..... DLB-287

Castile, Protest Poetry in DLB-286

Castile and Aragon, Vernacular Translations
in Crowns of 1352-1515 .... DLB-286

Castillejo, Cristóbal de 1490?-1550 ..... DLB-318

Castillo, Ana 1953- DLB-122, 227

Castillo, Rafael C. 1950- DLB-209

The Castle of Perseverance
circa 1400-1425 .... DLB-146

Castlemon, Harry (see Fosdick, Charles Austin)

Castro, Brian 1950- DLB-325

Castro, Consuelo de 1946- DLB-307

Castro Alves, Antônio de 1847-1871 .... DLB-307

Čašule, Kole 1921- DLB-181

Caswall, Edward 1814-1878 .... DLB-32

Catacalos, Rosemary 1944- DLB-122

Cather, Willa 1873-1947
.... DLB-9, 54, 78, 256; DS-1; CDALB-3

The Willa Cather Pioneer Memorial
and Education Foundation Y-00

Catherine II (Ekaterina Alekseevna), "The Great,"
Empress of Russia 1729-1796 .... DLB-150

Catherwood, Mary Hartwell 1847-1902... DLB-78

Catledge, Turner 1901-1983 .... DLB-127

Catlin, George 1796-1872 .... DLB-186, 189

Cato the Elder 234 B.C.-149 B.C. DLB-211

Cattafi, Bartolo 1922-1979 .... DLB-128

Catton, Bruce 1899-1978 .... DLB-17

Catullus circa 84 B.C.-54 B.C.
.... DLB-211; CDWLB-1

Causley, Charles 1917-2003 .... DLB-27

Caute, David 1936- DLB-14, 231

Cavendish, Duchess of Newcastle,
Margaret Lucas
1623?-1673 .... DLB-131, 252, 281

Cawein, Madison 1865-1914 .... DLB-54

William Caxton [publishing house] DLB-170

The Caxton Printers, Limited DLB-46

Caylor, O. P. 1849-1897 .... DLB-241

Caylus, Marthe-Marguerite de
1671-1729 .... DLB-313

Cayrol, Jean 1911-2005 .... DLB-83

Cecil, Lord David 1902-1986 .... DLB-155

Cela, Camilo José
1916-2002 .... DLB-322, 329; Y-89

Nobel Lecture 1989 .... Y-89

Celan, Paul 1920-1970 ...... DLB-69; CDWLB-2

Celati, Gianni 1937- DLB-196

Celaya, Gabriel 1911-1991 .... DLB-108

Céline, Louis-Ferdinand 1894-1961 ..... DLB-72

Celtis, Conrad 1459-1508 .... DLB-179

Cendrars, Blaise 1887-1961 .... DLB-258

The Steinbeck Centennial Y-02

Censorship
The Island Trees Case: A Symposium on
School Library Censorship Y-82

Center for Bibliographical Studies and
Research at the University of
California, Riverside Y-91

Center for Book Research Y-84

The Center for the Book in the Library
of Congress Y-93

A New Voice: The Center for the
Book's First Five Years............. Y-83

Centlivre, Susanna 1669?-1723 .... DLB-84

The Centre for Writing, Publishing and
Printing History at the University
of Reading Y-00

The Century Company DLB-49

A Century of Poetry, a Lifetime of Collecting:
J. M. Edelstein's Collection of
Twentieth-Century American Poetry Y-02

Cernuda, Luis 1902-1963 . . . . .DLB-134

Cerruto, Oscar 1912-1981 . . . . .DLB-283

Cervantes, Lorna Dee 1954- DLB-82

Césaire, Aimé 1913- DLB-321

de Céspedes, Alba 1911-1997 . . . . .DLB-264

Cetina, Gutierre de 1514-17?-1556 . . . . . .DLB-318

Ch., T. (see Marchenko, Anastasiia Iakovlevna)

Cha, Theresa Hak Kyung 1951-1982 . . . .DLB-312

Chaadaev, Petr Iakovlevich
   1794-1856 .DLB-198

Chabon, Michael 1963- DLB-278

Chacel, Rosa 1898-1994 . . . . .DLB-134, 322

Chacón, Eusebio 1869-1948 . . . . .DLB-82

Chacón, Felipe Maximiliano 1873-? DLB-82

Chadwick, Henry 1824-1908. . . . . .DLB-241

Chadwyck-Healey's Full-Text Literary Databases:
   Editing Commercial Databases of
   Primary Literary Texts Y-95

Challans, Eileen Mary (see Renault, Mary)

Chalmers, George 1742-1825. . . . . .DLB-30

Chaloner, Sir Thomas 1520-1565 . . . . . .DLB-167

Chamberlain, Samuel S. 1851-1916 . . . . . .DLB-25

Chamberland, Paul 1939- DLB-60

Chamberlin, William Henry 1897-1969. . . .DLB-29

Chambers, Charles Haddon 1860-1921 . . .DLB-10

Chambers, María Cristina (see Mena, María Cristina)

Chambers, Robert W. 1865-1933 . . . . . . .DLB-202

W. and R. Chambers
   [publishing house] DLB-106

Chambers, Whittaker 1901-1961 . . . . . . .DLB-303

Chamfort, Sébastien-Roch Nicolas de
   1740?-1794. .DLB-313

Chamisso, Adelbert von 1781-1838 . . . . . .DLB-90

Champfleury 1821-1889 . . . . .DLB-119

Champier, Symphorien 1472?-1539? DLB-327

Chan, Jeffery Paul 1942- DLB-312

Chandler, Harry 1864-1944. . . . . .DLB-29

Chandler, Norman 1899-1973 . . . . .DLB-127

Chandler, Otis 1927-2006. . . . . .DLB-127

Chandler, Raymond
   1888-1959 . . . .DLB-226, 253; DS-6; CDALB-5

   Raymond Chandler Centenary. Y-88

Chang, Diana 1934- DLB-312

Channing, Edward 1856-1931 . . . . .DLB-17

Channing, Edward Tyrrell
   1790-1856 . . . . .DLB-1, 59, 235

Channing, William Ellery
   1780-1842 . . . . .DLB-1, 59, 235

Channing, William Ellery, II
   1817-1901 . . . . .DLB-1, 223

Channing, William Henry
   1810-1884 . . . . .DLB-1, 59, 243

Chapelain, Jean 1595-1674. . . . . .DLB-268

Chaplin, Charlie 1889-1977 . . . . .DLB-44

Chapman, George
   1559 or 1560-1634 . . . . .DLB-62, 121

Chapman, Olive Murray 1892-1977 . . . . .DLB-195

Chapman, R. W. 1881-1960 . . . . .DLB-201

Chapman, William 1850-1917. . . . . .DLB-99

John Chapman [publishing house]. DLB-106

Chapman and Hall [publishing house] . . .DLB-106

Chappell, Fred 1936- DLB-6, 105

   "A Detail in a Poem" DLB-105

   Tribute to Peter Taylor Y-94

Chappell, William 1582-1649 . . . . .DLB-236

Char, René 1907-1988 . . . . .DLB-258

Charbonneau, Jean 1875-1960. . . . . .DLB-92

Charbonneau, Robert 1911-1967 . . . . .DLB-68

Charles, Gerda 1914-1996. . . . . .DLB-14

William Charles [publishing house]. DLB-49

Charles d'Orléans 1394-1465 . . . . .DLB-208

Charley (see Mann, Charles)

Charrière, Isabelle de 1740-1805 . . . . . . .DLB-313

Charskaia, Lidiia 1875-1937. . . . . .DLB-295

Charteris, Leslie 1907-1993 . . . . .DLB-77

Chartier, Alain circa 1385-1430 . . . . .DLB-208

Charyn, Jerome 1937- Y-83

Chase, Borden 1900-1971 . . . . .DLB-26

Chase, Edna Woolman 1877-1957 . . . . . . .DLB-91

Chase, James Hadley (René Raymond)
   1906-1985 . . . . .DLB-276

Chase, Mary Coyle 1907-1981. . . . . .DLB-228

Chase-Riboud, Barbara 1936- DLB-33

Chateaubriand, François-René de
   1768-1848 . . . . .DLB-119

Châtelet, Gabrielle-Emilie Du
   1706-1749 . . . . .DLB-313

Chatterjee, Upamanyu 1959- DLB-323

Chatterton, Thomas 1752-1770 . . . . .DLB-109

   Essay on Chatterton (1842), by
   Robert Browning DLB-32

Chatto and Windus DLB-106

Chatwin, Bruce 1940-1989 . . . . .DLB-194, 204

Chaucer, Geoffrey
   1340?-1400 . . . . .DLB-146; CDBLB-1

   New Chaucer Society Y-00

Chaudhuri, Amit 1962- DLB-267, 323

Chaudhuri, Nirad C. 1897-1999 . . . . . . .DLB-323

Chauncy, Charles 1705-1787 . . . . .DLB-24

Chauveau, Pierre-Joseph-Olivier
   1820-1890 . . . . .DLB-99

Chávez, Denise 1948- DLB-122

Chávez, Fray Angélico 1910-1996 . . . . . . .DLB-82

Chayefsky, Paddy 1923-1981. . . . .DLB-7, 44; Y-81

Cheesman, Evelyn 1881-1969 . . . . .DLB-195

Cheever, Ezekiel 1615-1708 . . . . .DLB-24

Cheever, George Barrell 1807-1890 . . . . . .DLB-59

Cheever, John 1912-1982
   . . . . . . .DLB-2, 102, 227; Y-80, 82; CDALB-1

Cheever, Susan 1943- Y-82

Cheke, Sir John 1514-1557 . . . . .DLB-132

Chekhov, Anton Pavlovich 1860-1904 . . .DLB-277

Chelsea House. .DLB-46

Chênedollé, Charles de 1769-1833 . . . . . .DLB-217

Cheney, Brainard
   Tribute to Caroline Gordon Y-81

Cheney, Ednah Dow 1824-1904 . . . . . .DLB-1, 223

Cheney, Harriet Vaughan 1796-1889. . . . . .DLB-99

Chénier, Marie-Joseph 1764-1811 . . . . . .DLB-192

Cheng Xiaoqing 1893-1976 . . . . .DLB-328

Cherny, Sasha 1880-1932 . . . . .DLB-317

Chernyshevsky, Nikolai Gavrilovich
   1828-1889 . . . . .DLB-238

Cherry, Kelly 1940- Y-83

Cherryh, C. J. 1942- Y-80

Chesebro', Caroline 1825-1873 . . . . .DLB-202

Chesney, Sir George Tomkyns
   1830-1895 . . . . .DLB-190

Chesnut, Mary Boykin 1823-1886. . . . . . .DLB-239

Chesnutt, Charles Waddell
   1858-1932 . . . . .DLB-12, 50, 78

Chesson, Mrs. Nora (see Hopper, Nora)

Chester, Alfred 1928-1971 . . . . .DLB-130

Chester, George Randolph 1869-1924 . . . .DLB-78

The Chester Plays circa 1505-1532;
   revisions until 1575 . . . . .DLB-146

Chesterfield, Philip Dormer Stanhope,
   Fourth Earl of 1694-1773. . . . . .DLB-104

Chesterton, G. K. 1874-1936
   . . DLB-10, 19, 34, 70, 98, 149, 178; CDBLB-6

   "The Ethics of Elfland" (1908) DLB-178

Chettle, Henry
   circa 1560-circa 1607 . . . . .DLB-136

Cheuse, Alan 1940- DLB-244

Chew, Ada Nield 1870-1945 . . . . .DLB-135

Cheyney, Edward P. 1861-1947. . . . . .DLB-47

Chiang Yee 1903-1977 . . . . .DLB-312

Chiara, Piero 1913-1986 . . . . .DLB-177

Chicanos
   Chicano History DLB-82

   Chicano Language DLB-82

   Chicano Literature: A Bibliography . .DLB-209

   A Contemporary Flourescence of Chicano
   Literature Y-84

   Literatura Chicanesca: The View From
   Without DLB-82

Child, Francis James 1825-1896. . . .DLB-1, 64, 235

Child, Lydia Maria 1802-1880 . . . .DLB-1, 74, 243

Child, Philip 1898-1978 . . . . .DLB-68

Childers, Erskine 1870-1922 . . . . .DLB-70

Children's Literature
   Afterword: Propaganda, Namby-Pamby,
   and Some Books of Distinction . . .DLB-52

Children's Book Awards and Prizes... DLB-61

Children's Book Illustration in the
  Twentieth Century DLB-61

Children's Illustrators, 1800-1880 ... DLB-163

The Harry Potter Phenomenon Y-99

Pony Stories, Omnibus
  Essay on DLB-160

The Reality of One Woman's Dream:
  The de Grummond Children's
  Literature Collection Y-99

School Stories, 1914-1960 .... DLB-160

The Year in Children's
  Books................ Y-92–96, 98–01

The Year in Children's Literature Y-97

Childress, Alice 1916-1994........DLB-7, 38, 249

Childress, Mark 1957- DLB-292

Childs, George W. 1829-1894 .... DLB-23

Chilton Book Company DLB-46

Chin, Frank 1940- DLB-206, 312

Chin, Justin 1969- DLB-312

Chin, Marilyn 1955- DLB-312

Chinweizu 1943- DLB-157

Chinnov, Igor' 1909-1996............ DLB-317

Chitham, Edward 1932- DLB-155

Chittenden, Hiram Martin 1858-1917 .... DLB-47

Chivers, Thomas Holley 1809-1858... DLB-3, 248

Chkhartishvili, Grigorii Shalvovich
  (see Akunin, Boris)

Chocano, José Santos 1875-1934 .... DLB-290

Cholmondeley, Mary 1859-1925 .... DLB-197

Chomsky, Noam 1928- DLB-246

Chopin, Kate 1850-1904... DLB-12, 78; CDALB-3

Chopin, René 1885-1953 .... DLB-92

Choquette, Adrienne 1915-1973....... DLB-68

Choquette, Robert 1905-1991 .... DLB-68

Choyce, Lesley 1951- DLB-251

Chrétien de Troyes
  circa 1140-circa 1190 .... DLB-208

Christensen, Inger 1935- DLB-214

Christensen, Lars Saabye 1953- DLB-297

The Christian Examiner DLB-1

The Christian Publishing Company...... DLB-49

Christie, Agatha
  1890-1976........DLB-13, 77, 245; CDBLB-6

Christine de Pizan
  circa 1365-circa 1431 .... DLB-208

Christopher, John (Sam Youd) 1922- .. DLB-255

Christus und die Samariterin circa 950 ..... DLB-148

Christy, Howard Chandler 1873-1952 ... DLB-188

Chu, Louis 1915-1970................. DLB-312

Chukovskaia, Lidiia 1907-1996....... DLB-302

Chulkov, Mikhail Dmitrievich
  1743?-1792................. DLB-150

Church, Benjamin 1734-1778 .... DLB-31

Church, Francis Pharcellus 1839-1906.... DLB-79

Church, Peggy Pond 1903-1986........ DLB-212

Church, Richard 1893-1972 .... DLB-191

Church, William Conant 1836-1917...... DLB-79

Churchill, Caryl 1938- DLB-13, 310

Churchill, Charles 1731-1764 .... DLB-109

Churchill, Winston 1871-1947 .... DLB-202

Churchill, Sir Winston
  1874-1965... DLB-100, 329; DS-16; CDBLB-5

Churchyard, Thomas 1520?-1604 ...... DLB-132

E. Churton and Company DLB-106

Chute, Marchette 1909-1994 .... DLB-103

Ciardi, John 1916-1986.............DLB-5; Y-86

Cibber, Colley 1671-1757 .... DLB-84

Cicero 106 B.C.-43 B.C......DLB-211, CDWLB-1

Cima, Annalisa 1941- DLB-128

Čingo, Živko 1935-1987............ DLB-181

Cioran, E. M. 1911-1995 .... DLB-220

Čipkus, Alfonsas (see Nyka-Niliūnas, Alfonsas)

Cirese, Eugenio 1884-1955............ DLB-114

Cīrulis, Jānis (see Bels, Alberts)

Cisneros, Antonio 1942- DLB-290

Cisneros, Sandra 1954- DLB-122, 152

City Lights Books.................... DLB-46

Civil War (1861–1865)
  Battles and Leaders of the Civil War....DLB-47
  Official Records of the Rebellion DLB-47
  Recording the Civil War DLB-47

Cixous, Hélène 1937- DLB-83, 242

Claire d'Albe, Sophie Cottin DLB-314

Clampitt, Amy 1920-1994 .... DLB-105

Tribute to Alfred A. Knopf............. Y-84

Clancy, Tom 1947- DLB-227

Clapper, Raymond 1892-1944 .... DLB-29

Clare, John 1793-1864 .... DLB-55, 96

Clarendon, Edward Hyde, Earl of
  1609-1674..................... DLB-101

Clark, Alfred Alexander Gordon
  (see Hare, Cyril)

Clark, Ann Nolan 1896-1995.......... DLB-52

Clark, C. E. Frazer, Jr. 1925-2001... DLB-187; Y-01

C. E. Frazer Clark Jr. and
  Hawthorne Bibliography....... DLB-269

The Publications of C. E. Frazer
  Clark Jr. DLB-269

Clark, Catherine Anthony 1892-1977..... DLB-68

Clark, Charles Heber 1841-1915 .... DLB-11

Clark, Davis Wasgatt 1812-1871......... DLB-79

Clark, Douglas 1919-1993 ....DLB-276

Clark, Eleanor 1913-1996............. DLB-6

Clark, J. P. 1935- DLB-117; CDWLB-3

Clark, Lewis Gaylord
  1808-1873.............DLB-3, 64, 73, 250

Clark, Mary Higgins 1929- DLB-306

Clark, Walter Van Tilburg
  1909-1971................. DLB-9, 206

Clark, William 1770-1838......... DLB-183, 186

Clark, William Andrews, Jr.
  1877-1934....................DLB-187

C. M. Clark Publishing Company DLB-46

Clarke, Sir Arthur C. 1917- DLB-261

Tribute to Theodore Sturgeon.......... Y-85

Clarke, Austin 1896-1974........... DLB-10, 20

Clarke, Austin C. 1934- DLB-53, 125

Clarke, Gillian 1937- DLB-40

Clarke, James Freeman
  1810-1888 .... DLB-1, 59, 235; DS-5

Clarke, John circa 1596-1658 .... DLB-281

Clarke, Lindsay 1939- DLB-231

Clarke, Marcus 1846-1881............ DLB-230

Clarke, Pauline 1921- DLB-161

Clarke, Rebecca Sophia 1833-1906 ...... DLB-42

Clarke, Samuel 1675-1729 .... DLB-252

Robert Clarke and Company........... DLB-49

Clarkson, Thomas 1760-1846.......... DLB-158

Claudel, Paul 1868-1955 ..... DLB-192, 258, 321

Claudius, Matthias 1740-1815 .... DLB-97

Clausen, Andy 1943- DLB-16

Claussen, Sophus 1865-1931 .... DLB-300

Clawson, John L. 1865-1933 ....DLB-187

Claxton, Remsen and Haffelfinger....... DLB-49

Clay, Cassius Marcellus 1810-1903 ...... DLB-43

Clayton, Richard (see Haggard, William)

Cleage, Pearl 1948- DLB-228

Cleary, Beverly 1916- DLB-52

Cleary, Kate McPhelim 1863-1905...... DLB-221

Cleaver, Vera 1919-1992 and
  Cleaver, Bill 1920-1981 .... DLB-52

Cleeve, Brian 1921-2003 ....DLB-276

Cleland, John 1710-1789 .... DLB-39

Clemens, Samuel Langhorne (Mark Twain)
  1835-1910 .... DLB-11, 12, 23, 64, 74,
                         186, 189; CDALB-3

Comments From Authors and Scholars on
  their First Reading of *Huck Finn* Y-85

Huck at 100: How Old Is
  Huckleberry Finn? Y-85

Mark Twain on Perpetual Copyright..... Y-92

A New Edition of *Huck Finn*............. Y-85

Clement, Hal 1922-2003 .... DLB-8

Clemo, Jack 1916-1994................ DLB-27

Clephane, Elizabeth Cecilia 1830-1869 .. DLB-199

Cleveland, John 1613-1658............ DLB-126

Cliff, Michelle 1946- DLB-157; CDWLB-3

Clifford, Lady Anne 1590-1676 .... DLB-151

Clifford, James L. 1901-1978 .... DLB-103

Clifford, Lucy 1853?-1929.....DLB-135, 141, 197

Clift, Charmian 1923-1969............DLB-260

Clifton, Lucille 1936-..............DLB-5, 41

Clines, Francis X. 1938-................DLB-185

Clive, Caroline (V) 1801-1873...........DLB-199

Edward J. Clode [publishing house].......DLB-46

Clough, Arthur Hugh 1819-1861........DLB-32

Cloutier, Cécile 1930-................DLB-60

Clouts, Sidney 1926-1982............DLB-225

Clutton-Brock, Arthur 1868-1924........DLB-98

Coates, Robert M.
 1897-1973.............DLB-4, 9, 102; DS-15

Coatsworth, Elizabeth 1893-1986........DLB-22

Cobb, Charles E., Jr. 1943-..............DLB-41

Cobb, Frank I. 1869-1923..............DLB-25

Cobb, Irvin S. 1876-1944.........DLB-11, 25, 86

Cobbe, Frances Power 1822-1904.......DLB-190

Cobbett, William 1763-1835....DLB-43, 107, 158

Cobbledick, Gordon 1898-1969.........DLB-171

Cochran, Thomas C. 1902-1999..........DLB-17

Cochrane, Elizabeth 1867-1922......DLB-25, 189

Cockerell, Sir Sydney 1867-1962........DLB-201

Cockerill, John A. 1845-1896............DLB-23

Cocteau, Jean 1889-1963........DLB-65, 258, 321

Coderre, Emile (see Jean Narrache)

Cody, Liza 1944-................DLB-276

Coe, Jonathan 1961-................DLB-231

Coetzee, J. M. 1940-.........DLB-225, 326, 329

Coffee, Lenore J. 1900?-1984............DLB-44

Coffin, Robert P. Tristram 1892-1955.....DLB-45

Coghill, Mrs. Harry (see Walker, Anna Louisa)

Cogswell, Fred 1917-................DLB-60

Cogswell, Mason Fitch 1761-1830........DLB-37

Cohan, George M. 1878-1942..........DLB-249

Cohen, Arthur A. 1928-1986............DLB-28

Cohen, Leonard 1934-................DLB-53

Cohen, Matt 1942-................DLB-53

Cohen, Morris Raphael 1880-1947.......DLB-270

Colasanti, Marina 1937-................DLB-307

Colbeck, Norman 1903-1987..........DLB-201

Colden, Cadwallader
 1688-1776................DLB-24, 30, 270

Colden, Jane 1724-1766..............DLB-200

Cole, Barry 1936-................DLB-14

Cole, George Watson 1850-1939..........DLB-140

Colegate, Isabel 1931-..........DLB-14, 231

Coleman, Emily Holmes 1899-1974........DLB-4

Coleman, Wanda 1946-................DLB-130

Coleridge, Hartley 1796-1849............DLB-96

Coleridge, Mary 1861-1907..........DLB-19, 98

Coleridge, Samuel Taylor
 1772-1834..........DLB-93, 107; CDBLB-3

Coleridge, Sara 1802-1852.............DLB-199

Colet, John 1467-1519................DLB-132

Colette 1873-1954....................DLB-65

Colette, Sidonie Gabrielle (see Colette)

Colinas, Antonio 1946-..............DLB-134

Coll, Joseph Clement 1881-1921........DLB-188

A Century of Poetry, a Lifetime of Collecting:
 J. M. Edelstein's Collection of
 Twentieth-Century American Poetry.....Y-02

Collier, John 1901-1980............DLB-77, 255

Collier, John Payne 1789-1883..........DLB-184

Collier, Mary 1690-1762...............DLB-95

Collier, Robert J. 1876-1918............DLB-91

P. F. Collier [publishing house]..........DLB-49

Collin and Small.....................DLB-49

Collingwood, R. G. 1889-1943..........DLB-262

Collingwood, W. G. 1854-1932..........DLB-149

Collins, An floruit circa 1653..........DLB-131

Collins, Anthony 1676-1729............DLB-252

Collins, Merle 1950-................DLB-157

Collins, Michael 1964-................DLB-267

Collins, Michael (see Lynds, Dennis)

Collins, Mortimer 1827-1876.........DLB-21, 35

Collins, Wilkie
 1824-1889........DLB-18, 70, 159; CDBLB-4

 "The Unknown Public" (1858)
 [excerpt]....................DLB-57

 The Wilkie Collins Society............Y-98

Collins, William 1721-1759............DLB-109

Isaac Collins [publishing house]..........DLB-49

William Collins, Sons and Company.....DLB-154

Collis, Maurice 1889-1973............DLB-195

Collyer, Mary 1716?-1763?.............DLB-39

Colman, Benjamin 1673-1747............DLB-24

Colman, George, the Elder 1732-1794.....DLB-89

Colman, George, the Younger
 1762-1836......................DLB-89

S. Colman [publishing house]............DLB-49

Colombo, John Robert 1936-............DLB-53

Colonial Literature....................DLB-307

Colquhoun, Patrick 1745-1820..........DLB-158

Colter, Cyrus 1910-2002................DLB-33

Colum, Padraic 1881-1972..............DLB-19

The Columbia History of the American Novel
 A Symposium on....................Y-92

Columbus, Christopher 1451-1506......DLB-318

Columella fl. first century A.D..........DLB-211

Colvin, Sir Sidney 1845-1927..........DLB-149

Colwin, Laurie 1944-1992........DLB-218; Y-80

Comden, Betty 1915- and
 Green, Adolph 1918-2002.......DLB-44, 265

Comi, Girolamo 1890-1968............DLB-114

Comisso, Giovanni 1895-1969..........DLB-264

Commager, Henry Steele 1902-1998......DLB-17

Commynes, Philippe de
 circa 1447-1511..................DLB-208

Compton, D. G. 1930-................DLB-261

Compton-Burnett, Ivy 1884?-1969.......DLB-36

Conan, Laure (Félicité Angers)
 1845-1924......................DLB-99

Concord, Massachusetts
 Concord History and Life..........DLB-223

 Concord: Literary History
 of a Town....................DLB-223

 The Old Manse, by Hawthorne.....DLB-223

 The Thoreauvian Pilgrimage: The
 Structure of an American Cult...DLB-223

Concrete Poetry.....................DLB-307

Conde, Carmen 1901-1996............DLB-108

Condillac, Etienne Bonnot de
 1714-1780.....................DLB-313

Condorcet, Marie-Jean-Antoine-Nicolas Caritat,
 marquis de 1743-1794.............DLB-313

"The Tenth Stage"..................DLB-314

Congreve, William
 1670-1729..........DLB-39, 84; CDBLB-2

 Preface to Incognita (1692)............DLB-39

W. B. Conkey Company................DLB-49

Conlon, Evelyn 1952-................DLB-319

Conn, Stewart 1936-................DLB-233

Connell, Evan S., Jr. 1924-.........DLB-2; Y-81

Connelly, Marc 1890-1980..........DLB-7; Y-80

Connolly, Cyril 1903-1974.............DLB-98

Connolly, James B. 1868-1957..........DLB-78

Connor, Ralph (Charles William Gordon)
 1860-1937......................DLB-92

Connor, Tony 1930-................DLB-40

Conquest, Robert 1917-................DLB-27

Conrad, Joseph
 1857-1924....DLB-10, 34, 98, 156; CDBLB-5

John Conrad and Company............DLB-49

Conroy, Jack 1899-1990..................Y-81

 A Tribute [to Nelson Algren]............Y-81

Conroy, Pat 1945-................DLB-6

The Conservationist, 1974 Booker Prize winner,
 Nadine Gordimer................DLB-326

Considine, Bob 1906-1975............DLB-241

Consolo, Vincenzo 1933-............DLB-196

Constable, Henry 1562-1613..........DLB-136

Archibald Constable and Company.....DLB-154

Constable and Company Limited.......DLB-112

Constant, Benjamin 1767-1830.........DLB-119

Constant de Rebecque, Henri-Benjamin de
 (see Constant, Benjamin)

Cumulative Index

Constantine, David 1944- DLB-40

Constantine, Murray (see Burdekin, Katharine)

Constantin-Weyer, Maurice 1881-1964.... DLB-92

Contempo (magazine)
Contempo Caravan:
Kites in a Windstorm Y-85

The Continental Publishing Company.... DLB-49

A Conversation between William Riggan
and Janette Turner Hospital........... Y-02

Conversations with Editors Y-95

Conway, Anne 1631-1679............. DLB-252

Conway, Moncure Daniel
1832-1907................... DLB-1, 223

Cook, Ebenezer circa 1667-circa 1732..... DLB-24

Cook, Edward Tyas 1857-1919......... DLB-149

Cook, Eliza 1818-1889 .... DLB-199

Cook, George Cram 1873-1924 .... DLB-266

Cook, Michael 1933-1994 .... DLB-53

David C. Cook Publishing Company..... DLB-49

Cooke, George Willis 1848-1923 .... DLB-71

Cooke, John Esten 1830-1886 .... DLB-3, 248

Cooke, Philip Pendleton
1816-1850................. DLB-3, 59, 248

Cooke, Rose Terry 1827-1892 .... DLB-12, 74

Increase Cooke and Company DLB-49

Cook-Lynn, Elizabeth 1930-.........DLB-175

Coolbrith, Ina 1841-1928 .... DLB-54, 186

Cooley, Peter 1940- DLB-105

"Into the Mirror" DLB-105

Coolidge, Clark 1939- DLB-193

Coolidge, Susan
(see Woolsey, Sarah Chauncy)

George Coolidge [publishing house]...... DLB-49

Coomaraswamy, Ananda 1877-1947..... DLB-323

Cooper, Anna Julia 1858-1964 .... DLB-221

Cooper, Edith Emma 1862-1913 .... DLB-240

Cooper, Giles 1918-1966 .... DLB-13

Cooper, J. California 19??- DLB-212

Cooper, James Fenimore
1789-1851....... DLB-3, 183, 250; CDALB-2

The Bicentennial of James Fenimore Cooper:
An International Celebration........ Y-89

The James Fenimore Cooper Society..... Y-01

Cooper, Kent 1880-1965............ DLB-29

Cooper, Susan 1935- DLB-161, 261

Cooper, Susan Fenimore 1813-1894..... DLB-239

William Cooper [publishing house] DLB-170

J. Coote [publishing house]........... DLB-154

Coover, Robert 1932- DLB-2, 227; Y-81

Tribute to Donald Barthelme........... Y-89

Tribute to Theodor Seuss Geisel Y-91

Copeland and Day DLB-49

Ćopić, Branko 1915-1984............. DLB-181

Copland, Robert 1470?-1548 .... DLB-136

Coppard, A. E. 1878-1957 .... DLB-162

Coppée, François 1842-1908 .... DLB-217

Coppel, Alfred 1921-2004 .... Y-83

Tribute to Jessamyn West............. Y-84

Coppola, Francis Ford 1939- DLB-44

Copway, George (Kah-ge-ga-gah-bowh)
1818-1869 ....DLB-175, 183

Copyright
The Development of the Author's
Copyright in Britain DLB-154

The Digital Millennium Copyright Act:
Expanding Copyright Protection in
Cyberspace and Beyond Y-98

Editorial: The Extension of Copyright ... Y-02

Mark Twain on Perpetual Copyright..... Y-92

Public Domain and the Violation
of Texts Y-97

The Question of American Copyright
in the Nineteenth Century
Preface, by George Haven Putnam
The Evolution of Copyright, by
Brander Matthews
Summary of Copyright Legislation in
the United States, by R. R. Bowker
Analysis of the Provisions of the
Copyright Law of 1891, by
George Haven Putnam
The Contest for International Copyright,
by George Haven Putnam
Cheap Books and Good Books,
by Brander Matthews DLB-49

Writers and Their Copyright Holders:
the WATCH Project Y-94

Corazzini, Sergio 1886-1907.......... DLB-114

Corbett, Richard 1582-1635.......... DLB-121

Corbière, Tristan 1845-1875.......... DLB-217

Corcoran, Barbara 1911- DLB-52

Cordelli, Franco 1943- DLB-196

Corelli, Marie 1855-1924 .... DLB-34, 156

Corle, Edwin 1906-1956................. Y-85

Corman, Cid 1924-2004............ DLB-5, 193

Cormier, Robert 1925-2000 ... DLB-52; CDALB-6

Tribute to Theodor Seuss Geisel Y-91

Corn, Alfred 1943- DLB-120, 282; Y-80

Corneille, Pierre 1606-1684............DLB-268

Cornford, Frances 1886-1960.......... DLB-240

Cornish, Sam 1935- DLB-41

Cornish, William
circa 1465-circa 1524 .... DLB-132

Cornwall, Barry (see Procter, Bryan Waller)

Cornwallis, Sir William, the Younger
circa 1579-1614.................. DLB-151

Cornwell, David John Moore (see le Carré, John)

Cornwell, Patricia 1956- DLB-306

Coronel Urtecho, José 1906-1994........ DLB-290

Corpi, Lucha 1945- DLB-82

Corrington, John William
1932-1988 .... DLB-6, 244

Corriveau, Monique 1927-1976 .... DLB-251

Corrothers, James D. 1869-1917......... DLB-50

Corso, Gregory 1930-2001.........DLB-5, 16, 237

Cortázar, Julio 1914-1984....DLB-113; CDWLB-3

Cortéz, Carlos 1923-2005............. DLB-209

Cortez, Jayne 1936- DLB-41

Corvinus, Gottlieb Siegmund
1677-1746 .... DLB-168

Corvo, Baron (see Rolfe, Frederick William)

Cory, Annie Sophie (see Cross, Victoria)

Cory, Desmond (Shaun Lloyd McCarthy)
1928- DLB-276

Cory, William Johnson 1823-1892....... DLB-35

Coryate, Thomas 1577?-1617.......DLB-151, 172

Ćosić, Dobrica 1921- DLB-181; CDWLB-4

Cosin, John 1595-1672 .... DLB-151, 213

Cosmopolitan Book Corporation........ DLB-46

Cossa, Roberto 1934- DLB-305

Costa, Maria Velho da (see The Three Marias:
A Landmark Case in Portuguese
Literary History)

Costain, Thomas B. 1885-1965 .... DLB-9

Coste, Donat (Daniel Boudreau)
1912-1957...................... DLB-88

Costello, Louisa Stuart 1799-1870....... DLB-166

Cota-Cárdenas, Margarita 1941- DLB-122

Côté, Denis 1954- DLB-251

Cotten, Bruce 1873-1954 ....DLB-187

Cotter, Joseph Seamon, Jr. 1895-1919..... DLB-50

Cotter, Joseph Seamon, Sr. 1861-1949 .... DLB-50

Cottin, Sophie 1770-1807 .... DLB-313

Claire d'Albe.................... DLB-314

Joseph Cottle [publishing house] DLB-154

Cotton, Charles 1630-1687............ DLB-131

Cotton, John 1584-1652................ DLB-24

Cotton, Sir Robert Bruce 1571-1631 .... DLB-213

Couani, Anna 1948- DLB-325

Coulter, John 1888-1980.............. DLB-68

Cournos, John 1881-1966............. DLB-54

Courteline, Georges 1858-1929 .... DLB-192

Cousins, Margaret 1905-1996 ....DLB-137

Cousins, Norman 1915-1990 ....DLB-137

Couvreur, Jessie (see Tasma)

Coventry, Francis 1725-1754........... DLB-39

Dedication, *The History of Pompey
the Little* (1751) DLB-39

Coverdale, Miles 1487 or 1488-1569 .... DLB-167

N. Coverly [publishing house] DLB-49

Covici-Friede DLB-46

Cowan, Peter 1914-2002.............. DLB-260

Coward, Noel
1899-1973.........DLB-10, 245; CDBLB-6

Coward, McCann and Geoghegan....... DLB-46

Cowles, Gardner 1861-1946 . . . . .DLB-29

Cowles, Gardner "Mike", Jr.
  1903-1985 . . . . DLB-127, 137

Cowley, Abraham 1618-1667 . . . . . .DLB-131, 151

Cowley, Hannah 1743-1809 . . . . .DLB-89

Cowley, Malcolm
  1898-1989 . . . . DLB-4, 48; DS-15; Y-81, 89

Cowper, Richard (John Middleton Murry Jr.)
  1926-2002 . . . . .DLB-261

Cowper, William 1731-1800 . . . . .DLB-104, 109

Cox, A. B. (see Berkeley, Anthony)

Cox, James McMahon 1903-1974 . . . . . . .DLB-127

Cox, James Middleton 1870-1957 . . . . . . .DLB-127

Cox, Leonard circa 1495-circa 1550 . . . . .DLB-281

Cox, Palmer 1840-1924 . . . . .DLB-42

Coxe, Louis 1918-1993 . . . . .DLB-5

Coxe, Tench 1755-1824 . . . . .DLB-37

Cozzens, Frederick S. 1818-1869 . . . . . . .DLB-202

Cozzens, James Gould 1903-1978 . . . .
  . . . . DLB-9, 294; Y-84; DS-2; CDALB-1

  Cozzens's *Michael Scarlett* Y-97

  Ernest Hemingway's Reaction to
    James Gould Cozzens Y-98

  James Gould Cozzens—A View
    from Afar Y-97

  James Gould Cozzens: How to
    Read Him Y-97

  James Gould Cozzens Symposium and
    Exhibition at the University of
    South Carolina, Columbia Y-00

  Mens Rea (or Something) Y-97

  Novels for Grown-Ups Y-97

Crabbe, George 1754-1832 . . . . .DLB-93

Crace, Jim 1946- DLB-231

Crackanthorpe, Hubert 1870-1896 . . . . . .DLB-135

Craddock, Charles Egbert (see Murfree, Mary N.)

Cradock, Thomas 1718-1770 . . . . .DLB-31

Craig, Daniel H. 1811-1895 . . . . .DLB-43

Craik, Dinah Maria 1826-1887 . . . . . . .DLB-35, 163

Cramer, Richard Ben 1950- DLB-185

Cranch, Christopher Pearse
  1813-1892 . . . . .DLB-1, 42, 243; DS-5

Crane, Hart 1899-1932 . . . . .DLB-4, 48; CDALB-4

  Nathan Asch Remembers Ford Madox
    Ford, Sam Roth, and Hart Crane Y-02

Crane, R. S. 1886-1967 . . . . .DLB-63

Crane, Stephen
  1871-1900 . . . . . . .DLB-12, 54, 78; CDALB-3

  Stephen Crane: A Revaluation, Virginia
    Tech Conference, 1989 . . . . .Y-89

  The Stephen Crane Society Y-98, 01

Crane, Walter 1845-1915 . . . . .DLB-163

Cranmer, Thomas 1489-1556 . . . . . .DLB-132, 213

Crapsey, Adelaide 1878-1914 . . . . .DLB-54

Crashaw, Richard 1612/1613-1649 . . . . . .DLB-126

Craven, Avery 1885-1980 . . . . .DLB-17

Crawford, Charles 1752-circa 1815 . . . . . . .DLB-31

Crawford, F. Marion 1854-1909 . . . . .DLB-71

Crawford, Isabel Valancy 1850-1887 . . . . . .DLB-92

Crawley, Alan 1887-1975 . . . . .DLB-68

Crayon, Geoffrey (see Irving, Washington)

Crayon, Porte (see Strother, David Hunter)

Creamer, Robert W. 1922- DLB-171

Creasey, John 1908-1973 . . . . .DLB-77

Creative Age Press DLB-46

Creative Nonfiction .Y-02

Crébillon, Claude-Prosper Jolyot de *fils*
  1707-1777 . . . . .DLB-313

Crébillon, Claude-Prosper Jolyot de *père*
  1674-1762 . . . . .DLB-313

William Creech [publishing house] DLB-154

Thomas Creede [publishing house] DLB-170

Creel, George 1876-1953 . . . . .DLB-25

Creeley, Robert 1926-2005
  . . . . DLB-5, 16, 169; DS-17

Creelman, James
  1859-1915 . . . . .DLB-23

Cregan, David 1931- DLB-13

Creighton, Donald 1902-1979 . . . . .DLB-88

Crémazie, Octave 1827-1879 . . . . .DLB-99

Crémer, Victoriano 1909?- DLB-108

Crenne, Hélisenne de (Marguerite de Briet)
  1510?-1560? DLB-327

Crescas, Hasdai circa 1340-1412? DLB-115

Crespo, Angel 1926-1995 . . . . .DLB-134

Cresset Press DLB-112

Cresswell, Helen 1934- DLB-161

Crèvecoeur, Michel Guillaume Jean de
  1735-1813 . . . . .DLB-37

Crewe, Candida 1964- DLB-207

Crews, Harry 1935- DLB-6, 143, 185

Crichton, Michael (John Lange, Jeffrey Hudson,
  Michael Douglas) 1942- DLB-292; Y-81

Crispin, Edmund (Robert Bruce Montgomery)
  1921-1978 . . . . .DLB-87

Cristofer, Michael 1946- DLB-7

Criticism
  Afro-American Literary Critics:
    An Introduction DLB-33

  The Consolidation of Opinion: Critical
    Responses to the Modernists DLB-36

  "Criticism in Relation to Novels"
    (1863), by G. H. Lewes DLB-21

  The Limits of Pluralism DLB-67

  Modern Critical Terms, Schools, and
    Movements DLB-67

  "Panic Among the Philistines":
    A Postscript, An Interview
    with Bryan Griffin Y-81

  The Recovery of Literature: Criticism
    in the 1990s: A Symposium Y-91

  The Stealthy School of Criticism (1871),
    by Dante Gabriel Rossetti DLB-35

Crnjanski, Miloš
  1893-1977 . . . . .DLB-147; CDWLB-4

Crocker, Hannah Mather 1752-1829 . . . . .DLB-200

Crockett, David (Davy)
  1786-1836 . . . . DLB-3, 11, 183, 248

Croft-Cooke, Rupert (see Bruce, Leo)

Crofts, Freeman Wills 1879-1957 . . . . .DLB-77

Croker, John Wilson 1780-1857 . . . . .DLB-110

Croly, George 1780-1860 . . . . .DLB-159

Croly, Herbert 1869-1930 . . . . .DLB-91

Croly, Jane Cunningham 1829-1901 . . . . . .DLB-23

Crompton, Richmal 1890-1969 . . . . .DLB-160

Cronin, A. J. 1896-1981 . . . . .DLB-191

Cros, Charles 1842-1888 . . . . .DLB-217

Crosby, Caresse 1892-1970 and
  Crosby, Harry 1898-1929 and . . DLB-4; DS-15

Crosby, Harry 1898-1929 . . . . .DLB-48

Crosland, Camilla Toulmin (Mrs. Newton
  Crosland) 1812-1895 . . . . .DLB-240

Cross, Amanda (Carolyn G. Heilbrun)
  1926-2003 . . . . .DLB-306

Cross, Gillian 1945- DLB-161

Cross, Victoria 1868-1952 . . . . .DLB-135, 197

Crossley-Holland, Kevin 1941- DLB-40, 161

Crothers, Rachel 1870-1958 . . . . DLB-7, 266

Thomas Y. Crowell Company DLB-49

Crowley, John 1942- Y-82

Crowley, Mart 1935- DLB-7, 266

Crown Publishers DLB-46

Crowne, John 1641-1712 . . . . .DLB-80

Crowninshield, Edward Augustus
  1817-1859 . . . . .DLB-140

Crowninshield, Frank 1872-1947 . . . . . . .DLB-91

Croy, Homer 1883-1965 . . . . .DLB-4

Crumley, James 1939- DLB-226; Y-84

Cruse, Mary Anne 1825?-1910 . . . . .DLB-239

Cruz, Migdalia 1958- DLB-249

Cruz, Sor Juana Inés de la 1651-1695 . . . .DLB-305

Cruz, Victor Hernández 1949- DLB-41

Cruz e Sousa, João 1861-1898 . . . . .DLB-307

Csokor, Franz Theodor 1885-1969 . . . . . .DLB-81

Csoóri, Sándor 1930- DLB-232; CDWLB-4

Cuadra, Pablo Antonio 1912-2002 . . . . . .DLB-290

Cuala Press DLB-112

Cudworth, Ralph 1617-1688 . . . . .DLB-252

Cueva, Juan de la 1543-1612 . . . . .DLB-318

Cugoano, Quobna Ottabah 1797?- Y-02

Cullen, Countee
  1903-1946 . . . . .DLB-4, 48, 51; CDALB-4

Culler, Jonathan D. 1944- DLB-67, 246

Cullinan, Elizabeth 1933- DLB-234

Culverwel, Nathaniel 1619?-1651? DLB-252

Cumberland, Richard 1732-1811 . . . . .DLB-89

Cumulative Index

Cummings, Constance Gordon
1837-1924 . . . . .DLB-174

Cummings, E. E.
1894-1962 . . . . DLB-4, 48; CDALB-5

    The E. E. Cummings Society Y-01

Cummings, Ray 1887-1957 . . . . DLB-8

Cummings and Hilliard DLB-49

Cummins, Maria Susanna 1827-1866 . . . . . DLB-42

Cumpián, Carlos 1953- DLB-209

Cunard, Nancy 1896-1965 . . . . DLB-240

Joseph Cundall [publishing house] DLB-106

Cuney, Waring 1906-1976 . . . . DLB-51

Cuney-Hare, Maude 1874-1936 . . . . DLB-52

Cunha, Euclides da 1866-1909 . . . . DLB-307

Cunningham, Allan
1784-1842 . . . . DLB-116, 144

Cunningham, J. V. 1911-1985 . . . . DLB-5

Cunningham, Michael 1952- DLB-292

Cunningham, Peter (Peter Lauder, Peter
Benjamin) 1947- DLB-267

Peter F. Cunningham
[publishing house] DLB-49

Cunqueiro, Alvaro 1911-1981 . . . . DLB-134

Cuomo, George 1929- Y-80

Cupples, Upham and Company DLB-49

Cupples and Leon DLB-46

Cuppy, Will 1884-1949 . . . . DLB-11

Curiel, Barbara Brinson 1956- DLB-209

Edmund Curll [publishing house] DLB-154

Currie, James 1756-1805 . . . . DLB-142

Currie, Mary Montgomerie Lamb Singleton,
Lady Currie (see Fane, Violet)

Cursor Mundi circa 1300 . . . . DLB-146

Curti, Merle E. 1897-1996 . . . . DLB-17

Curtis, Anthony 1926- DLB-155

Curtis, Cyrus H. K. 1850-1933 . . . . DLB-91

Curtis, George William
1824-1892 . . . . DLB-1, 43, 223

Curzon, Robert 1810-1873 . . . . DLB-166

Curzon, Sarah Anne 1833-1898 . . . . DLB-99

Cusack, Dymphna 1902-1981 . . . . DLB-260

Cushing, Eliza Lanesford
1794-1886 . . . . DLB-99

Cushing, Harvey 1869-1939 . . . . DLB-187

Custance, Olive (Lady Alfred Douglas)
1874-1944 . . . . DLB-240

Cynewulf circa 770-840 . . . . DLB-146

Cyrano de Bergerac, Savinien de
1619-1655 . . . . DLB-268

Czepko, Daniel 1605-1660 . . . . DLB-164

Czerniawski, Adam 1934- DLB-232

D

Dabit, Eugène 1898-1936 . . . . DLB-65

Daborne, Robert circa 1580-1628 . . . . DLB-58

Dąbrowska, Maria
1889-1965 . . . . DLB-215; CDWLB-4

Dacey, Philip 1939- DLB-105

    "Eyes Across Centuries:
Contemporary Poetry and 'That
Vision Thing,'" DLB-105

Dach, Simon 1605-1659 . . . . DLB-164

Dacier, Anne Le Fèvre 1647-1720 . . . . DLB-313

Dagerman, Stig 1923-1954 . . . . DLB-259

Daggett, Rollin M. 1831-1901 . . . . DLB-79

D'Aguiar, Fred 1960- DLB-157

Dahl, Roald 1916-1990 . . . . DLB-139, 255

    Tribute to Alfred A. Knopf Y-84

Dahlberg, Edward 1900-1977 . . . . DLB-48

Dahn, Felix 1834-1912 . . . . DLB-129

The Daily Worker DLB-303

Dal', Vladimir Ivanovich (Kazak Vladimir
Lugansky) 1801-1872 . . . . DLB-198

Dale, Peter 1938- DLB-40

Daley, Arthur 1904-1974 . . . . .DLB-171

Dall, Caroline Healey 1822-1912 . . . . . DLB-1, 235

Dallas, E. S. 1828-1879 . . . . DLB-55

    The Gay Science [excerpt](1866) DLB-21

The Dallas Theater Center DLB-7

D'Alton, Louis 1900-1951 . . . . DLB-10

Dalton, Roque 1935-1975 . . . . DLB-283

Daly, Carroll John 1889-1958 . . . . DLB-226

Daly, T. A. 1871-1948 . . . . DLB-11

Damon, S. Foster 1893-1971 . . . . DLB-45

William S. Damrell [publishing house] DLB-49

Dana, Charles A. 1819-1897 . . . . . . DLB-3, 23, 250

Dana, Richard Henry, Jr.
1815-1882 . . . . DLB-1, 183, 235

Dandridge, Ray Garfield 1882-1930 . . . . . . DLB-51

Dane, Clemence 1887-1965 . . . . .DLB-10, 197

Danforth, John 1660-1730 . . . . DLB-24

Danforth, Samuel, I 1626-1674 . . . . DLB-24

Danforth, Samuel, II 1666-1727 . . . . DLB-24

Dangerous Acquaintances, Pierre-Ambroise-François
Choderlos de Laclos DLB-314

Daniel, John M. 1825-1865 . . . . DLB-43

Daniel, Samuel 1562 or 1563-1619 . . . . DLB-62

Daniel Press DLB-106

Daniel', Iulii 1925-1988 . . . . DLB-302

Daniells, Roy 1902-1979 . . . . DLB-68

Daniels, Jim 1956- DLB-120

Daniels, Jonathan 1902-1981 . . . . DLB-127

Daniels, Josephus 1862-1948 . . . . DLB-29

Daniels, Sarah 1957- DLB-245

Danilevsky, Grigorii Petrovich
1829-1890 . . . . DLB-238

Dannay, Frederic 1905-1982 . . . . DLB-137

Danner, Margaret Esse 1915- DLB-41

John Danter [publishing house] DLB-170

Dantin, Louis (Eugene Seers)
1865-1945 . . . . DLB-92

Danto, Arthur C. 1924- DLB-279

Danzig, Allison 1898-1987 . . . . .DLB-171

D'Arcy, Ella circa 1857-1937 . . . . DLB-135

Darío, Rubén 1867-1916 . . . . DLB-290

Dark, Eleanor 1901-1985 . . . . DLB-260

Darke, Nick 1948- DLB-233

Darley, Felix Octavious Carr
1822-1888 . . . . DLB-188

Darley, George 1795-1846 . . . . DLB-96

Darmesteter, Madame James
(see Robinson, A. Mary F.)

Darrow, Clarence 1857-1938 . . . . DLB-303

Darwin, Charles 1809-1882 . . . . .DLB-57, 166

Darwin, Erasmus 1731-1802 . . . . DLB-93

Daryush, Elizabeth 1887-1977 . . . . DLB-20

Das, Kamala 1934- DLB-323

Dashkova, Ekaterina Romanovna
(née Vorontsova) 1743-1810 . . . . DLB-150

Dashwood, Edmée Elizabeth Monica de la Pasture
(see Delafield, E. M.)

Dattani, Mahesh 1958- DLB-323

Daudet, Alphonse 1840-1897 . . . . DLB-123

d'Aulaire, Edgar Parin 1898-1986 and
d'Aulaire, Ingri 1904-1980 . . . . DLB-22

Davenant, Sir William 1606-1668 . . . . DLB-58, 126

Davenport, Guy 1927-2005 . . . . DLB-130

    Tribute to John Gardner Y-82

Davenport, Marcia 1903-1996 . . . . DS-17

Davenport, Robert circa 17th century DLB-58

Daves, Delmer 1904-1977 . . . . DLB-26

Davey, Frank 1940- DLB-53

Davidson, Avram 1923-1993 . . . . DLB-8

Davidson, Donald 1893-1968 . . . . DLB-45

Davidson, Donald 1917-2003 . . . . .DLB-279

Davidson, John 1857-1909 . . . . DLB-19

Davidson, Lionel 1922- DLB-14, 276

Davidson, Robyn 1950- DLB-204

Davidson, Sara 1943- DLB-185

Davíð Stefánsson frá Fagraskógi
1895-1964 . . . . DLB-293

Davie, Donald 1922-1995 . . . . DLB-27

Davie, Elspeth 1919-1995 . . . . DLB-139

Davies, Sir John 1569-1626 . . . . .DLB-172

Davies, John, of Hereford 1565?-1618 . . . DLB-121

Davies, Rhys 1901-1978 . . . . DLB-139, 191

Davies, Robertson 1913-1995 . . . . DLB-68

Davies, Samuel 1723-1761 . . . . DLB-31

Davies, Thomas 1712?-1785 . . . . DLB-142, 154

Davies, W. H. 1871-1940 . . . . DLB-19, 174

Peter Davies Limited DLB-112

Davin, Nicholas Flood 1840?-1901 . . . . DLB-99

Daviot, Gordon 1896?-1952 . . . . DLB-10
(see also Tey, Josephine)

Davis, Arthur Hoey (see Rudd, Steele)

Davis, Benjamin J. 1903-1964 . . . . DLB-303

Davis, Charles A. (Major J. Downing) 1795-1867 . . . . DLB-11

Davis, Clyde Brion 1894-1962 . . . . DLB-9

Davis, Dick 1945- DLB-40, 282

Davis, Frank Marshall 1905-1987 . . . . DLB-51

Davis, H. L. 1894-1960 . . . . DLB-9, 206

Davis, Jack 1917-2000 . . . . DLB-325

Davis, John 1774-1854 . . . . DLB-37

Davis, Lydia 1947- DLB-130

Davis, Margaret Thomson 1926- DLB-14

Davis, Ossie 1917-2005 . . . . DLB-7, 38, 249

Davis, Owen 1874-1956 . . . . DLB-249

Davis, Paxton 1925-1994 . . . . Y-89

Davis, Rebecca Harding 1831-1910 . . . . DLB-74, 239

Davis, Richard Harding 1864-1916 . . . . DLB-12, 23, 78, 79, 189; DS-13

Davis, Samuel Cole 1764-1809 . . . . DLB-37

Davis, Samuel Post 1850-1918 . . . . DLB-202

Davison, Frank Dalby 1893-1970 . . . . DLB-260

Davison, Peter 1928- DLB-5

Davydov, Denis Vasil'evich 1784-1839 . . . . DLB-205

Davys, Mary 1674-1732 . . . . DLB-39

Preface to *The Works of Mrs. Davys* (1725) DLB-39

DAW Books DLB-46

Dawe, Bruce 1930- DLB-289

Dawson, Ernest 1882-1947 . . . . DLB-140; Y-02

Dawson, Fielding 1930- DLB-130

Dawson, Sarah Morgan 1842-1909 . . . . . . DLB-239

Dawson, William 1704-1752 . . . . DLB-31

Day, Angel fl. 1583-1599 . . . . DLB-167, 236

Day, Benjamin Henry 1810-1889 . . . . DLB-43

Day, Clarence 1874-1935 . . . . DLB-11

Day, Dorothy 1897-1980 . . . . DLB-29

Day, Frank Parker 1881-1950 . . . . DLB-92

Day, John circa 1574-circa 1640 . . . . DLB-62

Day, Marele 1947- DLB-325

Day, Thomas 1748-1789 . . . . DLB-39

John Day [publishing house] DLB-170

The John Day Company DLB-46

Mahlon Day [publishing house] DLB-49

Day Lewis, C. (see Blake, Nicholas)

Dazai Osamu 1909-1948 . . . . DLB-182

Deacon, William Arthur 1890-1977 . . . . . . DLB-68

Deal, Borden 1922-1985 . . . . DLB-6

de Angeli, Marguerite 1889-1987 . . . . DLB-22

De Angelis, Milo 1951- DLB-128

Debord, Guy 1931-1994 . . . . DLB-296

De Bow, J. D. B. 1820-1867 . . . . DLB-3, 79, 248

Debs, Eugene V. 1855-1926 . . . . DLB-303

de Bruyn, Günter 1926- DLB-75

de Camp, L. Sprague 1907-2000 . . . . DLB-8

De Carlo, Andrea 1952- DLB-196

De Casas, Celso A. 1944- DLB-209

Dechert, Robert 1895-1975 . . . . DLB-187

Declaration of the Rights of Man and of the Citizen DLB-314

Declaration of the Rights of Woman, Olympe de Gouges DLB-314

Dedications, Inscriptions, and Annotations Y-01–02

Dee, John 1527-1608 or 1609 . . . . . . DLB-136, 213

Deeping, George Warwick 1877-1950 . . . . DLB-153

Deffand, Marie de Vichy-Chamrond, marquise Du 1696-1780 . . . . DLB-313

Defoe, Daniel 1660-1731 . . . . DLB-39, 95, 101; CDBLB-2

Preface to *Colonel Jack* (1722) DLB-39

Preface to *The Farther Adventures of Robinson Crusoe* (1719) DLB-39

Preface to *Moll Flanders* (1722) DLB-39

Preface to *Robinson Crusoe* (1719) DLB-39

Preface to *Roxana* (1724) DLB-39

de Fontaine, Felix Gregory 1834-1896 . . . . DLB-43

De Forest, John William 1826-1906 . . . . DLB-12, 189

DeFrees, Madeline 1919- DLB-105

"The Poet's Kaleidoscope: The Element of Surprise in the Making of the Poem" DLB-105

DeGolyer, Everette Lee 1886-1956 . . . . . . DLB-187

de Graff, Robert 1895-1981 . . . . Y-81

de Graft, Joe 1924-1978 . . . . DLB-117

De Groen, Alma 1941- DLB-325

De Heinrico circa 980? DLB-148

Deighton, Len 1929- DLB-87; CDBLB-8

DeJong, Meindert 1906-1991 . . . . DLB-52

Dekker, Thomas circa 1572-1632 . . . . . . DLB-62, 172; CDBLB-1

Delacorte, George T., Jr. 1894-1991 . . . . . . DLB-91

Delafield, E. M. 1890-1943 . . . . DLB-34

Delahaye, Guy (Guillaume Lahaise) 1888-1969 . . . . DLB-92

de la Mare, Walter 1873-1956 . . . . DLB-19, 153, 162, 255; CDBLB-6

Deland, Margaret 1857-1945 . . . . DLB-78

Delaney, Shelagh 1939- DLB-13; CDBLB-8

Delano, Amasa 1763-1823 . . . . DLB-183

Delany, Martin Robinson 1812-1885 . . . . . . DLB-50

Delany, Samuel R. 1942- DLB-8, 33

de la Roche, Mazo 1879-1961 . . . . DLB-68

Delavigne, Jean François Casimir 1793-1843 . . . . DLB-192

Delbanco, Nicholas 1942- DLB-6, 234

Delblanc, Sven 1931-1992 . . . . DLB-257

Del Castillo, Ramón 1949- DLB-209

Deledda, Grazia 1871-1936 . . . . DLB-264, 329

De León, Nephtal 1945- DLB-82

Deleuze, Gilles 1925-1995 . . . . DLB-296

Delfini, Antonio 1907-1963 . . . . DLB-264

Delgado, Abelardo Barrientos 1931- DLB-82

Del Giudice, Daniele 1949- DLB-196

De Libero, Libero 1906-1981 . . . . DLB-114

Delibes, Miguel 1920- DLB-322

Delicado, Francisco circa 1475-circa 1540? DLB-318

DeLillo, Don 1936- DLB-6, 173

de Lint, Charles 1951- DLB-251

de Lisser H. G. 1878-1944 . . . . DLB-117

Dell, Floyd 1887-1969 . . . . DLB-9

Dell Publishing Company DLB-46

delle Grazie, Marie Eugene 1864-1931 . . . . DLB-81

Deloney, Thomas died 1600 . . . . DLB-167

Deloria, Ella C. 1889-1971 . . . . DLB-175

Deloria, Vine, Jr. 1933- DLB-175

del Rey, Lester 1915-1993 . . . . DLB-8

Del Vecchio, John M. 1947- DS-9

Del'vig, Anton Antonovich 1798-1831 . . . . DLB-205

de Man, Paul 1919-1983 . . . . DLB-67

DeMarinis, Rick 1934- DLB-218

Demby, William 1922- DLB-33

De Mille, James 1833-1880 . . . . DLB-99, 251

de Mille, William 1878-1955 . . . . DLB-266

Deming, Philander 1829-1915 . . . . DLB-74

Deml, Jakub 1878-1961 . . . . DLB-215

Demorest, William Jennings 1822-1895 . . . . DLB-79

De Morgan, William 1839-1917 . . . . DLB-153

Demosthenes 384 B.C.-322 B.C. DLB-176

Henry Denham [publishing house] DLB-170

Denham, Sir John 1615-1669 . . . . DLB-58, 126

Denison, Merrill 1893-1975 . . . . DLB-92

T. S. Denison and Company DLB-49

Dennery, Adolphe Philippe 1811-1899 . . . DLB-192

Dennie, Joseph 1768-1812 . . . . . DLB-37, 43, 59, 73

Dennis, C. J. 1876-1938 . . . . DLB-260

Dennis, John 1658-1734 . . . . DLB-101

Dennis, Nigel 1912-1989 . . . . DLB-13, 15, 233

Denslow, W. W. 1856-1915 . . . . DLB-188

Dent, J. M., and Sons DLB-112

Cumulative Index

Dent, Lester 1904-1959 .... DLB-306
Dent, Tom 1932-1998................. DLB-38
Denton, Daniel circa 1626-1703 .... DLB-24
DePaola, Tomie 1934- DLB-61
De Quille, Dan 1829-1898 .... DLB-186
De Quincey, Thomas
   1785-1859......... DLB-110, 144; CDBLB-3
   "Rhetoric" (1828; revised, 1859)
     [excerpt].................... DLB-57
   "Style" (1840; revised, 1859)
     [excerpt].................... DLB-57
Derby, George Horatio 1823-1861 .... DLB-11
J. C. Derby and Company DLB-49
Derby and Miller DLB-49
De Ricci, Seymour 1881-1942 .... DLB-201
Derleth, August 1909-1971 .... DLB-9; DS-17
Derrida, Jacques 1930-2004 .... DLB-242
The Derrydale Press.................. DLB-46
Derzhavin, Gavriil Romanovich
   1743-1816..................... DLB-150
Desai, Anita 1937- DLB-271, 323
Desani, G. V. 1909-2000.............. DLB-323
Desaulniers, Gonzalve 1863-1934........ DLB-92
Desbordes-Valmore, Marceline
   1786-1859..................... DLB-217
Descartes, René 1596-1650 .... DLB-268
Deschamps, Emile 1791-1871 .... DLB-217
Deschamps, Eustache 1340?-1404 ...... DLB-208
Desbiens, Jean-Paul 1927- DLB-53
des Forêts, Louis-Rene 1918-2001 .... DLB-83
Deshpande, Shashi 1938- DLB-323
Desiato, Luca 1941- DLB-196
Desjardins, Marie-Catherine
   (see Villedieu, Madame de)
Desnica, Vladan 1905-1967 .... DLB-181
Desnos, Robert 1900-1945 .... DLB-258
Des Périers, Bonaventure
   1510?-1543?.................... DLB-327
Desportes, Philippe 1546-1606 .... DLB-327
DesRochers, Alfred 1901-1978 .... DLB-68
Des Roches, Madeleine 1520?-1587? and
   Catherine des Roches 1542-1587?..... DLB-327
Des Roches, Madeleine
   1520?-1587?.................... DLB-327
Desrosiers, Léo-Paul 1896-1967 .... DLB-68
Dessaulles, Louis-Antoine 1819-1895 ..... DLB-99
Dessì, Giuseppe 1909-1977 ....DLB-177
Destouches, Louis-Ferdinand
   (see Céline, Louis-Ferdinand)
Desvignes, Lucette 1926- DLB-321
DeSylva, Buddy 1895-1950 .... DLB-265
De Tabley, Lord 1835-1895 .... DLB-35
Deutsch, Babette 1895-1982........... DLB-45

Deutsch, Niklaus Manuel
   (see Manuel, Niklaus)
André Deutsch Limited DLB-112
Devanny, Jean 1894-1962............. DLB-260
Deveaux, Alexis 1948- DLB-38
De Vere, Aubrey 1814-1902 .... DLB-35
Devereux, second Earl of Essex, Robert
   1565-1601 .... DLB-136
The Devin-Adair Company DLB-46
De Vinne, Theodore Low
   1828-1914 .... DLB-187
Devlin, Anne 1951- DLB-245
DeVoto, Bernard 1897-1955 .... DLB-9, 256
De Vries, Peter 1910-1993 ....DLB-6; Y-82
   Tribute to Albert Erskine............. Y-93
Dewart, Edward Hartley 1828-1903...... DLB-99
Dewdney, Christopher 1951- DLB-60
Dewdney, Selwyn 1909-1979 .... DLB-68
Dewey, John 1859-1952 ....DLB-246, 270
Dewey, Orville 1794-1882............. DLB-243
Dewey, Thomas B. 1915-1981 .... DLB-226
DeWitt, Robert M., Publisher DLB-49
DeWolfe, Fiske and Company DLB-49
Dexter, Colin 1930- DLB-87
de Young, M. H. 1849-1925 .... DLB-25
Dhlomo, H. I. E. 1903-1956........DLB-157, 225
Dhu al-Rummah (Abu al-Harith Ghaylan ibn 'Uqbah)
   circa 696-circa 735 .... DLB-311
Dhuoda circa 803-after 843 .... DLB-148
The Dial 1840-1844 .... DLB-223
The Dial Press DLB-46
"Dialogue entre un prêtre et un moribond,"
   Marquis de Sade................. DLB-314
Diamond, I. A. L. 1920-1988 .... DLB-26
Dias Gomes, Alfredo 1922-1999........ DLB-307
Díaz del Castillo, Bernal
   circa 1496-1584 .... DLB-318
Dibble, L. Grace 1902-1998 .... DLB-204
Dibdin, Thomas Frognall
   1776-1847..................... DLB-184
Di Cicco, Pier Giorgio 1949- DLB-60
Dick, Philip K. 1928-1982 .... DLB-8
Dick and Fitzgerald.................. DLB-49
Dickens, Charles 1812-1870
   .... DLB-21, 55, 70, 159,
               166; DS-5; CDBLB-4
Dickey, Eric Jerome 1961- DLB-292
Dickey, James 1923-1997 .... DLB-5, 193;
   Y-82, 93, 96, 97; DS-7, 19; CDALB-6
   James Dickey and Stanley Burnshaw
     Correspondence Y-02
   James Dickey at Seventy–A Tribute Y-93
   James Dickey, American Poet........... Y-96
   The James Dickey Society Y-99

   The Life of James Dickey: A Lecture to
     the Friends of the Emory Libraries,
     by Henry Hart................... Y-98
   Tribute to Archibald MacLeish Y-82
   Tribute to Malcolm Cowley Y-89
   Tribute to Truman Capote............. Y-84
   Tributes [to Dickey] Y-97
Dickey, William 1928-1994 .... DLB-5
Dickinson, Emily
   1830-1886 .... DLB-1, 243; CDALB-3
Dickinson, John 1732-1808.............. DLB-31
Dickinson, Jonathan 1688-1747 .... DLB-24
Dickinson, Patric 1914-1994............ DLB-27
Dickinson, Peter 1927- DLB-87, 161, 276
John Dicks [publishing house] DLB-106
Dickson, Gordon R. 1923-2001 .... DLB-8
Dictionary of Literary Biography
   Annual Awards for *Dictionary of
   Literary Biography* Editors and
   Contributors Y-98–02
*Dictionary of Literary Biography
   Yearbook* Awards...........Y-92–93, 97–02
The Dictionary of National Biography DLB-144
Diderot, Denis 1713-1784 .... DLB-313
   "The Encyclopedia"................ DLB-314
Didion, Joan 1934-
   .... DLB-2, 173, 185; Y-81, 86; CDALB-6
Di Donato, Pietro 1911-1992 .... DLB-9
Die Fürstliche Bibliothek Corvey Y-96
Diego, Gerardo 1896-1987 .... DLB-134
Dietz, Howard 1896-1983............. DLB-265
Díez, Luis Mateo 1942- DLB-322
Digby, Everard 1550?-1605 .... DLB-281
Digges, Thomas circa 1546-1595 .... DLB-136
The Digital Millennium Copyright Act:
   Expanding Copyright Protection in
   Cyberspace and Beyond Y-98
Diktonius, Elmer 1896-1961........... DLB-259
Dillard, Annie 1945- DLB-275, 278; Y-80
Dillard, R. H. W. 1937- DLB-5, 244
Charles T. Dillingham Company DLB-49
G. W. Dillingham Company........... DLB-49
Edward and Charles Dilly
   [publishing house] DLB-154
Dilthey, Wilhelm 1833-1911........... DLB-129
Dimitrova, Blaga 1922- DLB-181; CDWLB-4
Dimov, Dimitr 1909-1966............. DLB-181
Dimsdale, Thomas J. 1831?-1866....... DLB-186
Dinescu, Mircea 1950- DLB-232
Dinesen, Isak (see Blixen, Karen)
Ding Ling 1904-1986 .... DLB-328
Dingelstedt, Franz von 1814-1881 ...... DLB-133
Dinis, Júlio (Joaquim Guilherme
   Gomes Coelho) 1839-1871......... DLB-287
Dintenfass, Mark 1941- Y-84

Diogenes, Jr. (see Brougham, John)

Diogenes Laertius circa 200 . . . . DLB-176

DiPrima, Diane 1934- DLB-5, 16

Disch, Thomas M. 1940- DLB-8, 282

"Le Discours sur le style," Georges-Louis Leclerc de Buffon DLB-314

Disgrace, 1999 Booker Prize winner, J. M. Coetzee DLB-326

Diski, Jenny 1947- DLB-271

Disney, Walt 1901-1966 . . . . DLB-22

Disraeli, Benjamin 1804-1881 . . . . . . DLB-21, 55

D'Israeli, Isaac 1766-1848 . . . . DLB-107

DLB Award for Distinguished Literary Criticism Y-02

Ditlevsen, Tove 1917-1976 . . . . DLB-214

Ditzen, Rudolf (see Fallada, Hans)

Divakaruni, Chitra Banerjee 1956- DLB-323

Dix, Dorothea Lynde 1802-1887 . . . . . . DLB-1, 235

Dix, Dorothy (see Gilmer, Elizabeth Meriwether)

Dix, Edwards and Company DLB-49

Dix, Gertrude circa 1874-? DLB-197

Dixie, Florence Douglas 1857-1905 . . . . . DLB-174

Dixon, Ella Hepworth 1855 or 1857-1932 . . . . DLB-197

Dixon, Paige (see Corcoran, Barbara)

Dixon, Richard Watson 1833-1900 . . . . DLB-19

Dixon, Stephen 1936- DLB-130

DLB Award for Distinguished Literary Criticism Y-02

Dmitriev, Andrei Viktorovich 1956- DLB-285

Dmitriev, Ivan Ivanovich 1760-1837 . . . . . DLB-150

Dobell, Bertram 1842-1914 . . . . DLB-184

Dobell, Sydney 1824-1874 . . . . DLB-32

Dobie, J. Frank 1888-1964 . . . . DLB-212

Dobles Yzaguirre, Julieta 1943- DLB-283

Döblin, Alfred 1878-1957 . . . . . DLB-66; CDWLB-2

Dobroliubov, Nikolai Aleksandrovich 1836-1861 . . . . DLB-277

Dobson, Austin 1840-1921 . . . . DLB-35, 144

Dobson, Rosemary 1920- DLB-260

Doctorow, E. L. 1931- DLB-2, 28, 173; Y-80; CDALB-6

Dodd, Susan M. 1946- DLB-244

Dodd, William E. 1869-1940 . . . . DLB-17

Anne Dodd [publishing house] DLB-154

Dodd, Mead and Company DLB-49

Doderer, Heimito von 1896-1966 . . . . DLB-85

B. W. Dodge and Company DLB-46

Dodge, Mary Abigail 1833-1896 . . . . DLB-221

Dodge, Mary Mapes 1831?-1905 . . . . DLB-42, 79; DS-13

Dodge Publishing Company DLB-49

Dodgson, Charles Lutwidge (see Carroll, Lewis)

Dodsley, Robert 1703-1764 . . . . DLB-95

R. Dodsley [publishing house] DLB-154

Dodson, Owen 1914-1983 . . . . DLB-76

Dodwell, Christina 1951- DLB-204

Doesticks, Q. K. Philander, P. B. (see Thomson, Mortimer)

Doheny, Carrie Estelle 1875-1958 . . . . . . DLB-140

Doherty, John 1798?-1854 . . . . DLB-190

Doig, Ivan 1939- DLB-206

Doinaş, Ştefan Augustin 1922- DLB-232

Dolet, Etienne 1509-1546 . . . . DLB-327

Domínguez, Sylvia Maida 1935- DLB-122

Donaghy, Michael 1954- DLB-282

Patrick Donahoe [publishing house] DLB-49

Donald, David H. 1920- DLB-17; Y-87

Donaldson, Scott 1928- DLB-111

Doni, Rodolfo 1919- DLB-177

Donleavy, J. P. 1926- DLB-6, 173

Donnadieu, Marguerite (see Duras, Marguerite)

Donne, John 1572-1631 . . . . DLB-121, 151; CDBLB-1

Donnelly, Ignatius 1831-1901 . . . . DLB-12

R. R. Donnelley and Sons Company DLB-49

Donoghue, Emma 1969- DLB-267

Donohue and Henneberry DLB-49

Donoso, José 1924-1996 . . . . DLB-113; CDWLB-3

M. Doolady [publishing house] DLB-49

Dooley, Ebon (see Ebon)

Doolittle, Hilda 1886-1961 . . . . . DLB-4, 45; DS-15

Doplicher, Fabio 1938- DLB-128

Dor, Milo 1923- DLB-85

George H. Doran Company DLB-46

Dorat, Jean 1508-1588 . . . . DLB-327

Dorcey, Mary 1950- DLB-319

Dorgelès, Roland 1886-1973 . . . . DLB-65

Dorn, Edward 1929-1999 . . . . DLB-5

Dorr, Rheta Childe 1866-1948 . . . . DLB-25

Dorris, Michael 1945-1997 . . . . DLB-175

Dorset and Middlesex, Charles Sackville, Lord Buckhurst, Earl of 1643-1706 . . . . DLB-131

Dorsey, Candas Jane 1952- DLB-251

Dorst, Tankred 1925- DLB-75, 124

Dos Passos, John 1896-1970 . . . . DLB-4, 9, 316; DS-1, 15; CDALB-5

  John Dos Passos: A Centennial Commemoration Y-96

  John Dos Passos: Artist Y-99

  John Dos Passos Newsletter Y-00

  U.S.A. (Documentary) DLB-274

Dostoevsky, Fyodor 1821-1881 . . . . DLB-238

Doubleday and Company DLB-49

Doubrovsky, Serge 1928- DLB-299

Dougall, Lily 1858-1923 . . . . DLB-92

Doughty, Charles M. 1843-1926 . . . . DLB-19, 57, 174

Douglas, Lady Alfred (see Custance, Olive)

Douglas, Ellen (Josephine Ayres Haxton) 1921- DLB-292

Douglas, Gavin 1476-1522 . . . . DLB-132

Douglas, Keith 1920-1944 . . . . DLB-27

Douglas, Norman 1868-1952 . . . . DLB-34, 195

Douglass, Frederick 1817-1895 . . . . DLB-1, 43, 50, 79, 243; CDALB-2

  Frederick Douglass Creative Arts Center   Y-01

Douglass, William circa 1691-1752 . . . . . . DLB-24

Dourado, Autran 1926- DLB-145, 307

Dove, Arthur G. 1880-1946 . . . . DLB-188

Dove, Rita 1952- DLB-120; CDALB-7

Dover Publications DLB-46

Doves Press DLB-112

Dovlatov, Sergei Donatovich 1941-1990 . . . . DLB-285

Dowden, Edward 1843-1913 . . . . DLB-35, 149

Dowell, Coleman 1925-1985 . . . . DLB-130

Dowland, John 1563-1626 . . . . DLB-172

Downes, Gwladys 1915- DLB-88

Downing, J., Major (see Davis, Charles A.)

Downing, Major Jack (see Smith, Seba)

Dowriche, Anne before 1560-after 1613 . . . . DLB-172

Dowson, Ernest 1867-1900 . . . . DLB-19, 135

William Doxey [publishing house] DLB-49

Doyle, Sir Arthur Conan 1859-1930 . . . DLB-18, 70, 156, 178; CDBLB-5

  The Priory Scholars of New York Y-99

Doyle, Kirby 1932- DLB-16

Doyle, Roddy 1958- DLB-194, 326

Drabble, Margaret 1939- DLB-14, 155, 231; CDBLB-8

  Tribute to Graham Greene Y-91

Drach, Albert 1902-1995 . . . . DLB-85

Drachmann, Holger 1846-1908 . . . . DLB-300

Dracula (Documentary) DLB-304

Dragojević, Danijel 1934- DLB-181

Dragún, Osvaldo 1929-1999 . . . . DLB-305

Drake, Samuel Gardner 1798-1875 . . . . . . DLB-187

Drama (*See* Theater)

The Dramatic Publishing Company DLB-49

Dramatists Play Service DLB-46

Drant, Thomas early 1540s?-1578 . . . . DLB-167

Draper, John W. 1811-1882 . . . . DLB-30

Draper, Lyman C. 1815-1891 . . . . DLB-30

Drayton, Michael 1563-1631 . . . . DLB-121

Dreiser, Theodore 1871-1945 . . . . DLB-9, 12, 102, 137; DS-1; CDALB-3

491

Cumulative Index

The International Theodore Dreiser
Society........................... Y-01

Notes from the Underground
of *Sister Carrie*.................... Y-01

Dresser, Davis 1904-1977............. DLB-226

Drew, Elizabeth A.
"A Note on Technique" [excerpt]
(1926)....................... DLB-36

Drewe, Robert 1943-................. DLB-325

Drewitz, Ingeborg 1923-1986.......... DLB-75

Drieu La Rochelle, Pierre 1893-1945..... DLB-72

Drinker, Elizabeth 1735-1807.......... DLB-200

Drinkwater, John 1882-1937.....DLB-10, 19, 149

The Friends of the Dymock Poets....... Y-00

Droste-Hülshoff, Annette von
1797-1848............ DLB-133; CDWLB-2

The Drue Heinz Literature Prize
Excerpt from "Excerpts from a Report
of the Commission," in David
Bosworth's *The Death of Descartes*
An Interview with David Bosworth....... Y-82

Drummond, William, of Hawthornden
1585-1649................ DLB-121, 213

Drummond, William Henry 1854-1907... DLB-92

Drummond de Andrade, Carlos
1902-1987..................... DLB-307

Druzhinin, Aleksandr Vasil'evich
1824-1864..................... DLB-238

Druzhnikov, Yuri 1933-............... DLB-317

Dryden, Charles 1860?-1931...........DLB-171

Dryden, John
1631-1700...... DLB-80, 101, 131; CDBLB-2

Držić, Marin
circa 1508-1567........DLB-147; CDWLB-4

Duane, William 1760-1835............. DLB-43

Du Bartas, Guillaume 1544-1590....... DLB-327

Dubé, Marcel 1930-................. DLB-53

Dubé, Rodolphe (see Hertel, François)

Du Bellay, Joachim 1522?-1560........ DLB-327

Dubie, Norman 1945-................ DLB-120

Dubin, Al 1891-1945................. DLB-265

Du Boccage, Anne-Marie 1710-1802..... DLB-313

Dubois, Silvia 1788 or 1789?-1889....... DLB-239

Du Bois, W. E. B.
1868-1963....DLB-47, 50, 91, 246; CDALB-3

Du Bois, William Pène 1916-1993....... DLB-61

Dubrovina, Ekaterina Oskarovna
1846-1913..................... DLB-238

Dubus, Andre 1936-1999............. DLB-130

Tribute to Michael M. Rea............ Y-97

Dubus, Andre, III 1959-.............. DLB-292

Ducange, Victor 1783-1833............ DLB-192

Du Chaillu, Paul Belloni 1831?-1903.... DLB-189

Ducharme, Réjean 1941-.............. DLB-60

Dučić, Jovan 1871-1943.....DLB-147; CDWLB-4

Duck, Stephen 1705?-1756............. DLB-95

Gerald Duckworth and Company
Limited...................... DLB-112

Duclaux, Madame Mary (see Robinson, A. Mary F.)

Dudek, Louis 1918-2001.............. DLB-88

Dudintsev, Vladimir Dmitrievich
1918-1998..................... DLB-302

Dudley-Smith, Trevor (see Hall, Adam)

Duell, Sloan and Pearce.............. DLB-46

Duerer, Albrecht 1471-1528...........DLB-179

Duff Gordon, Lucie 1821-1869......... DLB-166

Dufferin, Helen Lady, Countess of Gifford
1807-1867..................... DLB-199

Duffield and Green.................. DLB-46

Duffy, Maureen 1933-............ DLB-14, 310

Dufief, Nicholas Gouin 1776-1834....... DLB-187

Dufresne, John 1948-................ DLB-292

Dugan, Alan 1923-2003............... DLB-5

Dugard, William 1606-1662........DLB-170, 281

William Dugard [publishing house]......DLB-170

Dugas, Marcel 1883-1947............. DLB-92

William Dugdale [publishing house]..... DLB-106

Du Guillet, Pernette 1520?-1545........ DLB-327

Duhamel, Georges 1884-1966.......... DLB-65

Dujardin, Edouard 1861-1949......... DLB-123

Dukes, Ashley 1885-1959............. DLB-10

Dumas, Alexandre *fils* 1824-1895....... DLB-192

Dumas, Alexandre *père* 1802-1870..... DLB-119, 192

Dumas, Henry 1934-1968............. DLB-41

du Maurier, Daphne 1907-1989........ DLB-191

Du Maurier, George 1834-1896.....DLB-153, 178

Dummett, Michael 1925-............ DLB-262

Dunbar, Paul Laurence
1872-1906........ DLB-50, 54, 78; CDALB-3

Introduction to *Lyrics of Lowly Life* (1896),
by William Dean Howells........ DLB-50

Dunbar, William
circa 1460-circa 1522......... DLB-132, 146

Duncan, Dave 1933-................ DLB-251

Duncan, David James 1952-.......... DLB-256

Duncan, Norman 1871-1916.......... DLB-92

Duncan, Quince 1940-............... DLB-145

Duncan, Robert 1919-1988........ DLB-5, 16, 193

Duncan, Ronald 1914-1982............ DLB-13

Duncan, Sara Jeannette 1861-1922....... DLB-92

Dunigan, Edward, and Brother........ DLB-49

Dunlap, John 1747-1812.............. DLB-43

Dunlap, William 1766-1839.......DLB-30, 37, 59

Dunlop, William "Tiger" 1792-1848...... DLB-99

Dunmore, Helen 1952-............... DLB-267

Dunn, Douglas 1942-................ DLB-40

Dunn, Harvey Thomas 1884-1952...... DLB-188

Dunn, Stephen 1939-................ DLB-105

"The Good, The Not So Good".... DLB-105

Dunne, Dominick 1925-............ DLB-306

Dunne, Finley Peter 1867-1936........ DLB-11, 23

Dunne, John Gregory 1932-............ Y-80

Dunne, Philip 1908-1992.............. DLB-26

Dunning, Ralph Cheever 1878-1930...... DLB-4

Dunning, William A. 1857-1922..........DLB-17

Duns Scotus, John circa 1266-1308..... DLB-115

Dunsany, Lord (Edward John Moreton
Drax Plunkett, Baron Dunsany)
1878-1957........ DLB-10, 77, 153, 156, 255

Dunton, W. Herbert 1878-1936........ DLB-188

John Dunton [publishing house]........DLB-170

Dupin, Amantine-Aurore-Lucile (see Sand, George)

Du Pont de Nemours, Pierre Samuel
1739-1817..................... DLB-313

Dupuy, Eliza Ann 1814-1880.......... DLB-248

Durack, Mary 1913-1994............. DLB-260

Durand, Lucile (see Bersianik, Louky)

Duranti, Francesca 1935-............ DLB-196

Duranty, Walter 1884-1957........... DLB-29

Duras, Marguerite (Marguerite Donnadieu)
1914-1996................ DLB-83, 321

Durfey, Thomas 1653-1723........... DLB-80

Durova, Nadezhda Andreevna
(Aleksandr Andreevich Aleksandrov)
1783-1866..................... DLB-198

Durrell, Lawrence 1912-1990
.... DLB-15, 27, 204; Y-90; CDBLB-7

William Durrell [publishing house]...... DLB-49

Dürrenmatt, Friedrich
1921-1990.........DLB-69, 124; CDWLB-2

Duston, Hannah 1657-1737............ DLB-200

Dutt, Toru 1856-1877................ DLB-240

E. P. Dutton and Company........... DLB-49

Duun, Olav 1876-1939............... DLB-297

Duvoisin, Roger 1904-1980............ DLB-61

Duyckinck, Evert Augustus
1816-1878................. DLB-3, 64, 250

Duyckinck, George L.
1823-1863.................. DLB-3, 250

Duyckinck and Company............. DLB-49

Dwight, John Sullivan 1813-1893..... DLB-1, 235

Dwight, Timothy 1752-1817............ DLB-37

America: or, A Poem on the Settlement
of the British Colonies, by
Timothy Dwight.............. DLB-37

Dybek, Stuart 1942-................. DLB-130

Tribute to Michael M. Rea............ Y-97

Dyer, Charles 1928-................. DLB-13

Dyer, Sir Edward 1543-1607...........DLB-136

Dyer, George 1755-1841.............. DLB-93

Dyer, John 1699-1757................ DLB-95

Dyk, Viktor 1877-1931............... DLB-215

Dylan, Bob 1941-................... DLB-16

E

Eager, Edward 1911-1964 . . . . .DLB-22

Eagleton, Terry 1943- DLB-242

Eames, Wilberforce
   1855-1937 . . . . .DLB-140

Earle, Alice Morse
   1853-1911 . . . . .DLB-221

Earle, John 1600 or 1601-1665 . . . . .DLB-151

James H. Earle and Company DLB-49

East Europe
   Independence and Destruction,
     1918-1941 .DLB-220

   Social Theory and Ethnography:
     Language and Ethnicity in
     Western versus Eastern Man DLB-220

Eastlake, William 1917-1997 . . . . .DLB-6, 206

Eastman, Carol ?- .DLB-44

Eastman, Charles A. (Ohiyesa)
   1858-1939 . . . . .DLB-175

Eastman, Max 1883-1969 . . . . .DLB-91

Eaton, Daniel Isaac 1753-1814 . . . . .DLB-158

Eaton, Edith Maude 1865-1914 . . . . .DLB-221, 312

Eaton, Winnifred 1875-1954 . . . . . . .DLB-221, 312

Eberhart, Richard 1904-2005 . . .DLB-48; CDALB-1

   Tribute to Robert Penn Warren Y-89

Ebner, Jeannie 1918-2004 . . . . .DLB-85

Ebner-Eschenbach, Marie von
   1830-1916 . . . . .DLB-81

Ebon 1942- DLB-41

E-Books' Second Act in Libraries Y-02

Ecbasis Captivi circa 1045 . . . . .DLB-148

Ecco Press DLB-46

Echegaray, José 1832-1916 . . . . .DLB-329

Eckhart, Meister circa 1260-circa 1328 . . .DLB-115

The Eclectic Review 1805-1868 . . . . .DLB-110

Eco, Umberto 1932- DLB-196, 242

Eddison, E. R. 1882-1945 . . . . .DLB-255

Edel, Leon 1907-1997 . . . . .DLB-103

Edelfeldt, Inger 1956- DLB-257

J. M. Edelstein's Collection of Twentieth-
   Century American Poetry (A Century of Poetry,
   a Lifetime of Collecting) Y-02

Edes, Benjamin 1732-1803 . . . . .DLB-43

Edgar, David 1948- DLB-13, 233

   Viewpoint: Politics and
     Performance DLB-13

Edgerton, Clyde 1944- DLB-278

Edgeworth, Maria
   1768-1849 . . . . .DLB-116, 159, 163

The Edinburgh Review 1802-1929 . . . . .DLB-110

Edinburgh University Press DLB-112

Editing
   Conversations with Editors Y-95

   Editorial Statements DLB-137

   The Editorial Style of Fredson Bowers Y-91

Editorial: The Extension of Copyright Y-02

   We See the Editor at Work Y-97

   Whose *Ulysses*? The Function of Editing . . .Y-97

The Editor Publishing Company DLB-49

Editorial Institute at Boston University Y-00

Edmonds, Helen Woods Ferguson
   (see Kavan, Anna)

Edmonds, Randolph 1900-1983 . . . . .DLB-51

Edmonds, Walter D. 1903-1998 . . . . .DLB-9

Edric, Robert (see Armitage, G. E.)

Edschmid, Kasimir 1890-1966 . . . . .DLB-56

Edson, Margaret 1961- DLB-266

Edson, Russell 1935- DLB-244

Edwards, Amelia Anne Blandford
   1831-1892 . . . . .DLB-174

Edwards, Dic 1953- DLB-245

Edwards, Edward 1812-1886 . . . . .DLB-184

Edwards, Jonathan 1703-1758 . . . . . .DLB-24, 270

Edwards, Jonathan, Jr. 1745-1801 . . . . . . .DLB-37

Edwards, Junius 1929- DLB-33

Edwards, Matilda Barbara Betham
   1836-1919 . . . . .DLB-174

Edwards, Richard 1524-1566 . . . . .DLB-62

Edwards, Sarah Pierpont 1710-1758 . . . . .DLB-200

James Edwards [publishing house] DLB-154

Effinger, George Alec 1947- DLB-8

Egerton, George 1859-1945 . . . . .DLB-135

Eggleston, Edward 1837-1902 . . . . .DLB-12

Eggleston, Wilfred 1901-1986 . . . . .DLB-92

Eglītis, Anšlavs 1906-1993 . . . . .DLB-220

Eguren, José María 1874-1942 . . . . .DLB-290

Ehrenreich, Barbara 1941- DLB-246

Ehrenstein, Albert 1886-1950 . . . . .DLB-81

Ehrhart, W. D. 1948- DS-9

Ehrlich, Gretel 1946- DLB-212, 275

Eich, Günter 1907-1972 . . . . .DLB-69, 124

Eichendorff, Joseph Freiherr von
   1788-1857 . . . . .DLB-90

Eifukumon'in 1271-1342 . . . . .DLB-203

Eigner, Larry 1926-1996 . . . . .DLB-5, 193

Eikon Basilike 1649 . . . . .DLB-151

Eilhart von Oberge
   circa 1140-circa 1195 . . . . .DLB-148

Einar Benediktsson 1864-1940 . . . . .DLB-293

Einar Kárason 1955- DLB-293

Einar Már Guðmundsson 1954- DLB-293

Einhard circa 770-840 . . . . .DLB-148

Eiseley, Loren 1907-1977 . . . . . . .DLB-275, DS-17

Eisenberg, Deborah 1945- DLB-244

Eisenreich, Herbert 1925-1986 . . . . .DLB-85

Eisner, Kurt 1867-1919 . . . . .DLB-66

Ekelöf, Gunnar 1907-1968 . . . . .DLB-259

Eklund, Gordon 1945- Y-83

Ekman, Kerstin 1933- DLB-257

Ekwensi, Cyprian 1921- . . .DLB-117; CDWLB-3

Elaw, Zilpha circa 1790-? DLB-239

George Eld [publishing house] DLB-170

Elder, Lonne, III 1931- DLB-7, 38, 44

Paul Elder and Company DLB-49

Eldershaw, Flora (M. Barnard Eldershaw)
   1897-1956 . . . . .DLB-260

Eldershaw, M. Barnard (see Barnard, Marjorie and
   Eldershaw, Flora)

The Elected Member, 1970 Booker Prize winner,
   Bernice Rubens DLB-326

The Electronic Text Center and the Electronic
   Archive of Early American Fiction at the
   University of Virginia Library Y-98

Eliade, Mircea 1907-1986 . . . .DLB-220; CDWLB-4

Elie, Robert 1915-1973 . . . . .DLB-88

Elin Pelin 1877-1949 . . . . .DLB-147; CDWLB-4

Eliot, George
   1819-1880 . . . . .DLB-21, 35, 55; CDBLB-4

   The George Eliot Fellowship Y-99

Eliot, John 1604-1690 . . . . .DLB-24

Eliot, T. S. 1888-1965
    . . . . . . DLB-7, 10, 45, 63, 245, 329; CDALB-5

   T. S. Eliot Centennial: The Return
     of the Old Possum Y-88

   The T. S. Eliot Society: Celebration and
     Scholarship, 1980-1999 . . . . .Y-99

Eliot's Court Press DLB-170

Elizabeth I 1533-1603 . . . . .DLB-136

Elizabeth von Nassau-Saarbrücken
   after 1393-1456 . . . . .DLB-179

Elizondo, Salvador 1932- DLB-145

Elizondo, Sergio 1930- DLB-82

Elkin, Stanley
   1930-1995 . . . . .DLB-2, 28, 218, 278; Y-80

Elles, Dora Amy (see Wentworth, Patricia)

Ellet, Elizabeth F. 1818?-1877 . . . . .DLB-30

Elliot, Ebenezer 1781-1849 . . . . .DLB-96, 190

Elliot, Frances Minto (Dickinson)
   1820-1898 . . . . .DLB-166

Elliott, Charlotte 1789-1871 . . . . .DLB-199

Elliott, George 1923- DLB-68

Elliott, George P. 1918-1980 . . . . .DLB-244

Elliott, Janice 1931-1995 . . . . .DLB-14

Elliott, Sarah Barnwell 1848-1928 . . . . . . .DLB-221

Elliott, Sumner Locke 1917-1991 . . . . . . .DLB-289

Elliott, Thomes and Talbot DLB-49

Elliott, William, III 1788-1863 . . . . .DLB-3, 248

Ellin, Stanley 1916-1986 . . . . .DLB-306

Ellis, Alice Thomas (Anna Margaret Haycraft)
   1932- DLB-194

Ellis, Bret Easton 1964- DLB-292

Ellis, Edward S. 1840-1916 . . . . .DLB-42

Cumulative Index DLB 329

Frederick Staridge Ellis
   [publishing house] DLB-106

Ellis, George E.
   "The New Controversy Concerning
   Miracles........................DS-5

The George H. Ellis Company......... DLB-49

Ellis, Havelock 1859-1939 .... DLB-190

Ellison, Harlan 1934- DLB-8

   Tribute to Isaac Asimov............... Y-92

Ellison, Ralph
   1914-1994.... DLB-2, 76, 227; Y-94; CDALB-1

Ellmann, Richard 1918-1987 ...... DLB-103; Y-87

Ellroy, James 1948- DLB-226; Y-91

   Tribute to John D. MacDonald Y-86

   Tribute to Raymond Chandler.......... Y-88

Eluard, Paul 1895-1952 .... DLB-258

Elyot, Thomas 1490?-1546............ DLB-136

Elytis, Odysseus 1911-1996 .... DLB-329

Emanuel, James Andrew 1921- DLB-41

Emecheta, Buchi 1944- DLB-117; CDWLB-3

Emerson, Ralph Waldo
   1803-1882 ..... DLB-1, 59, 73, 183, 223, 270;
   DS-5; CDALB-2

   Ralph Waldo Emerson in 1982 .... Y-82

   The Ralph Waldo Emerson Society...... Y-99

Emerson, William 1769-1811 .... DLB-37

Emerson, William R. 1923-1997............ Y-97

Emin, Fedor Aleksandrovich
   circa 1735-1770.................. DLB-150

Emmanuel, Pierre 1916-1984 .... DLB-258

Empedocles fifth century B.C...........DLB-176

Empson, William 1906-1984 .... DLB-20

Enchi Fumiko 1905-1986 .... DLB-182

"The Encyclopedia," Denis Diderot DLB-314

Ende, Michael 1929-1995.............. DLB-75

Endō Shūsaku 1923-1996............. DLB-182

Engel, Marian 1933-1985.............. DLB-53

Engel'gardt, Sof'ia Vladimirovna
   1828-1894 ....DLB-277

Engels, Friedrich 1820-1895 .... DLB-129

Engle, Paul 1908-1991 .... DLB-48

   Tribute to Robert Penn Warren Y-89

English, Thomas Dunn 1819-1902...... DLB-202

The English Patient, 1992 Booker Prize winner,
   Michael Ondaatje................. DLB-326

Ennius 239 B.C.-169 B.C. DLB-211

Enquist, Per Olov 1934- DLB-257

Enright, Anne 1962- DLB-267

Enright, D. J. 1920-2002............. DLB-27

Enright, Elizabeth 1909-1968 .... DLB-22

Enright, Nick 1950-2003............. DLB-325

Epic, The Sixteenth-Century Spanish.... DLB-318

Epictetus circa 55-circa 125-130 ....DLB-176

Epicurus 342/341 B.C.-271/270 B.C. DLB-176

d'Epinay, Louise (Louise-Florence-Pétronille Tardieu
   d'Esclavelles, marquise d'Epinay)
   1726-1783..................... DLB-313

Epps, Bernard 1936- DLB-53

Epshtein, Mikhail Naumovich 1950- .. DLB-285

Epstein, Julius 1909-2000 and
   Epstein, Philip 1909-1952.......... DLB-26

Epstein, Leslie 1938- DLB-299

Editors, Conversations with Y-95

Equiano, Olaudah
   circa 1745-1797....... DLB-37, 50; CDWLB-3

   Olaudah Equiano and Unfinished
   Journeys: The Slave-Narrative
   Tradition and Twentieth-Century
   Continuities..................DLB-117

Eragny Press...................... DLB-112

Erasmus, Desiderius 1467-1536 .... DLB-136

Erba, Luciano 1922- DLB-128

Erdman, Nikolai Robertovich
   1900-1970.....................DLB-272

Erdrich, Louise
   1954- DLB-152, 175, 206; CDALB-7

Erenburg, Il'ia Grigor'evich 1891-1967 ...DLB-272

Erichsen-Brown, Gwethalyn Graham
   (see Graham, Gwethalyn)

Eriugena, John Scottus circa 810-877 .... DLB-115

Ernst, Paul 1866-1933 .... DLB-66, 118

Erofeev, Venedikt Vasil'evich
   1938-1990 .... DLB-285

Erofeev, Viktor Vladimirovich 1947- ... DLB-285

Ershov, Petr Pavlovich 1815-1869....... DLB-205

Erskine, Albert 1911-1993 .... Y-93

   At Home with Albert Erskine Y-00

Erskine, John 1879-1951............. DLB-9, 102

Erskine, Mrs. Steuart ?-1948 .... DLB-195

Ertel', Aleksandr Ivanovich
   1855-1908 .... DLB-238

Ervine, St. John Greer 1883-1971........ DLB-10

Eschenburg, Johann Joachim
   1743-1820...................... DLB-97

Escofet, Cristina 1945- DLB-305

Escoto, Julio 1944- DLB-145

Esdaile, Arundell 1880-1956........... DLB-201

Esenin, Sergei Aleksandrovich
   1895-1925 .... DLB-295

Eshleman, Clayton 1935- DLB-5

Espaillat, Rhina P. 1932- DLB-282

Espanca, Florbela 1894-1930 .... DLB-287

Espriu, Salvador 1913-1985 .... DLB-134

Ess Ess Publishing Company DLB-49

Essex House Press DLB-112

Esson, Louis 1878-1943 .... DLB-260

Essop, Ahmed 1931- DLB-225

Esterházy, Péter 1950- DLB-232; CDWLB-4

Estes, Eleanor 1906-1988 .... DLB-22

Estes and Lauriat DLB-49

Estienne, Henri II (Henricus Stephanus)
   1531-1597 .... DLB-327

Estleman, Loren D. 1952- DLB-226

Eszterhas, Joe 1944- DLB-185

Etherege, George 1636-circa 1692 .... DLB-80

Ethridge, Mark, Sr. 1896-1981 ....DLB-127

Ets, Marie Hall 1893-1984 .... DLB-22

Etter, David 1928- DLB-105

Ettner, Johann Christoph 1654-1724 .... DLB-168

Eucken, Rudolf 1846-1926............ DLB-329

Eudora Welty Remembered in
   Two Exhibits Y-02

Eugene Gant's Projected Works Y-01

Eupolemius fl. circa 1095 .... DLB-148

Euripides circa 484 B.C.-407/406 B.C.
   ....DLB-176; CDWLB-1

Evans, Augusta Jane 1835-1909 .... DLB-239

Evans, Caradoc 1878-1945 .... DLB-162

Evans, Charles 1850-1935 ....DLB-187

Evans, Donald 1884-1921 .... DLB-54

Evans, George Henry 1805-1856........ DLB-43

Evans, Hubert 1892-1986.............. DLB-92

Evans, Mari 1923- DLB-41

Evans, Mary Ann (see Eliot, George)

Evans, Nathaniel 1742-1767 .... DLB-31

Evans, Sebastian 1830-1909 .... DLB-35

Evans, Ray 1915- DLB-265

M. Evans and Company................ DLB-46

Evaristi, Marcella 1953- DLB-233

Everett, Alexander Hill 1790-1847 .... DLB-59

Everett, Edward 1794-1865........ DLB-1, 59, 235

Everson, R. G. 1903- DLB-88

Everson, William 1912-1994 ......DLB-5, 16, 212

Evreinov, Nikolai 1879-1953 ....DLB-317

Ewald, Johannes 1743-1781 .... DLB-300

Ewart, Gavin 1916-1995............... DLB-40

Ewing, Juliana Horatia 1841-1885 ... DLB-21, 163

The Examiner 1808-1881 .... DLB-110

Exley, Frederick 1929-1992 ....DLB-143; Y-81

Editorial: The Extension of Copyright....... Y-02

von Eyb, Albrecht 1420-1475 ....DLB-179

Eyre and Spottiswoode DLB-106

Ezekiel, Nissim 1924-2004 .... DLB-323

Ezera, Regīna 1930- DLB-232

Ezzo ?-after 1065 .... DLB-148

F

Faber, Frederick William 1814-1863...... DLB-32

Faber and Faber Limited DLB-112

Faccio, Rena (see Aleramo, Sibilla)

Facsimiles
    The Uses of Facsimile: A Symposium.....Y-90

Fadeev, Aleksandr Aleksandrovich
    1901-1956......................DLB-272

Fagundo, Ana María 1938- DLB-134

Fainzil'berg, Il'ia Arnol'dovich
    (see Il'f, Il'ia and Petrov, Evgenii)

Fair, Ronald L. 1932- DLB-33

Fairfax, Beatrice (see Manning, Marie)

Fairlie, Gerard 1899-1983 ....DLB-77

Faldbakken, Knut 1941- DLB-297

Falkberget, Johan (Johan Petter Lillebakken)
    1879-1967 ....DLB-297

Fallada, Hans 1893-1947 ....DLB-56

The Famished Road, 1991 Booker Prize winner,
    Ben Okri......................DLB-326

Fancher, Betsy 1928- Y-83

Fane, Violet 1843-1905 ....DLB-35

Fanfrolico Press DLB-112

Fanning, Katherine 1927- DLB-127

Fanon, Frantz 1925-1961 ....DLB-296

Fanshawe, Sir Richard 1608-1666 ....DLB-126

Fantasy Press Publishers DLB-46

Fante, John 1909-1983 ....DLB-130; Y-83

Al-Farabi circa 870-950................DLB-115

Farabough, Laura 1949- DLB-228

Farah, Nuruddin 1945- DLB-125; CDWLB-3

Farber, Norma 1909-1984 ....DLB-61

A Farewell to Arms (Documentary).......DLB-308

Fargue, Léon-Paul 1876-1947..........DLB-258

Farigoule, Louis (see Romains, Jules)

Farjeon, Eleanor 1881-1965...........DLB-160

Farley, Harriet 1812-1907.............DLB-239

Farley, Walter 1920-1989.............DLB-22

Farmborough, Florence 1887-1978.......DLB-204

Farmer, Beverley 1941- DLB-325

Farmer, Penelope 1939- DLB-161

Farmer, Philip José 1918- DLB-8

Farnaby, Thomas 1575?-1647..........DLB-236

Farningham, Marianne (see Hearn, Mary Anne)

Farquhar, George circa 1677-1707........DLB-84

Farquharson, Martha (see Finley, Martha)

Farrar, Frederic William 1831-1903......DLB-163

Farrar, Straus and Giroux DLB-46

Farrar and Rinehart...................DLB-46

Farrell, J. G. 1935-1979 ....DLB-14, 271, 326

Farrell, James T. 1904-1979 ....DLB-4, 9, 86; DS-2

Fast, Howard 1914-2003 ....DLB-9

Faulkner, William 1897-1962 ....
    DLB-9, 11, 44, 102, 316; DS-2; Y-86; CDALB-5

    Faulkner and Yoknapatawpha
        Conference, Oxford, Mississippi......Y-97

    Faulkner Centennial Addresses...........Y-97

"Faulkner 100–Celebrating the Work,"
    University of South Carolina,
    Columbia Y-97

Impressions of William Faulkner.........Y-97

William Faulkner and the People-to-People
    Program Y-86

William Faulkner Centenary
    Celebrations Y-97

The William Faulkner Society..........Y-99

George Faulkner [publishing house].....DLB-154

Faulks, Sebastian 1953- DLB-207

Fauset, Jessie Redmon 1882-1961 ....DLB-51

Faust, Frederick Schiller (Max Brand)
    1892-1944 ....DLB-256

Faust, Irvin
    1924- DLB-2, 28, 218, 278; Y-80, 00

    I Wake Up Screaming [Response to
        Ken Auletta] Y-97

    Tribute to Bernard Malamud Y-86

    Tribute to Isaac Bashevis Singer Y-91

    Tribute to Meyer Levin...............Y-81

Fawcett, Edgar 1847-1904 ....DLB-202

Fawcett, Millicent Garrett 1847-1929 ....DLB-190

Fawcett Books DLB-46

Fay, Theodore Sedgwick 1807-1898......DLB-202

Fearing, Kenneth 1902-1961 ....DLB-9

Federal Writers' Project DLB-46

Federman, Raymond 1928- Y-80

Fedin, Konstantin Aleksandrovich
    1892-1977 ....DLB-272

Fedorov, Innokentii Vasil'evich
    (see Omulevsky, Innokentii Vasil'evich)

Feiffer, Jules 1929- DLB-7, 44

Feinberg, Charles E. 1899-1988....DLB-187; Y-88

Feind, Barthold 1678-1721 ....DLB-168

Feinstein, Elaine 1930- DLB-14, 40

Feirstein, Frederick 1940- DLB-282

Feiss, Paul Louis 1875-1952 ....DLB-187

Feldman, Irving 1928- DLB-169

Felipe, Carlos 1911-1975 ....DLB-305

Felipe, Léon 1884-1968 ....DLB-108

Fell, Frederick, Publishers DLB-46

Fellowship of Southern Writers Y-98

Felltham, Owen 1602?-1668 ....DLB-126, 151

Felman, Shoshana 1942- DLB-246

Fels, Ludwig 1946- DLB-75

Felton, Cornelius Conway
    1807-1862 ....DLB-1, 235

Fel'zen, Iurii (Nikolai Berngardovich Freidenshtein)
    1894?-1943 ....DLB-317

Mothe-Fénelon, François de Salignac de la
    1651-1715 ....DLB-268

Fenn, Harry 1837-1911 ....DLB-188

Fennario, David 1947- DLB-60

Fenner, Dudley 1558?-1587? DLB-236

Fenno, Jenny 1765?-1803.............DLB-200

Fenno, John 1751-1798................DLB-43

R. F. Fenno and Company.............DLB-49

Fenoglio, Beppe 1922-1963 ....DLB-177

Fenton, Geoffrey 1539?-1608..........DLB-136

Fenton, James 1949- DLB-40

    The Hemingway/Fenton
        Correspondence Y-02

Ferber, Edna 1885-1968.......DLB-9, 28, 86, 266

Ferdinand, Vallery, III (see Salaam, Kalamu ya)

Ferguson, Sir Samuel 1810-1886 ....DLB-32

Ferguson, William Scott 1875-1954 ......DLB-47

Fergusson, Robert 1750-1774 ....DLB-109

Ferland, Albert 1872-1943 ....DLB-92

Ferlinghetti, Lawrence
    1919- DLB-5, 16; CDALB-1

    Tribute to Kenneth Rexroth Y-82

Fermor, Patrick Leigh 1915- DLB-204

Fern, Fanny (see Parton, Sara Payson Willis)

Ferrars, Elizabeth (Morna Doris Brown)
    1907-1995 ....DLB-87

Ferré, Rosario 1942- DLB-145

Ferreira, Vergílio 1916-1996...........DLB-287

E. Ferret and Company DLB-49

Ferrier, Susan 1782-1854 ....DLB-116

Ferril, Thomas Hornsby 1896-1988......DLB-206

Ferrini, Vincent 1913- DLB-48

Ferron, Jacques 1921-1985 ....DLB-60

Ferron, Madeleine 1922- DLB-53

Ferrucci, Franco 1936- DLB-196

Fet, Afanasii Afanas'evich
    1820?-1892 ....DLB-277

Fetridge and Company DLB-49

Feuchtersleben, Ernst Freiherr von
    1806-1849 ....DLB-133

Feuchtwanger, Lion 1884-1958 ....DLB-66

Feuerbach, Ludwig 1804-1872 ....DLB-133

Feuillet, Octave 1821-1890............DLB-192

Feydeau, Georges 1862-1921 ....DLB-192

Fibiger, Mathilde 1830-1872...........DLB-300

Fichte, Johann Gottlieb 1762-1814 ....DLB-90

Ficke, Arthur Davison 1883-1945 ....DLB-54

Fiction
    American Fiction and the 1930s DLB-9

    Fiction Best-Sellers, 1910-1945 ....DLB-9

    Postmodern Holocaust Fiction DLB-299

    The Year in Fiction Y-84, 86, 89, 94–99

    The Year in Fiction: A Biased View Y-83

    The Year in U.S. Fiction Y-00, 01

    The Year's Work in Fiction: A Survey Y-82

Fiedler, Leslie A. 1917-2003 ....DLB-28, 67

    Tribute to Bernard Malamud Y-86

    Tribute to James Dickey Y-97

Field, Barron 1789-1846 . . . . DLB-230
Field, Edward 1924- DLB-105
Field, Eugene 1850-1895. . DLB-23, 42, 140; DS-13
Field, John 1545?-1588. . . . . DLB-167
Field, Joseph M. 1810-1856 . . . . DLB-248
Field, Marshall, III 1893-1956 . . . . DLB-127
Field, Marshall, IV 1916-1965 . . . . DLB-127
Field, Marshall, V 1941- DLB-127
Field, Michael (Katherine Harris Bradley)
   1846-1914. . . . . DLB-240
   "The Poetry File" DLB-105
Field, Nathan 1587-1619 or 1620 . . . . DLB-58
Field, Rachel 1894-1942 . . . . DLB-9, 22
Fielding, Helen 1958- DLB-231
Fielding, Henry
   1707-1754 . . . . DLB-39, 84, 101; CDBLB-2
   "Defense of *Amelia*" (1752) DLB-39
   The History of the Adventures of Joseph Andrews
     [excerpt] (1742) DLB-39
   Letter to [Samuel] Richardson on *Clarissa*
     (1748). DLB-39
   Preface to *Joseph Andrews* (1742) DLB-39
   Preface to Sarah Fielding's *Familiar
     Letters* (1747) [excerpt] DLB-39
   Preface to Sarah Fielding's *The
     Adventures of David Simple* (1744) . . . DLB-39
   Review of *Clarissa* (1748). DLB-39
   Tom Jones (1749) [excerpt] DLB-39
Fielding, Sarah 1710-1768 . . . . DLB-39
   Preface to *The Cry* (1754) DLB-39
Fields, Annie Adams 1834-1915 . . . . DLB-221
Fields, Dorothy 1905-1974 . . . . DLB-265
Fields, James T. 1817-1881 . . . . DLB-1, 235
Fields, Julia 1938- DLB-41
Fields, Osgood and Company DLB-49
Fields, W. C. 1880-1946 . . . . DLB-44
Fierstein, Harvey 1954- DLB-266
Figes, Eva 1932- DLB-14, 271
Figuera, Angela 1902-1984 . . . . DLB-108
Filmer, Sir Robert 1586-1653 . . . . DLB-151
Filson, John circa 1753-1788 . . . . DLB-37
Finch, Anne, Countess of Winchilsea
   1661-1720. . . . . DLB-95
Finch, Annie 1956- DLB-282
Finch, Robert 1900- DLB-88
Findley, Timothy 1930-2002 . . . . DLB-53
Finlay, Ian Hamilton 1925- DLB-40
Finley, Martha 1828-1909 . . . . DLB-42
Finn, Elizabeth Anne (McCaul)
   1825-1921 . . . . DLB-166
Finnegan, Seamus 1949- DLB-245
Finney, Jack 1911-1995. . . . . DLB-8
Finney, Walter Braden (see Finney, Jack)
Firbank, Ronald 1886-1926 . . . . DLB-36
Firmin, Giles 1615-1697 . . . . DLB-24
First Edition Library/Collectors'
   Reprints, Inc. Y-91

Fischart, Johann
   1546 or 1547-1590 or 1591 . . . . DLB-179
Fischer, Karoline Auguste Fernandine
   1764-1842. . . . . DLB-94
Fischer, Tibor 1959- DLB-231
Fish, Stanley 1938- DLB-67
Fishacre, Richard 1205-1248 . . . . DLB-115
Fisher, Clay (see Allen, Henry W.)
Fisher, Dorothy Canfield 1879-1958. . . DLB-9, 102
Fisher, Leonard Everett 1924- DLB-61
Fisher, Roy 1930- DLB-40
Fisher, Rudolph 1897-1934 . . . . DLB-51, 102
Fisher, Steve 1913-1980 . . . . DLB-226
Fisher, Sydney George 1856-1927 . . . . . . DLB-47
Fisher, Vardis 1895-1968. . . . . DLB-9, 206
Fiske, John 1608-1677. . . . . DLB-24
Fiske, John 1842-1901 . . . . DLB-47, 64
Fitch, Thomas circa 1700-1774 . . . . DLB-31
Fitch, William Clyde 1865-1909. . . . . DLB-7
FitzGerald, Edward 1809-1883. . . . . DLB-32
Fitzgerald, F. Scott 1896-1940
   . . . . DLB-4, 9, 86; Y-81, 92;
                 DS-1, 15, 16; CDALB-4
   F. Scott Fitzgerald: A Descriptive
     Bibliography, Supplement (2001) Y-01
   F. Scott Fitzgerald Centenary
     Celebrations Y-96
   F. Scott Fitzgerald Inducted into the
     American Poets' Corner at St. John
     the Divine; Ezra Pound Banned Y-99
   "F. Scott Fitzgerald: St. Paul's Native Son
     and Distinguished American Writer":
     University of Minnesota Conference,
     29-31 October 1982. . . . . Y-82
   First International F. Scott Fitzgerald
     Conference Y-92
   The Great Gatsby (Documentary). DLB-219
   Tender Is the Night (Documentary) DLB-273
Fitzgerald, Penelope
   1916-2000. . . . . DLB-14, 194, 326
Fitzgerald, Robert 1910-1985 . . . . Y-80
FitzGerald, Robert D. 1902-1987 . . . . . . DLB-260
Fitzgerald, Thomas 1819-1891 . . . . DLB-23
Fitzgerald, Zelda Sayre 1900-1948 . . . . Y-84
Fitzhugh, Louise 1928-1974 . . . . DLB-52
Fitzhugh, William circa 1651-1701 . . . . . . DLB-24
Flagg, James Montgomery 1877-1960. . . . DLB-188
Flanagan, Thomas 1923-2002 . . . . Y-80
Flanner, Hildegarde 1899-1987. . . . . DLB-48
Flanner, Janet 1892-1978 . . . . DLB-4; DS-15
Flannery, Peter 1951- DLB-233
Flaubert, Gustave 1821-1880 . . . . . . DLB-119, 301
Flavin, Martin 1883-1967 . . . . DLB-9
Fleck, Konrad (fl. circa 1220) DLB-138
Flecker, James Elroy 1884-1915 . . . . . . DLB-10, 19
Fleeson, Doris 1901-1970 . . . . DLB-29
Fleißer, Marieluise 1901-1974 . . . . . . DLB-56, 124

Fleischer, Nat 1887-1972 . . . . DLB-241
Fleming, Abraham 1552?-1607. . . . . DLB-236
Fleming, Ian 1908-1964 . . .DLB-87, 201; CDBLB-7
Fleming, Joan 1908-1980 . . . . .DLB-276
Fleming, May Agnes 1840-1880 . . . . DLB-99
Fleming, Paul 1609-1640 . . . . DLB-164
Fleming, Peter 1907-1971 . . . . DLB-195
Fletcher, Giles, the Elder 1546-1611 . . . . . DLB-136
Fletcher, Giles, the Younger
   1585 or 1586-1623. . . . . DLB-121
Fletcher, J. S. 1863-1935 . . . . DLB-70
Fletcher, John 1579-1625. . . . . DLB-58
Fletcher, John Gould 1886-1950. . . . . . DLB-4, 45
Fletcher, Phineas 1582-1650 . . . . DLB-121
Flieg, Helmut (see Heym, Stefan)
Flint, F. S. 1885-1960 . . . . DLB-19
Flint, Timothy 1780-1840 . . . . .DLB-73, 186
Fløgstad, Kjartan 1944- DLB-297
Florensky, Pavel Aleksandrovich
   1882-1937 . . . . DLB-295
Flores, Juan de fl. 1470-1500 . . . . DLB-286
Flores-Williams, Jason 1969- DLB-209
Florio, John 1553?-1625 . . . . .DLB-172
Fludd, Robert 1574-1637 . . . . DLB-281
Flynn, Elizabeth Gurley 1890-1964 . . . . . DLB-303
Fo, Dario 1926- Y-97
   Nobel Lecture 1997: Contra Jogulatores
     Obloquentes Y-97
Foden, Giles 1967- DLB-267
Fofanov, Konstantin Mikhailovich
   1862-1911 . . . . .DLB-277
Foix, J. V. 1893-1987. . . . . DLB-134
Foley, Martha 1897-1977 . . . . .DLB-137
Folger, Henry Clay 1857-1930 . . . . DLB-140
Folio Society DLB-112
Follain, Jean 1903-1971 . . . . DLB-258
Follen, Charles 1796-1840. . . . . DLB-235
Follen, Eliza Lee (Cabot) 1787-1860 . . . DLB-1, 235
Follett, Ken 1949- DLB-87; Y-81
Follett Publishing Company DLB-46
John West Folsom [publishing house] DLB-49
Folz, Hans
   between 1435 and 1440-1513 . . . . . . .DLB-179
Fonseca, Manuel da 1911-1993 . . . . DLB-287
Fonseca, Rubem 1925- DLB-307
Fontane, Theodor
   1819-1898 . . . . .DLB-129; CDWLB-2
Fontenelle, Bernard Le Bovier de
   1657-1757 . . . . .DLB-268, 313
Fontes, Montserrat 1940- DLB-209
Fonvisin, Denis Ivanovich
   1744 or 1745-1792 . . . . DLB-150
Foote, Horton 1916- DLB-26, 266

Foote, Mary Hallock
   1847-1938 ....DLB-186, 188, 202, 221
Foote, Samuel 1721-1777 ....DLB-89
Foote, Shelby 1916-2005 ....DLB-2, 17
Forbes, Calvin 1945- DLB-41
Forbes, Ester 1891-1967................DLB-22
Forbes, John 1950-1998..............DLB=325
Forbes, Rosita 1893?-1967..............DLB-195
Forbes and Company..................DLB-49
Force, Peter 1790-1868.................DLB-30
Forché, Carolyn 1950- DLB-5, 193
Ford, Charles Henri 1913-2002.......DLB-4, 48
Ford, Corey 1902-1969 ....DLB-11
Ford, Ford Madox
   1873-1939 ....DLB-34, 98, 162; CDBLB-6
   Nathan Asch Remembers Ford Madox
      Ford, Sam Roth, and Hart Crane Y-02
J. B. Ford and Company DLB-49
Ford, Jesse Hill 1928-1996................DLB-6
Ford, John 1586-?........... DLB-58; CDBLB-1
Ford, R. A. D. 1915-1998.................DLB-88
Ford, Richard 1944- DLB-227
Ford, Worthington C. 1858-1941.........DLB-47
Fords, Howard, and Hulbert DLB-49
Foreman, Carl 1914-1984 ....DLB-26
Forester, C. S. 1899-1966................DLB-191
   The C. S. Forester Society..............Y-00
Forester, Frank (see Herbert, Henry William)
Formalism, New
   Anthologizing New Formalism DLB-282
   The Little Magazines of the
      New Formalism................DLB-282
   The New Narrative Poetry DLB-282
   Presses of the New Formalism and
      the New Narrative DLB-282
   The Prosody of the New Formalism ..DLB-282
   Younger Women Poets of the
      New Formalism................DLB-282
Forman, Harry Buxton 1842-1917.......DLB-184
Fornés, María Irene 1930- DLB-7
Forrest, Leon 1937-1997.................DLB-33
Forsh, Ol'ga Dmitrievna 1873-1961......DLB-272
Forster, E. M. 1879-1970
   . DLB-34, 98, 162, 178, 195; DS-10; CDBLB-6
   "Fantasy," from Aspects of the Novel
      (1927) DLB-178
Forster, Georg 1754-1794 ....DLB-94
Forster, John 1812-1876 ....DLB-144
Forster, Margaret 1938- DLB-155, 271
Forsyth, Frederick 1938- DLB-87
Forsyth, William
   "Literary Style" (1857) [excerpt] DLB-57
Forten, Charlotte L. 1837-1914 ...DLB-50, 239
   Pages from Her Diary DLB-50
Fortini, Franco 1917-1994...............DLB-128

Fortune, Mary ca. 1833-ca. 1910........DLB-230
Fortune, T. Thomas 1856-1928..........DLB-23
Fosdick, Charles Austin 1842-1915........DLB-42
Fosse, Jon 1959- DLB-297
Foster, David 1944- DLB-289
Foster, Genevieve 1893-1979 ....DLB-61
Foster, Hannah Webster
   1758-1840 .... DLB-37, 200
Foster, John 1648-1681.................DLB-24
Foster, Michael 1904-1956................DLB-9
Foster, Myles Birket 1825-1899 ....DLB-184
Foster, William Z. 1881-1961...........DLB-303
Foucault, Michel 1926-1984.............DLB-242
Robert and Andrew Foulis
   [publishing house] DLB-154
Fouqué, Caroline de la Motte 1774-1831....DLB-90
Fouqué, Friedrich de la Motte
   1777-1843.........................DLB-90
Four Seas Company....................DLB-46
Four Winds Press......................DLB-46
Fournier, Henri Alban (see Alain-Fournier)
Fowler, Christopher 1953- DLB-267
Fowler, Connie May 1958- DLB-292
Fowler and Wells Company.............DLB-49
Fowles, John
   1926- DLB-14, 139, 207; CDBLB-8
Fox, John 1939- DLB-245
Fox, John, Jr. 1862 or 1863-1919 ....DLB-9; DS-13
Fox, Paula 1923- DLB-52
Fox, Richard Kyle 1846-1922...........DLB-79
Fox, William Price 1926- DLB-2; Y-81
   Remembering Joe Heller...............Y-99
Richard K. Fox [publishing house]........DLB-49
Foxe, John 1517-1587 ....DLB-132
Fraenkel, Michael 1896-1957 ....DLB-4
Frame, Ronald 1953- DLB-319
France, Anatole 1844-1924 ....DLB-123
France, Richard 1938- DLB-7
Francis, Convers 1795-1863...........DLB-1, 235
Francis, Dick 1920- DLB-87; CDBLB-8
Francis, Sir Frank 1901-1988...........DLB-201
Francis, Jeffrey, Lord 1773-1850.........DLB-107
C. S. Francis [publishing house]..........DLB-49
Franck, Sebastian 1499-1542 ....DLB-179
Francke, Kuno 1855-1930 ....DLB-71
Françoise (Robertine Barry) 1863-1910....DLB-92
François, Louise von 1817-1893.........DLB-129
Frank, Bruno 1887-1945 ....DLB-118
Frank, Leonhard 1882-1961 ....DLB-56, 118
Frank, Melvin 1913-1988................DLB-26
Frank, Waldo 1889-1967 ....DLB-9, 63

Franken, Rose 1895?-1988 .... DLB-228, Y-84
Franklin, Benjamin
   1706-1790 ....DLB-24, 43, 73, 183; CDALB-2
Franklin, James 1697-1735 ....DLB-43
Franklin, John 1786-1847................DLB-99
Franklin, Miles 1879-1954 ....DLB-230
Franklin Library DLB-46
Frantz, Ralph Jules 1902-1979 ....DLB-4
Franzos, Karl Emil 1848-1904 ....DLB-129
Fraser, Antonia 1932- DLB-276
Fraser, G. S. 1915-1980 ....DLB-27
Fraser, Kathleen 1935- DLB-169
Frattini, Alberto 1922- DLB-128
Frau Ava ?-1127......................DLB-148
Fraunce, Abraham 1558?-1592 or 1593 ..DLB-236
Frayn, Michael 1933- DLB-13, 14, 194, 245
Frazier, Charles 1950- DLB-292
Fréchette, Louis-Honoré 1839-1908 ......DLB-99
Frederic, Harold 1856-1898....DLB-12, 23; DS-13
Freed, Arthur 1894-1973 ....DLB-265
Freeling, Nicolas 1927-2003 ....DLB-87
   Tribute to Georges Simenon............Y-89
Freeman, Douglas Southall
   1886-1953 .... DLB-17; DS-17
Freeman, Joseph 1897-1965 ....DLB-303
Freeman, Judith 1946- DLB-256
Freeman, Legh Richmond 1842-1915 .....DLB-23
Freeman, Mary E. Wilkins
   1852-1930 .... DLB-12, 78, 221
Freeman, R. Austin 1862-1943 ....DLB-70
Freidank circa 1170-circa 1233..........DLB-138
Freiligrath, Ferdinand 1810-1876 ....DLB-133
Fremlin, Celia 1914- DLB-276
Frémont, Jessie Benton 1834-1902.......DLB-183
Frémont, John Charles
   1813-1890 .... DLB-183, 186
French, Alice 1850-1934 .... DLB-74; DS-13
French, David 1939- DLB-53
French, Evangeline 1869-1960...........DLB-195
French, Francesca 1871-1960 ....DLB-195
James French [publishing house] DLB-49
Samuel French [publishing house] DLB-49
Samuel French, Limited................DLB-106
French Literature
   Georges-Louis Leclerc de Buffon, "Le Discours
      sur le style"..................DLB-314
   Marie-Jean-Antoine-Nicolas Caritat, marquis de
      Condorcet, "The Tenth Stage"...DLB-314
   Sophie Cottin, Claire d'Albe DLB-314
   Declaration of the Rights of Man and of
      the Citizen DLB-314
   Denis Diderot, "The Encyclopedia" ..DLB-314
   Epic and Beast Epic................DLB-208

French Arthurian Literature........ DLB-208

Olympe de Gouges, *Declaration of the Rights of Woman*................... DLB-314

Françoise d'Issembourg de Graffigny, *Letters from a Peruvian Woman*............. DLB-314

Claude-Adrien Helvétius, *The Spirit of Laws*................... DLB-314

Paul Henri Thiry, baron d'Holbach (writing as Jean-Baptiste de Mirabaud), *The System of Nature*................... DLB-314

Pierre-Ambroise-François Choderlos de Laclos, *Dangerous Acquaintances*......... DLB-314

Lyric Poetry DLB-268

Louis-Sébastien Mercier, *Le Tableau de Paris*................... DLB-314

Charles-Louis de Secondat, baron de Montesquieu, *The Spirit of Laws*.. DLB-314

Other Poets DLB-217

Poetry in Nineteenth-Century France: Cultural Background and Critical Commentary DLB-217

Roman de la Rose: Guillaume de Lorris 1200 to 1205-circa 1230, Jean de Meun 1235/1240-circa 1305 .... DLB-208

Jean-Jacques Rousseau, *The Social Contract*.................... DLB-314

Marquis de Sade, "Dialogue entre un prêtre et un moribond" DLB-314

Saints' Lives DLB-208

Troubadours, *Trobairitz*, and Trouvères................... DLB-208

Anne-Robert-Jacques Turgot, baron de l'Aulne, "Memorandum on Local Government"................ DLB-314

Voltaire, "An account of the death of the chevalier de La Barre" DLB-314

Voltaire, *Candide* DLB-314

Voltaire, *Philosophical Dictionary* DLB-314

French Theater
  Medieval French Drama DLB-208
  Parisian Theater, Fall 1984: Toward a New Baroque Y-85

Freneau, Philip 1752-1832............DLB-37, 43
  The Rising Glory of America........ DLB-37

Freni, Melo 1934- DLB-128

Fréron, Elie Catherine 1718-1776 .... DLB-313

Freshfield, Douglas W. 1845-1934 ....DLB-174

Freud, Sigmund 1856-1939............ DLB-296

Freytag, Gustav 1816-1895............ DLB-129

Frída Á. Sigurðardóttir 1940- DLB-293

Fridegård, Jan 1897-1968 .... DLB-259

Fried, Erich 1921-1988................. DLB-85

Friedan, Betty 1921-2006............ DLB-246

Friedman, Bruce Jay 1930- DLB-2, 28, 244

Friedman, Carl 1952- DLB-299

Friedman, Kinky 1944- DLB-292

Friedrich von Hausen circa 1171-1190 ... DLB-138

Friel, Brian 1929- DLB-13, 319

Friend, Krebs 1895?-1967?.............. DLB-4

Fries, Fritz Rudolf 1935- DLB-75

Frisch, Max 1911-1991 ....DLB-69, 124; CDWLB-2

Frischlin, Nicodemus 1547-1590.........DLB-179

Frischmuth, Barbara 1941- DLB-85

Fritz, Jean 1915- DLB-52

Froissart, Jean circa 1337-circa 1404 ..... DLB-208

Fromm, Erich 1900-1980 .... DLB-296

Fromentin, Eugene 1820-1876 .... DLB-123

Frontinus circa A.D. 35-A.D. 103/104..... DLB-211

Frost, A. B. 1851-1928 .... DLB-188; DS-13

Frost, Robert 1874-1963......... DLB-54; DS-7; CDALB-4

The Friends of the Dymock Poets Y-00

Frostenson, Katarina 1953- DLB-257

Frothingham, Octavius Brooks 1822-1895 .... DLB-1, 243

Froude, James Anthony 1818-1894 ....DLB-18, 57, 144

Fruitlands 1843-1844 .... DLB-1, 223; DS-5

Fry, Christopher 1907-2005 .... DLB-13
  Tribute to John Betjeman.............. Y-84

Fry, Roger 1866-1934.................DS-10

Fry, Stephen 1957- DLB-207

Frye, Northrop 1912-1991 ....DLB-67, 68, 246

Fuchs, Daniel 1909-1993 .....DLB-9, 26, 28; Y-93
  Tribute to Isaac Bashevis Singer......... Y-91

Fuentes, Carlos 1928- DLB-113; CDWLB-3

Fuertes, Gloria 1918-1998 .... DLB-108

Fugard, Athol 1932- DLB-225

The Fugitives and the Agrarians: The First Exhibition.................. Y-85

Fujiwara no Shunzei 1114-1204 .... DLB-203

Fujiwara no Tameaki 1230s?-1290s? DLB-203

Fujiwara no Tameie 1198-1275 .... DLB-203

Fujiwara no Teika 1162-1241 .... DLB-203

Fuks, Ladislav 1923-1994............. DLB-299

Fulbecke, William 1560-1603?.........DLB-172

Fuller, Charles 1939- DLB-38, 266

Fuller, Henry Blake 1857-1929 .... DLB-12

Fuller, John 1937- DLB-40

Fuller, Margaret (see Fuller, Sarah)

Fuller, Roy 1912-1991............. DLB-15, 20
  Tribute to Christopher Isherwood....... Y-86

Fuller, Samuel 1912-1997 .... DLB-26

Fuller, Sarah 1810-1850 .... DLB-1, 59, 73, 183, 223, 239; DS-5; CDALB-2

Fuller, Thomas 1608-1661 .... DLB-151

Fullerton, Hugh 1873-1945.............DLB-171

Fullwood, William fl. 1568............ DLB-236

Fulton, Alice 1952- DLB-193

Fulton, Len 1934- Y-86

Fulton, Robin 1937- DLB-40

Furbank, P. N. 1920- DLB-155

Furetière, Antoine 1619-1688............DLB-268

Furman, Laura 1945- Y-86

Furmanov, Dmitrii Andreevich 1891-1926 ....DLB-272

Furness, Horace Howard 1833-1912 ..... DLB-64

Furness, William Henry 1802-1896 .... DLB-1, 235

Furnivall, Frederick James 1825-1910.... DLB-184

Furphy, Joseph (Tom Collins) 1843-1912 .... DLB-230

Furthman, Jules 1888-1966............. DLB-26
  Shakespeare and Montaigne: A Symposium by Jules Furthman Y-02

Furui Yoshikichi 1937- DLB-182

Fushimi, Emperor 1265-1317 .... DLB-203

Futabatei Shimei (Hasegawa Tatsunosuke) 1864-1909 .... DLB-180

Fyleman, Rose 1877-1957 .... DLB-160

G

G., 1972 Booker Prize winner, John Berger DLB-326

Gaarder, Jostein 1952- DLB-297

Gadallah, Leslie 1939- DLB-251

Gadamer, Hans-Georg 1900-2002 ...... DLB-296

Gadda, Carlo Emilio 1893-1973.........DLB-177

Gaddis, William 1922-1998 ....DLB-2, 278
  William Gaddis: A Tribute Y-99

Gág, Wanda 1893-1946 .... DLB-22

Gagarin, Ivan Sergeevich 1814-1882 .... DLB-198

Gagnon, Madeleine 1938- DLB-60

Gaiman, Neil 1960- DLB-261

Gaine, Hugh 1726-1807 .... DLB-43

Hugh Gaine [publishing house] DLB-49

Gaines, Ernest J. 1933- DLB-2, 33, 152; Y-80; CDALB-6

Gaiser, Gerd 1908-1976 .... DLB-69

Gaitskill, Mary 1954- DLB-244

Galarza, Ernesto 1905-1984 .... DLB-122

Galaxy Science Fiction Novels DLB-46

Galbraith, Robert (or Caubraith) circa 1483-1544 .... DLB-281

Gale, Zona 1874-1938............DLB-9, 228, 78

Galen of Pergamon 129-after 210 ....DLB-176

Gales, Winifred Marshall 1761-1839 .... DLB-200

Galich, Aleksandr 1918-1977 ....DLB-317

Medieval Galician-Portuguese Poetry.... DLB-287

Gall, Louise von 1815-1855 .... DLB-133

Gallagher, Tess 1943- DLB-120, 212, 244

Gallagher, Wes 1911-1997 ....DLB-127

Gallagher, William Davis 1808-1894 ..... DLB-73

Gallant, Mavis 1922- DLB-53
Gallegos, María Magdalena 1935- DLB-209
Gallico, Paul 1897-1976 ....DLB-9, 171
Gallop, Jane 1952- DLB-246
Galloway, Grace Growden 1727-1782.....DLB-200
Galloway, Janice 1956- DLB-319
Gallup, Donald 1913-2000............DLB-187
Galsworthy, John 1867-1933
......DLB-10, 34, 98, 162; DS-16; CDBLB-5
Galt, John 1779-1839 ....DLB-99, 116, 159
Galton, Sir Francis 1822-1911 ....DLB-166
Galvin, Brendan 1938- DLB-5
Gambaro, Griselda 1928- DLB-305
Gambit..............................DLB-46
Gamboa, Reymundo 1948- DLB-122
Gammer Gurton's Needle DLB-62
Gan, Elena Andreevna (Zeneida R-va)
1814-1842 ....DLB-198
Gandhi, Mohandas Karamchand
1869-1948 ....DLB-323
Gandlevsky, Sergei Markovich
1952- DLB-285
Gannett, Frank E. 1876-1957 ....DLB-29
Gant, Eugene: Projected Works.........Y-01
Gao Xingjian 1940- Y-00
Nobel Lecture 2000: "The Case for
Literature" Y-00
Gaos, Vicente 1919-1980..............DLB-134
García, Andrew 1854?-1943 ....DLB-209
García, Cristina 1958- DLB-292
García, Lionel G. 1935- DLB-82
García, Richard 1941- DLB-209
García, Santiago 1928- DLB-305
García Márquez, Gabriel
1928- DLB-113; Y-82; CDWLB-3
The Magical World of Macondo.........Y-82
Nobel Lecture 1982: The Solitude of
Latin America...................Y-82
A Tribute to Gabriel García Márquez Y-82
García Marruz, Fina 1923- DLB-283
García-Camarillo, Cecilio 1943- DLB-209
Garcilaso de la Vega circa 1503-1536.....DLB-318
Garcilaso de la Vega, Inca 1539-1616 ....DLB-318
Gardam, Jane 1928- DLB-14, 161, 231
Gardell, Jonas 1963- DLB-257
Garden, Alexander circa 1685-1756......DLB-31
Gardiner, John Rolfe 1936- DLB-244
Gardiner, Margaret Power Farmer
(see Blessington, Marguerite, Countess of)
Gardner, John
1933-1982 ....DLB-2; Y-82; CDALB-7
Garfield, Leon 1921-1996 ....DLB-161
Garis, Howard R. 1873-1962 ....DLB-22
Garland, Hamlin 1860-1940 .. DLB-12, 71, 78, 186

The Hamlin Garland Society Y-01
Garneau, François-Xavier 1809-1866 .....DLB-99
Garneau, Hector de Saint-Denys
1912-1943 ....DLB-88
Garneau, Michel 1939- DLB-53
Garner, Alan 1934- DLB-161, 261
Garner, Helen 1942- DLB-325
Garner, Hugh 1913-1979 ....DLB-68
Garnett, David 1892-1981 ....DLB-34
Garnett, Eve 1900-1991 ....DLB-160
Garnett, Richard 1835-1906 ....DLB-184
Garnier, Robert 1545?-1590 ....DLB-327
Garrard, Lewis H. 1829-1887 ....DLB-186
Garraty, John A. 1920- DLB-17
Garrett, Almeida (João Baptista da Silva
Leitão de Almeida Garrett)
1799-1854 ....DLB-287
Garrett, George
1929- DLB-2, 5, 130, 152; Y-83
Literary Prizes......................Y-00
My Summer Reading Orgy: Reading
for Fun and Games: One Reader's
Report on the Summer of 2001 ......Y-01
A Summing Up at Century's End Y-99
Tribute to James Dickey Y-97
Tribute to Michael M. Rea Y-97
Tribute to Paxton Davis Y-94
Tribute to Peter Taylor Y-94
Tribute to William Goyen Y-83
A Writer Talking: A Collage Y-00
Garrett, John Work 1872-1942.........DLB-187
Garrick, David 1717-1779 ....DLB-84, 213
Garrison, William Lloyd
1805-1879 ....DLB-1, 43, 235; CDALB-2
Garro, Elena 1920-1998...............DLB-145
Garshin, Vsevolod Mikhailovich
1855-1888 ....DLB-277
Garth, Samuel 1661-1719..............DLB-95
Garve, Andrew 1908-2001..............DLB-87
Gary, Romain 1914-1980 ....DLB-83, 299
Gascoigne, George 1539?-1577 ....DLB-136
Gascoyne, David 1916-2001 ....DLB-20
Gash, Jonathan (John Grant) 1933- DLB-276
Gaskell, Elizabeth Cleghorn
1810-1865 .....DLB-21, 144, 159; CDBLB-4
The Gaskell Society Y-98
Gaskell, Jane 1941- DLB-261
Gaspey, Thomas 1788-1871 ....DLB-116
Gass, William H. 1924- DLB-2, 227
Gates, Doris 1901-1987 ....DLB-22
Gates, Henry Louis, Jr. 1950- DLB-67
Gates, Lewis E. 1860-1924 ....DLB-71
Gatto, Alfonso 1909-1976 ....DLB-114
Gault, William Campbell 1910-1995.....DLB-226

Tribute to Kenneth Millar.............Y-83
Gaunt, Mary 1861-1942 ....DLB-174, 230
Gautier, Théophile 1811-1872 ....DLB-119
Gautreaux, Tim 1947- DLB-292
Gauvreau, Claude 1925-1971 ....DLB-88
The *Gawain*-Poet
fl. circa 1350-1400..................DLB-146
Gawsworth, John (Terence Ian Fytton
Armstrong) 1912-1970............DLB-255
Gay, Ebenezer 1696-1787..............DLB-24
Gay, John 1685-1732 ....DLB-84, 95
Gayarré, Charles E. A. 1805-1895.......DLB-30
Charles Gaylord [publishing house]......DLB-49
Gaylord, Edward King 1873-1974 ......DLB-127
Gaylord, Edward Lewis 1919-2003 .....DLB-127
Gazdanov, Gaito 1903-1971............DLB-317
Gébler, Carlo 1954- DLB-271
Geda, Sigitas 1943- DLB-232
Geddes, Gary 1940- DLB-60
Geddes, Virgil 1897-1989..............DLB-4
Gedeon (Georgii Andreevich Krinovsky)
circa 1730-1763 ....DLB-150
Gee, Maggie 1948- DLB-207
Gee, Shirley 1932- DLB-245
Geibel, Emanuel 1815-1884............DLB-129
Geiogamah, Hanay 1945- DLB-175
Geis, Bernard, Associates...............DLB-46
Geisel, Theodor Seuss 1904-1991 ... DLB-61; Y-91
Gelb, Arthur 1924- DLB-103
Gelb, Barbara 1926- DLB-103
Gelber, Jack 1932- DLB-7, 228
Gélinas, Gratien 1909-1999............DLB-88
Gellert, Christian Füerchtegott
1715-1769 ....DLB-97
Gellhorn, Martha 1908-1998...........Y-82, 98
Gems, Pam 1925- DLB-13
Genet, Jean 1910-1986 ....DLB-72, 321; Y-86
Genette, Gérard 1930- DLB-242
Genevoix, Maurice 1890-1980..........DLB-65
Genis, Aleksandr Aleksandrovich
1953- DLB-285
Genlis, Stéphanie-Félicité Ducrest, comtesse de
1746-1830 ....DLB-313
Genovese, Eugene D. 1930- DLB-17
Gent, Peter 1942- Y-82
Geoffrey of Monmouth
circa 1100-1155....................DLB-146
George, Elizabeth 1949- DLB-306
George, Henry 1839-1897 ....DLB-23
George, Jean Craighead 1919- DLB-52
George, W. L. 1882-1926 ....DLB-197
George III, King of Great Britain
and Ireland 1738-1820 ....DLB-213

Georgslied 896? DLB-148
Gerber, Merrill Joan 1938- DLB-218
Gerhardie, William 1895-1977 .... DLB-36
Gerhardt, Paul 1607-1676 .... DLB-164
Gérin, Winifred 1901-1981 .... DLB-155
Gérin-Lajoie, Antoine 1824-1882 .... DLB-99
German Literature
   A Call to Letters and an Invitation
     to the Electric Chair DLB-75
   The Conversion of an Unpolitical
     Man DLB-66
   The German Radio Play DLB-124
   The German Transformation from the
     Baroque to the Enlightenment DLB-97
   Germanophilism DLB-66
   A Letter from a New Germany Y-90
   The Making of a People DLB-66
   The Novel of Impressionism DLB-66
   Pattern and Paradigm: History as
     Design DLB-75
   Premisses DLB-66
   The 'Twenties and Berlin DLB-66
   Wolfram von Eschenbach's *Parzival:*
     Prologue and Book 3 .... DLB-138
   Writers and Politics: 1871-1918 ...... DLB-66
German Literature, Middle Ages
   Abrogans circa 790-800 .... DLB-148
   Annolied between 1077 and 1081 ..... DLB-148
   The Arthurian Tradition and
     Its European Context DLB-138
   Cambridge Songs (Carmina Cantabrigensia)
     circa 1050 .... DLB-148
   Christus und die Samariterin circa 950 ... DLB-148
   De Heinrico circa 980? DLB-148
   Ecbasis Captivi circa 1045 .... DLB-148
   Georgslied 896? DLB-148
   German Literature and Culture from
     Charlemagne to the Early Courtly
     Period DLB-148; CDWLB-2
   The Germanic Epic and Old English
     Heroic Poetry: *Widsith, Waldere,*
     and *The Fight at Finnsburg* DLB-146
   Graf Rudolf between circa
     1170 and circa 1185 .... DLB-148
   Heliand circa 850 .... DLB-148
   Das Hildesbrandslied
     circa 820 .... DLB-148; CDWLB-2
   Kaiserchronik circa 1147 .... DLB-148
   The Legends of the Saints and a
     Medieval Christian
     Worldview DLB-148
   Ludus de Antichristo circa 1160 .... DLB-148
   Ludwigslied 881 or 882 .... DLB-148
   Muspilli circa 790-circa 850 .... DLB-148
   Old German Genesis and *Old German*
     Exodus circa 1050-circa 1130 .... DLB-148
   Old High German Charms
     and Blessings DLB-148; CDWLB-2
   The *Old High German Isidor*
     circa 790-800 .... DLB-148

Petruslied circa 854? DLB-148
Physiologus circa 1070-circa 1150 ..... DLB-148
Ruodlieb circa 1050-1075 .... DLB-148
"Spielmannsepen" (circa 1152
   circa 1500) DLB-148
The Strasbourg Oaths 842 .... DLB-148
Tatian circa 830 .... DLB-148
Waltharius circa 825 .... DLB-148
Wessobrunner Gebet circa 787-815 ..... DLB-148
German Theater
   German Drama 800-1280 .... DLB-138
   German Drama from Naturalism
     to Fascism: 1889-1933 .... DLB-118
Gernsback, Hugo 1884-1967 .... DLB-8, 137
Gerould, Katharine Fullerton
   1879-1944 .... DLB-78
Samuel Gerrish [publishing house] DLB-49
Gerrold, David 1944- DLB-8
Gersão, Teolinda 1940- DLB-287
Gershon, Karen 1923-1993 .... DLB-299
Gershwin, Ira 1896-1983 .... DLB-265
   The Ira Gershwin Centenary Y-96
Gerson, Jean 1363-1429 .... DLB-208
Gersonides 1288-1344 .... DLB-115
Gerstäcker, Friedrich 1816-1872 .... DLB-129
Gertsen, Aleksandr Ivanovich
   (see Herzen, Alexander)
Gerstenberg, Heinrich Wilhelm von
   1737-1823 .... DLB-97
Gervinus, Georg Gottfried
   1805-1871 .... DLB-133
Gery, John 1953- DLB-282
Geßner, Solomon 1730-1788 .... DLB-97
Geston, Mark S. 1946- DLB-8
Al-Ghazali 1058-1111 .... DLB-115
Ghelderode, Michel de (Adolphe-Adhémar Martens)
   1898-1962 .... DLB-321
Ghose, Zulfikar 1935- DLB-323
Ghosh, Amitav 1956- DLB-323
The Ghost Road, 1995 Booker Prize winner,
   Pat Barker DLB-326
Gibbings, Robert 1889-1958 .... DLB-195
Gibbon, Edward 1737-1794 .... DLB-104
Gibbon, John Murray 1875-1952 .... DLB-92
Gibbon, Lewis Grassic (see Mitchell, James Leslie)
Gibbons, Floyd 1887-1939 .... DLB-25
Gibbons, Kaye 1960- DLB-292
Gibbons, Reginald 1947- DLB-120
Gibbons, William eighteenth century DLB-73
Gibson, Charles Dana
   1867-1944 .... DLB-188; DS-13
Gibson, Graeme 1934- DLB-53
Gibson, Margaret 1944- DLB-120
Gibson, Margaret Dunlop 1843-1920 .... DLB-174
Gibson, Wilfrid 1878-1962 .... DLB-19

The Friends of the Dymock Poets Y-00
Gibson, William 1914- DLB-7
Gibson, William 1948- DLB-251
Gide, André 1869-1951 .... DLB-65, 321
Giguère, Diane 1937- DLB-53
Giguère, Roland 1929- DLB-60
Gil de Biedma, Jaime 1929-1990 .... DLB-108
Gil-Albert, Juan 1906-1994 .... DLB-134
Gilbert, Anthony 1899-1973 .... DLB-77
Gilbert, Elizabeth 1969- DLB-292
Gilbert, Sir Humphrey 1537-1583 ...... DLB-136
Gilbert, Michael 1912- DLB-87
Gilbert, Sandra M. 1936- DLB-120, 246
Gilchrist, Alexander 1828-1861 .... DLB-144
Gilchrist, Ellen 1935- DLB-130
Gilder, Jeannette L. 1849-1916 .... DLB-79
Gilder, Richard Watson 1844-1909 .... DLB-64, 79
Gildersleeve, Basil 1831-1924 .... DLB-71
Giles, Henry 1809-1882 .... DLB-64
Giles of Rome circa 1243-1316 .... DLB-115
Gilfillan, George 1813-1878 .... DLB-144
Gill, Eric 1882-1940 .... DLB-98
Gill, Sarah Prince 1728-1771 .... DLB-200
William F. Gill Company DLB-49
Gillespie, A. Lincoln, Jr. 1895-1950 .... DLB-4
Gillespie, Haven 1883-1975 .... DLB-265
Gilliam, Florence fl. twentieth century DLB-4
Gilliatt, Penelope 1932-1993 .... DLB-14
Gillott, Jacky 1939-1980 .... DLB-14
Gilman, Caroline H. 1794-1888 .... DLB-3, 73
Gilman, Charlotte Perkins 1860-1935 ... DLB-221
   The Charlotte Perkins Gilman Society ... Y-99
W. and J. Gilman [publishing house] DLB-49
Gilmer, Elizabeth Meriwether
   1861-1951 .... DLB-29
Gilmer, Francis Walker 1790-1826 .... DLB-37
Gilmore, Mary 1865-1962 .... DLB-260
Gilroy, Frank D. 1925- DLB-7
Gimferrer, Pere (Pedro) 1945- DLB-134
Ginger, Aleksandr S. 1897-1965 .... DLB-317
Gingrich, Arnold 1903-1976 .... DLB-137
   Prospectus From the Initial Issue of
     Esquire (Autumn 1933) DLB-137
   "With the Editorial Ken," Prospectus
     From the Initial Issue of *Ken*
     (7 April 1938) DLB-137
Ginibi, Ruby Langford 1934- DLB-325
Ginsberg, Allen
   1926-1997 .... DLB-5, 16, 169, 237; CDALB-1
Ginzburg, Evgeniia
   1904-1977 .... DLB-302
Ginzburg, Lidiia Iakovlevna
   1902-1990 .... DLB-302

Ginzburg, Natalia 1916-1991 . . . . DLB-177	*The God of Small Things,* 1997 Booker Prize winner, Arundhati Roy DLB-326	Goldstein, Richard 1944- DLB-185
Ginzkey, Franz Karl 1871-1963 . . . . DLB-81	Godber, John 1956- DLB-233	Goldsworthy, Peter 1951- DLB-325
Gioia, Dana 1950- DLB-120, 282	Godbout, Jacques 1933- DLB-53	Gollancz, Sir Israel 1864-1930 . . . . DLB-201
Giono, Jean 1895-1970 . . . . DLB-72, 321	Goddard, Morrill 1865-1937 . . . . DLB-25	Victor Gollancz Limited DLB-112
Giotti, Virgilio 1885-1957 . . . . DLB-114	Goddard, William 1740-1817 . . . . DLB-43	Gomberville, Marin Le Roy, sieur de 1600?-1674 . . . . DLB-268
Giovanni, Nikki 1943- DLB-5, 41; CDALB-7	Godden, Rumer 1907-1998 . . . . DLB-161	Gombrowicz, Witold 1904-1969 . . . . DLB-215; CDWLB-4
Giovannitti, Arturo 1884-1959 . . . . DLB-303	Godey, Louis A. 1804-1878 . . . . DLB-73	Gomez, Madeleine-Angélique Poisson de 1684-1770 . . . . DLB-313
Gipson, Lawrence Henry 1880-1971 . . . . . . DLB-17	Godey and McMichael DLB-49	Gómez de Ciudad Real, Alvar (Alvar Gómez de Guadalajara) 1488-1538 . . . . DLB-318
Girard, Rodolphe 1879-1956 . . . . DLB-92	Godfrey, Dave 1938- DLB-60	Gómez-Quiñones, Juan 1942- DLB-122
Giraudoux, Jean 1882-1944 . . . . DLB-65, 321	Godfrey, Thomas 1736-1763 . . . . DLB-31	Laurence James Gomme [publishing house] DLB-46
Girondo, Oliverio 1891-1967 . . . . DLB-283	Godine, David R., Publisher DLB-46	Gompers, Samuel 1850-1924 . . . . DLB-303
Gissing, George 1857-1903 . . . . . DLB-18, 135, 184	Godkin, E. L. 1831-1902 . . . . DLB-79	Gonçalves Dias, Antônio 1823-1864 . . . . . DLB-307
The Place of Realism in Fiction (1895) . . . DLB-18	Godolphin, Sidney 1610-1643 . . . . DLB-126	Goncharov, Ivan Aleksandrovich 1812-1891 . . . . DLB-238
Giudici, Giovanni 1924- DLB-128	M. J. Godwin and Company DLB-154	Goncourt, Edmond de 1822-1896 . . . . . . DLB-123
Giuliani, Alfredo 1924- DLB-128	Godwin, Mary Jane Clairmont 1766-1841 . . . . DLB-163	Goncourt, Jules de 1830-1870 . . . . DLB-123
Gjellerup, Karl 1857-1919 . . . . DLB-300	Godwin, Parke 1816-1904 . . . . DLB-3, 64, 250	Gonzales, Rodolfo "Corky" 1928- DLB-122
Glackens, William J. 1870-1938 . . . . DLB-188	Godwin, William 1756-1836 . . . . . . DLB-39, 104, 142, 158, 163, 262; CDBLB-3	Gonzales-Berry, Erlinda 1942- DLB-209
Gladilin, Anatolii Tikhonovich 1935- DLB-302	Preface to *St. Leon* (1799) DLB-39	"Chicano Language" DLB-82
Gladkov, Fedor Vasil'evich 1883-1958 . . . . DLB-272	Goering, Reinhard 1887-1936 . . . . DLB-118	González, Angel 1925- DLB-108
Gladstone, William Ewart 1809-1898 . . . . DLB-57, 184	Goes, Albrecht 1908- DLB-69	Gonzalez, Genaro 1949- DLB-122
Glaeser, Ernst 1902-1963 . . . . DLB-69	Goethe, Johann Wolfgang von 1749-1832 . . . . DLB-94; CDWLB-2	Gonzalez, N. V. M. 1915-1999 . . . . DLB-312
Glancy, Diane 1941- DLB-175	Goetz, Curt 1888-1960 . . . . DLB-124	González, Otto-Raúl 1921- DLB-290
Glanvill, Joseph 1636-1680 . . . . DLB-252	Goffe, Thomas circa 1592-1629 . . . . DLB-58	Gonzalez, Ray 1952- DLB-122
Glanville, Brian 1931- DLB-15, 139	Goffstein, M. B. 1940- DLB-61	González de Mireles, Jovita 1899-1983 . . . . DLB-122
Glapthorne, Henry 1610-1643? DLB-58	Gogarty, Oliver St. John 1878-1957 . . . . DLB-15, 19	González Martínez, Enrique 1871-1952 . . . DLB-290
Glasgow, Ellen 1873-1945 . . . . DLB-9, 12	Gogol, Nikolai Vasil'evich 1809-1852 . . . . DLB-198	González-T., César A. 1931- DLB-82
The Ellen Glasgow Society Y-01	Goines, Donald 1937-1974 . . . . DLB-33	Goodis, David 1917-1967 . . . . DLB-226
Glasier, Katharine Bruce 1867-1950 . . . . . DLB-190	Gold, Herbert 1924- DLB-2; Y-81	Goodison, Lorna 1947- DLB-157
Glaspell, Susan 1876-1948 . . . . . . DLB-7, 9, 78, 228	Tribute to William Saroyan Y-81	Goodman, Allegra 1967- DLB-244
Glass, Montague 1877-1934 . . . . DLB-11	Gold, Michael 1893-1967 . . . . DLB-9, 28	Goodman, Nelson 1906-1998 . . . . DLB-279
Glassco, John 1909-1981 . . . . DLB-68	Goldbarth, Albert 1948- DLB-120	Goodman, Paul 1911-1972 . . . . DLB-130, 246
Glauser, Friedrich 1896-1938 . . . . DLB-56	Goldberg, Dick 1947- DLB-7	The Goodman Theatre DLB-7
Glavin, Anthony 1946- DLB-319	Golden Cockerel Press DLB-112	Goodrich, Frances 1891-1984 and Hackett, Albert 1900-1995 . . . . DLB-26
F. Gleason's Publishing Hall DLB-49	Golding, Arthur 1536-1606 . . . . DLB-136	Goodrich, Samuel Griswold 1793-1860 . . . . DLB-1, 42, 73, 243
Gleim, Johann Wilhelm Ludwig 1719-1803 . . . . DLB-97	Golding, Louis 1895-1958 . . . . DLB-195	S. G. Goodrich [publishing house] DLB-49
Glendinning, Robin 1938- DLB-310	Golding, William 1911-1993 . . . . . DLB-15, 100, 255, 326; Y-83; CDBLB-7	C. E. Goodspeed and Company DLB-49
Glendinning, Victoria 1937- DLB-155	Nobel Lecture 1993 . . . . Y-83	Goodwin, Stephen 1943- Y-82
Glidden, Frederick Dilley (Luke Short) 1908-1975 . . . . DLB-256	The Stature of William Golding Y-83	Googe, Barnabe 1540-1594 . . . . DLB-132
Glinka, Fedor Nikolaevich 1786-1880 . . . . DLB-205	Goldman, Emma 1869-1940 . . . . DLB-221	Gookin, Daniel 1612-1687 . . . . DLB-24
Glover, Keith 1966- DLB-249	Goldman, William 1931- DLB-44	Gopegui, Belén 1963- DLB-322
Glover, Richard 1712-1785 . . . . DLB-95	Goldring, Douglas 1887-1960 . . . . DLB-197	Goran, Lester 1928- DLB-244
Glover, Sue 1943- DLB-310	Goldschmidt, Meir Aron 1819-1887 . . . . . DLB-300	Gordimer, Nadine 1923- DLB-225, 326; Y-91
Glück, Louise 1943- DLB-5	Goldsmith, Oliver 1730?-1774 . . . . . . DLB-39, 89, 104, 109, 142; CDBLB-2	Nobel Lecture 1991 . . . . Y-91
Glyn, Elinor 1864-1943 . . . . DLB-153	Goldsmith, Oliver 1794-1861 . . . . DLB-99	
Gnedich, Nikolai Ivanovich 1784-1833 . . . DLB-205	Goldsmith Publishing Company DLB-46	Gordon, Adam Lindsay 1833-1870 . . . . . DLB-230
Gobineau, Joseph-Arthur de 1816-1882 . . . . DLB-123		

Cumulative Index

Gordon, Caroline
1895-1981 .... DLB-4, 9, 102; DS-17; Y-81

Gordon, Charles F. (see OyamO)

Gordon, Charles William (see Connor, Ralph)

Gordon, Giles 1940- DLB-14, 139, 207

Gordon, Helen Cameron, Lady Russell
1867-1949..................... DLB-195

Gordon, Lyndall 1941- DLB-155

Gordon, Mack 1904-1959............. DLB-265

Gordon, Mary 1949- DLB-6; Y-81

Gordone, Charles 1925-1995 .... DLB-7

Gore, Catherine 1800-1861 .... DLB-116

Gore-Booth, Eva 1870-1926 .... DLB-240

Gores, Joe 1931- DLB-226; Y-02

    Tribute to Kenneth Millar Y-83

    Tribute to Raymond Chandler.......... Y-88

Gorey, Edward 1925-2000 .... DLB-61

Gorgias of Leontini
circa 485 B.C.-376 B.C. DLB-176

Gor'ky, Maksim 1868-1936 .... DLB-295

Gorodetsky, Sergei Mitrofanovich
1884-1967..................... DLB-295

Gorostiza, José 1901-1979............. DLB-290

Görres, Joseph 1776-1848 .... DLB-90

Gosse, Edmund 1849-1928...... DLB-57, 144, 184

Gosson, Stephen 1554-1624 .... DLB-172

    The Schoole of Abuse (1579) DLB-172

Gotanda, Philip Kan 1951- DLB-266

Gotlieb, Phyllis 1926- DLB-88, 251

Go-Toba 1180-1239.................. DLB-203

Gottfried von Straßburg
died before 1230 ...... DLB-138; CDWLB-2

Gotthelf, Jeremias 1797-1854............ DLB-133

Gottschalk circa 804/808-869 .... DLB-148

Gottsched, Johann Christoph
1700-1766..................... DLB-97

Götz, Johann Nikolaus 1721-1781........ DLB-97

Goudge, Elizabeth 1900-1984.......... DLB-191

Gouges, Olympe de 1748-1793......... DLB-313

    Declaration of the Rights of Woman...... DLB-314

Gough, John B. 1817-1886 .... DLB-243

Gould, Wallace 1882-1940 .... DLB-54

Gournay, Marie de 1565-1645 .... DLB-327

Govoni, Corrado 1884-1965........... DLB-114

Govrin, Michal 1950- DLB-299

Gower, John circa 1330-1408 .... DLB-146

Goyen, William 1915-1983......DLB-2, 218; Y-83

Goytisolo, José Augustín 1928- DLB-134

Goytisolo, Juan 1931- DLB-322

Goytisolo, Luis 1935- DLB-322

Gozzano, Guido 1883-1916 .... DLB-114

Grabbe, Christian Dietrich 1801-1836 ... DLB-133

Gracq, Julien (Louis Poirier) 1910- DLB-83

Grady, Henry W. 1850-1889 .... DLB-23

Graf, Oskar Maria 1894-1967 .... DLB-56

Graf Rudolf between circa 1170 and
circa 1185..................... DLB-148

Graff, Gerald 1937- DLB-246

Graffigny, Françoise d'Issembourg de
1695-1758..................... DLB-313

    Letters from a Peruvian Woman DLB-314

Richard Grafton [publishing house] DLB-170

Grafton, Sue 1940- DLB-226

Graham, Frank 1893-1965 .... DLB-241

Graham, George Rex 1813-1894 .... DLB-73

Graham, Gwethalyn (Gwethalyn Graham
Erichsen-Brown) 1913-1965......... DLB-88

Graham, Jorie 1951- DLB-120

Graham, Katharine 1917-2001 .... DLB-127

Graham, Lorenz 1902-1989 .... DLB-76

Graham, Philip 1915-1963 .... DLB-127

Graham, R. B. Cunninghame
1852-1936 ....DLB-98, 135, 174

Graham, Shirley 1896-1977 .... DLB-76

Graham, Stephen 1884-1975............ DLB-195

Graham, W. S. 1918-1986 .... DLB-20

William H. Graham [publishing house] ... DLB-49

Graham, Winston 1910-2003........... DLB-77

Grahame, Kenneth 1859-1932 ...DLB-34, 141, 178

Grainger, Martin Allerdale 1874-1941 .... DLB-92

Gramatky, Hardie 1907-1979 .... DLB-22

Gramcko, Ida 1924-1994 .... DLB-290

Gramsci, Antonio 1891-1937 .... DLB-296

Granada, Fray Luis de 1504-1588 ...... DLB-318

Grand, Sarah 1854-1943..........DLB-135, 197

Grandbois, Alain 1900-1975........... DLB-92

Grandson, Oton de circa 1345-1397..... DLB-208

Grange, John circa 1556-?............. DLB-136

Granger, Thomas 1578-1627........... DLB-281

Granich, Irwin (see Gold, Michael)

Granin, Daniil 1918- DLB-302

Granovsky, Timofei Nikolaevich
1813-1855 .... DLB-198

Grant, Anne MacVicar 1755-1838 .... DLB-200

Grant, Duncan 1885-1978 ....DS-10

Grant, George 1918-1988.............. DLB-88

Grant, George Monro 1835-1902 .... DLB-99

Grant, Harry J. 1881-1963 .... DLB-29

Grant, James Edward 1905-1966 .... DLB-26

Grant, John (see Gash, Jonathan)

War of the Words (and Pictures): The Creation
of a Graphic Novel Y-02

Grass, Günter 1927- ...DLB-75, 124; CDWLB-2

    Nobel Lecture 1999:
"To Be Continued..." Y-99

Tribute to Helen Wolff................ Y-94

Grasty, Charles H. 1863-1924 .... DLB-25

Grau, Shirley Ann 1929- DLB-2, 218

Graves, John 1920- Y-83

Graves, Richard 1715-1804............. DLB-39

Graves, Robert 1895-1985
...DLB-20, 100, 191; DS-18; Y-85; CDBLB-6

    The St. John's College
Robert Graves Trust Y-96

Gray, Alasdair 1934- DLB-194, 261, 319

Gray, Asa 1810-1888 .... DLB-1, 235

Gray, David 1838-1861 .... DLB-32

Gray, Simon 1936- DLB-13

Gray, Robert 1945- DLB-325

Gray, Thomas 1716-1771 .... DLB-109; CDBLB-2

Grayson, Richard 1951- DLB-234

Grayson, William J. 1788-1863.... DLB-3, 64, 248

The Great Bibliographers Series............ Y-93

The Great Gatsby (Documentary) DLB-219

"The Greatness of Southern Literature":
League of the South Institute for the
Study of Southern Culture and History
.... Y-02

Grech, Nikolai Ivanovich 1787-1867 ..... DLB-198

Greeley, Horace 1811-1872....DLB-3, 43, 189, 250

Green, Adolph 1915-2002 .... DLB-44, 265

Green, Anna Katharine
1846-1935 .... DLB-202, 221

Green, Duff 1791-1875 .... DLB-43

Green, Elizabeth Shippen 1871-1954 .... DLB-188

Green, Gerald 1922- DLB-28

Green, Henry 1905-1973 .... DLB-15

Green, Jonas 1712-1767................ DLB-31

Green, Joseph 1706-1780............... DLB-31

Green, Julien 1900-1998............. DLB-4, 72

Green, Paul 1894-1981....... DLB-7, 9, 249; Y-81

Green, T. H. 1836-1882 .... DLB-190, 262

Green, Terence M. 1947- DLB-251

T. and S. Green [publishing house]....... DLB-49

Green Tiger Press.................... DLB-46

Timothy Green [publishing house]........ DLB-49

Greenaway, Kate 1846-1901 .... DLB-141

Greenberg: Publisher DLB-46

Greene, Asa 1789-1838................ DLB-11

Greene, Belle da Costa 1883-1950 .....DLB-187

Greene, Graham 1904-1991
..........DLB-13, 15, 77, 100, 162, 201, 204;
Y-85, 91; CDBLB-7

    Tribute to Christopher Isherwood........ Y-86

Greene, Robert 1558-1592 ....DLB-62, 167

Greene, Robert Bernard (Bob), Jr.
1947- DLB-185

Benjamin H Greene [publishing house] ... DLB-49

Greenfield, George 1917-2000 .... Y-91, 00

Derek Robinson's Review of George
    Greenfield's *Rich Dust* Y-02
Greenhow, Robert 1800-1854 ....DLB-30
Greenlee, William B. 1872-1953 ....DLB-187
Greenough, Horatio 1805-1852 ....DLB-1, 235
Greenwell, Dora 1821-1882 ....DLB-35, 199
Greenwillow Books DLB-46
Greenwood, Grace (see Lippincott, Sara Jane Clarke)
Greenwood, Walter 1903-1974 ....DLB-10, 191
Greer, Ben 1948- DLB-6
Greflinger, Georg 1620?-1677 ....DLB-164
Greg, W. R. 1809-1881 ....DLB-55
Greg, W. W. 1875-1959 ....DLB-201
Gregg, Josiah 1806-1850 ....DLB-183, 186
Gregg Press DLB-46
Gregory, Horace 1898-1982 ....DLB-48
Gregory, Isabella Augusta Persse, Lady
    1852-1932 ....DLB-10
Gregory of Rimini circa 1300-1358 .....DLB-115
Gregynog Press DLB-112
Greiff, León de 1895-1976 ....DLB-283
Greiffenberg, Catharina Regina von
    1633-1694 ....DLB-168
Greig, Noël 1944- DLB-245
Grekova, Irina (Elena Sergeevna Venttsel')
    1907-2002 ....DLB-302
Grenfell, Wilfred Thomason
    1865-1940 ....DLB-92
Grenville, Kate 1950- DLB-325
Gress, Elsa 1919-1988 ....DLB-214
Greve, Felix Paul (see Grove, Frederick Philip)
Greville, Fulke, First Lord Brooke
    1554-1628 ....DLB-62, 172
Grey, Sir George, K.C.B. 1812-1898 .....DLB-184
Grey, Lady Jane 1537-1554 ....DLB-132
Grey, Zane 1872-1939 ....DLB-9, 212
    Zane Grey's West Society Y-00
Grey Owl (Archibald Stansfeld Belaney)
    1888-1938 ....DLB-92; DS-17
Grey Walls Press DLB-112
Griboedov, Aleksandr Sergeevich
    1795?-1829 ....DLB-205
Grice, Paul 1913-1988 ....DLB-279
Grier, Eldon 1917- DLB-88
Grieve, C. M. (see MacDiarmid, Hugh)
Griffin, Bartholomew fl. 1596 ....DLB-172
Griffin, Bryan
    "Panic Among the Philistines":
    A Postscript, An Interview
    with Bryan Griffin Y-81
Griffin, Gerald 1803-1840 ....DLB-159
The Griffin Poetry Prize Y-00
Griffith, Elizabeth 1727?-1793 ....DLB-39, 89
    Preface to *The Delicate Distress* (1769) ...DLB-39

Griffith, George 1857-1906 ....DLB-178
Ralph Griffiths [publishing house] DLB-154
Griffiths, Trevor 1935- DLB-13, 245
S. C. Griggs and Company DLB-49
Griggs, Sutton Elbert 1872-1930 ....DLB-50
Grignon, Claude-Henri 1894-1976 ....DLB-68
Grigor'ev, Apollon Aleksandrovich
    1822-1864 ....DLB-277
Grigorovich, Dmitrii Vasil'evich
    1822-1899 ....DLB-238
Grigson, Geoffrey 1905-1985 ....DLB-27
Grillparzer, Franz
    1791-1872 ....DLB-133; CDWLB-2
Grimald, Nicholas
    circa 1519-circa 1562 ....DLB-136
Grimké, Angelina Weld 1880-1958 ....DLB-50, 54
Grimké, Sarah Moore 1792-1873 ....DLB-239
Grimm, Frédéric Melchior 1723-1807 ....DLB-313
Grimm, Hans 1875-1959 ....DLB-66
Grimm, Jacob 1785-1863 ....DLB-90
Grimm, Wilhelm
    1786-1859 ....DLB-90; CDWLB-2
Grimmelshausen, Johann Jacob Christoffel von
    1621 or 1622-1676 ....DLB-168; CDWLB-2
Grimshaw, Beatrice Ethel 1871-1953 .....DLB-174
Grímur Thomsen 1820-1896 ....DLB-293
Grin, Aleksandr Stepanovich
    1880-1932 ....DLB-272
Grindal, Edmund 1519 or 1520-1583 ....DLB-132
Gripe, Maria (Kristina) 1923- DLB-257
Griswold, Rufus Wilmot
    1815-1857 ....DLB-3, 59, 250
Gronlund, Laurence 1846-1899 ....DLB-303
Grosart, Alexander Balloch 1827-1899 ...DLB-184
Grosholz, Emily 1950- DLB-282
Gross, Milt 1895-1953 ....DLB-11
Grosset and Dunlap DLB-49
Grosseteste, Robert circa 1160-1253 .....DLB-115
Grossman, Allen 1932- DLB-193
Grossman, David 1954- DLB-299
Grossman, Vasilii Semenovich
    1905-1964 ....DLB-272
Grossman Publishers DLB-46
Grosvenor, Gilbert H. 1875-1966 ....DLB-91
Groth, Klaus 1819-1899 ....DLB-129
Groulx, Lionel 1878-1967 ....DLB-68
Grove, Frederick Philip (Felix Paul Greve)
    1879-1948 ....DLB-92
Grove Press DLB-46
Groys, Boris Efimovich 1947- DLB-285
Grubb, Davis 1919-1980 ....DLB-6
Gruelle, Johnny 1880-1938 ....DLB-22
von Grumbach, Argula
    1492-after 1563? DLB-179

Grundtvig, N. F. S. 1783-1872 ....DLB-300
Grymeston, Elizabeth
    before 1563-before 1604 ....DLB-136
Grynberg, Henryk 1936- DLB-299
Gryphius, Andreas
    1616-1664 ....DLB-164; CDWLB-2
Gryphius, Christian 1649-1706 ....DLB-168
Guare, John 1938- DLB-7, 249
Guarnieri, Gianfrancesco 1934- DLB-307
Guberman, Igor Mironovich 1936- DLB-285
Guðbergur Bergsson 1932- DLB-293
Guðmundur Böðvarsson 1904-1974 .....DLB-293
Guðmundur Gíslason Hagalín
    1898-1985 ....DLB-293
Guðmundur Magnússon (see Jón Trausti)
Guerra, Tonino 1920- DLB-128
Guest, Barbara 1920- DLB-5, 193
Guevara, Fray Antonio de 1480?-1545 ...DLB-318
Guèvremont, Germaine 1893-1968 ....DLB-68
Guglielminetti, Amalia 1881-1941 ....DLB-264
Guidacci, Margherita 1921-1992 ....DLB-128
Guillén, Jorge 1893-1984 ....DLB-108
Guillén, Nicolás 1902-1989 ....DLB-283
Guilloux, Louis 1899-1980 ....DLB-72
Guilpin, Everard
    circa 1572-after 1608? DLB-136
Guiney, Louise Imogen 1861-1920 ....DLB-54
Guiterman, Arthur 1871-1943 ....DLB-11
Gul', Roman 1896-1986 ....DLB-317
Gumilev, Nikolai Stepanovich
    1886-1921 ....DLB-295
Günderrode, Caroline von
    1780-1806 ....DLB-90
Gundulić, Ivan 1589-1638 ...DLB-147; CDWLB-4
Gunesekera, Romesh 1954- DLB-267, 323
Gunn, Bill 1934-1989 ....DLB-38
Gunn, James E. 1923- DLB-8
Gunn, Neil M. 1891-1973 ....DLB-15
Gunn, Thom 1929- DLB-27; CDBLB-8
Gunnar Gunnarsson 1889-1975 ....DLB-293
Gunnars, Kristjana 1948- DLB-60
Günther, Johann Christian 1695-1723 ....DLB-168
Gupta, Sunetra 1965- DLB-323
Gurik, Robert 1932- DLB-60
Gurney, A. R. 1930- DLB-266
Gurney, Ivor 1890-1937 ....Y-02
    The Ivor Gurney Society Y-98
Guro, Elena Genrikhovna 1877-1913 .....DLB-295
Gustafson, Ralph 1909-1995 ....DLB-88
Gustafsson, Lars 1936- DLB-257
Gütersloh, Albert Paris 1887-1973 ....DLB-81
Guterson, David 1956- DLB-292

Cumulative Index

Guthrie, A. B., Jr. 1901-1991 . . . . DLB-6, 212
Guthrie, Ramon 1896-1973 . . . . DLB-4
Guthrie, Thomas Anstey (see Anstey, FC)
Guthrie, Woody 1912-1967 . . . . DLB-303
The Guthrie Theater DLB-7
Gutiérrez Nájera, Manuel 1859-1895 . . . . DLB-290
Guttormur J. Guttormsson 1878-1966 . . . DLB-293
Gutzkow, Karl 1811-1878 . . . . DLB-133
Guy, Ray 1939- DLB-60
Guy, Rosa 1925- DLB-33
Guyot, Arnold 1807-1884 . . . . DS-13
Gwynn, R. S. 1948- DLB-282
Gwynne, Erskine 1898-1948 . . . . DLB-4
Gyles, John 1680-1755 . . . . DLB-99
Gyllembourg, Thomasine 1773-1856 . . . . DLB-300
Gyllensten, Lars 1921- DLB-257
Gyrðir Elíasson 1961- DLB-293
Gysin, Brion 1916-1986 . . . . DLB-16

H

H.D. (see Doolittle, Hilda)
Habermas, Jürgen 1929- DLB-242
Habington, William 1605-1654 . . . . DLB-126
Hacker, Marilyn 1942- DLB-120, 282
Hackett, Albert 1900-1995 . . . . DLB-26
Hacks, Peter 1928- DLB-124
Hadas, Rachel 1948- DLB-120, 282
Hadden, Briton 1898-1929 . . . . DLB-91
Hagedorn, Friedrich von 1708-1754 . . . . . DLB-168
Hagedorn, Jessica Tarahata 1949- DLB-312
Hagelstange, Rudolf 1912-1984 . . . . DLB-69
Hagerup, Inger 1905-1985 . . . . DLB-297
Haggard, H. Rider
 1856-1925 . . . . DLB-70, 156, 174, 178
Haggard, William (Richard Clayton)
 1907-1993 . . . . DLB-276; Y-93
Hagy, Alyson 1960- DLB-244
Hahn-Hahn, Ida Gräfin von 1805-1880 . . DLB-133
Haig-Brown, Roderick 1908-1976 . . . . DLB-88
Haight, Gordon S. 1901-1985 . . . . DLB-103
Hailey, Arthur 1920-2004 . . . . DLB-88; Y-82
Haines, John 1924- DLB-5, 212
Hake, Edward fl. 1566-1604 . . . . DLB-136
Hake, Thomas Gordon 1809-1895 . . . . . . DLB-32
Hakluyt, Richard 1552?-1616 . . . . DLB-136
Halas, František 1901-1949 . . . . DLB-215
Halbe, Max 1865-1944 . . . . DLB-118
Halberstam, David 1934- DLB-241
Haldane, Charlotte 1894-1969 . . . . DLB-191
Haldane, J. B. S. 1892-1964 . . . . DLB-160
Haldeman, Joe 1943- DLB-8

Haldeman-Julius Company DLB-46
Hale, E. J., and Son DLB-49
Hale, Edward Everett
 1822-1909 . . . . DLB-1, 42, 74, 235
Hale, Janet Campbell 1946- DLB-175
Hale, Kathleen 1898-2000 . . . . DLB-160
Hale, Leo Thomas (see Ebon)
Hale, Lucretia Peabody 1820-1900 . . . . . . DLB-42
Hale, Nancy
 1908-1988 . . . . DLB-86; DS-17; Y-80, 88
Hale, Sarah Josepha (Buell)
 1788-1879 . . . . DLB-1, 42, 73, 243
Hale, Susan 1833-1910 . . . . DLB-221
Hales, John 1584-1656 . . . . DLB-151
Halévy, Ludovic 1834-1908 . . . . DLB-192
Haley, Alex 1921-1992 . . . . DLB-38; CDALB-7
Haliburton, Thomas Chandler
 1796-1865 . . . . DLB-11, 99
Hall, Adam (Trevor Dudley-Smith)
 1920-1995 . . . . DLB-276
Hall, Anna Maria 1800-1881 . . . . DLB-159
Hall, Donald 1928- DLB-5
Hall, Edward 1497-1547 . . . . DLB-132
Hall, Halsey 1898-1977 . . . . DLB-241
Hall, James 1793-1868 . . . . DLB-73, 74
Hall, Joseph 1574-1656 . . . . DLB-121, 151
Hall, Radclyffe 1880-1943 . . . . DLB-191
Hall, Rodney 1935- DLB-289
Hall, Sarah Ewing 1761-1830 . . . . DLB-200
Hall, Stuart 1932- DLB-242
Samuel Hall [publishing house] DLB-49
al-Hallaj 857-922 . . . . DLB-311
Hallam, Arthur Henry 1811-1833 . . . . DLB-32
 On Some of the Characteristics of
 Modern Poetry and On the
 Lyrical Poems of Alfred
 Tennyson (1831) DLB-32
Halldór Laxness (Halldór Guðjónsson)
 1902-1998 . . . . DLB-293
Halleck, Fitz-Greene 1790-1867 . . . . . . DLB-3, 250
Haller, Albrecht von 1708-1777 . . . . DLB-168
Halliday, Brett (see Dresser, Davis)
Halligan, Marion 1940- DLB-325
Halliwell-Phillipps, James Orchard
 1820-1889 . . . . DLB-184
Hallmann, Johann Christian
 1640-1704 or 1716? DLB-168
Hallmark Editions DLB-46
Halper, Albert 1904-1984 . . . . DLB-9
Halperin, John William 1941- DLB-111
Halstead, Murat 1829-1908 . . . . DLB-23
Hamann, Johann Georg 1730-1788 . . . . . . DLB-97
Hamburger, Michael 1924- DLB-27
Hamilton, Alexander 1712-1756 . . . . DLB-31

Hamilton, Alexander 1755?-1804 . . . . DLB-37
Hamilton, Cicely 1872-1952 . . . . DLB-10, 197
Hamilton, Edmond 1904-1977 . . . . DLB-8
Hamilton, Elizabeth 1758-1816 . . . . . DLB-116, 158
Hamilton, Gail (see Corcoran, Barbara)
Hamilton, Gail (see Dodge, Mary Abigail)
Hamish Hamilton Limited DLB-112
Hamilton, Hugo 1953- DLB-267
Hamilton, Ian 1938-2001 . . . . DLB-40, 155
Hamilton, Janet 1795-1873 . . . . DLB-199
Hamilton, Mary Agnes 1884-1962 . . . . . . DLB-197
Hamilton, Patrick 1904-1962 . . . . DLB-10, 191
Hamilton, Virginia 1936-2002 . . . DLB-33, 52; Y-01
Hamilton, Sir William 1788-1856 . . . . . . DLB-262
Hamilton-Paterson, James 1941- DLB-267
Hammerstein, Oscar, 2nd 1895-1960 . . . . DLB-265
Hammett, Dashiell
 1894-1961 . . . . DLB-226; DS-6; CDALB-5
 An Appeal in *TAC* Y-91
 The Glass Key and Other Dashiell
 Hammett Mysteries Y-96
 Knopf to Hammett: The Editoral
 Correspondence Y-00
 The Maltese Falcon (Documentary) DLB-280
Hammon, Jupiter 1711-died between
 1790 and 1806 . . . . DLB-31, 50
Hammond, John ?-1663 . . . . DLB-24
Hamner, Earl 1923- DLB-6
Hampson, John 1901-1955 . . . . DLB-191
Hampton, Christopher 1946- DLB-13
Hamsun, Knut 1859-1952 . . . . DLB-297
Handel-Mazzetti, Enrica von 1871-1955 . . DLB-81
Handke, Peter 1942- DLB-85, 124
Handlin, Oscar 1915- DLB-17
Hankin, St. John 1869-1909 . . . . DLB-10
Hanley, Clifford 1922- DLB-14
Hanley, James 1901-1985 . . . . DLB-191
Hannah, Barry 1942- DLB-6, 234
Hannay, James 1827-1873 . . . . DLB-21
Hannes Hafstein 1861-1922 . . . . DLB-293
Hano, Arnold 1922- DLB-241
Hanrahan, Barbara 1939-1991 . . . . DLB-289
Hansberry, Lorraine
 1930-1965 . . . . DLB-7, 38; CDALB-1
Hansen, Joseph 1923-2004 . . . . DLB-226
Hansen, Martin A. 1909-1955 . . . . DLB-214
Hansen, Thorkild 1927-1989 . . . . DLB-214
Hanson, Elizabeth 1684-1737 . . . . DLB-200
Hapgood, Norman 1868-1937 . . . . DLB-91
Happel, Eberhard Werner 1647-1690 . . . . DLB-168
Haq, Kaiser 1950- DLB-323
Harbach, Otto 1873-1963 . . . . DLB-265

The Harbinger 1845-1849 . . . . DLB-1, 223

Harburg, E. Y. "Yip" 1896-1981 . . . . DLB-265

Harcourt Brace Jovanovich DLB-46

Hardenberg, Friedrich von (see Novalis)

Harding, Walter 1917-1996 . . . . DLB-111

Hardwick, Elizabeth 1916- DLB-6

Hardy, Alexandre 1572?-1632 . . . . DLB-268

Hardy, Frank 1917-1994 . . . . DLB-260

Hardy, Thomas
  1840-1928 . . . . DLB-18, 19, 135; CDBLB-5

  "Candour in English Fiction" (1890) . . . DLB-18

Hare, Cyril 1900-1958 . . . . DLB-77

Hare, David 1947- DLB-13, 310

Hare, R. M. 1919-2002 . . . . DLB-262

Hargrove, Marion 1919-2003 . . . . DLB-11

Häring, Georg Wilhelm Heinrich
  (see Alexis, Willibald)

Harington, Donald 1935- DLB-152

Harington, Sir John 1560-1612 . . . . DLB-136

Harjo, Joy 1951- DLB-120, 175

Harkness, Margaret (John Law)
  1854-1923 . . . . DLB-197

Harley, Edward, second Earl of Oxford
  1689-1741 . . . . DLB-213

Harley, Robert, first Earl of Oxford
  1661-1724 . . . . DLB-213

Harlow, Robert 1923- DLB-60

Harman, Thomas fl. 1566-1573 . . . . DLB-136

Harness, Charles L. 1915- DLB-8

Harnett, Cynthia 1893-1981 . . . . DLB-161

Harnick, Sheldon 1924- DLB-265

  Tribute to Ira Gershwin Y-96

  Tribute to Lorenz Hart Y-95

Harper, Edith Alice Mary (see Wickham, Anna)

Harper, Fletcher 1806-1877 . . . . DLB-79

Harper, Frances Ellen Watkins
  1825-1911 . . . . DLB-50, 221

Harper, Michael S. 1938- DLB-41

Harper and Brothers DLB-49

Harpur, Charles 1813-1868 . . . . DLB-230

Harraden, Beatrice 1864-1943 . . . . DLB-153

George G. Harrap and Company
  Limited DLB-112

Harriot, Thomas 1560-1621 . . . . DLB-136

Harris, Alexander 1805-1874 . . . . DLB-230

Harris, Benjamin ?-circa 1720 . . . . DLB-42, 43

Harris, Christie 1907-2002 . . . . DLB-88

Harris, Errol E. 1908- DLB-279

Harris, Frank 1856-1931 . . . . DLB-156, 197

Harris, George Washington
  1814-1869 . . . . DLB-3, 11, 248

Harris, Joanne 1964- DLB-271

Harris, Joel Chandler
  1848-1908 . . . . DLB-11, 23, 42, 78, 91

The Joel Chandler Harris Association Y-99

Harris, Mark 1922- DLB-2; Y-80

  Tribute to Frederick A. Pottle Y-87

Harris, William Torrey 1835-1909 . . . . DLB-270

Harris, Wilson 1921- DLB-117; CDWLB-3

Harrison, Mrs. Burton
  (see Harrison, Constance Cary)

Harrison, Charles Yale 1898-1954 . . . . DLB-68

Harrison, Constance Cary 1843-1920 . . . . DLB-221

Harrison, Frederic 1831-1923 . . . . DLB-57, 190

  "On Style in English Prose" (1898) DLB-57

Harrison, Harry 1925- DLB-8

James P. Harrison Company DLB-49

Harrison, Jim 1937- Y-82

Harrison, M. John 1945- DLB-261

Harrison, Mary St. Leger Kingsley
  (see Malet, Lucas)

Harrison, Paul Carter 1936- DLB-38

Harrison, Susan Frances 1859-1935 . . . . . . DLB-99

Harrison, Tony 1937- DLB-40, 245

Harrison, William 1535-1593 . . . . DLB-136

Harrison, William 1933- DLB-234

Harrisse, Henry 1829-1910 . . . . DLB-47

Harry, J. S. 1939- DLB-325

The Harry Ransom Humanities Research Center
  at the University of Texas at Austin Y-00

Harryman, Carla 1952- DLB-193

Harsdörffer, Georg Philipp 1607-1658 . . . . DLB-164

Harsent, David 1942- DLB-40

Hart, Albert Bushnell 1854-1943 . . . . DLB-17

Hart, Anne 1768-1834 . . . . DLB-200

Hart, Elizabeth 1771-1833 . . . . DLB-200

Hart, Julia Catherine 1796-1867 . . . . DLB-99

Hart, Kevin 1954- DLB-325

Hart, Lorenz 1895-1943 . . . . DLB-265

  Larry Hart: Still an Influence Y-95

  Lorenz Hart: An American Lyricist Y-95

  The Lorenz Hart Centenary Y-95

Hart, Moss 1904-1961 . . . . DLB-7, 266

Hart, Oliver 1723-1795 . . . . DLB-31

Rupert Hart-Davis Limited DLB-112

Harte, Bret 1836-1902
  . . . . DLB-12, 64, 74, 79, 186; CDALB-3

Harte, Edward Holmead 1922- DLB-127

Harte, Houston Harriman 1927- DLB-127

Harte, Jack 1944- DLB-319

Hartlaub, Felix 1913-1945 . . . . DLB-56

Hartlebon, Otto Erich 1864-1905 . . . . DLB-118

Hartley, David 1705-1757 . . . . DLB-252

Hartley, L. P. 1895-1972 . . . . DLB-15, 139

Hartley, Marsden 1877-1943 . . . . DLB-54

Hartling, Peter 1933- DLB-75

Hartman, Geoffrey H. 1929- DLB-67

Hartmann, Sadakichi 1867-1944 . . . . DLB-54

Hartmann von Aue
  circa 1160-circa 1205 . . . . DLB-138; CDWLB-2

Hartshorne, Charles 1897-2000 . . . . DLB-270

Haruf, Kent 1943- DLB-292

Harvey, Gabriel 1550?-1631 . . . DLB-167, 213, 281

Harvey, Jack (see Rankin, Ian)

Harvey, Jean-Charles 1891-1967 . . . . DLB-88

Harvill Press Limited DLB-112

Harwood, Gwen 1920-1995 . . . . DLB-289

Harwood, Lee 1939- DLB-40

Harwood, Ronald 1934- DLB-13

al-Hasan al-Basri 642-728 . . . . DLB-311

Hašek, Jaroslav 1883-1923 . . . DLB-215; CDWLB-4

Haskins, Charles Homer 1870-1937 . . . . . . DLB-47

Haslam, Gerald 1937- DLB-212

Hass, Robert 1941- DLB-105, 206

Hasselstrom, Linda M. 1943- DLB-256

Hastings, Michael 1938- DLB-233

Hatar, Győző 1914- DLB-215

The Hatch-Billops Collection DLB-76

Hathaway, William 1944- DLB-120

Hatherly, Ana 1929- DLB-287

Hauch, Carsten 1790-1872 . . . . DLB-300

Hauff, Wilhelm 1802-1827 . . . . DLB-90

Hauge, Olav H. 1908-1994 . . . . DLB-297

Haugen, Paal-Helge 1945- DLB-297

Haugwitz, August Adolph von
  1647-1706 . . . . DLB-168

Hauptmann, Carl 1858-1921 . . . . DLB-66, 118

Hauptmann, Gerhart
  1862-1946 . . . . DLB-66, 118; CDWLB-2

Hauser, Marianne 1910- Y-83

Havel, Václav 1936- DLB-232; CDWLB-4

Haven, Alice B. Neal 1827-1863 . . . . DLB-250

Havergal, Frances Ridley 1836-1879 . . . . . DLB-199

Hawes, Stephen 1475?-before 1529 . . . . . . DLB-132

Hawker, Robert Stephen 1803-1875 . . . . . . DLB-32

Hawkes, John
  1925-1998 . . . . DLB-2, 7, 227; Y-80, Y-98

  John Hawkes: A Tribute Y-98

  Tribute to Donald Barthelme Y-89

Hawkesworth, John 1720-1773 . . . . DLB-142

Hawkins, Sir Anthony Hope (see Hope, Anthony)

Hawkins, Sir John 1719-1789 . . . . DLB-104, 142

Hawkins, Walter Everette 1883-? DLB-50

Hawthorne, Nathaniel 1804-1864
  . . . DLB-1, 74, 183, 223, 269; DS-5; CDALB-2

  The Nathaniel Hawthorne Society Y-00

  The Old Manse DLB-223

Cumulative Index

Hawthorne, Sophia Peabody
   1809-1871................... DLB-183, 239

Hay, John 1835-1905 ....DLB-12, 47, 189

Hay, John 1915- DLB-275

Hayashi Fumiko 1903-1951 .... DLB-180

Haycox, Ernest 1899-1950 .... DLB-206

Haycraft, Anna Margaret (see Ellis, Alice Thomas)

Hayden, Robert
   1913-1980............ DLB-5, 76; CDALB-1

Haydon, Benjamin Robert 1786-1846 ... DLB-110

Hayes, John Michael 1919- DLB-26

Hayley, William 1745-1820......... DLB-93, 142

Haym, Rudolf 1821-1901 .... DLB-129

Hayman, Robert 1575-1629 .... DLB-99

Hayman, Ronald 1932- DLB-155

Hayne, Paul Hamilton
   1830-1886 ....DLB-3, 64, 79, 248

Hays, Mary 1760-1843 .... DLB-142, 158

Hayslip, Le Ly 1949- DLB-312

Hayward, John 1905-1965 .... DLB-201

Haywood, Eliza 1693?-1756 .... DLB-39

   Dedication of *Lasselia* [excerpt]
   (1723)..................... DLB-39

   Preface to *The Disguis'd Prince*
   [excerpt] (1723) DLB-39

   The Tea-Table [excerpt]............. DLB-39

Haywood, William D. 1869-1928....... DLB-303

Willis P. Hazard [publishing house] DLB-49

Hazlitt, William 1778-1830 .... DLB-110, 158

Hazzard, Shirley 1931- DLB-289; Y-82

Head, Bessie
   1937-1986......... DLB-117, 225; CDWLB-3

Headley, Joel T. 1813-1897... DLB-30, 183; DS-13

Heaney, Seamus 1939- .. DLB-40; Y-95; CDBLB-8

   Nobel Lecture 1994: Crediting Poetry.... Y-95

Heard, Nathan C. 1936- DLB-33

Hearn, Lafcadio 1850-1904 ......DLB-12, 78, 189

Hearn, Mary Anne (Marianne Farningham,
   Eva Hope) 1834-1909 .... DLB-240

Hearne, John 1926- DLB-117

Hearne, Samuel 1745-1792 .... DLB-99

Hearne, Thomas 1678?-1735 .... DLB-213

Hearst, William Randolph 1863-1951 .... DLB-25

Hearst, William Randolph, Jr.
   1908-1993 .... DLB-127

Heartman, Charles Frederick
   1883-1953 .... DLB-187

Heat and Dust, 1975 Booker Prize winner,
   Ruth Prawer Jhabvala............. DLB-326

Heath, Catherine 1924- DLB-14

Heath, James Ewell 1792-1862 .... DLB-248

Heath, Roy A. K. 1926- DLB-117

Heath-Stubbs, John 1918- DLB-27

Heavysege, Charles 1816-1876 .... DLB-99

Hebbel, Friedrich
   1813-1863 .... DLB-129; CDWLB-2

Hebel, Johann Peter 1760-1826.......... DLB-90

Heber, Richard 1774-1833 .... DLB-184

Hébert, Anne 1916-2000 .... DLB-68

Hébert, Jacques 1923- DLB-53

Hebreo, León circa 1460-1520 .... DLB-318

Hecht, Anthony 1923- DLB-5, 169

Hecht, Ben 1894-1964 ....DLB-7, 9, 25, 26, 28, 86

Hecker, Isaac Thomas 1819-1888..... DLB-1, 243

Hedge, Frederic Henry
   1805-1890 .... DLB-1, 59, 243; DS-5

Hefner, Hugh M. 1926- DLB-137

Hegel, Georg Wilhelm Friedrich
   1770-1831..................... DLB-90

Heiberg, Johan Ludvig 1791-1860 ...... DLB-300

Heiberg, Johanne Luise 1812-1890...... DLB-300

Heide, Robert 1939- DLB-249

Heidegger, Martin 1889-1976 .... DLB-296

Heidish, Marcy 1947- Y-82

Heißenbüttel, Helmut 1921-1996........ DLB-75

Heike monogatari.................... DLB-203

Hein, Christoph 1944- ... DLB-124; CDWLB-2

Hein, Piet 1905-1996 .... DLB-214

Heine, Heinrich 1797-1856 ... DLB-90; CDWLB-2

Heinemann, Larry 1944- DS-9

William Heinemann Limited DLB-112

Heinesen, William 1900-1991.......... DLB-214

Heinlein, Robert A. 1907-1988 .... DLB-8

Heinrich, Willi 1920- DLB-75

Heinrich Julius of Brunswick|
   1564-1613 .... DLB-164

Heinrich von dem Türlîn
   fl. circa 1230..................... DLB-138

Heinrich von Melk
   fl. after 1160 .... DLB-148

Heinrich von Veldeke
   circa 1145-circa 1190 .... DLB-138

Heinse, Wilhelm 1746-1803 .... DLB-94

Heinz, W. C. 1915- DLB-171

Heiskell, John 1872-1972............... DLB-127

Hejinian, Lyn 1941- DLB-165

Helder, Herberto 1930- DLB-287

Heliand circa 850 .... DLB-148

Heller, Joseph
   1923-1999 .... DLB-2, 28, 227; Y-80, 99, 02

   Excerpts from Joseph Heller's
   USC Address, "The Literature
   of Despair"...................... Y-96

   Remembering Joe Heller, by William
   Price Fox Y-99

   A Tribute to Joseph Heller Y-99

Heller, Michael 1937- DLB-165

Hellman, Lillian 1906-1984 ..... DLB-7, 228; Y-84

Hellwig, Johann 1609-1674............ DLB-164

Helprin, Mark 1947- Y-85; CDALB-7

Helvétius, Claude-Adrien 1715-1771..... DLB-313

   The Spirit of Laws................. DLB-314

Helwig, David 1938- DLB-60

Hemans, Felicia 1793-1835 .... DLB-96

Hemenway, Abby Maria 1828-1890..... DLB-243

Hemingway, Ernest 1899-1961....DLB-4, 9, 102,
   210, 316; Y-81, 87, 99; DS-1, 15, 16; CDALB-4

   A Centennial Celebration Y-99

   Come to Papa Y-99

   The Ernest Hemingway Collection at
   the John F. Kennedy Library........ Y-99

   Ernest Hemingway Declines to
   Introduce *War and Peace* Y-01

   Ernest Hemingway's Reaction to
   James Gould Cozzens Y-98

   Ernest Hemingway's Toronto Journalism
   Revisited: With Three Previously
   Unrecorded Stories Y-92

   Falsifying Hemingway Y-96

   A Farewell to Arms (Documentary).... DLB-308

   Hemingway Centenary Celebration
   at the JFK Library................ Y-99

   The Hemingway/Fenton
   Correspondence Y-02

   Hemingway in the JFK Y-99

   The Hemingway Letters Project
   Finds an Editor Y-02

   Hemingway Salesmen's Dummies Y-00

   Hemingway: Twenty-Five Years Later Y-85

   A Literary Archaeologist Digs On:
   A Brief Interview with Michael
   Reynolds Y-99

   Not Immediately Discernible... but
   Eventually Quite Clear: The *First
   Light* and *Final Years* of
   Hemingway's Centenary Y-99

   Packaging Papa: *The Garden of Eden* Y-86

   Second International Hemingway
   Colloquium: Cuba Y-98

Hémon, Louis 1880-1913............. DLB-92

Hempel, Amy 1951- DLB-218

Hempel, Carl G. 1905-1997 ....DLB-279

Hemphill, Paul 1936- Y-87

Hénault, Gilles 1920-1996 .... DLB-88

Henchman, Daniel 1689-1761 .... DLB-24

Henderson, Alice Corbin 1881-1949 ..... DLB-54

Henderson, Archibald 1877-1963 .... DLB-103

Henderson, David 1942- DLB-41

Henderson, George Wylie 1904-1965 .... DLB-51

Henderson, Zenna 1917-1983 .... DLB-8

Henighan, Tom 1934- DLB-251

Henisch, Peter 1943- DLB-85

Henley, Beth 1952- Y-86

Henley, William Ernest 1849-1903........ DLB-19

Henniker, Florence 1855-1923 .... DLB-135

Henning, Rachel 1826-1914 . . . . .DLB-230	Herodotus circa 484 B.C.-circa 420 B.C. DLB-176; CDWLB-1	Hidalgo, José Luis 1919-1947 . . . . DLB-108
Henningsen, Agnes 1868-1962 . . . . .DLB-214	Héroët, Antoine 1490?-1567? DLB-327	Hiebert, Paul 1892-1987 . . . . DLB-68
Henry, Alexander 1739-1824 . . . . .DLB-99	Heron, Robert 1764-1807 . . . . DLB-142	Hieng, Andrej 1925- DLB-181
Henry, Buck 1930- DLB-26	Herr, Michael 1940- DLB-185	Hierro, José 1922-2002 . . . . DLB-108
Henry, Marguerite 1902-1997 . . . . .DLB-22	Herrera, Darío 1870-1914 . . . . DLB-290	Higgins, Aidan 1927- DLB-14
Henry, O. (see Porter, William Sydney)	Herrera, Fernando de 1534?-1597 . . . . . . DLB-318	Higgins, Colin 1941-1988 . . . . DLB-26
Henry, Robert Selph 1889-1970 . . . . .DLB-17	Herrera, Juan Felipe 1948- DLB-122	Higgins, George V. 1939-1999 . . . . DLB-2; Y-81, 98–99
Henry, Will (see Allen, Henry W.)	E. R. Herrick and Company DLB-49	Afterword [in response to Cozzen's *Mens Rea* (or Something)] Y-97
Henry VIII of England 1491-1547 . . . . . .DLB-132	Herrick, Robert 1591-1674 . . . . .DLB-126	
Henry of Ghent circa 1217-1229 - 1293 . . . . .DLB-115	Herrick, Robert 1868-1938 . . . . DLB-9, 12, 78	*At End of Day*: The Last George V. Higgins Novel .Y-99
Henryson, Robert 1420s or 1430s-circa 1505 . . . . .DLB-146	Herrick, William 1915-2004 . . . . .Y-83	The Books of George V. Higgins: A Checklist of Editions and Printings .Y-00
Henschke, Alfred (see Klabund)	Herrmann, John 1900-1959 . . . . .DLB-4	
Hensher, Philip 1965- DLB-267	Hersey, John 1914-1993 . . . DLB-6, 185, 278, 299; CDALB-7	George V. Higgins in Class Y-02
Hensley, Sophie Almon 1866-1946 . . . . . . .DLB-99	Hertel, François 1905-1985 . . . . DLB-68	Tribute to Alfred A. Knopf Y-84
Henson, Lance 1944- DLB-175	Hervé-Bazin, Jean Pierre Marie (see Bazin, Hervé)	Tributes to George V. Higgins Y-99
Henty, G. A. 1832-1902 . . . . .DLB-18, 141	Hervey, John, Lord 1696-1743 . . . . DLB-101	"What You Lose on the Swings You Make Up on the Merry-Go-Round" Y-99
The Henty Society Y-98	Herwig, Georg 1817-1875 . . . . DLB-133	
Hentz, Caroline Lee 1800-1856 . . . . . . .DLB-3, 248	Herzen, Alexander (Aleksandr Ivanovich Gersten) 1812-1870 . . . . DLB-277	Higginson, Thomas Wentworth 1823-1911 . . . . .DLB-1, 64, 243
Heraclitus fl. circa 500 B.C. DLB-176	Herzog, Emile Salomon Wilhelm (see Maurois, André)	Highsmith, Patricia 1921-1995 . . . . .DLB-306
Herbert, Agnes circa 1880-1960 . . . . .DLB-174	Hesiod eighth century B.C. DLB-176	Highwater, Jamake 1942?- DLB-52; Y-85
Herbert, Alan Patrick 1890-1971 . . . . .DLB-10, 191	Hesse, Hermann 1877-1962 . . . . DLB-66; CDWLB-2	Hijuelos, Oscar 1951- DLB-145
Herbert, Edward, Lord, of Cherbury 1582-1648 . . . . DLB-121, 151, 252		Hildegard von Bingen 1098-1179 . . . . .DLB-148
Herbert, Frank 1920-1986 . . . . . .DLB-8; CDALB-7	Hessus, Eobanus 1488-1540 . . . . DLB-179	*Das Hildesbrandslied* circa 820 . . . . DLB-148; CDWLB-2
Herbert, George 1593-1633 . . DLB-126; CDBLB-1	Heureka! (see Kertész, Imre and Nobel Prize in Literature: 2002) Y-02	
Herbert, Henry William 1807-1858 . . . . .DLB-3, 73	Hewat, Alexander circa 1743-circa 1824 . . . DLB-30	Hildesheimer, Wolfgang 1916-1991 . . .DLB-69, 124
Herbert, John 1926-2001 . . . . .DLB-53	Hewett, Dorothy 1923-2002 . . . . DLB-289	Hildreth, Richard 1807-1865 . . . DLB-1, 30, 59, 235
Herbert, Mary Sidney, Countess of Pembroke (see Sidney, Mary)	Hewitt, John 1907-1987 . . . . DLB-27	Hill, Aaron 1685-1750 . . . . DLB-84
	Hewlett, Maurice 1861-1923 . . . . .DLB-34, 156	Hill, Geoffrey 1932- DLB-40; CDBLB-8
Herbert, Xavier 1901-1984 . . . . .DLB-260	Heyen, William 1940- DLB-5	George M. Hill Company DLB-49
Herbert, Zbigniew 1924-1998 . . . . .DLB-232; CDWLB-4	Heyer, Georgette 1902-1974 . . . . DLB-77, 191	Hill, "Sir" John 1714?-1775 . . . . DLB-39
	Heym, Stefan 1913-2001 . . . . DLB-69	Lawrence Hill and Company, Publishers DLB-46
Herbst, Josephine 1892-1969 . . . . .DLB-9	Heyse, Paul 1830-1914 . . . . DLB-129	
Herburger, Gunter 1932- DLB-75, 124	Heytesbury, William circa 1310-1372 or 1373 . . . . DLB-115	Hill, Joe 1879-1915 . . . . .DLB-303
Herculano, Alexandre 1810-1877 . . . . . . .DLB-287		Hill, Leslie 1880-1960 . . . . DLB-51
Hercules, Frank E. M. 1917-1996 . . . . .DLB-33	Heyward, Dorothy 1890-1961 . . . . DLB-7, 249	Hill, Reginald 1936- DLB-276
Herder, Johann Gottfried 1744-1803 . . . . . .DLB-97	Heyward, DuBose 1885-1940 . . . DLB-7, 9, 45, 249	Hill, Susan 1942- DLB-14, 139
B. Herder Book Company DLB-49	Heywood, John 1497?-1580? DLB-136	Hill, Walter 1942- DLB-44
Heredia, José-María de 1842-1905 . . . . . . .DLB-217	Heywood, Thomas 1573 or 1574-1641 . . . .DLB-62	Hill and Wang DLB-46
Herford, Charles Harold 1853-1931 . . . . .DLB-149	Hiaasen, Carl 1953- DLB-292	Hillberry, Conrad 1928- DLB-120
Hergesheimer, Joseph 1880-1954 . . . . . .DLB-9, 102	Hibberd, Jack 1940- DLB-289	Hillerman, Tony 1925- DLB-206, 306
Heritage Press DLB-46	Hibbs, Ben 1901-1975 . . . . DLB-137	Hilliard, Gray and Company DLB-49
Hermann the Lame 1013-1054 . . . . DLB-148	"The Saturday Evening Post reaffirms a policy," Ben Hibb's Statement in *The Saturday Evening Post* (16 May 1942) DLB-137	Hills, Lee 1906-2000 . . . . .DLB-127
Hermes, Johann Timotheu 1738-1821 . . . . .DLB-97		Hillyer, Robert 1895-1961 . . . . DLB-54
Hermlin, Stephan 1915-1997 . . . . .DLB-69		Hilsenrath, Edgar 1926- DLB-299
Hernández, Alfonso C. 1938- DLB-122		Hilton, James 1900-1954 . . . . .DLB-34, 77
Hernández, Inés 1947- DLB-122	Hichens, Robert S. 1864-1950 . . . . DLB-153	Hilton, Walter died 1396 . . . . DLB-146
Hernández, Miguel 1910-1942 . . . . DLB-134	Hickey, Emily 1845-1924 . . . . DLB-199	Hilton and Company DLB-49
Hernton, Calvin C. 1932- DLB-38	Hickman, William Albert 1877-1957 . . . . . .DLB-92	Himes, Chester 1909-1984 . . . DLB-2, 76, 143, 226
	Hicks, Granville 1901-1982 . . . . DLB-246	Joseph Hindmarsh [publishing house] DLB-170
		Hine, Daryl 1936- DLB-60

Cumulative Index   DLB 329

Hingley, Ronald 1920- DLB-155

Hinojosa-Smith, Rolando 1929- DLB-82

Hinton, S. E. 1948- CDALB-7

Hippel, Theodor Gottlieb von 1741-1796..................... DLB-97

Hippius, Zinaida Nikolaevna 1869-1945 .... DLB-295

Hippocrates of Cos fl. circa 425 B.C.............DLB-176; CDWLB-1

Hirabayashi Taiko 1905-1972 .... DLB-180

Hirsch, E. D., Jr. 1928- DLB-67

Hirsch, Edward 1950- DLB-120

"Historical Novel," The Holocaust...... DLB-299

Hoagland, Edward 1932- DLB-6

Hoagland, Everett H., III 1942- DLB-41

Hoban, Russell 1925- DLB-52; Y-90

Hobbes, Thomas 1588-1679... DLB-151, 252, 281

Hobby, Oveta 1905-1995 .... DLB-127

Hobby, William 1878-1964............ DLB-127

Hobsbaum, Philip 1932- DLB-40

Hobsbawm, Eric (Francis Newton) 1917- DLB-296

Hobson, Laura Z. 1900-1986 .... DLB-28

Hobson, Sarah 1947- DLB-204

Hoby, Thomas 1530-1566 .... DLB-132

Hoccleve, Thomas circa 1368-circa 1437 .... DLB-146

Hoch, Edward D. 1930- DLB-306

Hochhuth, Rolf 1931- DLB-124

Hochman, Sandra 1936- DLB-5

Hocken, Thomas Morland 1836-1910 ... DLB-184

Hocking, William Ernest 1873-1966......DLB-270

Hodder and Stoughton, Limited........ DLB-106

Hodgins, Jack 1938- DLB-60

Hodgman, Helen 1945- DLB-14

Hodgskin, Thomas 1787-1869 .... DLB-158

Hodgson, Ralph 1871-1962 .... DLB-19

Hodgson, William Hope 1877-1918............DLB-70, 153, 156, 178

Hoe, Robert, III 1839-1909 .... DLB-187

Hoeg, Peter 1957- DLB-214

Hoel, Sigurd 1890-1960 .... DLB-297

Hoem, Edvard 1949- DLB-297

Hoffenstein, Samuel 1890-1947 .... DLB-11

Hoffman, Alice 1952- DLB-292

Hoffman, Charles Fenno 1806-1884... DLB-3, 250

Hoffman, Daniel 1923- DLB-5

   Tribute to Robert Graves.............. Y-85

Hoffmann, E. T. A. 1776-1822............ DLB-90; CDWLB-2

Hoffman, Frank B. 1888-1958 .... DLB-188

Hoffman, William 1925- DLB-234

   Tribute to Paxton Davis............... Y-94

Hoffmanswaldau, Christian Hoffman von 1616-1679..................... DLB-168

Hofmann, Michael 1957- DLB-40

Hofmannsthal, Hugo von 1874-1929..........DLB-81, 118; CDWLB-2

Hofmo, Gunvor 1921-1995 .... DLB-297

Hofstadter, Richard 1916-1970 ....DLB-17, 246

Hogan, Desmond 1950- DLB-14, 319

Hogan, Linda 1947- DLB-175

Hogan and Thompson................ DLB-49

Hogarth Press................. DLB-112; DS-10

Hogg, James 1770-1835.........DLB-93, 116, 159

Hohberg, Wolfgang Helmhard Freiherr von 1612-1688 .... DLB-168

von Hohenheim, Philippus Aureolus Theophrastus Bombastus (see Paracelsus)

Hohl, Ludwig 1904-1980 .... DLB-56

Højholt, Per 1928- DLB-214

Holan, Vladimir 1905-1980 .... DLB-215

d'Holbach, Paul Henri Thiry, baron 1723-1789..................... DLB-313

   The System of Nature (as Jean-Baptiste de Mirabaud) DLB-314

Holberg, Ludvig 1684-1754 .... DLB-300

Holbrook, David 1923- DLB-14, 40

Holcroft, Thomas 1745-1809 .... DLB-39, 89, 158

   Preface to *Alwyn* (1780)............. DLB-39

Holden, Jonathan 1941- DLB-105

   "Contemporary Verse Story-telling"... DLB-105

Holden, Molly 1927-1981 .... DLB-40

Hölderlin, Friedrich 1770-1843............ DLB-90; CDWLB-2

Holdstock, Robert 1948- DLB-261

Holiday, 1974 Booker Prize winner, Stanley Middleton DLB-326

Holiday House..................... DLB-46

Holinshed, Raphael died 1580 .... DLB-167

Holland, J. G. 1819-1881 ....DS-13

Holland, Norman N. 1927- DLB-67

Hollander, John 1929- DLB-5

Holley, Marietta 1836-1926 .... DLB-11

Hollinghurst, Alan 1954- DLB-207, 326

Hollingsworth, Margaret 1940- DLB-60

Hollo, Anselm 1934- DLB-40

Holloway, Emory 1885-1977 ....DLB-103

Holloway, John 1920- DLB-27

Holloway House Publishing Company ... DLB-46

Holme, Constance 1880-1955 .... DLB-34

Holmes, Abraham S. 1821?-1908........ DLB-99

Holmes, John Clellon 1926-1988 .....DLB-16, 237

   "Four Essays on the Beat Generation".................. DLB-16

Holmes, Mary Jane 1825-1907 ..... DLB-202, 221

Holmes, Oliver Wendell 1809-1894 ...... DLB-1, 189, 235; CDALB-2

Holmes, Richard 1945- DLB-155

Holmes, Thomas James 1874-1959.......DLB-187

The Holocaust "Historical Novel" DLB-299

Holocaust Fiction, Postmodern......... DLB-299

Holocaust Novel, The "Second-Generation" DLB-299

Holroyd, Michael 1935- DLB-155; Y-99

Holst, Hermann E. von 1841-1904 ...... DLB-47

Holt, John 1721-1784 .... DLB-43

Henry Holt and Company DLB-49, 284

Holt, Rinehart and Winston............ DLB-46

Holtby, Winifred 1898-1935........... DLB-191

Holthusen, Hans Egon 1913-1997 .... DLB-69

Hölty, Ludwig Christoph Heinrich 1748-1776..................... DLB-94

Holub, Miroslav 1923-1998 .... DLB-232; CDWLB-4

Holz, Arno 1863-1929 .... DLB-118

Home, Henry, Lord Kames (see Kames, Henry Home, Lord)

Home, John 1722-1808................ DLB-84

Home, William Douglas 1912-1992 ...... DLB-13

Home Publishing Company DLB-49

Homer circa eighth-seventh centuries B.C. DLB-176; CDWLB-1

Homer, Winslow 1836-1910........... DLB-188

Homes, Geoffrey (see Mainwaring, Daniel)

Honan, Park 1928- DLB-111

Hone, William 1780-1842..........DLB-110, 158

Hongo, Garrett Kaoru 1951- DLB-120, 312

Honig, Edwin 1919- DLB-5

Hood, Hugh 1928-2000 .... DLB-53

Hood, Mary 1946- DLB-234

Hood, Thomas 1799-1845 .... DLB-96

Hook, Sidney 1902-1989 ....DLB-279

Hook, Theodore 1788-1841 .... DLB-116

Hooker, Jeremy 1941- DLB-40

Hooker, Richard 1554-1600 .... DLB-132

Hooker, Thomas 1586-1647 .... DLB-24

hooks, bell 1952- DLB-246

Hooper, Johnson Jones 1815-1862 .... DLB-3, 11, 248

Hope, A. D. 1907-2000................ DLB-289

Hope, Anthony 1863-1933........ DLB-153, 156

Hope, Christopher 1944- DLB-225

Hope, Eva (see Hearn, Mary Anne)

Hope, Laurence (Adela Florence Cory Nicolson) 1865-1904.......... DLB-240

Hopkins, Ellice 1836-1904 .... DLB-190

Hopkins, Gerard Manley 1844-1889 .... DLB-35, 57; CDBLB-5

508

Hopkins, John ?-1570 . . . . DLB-132
Hopkins, John H., and Son DLB-46
Hopkins, Lemuel 1750-1801 . . . . DLB-37
Hopkins, Pauline Elizabeth 1859-1930 . . . . DLB-50
Hopkins, Samuel 1721-1803 . . . . DLB-31
Hopkinson, Francis 1737-1791 . . . . DLB-31
Hopkinson, Nalo 1960- DLB-251
Hopper, Nora (Mrs. Nora Chesson)
 1871-1906 . . . . DLB-240
Hoppin, Augustus 1828-1896 . . . . DLB-188
Hora, Josef 1891-1945 . . . . . . DLB-215; CDWLB-4
Horace 65 B.C.-8 B.C. DLB-211; CDWLB-1
Horgan, Paul 1903-1995 . . . . . DLB-102, 212; Y-85
 Tribute to Alfred A. Knopf Y-84
Horizon Press DLB-46
Horkheimer, Max 1895-1973 . . . . DLB-296
Hornby, C. H. St. John 1867-1946 . . . . . . DLB-201
Hornby, Nick 1957- DLB-207
Horne, Frank 1899-1974 . . . . DLB-51
Horne, Richard Henry (Hengist)
 1802 or 1803-1884 . . . . DLB-32
Horne, Thomas 1608-1654 . . . . DLB-281
Horney, Karen 1885-1952 . . . . DLB-246
Hornung, E. W. 1866-1921 . . . . DLB-70
Horovitz, Israel 1939- DLB-7
Horta, Maria Teresa (see The Three Marias:
 A Landmark Case in Portuguese
 Literary History)
Horton, George Moses 1797?-1883? DLB-50
 George Moses Horton Society Y-99
Horváth, Ödön von 1901-1938 . . . . . . DLB-85, 124
Horwood, Harold 1923- DLB-60
E. and E. Hosford [publishing house] DLB-49
Hoskens, Jane Fenn 1693-1770? DLB-200
Hoskyns, John circa 1566-1638 . . . . . DLB-121, 281
Hosokawa Yūsai 1535-1610 . . . . DLB-203
Hospers, John 1918- DLB-279
Hospital, Janette Turner 1942- DLB-325
Hostovský, Egon 1908-1973 . . . . DLB-215
Hotchkiss and Company DLB-49
Hotel du Lac, 1984 Booker Prize winner,
 Anita Brookner DLB-326
Hough, Emerson 1857-1923 . . . . DLB-9, 212
Houghton, Stanley 1881-1913 . . . . DLB-10
Houghton Mifflin Company DLB-49
Hours at Home DS-13
Household, Geoffrey 1900-1988 . . . . DLB-87
Housman, A. E. 1859-1936 . . . DLB-19; CDBLB-5
Housman, Laurence 1865-1959 . . . . DLB-10
Houston, Pam 1962- DLB-244
Houwald, Ernst von 1778-1845 . . . . DLB-90
Hovey, Richard 1864-1900 . . . . DLB-54

How Late It Was, How Late, 1994 Booker Prize winner,
 James Kelman DLB-326
Howard, Donald R. 1927-1987 . . . . DLB-111
Howard, Maureen 1930- Y-83
Howard, Richard 1929- DLB-5
Howard, Roy W. 1883-1964 . . . . DLB-29
Howard, Sidney 1891-1939 . . . . . . DLB-7, 26, 249
Howard, Thomas, second Earl of Arundel
 1585-1646 . . . . DLB-213
Howe, E. W. 1853-1937 . . . . DLB-12, 25
Howe, Henry 1816-1893 . . . . DLB-30
Howe, Irving 1920-1993 . . . . DLB-67
Howe, Joseph 1804-1873 . . . . DLB-99
Howe, Julia Ward 1819-1910 . . . . . DLB-1, 189, 235
Howe, Percival Presland 1886-1944 . . . . . . DLB-149
Howe, Susan 1937- DLB-120
Howell, Clark, Sr. 1863-1936 . . . . DLB-25
Howell, Evan P. 1839-1905 . . . . DLB-23
Howell, James 1594?-1666 . . . . DLB-151
Howell, Soskin and Company DLB-46
Howell, Warren Richardson
 1912-1984 . . . . DLB-140
Howells, William Dean 1837-1920
 . . . . DLB-12, 64, 74, 79, 189; CDALB-3
 Introduction to Paul Laurence
 Dunbar's *Lyrics of Lowly Life*
 (1896) DLB-50
 The William Dean Howells Society Y-01
Howitt, Mary 1799-1888 . . . . DLB-110, 199
Howitt, William 1792-1879 . . . . DLB-110
Hoyem, Andrew 1935- DLB-5
Hoyers, Anna Ovena 1584-1655 . . . . DLB-164
Hoyle, Fred 1915-2001 . . . . DLB-261
Hoyos, Angela de 1940- DLB-82
Henry Hoyt [publishing house] DLB-49
Hoyt, Palmer 1897-1979 . . . . DLB-127
Hrabal, Bohumil 1914-1997 . . . . DLB-232
Hrabanus Maurus 776?-856 . . . . DLB-148
Hronský, Josef Cíger 1896-1960 . . . . DLB-215
Hrotsvit of Gandersheim
 circa 935-circa 1000 . . . . DLB-148
Hubbard, Elbert 1856-1915 . . . . DLB-91
Hubbard, Kin 1868-1930 . . . . DLB-11
Hubbard, William circa 1621-1704 . . . . DLB-24
Huber, Therese 1764-1829 . . . . DLB-90
Huch, Friedrich 1873-1913 . . . . DLB-66
Huch, Ricarda 1864-1947 . . . . DLB-66
Huddle, David 1942- DLB-130
Hudgins, Andrew 1951- DLB-120, 282
Hudson, Henry Norman 1814-1886 . . . . . . DLB-64
Hudson, Stephen 1868?-1944 . . . . DLB-197
Hudson, W. H. 1841-1922 . . . . . DLB-98, 153, 174
Hudson and Goodwin DLB-49

Huebsch, B. W., oral history Y-99
B. W. Huebsch [publishing house] DLB-46
Hueffer, Oliver Madox 1876-1931 . . . . DLB-197
Huet, Pierre Daniel
 Preface to *The History of Romances*
 (1715) DLB-39
Hugh of St. Victor circa 1096-1141 . . . . . . DLB-208
Hughes, David 1930- DLB-14
Hughes, Dusty 1947- DLB-233
Hughes, Hatcher 1881-1945 . . . . DLB-249
Hughes, John 1677-1720 . . . . DLB-84
Hughes, Langston 1902-1967 . . . . . . DLB-4, 7, 48,
 51, 86, 228, 315; DS-15; CDALB-5
Hughes, Richard 1900-1976 . . . . DLB-15, 161
Hughes, Ted 1930-1998 . . . . DLB-40, 161
Hughes, Thomas 1822-1896 . . . . DLB-18, 163
Hugo, Richard 1923-1982 . . . . DLB-5, 206
Hugo, Victor 1802-1885 . . . . . DLB-119, 192, 217
Hugo Awards and Nebula Awards DLB-8
Huidobro, Vicente 1893-1948 . . . . DLB-283
Hull, Richard 1896-1973 . . . . DLB-77
Hulda (Unnur Benediktsdóttir Bjarklind)
 1881-1946 . . . . DLB-293
Hulme, Keri 1947- DLB-326
Hulme, T. E. 1883-1917 . . . . DLB-19
Hulton, Anne ?-1779? DLB-200
Humanism, Sixteenth-Century
 Spanish DLB-318
Humboldt, Alexander von 1769-1859 . . . . . DLB-90
Humboldt, Wilhelm von 1767-1835 . . . . . . DLB-90
Hume, David 1711-1776 . . . . DLB-104, 252
Hume, Fergus 1859-1932 . . . . DLB-70
Hume, Sophia 1702-1774 . . . . DLB-200
Hume-Rothery, Mary Catherine
 1824-1885 . . . . DLB-240
Humishuma
 (see Mourning Dove)
Hummer, T. R. 1950- DLB-120
Humor
 American Humor: A Historical
 Survey DLB-11
 American Humor Studies Association Y-99
 The Comic Tradition Continued
 [in the British Novel] DLB-15
 Humorous Book Illustration DLB-11
 International Society for Humor Studies . . . Y-99
 Newspaper Syndication of American
 Humor DLB-11
 Selected Humorous Magazines
 (1820-1950) DLB-11
Bruce Humphries [publishing house] DLB-46
Humphrey, Duke of Gloucester
 1391-1447 . . . . DLB-213
Humphrey, William
 1924-1997 . . . . DLB-6, 212, 234, 278
Humphreys, David 1752-1818 . . . . DLB-37

Humphreys, Emyr 1919- DLB-15	Hyde, Mary 1912-2003............... DLB-187	Indiana University Press.................. Y-02
Humphreys, Josephine 1945- DLB-292	Hyman, Trina Schart 1939- DLB-61	Ingamells, Rex 1913-1955 .... DLB-260
Hunayn ibn Ishaq 809-873 or 877....... DLB-311	**I**	Inge, William 1913-1973....DLB-7, 249; CDALB-1
Huncke, Herbert 1915-1996........... DLB-16		Ingelow, Jean 1820-1897 .... DLB-35, 163
Huneker, James Gibbons 1857-1921..................... DLB-71	Iavorsky, Stefan 1658-1722............ DLB-150	Ingemann, B. S. 1789-1862............ DLB-300
Hunold, Christian Friedrich 1681-1721.................... DLB-168	Iazykov, Nikolai Mikhailovich 1803-1846 .... DLB-205	Ingersoll, Ralph 1900-1985............DLB-127
Hunt, Irene 1907- DLB-52	Ibáñez, Armando P. 1949- DLB-209	The Ingersoll Prizes Y-84
Hunt, Leigh 1784-1859........DLB-96, 110, 144	Ibáñez, Sara de 1909-1971 .... DLB-290	Ingoldsby, Thomas (see Barham, Richard Harris)
Hunt, Violet 1862-1942 ....DLB-162, 197	Ibarbourou, Juana de 1892-1979....... DLB-290	Ingraham, Joseph Holt 1809-1860 .... DLB-3, 248
Hunt, William Gibbes 1791-1833 .... DLB-73	Ibn Abi Tahir Tayfur 820-893 .... DLB-311	Inman, John 1805-1850 .... DLB-73
Hunter, Evan (Ed McBain) 1926-2005 ....DLB-306; Y-82	Ibn Qutaybah 828-889 .... DLB-311	Innerhofer, Franz 1944- DLB-85
Tribute to John D. MacDonald Y-86	Ibn al-Rumi 836-896................. DLB-311	Innes, Michael (J. I. M. Stewart) 1906-1994 ....DLB-276
Hunter, Jim 1939- DLB-14	Ibn Sa'd 784-845..................... DLB-311	Innis, Harold Adams 1894-1952......... DLB-88
Hunter, Kristin 1931- DLB-33	Ibrahim al-Mawsili 742 or 743-803 or 804 DLB-311	Innis, Mary Quayle 1899-1972.......... DLB-88
Tribute to Julian Mayfield Y-84	Ibn Bajja circa 1077-1138.............. DLB-115	Inō Sōgi 1421-1502................... DLB-203
Hunter, Mollie 1922- DLB-161	Ibn Gabirol, Solomon circa 1021-circa 1058 .... DLB-115	Inoue Yasushi 1907-1991 .... DLB-182
Hunter, N. C. 1908-1971 .... DLB-10	Ibn al-Muqaffa' circa 723-759 .... DLB-311	"The Greatness of Southern Literature": League of the South Institute for the Study of Southern Culture and History Y-02
Hunter-Duvar, John 1821-1899 .... DLB-99	Ibn al-Mu'tazz 861-908................. DLB-311	
Huntington, Henry E. 1850-1927....... DLB-140	Ibuse Masuji 1898-1993 .... DLB-180	
The Henry E. Huntington Library Y-92	Ichijō Kanera (see Ichijō Kaneyoshi)	International Publishers Company DLB-46
Huntington, Susan Mansfield 1791-1823..................... DLB-200	Ichijō Kaneyoshi (Ichijō Kanera) 1402-1481 .... DLB-203	Internet (publishing and commerce) Author Websites.................... Y-97
Hurd and Houghton.................. DLB-49	Iffland, August Wilhelm 1759-1814..................... DLB-94	The Book Trade and the Internet Y-00
Hurst, Fannie 1889-1968 .... DLB-86		E-Books Turn the Corner Y-98
Hurst and Blackett DLB-106	Iggulden, John 1917- DLB-289	The E-Researcher: Possibilities and Pitfalls....................... Y-00
Hurst and Company................... DLB-49	Ignatieff, Michael 1947- DLB-267	Interviews on E-publishing............. Y-00
Hurston, Zora Neale 1901?-1960......... DLB-51, 86; CDALB-7	Ignatow, David 1914-1997 .... DLB-5	John Updike on the Internet Y-97
Husserl, Edmund 1859-1938 .... DLB-296	Ike, Chukwuemeka 1931- DLB-157	LitCheck Website.................... Y-01
Husson, Jules-François-Félix (see Champfleury)	Ikkyū Sōjun 1394-1481................ DLB-203	Virtual Books and Enemies of Books..... Y-00
Huston, John 1906-1987............... DLB-26	Iles, Francis (see Berkeley, Anthony)	Interviews Adoff, Arnold...................... Y-01
Hutcheson, Francis 1694-1746 ...... DLB-31, 252	Il'f, Il'ia (Il'ia Arnol'dovich Fainzil'berg) 1897-1937......................DLB-272	Aldridge, John W................... Y-91
Hutchinson, Ron 1947- DLB-245		Anastas, Benjamin Y-98
Hutchinson, R. C. 1907-1975 .... DLB-191	Illich, Ivan 1926-2002 .... DLB-242	Baker, Nicholson Y-00
Hutchinson, Thomas 1711-1780 ...... DLB-30, 31	Illustration Children's Book Illustration in the Twentieth Century DLB-61	Bank, Melissa Y-98
Hutchinson and Company (Publishers) Limited.............. DLB-112		Bass, T. J......................... Y-80
	Children's Illustrators, 1800-1880 ... DLB-163	Bernstein, Harriet.................... Y-82
Huth, Angela 1938- DLB-271	Early American Book Illustration DLB-49	Betts, Doris Y-82
Hutton, Richard Holt 1826-1897..................... DLB-57	The Iconography of Science-Fiction Art........................ DLB-8	Bosworth, David Y-82
von Hutten, Ulrich 1488-1523 ....DLB-179	The Illustration of Early German Literary Manuscripts, circa 1150-circa 1300 .... DLB-148	Bottoms, David Y-83
Huxley, Aldous 1894-1963 ...... DLB-36, 100, 162, 195, 255; CDBLB-6		Bowers, Fredson.................... Y-80
		Burnshaw, Stanley Y-97
Huxley, Elspeth Josceline 1907-1997...................DLB-77, 204	Minor Illustrators, 1880-1914 .... DLB-141	Carpenter, Humphrey Y-84, 99
	Illyés, Gyula 1902-1983 .... DLB-215; CDWLB-4	Carr, Virginia Spencer Y-00
Huxley, T. H. 1825-1895 .... DLB-57	Imbs, Bravig 1904-1946 .... DLB-4; DS-15	Carver, Raymond Y-83
Huyghue, Douglas Smith 1816-1891 ..... DLB-99	Imbuga, Francis D. 1947- DLB-157	Cherry, Kelly Y-83
Huysmans, Joris-Karl 1848-1907 ...... DLB-123	Immermann, Karl 1796-1840 .... DLB-133	Conroy, Jack Y-81
Hwang, David Henry 1957- DLB-212, 228, 312	Imru' al-Qays circa 526-circa 565 .... DLB-311	Coppel, Alfred Y-83
	In a Free State, 1971 Booker Prize winner, V. S. Naipaul DLB-326	Cowley, Malcolm Y-81
		Davis, Paxton..................... Y-89
Hyde, Donald 1909-1966 .... DLB-187	Inchbald, Elizabeth 1753-1821 .... DLB-39, 89	Devito, Carlo Y-94
		De Vries, Peter Y-82

Dickey, James Y-82	Potok, Chaim Y-84	Islas, Arturo 1938-1991 .... DLB-122
Donald, David Herbert Y-87	Powell, Padgett Y-01	Issit, Debbie 1966- DLB-233
Editors, Conversations with Y-95	Prescott, Peter S. Y-86	Ivanišević, Drago 1907-1981 .... DLB-181
Ellroy, James Y-91	Rabe, David Y-91	Ivanov, Georgii 1894-1954 .... DLB-317
Fancher, Betsy Y-83	Rechy, John Y-82	Ivanov, Viacheslav Ivanovich 1866-1949 .... DLB-295
Faust, Irvin Y-00	Reid, B. L. Y-83	Ivanov, Vsevolod Viacheslavovich 1895-1963 .... DLB-272
Fulton, Len Y-86	Reynolds, Michael Y-95, 99	Ivask, Yuri 1907-1986 .... DLB-317
Furst, Alan Y-01	Robinson, Derek Y-02	Ivaska, Astrīde 1926- DLB-232
Garrett, George Y-83	Rollyson, Carl Y-97	M. J. Ivers and Company DLB-49
Gelfman, Jane Y-93	Rosset, Barney Y-02	Iwaniuk, Wacław 1915-2001 .... DLB-215
Goldwater, Walter Y-93	Schlafly, Phyllis Y-82	Iwano Hōmei 1873-1920 .... DLB-180
Gores, Joe Y-02	Schroeder, Patricia Y-99	Iwaszkiewicz, Jarosław 1894-1980 .... DLB-215
Greenfield, George Y-91	Schulberg, Budd Y-81, 01	Iyayi, Festus 1947- DLB-157
Griffin, Bryan Y-81	Scribner, Charles, III. Y-94	Izumi Kyōka 1873-1939 .... DLB-180
Groom, Winston Y-01	Sipper, Ralph Y-94	
Guilds, John Caldwell Y-92	Smith, Cork Y-95	
Hamilton, Virginia Y-01	Staley, Thomas F. Y-00	**J**
Hardin, James Y-92	Styron, William Y-80	Jackmon, Marvin E. (see Marvin X)
Harris, Mark Y-80	Talese, Nan Y-94	Jacks, L. P. 1860-1955 .... DLB-135
Harrison, Jim Y-82	Thornton, John Y-94	Jackson, Angela 1951- DLB-41
Hazzard, Shirley Y-82	Toth, Susan Allen Y-86	Jackson, Charles 1903-1968 .... DLB-234
Herrick, William Y-01	Tyler, Anne Y-82	Jackson, Helen Hunt 1830-1885 .... DLB-42, 47, 186, 189
Higgins, George V. Y-98	Vaughan, Samuel Y-97	Jackson, Holbrook 1874-1948 .... DLB-98
Hoban, Russell Y-90	Von Ogtrop, Kristin Y-92	Jackson, Laura Riding 1901-1991 .... DLB-48
Holroyd, Michael Y-99	Wallenstein, Barry Y-92	Jackson, Shirley 1916-1965 .... DLB-6, 234; CDALB-1
Horowitz, Glen Y-90	Weintraub, Stanley Y-82	Jacob, Max 1876-1944 .... DLB-258
Iggulden, John Y-01	Williams, J. Chamberlain Y-84	Jacob, Naomi 1884?-1964 .... DLB-191
Jakes, John Y-83	Into the Past: William Jovanovich's Reflections in Publishing Y-02	Jacob, Piers Anthony Dillingham (see Anthony, Piers)
Jenkinson, Edward B. Y-82	Ionesco, Eugène 1909-1994 .... DLB-321	Jacob, Violet 1863-1946 .... DLB-240
Jenks, Tom Y-86	Ireland, David 1927- DLB-289	Jacobi, Friedrich Heinrich 1743-1819 ...... DLB-94
Kaplan, Justin Y-86	The National Library of Ireland's New James Joyce Manuscripts Y-02	Jacobi, Johann Georg 1740-1841 .... DLB-97
King, Florence Y-85	Irigaray, Luce 1930- DLB-296	George W. Jacobs and Company DLB-49
Klopfer, Donald S. Y-97	Irving, John 1942- DLB-6, 278; Y-82	Jacobs, Harriet 1813-1897 .... DLB-239
Krug, Judith Y-82	Irving, Washington 1783-1859 .... DLB-3, 11, 30, 59, 73, 74, 183, 186, 250; CDALB-2	Jacobs, Joseph 1854-1916 .... DLB-141
Lamm, Donald Y-95		Jacobs, W. W. 1863-1943 .... DLB-135
Laughlin, James Y-96	Irwin, Grace 1907- DLB-68	The W. W. Jacobs Appreciation Society ... Y-98
Lawrence, Starling Y-95	Irwin, Will 1873-1948 .... DLB-25	Jacobsen, J. P. 1847-1885 .... DLB-300
Lindsay, Jack Y-84	Isaksson, Ulla 1916-2000 .... DLB-257	Jacobsen, Jørgen-Frantz 1900-1938 ...... DLB-214
Mailer, Norman Y-97	Iser, Wolfgang 1926- DLB-242	Jacobsen, Josephine 1908- DLB-244
Manchester, William Y-85	Isherwood, Christopher 1904-1986 .... DLB-15, 195; Y-86	Jacobsen, Rolf 1907-1994 .... DLB-297
Max, D. T. Y-94		Jacobson, Dan 1929- DLB-14, 207, 225, 319
McCormack, Thomas Y-98	The Christopher Isherwood Archive, The Huntington Library Y-99	Jacobson, Howard 1942- DLB-207
McNamara, Katherine Y-97	Ishiguro, Kazuo 1954- DLB-194, 326	Jacques de Vitry circa 1160/1170-1240 .... DLB-208
Mellen, Joan Y-94	Ishikawa Jun 1899-1987 .... DLB-182	Jæger, Frank 1926-1977 .... DLB-214
Menaker, Daniel Y-97	Iskander, Fazil' Abdulevich 1929- DLB-302	Ja'far al-Sadiq circa 702-765 .... DLB-311
Mooneyham, Lamarr Y-82	The Island Trees Case: A Symposium on School Library Censorship An Interview with Judith Krug An Interview with Phyllis Schlafly An Interview with Edward B. Jenkinson An Interview with Lamarr Mooneyham An Interview with Harriet Bernstein Y-82	William Jaggard [publishing house] DLB-170
Murray, Les Y-01		Jahier, Piero 1884-1966 .... DLB-114, 264
Nosworth, David Y-82		al-Jahiz circa 776-868 or 869 .... DLB-311
O'Connor, Patrick Y-84, 99		
Ozick, Cynthia Y-83		
Penner, Jonathan Y-83		
Pennington, Lee Y-82		
Penzler, Otto Y-96		
Plimpton, George Y-99		

Jahnn, Hans Henny 1894-1959 ..... DLB-56, 124

Jaimes, Freyre, Ricardo 1866?-1933 ..... DLB-283

Jakes, John 1932- DLB-278; Y-83

    Tribute to John Gardner Y-82

    Tribute to John D. MacDonald Y-86

Jakobína Johnson (Jakobína Sigurbjarnardóttir) 1883-1977................. DLB-293

Jakobson, Roman 1896-1982 .... DLB-242

James, Alice 1848-1892............... DLB-221

James, C. L. R. 1901-1989 .... DLB-125

James, Clive 1939- DLB-325

James, George P. R. 1801-1860 .... DLB-116

James, Henry 1843-1916
......DLB-12, 71, 74, 189; DS-13; CDALB-3

    "The Future of the Novel" (1899) DLB-18

    "The Novel in [Robert Browning's] 'The Ring and the Book'" (1912) DLB-32

James, John circa 1633-1729 .... DLB-24

James, M. R. 1862-1936 .... DLB-156, 201

James, Naomi 1949- DLB-204

James, P. D. (Phyllis Dorothy James White) 1920- DLB-87, 276; DS-17; CDBLB-8

    Tribute to Charles Scribner Jr........... Y-95

James, Thomas 1572?-1629 .... DLB-213

U. P. James [publishing house] DLB-49

James, Will 1892-1942 .... DS-16

James, William 1842-1910 ....DLB-270

James VI of Scotland, I of England 1566-1625 ....DLB-151, 172

Ane Schort Treatise Conteining Some Revlis and Cautelis to Be Obseruit and Eschewit in Scottis Poesi (1584)......DLB-172

Jameson, Anna 1794-1860.......... DLB-99, 166

Jameson, Fredric 1934- DLB-67

Jameson, J. Franklin 1859-1937 .... DLB-17

Jameson, Storm 1891-1986.............. DLB-36

Jančar, Drago 1948- DLB-181

Janés, Clara 1940- DLB-134

Janevski, Slavko 1920-2000 . DLB-181; CDWLB-4

Janowitz, Tama 1957- DLB-292

Jansson, Tove 1914-2001 .... DLB-257

Janvier, Thomas 1849-1913 .... DLB-202

Japan
    "The Development of Meiji Japan" .. DLB-180

    "Encounter with the West"........... DLB-180

Japanese Literature
    Letter from Japan................. Y-94, 98

    Medieval Travel Diaries........... DLB-203

    Surveys: 1987-1995 .... DLB-182

Jaramillo, Cleofas M. 1878-1956........ DLB-122

Jaramillo Levi, Enrique 1944- DLB-290

Jarir after 650-circa 730................ DLB-311

Jarman, Mark 1952- DLB-120, 282

Jarrell, Randall 1914-1965 .... DLB-48, 52; CDALB-1

Jarrold and Sons.................. DLB-106

Jarry, Alfred 1873-1907.......... DLB-192, 258

Jarves, James Jackson 1818-1888 .... DLB-189

Jasmin, Claude 1930- DLB-60

Jaunsudrabiņš, Jānis 1877-1962......... DLB-220

Jay, John 1745-1829................... DLB-31

Jean de Garlande (see John of Garland)

Jefferies, Richard 1848-1887........ DLB-98, 141

    The Richard Jefferies Society........... Y-98

Jeffers, Lance 1919-1985............... DLB-41

Jeffers, Robinson 1887-1962.......... DLB-45, 212; CDALB-4

Jefferson, Thomas 1743-1826.......... DLB-31, 183; CDALB-2

Jégé 1866-1940 .... DLB-215

Jelinek, Elfriede 1946- DLB-85

Jellicoe, Ann 1927- DLB-13, 233

Jemison, Mary circa 1742-1833......... DLB-239

Jen, Gish 1955- DLB-312

Jenkins, Dan 1929- DLB-241

Jenkins, Elizabeth 1905- DLB-155

Jenkins, Robin 1912-2005...........DLB-14, 271

Jenkins, William Fitzgerald (see Leinster, Murray)

Herbert Jenkins Limited.............. DLB-112

Jennings, Elizabeth 1926- DLB-27

Jens, Walter 1923- DLB-69

Jensen, Axel 1932-2003 .... DLB-297

Jensen, Johannes V. 1873-1950 .... DLB-214

Jensen, Merrill 1905-1980.............. DLB-17

Jensen, Thit 1876-1957 .... DLB-214

Jephson, Robert 1736-1803............. DLB-89

Jerome, Jerome K. 1859-1927 .....DLB-10, 34, 135

    The Jerome K. Jerome Society.......... Y-98

Jerome, Judson 1927-1991.............. DLB-105

    "Reflections: After a Tornado"...... DLB-105

Jerrold, Douglas 1803-1857 .... DLB-158, 159

Jersild, Per Christian 1935- DLB-257

Jesse, F. Tennyson 1888-1958........... DLB-77

Jewel, John 1522-1571................ DLB-236

John P. Jewett and Company DLB-49

Jewett, Sarah Orne 1849-1909 ....DLB-12, 74, 221

The Jewish Publication Society.......... DLB-49

Studies in American Jewish Literature Y-02

Jewitt, John Rodgers 1783-1821 .... DLB-99

Jewsbury, Geraldine 1812-1880 .... DLB-21

Jewsbury, Maria Jane 1800-1833 .... DLB-199

Jhabvala, Ruth Prawer 1927- DLB-139, 194, 323, 326

Jiang Guangci 1901-1931 .... DLB-328

Jiménez, Juan Ramón 1881-1958 .... DLB-134

Jin, Ha 1956- DLB-244, 292

Joans, Ted 1928-2003 .... DLB-16, 41

Jodelle, Estienne 1532?-1573............ DLB-327

Jōha 1525-1602..................... DLB-203

Jóhann Sigurjónsson 1880-1919 .... DLB-293

Jóhannes úr Kötlum 1899-1972 .... DLB-293

Johannis de Garlandia (see John of Garland)

John, Errol 1924-1988 .... DLB-233

John, Eugenie (see Marlitt, E.)

John of Dumbleton circa 1310-circa 1349 .... DLB-115

John of Garland (Jean de Garlande, Johannis de Garlandia) circa 1195-circa 1272 .... DLB-208

The John Reed Clubs................. DLB-303

Johns, Captain W. E. 1893-1968 .... DLB-160

Johnson, Mrs. A. E. ca. 1858-1922...... DLB-221

Johnson, Amelia (see Johnson, Mrs. A. E.)

Johnson, B. S. 1933-1973 .... DLB-14, 40

Johnson, Charles 1679-1748 .... DLB-84

Johnson, Charles 1948- DLB-33, 278

Johnson, Charles S. 1893-1956....... DLB-51, 91

Johnson, Colin (Mudrooroo) 1938- ... DLB-289

Johnson, Denis 1949- DLB-120

Johnson, Diane 1934- Y-80

Johnson, Dorothy M. 1905–1984 .... DLB-206

Johnson, E. Pauline (Tekahionwake) 1861-1913 ....DLB-175

Johnson, Edgar 1901-1995 .... DLB-103

Johnson, Edward 1598-1672............ DLB-24

Johnson, Eyvind 1900-1976 .... DLB-259

Johnson, Fenton 1888-1958 .... DLB-45, 50

Johnson, Georgia Douglas 1877?-1966.................. DLB-51, 249

Johnson, Gerald W. 1890-1980 .... DLB-29

Johnson, Greg 1953- DLB-234

Johnson, Helene 1907-1995 .... DLB-51

Jacob Johnson and Company DLB-49

Johnson, James Weldon 1871-1938............... DLB-51; CDALB-4

Johnson, John H. 1918-2005...........DLB-137

    "Backstage," Statement From the Initial Issue of *Ebony* (November 1945...............DLB-137

Johnson, Joseph [publishing house] DLB-154

Johnson, Linton Kwesi 1952- DLB-157

Johnson, Lionel 1867-1902 .... DLB-19

Johnson, Nunnally 1897-1977........... DLB-26

Johnson, Owen 1878-1952 .... Y-87

Johnson, Pamela Hansford 1912-1981 .... DLB-15

Johnson, Pauline 1861-1913 .... DLB-92

Johnson, Ronald 1935-1998 .... DLB-169

Johnson, Samuel 1696-1772 ... DLB-24; CDBLB-2

Johnson, Samuel
    1709-1784. . . . . DLB-39, 95, 104, 142, 213
    Rambler, no. 4 (1750) [excerpt] DLB-39
The BBC Four Samuel Johnson Prize
    for Non-fiction. Y-02
Johnson, Samuel 1822-1882. . . . . .DLB-1, 243
Johnson, Susanna 1730-1810 . . . . .DLB-200
Johnson, Terry 1955- DLB-233
Johnson, Uwe 1934-1984. . . . . DLB-75; CDWLB-2
Benjamin Johnson [publishing house] DLB-49
Benjamin, Jacob, and Robert Johnson
    [publishing house] DLB-49
Johnston, Annie Fellows 1863-1931. . . . . . .DLB-42
Johnston, Basil H. 1929- DLB-60
Johnston, David Claypole 1798?-1865. . . .DLB-188
Johnston, Denis 1901-1984 . . . . .DLB-10
Johnston, Ellen 1835-1873 . . . . .DLB-199
Johnston, George 1912-1970 . . . . .DLB-260
Johnston, George 1913-1970 . . . . .DLB-88
Johnston, Sir Harry 1858-1927 . . . . .DLB-174
Johnston, Jennifer 1930- DLB-14
Johnston, Mary 1870-1936. . . . . .DLB-9
Johnston, Richard Malcolm 1822-1898 . . . .DLB-74
Johnstone, Charles 1719?-1800?. DLB-39
Johst, Hanns 1890-1978 . . . . .DLB-124
Jökull Jakobsson 1933-1978 . . . . .DLB-293
Jolas, Eugene 1894-1952 . . . . .DLB-4, 45
Jolley, Elizabeth 1923- DLB-325
Jón Stefán Sveinsson or Svensson (see Nonni)
Jón Trausti (Guðmundur Magnússon)
    1873-1918 . . . . .DLB-293
Jón úr Vör (Jón Jónsson) 1917-2000 . . . .DLB-293
Jónas Hallgrímsson 1807-1845. . . . . .DLB-293
Jones, Alice C. 1853-1933 . . . . .DLB-92
Jones, Charles C., Jr. 1831-1893 . . . . .DLB-30
Jones, D. G. 1929- DLB-53
Jones, David 1895-1974 . . .DLB-20, 100; CDBLB-7
Jones, Diana Wynne 1934- DLB-161
Jones, Ebenezer 1820-1860 . . . . .DLB-32
Jones, Ernest 1819-1868. . . . . .DLB-32
Jones, Gayl 1949- DLB-33, 278
Jones, George 1800-1870 . . . . .DLB-183
Jones, Glyn 1905-1995. . . . . .DLB-15
Jones, Gwyn 1907- DLB-15, 139
Jones, Henry Arthur 1851-1929. . . . . .DLB-10
Jones, Hugh circa 1692-1760 . . . . .DLB-24
Jones, James 1921-1977 . . . . . . .DLB-2, 143; DS-17
    James Jones Papers in the Handy
        Writers' Colony Collection at
        the University of Illinois at
        Springfield. Y-98
    The James Jones Society Y-92
Jones, Jenkin Lloyd 1911-2004. . . . . .DLB-127

Jones, John Beauchamp 1810-1866 . . . . . .DLB-202
Jones, Joseph, Major
    (see Thompson, William Tappan)
Jones, LeRoi (see Baraka, Amiri)
Jones, Lewis 1897-1939 . . . . .DLB-15
Jones, Madison 1925- DLB-152
Jones, Marie 1951- DLB-233
Jones, Preston 1936-1979 . . . . .DLB-7
Jones, Rodney 1950- DLB-120
Jones, Thom 1945- DLB-244
Jones, Sir William 1746-1794 . . . . .DLB-109
Jones, William Alfred 1817-1900 . . . . .DLB-59
Jones's Publishing House. DLB-49
Jong, Erica 1942- DLB-2, 5, 28, 152
Jonke, Gert F. 1946- DLB-85
Jonson, Ben
    1572?-1637 . . . . .DLB-62, 121; CDBLB-1
Jonsson, Tor 1916-1951 . . . . .DLB-297
Jordan, June 1936- DLB-38
Jorgensen, Johannes 1866-1956 . . . . .DLB-300
Jose, Nicholas 1952- DLB-325
Joseph, Jenny 1932- DLB-40
Joseph and George. Y-99
Michael Joseph Limited DLB-112
Josephson, Matthew 1899-1978 . . . . .DLB-4
Josephus, Flavius 37-100. . . . . .DLB-176
Josephy, Alvin M., Jr.
    Tribute to Alfred A. Knopf Y-84
Josiah Allen's Wife (see Holley, Marietta)
Josipovici, Gabriel 1940- DLB-14, 319
Josselyn, John ?-1675 . . . . .DLB-24
Joudry, Patricia 1921-2000 . . . . .DLB-88
Jouve, Pierre Jean 1887-1976 . . . . .DLB-258
Jovanovich, William 1920-2001 . . . . .Y-01
    Into the Past: William Jovanovich's
        Reflections on Publishing Y-02
    [Response to Ken Auletta]. Y-97
    The Temper of the West: William
        Jovanovich Y-02
    Tribute to Charles Scribner Jr.. . . . . .Y-95
Jovine, Francesco 1902-1950 . . . . .DLB-264
Jovine, Giuseppe 1922- DLB-128
Joyaux, Philippe (see Sollers, Philippe)
Joyce, Adrien (see Eastman, Carol)
Joyce, James 1882-1941
    . . . . .DLB-10, 19, 36, 162, 247; CDBLB-6
    Danis Rose and the Rendering of *Ulysses*. . . .Y-97
    James Joyce Centenary: Dublin, 1982. . . . .Y-82
    James Joyce Conference Y-85
    A Joyce (Con)Text: Danis Rose and the
        Remaking of *Ulysses*. Y-97
    The National Library of Ireland's
        New James Joyce Manuscripts Y-02
    The New *Ulysses*. Y-84

Public Domain and the Violation of
    Texts. Y-97
The Quinn Draft of James Joyce's
    Circe Manuscript Y-00
Stephen Joyce's Letter to the Editor of
    The Irish Times Y-97
Ulysses, Reader's Edition: First Reactions. . .Y-97
We See the Editor at Work Y-97
Whose *Ulysses?* The Function of Editing. . .Y-97
Jozsef, Attila 1905-1937 . . . . . DLB-215; CDWLB-4
San Juan de la Cruz 1542-1591 . . . . .DLB-318
Juarroz, Roberto 1925-1995. . . . . .DLB-283
Orange Judd Publishing Company DLB-49
Judd, Sylvester 1813-1853 . . . . .DLB-1, 243
Judith circa 930 . . . . .DLB-146
Juel-Hansen, Erna 1845-1922 . . . . .DLB-300
Julian of Norwich 1342-circa 1420. . . . . .DLB-1146
Julius Caesar
    100 B.C.-44 B.C.. . . . . DLB-211; CDWLB-1
June, Jennie
    (see Croly, Jane Cunningham)
Jung, Carl Gustav 1875-1961. . . . . .DLB-296
Jung, Franz 1888-1963. . . . . .DLB-118
Jünger, Ernst 1895-1998. . . . . DLB-56; CDWLB-2
Der jüngere Titurel circa 1275 . . . . .DLB-138
Jung-Stilling, Johann Heinrich
    1740-1817. . . . . .DLB-94
Junqueiro, Abílio Manuel Guerra
    1850-1923 . . . . .DLB-287
Justice, Donald 1925- Y-83
Juvenal circa A.D. 60-circa A.D. 130
    . . . . DLB-211; CDWLB-1
The Juvenile Library
    (see M. J. Godwin and Company)

K

Kacew, Romain (see Gary, Romain)
Kafka, Franz 1883-1924. . . . . . DLB-81; CDWLB-2
Kahn, Gus 1886-1941 . . . . .DLB-265
Kahn, Roger 1927- DLB-171
Kaikō Takeshi 1939-1989 . . . . .DLB-182
Káinn (Kristján Níels Jónsson/Kristjan
    Niels Julius) 1860-1936. . . . . .DLB-293
Kaiser, Georg 1878-1945 . . . . DLB-124; CDWLB-2
Kaiserchronik circa 1147 . . . . .DLB-148
Kaleb, Vjekoslav 1905- DLB-181
Kalechofsky, Roberta 1931- DLB-28
Kaler, James Otis 1848-1912 . . . . .DLB-12, 42
Kalmar, Bert 1884-1947. . . . . .DLB-265
Kamensky, Vasilii Vasil'evich
    1884-1961 . . . . .DLB-295
Kames, Henry Home, Lord
    1696-1782 . . . . .DLB-31, 104
Kamo no Chōmei (Kamo no Nagaakira)
    1153 or 1155-1216 . . . . .DLB-203
Kamo no Nagaakira (see Kamo no Chōmei)

Cumulative Index

Kampmann, Christian 1939-1988....... DLB-214

Kandel, Lenore 1932- DLB-16

Kane, Sarah 1971-1999............... DLB-310

Kaneko, Lonny 1939- DLB-312

Kang, Younghill 1903-1972........... DLB-312

Kanin, Garson 1912-1999............. DLB-7

    A Tribute (to Marc Connelly) Y-80

Kaniuk, Yoram 1930- DLB-299

Kant, Hermann 1926- DLB-75

Kant, Immanuel 1724-1804........... DLB-94

Kantemir, Antiokh Dmitrievich
    1708-1744.................... DLB-150

Kantor, MacKinlay 1904-1977 .... DLB-9, 102

Kanze Kōjirō Nobumitsu 1435-1516 .... DLB-203

Kanze Motokiyo (see Zeimi)

Kaplan, Fred 1937- DLB-111

Kaplan, Johanna 1942- DLB-28

Kaplan, Justin 1925- DLB-111; Y-86

Kaplinski, Jaan 1941- DLB-232

Kapnist, Vasilii Vasilevich 1758?-1823 ... DLB-150

Karadžić, Vuk Stefanović
    1787-1864 ....DLB-147; CDWLB-4

Karamzin, Nikolai Mikhailovich
    1766-1826.................... DLB-150

Karinthy, Frigyes 1887-1938 .... DLB-215

Karmel, Ilona 1925-2000 .... DLB-299

Karnad, Girish 1938- DLB-323

Karsch, Anna Louisa 1722-1791 .... DLB-97

Kasack, Hermann 1896-1966 .... DLB-69

Kasai Zenzō 1887-1927 .... DLB-180

Kaschnitz, Marie Luise 1901-1974 ..... DLB-69

Kassák, Lajos 1887-1967 .... DLB-215

Kaštelan, Jure 1919-1990 .... DLB-147

Kästner, Erich 1899-1974 .... DLB-56

Kataev, Evgenii Petrovich
    (see Il'f, Il'ia and Petrov, Evgenii)

Kataev, Valentin Petrovich 1897-1986.... DLB-272

Katenin, Pavel Aleksandrovich
    1792-1853.................... DLB-205

Kattan, Naim 1928- DLB-53

Katz, Steve 1935- Y-83

Ka-Tzetnik 135633 (Yehiel Dinur)
    1909-2001 .... DLB-299

Kauffman, Janet 1945- DLB-218; Y-86

Kauffmann, Samuel 1898-1971........ DLB-127

Kaufman, Bob 1925-1986............ DLB-16, 41

Kaufman, George S. 1889-1961 .... DLB-7

Kaufmann, Walter 1921-1980..........DLB-279

Kavan, Anna (Helen Woods Ferguson
    Edmonds) 1901-1968............. DLB-255

Kavanagh, P. J. 1931- DLB-40

Kavanagh, Patrick 1904-1967 .... DLB-15, 20

Kaverin, Veniamin Aleksandrovich
    (Veniamin Aleksandrovich Zil'ber)
    1902-1989 ....DLB-272

Kawabata Yasunari 1899-1972 .... DLB-180

Kay, Guy Gavriel 1954- DLB-251

Kaye-Smith, Sheila 1887-1956........... DLB-36

Kazakov, Iurii Pavlovich 1927-1982 ..... DLB-302

Kazin, Alfred 1915-1998............... DLB-67

Keane, John B. 1928-2002 .... DLB-13

Keary, Annie 1825-1879 .... DLB-163

Keary, Eliza 1827-1918 .... DLB-240

Keating, H. R. F. 1926- DLB-87

Keatley, Charlotte 1960- DLB-245

Keats, Ezra Jack 1916-1983............ DLB-61

Keats, John 1795-1821 ... DLB-96, 110; CDBLB-3

Keble, John 1792-1866 .... DLB-32, 55

Keckley, Elizabeth 1818?-1907 .... DLB-239

Keeble, John 1944- Y-83

Keeffe, Barrie 1945- DLB-13, 245

Keeley, James 1867-1934............... DLB-25

W. B. Keen, Cooke and Company....... DLB-49

The Mystery of Carolyn Keene Y-02

Kefala, Antigone 1935- DLB-289

Keillor, Garrison 1942- Y-87

Keith, Marian (Mary Esther MacGregor)
    1874?-1961..................... DLB-92

Keller, Gary D. 1943- DLB-82

Keller, Gottfried
    1819-1890 .... DLB-129; CDWLB-2

Keller, Helen 1880-1968 .... DLB-303

Kelley, Edith Summers 1884-1956 .... DLB-9

Kelley, Emma Dunham ?-? DLB-221

Kelley, Florence 1859-1932........... DLB-303

Kelley, William Melvin 1937- DLB-33

Kellogg, Ansel Nash 1832-1886 .... DLB-23

Kellogg, Steven 1941- DLB-61

Kelly, George E. 1887-1974 ....DLB-7, 249

Kelly, Hugh 1739-1777 .... DLB-89

Kelly, Piet and Company DLB-49

Kelly, Robert 1935- DLB-5, 130, 165

Kelman, James 1946- DLB-194, 319, 326

Kelmscott Press..................... DLB-112

Kelton, Elmer 1926- DLB-256

Kemble, E. W. 1861-1933............ DLB-188

Kemble, Fanny 1809-1893 .... DLB-32

Kemelman, Harry 1908-1996 .... DLB-28

Kempe, Margery circa 1373-1438....... DLB-146

Kempinski, Tom 1938- DLB-310

Kempner, Friederike 1836-1904 .... DLB-129

Kempowski, Walter 1929- DLB-75

Kenan, Randall 1963- DLB-292

Claude Kendall [publishing company] DLB-46

Kendall, Henry 1839-1882............ DLB-230

Kendall, May 1861-1943 .... DLB-240

Kendell, George 1809-1867 .... DLB-43

Keneally, Thomas 1935- DLB-289, 299, 326

Kenedy, P. J., and Sons............... DLB-49

Kenkō circa 1283-circa 1352........... DLB-203

Kenna, Peter 1930-1987 .... DLB-289

Kennan, George 1845-1924 .... DLB-189

Kennedy, A. L. 1965- DLB-271

Kennedy, Adrienne 1931- DLB-38

Kennedy, John Pendleton 1795-1870... DLB-3, 248

Kennedy, Leo 1907-2000.............. DLB-88

Kennedy, Margaret 1896-1967 .... DLB-36

Kennedy, Patrick 1801-1873 .... DLB-159

Kennedy, Richard S. 1920- DLB-111; Y-02

Kennedy, William 1928- DLB-143; Y-85

Kennedy, X. J. 1929- DLB-5

    Tribute to John Ciardi Y-86

Kennelly, Brendan 1936- DLB-40

Kenner, Hugh 1923-2003 .... DLB-67

    Tribute to Cleanth Brooks Y-80

Mitchell Kennerley [publishing house] DLB-46

Kenny, Maurice 1929- DLB-175

Kent, Frank R. 1877-1958 .... DLB-29

Kenyon, Jane 1947-1995 .... DLB-120

Kenzheev, Bakhyt Shkurullaevich
    1950- DLB-285

Keough, Hugh Edmund 1864-1912 ......DLB-171

Keppler and Schwartzmann DLB-49

Ker, John, third Duke of Roxburghe
    1740-1804................... DLB-213

Ker, N. R. 1908-1982 .... DLB-201

Keralio-Robert, Louise-Félicité de
    1758-1822 .... DLB-313

Kerlan, Irvin 1912-1963 ....DLB-187

Kermode, Frank 1919- DLB-242

Kern, Jerome 1885-1945 ....DLB-187

Kernaghan, Eileen 1939- DLB-251

Kerner, Justinus 1786-1862 .... DLB-90

Kerouac, Jack
    1922-1969 .. DLB-2, 16, 237; DS-3; CDALB-1

    Auction of Jack Kerouac's
        On the Road Scroll............. Y-01

    The Jack Kerouac Revival Y-95

    "Re-meeting of Old Friends":
        The Jack Kerouac Conference....... Y-82

    Statement of Correction to "The Jack
        Kerouac Revival" Y-96

Kerouac, Jan 1952-1996 .... DLB-16

Charles H. Kerr and Company DLB-49

Kerr, Orpheus C. (see Newell, Robert Henry)

Kersh, Gerald 1911-1968 .... DLB-255

Kertész, Imre DLB-299; Y-02
Kesey, Ken 1935-2001 . . . . DLB-2, 16, 206; CDALB-6
Kessel, Joseph 1898-1979 . . . . DLB-72
Kessel, Martin 1901-1990 . . . . DLB-56
Kesten, Hermann 1900-1996 . . . . DLB-56
Keun, Irmgard 1905-1982 . . . . DLB-69
Key, Ellen 1849-1926 . . . . DLB-259
Key and Biddle DLB-49
Keynes, Sir Geoffrey 1887-1982 . . . . DLB-201
Keynes, John Maynard 1883-1946 . . . . DS-10
Keyserling, Eduard von 1855-1918 . . . . DLB-66
al-Khalil ibn Ahmad circa 718-791 . . . . DLB-311
Khan, Adib 1949- DLB-323
Khan, Ismith 1925-2002 . . . . DLB-125
al-Khansa' fl. late sixth-mid seventh centuries DLB-311
Kharitonov, Evgenii Vladimirovich 1941-1981 . . . . DLB-285
Kharitonov, Mark Sergeevich 1937- DLB-285
Khaytov, Nikolay 1919- DLB-181
Khemnitser, Ivan Ivanovich 1745-1784 . . . . DLB-150
Kheraskov, Mikhail Matveevich 1733-1807 . . . . DLB-150
Khlebnikov, Velimir 1885-1922 . . . . DLB-295
Khodasevich, Vladislav 1886-1939 . . . . . . DLB-317
Khomiakov, Aleksei Stepanovich 1804-1860 . . . . DLB-205
Khristov, Boris 1945- DLB-181
Khvoshchinskaia, Nadezhda Dmitrievna 1824-1889 . . . . DLB-238
Khvostov, Dmitrii Ivanovich 1757-1835 . . . . DLB-150
Kibirov, Timur Iur'evich (Timur Iur'evich Zapoev) 1955- DLB-285
Kidd, Adam 1802?-1831 . . . . DLB-99
William Kidd [publishing house] DLB-106
Kidde, Harald 1878-1918 . . . . DLB-300
Kidder, Tracy 1945- DLB-185
Kiely, Benedict 1919- DLB-15, 319
Kieran, John 1892-1981 . . . . DLB-171
Kierkegaard, Søren 1813-1855 . . . . DLB-300
Kies, Marietta 1853-1899 . . . . DLB-270
Kiggins and Kellogg DLB-49
Kiley, Jed 1889-1962 . . . . DLB-4
Kilgore, Bernard 1908-1967 . . . . DLB-127
Kilian, Crawford 1941- DLB-251
Killens, John Oliver 1916-1987 . . . . DLB-33
    Tribute to Julian Mayfield Y-84
Killigrew, Anne 1660-1685 . . . . DLB-131
Killigrew, Thomas 1612-1683 . . . . DLB-58
Kilmer, Joyce 1886-1918 . . . . DLB-45

Kilroy, Thomas 1934- DLB-233
Kilwardby, Robert circa 1215-1279 . . . . . . DLB-115
Kilworth, Garry 1941- DLB-261
Kim, Anatolii Andreevich 1939- DLB-285
Kimball, Richard Burleigh 1816-1892 . . . . DLB-202
Kincaid, Jamaica 1949- DLB-157, 227; CDALB-7; CDWLB-3
Kinck, Hans Ernst 1865-1926 . . . . DLB-297
King, Charles 1844-1933 . . . . DLB-186
King, Clarence 1842-1901 . . . . DLB-12
King, Florence 1936- Y-85
King, Francis 1923- DLB-15, 139
King, Grace 1852-1932 . . . . DLB-12, 78
King, Harriet Hamilton 1840-1920 . . . . . . DLB-199
King, Henry 1592-1669 . . . . DLB-126
Solomon King [publishing house] DLB-49
King, Stephen 1947- DLB-143; Y-80
King, Susan Petigru 1824-1875 . . . . DLB-239
King, Thomas 1943- DLB-175
King, Woodie, Jr. 1937- DLB-38
Kinglake, Alexander William 1809-1891 . . . . DLB-55, 166
Kingo, Thomas 1634-1703 . . . . DLB-300
Kingsbury, Donald 1929- DLB-251
Kingsley, Charles 1819-1875 . . . . DLB-21, 32, 163, 178, 190
Kingsley, Henry 1830-1876 . . . . DLB-21, 230
Kingsley, Mary Henrietta 1862-1900 . . . . . DLB-174
Kingsley, Sidney 1906-1995 . . . . DLB-7
Kingsmill, Hugh 1889-1949 . . . . DLB-149
Kingsolver, Barbara 1955- DLB-206; CDALB-7
Kingston, Maxine Hong 1940- . . DLB-173, 212, 312; Y-80; CDALB-7
Kingston, William Henry Giles 1814-1880 . . . . DLB-163
Kinnan, Mary Lewis 1763-1848 . . . . DLB-200
Kinnell, Galway 1927- DLB-5; Y-87
Kinsella, John 1963- DLB-325
Kinsella, Thomas 1928- DLB-27
Kipling, Rudyard 1865-1936 . . . . DLB-19, 34, 141, 156; CDBLB-5
Kipphardt, Heinar 1922-1982 . . . . DLB-124
Kirby, William 1817-1906 . . . . DLB-99
Kircher, Athanasius 1602-1680 . . . . DLB-164
Kireevsky, Ivan Vasil'evich 1806-1856 . . . . DLB-198
Kireevsky, Petr Vasil'evich 1808-1856 . . . . DLB-205
Kirk, Hans 1898-1962 . . . . DLB-214
Kirk, John Foster 1824-1904 . . . . DLB-79
Kirkconnell, Watson 1895-1977 . . . . DLB-68
Kirkland, Caroline M. 1801-1864 . . . . DLB-3, 73, 74, 250; DS-13
Kirkland, Joseph 1830-1893 . . . . DLB-12

Francis Kirkman [publishing house] DLB-170
Kirkpatrick, Clayton 1915-2004 . . . . DLB-127
Kirkup, James 1918- DLB-27
Kirouac, Conrad (see Marie-Victorin, Frère)
Kirsch, Sarah 1935- DLB-75
Kirst, Hans Hellmut 1914-1989 . . . . DLB-69
Kiš, Danilo 1935-1989 . . . . . . DLB-181; CDWLB-4
Kita Morio 1927- DLB-182
Kitcat, Mabel Greenhow 1859-1922 . . . . . DLB-135
Kitchin, C. H. B. 1895-1967 . . . . DLB-77
Kittredge, William 1932- DLB-212, 244
Kiukhel'beker, Vil'gel'm Karlovich 1797-1846 . . . . DLB-205
Kizer, Carolyn 1925- DLB-5, 169
Kjaerstad, Jan 1953- DLB-297
Klabund 1890-1928 . . . . DLB-66
Klaj, Johann 1616-1656 . . . . DLB-164
Klappert, Peter 1942- DLB-5
Klass, Philip (see Tenn, William)
Klein, A. M. 1909-1972 . . . . DLB-68
Kleist, Ewald von 1715-1759 . . . . DLB-97
Kleist, Heinrich von 1777-1811 . . . . DLB-90; CDWLB-2
Klíma, Ivan 1931- DLB-232; CDWLB-4
Klimentev, Andrei Platonovic (see Platonov, Andrei Platonovich)
Klinger, Friedrich Maximilian 1752-1831 . . . . DLB-94
Kliuev, Nikolai Alekseevich 1884-1937 . . . DLB-295
Kliushnikov, Viktor Petrovich 1841-1892 . . . . DLB-238
Klopfer, Donald S.
    Impressions of William Faulkner Y-97
    Oral History Interview with Donald S. Klopfer Y-97
    Tribute to Alfred A. Knopf Y-84
Klopstock, Friedrich Gottlieb 1724-1803 . . . . DLB-97
Klopstock, Meta 1728-1758 . . . . DLB-97
Kluge, Alexander 1932- DLB-75
Kluge, P. F. 1942- Y-02
Knapp, Joseph Palmer 1864-1951 . . . . DLB-91
Knapp, Samuel Lorenzo 1783-1838 . . . . . . DLB-59
J. J. and P. Knapton [publishing house] . . . DLB-154
Kniazhnin, Iakov Borisovich 1740-1791 . . . . DLB-150
Knickerbocker, Diedrich (see Irving, Washington)
Knigge, Adolph Franz Friedrich Ludwig, Freiherr von 1752-1796 . . . . DLB-94
Charles Knight and Company DLB-106
Knight, Damon 1922-2002 . . . . DLB-8
Knight, Etheridge 1931-1992 . . . . DLB-41
Knight, John S. 1894-1981 . . . . DLB-29
Knight, Sarah Kemble 1666-1727 . . . . DLB-24, 200

Cumulative Index

Knight-Bruce, G. W. H. 1852-1896 ...... DLB-174

Knister, Raymond 1899-1932 .... DLB-68

Knoblock, Edward 1874-1945 .... DLB-10

Knopf, Alfred A. 1892-1984 .... Y-84

    Knopf to Hammett: The Editoral Correspondence Y-00

Alfred A. Knopf [publishing house] DLB-46

Knorr von Rosenroth, Christian 1636-1689 .... DLB-168

Knowles, John 1926-2001 ...... DLB-6; CDALB-6

Knox, Frank 1874-1944 .... DLB-29

Knox, John circa 1514-1572 .... DLB-132

Knox, John Armoy 1850-1906 .... DLB-23

Knox, Lucy 1845-1884 .... DLB-240

Knox, Ronald Arbuthnott 1888-1957 ..... DLB-77

Knox, Thomas Wallace 1835-1896 ...... DLB-189

Knudsen, Jakob 1858-1917 .... DLB-300

Knut, Dovid 1900-1955 .... DLB-317

Kobayashi Takiji 1903-1933 .... DLB-180

Kober, Arthur 1900-1975 .... DLB-11

Kobiakova, Aleksandra Petrovna 1823-1892 .... DLB-238

Kocbek, Edvard 1904-1981 ...DLB-147; CDWLB-4

Koch, C. J. 1932- DLB-289

Koch, Howard 1902-1995 .... DLB-26

Koch, Kenneth 1925-2002 .... DLB-5

Kōda Rohan 1867-1947 .... DLB-180

Koehler, Ted 1894-1973 .... DLB-265

Koenigsberg, Moses 1879-1945 .... DLB-25

Koeppen, Wolfgang 1906-1996 .... DLB-69

Koertge, Ronald 1940- DLB-105

Koestler, Arthur 1905-1983 ...... Y-83; CDBLB-7

Kohn, John S. Van E. 1906-1976 .... DLB-187

Kokhanovskaia (see Sokhanskaia, Nadezhda Stepanova)

Kokoschka, Oskar 1886-1980 .... DLB-124

Kolatkar, Arun 1932-2004 .... DLB-323

Kolb, Annette 1870-1967 .... DLB-66

Kolbenheyer, Erwin Guido 1878-1962 .... DLB-66, 124

Kolleritsch, Alfred 1931- DLB-85

Kolodny, Annette 1941- DLB-67

Koltès, Bernard-Marie 1948-1989 .... DLB-321

Kol'tsov, Aleksei Vasil'evich 1809-1842 .... DLB-205

Komarov, Matvei circa 1730-1812 ...... DLB-150

Komroff, Manuel 1890-1974 .... DLB-4

Komunyakaa, Yusef 1947- DLB-120

Kondoleon, Harry 1955-1994 .... DLB-266

Koneski, Blaže 1921-1993 ... DLB-181; CDWLB-4

Konigsburg, E. L. 1930- DLB-52

Konparu Zenchiku 1405-1468? DLB-203

Konrád, György 1933- DLB-232; CDWLB-4

Konrad von Würzburg circa 1230-1287 .... DLB-138

Konstantinov, Aleko 1863-1897 .... DLB-147

Konwicki, Tadeusz 1926- DLB-232

Koontz, Dean 1945- DLB-292

Kooser, Ted 1939- DLB-105

Kopit, Arthur 1937- DLB-7

Kops, Bernard 1926?- DLB-13

Kornbluth, C. M. 1923-1958 .... DLB-8

Körner, Theodor 1791-1813 .... DLB-90

Kornfeld, Paul 1889-1942 .... DLB-118

Korolenko, Vladimir Galaktionovich 1853-1921 .... DLB-277

Kosinski, Jerzy 1933-1991 .... DLB-2, 299; Y-82

Kosmač, Ciril 1910-1980 .... DLB-181

Kosovel, Srečko 1904-1926 .... DLB-147

Kostrov, Ermil Ivanovich 1755-1796 ..... DLB-150

Kotzebue, August von 1761-1819 .... DLB-94

Kotzwinkle, William 1938- DLB-173

Kovačić, Ante 1854-1889 .... DLB-147

Kovalevskaia, Sof'ia Vasil'evna 1850-1891 .... DLB-277

Kovič, Kajetan 1931- DLB-181

Kozlov, Ivan Ivanovich 1779-1840 .... DLB-205

Kracauer, Siegfried 1889-1966 .... DLB-296

Kraf, Elaine 1946- Y-81

Kramer, Jane 1938- DLB-185

Kramer, Larry 1935- DLB-249

Kramer, Mark 1944- DLB-185

Kranjčević, Silvije Strahimir 1865-1908 .. DLB-147

Krasko, Ivan 1876-1958 .... DLB-215

Krasna, Norman 1909-1984 .... DLB-26

Kraus, Hans Peter 1907-1988 .... DLB-187

Kraus, Karl 1874-1936 .... DLB-118

Krause, Herbert 1905-1976 .... DLB-256

Krauss, Ruth 1911-1993 .... DLB-52

Krauth, Nigel 1949- DLB-325

Kreisel, Henry 1922-1991 .... DLB-88

Krestovsky V. (see Khvoshchinskaia, Nadezhda Dmitrievna)

Krestovsky, Vsevolod Vladimirovich 1839-1895 .... DLB-238

Kreuder, Ernst 1903-1972 .... DLB-69

Krėvė-Mickevičius, Vincas 1882-1954 ... DLB-220

Kreymborg, Alfred 1883-1966 .... DLB-4, 54

Krieger, Murray 1923-2000 .... DLB-67

Krim, Seymour 1922-1989 .... DLB-16

Kripke, Saul 1940- DLB-279

Kristensen, Tom 1893-1974 .... DLB-214

Kristeva, Julia 1941- DLB-242

Kristján Níels Jónsson/Kristjan Niels Julius (see Káinn)

Kritzer, Hyman W. 1918-2002 .... Y-02

Krivulin, Viktor Borisovich 1944-2001... DLB-285

Krleža, Miroslav 1893-1981 .... DLB-147; CDWLB-4

Krock, Arthur 1886-1974 .... DLB-29

Kroetsch, Robert 1927- DLB-53

Kropotkin, Petr Alekseevich 1842-1921 ...DLB-277

Kross, Jaan 1920- DLB-232

Kruchenykh, Aleksei Eliseevich 1886-1968 .... DLB-295

Krúdy, Gyula 1878-1933 .... DLB-215

Krutch, Joseph Wood 1893-1970 .... DLB-63, 206, 275

Krylov, Ivan Andreevich 1769-1844 ..... DLB-150

Krymov, Iurii Solomonovich (Iurii Solomonovich Beklemishev) 1908-1941 .... DLB-272

Kubin, Alfred 1877-1959 .... DLB-81

Kubrick, Stanley 1928-1999 .... DLB-26

Kudrun circa 1230-1240 .... DLB-138

Kuffstein, Hans Ludwig von 1582-1656.. DLB-164

Kuhlmann, Quirinus 1651-1689 .... DLB-168

Kuhn, Thomas S. 1922-1996 .... DLB-279

Kuhnau, Johann 1660-1722 .... DLB-168

Kukol'nik, Nestor Vasil'evich 1809-1868 .... DLB-205

Kukučín, Martin 1860-1928 .... DLB-215; CDWLB-4

Kumin, Maxine 1925- DLB-5

Kuncewicz, Maria 1895-1989 .... DLB-215

Kundera, Milan 1929- DLB-232; CDWLB-4

Kunene, Mazisi 1930- DLB-117

Kunikida Doppo 1869-1908 .... DLB-180

Kunitz, Stanley 1905-2006 .... DLB-48

Kunjufu, Johari M. (see Amini, Johari M.)

Kunnert, Gunter 1929- DLB-75

Kunze, Reiner 1933- DLB-75

Kuo, Helena 1911-1999 .... DLB-312

Kupferberg, Tuli 1923- DLB-16

Kuprin, Aleksandr Ivanovich 1870-1938 .... DLB-295

Kuraev, Mikhail Nikolaevich 1939- ... DLB-285

Kurahashi Yumiko 1935- DLB-182

Kureishi, Hanif 1954- DLB-194, 245

Kürnberger, Ferdinand 1821-1879 ...... DLB-129

Kurz, Isolde 1853-1944 .... DLB-66

Kusenberg, Kurt 1904-1983 .... DLB-69

Kushchevsky, Ivan Afanas'evich 1847-1876 .... DLB-238

Kushner, Tony 1956- DLB-228

Kuttner, Henry 1915-1958 .... DLB-8

Kuzmin, Mikhail Alekseevich 1872-1936 ... DLB-295
Kuznetsov, Anatoli 1929-1979 ... DLB-299, 302
Kyd, Thomas 1558-1594 ... DLB-62
Kyffin, Maurice circa 1560?-1598 ... DLB-136
Kyger, Joanne 1934- ... DLB-16
Kyne, Peter B. 1880-1957 ... DLB-78
Kyōgoku Tamekane 1254-1332 ... DLB-203
Kyrklund, Willy 1921- ... DLB-257

L

L. E. L. (see Landon, Letitia Elizabeth)
Labé, Louise 1520?-1566 ... DLB-327
Laberge, Albert 1871-1960 ... DLB-68
Laberge, Marie 1950- ... DLB-60
Labiche, Eugène 1815-1888 ... DLB-192
Labrunie, Gerard (see Nerval, Gerard de)
La Bruyère, Jean de 1645-1696 ... DLB-268
La Calprenède 1609?-1663 ... DLB-268
Lacan, Jacques 1901-1981 ... DLB-296
La Capria, Raffaele 1922- ... DLB-196
La Ceppède, Jean de 1550?-1623 ... DLB-327
La Chaussée, Pierre-Claude Nivelle de 1692-1754 ... DLB-313
Laclos, Pierre-Ambroise-François Choderlos de 1741-1803 ... DLB-313
Dangerous Acquaintances ... DLB-314
Lacombe, Patrice (see Trullier-Lacombe, Joseph Patrice)
Lacretelle, Jacques de 1888-1985 ... DLB-65
Lacy, Ed 1911-1968 ... DLB-226
Lacy, Sam 1903- ... DLB-171
Ladd, Joseph Brown 1764-1786 ... DLB-37
La Farge, Oliver 1901-1963 ... DLB-9
Lafayette, Marie-Madeleine, comtesse de 1634-1693 ... DLB-268
Laffan, Mrs. R. S. de Courcy (see Adams, Bertha Leith)
Lafferty, R. A. 1914-2002 ... DLB-8
La Flesche, Francis 1857-1932 ... DLB-175
La Fontaine, Jean de 1621-1695 ... DLB-268
Laforet, Carmen 1921-2004 ... DLB-322
Laforge, Jules 1860-1887 ... DLB-217
Lagerkvist, Pär 1891-1974 ... DLB-259
Lagerlöf, Selma 1858-1940 ... DLB-259
Lagorio, Gina 1922- ... DLB-196
La Guma, Alex 1925-1985 ... DLB-117, 225; CDWLB-3
Lahaise, Guillaume (see Delahaye, Guy)
La Harpe, Jean-François de 1739-1803 ... DLB-313
Lahiri, Jhumpa 1967- ... DLB-323

Lahontan, Louis-Armand de Lom d'Arce, Baron de 1666-1715? ... DLB-99
Lai He 1894-1943 ... DLB-328
Laing, Kojo 1946- ... DLB-157
Laird, Carobeth 1895-1983 ... Y-82
Laird and Lee ... DLB-49
Lake, Paul 1951- ... DLB-282
Lalić, Ivan V. 1931-1996 ... DLB-181
Lalić, Mihailo 1914-1992 ... DLB-181
Lalonde, Michèle 1937- ... DLB-60
Lamantia, Philip 1927- ... DLB-16
Lamartine, Alphonse de 1790-1869 ... DLB-217
Lamb, Lady Caroline 1785-1828 ... DLB-116
Lamb, Charles 1775-1834 ... DLB-93, 107, 163; CDBLB-3
Lamb, Mary 1764-1874 ... DLB-163
Lambert, Angela 1940- ... DLB-271
Lambert, Anne-Thérèse de (Anne-Thérèse de Marguenat de Courcelles, marquise de Lambert) 1647-1733 ... DLB-313
Lambert, Betty 1933-1983 ... DLB-60
La Mettrie, Julien Offroy de 1709-1751 ... DLB-313
Lamm, Donald
Goodbye, Gutenberg? A Lecture at the New York Public Library, 18 April 1995 ... Y-95
Lamming, George 1927- ... DLB-125; CDWLB-3
La Mothe Le Vayer, François de 1588-1672 ... DLB-268
L'Amour, Louis 1908-1988 ... DLB-206; Y-80
Lampman, Archibald 1861-1899 ... DLB-92
Lamson, Wolffe and Company ... DLB-49
Lancer Books ... DLB-46
Lanchester, John 1962- ... DLB-267
Lander, Peter (see Cunningham, Peter)
Landesman, Jay 1919- and Landesman, Fran 1927- ... DLB-16
Landolfi, Tommaso 1908-1979 ... DLB-177
Landon, Letitia Elizabeth 1802-1838 ... DLB-96
Landor, Walter Savage 1775-1864 ... DLB-93, 107
Landry, Napoléon-P. 1884-1956 ... DLB-92
Landvik, Lorna 1954- ... DLB-292
Lane, Charles 1800-1870 ... DLB-1, 223; DS-5
Lane, F. C. 1885-1984 ... DLB-241
Lane, Laurence W. 1890-1967 ... DLB-91
Lane, M. Travis 1934- ... DLB-60
Lane, Patrick 1939- ... DLB-53
Lane, Pinkie Gordon 1923- ... DLB-41
John Lane Company ... DLB-49
Laney, Al 1896-1988 ... DLB-4, 171
Lang, Andrew 1844-1912 ... DLB-98, 141, 184
Langer, Susanne K. 1895-1985 ... DLB-270

Langevin, André 1927- ... DLB-60
Langford, David 1953- ... DLB-261
Langgässer, Elisabeth 1899-1950 ... DLB-69
Langhorne, John 1735-1779 ... DLB-109
Langland, William circa 1330-circa 1400 ... DLB-146
Langton, Anna 1804-1893 ... DLB-99
Lanham, Edwin 1904-1979 ... DLB-4
Lanier, Sidney 1842-1881 ... DLB-64; DS-13
Lanyer, Aemilia 1569-1645 ... DLB-121
Lao She 1899-1966 ... DLB-328
Lapointe, Gatien 1931-1983 ... DLB-88
Lapointe, Paul-Marie 1929- ... DLB-88
La Ramée, Pierre de (Petrus Ramus, Peter Ramus) 1515-1572 ... DLB-327
Larcom, Lucy 1824-1893 ... DLB-221, 243
Lardner, John 1912-1960 ... DLB-171
Lardner, Ring 1885-1933 ... DLB-11, 25, 86, 171; DS-16; CDALB-4
Lardner 100: Ring Lardner Centennial Symposium ... Y-85
Lardner, Ring, Jr. 1915-2000 ... DLB-26, Y-00
Larivey, Pierre de 1541-1619 ... DLB-327
Larkin, Philip 1922-1985 ... DLB-27; CDBLB-8
The Philip Larkin Society ... Y-99
La Roche, Sophie von 1730-1807 ... DLB-94
La Rochefoucauld, François duc de 1613-1680 ... DLB-268
La Rocque, Gilbert 1943-1984 ... DLB-60
Laroque de Roquebrune, Robert (see Roquebrune, Robert de)
Larrick, Nancy 1910-2004 ... DLB-61
Lars, Claudia 1899-1974 ... DLB-283
Larsen, Nella 1893-1964 ... DLB-51
Larsen, Thøger 1875-1928 ... DLB-300
Larson, Clinton F. 1919-1994 ... DLB-256
La Sale, Antoine de circa 1386-1460/1467 ... DLB-208
Las Casas, Fray Bartolomé de 1474-1566 ... DLB-318
Lasch, Christopher 1932-1994 ... DLB-246
Lasdun, James 1958- ... DLB-319
Lasker-Schüler, Else 1869-1945 ... DLB-66, 124
Lasnier, Rina 1915-1997 ... DLB-88
Lassalle, Ferdinand 1825-1864 ... DLB-129
Last Orders, 1996 Booker Prize winner, Graham Swift ... DLB-326
La Taille, Jean de 1534?-1611? ... DLB-327
Late-Medieval Castilian Theater ... DLB-286
Latham, Robert 1912-1995 ... DLB-201
Lathan, Emma (Mary Jane Latsis [1927-1997] and Martha Henissart [1929-]) ... DLB-306
Lathrop, Dorothy P. 1891-1980 ... DLB-22
Lathrop, George Parsons 1851-1898 ... DLB-71

Cumulative Index

Lathrop, John, Jr. 1772-1820............DLB-37
Latimer, Hugh 1492?-1555............DLB-136
Latimore, Jewel Christine McLawler (see Amini, Johari M.)
Latin Literature, The Uniqueness of....DLB-211
La Tour du Pin, Patrice de 1911-1975....DLB-258
Latymer, William 1498-1583..........DLB-132
Laube, Heinrich 1806-1884...........DLB-133
Laud, William 1573-1645.............DLB-213
Laughlin, James 1914-1997......DLB-48; Y-96, 97
   A Tribute [to Henry Miller]............Y-80
   Tribute to Albert Erskine..............Y-93
   Tribute to Kenneth Rexroth............Y-82
   Tribute to Malcolm Cowley............Y-89
Laumer, Keith 1925-1993...............DLB-8
Lauremberg, Johann 1590-1658........DLB-164
Laurence, Margaret 1926-1987.........DLB-53
Laurentius von Schnüffis 1633-1702.....DLB-168
Laurents, Arthur 1918-................DLB-26
Laurie, Annie (see Black, Winifred)
Laut, Agnes Christiana 1871-1936.......DLB-92
Lauterbach, Ann 1942-................DLB-193
Lautréamont, Isidore Lucien Ducasse, Comte de 1846-1870.............DLB-217
Lavater, Johann Kaspar 1741-1801.......DLB-97
Lavin, Mary 1912-1996............DLB-15, 319
Law, John (see Harkness, Margaret)
Lawes, Henry 1596-1662..............DLB-126
Lawler, Ray 1922-....................DLB-289
Lawless, Anthony (see MacDonald, Philip)
Lawless, Emily (The Hon. Emily Lawless) 1845-1913.....................DLB-240
Lawrence, D. H. 1885-1930 .....DLB-10, 19, 36, 98, 162, 195; CDBLB-6
   The D. H. Lawrence Society of North America...................Y-00
Lawrence, David 1888-1973...........DLB-29
Lawrence, Jerome 1915-2004..........DLB-228
Lawrence, Seymour 1926-1994..........Y-94
   Tribute to Richard Yates...............Y-92
Lawrence, T. E. 1888-1935...........DLB-195
   The T. E. Lawrence Society............Y-98
Lawson, George 1598-1678...........DLB-213
Lawson, Henry 1867-1922............DLB-230
Lawson, John ?-1711..................DLB-24
Lawson, John Howard 1894-1977.......DLB-228
Lawson, Louisa Albury 1848-1920......DLB-230
Lawson, Robert 1892-1957.............DLB-22
Lawson, Victor F. 1850-1925...........DLB-25
Layard, Austen Henry 1817-1894......DLB-166
Layton, Irving 1912-..................DLB-88
LaZamon fl. circa 1200...............DLB-146

Lazarević, Laza K. 1851-1890..........DLB-147
Lazarus, George 1904-1997...........DLB-201
Lazhechnikov, Ivan Ivanovich 1792-1869....................DLB-198
Lea, Henry Charles 1825-1909.........DLB-47
Lea, Sydney 1942-...............DLB-120, 282
Lea, Tom 1907-2001...................DLB-6
Leacock, John 1729-1802..............DLB-31
Leacock, Stephen 1869-1944...........DLB-92
Lead, Jane Ward 1623-1704...........DLB-131
Leadenhall Press....................DLB-106
"The Greatness of Southern Literature": League of the South Institute for the Study of Southern Culture and History Y-02
Leakey, Caroline Woolmer 1827-1881....DLB-230
Leapor, Mary 1722-1746..............DLB-109
Lear, Edward 1812-1888.......DLB-32, 163, 166
Leary, Timothy 1920-1996............DLB-16
W. A. Leary and Company............DLB-49
Léautaud, Paul 1872-1956.............DLB-65
Leavis, F. R. 1895-1978..............DLB-242
Leavitt, David 1961-.................DLB-130
Leavitt and Allen....................DLB-49
Le Blond, Mrs. Aubrey 1861-1934.......DLB-174
le Carré, John (David John Moore Cornwell) 1931-................DLB-87; CDBLB-8
   Tribute to Graham Greene.............Y-91
   Tribute to George Greenfield..........Y-00
Lécavelé, Roland (see Dorgeles, Roland)
Lechlitner, Ruth 1901-................DLB-48
Leclerc, Félix 1914-1988..............DLB-60
Le Clézio, J. M. G. 1940-.............DLB-83
Leder, Rudolf (see Hermlin, Stephan)
Lederer, Charles 1910-1976............DLB-26
Ledwidge, Francis 1887-1917..........DLB-20
Lee, Chang-rae 1965-................DLB-312
Lee, Cherylene 1953-................DLB-312
Lee, Dennis 1939-...................DLB-53
Lee, Don L. (see Madhubuti, Haki R.)
Lee, George W. 1894-1976............DLB-51
Lee, Gus 1946-.....................DLB-312
Lee, Harper 1926-..........DLB-6; CDALB-1
Lee, Harriet 1757-1851 and Lee, Sophia 1750-1824............DLB-39
Lee, Laurie 1914-1997................DLB-27
Lee, Leslie 1935-....................DLB-266
Lee, Li-Young 1957-.............DLB-165, 312
Lee, Manfred B. 1905-1971............DLB-137
Lee, Nathaniel circa 1645-1692.........DLB-80
Lee, Robert E. 1918-1994.............DLB-228
Lee, Sir Sidney 1859-1926.........DLB-149, 184

"Principles of Biography," in *Elizabethan and Other Essays*......DLB-149
Lee, Tanith 1947-...................DLB-261
Lee, Vernon 1856-1935........DLB-57, 153, 156, 174, 178
Lee and Shepard....................DLB-49
Le Fanu, Joseph Sheridan 1814-1873............DLB-21, 70, 159, 178
Lefèvre d'Etaples, Jacques 1460?-1536....................DLB-327
Leffland, Ella 1931-..................Y-84
le Fort, Gertrud von 1876-1971.........DLB-66
Le Gallienne, Richard 1866-1947........DLB-4
Legaré, Hugh Swinton 1797-1843.............DLB-3, 59, 73, 248
Legaré, James Mathewes 1823-1859....DLB-3, 248
Léger, Antoine-J. 1880-1950...........DLB-88
Leggett, William 1801-1839...........DLB-250
Le Guin, Ursula K. 1929-......DLB-8, 52, 256, 275; CDALB-6
Lehman, Ernest 1920-................DLB-44
Lehmann, John 1907-1989.........DLB-27, 100
John Lehmann Limited..............DLB-112
Lehmann, Rosamond 1901-1990........DLB-15
Lehmann, Wilhelm 1882-1968..........DLB-56
Leiber, Fritz 1910-1992.................DLB-8
Leibniz, Gottfried Wilhelm 1646-1716...DLB-168
Leicester University Press............DLB-112
Leigh, Carolyn 1926-1983.............DLB-265
Leigh, W. R. 1866-1955...............DLB-188
Leinster, Murray 1896-1975.............DLB-8
Leiser, Bill 1898-1965.................DLB-241
Leisewitz, Johann Anton 1752-1806......DLB-94
Leitch, Maurice 1933-................DLB-14
Leithauser, Brad 1943-...........DLB-120, 282
Leland, Charles G. 1824-1903..........DLB-11
Leland, John 1503?-1552..............DLB-136
Lemaire de Belges, Jean 1473-?.........DLB-327
Lemay, Pamphile 1837-1918...........DLB-99
Lemelin, Roger 1919-1992.............DLB-88
Lemercier, Louis-Jean-Népomucène 1771-1840......................DLB-192
Le Moine, James MacPherson 1825-1912 . DLB-99
Lemon, Mark 1809-1870..............DLB-163
Le Moyne, Jean 1913-1996............DLB-88
Lemperly, Paul 1858-1939.............DLB-187
Leñero, Vicente 1933-................DLB-305
L'Engle, Madeleine 1918-..............DLB-52
Lennart, Isobel 1915-1971..............DLB-44
Lennox, Charlotte 1729 or 1730-1804....DLB-39
Lenox, James 1800-1880..............DLB-140
Lenski, Lois 1893-1974.................DLB-22
Lentricchia, Frank 1940-..............DLB-246

Lenz, Hermann 1913-1998 . . . . DLB-69

Lenz, J. M. R. 1751-1792 . . . . DLB-94

Lenz, Siegfried 1926- DLB-75

León, Fray Luis de 1527-1591 . . . . DLB-318

Leonard, Elmore 1925- DLB-173, 226

Leonard, Hugh 1926- DLB-13

Leonard, William Ellery 1876-1944 . . . . . . DLB-54

Leong, Russell C. 1950- DLB-312

Leonov, Leonid Maksimovich
   1899-1994. . . . . DLB-272

Leonowens, Anna 1834-1914. . . . . . . DLB-99, 166

Leont'ev, Konstantin Nikolaevich
   1831-1891 . . . . DLB-277

Leopold, Aldo 1887-1948. . . . . DLB-275

LePan, Douglas 1914-1998 . . . . DLB-88

Lepik, Kalju 1920-1999 . . . . DLB-232

Leprohon, Rosanna Eleanor 1829-1879. . . . DLB-99

Le Queux, William 1864-1927. . . . . DLB-70

Lermontov, Mikhail Iur'evich
   1814-1841 . . . . DLB-205

Lerner, Alan Jay 1918-1986 . . . . DLB-265

Lerner, Max 1902-1992 . . . . DLB-29

Lernet-Holenia, Alexander 1897-1976 . . . . DLB-85

Le Rossignol, James 1866-1969 . . . . DLB-92

Lesage, Alain-René 1668-1747 . . . . DLB-313

Lescarbot, Marc circa 1570-1642 . . . . DLB-99

LeSeur, William Dawson 1840-1917 . . . . . DLB-92

LeSieg, Theo. (see Geisel, Theodor Seuss)

Leskov, Nikolai Semenovich
   1831-1895 . . . . DLB-238

Leslie, Doris before 1902-1982 . . . . DLB-191

Leslie, Eliza 1787-1858 . . . . DLB-202

Leslie, Frank (Henry Carter)
   1821-1880 . . . . DLB-43, 79

Frank Leslie [publishing house] DLB-49

Leśmian, Bolesław 1878-1937 . . . . DLB-215

Lesperance, John 1835?-1891 . . . . DLB-99

Lespinasse, Julie de 1732-1776 . . . . DLB-313

Lessing, Bruno 1870-1940 . . . . DLB-28

Lessing, Doris
   1919- DLB-15, 139; Y-85; CDBLB-8

Lessing, Gotthold Ephraim
   1729-1781 . . . . DLB-97; CDWLB-2

   The Lessing Society Y-00

L'Estoile, Pierre de 1546-1611 . . . . DLB-327

Le Sueur, Meridel 1900-1996 . . . . DLB-303

Lettau, Reinhard 1929-1996 . . . . DLB-75

Letters from a Peruvian Woman, Françoise d'Issembourg
   de Graffigny DLB-314

The Hemingway Letters Project Finds
   an Editor Y-02

Lever, Charles 1806-1872. . . . . DLB-21

Lever, Ralph ca. 1527-1585 . . . . DLB-236

Leverson, Ada 1862-1933 . . . . DLB-153

Levertov, Denise
   1923-1997 . . . . DLB-5, 165; CDALB-7

Levi, Peter 1931-2000 . . . . DLB-40

Levi, Primo 1919-1987. . . . . DLB-177, 299

Levien, Sonya 1888-1960. . . . . DLB-44

Levin, Meyer 1905-1981 . . . . DLB-9, 28; Y-81

Levin, Phillis 1954- DLB-282

Lévinas, Emmanuel 1906-1995 . . . . DLB-296

Levine, Norman 1923- DLB-88

Levine, Philip 1928- DLB-5

Levis, Larry 1946- DLB-120

Lévi-Strauss, Claude 1908- DLB-242

Levitov, Aleksandr Ivanovich
   1835?-1877 . . . . DLB-277

Levy, Amy 1861-1889 . . . . DLB-156, 240

Levy, Benn Wolfe 1900-1973 . . . . . . DLB-13; Y-81

Levy, Deborah 1959- DLB-310

Lewald, Fanny 1811-1889 . . . . DLB-129

Lewes, George Henry 1817-1878 . . . . . DLB-55, 144

   "Criticism in Relation to Novels"
   (1863) DLB-21

   The Principles of Success in Literature
   (1865) [excerpt]. DLB-57

Lewis, Agnes Smith 1843-1926 . . . . DLB-174

Lewis, Alfred H. 1857-1914 . . . . DLB-25, 186

Lewis, Alun 1915-1944 . . . . DLB-20, 162

Lewis, C. Day (see Day Lewis, C.)

Lewis, C. I. 1883-1964. . . . . DLB-270

Lewis, C. S. 1898-1963
   . . . . DLB-15, 100, 160, 255; CDBLB-7

   The New York C. S. Lewis Society Y-99

Lewis, Charles B. 1842-1924 . . . . DLB-11

Lewis, David 1941-2001 . . . . DLB-279

Lewis, Henry Clay 1825-1850 . . . . DLB-3, 248

Lewis, Janet 1899-1999 . . . . Y-87

   Tribute to Katherine Anne Porter Y-80

Lewis, Matthew Gregory
   1775-1818 . . . . DLB-39, 158, 178

Lewis, Meriwether 1774-1809 . . . . . . DLB-183, 186

Lewis, Norman 1908-2003 . . . . DLB-204

Lewis, R. W. B. 1917-2002. . . . . DLB-111

Lewis, Richard circa 1700-1734 . . . . DLB-24

Lewis, Saunders 1893-1985 . . . . DLB-310

Lewis, Sinclair
   1885-1951 . . . . . . DLB-9, 102; DS-1; CDALB-4

   Sinclair Lewis Centennial Conference. Y-85

   The Sinclair Lewis Society Y-99

Lewis, Wilmarth Sheldon 1895-1979 . . . . DLB-140

Lewis, Wyndham 1882-1957 . . . . DLB-15

   Time and Western Man
   [excerpt] (1927) DLB-36

Lewisohn, Ludwig 1882-1955 . . . DLB-4, 9, 28, 102

Leyendecker, J. C. 1874-1951. . . . . DLB-188

Leyner, Mark 1956- DLB-292

Lezama Lima, José 1910-1976 . . . . . . DLB-113, 283

Lézardière, Marie-Charlotte-Pauline Robert de
   1754-1835 . . . . DLB-313

L'Heureux, John 1934- DLB-244

Libbey, Laura Jean 1862-1924 . . . . DLB-221

Libedinsky, Iurii Nikolaevich
   1898-1959 . . . . DLB-272

The Liberator DLB-303

Library History Group Y-01

E-Books' Second Act in Libraries Y-02

The Library of America. DLB-46

The Library of America: An Assessment
   After Two Decades Y-02

Licensing Act of 1737. . . . . DLB-84

Leonard Lichfield I [publishing house] . . . DLB-170

Lichtenberg, Georg Christoph
   1742-1799 . . . . DLB-94

The Liddle Collection Y-97

Lidman, Sara 1923-2004 . . . . DLB-257

Lieb, Fred 1888-1980. . . . . DLB-171

Liebling, A. J. 1904-1963 . . . . DLB-4, 171

Lieutenant Murray (see Ballou, Maturin Murray)

Life and Times of Michael K, 1983 Booker Prize winner,
   J. M. Coetzee. DLB-326

Life of Pi, 2002 Booker Prize winner,
   Yann Martel DLB-326

Lighthall, William Douw 1857-1954 . . . . . . DLB-92

Lihn, Enrique 1929-1988. . . . . DLB-283

Lilar, Françoise (see Mallet-Joris, Françoise)

Lili'uokalani, Queen 1838-1917 . . . . DLB-221

Lillo, George 1691-1739. . . . . DLB-84

Lilly, J. K., Jr. 1893-1966 . . . . DLB-140

Lilly, Wait and Company DLB-49

Lily, William circa 1468-1522 . . . . DLB-132

Lim, Shirley Geok-lin 1944- DLB-312

Lima, Jorge de 1893-1953 . . . . DLB-307

Lima Barreto, Afonso Henriques de
   1881-1922 . . . . DLB-307

Limited Editions Club DLB-46

Limón, Graciela 1938- DLB-209

Limonov, Eduard 1943- DLB-317

Lincoln and Edmands DLB-49

Lind, Jakov 1927- DLB-299

Linda Vilhjálmsdóttir 1958- DLB-293

Lindesay, Ethel Forence
   (see Richardson, Henry Handel)

Lindgren, Astrid 1907-2002 . . . . DLB-257

Lindgren, Torgny 1938- DLB-257

Lindsay, Alexander William, Twenty-fifth
   Earl of Crawford 1812-1880 . . . . DLB-184

Lindsay, Sir David circa 1485-1555 . . . . . . DLB-132

Lindsay, David 1878-1945. . . . . DLB-255

Lindsay, Jack 1900-1990 . . . . Y-84

Lindsay, Lady (Caroline Blanche
   Elizabeth Fitzroy Lindsay)
   1844-1912. . . . . DLB-199

Lindsay, Norman 1879-1969. . . . . DLB-260

Lindsay, Vachel
   1879-1931 . . . . DLB-54; CDALB-3

The Line of Beauty, 2004 Booker Prize winner,
   Alan Hollinghurst DLB-326

Linebarger, Paul Myron Anthony
   (see Smith, Cordwainer)

Ling Shuhua 1900-1990 . . . . DLB-328

Link, Arthur S. 1920-1998 . . . . DLB-17

Linn, Ed 1922-2000 . . . . DLB-241

Linn, John Blair 1777-1804 . . . . DLB-37

Lins, Osman 1924-1978 . . . . DLB-145, 307

Linton, Eliza Lynn 1822-1898 . . . . DLB-18

Linton, William James 1812-1897. . . . . . . DLB-32

Barnaby Bernard Lintot
   [publishing house] DLB-170

Lion Books DLB-46

Lionni, Leo 1910-1999 . . . . DLB-61

Lippard, George 1822-1854 . . . . DLB-202

Lippincott, Sara Jane Clarke
   1823-1904 . . . . DLB-43

J. B. Lippincott Company DLB-49

Lippmann, Walter 1889-1974 . . . . DLB-29

Lipton, Lawrence 1898-1975. . . . . DLB-16

Lisboa, Irene 1892-1958 . . . . DLB-287

Liscow, Christian Ludwig
   1701-1760 . . . . DLB-97

Lish, Gordon 1934- DLB-130

   Tribute to Donald Barthelme Y-89

   Tribute to James Dickey. Y-97

Lisle, Charles-Marie-René Leconte de
   1818-1894. . . . . DLB-217

Lispector, Clarice
   1925?-1977 . . . . DLB-113, 307; CDWLB-3

LitCheck Website Y-01

Literary Awards and Honors Y-81–02

   Booker Prize. Y-86, 96–98

   The Drue Heinz Literature Prize Y-82

   The Elmer Holmes Bobst Awards
      in Arts and Letters. Y-87

   The Griffin Poetry Prize. Y-00

   Literary Prizes [British]. DLB-15, 207

   National Book Critics Circle
      Awards Y-00–01

   The National Jewish
      Book Awards. Y-85

   Nobel Prize. Y-80–02

   Winning an Edgar Y-98

The Literary Chronicle and Weekly Review
   1819-1828 . . . . DLB-110

Literary Periodicals:

Callaloo Y-87

Expatriates in Paris DS-15

New Literary Periodicals:
   A Report for 1987 . . . . Y-87

   A Report for 1988 . . . . Y-88

   A Report for 1989 . . . . Y-89

   A Report for 1990 . . . . Y-90

   A Report for 1991 . . . . Y-91

   A Report for 1992 . . . . Y-92

   A Report for 1993 . . . . Y-93

Literary Research Archives

   The Anthony Burgess Archive at
      the Harry Ransom Humanities
      Research Center Y-98

   Archives of Charles Scribner's Sons. DS-17

   Berg Collection of English and
      American Literature of the
      New York Public Library. Y-83

   The Bobbs-Merrill Archive at the
      Lilly Library, Indiana University. . . . Y-90

   Die Fürstliche Bibliothek Corvey. Y-96

   Guide to the Archives of Publishers,
      Journals, and Literary Agents in
      North American Libraries Y-93

   The Henry E. Huntington Library Y-92

   The Humanities Research Center,
      University of Texas Y-82

   The John Carter Brown Library Y-85

   Kent State Special Collections Y-86

   The Lilly Library. Y-84

   The Modern Literary Manuscripts
      Collection in the Special
      Collections of the Washington
      University Libraries. Y-87

   A Publisher's Archives: G. P. Putnam . . . Y-92

   Special Collections at Boston
      University Y-99

   The University of Virginia Libraries Y-91

   The William Charvat American Fiction
      Collection at the Ohio State
      University Libraries. Y-92

Literary Societies Y-98–02

   The Margery Allingham Society Y-98

   The American Studies Association
      of Norway Y-00

   The Arnold Bennett Society. Y-98

   The Association for the Study of
      Literature and Environment
      (ASLE) Y-99

   Belgian Luxembourg American Studies
      Association Y-01

   The E. F. Benson Society. Y-98

   The Elizabeth Bishop Society. Y-01

   The [Edgar Rice] Burroughs
      Bibliophiles Y-98

   The Byron Society of America. Y-00

   The Lewis Carroll Society
      of North America Y-00

   The Willa Cather Pioneer Memorial
      and Education Foundation Y-00

   New Chaucer Society. Y-00

   The Wilkie Collins Society Y-98

   The James Fenimore Cooper Society Y-01

   The Stephen Crane Society Y-98, 01

   The E. E. Cummings Society. Y-01

   The James Dickey Society Y-99

   John Dos Passos Newsletter. Y-00

   The Priory Scholars [Sir Arthur Conan
      Doyle] of New York. Y-99

   The International Theodore Dreiser
      Society Y-01

   The Friends of the Dymock Poets Y-00

   The George Eliot Fellowship Y-99

   The T. S. Eliot Society: Celebration and
      Scholarship, 1980-1999 . . . . Y-99

   The Ralph Waldo Emerson Society. Y-99

   The William Faulkner Society Y-99

   The C. S. Forester Society Y-00

   The Hamlin Garland Society Y-01

   The [Elizabeth] Gaskell Society Y-98

   The Charlotte Perkins Gilman Society . . . Y-99

   The Ellen Glasgow Society Y-01

   Zane Grey's West Society. Y-00

   The Ivor Gurney Society Y-98

   The Joel Chandler Harris Association Y-99

   The Nathaniel Hawthorne Society. Y-00

   The [George Alfred] Henty Society Y-98

   George Moses Horton Society Y-99

   The William Dean Howells Society. Y-01

   WW2 HMSO Paperbacks Society Y-98

   American Humor Studies Association Y-99

   International Society for Humor Studies . . . Y-99

   The W. W. Jacobs Appreciation Society . . Y-98

   The Richard Jefferies Society Y-98

   The Jerome K. Jerome Society Y-98

   The D. H. Lawrence Society of
      North America Y-00

   The T. E. Lawrence Society Y-98

   The [Gotthold] Lessing Society Y-00

   The New York C. S. Lewis Society Y-99

   The Sinclair Lewis Society. Y-99

   The Jack London Research Center Y-00

   The Jack London Society. Y-99

   The Cormac McCarthy Society. Y-99

   The Melville Society Y-01

   The Arthur Miller Society Y-01

   The Milton Society of America Y-00

   International Marianne Moore Society . . . Y-98

   International Nabokov Society. Y-99

   The Vladimir Nabokov Society. Y-01

   The Flannery O'Connor Society Y-99

   The Wilfred Owen Association Y-98

   Penguin Collectors' Society Y-98

   The [E. A.] Poe Studies Association. Y-99

   The Katherine Anne Porter Society Y-01

   The Beatrix Potter Society Y-98

   The Ezra Pound Society. Y-01

The Powys Society Y-98	Liyong, Taban lo (see Taban lo Liyong)	Long, David 1948- DLB-244
Proust Society of America Y-00	Lizárraga, Sylvia S. 1925- DLB-82	Long, H., and Brother DLB-49
The Dorothy L. Sayers Society Y-98	Llamazares, Julio 1955- DLB-322	Long, Haniel 1888-1956 . . . . DLB-45
The Bernard Shaw Society Y-99	Llewellyn, Kate 1936- DLB-325	Long, Ray 1878-1935. . . . . DLB-137
The Society for the Study of Southern Literature. Y-00	Llewellyn, Richard 1906-1983 . . . . DLB-15	Longfellow, Henry Wadsworth 1807-1882 . . . . DLB-1, 59, 235; CDALB-2
The Wallace Stevens Society Y-99	Lloréns Torres, Luis 1876-1944 . . . . DLB-290	Longfellow, Samuel 1819-1892 . . . . DLB-1
The Harriet Beecher Stowe Center Y-00	Edward Lloyd [publishing house] DLB-106	Longford, Elizabeth 1906-2002 . . . . DLB-155
The R. S. Surtees Society Y-98	Lobato, José Bento Monteiro 1882-1948 . . . . DLB-307	Tribute to Alfred A. Knopf Y-84
The Thoreau Society. Y-99	Lobel, Arnold 1933- DLB-61	Longinus circa first century DLB-176
The Tilling [E. F. Benson] Society. Y-98	Lochhead, Liz 1947- DLB-310	Longley, Michael 1939- DLB-40
The Trollope Societies Y-00	Lochridge, Betsy Hopkins (see Fancher, Betsy)	T. Longman [publishing house] DLB-154
H. G. Wells Society Y-98	Locke, Alain 1886-1954. . . . . DLB-51	Longmans, Green and Company DLB-49
The Western Literature Association Y-99	Locke, David Ross 1833-1888 . . . . DLB-11, 23	Longmore, George 1793?-1867 . . . . DLB-99
The William Carlos Williams Society Y-99	Locke, John 1632-1704. . . . . DLB-31, 101, 213, 252	Longstreet, Augustus Baldwin 1790-1870 . . . . DLB-3, 11, 74, 248
The Henry Williamson Society Y-98	Locke, Richard Adams 1800-1871 . . . . DLB-43	D. Longworth [publishing house] DLB-49
The [Nero] Wolfe Pack Y-99	Locker-Lampson, Frederick 1821-1895 . . . . DLB-35, 184	Lønn, Øystein 1936- DLB-297
The Thomas Wolfe Society. Y-99	Lockhart, John Gibson 1794-1854 . . . . DLB-110, 116 144	Lonsdale, Frederick 1881-1954 . . . . DLB-10
Worldwide Wodehouse Societies. Y-98	Lockridge, Francis 1896-1963 . . . . DLB-306	Loos, Anita 1893-1981. . . . . DLB-11, 26, 228; Y-81
The W. B. Yeats Society of N.Y. Y-99	Lockridge, Richard 1898-1982. . . . . DLB-306	Lopate, Phillip 1943- Y-80
The Charlotte M. Yonge Fellowship Y-98	Lockridge, Ross, Jr. 1914-1948 . . . . DLB-143; Y-80	Lope de Rueda 1510?-1565? DLB-318
Literary Theory The Year in Literary Theory. Y-92–Y-93	*Locrine and Selimus* DLB-62	Lopes, Fernão 1380/1390?-1460? DLB-287
Literature at Nurse, or Circulating Morals (1885), by George Moore DLB-18	Lodge, David 1935- DLB-14, 194	Lopez, Barry 1945- DLB-256, 275
Litt, Toby 1968- DLB-267, 319	Lodge, George Cabot 1873-1909 . . . . DLB-54	López, Diana (see Isabella, Ríos)
Littell, Eliakim 1797-1870 . . . . DLB-79	Lodge, Henry Cabot 1850-1924 . . . . DLB-47	López, Josefina 1969- DLB-209
Littell, Robert S. 1831-1896. . . . . DLB-79	Lodge, Thomas 1558-1625 . . . . DLB-172	López de Mendoza, Íñigo (see Santillana, Marqués de)
Little, Brown and Company DLB-49	*Defence of Poetry* (1579) [excerpt] DLB-172	López Velarde, Ramón 1888-1921 . . . . . . DLB-290
Little Magazines and Newspapers DS-15	Loeb, Harold 1891-1974 . . . . DLB-4; DS-15	Loranger, Jean-Aubert 1896-1942 . . . . DLB-92
Selected English-Language Little Magazines and Newspapers [France, 1920-1939] DLB-4	Loeb, William 1905-1981 . . . . DLB-127	Lorca, Federico García 1898-1936 . . . . . . DLB-108
	Loesser, Frank 1910-1969 . . . . DLB-265	Lord, John Keast 1818-1872. . . . . DLB-99
The Little Magazines of the New Formalism DLB-282	Lofting, Hugh 1886-1947. . . . . DLB-160	Lorde, Audre 1934-1992 . . . . DLB-41
The Little Review 1914-1929 . . . . DS-15	Logan, Deborah Norris 1761-1839 . . . . . . DLB-200	Lorimer, George Horace 1867-1937 . . . . . . DLB-91
Littlewood, Joan 1914-2002 . . . . DLB-13	Logan, James 1674-1751. . . . . DLB-24, 140	A. K. Loring [publishing house] DLB-49
Liu, Aimee E. 1953- DLB-312	Logan, John 1923-1987 . . . . DLB-5	Loring and Mussey DLB-46
Liu E 1857-1909. DLB-328	Logan, Martha Daniell 1704?-1779 . . . . . . DLB-200	Lorris, Guillaume de (see *Roman de la Rose*)
Lively, Penelope 1933- . . . DLB-14, 161, 207, 326	Logan, William 1950- DLB-120	Lossing, Benson J. 1813-1891 . . . . DLB-30
Liverpool University Press. DLB-112	Logau, Friedrich von 1605-1655 . . . . DLB-164	Lothar, Ernst 1890-1974. . . . . DLB-81
The Lives of the Poets (1753) DLB-142	Logue, Christopher 1926- DLB-27	D. Lothrop and Company DLB-49
Livesay, Dorothy 1909-1996 . . . . DLB-68	Lohenstein, Daniel Casper von 1635-1683 . . . . DLB-168	Lothrop, Harriet M. 1844-1924 . . . . DLB-42
Livesay, Florence Randal 1874-1953 . . . . . DLB-92	Lohrey, Amanda 1947- DLB-325	Loti, Pierre 1850-1923 . . . . DLB-123
Livings, Henry 1929-1998 . . . . DLB-13	Lo-Johansson, Ivar 1901-1990 . . . . DLB-259	Lotichius Secundus, Petrus 1528-1560. . . . DLB-179
Livingston, Anne Howe 1763-1841 . . . DLB-37, 200	Lokert, George (or Lockhart) circa 1485-1547 . . . . DLB-281	Lott, Emmeline fl. nineteenth century DLB-166
Livingston, Jay 1915-2001 . . . . DLB-265	Lomonosov, Mikhail Vasil'evich 1711-1765. . . . . DLB-150	Louisiana State University Press Y-97
Livingston, Myra Cohn 1926-1996 . . . . . . DLB-61	London, Jack 1876-1916 . . . . . DLB-8, 12, 78, 212; CDALB-3	Lounsbury, Thomas R. 1838-1915 . . . . DLB-71
Livingston, William 1723-1790. . . . . DLB-31		Louÿs, Pierre 1870-1925 . . . . DLB-123
Livingstone, David 1813-1873 . . . . DLB-166	The Jack London Research Center Y-00	Løveid, Cecile 1951- DLB-297
Livingstone, Douglas 1932-1996 . . . . DLB-225	The Jack London Society Y-99	Lovejoy, Arthur O. 1873-1962 . . . . DLB-270
Livshits, Benedikt Konstantinovich 1886-1938 or 1939 . . . . DLB-295	*The London Magazine* 1820-1829 . . . . DLB-110	Lovelace, Earl 1935- DLB-125; CDWLB-3
Livy 59 B.C.-A.D. 17 . . . . DLB-211; CDWLB-1		Lovelace, Richard 1618-1657 . . . . DLB-131

John W. Lovell Company DLB-49

Lovell, Coryell and Company DLB-49

Lover, Samuel 1797-1868 . . . . DLB-159, 190

Lovesey, Peter 1936- DLB-87

    Tribute to Georges Simenon Y-89

Lovinescu, Eugen
1881-1943 . . . . DLB-220; CDWLB-4

Lovingood, Sut
(see Harris, George Washington)

Low, Samuel 1765-? DLB-37

Lowell, Amy 1874-1925 . . . . DLB-54, 140

Lowell, James Russell 1819-1891
. . . . . . .DLB-1, 11, 64, 79, 189, 235; CDALB-2

Lowell, Robert
1917-1977 . . . . DLB-5, 169; CDALB-7

Lowenfels, Walter 1897-1976 . . . . DLB-4

Lowndes, Marie Belloc 1868-1947 . . . . DLB-70

Lowndes, William Thomas 1798-1843 . . . DLB-184

Humphrey Lownes [publishing house] DLB-170

Lowry, Lois 1937- DLB-52

Lowry, Malcolm 1909-1957 . . . DLB-15; CDBLB-7

Lowther, Pat 1935-1975 . . . . DLB-53

Loy, Mina 1882-1966 . . . . DLB-4, 54

Loynaz, Dulce María 1902-1997 . . . . DLB-283

Lozeau, Albert 1878-1924 . . . . DLB-92

Lu Ling 1923-1994 . . . . DLB-328

Lu Xun 1881-1936 . . . . DLB-328

Lu Yin 1898?-1934 . . . . DLB-328

Lubbock, Percy 1879-1965 . . . . DLB-149

Lucan A.D. 39-A.D. 65 . . . . DLB-211

Lucas, E. V. 1868-1938 . . . . DLB-98, 149, 153

Fielding Lucas Jr. [publishing house] DLB-49

Luce, Clare Booth 1903-1987 . . . . DLB-228

Luce, Henry R. 1898-1967 . . . . DLB-91

John W. Luce and Company DLB-46

Lucena, Juan de ca. 1430-1501 . . . . DLB-286

Lucian circa 120-180 . . . . .DLB-176

Lucie-Smith, Edward 1933- DLB-40

Lucilius circa 180 B.C.-102/101 B.C. DLB-211

Lucini, Gian Pietro 1867-1914 . . . . DLB-114

Luco Cruchaga, Germán 1894-1936 . . . . DLB-305

Lucretius circa 94 B.C.-circa 49 B.C.
. . . . DLB-211; CDWLB-1

Luder, Peter circa 1415-1472 . . . . .DLB-179

Ludlam, Charles 1943-1987 . . . . DLB-266

Ludlum, Robert 1927-2001 . . . . Y-82

Ludus de Antichristo circa 1160 . . . . DLB-148

Ludvigson, Susan 1942- DLB-120

Ludwig, Jack 1922- DLB-60

Ludwig, Otto 1813-1865 . . . . DLB-129

Ludwigslied 881 or 882 . . . . DLB-148

Luera, Yolanda 1953- DLB-122

Luft, Lya 1938- DLB-145

Lugansky, Kazak Vladimir
(see Dal', Vladimir Ivanovich)

Lugn, Kristina 1948- DLB-257

Lugones, Leopoldo 1874-1938 . . . . DLB-283

Luhan, Mabel Dodge 1879-1962 . . . . DLB-303

Lukács, Georg (see Lukács, György)

Lukács, György
1885-1971 . . . . .DLB-215, 242; CDWLB-4

Luke, Peter 1919-1995 . . . . DLB-13

Lummis, Charles F. 1859-1928 . . . . DLB-186

Lundkvist, Artur 1906-1991 . . . . DLB-259

Lunts, Lev Natanovich
1901-1924 . . . . .DLB-272

F. M. Lupton Company DLB-49

Lupus of Ferrières
circa 805-circa 862 . . . . DLB-148

Lurie, Alison 1926- DLB-2

Lussu, Emilio 1890-1975 . . . . DLB-264

Lustig, Arnošt 1926- DLB-232, 299

Luther, Martin
1483-1546 . . . . .DLB-179; CDWLB-2

Luzi, Mario 1914-2005 . . . . DLB-128

L'vov, Nikolai Aleksandrovich
1751-1803 . . . . DLB-150

Lyall, Gavin 1932-2003 . . . . DLB-87

Lydgate, John circa 1370-1450 . . . . DLB-146

Lyly, John circa 1554-1606 . . . . DLB-62, 167

Lynch, Martin 1950- DLB-310

Lynch, Patricia 1898-1972 . . . . DLB-160

Lynch, Richard fl. 1596-1601 . . . . .DLB-172

Lynd, Robert 1879-1949 . . . . DLB-98

Lynds, Dennis (Michael Collins)
1924- DLB-306

    Tribute to John D. MacDonald Y-86

    Tribute to Kenneth Millar Y-83

    Why I Write Mysteries: Night and Day . . . Y-85

Lyon, Matthew 1749-1822 . . . . DLB-43

Lyotard, Jean-François 1924-1998 . . . . DLB-242

Lyricists
    Additional Lyricists: 1920-1960 . . . . . DLB-265

Lysias circa 459 B.C.-circa 380 B.C. DLB-176

Lytle, Andrew 1902-1995 . . . . .DLB-6; Y-95

    Tribute to Caroline Gordon Y-81

    Tribute to Katherine Anne Porter Y-80

Lytton, Edward
(see Bulwer-Lytton, Edward)

Lytton, Edward Robert Bulwer
1831-1891 . . . . DLB-32

M

Maass, Joachim 1901-1972 . . . . DLB-69

Mabie, Hamilton Wright 1845-1916 . . . . . . DLB-71

Mac A'Ghobhainn, Iain (see Smith, Iain Crichton)

MacArthur, Charles 1895-1956 . . . . .DLB-7, 25, 44

Macaulay, Catherine 1731-1791 . . . . DLB-104

Macaulay, David 1945- DLB-61

Macaulay, Rose 1881-1958 . . . . DLB-36

Macaulay, Thomas Babington
1800-1859 . . . . DLB-32, 55; CDBLB-4

Macaulay Company DLB-46

MacBeth, George 1932-1992 . . . . DLB-40

Macbeth, Madge 1880-1965 . . . . DLB-92

MacCaig, Norman 1910-1996 . . . . DLB-27

MacDiarmid, Hugh
1892-1978 . . . . DLB-20; CDBLB-7

MacDonald, Cynthia 1928- DLB-105

MacDonald, George 1824-1905 . . . . DLB-18, 163, 178

MacDonald, John D.
1916-1986 . . . . .DLB-8, 306; Y-86

MacDonald, Philip 1899?-1980 . . . . DLB-77

Macdonald, Ross (see Millar, Kenneth)

Macdonald, Sharman 1951- DLB-245

MacDonald, Wilson 1880-1967 . . . . DLB-92

Macdonald and Company (Publishers) . . DLB-112

MacEwen, Gwendolyn 1941-1987 . . . DLB-53, 251

Macfadden, Bernarr 1868-1955 . . . . . . DLB-25, 91

MacGregor, John 1825-1892 . . . . DLB-166

MacGregor, Mary Esther (see Keith, Marian)

Macherey, Pierre 1938- DLB-296

Machado, Antonio 1875-1939 . . . . DLB-108

Machado, Manuel 1874-1947 . . . . DLB-108

Machado de Assis, Joaquim Maria
1839-1908 . . . . DLB-307

Machar, Agnes Maule 1837-1927 . . . . DLB-92

Machaut, Guillaume de
circa 1300-1377 . . . . DLB-208

Machen, Arthur Llewelyn Jones
1863-1947 . . . . .DLB-36, 156, 178

MacIlmaine, Roland fl. 1574 . . . . DLB-281

MacInnes, Colin 1914-1976 . . . . DLB-14

MacInnes, Helen 1907-1985 . . . . DLB-87

Mac Intyre, Tom 1931- DLB-245

Mačiulis, Jonas (see Maironis, Jonas)

Mack, Maynard 1909-2001 . . . . DLB-111

Mackall, Leonard L. 1879-1937 . . . . DLB-140

MacKay, Isabel Ecclestone 1875-1928 . . . . . DLB-92

Mackay, Shena 1944- DLB-231, 319

MacKaye, Percy 1875-1956 . . . . DLB-54

Macken, Walter 1915-1967 . . . . DLB-13

MacKenna, John 1952- DLB-319

Mackenzie, Alexander 1763-1820 . . . . DLB-99

Mackenzie, Alexander Slidell
1803-1848 . . . . DLB-183

Mackenzie, Compton 1883-1972 . . . . .DLB-34, 100

Mackenzie, Henry 1745-1831 . . . . DLB-39

    The Lounger, no. 20 (1785) DLB-39

Mackenzie, Kenneth (Seaforth Mackenzie) 1913-1955 . . . . DLB-260	Magee, David 1905-1977 . . . . DLB-187	Malerba, Luigi 1927- DLB-196
Mackenzie, William 1758-1828 . . . . DLB-187	Maginn, William 1794-1842. . . . . DLB-110, 159	Malet, Lucas 1852-1931. . . . . DLB-153
Mackey, Nathaniel 1947- DLB-169	Magoffin, Susan Shelby 1827-1855 . . . . . . DLB-239	Malherbe, François de 1555-1628 . . . . DLB-327
Mackey, William Wellington 1937- DLB-38	Mahan, Alfred Thayer 1840-1914 . . . . DLB-47	Mallarmé, Stéphane 1842-1898 . . . . DLB-217
Mackintosh, Elizabeth (see Tey, Josephine)	Mahapatra, Jayanta 1928- DLB-323	Malleson, Lucy Beatrice (see Gilbert, Anthony)
Mackintosh, Sir James 1765-1832 . . . . DLB-158	Maheux-Forcier, Louise 1929- DLB-60	Mallet-Joris, Françoise (Françoise Lilar) 1930- DLB-83
Macklin, Charles 1699-1797. . . . . DLB-89	Mahin, John Lee 1902-1984 . . . . DLB-44	Mallock, W. H. 1849-1923 . . . . DLB-18, 57
Maclaren, Ian (see Watson, John)	Mahon, Derek 1941- DLB-40	"Every Man His Own Poet; or, The Inspired Singer's Recipe Book" (1877). DLB-35
Maclaren-Ross, Julian 1912-1964. . . . . DLB-319	Maiakovsky, Vladimir Vladimirovich 1893-1930 . . . . DLB-295	
MacLaverty, Bernard 1942- DLB-267	Maikov, Apollon Nikolaevich 1821-1897 . . . . DLB-277	"Le Style c'est l'homme" (1892) DLB-57
MacLean, Alistair 1922-1987 . . . . DLB-276		Memoirs of Life and Literature (1920), [excerpt] DLB-57
MacLean, Katherine Anne 1925- DLB-8	Maikov, Vasilii Ivanovich 1728-1778 . . . . . DLB-150	Malone, Dumas 1892-1986 . . . . DLB-17
Maclean, Norman 1902-1990 . . . . DLB-206	Mailer, Norman 1923- DLB-2, 16, 28, 185, 278; Y-80, 83, 97; DS-3; CDALB-6	Malone, Edmond 1741-1812 . . . . DLB-142
MacLeish, Archibald 1892-1982 . . . . DLB-4, 7, 45; Y-82; DS-15; CDALB-7		Malory, Sir Thomas circa 1400-1410 - 1471 . . . . DLB-146; CDBLB-1
MacLennan, Hugh 1907-1990 . . . . DLB-68	Tribute to Isaac Bashevis Singer Y-91	Malouf, David 1934- DLB-289
MacLeod, Alistair 1936- DLB-60	Tribute to Meyer Levin. Y-81	Malpede, Karen 1945- DLB-249
Macleod, Fiona (see Sharp, William)	Maillart, Ella 1903-1997 . . . . DLB-195	Malraux, André 1901-1976 . . . . DLB-72
Macleod, Norman 1906-1985 . . . . DLB-4	Maillet, Adrienne 1885-1963 . . . . DLB-68	The Maltese Falcon (Documentary). DLB-280
Mac Low, Jackson 1922-2004 . . . . DLB-193	Maillet, Antonine 1929- DLB-60	Malthus, Thomas Robert 1766-1834 . . . . DLB-107, 158
MacMahon, Bryan 1909-1998 . . . . DLB-319	Maillu, David G. 1939- DLB-157	
Macmillan and Company DLB-106	Maimonides, Moses 1138-1204 . . . . DLB-115	Maltz, Albert 1908-1985 . . . . DLB-102
The Macmillan Company DLB-49	Main Selections of the Book-of-the-Month Club, 1926-1945 . . . . DLB-9	Malzberg, Barry N. 1939- DLB-8
Macmillan's English Men of Letters, First Series (1878-1892) DLB-144		Mamet, David 1947- DLB-7
	Mainwaring, Daniel 1902-1977 . . . . DLB-44	Mamin, Dmitrii Narkisovich 1852-1912 . . . . DLB-238
MacNamara, Brinsley 1890-1963 . . . . DLB-10	Mair, Charles 1838-1927 . . . . DLB-99	
MacNeice, Louis 1907-1963 . . . . DLB-10, 20	Mair, John circa 1467-1550. . . . . DLB-281	Manaka, Matsemela 1956- DLB-157
Macphail, Andrew 1864-1938 . . . . DLB-92	Maironis, Jonas 1862-1932 . . DLB-220; CDWLB-4	Mañas, José Ángel 1971- DLB-322
Macpherson, James 1736-1796 . . . . DLB-109	Mais, Roger 1905-1955 . . . . . DLB-125; CDWLB-3	Manchester University Press DLB-112
Macpherson, Jay 1931- DLB-53	Maitland, Sara 1950- DLB-271	Mandel, Eli 1922-1992. . . . . DLB-53
Macpherson, Jeanie 1884-1946 . . . . DLB-44	Major, Andre 1942- DLB-60	Mandel'shtam, Nadezhda Iakovlevna 1899-1980 . . . . DLB-302
Macrae Smith Company DLB-46	Major, Charles 1856-1913 . . . . DLB-202	
MacRaye, Lucy Betty (see Webling, Lucy)	Major, Clarence 1936- DLB-33	Mandel'shtam, Osip Emil'evich 1891-1938 . . . . DLB-295
John Macrone [publishing house]. DLB-106	Major, Kevin 1949- DLB-60	
MacShane, Frank 1927-1999 . . . . DLB-111	Major Books DLB-46	Mandeville, Bernard 1670-1733 . . . . DLB-101
Macy-Masius DLB-46	Makanin, Vladimir Semenovich 1937- DLB-285	Mandeville, Sir John mid fourteenth century DLB-146
Madden, David 1933- DLB-6		
Madden, Sir Frederic 1801-1873 . . . . DLB-184	Makarenko, Anton Semenovich 1888-1939 . . . . DLB-272	Mandiargues, André Pieyre de 1909-1991 . . . . DLB-83
Maddow, Ben 1909-1992. . . . . DLB-44		
Maddux, Rachel 1912-1983 . . . . DLB-234; Y-93	Makemie, Francis circa 1658-1708 . . . . DLB-24	Manea, Norman 1936- DLB-232
Madgett, Naomi Long 1923- DLB-76	The Making of Americans Contract Y-98	Manfred, Frederick 1912-1994 . . . . DLB-6, 212, 227
Madhubuti, Haki R. 1942- DLB-5, 41; DS-8	Makovsky, Sergei 1877-1962 . . . . DLB-317	Manfredi, Gianfranco 1948- DLB-196
Madison, James 1751-1836. . . . . DLB-37	Maksimov, Vladimir Emel'ianovich 1930-1995 . . . . DLB-302	Mangan, Sherry 1904-1961 . . . . DLB-4
Madsen, Svend Åge 1939- DLB-214		Manganelli, Giorgio 1922-1990 . . . . DLB-196
Madrigal, Alfonso Fernández de (El Tostado) ca. 1405-1455 . . . . DLB-286	Maksimović, Desanka 1898-1993 . . . . DLB-147; CDWLB-4	Manilius fl. first century A.D. DLB-211
		Mankiewicz, Herman 1897-1953 . . . . DLB-26
Maeterlinck, Maurice 1862-1949 . . . . DLB-192	Malamud, Bernard 1914-1986 . . . . DLB-2, 28, 152; Y-80, 86; CDALB-1	Mankiewicz, Joseph L. 1909-1993 . . . . DLB-44
Mafūz, Najīb 1911- Y-88		Mankowitz, Wolf 1924-1998 . . . . DLB-15
Nobel Lecture 1988. . . . . Y-88	Bernard Malamud Archive at the Harry Ransom Humanities Research Center Y-00	Manley, Delarivière 1672?-1724 . . . . DLB-39, 80
The Little Magazines of the New Formalism DLB-282		
	Mălăncioiu, Ileana 1940- DLB-232	Preface to The Secret History, of Queen Zarah, and the Zarazians (1705) DLB-39
	Malaparte, Curzio (Kurt Erich Suckert) 1898-1957. . . . . . DLB-264	Mann, Abby 1927- DLB-44

Cumulative Index

Mann, Charles 1929-1998 .... Y-98

Mann, Emily 1952- DLB-266

Mann, Heinrich 1871-1950 .... DLB-66, 118

Mann, Horace 1796-1859 .... DLB-1, 235

Mann, Klaus 1906-1949 .... DLB-56

Mann, Mary Peabody 1806-1887 .... DLB-239

Mann, Thomas 1875-1955 ... DLB-66; CDWLB-2

Mann, William D'Alton 1839-1920 ..... DLB-137

Mannin, Ethel 1900-1984 .... DLB-191, 195

Manning, Emily (see Australie)

Manning, Frederic 1882-1935.......... DLB-260

Manning, Laurence 1899-1972 .... DLB-251

Manning, Marie 1873?-1945............ DLB-29

Manning and Loring.................. DLB-49

Mannyng, Robert fl. 1303-1338 .... DLB-146

Mano, D. Keith 1942- DLB-6

Manor Books DLB-46

Manrique, Gómez 1412?-1490 .... DLB-286

Manrique, Jorge ca. 1440-1479 .... DLB-286

Mansfield, Katherine 1888-1923........ DLB-162

Mantel, Hilary 1952- DLB-271

Manuel, Niklaus circa 1484-1530 ....DLB-179

Manzini, Gianna 1896-1974 ....DLB-177

Mao Dun 1896-1981 .... DLB-328

Mapanje, Jack 1944- DLB-157

Maraini, Dacia 1936- DLB-196

Maraise, Marie-Catherine-Renée Darcel de 1737-1822 .... DLB-314

Maramzin, Vladimir Rafailovich 1934- DLB-302

March, William (William Edward Campbell) 1893-1954 .... DLB-9, 86, 316

Marchand, Leslie A. 1900-1999 .... DLB-103

Marchant, Bessie 1862-1941........... DLB-160

Marchant, Tony 1959- DLB-245

Marchenko, Anastasiia Iakovlevna 1830-1880 .... DLB-238

Marchessault, Jovette 1938- DLB-60

Marcinkevičius, Justinas 1930- DLB-232

Marcos, Plínio (Plínio Marcos de Barros) 1935-1999 .... DLB-307

Marcus, Frank 1928- DLB-13

Marcuse, Herbert 1898-1979 .... DLB-242

Marden, Orison Swett 1850-1924....... DLB-137

Marechera, Dambudzo 1952-1987 ...... DLB-157

Marek, Richard, Books................ DLB-46

Mares, E. A. 1938- DLB-122

Marguerite de Navarre 1492-1549 ...... DLB-327

Margulies, Donald 1954- DLB-228

Mariana, Juan de 1535 or 1536-1624 .... DLB-318

Mariani, Paul 1940- DLB-111

Marías, Javier 1951- DLB-322

Marie de France fl. 1160-1178.......... DLB-208

Marie-Victorin, Frère (Conrad Kirouac) 1885-1944 .... DLB-92

Marin, Biagio 1891-1985 .... DLB-128

Marinetti, Filippo Tommaso 1876-1944.................. DLB-114, 264

Marinina, Aleksandra (Marina Anatol'evna Alekseeva) 1957- DLB-285

Marinković, Ranko 1913-2001 ....DLB-147; CDWLB-4

Marion, Frances 1886-1973 .... DLB-44

Marius, Richard C. 1933-1999............ Y-85

Marivaux, Pierre Carlet de Chamblain de 1688-1763 .... DLB-314

Markandaya, Kamala 1924-2004 .... DLB-323

Markevich, Boleslav Mikhailovich 1822-1884 .... DLB-238

Markfield, Wallace 1926-2002 .... DLB-2, 28

Markham, E. A. 1939- DLB-319

Markham, Edwin 1852-1940 .... DLB-54, 186

Markish, David 1938- DLB-317

Markle, Fletcher 1921-1991 ....DLB-68; Y-91

Marlatt, Daphne 1942- DLB-60

Marlitt, E. 1825-1887 .... DLB-129

Marlowe, Christopher 1564-1593 .... DLB-62; CDBLB-1

Marlyn, John 1912-1985............... DLB-88

Marmion, Shakerley 1603-1639 .... DLB-58

Marmontel, Jean-François 1723-1799 .... DLB-314

Der Marner before 1230-circa 1287 ..... DLB-138

Marnham, Patrick 1943- DLB-204

Marot, Clément 1496-1544............ DLB-327

The Marprelate Tracts 1588-1589 .... DLB-132

Marquand, John P. 1893-1960 .... DLB-9, 102

Marques, Helena 1935- DLB-287

Marqués, René 1919-1979 .... DLB-113, 305

Marquis, Don 1878-1937 .... DLB-11, 25

Marriott, Anne 1913-1997 .... DLB-68

Marryat, Frederick 1792-1848 .... DLB-21, 163

Marsé, Juan 1933- DLB-322

Marsh, Capen, Lyon and Webb DLB-49

Marsh, George Perkins 1801-1882 .... DLB-1, 64, 243

Marsh, James 1794-1842............. DLB-1, 59

Marsh, Narcissus 1638-1713 .... DLB-213

Marsh, Ngaio 1899-1982 .... DLB-77

Marshall, Alan 1902-1984 .... DLB-260

Marshall, Edison 1894-1967 .... DLB-102

Marshall, Edward 1932- DLB-16

Marshall, Emma 1828-1899 .... DLB-163

Marshall, James 1942-1992 .... DLB-61

Marshall, Joyce 1913- DLB-88

Marshall, Paule 1929- DLB-33, 157, 227

Marshall, Tom 1938-1993............. DLB-60

Marsilius of Padua circa 1275-circa 1342 .... DLB-115

Mars-Jones, Adam 1954- DLB-207, 319

Marson, Una 1905-1965................DLB-157

Marston, John 1576-1634 ....DLB-58, 172

Marston, Philip Bourke 1850-1887....... DLB-35

Martel, Yann 1963- DLB-326

Martens, Kurt 1870-1945 .... DLB-66

Martí, José 1853-1895................. DLB-290

Martial circa A.D. 40-circa A.D. 103 ....DLB-211; CDWLB-1

William S. Martien [publishing house] DLB-49

Martin, Abe (see Hubbard, Kin)

Martin, Catherine ca. 1847-1937........ DLB-230

Martin, Charles 1942- DLB-120, 282

Martin, Claire 1914- DLB-60

Martin, David 1915-1997 .... DLB-260

Martin, Jay 1935- DLB-111

Martin, Johann (see Laurentius von Schnüffis)

Martin, Thomas 1696-1771 .... DLB-213

Martin, Violet Florence (see Ross, Martin)

Martin du Gard, Roger 1881-1958....... DLB-65

Martineau, Harriet 1802-1876.....DLB-21, 55, 159, 163, 166, 190

Martínez, Demetria 1960- DLB-209

Martínez de Toledo, Alfonso 1398?-1468..................... DLB-286

Martínez, Eliud 1935- DLB-122

Martínez, Max 1943- DLB-82

Martínez, Rubén 1962- DLB-209

Martín Gaite, Carmen 1925-2000 ...... DLB-322

Martín-Santos, Luis 1924-1964........ DLB-322

Martinson, Harry 1904-1978 .... DLB-259

Martinson, Moa 1890-1964 .... DLB-259

Martone, Michael 1955- DLB-218

Martyn, Edward 1859-1923 .... DLB-10

Marvell, Andrew 1621-1678............. DLB-131; CDBLB-2

Marvin X 1944- DLB-38

Marx, Karl 1818-1883 .... DLB-129

Marzials, Theo 1850-1920 .... DLB-35

Masefield, John 1878-1967 .... DLB-10, 19, 153, 160; CDBLB-5

Masham, Damaris Cudworth, Lady 1659-1708..................... DLB-252

Masino, Paola 1908-1989 .... DLB-264

Mason, A. E. W. 1865-1948 .... DLB-70

Mason, Bobbie Ann 1940- DLB-173; Y-87; CDALB-7

Mason, F. van Wyck (Geoffrey Coffin, Frank W. Mason, Ward Weaver) 1901-1978 .... DLB-306

Mason, William 1725-1797.............DLB-142	Maugham, W. Somerset 1874-1965 .... DLB-10, 36, 77, 100, 162, 195; CDBLB-6	McCay, Winsor 1871-1934.............DLB-22
Mason Brothers......................DLB-49	Maupassant, Guy de 1850-1893........DLB-123	McClane, Albert Jules 1922-1991.......DLB-171
The Massachusetts Quarterly Review 1847-1850........................DLB-1	Maupertuis, Pierre-Louis Moreau de 1698-1759......................DLB-314	McClatchy, C. K. 1858-1936............DLB-25
The Masses.........................DLB-303	Maupin, Armistead 1944- DLB-278	McClellan, George Marion 1860-1934....DLB-50
Massey, Gerald 1828-1907..............DLB-32	Mauriac, Claude 1914-1996.............DLB-83	"The Negro as a Writer"............DLB-50
Massey, Linton R. 1900-1974..........DLB-187	Mauriac, François 1885-1970............DLB-65	McCloskey, Robert 1914-2003 ....DLB-22
Massie, Allan 1938- DLB-271	Maurice, Frederick Denison 1805-1872....DLB-55	McCloy, Helen 1904-1992..............DLB-306
Massinger, Philip 1583-1640 ....DLB-58	Maurois, André 1885-1967 ....DLB-65	McClung, Nellie Letitia 1873-1951 ....DLB-92
Masson, David 1822-1907.............DLB-144	Maury, James 1718-1769 ....DLB-31	McClure, James 1939- DLB-276
Masters, Edgar Lee 1868-1950..............DLB-54; CDALB-3	Mavor, Elizabeth 1927- DLB-14	McClure, Joanna 1930- DLB-16
Masters, Hilary 1928- DLB-244	Mavor, Osborne Henry (see Bridie, James)	McClure, Michael 1932- DLB-16
Masters, Olga 1919-1986..............DLB-325	Maxwell, Gavin 1914-1969 ....DLB-204	McClure, Phillips and Company.........DLB-46
Mastronardi, Lucio 1930-1979..........DLB-177	Maxwell, William 1908-2000........... DLB-218, 278; Y-80	McClure, S. S. 1857-1949..............DLB-91
Mat' Maria (Elizaveta Kuz'mina-Karavdeva Skobtsova, née Pilenko) 1891-1945 .... DLB-317	Tribute to Nancy Hale Y-88	A. C. McClurg and Company...........DLB-49
Matevski, Mateja 1929- ...DLB-181; CDWLB-4	H. Maxwell [publishing house] DLB-49	McCluskey, John A., Jr. 1944- DLB-33
Mather, Cotton 1663-1728.......DLB-24, 30, 140; CDALB-2	John Maxwell [publishing house].......DLB-106	McCollum, Michael A. 1946- Y-87
Mather, Increase 1639-1723.............DLB-24	May, Elaine 1932- DLB-44	McConnell, William C. 1917- DLB-88
Mather, Richard 1596-1669.............DLB-24	May, Karl 1842-1912..................DLB-129	McCord, David 1897-1997..............DLB-61
Matheson, Annie 1853-1924 ....DLB-240	May, Thomas 1595/1596-1650 ....DLB-58	McCord, Louisa S. 1810-1879 ....DLB-248
Matheson, Richard 1926- DLB-8, 44	Mayer, Bernadette 1945- DLB-165	McCorkle, Jill 1958- DLB-234; Y-87
Matheus, John F. 1887-1986.............DLB-51	Mayer, Mercer 1943- DLB-61	McCorkle, Samuel Eusebius 1746-1811....DLB-37
Mathews, Aidan 1956- DLB-319	Mayer, O. B. 1818-1891.............DLB-3, 248	McCormick, Anne O'Hare 1880-1954 ....DLB-29
Mathews, Cornelius 1817?-1889 ...DLB-3, 64, 250	Mayes, Herbert R. 1900-1987 ....DLB-137	McCormick, Kenneth Dale 1906-1997 ....Y-97
Elkin Mathews [publishing house].......DLB-112	Mayes, Wendell 1919-1992 ....DLB-26	McCormick, Robert R. 1880-1955 ....DLB-29
Mathews, John Joseph 1894-1979 ....DLB-175	Mayfield, Julian 1928-1984 .... DLB-33; Y-84	McCourt, Edward 1907-1972..........DLB-88
Mathias, Roland 1915- DLB-27	Mayhew, Henry 1812-1887 ...... DLB-18, 55, 190	McCoy, Horace 1897-1955 ....DLB-9
Mathis, June 1892-1927................DLB-44	Mayhew, Jonathan 1720-1766 ....DLB-31	McCrae, Hugh 1876-1958.............DLB-260
Mathis, Sharon Bell 1937- DLB-33	Mayne, Ethel Colburn 1865-1941 ....DLB-197	McCrae, John 1872-1918...............DLB-92
Matković, Marijan 1915-1985 ....DLB-181	Mayne, Jasper 1604-1672...............DLB-126	McCrumb, Sharyn 1948- DLB-306
Matoš, Antun Gustav 1873-1914 ....DLB-147	Mayne, Seymour 1944- DLB-60	McCullagh, Joseph B. 1842-1896 ....DLB-23
Matos Paoli, Francisco 1915-2000 ....DLB-290	Mayor, Flora Macdonald 1872-1932 .....DLB-36	McCullers, Carson 1917-1967..... DLB-2, 7, 173, 228; CDALB-1
Matsumoto Seichō 1909-1992 ....DLB-182	Mayröcker, Friederike 1924- DLB-85	McCulloch, Thomas 1776-1843..........DLB-99
The Matter of England 1240-1400.......DLB-146	Mazrui, Ali A. 1933- DLB-125	McCunn, Ruthanne Lum 1946- DLB-312
The Matter of Rome early twelfth to late fifteenth century DLB-146	Mažuranić, Ivan 1814-1890 ....DLB-147	McDermott, Alice 1953- DLB-292
Matthew of Vendôme circa 1130-circa 1200...............DLB-208	Mazursky, Paul 1930- DLB-44	McDonald, Forrest 1927- DLB-17
Matthews, Brander 1852-1929.. DLB-71, 78; DS-13	McAlmon, Robert 1896-1956 ...DLB-4, 45; DS-15	McDonald, Walter 1934- DLB-105, DS-9
Matthews, Brian 1936- DLB-325	"A Night at Bricktop's" Y-01	"Getting Started: Accepting the Regions You Own-or Which Own You"..................DLB-105
Matthews, Jack 1925- DLB-6	McArthur, Peter 1866-1924 ....DLB-92	Tribute to James Dickey Y-97
Matthews, Victoria Earle 1861-1907 .....DLB-221	McAuley, James 1917-1976.............DLB-260	McDougall, Colin 1917-1984............DLB-68
Matthews, William 1942-1997 ....DLB-5	Robert M. McBride and Company DLB-46	McDowell, Katharine Sherwood Bonner 1849-1883..................DLB-202, 239
Matthías Jochumsson 1835-1920 ....DLB-293	McCabe, Patrick 1955- DLB-194	Obolensky McDowell [publishing house]..................DLB-46
Matthías Johannessen 1930- DLB-293	McCafferty, Owen 1961- DLB-310	McEwan, Ian 1948- DLB-14, 194, 319, 326
Matthiessen, F. O. 1902-1950 ....DLB-63	McCaffrey, Anne 1926- DLB-8	McFadden, David 1940- DLB-60
Matthiessen, Peter 1927- DLB-6, 173, 275	McCann, Colum 1965- DLB-267	McFall, Frances Elizabeth Clarke (see Grand, Sarah)
Maturin, Charles Robert 1780-1824 ..... DLB-178	McCarthy, Cormac 1933- DLB-6, 143, 256	McFarland, Ron 1942- DLB-256
Matute, Ana María 1926- DLB-322	The Cormac McCarthy Society Y-99	McFarlane, Leslie 1902-1977 ....DLB-88
	McCarthy, Mary 1912-1989 .... DLB-2; Y-81	
	McCarthy, Shaun Lloyd (see Cory, Desmond)	

Cumulative Index

McFee, William 1881-1966 . . . . DLB-153

McGahan, Andrew 1966- DLB-325

McGahern, John 1934- DLB-14, 231, 319

McGee, Thomas D'Arcy 1825-1868 . . . . . . DLB-99

McGeehan, W. O. 1879-1933 . . . . DLB-25, 171

McGill, Ralph 1898-1969 . . . . DLB-29

McGinley, Phyllis 1905-1978 . . . . DLB-11, 48

McGinniss, Joe 1942- DLB-185

McGirt, James E. 1874-1930 . . . . DLB-50

McGlashan and Gill DLB-106

McGough, Roger 1937- DLB-40

McGrath, John 1935- DLB-233

McGrath, Patrick 1950- DLB-231

McGraw-Hill DLB-46

McGuane, Thomas 1939- DLB-2, 212; Y-80

    Tribute to Seymour Lawrence Y-94

McGuckian, Medbh 1950- DLB-40

McGuffey, William Holmes 1800-1873 . . . . DLB-42

McGuinness, Frank 1953- DLB-245

McHenry, James 1785-1845 . . . . DLB-202

McIlvanney, William 1936- DLB-14, 207

McIlwraith, Jean Newton 1859-1938 . . . . . DLB-92

McInerney, Jay 1955- DLB-292

McInerny, Ralph 1929- DLB-306

McIntosh, Maria Jane 1803-1878 . . . DLB-239, 248

McIntyre, James 1827-1906 . . . . DLB-99

McIntyre, O. O. 1884-1938 . . . . DLB-25

McKay, Claude 1889-1948 . . . . . DLB-4, 45, 51, 117

The David McKay Company DLB-49

McKean, William V. 1820-1903 . . . . DLB-23

McKenna, Stephen 1888-1967 . . . . DLB-197

The McKenzie Trust Y-96

McKerrow, R. B. 1872-1940 . . . . DLB-201

McKinley, Robin 1952- DLB-52

McKnight, Reginald 1956- DLB-234

McLachlan, Alexander 1818-1896 . . . . DLB-99

McLaren, Floris Clark 1904-1978 . . . . DLB-68

McLaverty, Michael 1907-1992 . . . . DLB-15

McLean, Duncan 1964- DLB-267

McLean, John R. 1848-1916 . . . . DLB-23

McLean, William L. 1852-1931 . . . . DLB-25

McLennan, William 1856-1904 . . . . DLB-92

McLoughlin Brothers DLB-49

McLuhan, Marshall 1911-1980 . . . . DLB-88

McMaster, John Bach 1852-1932 . . . . DLB-47

McMillan, Terri 1951- DLB-292

McMurtry, Larry 1936-
    . . . . DLB-2, 143, 256; Y-80, 87; CDALB-6

McNally, Terrence 1939- DLB-7, 249

McNeil, Florence 1937- DLB-60

McNeile, Herman Cyril 1888-1937 . . . . . . DLB-77

McNickle, D'Arcy 1904-1977 . . . . DLB-175, 212

McPhee, John 1931- DLB-185, 275

McPherson, James Alan 1943- DLB-38, 244

McPherson, Sandra 1943- Y-86

McTaggart, J. M. E. 1866-1925 . . . . DLB-262

McWhirter, George 1939- DLB-60

McWilliam, Candia 1955- DLB-267

McWilliams, Carey 1905-1980 . . . . DLB-137

    "*The Nation's* Future," Carey
    McWilliams's Editorial Policy
    in *Nation* DLB-137

Mda, Zakes 1948- DLB-225

Mead, George Herbert 1863-1931 . . . . . . DLB-270

Mead, L. T. 1844-1914 . . . . DLB-141

Mead, Matthew 1924- DLB-40

Mead, Taylor circa 1931- DLB-16

Meany, Tom 1903-1964 . . . . DLB-171

Mears, Gillian 1964- DLB-325

Mechthild von Magdeburg
    circa 1207-circa 1282 . . . . DLB-138

Medieval Galician-Portuguese Poetry DLB-287

Medill, Joseph 1823-1899 . . . . DLB-43

Medoff, Mark 1940- DLB-7

Meek, Alexander Beaufort
    1814-1865 . . . . DLB-3, 248

Meeke, Mary ?-1816 . . . . DLB-116

Mehta, Ved 1934- DLB-323

Mei, Lev Aleksandrovich 1822-1862 . . . . . DLB-277

Meinke, Peter 1932- DLB-5

Meireles, Cecília 1901-1964 . . . . DLB-307

Mejía, Pedro 1497-1551 . . . . DLB-318

Mejia Vallejo, Manuel 1923- DLB-113

Melanchthon, Philipp 1497-1560 . . . . . . DLB-179

Melançon, Robert 1947- DLB-60

Mell, Max 1882-1971 . . . . DLB-81, 124

Mellow, James R. 1926-1997 . . . . DLB-111

Mel'nikov, Pavel Ivanovich 1818-1883 . . . DLB-238

Meltzer, David 1937- DLB-16

Meltzer, Milton 1915- DLB-61

Melville, Elizabeth, Lady Culross
    circa 1585-1640 . . . . DLB-172

Melville, Herman
    1819-1891 . . . . DLB-3, 74, 250; CDALB-2

    The Melville Society Y-01

Melville, James
    (Roy Peter Martin) 1931- DLB-276

"Memorandum on Local Government," Anne-
    Robert-Jacques Turgot, bacon de
    l'Aulne DLB-314

Mena, Juan de 1411-1456 . . . . DLB-286

Mena, María Cristina 1893-1965 . . . DLB-209, 221

Menander 342-341 B.C.-circa 292-291 B.C.
    . . . . DLB-176; CDWLB-1

Menantes (see Hunold, Christian Friedrich)

Mencke, Johann Burckhard 1674-1732 . . . DLB-168

Mencken, H. L. 1880-1956
    . . . . DLB-11, 29, 63, 137, 222; CDALB-4

    "Berlin, February, 1917" Y-00

    From the Initial Issue of *American Mercury*
    (January 1924) DLB-137

    Mencken and Nietzsche: An
    Unpublished Excerpt from H. L.
    Mencken's *My Life as Author and
    Editor* Y-93

Mendelssohn, Moses 1729-1786 . . . . DLB-97

Mendes, Catulle 1841-1909 . . . . DLB-217

Méndez M., Miguel 1930- DLB-82

Mendoza, Diego Hurtado de
    1504-1575 . . . . DLB-318

Mendoza, Eduardo 1943- DLB-322

The Mercantile Library of New York Y-96

Mercer, Cecil William (see Yates, Dornford)

Mercer, David 1928-1980 . . . . DLB-13, 310

Mercer, John 1704-1768 . . . . DLB-31

Mercer, Johnny 1909-1976 . . . . DLB-265

Mercier, Louis-Sébastien 1740-1814 . . . . . DLB-314

    Le Tableau de Paris DLB-314

Meredith, George
    1828-1909 . . . . DLB-18, 35, 57, 159; CDBLB-4

Meredith, Louisa Anne 1812-1895 . . DLB-166, 230

Meredith, Owen
    (see Lytton, Edward Robert Bulwer)

Meredith, William 1919- DLB-5

Meres, Francis
    Palladis Tamia, Wits Treasurie (1598)
    [excerpt] DLB-172

Merezhkovsky, Dmitrii Sergeevich
    1865-1941 . . . . DLB-295

Mergerle, Johann Ulrich
    (see Abraham ä Sancta Clara)

Mérimée, Prosper 1803-1870 . . . . DLB-119, 192

Merino, José María 1941- DLB-322

Merivale, John Herman 1779-1844 . . . . . . DLB-96

Meriwether, Louise 1923- DLB-33

Merleau-Ponty, Maurice 1908-1961 . . . . . DLB-296

Merlin Press DLB-112

Merriam, Eve 1916-1992 . . . . DLB-61

The Merriam Company DLB-49

Merril, Judith 1923-1997 . . . . DLB-251

    Tribute to Theodore Sturgeon Y-85

Merrill, James 1926-1995 . . . . . . DLB-5, 165; Y-85

Merrill and Baker DLB-49

The Mershon Company DLB-49

Merton, Thomas 1915-1968 . . . . DLB-48; Y-81

Merwin, W. S. 1927- DLB-5, 169

Julian Messner [publishing house] DLB-46

Mészöly, Miklós 1921- DLB-232

J. Metcalf [publishing house] DLB-49

Metcalf, John 1938- DLB-60

The Methodist Book Concern..........DLB-49

Methuen and Company...............DLB-112

Meun, Jean de (see *Roman de la Rose*)

Mew, Charlotte 1869-1928 ....DLB-19, 135

Mewshaw, Michael 1943- Y-80

Tribute to Albert Erskine Y-93

Meyer, Conrad Ferdinand 1825-1898 ....DLB-129

Meyer, E. Y. 1946- DLB-75

Meyer, Eugene 1875-1959 ....DLB-29

Meyer, Michael 1921-2000.............DLB-155

Meyers, Jeffrey 1939- DLB-111

Meynell, Alice 1847-1922............DLB-19, 98

Meynell, Viola 1885-1956 ....DLB-153

Meyrink, Gustav 1868-1932 ....DLB-81

Mézières, Philipe de circa 1327-1405 .....DLB-208

Michael, Ib 1945- DLB-214

Michael, Livi 1960- DLB-267

Michaëlis, Karen 1872-1950...........DLB-214

Michaels, Anne 1958- DLB-299

Michaels, Leonard 1933-2003 ....DLB-130

Michaux, Henri 1899-1984 ....DLB-258

Micheaux, Oscar 1884-1951 ....DLB-50

Michel of Northgate, Dan
  circa 1265-circa 1340................DLB-146

Micheline, Jack 1929-1998..............DLB-16

Michener, James A. 1907?-1997 ....DLB-6

Micklejohn, George circa 1717-1818.......DLB-31

Middle Hill Press DLB-106

Middleton, Christopher 1926- DLB-40

Middleton, Richard 1882-1911 ....DLB-156

Middleton, Stanley 1919- DLB-14, 326

Middleton, Thomas 1580-1627 ....DLB-58

Midnight's Children, 1981 Booker Prize winner,
  Salman Rushdie..................DLB-326

Miegel, Agnes 1879-1964..............DLB-56

Miežalaitis, Eduardas 1919-1997 ....DLB-220

Miguéis, José Rodrigues 1901-1980......DLB-287

Mihailović, Dragoslav 1930- DLB-181

Mihalić, Slavko 1928- DLB-181

Mikhailov, A.
  (see Sheller, Aleksandr Konstantinovich)

Mikhailov, Mikhail Larionovich
  1829-1865.....................DLB-238

Mikhailovsky, Nikolai Konstantinovich
  1842-1904.....................DLB-277

Miles, Josephine 1911-1985 ....DLB-48

Miles, Susan (Ursula Wyllie Roberts)
  1888-1975.....................DLB-240

Miliković, Branko 1934-1961............DLB-181

Milius, John 1944- DLB-44

Mill, James 1773-1836 ....DLB-107, 158, 262

Mill, John Stuart
  1806-1873 ......DLB-55, 190, 262; CDBLB-4

Thoughts on Poetry and Its Varieties
  (1833) DLB-32

Andrew Millar [publishing house] DLB-154

Millar, Kenneth
  1915-1983 ....DLB-2, 226; Y-83; DS-6

Millás, Juan José 1946- DLB-322

Millay, Edna St. Vincent
  1892-1950 ....DLB-45, 249; CDALB-4

Millen, Sarah Gertrude 1888-1968 ......DLB-225

Miller, Andrew 1960- DLB-267

Miller, Arthur 1915-2005 ...DLB-7, 266; CDALB-1

The Arthur Miller Society..............Y-01

Miller, Caroline 1903-1992 ....DLB-9

Miller, Eugene Ethelbert 1950- DLB-41

Tribute to Julian Mayfield Y-84

Miller, Heather Ross 1939- DLB-120

Miller, Henry
  1891-1980 ....DLB-4, 9; Y-80; CDALB-5

Miller, Hugh 1802-1856...............DLB-190

Miller, J. Hillis 1928- DLB-67

Miller, Jason 1939- DLB-7

Miller, Joaquin 1839-1913 ....DLB-186

Miller, May 1899-1995................DLB-41

Miller, Paul 1906-1991................DLB-127

Miller, Perry 1905-1963 ....DLB-17, 63

Miller, Sue 1943- DLB-143

Miller, Vassar 1924-1998 ....DLB-105

Miller, Walter M., Jr. 1923-1996 ....DLB-8

Miller, Webb 1892-1940...............DLB-29

James Miller [publishing house].........DLB-49

Millett, Kate 1934- DLB-246

Millhauser, Steven 1943- DLB-2

Millican, Arthenia J. Bates 1920- DLB-38

Milligan, Alice 1866-1953 ....DLB-240

Mills, Magnus 1954- DLB-267

Mills and Boon DLB-112

Milman, Henry Hart 1796-1868 ....DLB-96

Milne, A. A. 1882-1956 .....DLB-10, 77, 100, 160

Milner, Ron 1938- DLB-38

William Milner [publishing house].......DLB-106

Milnes, Richard Monckton (Lord Houghton)
  1809-1885 ....DLB-32, 184

Milton, John
  1608-1674 .....DLB-131, 151, 281; CDBLB-2

The Milton Society of America..........Y-00

Miłosz, Czesław
  1911-2004 ....DLB-215; CDWLB-4

Minakami Tsutomu 1919- DLB-182

Minamoto no Sanetomo 1192-1219.....DLB-203

Minco, Marga 1920- DLB-299

The Minerva Press..................DLB-154

Minnesang circa 1150-1280 ....DLB-138

The Music of *Minnesang* DLB-138

Minns, Susan 1839-1938 ....DLB-140

Minsky, Nikolai 1855-1937 ....DLB-317

Minton, Balch and Company DLB-46

Minyana, Philippe 1946- DLB-321

Mirbeau, Octave 1848-1917........DLB-123, 192

Mirikitani, Janice 1941- DLB-312

Mirk, John died after 1414?...........DLB-146

Miró, Gabriel 1879-1930 ....DLB-322

Miró, Ricardo 1883-1940...............DLB-290

Miron, Gaston 1928-1996 ....DLB-60

A Mirror for Magistrates DLB-167

Mirsky, D. S. 1890-1939 ....DLB-317

Mishima Yukio 1925-1970 ....DLB-182

Mistral, Gabriela 1889-1957 ....DLB-283

Mitchel, Jonathan 1624-1668...........DLB-24

Mitchell, Adrian 1932- DLB-40

Mitchell, Donald Grant
  1822-1908..............DLB-1, 243; DS-13

Mitchell, Gladys 1901-1983.............DLB-77

Mitchell, James Leslie 1901-1935.........DLB-15

Mitchell, John (see Slater, Patrick)

Mitchell, John Ames 1845-1918..........DLB-79

Mitchell, Joseph 1908-1996 ......DLB-185; Y-96

Mitchell, Julian 1935- DLB-14

Mitchell, Ken 1940- DLB-60

Mitchell, Langdon 1862-1935 ....DLB-7

Mitchell, Loften 1919-2001 ....DLB-38

Mitchell, Margaret 1900-1949 ...DLB-9; CDALB-7

Mitchell, S. Weir 1829-1914............DLB-202

Mitchell, W. J. T. 1942- DLB-246

Mitchell, W. O. 1914-1998 ....DLB-88

Mitchison, Naomi Margaret (Haldane)
  1897-1999 ....DLB-160, 191, 255, 319

Mitford, Mary Russell 1787-1855....DLB-110, 116

Mitford, Nancy 1904-1973............DLB-191

Mittelholzer, Edgar
  1909-1965............DLB-117; CDWLB-3

Mitterer, Erika 1906-2001 ....DLB-85

Mitterer, Felix 1948- DLB-124

Mitternacht, Johann Sebastian
  1613-1679 ....DLB-168

Miyamoto Yuriko 1899-1951...........DLB-180

Mizener, Arthur 1907-1988 ....DLB-103

Mo, Timothy 1950- DLB-194

Moberg, Vilhelm 1898-1973 ....DLB-259

Modern Age Books DLB-46

Modern Language Association of America
  The Modern Language Association of
  America Celebrates Its Centennial ...Y-84

The Modern Library.................DLB-46

Cumulative Index

Modiano, Patrick 1945- DLB-83, 299

Modjeska, Drusilla 1946- DLB-325

Moffat, Yard and Company DLB-46

Moffet, Thomas 1553-1604 . . . . DLB-136

Mofolo, Thomas 1876-1948 . . . . DLB-225

Mohr, Nicholasa 1938- DLB-145

Moix, Ana María 1947- DLB-134

Molesworth, Louisa 1839-1921 . . . . DLB-135

Molière (Jean-Baptiste Poquelin) 1622-1673 . . . . DLB-268

Møller, Poul Martin 1794-1838 . . . . DLB-300

Möllhausen, Balduin 1825-1905 . . . . DLB-129

Molnár, Ferenc 1878-1952 . . . DLB-215; CDWLB-4

Molnár, Miklós (see Mészöly, Miklós)

Momaday, N. Scott 1934- DLB-143, 175, 256; CDALB-7

Monkhouse, Allan 1858-1936. . . . . DLB-10

Monro, Harold 1879-1932 . . . . DLB-19

Monroe, Harriet 1860-1936 . . . . DLB-54, 91

Monsarrat, Nicholas 1910-1979 . . . . DLB-15

Montagu, Lady Mary Wortley 1689-1762. . . . . DLB-95, 101

Montague, C. E. 1867-1928 . . . . DLB-197

Montague, John 1929- DLB-40

Montaigne, Michel de 1533-1592 . . . . DLB-327

Montale, Eugenio 1896-1981 . . . . DLB-114

Montalvo, Garci Rodríguez de ca. 1450?-before 1505 . . . . DLB-286

Montalvo, José 1946-1994 . . . . DLB-209

Montemayor, Jorge de 1521?-1561? DLB-318

Montero, Rosa 1951- DLB-322

Monterroso, Augusto 1921-2003 . . . . DLB-145

Montesquieu, Charles-Louis de Secondat, baron de 1689-1755. . . . . DLB-314

The Spirit of Laws. DLB-314

Montesquiou, Robert de 1855-1921 . . . . . DLB-217

Montgomerie, Alexander circa 1550?-1598 . . . . DLB-167

Montgomery, James 1771-1854 . . . . . . DLB-93, 158

Montgomery, John 1919- DLB-16

Montgomery, Lucy Maud 1874-1942. . . . . DLB-92; DS-14

Montgomery, Marion 1925- DLB-6

Montgomery, Robert Bruce (see Crispin, Edmund)

Montherlant, Henry de 1896-1972 . . . DLB-72, 321

The Monthly Review 1749-1844 . . . . DLB-110

Monti, Ricardo 1944- DLB-305

Montigny, Louvigny de 1876-1955 . . . . . . DLB-92

Montoya, José 1932- DLB-122

Moodie, John Wedderburn Dunbar 1797-1869 . . . . DLB-99

Moodie, Susanna 1803-1885 . . . . DLB-99

Moody, Joshua circa 1633-1697 . . . . DLB-24

Moody, William Vaughn 1869-1910 . . . . . DLB-7, 54

Moon Tiger, 1987 Booker Prize winner, Penelope Lively DLB-326

Moorcock, Michael 1939- . . DLB-14, 231, 261, 319

Moore, Alan 1953- DLB-261

Moore, Brian 1921-1999. . . . . DLB-251

Moore, Catherine L. 1911-1987 . . . . DLB-8

Moore, Clement Clarke 1779-1863 . . . . . . DLB-42

Moore, Dora Mavor 1888-1979 . . . . DLB-92

Moore, G. E. 1873-1958 . . . . DLB-262

Moore, George 1852-1933 . . . DLB-10, 18, 57, 135

Literature at Nurse, or Circulating Morals (1885) DLB-18

Moore, Lorrie 1957- DLB-234

Moore, Marianne 1887-1972 . . . . DLB-45; DS-7; CDALB-5

International Marianne Moore Society . . . Y-98

Moore, Mavor 1919- DLB-88

Moore, Richard 1927- DLB-105

"The No Self, the Little Self, and the Poets". DLB-105

Moore, T. Sturge 1870-1944 . . . . DLB-19

Moore, Thomas 1779-1852 . . . . DLB-96, 144

Moore, Ward 1903-1978 . . . . DLB-8

Moore, Wilstach, Keys and Company DLB-49

Moorehead, Alan 1901-1983 . . . . DLB-204

Moorhouse, Frank 1938- DLB-289

Moorhouse, Geoffrey 1931- DLB-204

Moorish Novel of the Sixteenth Century, The DLB-318

The Moorland-Spingarn Research Center DLB-76

Moorman, Mary C. 1905-1994 . . . . DLB-155

Mora, Pat 1942- DLB-209

Moraes, Dom 1938-2004 . . . . DLB-323

Moraes, Vinicius de 1913-1980 . . . . DLB-307

Moraga, Cherríe 1952- DLB-82, 249

Morales, Alejandro 1944- DLB-82

Morales, Mario Roberto 1947- DLB-145

Morales, Rafael 1919- DLB-108

Morality Plays: *Mankind* circa 1450-1500 and *Everyman* circa 1500 . . . . DLB-146

Morand, Paul (1888-1976) DLB-65

Morante, Elsa 1912-1985 . . . . DLB-177

Morata, Olympia Fulvia 1526-1555 . . . . . DLB-179

Moravia, Alberto 1907-1990 . . . . DLB-177

Mordaunt, Elinor 1872-1942 . . . . DLB-174

Mordovtsev, Daniil Lukich 1830-1905 . . . DLB-238

More, Hannah 1745-1833. . . . . DLB-107, 109, 116, 158

More, Henry 1614-1687 . . . . DLB-126, 252

More, Sir Thomas 1477/1478-1535 . . . . DLB-136, 281

Morejón, Nancy 1944- DLB-283

Morellet, André 1727-1819 . . . . DLB-314

Morency, Pierre 1942- DLB-60

Moreno, Dorinda 1939- DLB-122

Moretti, Marino 1885-1979. . . . . . . DLB-114, 264

Morgan, Berry 1919-2002 . . . . DLB-6

Morgan, Charles 1894-1958. . . . . DLB-34, 100

Morgan, Edmund S. 1916- DLB-17

Morgan, Edwin 1920- DLB-27

Morgan, John Pierpont 1837-1913 . . . . . . DLB-140

Morgan, John Pierpont, Jr. 1867-1943 . . . DLB-140

Morgan, Robert 1944- DLB-120, 292

Morgan, Sally 1951- DLB-325

Morgan, Sydney Owenson, Lady 1776?-1859. . . . . DLB-116, 158

Morgner, Irmtraud 1933-1990 . . . . DLB-75

Morhof, Daniel Georg 1639-1691 . . . . . . DLB-164

Mori, Kyoko 1957- DLB-312

Mori Ōgai 1862-1922 . . . . DLB-180

Mori, Toshio 1910-1980 . . . . DLB-312

Móricz, Zsigmond 1879-1942 . . . . DLB-215

Morier, James Justinian 1782 or 1783?-1849 . . . . DLB-116

Mörike, Eduard 1804-1875 . . . . DLB-133

Morin, Paul 1889-1963. . . . . DLB-92

Morison, Richard 1514?-1556 . . . . DLB-136

Morison, Samuel Eliot 1887-1976 . . . . DLB-17

Morison, Stanley 1889-1967 . . . . DLB-201

Moritz, Karl Philipp 1756-1793 . . . . DLB-94

Moriz von Craûn circa 1220-1230 . . . . DLB-138

Morley, Christopher 1890-1957 . . . . DLB-9

Morley, John 1838-1923 . . . . DLB-57, 144, 190

Moro, César 1903-1956 . . . . DLB-290

Morris, George Pope 1802-1864 . . . . DLB-73

Morris, James Humphrey (see Morris, Jan)

Morris, Jan 1926- DLB-204

Morris, Lewis 1833-1907 . . . . DLB-35

Morris, Margaret 1737-1816 . . . . DLB-200

Morris, Mary McGarry 1943- DLB-292

Morris, Richard B. 1904-1989 . . . . DLB-17

Morris, William 1834-1896 . . . . . DLB-18, 35, 57, 156, 178, 184; CDBLB-4

Morris, Willie 1934-1999 . . . . Y-80

Tribute to Irwin Shaw Y-84

Tribute to James Dickey. Y-97

Morris, Wright 1910-1998 . . . . DLB-2, 206, 218; Y-81

Morrison, Arthur 1863-1945 . . . . DLB-70, 135, 197

Morrison, Charles Clayton 1874-1966 . . . . DLB-91

Morrison, John 1904-1998 . . . . DLB-260

Morrison, Toni 1931- DLB-6, 33, 143; Y-81, 93; CDALB-6

Nobel Lecture 1993 . . . . Y-93

Morrissy, Mary 1957- DLB-267

William Morrow and Company DLB-46

Morse, James Herbert 1841-1923 ....DLB-71

Morse, Jedidiah 1761-1826.............DLB-37

Morse, John T., Jr. 1840-1937 ....DLB-47

Morselli, Guido 1912-1973.............DLB-177

Morte Arthure, the *Alliterative* and the
 Stanzaic circa 1350-1400............DLB-146

Mortimer, Favell Lee 1802-1878.........DLB-163

Mortimer, John
 1923- DLB-13, 245, 271; CDBLB-8

Morton, Carlos 1942- DLB-122

Morton, H. V. 1892-1979..............DLB-195

John P. Morton and Company DLB-49

Morton, Nathaniel 1613-1685 ....DLB-24

Morton, Sarah Wentworth 1759-1846 .....DLB-37

Morton, Thomas circa 1579-circa 1647 ....DLB-24

Moscherosch, Johann Michael
 1601-1669 ....DLB-164

Humphrey Moseley
 [publishing house] DLB-170

Möser, Justus 1720-1794................DLB-97

Mosley, Nicholas 1923- DLB-14, 207

Mosley, Walter 1952- DLB-306

Moss, Arthur 1889-1969 ....DLB-4

Moss, Howard 1922-1987 ....DLB-5

Moss, Thylias 1954- DLB-120

Motion, Andrew 1952- DLB-40

Motley, John Lothrop
 1814-1877 ....DLB-1, 30, 59, 235

Motley, Willard 1909-1965 ....DLB-76, 143

Mott, Lucretia 1793-1880.............DLB-239

Benjamin Motte Jr.
 [publishing house] DLB-154

Motteux, Peter Anthony 1663-1718......DLB-80

Mottram, R. H. 1883-1971.............DLB-36

Mount, Ferdinand 1939- DLB-231

Mouré, Erin 1955- DLB-60

Mourning Dove (Humishuma) between
 1882 and 1888?-1936 ....DLB-175, 221

Movies
 Fiction into Film, 1928-1975: A List
 of Movies Based on the Works
 of Authors in British Novelists,
 1930-1959....................DLB-15

 Movies from Books, 1920-1974.......DLB-9

Mowat, Farley 1921- DLB-68

A. R. Mowbray and Company,
 Limited DLB-106

Mowrer, Edgar Ansel 1892-1977 ......DLB-29

Mowrer, Paul Scott 1887-1971 ....DLB-29

Edward Moxon [publishing house] DLB-106

Joseph Moxon [publishing house] DLB-170

Moyes, Patricia 1923-2000.............DLB-276

Mphahlele, Es'kia (Ezekiel)
 1919- DLB-125, 225; CDWLB-3

Mrożek, Sławomir 1930- ...DLB-232; CDWLB-4

Mtshali, Oswald Mbuyiseni
 1940- DLB-125, 225

Mu Shiying 1912-1940................DLB-328

al-Mubarrad 826-898 or 899..........DLB-311

Mucedorus.........................DLB-62

Mudford, William 1782-1848..........DLB-159

Mudrooroo (see Johnson, Colin)

Mueller, Lisel 1924- DLB-105

Muhajir, El (see Marvin X)

Muhajir, Nazzam Al Fitnah (see Marvin X)

Muhammad the Prophet circa 570-632 ...DLB-311

Mühlbach, Luise 1814-1873.............DLB-133

Muir, Edwin 1887-1959 ....DLB-20, 100, 191

Muir, Helen 1937- DLB-14

Muir, John 1838-1914 ....DLB-186, 275

Muir, Percy 1894-1979...............DLB-201

Mujū Ichien 1226-1312 ....DLB-203

Mukherjee, Bharati 1940- DLB-60, 218, 323

Mulcaster, Richard 1531 or 1532-1611 ...DLB-167

Muldoon, Paul 1951- DLB-40

Mulisch, Harry 1927- DLB-299

Mulkerns, Val 1925- DLB-319

Müller, Friedrich (see Müller, Maler)

Müller, Heiner 1929-1995 ....DLB-124

Müller, Maler 1749-1825 ....DLB-94

Muller, Marcia 1944- DLB-226

Müller, Wilhelm 1794-1827 ....DLB-90

Mumford, Lewis 1895-1990 ....DLB-63

Munby, A. N. L. 1913-1974 ....DLB-201

Munby, Arthur Joseph 1828-1910 ....DLB-35

Munday, Anthony 1560-1633 ....DLB-62, 172

Mundt, Clara (see Mühlbach, Luise)

Mundt, Theodore 1808-1861 ....DLB-133

Munford, Robert circa 1737-1783.........DLB-31

Mungoshi, Charles 1947- DLB-157

Munk, Kaj 1898-1944 ....DLB-214

Munonye, John 1929- DLB-117

Muñoz Molina, Antonio 1956- DLB-322

Munro, Alice 1931- DLB-53

George Munro [publishing house]........DLB-49

Munro, H. H.
 1870-1916 ....DLB-34, 162; CDBLB-5

Munro, Neil 1864-1930 ....DLB-156

Norman L. Munro [publishing house].....DLB-49

Munroe, Kirk 1850-1930...............DLB-42

Munroe and Francis..................DLB-49

James Munroe and Company DLB-49

Joel Munsell [publishing house] DLB-49

Munsey, Frank A. 1854-1925 ....DLB-25, 91

Frank A. Munsey and Company.........DLB-49

Mura, David 1952- DLB-312

Murakami Haruki 1949- DLB-182

Muratov, Pavel 1881-1950.............DLB-317

Murayama, Milton 1923- DLB-312

Murav'ev, Mikhail Nikitich 1757-1807....DLB-150

Murdoch, Iris 1919-1999
 ....DLB-14, 194, 233, 326; CDBLB-8

Murdock, James
 From *Sketches of Modern Philosophy*........ DS-5

Murdoch, Rupert 1931- DLB-127

Murfree, Mary N. 1850-1922 ....DLB-12, 74

Murger, Henry 1822-1861..............DLB-119

Murger, Louis-Henri (see Murger, Henry)

Murnane, Gerald 1939- DLB-289

Murner, Thomas 1475-1537.............DLB-179

Muro, Amado 1915-1971...............DLB-82

Murphy, Arthur 1727-1805 ....DLB-89, 142

Murphy, Beatrice M. 1908-1992 ....DLB-76

Murphy, Dervla 1931- DLB-204

Murphy, Emily 1868-1933..............DLB-99

Murphy, Jack 1923-1980 ....DLB-241

John Murphy and Company DLB-49

Murphy, John H., III 1916- DLB-127

Murphy, Richard 1927-1993 ....DLB-40

Murphy, Tom 1935- DLB-310

Murray, Albert L. 1916- DLB-38

Murray, Gilbert 1866-1957 ....DLB-10

Murray, Jim 1919-1998 ....DLB-241

John Murray [publishing house] DLB-154

Murray, Judith Sargent
 1751-1820 ....DLB-37, 200

Murray, Les 1938- DLB-289

Murray, Pauli 1910-1985 ....DLB-41

Murry, John Middleton 1889-1957 ......DLB-149

 "The Break-Up of the Novel"
 (1922).....................DLB-36

Murry, John Middleton, Jr. (see Cowper, Richard)

Musäus, Johann Karl August
 1735-1787.....................DLB-97

Muschg, Adolf 1934- DLB-75

Musil, Robert
 1880-1942..........DLB-81, 124; CDWLB-2

Muspilli circa 790-circa 850.............DLB-148

Musset, Alfred de 1810-1857 ....DLB-192, 217

Benjamin B. Mussey
 and Company....................DLB-49

Muste, A. J. 1885-1967 ....DLB-303

Mutafchieva, Vera 1929- DLB-181

Mutis, Alvaro 1923-..................DLB-283

Mwangi, Meja 1948- DLB-125

Cumulative Index

Myers, Frederic W. H.
1843-1901 .... DLB-190

Myers, Gustavus 1872-1942 .... DLB-47

Myers, L. H. 1881-1944 .... DLB-15

Myers, Walter Dean 1937- DLB-33

Myerson, Julie 1960- DLB-267

Mykle, Agnar 1915-1994 .... DLB-297

Mykolaitis-Putinas,
Vincas 1893-1967................ DLB-220

Myles, Eileen 1949- DLB-193

Myrdal, Jan 1927- DLB-257

Mystery
1985: The Year of the Mystery:
A Symposium Y-85

Comments from Other Writers Y-85

The Second Annual New York Festival
of Mystery..................... Y-00

Why I Read Mysteries................ Y-85

Why I Write Mysteries: Night and Day,
by Michael Collins................ Y-85

N

Na Prous Boneta circa 1296-1328....... DLB-208

Nabl, Franz 1883-1974 .... DLB-81

Nabakov, Véra 1902-1991 .... Y-91

Nabokov, Vladimir 1899-1977 .... DLB-2, 244,
278, 317; Y-80, 91; DS-3; CDALB-1
International Nabokov Society.......... Y-99

An Interview [On Nabokov], by
Fredson Bowers.................. Y-80

Nabokov Festival at Cornell............ Y-83

The Vladimir Nabokov Archive in the
Berg Collection of the New York
Public Library: An Overview Y-91

The Vladimir Nabokov Society Y-01

Nádaši, Ladislav (see Jégé)

Naden, Constance 1858-1889.......... DLB-199

Nadezhdin, Nikolai Ivanovich
1804-1856 .... DLB-198

Nadson, Semen Iakovlevich 1862-1887 ...DLB-277

Naevius circa 265 B.C.-201 B.C. DLB-211

Nafis and Cornish..................... DLB-49

Nagai Kafū 1879-1959 .... DLB-180

Nagel, Ernest 1901-1985...............DLB-279

Nagibin, Iurii Markovich 1920-1994 .... DLB-302

Nagrodskaia, Evdokiia Apollonovna
1866-1930 .... DLB-295

Naipaul, Shiva 1945-1985..........DLB-157; Y-85

Naipaul, V. S. 1932-   ... DLB-125, 204, 207, 326;
Y-85, Y-01; CDBLB-8; CDWLB-3

Nobel Lecture 2001: "Two Worlds"...... Y-01

Nakagami Kenji 1946-1992 .... DLB-182

Nakano-in Masatada no Musume (see Nijō, Lady)

Nałkowska, Zofia 1884-1954 .... DLB-215

Namora, Fernando 1919-1989 .... DLB-287

Joseph Nancrede [publishing house]...... DLB-49

Naranjo, Carmen 1930- DLB-145

Narayan, R. K. 1906-2001 .... DLB-323

Narbikova, Valeriia Spartakovna
1958- DLB-285

Narezhny, Vasilii Trofimovich
1780-1825..................... DLB-198

Narrache, Jean (Emile Coderre)
1893-1970..................... DLB-92

Nasby, Petroleum Vesuvius (see Locke, David Ross)

Eveleigh Nash [publishing house]....... DLB-112

Nash, Ogden 1902-1971 .... DLB-11

Nashe, Thomas 1567-1601? DLB-167

Nason, Jerry 1910-1986 .... DLB-241

Nasr, Seyyed Hossein 1933- DLB-279

Nast, Condé 1873-1942 .... DLB-91

Nast, Thomas 1840-1902 .... DLB-188

Nastasijević, Momčilo 1894-1938....... DLB-147

Nathan, George Jean 1882-1958........ DLB-137

Nathan, Robert 1894-1985............. DLB-9

Nation, Carry A. 1846-1911........... DLB-303

National Book Critics Circle Awards Y-00–01

The National Jewish Book Awards......... Y-85

Natsume Sōseki 1867-1916 .... DLB-180

Naughton, Bill 1910-1992............. DLB-13

Nava, Michael 1954- DLB-306

Navarro, Joe 1953- DLB-209

Naylor, Gloria 1950- DLB-173

Nazor, Vladimir 1876-1949........... DLB-147

Ndebele, Njabulo 1948- DLB-157, 225

Neagoe, Peter 1881-1960 .... DLB-4

Neal, John 1793-1876 .... DLB-1, 59, 243

Neal, Joseph C. 1807-1847 .... DLB-11

Neal, Larry 1937-1981 .... DLB-38

The Neale Publishing Company......... DLB-49

Nearing, Scott 1883-1983 .... DLB-303

Nebel, Frederick 1903-1967 .... DLB-226

Nebrija, Antonio de 1442 or 1444-1522.. DLB-286

Nedreaas, Torborg 1906-1987 .... DLB-297

F. Tennyson Neely [publishing house] DLB-49

Negoițescu, Ion 1921-1993 .... DLB-220

Negri, Ada 1870-1945 .... DLB-114

Nehru, Pandit Jawaharlal 1889-1964 .... DLB-323

Neihardt, John G. 1881-1973 ..... DLB-9, 54, 256

Neidhart von Reuental
circa 1185-circa 1240 .... DLB-138

Neilson, John Shaw 1872-1942 .... DLB-230

Nekrasov, Nikolai Alekseevich
1821-1877.....................DLB-277

Nekrasov, Viktor Platonovich
1911-1987..................... DLB-302

Neledinsky-Meletsky, Iurii Aleksandrovich
1752-1828..................... DLB-150

Nelligan, Emile 1879-1941 .... DLB-92

Nelson, Alice Moore Dunbar 1875-1935 .. DLB-50

Nelson, Antonya 1961- DLB-244

Nelson, Kent 1943- DLB-234

Nelson, Richard K. 1941- DLB-275

Nelson, Thomas, and Sons [U.K.] DLB-106

Nelson, Thomas, and Sons [U.S.]........ DLB-49

Nelson, William 1908-1978............ DLB-103

Nelson, William Rockhill 1841-1915 ..... DLB-23

Nemerov, Howard 1920-1991 ....DLB-5, 6; Y-83

Németh, László 1901-1975 .... DLB-215

Nepos circa 100 B.C.-post 27 B.C. DLB-211

Nėris, Salomėja 1904-1945 .. DLB-220; CDWLB-4

Neruda, Pablo 1904-1973 .... DLB-283

Nerval, Gérard de 1808-1855 ....DLB-217

Nervo, Amado 1870-1919............. DLB-290

Nesbit, E. 1858-1924 ....DLB-141, 153, 178

Ness, Evaline 1911-1986................ DLB-61

Nestroy, Johann 1801-1862............ DLB-133

Nettleship, R. L. 1846-1892 .... DLB-262

Neugeboren, Jay 1938- DLB-28

Neukirch, Benjamin 1655-1729......... DLB-168

Neumann, Alfred 1895-1952 .... DLB-56

Neumann, Ferenc (see Molnár, Ferenc)

Neumark, Georg 1621-1681........... DLB-164

Neumeister, Erdmann 1671-1756 .... DLB-168

Nevins, Allan 1890-1971..........DLB-17; DS-17

Nevinson, Henry Woodd 1856-1941 .... DLB-135

The New American Library............ DLB-46

New Directions Publishing Corporation... DLB-46

The New Monthly Magazine 1814-1884 .... DLB-110

New York Times Book Review Y-82

John Newbery [publishing house]....... DLB-154

Newbolt, Henry 1862-1938 .... DLB-19

Newbound, Bernard Slade (see Slade, Bernard)

Newby, Eric 1919- DLB-204

Newby, P. H. 1918-1997 .... DLB-15, 326

Thomas Cautley Newby
[publishing house] DLB-106

Newcomb, Charles King 1820-1894... DLB-1, 223

Newell, Peter 1862-1924................ DLB-42

Newell, Robert Henry 1836-1901 .... DLB-11

Newhouse, Samuel I. 1895-1979.........DLB-127

Newman, Cecil Earl 1903-1976 ....DLB-127

Newman, David 1937- DLB-44

Newman, Frances 1883-1928............. Y-80

Newman, Francis William 1805-1897.... DLB-190

Newman, G. F. 1946- DLB-310

Newman, John Henry
1801-1890 .... DLB-18, 32, 55

Mark Newman [publishing house] DLB-49

Newmarch, Rosa Harriet 1857-1940..... DLB-240

George Newnes Limited DLB-112

Newsome, Effie Lee 1885-1979 . . . . DLB-76

Newton, A. Edward 1864-1940 . . . . DLB-140

Newton, Sir Isaac 1642-1727 . . . . DLB-252

Nexø, Martin Andersen 1869-1954 . . . . . . DLB-214

Nezval, Vítěslav
1900-1958 . . . . DLB-215; CDWLB-4

Ngugi wa Thiong'o
1938- DLB-125; CDWLB-3

Niatum, Duane 1938- DLB-175

The *Nibelungenlied* and the *Klage*
circa 1200 . . . . DLB-138

Nichol, B. P. 1944-1988 . . . . DLB-53

Nicholas of Cusa 1401-1464 . . . . DLB-115

Nichols, Ann 1891?-1966. . . . . DLB-249

Nichols, Beverly 1898-1983 . . . . DLB-191

Nichols, Dudley 1895-1960 . . . . DLB-26

Nichols, Grace 1950- DLB-157

Nichols, John 1940- Y-82

Nichols, Mary Sargeant (Neal) Gove
1810-1884 . . . . DLB-1, 243

Nichols, Peter 1927- DLB-13, 245

Nichols, Roy F. 1896-1973 . . . . DLB-17

Nichols, Ruth 1948- DLB-60

Nicholson, Edward Williams Byron
1849-1912 . . . . DLB-184

Nicholson, Geoff 1953- DLB-271

Nicholson, Norman 1914-1987 . . . . DLB-27

Nicholson, William 1872-1949. . . . . DLB-141

Ní Chuilleanáin, Eiléan 1942- DLB-40

Nicol, Eric 1919- DLB-68

Nicolai, Friedrich 1733-1811 . . . . DLB-97

Nicolas de Clamanges circa 1363-1437 . . . DLB-208

Nicolay, John G. 1832-1901 and
Hay, John 1838-1905. . . . . DLB-47

Nicole, Pierre 1625-1695 . . . . DLB-268

Nicolson, Adela Florence Cory (see Hope, Laurence)

Nicolson, Harold 1886-1968 . . . . DLB-100, 149

"The Practice of Biography," in
*The English Sense of Humour and
Other Essays* DLB-149

Nicolson, Nigel 1917-2004 . . . . DLB-155

Ní Dhuibhne, Éilís 1954- DLB-319

Niebuhr, Reinhold 1892-1971 . . . . . DLB-17; DS-17

Niedecker, Lorine 1903-1970 . . . . DLB-48

Nieman, Lucius W. 1857-1935 . . . . DLB-25

Nietzsche, Friedrich
1844-1900 . . . . DLB-129; CDWLB-2

Mencken and Nietzsche: An Unpublished
Excerpt from H. L. Mencken's *My Life
as Author and Editor* Y-93

Nievo, Stanislao 1928- DLB-196

Niggli, Josefina 1910-1983 . . . . Y-80

Nightingale, Florence 1820-1910 . . . . DLB-166

Nijō, Lady (Nakano-in Masatada no Musume)
1258-after 1306 . . . . DLB-203

Nijō Yoshimoto 1320-1388. . . . . DLB-203

Nikitin, Ivan Savvich 1824-1861 . . . . DLB-277

Nikitin, Nikolai Nikolaevich 1895-1963 . . DLB-272

Nikolev, Nikolai Petrovich 1758-1815 . . . . DLB-150

Niles, Hezekiah 1777-1839 . . . . DLB-43

Nims, John Frederick 1913-1999 . . . . DLB-5

Tribute to Nancy Hale Y-88

Nin, Anaïs 1903-1977. . . . . DLB-2, 4, 152

Nína Björk Árnadóttir 1941-2000 . . . . DLB-293

Niño, Raúl 1961- DLB-209

Nissenson, Hugh 1933- DLB-28

Niven, Frederick John 1878-1944. . . . . DLB-92

Niven, Larry 1938- DLB-8

Nixon, Howard M. 1909-1983 . . . . DLB-201

Nizan, Paul 1905-1940. . . . . DLB-72

Njegoš, Petar II Petrović
1813-1851 . . . . DLB-147; CDWLB-4

Nkosi, Lewis 1936- DLB-157, 225

Noah, Mordecai M. 1785-1851 . . . . DLB-250

Noailles, Anna de 1876-1933 . . . . DLB-258

Nobel Peace Prize
The Nobel Prize and Literary Politics Y-88
Elie Wiesel Y-86

Nobel Prize in Literature
Shmuel Yosef Agnon DLB-329
Vicente Aleixandre DLB-108, 329
Ivo Andrić DLB-147, 329; CDWLB-4
Miguel Ángel Asturias DLB-113, 290,
329; CDWLB-3
Samuel Beckett DLB-13, 15, 233, 319,
321, 329; Y-90; CDBLB-7
Saul Bellow DLB-2, 28, 299, 329;
Y-82; DS-3; CDALB-1
Jacinto Benevente DLB-329
Henri Bergson DLB-329
Bjørnstjerne Bjørnson DLB-329
Heinrich Böll . . . DLB-69, 329; Y-85; CDWLB-2
Joseph Brodsky DLB-285, 329; Y-87
Pearl S. Buck DLB-9, 102, 329; CDALB-7
Ivan Bunin. DLB-317, 329
Albert Camus DLB-72, 321, 329
Elias Canetti . . . DLB-85, 124, 329; CDWLB-2
Giosuè Carducci DLB-329
Camilo José Cela DLB-322, 329; Y-89
Sir Winston Churchill DLB-100, 329;
DS-16; CDBLB-5
J. M. Coetzee. DLB-225, 326, 329
Grazia Deledda DLB-264, 329
Jose Echegaray DLB-329
T. S. Eliot DLB-7, 10, 45, 63, 245, 329;
Y-88, 99; CDALB-5
Odysseus Elytis DLB-329
Rudolf Eucken DLB-329

Dario Fo Y-97
Gabriel García Márquez Y-82
William Golding Y-83
Nadine Gordimer Y-91
Günter Grass. Y-99
Seamus Heaney. Y-95
Imre Kertész Y-02
Najīb Mahfūz Y-88
Toni Morrison. Y-93
V. S. Naipaul Y-01
Kenzaburō Ōe Y-94
Octavio Paz Y-90
José Saramago Y-98
Jaroslav Seifert. Y-84
Claude Simon Y-85
Wole Soyinka Y-86
Wisława Szymborska Y-96
Derek Walcott Y-92
Gao Xingjian. Y-00

Nobre, António 1867-1900. . . . . DLB-287

Nodier, Charles 1780-1844 . . . . DLB-119

Noël, Marie (Marie Mélanie Rouget)
1883-1967 . . . . DLB-258

Noel, Roden 1834-1894. . . . . DLB-35

Nogami Yaeko 1885-1985 . . . . DLB-180

Nogo, Rajko Petrov 1945- DLB-181

Nolan, William F. 1928- DLB-8
Tribute to Raymond Chandler Y-88

Noland, C. F. M. 1810?-1858 . . . . DLB-11

Noma Hiroshi 1915-1991 . . . . DLB-182

Nonesuch Press DLB-112

Creative Nonfiction Y-02

Nonni (Jón Stefán Sveinsson or Svensson)
1857-1944 . . . . DLB-293

Noon, Jeff 1957- DLB-267

Noonan, Robert Phillipe (see Tressell, Robert)

Noonday Press. DLB-46

Noone, John 1936- DLB-14

Nora, Eugenio de 1923- DLB-134

Nordan, Lewis 1939- DLB-234

Nordbrandt, Henrik 1945- DLB-214

Nordhoff, Charles 1887-1947 . . . . DLB-9

Norén, Lars 1944- DLB-257

Norfolk, Lawrence 1963- DLB-267

Norman, Charles 1904-1996 . . . . DLB-111

Norman, Marsha 1947- DLB-266; Y-84

Norris, Charles G. 1881-1945 . . . . DLB-9

Norris, Frank
1870-1902 . . . . DLB-12, 71, 186; CDALB-3

Norris, Helen 1916- DLB-292

Norris, John 1657-1712 . . . . DLB-252

Norris, Leslie 1921- DLB-27, 256

Norse, Harold 1916- DLB-16

Norte, Marisela 1955- DLB-209

North, Marianne 1830-1890............DLB-174

North Point Press DLB-46

Nortje, Arthur 1942-1970 .... DLB-125, 225

Norton, Alice Mary (see Norton, Andre)

Norton, Andre 1912-2005............ DLB-8, 52

Norton, Andrews 1786-1853.... DLB-1, 235; DS-5

Norton, Caroline 1808-1877 ... DLB-21, 159, 199

Norton, Charles Eliot 1827-1908 .. DLB-1, 64, 235

Norton, John 1606-1663................ DLB-24

Norton, Mary 1903-1992 .... DLB-160

Norton, Thomas 1532-1584............ DLB-62

W. W. Norton and Company........... DLB-46

Norwood, Robert 1874-1932 .... DLB-92

Nosaka Akiyuki 1930- DLB-182

Nossack, Hans Erich 1901-1977 .... DLB-69

Notker Balbulus circa 840-912 .... DLB-148

Notker III of Saint Gall
 circa 950-1022 .... DLB-148

Notker von Zweifalten ?-1095......... DLB-148

Nourse, Alan E. 1928-1992 .... DLB-8

Novak, Slobodan 1924- DLB-181

Novak, Vjenceslav 1859-1905 .... DLB-147

Novakovich, Josip 1956- DLB-244

Novalis 1772-1801.......... DLB-90; CDWLB-2

Novaro, Mario 1868-1944 .... DLB-114

Novás Calvo, Lino 1903-1983 .... DLB-145

Novelists
 Library Journal Statements and
  Questionnaires from First Novelists Y-87

Novels
 The Columbia History of the American Novel
  A Symposium on................. Y-92
 The Great Modern Library Scam Y-98
 Novels for Grown-Ups................. Y-97
 The Proletarian Novel DLB-9
 Novel, The "Second-Generation" Holocaust
  .... DLB-299
 The Year in the Novel Y-87–88, Y-90–93

Novels, British
 "The Break-Up of the Novel" (1922),
  by John Middleton Murry........ DLB-36
 The Consolidation of Opinion: Critical
  Responses to the Modernists..... DLB-36
 "Criticism in Relation to Novels"
  (1863), by G. H. Lewes DLB-21
 "Experiment in the Novel" (1929)
  [excerpt], by John D. Beresford ... DLB-36
 "The Future of the Novel" (1899), by
  Henry James DLB-18
 The Gay Science (1866), by E. S. Dallas
  [excerpt]..................... DLB-21
 A Haughty and Proud Generation
  (1922), by Ford Madox Hueffer .. DLB-36
 Literary Effects of World War II DLB-15
 "Modern Novelists –Great and Small"
  (1855), by Margaret Oliphant DLB-21

The Modernists (1932),
 by Joseph Warren Beach DLB-36

A Note on Technique (1926), by
 Elizabeth A. Drew [excerpts] DLB-36

Novel-Reading: *The Works of Charles
 Dickens; The Works of W. Makepeace
 Thackeray* (1879),
 by Anthony Trollope DLB-21

Novels with a Purpose (1864), by
 Justin M'Carthy DLB-21

"On Art in Fiction" (1838),
 by Edward Bulwer............. DLB-21

The Present State of the English Novel
 (1892), by George Saintsbury DLB-18

Representative Men and Women:
 A Historical Perspective on
 the British Novel, 1930-1960..... DLB-15

"The Revolt" (1937), by Mary Colum
 [excerpts] DLB-36

"Sensation Novels" (1863), by
 H. L. Manse DLB-21

Sex, Class, Politics, and Religion [in
 the British Novel, 1930-1959] DLB-15

Time and Western Man (1927),
 by Wyndham Lewis [excerpts] ... DLB-36

Noventa, Giacomo 1898-1960 .... DLB-114

Novikov, Nikolai Ivanovich
 1744-1818..................... DLB-150

Novomeský, Laco 1904-1976 .... DLB-215

Nowlan, Alden 1933-1983 .... DLB-53

Nowra, Louis 1950- DLB-325

Noyes, Alfred 1880-1958 .... DLB-20

Noyes, Crosby S. 1825-1908.......... DLB-23

Noyes, Nicholas 1647-1717 .... DLB-24

Noyes, Theodore W. 1858-1946......... DLB-29

Nozick, Robert 1938-2002 ....DLB-279

N-Town Plays circa 1468 to early
 sixteenth century................ DLB-146

Nugent, Frank 1908-1965.............. DLB-44

Nunez, Sigrid 1951- DLB-312

Nušić, Branislav
 1864-1938............DLB-147; CDWLB-4

David Nutt [publishing house] DLB-106

Nwapa, Flora
 1931-1993 .... DLB-125; CDWLB-3

Nye, Edgar Wilson (Bill)
 1850-1896 .... DLB-11, 23, 186

Nye, Naomi Shihab 1952- DLB-120

Nye, Robert 1939- DLB-14, 271

Nyka-Niliūnas, Alfonsas 1919- DLB-220

O

Oakes, Urian circa 1631-1681 .... DLB-24

Oakes Smith, Elizabeth
 1806-1893 .... DLB-1, 239, 243

Oakley, Violet 1874-1961 .... DLB-188

Oates, Joyce Carol 1938-
 ....DLB-2, 5, 130; Y-81; CDALB-6

Tribute to Michael M. Rea............ Y-97

Ōba Minako 1930- DLB-182

Ober, Frederick Albion 1849-1913 ...... DLB-189

Ober, William 1920-1993................ Y-93

Oberholtzer, Ellis Paxson 1868-1936 ..... DLB-47

The Obituary as Literary Form Y-02

Obradović, Dositej 1740?-1811..........DLB-147

O'Brien, Charlotte Grace 1845-1909 .... DLB-240

O'Brien, Edna 1932- DLB-14, 231, 319; CDBLB-8

O'Brien, Fitz-James 1828-1862 .... DLB-74

O'Brien, Flann (see O'Nolan, Brian)

O'Brien, Kate 1897-1974............... DLB-15

O'Brien, Tim
 1946- DLB-152; Y-80; DS-9; CDALB-7

Ó Cadhain, Máirtín 1905-1970......... DLB-319

O'Casey, Sean 1880-1964..... DLB-10; CDBLB-6

Occom, Samson 1723-1792............DLB-175

Occomy, Marita Bonner 1899-1971 ...... DLB-51

Ochs, Adolph S. 1858-1935 .... DLB-25

Ochs-Oakes, George Washington
 1861-1931 ....DLB-137

O'Connor, Flannery 1925-1964
 ....DLB-2, 152; Y-80; DS-12; CDALB-1

The Flannery O'Connor Society Y-99

O'Connor, Frank 1903-1966 .... DLB-162

O'Connor, Joseph 1963- DLB-267

Octopus Publishing Group............ DLB-112

Oda Sakunosuke 1913-1947 .... DLB-182

Odell, Jonathan 1737-1818 .... DLB-31, 99

O'Dell, Scott 1903-1989 .... DLB-52

Odets, Clifford 1906-1963 ....DLB-7, 26

Odhams Press Limited DLB-112

Odio, Eunice 1922-1974 .... DLB-283

Odoevsky, Aleksandr Ivanovich
 1802-1839 .... DLB-205

Odoevsky, Vladimir Fedorovich
 1804 or 1803-1869............... DLB-198

Odoevtseva, Irina 1895-1990 ....DLB-317

O'Donnell, Peter 1920- DLB-87

O'Donovan, Michael (see O'Connor, Frank)

O'Dowd, Bernard 1866-1953 .... DLB-230

Ōe, Kenzaburō 1935- DLB-182; Y-94

Nobel Lecture 1994: Japan, the
 Ambiguous, and Myself Y-94

Oehlenschläger, Adam 1779-1850...... DLB-300

O'Faolain, Julia 1932- DLB-14, 231, 319

O'Faolain, Sean 1900-1991......... DLB-15, 162

Off-Loop Theatres DLB-7

Offord, Carl Ruthven 1910-1990 .... DLB-76

Offshore, 1979 Booker Prize winner,
 Penelope Fitzgerald DLB-326

O'Flaherty, Liam 1896-1984.... DLB-36, 162; Y-84

Ogarev, Nikolai Platonovich 1813-1877 ...DLB-277

J. S. Ogilvie and Company............ DLB-49

Ogilvy, Eliza 1822-1912...............DLB-199

Ogot, Grace 1930- DLB-125

O'Grady, Desmond 1935- DLB-40

Ogunyemi, Wale 1939- DLB-157

O'Hagan, Howard 1902-1982..........DLB-68

O'Hara, Frank 1926-1966........DLB-5, 16, 193

O'Hara, John
1905-1970...DLB-9, 86, 324; DS-2; CDALB-5

John O'Hara's Pottsville Journalism.......Y-88

O'Hare, Kate Richards 1876-1948.......DLB-303

O'Hegarty, P. S. 1879-1955............DLB-201

Ohio State University
The William Charvat American Fiction
Collection at the Ohio State
University Libraries...............Y-92

Okada, John 1923-1971...............DLB-312

Okara, Gabriel 1921- DLB-125; CDWLB-3

O'Keeffe, John 1747-1833.............DLB-89

Nicholas Okes [publishing house].......DLB-170

Okigbo, Christopher
1930-1967............DLB-125; CDWLB-3

Okot p'Bitek 1931-1982.....DLB-125; CDWLB-3

Okpewho, Isidore 1941- DLB-157

Okri, Ben 1959- DLB-157, 231, 319, 326

Ólafur Jóhann Sigurðsson 1918-1988....DLB-293

The Old Devils, 1986 Booker Prize winner,
Kingsley Amis...................DLB-326

Old Dogs / New Tricks? New Technologies,
the Canon, and the Structure of
the Profession.....................Y-02

Old Franklin Publishing House..........DLB-49

Old German Genesis and *Old German Exodus*
circa 1050-circa 1130..............DLB-148

The *Old High German Isidor*
circa 790-800....................DLB-148

Older, Fremont 1856-1935..............DLB-25

Oldham, John 1653-1683...............DLB-131

Oldman, C. B. 1894-1969..............DLB-201

Olds, Sharon 1942- DLB-120

Olearius, Adam 1599-1671............DLB-164

O'Leary, Ellen 1831-1889............DLB-240

O'Leary, Juan E. 1879-1969...........DLB-290

Olesha, Iurii Karlovich 1899-1960.......DLB-272

Oliphant, Laurence 1829?-1888......DLB-18, 166

Oliphant, Margaret 1828-1897...DLB-18, 159, 190

"Modern Novelists–Great and Small"
(1855).......................DLB-21

Oliveira, Carlos de 1921-1981.........DLB-287

Oliver, Chad 1928-1993................DLB-8

Oliver, Mary 1935- DLB-5, 193

Ollier, Claude 1922- DLB-83

Olsen, Tillie 1912/1913-
............DLB-28, 206; Y-80; CDALB-7

Olson, Charles 1910-1970........DLB-5, 16, 193

Olson, Elder 1909-1992...........DLB-48, 63

Olson, Sigurd F. 1899-1982............DLB-275

The Omega Workshops.................DS-10

Omotoso, Kole 1943- DLB-125

Omulevsky, Innokentii Vasil'evich
1836 [or 1837]-1883...............DLB-238

Ondaatje, Michael 1943- DLB-60, 323, 326

O'Neill, Eugene 1888-1953.....DLB-7; CDALB-5

Eugene O'Neill Memorial Theater
Center.......................DLB-7

Eugene O'Neill's Letters: A Review......Y-88

Onetti, Juan Carlos
1909-1994............DLB-113; CDWLB-3

Onions, George Oliver 1872-1961.......DLB-153

Onofri, Arturo 1885-1928.............DLB-114

O'Nolan, Brian 1911-1966.............DLB-231

Oodgeroo of the Tribe Noonuccal
(Kath Walker) 1920-1993............DLB-289

Opie, Amelia 1769-1853..........DLB-116, 159

Opitz, Martin 1597-1639..............DLB-164

Oppen, George 1908-1984..........DLB-5, 165

Oppenheim, E. Phillips 1866-1946......DLB-70

Oppenheim, James 1882-1932..........DLB-28

Oppenheimer, Joel 1930-1988........DLB-5, 193

Optic, Oliver (see Adams, William Taylor)

Orczy, Emma, Baroness 1865-1947......DLB-70

Oregon Shakespeare Festival..............Y-00

Origo, Iris 1902-1988................DLB-155

O'Riordan, Kate 1960- DLB-267

Orlovitz, Gil 1918-1973..............DLB-2, 5

Orlovsky, Peter 1933- DLB-16

Ormond, John 1923- DLB-27

Ornitz, Samuel 1890-1957..........DLB-28, 44

O'Rourke, P. J. 1947- DLB-185

Orozco, Olga 1920-1999..............DLB-283

Orten, Jiří 1919-1941...............DLB-215

Ortese, Anna Maria 1914- DLB-177

Ortiz, Lourdes 1943- DLB-322

Ortiz, Simon J. 1941- DLB-120, 175, 256

Ortnit and *Wolfdietrich* circa 1225-1250.....DLB-138

Orton, Joe 1933-1967.....DLB-13, 310; CDBLB-8

Orwell, George (Eric Arthur Blair)
1903-1950...DLB-15, 98, 195, 255; CDBLB-7

The Orwell Year.....................Y-84

(Re-)Publishing Orwell................Y-86

Ory, Carlos Edmundo de 1923- DLB-134

Osbey, Brenda Marie 1957- DLB-120

Osbon, B. S. 1827-1912...............DLB-43

Osborn, Sarah 1714-1796.............DLB-200

Osborne, John 1929-1994.....DLB-13; CDBLB-7

Oscar and Lucinda, 1988 Booker Prize winner,
Peter Carey....................DLB-326

Osgood, Frances Sargent 1811-1850.....DLB-250

Osgood, Herbert L. 1855-1918..........DLB-47

James R. Osgood and Company........DLB-49

Osgood, McIlvaine and Company.......DLB-112

O'Shaughnessy, Arthur 1844-1881.......DLB-35

Patrick O'Shea [publishing house].....DLB-49

Osipov, Nikolai Petrovich 1751-1799.....DLB-150

Oskison, John Milton 1879-1947........DLB-175

Osler, Sir William 1849-1919..........DLB-184

Osofisan, Femi 1946- DLB-125; CDWLB-3

Ostenso, Martha 1900-1963.............DLB-92

Ostrauskas, Kostas 1926- DLB-232

Ostriker, Alicia 1937- DLB-120

Ostrovsky, Aleksandr Nikolaevich
1823-1886.....................DLB-277

Ostrovsky, Nikolai Alekseevich
1904-1936.....................DLB-272

Osundare, Niyi 1947- DLB-157; CDWLB-3

Oswald, Eleazer 1755-1795............DLB-43

Oswald von Wolkenstein
1376 or 1377-1445................DLB-179

Otero, Blas de 1916-1979.............DLB-134

Otero, Miguel Antonio 1859-1944......DLB-82

Otero, Nina 1881-1965...............DLB-209

Otero Silva, Miguel 1908-1985.........DLB-145

Otfried von Weißenburg
circa 800-circa 875?..............DLB-148

Otis, Broaders and Company..........DLB-49

Otis, James (see Kaler, James Otis)

Otis, James, Jr. 1725-1783.............DLB-31

Otsup, Nikolai 1894-1958.............DLB-317

Ottaway, James 1911-2000............DLB-127

Ottendorfer, Oswald 1826-1900........DLB-23

Ottieri, Ottiero 1924-2002............DLB-177

Otto-Peters, Louise 1819-1895.........DLB-129

Otway, Thomas 1652-1685.............DLB-80

Ouellette, Fernand 1930- DLB-60

Ouida 1839-1908..................DLB-18, 156

Outing Publishing Company..........DLB-46

Overbury, Sir Thomas
circa 1581-1613..................DLB-151

The Overlook Press..................DLB-46

Ovid 43 B.C.-A.D. 17....... DLB-211; CDWLB-1

Oviedo, Gonzalo Fernández de
1478-1557......................DLB-318

Owen, Guy 1925-1981..................DLB-5

Owen, John 1564-1622................DLB-121

John Owen [publishing house]..........DLB-49

Peter Owen Limited..................DLB-112

Owen, Robert 1771-1858.........DLB-107, 158

Owen, Wilfred
1893-1918........DLB-20; DS-18; CDBLB-6

A Centenary Celebration..............Y-93

The Wilfred Owen Association.........Y-98

The Owl and the Nightingale
circa 1189-1199 .... DLB-146

Owsley, Frank L. 1890-1956............ DLB-17

Oxford, Seventeenth Earl of, Edward
de Vere 1550-1604 ....DLB-172

OyamO (Charles F. Gordon)
1943- DLB-266

Ozerov, Vladislav Aleksandrovich
1769-1816.................... DLB-150

Ozick, Cynthia 1928- ...DLB-28, 152, 299; Y-82

   First Strauss "Livings" Awarded
to Cynthia Ozick and
Raymond Carver
An Interview with Cynthia Ozick Y-83

   Tribute to Michael M. Rea............ Y-97

P

Pace, Richard 1482?-1536............. DLB-167

Pacey, Desmond 1917-1975 .... DLB-88

Pacheco, José Emilio 1939- DLB-290

Pack, Robert 1929- DLB-5

Paddy Clarke Ha Ha Ha, 1993 Booker Prize winner,
Roddy Doyle DLB-326

Padell Publishing Company DLB-46

Padgett, Ron 1942- DLB-5

Padilla, Ernesto Chávez 1944- DLB-122

L. C. Page and Company DLB-49

Page, Louise 1955- DLB-233

Page, P. K. 1916- DLB-68

Page, Thomas Nelson
1853-1922 ....DLB-12, 78; DS-13

Page, Walter Hines 1855-1918 .... DLB-71, 91

Paget, Francis Edward 1806-1882...... DLB-163

Paget, Violet (see Lee, Vernon)

Pagliarani, Elio 1927- DLB-128

Pagnol, Marcel 1895-1974............. DLB-321

Pain, Barry 1864-1928 ....DLB-135, 197

Pain, Philip ?-circa 1666 .... DLB-24

Paine, Robert Treat, Jr. 1773-1811 .... DLB-37

Paine, Thomas
1737-1809 .... DLB-31, 43, 73, 158; CDALB-2

Painter, George D. 1914- DLB-155

Painter, William 1540?-1594........... DLB-136

Palazzeschi, Aldo 1885-1974....... DLB-114, 264

Palei, Marina Anatol'evna 1955- DLB-285

Palencia, Alfonso de 1424-1492 .... DLB-286

Palés Matos, Luis 1898-1959 .... DLB-290

Paley, Grace 1922- DLB-28, 218

Paley, William 1743-1805 .... DLB-252

Palfrey, John Gorham
1796-1881................ DLB-1, 30, 235

Palgrave, Francis Turner 1824-1897 ...... DLB-35

Palissy, Bernard 1510?-1590?.......... DLB-327

Palmer, Joe H. 1904-1952 ....DLB-171

Palmer, Michael 1943- DLB-169

Palmer, Nettie 1885-1964 .... DLB-260

Palmer, Vance 1885-1959 .... DLB-260

Paltock, Robert 1697-1767............. DLB-39

Paludan, Jacob 1896-1975............. DLB-214

Paludin-Müller, Frederik 1809-1876 .... DLB-300

Pan Books Limited DLB-112

Panaev, Ivan Ivanovich 1812-1862 ...... DLB-198

Panaeva, Avdot'ia Iakovlevna
1820-1893 .... DLB-238

Panama, Norman 1914-2003 and
Frank, Melvin 1913-1988.......... DLB-26

Pancake, Breece D'J 1952-1979......... DLB-130

Panduro, Leif 1923-1977............. DLB-214

Panero, Leopoldo 1909-1962 .... DLB-108

Pangborn, Edgar 1909-1976 .... DLB-8

Panizzi, Sir Anthony 1797-1879 .... DLB-184

Panneton, Philippe (see Ringuet)

Panova, Vera Fedorovna 1905-1973 ..... DLB-302

Panshin, Alexei 1940- DLB-8

Pansy (see Alden, Isabella)

Pantheon Books DLB-46

Papadat-Bengescu, Hortensia
1876-1955..................... DLB-220

Papantonio, Michael 1907-1976 .... DLB-187

Paperback Library DLB-46

Paperback Science Fiction.............. DLB-8

Papini, Giovanni 1881-1956 .... DLB-264

Paquet, Alfons 1881-1944 .... DLB-66

Paracelsus 1493-1541 ....DLB-179

Paradis, Suzanne 1936- DLB-53

Páral, Vladimír, 1932- DLB-232

Pardoe, Julia 1804-1862 .... DLB-166

Paré, Ambroise 1510 or 1517?-1590..... DLB-327

Paredes, Américo 1915-1999 .... DLB-209

Pareja Diezcanseco, Alfredo 1908-1993 .. DLB-145

Parents' Magazine Press DLB-46

Paretsky, Sara 1947- DLB-306

Parfit, Derek 1942- DLB-262

Parise, Goffredo 1929-1986 ....DLB-177

Parish, Mitchell 1900-1993 .... DLB-265

Parizeau, Alice 1930-1990 .... DLB-60

Park, Ruth 1923?- DLB-260

Parke, John 1754-1789 .... DLB-31

Parker, Dan 1893-1967 .... DLB-241

Parker, Dorothy 1893-1967 ...... DLB-11, 45, 86

Parker, Gilbert 1860-1932............. DLB-99

Parker, James 1714-1770 .... DLB-43

Parker, John [publishing house] DLB-106

Parker, Matthew 1504-1575 .... DLB-213

Parker, Robert B. 1932- DLB-306

Parker, Stewart 1941-1988 .... DLB-245

Parker, Theodore 1810-1860 ... DLB-1, 235; DS-5

Parker, William Riley 1906-1968 .... DLB-103

J. H. Parker [publishing house]......... DLB-106

Parkes, Bessie Rayner (Madame Belloc)
1829-1925 .... DLB-240

Parkman, Francis
1823-1893 ....DLB-1, 30, 183, 186, 235

Parks, Gordon 1912- DLB-33

Parks, Tim 1954- DLB-231

Parks, William 1698-1750............. DLB-43

William Parks [publishing house]........ DLB-49

Parley, Peter (see Goodrich, Samuel Griswold)

Parmenides late sixth-fifth century B.C. DLB-176

Parnell, Thomas 1679-1718............. DLB-95

Parnicki, Teodor 1908-1988 .... DLB-215

Parnok, Sofiia Iakovlevna (Parnokh)
1885-1933 .... DLB-295

Parr, Catherine 1513?-1548 .... DLB-136

Parra, Nicanor 1914- DLB-283

Parrington, Vernon L. 1871-1929 ...... DLB-17, 63

Parrish, Maxfield 1870-1966........... DLB-188

Parronchi, Alessandro 1914- DLB-128

Parshchikov, Aleksei Maksimovich
(Raiderman) 1954- DLB-285

Partisan Review DLB-303

Parton, James 1822-1891 .... DLB-30

Parton, Sara Payson Willis
1811-1872.................DLB-43, 74, 239

S. W. Partridge and Company DLB-106

Parun, Vesna 1922- DLB-181; CDWLB-4

Pascal, Blaise 1623-1662................DLB-268

Pasinetti, Pier Maria 1913- DLB-177

   Tribute to Albert Erskine.............. Y-93

Pasolini, Pier Paolo 1922-1975 ......DLB-128, 177

Pastan, Linda 1932- DLB-5

Pasternak, Boris
1890-1960 .... DLB-302

Paston, George (Emily Morse Symonds)
1860-1936 ....DLB-149, 197

The Paston Letters 1422-1509............ DLB-146

Pastoral Novel of the Sixteenth
Century, The................... DLB-318

Pastorius, Francis Daniel
1651-circa 1720 .... DLB-24

Patchen, Kenneth 1911-1972 .... DLB-16, 48

Pater, Walter 1839-1894 ...DLB-57, 156; CDBLB-4

   Aesthetic Poetry (1873) DLB-35

   "Style" (1888) [excerpt] DLB-57

Paterson, A. B. "Banjo" 1864-1941...... DLB-230

Paterson, Katherine 1932- DLB-52

Patmore, Coventry 1823-1896 .... DLB-35, 98

Paton, Alan 1903-1988..........DLB-225; DS-17

Paton, Joseph Noel 1821-1901 .... DLB-35

Paton Walsh, Jill 1937- DLB-161

Patrick, Edwin Hill ("Ted") 1901-1964 ... DLB-137
Patrick, John 1906-1995 ... DLB-7
Pattee, Fred Lewis 1863-1950 ... DLB-71
Patterson, Alicia 1906-1963 ... DLB-127
Patterson, Eleanor Medill 1881-1948 ... DLB-29
Patterson, Eugene 1923- ... DLB-127
Patterson, Joseph Medill 1879-1946 ... DLB-29
Pattillo, Henry 1726-1801 ... DLB-37
Paul, Elliot 1891-1958 ... DLB-4; DS-15
Paul, Jean (see Richter, Johann Paul Friedrich)
Paul, Kegan, Trench, Trubner and Company Limited ... DLB-106
Peter Paul Book Company ... DLB-49
Stanley Paul and Company Limited ... DLB-112
Paulding, James Kirke 1778-1860 ... DLB-3, 59, 74, 250
Paulin, Tom 1949- ... DLB-40
Pauper, Peter, Press ... DLB-46
Paustovsky, Konstantin Georgievich 1892-1968 ... DLB-272
Pavese, Cesare 1908-1950 ... DLB-128, 177
Pavić, Milorad 1929- ... DLB-181; CDWLB-4
Pavlov, Konstantin 1933- ... DLB-181
Pavlov, Nikolai Filippovich 1803-1864 ... DLB-198
Pavlova, Karolina Karlovna 1807-1893 ... DLB-205
Pavlović, Miodrag 1928- ... DLB-181; CDWLB-4
Pavlovsky, Eduardo 1933- ... DLB-305
Paxton, John 1911-1985 ... DLB-44
Payn, James 1830-1898 ... DLB-18
Payne, John 1842-1916 ... DLB-35
Payne, John Howard 1791-1852 ... DLB-37
Payson and Clarke ... DLB-46
Paz, Octavio 1914-1998 ... DLB-290; Y-90, 98
Nobel Lecture 1990 ... Y-90
Pazzi, Roberto 1946- ... DLB-196
Pea, Enrico 1881-1958 ... DLB-264
Peabody, Elizabeth Palmer 1804-1894 ... DLB-1, 223
Preface to *Record of a School: Exemplifying the General Principles of Spiritual Culture* ... DS-5
Elizabeth Palmer Peabody [publishing house] ... DLB-49
Peabody, Josephine Preston 1874-1922 ... DLB-249
Peabody, Oliver William Bourn 1799-1848 ... DLB-59
Peace, Roger 1899-1968 ... DLB-127
Peacham, Henry 1578-1644? ... DLB-151
Peacham, Henry, the Elder 1547-1634 ... DLB-172, 236
Peachtree Publishers, Limited ... DLB-46
Peacock, Molly 1947- ... DLB-120
Peacock, Thomas Love 1785-1866 ... DLB-96, 116

Pead, Deuel ?-1727 ... DLB-24
Peake, Mervyn 1911-1968 ... DLB-15, 160, 255
Peale, Rembrandt 1778-1860 ... DLB-183
Pear Tree Press ... DLB-112
Pearce, Philippa 1920- ... DLB-161
H. B. Pearson [publishing house] ... DLB-49
Pearson, Hesketh 1887-1964 ... DLB-149
Peattie, Donald Culross 1898-1964 ... DLB-275
Pechersky, Andrei (see Mel'nikov, Pavel Ivanovich)
Peck, George W. 1840-1916 ... DLB-23, 42
H. C. Peck and Theo. Bliss [publishing house] ... DLB-49
Peck, Harry Thurston 1856-1914 ... DLB-71, 91
Peden, William 1913-1999 ... DLB-234
Tribute to William Goyen ... Y-83
Peele, George 1556-1596 ... DLB-62, 167
Pegler, Westbrook 1894-1969 ... DLB-171
Péguy, Charles 1873-1914 ... DLB-258
Peirce, Charles Sanders 1839-1914 ... DLB-270
Pekić, Borislav 1930-1992 ... DLB-181; CDWLB-4
Pelecanos, George P. 1957- ... DLB-306
Peletier du Mans, Jacques 1517-1582 ... DLB-327
Pelevin, Viktor Olegovich 1962- ... DLB-285
Pellegrini and Cudahy ... DLB-46
Pelletier, Aimé (see Vac, Bertrand)
Pelletier, Francine 1959- ... DLB-251
Pellicer, Carlos 1897?-1977 ... DLB-290
Pemberton, Sir Max 1863-1950 ... DLB-70
de la Peña, Terri 1947- ... DLB-209
Penfield, Edward 1866-1925 ... DLB-188
Penguin Books [U.K.] ... DLB-112
Fifty Penguin Years ... Y-85
Penguin Collectors' Society ... Y-98
Penguin Books [U.S.] ... DLB-46
Penn, William 1644-1718 ... DLB-24
Penn Publishing Company ... DLB-49
Penna, Sandro 1906-1977 ... DLB-114
Pennell, Joseph 1857-1926 ... DLB-188
Penner, Jonathan 1940- ... Y-83
Pennington, Lee 1939- ... Y-82
Penton, Brian 1904-1951 ... DLB-260
Pepper, Stephen C. 1891-1972 ... DLB-270
Pepys, Samuel 1633-1703 ... DLB-101, 213; CDBLB-2
Percy, Thomas 1729-1811 ... DLB-104
Percy, Walker 1916-1990 ... DLB-2; Y-80, 90
Tribute to Caroline Gordon ... Y-81
Percy, William 1575-1648 ... DLB-172
Perec, Georges 1936-1982 ... DLB-83, 299
Perelman, Bob 1947- ... DLB-193
Perelman, S. J. 1904-1979 ... DLB-11, 44

Perez, Raymundo "Tigre" 1946- ... DLB-122
Pérez de Ayala, Ramón 1880-1962 ... DLB-322
Pérez de Guzmán, Fernán ca. 1377-ca. 1460 ... DLB-286
Pérez-Reverte, Arturo 1951- ... DLB-322
Peri Rossi, Cristina 1941- ... DLB-145, 290
Perkins, Eugene 1932- ... DLB-41
Perkins, Maxwell
The Claims of Business and Literature: An Undergraduate Essay ... Y-01
Perkins, William 1558-1602 ... DLB-281
Perkoff, Stuart Z. 1930-1974 ... DLB-16
Perley, Moses Henry 1804-1862 ... DLB-99
Permabooks ... DLB-46
Perovsky, Aleksei Alekseevich (Antonii Pogorel'sky) 1787-1836 ... DLB-198
Perrault, Charles 1628-1703 ... DLB-268
Perri, Henry 1561-1617 ... DLB-236
Perrin, Alice 1867-1934 ... DLB-156
Perry, Anne 1938- ... DLB-276
Perry, Bliss 1860-1954 ... DLB-71
Perry, Eleanor 1915-1981 ... DLB-44
Perry, Henry (see Perri, Henry)
Perry, Matthew 1794-1858 ... DLB-183
Perry, Sampson 1747-1823 ... DLB-158
Perse, Saint-John 1887-1975 ... DLB-258
Persius A.D. 34-A.D. 62 ... DLB-211
Perutz, Leo 1882-1957 ... DLB-81
Pesetsky, Bette 1932- ... DLB-130
Pessanha, Camilo 1867-1926 ... DLB-287
Pessoa, Fernando 1888-1935 ... DLB-287
Pestalozzi, Johann Heinrich 1746-1827 ... DLB-94
Peter, Laurence J. 1919-1990 ... DLB-53
Peter of Spain circa 1205-1277 ... DLB-115
Peterkin, Julia 1880-1961 ... DLB-9
Peters, Ellis (Edith Pargeter) 1913-1995 ... DLB-276
Peters, Lenrie 1932- ... DLB-117
Peters, Robert 1924- ... DLB-105
"Foreword to *Ludwig of Baviria*" ... DLB-105
Petersham, Maud 1889-1971 and Petersham, Miska 1888-1960 ... DLB-22
Peterson, Charles Jacobs 1819-1887 ... DLB-79
Peterson, Len 1917- ... DLB-88
Peterson, Levi S. 1933- ... DLB-206
Peterson, Louis 1922-1998 ... DLB-76
Peterson, T. B., and Brothers ... DLB-49
Petitclair, Pierre 1813-1860 ... DLB-99
Petrescu, Camil 1894-1957 ... DLB-220
Petronius circa A.D. 20-A.D. 66 ... DLB-211; CDWLB-1
Petrov, Aleksandar 1938- ... DLB-181

Cumulative Index

Petrov, Evgenii (Evgenii Petrovich Kataev)
  1903-1942 .... DLB-272
Petrov, Gavriil 1730-1801 .... DLB-150
Petrov, Valeri 1920- DLB-181
Petrov, Vasilii Petrovich 1736-1799 ...... DLB-150
Petrović, Rastko
  1898-1949 .... DLB-147; CDWLB-4
Petrushevskaia, Liudmila Stefanovna
  1938- DLB-285
Petruslied circa 854? DLB-148
Petry, Ann 1908-1997 .... DLB-76
Pettie, George circa 1548-1589 .... DLB-136
Pétur Gunnarsson 1947- DLB-293
Peyton, K. M. 1929- DLB-161
Pfaffe Konrad fl. circa 1172 .... DLB-148
Pfaffe Lamprecht fl. circa 1150 .... DLB-148
Pfeiffer, Emily 1827-1890 .... DLB-199
Pforzheimer, Carl H. 1879-1957 .... DLB-140
Phaedrus circa 18 B.C.-circa A.D. 50 ..... DLB-211
Phaer, Thomas 1510?-1560 .... DLB-167
Phaidon Press Limited DLB-112
Pharr, Robert Deane 1916-1992 .... DLB-33
Phelps, Elizabeth Stuart 1815-1852 ...... DLB-202
Phelps, Elizabeth Stuart 1844-1911 ... DLB-74, 221
Philander von der Linde
  (see Mencke, Johann Burckhard)
Philby, H. St. John B. 1885-1960 .... DLB-195
Philip, Marlene Nourbese 1947- DLB-157
Philippe, Charles-Louis 1874-1909 .... DLB-65
Philips, John 1676-1708 .... DLB-95
Philips, Katherine 1632-1664 .... DLB-131
Phillipps, Sir Thomas 1792-1872 .... DLB-184
Phillips, Caryl 1958- DLB-157
Phillips, David Graham
  1867-1911 .... DLB-9, 12, 303
Phillips, Jayne Anne 1952- DLB-292; Y-80
  Tribute to Seymour Lawrence Y-94
Phillips, Robert 1938- DLB-105
  "Finding, Losing, Reclaiming: A Note
    on My Poems" DLB-105
  Tribute to William Goyen Y-83
Phillips, Stephen 1864-1915 .... DLB-10
Phillips, Ulrich B. 1877-1934............ DLB-17
Phillips, Wendell 1811-1884 .... DLB-235
Phillips, Willard 1784-1873 .... DLB-59
Phillips, William 1907-2002 .... DLB-137
Phillips, Sampson and Company DLB-49
Phillpotts, Adelaide Eden (Adelaide Ross)
  1896-1993 .... DLB-191
Phillpotts, Eden 1862-1960...DLB-10, 70, 135, 153
Philo circa 20-15 B.C.-circa A.D. 50 ....DLB-176
Philosophical Dictionary, Voltaire DLB-314
Philosophical Library DLB-46

Philosophy
  Eighteenth-Century Philosophical
    Background................. DLB-31
  Philosophic Thought in Boston DLB-235
  Translators of the Twelfth Century:
    Literary Issues Raised and
    Impact Created DLB-115
Elihu Phinney [publishing house]........ DLB-49
Phoenix, John (see Derby, George Horatio)
PHYLON (Fourth Quarter, 1950),
  The Negro in Literature:
  The Current Scene................ DLB-76
Physiologus circa 1070-circa 1150......... DLB-148
Π.Ο. (Pi O, Peter Oustabasides)
  1951- DLB-325
Piccolo, Lucio 1903-1969 .... DLB-114
Pichette, Henri 1924-2000 .... DLB-321
Pickard, Tom 1946- DLB-40
William Pickering [publishing house].... DLB-106
Pickthall, Marjorie 1883-1922. .... DLB-92
Picoult, Jodi 1966- DLB-292
Pictorial Printing Company DLB-49
Piel, Gerard 1915-2004................ DLB-137
  "An Announcement to Our Readers,"
    Gerard Piel's Statement in *Scientific
    American* (April 1948) DLB-137
Pielmeier, John 1949- DLB-266
Piercy, Marge 1936- DLB-120, 227
Pierre, DBC 1961- DLB-326
Pierro, Albino 1916-1995 .... DLB-128
Pignotti, Lamberto 1926- DLB-128
Pike, Albert 1809-1891................. DLB-74
Pike, Zebulon Montgomery 1779-1813... DLB-183
Pillat, Ion 1891-1945.................. DLB-220
Pil'niak, Boris Andreevich (Boris Andreevich
  Vogau) 1894-1938 ....DLB-272
Pilon, Jean-Guy 1930- DLB-60
Pinar, Florencia fl. ca. late
  fifteenth century.................. DLB-286
Pinckney, Eliza Lucas 1722-1793......... DLB-200
Pinckney, Josephine 1895-1957........... DLB-6
Pindar circa 518 B.C.-circa 438 B.C.
  .... DLB-176; CDWLB-1
Pindar, Peter (see Wolcot, John)
Pineda, Cecile 1942- DLB-209
Pinero, Arthur Wing 1855-1934.......... DLB-10
Piñero, Miguel 1946-1988............... DLB-266
Pinget, Robert 1919-1997 .... DLB-83
Pinkney, Edward Coote
  1802-1828 .... DLB-248
Pinnacle Books...................... DLB-46
Piñon, Nélida 1935- DLB-145, 307
Pinsky, Robert 1940- Y-82
  Reappointed Poet Laureate Y-98
Pinter, Harold 1930- ... DLB-13, 310; CDBLB-8

Writing for the Theatre DLB-13
Pinto, Fernão Mendes 1509/1511?-1583.. DLB-287
Piontek, Heinz 1925- DLB-75
Piozzi, Hester Lynch [Thrale]
  1741-1821.................DLB-104, 142
Piper, H. Beam 1904-1964 .... DLB-8
Piper, Watty DLB-22
Pirandello, Luigi 1867-1936 .... DLB-264
Pirckheimer, Caritas 1467-1532 ......DLB-179
Pirckheimer, Willibald 1470-1530.......DLB-179
Pires, José Cardoso 1925-1998 .... DLB-287
Pisar, Samuel 1929- Y-83
Pisarev, Dmitrii Ivanovich 1840-1868.....DLB-277
Pisemsky, Aleksei Feofilaktovich
  1821-1881 .... DLB-238
Pitkin, Timothy 1766-1847............. DLB-30
Pitter, Ruth 1897-1992 .... DLB-20
Pix, Mary 1666-1709 .... DLB-80
Pixerécourt, René Charles Guilbert de
  1773-1844..................... DLB-192
Pizarnik, Alejandra 1936-1972 .... DLB-283
Plá, Josefina 1909-1999................ DLB-290
Plaatje, Sol T. 1876-1932.......... DLB-125, 225
Planchon, Roger 1931- DLB-321
Plante, David 1940- Y-83
Plantinga, Alvin 1932- DLB-279
Platen, August von 1796-1835 .... DLB-90
Plath, Sylvia
  1932-1963 .... DLB-5, 6, 152; CDALB-1
Plato circa 428 B.C.-348-347 B.C.
  ....DLB-176; CDWLB-1
Plato, Ann 1824-?.................... DLB-239
Platon 1737-1812..................... DLB-150
Platonov, Andrei Platonovich (Andrei
  Platonovich Klimentev)
  1899-1951 ....DLB-272
Platt, Charles 1945- DLB-261
Platt and Munk Company DLB-46
Plautus circa 254 B.C.-184 B.C.
  ....DLB-211; CDWLB-1
Playboy Press DLB-46
John Playford [publishing house] DLB-170
Der Pleier fl. circa 1250 .... DLB-138
Pleijel, Agneta 1940- DLB-257
Plenzdorf, Ulrich 1934- DLB-75
Pleshcheev, Aleksei Nikolaevich
  1825?-1893.....................DLB-277
Plessen, Elizabeth 1944- DLB-75
Pletnev, Petr Aleksandrovich
  1792-1865..................... DLB-205
Pliekšāne, Elza Rozenberga (see Aspazija)
Pliekšāns, Jānis (see Rainis, Jānis)
Plievier, Theodor 1892-1955 .... DLB-69
Plimpton, George 1927-2003 ..DLB-185, 241; Y-99

Pliny the Elder A.D. 23/24-A.D. 79 . . . . . . .DLB-211

Pliny the Younger
circa A.D. 61-A.D. 112 . . . . .DLB-211

Plomer, William
1903-1973 . . . . .DLB-20, 162, 191, 225

Plotinus 204-270. . . . . DLB-176; CDWLB-1

Plowright, Teresa 1952- DLB-251

Plume, Thomas 1630-1704 . . . . .DLB-213

Plumly, Stanley 1939- DLB-5, 193

Plumpp, Sterling D. 1940- DLB-41

Plunkett, James 1920-2003. . . . . .DLB-14

Plutarch
circa 46-circa 120. . . . . . . DLB-176; CDWLB-1

Plymell, Charles 1935- DLB-16

Pocket Books DLB-46

Podestá, José J. 1858-1937 . . . . .DLB-305

Poe, Edgar Allan 1809-1849
. . . . DLB-3, 59, 73, 74, 248; CDALB-2

The Poe Studies Association Y-99

Poe, James 1921-1980 . . . . .DLB-44

The Poet Laureate of the United States Y-86

Statements from Former Consultants
in Poetry Y-86

Poetry
Aesthetic Poetry (1873) DLB-35

A Century of Poetry, a Lifetime of
Collecting: J. M. Edelstein's
Collection of Twentieth-
Century American Poetry. Y-02

"Certain Gifts," by Betty Adcock DLB-105

Concrete Poetry. DLB-307

Contempo Caravan: Kites in a
Windstorm .Y-85

"Contemporary Verse Story-telling,"
by Jonathan Holden DLB-105

"A Detail in a Poem," by Fred
Chappell DLB-105

"The English Renaissance of Art"
(1908), by Oscar Wilde. DLB-35

"Every Man His Own Poet; or,
The Inspired Singer's Recipe
Book" (1877), by
H. W. Mallock DLB-35

"Eyes Across Centuries: Contemporary
Poetry and 'That Vision Thing,'"
by Philip Dacey. DLB-105

A Field Guide to Recent Schools
of American Poetry. Y-86

"Finding, Losing, Reclaiming:
A Note on My Poems,
by Robert Phillips" DLB-105

"The Fleshly School of Poetry and Other
Phenomena of the Day" (1872). . . .DLB-35

"The Fleshly School of Poetry:
Mr. D. G. Rossetti" (1871) DLB-35

The G. Ross Roy Scottish Poetry Collection
at the University of South Carolina . . .Y-89

"Getting Started: Accepting the Regions
You Own—or Which Own You,"
by Walter McDonald DLB-105

"The Good, The Not So Good," by
Stephen Dunn. DLB-105

The Griffin Poetry Prize Y-00

The Hero as Poet. Dante; Shakspeare
(1841), by Thomas Carlyle. DLB-32

"Images and 'Images,'" by Charles
Simic. DLB-105

"Into the Mirror," by Peter Cooley . . .DLB-105

"Knots into Webs: Some Autobiographical
Sources," by Dabney Stuart DLB-105

"L'Envoi" (1882), by Oscar Wilde DLB-35

"Living in Ruin," by Gerald Stern. . . .DLB-105

Looking for the Golden Mountain:
Poetry Reviewing Y-89

Lyric Poetry (French) DLB-268

Medieval Galician-Portuguese
Poetry DLB-287

"The No Self, the Little Self, and the
Poets," by Richard Moore. DLB-105

On Some of the Characteristics of Modern
Poetry and On the Lyrical Poems of
Alfred Tennyson (1831) DLB-32

The Pitt Poetry Series: Poetry Publishing
Today Y-85

"The Poetry File," by Edward
Field DLB-105

Poetry in Nineteenth-Century France:
Cultural Background and Critical
Commentary DLB-217

The Poetry of Jorge Luis Borges Y-86

"The Poet's Kaleidoscope: The Element
of Surprise in the Making of the
Poem" by Madeline DeFrees. DLB-105

The Pre-Raphaelite Controversy. DLB-35

Protest Poetry in Castile DLB-286

"Reflections: After a Tornado,"
by Judson Jerome DLB-105

Statements from Former Consultants
in Poetry Y-86

Statements on the Art of Poetry DLB-54

The Study of Poetry (1880), by
Matthew Arnold. DLB-35

A Survey of Poetry Anthologies,
1879-1960 . . . . .DLB-54

Thoughts on Poetry and Its Varieties
(1833), by John Stuart Mill DLB-32

Under the Microscope (1872), by
A. C. Swinburne. DLB-35

The Unterberg Poetry Center of the
92nd Street Y Y-98

Victorian Poetry: Five Critical
Views DLBV-35

Year in Poetry Y-83–92, 94–01

Year's Work in American Poetry Y-82

Poets
The Lives of the Poets (1753) DLB-142

Minor Poets of the Earlier
Seventeenth Century DLB-121

Other British Poets Who Fell
in the Great War. DLB-216

Other Poets [French] DLB-217

Second-Generation Minor Poets of
the Seventeenth Century DLB-126

Third-Generation Minor Poets of
the Seventeenth Century DLB-131

Pogodin, Mikhail Petrovich 1800-1875. . . .DLB-198

Pogorel'sky, Antonii
(see Perovsky, Aleksei Alekseevich)

Pohl, Frederik 1919- DLB-8

Tribute to Isaac Asimov Y-92

Tribute to Theodore Sturgeon Y-85

Poirier, Louis (see Gracq, Julien)

Poláček, Karel 1892-1945 . . . DLB-215; CDWLB-4

Polanyi, Michael 1891-1976. . . . . .DLB-100

Pole, Reginald 1500-1558 . . . . .DLB-132

Polevoi, Nikolai Alekseevich 1796-1846. . .DLB-198

Polezhaev, Aleksandr Ivanovich
1804-1838 . . . . .DLB-205

Poliakoff, Stephen 1952- DLB-13

Polidori, John William 1795-1821 . . . . . . .DLB-116

Polite, Carlene Hatcher 1932- DLB-33

Pollard, Alfred W. 1859-1944 . . . . .DLB-201

Pollard, Edward A. 1832-1872. . . . . .DLB-30

Pollard, Graham 1903-1976 . . . . .DLB-201

Pollard, Percival 1869-1911 . . . . .DLB-71

Pollard and Moss. DLB-49

Pollock, Sharon 1936- DLB-60

Polonsky, Abraham 1910-1999 . . . . .DLB-26

Polonsky, Iakov Petrovich 1819-1898 . . . .DLB-277

Polotsky, Simeon 1629-1680 . . . . .DLB-150

Polybius circa 200 B.C.-118 B.C.. . . . . .DLB-176

Pomialovsky, Nikolai Gerasimovich
1835-1863 . . . . .DLB-238

Pomilio, Mario 1921-1990 . . . . .DLB-177

Pompéia, Raul (Raul d'Avila Pompéia)
1863-1895 . . . . .DLB-307

Ponce, Mary Helen 1938- DLB-122

Ponce-Montoya, Juanita 1949- DLB-122

Ponet, John 1516?-1556 . . . . .DLB-132

Ponge, Francis 1899-1988 . . . . DLB-258; Y-02

Poniatowska, Elena
1933- DLB-113; CDWLB-3

Ponsard, François 1814-1867 . . . . .DLB-192

William Ponsonby [publishing house] DLB-170

Pontiggia, Giuseppe 1934- DLB-196

Pontoppidan, Henrik 1857-1943 . . . . . . .DLB-300

Pony Stories, Omnibus Essay on DLB-160

Poole, Ernest 1880-1950 . . . . .DLB-9

Poole, Sophia 1804-1891 . . . . .DLB-166

Poore, Benjamin Perley 1820-1887 . . . . . .DLB-23

Popa, Vasko 1922-1991 . . . . . DLB-181; CDWLB-4

Pope, Abbie Hanscom 1858-1894 . . . . . . .DLB-140

Pope, Alexander
1688-1744 . . . . . .DLB-95, 101, 213; CDBLB-2

Poplavsky, Boris 1903-1935 . . . . .DLB-317

Popov, Aleksandr Serafimovich
(see Serafimovich, Aleksandr Serafimovich)

Popov, Evgenii Anatol'evich 1946- DLB-285

Cumulative Index

Popov, Mikhail Ivanovich
 1742-circa 1790.................DLB-150

Popović, Aleksandar 1929-1996........DLB-181

Popper, Karl 1902-1994..............DLB-262

Popular Culture Association/
 American Culture Association.......Y-99

Popular Library....................DLB-46

Poquelin, Jean-Baptiste (see Molière)

Porete, Marguerite ?-1310...........DLB-208

Porlock, Martin (see MacDonald, Philip)

Porpoise Press.....................DLB-112

Porta, Antonio 1935-1989............DLB-128

Porter, Anna Maria 1780-1832.....DLB-116, 159

Porter, Cole 1891-1964..............DLB-265

Porter, David 1780-1843.............DLB-183

Porter, Dorothy 1954-...............DLB-325

Porter, Eleanor H. 1868-1920...........DLB-9

Porter, Gene Stratton (see Stratton-Porter, Gene)

Porter, Hal 1911-1984...............DLB-260

Porter, Henry circa sixteenth century.....DLB-62

Porter, Jane 1776-1850..........DLB-116, 159

Porter, Katherine Anne 1890-1980
 ......DLB-4, 9, 102; Y-80; DS-12; CDALB-7

 The Katherine Anne Porter Society.......Y-01

Porter, Peter 1929-..............DLB-40, 289

Porter, William Sydney (O. Henry)
 1862-1910........DLB-12, 78, 79; CDALB-3

Porter, William T. 1809-1858.....DLB-3, 43, 250

Porter and Coates...................DLB-49

Portillo Trambley, Estela 1927-1998.....DLB-209

Portis, Charles 1933-................DLB-6

Medieval Galician-Portuguese Poetry....DLB-287

Posey, Alexander 1873-1908...........DLB-175

Possession, 1990 Booker Prize winner,
 A. S. Byatt......................DLB-326

Postans, Marianne circa 1810-1865......DLB-166

Postgate, Raymond 1896-1971..........DLB-276

Postl, Carl (see Sealsfield, Carl)

Postmodern Holocaust Fiction.........DLB-299

Poston, Ted 1906-1974...............DLB-51

Potekhin, Aleksei Antipovich
 1829-1908.....................DLB-238

Potok, Chaim 1929-2002..........DLB-28, 152

 A Conversation with Chaim Potok.......Y-84

 Tribute to Bernard Malamud..........Y-86

Potter, Beatrix 1866-1943............DLB-141

 The Beatrix Potter Society............Y-98

Potter, David M. 1910-1971............DLB-17

Potter, Dennis 1935-1994.............DLB-233

John E. Potter and Company............DLB-49

Pottle, Frederick A. 1897-1987.....DLB-103; Y-87

Poulin, Jacques 1937-................DLB-60

Pound, Ezra 1885-1972
 ....DLB-4, 45, 63; DS-15; CDALB-4

 The Cost of the *Cantos:* William Bird
  to Ezra Pound...................Y-01

 The Ezra Pound Society..............Y-01

Poverman, C. E. 1944-..............DLB-234

Povey, Meic 1950-..................DLB-310

Povich, Shirley 1905-1998............DLB-171

Powell, Anthony 1905-2000...DLB-15; CDBLB-7

 The Anthony Powell Society: Powell and
  the First Biennial Conference.......Y-01

Powell, Dawn 1897-1965
 Dawn Powell, Where Have You Been
  All Our Lives?....................Y-97

Powell, John Wesley 1834-1902........DLB-186

Powell, Padgett 1952-...............DLB-234

Powers, J. F. 1917-1999..............DLB-130

Powers, Jimmy 1903-1995.............DLB-241

Pownall, David 1938-................DLB-14

Powys, John Cowper 1872-1963.....DLB-15, 255

Powys, Llewelyn 1884-1939............DLB-98

Powys, T. F. 1875-1953...........DLB-36, 162

 The Powys Society...................Y-98

Poynter, Nelson 1903-1978............DLB-127

Prada, Juan Manuel de 1970-..........DLB-322

Prado, Adélia 1935-.................DLB-307

Prado, Pedro 1886-1952..............DLB-283

Prados, Emilio 1899-1962.............DLB-134

Praed, Mrs. Caroline (see Praed, Rosa)

Praed, Rosa (Mrs. Caroline Praed)
 1851-1935.....................DLB-230

Praed, Winthrop Mackworth 1802-1839..DLB-96

Praeger Publishers...................DLB-46

Praetorius, Johannes 1630-1680........DLB-168

Pratolini, Vasco 1913-1991............DLB-177

Pratt, E. J. 1882-1964................DLB-92

Pratt, Samuel Jackson 1749-1814........DLB-39

Preciado Martin, Patricia 1939-.......DLB-209

Préfontaine, Yves 1937-...............DLB-53

Prelutsky, Jack 1940-.................DLB-61

Prentice, George D. 1802-1870.........DLB-43

Prentice-Hall......................DLB-46

Prescott, Orville 1906-1996...........Y-96

Prescott, William Hickling
 1796-1859..............DLB-1, 30, 59, 235

Prešeren, France
 1800-1849.............DLB-147; CDWLB-4

Presses (*See also* Publishing)
 Small Presses in Great Britain and
  Ireland, 1960-1985..............DLB-40

 Small Presses I: Jargon Society..........Y-84

 Small Presses II: The Spirit That Moves
  Us Press.......................Y-85

 Small Presses III: Pushcart Press........Y-87

Preston, Margaret Junkin
 1820-1897.................DLB-239, 248

Preston, May Wilson 1873-1949........DLB-188

Preston, Thomas 1537-1598............DLB-62

Prévert, Jacques 1900-1977...........DLB-258

Prévost d'Exiles, Antoine François
 1697-1763.....................DLB-314

Price, Anthony 1928-................DLB-276

Price, Reynolds 1933-........DLB-2, 218, 278

Price, Richard 1723-1791.............DLB-158

Price, Richard 1949-.................Y-81

Prichard, Katharine Susannah
 1883-1969.....................DLB-260

Prideaux, John 1578-1650............DLB-236

Priest, Christopher 1943-.....DLB-14, 207, 261

Priestley, J. B. 1894-1984
 ....DLB-10, 34, 77, 100, 139; Y-84; CDBLB-6

Priestley, Joseph 1733-1804...........DLB-252

Prigov, Dmitrii Aleksandrovich 1940-...DLB-285

Prime, Benjamin Young 1733-1791........DLB-31

Primrose, Diana floruit circa 1630......DLB-126

Prince, F. T. 1912-2003...............DLB-20

Prince, Nancy Gardner
 1799-circa 1856..................DLB-239

Prince, Thomas 1687-1758.........DLB-24, 140

Pringle, Thomas 1789-1834............DLB-225

Printz, Wolfgang Casper 1641-1717......DLB-168

Prior, Matthew 1664-1721..............DLB-95

Prisco, Michele 1920-2003............DLB-177

Prishvin, Mikhail Mikhailovich
 1873-1954.....................DLB-272

Pritchard, William H. 1932-..........DLB-111

Pritchett, V. S. 1900-1997........DLB-15, 139

Probyn, May 1856 or 1857-1909........DLB-199

Procter, Adelaide Anne 1825-1864...DLB-32, 199

Procter, Bryan Waller 1787-1874.....DLB-96, 144

Proctor, Robert 1868-1903............DLB-184

Prokopovich, Feofan 1681?-1736.......DLB-150

Prokosch, Frederic 1906-1989..........DLB-48

Pronzini, Bill 1943-.................DLB-226

Propertius circa 50 B.C.-post 16 B.C.
 ....DLB-211; CDWLB-1

Propper, Dan 1937-..................DLB-16

Prose, Francine 1947-...............DLB-234

Protagoras circa 490 B.C.-420 B.C........DLB-176

Protest Poetry in Castile
 ca. 1445-ca. 1506................DLB-286

Proud, Robert 1728-1813..............DLB-30

Proust, Marcel 1871-1922.............DLB-65

 Marcel Proust at 129 and the Proust
  Society of America................Y-00

 Marcel Proust's *Remembrance of Things Past:*
  The Rediscovered Galley Proofs.....Y-00

Prutkov, Koz'ma Petrovich
   1803-1863 . . . . DLB-277

Prynne, J. H. 1936- DLB-40

Przybyszewski, Stanislaw 1868-1927 . . . . . . DLB-66

Pseudo-Dionysius the Areopagite floruit
   circa 500 . . . . DLB-115

Public Lending Right in America
   PLR and the Meaning of Literary
     Property Y-83
   Statement by Sen. Charles
     McC. Mathias, Jr. PLR Y-83
   Statements on PLR by American Writers . . . Y-83

Public Lending Right in the United Kingdom
   The First Year in the United Kingdom Y-83

Publishers [listed by individual names]
   Publishers, Conversations with:
     An Interview with Charles Scribner III . . . Y-94
     An Interview with Donald Lamm Y-95
     An Interview with James Laughlin Y-96
     An Interview with Patrick O'Connor Y-84

Publishing
   The Art and Mystery of Publishing:
     Interviews Y-97
   Book Publishing Accounting: Some Basic
     Concepts Y-98
   1873 Publishers' Catalogues DLB-49
   The Literary Scene 2002: Publishing, Book
     Reviewing, and Literary Journalism . . . Y-02
   Main Trends in Twentieth-Century
     Book Clubs DLB-46
   Overview of U.S. Book Publishing,
     1910-1945 . . . . DLB-9
   The Pitt Poetry Series: Poetry Publishing
     Today Y-85
   Publishing Fiction at LSU Press Y-87
   The Publishing Industry in 1998:
     Sturm-und-drang.com Y-98
   The Publishing Industry in 1999 . . . . Y-99
   Publishers and Agents: The Columbia
     Connection Y-87
   Responses to Ken Auletta Y-97
   Southern Writers Between the Wars DLB-9
   The State of Publishing Y-97
   Trends in Twentieth-Century
     Mass Market Publishing DLB-46
   The Year in Book Publishing Y-86

Pückler-Muskau, Hermann von
   1785-1871 . . . . DLB-133

Puértolas, Soledad 1947- DLB-322

Pufendorf, Samuel von 1632-1694 . . . . DLB-168

Pugh, Edwin William 1874-1930 . . . . DLB-135

Pugin, A. Welby 1812-1852 . . . . DLB-55

Puig, Manuel 1932-1990 . . . . DLB-113; CDWLB-3

Puisieux, Madeleine d'Arsant de
   1720-1798 . . . . DLB-314

Pulgar, Hernando del (Fernando del Pulgar)
   ca. 1436-ca. 1492 . . . . DLB-286

Pulitzer, Joseph 1847-1911 . . . . DLB-23

Pulitzer, Joseph, Jr. 1885-1955 . . . . DLB-29

Pulitzer Prizes for the Novel, 1917-1945 . . . . DLB-9

Pulliam, Eugene 1889-1975 . . . . DLB-127

Purcell, Deirdre 1945- DLB-267

Purchas, Samuel 1577?-1626 . . . . DLB-151

Purdy, Al 1918-2000 . . . . DLB-88

Purdy, James 1923- DLB-2, 218

Purdy, Ken W. 1913-1972 . . . . DLB-137

Pusey, Edward Bouverie 1800-1882 . . . . . . DLB-55

Pushkin, Aleksandr Sergeevich
   1799-1837 . . . . DLB-205

Pushkin, Vasilii L'vovich
   1766-1830 . . . . DLB-205

Putnam, George Palmer
   1814-1872 . . . . DLB-3, 79, 250, 254

G. P. Putnam [publishing house] DLB-254

G. P. Putnam's Sons [U.K.] DLB-106

G. P. Putnam's Sons [U.S.] DLB-49

   A Publisher's Archives: G. P. Putnam Y-92

Putnam, Hilary 1926- DLB-279

Putnam, Samuel 1892-1950 . . . . DLB-4; DS-15

Puttenham, George 1529?-1590 . . . . DLB-281

Puzo, Mario 1920-1999 . . . . DLB-6

Pyle, Ernie 1900-1945 . . . . DLB-29

Pyle, Howard
   1853-1911 . . . . DLB-42, 188; DS-13

Pyle, Robert Michael 1947- DLB-275

Pym, Barbara 1913-1980 . . . . . . DLB-14, 207; Y-87

Pynchon, Thomas 1937- DLB-2, 173

Pyramid Books DLB-46

Pyrnelle, Louise-Clarke 1850-1907 . . . . DLB-42

Pythagoras circa 570 B.C.-? DLB-176

Q

Qays ibn al-Mulawwah circa 680-710 . . . . DLB-311

Qian Zhongshu 1910-1998 . . . . DLB-328

Quad, M. (see Lewis, Charles B.)

Quaritch, Bernard 1819-1899 . . . . DLB-184

Quarles, Francis 1592-1644 . . . . DLB-126

The Quarterly Review 1809-1967 . . . . DLB-110

Quasimodo, Salvatore 1901-1968 . . . . DLB-114

Queen, Ellery (see Dannay, Frederic, and
   Manfred B. Lee)

Queen, Frank 1822-1882 . . . . DLB-241

The Queen City Publishing House DLB-49

Queirós, Eça de 1845-1900 . . . . DLB-287

Queneau, Raymond 1903-1976 . . . . . DLB-72, 258

Quennell, Peter 1905-1993 . . . . DLB-155, 195

Quental, Antero de
   1842-1891 . . . . DLB-287

Quesada, José Luis 1948- DLB-290

Quesnel, Joseph 1746-1809 . . . . DLB-99

Quiller-Couch, Sir Arthur Thomas
   1863-1944 . . . . DLB-135, 153, 190

Quin, Ann 1936-1973 . . . . DLB-14, 231

Quinault, Philippe 1635-1688 . . . . DLB-268

Quincy, Samuel, of Georgia
   fl. eighteenth century DLB-31

Quincy, Samuel, of Massachusetts
   1734-1789 . . . . DLB-31

Quindlen, Anna 1952- DLB-292

Quine, W. V. 1908-2000 . . . . DLB-279

Quinn, Anthony 1915-2001 . . . . DLB-122

Quinn, John 1870-1924 . . . . DLB-187

Quiñónez, Naomi 1951- DLB-209

Quintana, Leroy V. 1944- DLB-82

Quintana, Miguel de 1671-1748
   A Forerunner of Chicano
     Literature DLB-122

Quintilian circa A.D. 40-circa A.D. 96 . . . . DLB-211

Quintus Curtius Rufus
   fl. A.D. 35 . . . . DLB-211

Harlin Quist Books DLB-46

Quoirez, Françoise (see Sagan, Françoise)

R

Raabe, Wilhelm 1831-1910 . . . . DLB-129

Raban, Jonathan 1942- DLB-204

Rabe, David 1940- DLB-7, 228; Y-91

Rabelais, François 1494?-1593 . . . . DLB-327

Rabi'ah al-'Adawiyyah circa 720-801 . . . . . DLB-311

Raboni, Giovanni 1932- DLB-128

Rachilde 1860-1953 . . . . DLB-123, 192

Racin, Kočo 1908-1943 . . . . DLB-147

Racine, Jean 1639-1699 . . . . DLB-268

Rackham, Arthur 1867-1939 . . . . DLB-141

Raczymow, Henri 1948- DLB-299

Radauskas, Henrikas
   1910-1970 . . . . DLB-220; CDWLB-4

Radcliffe, Ann 1764-1823 . . . . DLB-39, 178

Raddall, Thomas 1903-1994 . . . . DLB-68

Radford, Dollie 1858-1920 . . . . DLB-240

Radichkov, Yordan 1929-2004 . . . . DLB-181

Radiguet, Raymond 1903-1923 . . . . DLB-65

Radishchev, Aleksandr Nikolaevich
   1749-1802 . . . . DLB-150

Radnóti, Miklós
   1909-1944 . . . . DLB-215; CDWLB-4

Radrigán, Juan 1937- DLB-305

Radványi, Netty Reiling (see Seghers, Anna)

Rafat, Taufiq 1927-1998 . . . . DLB-323

Rahv, Philip 1908-1973 . . . . DLB-137

Raich, Semen Egorovich 1792-1855 . . . . . DLB-205

Raičković, Stevan 1928- DLB-181

Raiderman (see Parshchikov, Aleksei Maksimovich)

Raimund, Ferdinand Jakob 1790-1836 . . . . DLB-90

Raine, Craig 1944- DLB-40

Raine, Kathleen 1908-2003 . . . . DLB-20

Rainis, Jānis 1865-1929..... DLB-220; CDWLB-4

Rainolde, Richard circa 1530-1606 .... DLB-136, 236

Rainolds, John 1549-1607............. DLB-281

Rakić, Milan 1876-1938 ..... DLB-147; CDWLB-4

Rakosi, Carl 1903-2004 .... DLB-193

Ralegh, Sir Walter 1554?-1618............ DLB-172; CDBLB-1

Raleigh, Walter
Style (1897) [excerpt]............... DLB-57

Ralin, Radoy 1923-2004.............. DLB-181

Ralph, Julian 1853-1903 .... DLB-23

Ramanujan, A. K. 1929-1993 .... DLB-323

Ramat, Silvio 1939- DLB-128

Ramée, Marie Louise de la (see Ouida)

Ramírez, Sergio 1942- DLB-145

Ramke, Bin 1947- DLB-120

Ramler, Karl Wilhelm 1725-1798 .... DLB-97

Ramon Ribeyro, Julio 1929-1994 ...... DLB-145

Ramos, Graciliano 1892-1953 .... DLB-307

Ramos, Manuel 1948- DLB-209

Ramos Sucre, José Antonio 1890-1930... DLB-290

Ramous, Mario 1924- DLB-128

Rampersad, Arnold 1941- DLB-111

Ramsay, Allan 1684 or 1685-1758 .... DLB-95

Ramsay, David 1749-1815.............. DLB-30

Ramsay, Martha Laurens 1759-1811..... DLB-200

Ramsey, Frank P. 1903-1930 .... DLB-262

Ranch, Hieronimus Justesen 1539-1607...................... DLB-300

Ranck, Katherine Quintana 1942- DLB-122

Rand, Avery and Company DLB-49

Rand, Ayn 1905-1982.... DLB-227, 279; CDALB-7

Rand McNally and Company DLB-49

Randall, David Anton 1905-1975 .... DLB-140

Randall, Dudley 1914-2000 .... DLB-41

Randall, Henry S. 1811-1876 .... DLB-30

Randall, James G. 1881-1953 .... DLB-17

The Randall Jarrell Symposium: A Small Collection of Randall Jarrells........ Y-86

Excerpts From Papers Delivered at the Randall Jarrel Symposium Y-86

Randall, John Herman, Jr. 1899-1980.....DLB-279

Randolph, A. Philip 1889-1979.......... DLB-91

Anson D. F. Randolph [publishing house] DLB-49

Randolph, Thomas 1605-1635 ...... DLB-58, 126

Random House...................... DLB-46

Rankin, Ian (Jack Harvey) 1960- DLB-267

Henry Ranlet [publishing house] DLB-49

Ransom, Harry 1908-1976 .... DLB-187

Ransom, John Crowe 1888-1974........... DLB-45, 63; CDALB-7

Ransome, Arthur 1884-1967 .... DLB-160

Rao, Raja 1908- DLB-323

Raphael, Frederic 1931- DLB-14, 319

Raphaelson, Samson 1896-1983 .... DLB-44

Rare Book Dealers
Bertram Rota and His Bookshop........ Y-91
An Interview with Glenn Horowitz Y-90
An Interview with Otto Penzler Y-96
An Interview with Ralph Sipper....... Y-94
New York City Bookshops in the 1930s and 1940s: The Recollections of Walter Goldwater Y-93

Rare Books
Research in the American Antiquarian Book Trade Y-97
Two Hundred Years of Rare Books and Literary Collections at the University of South Carolina Y-00

Rascón Banda, Víctor Hugo 1948- DLB-305

Rashi circa 1040-1105................. DLB-208

Raskin, Ellen 1928-1984............... DLB-52

Rasputin, Valentin Grigor'evich 1937- DLB-302

Rastell, John 1475?-1536............DLB-136, 170

Rattigan, Terence 1911-1977.............. DLB-13; CDBLB-7

Raven, Simon 1927-2001 ....DLB-271

Ravenhill, Mark 1966- DLB-310

Ravnkilde, Adda 1862-1883........... DLB-300

Rawicz, Piotr 1919-1982............... DLB-299

Rawlings, Marjorie Kinnan 1896-1953 .... DLB-9, 22, 102; DS-17; CDALB-7

Rawlinson, Richard 1690-1755......... DLB-213

Rawlinson, Thomas 1681-1725 .... DLB-213

Rawls, John 1921-2002...............DLB-279

Raworth, Tom 1938- DLB-40

Ray, David 1932- DLB-5

Ray, Gordon Norton 1915-1986.... DLB-103, 140

Ray, Henrietta Cordelia 1849-1916 ...... DLB-50

Raymond, Ernest 1888-1974............ DLB-191

Raymond, Henry J. 1820-1869....... DLB-43, 79

Raymond, René (see Chase, James Hadley)

Razaf, Andy 1895-1973............... DLB-265

al-Razi 865?-925? DLB-311

Rea, Michael 1927-1996 .... Y-97

Michael M. Rea and the Rea Award for the Short Story Y-97

Reach, Angus 1821-1856 .... DLB-70

Read, Herbert 1893-1968.......... DLB-20, 149

Read, Martha Meredith fl. nineteenth century DLB-200

Read, Opie 1852-1939 .... DLB-23

Read, Piers Paul 1941- DLB-14

Reade, Charles 1814-1884 .... DLB-21

Reader's Digest Condensed Books....... DLB-46

Readers Ulysses Symposium................ Y-97

Reading, Peter 1946- DLB-40

Reading Series in New York City........... Y-96

Reaney, James 1926- DLB-68

Rebhun, Paul 1500?-1546..............DLB-179

Rèbora, Clemente 1885-1957 .... DLB-114

Rebreanu, Liviu 1885-1944 .... DLB-220

Rechy, John 1934- DLB-122, 278; Y-82

Redding, J. Saunders 1906-1988.......DLB-63, 76

J. S. Redfield [publishing house] DLB-49

Redgrove, Peter 1932-2003............. DLB-40

Redmon, Anne 1943- Y-86

Redmond, Eugene B. 1937- DLB-41

Redol, Alves 1911-1969 .... DLB-287

James Redpath [publishing house] DLB-49

Reed, Henry 1808-1854............... DLB-59

Reed, Henry 1914-1986............... DLB-27

Reed, Ishmael 1938- DLB-2, 5, 33, 169, 227; DS-8

Reed, Rex 1938- DLB-185

Reed, Sampson 1800-1880 .... DLB-1, 235

Reed, Talbot Baines 1852-1893 .... DLB-141

Reedy, William Marion 1862-1920 ...... DLB-91

Reese, Lizette Woodworth 1856-1935 .... DLB-54

Reese, Thomas 1742-1796 .... DLB-37

Reeve, Clara 1729-1807 .... DLB-39

Preface to *The Old English Baron* (1778)..................... DLB-39

The Progress of Romance (1785) [excerpt]..................... DLB-39

Reeves, James 1909-1978 .... DLB-161

Reeves, John 1926- DLB-88

Reeves-Stevens, Garfield 1953- DLB-251

Régio, José (José Maria dos Reis Pereira) 1901-1969 .... DLB-287

Henry Regnery Company DLB-46

Rêgo, José Lins do 1901-1957 .... DLB-307

Rehberg, Hans 1901-1963 .... DLB-124

Rehfisch, Hans José 1891-1960 .... DLB-124

Reich, Ebbe Kløvedal 1940- DLB-214

Reid, Alastair 1926- DLB-27

Reid, B. L. 1918-1990................ DLB-111

Reid, Christopher 1949- DLB-40

Reid, Forrest 1875-1947 .... DLB-153

Reid, Helen Rogers 1882-1970 ....DLB-29

Reid, James fl. eighteenth century DLB-31

Reid, Mayne 1818-1883 .... DLB-21, 163

Reid, Thomas 1710-1796 .... DLB-31, 252

Reid, V. S. (Vic) 1913-1987............ DLB-125

Reid, Whitelaw 1837-1912 .... DLB-23

Reilly and Lee Publishing Company DLB-46

Reimann, Brigitte 1933-1973 .... DLB-75

Reinmar der Alte circa 1165-circa 1205 . . . DLB-138

Reinmar von Zweter
circa 1200-circa 1250 . . . . DLB-138

Reisch, Walter 1903-1983 . . . . DLB-44

Reizei Family DLB-203

Religion
A Crisis of Culture: The Changing
Role of Religion in the
New Republic DLB-37

The Remains of the Day, 1989 Booker Prize winner,
Kazuo Ishiguro DLB-326

Remarque, Erich Maria
1898-1970 . . . . DLB-56; CDWLB-2

Remington, Frederic
1861-1909 . . . . DLB-12, 186, 188

Remizov, Aleksei Mikhailovich
1877-1957 . . . . DLB-295

Renaud, Jacques 1943- DLB-60

Renault, Mary 1905-1983 . . . . Y-83

Rendell, Ruth (Barbara Vine)
1930- DLB-87, 276

Rensselaer, Maria van Cortlandt van
1645-1689 . . . . DLB-200

Repplier, Agnes 1855-1950 . . . . DLB-221

Reshetnikov, Fedor Mikhailovich
1841-1871 . . . . DLB-238

Restif (Rétif) de La Bretonne, Nicolas-Edme
1734-1806 . . . . DLB-314

Rettenbacher, Simon 1634-1706 . . . . DLB-168

Retz, Jean-François-Paul de Gondi,
cardinal de 1613-1679 . . . . DLB-268

Reuchlin, Johannes 1455-1522 . . . . DLB-179

Reuter, Christian 1665-after 1712 . . . . DLB-168

Fleming H. Revell Company DLB-49

Reverdy, Pierre 1889-1960 . . . . DLB-258

Reuter, Fritz 1810-1874 . . . . DLB-129

Reuter, Gabriele 1859-1941 . . . . DLB-66

Reventlow, Franziska Gräfin zu
1871-1918 . . . . DLB-66

Review of Reviews Office DLB-112

Rexroth, Kenneth 1905-1982
. . . . . . DLB-16, 48, 165, 212; Y-82; CDALB-1

The Commercialization of the Image
of Revolt DLB-16

Rey, H. A. 1898-1977 . . . . DLB-22

Reyes, Carlos José 1941- DLB-305

Reynal and Hitchcock DLB-46

Reynolds, G. W. M. 1814-1879 . . . . DLB-21

Reynolds, John Hamilton
1794-1852 . . . . DLB-96

Reynolds, Sir Joshua 1723-1792 . . . . DLB-104

Reynolds, Mack 1917-1983 . . . . DLB-8

Reza, Yazmina 1959- DLB-321

Reznikoff, Charles 1894-1976 . . . . DLB-28, 45

Rhetoric
Continental European Rhetoricians,
1400-1600, and Their Influence
in Reaissance England DLB-236

A Finding Guide to Key Works on
Microfilm DLB-236

Glossary of Terms and Definitions of
Rhetoic and Logic DLB-236

Rhett, Robert Barnwell 1800-1876 . . . . DLB-43

Rhode, John 1884-1964 . . . . DLB-77

Rhodes, Eugene Manlove 1869-1934 . . . . DLB-256

Rhodes, James Ford 1848-1927 . . . . DLB-47

Rhodes, Richard 1937- DLB-185

Rhys, Jean 1890-1979
. . . . DLB-36, 117, 162; CDBLB-7; CDWLB-3

Ribeiro, Bernadim
fl. ca. 1475/1482-1526/1544 . . . . DLB-287

Ricardo, David 1772-1823 . . . . DLB-107, 158

Ricardou, Jean 1932- DLB-83

Riccoboni, Marie-Jeanne (Marie-Jeanne de
Heurles Laboras de Mézières Riccoboni)
1713-1792 . . . . DLB-314

Rice, Anne (A. N. Roquelare, Anne Rampling)
1941- DLB-292

Rice, Christopher 1978- DLB-292

Rice, Elmer 1892-1967 . . . . DLB-4, 7

Rice, Grantland 1880-1954 . . . . DLB-29, 171

Rich, Adrienne 1929- DLB-5, 67; CDALB-7

Richard, Mark 1955- DLB-234

Richard de Fournival
1201-1259 or 1260 . . . . DLB-208

Richards, David Adams 1950- DLB-53

Richards, George circa 1760-1814 . . . . DLB-37

Richards, I. A. 1893-1979 . . . . DLB-27

Richards, Laura E. 1850-1943 . . . . DLB-42

Richards, William Carey 1818-1892 . . . . . . DLB-73

Grant Richards [publishing house] DLB-112

Richardson, Charles F. 1851-1913 . . . . DLB-71

Richardson, Dorothy M. 1873-1957 . . . . . . DLB-36

The Novels of Dorothy Richardson
(1918), by May Sinclair DLB-36

Richardson, Henry Handel
(Ethel Florence Lindesay Robertson)
1870-1946 . . . . DLB-197, 230

Richardson, Jack 1935- DLB-7

Richardson, John 1796-1852 . . . . DLB-99

Richardson, Samuel
1689-1761 . . . . DLB-39, 154; CDBLB-2

Introductory Letters from the Second
Edition of *Pamela* (1741) DLB-39

Postscript to [the Third Edition of]
Clarissa (1751) DLB-39

Preface to the First Edition of
Pamela (1740) DLB-39

Preface to the Third Edition of
Clarissa (1751) [excerpt] DLB-39

Preface to Volume 1 of *Clarissa*
(1747) DLB-39

Preface to Volume 3 of *Clarissa*
(1748) DLB-39

Richardson, Willis 1889-1977 . . . . DLB-51

Riche, Barnabe 1542-1617 . . . . DLB-136

Richepin, Jean 1849-1926 . . . . DLB-192

Richler, Mordecai 1931-2001 . . . . DLB-53

Richter, Conrad 1890-1968 . . . . DLB-9, 212

Richter, Hans Werner 1908-1993 . . . . DLB-69

Richter, Johann Paul Friedrich
1763-1825 . . . . DLB-94; CDWLB-2

Joseph Rickerby [publishing house] DLB-106

Rickword, Edgell 1898-1982 . . . . DLB-20

Riddell, Charlotte 1832-1906 . . . . DLB-156

Riddell, John (see Ford, Corey)

Ridge, John Rollin 1827-1867 . . . . DLB-175

Ridge, Lola 1873-1941 . . . . DLB-54

Ridge, William Pett 1859-1930 . . . . DLB-135

Riding, Laura (see Jackson, Laura Riding)

Ridler, Anne 1912-2001 . . . . DLB-27

Ridruego, Dionisio 1912-1975 . . . . DLB-108

Riel, Louis 1844-1885 . . . . DLB-99

Riemer, Johannes 1648-1714 . . . . DLB-168

Riera, Carme 1948- DLB-322

Rifbjerg, Klaus 1931- DLB-214

Riffaterre, Michael 1924- DLB-67

A Conversation between William Riggan
and Janette Turner Hospital Y-02

Riggs, Lynn 1899-1954 . . . . DLB-175

Riis, Jacob 1849-1914 . . . . DLB-23

John C. Riker [publishing house] DLB-49

Riley, James 1777-1840 . . . . DLB-183

Riley, John 1938-1978 . . . . DLB-40

Rilke, Rainer Maria
1875-1926 . . . . DLB-81; CDWLB-2

Rimanelli, Giose 1926- DLB-177

Rimbaud, Jean-Nicolas-Arthur
1854-1891 . . . . DLB-217

Rinehart and Company DLB-46

Ringuet 1895-1960 . . . . DLB-68

Ringwood, Gwen Pharis 1910-1984 . . . . . . DLB-88

Rinser, Luise 1911-2002 . . . . DLB-69

Ríos, Alberto 1952- DLB-122

Ríos, Isabella 1948- DLB-82

Ripley, Arthur 1895-1961 . . . . DLB-44

Ripley, George 1802-1880 . . . . . DLB-1, 64, 73, 235

The Rising Glory of America:
Three Poems DLB-37

The Rising Glory of America: Written in 1771
(1786), by Hugh Henry Brackenridge
and Philip Freneau DLB-37

Riskin, Robert 1897-1955 . . . . DLB-26

Risse, Heinz 1898-1989 . . . . DLB-69

Rist, Johann 1607-1667 . . . . DLB-164

Ristikivi, Karl 1912-1977 . . . . DLB-220

Ritchie, Anna Mowatt 1819-1870 . . . . . DLB-3, 250

Ritchie, Anne Thackeray 1837-1919 . . . . . . DLB-18

Cumulative Index

Ritchie, Thomas 1778-1854 .... DLB-43

Rites of Passage, 1980 Booker Prize winner, William Golding DLB-326

The Ritz Paris Hemingway Award Y-85

    Mario Varga Llosa's Acceptance Speech .. Y-85

Rivard, Adjutor 1868-1945 .... DLB-92

Rive, Richard 1931-1989 .... DLB-125, 225

Rivera, José 1955- DLB-249

Rivera, Marina 1942- DLB-122

Rivera, Tomás 1935-1984 .... DLB-82

Rivers, Conrad Kent 1933-1968 .... DLB-41

Riverside Press DLB-49

Rivington, James circa 1724-1802 .... DLB-43

Charles Rivington [publishing house] DLB-154

Rivkin, Allen 1903-1990 .... DLB-26

Roa Bastos, Augusto 1917-2005 .... DLB-113

Robbe-Grillet, Alain 1922- DLB-83

Robbins, Tom 1936- Y-80

Roberts, Charles G. D. 1860-1943 ...... DLB-92

Roberts, Dorothy 1906-1993 .... DLB-88

Roberts, Elizabeth Madox 1881-1941 .... DLB-9, 54, 102

Roberts, John (see Swynnerton, Thomas)

Roberts, Kate 1891-1985 .... DLB-319

Roberts, Keith 1935-2000 .... DLB-261

Roberts, Kenneth 1885-1957 .... DLB-9

Roberts, Michèle 1949- DLB-231

Roberts, Theodore Goodridge 1877-1953 .... DLB-92

Roberts, Ursula Wyllie (see Miles, Susan)

Roberts, William 1767-1849 .... DLB-142

James Roberts [publishing house] DLB-154

Roberts Brothers DLB-49

A. M. Robertson and Company DLB-49

Robertson, Ethel Florence Lindesay (see Richardson, Henry Handel)

Robertson, William 1721-1793 .... DLB-104

Robin, Leo 1895-1984 .... DLB-265

Robins, Elizabeth 1862-1952 .... DLB-197

Robinson, A. Mary F. (Madame James Darmesteter, Madame Mary Duclaux) 1857-1944 .... DLB-240

Robinson, Casey 1903-1979 .... DLB-44

Robinson, Derek 1932- Y-02

Robinson, Edwin Arlington 1869-1935 .... DLB-54; CDALB-3

    Review by Derek Robinson of George Greenfield's *Rich Dust* Y-02

Robinson, Henry Crabb 1775-1867 ..... DLB-107

Robinson, James Harvey 1863-1936 ..... DLB-47

Robinson, Lennox 1886-1958 .... DLB-10

Robinson, Mabel Louise 1874-1962 ..... DLB-22

Robinson, Marilynne 1943- DLB-206

Robinson, Mary 1758-1800 .... DLB-158

Robinson, Richard circa 1545-1607 ..... DLB-167

Robinson, Therese 1797-1870 .... DLB-59, 133

Robison, Mary 1949- DLB-130

Roblès, Emmanuel 1914-1995 .... DLB-83

Roccatagliata Ceccardi, Ceccardo 1871-1919 .... DLB-114

Rocha, Adolfo Correira da (see Torga, Miguel)

Roche, Billy 1949- DLB-233

Rochester, John Wilmot, Earl of 1647-1680 .... DLB-131

Rochon, Esther 1948- DLB-251

Rock, Howard 1911-1976 .... DLB-127

Rockwell, Norman Perceval 1894-1978 .. DLB-188

Rodgers, Carolyn M. 1945- DLB-41

Rodgers, W. R. 1909-1969 .... DLB-20

Rodney, Lester 1911- DLB-241

Rodoreda, Mercé 1908-1983 .... DLB-322

Rodrigues, Nelson 1912-1980 .... DLB-307

Rodríguez, Claudio 1934-1999 .... DLB-134

Rodríguez, Joe D. 1943- DLB-209

Rodriguez, Judith 1936- DLB-325

Rodríguez, Luis J. 1954- DLB-209

Rodriguez, Richard 1944- DLB-82, 256

Rodríguez Julia, Edgardo 1946- DLB-145

Roe, E. P. 1838-1888 .... DLB-202

Roethke, Theodore 1908-1963 .... DLB-5, 206; CDALB-1

Rogers, Jane 1952- DLB-194

Rogers, Pattiann 1940- DLB-105

Rogers, Samuel 1763-1855 .... DLB-93

Rogers, Will 1879-1935 .... DLB-11

Rohmer, Sax 1883-1959 .... DLB-70

Roig, Montserrat 1946-1991 .... DLB-322

Roiphe, Anne 1935- Y-80

Rojas, Arnold R. 1896-1988 .... DLB-82

Rojas, Fernando de ca. 1475-1541 ..... DLB-286

Roland de la Platière, Marie-Jeanne (Madame Roland) 1754-1793 .... DLB-314

Rolfe, Edwin (Solomon Fishman) 1909-1954 .... DLB-303

Rolfe, Frederick William 1860-1913 .... DLB-34, 156

Rolland, Romain 1866-1944 .... DLB-65

Rolle, Richard circa 1290-1300 - 1349 ... DLB-146

Rölvaag, O. E. 1876-1931 .... DLB-9, 212

Romains, Jules 1885-1972 .... DLB-65, 321

A. Roman and Company DLB-49

Roman de la Rose: Guillaume de Lorris 1200/1205-circa 1230, Jean de Meun 1235-1240-circa 1305 .... DLB-208

Romano, Lalla 1906-2001 .... DLB-177

Romano, Octavio 1923- DLB-122

Rome, Harold 1908-1993 .... DLB-265

Romero, Leo 1950- DLB-122

Romero, Lin 1947- DLB-122

Romero, Orlando 1945- DLB-82

Ronsard, Pierre de 1524-1585 .... DLB-327

Rook, Clarence 1863-1915 .... DLB-135

Roosevelt, Theodore 1858-1919 .... DLB-47, 186, 275

Root, Waverley 1903-1982 .... DLB-4

Root, William Pitt 1941- DLB-120

Roquebrune, Robert de 1889-1978 ...... DLB-68

Rorty, Richard 1931- DLB-246, 279

Rosa, João Guimarães 1908-1967 ... DLB-113, 307

Rosales, Luis 1910-1992 .... DLB-134

Roscoe, William 1753-1831 .... DLB-163

Rose, Dilys 1954- DLB-319

Rose, Reginald 1920-2002 .... DLB-26

Rose, Wendy 1948- DLB-175

Rosegger, Peter 1843-1918 .... DLB-129

Rosei, Peter 1946- DLB-85

Rosen, Norma 1925- DLB-28

Rosenbach, A. S. W. 1876-1952 ...... DLB-140

Rosenbaum, Ron 1946- DLB-185

Rosenbaum, Thane 1960- DLB-299

Rosenberg, Isaac 1890-1918 ...... DLB-20, 216

Rosenfeld, Isaac 1918-1956 .... DLB-28

Rosenthal, Harold 1914-1999 .... DLB-241

    Jimmy, Red, and Others: Harold Rosenthal Remembers the Stars of the Press Box Y-01

Rosenthal, M. L. 1917-1996 .... DLB-5

Rosenwald, Lessing J. 1891-1979 ...... DLB-187

Ross, Alexander 1591-1654 .... DLB-151

Ross, Harold 1892-1951 .... DLB-137

Ross, Jerry 1926-1955 .... DLB-265

Ross, Leonard Q. (see Rosten, Leo)

Ross, Lillian 1927- DLB-185

Ross, Martin 1862-1915 .... DLB-135

Ross, Sinclair 1908-1996 .... DLB-88

Ross, W. W. E. 1894-1966 .... DLB-88

Rosselli, Amelia 1930-1996 .... DLB-128

Rossen, Robert 1908-1966 .... DLB-26

Rosset, Barney 1922- Y-02

Rossetti, Christina 1830-1894 ... DLB-35, 163, 240

Rossetti, Dante Gabriel 1828-1882 .... DLB-35; CDBLB-4

    The Stealthy School of Criticism (1871) DLB-35

Rossner, Judith 1935- DLB-6

Rostand, Edmond 1868-1918 .... DLB-192

Rosten, Leo 1908-1997 .... DLB-11

Rostenberg, Leona 1908-2005 .... DLB-140

DLB 329   Cumulative Index

Rostopchina, Evdokiia Petrovna 1811-1858 .... DLB-205

Rostovsky, Dimitrii 1651-1709 .... DLB-150

Rota, Bertram 1903-1966 .... DLB-201

    Bertram Rota and His Bookshop Y-91

Roth, Gerhard 1942- DLB-85, 124

Roth, Henry 1906?-1995 .... DLB-28

Roth, Joseph 1894-1939 .... DLB-85

Roth, Philip 1933- DLB-2, 28, 173; Y-82; CDALB-6

Rothenberg, Jerome 1931- DLB-5, 193

Rothschild Family DLB-184

Rotimi, Ola 1938- DLB-125

Rotrou, Jean 1609-1650 .... DLB-268

Rousseau, Jean-Jacques 1712-1778 .... DLB-314

    The Social Contract DLB-314

Routhier, Adolphe-Basile 1839-1920 ..... DLB-99

Routier, Simone 1901-1987 .... DLB-88

George Routledge and Sons DLB-106

Roversi, Roberto 1923- DLB-128

Rowe, Elizabeth Singer 1674-1737 ..... DLB-39, 95

Rowe, Nicholas 1674-1718 .... DLB-84

Rowlands, Ian 1964- DLB-310

Rowlands, Samuel circa 1570-1630 ...... DLB-121

Rowlandson, Mary circa 1637-circa 1711 .... DLB-24, 200

Rowley, William circa 1585-1626 .... DLB-58

Rowling, J. K. The Harry Potter Phenomenon Y-99

Rowse, A. L. 1903-1997 .... DLB-155

Rowson, Susanna Haswell circa 1762-1824 .... DLB-37, 200

Roy, Arundhati 1961- DLB-323, 326

Roy, Camille 1870-1943 .... DLB-92

The G. Ross Roy Scottish Poetry Collection at the University of South Carolina Y-89

Roy, Gabrielle 1909-1983 .... DLB-68

Roy, Jules 1907-2000 .... DLB-83

The Royal Court Theatre and the English Stage Company DLB-13

The Royal Court Theatre and the New Drama DLB-10

The Royal Shakespeare Company at the Swan Y-88

Royall, Anne Newport 1769-1854 .... DLB-43, 248

Royce, Josiah 1855-1916 .... DLB-270

The Roycroft Printing Shop DLB-49

Royde-Smith, Naomi 1875-1964 .... DLB-191

Royster, Vermont 1914-1996 .... DLB-127

Richard Royston [publishing house] DLB-170

Rozanov, Vasilii Vasil'evich 1856-1919 .... DLB-295

Różewicz, Tadeusz 1921- DLB-232

Ruark, Gibbons 1941- DLB-120

Ruban, Vasilii Grigorevich 1742-1795 .... DLB-150

Rubens, Bernice 1928-2004 ..... DLB-14, 207, 326

Rubião, Murilo 1916-1991 .... DLB-307

Rubina, Dina Il'inichna 1953- DLB-285

Rubinshtein, Lev Semenovich 1947- ... DLB-285

Rudd and Carleton DLB-49

Rudd, Steele (Arthur Hoey Davis) DLB-230

Rudkin, David 1936- DLB-13

Rudnick, Paul 1957- DLB-266

Rudnicki, Adolf 1909-1990 .... DLB-299

Rudolf von Ems circa 1200-circa 1254 ... DLB-138

Ruffin, Josephine St. Pierre 1842-1924 ..... DLB-79

Rufo, Juan Gutiérrez 1547?-1620? DLB-318

Ruganda, John 1941- DLB-157

Ruggles, Henry Joseph 1813-1906 .... DLB-64

Ruiz de Burton, María Amparo 1832-1895 .... DLB-209, 221

Rukeyser, Muriel 1913-1980 .... DLB-48

Rule, Jane 1931- DLB-60

Rulfo, Juan 1918-1986 ...... DLB-113; CDWLB-3

Rumaker, Michael 1932- DLB-16

Rumens, Carol 1944- DLB-40

Rummo, Paul-Eerik 1942- DLB-232

Runyon, Damon 1880-1946 .... DLB-11, 86, 171

Ruodlieb circa 1050-1075 .... DLB-148

Rush, Benjamin 1746-1813 .... DLB-37

Rush, Rebecca 1779-? DLB-200

Rushdie, Salman 1947- DLB-194, 323, 326

Rusk, Ralph L. 1888-1962 .... DLB-103

Ruskin, John 1819-1900 ...... DLB-55, 163, 190; CDBLB-4

Russ, Joanna 1937- DLB-8

Russell, Benjamin 1761-1845 .... DLB-43

Russell, Bertrand 1872-1970 .... DLB-100, 262

Russell, Charles Edward 1860-1941 ...... DLB-25

Russell, Charles M. 1864-1926 .... DLB-188

Russell, Eric Frank 1905-1978 .... DLB-255

Russell, Fred 1906-2003 .... DLB-241

Russell, George William (see AE)

Russell, Countess Mary Annette Beauchamp (see Arnim, Elizabeth von)

Russell, Willy 1947- DLB-233

B. B. Russell and Company DLB-49

R. H. Russell and Son DLB-49

Rutebeuf fl.1249-1277 .... DLB-208

Rutherford, Mark 1831-1913 .... DLB-18

Ruxton, George Frederick 1821-1848 .... DLB-186

R-va, Zeneida (see Gan, Elena Andreevna)

Ryan, Gig 1956- DLB-325

Ryan, James 1952- DLB-267

Ryan, Michael 1946- Y-82

Ryan, Oscar 1904- DLB-68

Rybakov, Anatolii Naumovich 1911-1994 .... DLB-302

Ryder, Jack 1871-1936 .... DLB-241

Ryga, George 1932-1987 .... DLB-60

Rylands, Enriqueta Augustina Tennant 1843-1908 .... DLB-184

Rylands, John 1801-1888 .... DLB-184

Ryle, Gilbert 1900-1976 .... DLB-262

Ryleev, Kondratii Fedorovich 1795-1826 .... DLB-205

Rymer, Thomas 1643?-1713 .... DLB-101

Ryskind, Morrie 1895-1985 .... DLB-26

Rzhevsky, Aleksei Andreevich 1737-1804 .... DLB-150

S

The Saalfield Publishing Company DLB-46

Saba, Umberto 1883-1957 .... DLB-114

Sábato, Ernesto 1911- DLB-145; CDWLB-3

Saberhagen, Fred 1930- DLB-8

Sabin, Joseph 1821-1881 .... DLB-187

Sabino, Fernando (Fernando Tavares Sabino) 1923-2004 .... DLB-307

Sacer, Gottfried Wilhelm 1635-1699 ..... DLB-168

Sachs, Hans 1494-1576 ..... DLB-179; CDWLB-2

Sá-Carneiro, Mário de 1890-1916 .... DLB-287

Sack, John 1930-2004 .... DLB-185

Sackler, Howard 1929-1982 .... DLB-7

Sackville, Lady Margaret 1881-1963 ..... DLB-240

Sackville, Thomas 1536-1608 and Norton, Thomas 1532-1584 .... DLB-62

Sackville, Thomas 1536-1608 .... DLB-132

Sackville-West, Edward 1901-1965 ...... DLB-191

Sackville-West, Vita 1892-1962 ...... DLB-34, 195

Sacred Hunger, 1992 Booker Prize winner, Barry Unsworth DLB-326

Sá de Miranda, Francisco de 1481-1588? DLB-287

Sade, Marquis de (Donatien-Alphonse-François, comte de Sade) 1740-1814 .... DLB-314

    "Dialogue entre un prêtre et un moribond" DLB-314

Sadlier, Mary Anne 1820-1903 .... DLB-99

D. and J. Sadlier and Company DLB-49

Sadoff, Ira 1945- DLB-120

Sadoveanu, Mihail 1880-1961 .... DLB-220

Sadur, Nina Nikolaevna 1950- DLB-285

Sáenz, Benjamin Alire 1954- DLB-209

Saenz, Jaime 1921-1986 .... DLB-145, 283

Saffin, John circa 1626-1710 .... DLB-24

Sagan, Françoise 1935- DLB-83

Sage, Robert 1899-1962 .... DLB-4

Cumulative Index

Sagel, Jim 1947- DLB-82
Sagendorph, Robb Hansell 1900-1970 ... DLB-137
Sahagún, Carlos 1938- DLB-108
Sahgal, Nayantara 1927- DLB-323
Sahkomaapii, Piitai (see Highwater, Jamake)
Sahl, Hans 1902-1993................ DLB-69
Said, Edward W. 1935- DLB-67
Saigyō 1118-1190 .... DLB-203
Saijo, Albert 1926- DLB-312
Saiko, George 1892-1962 .... DLB-85
Sainte-Beuve, Charles-Augustin
   1804-1869 .... DLB-217
Saint-Exupéry, Antoine de 1900-1944..... DLB-72
Saint-Gelais, Mellin de 1490?-1558...... DLB-327
St. John, J. Allen 1872-1957.......... DLB-188
St John, Madeleine 1942- DLB-267
St. Johns, Adela Rogers 1894-1988...... DLB-29
St. Omer, Garth 1931- DLB-117
Saint Pierre, Michel de 1916-1987 .... DLB-83
Saintsbury, George 1845-1933 ....DLB-57, 149
   "Modern English Prose" (1876) DLB-57
   The Present State of the English
     Novel (1892),................. DLB-18
Saint-Simon, Louis de Rouvroy, duc de
   1675-1755..................... DLB-314
St. Dominic's Press DLB-112
The St. John's College Robert Graves Trust... Y-96
St. Martin's Press DLB-46
St. Nicholas 1873-1881 ....DS-13
Saiokuken Sōchō 1448-1532.......... DLB-203
Saki (see Munro, H. H.)
Salaam, Kalamu ya 1947- DLB-38
Salacrou, Armand 1899-1989 .... DLB-321
Šalamun, Tomaž 1941- ... DLB-181; CDWLB-4
Salas, Floyd 1931- DLB-82
Sálaz-Marquez, Rubén 1935- DLB-122
Salcedo, Hugo 1964- DLB-305
Salemson, Harold J. 1910-1988.......... DLB-4
Salesbury, William 1520?-1584?........ DLB-281
Salinas, Luis Omar 1937- DLB-82
Salinas, Pedro 1891-1951 .... DLB-134
Salinger, J. D.
   1919- DLB-2, 102, 173; CDALB-1
Salkey, Andrew 1928-1995 .... DLB-125
Sallust circa 86 B.C.-35 B.C.
   .... DLB-211; CDWLB-1
Salt, Waldo 1914-1987 .... DLB-44
Salter, James 1925- DLB-130
Salter, Mary Jo 1954- DLB-120
Saltus, Edgar 1855-1921............. DLB-202
Saltykov, Mikhail Evgrafovich
   1826-1889 .... DLB-238

Salustri, Carlo Alberto (see Trilussa)
Salverson, Laura Goodman 1890-1970.... DLB-92
Samain, Albert 1858-1900 .... DLB-217
Sampson, Richard Henry (see Hull, Richard)
Samuels, Ernest 1903-1996............ DLB-111
Sanborn, Franklin Benjamin
   1831-1917................... DLB-1, 223
Sánchez, Florencio 1875-1910.......... DLB-305
Sánchez, Luis Rafael 1936- DLB-145, 305
Sánchez, Philomeno "Phil" 1917- DLB-122
Sánchez, Ricardo 1941-1995........... DLB-82
Sánchez, Saúl 1943- DLB-209
Sanchez, Sonia 1934- DLB-41; DS-8
Sánchez de Arévalo, Rodrigo
   1404-1470.................... DLB-286
Sánchez de Badajoz, Diego ?-1552? DLB-318
Sánchez Ferlosio, Rafael 1927- DLB-322
Sand, George 1804-1876 .... DLB-119, 192
Sandburg, Carl
   1878-1967.........DLB-17, 54; CDALB-3
Sandel, Cora (Sara Fabricius)
   1880-1974.................... DLB-297
Sandemose, Aksel 1899-1965 .... DLB-297
Sanders, Edward 1939- DLB-16, 244
Sanderson, Robert 1587-1663.......... DLB-281
Sandoz, Mari 1896-1966............ DLB-9, 212
Sandwell, B. K. 1876-1954 .... DLB-92
Sandy, Stephen 1934- DLB-165
Sandys, George 1578-1644 .... DLB-24, 121
Sangster, Charles 1822-1893........... DLB-99
Sanguineti, Edoardo 1930- DLB-128
Sanjōnishi Sanetaka 1455-1537......... DLB-203
San Pedro, Diego de fl. ca. 1492....... DLB-286
Sansay, Leonora ?-after 1823 .... DLB-200
Sansom, William 1912-1976 .... DLB-139
Sant'Anna, Affonso Romano de
   1937- DLB-307
Santayana, George
   1863-1952......DLB-54, 71, 246, 270; DS-13
Santiago, Danny 1911-1988 .... DLB-122
Santillana, Marqués de (Íñigo López de Mendoza)
   1398-1458 .... DLB-286
Santmyer, Helen Hooven 1895-1986 .... Y-84
Santos, Bienvenido 1911-1996 .... DLB-312
Sanvitale, Francesca 1928- DLB-196
Sapidus, Joannes 1490-1561 ....DLB-179
Sapir, Edward 1884-1939 .... DLB-92
Sapper (see McNeile, Herman Cyril)
Sappho circa 620 B.C.-circa 550 B.C.
   ....DLB-176; CDWLB-1
Saramago, José 1922- DLB-287; Y-98
   Nobel Lecture 1998: How Characters
     Became the Masters and the Author
     Their Apprentice................ Y-98

Sarban (John W. Wall) 1910-1989 ...... DLB-255
Sardou, Victorien 1831-1908 .... DLB-192
Sarduy, Severo 1937-1993............. DLB-113
Sargent, Pamela 1948- DLB-8
Saro-Wiwa, Ken 1941- DLB-157
Saroyan, Aram
   Rites of Passage [on William Saroyan].... Y-83
Saroyan, William
   1908-1981 .....DLB-7, 9, 86; Y-81; CDALB-7
Sarraute, Nathalie 1900-1999 .... DLB-83, 321
Sarrazin, Albertine 1937-1967........... DLB-83
Sarris, Greg 1952- DLB-175
Sarton, May 1912-1995 ....DLB-48; Y-81
Sartre, Jean-Paul 1905-1980 .....DLB-72, 296, 321
Sassoon, Siegfried
   1886-1967 .... DLB-20, 191; DS-18
   A Centenary Essay................. Y-86
   Tributes from Vivien F. Clarke and
     Michael Thorpe................. Y-86
Sata Ineko 1904-1998................ DLB-180
Saturday Review Press DLB-46
Saunders, James 1925-2004 .... DLB-13
Saunders, John Monk 1897-1940 .... DLB-26
Saunders, Margaret Marshall
   1861-1947 .... DLB-92
Saunders and Otley DLB-106
Saussure, Ferdinand de 1857-1913 ...... DLB-242
Savage, James 1784-1873.............. DLB-30
Savage, Marmion W. 1803?-1872 .... DLB-21
Savage, Richard 1697?-1743 .... DLB-95
Savard, Félix-Antoine 1896-1982 .... DLB-68
Savery, Henry 1791-1842 .... DLB-230
Saville, (Leonard) Malcolm 1901-1982... DLB-160
Saville, 1976 Booker Prize winner,
   David Storey DLB-326
Savinio, Alberto 1891-1952 .... DLB-264
Sawyer, Robert J. 1960- DLB-251
Sawyer, Ruth 1880-1970............... DLB-22
Sayer, Mandy 1963- DLB-325
Sayers, Dorothy L.
   1893-1957 ....DLB-10, 36, 77, 100; CDBLB-6
   The Dorothy L. Sayers Society Y-98
Sayle, Charles Edward 1864-1924 ...... DLB-184
Sayles, John Thomas 1950- DLB-44
Sbarbaro, Camillo 1888-1967.......... DLB-114
Scalapino, Leslie 1947- DLB-193
Scannell, Vernon 1922- DLB-27
Scarry, Richard 1919-1994 .... DLB-61
Scève, Maurice circa 1502-circa 1564.... DLB-327
Schack, Hans Egede 1820-1859 .... DLB-300
Schaefer, Jack 1907-1991............. DLB-212
Schaeffer, Albrecht 1885-1950 .... DLB-66
Schaeffer, Susan Fromberg 1941- .. DLB-28, 299

Schaff, Philip 1819-1893................DS-13	Schouler, James 1839-1920............DLB-47	Scott, Dennis 1939-1991............DLB-125
Schaper, Edzard 1908-1984............DLB-69	Schoultz, Solveig von 1907-1996........DLB-259	Scott, Dixon 1881-1915..............DLB-98
Scharf, J. Thomas 1843-1898...........DLB-47	Schrader, Paul 1946-................DLB-44	Scott, Duncan Campbell 1862-1947......DLB-92
Schede, Paul Melissus 1539-1602.......DLB-179	Schreiner, Olive 1855-1920.........DLB-18, 156, 190, 225	Scott, Evelyn 1893-1963............DLB-9, 48
Scheffel, Joseph Viktor von 1826-1886...DLB-129	Schroeder, Andreas 1946-............DLB-53	Scott, F. R. 1899-1985..............DLB-88
Scheffler, Johann 1624-1677...........DLB-164	Schubart, Christian Friedrich Daniel 1739-1791...................DLB-97	Scott, Frederick George 1861-1944......DLB-92
Schéhadé, Georges 1905-1999..........DLB-321	Schubert, Gotthilf Heinrich 1780-1860....DLB-90	Scott, Geoffrey 1884-1929............DLB-149
Schelling, Friedrich Wilhelm Joseph von 1775-1854.....................DLB-90	Schücking, Levin 1814-1883...........DLB-133	Scott, Harvey W. 1838-1910............DLB-23
Scherer, Wilhelm 1841-1886............DLB-129	Schulberg, Budd 1914-.....DLB-6, 26, 28; Y-81	Scott, John 1948-................DLB-325
Scherfig, Hans 1905-1979..............DLB-214	Excerpts from USC Presentation [on F. Scott Fitzgerald]............Y-96	Scott, Lady Jane (see Scott, Alicia Anne)
Schickele, René 1883-1940.............DLB-66	F. J. Schulte and Company..............DLB-49	Scott, Paul 1920-1978..........DLB-14, 207, 326
Schiff, Dorothy 1903-1989..............DLB-127	Schulz, Bruno 1892-1942....DLB-215; CDWLB-4	Scott, Sarah 1723-1795...............DLB-39
Schiller, Friedrich 1759-1805..............DLB-94; CDWLB-2	Schulze, Hans (see Praetorius, Johannes)	Scott, Tom 1918-1995................DLB-27
Schindler's Ark, 1982 Booker Prize winner, Thomas Keneally................DLB-326	Schupp, Johann Balthasar 1610-1661.....DLB-164	Scott, Sir Walter 1771-1832 ......DLB-93, 107, 116, 144, 159; CDBLB-3
Schirmer, David 1623-1687............DLB-164	Schurz, Carl 1829-1906...............DLB-23	Scott, William Bell 1811-1890............DLB-32
Schlaf, Johannes 1862-1941............DLB-118	Schuyler, George S. 1895-1977.........DLB-29, 51	Walter Scott Publishing Company Limited......................DLB-112
Schlegel, August Wilhelm 1767-1845......DLB-94	Schuyler, James 1923-1991............DLB-5, 169	William R. Scott [publishing house].......DLB-46
Schlegel, Dorothea 1763-1839...........DLB-90	Schwartz, Delmore 1913-1966........DLB-28, 48	Scott-Heron, Gil 1949-................DLB-41
Schlegel, Friedrich 1772-1829...........DLB-90	Schwartz, Jonathan 1938-................Y-82	Scribe, Eugene 1791-1861.............DLB-192
Schleiermacher, Friedrich 1768-1834......DLB-90	Schwartz, Lynne Sharon 1939-.......DLB-218	Scribner, Arthur Hawley 1859-1932....DS-13, 16
Schlesinger, Arthur M., Jr. 1917-........DLB-17	Schwarz, Sibylle 1621-1638............DLB-164	Scribner, Charles 1854-1930..........DS-13, 16
Schlumberger, Jean 1877-1968..........DLB-65	Schwarz-Bart, Andre 1928-...........DLB-299	Scribner, Charles, Jr. 1921-1995............Y-95
Schmid, Eduard Hermann Wilhelm (see Edschmid, Kasimir)	Schwerner, Armand 1927-1999.........DLB-165	Reminiscences.....................DS-17
Schmidt, Arno 1914-1979...............DLB-69	Schwob, Marcel 1867-1905............DLB-123	Charles Scribner's Sons....DLB-49; DS-13, 16, 17
Schmidt, Johann Kaspar (see Stirner, Max)	Sciascia, Leonardo 1921-1989..........DLB-177	Archives of Charles Scribner's Sons....DS-17
Schmidt, Michael 1947-................DLB-40	Science Fiction and Fantasy Documents in British Fantasy and Science Fiction................DLB-178	Scribner's Magazine.....................DS-13
Schmidtbonn, Wilhelm August 1876-1952.....................DLB-118	Hugo Awards and Nebula Awards.....DLB-8	Scribner's Monthly......................DS-13
Schmitz, Aron Hector (see Svevo, Italo)	The Iconography of Science-Fiction Art.........................DLB-8	Scripps, E. W. 1854-1926................DLB-25
Schmitz, James H. 1911-1981.............DLB-8	The New Wave....................DLB-8	Scudder, Horace Elisha 1838-1902....DLB-42, 71
Schnabel, Johann Gottfried 1692-1760....DLB-168	Paperback Science Fiction..........DLB-8	Scudder, Vida Dutton 1861-1954........DLB-71
Schnackenberg, Gjertrud 1953-........DLB-120	Science Fantasy...................DLB-8	Scudéry, Madeleine de 1607-1701.........DLB-268
Schnitzler, Arthur 1862-1931..........DLB-81, 118; CDWLB-2	Science-Fiction Fandom and Conventions...................DLB-8	Scupham, Peter 1933-................DLB-40
Schnurre, Wolfdietrich 1920-1989........DLB-69	Science-Fiction Fanzines: The Time Binders......................DLB-8	The Sea, 2005 Booker Prize winner, John Banville...................DLB-326
Schocken Books....................DLB-46	Science-Fiction Films.................DLB-8	The Sea, The Sea, 1978 Booker Prize winner, Iris Murdoch....................DLB-326
Scholartis Press.....................DLB-112	Science Fiction Writers of America and the Nebula Award...........DLB-8	Seabrook, William 1886-1945............DLB-4
Scholderer, Victor 1880-1971............DLB-201	Selected Science-Fiction Magazines and Anthologies....................DLB-8	Seabury, Samuel 1729-1796.............DLB-31
The Schomburg Center for Research in Black Culture..................DLB-76	A World Chronology of Important Science Fiction Works (1818-1979)........DLB-8	Seacole, Mary Jane Grant 1805-1881....DLB-166
Schönbeck, Virgilio (see Giotti, Virgilio)	The Year in Science Fiction and Fantasy...................Y-00, 01	The Seafarer circa 970.................DLB-146
Schönherr, Karl 1867-1943............DLB-118	Scot, Reginald circa 1538-1599........DLB-136	Sealsfield, Charles (Carl Postl) 1793-1864...................DLB-133, 186
Schoolcraft, Jane Johnston 1800-1841....DLB-175	Scotellaro, Rocco 1923-1953...........DLB-128	Searle, John R. 1932-................DLB-279
School Stories, 1914-1960..............DLB-160	Scott, Alicia Anne (Lady John Scott) 1810-1900....................DLB-240	Sears, Edward I. 1819?-1876............DLB-79
Schopenhauer, Arthur 1788-1860.........DLB-90	Scott, Catharine Amy Dawson 1865-1934....................DLB-240	Sears Publishing Company............DLB-46
Schopenhauer, Johanna 1766-1838.......DLB-90		Seaton, George 1911-1979..............DLB-44
Schorer, Mark 1908-1977..............DLB-103		Seaton, William Winston 1785-1866......DLB-43
Schottelius, Justus Georg 1612-1676.....DLB-164		Sebillet, Thomas 1512-1589............DLB-327
		Martin Secker [publishing house]........DLB-112
		Martin Secker, and Warburg Limited....DLB-112

Cumulative Index

The "Second Generation" Holocaust Novel DLB-299

Sedgwick, Arthur George 1844-1915 ..... DLB-64

Sedgwick, Catharine Maria 1789-1867 .... DLB-1, 74, 183, 239, 243

Sedgwick, Ellery 1872-1960 .... DLB-91

Sedgwick, Eve Kosofsky 1950- DLB-246

Sedley, Sir Charles 1639-1701 .... DLB-131

Seeberg, Peter 1925-1999 .... DLB-214

Seeger, Alan 1888-1916 .... DLB-45

Seers, Eugene (see Dantin, Louis)

Segal, Erich 1937- Y-86

Segal, Lore 1928- DLB-299

Šegedin, Petar 1909-1998 .... DLB-181

Seghers, Anna 1900-1983 .... DLB-69; CDWLB-2

Seid, Ruth (see Sinclair, Jo)

Seidel, Frederick Lewis 1936- Y-84

Seidel, Ina 1885-1974 .... DLB-56

Seifert, Jaroslav 1901-1986 .... DLB-215; Y-84; CDWLB-4

    Jaroslav Seifert Through the Eyes of the English-Speaking Reader Y-84

    Three Poems by Jaroslav Seifert Y-84

Seifullina, Lidiia Nikolaevna 1889-1954 .. DLB-272

Seigenthaler, John 1927- DLB-127

Seizin Press DLB-112

Séjour, Victor 1817-1874 .... DLB-50

Séjour Marcou et Ferrand, Juan Victor (see Séjour, Victor)

Sekowski, Józef-Julian, Baron Brambeus (see Senkovsky, Osip Ivanovich)

Selby, Bettina 1934- DLB-204

Selby, Hubert Jr. 1928-2004 .... DLB-2, 227

Selden, George 1929-1989 .... DLB-52

Selden, John 1584-1654 .... DLB-213

Selenić, Slobodan 1933-1995 .... DLB-181

Self, Edwin F. 1920- DLB-137

Self, Will 1961- DLB-207

Seligman, Edwin R. A. 1861-1939 .... DLB-47

Selimović, Meša 1910-1982 .... DLB-181; CDWLB-4

Sellars, Wilfrid 1912-1989 .... DLB-279

Sellings, Arthur (Arthur Gordon Ley) 1911-1968 .... DLB-261

Selous, Frederick Courteney 1851-1917 .. DLB-174

Seltzer, Chester E. (see Muro, Amado)

Thomas Seltzer [publishing house] DLB-46

Selvadurai, Shyam 1965- DLB-323

Selvon, Sam 1923-1994 ..... DLB-125; CDWLB-3

Semel, Nava 1954- DLB-299

Semmes, Raphael 1809-1877 .... DLB-189

Senancour, Etienne de 1770-1846 .... DLB-119

Sena, Jorge de 1919-1978 .... DLB-287

Sendak, Maurice 1928- DLB-61

Sender, Ramón J. 1901-1982 .... DLB-322

Seneca the Elder circa 54 B.C.-circa A.D. 40 .... DLB-211

Seneca the Younger circa 1 B.C.-A.D. 65 ..... DLB-211; CDWLB-1

Senécal, Eva 1905-1988 .... DLB-92

Sengstacke, John 1912-1997 .... DLB-127

Senior, Olive 1941- DLB-157

Senkovsky, Osip Ivanovich (Józef-Julian Sekowski, Baron Brambeus) 1800-1858 .... DLB-198

Šenoa, August 1838-1881 .... DLB-147; CDWLB-4

Sentimental Fiction of the Sixteenth Century DLB-318

Sepamla, Sipho 1932- DLB-157, 225

Serafimovich, Aleksandr Serafimovich (Aleksandr Serafimovich Popov) 1863-1949 .... DLB-272

Serao, Matilde 1856-1927 .... DLB-264

Seredy, Kate 1899-1975 .... DLB-22

Sereni, Vittorio 1913-1983 .... DLB-128

William Seres [publishing house] DLB-170

Sergeev-Tsensky, Sergei Nikolaevich (Sergei Nikolaevich Sergeev) 1875-1958 ..... DLB-272

Serling, Rod 1924-1975 .... DLB-26

Sernine, Daniel 1955- DLB-251

Serote, Mongane Wally 1944- DLB-125, 225

Serraillier, Ian 1912-1994 .... DLB-161

Serrano, Nina 1934- DLB-122

Service, Robert 1874-1958 .... DLB-92

Sessler, Charles 1854-1935 .... DLB-187

Seth, Vikram 1952- DLB-120, 271, 323

Seton, Elizabeth Ann 1774-1821 .... DLB-200

Seton, Ernest Thompson 1860-1942 .... DLB-92; DS-13

Seton, John circa 1509-1567 .... DLB-281

Setouchi Harumi 1922- DLB-182

Settle, Mary Lee 1918- DLB-6

Seume, Johann Gottfried 1763-1810 ...... DLB-94

Seuse, Heinrich 1295?-1366 .... DLB-179

Seuss, Dr. (see Geisel, Theodor Seuss)

Severianin, Igor' 1887-1941 .... DLB-295

Severin, Timothy 1940- DLB-204

Sévigné, Marie de Rabutin Chantal, Madame de 1626-1696 .... DLB-268

Sewall, Joseph 1688-1769 .... DLB-24

Sewall, Richard B. 1908-2003 .... DLB-111

Sewall, Samuel 1652-1730 .... DLB-24

Sewell, Anna 1820-1878 .... DLB-163

Sewell, Stephen 1953- DLB-325

Sexton, Anne 1928-1974 ... DLB-5, 169; CDALB-1

Seymour-Smith, Martin 1928-1998 ...... DLB-155

Sgorlon, Carlo 1930- DLB-196

Shaara, Michael 1929-1988 .... Y-83

Shabel'skaia, Aleksandra Stanislavovna 1845-1921 .... DLB-238

Shadwell, Thomas 1641?-1692 .... DLB-80

Shaffer, Anthony 1926-2001 .... DLB-13

Shaffer, Peter 1926- DLB-13, 233; CDBLB-8

Muhammad ibn Idris al-Shafi'i 767-820 .. DLB-311

Shaftesbury, Anthony Ashley Cooper, Third Earl of 1671-1713 .... DLB-101

Shaginian, Marietta Sergeevna 1888-1982 .... DLB-272

Shairp, Mordaunt 1887-1939 .... DLB-10

Shakespeare, Nicholas 1957- DLB-231

Shakespeare, William 1564-1616 ..... DLB-62, 172, 263; CDBLB-1

    The New Variorum Shakespeare Y-85

    Shakespeare and Montaigne: A Symposium by Jules Furthman Y-02

    $6,166,000 for a *Book*! Observations on *The Shakespeare First Folio: The History of the Book* Y-01

    Taylor-Made Shakespeare? Or Is "Shall I Die?" the Long-Lost Text of Bottom's Dream? Y-85

The Shakespeare Globe Trust Y-93

Shakespeare Head Press DLB-112

Shakhova, Elisaveta Nikitichna 1822-1899 .... DLB-277

Shakhovskoi, Aleksandr Aleksandrovich 1777-1846 .... DLB-150

Shalamov, Varlam Tikhonovich 1907-1982 .... DLB-302

al-Shanfara fl. sixth century DLB-311

Shange, Ntozake 1948- DLB-38, 249

Shapcott, Thomas W. 1935- DLB-289

Shapir, Ol'ga Andreevna 1850-1916 ..... DLB-295

Shapiro, Karl 1913-2000 .... DLB-48

Sharon Publications DLB-46

Sharov, Vladimir Aleksandrovich 1952- DLB-285

Sharp, Margery 1905-1991 .... DLB-161

Sharp, William 1855-1905 .... DLB-156

Sharpe, Tom 1928- DLB-14, 231

Shaw, Albert 1857-1947 .... DLB-91

Shaw, George Bernard 1856-1950 .... DLB-10, 57, 190, CDBLB-6

    The Bernard Shaw Society Y-99

    "Stage Censorship: The Rejected Statement" (1911) [excerpts] DLB-10

Shaw, Henry Wheeler 1818-1885 .... DLB-11

Shaw, Irwin 1913-1984 .... DLB-6, 102; Y-84; CDALB-1

Shaw, Joseph T. 1874-1952 .... DLB-137

    "As I Was Saying," Joseph T. Shaw's Editorial Rationale in *Black Mask* (January 1927) DLB-137

Shaw, Mary 1854-1929 .... DLB-228

Shaw, Robert 1927-1978 . . . . .DLB-13, 14

Shaw, Robert B. 1947- DLB-120

Shawn, Wallace 1943- DLB-266

Shawn, William 1907-1992. . . . . .DLB-137

Frank Shay [publishing house] DLB-46

Shchedrin, N. (see Saltykov, Mikhail Evgrafovich)

Shcherbakova, Galina Nikolaevna
1932- DLB-285

Shcherbina, Nikolai Fedorovich
1821-1869 . . . . .DLB-277

Shea, John Gilmary 1824-1892 . . . . .DLB-30

Sheaffer, Louis 1912-1993 . . . . .DLB-103

Sheahan, Henry Beston (see Beston, Henry)

Shearing, Joseph 1886-1952 . . . . .DLB-70

Shebbeare, John 1709-1788. . . . . .DLB-39

Sheckley, Robert 1928- DLB-8

Shedd, William G. T. 1820-1894 . . . . .DLB-64

Sheed, Wilfrid 1930- DLB-6

Sheed and Ward [U.S.] DLB-46

Sheed and Ward Limited [U.K.] DLB-112

Sheldon, Alice B. (see Tiptree, James, Jr.)

Sheldon, Edward 1886-1946 . . . . .DLB-7

Sheldon and Company DLB-49

Sheller, Aleksandr Konstantinovich
1838-1900 . . . . .DLB-238

Shelley, Mary Wollstonecraft 1797-1851
. . . . DLB-110, 116, 159, 178; CDBLB-3

Preface to *Frankenstein; or, The
Modern Prometheus* (1818) DLB-178

Shelley, Percy Bysshe
1792-1822 . . . . . .DLB-96, 110, 158; CDBLB-3

Shelnutt, Eve 1941- DLB-130

Shen Congwen 1902-1988 . . . . .DLB-328

Shenshin (see Fet, Afanasii Afanas'evich)

Shenstone, William 1714-1763 . . . . .DLB-95

Shepard, Clark and Brown DLB-49

Shepard, Ernest Howard 1879-1976 . . . . . .DLB-160

Shepard, Sam 1943- DLB-7, 212

Shepard, Thomas I, 1604 or 1605-1649 . . .DLB-24

Shepard, Thomas, II, 1635-1677 . . . . .DLB-24

Shepherd, Luke fl. 1547-1554 . . . . .DLB-136

Sherburne, Edward 1616-1702 . . . . .DLB-131

Sheridan, Frances 1724-1766 . . . . .DLB-39, 84

Sheridan, Richard Brinsley
1751-1816 . . . . DLB-89; CDBLB-2

Sherman, Francis 1871-1926 . . . . .DLB-92

Sherman, Martin 1938- DLB-228

Sherriff, R. C. 1896-1975 . . . . . DLB-10, 191, 233

Sherrod, Blackie 1919- DLB-241

Sherry, Norman 1935- DLB-155

Tribute to Graham Greene Y-91

Sherry, Richard 1506-1551 or 1555 . . . . . .DLB-236

Sherwood, Mary Martha 1775-1851 . . . . . .DLB-163

Sherwood, Robert E. 1896-1955 . . . DLB-7, 26, 249

Shevyrev, Stepan Petrovich
1806-1864 . . . . .DLB-205

Shi Tuo (Lu Fen) 1910-1988 . . . . .DLB-328

Shiel, M. P. 1865-1947 . . . . .DLB-153

Shiels, George 1886-1949 . . . . .DLB-10

Shiga Naoya 1883-1971 . . . . .DLB-180

Shiina Rinzō 1911-1973 . . . . .DLB-182

Shikishi Naishinnō 1153?-1201 . . . . .DLB-203

Shillaber, Benjamin Penhallow
1814-1890 . . . . .DLB-1, 11, 235

Shimao Toshio 1917-1986 . . . . .DLB-182

Shimazaki Tōson 1872-1943 . . . . .DLB-180

Shimose, Pedro 1940- DLB-283

Shine, Ted 1931- .DLB-38

Shinkei 1406-1475 . . . . .DLB-203

Ship, Reuben 1915-1975 . . . . .DLB-88

Shirer, William L. 1904-1993 . . . . .DLB-4

Shirinsky-Shikhmatov, Sergii Aleksandrovich
1783-1837 . . . . .DLB-150

Shirley, James 1596-1666 . . . . .DLB-58

Shishkov, Aleksandr Semenovich
1753-1841 . . . . .DLB-150

Shmelev, I. S. 1873-1950 . . . . .DLB-317

Shockley, Ann Allen 1927- DLB-33

Sholokhov, Mikhail Aleksandrovich
1905-1984 . . . . .DLB-272

Shōno Junzō 1921- DLB-182

Shore, Arabella 1820?-1901 . . . . .DLB-199

Shore, Louisa 1824-1895 . . . . .DLB-199

Short, Luke (see Glidden, Frederick Dilley)

Peter Short [publishing house] DLB-170

Shorter, Dora Sigerson 1866-1918 . . . . . . .DLB-240

Shorthouse, Joseph Henry 1834-1903 . . . . .DLB-18

Short Stories
Michael M. Rea and the Rea Award
for the Short Story Y-97

The Year in Short Stories Y-87

The Year in the Short Story Y-88, 90–93

Shōtetsu 1381-1459 . . . . .DLB-203

Showalter, Elaine 1941- DLB-67

Shreve, Anita 1946- DLB-292

Shteiger, Anatolii 1907-1944 . . . . .DLB-317

Shukshin, Vasilii Makarovich
1929-1974 . . . . .DLB-302

Shulevitz, Uri 1935- DLB-61

Shulman, Max 1919-1988 . . . . .DLB-11

Shute, Henry A. 1856-1943 . . . . .DLB-9

Shute, Nevil (Nevil Shute Norway)
1899-1960 . . . . .DLB-255

Shuttle, Penelope 1947- DLB-14, 40

Shvarts, Evgenii L'vovich 1896-1958 . . . . . .DLB-272

Sibawayhi circa 750-circa 795 . . . . .DLB-311

Sibbes, Richard 1577-1635 . . . . .DLB-151

Sibiriak, D. (see Mamin, Dmitrii Narkisovich)

Siddal, Elizabeth Eleanor 1829-1862 . . . . .DLB-199

Sidgwick, Ethel 1877-1970 . . . . .DLB-197

Sidgwick, Henry 1838-1900. . . . . .DLB-262

Sidgwick and Jackson Limited DLB-112

Sidhwa, Bapsi 1939- DLB-323

Sidney, Margaret (see Lothrop, Harriet M.)

Sidney, Mary 1561-1621 . . . . .DLB-167

Sidney, Sir Philip
1554-1586 . . . . .DLB-167; CDBLB-1

An *Apologie for Poetrie* (the Olney edition,
1595, of *Defence of Poesie*) DLB-167

Sidney's Press DLB-49

The Siege of Krishnapur, 1973 Booker Prize winner,
J. G. Farrell .DLB-326

Sierra, Rubén 1946- DLB-122

Sierra Club Books .DLB-49

Siger of Brabant circa 1240-circa 1284 . . . .DLB-115

Sigourney, Lydia Huntley
1791-1865 . . . . . . DLB-1, 42, 73, 183, 239, 243

Silkin, Jon 1930-1997 . . . . .DLB-27

Silko, Leslie Marmon
1948- DLB-143, 175, 256, 275

Silliman, Benjamin 1779-1864 . . . . .DLB-183

Silliman, Ron 1946- DLB-169

Silliphant, Stirling 1918-1996 . . . . .DLB-26

Sillitoe, Alan 1928- DLB-14, 139; CDBLB-8

Tribute to J. B. Priestly Y-84

Silman, Roberta 1934- DLB-28

Silone, Ignazio (Secondino Tranquilli)
1900-1978 . . . . .DLB-264

Silva, Beverly 1930- DLB-122

Silva, Clara 1905-1976 . . . . .DLB-290

Silva, José Asunció 1865-1896 . . . . .DLB-283

Silverberg, Robert 1935- DLB-8

Silverman, Kaja 1947- DLB-246

Silverman, Kenneth 1936- DLB-111

Simak, Clifford D. 1904-1988 . . . . .DLB-8

Simcoe, Elizabeth 1762-1850 . . . . .DLB-99

Simcox, Edith Jemima 1844-1901 . . . . .DLB-190

Simcox, George Augustus 1841-1905 . . . . .DLB-35

Sime, Jessie Georgina 1868-1958 . . . . .DLB-92

Simenon, Georges 1903-1989 . . . . . DLB-72; Y-89

Simic, Charles 1938- DLB-105

"Images and 'Images'" DLB-105

Simionescu, Mircea Horia 1928- DLB-232

Simmel, Georg 1858-1918 . . . . .DLB-296

Simmel, Johannes Mario 1924- DLB-69

Valentine Simmes [publishing house] DLB-170

Simmons, Ernest J. 1903-1972 . . . . .DLB-103

Simmons, Herbert Alfred 1930- DLB-33

Simmons, James 1933- DLB-40

Cumulative Index

Simms, William Gilmore 1806-1870 .... DLB-3, 30, 59, 73, 248

Simms and M'Intyre DLB-106

Simon, Claude 1913-2005 .... DLB-83; Y-85

 Nobel Lecture Y-85

Simon, Neil 1927- DLB-7, 266

Simon and Schuster DLB-46

Simonov, Konstantin Mikhailovich 1915-1979 .... DLB-302

Simons, Katherine Drayton Mayrant 1890-1969 .... Y-83

Simović, Ljubomir 1935- DLB-181

Simpkin and Marshall [publishing house] DLB-154

Simpson, Helen 1897-1940 .... DLB-77

Simpson, Louis 1923- DLB-5

Simpson, N. F. 1919- DLB-13

Sims, George 1923-1999 .... DLB-87; Y-99

Sims, George Robert 1847-1922 .. DLB-35, 70, 135

Sinán, Rogelio 1902-1994 .... DLB-145, 290

Sinclair, Andrew 1935- DLB-14

Sinclair, Bertrand William 1881-1972 ..... DLB-92

Sinclair, Catherine 1800-1864 .... DLB-163

Sinclair, Clive 1948- DLB-319

Sinclair, Jo 1913-1995 .... DLB-28

Sinclair, Lister 1921- DLB-88

Sinclair, May 1863-1946 .... DLB-36, 135

 The Novels of Dorothy Richardson (1918) DLB-36

Sinclair, Upton 1878-1968 ...... DLB-9; CDALB-5

Upton Sinclair [publishing house] DLB-46

Singer, Isaac Bashevis 1904-1991 .... DLB-6, 28, 52, 278; Y-91; CDALB-1

Singer, Mark 1950- DLB-185

Singh, Khushwant 1915- DLB-323

Singmaster, Elsie 1879-1958 .... DLB-9

Siniavsky, Andrei (Abram Tertz) 1925-1997 .... DLB-302

Sinisgalli, Leonardo 1908-1981 .... DLB-114

Siodmak, Curt 1902-2000 .... DLB-44

Sîrbu, Ion D. 1919-1989 .... DLB-232

Siringo, Charles A. 1855-1928 .... DLB-186

Sissman, L. E. 1928-1976 .... DLB-5

Sisson, C. H. 1914-2003 .... DLB-27

Sitwell, Edith 1887-1964 ...... DLB-20; CDBLB-7

Sitwell, Osbert 1892-1969 .... DLB-100, 195

Sivanandan, Ambalavaner 1923- DLB-323

Sixteenth-Century Spanish Epic, The DLB-318

Skácel, Jan 1922-1989 .... DLB-232

Skalbe, Kārlis 1879-1945 .... DLB-220

Skármeta, Antonio 1940- DLB-145; CDWLB-3

Skavronsky, A. (see Danilevsky, Grigorii Petrovich)

Skeat, Walter W. 1835-1912 .... DLB-184

William Skeffington [publishing house] .. DLB-106

Skelton, John 1463-1529 .... DLB-136

Skelton, Robin 1925-1997 .... DLB-27, 53

Škėma, Antanas 1910-1961 .... DLB-220

Skinner, Constance Lindsay 1877-1939 .... DLB-92

Skinner, John Stuart 1788-1851 .... DLB-73

Skipsey, Joseph 1832-1903 .... DLB-35

Skou-Hansen, Tage 1925- DLB-214

Skrzynecki, Peter 1945- DLB-289

Škvorecký, Josef 1924- DLB-232; CDWLB-4

Slade, Bernard 1930- DLB-53

Slamnig, Ivan 1930- DLB-181

Slančeková, Božena (see Timrava)

Slataper, Scipio 1888-1915 .... DLB-264

Slater, Patrick 1880-1951 .... DLB-68

Slaveykov, Pencho 1866-1912 .... DLB-147

Slaviček, Milivoj 1929- DLB-181

Slavitt, David 1935- DLB-5, 6

Sleigh, Burrows Willcocks Arthur 1821-1869 .... DLB-99

Sleptsov, Vasilii Alekseevich 1836-1878 ... DLB-277

Slesinger, Tess 1905-1945 .... DLB-102

Slessor, Kenneth 1901-1971 .... DLB-260

Slick, Sam (see Haliburton, Thomas Chandler)

Sloan, John 1871-1951 .... DLB-188

Sloane, William, Associates DLB-46

Slonimsky, Mikhail Leonidovich 1897-1972 .... DLB-272

Sluchevsky, Konstantin Konstantinovich 1837-1904 .... DLB-277

Small, Maynard and Company DLB-49

Smart, Christopher 1722-1771 .... DLB-109

Smart, David A. 1892-1957 .... DLB-137

Smart, Elizabeth 1913-1986 .... DLB-88

Smart, J. J. C. 1920- DLB-262

Smedley, Menella Bute 1820?-1877 ...... DLB-199

William Smellie [publishing house] DLB-154

Smiles, Samuel 1812-1904 .... DLB-55

Smiley, Jane 1949- DLB-227, 234

Smith, A. J. M. 1902-1980 .... DLB-88

Smith, Adam 1723-1790 .... DLB-104, 252

Smith, Adam (George Jerome Waldo Goodman) 1930- DLB-185

Smith, Alexander 1829-1867 .... DLB-32, 55

 "On the Writing of Essays" (1862) ... DLB-57

Smith, Amanda 1837-1915 .... DLB-221

Smith, Betty 1896-1972 .... Y-82

Smith, Carol Sturm 1938- Y-81

Smith, Charles Henry 1826-1903 .... DLB-11

Smith, Charlotte 1749-1806 .... DLB-39, 109

Smith, Chet 1899-1973 .... DLB-171

Smith, Cordwainer 1913-1966 .... DLB-8

Smith, Dave 1942- DLB-5

 Tribute to James Dickey Y-97

 Tribute to John Gardner Y-82

Smith, Dodie 1896-1990 .... DLB-10

Smith, Doris Buchanan 1934-2002 .... DLB-52

Smith, E. E. 1890-1965 .... DLB-8

Smith, Elihu Hubbard 1771-1798 .... DLB-37

Smith, Elizabeth Oakes (Prince) (see Oakes Smith, Elizabeth)

Smith, Eunice 1757-1823 .... DLB-200

Smith, F. Hopkinson 1838-1915 .... DS-13

Smith, George D. 1870-1920 .... DLB-140

Smith, George O. 1911-1981 .... DLB-8

Smith, Goldwin 1823-1910 .... DLB-99

Smith, H. Allen 1907-1976 .... DLB-11, 29

Smith, Harry B. 1860-1936 .... DLB-187

Smith, Hazel Brannon 1914-1994 .... DLB-127

Smith, Henry circa 1560-circa 1591 ..... DLB-136

Smith, Horatio (Horace) 1779-1849 .... DLB-96, 116

Smith, Iain Crichton (Iain Mac A'Ghobhainn) 1928-1998 .... DLB-40, 139, 319

Smith, J. Allen 1860-1924 .... DLB-47

Smith, James 1775-1839 .... DLB-96

Smith, Jessie Willcox 1863-1935 .... DLB-188

Smith, John 1580-1631 .... DLB-24, 30

Smith, John 1618-1652 .... DLB-252

Smith, Josiah 1704-1781 .... DLB-24

Smith, Ken 1938- DLB-40

Smith, Lee 1944- DLB-143; Y-83

Smith, Logan Pearsall 1865-1946 .... DLB-98

Smith, Margaret Bayard 1778-1844 ..... DLB-248

Smith, Mark 1935- Y-82

Smith, Michael 1698-circa 1771 .... DLB-31

Smith, Pauline 1882-1959 .... DLB-225

Smith, Red 1905-1982 .... DLB-29, 171

Smith, Roswell 1829-1892 .... DLB-79

Smith, Samuel Harrison 1772-1845 ...... DLB-43

Smith, Samuel Stanhope 1751-1819 ...... DLB-37

Smith, Sarah (see Stretton, Hesba)

Smith, Sarah Pogson 1774-1870 .... DLB-200

Smith, Seba 1792-1868 .... DLB-1, 11, 243

Smith, Stevie 1902-1971 .... DLB-20

Smith, Sydney 1771-1845 .... DLB-107

Smith, Sydney Goodsir 1915-1975 .... DLB-27

Smith, Sir Thomas 1513-1577 .... DLB-132

Smith, Vivian 1933- DLB-325

Smith, W. Gordon 1928-1996 .... DLB-310

Smith, Wendell 1914-1972 .... DLB-171

Smith, William fl. 1595-1597 . . . . DLB-136	Solmi, Sergio 1899-1981 . . . . DLB-114	"The Greatness of Southern Literature": League of the South Institute for the Study of Southern Culture and History Y-02
Smith, William 1727-1803 . . . . DLB-31	Sologub, Fedor 1863-1927 . . . . DLB-295	
A General Idea of the College of Mirania (1753) [excerpts] DLB-31	Solomon, Carl 1928- DLB-16	
	Solórzano, Carlos 1922- DLB-305	The Society for the Study of Southern Literature Y-00
Smith, William 1728-1793 . . . . DLB-30	Soloukhin, Vladimir Alekseevich 1924-1997 . . . . DLB-302	
Smith, William Gardner 1927-1974 . . . . . . DLB-76		Southern Writers Between the Wars DLB-9
Smith, William Henry 1808-1872 . . . . DLB-159	Solov'ev, Sergei Mikhailovich 1885-1942 . . . . DLB-295	Southerne, Thomas 1659-1746 . . . . DLB-80
Smith, William Jay 1918- DLB-5		Southey, Caroline Anne Bowles 1786-1854 . . . . DLB-116
Smith, Elder and Company DLB-154	Solov'ev, Vladimir Sergeevich 1853-1900 . . . . DLB-295	
Harrison Smith and Robert Haas [publishing house] DLB-46	Solstad, Dag 1941- DLB-297	Southey, Robert 1774-1843 . . . . . DLB-93, 107, 142
		Southwell, Robert 1561?-1595 . . . . DLB-167
J. Stilman Smith and Company DLB-49	Solway, David 1941- DLB-53	Southworth, E. D. E. N. 1819-1899 . . . . . . DLB-239
W. B. Smith and Company DLB-49	Solzhenitsyn, Aleksandr 1918- DLB-302	Sowande, Bode 1948- DLB-157
W. H. Smith and Son DLB-106	Solzhenitsyn and America Y-85	Tace Sowle [publishing house] DLB-170
Leonard Smithers [publishing house] DLB-112	Some Basic Notes on Three Modern Genres: Interview, Blurb, and Obituary Y-02	Soyfer, Jura 1912-1939 . . . . DLB-124
Smollett, Tobias 1721-1771 . . . . DLB-39, 104; CDBLB-2		Soyinka, Wole 1934- DLB-125; Y-86, Y-87; CDWLB-3
	Somerville, Edith Œnone 1858-1949 . . . . . DLB-135	
Dedication to *Ferdinand Count Fathom* (1753) DLB-39	*Something to Answer For,* 1969 Booker Prize winner, P. H. Newby DLB-326	Nobel Lecture 1986: This Past Must Address Its Present Y-86
Preface to *Ferdinand Count Fathom* (1753) DLB-39	Somov, Orest Mikhailovich 1793-1833 . . . DLB-198	Spacks, Barry 1931- DLB-105
	Sønderby, Knud 1909-1966 . . . . DLB-214	Spalding, Frances 1950- DLB-155
Preface to *Roderick Random* (1748) DLB-39	Sone, Monica 1919- DLB-312	Spanish Byzantine Novel, The DLB-318
Smythe, Francis Sydney 1900-1949 . . . . . . DLB-195	Song, Cathy 1955- DLB-169, 312	Spanish Travel Writers of the Late Middle Ages DLB-286
Snelling, William Joseph 1804-1848 . . . . . . DLB-202	Sonnevi, Göran 1939- DLB-257	
Snellings, Rolland (see Touré, Askia Muhammad)	Sono Ayako 1931- DLB-182	Spark, Muriel 1918- DLB-15, 139; CDBLB-7
Snodgrass, W. D. 1926- DLB-5	Sontag, Susan 1933-2004 . . . . DLB-2, 67	Michael Sparke [publishing house] DLB-170
Snorri Hjartarson 1906-1986 . . . . DLB-293	Sophocles 497/496 B.C.-406/405 B.C. DLB-176; CDWLB-1	Sparks, Jared 1789-1866 . . . . DLB-1, 30, 235
Snow, C. P. 1905-1980 . . . . . DLB-15, 77; DS-17; CDBLB-7		Sparshott, Francis 1926- DLB-60
	Šopov, Aco 1923-1982 . . . . DLB-181	Späth, Gerold 1939- DLB-75
Snyder, Gary 1930- DLB-5, 16, 165, 212, 237, 275	Sorel, Charles ca.1600-1674 . . . . DLB-268	Spatola, Adriano 1941-1988 . . . . DLB-128
	Sørensen, Villy 1929- DLB-214	Spaziani, Maria Luisa 1924- DLB-128
Sobiloff, Hy 1912-1970 . . . . DLB-48	Sorensen, Virginia 1912-1991 . . . . DLB-206	*Specimens of Foreign Standard Literature* 1838-1842 . . . . DLB-1
The Social Contract, Jean-Jacques Rousseau DLB-314	Sorge, Reinhard Johannes 1892-1916 . . . . DLB-118	
	Sorokin, Vladimir Georgievich 1955- DLB-285	*The Spectator* 1828- DLB-110
The Society for Textual Scholarship and *TEXT* Y-87		Spedding, James 1808-1881 . . . . DLB-144
	Sorrentino, Gilbert 1929- DLB-5, 173; Y-80	Spee von Langenfeld, Friedrich 1591-1635 . . . . DLB-164
The Society for the History of Authorship, Reading and Publishing Y-92	Sosa, Roberto 1930- DLB-290	
	Sotheby, James 1682-1742 . . . . DLB-213	Speght, Rachel 1597-after 1630 . . . . DLB-126
Söderberg, Hjalmar 1869-1941 . . . . DLB-259	Sotheby, John 1740-1807 . . . . DLB-213	Speke, John Hanning 1827-1864 . . . . DLB-166
Södergran, Edith 1892-1923 . . . . DLB-259	Sotheby, Samuel 1771-1842 . . . . DLB-213	Spellman, A. B. 1935- DLB-41
Soffici, Ardengo 1879-1964 . . . . DLB-114, 264	Sotheby, Samuel Leigh 1805-1861 . . . . . . DLB-213	Spence, Catherine Helen 1825-1910 . . . . . DLB-230
Sofola, 'Zulu 1938- DLB-157	Sotheby, William 1757-1833 . . . . DLB-93, 213	Spence, Thomas 1750-1814 . . . . DLB-158
Sokhanskaia, Nadezhda Stepanovna (Kokhanovskaia) 1823?-1884 . . . . DLB-277	Soto, Gary 1952- DLB-82	Spencer, Anne 1882-1975 . . . . DLB-51, 54
	Soueif, Ahdaf 1950- DLB-267	Spencer, Charles, third Earl of Sunderland 1674-1722 . . . . DLB-213
Sokolov, Sasha (Aleksandr Vsevolodovich Sokolov) 1943- DLB-285	Souster, Raymond 1921- DLB-88	
	The *South English Legendary* circa thirteenth-fifteenth centuries DLB-146	Spencer, Elizabeth 1921- DLB-6, 218
Solano, Solita 1888-1975 . . . . DLB-4		Spencer, George John, Second Earl Spencer 1758-1834 . . . . DLB-184
Soldati, Mario 1906-1999 . . . . DLB-177	Southerland, Ellease 1943- DLB-33	
Soledad (see Zamudio, Adela)	Southern, Terry 1924-1995 . . . . DLB-2	Spencer, Herbert 1820-1903 . . . . DLB-57, 262
Šoljan, Antun 1932-1993 . . . . DLB-181	Southern Illinois University Press Y-95	"The Philosophy of Style" (1852) DLB-57
Sollers, Philippe (Philippe Joyaux) 1936- DLB-83	Southern Literature Fellowship of Southern Writers Y-98	Spencer, Scott 1945- Y-86
		Spender, J. A. 1862-1942 . . . . DLB-98
Sollogub, Vladimir Aleksandrovich 1813-1882 . . . . DLB-198	The Fugitives and the Agrarians: The First Exhibition Y-85	Spender, Stephen 1909-1995 . . . DLB-20; CDBLB-7
Sollors, Werner 1943- DBL-246		Spener, Philipp Jakob 1635-1705 . . . . DLB-164

Spenser, Edmund
circa 1552-1599 .... DLB-167; CDBLB-1

   Envoy from *The Shepheardes Calender*.... DLB-167

   "The Generall Argument of the
Whole Booke," from
The Shepheardes Calender DLB-167

   "A Letter of the Authors Expounding
His Whole Intention in the Course
of this Worke: Which for that It
Giueth Great Light to the Reader,
for the Better Vnderstanding
Is Hereunto Annexed,"
from *The Faerie Queene* (1590).... DLB-167

   "To His Booke," from
The Shepheardes Calender (1579) ... DLB-167

   "To the Most Excellent and Learned
Both Orator and Poete, Mayster
Gabriell Haruey, His Verie Special
and Singular Good Frend E. K.
Commendeth the Good Lyking of
This His Labour, and the Patronage
of the New Poete," from
The Shepheardes Calender DLB-167

Sperr, Martin 1944- DLB-124

Spewack, Bella Cowen 1899-1990 ...... DLB-266

Spewack, Samuel 1899-1971 .... DLB-266

Spicer, Jack 1925-1965 .... DLB-5, 16, 193

Spiegelman, Art 1948- DLB-299

Spielberg, Peter 1929- Y-81

Spielhagen, Friedrich 1829-1911........ DLB-129

"Spielmannsepen" (circa 1152-circa 1500)... DLB-148

Spier, Peter 1927- DLB-61

Spillane, Mickey 1918-2006 .... DLB-226

Spink, J. G. Taylor 1888-1962......... DLB-241

Spinrad, Norman 1940- DLB-8

   Tribute to Isaac Asimov Y-92

Spires, Elizabeth 1952- DLB-120

The Spirit of Laws, Claude-Adrien
Helvétius DLB-314

The Spirit of Laws, Charles-Louis de Secondat, baron
de Montesquieu DLB-314

Spitteler, Carl 1845-1924 .... DLB-129

Spivak, Lawrence E. 1900-1994 .... DLB-137

Spofford, Harriet Prescott
1835-1921 .... DLB-74, 221

Sponde, Jean de 1557-1595 .... DLB-327

Sports
   Jimmy, Red, and Others: Harold
Rosenthal Remembers the Stars
of the Press Box.................. Y-01

   The Literature of Boxing in England
through Arthur Conan Doyle Y-01

   Notable Twentieth-Century Books
about Sports DLB-241

Sprigge, Timothy L. S. 1932- DLB-262

Spring, Howard 1889-1965........... DLB-191

Springs, Elliott White 1896-1959 .... DLB-316

Squibob (see Derby, George Horatio)

Squier, E. G. 1821-1888 .... DLB-189

Staal-Delaunay, Marguerite-Jeanne Cordier de
1684-1750..................... DLB-314

Stableford, Brian 1948- DLB-261

Stacpoole, H. de Vere 1863-1951 .... DLB-153

Staël, Germaine de 1766-1817...... DLB-119, 192

Staël-Holstein, Anne-Louise Germaine de
(see Staël, Germaine de)

Staffeldt, Schack 1769-1826........... DLB-300

Stafford, Jean 1915-1979 .... DLB-2, 173

Stafford, William 1914-1993......... DLB-5, 206

Stallings, Laurence 1894-1968 .....DLB-7, 44, 316

Stallworthy, Jon 1935- DLB-40

Stampp, Kenneth M. 1912- DLB-17

Stănescu, Nichita 1933-1983.......... DLB-232

Stanev, Emiliyan 1907-1979............ DLB-181

Stanford, Ann 1916-1987 .... DLB-5

Stangerup, Henrik 1937-1998 .... DLB-214

Stanihurst, Richard 1547-1618 .... DLB-281

Stanitsky, N. (see Panaeva, Avdot'ia Iakovlevna)

Stankevich, Nikolai Vladimirovich
1813-1840 .... DLB-198

Stanković, Borisav ("Bora")
1876-1927............DLB-147; CDWLB-4

Stanley, Henry M. 1841-1904.... DLB-189; DS-13

Stanley, Thomas 1625-1678 .... DLB-131

Stannard, Martin 1947- DLB-155

William Stansby [publishing house] DLB-170

Stanton, Elizabeth Cady 1815-1902 ..... DLB-79

Stanton, Frank L. 1857-1927........... DLB-25

Stanton, Maura 1946- DLB-120

Stapledon, Olaf 1886-1950 .... DLB-15, 255

Star Spangled Banner Office........... DLB-49

Stark, Freya 1893-1993............... DLB-195

Starkey, Thomas circa 1499-1538....... DLB-132

Starkie, Walter 1894-1976............. DLB-195

Starkweather, David 1935- DLB-7

Starrett, Vincent 1886-1974............ DLB-187

Stationers' Company of London, The DLB-170

Statius circa A.D. 45-A.D. 96 .... DLB-211

Staying On, 1977 Booker Prize winner,
Paul Scott..................... DLB-326

Stead, Christina 1902-1983........... DLB-260

Stead, Robert J. C. 1880-1959 .... DLB-92

Steadman, Mark 1930- DLB-6

Stearns, Harold E. 1891-1943...... DLB-4; DS-15

Stebnitsky, M. (see Leskov, Nikolai Semenovich)

Stedman, Edmund Clarence 1833-1908 ... DLB-64

Steegmuller, Francis 1906-1994 .... DLB-111

Steel, Flora Annie 1847-1929 ...... DLB-153, 156

Steele, Max 1922-2005 .... Y-80

Steele, Richard
1672-1729......... DLB-84, 101; CDBLB-2

Steele, Timothy 1948- DLB-120

Steele, Wilbur Daniel 1886-1970........ DLB-86

Wallace Markfield's "Steeplechase" Y-02

Steere, Richard circa 1643-1721 .... DLB-24

Stefán frá Hvítadal (Stefán Sigurðsson)
1887-1933..................... DLB-293

Stefán Guðmundsson (see Stephan G. Stephansson)

Stefán Hörður Grímsson
1919 or 1920-2002............... DLB-293

Steffens, Lincoln 1866-1936 .... DLB-303

Stefanovski, Goran 1952- DLB-181

Stegner, Wallace
1909-1993 .... DLB-9, 206, 275; Y-93

Stehr, Hermann 1864-1940............. DLB-66

Steig, William 1907-2003 .... DLB-61

Stein, Gertrude 1874-1946
.... DLB-4, 54, 86, 228; DS-15; CDALB-4

Stein, Leo 1872-1947.................. DLB-4

Stein and Day Publishers DLB-46

Steinbeck, John 1902-1968
.... DLB-7, 9, 212, 275, 309; DS-2; CDALB-5

   John Steinbeck Research Center,
San Jose State University........... Y-85

   The Steinbeck Centennial Y-02

Steinem, Gloria 1934- DLB-246

Steiner, George 1929- DLB-67, 299

Steinhoewel, Heinrich 1411/1412-1479....DLB-179

Steinn Steinarr (Aðalsteinn Kristmundsson)
1908-1958 .... DLB-293

Steinunn Sigurðardóttir 1950- DLB-293

Steloff, Ida Frances 1887-1989 ....DLB-187

Stendhal 1783-1842.................. DLB-119

Stephan G. Stephansson (Stefán Guðmundsson)
1853-1927 .... DLB-293

Stephen, Leslie 1832-1904 ...... DLB-57, 144, 190

Stephen Family (Bloomsbury Group).......DS-10

Stephens, A. G. 1865-1933............. DLB-230

Stephens, Alexander H. 1812-1883 ...... DLB-47

Stephens, Alice Barber 1858-1932 ...... DLB-188

Stephens, Ann 1810-1886.........DLB-3, 73, 250

Stephens, Charles Asbury 1844?-1931 .... DLB-42

Stephens, James 1882?-1950.....DLB-19, 153, 162

Stephens, John Lloyd 1805-1852 ... DLB-183, 250

Stephens, Michael 1946- DLB-234

Stephensen, P. R. 1901-1965 .... DLB-260

Sterling, George 1869-1926 .... DLB-54

Sterling, James 1701-1763 .... DLB-24

Sterling, John 1806-1844 .... DLB-116

Stern, Gerald 1925- DLB-105

   "Living in Ruin" DLB-105

Stern, Gladys B. 1890-1973 ....DLB-197

Stern, Madeleine B. 1912- DLB-111, 140

Stern, Richard 1928- DLB-218; Y-87

Stern, Stewart 1922- DLB-26

Sterne, Laurence 1713-1768 ... DLB-39; CDBLB-2

Sternheim, Carl 1878-1942..........DLB-56, 118

Sternhold, Thomas ?-1549.............DLB-132

Steuart, David 1747-1824..............DLB-213

Stevens, Henry 1819-1886.............DLB-140

Stevens, Wallace 1879-1955....DLB-54; CDALB-5

    The Wallace Stevens Society............Y-99

Stevenson, Anne 1933- DLB-40

Stevenson, D. E. 1892-1973............DLB-191

Stevenson, Lionel 1902-1973...........DLB-155

Stevenson, Robert Louis
1850-1894........DLB-18, 57, 141, 156, 174;
DS-13; CDBLB-5
    "On Style in Literature:
    Its Technical Elements" (1885)....DLB-57

Stewart, Donald Ogden
1894-1980............DLB-4, 11, 26; DS-15

Stewart, Douglas 1913-1985 ....DLB-260

Stewart, Dugald 1753-1828 ....DLB-31

Stewart, George, Jr. 1848-1906 ....DLB-99

Stewart, George R. 1895-1980...........DLB-8

Stewart, Harold 1916-1995 ....DLB-260

Stewart, J. I. M. (see Innes, Michael)

Stewart, Maria W. 1803?-1879.........DLB-239

Stewart, Randall 1896-1964............DLB-103

Stewart, Sean 1965- DLB-251

Stewart and Kidd Company DLB-46

Sthen, Hans Christensen 1544-1610.....DLB-300

Stickney, Trumbull 1874-1904 ....DLB-54

Stieler, Caspar 1632-1707.............DLB-164

Stifter, Adalbert
1805-1868............DLB-133; CDWLB-2

Stiles, Ezra 1727-1795 ....DLB-31

Still, James 1906-2001 ....DLB-9; Y-01

Stirling, S. M. 1953- DLB-251

Stirner, Max 1806-1856 ....DLB-129

Stith, William 1707-1755..............DLB-31

Stivens, Dal 1911-1997...............DLB-260

Elliot Stock [publishing house].........DLB-106

Stockton, Annis Boudinot 1736-1801....DLB-200

Stockton, Frank R.
1834-1902...............DLB-42, 74; DS-13

Stockton, J. Roy 1892-1972 ....DLB-241

Ashbel Stoddard [publishing house].......DLB-49

Stoddard, Charles Warren 1843-1909....DLB-186

Stoddard, Elizabeth 1823-1902 ....DLB-202

Stoddard, Richard Henry
1825-1903..........DLB-3, 64, 250; DS-13

Stoddard, Solomon 1643-1729..........DLB-24

Stoker, Bram
1847-1912.......DLB-36, 70, 178; CDBLB-5
    On Writing *Dracula,* from the
    Introduction to *Dracula* (1897)....DLB-178
    Dracula (Documentary)...........DLB-304

Frederick A. Stokes Company..........DLB-49

Stokes, Thomas L. 1898-1958..........DLB-29

Stokesbury, Leon 1945- DLB-120

Stolberg, Christian Graf zu 1748-1821.....DLB-94

Stolberg, Friedrich Leopold Graf zu
1750-1819......................DLB-94

Stone, Lucy 1818-1893..........DLB-79, 239

Stone, Melville 1848-1929..............DLB-25

Stone, Robert 1937- DLB-152

Stone, Ruth 1915- DLB-105

Stone, Samuel 1602-1663...............DLB-24

Stone, William Leete 1792-1844........DLB-202

Herbert S. Stone and Company..........DLB-49

Stone and Kimball.....................DLB-49

Stoppard, Tom
1937- DLB-13, 233; Y-85; CDBLB-8
    Playwrights and Professors DLB-13

Storey, Anthony 1928- DLB-14

Storey, David 1933- ..DLB-13, 14, 207, 245, 326

Storm, Theodor
1817-1888............DLB-129; CDWLB-2

Storni, Alfonsina 1892-1938 ....DLB-283

Story, Thomas circa 1670-1742 ....DLB-31

Story, William Wetmore 1819-1895....DLB-1, 235

Storytelling: A Contemporary Renaissance....Y-84

Stoughton, William 1631-1701..........DLB-24

Stout, Rex 1886-1975.................DLB-306

Stow, John 1525-1605 ....DLB-132

Stow, Randolph 1935- DLB-260

Stowe, Harriet Beecher 1811-1896......DLB-1,12,
42, 74, 189, 239, 243; CDALB-3
    The Harriet Beecher Stowe Center.......Y-00

Stowe, Leland 1899-1994............DLB-29

Stoyanov, Dimitr Ivanov (see Elin Pelin)

Strabo 64/63 B.C.-circa A.D. 25..........DLB-176

Strachey, Lytton 1880-1932......DLB-149; DS-10
    Preface to *Eminent Victorians* DLB-149

William Strahan [publishing house]......DLB-154

Strahan and Company..............DLB-106

Strand, Mark 1934- DLB-5

The Strasbourg Oaths 842.............DLB-148

Stratemeyer, Edward 1862-1930 ....DLB-42

Strati, Saverio 1924- DLB-177

Stratton and Barnard....................DLB-49

Stratton-Porter, Gene
1863-1924................DLB-221; DS-14

Straub, Peter 1943- Y-84

Strauß, Botho 1944- DLB-124

Strauß, David Friedrich 1808-1874........DLB-133

Strauss, Jennifer 1933- DLB-325

The Strawberry Hill Press..............DLB-154

Strawson, P. F. 1919- DLB-262

Streatfeild, Noel 1895-1986 ....DLB-160

Street, Cecil John Charles (see Rhode, John)

Street, G. S. 1867-1936................DLB-135

Street and Smith......................DLB-49

Streeter, Edward 1891-1976.............DLB-11

Streeter, Thomas Winthrop 1883-1965...DLB-140

Stretton, Hesba 1832-1911..........DLB-163, 190

Stribling, T. S. 1881-1965 ....DLB-9

Der Stricker circa 1190-circa 1250.......DLB-138

Strickland, Samuel 1804-1867 ....DLB-99

Strindberg, August 1849-1912..........DLB-259

Stringer, Arthur 1874-1950 ....DLB-92

Stringer and Townsend DLB-49

Strittmatter, Erwin 1912-1994 ....DLB-69

Strniša, Gregor 1930-1987..............DLB-181

Strode, William 1630-1645 ....DLB-126

Strong, L. A. G. 1896-1958 ....DLB-191

Strother, David Hunter (Porte Crayon)
1816-1888....................DLB-3, 248

Strouse, Jean 1945- DLB-111

Strugatsky, Arkadii Natanovich
1925- DLB-302

Strugatsky, Boris Natanovich 1933- DLB-302

Stuart, Dabney 1937- DLB-105
    "Knots into Webs: Some
    Autobiographical Sources"......DLB-105

Stuart, Jesse 1906-1984.....DLB-9, 48, 102; Y-84

Lyle Stuart [publishing house]...........DLB-46

Stuart, Ruth McEnery 1849?-1917......DLB-202

Stub, Ambrosius 1705-1758.............DLB-300

Stubbs, Harry Clement (see Clement, Hal)

Stubenberg, Johann Wilhelm von
1619-1663......................DLB-164

Stuckenberg, Viggo 1763-1905..........DLB-300

Studebaker, William V. 1947- DLB-256

Studies in American Jewish Literature........Y-02

Studio..............................DLB-112

Stump, Al 1916-1995.................DLB-241

Sturgeon, Theodore
1918-1985 .... DLB-8; Y-85

Sturges, Preston 1898-1959 ....DLB-26

Styron, William
1925- DLB-2, 143, 299; Y-80; CDALB-6
    Tribute to James Dickey Y-97

Suard, Jean-Baptiste-Antoine
1732-1817 ....DLB-314

Suárez, Clementina 1902-1991 ....DLB-290

Suárez, Mario 1925- DLB-82

Suassuna, Ariano 1927- DLB-307

Such, Peter 1939- DLB-60

Suckling, Sir John 1609-1641?.......DLB-58, 126

Suckow, Ruth 1892-1960...........DLB-9, 102

Sudermann, Hermann 1857-1928.......DLB-118

Sue, Eugène 1804-1857................DLB-119

Cumulative Index

Sue, Marie-Joseph (see Sue, Eugène)

Suetonius circa A.D. 69-post A.D. 122 .... DLB-211

Suggs, Simon (see Hooper, Johnson Jones)

Sui Sin Far (see Eaton, Edith Maude)

Suits, Gustav 1883-1956.... DLB-220; CDWLB-4

Sukenick, Ronald 1932-2004 ...... DLB-173; Y-81

    An Author's Response Y-82

Sukhovo-Kobylin, Aleksandr Vasil'evich
1817-1903..................... DLB-277

Suknaski, Andrew 1942- DLB-53

Sullivan, Alan 1868-1947 .... DLB-92

Sullivan, C. Gardner 1886-1965........ DLB-26

Sullivan, Frank 1892-1976 .... DLB-11

Sulte, Benjamin 1841-1923............ DLB-99

Sulzberger, Arthur Hays 1891-1968 ..... DLB-127

Sulzberger, Arthur Ochs 1926- DLB-127

Sulzer, Johann Georg 1720-1779 .... DLB-97

Sumarokov, Aleksandr Petrovich
1717-1777 .... DLB-150

Summers, Hollis 1916-1987 .... DLB-6

Sumner, Charles 1811-1874 .... DLB-235

Sumner, William Graham 1840-1910..... DLB-270

Henry A. Sumner
[publishing house] DLB-49

Sundman, Per Olof 1922-1992 .... DLB-257

Supervielle, Jules 1884-1960 .... DLB-258

Surtees, Robert Smith 1803-1864 .... DLB-21

    The R. S. Surtees Society.............. Y-98

Sutcliffe, Matthew 1550?-1629 .... DLB-281

Sutcliffe, William 1971- DLB-271

Sutherland, Efua Theodora 1924-1996... DLB-117

Sutherland, John 1919-1956 .... DLB-68

Sutro, Alfred 1863-1933 .... DLB-10

Svava Jakobsdóttir 1930- DLB-293

Svendsen, Hanne Marie 1933- DLB-214

Svevo, Italo (Ettore Schmitz)
1861-1928 .... DLB-264

Swados, Harvey 1920-1972............. DLB-2

Swain, Charles 1801-1874............. DLB-32

Swallow Press DLB-46

Swan Sonnenschein Limited.......... DLB-106

Swanberg, W. A. 1907-1992 .... DLB-103

Swedish Literature
The Literature of the Modern
Breakthrough................ DLB-259

Swenson, May 1919-1989 .... DLB-5

Swerling, Jo 1897-1964 .... DLB-44

Swift, Graham 1949- DLB-194, 326

Swift, Jonathan
1667-1745 .... DLB-39, 95, 101; CDBLB-2

Swinburne, A. C.
1837-1909 .... DLB-35, 57; CDBLB-4

    Under the Microscope (1872)........ DLB-35

Swineshead, Richard floruit circa 1350... DLB-115

Swinnerton, Frank 1884-1982........... DLB-34

Swisshelm, Jane Grey 1815-1884 .... DLB-43

Swope, Herbert Bayard 1882-1958....... DLB-25

Swords, James ?-1844 .... DLB-73

Swords, Thomas 1763-1843 .... DLB-73

T. and J. Swords and Company DLB-49

Swynnerton, Thomas (John Roberts)
circa 1500-1554 .... DLB-281

Sykes, Ella C. ?-1939 .... DLB-174

Sylvester, Josuah 1562 or 1563-1618 .... DLB-121

Symonds, Emily Morse (see Paston, George)

Symonds, John Addington
1840-1893 .... DLB-57, 144

    "Personal Style" (1890) DLB-57

Symons, A. J. A. 1900-1941 .... DLB-149

Symons, Arthur 1865-1945........ DLB-19, 57, 149

Symons, Julian 1912-1994...... DLB-87, 155; Y-92

    Julian Symons at Eighty............... Y-92

Symons, Scott 1933- DLB-53

Synge, John Millington
1871-1909 .... DLB-10, 19; CDBLB-5

Synge Summer School: J. M. Synge
and the Irish Theater, Rathdrum,
County Wiclow, Ireland Y-93

Syrett, Netta 1865-1943 .... DLB-135, 197

The System of Nature, Paul Henri Thiry,
baron d'Holbach (as Jean-Baptiste
de Mirabaud).................. DLB-314

Szabó, Lőrinc 1900-1957 .... DLB-215

Szabó, Magda 1917- DLB-215

Szymborska, Wisława
1923- DLB-232, Y-96; CDWLB-4

    Nobel Lecture 1996:
The Poet and the World Y-96

T

Taban lo Liyong 1939?- DLB-125

al-Tabari 839-923 .... DLB-311

Tablada, José Juan 1871-1945.......... DLB-290

Le Tableau de Paris, Louis-Sébastien
Mercier..................... DLB-314

Tabori, George 1914- DLB-245

Tabucchi, Antonio 1943- DLB-196

Taché, Joseph-Charles 1820-1894........ DLB-99

Tachihara Masaaki 1926-1980 .... DLB-182

Tacitus circa A.D. 55-circa A.D. 117
.... DLB-211; CDWLB-1

Tadijanović, Dragutin 1905- DLB-181

Tafdrup, Pia 1952- DLB-214

Tafolla, Carmen 1951- DLB-82

Taggard, Genevieve 1894-1948 .... DLB-45

Taggart, John 1942- DLB-193

Tagger, Theodor (see Bruckner, Ferdinand)

Tagore, Rabindranath 1861-1941 ...... DLB-323

Taiheiki late fourteenth century DLB-203

Tait, J. Selwin, and Sons DLB-49

Tait's Edinburgh Magazine 1832-1861...... DLB-110

The Takarazaka Revue Company Y-91

Talander (see Bohse, August)

Talese, Gay 1932- DLB-185

    Tribute to Irwin Shaw Y-84

Talev, Dimitr 1898-1966.............. DLB-181

Taliaferro, H. E. 1811-1875............ DLB-202

Tallent, Elizabeth 1954- DLB-130

TallMountain, Mary 1918-1994........ DLB-193

Talvj 1797-1870 .... DLB-59, 133

Tamási, Áron 1897-1966.............. DLB-215

Tammsaare, A. H.
1878-1940............ DLB-220; CDWLB-4

Tan, Amy 1952- DLB-173, 312; CDALB-7

Tandori, Dezső 1938- DLB-232

Tanner, Thomas 1673/1674-1735 ...... DLB-213

Tanizaki Jun'ichirō 1886-1965 .... DLB-180

Tapahonso, Luci 1953- DLB-175

The Mark Taper Forum DLB-7

Taradash, Daniel 1913-2003............ DLB-44

Tarasov-Rodionov, Aleksandr Ignat'evich
1885-1938 .... DLB-272

Tarbell, Ida M. 1857-1944.............. DLB-47

Tardieu, Jean 1903-1995............... DLB-321

Tardivel, Jules-Paul 1851-1905 .... DLB-99

Targan, Barry 1932- DLB-130

    Tribute to John Gardner Y-82

Tarkington, Booth 1869-1946......... DLB-9, 102

Tashlin, Frank 1913-1972 .... DLB-44

Tasma (Jessie Couvreur) 1848-1897 .... DLB-230

Tate, Allen 1899-1979........DLB-4, 45, 63; DS-17

Tate, James 1943- DLB-5, 169

Tate, Nahum circa 1652-1715 .... DLB-80

Tatian circa 830 .... DLB-148

Taufer, Veno 1933- DLB-181

Tauler, Johannes circa 1300-1361 ......DLB-179

Tavares, Salette 1922-1994 .... DLB-287

Tavčar, Ivan 1851-1923 ....DLB-147

Taverner, Richard ca. 1505-1575 ...... DLB-236

Taylor, Ann 1782-1866 .... DLB-163

Taylor, Bayard 1825-1878 ..... DLB-3, 189, 250

Taylor, Bert Leston 1866-1921 .... DLB-25

Taylor, Charles H. 1846-1921 .... DLB-25

Taylor, Edward circa 1642-1729 .... DLB-24

Taylor, Elizabeth 1912-1975 .... DLB-139

Taylor, Sir Henry 1800-1886 .... DLB-32

Taylor, Henry 1942- DLB-5

    Who Owns American Literature Y-94

Taylor, Jane 1783-1824 .... DLB-163

Taylor, Jeremy circa 1613-1667 . . . . DLB-151	Thacher, James 1754-1844 . . . . DLB-37	Politics and the Theater DLB-263
Taylor, John 1577 or 1578 - 1653 . . . . DLB-121	Thacher, John Boyd 1847-1909 . . . . DLB-187	Practical Matters DLB-263
Taylor, Mildred D. 1943- DLB-52	Thackeray, William Makepeace 1811-1863 . . . DLB-21, 55, 159, 163; CDBLB-4	Prologues, Epilogues, Epistles to Readers, and Excerpts from Plays DLB-263
Taylor, Peter 1917-1994 . . . DLB-218, 278; Y-81, 94	Thames and Hudson Limited DLB-112	
Taylor, Susie King 1848-1912 . . . . DLB-221	Thanet, Octave (see French, Alice)	The Publication of English Renaissance Plays DLB-62
Taylor, William Howland 1901-1966 . . . . . DLB-241	Thaxter, Celia Laighton 1835-1894 . . . . DLB-239	
William Taylor and Company DLB-49		Regulations for the Theater DLB-263
Teale, Edwin Way 1899-1980 . . . . DLB-275	Thayer, Caroline Matilda Warren 1785-1844 . . . . DLB-200	Sources for the Study of Tudor and Stuart Drama DLB-62
Teasdale, Sara 1884-1933 . . . . DLB-45		Stage Censorship: "The Rejected Statement" (1911), by Bernard Shaw [excerpts] DLB-10
Teffi, Nadezhda 1872-1952 . . . . DLB-317	Thayer, Douglas H. 1929- DLB-256	
Teillier, Jorge 1935-1996 . . . . DLB-283	Theater Black Theatre: A Forum [excerpts] DLB-38	
Telles, Lygia Fagundes 1924- DLB-113, 307		Synge Summer School: J. M. Synge and the Irish Theater, Rathdrum, County Wiclow, Ireland Y-93
The Temper of the West: William Jovanovich Y-02	Community and Commentators: Black Theatre and Its Critics DLB-38	
Temple, Sir William 1555?-1627 . . . . DLB-281	German Drama from Naturalism to Fascism: 1889-1933 . . . . DLB-118	The Theater in Shakespeare's Time . . . DLB-62
Temple, Sir William 1628-1699 . . . . DLB-101		The Theatre Guild DLB-7
Temple, William F. 1914-1989 . . . . DLB-255	A Look at the Contemporary Black Theatre Movement DLB-38	The Townely Plays fifteenth and sixteenth centuries DLB-146
Temrizov, A. (see Marchenko, Anastasia Iakovlevna)	The Lord Chamberlain's Office and Stage Censorship in England DLB-10	The Year in British Drama Y-99–01
Tench, Watkin ca. 1758-1833 . . . . DLB-230		The Year in Drama: London Y-90
Tencin, Alexandrine-Claude Guérin de 1682-1749 . . . . DLB-314	New Forces at Work in the American Theatre: 1915-1925 . . . . DLB-7	The Year in London Theatre Y-92
	Off Broadway and Off-Off Broadway . . . DLB-7	*A Yorkshire Tragedy* DLB-58
Tender Is the Night (Documentary) DLB-273	Oregon Shakespeare Festival Y-00	Theaters
Tendriakov, Vladimir Fedorovich 1923-1984 . . . . DLB-302	Plays, Playwrights, and Playgoers DLB-84	The Abbey Theatre and Irish Drama, 1900-1945 . . . . DLB-10
	Playwrights on the Theater DLB-80	
Tenn, William 1919- DLB-8	Playwrights and Professors DLB-13	Actors Theatre of Louisville DLB-7
Tennant, Emma 1937- DLB-14	Producing *Dear Bunny, Dear Volodya: The Friendship and the Feud* Y-97	American Conservatory Theatre DLB-7
Tenney, Tabitha Gilman 1762-1837 . . . DLB-37, 200		Arena Stage DLB-7
Tennyson, Alfred 1809-1892 . . DLB-32; CDBLB-4	Viewpoint: Politics and Performance, by David Edgar DLB-13	Black Theaters and Theater Organizations in America, 1961-1982: A Research List DLB-38
On Some of the Characteristics of Modern Poetry and On the Lyrical Poems of Alfred Tennyson (1831) DLB-32	Writing for the Theatre, by Harold Pinter DLB-13	
		The Dallas Theater Center DLB-7
	The Year in Drama Y-82–85, 87–98	Eugene O'Neill Memorial Theater Center DLB-7
Tennyson, Frederick 1807-1898 . . . . DLB-32	The Year in U.S. Drama Y-00	
Tenorio, Arthur 1924- DLB-209	Theater, English and Irish Anti-Theatrical Tracts DLB-263	The Goodman Theatre DLB-7
"The Tenth Stage," Marie-Jean-Antoine-Nicolas Caritat, marquis de Condorcet DLB-314		The Guthrie Theater DLB-7
	The Chester Plays circa 1505-1532; revisions until 1575 . . . . DLB-146	The Mark Taper Forum DLB-7
Tepl, Johannes von circa 1350-1414/1415 . . . . DLB-179	Dangerous Years: London Theater, 1939-1945 . . . . DLB-10	The National Theatre and the Royal Shakespeare Company: The National Companies DLB-13
Tepliakov, Viktor Grigor'evich 1804-1842 . . . . DLB-205		
	A Defense of Actors DLB-263	Off-Loop Theatres DLB-7
Terence circa 184 B.C.-159 B.C. or after DLB-211; CDWLB-1	The Development of Lighting in the Staging of Drama, 1900-1945 . . . . DLB-10	The Royal Court Theatre and the English Stage Company DLB-13
St. Teresa of Ávila 1515-1582 . . . . DLB-318	Education DLB-263	The Royal Court Theatre and the New Drama DLB-10
Terhune, Albert Payson 1872-1942 . . . . DLB-9	The End of English Stage Censorship, 1945-1968 . . . . DLB-13	
Terhune, Mary Virginia 1830-1922 . . . . DS-13		The Takarazaka Revue Company Y-91
Terpigorev, Sergei Nikolaevich (S. Atava) 1841-1895 . . . . DLB-277	Epigrams and Satires DLB-263	Thegan and the Astronomer fl. circa 850 . . . . DLB-148
	Eyewitnesses and Historians DLB-263	
Terry, Megan 1932- DLB-7, 249	Fringe and Alternative Theater in Great Britain DLB-13	Thelwall, John 1764-1834 . . . . DLB-93, 158
Terson, Peter 1932- DLB-13		Theocritus circa 300 B.C.-260 B.C. DLB-176
Tesich, Steve 1943-1996 . . . . Y-83	The Great War and the Theater, 1914-1918 [Great Britain] DLB-10	Theodorescu, Ion N. (see Arghezi, Tudor)
Tessa, Delio 1886-1939 . . . . DLB-114		Theodulf circa 760-circa 821 . . . . DLB-148
Testori, Giovanni 1923-1993 . . . . DLB-128, 177	Licensing Act of 1737 . . . . DLB-84	Theophrastus circa 371 B.C.-287 B.C. DLB-176
	Morality Plays: *Mankind* circa 1450-1500 and *Everyman* circa 1500 . . . . DLB-146	Thériault, Yves 1915-1983 . . . . DLB-88
Texas The Year in Texas Literature Y-98		Thério, Adrien 1925- DLB-53
	The New Variorum Shakespeare Y-85	Theroux, Paul 1941- DLB-2, 218; CDALB-7
Tey, Josephine 1896?-1952 . . . . DLB-77	N-Town Plays circa 1468 to early sixteenth century DLB-146	Thesiger, Wilfred 1910-2003 . . . . DLB-204

Cumulative Index

They All Came to Paris DS-15

Thibaudeau, Colleen 1925- DLB-88

Thiele, Colin 1920- DLB-289

Thielen, Benedict 1903-1965 . . . . DLB-102

Thiong'o Ngugi wa (see Ngugi wa Thiong'o)

Thiroux d'Arconville, Marie-Geneviève 1720-1805. . . . . DLB-314

This Quarter 1925-1927, 1929-1932 . . . . DS-15

Thoma, Ludwig 1867-1921. . . . . DLB-66

Thoma, Richard 1902-1974 . . . . DLB-4

Thomas, Audrey 1935- DLB-60

Thomas, D. M. 1935- . . . DLB-40, 207, 299; Y-82; CDBLB-8

    The Plagiarism Controversy Y-82

Thomas, Dylan 1914-1953. . . . . . . DLB-13, 20, 139; CDBLB-7

    The Dylan Thomas Celebration Y-99

Thomas, Ed 1961- DLB-310

Thomas, Edward 1878-1917. . . . . .DLB-19, 98, 156, 216

    The Friends of the Dymock Poets Y-00

Thomas, Frederick William 1806-1866 . . DLB-202

Thomas, Gwyn 1913-1981. . . . . DLB-15, 245

Thomas, Isaiah 1750-1831 . . . . . . .DLB-43, 73, 187

Thomas, Johann 1624-1679 . . . . DLB-168

Thomas, John 1900-1932 . . . . DLB-4

Thomas, Joyce Carol 1938- DLB-33

Thomas, Lewis 1913-1993 . . . . .DLB-275

Thomas, Lorenzo 1944- DLB-41

Thomas, Norman 1884-1968 . . . . DLB-303

Thomas, R. S. 1915-2000 . . . . . DLB-27; CDBLB-8

Isaiah Thomas [publishing house] DLB-49

Thomasîn von Zerclære circa 1186-circa 1259 . . . . DLB-138

Thomason, George 1602?-1666 . . . . DLB-213

Thomasius, Christian 1655-1728 . . . . DLB-168

Thompson, Daniel Pierce 1795-1868 . . . . DLB-202

Thompson, David 1770-1857 . . . . DLB-99

Thompson, Dorothy 1893-1961 . . . . DLB-29

Thompson, E. P. 1924-1993 . . . . DLB-242

Thompson, Flora 1876-1947 . . . . DLB-240

Thompson, Francis 1859-1907. . . . . DLB-19; CDBLB-5

Thompson, George Selden (see Selden, George)

Thompson, Henry Yates 1838-1928 . . . . . DLB-184

Thompson, Hunter S. 1939-2005 . . . . DLB-185

Thompson, Jim 1906-1977 . . . . DLB-226

Thompson, John 1938-1976 . . . . DLB-60

Thompson, John R. 1823-1873 . . . . DLB-3, 73, 248

Thompson, Lawrance 1906-1973 . . . . DLB-103

Thompson, Maurice 1844-1901 . . . . .DLB-71, 74

Thompson, Ruth Plumly 1891-1976 . . . . . DLB-22

Thompson, Thomas Phillips 1843-1933 . . . DLB-99

Thompson, William 1775-1833 . . . . DLB-158

Thompson, William Tappan 1812-1882 . . . . DLB-3, 11, 248

Thomson, Cockburn "Modern Style" (1857) [excerpt] DLB-57

Thomson, Edward William 1849-1924 . . . DLB-92

Thomson, James 1700-1748 . . . . DLB-95

Thomson, James 1834-1882 . . . . DLB-35

Thomson, Joseph 1858-1895 . . . . .DLB-174

Thomson, Mortimer 1831-1875 . . . . DLB-11

Thomson, Rupert 1955- DLB-267

Thon, Melanie Rae 1957- DLB-244

Thor Vilhjálmsson 1925- DLB-293

Þórarinn Eldjárn 1949- DLB-293

Þórbergur Þórðarson 1888-1974. . . . . DLB-293

Thoreau, Henry David 1817-1862 . . . . DLB-1, 183, 223, 270, 298; DS-5; CDALB-2

    The Thoreau Society Y-99

    The Thoreauvian Pilgrimage: The Structure of an American Cult . . DLB-223

Thorne, William 1568?-1630 . . . . DLB-281

Thornton, John F. [Repsonse to Ken Auletta] Y-97

Thorpe, Adam 1956- DLB-231

Thorpe, Thomas Bangs 1815-1878. . . . . DLB-3, 11, 248

Thorup, Kirsten 1942- DLB-214

Thotl, Birgitte 1610-1662 . . . . DLB-300

Thrale, Hester Lynch (see Piozzi, Hester Lynch [Thrale])

The Three Marias: A Landmark Case in Portuguese Literary History (Maria Isabel Barreno, 1939- ; Maria Teresa Horta, 1937- ; Maria Velho da Costa, 1938-) DLB-287

Thubron, Colin 1939- DLB-204, 231

Thucydides circa 455 B.C.-circa 395 B.C. DLB-176

Thulstrup, Thure de 1848-1930 . . . . DLB-188

Thümmel, Moritz August von 1738-1817 . . . . DLB-97

Thurber, James 1894-1961 . . . . DLB-4, 11, 22, 102; CDALB-5

Thurman, Wallace 1902-1934 . . . . DLB-51

    "Negro Poets and Their Poetry" DLB-50

Thwaite, Anthony 1930- DLB-40

    The Booker Prize, Address Y-86

Thwaites, Reuben Gold 1853-1913 . . . . . . DLB-47

Tibullus circa 54 B.C.-circa 19 B.C. DLB-211

Ticknor, George 1791-1871 . . . . .DLB-1, 59, 140, 235

Ticknor and Fields DLB-49

Ticknor and Fields (revived) DLB-46

Tieck, Ludwig 1773-1853 . . . . DLB-90; CDWLB-2

Tietjens, Eunice 1884-1944 . . . . DLB-54

Tikkanen, Märta 1935- DLB-257

Tilghman, Christopher circa 1948 . . . . . . DLB-244

Tilney, Edmund circa 1536-1610 . . . . DLB-136

Charles Tilt [publishing house] DLB-106

J. E. Tilton and Company DLB-49

Time-Life Books DLB-46

Times Books DLB-46

Timothy, Peter circa 1725-1782 . . . . DLB-43

Timrava 1867-1951 . . . . DLB-215

Timrod, Henry 1828-1867 . . . . DLB-3, 248

Tindal, Henrietta 1818?-1879 . . . . DLB-199

Tinker, Chauncey Brewster 1876-1963 . . . . DLB-140

Tinsley Brothers DLB-106

Tiptree, James, Jr. 1915-1987 . . . . DLB-8

Tišma, Aleksandar 1924-2003 . . . . DLB-181

Titus, Edward William 1870-1952 . . . . DLB-4; DS-15

Tiutchev, Fedor Ivanovich 1803-1873 . . . . DLB-205

Tlali, Miriam 1933- DLB-157, 225

Todd, Barbara Euphan 1890-1976 . . . . . . DLB-160

Todorov, Tzvetan 1939- DLB-242

Tofte, Robert 1561 or 1562-1619 or 1620 . . . . .DLB-172

Tóibín, Colm 1955- DLB-271

Toklas, Alice B. 1877-1967 . . . . DLB-4; DS-15

Tokuda Shūsei 1872-1943 . . . . DLB-180

Toland, John 1670-1722 . . . . DLB-252

Tolkien, J. R. R. 1892-1973 . . . . . . DLB-15, 160, 255; CDBLB-6

Toller, Ernst 1893-1939 . . . . DLB-124

Tollet, Elizabeth 1694-1754 . . . . DLB-95

Tolson, Melvin B. 1898-1966 . . . . .DLB-48, 76

Tolstaya, Tatyana 1951- DLB-285

Tolstoy, Aleksei Konstantinovich 1817-1875 . . . . .DLB-238

Tolstoy, Aleksei Nikolaevich 1883-1945 . . .DLB-272

Tolstoy, Leo 1828-1910 . . . . DLB-238

Tomalin, Claire 1933- DLB-155

Tómas Guðmundsson 1901-1983 . . . . DLB-293

Tomasi di Lampedusa, Giuseppe 1896-1957 . . . . .DLB-177

Tomlinson, Charles 1927- DLB-40

Tomlinson, H. M. 1873-1958 . . . .DLB-36, 100, 195

Abel Tompkins [publishing house] DLB-49

Tompson, Benjamin 1642-1714 . . . . DLB-24

Tomson, Graham R. (see Watson, Rosamund Marriott)

Ton'a 1289-1372 . . . . DLB-203

Tondelli, Pier Vittorio 1955-1991 . . . . DLB-196

Tonks, Rosemary 1932- DLB-14, 207

Tonna, Charlotte Elizabeth 1790-1846 . . . DLB-163

Jacob Tonson the Elder [publishing house] DLB-170

Toole, John Kennedy 1937-1969 . . . . Y-81

Toomer, Jean
 1894-1967 . . . . .DLB-45, 51; CDALB-4

Topsoe, Vilhelm 1840-1881 . . . . .DLB-300

Tor Books DLB-46

Torberg, Friedrich 1908-1979. . . . . .DLB-85

Torga, Miguel (Adolfo Correira da Rocha)
 1907-1995 . . . . .DLB-287

Torre, Francisco de la ?-? DLB-318

Torrence, Ridgely 1874-1950 . . . . .DLB-54, 249

Torrente Ballester, Gonzalo
 1910-1999 . . . . .DLB-322

Torres-Metzger, Joseph V. 1933- DLB-122

Torres Naharro, Bartolomé de
 1485?-1523? .DLB-318

El Tostado (see Madrigal, Alfonso Fernández de)

Toth, Susan Allen 1940- Y-86

Richard Tottell [publishing house] DLB-170

"The Printer to the Reader,"
 (1557) DLB-167

Tough-Guy Literature DLB-9

Touré, Askia Muhammad 1938- DLB-41

Tourgée, Albion W. 1838-1905 . . . . .DLB-79

Tournemir, Elizaveta Sailhas de (see Tur, Evgeniia)

Tourneur, Cyril circa 1580-1626 . . . . .DLB-58

Tournier, Michel 1924- DLB-83

Frank Tousey [publishing house] DLB-49

Tower Publications. DLB-46

Towne, Benjamin circa 1740-1793 . . . . . . .DLB-43

Towne, Robert 1936- DLB-44

The Townely Plays fifteenth and sixteenth
 centuries DLB-146

Townsend, Sue 1946- DLB-271

Townshend, Aurelian
 by 1583-circa 1651 . . . . .DLB-121

Toy, Barbara 1908-2001. . . . . .DLB-204

Tozzi, Federigo 1883-1920 . . . . .DLB-264

Tracy, Honor 1913-1989 . . . . .DLB-15

Traherne, Thomas 1637?-1674 . . . . .DLB-131

Traill, Catharine Parr 1802-1899 . . . . .DLB-99

Train, Arthur 1875-1945 . . . . .DLB-86; DS-16

Tranquilli, Secondino (see Silone, Ignazio)

The Transatlantic Publishing Company . . .DLB-49

The Transatlantic Review 1924-1925 . . . . DS-15

The Transcendental Club
 1836-1840 . . . . DLB-1; DLB-223

Transcendentalism DLB-1; DLB-223; DS-5

 "A Response from America," by
  John A. Heraud DS-5

 Publications and Social Movements DLB-1

 The Rise of Transcendentalism,
  1815-1860. . . . . DS-5

 Transcendentalists, American DS-5

 "What Is Transcendentalism? By a
  Thinking Man," by James
  Kinnard Jr. DS-5

transition 1927-1938 . . . . DS-15

Translations (Vernacular) in the Crowns of
 Castile and Aragon 1352-1515 . . . . . .DLB-286

Tranströmer, Tomas 1931- DLB-257

Tranter, John 1943- DLB-289

Travel Writing

 American Travel Writing, 1776-1864
  (checklist) DLB-183

 British Travel Writing, 1940-1997
  (checklist) DLB-204

 Travel Writers of the Late
  Middle Ages DLB-286

 (1876-1909. DLB-174

 (1837-1875 . . . . DLB-166

 (1910-1939 . . . . DLB-195

Traven, B. 1882?/1890?-1969?. DLB-9, 56

Travers, Ben 1886-1980 . . . . .DLB-10, 233

Travers, P. L. (Pamela Lyndon)
 1899-1996 . . . . .DLB-160

Trediakovsky, Vasilii Kirillovich
 1703-1769 . . . . .DLB-150

Treece, Henry 1911-1966. . . . . .DLB-160

Treitel, Jonathan 1959- DLB-267

Trejo, Ernesto 1950-1991. . . . . .DLB-122

Trelawny, Edward John
 1792-1881 . . . . DLB-110, 116, 144

Tremain, Rose 1943- DLB-14, 271

Tremblay, Michel 1942- DLB-60

Trent, William P. 1862-1939 . . . . DLB-47, 71

Trescot, William Henry 1822-1898 . . . . . . .DLB-30

Tressell, Robert (Robert Phillipe Noonan)
 1870-1911 . . . . .DLB-197

Trevelyan, Sir George Otto
 1838-1928 . . . . .DLB-144

Trevisa, John circa 1342-circa 1402 . . . . . .DLB-146

Trevisan, Dalton 1925- DLB-307

Trevor, William 1928- DLB-14, 139

Triana, José 1931- DLB-305

Trierer Floyris circa 1170-1180 . . . . .DLB-138

Trifonov, Iurii Valentinovich
 1925-1981 . . . . .DLB-302

Trillin, Calvin 1935- DLB-185

Trilling, Lionel 1905-1975 . . . . .DLB-28, 63

Trilussa 1871-1950 . . . . .DLB-114

Trimmer, Sarah 1741-1810 . . . . .DLB-158

Triolet, Elsa 1896-1970. . . . . .DLB-72

Tripp, John 1927- DLB-40

Trocchi, Alexander 1925-1984. . . . . .DLB-15

Troisi, Dante 1920-1989 . . . . .DLB-196

Trollope, Anthony
 1815-1882 . . . . DLB-21, 57, 159; CDBLB-4

 Novel-Reading: *The Works of Charles
  Dickens; The Works of W. Makepeace
  Thackeray* (1879) DLB-21

 The Trollope Societies. Y-00

Trollope, Frances 1779-1863. . . . . .DLB-21, 166

Trollope, Joanna 1943- DLB-207

Troop, Elizabeth 1931- DLB-14

Tropicália. DLB-307

Trotter, Catharine 1679-1749 . . . . .DLB-84, 252

Trotti, Lamar 1898-1952 . . . . .DLB-44

Trottier, Pierre 1925- DLB-60

Trotzig, Birgitta 1929- DLB-257

Troupe, Quincy Thomas, Jr. 1943- DLB-41

John F. Trow and Company DLB-49

Trowbridge, John Townsend 1827-1916. . .DLB-202

Trudel, Jean-Louis 1967- DLB-251

True History of the Kelly Gang, 2001 Booker Prize winner,
 Peter Carey DLB-326

Truillier-Lacombe, Joseph-Patrice
 1807-1863 . . . . .DLB-99

Trumbo, Dalton 1905-1976 . . . . .DLB-26

Trumbull, Benjamin 1735-1820 . . . . .DLB-30

Trumbull, John 1750-1831 . . . . .DLB-31

Trumbull, John 1756-1843 . . . . .DLB-183

Truth, Sojourner 1797?-1883 . . . . .DLB-239

Tscherning, Andreas 1611-1659 . . . . .DLB-164

Tsubouchi Shōyō 1859-1935 . . . . .DLB-180

Tsvetaeva, Marina Ivanovna
 1892-1941 . . . . .DLB-295

Tuchman, Barbara W.
 Tribute to Alfred A. Knopf Y-84

Tucholsky, Kurt 1890-1935 . . . . .DLB-56

Tucker, Charlotte Maria
 1821-1893 . . . . .DLB-163, 190

Tucker, George 1775-1861 . . . . .DLB-3, 30, 248

Tucker, James 1808?-1866? DLB-230

Tucker, Nathaniel Beverley
 1784-1851 .DLB-3, 248

Tucker, St. George 1752-1827 . . . . .DLB-37

Tuckerman, Frederick Goddard
 1821-1873 . . . . .DLB-243

Tuckerman, Henry Theodore 1813-1871. . . . .DLB-64

Tumas, Juozas (see Vaizgantas)

Tunis, John R. 1889-1975. . . . . DLB-22, 171

Tunstall, Cuthbert 1474-1559 . . . . .DLB-132

Tunström, Göran 1937-2000 . . . . .DLB-257

Tuohy, Frank 1925- DLB-14, 139

Tupper, Martin F. 1810-1889 . . . . .DLB-32

Tur, Evgeniia 1815-1892 . . . . .DLB-238

Turbyfill, Mark 1896-1991. . . . . .DLB-45

Turco, Lewis 1934- Y-84

 Tribute to John Ciardi. Y-86

Turgenev, Aleksandr Ivanovich
 1784-1845 . . . . .DLB-198

Turgenev, Ivan Sergeevich
 1818-1883 . . . . .DLB-238

Turgot, baron de l'Aulne, Anne-Robert-Jacques
 1727-1781 . . . . .DLB-314

Cumulative Index

"Memorandum on Local Government" DLB-314
Turnbull, Alexander H. 1868-1918 ...... DLB-184
Turnbull, Andrew 1921-1970 .... DLB-103
Turnbull, Gael 1928- DLB-40
Turnèbe, Odet de 1552-1581 .... DLB-327
Turner, Arlin 1909-1980 .... DLB-103
Turner, Charles (Tennyson) 1808-1879 .... DLB-32
Turner, Ethel 1872-1958 .... DLB-230
Turner, Frederick 1943- DLB-40
Turner, Frederick Jackson 1861-1932 .... DLB-17, 186
A Conversation between William Riggan and Janette Turner Hospital Y-02
Turner, Joseph Addison 1826-1868 ...... DLB-79
Turpin, Waters Edward 1910-1968 ...... DLB-51
Turrini, Peter 1944- DLB-124
Tusquets, Esther 1936- DLB-322
Tutuola, Amos 1920-1997 ... DLB-125; CDWLB-3
Twain, Mark (see Clemens, Samuel Langhorne)
Tweedie, Ethel Brilliana circa 1860-1940 .... DLB-174
A Century of Poetry, a Lifetime of Collecting: J. M. Edelstein's Collection of Twentieth-Century American Poetry YB-02
Twombly, Wells 1935-1977 .... DLB-241
Twysden, Sir Roger 1597-1672 .... DLB-213
Tyard, Pontus de 1521?-1605 .... DLB-327
Ty-Casper, Linda 1931- DLB-312
Tyler, Anne 1941- DLB-6, 143; Y-82; CDALB-7
Tyler, Mary Palmer 1775-1866 .... DLB-200
Tyler, Moses Coit 1835-1900 .... DLB-47, 64
Tyler, Royall 1757-1826 .... DLB-37
Tylor, Edward Burnett 1832-1917 ...... DLB-57
Tynan, Katharine 1861-1931 ...... DLB-153, 240
Tyndale, William circa 1494-1536 ...... DLB-132
Tyree, Omar 1969- DLB-292

U

Uchida, Yoshiko 1921-1992 .. DLB-312; CDALB-7
Udall, Nicholas 1504-1556 .... DLB-62
Ugrešić, Dubravka 1949- DLB-181
Uhland, Ludwig 1787-1862 .... DLB-90
Uhse, Bodo 1904-1963 .... DLB-69
Ujević, Augustin "Tin" 1891-1955 .... DLB-147
Ulenhart, Niclas fl. circa 1600 .... DLB-164
Ulfeldt, Leonora Christina 1621-1698 ... DLB-300
Ulibarrí, Sabine R. 1919-2003 .... DLB-82
Ulica, Jorge 1870-1926 .... DLB-82
Ulitskaya, Liudmila Evgen'evna 1943- DLB-285

Ulivi, Ferruccio 1912- DLB-196
Ulizio, B. George 1889-1969 .... DLB-140
Ulrich von Liechtenstein circa 1200-circa 1275 .... DLB-138
Ulrich von Zatzikhoven before 1194-after 1214 .... DLB-138
'Umar ibn Abi Rabi'ah 644-712 or 721 .. DLB-311
Unaipon, David 1872-1967 .... DLB-230
Unamuno, Miguel de 1864-1936 ... DLB-108, 322
Under, Marie 1883-1980 ... DLB-220; CDWLB-4
Underhill, Evelyn 1875-1941 .... DLB-240
Undset, Sigrid 1882-1949 .... DLB-297
Ungaretti, Giuseppe 1888-1970 .... DLB-114
Unger, Friederike Helene 1741-1813 .... DLB-94
United States Book Company DLB-49
Universal Publishing and Distributing Corporation DLB-46
University of Colorado Special Collections at the University of Colorado at Boulder Y-98
Indiana University Press Y-02
The University of Iowa Writers' Workshop Golden Jubilee Y-86
University of Missouri Press Y-01
University of South Carolina The G. Ross Roy Scottish Poetry Collection Y-89
Two Hundred Years of Rare Books and Literary Collections at the University of South Carolina Y-00
The University of South Carolina Press Y-94
University of Virginia The Book Arts Press at the University of Virginia Y-96
The Electronic Text Center and the Electronic Archive of Early American Fiction at the University of Virginia Library Y-98
University of Virginia Libraries Y-91
University of Wales Press DLB-112
University Press of Florida Y-00
University Press of Kansas Y-98
University Press of Mississippi Y-99
Unnur Benediktsdóttir Bjarklind (see Hulda)
Uno Chiyo 1897-1996 .... DLB-180
Unruh, Fritz von 1885-1970 .... DLB-56, 118
Unsworth, Barry 1930- DLB-194, 326
Unt, Mati 1944- DLB-232
The Unterberg Poetry Center of the 92nd Street Y Y-98
Untermeyer, Louis 1885-1977 .... DLB-303
T. Fisher Unwin [publishing house] DLB-106
Upchurch, Boyd B. (see Boyd, John)
Updike, John 1932- DLB-2, 5, 143, 218, 227; Y-80, 82; DS-3; CDALB-6
John Updike on the Internet Y-97

Tribute to Alfred A. Knopf Y-84
Tribute to John Ciardi Y-86
Upīts, Andrejs 1877-1970 .... DLB-220
Uppdal, Kristofer 1878-1961 .... DLB-297
Upton, Bertha 1849-1912 .... DLB-141
Upton, Charles 1948- DLB-16
Upton, Florence K. 1873-1922 .... DLB-141
Upward, Allen 1863-1926 .... DLB-36
Urban, Milo 1904-1982 .... DLB-215
Ureña de Henríquez, Salomé 1850-1897 . DLB-283
Urfé, Honoré d' 1567-1625 .... DLB-268
Urista, Alberto Baltazar (see Alurista)
Urquhart, Fred 1912-1995 .... DLB-139
Urrea, Luis Alberto 1955- DLB-209
Urzidil, Johannes 1896-1970 .... DLB-85
U.S.A. (Documentary) DLB-274
Usigli, Rodolfo 1905-1979 .... DLB-305
Usk, Thomas died 1388 .... DLB-146
Uslar Pietri, Arturo 1906-2001 .... DLB-113
Uspensky, Gleb Ivanovich 1843-1902 .... DLB-277
Ussher, James 1581-1656 .... DLB-213
Ustinov, Peter 1921-2004 .... DLB-13
Uttley, Alison 1884-1976 .... DLB-160
Uz, Johann Peter 1720-1796 .... DLB-97

V

Vadianus, Joachim 1484-1551 .... DLB-179
Vac, Bertrand (Aimé Pelletier) 1914- DLB-88
Vācietis, Ojārs 1933-1983 .... DLB-232
Vaculík, Ludvík 1926- DLB-232
Vaičiulaitis, Antanas 1906-1992 .... DLB-220
Vaičiūnaite, Judita 1937- DLB-232
Vail, Laurence 1891-1968 .... DLB-4
Vail, Petr L'vovich 1949- DLB-285
Vailland, Roger 1907-1965 .... DLB-83
Vaižgantas 1869-1933 .... DLB-220
Vajda, Ernest 1887-1954 .... DLB-44
Valdés, Alfonso de circa 1490?-1532 .... DLB-318
Valdés, Gina 1943- DLB-122
Valdes, Juan de 1508-1541 .... DLB-318
Valdez, Luis Miguel 1940- DLB-122
Valduga, Patrizia 1953- DLB-128
Vale Press DLB-112
Valente, José Angel 1929-2000 .... DLB-108
Valenzuela, Luisa 1938- ... DLB-113; CDWLB-3
Valera, Diego de 1412-1488 .... DLB-286
Valeri, Diego 1887-1976 .... DLB-128
Valerius Flaccus fl. circa A.D. 92 .... DLB-211
Valerius Maximus fl. circa A.D. 31 ...... DLB-211
Valéry, Paul 1871-1945 .... DLB-258

Valesio, Paolo 1939- DLB-196	Vasiliu, George (see Bacovia, George)	Vidal, Gore 1925- DLB-6, 152; CDALB-7
Valgardson, W. D. 1939- DLB-60	Vásquez, Richard 1928- DLB-209	Vidal, Mary Theresa 1815-1873 ....DLB-230
Valle, Luz 1899-1971 ....DLB-290	Vassa, Gustavus (see Equiano, Olaudah)	Vidmer, Richards 1898-1978 ....DLB-241
Valle, Víctor Manuel 1950- DLB-122	Vassalli, Sebastiano 1941- DLB-128, 196	Viebig, Clara 1860-1952 ....DLB-66
Valle-Inclán, Ramón del 1866-1936 ....DLB-134, 322	Vaugelas, Claude Favre de 1585-1650 ....DLB-268	Vieira, António, S. J. (Antonio Vieyra) 1608-1697 ....DLB-307
Vallejo, Armando 1949- DLB-122	Vaughan, Henry 1621-1695............DLB-131	Viereck, George Sylvester 1884-1962 .....DLB-54
Vallejo, César Abraham 1892-1938 ......DLB-290	Vaughan, Thomas 1621-1666 ....DLB-131	Viereck, Peter 1916- DLB-5
Vallès, Jules 1832-1885.................DLB-123	Vaughn, Robert 1592?-1667 ....DLB-213	Vietnam War (ended 1975) Resources for the Study of Vietnam War Literature DLB-9
Vallette, Marguerite Eymery (see Rachilde)	Vaux, Thomas, Lord 1509-1556 ....DLB-132	
Valverde, José María 1926-1996 ....DLB-108	Vazov, Ivan 1850-1921...... DLB-147; CDWLB-4	Viets, Roger 1738-1811 ....DLB-99
Vampilov, Aleksandr Valentinovich (A. Sanin) 1937-1972.....................DLB-302	Vázquez Montalbán, Manuel 1939- DLB-134, 322	Vigil-Piñon, Evangelina 1949- DLB-122
	Véa, Alfredo, Jr. 1950- DLB-209	Vigneault, Gilles 1928- DLB-60
Van Allsburg, Chris 1949- DLB-61	Veblen, Thorstein 1857-1929 ....DLB-246	Vigny, Alfred de 1797-1863 .... DLB-119, 192, 217
Van Anda, Carr 1864-1945 ....DLB-25	Vedel, Anders Sørensen 1542-1616 ......DLB-300	Vigolo, Giorgio 1894-1983 ....DLB-114
Vanbrugh, Sir John 1664-1726..........DLB-80	Vega, Janine Pommy 1942- DLB-16	Vik, Bjorg 1935- DLB-297
Vance, Jack 1916?- DLB-8	Veiller, Anthony 1903-1965............DLB-44	The Viking Press DLB-46
Vančura, Vladislav 1891-1942............DLB-215; CDWLB-4	Velásquez-Trevino, Gloria 1949- DLB-122	Vila-Matas, Enrique 1948- DLB-322
	Veley, Margaret 1843-1887 ....DLB-199	Vilde, Eduard 1865-1933...............DLB-220
van der Post, Laurens 1906-1996........DLB-204	Velleius Paterculus circa 20 B.C.-circa A.D. 30 ....DLB-211	Vilinskaia, Mariia Aleksandrovna (see Vovchok, Marko)
Van Dine, S. S. (see Wright, Willard Huntington)		
Van Doren, Mark 1894-1972............DLB-45	Veloz Maggiolo, Marcio 1936- DLB-145	Villa, José García 1908-1997 ....DLB-312
van Druten, John 1901-1957 ....DLB-10	Vel'tman, Aleksandr Fomich 1800-1870 ....DLB-198	Villanueva, Alma Luz 1944- DLB-122
Van Duyn, Mona 1921-2004 ....DLB-5		Villanueva, Tino 1941- DLB-82
Tribute to James Dickey Y-97	Venegas, Daniel ?-? DLB-82	Villard, Henry 1835-1900 ....DLB-23
Van Dyke, Henry 1852-1933...... DLB-71; DS-13	Venevitinov, Dmitrii Vladimirovich 1805-1827.....................DLB-205	Villard, Oswald Garrison 1872-1949 ...DLB-25, 91
Van Dyke, Henry 1928- DLB-33		Villarreal, Edit 1944- DLB-209
Van Dyke, John C. 1856-1932..........DLB-186	Verbitskaia, Anastasiia Alekseevna 1861-1928 ....DLB-295	Villarreal, José Antonio 1924- DLB-82
Vane, Sutton 1888-1963.................DLB-10		Villaseñor, Victor 1940- DLB-209
Van Gieson, Judith 1941- DLB-306	Verde, Cesário 1855-1886 ....DLB-287	Villedieu, Madame de (Marie-Catherine Desjardins) 1640?-1683 ....DLB-268
Vanguard Press DLB-46	Vergil, Polydore circa 1470-1555 ....DLB-132	
van Gulik, Robert Hans 1910-1967 .... DS-17	Veríssimo, Erico 1905-1975 .... DLB-145, 307	Villegas, Antonio de ?-? DLB-318
van Itallie, Jean-Claude 1936- DLB-7	Verlaine, Paul 1844-1896...............DLB-217	Villegas de Magnón, Leonor 1876-1955 ....DLB-122
Van Loan, Charles E. 1876-1919 ....DLB-171	Vernacular Translations in the Crowns of Castile and Aragon 1352-1515 .....DLB-286	
Vann, Robert L. 1879-1940 ....DLB-29		Villehardouin, Geoffroi de circa 1150-1215 ....DLB-208
Van Rensselaer, Mariana Griswold 1851-1934 ....DLB-47	Verne, Jules 1828-1905 ....DLB-123	
	Vernon God Little, 2003 Booker Prize winner, DBC Pierre.....................DLB-326	Villemaire, Yolande 1949- DLB-60
Van Rensselaer, Mrs. Schuyler (see Van Rensselaer, Mariana Griswold)		Villena, Enrique de ca. 1382/84-1432.................DLB-286
	Verplanck, Gulian C. 1786-1870 ....DLB-59	
Van Vechten, Carl 1880-1964 .... DLB-4, 9, 51	Vertinsky, Aleksandr 1889-1957 .... DLB-317	Villena, Luis Antonio de 1951- DLB-134
van Vogt, A. E. 1912-2000............DLB-8, 251	Very, Jones 1813-1880 ....DLB-1, 243; DS-5	Villiers, George, Second Duke of Buckingham 1628-1687............DLB-80
Varela, Blanca 1926- DLB-290	Vesaas, Halldis Moren 1907-1995 ....DLB-297	
Vargas Llosa, Mario 1936- DLB-145; CDWLB-3	Vesaas, Tarjei 1897-1970...............DLB-297	Villiers de l'Isle-Adam, Jean-Marie Mathias Philippe-Auguste, Comte de 1838-1889..........DLB-123, 192
	Vian, Boris 1920-1959..............DLB-72, 321	
Acceptance Speech for the Ritz Paris Hemingway Award................Y-85	Viazemsky, Petr Andreevich 1792-1878 ....DLB-205	Villon, François 1431-circa 1463? DLB-208
Varley, John 1947- Y-81	Vicars, Thomas 1591-1638 ....DLB-236	Vinaver, Michel (Michel Grinberg) 1927- DLB-321
Varnhagen von Ense, Karl August 1785-1858 ....DLB-90	Vicente, Gil 1465-1536/1540? DLB-287, 318	
	Vickers, Roy 1888?-1965...............DLB-77	Vine Press DLB-112
Varnhagen von Ense, Rahel 1771-1833 ....DLB-90	Vickery, Sukey 1779-1821 ....DLB-200	Viorst, Judith 1931- DLB-52
	Victoria 1819-1901....................DLB-55	Vipont, Elfrida (Elfrida Vipont Foulds, Charles Vipont) 1902-1992.........DLB-160
Varro 116 B.C.-27 B.C. DLB-211	Victoria Press......................DLB-106	
Vasilenko, Svetlana Vladimirovna 1956- DLB-285	La vida de Lazarillo de Tormes DLB-318	Viramontes, Helena María 1954- DLB-122
		Virgil 70 B.C.-19 B.C. DLB-211; CDWLB-1

Cumulative Index

Vischer, Friedrich Theodor 1807-1887 ... DLB-133
Vitier, Cintio 1921- DLB-283
Vitrac, Roger 1899-1952. .... DLB-321
Vitruvius circa 85 B.C.-circa 15 B.C. DLB-211
Vitry, Philippe de 1291-1361 .... DLB-208
Vittorini, Elio 1908-1966 .... DLB-264
Vivanco, Luis Felipe 1907-1975........ DLB-108
Vives, Juan Luis 1493-1540 .... DLB-318
Vivian, E. Charles (Charles Henry Cannell,
   Charles Henry Vivian, Jack Mann,
   Barry Lynd) 1882-1947 .... DLB-255
Viviani, Cesare 1947- DLB-128
Vivien, Renée 1877-1909. .... DLB-217
Vizenor, Gerald 1934- DLB-175, 227
Vizetelly and Company DLB-106
Vladimov, Georgii
   1931-2003 .... DLB-302
Voaden, Herman 1903-1991............ DLB-88
Voß, Johann Heinrich 1751-1826 .... DLB-90
Vogau, Boris Andreevich
   (see Pil'niak, Boris Andreevich)
Voigt, Ellen Bryant 1943- DLB-120
Voinovich, Vladimir Nikolaevich
   1932- DLB-302
Vojnović, Ivo 1857-1929 .....DLB-147; CDWLB-4
Vold, Jan Erik 1939- DLB-297
Volkoff, Vladimir 1932- DLB-83
P. F. Volland Company................ DLB-46
Vollbehr, Otto H. F.
   1872?-1945 or 1946 .... DLB-187
Vologdin (see Zasodimsky, Pavel Vladimirovich)
Voloshin, Maksimilian Aleksandrovich
   1877-1932..................... DLB-295
Volponi, Paolo 1924-1994.............DLB-177
Voltaire (François-Marie Arouet)
   1694-1778..................... DLB-314
   "An account of the death of the chevalier de
   La Barre".................. DLB-314
   Candide DLB-314
   Philosophical Dictionary............... DLB-314
Vonarburg, Élisabeth 1947- DLB-251
von der Grün, Max 1926- DLB-75
Vonnegut, Kurt 1922- DLB-2, 8, 152;
   Y-80; DS-3; CDALB-6
   Tribute to Isaac Asimov Y-92
   Tribute to Richard Brautigan Y-84
Voranc, Prežihov 1893-1950 .... DLB-147
Voronsky, Aleksandr Konstantinovich
   1884-1937..................... DLB-272
Vorse, Mary Heaton 1874-1966 .... DLB-303
Vovchok, Marko 1833-1907 .... DLB-238
Voynich, E. L. 1864-1960............. DLB-197
Vroman, Mary Elizabeth
   circa 1924-1967 .... DLB-33

W

Wace, Robert ("Maistre")
   circa 1100-circa 1175 .... DLB-146
Wackenroder, Wilhelm Heinrich
   1773-1798..................... DLB-90
Wackernagel, Wilhelm 1806-1869 ...... DLB-133
Waddell, Helen 1889-1965........... DLB-240
Waddington, Miriam 1917-2004......... DLB-68
Wade, Henry 1887-1969............... DLB-77
Wagenknecht, Edward 1900-2004 ...... DLB-103
Wägner, Elin 1882-1949................ DLB-259
Wagner, Heinrich Leopold 1747-1779 ..... DLB-94
Wagner, Henry R. 1862-1957........... DLB-140
Wagner, Richard 1813-1883........... DLB-129
Wagoner, David 1926- DLB-5, 256
Wah, Fred 1939- DLB-60
Waiblinger, Wilhelm 1804-1830......... DLB-90
Wain, John
   1925-1994 ...DLB-15, 27, 139, 155; CDBLB-8
   Tribute to J. B. Priestly................ Y-84
Wainwright, Jeffrey 1944- DLB-40
Waite, Peirce and Company DLB-49
Wakeman, Stephen H. 1859-1924 ...... DLB-187
Wakoski, Diane 1937- DLB-5
Walahfrid Strabo circa 808-849 .... DLB-148
Henry Z. Walck [publishing house] DLB-46
Walcott, Derek
   1930- DLB-117; Y-81, 92; CDWLB-3
   Nobel Lecture 1992: The Antilles:
   Fragments of Epic Memory......... Y-92
Robert Waldegrave [publishing house]....DLB-170
Waldis, Burkhard circa 1490-1556?......DLB-178
Waldman, Anne 1945- DLB-16
Waldrop, Rosmarie 1935- DLB-169
Walker, Alice 1900-1982............. DLB-201
Walker, Alice
   1944- DLB-6, 33, 143; CDALB-6
Walker, Annie Louisa (Mrs. Harry Coghill)
   circa 1836-1907 .... DLB-240
Walker, George F. 1947- DLB-60
Walker, John Brisben 1847-1931......... DLB-79
Walker, Joseph A. 1935- DLB-38
Walker, Kath (see Oodgeroo of the Tribe Noonuccal)
Walker, Margaret 1915-1998 ....DLB-76, 152
Walker, Obadiah 1616-1699............ DLB-281
Walker, Ted 1934- DLB-40
Walker, Evans and Cogswell Company ... DLB-49
Wall, John F. (see Sarban)
Wallace, Alfred Russel 1823-1913 .... DLB-190
Wallace, Dewitt 1889-1981............. DLB-137
Wallace, Edgar 1875-1932 .... DLB-70
Wallace, Lew 1827-1905............... DLB-202

Wallace, Lila Acheson 1889-1984........DLB-137
   "A Word of Thanks," From the Initial
   Issue of Reader's Digest
   (February 1922)................DLB-137
Wallace, Naomi 1960- DLB-249
Wallace Markfield's "Steeplechase" Y-02
Wallace-Crabbe, Chris 1934- DLB-289
Wallant, Edward Lewis
   1926-1962 ....DLB-2, 28, 143, 299
Waller, Edmund 1606-1687 .... DLB-126
Walpole, Horace 1717-1797......DLB-39, 104, 213
   Preface to the First Edition of
   The Castle of Otranto (1764) DLB-39, 178
   Preface to the Second Edition of
   The Castle of Otranto (1765) DLB-39, 178
Walpole, Hugh 1884-1941 .... DLB-34
Walrond, Eric 1898-1966 .... DLB-51
Walser, Martin 1927- DLB-75, 124
Walser, Robert 1878-1956............. DLB-66
Walsh, Ernest 1895-1926 .... DLB-4, 45
Walsh, Robert 1784-1859 .... DLB-59
Walters, Henry 1848-1931 .... DLB-140
Waltharius circa 825 .... DLB-148
Walther von der Vogelweide
   circa 1170-circa 1230 .... DLB-138
Walton, Izaak
   1593-1683 .... DLB-151, 213; CDBLB-1
Walwicz, Ania 1951- DLB-325
Wambaugh, Joseph 1937- DLB-6; Y-83
Wand, Alfred Rudolph 1828-1891...... DLB-188
Wandor, Michelene 1940- DLB-310
Waniek, Marilyn Nelson 1946- DLB-120
Wanley, Humphrey 1672-1726 .... DLB-213
War of the Words (and Pictures):
   The Creation of a Graphic Novel Y-02
Warburton, William 1698-1779 .... DLB-104
Ward, Aileen 1919- DLB-111
Ward, Artemus (see Browne, Charles Farrar)
Ward, Arthur Henry Sarsfield (see Rohmer, Sax)
Ward, Douglas Turner 1930- DLB-7, 38
Ward, Mrs. Humphry 1851-1920......... DLB-18
Ward, James 1843-1925 .... DLB-262
Ward, Lynd 1905-1985 .... DLB-22
Ward, Lock and Company............ DLB-106
Ward, Nathaniel circa 1578-1652 .... DLB-24
Ward, Theodore 1902-1983 .... DLB-76
Wardle, Ralph 1909-1988.............. DLB-103
Ware, Henry, Jr. 1794-1843............ DLB-235
Ware, William 1797-1852 .... DLB-1, 235
Warfield, Catherine Ann 1816-1877........DLB-248
Waring, Anna Letitia 1823-1910 ....DLB-240
Frederick Warne and Company [U.K.] DLB-106
Frederick Warne and Company [U.S.] DLB-49

Warner, Anne 1869-1913 . . . . .DLB-202

Warner, Charles Dudley 1829-1900 . . . . . .DLB-64

Warner, Marina 1946- DLB-194

Warner, Rex 1905-1986 . . . . .DLB-15

Warner, Susan 1819-1885 . . . .DLB-3, 42, 239, 250

Warner, Sylvia Townsend
1893-1978 . . . . .DLB-34, 139

Warner, William 1558-1609 . . . . .DLB-172

Warner Books DLB-46

Warr, Bertram 1917-1943 . . . . .DLB-88

Warren, John Byrne Leicester
(see De Tabley, Lord)

Warren, Lella 1899-1982 . . . . .Y-83

Warren, Mercy Otis 1728-1814 . . . . . .DLB-31, 200

Warren, Robert Penn 1905-1989 . . . . . DLB-2, 48,
152, 320; Y-80, 89; CDALB-6

Tribute to Katherine Anne Porter Y-80

Warren, Samuel 1807-1877 . . . . .DLB-190

Die Wartburgkrieg circa 1230-circa 1280 . . . .DLB-138

Warton, Joseph 1722-1800 . . . . .DLB-104, 109

Warton, Thomas 1728-1790 . . . . . . .DLB-104, 109

Warung, Price (William Astley)
1855-1911 . . . . .DLB-230

Washington, George 1732-1799 . . . . .DLB-31

Washington, Ned 1901-1976 . . . . .DLB-265

Wassermann, Jakob 1873-1934 . . . . .DLB-66

Wasserstein, Wendy 1950-2006 . . . . .DLB-228

Wassmo, Herbjorg 1942- DLB-297

Wasson, David Atwood 1823-1887 . . . .DLB-1, 223

Watanna, Onoto (see Eaton, Winnifred)

Waten, Judah 1911?-1985 . . . . .DLB-289

Waterhouse, Keith 1929- DLB-13, 15

Waterman, Andrew 1940- DLB-40

Waters, Frank 1902-1995 . . . . DLB-212; Y-86

Waters, Michael 1949- DLB-120

Watkins, Tobias 1780-1855 . . . . .DLB-73

Watkins, Vernon 1906-1967 . . . . .DLB-20

Watmough, David 1926- DLB-53

Watson, Colin 1920-1983 . . . . .DLB-276

Watson, Ian 1943- DLB-261

Watson, James Wreford (see Wreford, James)

Watson, John 1850-1907 . . . . .DLB-156

Watson, Rosamund Marriott
(Graham R. Tomson) 1860-1911 . . . . .DLB-240

Watson, Sheila 1909-1998 . . . . .DLB-60

Watson, Thomas 1545?-1592 . . . . .DLB-132

Watson, Wilfred 1911-1998 . . . . .DLB-60

W. J. Watt and Company DLB-46

Watten, Barrett 1948- DLB-193

Watterson, Henry 1840-1921 . . . . .DLB-25

Watts, Alan 1915-1973 . . . . .DLB-16

Watts, Isaac 1674-1748 . . . . .DLB-95

Franklin Watts [publishing house] DLB-46

Waugh, Alec 1898-1981 . . . . .DLB-191

Waugh, Auberon 1939-2000 . . . DLB-14, 194; Y-00

Waugh, Evelyn 1903-1966
. . . . .DLB-15, 162, 195; CDBLB-6

Way and Williams .DLB-49

Wayman, Tom 1945- DLB-53

Wearne, Alan 1948- DLB-325

Weatherly, Tom 1942- DLB-41

Weaver, Gordon 1937- DLB-130

Weaver, Robert 1921- DLB-88

Webb, Beatrice 1858-1943 . . . . .DLB-190

Webb, Francis 1925-1973 . . . . .DLB-260

Webb, Frank J. fl. 1857 . . . . .DLB-50

Webb, James Watson 1802-1884 . . . . .DLB-43

Webb, Mary 1881-1927 . . . . .DLB-34

Webb, Phyllis 1927- DLB-53

Webb, Sidney 1859-1947 . . . . .DLB-190

Webb, Walter Prescott 1888-1963 . . . . .DLB-17

Webbe, William ?-1591 . . . . .DLB-132

Webber, Charles Wilkins
1819-1856? DLB-202

Weber, Max 1864-1920 . . . . .DLB-296

Webling, Lucy (Lucy Betty MacRaye)
1877-1952 . . . . .DLB-240

Webling, Peggy (Arthur Weston)
1871-1949 . . . . .DLB-240

Webster, Augusta 1837-1894 . . . . . . .DLB-35, 240

Webster, John
1579 or 1580-1634? DLB-58; CDBLB-1

The Melbourne Manuscript Y-86

Webster, Noah
1758-1843 . . . . DLB-1, 37, 42, 43, 73, 243

Webster, Paul Francis 1907-1984 . . . . .DLB-265

Charles L. Webster and Company DLB-49

Weckherlin, Georg Rodolf 1584-1653 . . . .DLB-164

Wedekind, Frank
1864-1918 . . . . DLB-118; CDWLB-2

Weeks, Edward Augustus, Jr.
1898-1989 . . . . .DLB-137

Weeks, Stephen B. 1865-1918 . . . . .DLB-187

Weems, Mason Locke 1759-1825 . . . DLB-30, 37, 42

Weerth, Georg 1822-1856 . . . . .DLB-129

Weidenfeld and Nicolson DLB-112

Weidman, Jerome 1913-1998 . . . . .DLB-28

Weigl, Bruce 1949- DLB-120

Weil, Jiří 1900-1959 . . . . .DLB-299

Weinbaum, Stanley Grauman
1902-1935 . . . . .DLB-8

Weiner, Andrew 1949- DLB-251

Weintraub, Stanley 1929- DLB-111; Y82

Weise, Christian 1642-1708 . . . . .DLB-168

Weisenborn, Gunther 1902-1969 . . . . .DLB-69, 124

Weiss, John 1818-1879 . . . . .DLB-1, 243

Weiss, Paul 1901-2002 . . . . .DLB-279

Weiss, Peter 1916-1982 . . . . .DLB-69, 124

Weiss, Theodore 1916-2003 . . . . .DLB-5

Weiß, Ernst 1882-1940 . . . . .DLB-81

Weiße, Christian Felix 1726-1804 . . . . .DLB-97

Weitling, Wilhelm 1808-1871 . . . . .DLB-129

Welch, Denton 1915-1948 . . . . .DLB-319

Welch, James 1940- DLB-175, 256

Welch, Lew 1926-1971? DLB-16

Weldon, Fay 1931- . .DLB-14, 194, 319; CDBLB-8

Wellek, René 1903-1995 . . . . .DLB-63

Weller, Archie 1957- DLB-325

Wells, Carolyn 1862-1942 . . . . .DLB-11

Wells, Charles Jeremiah
circa 1800-1879 . . . . .DLB-32

Wells, Gabriel 1862-1946 . . . . .DLB-140

Wells, H. G. 1866-1946
. . . . DLB-34, 70, 156, 178; CDBLB-6

H. G. Wells Society Y-98

Preface to *The Scientific Romances of
H. G. Wells* (1933) DLB-178

Wells, Helena 1758?-1824 . . . . .DLB-200

Wells, Rebecca 1952- DLB-292

Wells, Robert 1947- DLB-40

Wells-Barnett, Ida B. 1862-1931 . . . . .DLB-23, 221

Welsh, Irvine 1958- DLB-271

Welty, Eudora 1909-2001 . . . . . . DLB-2, 102, 143;
Y-87, 01; DS-12; CDALB-1

Eudora Welty: Eye of the Storyteller Y-87

Eudora Welty Newsletter Y-99

Eudora Welty's Funeral Y-01

Eudora Welty's Ninetieth Birthday Y-99

Eudora Welty Remembered in
Two Exhibits .Y-02

Wendell, Barrett 1855-1921 . . . . .DLB-71

Wentworth, Patricia 1878-1961 . . . . .DLB-77

Wentworth, William Charles
1790-1872 . . . . .DLB-230

Wenzel, Jean-Paul 1947- DLB-321

Werder, Diederich von dem 1584-1657 . . .DLB-164

Werfel, Franz 1890-1945 . . . . .DLB-81, 124

Werner, Zacharias 1768-1823 . . . . .DLB-94

The Werner Company DLB-49

Wersba, Barbara 1932- DLB-52

Wescott, Glenway
1901-1987 . . . . .DLB-4, 9, 102; DS-15

Wesker, Arnold
1932- DLB-13, 310, 319; CDBLB-8

Wesley, Charles 1707-1788 . . . . .DLB-95

Wesley, John 1703-1791 . . . . .DLB-104

Wesley, Mary 1912-2002 . . . . .DLB-231

Wesley, Richard 1945- DLB-38

Wessel, Johan Herman 1742-1785 . . . . . . .DLB-300

A. Wessels and Company DLB-46

Cumulative Index

Wessobrunner Gebet circa 787-815 . . . . DLB-148	Whetstone, George 1550-1587 . . . . DLB-136	Whitney, Isabella fl. 1566-1573. . . . . DLB-136
West, Anthony 1914-1988 . . . . DLB-15	Whetstone, Colonel Pete (see Noland, C. F. M.)	Whitney, John Hay 1904-1982. . . . . .DLB-127
Tribute to Liam O'Flaherty Y-84	Whewell, William 1794-1866 . . . . DLB-262	Whittemore, Reed 1919-1995. . . . . DLB-5
West, Cheryl L. 1957- DLB-266	Whichcote, Benjamin 1609?-1683 . . . . . . DLB-252	Whittier, John Greenleaf 1807-1892. . . . . DLB-1, 243; CDALB-2
West, Cornel 1953- DLB-246	Whicher, Stephen E. 1915-1961 . . . . DLB-111	
West, Dorothy 1907-1998 . . . . DLB-76	Whipple, Edwin Percy 1819-1886 . . . . . DLB-1, 64	Whittlesey House. DLB-46
West, Jessamyn 1902-1984 . . . . .DLB-6; Y-84	Whitaker, Alexander 1585-1617 . . . . DLB-24	Wickham, Anna (Edith Alice Mary Harper) 1884-1947 . . . . DLB-240
West, Mae 1892-1980. . . . . DLB-44	Whitaker, Daniel K. 1801-1881 . . . . DLB-73	
West, Michael Lee 1953- DLB-292	Whitcher, Frances Miriam 1812-1852 . . . . DLB-11, 202	Wickram, Georg circa 1505-circa 1561 . . .DLB-179
West, Michelle Sagara 1963- DLB-251		Wicomb, Zoë 1948- DLB-225
West, Morris 1916-1999 . . . . DLB-289	White, Andrew 1579-1656 . . . . DLB-24	Wideman, John Edgar 1941- DLB-33, 143
West, Nathanael 1903-1940 . . . . DLB-4, 9, 28; CDALB-5	White, Andrew Dickson 1832-1918 . . . . . . DLB-47	Widener, Harry Elkins 1885-1912 . . . . . . DLB-140
	White, E. B. 1899-1985 . . . DLB-11, 22; CDALB-7	Wiebe, Rudy 1934- DLB-60
West, Paul 1930- DLB-14	White, Edgar B. 1947- DLB-38	Wiechert, Ernst 1887-1950 . . . . DLB-56
West, Rebecca 1892-1983. . . . . .DLB-36; Y-83	White, Edmund 1940- DLB-227	Wied, Gustav 1858-1914 . . . . DLB-300
West, Richard 1941- DLB-185	White, Ethel Lina 1887-1944 . . . . DLB-77	Wied, Martina 1882-1957. . . . . DLB-85
West and Johnson. DLB-49	White, Hayden V. 1928- DLB-246	Wiehe, Evelyn May Clowes (see Mordaunt, Elinor)
Westcott, Edward Noyes 1846-1898 . . . . . DLB-202	White, Henry Kirke 1785-1806 . . . . DLB-96	Wieland, Christoph Martin 1733-1813. . . . DLB-97
The Western Literature Association Y-99	White, Horace 1834-1916 . . . . DLB-23	Wienbarg, Ludolf 1802-1872 . . . . DLB-133
The Western Messenger 1835-1841 . . . . DLB-1; DLB-223	White, James 1928-1999. . . . . DLB-261	Wieners, John 1934- DLB-16
	White, Patrick 1912-1990. . . . . DLB-260	Wier, Ester 1910-2000 . . . . DLB-52
Western Publishing Company DLB-46	White, Phyllis Dorothy James (see James, P. D.)	Wiesel, Elie 1928- DLB-83, 299; Y-86, 87; CDALB-7
Western Writers of America Y-99	White, Richard Grant 1821-1885 . . . . DLB-64	
The Westminster Review 1824-1914 . . . . DLB-110	White, T. H. 1906-1964 . . . . DLB-160, 255	Nobel Lecture 1986: Hope, Despair and Memory Y-86
Weston, Arthur (see Webling, Peggy)	White, Walter 1893-1955 . . . . DLB-51	
Weston, Elizabeth Jane circa 1582-1612 . . .DLB-172	Wilcox, James 1949- DLB-292	Wiggin, Kate Douglas 1856-1923. . . . . DLB-42
Wetherald, Agnes Ethelwyn 1857-1940 . . . DLB-99	William White and Company DLB-49	Wigglesworth, Michael 1631-1705 . . . . DLB-24
Wetherell, Elizabeth (see Warner, Susan)	White, William Allen 1868-1944 . . . . . . DLB-9, 25	Wilberforce, William 1759-1833. . . . . DLB-158
Wetherell, W. D. 1948- DLB-234	White, William Anthony Parker (see Boucher, Anthony)	Wilbrandt, Adolf 1837-1911 . . . . DLB-129
Wetzel, Friedrich Gottlob 1779-1819. . . . . . DLB-90		Wilbur, Richard 1921- . . DLB-5, 169; CDALB-7
Weyman, Stanley J. 1855-1928 . . . . . DLB-141, 156	White, William Hale (see Rutherford, Mark)	Tribute to Robert Penn Warren Y-89
Wezel, Johann Karl 1747-1819. . . . . DLB-94	Whitechurch, Victor L. 1868-1933. . . . . . . DLB-70	Wilcox, James 1949- DLB-292
Whalen, Philip 1923-2002 . . . . DLB-16	Whitehead, Alfred North 1861-1947. . . . . DLB-100, 262	Wild, Peter 1940- DLB-5
Whalley, George 1915-1983 . . . . DLB-88		Wilde, Lady Jane Francesca Elgee 1821?-1896. DLB-199
Wharton, Edith 1862-1937. . . . . DLB-4, 9, 12, 78, 189; DS-13; CDALB-3	Whitehead, E. A. (Ted Whitehead) 1933- DLB-310	
		Wilde, Oscar 1854-1900 . . DLB-10, 19, 34, 57, 141, 156, 190; CDBLB-5
Wharton, William 1925- Y-80	Whitehead, James 1936- Y-81	"The Critic as Artist" (1891) DLB-57
Whately, Mary Louisa 1824-1889 . . . . . . DLB-166	Whitehead, William 1715-1785. . . . . . DLB-84, 109	"The Decay of Lying" (1889) DLB-18
Whately, Richard 1787-1863. . . . . DLB-190	Whitfield, James Monroe 1822-1871 . . . . . DLB-50	"The English Renaissance of Art" (1908) DLB-35
Elements of Rhetoric (1828; revised, 1846) [excerpt] DLB-57	Whitfield, Raoul 1898-1945 . . . . DLB-226	
	Whitgift, John circa 1533-1604. . . . . DLB-132	"L'Envoi" (1882) DLB-35
Wheatley, Dennis 1897-1977. . . . . . . .DLB-77, 255	Whiting, John 1917-1963 . . . . DLB-13	Oscar Wilde Conference at Hofstra University Y-00
Wheatley, Phillis circa 1754-1784. . . . . . . DLB-31, 50; CDALB-2	Whiting, Samuel 1597-1679 . . . . DLB-24	
	Whitlock, Brand 1869-1934 . . . . DLB-12	Wilde, Richard Henry 1789-1847 . . . . . . DLB-3, 59
Wheeler, Anna Doyle 1785-1848? DLB-158	Whitman, Albery Allson 1851-1901. . . . . . DLB-50	W. A. Wilde Company. DLB-49
Wheeler, Charles Stearns 1816-1843 . . DLB-1, 223	Whitman, Alden 1913-1990. . . . . Y-91	Wilder, Billy 1906-2002 . . . . DLB-26
Wheeler, Monroe 1900-1988 . . . . DLB-4	Whitman, Sarah Helen (Power) 1803-1878. . . . . DLB-1, 243	Wilder, Laura Ingalls 1867-1957. . . . . DLB-22, 256
Wheelock, John Hall 1886-1978 . . . . DLB-45		Wilder, Thornton 1897-1975 . . . . . . .DLB-4, 7, 9, 228; CDALB-7
From John Hall Wheelock's Oral Memoir Y-01	Whitman, Walt 1819-1892 . . . DLB-3, 64, 224, 250; CDALB-2	
	Albert Whitman and Company DLB-46	Thornton Wilder Centenary at Yale Y-97
Wheelwright, J. B. 1897-1940 . . . . DLB-45	Whitman Publishing Company DLB-46	Wildgans, Anton 1881-1932. . . . . DLB-118
Wheelwright, John circa 1592-1679 . . . . . . DLB-24	Whitney, Geoffrey 1548 or 1552?-1601 . . . . DLB-136	Wilding, Michael 1942- DLB-325
		Wiley, Bell Irvin 1906-1980 . . . . .DLB-17
		John Wiley and Sons DLB-49
		Wilhelm, Kate 1928- DLB-8

Wilkes, Charles 1798-1877 . . . . DLB-183

Wilkes, George 1817-1885 . . . . DLB-79

Wilkins, John 1614-1672 . . . . DLB-236

Wilkinson, Anne 1910-1961 . . . . DLB-88

Wilkinson, Christopher 1941- DLB-310

Wilkinson, Eliza Yonge
1757-circa 1813 . . . . DLB-200

Wilkinson, Sylvia 1940- Y-86

Wilkinson, William Cleaver 1833-1920 . . . . DLB-71

Willard, Barbara 1909-1994 . . . . DLB-161

Willard, Emma 1787-1870 . . . . DLB-239

Willard, Frances E. 1839-1898 . . . . DLB-221

Willard, Nancy 1936- DLB-5, 52

Willard, Samuel 1640-1707 . . . . DLB-24

L. Willard [publishing house] DLB-49

Willeford, Charles 1919-1988 . . . . DLB-226

William of Auvergne 1190-1249 . . . . DLB-115

William of Conches
circa 1090-circa 1154 . . . . DLB-115

William of Ockham circa 1285-1347 . . . . . DLB-115

William of Sherwood
1200/1205-1266/1271 . . . . DLB-115

The William Charvat American Fiction
Collection at the Ohio State
University Libraries Y-92

Williams, Ben Ames 1889-1953 . . . . DLB-102

Williams, C. K. 1936- DLB-5

Williams, Chancellor 1905-1992 . . . . DLB-76

Williams, Charles 1886-1945 . . . DLB-100, 153, 255

Williams, Denis 1923-1998 . . . . DLB-117

Williams, Emlyn 1905-1987 . . . . DLB-10, 77

Williams, Garth 1912-1996 . . . . DLB-22

Williams, George Washington
1849-1891 . . . . DLB-47

Williams, Heathcote 1941- DLB-13

Williams, Helen Maria 1761-1827 . . . . . . DLB-158

Williams, Hugo 1942- DLB-40

Williams, Isaac 1802-1865 . . . . DLB-32

Williams, Joan 1928- DLB-6

Williams, Joe 1889-1972 . . . . DLB-241

Williams, John A. 1925- DLB-2, 33

Williams, John E. 1922-1994 . . . . DLB-6

Williams, Jonathan 1929- DLB-5

Williams, Miller 1930- DLB-105

Williams, Nigel 1948- DLB-231

Williams, Raymond
1921-1988 . . . . DLB-14, 231, 242

Williams, Roger circa 1603-1683 . . . . DLB-24

Williams, Rowland 1817-1870 . . . . DLB-184

Williams, Samm-Art 1946- DLB-38

Williams, Sherley Anne 1944-1999 . . . . . . DLB-41

Williams, T. Harry 1909-1979 . . . . DLB-17

Williams, Tennessee
1911-1983 . . . . . DLB-7; Y-83; DS-4; CDALB-1

Williams, Terry Tempest 1955- . . . DLB-206, 275

Williams, Ursula Moray 1911- DLB-160

Williams, Valentine 1883-1946 . . . . DLB-77

Williams, William Appleman 1921-1990 . . . DLB-17

Williams, William Carlos
1883-1963 . . . . . . DLB-4, 16, 54, 86; CDALB-4

The William Carlos Williams Society Y-99

Williams, Wirt 1921-1986 . . . . DLB-6

A. Williams and Company DLB-49

Williams Brothers DLB-49

Williamson, David 1942- DLB-289

Williamson, Henry 1895-1977 . . . . DLB-191

The Henry Williamson Society Y-98

Williamson, Jack 1908- DLB-8

Willingham, Calder Baynard, Jr.
1922-1995 . . . . DLB-2, 44

Williram of Ebersberg circa 1020-1085 . . . DLB-148

Willis, John circa 1572-1625 . . . . DLB-281

Willis, Nathaniel Parker 1806-1867
. . . . DLB-3, 59, 73, 74, 183, 250; DS-13

Willis, Ted 1918-1992 . . . . DLB-310

Willkomm, Ernst 1810-1886 . . . . DLB-133

Wills, Garry 1934- DLB-246

Tribute to Kenneth Dale McCormick Y-97

Willson, Meredith 1902-1984 . . . . DLB-265

Willumsen, Dorrit 1940- DLB-214

Wilmer, Clive 1945- DLB-40

Wilson, A. N. 1950- DLB-14, 155, 194

Wilson, Angus 1913-1991 . . . . . . DLB-15, 139, 155

Wilson, Arthur 1595-1652 . . . . DLB-58

Wilson, August 1945-2005 . . . . DLB-228

Wilson, Augusta Jane Evans 1835-1909 . . . DLB-42

Wilson, Colin 1931- DLB-14, 194

Tribute to J. B. Priestly Y-84

Wilson, Edmund 1895-1972 . . . . DLB-63

Wilson, Ethel 1888-1980 . . . . DLB-68

Wilson, F. P. 1889-1963 . . . . DLB-201

Wilson, Harriet E.
1827/1828?-1863? DLB-50, 239, 243

Wilson, Harry Leon 1867-1939 . . . . DLB-9

Wilson, John 1588-1667 . . . . DLB-24

Wilson, John 1785-1854 . . . . DLB-110

Wilson, John Anthony Burgess
(see Burgess, Anthony)

Wilson, John Dover 1881-1969 . . . . DLB-201

Wilson, Lanford 1937- DLB-7

Wilson, Margaret 1882-1973 . . . . DLB-9

Wilson, Michael 1914-1978 . . . . DLB-44

Wilson, Mona 1872-1954 . . . . DLB-149

Wilson, Robert Charles 1953- DLB-251

Wilson, Robert McLiam 1964- DLB-267

Wilson, Robley 1930- DLB-218

Wilson, Romer 1891-1930 . . . . DLB-191

Wilson, Thomas 1524-1581 . . . . DLB-132, 236

Wilson, Woodrow 1856-1924 . . . . DLB-47

Effingham Wilson [publishing house] DLB-154

Wimpfeling, Jakob 1450-1528 . . . . DLB-179

Wimsatt, William K., Jr. 1907-1975 . . . . . . DLB-63

Winchell, Walter 1897-1972 . . . . DLB-29

J. Winchester [publishing house] DLB-49

Winckelmann, Johann Joachim
1717-1768 . . . . DLB-97

Winckler, Paul 1630-1686 . . . . DLB-164

Wind, Herbert Warren 1916-2005 . . . . . . DLB-171

John Windet [publishing house] DLB-170

Windham, Donald 1920- DLB-6

Windsor, Gerard 1944- DLB-325

Wing, Donald Goddard 1904-1972 . . . . . . DLB-187

Wing, John M. 1844-1917 . . . . DLB-187

Allan Wingate [publishing house] DLB-112

Winnemucca, Sarah 1844-1921 . . . . DLB-175

Winnifrith, Tom 1938- DLB-155

Winsloe, Christa 1888-1944 . . . . DLB-124

Winslow, Anna Green 1759-1780 . . . . DLB-200

Winsor, Justin 1831-1897 . . . . DLB-47

John C. Winston Company DLB-49

Winters, Yvor 1900-1968 . . . . DLB-48

Winterson, Jeanette 1959- DLB-207, 261

Winther, Christian 1796-1876 . . . . DLB-300

Winthrop, John 1588-1649 . . . . DLB-24, 30

Winthrop, John, Jr. 1606-1676 . . . . DLB-24

Winthrop, Margaret Tyndal
1591-1647 . . . . DLB-200

Winthrop, Theodore
1828-1861 . . . . DLB-202

Winton, Tim 1960- DLB-325

Wirt, William 1772-1834 . . . . DLB-37

Wise, John 1652-1725 . . . . DLB-24

Wise, Thomas James 1859-1937 . . . . DLB-184

Wiseman, Adele 1928-1992 . . . . DLB-88

Wishart and Company DLB-112

Wisner, George 1812-1849 . . . . DLB-43

Wister, Owen 1860-1938 . . . . DLB-9, 78, 186

Wister, Sarah 1761-1804 . . . . DLB-200

Wither, George 1588-1667 . . . . DLB-121

Witherspoon, John 1723-1794 . . . . DLB-31

The Works of the Rev. John Witherspoon
(1800-1801) [excerpts] DLB-31

Withrow, William Henry 1839-1908 . . . . . DLB-99

Witkacy (see Witkiewicz, Stanisław Ignacy)

Witkiewicz, Stanisław Ignacy
1885-1939 . . . . DLB-215; CDWLB-4

Wittenwiler, Heinrich before 1387-
circa 1414? DLB-179

Wittgenstein, Ludwig 1889-1951 . . . . DLB-262

Wittig, Monique 1935- DLB-83

Witting, Amy (Joan Austral Levick, née Fraser)
1918-2001 . . . . DLB-325

Wodehouse, P. G. 1881-1975.......... DLB-34, 162; CDBLB-6
    Worldwide Wodehouse Societies........ Y-98
Wohmann, Gabriele 1932-........... DLB-75
Woiwode, Larry 1941-............... DLB-6
    Tribute to John Gardner.............. Y-82
Wolcot, John 1738-1819.............. DLB-109
Wolcott, Roger 1679-1767............. DLB-24
Wolf, Christa 1929-........DLB-75; CDWLB-2
Wolf, Friedrich 1888-1953............ DLB-124
Wolfe, Gene 1931-.................. DLB-8
Wolfe, Thomas 1900-1938....................
    DLB-9, 102, 229; Y-85; DS-2, DS-16; CDALB-5
    "All the Faults of Youth and Inexperience":
    A Reader's Report on
    Thomas Wolfe's *O Lost*............ Y-01
    Emendations for *Look Homeward, Angel*.... Y-00
    Eugene Gant's Projected Works........ Y-01
    Fire at the Old Kentucky Home
    [Thomas Wolfe Memorial]......... Y-98
    Thomas Wolfe Centennial
    Celebration in Asheville........... Y-00
    The Thomas Wolfe Collection at
    the University of North Carolina
    at Chapel Hill................... Y-97
    The Thomas Wolfe Society......... Y-97, 99
Wolfe, Tom 1931-............. DLB-152, 185
John Wolfe [publishing house].........DLB-170
Reyner (Reginald) Wolfe
    [publishing house]................DLB-170
Wolfenstein, Martha 1869-1906........ DLB-221
Wolff, David (see Maddow, Ben)
Wolff, Egon 1926-.................. DLB-305
Wolff, Helen 1906-1994.................. Y-94
Wolff, Tobias 1945-................. DLB-130
    Tribute to Michael M. Rea............ Y-97
    Tribute to Raymond Carver............ Y-88
Wolfram von Eschenbach
    circa 1170-after 1220.... DLB-138; CDWLB-2
    Wolfram von Eschenbach's *Parzival*:
    Prologue and Book 3.......... DLB-138
Wolker, Jiří 1900-1924.............. DLB-215
Wollstonecraft, Mary 1759-1797
    .... DLB-39, 104, 158, 252; CDBLB-3
Women
    Women's Work, Women's Sphere:
    Selected Comments from Women
    Writers.................... DLB-200
Women Writers in Sixteenth-Century
    Spain....................... DLB-318
Wondratschek, Wolf 1943-........... DLB-75
Wong, Elizabeth 1958-.............. DLB-266
Wong, Nellie 1934-................ DLB-312
Wong, Shawn 1949-................ DLB-312
Wongar, B. (Sreten Bozic) 1932-...... DLB-325
Wood, Anthony à 1632-1695.......... DLB-213
Wood, Benjamin 1820-1900.......... DLB-23
Wood, Charles 1932-1980............ DLB-13

The Charles Wood Affair:
    A Playwright Revived............. Y-83
Wood, Mrs. Henry 1814-1887......... DLB-18
Wood, Joanna E. 1867-1927........... DLB-92
Wood, Sally Sayward Barrell Keating
    1759-1855..................... DLB-200
Wood, William fl. seventeenth century.... DLB-24
Samuel Wood [publishing house]........ DLB-49
Woodberry, George Edward
    1855-1930...................DLB-71, 103
Woodbridge, Benjamin 1622-1684....... DLB-24
Woodbridge, Frederick J. E. 1867-1940...DLB-270
Woodcock, George 1912-1995......... DLB-88
Woodhull, Victoria C. 1838-1927........ DLB-79
Woodmason, Charles circa 1720-?....... DLB-31
Woodress, James Leslie, Jr. 1916-..... DLB-111
Woods, Margaret L. 1855-1945........ DLB-240
Woodson, Carter G. 1875-1950......... DLB-17
Woodward, C. Vann 1908-1999......... DLB-17
Woodward, Stanley 1895-1965.........DLB-171
Woodworth, Samuel 1785-1842........ DLB-250
Wooler, Thomas 1785 or 1786-1853..... DLB-158
Woolf, David (see Maddow, Ben)
Woolf, Douglas 1922-1992............ DLB-244
Woolf, Leonard 1880-1969.......DLB-100; DS-10
Woolf, Virginia 1882-1941
    .... DLB-36, 100, 162; DS-10; CDBLB-6
    "The New Biography," *New York Herald
    Tribune*, 30 October 1927....... DLB-149
Woollcott, Alexander 1887-1943......... DLB-29
Woolman, John 1720-1772............ DLB-31
Woolner, Thomas 1825-1892.......... DLB-35
Woolrich, Cornell 1903-1968.......... DLB-226
Woolsey, Sarah Chauncy 1835-1905..... DLB-42
Woolson, Constance Fenimore
    1840-1894............DLB-12, 74, 189, 221
Worcester, Joseph Emerson
    1784-1865.................... DLB-1, 235
Wynkyn de Worde [publishing house]....DLB-170
Wordsworth, Christopher 1807-1885.... DLB-166
Wordsworth, Dorothy 1771-1855........DLB-107
Wordsworth, Elizabeth
    1840-1932..................... DLB-98
Wordsworth, William
    1770-1850.......... DLB-93, 107; CDBLB-3
Workman, Fanny Bullock
    1859-1925.................... DLB-189
World Literatue Today: A Journal for the
    New Millennium.................. Y-01
World Publishing Company........... DLB-46
World War I (1914-1918)................DS-18
    The Great War Exhibit and Symposium
    at the University of South Carolina... Y-97
    The Liddle Collection and First World
    War Research................. Y-97
    Other British Poets Who Fell
    in the Great War............. DLB-216

    The Seventy-Fifth Anniversary of
    the Armistice: The Wilfred Owen
    Centenary and the Great War Exhibit
    at the University of Virginia........ Y-93
World War II (1939–1945)
    Literary Effects of World War II..... DLB-15
    World War II Writers Symposium
    at the University of South Carolina,
    12–14 April 1995................ Y-95
    WW2 HMSO Paperbacks Society...... Y-98
R. Worthington and Company.......... DLB-49
Wotton, Sir Henry 1568-1639......... DLB-121
Wouk, Herman 1915-........ Y-82; CDALB-7
    Tribute to James Dickey............ Y-97
Wreford, James 1915-1990............ DLB-88
Wren, Sir Christopher 1632-1723....... DLB-213
Wren, Percival Christopher 1885-1941.. DLB-153
Wrenn, John Henry 1841-1911........ DLB-140
Wright, C. D. 1949-................ DLB-120
Wright, Charles 1935-..........DLB-165; Y-82
Wright, Charles Stevenson 1932-...... DLB-33
Wright, Chauncey 1830-1875..........DLB-270
Wright, Frances 1795-1852............ DLB-73
Wright, Harold Bell 1872-1944.......... DLB-9
Wright, James 1927-1980
    .... DLB-5, 169; CDALB-7
Wright, Jay 1935-.................. DLB-41
Wright, Judith 1915-2000............. DLB-260
Wright, Louis B. 1899-1984............DLB-17
Wright, Richard
    1908-1960.... DLB-76, 102; DS-2; CDALB-5
Wright, Richard B. 1937-............ DLB-53
Wright, S. Fowler 1874-1965........... DLB-255
Wright, Sarah Elizabeth 1928-........ DLB-33
Wright, T. H. "Style" (1877) [excerpt].... DLB-57
Wright, Willard Huntington (S. S. Van Dine)
    1887-1939................ DLB-306; DS-16
Wrightson, Patricia 1921-........... DLB-289
Wrigley, Robert 1951-............... DLB-256
Writers' Forum......................... Y-85
Writing
    A Writing Life..................... Y-02
    On Learning to Write............... Y-88
    The Profession of Authorship:
    Scribblers for Bread............... Y-89
    A Writer Talking: A Collage.......... Y-00
Wroth, Lawrence C. 1884-1970.........DLB-187
Wroth, Lady Mary 1587-1653......... DLB-121
Wu Jianren (Wo Foshanren)
    1866-1910.................... DLB-328
Wu Zuxiang 1908-1994.............. DLB-328
Wumingshi (Bu Baonan) 1917-2002..... DLB-328
Wurlitzer, Rudolph 1937-............DLB-173
Wyatt, Sir Thomas circa 1503-1542..... DLB-132
Wycherley, William
    1641-1715............. DLB-80; CDBLB-2
Wyclif, John circa 1335-1384.......... DLB-146

Wyeth, N. C. 1882-1945 . . . . DLB-188; DS-16

Wyle, Niklas von circa 1415-1479 . . . . DLB-179

Wylie, Elinor 1885-1928 . . . . DLB-9, 45

Wylie, Philip 1902-1971 . . . . DLB-9

Wyllie, John Cook 1908-1968 . . . . DLB-140

Wyman, Lillie Buffum Chace
    1847-1929 . . . . DLB-202

Wymark, Olwen 1934- DLB-233

Wynd, Oswald Morris (see Black, Gavin)

Wyndham, John (John Wyndham Parkes
    Lucas Beynon Harris) 1903-1969 . . . . DLB-255

Wynne-Tyson, Esmé 1898-1972 . . . . DLB-191

X

Xenophon circa 430 B.C.-circa 356 B.C. DLB-176

Xiang Kairan (Pingjiang Buxiaoshengj Buxiaosheng)
    1890-1957 . . . . DLB-328

Xiao Hong 1911-1942 . . . . DLB-328

Xu Dishan (Luo Huasheng)
    1893-1941 . . . . DLB-328

Xu Zhenya 1889-1937 . . . . DLB-328

Y

Yahp, Beth 1964- DLB-325

Yamamoto, Hisaye 1921- DLB-312

Yamanaka, Lois-Ann 1961- DLB-312

Yamashita, Karen Tei 1951- DLB-312

Yamauchi, Wakako 1924- DLB-312

Yang Kui 1905-1985. . . . . DLB-328

Yasuoka Shōtarō 1920- DLB-182

Yates, Dornford 1885-1960 . . . . DLB-77, 153

Yates, J. Michael 1938- DLB-60

Yates, Richard 1926-1992. . . . DLB-2, 234; Y-81, 92

Yau, John 1950- DLB-234, 312

Yavorov, Peyo 1878-1914 . . . . DLB-147

Ye Shaojun (Ye Shengtao) 1894-1988 . . . . DLB-328

Yearsley, Ann 1753-1806 . . . . DLB-109

Yeats, William Butler
    1865-1939 . . . . DLB-10, 19, 98, 156; CDBLB-5

    The W. B. Yeats Society of N.Y. Y-99

Yellen, Jack 1892-1991 . . . . DLB-265

Yep, Laurence 1948- DLB-52, 312

Yerby, Frank 1916-1991 . . . . DLB-76

Yezierska, Anzia 1880-1970 . . . . DLB-28, 221

Yolen, Jane 1939- DLB-52

Yonge, Charlotte Mary 1823-1901 . . . . DLB-18, 163

    The Charlotte M. Yonge Fellowship Y-98

The York Cycle circa 1376-circa 1569 . . . . DLB-146

A Yorkshire Tragedy DLB-58

Thomas Yoseloff [publishing house] DLB-46

Youd, Sam (see Christopher, John)

Young, A. S. "Doc" 1919-1996 . . . . DLB-241

Young, Al 1939- DLB-33

Young, Arthur 1741-1820 . . . . DLB-158

Young, Dick 1917 or 1918-1987 . . . . DLB-171

Young, Edward 1683-1765 . . . . DLB-95

Young, Frank A. "Fay" 1884-1957 . . . . . . DLB-241

Young, Francis Brett 1884-1954 . . . . DLB-191

Young, Gavin 1928- DLB-204

Young, Stark 1881-1963 . . . . DLB-9, 102; DS-16

Young, Waldeman 1880-1938 . . . . DLB-26

William Young [publishing house] DLB-49

Young Bear, Ray A. 1950- DLB-175

Yourcenar, Marguerite 1903-1987 . . . DLB-72; Y-88

Yovkov, Yordan 1880-1937 . . . . DLB-147; CDWLB-4

Yu Dafu 1896-1945 . . . . DLB-328

Yushkevich, Semen 1868-1927 . . . . DLB-317

Yver, Jacques 1520?-1570? DLB-327

Z

Zachariä, Friedrich Wilhelm 1726-1777 . . . . DLB-97

Zagajewski, Adam 1945- DLB-232

Zagoskin, Mikhail Nikolaevich
    1789-1852 . . . . DLB-198

Zaitsev, Boris 1881-1972 . . . . DLB-317

Zajc, Dane 1929- DLB-181

Zālīte, Māra 1952- DLB-232

Zalygin, Sergei Pavlovich 1913-2000 . . . . . DLB-302

Zamiatin, Evgenii Ivanovich 1884-1937 . . . DLB-272

Zamora, Bernice 1938- DLB-82

Zamudio, Adela (Soledad) 1854-1928 . . . . DLB-283

Zand, Herbert 1923-1970 . . . . DLB-85

Zangwill, Israel 1864-1926 . . . . . . DLB-10, 135, 197

Zanzotto, Andrea 1921- DLB-128

Zapata Olivella, Manuel 1920- DLB-113

Zapoev, Timur Iur'evich
    (see Kibirov, Timur Iur'evich)

Zasodimsky, Pavel Vladimirovich
    1843-1912 . . . . DLB-238

Zebra Books DLB-46

Zebrowski, George 1945- DLB-8

Zech, Paul 1881-1946 . . . . DLB-56

Zeidner, Lisa 1955- DLB-120

Zeidonis, Imants 1933- DLB-232

Zeimi (Kanze Motokiyo) 1363-1443 . . . . . DLB-203

Zelazny, Roger 1937-1995 . . . . DLB-8

Zeng Pu 1872-1935 . . . . DLB-328

Zenger, John Peter 1697-1746 . . . . DLB-24, 43

Zepheria DLB-172

Zernova, Ruf' 1919-2004 . . . . DLB-317

Zesen, Philipp von 1619-1689 . . . . DLB-164

Zhadovskaia, Iuliia Valerianovna
    1824-1883 . . . . DLB-277

Zhang Ailing (Eileen Chang)
    1920-1995 . . . . DLB-328

Zhang Henshui 1895-1967 . . . . DLB-328

Zhang Tianyi 1906-1985 . . . . DLB-328

Zhao Shuli 1906-1970 . . . . DLB-328

Zhukova, Mar'ia Semenovna
    1805-1855 . . . . DLB-277

Zhukovsky, Vasilii Andreevich
    1783-1852 . . . . DLB-205

Zhvanetsky, Mikhail Mikhailovich
    1934- DLB-285

G. B. Zieber and Company DLB-49

Ziedonis, Imants 1933- CDWLB-4

Zieroth, Dale 1946- DLB-60

Zigler und Kliphausen, Heinrich
    Anshelm von 1663-1697 . . . . DLB-168

Zil'ber, Veniamin Aleksandrovich
    (see Kaverin, Veniamin Aleksandrovich)

Zimmer, Paul 1934- DLB-5

Zinberg, Len (see Lacy, Ed)

Zincgref, Julius Wilhelm 1591-1635 . . . . . DLB-164

Zindel, Paul 1936- DLB-7, 52; CDALB-7

Zinnes, Harriet 1919- DLB-193

Zinov'ev, Aleksandr Aleksandrovich
    1922- DLB-302

Zinov'eva-Annibal, Lidiia Dmitrievna
    1865 or 1866-1907 . . . . DLB-295

Zinzendorf, Nikolaus Ludwig von
    1700-1760 . . . . DLB-168

Zitkala-Ša 1876-1938 . . . . DLB-175

Zīverts, Mārtiņš 1903-1990 . . . . DLB-220

Zlatovratsky, Nikolai Nikolaevich
    1845-1911 . . . . DLB-238

Zola, Emile 1840-1902 . . . . DLB-123

Zolla, Elémire 1926- DLB-196

Zolotow, Charlotte 1915- DLB-52

Zoshchenko, Mikhail Mikhailovich
    1895-1958 . . . . DLB-272

Zschokke, Heinrich 1771-1848 . . . . DLB-94

Zubly, John Joachim 1724-1781 . . . . DLB-31

Zu-Bolton, Ahmos, II 1936- DLB-41

Zuckmayer, Carl 1896-1977 . . . . DLB-56, 124

Zukofsky, Louis 1904-1978 . . . . DLB-5, 165

Zupan, Vitomil 1914-1987 . . . . DLB-181

Župančič, Oton 1878-1949 . . . DLB-147; CDWLB-4

zur Mühlen, Hermynia 1883-1951 . . . . DLB-56

Zweig, Arnold 1887-1968 . . . . DLB-66

Zweig, Stefan 1881-1942 . . . . DLB-81, 118

Zwicky, Fay 1933- DLB-325

Zwinger, Ann 1925- DLB-275

Zwingli, Huldrych 1484-1531 . . . . DLB-179

Ø

Øverland, Arnulf 1889-1968 . . . . DLB-297

ISBN-13: 978-0-7876-8147-0
ISBN-10: 0-7876-8147-4

PN
171
.P75
N58

2007
pt.1